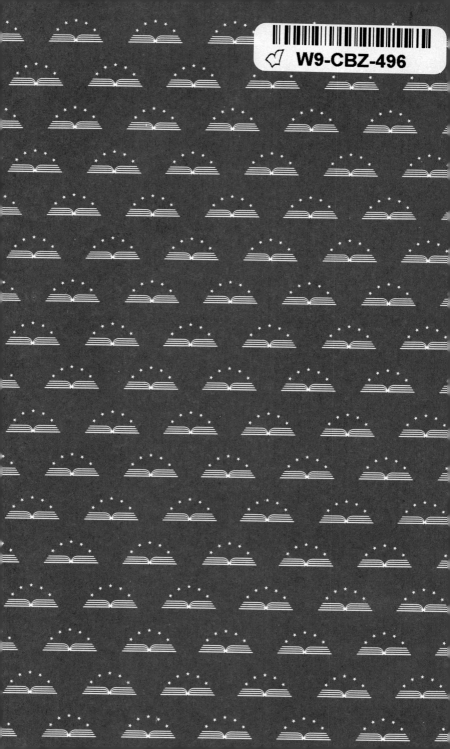

TENNESSEE WILLIAMS

Tennessee Williams

PLAYS 1937–1955

THE LIBRARY OF AMERICA

Published by arrangement with New Directions Publishing
Corporation, New York, Publisher of the plays of Tennessee
Williams, and The University of the South, copyright proprietor of
the works of Tennessee Williams. For copyrights, see page 1036.

The paper used in this publication meets the
minimum requirements of the American National Standard for
Information Sciences—Permanence of Paper for Printed
Library Materials, ANSI Z39.48—1984.

Distributed to the trade in the United States
by Penguin Putnam Inc.
and in Canada by Penguin Books Canada Ltd.

Library of Congress Catalog Number: 00–030190
For cataloging information, see end of Notes.
ISBN 1–883011–86–8

First Printing
The Library of America—119

Manufactured in the United States of America

MEL GUSSOW AND KENNETH HOLDICH
SELECTED THE CONTENTS AND WROTE THE NOTES
FOR THIS VOLUME

Tennessee Williams' *Plays 1937–1955*
is kept in print in memory of

RICHARD SANTINO
(1946–1994)

by a gift from

Richard Poirier

to the Guardians of American Letters Fund,
established by The Library of America
to ensure that every volume in the series
will be permanently available.

Contents

SPRING STORM

PLACE: Port Tyler, a small Mississippi town on the Mississippi River

TIME: Spring, 1937

ACT ONE: A high bluff overlooking the Mississippi River on a
spring afternoon

ACT TWO:
Scene One: The Critchfield home, the afternoon of Friday, the
same week
Scene Two: Same, that evening
Scene Three: Same, three in the morning

ACT THREE:
Scene One: Lawn of the Lamphrey residence, the next evening
(Saturday), a party is in full swing
Scene Two: The Port Tyler Carnegie Public Library, the same
evening
Scene Three: The Critchfield home, late afternoon toward
evening of the next day (Sunday)

ACT ONE

SCENE ONE

The house lights go down. Children's voices are heard singing "Here We Go Round the Mulberry Bush," interspersed with laughter and shouting.

The curtain rises to reveal a high, windy bluff over the Mississippi River. It is called Lover's Leap. On its verge are two old trees whose leafless branches have been grotesquely twisted by the winds. At first the scene has a mellow quality, the sky flooded with deep amber light from the sunset. But as it progresses, it changes to one of stormy violence to form a dramatic contrast between Heavenly's scene and Hertha's. The atmospheric change is caused by the approach of the spring storm which breaks at the scene's culmination.

Dick is discovered alone on the bluff. He is a good-looking boy, say about twenty-three or four, tall and athletic in build, with a fund of restless energy and imagination which prevents him from fitting into the conventional social pattern. Out of ten such men, or maybe a hundred, one becomes an Abraham Lincoln or a Clarence Darrow, and the rest live out their lives in frustrated rebellion. Maybe Dick will be the chosen one or maybe he'll just be one of the ninety-nine: that will depend upon future accidents of life which his author will not pretend to foresee.

The singing continues from below, then fades out in scattered shouting.

Heavenly enters. The important thing about Heavenly is that she is physically attractive. She has the natural and yet highly-developed charm that is characteristic of girls of pure southern stock. She is frankly sensuous without being coarse, fiery-tempered and yet disarmingly sweet. Her nature is confusing to herself and to all who know her. She wears a white skirt and sweater with a bright-colored scarf.

HEAVENLY: Dick! What are you doing up here?

DICK: Watchin' the rivuh. She's risen plenty since mawnin'. See how she's pushed up Wild Hoss Crick up there no'th o' Sutters? Ole man Sutter's gonna go to bed some night in the state o' Mississippi and wake up in Arkansaw. That is,

3

if he's lucky. If he isn't lucky he's gonna wake up a hell of a lot fu'ther south'n *any* state in the Union. Now if they'd just put that breakwater ha'f a mile fu'ther—

HEAVENLY (*exasperated*): Dick!

DICK: Yeah?

HEAVENLY: Why do you walk off by yourself like this, honey? It looks peculiuh to people.

DICK: Does it?

HEAVENLY: Of cou'se it does!

DICK: I'm sorry. I stuck it out as long's I could. But those guessin' games got my goat—lissen to that! I used my five words in one sentence beginnin' with 'g'—games got my goat! No, that's just four.

HEAVENLY: That's remarkable, honey—you're a remarkable man, but I wish you'd pay some attention to what I'm sayin!

DICK: What're you sayin?

HEAVENLY: I'm sayin it looks peculiuh to people when you come up here by yourself and leave me down there.

DICK: Well, why don't you come up here, too?

HEAVENLY: Because I can't. It's impolite, Dick.

DICK: Aw, politeness! Bein' a damn hypocrite, that's politeness!—Me, I don't truck with politeness, I do like I please!

HEAVENLY: Dick, you're tryin' to aggravate me!

DICK (*laughing*): Sure I'm tryin to aggravate you. Honey, I like to aggravate you.

HEAVENLY: I know you do. You take the greatest delight in getting me aggravated.

DICK: Sure I do. Cause when you get aggravated you're just as cute as a nine-tailed catawampus— Lookit that nigger down there in a flatboat tryin' to pull into shore. Bet he don't make it! Lookit by God! He's lost an oar!

HEAVENLY: Never mind that nigger. You come on down to the picnic.

DICK: Guessin' game over yet?

HEAVENLY: An hour ago.

DICK: I hope so. There's some things a grown man in his right senses can't put up with an' one of 'em's havin' some ole maid ask him what she's thinkin' of that's red, white, an' blue and begins with 'f'— I felt like sayin' "Your fanny!"

HEAVENLY: Dick!

DICK (*grinning slowly*): She wouldn't have understood. She would have said, "No, suh! My name is Agnes!"—That's her now comin' up the hill with that balmy sky-rider.

HEAVENLY: Shh, Dick!—That's Miss Peabody an' Reverend Hooker!

(*These two appear from below, a conventional, affable Episcopal clergyman and a coquettish spinster bubbling with animation.*)

AGNES: I told her it was strongly reminiscent of something I'd seen in the *Atlantic Monthly*. Not that I'm accusing you of plagiarism, I said, but when there is such a startling similarity—

DR. HOOKER (*ignoring her prattle, heartily*): Well, Richard, my boy, why aren't you down there participating in some of the big athletic events?

(*Everybody speaks simultaneously—confused chatter with a background of singing.*)

AGNES: Of course there was nothing I could do about it. Her parents were furious—

HEAVENLY: Hello, Dr. Hooker.

DR. HOOKER: How are you dear? If I remember correctly this young man of yours was quite a power on the high school football team back in—when did you graduate, Richard?

RICHARD: Thirty-two.

DR. HOOKER: Your laurels are still green, my lad, your laurels are still green—glorious sunset, Heavenly, glorious.

AGNES: Dr. Hooker, look at those clouds!

DR. HOOKER: And how does it happen your mother isn't with us this afternoon?

AGNES: Those clouds, Dr. Hooker.

HEAVENLY: Mother was very skeptical about the weather.

DR. HOOKER: Yes, storm clouds— "Swear not by the inconstant—April! Her moods are various—"

AGNES: Yes, but, Dr. Hooker—

HEAVENLY: I hope the picnic's a financial success.

AGNES: Yes but—

DR. HOOKER: Oh, indeed, yes. Richard, we're going to have the cake sale.

AGNES: Yes, but from the purely esthetic point of—

DICK (*indifferently*): Yeah?

DR. HOOKER: Purely esthetic, yes!

AGNES: Such a beautiful cumulus formation in all my life!

DR. HOOKER: I presume you'll wish to make a bid for the young lady's culinary masterpiece! (*He laughs.*)

VOICE BELOW: Dr. Hooker!

AGNES: Oh, they're calling you Dr. Hooker!

DR. HOOKER: Coming! Coming!

AGNES (*following him off*): It's the potato race, they're going to have the potato race! Wait for me, wait for Dr. Hookuh!

(*Exeunt. Dick has turned his back to the others and is still looking out from the bluff.*)

HEAVENLY (*slipping her arm through his*): Still watching the river?

DICK: Sure. (*Dick turns around and moves back up to look at the river.*)

HEAVENLY: Can't I compete with the river?

DICK: Not right now.

HEAVENLY: Why not?

DICK: It's goin' somewhere.

HEAVENLY: Oh! So'm I. (*She starts off. He grabs her arm.*)

DICK: No, you're a woman. Women never go anywhere unless a man makes 'em. Don't you know what's the real diff'rence between the sexes?

HEAVENLY: Yes, I mean, no. I don't want to hear any dirty jokes.

DICK: This isn't dirty, this is scientific. Set down an' I'll tell you. The real diff'rence is that a man knows that legs're made to move on but a woman thinks they're just for wearin' silk stockin's.

HEAVENLY: You're crazy. I haven't got any stockings on mine.

DICK: Naw. But as Agnes would say they're "purely exthetic!" Ornamental—ain't that what she means?

HEAVENLY: Why shouldn't they be?

DICK: That's right. Why shouldn't they be?

HEAVENLY: You'd be the first to complain if they weren't.

DICK: Sure— But don't you get restless sometimes. Don't that river-wind ever slap you in the face an' say, "Git movin', yuh damn l'il goober digger, git movin'!"?

HEAVENLY: No.

DICK: It does me.

HEAVENLY: You're gettin' one of your restless spells?

DICK: I'd like to follow that river down there—find out where she's goin'.

HEAVENLY: I know where it's goin' an' I'm not anxious to follow. Gulf of Mexico's the scummiest body of water I ever refused to put my feet in. Crawdads an' stingarees an'—

DICK: Aw, is 'at where it's goin'? I thought it was goin' further'n that. I thought it was goin' way on out to th' Caribbean an' then some. I didn't think it would stop till it got clear round th' Straits o' Magellan!

HEAVENLY: What is this? A geography lesson?

DICK: Naw. It hasn't got a damn thing to do with geography.

HEAVENLY: Oh. You're speaking symbolically about the Gypsy in you or something. Every spring you get restless like this and talk about goin' off places.

DICK: Time I got started.

HEAVENLY: You mean it's time you stopped. It's gettin damned monotonous.—Even way back in grade school you had spells like this. Used to make me play hooky so we could watch the trains coming in.

(*Pause. The children are playing another singing game. Their voices float up with a melancholy sweetness.*)

DICK: That was fun, huh?

HEAVENLY: Not for me. I was terribly bored.

DICK: Then what did you tag along for?

HEAVENLY: Because I was crazy about you just like I am now. I was always secretly hoping that you'd get romantic and try to kiss me or something, but you never did. You were never interested in anything but trains, trains! I tried everything I could to distract you, even hid behind cotton bales to make you look for me, but it never did any good.

DICK: Was that why you kept hiding from me?

HEAVENLY: I'd been reading *The Sheik*—I wanted to be pursued an' captured an' made a slave to passion!

DICK: On a station platform?

HEAVENLY: Anywhere. I was very romantic in those days.

DICK: Sort of precocious for thirteen.

HEAVENLY: But you weren't a damn bit. It was two years before you finally kissed me.

DICK: An' then you didn't like it.

HEAVENLY: Not the first time. It was an awful anticlimax to what I'd expected. (*She kisses him, he suddenly draws her against him with real passion.*) —Mmmm. Your technique has improved a little since then. (*She wipes the lipstick off his mouth.*)

DICK: So's yours.

HEAVENLY: I couldn't have been so bad even then. I made you stop looking at trains.

DICK: Yes, you did that.

HEAVENLY: And now I've made you stop watchin' the rivuh—haven't I?

DICK: Not quite.

HEAVENLY: Liuh!

DICK: I still like to watch things goin' places.

HEAVENLY: My idea of goin' places is to make a success of things where you are.

DICK: Sure. Provided you're in the right place.

(*He rises and stretches. The singing has ended. An excited woman's voice—*)

MRS. ASBURY (*off-stage*): Ronald! Oh, Ron-*ald*! (*She appears, a dumpy little matron in slacks.*) Oh Heavenly! Have you seen my child? Hertha Neilson's getting ready to tell the children one of her charming little fairy stories, and I don't want Ronald to miss it.

HEAVENLY: Sorry but I haven't seen him.

DICK: Is he a short fat kid with buck teeth wearin' glasses?

MRS. ASBURY (*outraged*): Why, no!! —I mean—uh— (*She tries to laugh.*) That's not a very flattering description! Which way did he go?

DICK: Down that-away. Tow'd the Devil's Icebox.

MRS. ASBURY: The Devil's—? Oh, Heavens! (*She goes off shrieking her son's name.*)

HEAVENLY: You should've offuhed to help her find him.

DICK: Hell. She needs to run some a' the lard off that carcass of hers.

HEAVENLY: Dick!—Dick, you know we've got to have some kind of social position when we get married, and we can't without bein' nice to people like Mrs. Asbury.

DICK: That's what I'm scahed of.

HEAVENLY: You mean you're scahed of marriage?

DICK: You remembuh that high-school play we acted in? Honey?

HEAVENLY: *Satuhday's Children*?

DICK: Yeah, there was one swell line in that play.

HEAVENLY: What's that?

DICK: Marriage is last year's love affair.

HEAVENLY: Oh! You don't want marriage!

DICK: Not the kind that ties ropes around people. (*He goes to the edge of the bluff.*) Listen to those whistles blowin'. They're gettin' out now. Pretty soon they'll be settlin' down in their overstuffed chairs t' look at the evenin' papers. Gettin' the news of the day. Who went to Mrs. Smith's afternoon tea. What happened in Czechoslovakia at eleven A.M. Who's runnin' for gov'nor in the state of Arkansas. Ain't that somethin' for you, you bastards, you poor beer guzzlers. Tomorrow you'll wake up at half past six with alarm clocks janglin' like hell's own beautiful bells in your ears. The little woman will get her fat shanks out of bed an' put on the coffee to boil. At a quarter past seven you'll kiss her good-bye, you'll give her a cold eggy smack on the kisser. She'll tell you to remember your overshoes. Or to stop at the West End butcher's for a pound o' calves' liver. Don't forget, Papa. Papa, for God's sake don't forget to bring home that thirty cents worth of calves' liver. That's good, that's sweet of you, Papa. —Bye-bye! (*He turns slowly back to Heavenly.*) And they call that *livin'* down there. I got another word for it, Heavenly, and it don't commence with an "l"!

(*Mrs. Asbury's voice is heard calling Ronald. Dick continues, mocking.*)

"Ronald, oh, Ron-*ald*!"—don't fall an' break your fat little neck! —Christ, Heavenly, I want to get away from that sort of stuff down there. That's what I mean when I say I want to go places!

HEAVENLY: I know. You talk just as though I didn't exist.

DICK: Oh, I know you exist.

HEAVENLY: No you don't. You think I'm completely out of the picture. But I'm not. I think I'm pretty much involved in your plans for the future whether you know it or not.

DICK: I haven't got any plans for the future.

HEAVENLY: Yes, you have. I've got some for you.

DICK: Yeah?

HEAVENLY: I was talking to Dad last night. He says Mr. Kramer's willing to put you on at his office as soon as buying picks up.

DICK: Tell your Dad I'm much obliged but I don't want a job in Mr. Kramer's office or anybody else's. I don't want a white-collar job.

HEAVENLY: You prefer to work around a drugstore?

DICK: No, I prefer to get the hell out of here.

HEAVENLY: You want to go on the bum?

DICK: I want to do something worthwhile.

HEAVENLY: What is worthwhile in your opinion?

DICK: I don't know. Maybe if I did some traveling I'd find out.

HEAVENLY: All right. Let's take a round-the-world cruise.

DICK: I'd rather take a cattleboat to South America. (*He quickly rationalizes his impulse.*) There's lots of business opportunities down there. I could get into radio or engineering or—

HEAVENLY: Oh. Don't let me stop you!

DICK: Don't worry, it's just a pipe dream.

HEAVENLY: Worry? Not me! I guess you think I'd be sitting at home knitting socks till you came back with a long white beard to reward my patience. No, not me! "Faithful unto death" isn't the sort of thing I want carved on my tombstone.

(*Enter Susan Lamphrey, a fat girl of Heavenly's age.*)

SUSAN: Heavenly, you missed it!

HEAVENLY: Missed what?

SUSAN: The auction! Guess who bought your cake?

HEAVENLY: Who bought it?

SUSAN: Arthur Shannon. Paid eighty dollars for it.

HEAVENLY: You're foolin'!

SUSAN: I hope to fall dead if I am. I nearly did anow. And he came with that girl who works at the library. Hertha Neilson. I wonder how *she* felt?—Hello, Richard. Goodness, you are the exclusive Mr. Somebody! I didn't even know you'd come to the picnic! Oh, what I wanted to ask you—before I forget—I'm givin' a little lawn party in honor of Arthur Shannon this Saturday evenin' an' want you to come, Heavenly—an' bring along Dick!

HEAVENLY: Thanks. We'll come.

SUSAN: I've got to rush down there an' help pack things up. Bye-bye! (*She rushes off.*)

DICK: You can count me out.

HEAVENLY: Dick.

DICK: You know I don't mix with those kind of people.

HEAVENLY: All right. Don't put yourself out. I'll go with Arthur Shannon. He deserves some reward, anyway, for payin' eighty dollars for that little coconut cake! (*Dick turns his back.*) Saturday Arthuh will take me to the Lamphrey's lawn party.

DICK: Is he?

HEAVENLY: Yes. And Sunday evenin' we're going to the Country Club for supper. (*There is a tense pause.*) An' on the way home he'll ask me to marry him.

DICK: —Will he?

HEAVENLY: Yes! I know how to work those things.

DICK: Yes. You're very clever.

HEAVENLY (*bursting out*): And you, you can take that river barge down to New Orleans an' ship out on a cattleboat if you want to. You can go clear down to the Straits of whatever-you-call-it 's far's I'm concerned! If you're restless, if you want to get rid of me so bad, don't think I'm gonna stand in your way! (*She turns away, sobbing convulsively.*)

DICK (*slowly*): You know that's not true. You can't make me jealous about that little milk-fed millionaire's brat. Suckin' a sugar-tit all his life. I remember him in grade school before he went off to Europe. God, what a sissy! His chauffeur brought him to school an' called for him afterwards an' at recess he used to sit in a corner of the play yard

readin' *The Wizard of Oz.* Remember how we used to ser-
enade him when he drove up to school in his limousine?

　　Artie, Smartie, went to a party!

　　What did he go for? To play with his dolly!

HEAVENLY: Oh, you're disgusting!

DICK: You used to sing it yourself. I guess that's what gave
him the nervous breakdown so he had to quit school an' be
shipped abroad. He was kind of stuck on you even then,
wasn't he? We used to kid you about the way he kept
hangin' around you.

HEAVENLY: With Arthur Shannon's prospects he can afford to
have some faults.

DICK: Meaning I can't?

HEAVENLY: Exactly! Meaning just that. I've given up plenty of
chances for you. In hopes you'd turn over a new leaf an'
amount to something. Now I see that you never will.
Arthur Shannon's going to ask me to marry him, and I'm
going to do it.

DICK: You won't.

HEAVENLY: You just think I won't.

(*He grabs her shoulders.*)

Let go of me, damn you!

(*She strikes him across the face. He draws back. They stand
facing each other in the deepening dusk.—From below them
comes the sound of the closing hymns at the church picnic—*

　　　　　　　Now the day is over
　　　　　　　Night is drawing nigh,
　　　　　　　Shadows of the evening
　　　　　　　Steal across the sky.

*The soft poignant quality of the hymn penetrates their mood
and softens them both. Heavenly turns away, crying. Dick
comes to her and embraces her gently. His voice is very low—*)

DICK: Listen Heavenly! Honey, listen! You don't mean none
of those things you just said. Why you couldn't shake me
off anymore than you could your own skin. An' I couldn't
either.—I've had my talk out. I'm always blowin' off my
damn fool head about somethin'. But that's all over.

Understan'? You and me, we'll get married this summer! Yeah. We'll have one a them June weddin's you see written up in sassiety columns with everything white an' sweet smellin' an' candles an' lilies an' yards an' yards of white lace for you to walk down like a queen with that new pipe organ playin' "I Love You Truly." An' me, I'll take that job of Mr. Kramer's!

HEAVENLY: Dick!

DICK: Sure . . . See those lights goin' on down there? One of them'll be ours! A little one off at the side—

(*He laughs gently. The closing hymn ends. There are sounds of general departure. Mrs. Lamphrey appears calling, "Ethel!"*)

MRS. LAMPHREY: Heavenly. Have you seen Mrs. Asbury? She's going home in our car.

HEAVENLY: She's gone after Ronald. He's exploring the Devil's Icebox.

MRS. LAMPHREY: Oh, that boy. Everybody's leaving; it looks so threatening!

HEAVENLY: Dick. Won't you hunt them up for Mrs. Lamphrey? I can't imagine what's keeping them so long.

MRS. LAMPHREY: Oh, I'd be so much obliged, Mr. Miles. (*She turns to Heavenly as Dick goes off.*) Richard is such a nice boy. I don't blame you, Heavenly.

HEAVENLY: For what?

MRS. LAMPHREY: For finding him irresistible. He has that— that sort of—primitive masculinity that's enough to make a girl lose her head!

HEAVENLY: Oh, I think I've kept mine.

MRS. LAMPHREY (*archly*): Oh, do you? Good heavens, the storm's going to break any minute. And here comes Arthur Shannon with that Neilson girl. (*Calling.*) Arthur, did you ever see such a sky?

(*Arthur enters, followed by Hertha. He is a good-looking es-thetic young man, about twenty-four. He wears white flan-nels, a sports coat, and a scarf about his throat. Hertha is thin and dark, about twenty-eight. Without money or social posi-tion, she has to depend upon a feverish animation and clever-ness to make her place among people. She has an original mind with a distinct gift for creative work. She is probably the most sensitive and intelligent person in Port Tyler, Mississippi. Much of the dialogue following is simultaneous.*)

ARTHUR: Marvelous, isn't it? We're coming up to a better view. (*To Heavenly.*) Hello!

MRS. LAMPHREY (*to Hertha*): Oh, Miss Neilson, I enjoyed your little story so much. It was charming. Did you make it up yourself? Goodness! What wind! What wind!

HEAVENLY: Oh, is that my cake Arthur? It was sweet of you to buy it.

MRS. LAMPHREY: Heavenly! Hadn't we better go down? This wind is terrific.

HEAVENLY: I would have taken more pains if I thought it was going to bring such a big price. What is it Mrs. Lamphrey?

MRS. LAMPHREY: Don't you think we'd better go down?

ARTHUR: You won't forget about our dinner Sunday?

HEAVENLY: Oh, no. Yes, Mrs. Lamphrey! I'm coming.

MRS. LAMPHREY (*calling back to Hertha*): Oh, Miss Neilson. Would you please remind your mother about those alterations to Susan's little pink blouse?

(*Hertha says nothing. Heavenly and Mrs. Lamphrey exeunt.*)

ARTHUR: Tired?

HERTHA: A little.

ARTHUR: It's your own fault. You would keep on climbing.

HERTHA: I wanted to reach the top.

ARTHUR: Well, now you're there.

HERTHA (*panting*): Not quite. I'm going to save the rest till later. I'm going to wait till it's just the right color and then I'm going to go up the rest of the way—and then you'll probably hear me shouting "hello" to God!

ARTHUR: It *is* nice up here.

HERTHA: Lovely. I hate living on a flat surface. It's bad for you, Arthur.

ARTHUR: Is it?

HERTHA: Yes, you don't know how bad it is till you get up on a high place like this and see how your spirit expands.

ARTHUR: Is your spirit expanding?

HERTHA: Enormously, enormously! Don't you see how it's filling up the whole sky?

ARTHUR: Oh, is that your spirit?

HERTHA (*laughing*): Yes!

ARTHUR: Congratulations! I haven't seen such a pyrotechnical display since July 14th, at Versailles!

(*Dick returns followed by the straggling Asburys.*)

RONALD: Aw, hell, Ma—

MRS. ASBURY: What did you say, Ronald?

RONALD: Nothing.

MRS. ASBURY: I'm afraid your father will be very angry when he hears about this. (*To Dick.*) Oh, Mr. Miles. I'm so grateful to you.—I hope you haven't lost Heavenly!

DICK: I reckon she's gone on with the others.

(*Exeunt all three.*)

HERTHA: We seem to be the sole survivors.

ARTHUR: Yes, thank heavens. I get so bored with those people.

HERTHA: Why do you bother with them?

ARTHUR: Have to. It's in the line of duty. I'm being groomed for the Planter's State Bank, so I have to make myself agreeable to depositors.

HERTHA (*seating herself on the hillside*): Oh.

ARTHUR (*sitting beside her*): Why do *you* bother with them?

HERTHA: I sort of—*belong* to them!

ARTHUR: How do you mean?

HERTHA: The Storybook Lady's a public institution.

ARTHUR: What?

HERTHA: The Storybook Lady—that's me! Every Tuesday, Thursday, and Saturday mornings, ten o'clock at the Carnegie Public Library. Have you ever heard what happened to the dark-haired princess in the magic tower when the handsome young prince went out to look for adventure? (*They both laugh.*) Oh, I don't mind that part of it. I like to make-believe as much as any of the kids. It's the old women that I can't stand, the ones like Mrs. Lamphrey who're so afraid that you'll forget your mother's a seamstress and your father's a night watchman at the lumberyard who gets notoriously drunk every Saturday night! —Oh, they're very sweet to me, call me darling and send me flowers when I'm sick, but they take every precaution

to see that I don't forget my social limitations— Did you
hear Mrs. Lamphrey remind me about Susan's little pink
blouse? Size forty-eight?—Know why she did that? She's
worried you didn't know that mother took in sewing. She's
worried about you and me—she thinks I'm trying to capti-
vate you or something! (*She laughs.*) Of course things like
that are only *amusing*, that's all!

(*Pause. Arthur lights a cigarette.*)

ARTHUR: You ought to get away from this place.

HERTHA: How could I?

ARTHUR: I don't know but there must be some way. You've
got lots of talent and you're wasting it here.

HERTHA: So are you, wasting yours—at the Planter's State
Bank.

ARTHUR (*lightly but with bitterness*): No, I'm not wasting anything. In literature I'm one of those tragic "not quites"!

HERTHA: That's silly. You're terribly young still.

ARTHUR: I know my limitations. I haven't got it in me to be
anything but a good amateur, I know that. You see, my
poetry, it isn't a terrific volcanic eruption— No—it's just a
little bonfire of dry leaves and dead branches. (*He laughs
harshly.*) This morning I received an invitation to join the
Junior Chamber of Commerce.

HERTHA (*pausing*): Of course you refused?

ARTHUR: No. Accepted.

HERTHA: Arthur!

ARTHUR: Why not? Father was tickled pink—slapped me on
the back three times and told me I was going places!

HERTHA: Did he tell you what places you were going?

ARTHUR: No. (*He laughs.*) There's no necessity for being
explicit about such things—going places is just going
places.

HERTHA: I see. (*Pause.*) Sometimes I wonder if anybody's
ever gone anyplace—or do we always just go back to where
we started?—I guess there's something significant about
the fact that the world is round and all of the planets are
round and all of them are going round and round the sun!
(*She laughs.*) The whole damned universe seems to be laid
out on a more or less elliptical plan. (*She rises.*) But I can't

get used to it, Arthur. I can't adjust myself to it like you're doing— (*She gropes for words.*) —You see I can't get over the idea that it might be possible for somebody—sometime —somewhere—to follow a straight line upwards and get some place that nobody's ever been yet! (*Pause.*)

ARTHUR (*looking up at her with a slight smile*): You mean to Paradise, don't you?

HERTHA: You're laughing at me. You think it's foolish.

ARTHUR (*slowly*): I know what you mean. But I don't believe in it. I think it's just one of those romantic fallacies that everybody gets knocked out of him in the course of time. —Where are you going?

HERTHA: I'm going on up the rest of the way.

ARTHUR: To see God?

HERTHA: Yes. (*Arthur laughs.*) Don't you think I'll find him up there?

ARTHUR: Oh, you might! And then you *might* just find the other side of the hill!

HERTHA: Coming?

ARTHUR: No! I hate steep places. They make me feel like falling.

HERTHA: I love them. They make me feel like flying!

(*She climbs slowly up the hillside, Arthur remaining below. When she reaches the top, she stands there silently, silhouetted between the two dead trees. It has grown almost dark except for the magenta streaks of color in the fading sunset. The wind is beginning to rise, and there is a fitful glimmer of lightning.*)

ARTHUR: Well, have you found Him? (*Pause.*)

HERTHA: Yes!

ARTHUR: What does he have to say?

HERTHA: Oh, he doesn't say anything, he doesn't use any words—just a lot of beautiful gestures which I can't understand.

ARTHUR: What does he look like? The fatherly type?

HERTHA: No!—He's a very vague sort of person. He reminds me a little bit of an old Irishman who used to get drunk with my father on Saturday nights.

ARTHUR (*laughing*): Yes?

HERTHA: An awfully funny old fellow— He never said much but he had a beautiful smile—especially when he was playing pinochle.

(*Arthur laughs.*)

You should come up and look at the river! It's marvelous! It's like a big yellow sea! (*Pause.*)

(*Arthur rises.*)

ARTHUR: That wind's too cold!
HERTHA: I like the taste of it.
ARTHUR: What does it taste like?
HERTHA: The outer edge of space. It's got the cold flavor of stars in it.
ARTHUR: That's the pine trees! You'd better come down and get into my trench coat, Miss Neilson.
HERTHA: I want to stay up here. I'm never coming down.
ARTHUR: Do I have to come up there and get you?
HERTHA: Yes, if you want me!

(*Arthur joins her above. The wind rises and blows Hertha's hair loose. They both point at things in the distance, talking and laughing, but the wind drowns their voices. Suddenly Hertha points upwards with a loud cry.*)

Wild geese!

(*If possible a faint honking should be heard as the geese pass over.*)

ARTHUR: Yes.
HERTHA: They're going up north to the lakes.—Why don't they take me with them?
ARTHUR: You're not a wild goose.
HERTHA: But I could be one—I could be anything that flies!

(*The wind roars about them.*)

ARTHUR: We'd better get down from here before we're blown down.
HERTHA: Not yet!
ARTHUR: Yes. Right now!

(*He jumps to the lower level, catches her waist and lifts her down with him. They descend to a lower level and seat themselves on the rocks. Arthur wraps his coat carefully about her. She looks at him silently—the wind falls.*)

HERTHA: Maybe the storm's blown over.

ARTHUR: No. This is just the traditional hush before it gets started.

HERTHA: If it storms let's stay up here! I love spring storms!

ARTHUR: If you caught your death of cold the kiddies would blame it on me—they'd say that I killed their Storybook Lady.

HERTHA: I'd like to die in a storm!

ARTHUR: Why would you?

HERTHA: I don't know. I think it's a good way of dying—Paul Cezanne died from painting in a storm.

ARTHUR: Did he?

HERTHA: Yes. I think that's the noblest death I ever heard of.

ARTHUR (*rising with a laugh*): Hertha! You're getting morbid —we'd better go back down.

HERTHA: Give me a few more minutes!

ARTHUR: Gosh. (*She sits back down.*) You sound like Mme. Du Barry at the foot of the guillotine.

HERTHA: Did she say that? Poor thing. I know just how she felt— She had her head chopped off and tomorrow I'll be back at the Carnegie Public Library!

ARTHUR: You're terribly dissatisfied with things, aren't you?

HERTHA: Why wouldn't I be?

ARTHUR (*carefully*): I wonder if it isn't because—

HERTHA: Because what?

ARTHUR: I knew a girl in London when I was going to school over there and she was terribly dissatisfied with things, too. We had a love affair.

HERTHA: Oh.

ARTHUR: It was her first experience and mine, too. It did us both good. We were both slightly crazy before it happened, and afterwards we were perfectly sane.

HERTHA: Why did you tell me that?

ARTHUR (*uncomfortably*): I don't know exactly.

HERTHA: Did you think that my case corresponded to hers?

ARTHUR: No.

HERTHA: Did you suppose that fornication was the straight line upwards that I'd been trying to find?

ARTHUR: I didn't think I was putting it quite that crudely.

HERTHA: I'm sorry. You were trying to be very delicate about it.

ARTHUR: It just popped out.

HERTHA: I see

ARTHUR: We talk about things so frankly in Europe. I forgot that your southern puritanism might rise up in arms at anything too boldly stated.

HERTHA: I'm not offended. No I want to thank you for being so honest with me, Arthur.—How did this idyllic affair of yours turn out?

ARTHUR: The way you'd expect. We were both disappointed to find out that the world didn't burst into a million glittering stars simply because a man and a woman shared the same bed. But we got over that. She was very practical about it. She said it was in the interest of science or something, and the next summer she married a young M.P.

HERTHA: So now you're in mourning for her?

ARTHUR: No. Not for her.

HERTHA: For somebody else?

ARTHUR: Yes. A funny thing happened to me. I've just described one of those vicious circles that you were complaining about. I've come back to something that I went away from.

HERTHA: What's that?

ARTHUR: The girl in the white skirt.

HERTHA: Heavenly Critchfield?

ARTHUR: Yes.

HERTHA: What do you mean?

ARTHUR: I loved her a long time ago. When we were in grade school.

HERTHA: That long ago?

ARTHUR: Yes. It doesn't sound possible, but it's true. I was terribly shy and one day she laughed at me. After that I couldn't go back to school anymore. They had to send me to Europe.

HERTHA: Because she laughed at you?

ARTHUR: Yes. I thought I'd forgotten about it. But now I'm beginning to see she's been in me all the time, laughing at me—and everything that I've done since then has been a sort of desperate effort to—to—

HERTHA: To compensate for her laughing at you?

ARTHUR: Yes, that's it!

HERTHA: But now that you *do* understand it, you ought to be able to get away from it.

ARTHUR: That's the funny thing. I can't. I don't think I'll be able to get away from it until I've possessed her.

HERTHA: And made her stop laughing!

ARTHUR: Yes—yes, made her stop laughing.

HERTHA: And to do that you think you will have to possess her?

ARTHUR: Yes. Or somebody else!!

HERTHA: Somebody else.

ARTHUR: Who could make me stop thinking about her.

HERTHA: Do you think that anyone could?

ARTHUR: I don't know. . . .

HERTHA: Neither do I. . . . (*She rises.*) When did we start being serious?

ARTHUR: I don't know.

HERTHA: We shouldn't be. This isn't the serious season. It's the season for green things and frivolity and—

ARTHUR (*trying to catch her mood*): And catching colds in the head.

HERTHA: Yes, the modern twist! The whimsical anticlimax! (*She jumps up to the second level.*)

ARTHUR: Where are you going?

HERTHA (*pointing gaily*): You see those two old trees up there? I used to call them the two weird sisters—they look like they're putting a curse on the town!

(*The wind rises again with great force. There is lightning and a rumble of thunder.*)

ARTHUR: Hertha. Come down from there! It's starting to rain—the storm's breaking!

(*She waves to him gaily from the summit.*)

HERTHA: Look, Arthur! There's three of us now! We're putting a curse on the town. (*She laughs wildly.*)

(*Lightning outlines her figure between the two dead trees. There is a crescendo of wind and thunder—*)

Curtain

ACT TWO

SCENE ONE

The curtain rises on the living room of the Critchfield home. We leave the practical arrangement of this room to the scene designer with these suggestions:

It is furnished in good taste with the impediment of very limited funds and a passion for antiques that are not too well-preserved. Nevertheless the room has charm. It should have a pastel spring-like quality which should be accomplished by the use of light wallpaper with a floral pattern and a pleasing combination of pastel shades in the furnishings. Mrs. Critchfield is a foolish woman, but she has made a conscientious study of the women's fashion and home magazines.

There are a few essential features: a sofa with a table lamp on a table directly beside it; a large military-equestrian portrait of a Civil War hero hung prominently on the wall, preferably in a position that seems to command the whole room; a pair of French doors with white or cream curtains; a big chair with a floor lamp beside it; a bookcase or "secretary" and a radio cabinet.

As the scene opens, Aunt Lila is seated in her rocker close to the radio. It is important that this rocker should squeak audibly when in motion. Aunt Lila is a spinster with humor and charm. She shows evidence of having been beautiful in her youth and is by no means a conventional old maid. The doorbell sounds.

MESSENGER BOY (*offstage*): Cutrere's.
MRS. CRITCHFIELD (*in the hall*): Flowers? How lovely!

(*The door is closed. After a few moments, Mrs. Critchfield enters with a light blue vase of talisman roses which she sets down*) *on the radio cabinet. Mrs. Critchfield is a woman with large hips, pearl eardrops, and pince-nez. Walking she always leans slightly forward from her hips like a kangaroo. Her mobile hands and quick jerky movements serve to emphasize this resemblance. She has a loud "cultured" voice and a manner that seems to be derived from a long career of presiding over women's clubs. On her breast are pinned emblems of the D.A.R. and D.O.C. She is always subconsciously aware of Colonel Wayne's presence in her domestic sphere and many times during the play we catch her glancing at his portrait as a source of continual moral support.)*

MRS. CRITCHFIELD (*bustling into the room*): A dozen roses from Cutrere's!

LILA: That Shannon boy send 'em?

MRS. CRITCHFIELD (*arranging*): Of course!

LILA: What did you do with the old ones?

MRS. CRITCHFIELD: Threw them out.

LILA: When I was a girl I used to save the petals and make sachets.

MRS. CRITCHFIELD: Heavenly isn't quite that sentimental. (*She plumps down on the sofa with her sewing and a copy of* Vogue) Where is Heavenly?

LILA: Out.

MRS. CRITCHFIELD: I knew that much.

LILA: Well, that's all I can tell you.

MRS. CRITCHFIELD: Lila, what is that you're working on?

LILA: Some goods I got at Power's spring sale. It looked like a good buy so I bought it.

MRS. CRITCHFIELD: Your dividend come in from the compress stock?

LILA: It did.

MRS. CRITCHFIELD: My dear! Don't you think you might spend it a little more judiciously?

LILA: It's mine. I can spend it the way I want to.

MRS. CRITCHFIELD: Of course you can, my dear! But you might think of better ways than buying goods that will make you look like a holiday at the races.

LILA: This is for Heavenly to wear to Susan Lamphrey's lawn party.

MRS. CRITCHFIELD: Oh, now, that's sweet of you, Lila. But Heavenly's going to wear her white organdy.

LILA: What organdy?

MRS. CRITCHFIELD: Why, the one she wore at her high school commencement.

LILA: Land of Goshen. You can think of more ways to cheat the moths.

MRS. CRITCHFIELD: The material's perfectly good. I'm making it over by this new pattern in *Vogue*. (*She hands Lila the magazine.*) Princess sleeves with a little circular cape effect round the shoulders.

LILA: April's too early for organdy.

MRS. CRITCHFIELD: Not necessarily.—Everybody will be wearing summer formals.

LILA: Who said so?

MRS. CRITCHFIELD: Mrs. Lamphrey said so herself.

LILA: She just wants Heavenly to come looking peculiar so that fat Susan of hers won't show up so bad in comparison.

MRS. CRITCHFIELD: Now Lila. Why do you always attribute such awful motives to people?

LILA: Because I know 'em.

MRS. CRITCHFIELD: Know them nothing. You practically never go out of the house anymore. All you know is what Agnes Peabody tells you over the phone.

LILA: She tells me enough.

MRS. CRITCHFIELD: Yes, I'll have to admit she keeps well-informed.

LILA: Yes, speaking of information, she told me this morning that Mary Louise Shumaker's expecting another.

MRS. CRITCHFIELD: When?

LILA: Next October. I bet you Mary Louise hasn't found it out herself yet.—You'd think that Agnes was taking mail orders for the stork the way she scoops the town on things like that.

MRS. CRITCHFIELD: Lila, dear, can you see to thread this needle? I'm so nervous I can't hold it still.—Well, if I don't get finished I suppose she could wear her blue knitted suit.

LILA: That would be more sensible. April really is too early for organdy.

MRS. CRITCHFIELD: Everything's early this spring. (*She takes the needle.*) Thank you, dear. The crepe myrtle's been out a week.

LILA: What's that got to do with it?

MRS. CRITCHFIELD: I always start wearing white when the crepe myrtle's out. The boys are wearing white flannels. I saw Arthur Shannon in the public library this morning wearing white flannel pants and white shoes and a white sweater.

LILA: Trust him to do the outlandish!

MRS. CRITCHFIELD: I said to him, "My, my but you're all in white this morning!"

LILA: What did he say?

MRS. CRITCHFIELD: He said, "Yes, it's good cricket weather!" (*She bites off the end of the thread.*)

LILA: Cricket! What is cricket anyhow?

MRS. CRITCHFIELD: A game they play at Oxford. Terribly stylish.

LILA: Somehow I can't picture that boy playing anything more strenuous than checkers, and even then he'd probably have his chauffeur or valet or something to push 'em around for him.

MRS. CRITCHFIELD: Lila, dear, I want to ask you as a special favor to me to please desist from making those sarcastic remarks about Arthur Shannon and his parents, especially when Heavenly's around.

LILA: Why, I scarcely mention the Shannons! I haven't for twenty years! But why should I anyhow?

MRS. CRITCHFIELD: I'm hoping they'll make a match of it.

LILA: Heavenly and Arthur Shannon?

MRS. CRITCHFIELD: Yes. Do you have any objections?

LILA: —No. But I think Heavenly has.

MRS. CRITCHFIELD: Not if she's got any sense. Lila, you surely don't want her to make your mistake.

LILA: Which mistake do you mean?

MRS. CRITCHFIELD: Everybody expected you to make a brilliant marriage when you were a girl, but you spoiled all your chances by being a sentimental fool. You had a dozen good chances that you simply threw to the wind.

LILA: There was only one that I wanted.

MRS. CRITCHFIELD: You could have had *him*. You could have been sitting up there right now in the biggest house in town.

LILA: Yes, if I'd wanted to hold him against his will.

MRS. CRITCHFIELD: Let's not discuss that affair. It's one of those things that are better forgotten, especially when there's a young girl in the house.

LILA: You brought it up. I didn't. Don't think I'm turned against the boy on account of his father. If anything I'm holding *that* in his favor. I've still got lots of respect for Gale Shannon. The point I'm making is simply that Heavenly's been going with Richard Miles too long to switch to another.

MRS. CRITCHFIELD (*looking at her sharply*): What do you mean?

LILA: Nothing but what I said.

MRS. CRITCHFIELD (*uneasily after a pause*): I'm afraid there's been some gossip about Heavenly and that Miles boy. Mrs. Lamphrey said something right funny at the D.A.R. board meeting. She said she was glad that Susan hadn't centered her affections too definitely on any one boy, and she gave me the most pointed look, as if it had some special application to me or to Heavenly.

LILA: Centered her affections! That's good. The only thing that girl has ever centered is fat in the wrong places.

MRS. CRITCHFIELD: Lila!

LILA: Well, it's the truth.

MRS. CRITCHFIELD: It's painfully obvious that people are beginning to talk. And you can't altogether blame them. Heavenly is sometimes terribly indiscreet.

LILA: Is she?

MRS. CRITCHFIELD: You know that she is. And the Miles boy doesn't have a nice reputation. Didn't even get through high school and he's never been known to hold a job for more than two months at a time. One of these congenital loafers, that's what he is. Is that the kind of boy I want my daughter's name to be associated with? No, it is not!

LILA: I'm not saying that I approve of Dick Miles either. But love is something it's a mistake to interfere with.

MRS. CRITCHFIELD: Love!—If I were a girl I'd be thrilled by Arthur's attentions. He's got looks, money, social position —everything!

LILA: Except a backbone.

MRS. CRITCHFIELD: You're prejudiced against him, you're holding a grudge.

LILA: I'm holding no grudge. Arthur bores the girl to death sitting here reading poetry to her and talking about—

MRS. CRITCHFIELD: Is there anything wrong with having intellectual interests?

LILA: Not if they're reasonably unobtrusive. Oh, he's nice enough I suppose. But I wouldn't put too much stock in him as a prospective son-in-law.

MRS. CRITCHFIELD: Didn't he pay eighty dollars for Heavenly's cake at that church affair?

LILA: He doesn't know eighty dollars from eighty cents. Agnes Peabody says he's taken a notion to that librarian, Hertha What's-her-name, that went to the picnic with him.

MRS. CRITCHFIELD: Hertha Neilson? That girl's peculiar!

LILA: Is she?

MRS. CRITCHFIELD: Yes! She paints very odd pictures.— Wears her hair in braids like a schoolgirl and she's easily twenty-eight or thirty.

LILA: Anything else wrong with her?

MRS. CRITCHFIELD: Indeed there is. Her father's a drunkard and her mother takes in sewing.—You can imagine the Shannons allowing their son to get himself mixed up with that kind of trash.

LILA: Well, they're both artistic and Heavenly isn't.

MRS. CRITCHFIELD: Heavenly is quite artistic. Those teacups she painted in the eighth grade. Absolutely remarkable! What's happened to them?

LILA: Don't you remember? You gave them to Ozzie.

MRS. CRITCHFIELD: I didn't.—She must have acquired them in her usual way.—Arthur is just being nice to the Neilson girl because of her pitiful circumstances.

(*The phone rings. Mrs. Critchfield rushes into the hall and can be heard answering phone in her flute-like company voice.*)

Mr. Critchfield's residence— No. Heavenly is not in at the moment. Who's calling, please? Oh! (*Her tone becomes icy.*) No, she's out and I hardly believe she'll be in the rest of the evening. (*She hangs up with a bang and re-enters living room.*)

LILA: Richard Miles?

MRS. CRITCHFIELD: Yes.—Disgusting!

LILA: You shouldn't have cut him off so short!

MRS. CRITCHFIELD: Why shouldn't I? I'm sick and tired of that boy monopolizing Heavenly's time. (*She speaks from the window.*) There she comes up the walk now without any hat on and the rain just pouring. (*She crosses to the hall.*) I guess she thinks we haven't got worries enough without— Heavenly!

(*Mrs. Critchfield exits. Lila turns on the radio.*)

ANNOUNCER'S VOICE: —And for his first selection, your old friend and neighbor would like to read you a little poem by Sara Teasdale which seems especially appropriate to a rainy spring afternoon—

(*A recitation with organ background follows.*)

When I am dead and over me bright April
Shakes out her rain-drenched hair
Though you should lean above me broken-hearted
I shall not care

I shall have peace as leafy trees are peaceful
When rain bends down the bough
And I shall be more silent and cold-hearted
Than you are now!

(*Mrs. Critchfield re-enters near the close of the poem.*)

MRS. CRITCHFIELD (*referring to some act of Heavenly's*) Insolence! What is that sob-stuff you're listening to?

LILA: The Village Rhymester.

MRS. CRITCHFIELD: Please use the earphones! (*She switches off the radio.*) Sentimentality is something that turns my stomach.

(*Aunt Lila quietly adjusts earphones and turns the radio back on. During the dialogue between Heavenly and Mrs.*

Critchfield, Aunt Lila is seen dissolving into tears as she listens to this, her favorite program—she dabs her eyes and her nostrils and looks dreamily at the ceiling—she finally blows her nose—it is evident that the Village Rhymester is giving his audience a thorough workout. Heavenly enters immediately after Mrs. Critchfield's speech directly above. Mrs. Critchfield continues.)

What do you mean by running upstairs when I ask you a question?

HEAVENLY: Did you want me to stand there dripping rain all over the carpet?

MRS. CRITCHFIELD: Where have you been—the drugstore?

HEAVENLY: Yes.

MRS. CRITCHFIELD: What for?

HEAVENLY: A Coke.

MRS. CRITCHFIELD: We've got bottled Cokes in the basement.

HEAVENLY: I like fountain Cokes, Mother.

MRS. CRITCHFIELD: What was that package you were trying to hide in your slicker?

HEAVENLY: I wasn't hiding it, I was trying to keep it dry.

MRS. CRITCHFIELD: What was it?

HEAVENLY: Perfume.

MRS. CRITCHFIELD: Perfume!

HEAVENLY: One ounce of *Quelques Fleurs.* I didn't have a drop left.

MRS. CRITCHFIELD: Did you charge it?

HEAVENLY: Of course I charged it, Mother.

MRS. CRITCHFIELD: Well, I suppose I shall have to have that account discontinued.

HEAVENLY: Suit yourself about that.

MRS. CRITCHFIELD: You don't seem to realize the financial condition this family's in.

HEAVENLY: Don't I?

MRS. CRITCHFIELD: No. For a girl of your age you show remarkably little sense about our account at Mungers. When I was twenty-two, I was married and keeping house. And believe me, I learned the value of every cent.

HEAVENLY: Yes, Mother.—Did anyone call?

MRS. CRITCHFIELD: Arthur called.

HEAVENLY: Who else?

(*Mrs. Critchfield says nothing.*)

I was expecting a call from Dick.

MRS. CRITCHFIELD: Didn't you see him at the drugstore?

HEAVENLY: No. He was out.

MRS. CRITCHFIELD: Imagine! A delivery boy.

HEAVENLY: He's not a delivery boy. He's assistant pharmacist.

MRS. CRITCHFIELD: Soda jerker.

LILA: Dick has never jerked a soda in his life. Besides, it's only a temporary job—Mr. Kramer's promised him something.

MRS. CRITCHFIELD: Did your father do that?

HEAVENLY: Yes.

MRS. CRITCHFIELD: Your father will just get himself in bad with Mr. Kramer. That Miles boy will never be able to hold a job.

HEAVENLY: He's going to hold this one.

MRS. CRITCHFIELD: You have a dinner engagement with Arthur, you know.

HEAVENLY: Yes, I know. Sunday night.

MRS. CRITCHFIELD: I think you should wear your blue knitted suit. It's really more stylish than ever. (*Heavenly rises.*) Where are you going?

HEAVENLY: I'm going to phone Dick.

MRS. CRITCHFIELD: Listen, Heavenly—

HEAVENLY: What?

MRS. CRITCHFIELD: If you let a chance like this slip through your fingers—

HEAVENLY: What chance are you talking about?

MRS. CRITCHFIELD: Arthur Shannon.

HEAVENLY (*smiling wryly*): Oh. (*She starts to leave.*)

MRS. CRITCHFIELD: Heavenly, come back here. I want to talk to you—you can call that boy later.

AUNT LILA (*huskily as she removes earphones*): "—But only God can make a tree!" (*She rises and dabs her eyes.*) Shall I make tea for anyone else? Heavenly? Esmeralda?

HEAVENLY: No, thanks, Aunty.

MRS. CRITCHFIELD: No.

(*Lila goes out, still under emotional spell of the Village Rhymester.*)

MRS. CRITCHFIELD (*after a short, uncomfortable pause*): How have you been feeling, dear?

HEAVENLY: Perfectly well, Mother.

MRS. CRITCHFIELD: I believe you've fallen off some.

HEAVENLY: Is that what you wanted to talk about?

MRS. CRITCHFIELD: No, it is not. When you assume that defensive attitude toward your mother, it makes it very difficult for her to discuss things with you. (*Heavenly lights a cigarette.*) You're smoking too much, Heavenly. It makes you nervous and cross and discolors your teeth.—Now what I wanted to say is—

HEAVENLY: Arthur Shannon?

MRS. CRITCHFIELD: Yes.

HEAVENLY: Please don't. (*She rises abruptly and crosses to the French window.*)

(*During this following speech, Mrs. Critchfield should acquire a certain dignity and force. She is talking about something she feels keenly which is the very core of her existence.*)

MRS. CRITCHFIELD: Don't you think that having the finest blood in America imposes on you some obligations? I'm sure that you do. It's a question of self-respect. But it's also a question of something deeper than that. Maybe I'm being old-fashioned. Hanging on to something that's lost its meaning. I know that some people say so. But they're people who never had anything worth hanging onto. You're not one of them, Heavenly. A girl whose name is listed under five or six different headings in Zella Armstrong's *Notable Families* and every other good southern genealogy couldn't help but feel it her sacred duty to live up to the best that's in her. The Waynes, the Critchfields, the Tylers, the Hallidays, and the Brookes. You've got them in you, Heavenly. You can't get them out. And they're going to fight you to the last wall if you try to mix their blood with ditchwater!

HEAVENLY (*turning furiously*): What do you mean?

MRS. CRITCHFIELD (*breathing heavily*): I mean that Arthur Shannon comes from your kind of people and the other one doesn't. You're not going to throw him over for a boy whose people are so low, so common that—!

HEAVENLY (*screaming*): Stop it! I won't listen to it!

MRS. CRITCHFIELD: You sit right back down there, young lady, and wait till I'm finished! There are certain practical considerations that I don't like to mention. You know what they are. The Shannons are the wealthiest family in the Delta. They own fifteen thousand acres of land and Gale Shannon's President of the Planter's State Bank. I know that sounds cheap and crude and mercenary, and I could hardly force myself to say it. But I had to. You forced me to, Heavenly.—Your father's health is uncertain. I was talking to Dr. Gray about his last examination and it seems it was not as favorable as it might have been.

HEAVENLY: Nobody pays any attention to Dr. Gray.

MRS. CRITCHFIELD: No? He brought us into the world. He's been our family physician for nearly sixty years.

HEAVENLY: He's in his dotage.

MRS. CRITCHFIELD: Very well, just ignore my warnings.— Some day you'll have a sad awakening, young lady.

HEAVENLY: Oh, mother, I know, I know!

MRS. CRITCHFIELD: You *don't* know. But under the circumstances I think it best you *should*.

HEAVENLY: Know what?

MRS. CRITCHFIELD: Dr. Gray intimated that your father does not have much longer to live.

(*A pause: Heavenly is slightly stunned.*)

HEAVENLY: I don't believe it.

MRS. CRITCHFIELD: I've kept this from you all. I've borne it alone— Your father's hypertensive condition has been aggravated by business worries. It's taken a serious turn. And if something should happen on top of everything else—

HEAVENLY: You mean if Dick and I should get married?

MRS. CRITCHFIELD: Yes! Precisely! Would you be willing to sign your father's death warrant? And mine, too? Do you know that we haven't managed to put by a single dollar since the stock crash, and now with this business recession— Our account's been cut off at Mungers— It's not at all unlikely that we'll have to go on relief next winter.

HEAVENLY (*in a quiet strained voice*): If you want me to marry Arthur Shannon, you might as well know right now that it isn't possible.

MRS. CRITCHFIELD: What do you mean?

HEAVENLY: I mean it isn't possible. (*She averts her face.*)

(*A pause while this penetrates Mrs. Critchfield's shocked brain.*)

MRS. CRITCHFIELD (*gasping*): Heavenly! (*Then she speaks slowly.*) Has there been—? Have you—?

HEAVENLY: Yes. I *have*. That's the answer.

(*A strangling sound comes from Mrs. Critchfield's throat. Her suffering is too acute to be ludicrous—she looks desperately about the room, her antiques, her heirlooms, even Colonel Wayne's portrait, fail to support her in this moment. Heavenly lights a cigarette.*)

MRS. CRITCHFIELD (*choked*): You dare to come into this house, in my presence and make that shameful confession?!

HEAVENLY (*with some of Colonel Wayne's courage*): You asked for it and I'm not ashamed. We love each other. God knows that's not as immoral as what you want me to do! And I'm not going to do it.

MRS. CRITCHFIELD: I—I feel sick.—No, it isn't the truth, you've made this up, it's a lie!

HEAVENLY: It's not a lie, mother.

MRS. CRITCHFIELD (*because she can't face it.*): It's got to be! Don't you understand? It's got to be— (*She sinks weakly on the sofa and looks at Colonel Wayne's portrait.*) You're never going to see him again.

HEAVENLY: Didn't you hear what I told you? We already belong to each other.

MRS. CRITCHFIELD: No. Not one more word! Or I'll report the whole thing to your father, even if it kills him.—So it *is* true. But I suppose it isn't too late?!

HEAVENLY: What do you mean?

MRS. CRITCHFIELD (*anxiously*): Nothing's happened! You haven't gotten yourself in trouble, have you?!

HEAVENLY (*turning away in distaste*): No.

MRS. CRITCHFIELD: Then it *isn't* too late. It can still be covered up.

HEAVENLY: Covered up?

MRS. CRITCHFIELD: Yes. You can leave town for awhile. Visit Aunt Clara down in Biloxi, in a month or two you'll—

HEAVENLY: I'm not going to give Dick up.

MRS. CRITCHFIELD: You've got to.

HEAVENLY: I can't. I'm not going to be an old maid.

MRS. CRITCHFIELD: You don't have to be an old maid.

HEAVENLY: Oh. You think Arthur Shannon would be willing to take me secondhand?

MRS. CRITCHFIELD: Does Arthur know?

HEAVENLY: I'd tell him.

MRS. CRITCHFIELD: No, you couldn't. You wouldn't have to. There's precious few girls that get married nowadays without having had one or two love affairs in the past.

HEAVENLY: Maybe not. But I've got a sense of decency.

MRS. CRITCHFIELD: *You* talk about *decency*!

HEAVENLY: Yes, I do.

MRS. CRITCHFIELD: You don't know what the word means.

HEAVENLY: It's you that don't know what it means. It's you that wants to make a prostitute of me.

MRS. CRITCHFIELD: Shut up! You dare to stand in front of me and say things like that. I don't know why I should let you kill me, you mean, despicable girl!

HEAVENLY: I haven't done anything terribly wrong. Dick and I loved each other—so much that—whatever happened it really wasn't our fault.

MRS. CRITCHFIELD: How long has it been going on?

HEAVENLY: For a year. Ever since last spring. I couldn't help it. I don't know how to explain. He lost his job at the planing mill and he was going to leave town—he was feeling so discouraged and restless and all—I couldn't bear it—I couldn't give him up—

MRS. CRITCHFIELD: And so to hold him you—

HEAVENLY: Yes. To hold him.

MRS. CRITCHFIELD: Without any shame you come to me and say that?

HEAVENLY: Yes. Without any shame.

MRS. CRITCHFIELD: You horrible, shameless, ungrateful girl!

HEAVENLY: Yes. (*She turns to leave.*)

MRS. CRITCHFIELD: Heavenly! (*Then with real feeling.*) Oh, my poor, poor daughter! (*She breaks down sobbing.*)

HEAVENLY (*slightly moved*): I'm sorry mother. (*Pause.*)

MRS. CRITCHFIELD (*sobbing*): When you were a little girl and did something wrong—I used to make you come in here and apologize to Colonel Wayne's portrait—don't you remember, Heavenly?

HEAVENLY: Yes.

MRS. CRITCHFIELD: That was because I wanted you to understand the responsibility of having fine blood in you. Heavenly —I want you to do that now. I want you to stand here in front of your great-grandfather's picture and beg his forgiveness for the first disgrace that's ever come to his name.

HEAVENLY (*stiffening*): I won't do it.

MRS. CRITCHFIELD: You've got to. Your family's all you've got left, you poor girl. If you don't respect that you've got nothing.—You come here and tell Colonel Wayne you're sorry for those awful things you talked about in his presence— *Heavenly!*

HEAVENLY (*dully*): Yes. (*She walks stiffly up to the portrait, stands before it, sobbing—then suddenly blurts out.*) Aw, go back to Gettysburg you big palooka!

(*She runs out of the room sobbing.*)

Curtain

SCENE TWO

Dinner has just been concluded. Mr. Critchfield slouches into the living room, thoughtfully manipulating a toothpick. He removes his coat and shoes and loosens his tie; he flops wearily into the big chair under the floor lamp and unfolds his evening paper to the market reports. As Lila enters, he mechanically extends a section of the paper to her with a muffled grunt.

LILA: No thanks, Oliver. I misplaced my glasses. (*She settles into her usual place by radio and picks up her sewing.*) How's cotton?

OLIVER: Off two points on the Memphis curb. One at New Orleans.

LILA (*glancing at him*): Well, did you go to the clinic today?

OLIVER: Huh?—Yes. I went.

LILA: What did they tell you?

OLIVER (*sheepishly*): Nothing wrong with my heart. Just gas on the stomach.

LILA (*relieved*): I knew it! I get palpitations myself when I eat too many starchy things. Nervous stomach's the curse of the Critchfields. Alf struggled against it for years, so did Cousin Rachel.

(*From the dining room across the hall Mrs. Critchfield's strident voice is heard directing the colored servant.*)

MRS. CRITCHFIELD: Hurry up, get this table cleared off. I want the place to look decent in case Mr. Shannon comes in. No, no, you've been in the house twenty years and you still don't know where the percolator sits! No, take the dishes, take the dishes, I'll take care of the silver! Ozzie, be careful. Don't try to carry three things off at once, here, you let me—

(*There is a startled outcry from Ozzie and a crash of broken china. Mrs. Critchfield screams in agony.*)

MRS. CRITCHFIELD: Oh, my good— *Ooooh!*

LILA (*with fatalistic calm*): She broke another piece of the Havilland.

MRS. CRITCHFIELD: Get out of here, you trifling nigger, get on back to the kitchen.

OZZIE: Yes'm, Mizz Critchfield.

LILA (*calling*): What happened in there?

MRS. CRITCHFIELD: She broke another piece of the Havilland.

LILA (*sotto voce*): It's no wonder. The way she devils that girl would drive a saint to distraction. (*She rubs her forearms.*) It's chilly, I've got goose pimples— (*She takes a few more stitches.*) Somebody must be walking over my grave . . .

(*Mrs. Critchfield charges into the front room. She stands stage center, her eyes shooting Olympian bolts at her husband's*) *oblivious figure. She suddenly swoops down on him like a predatory hawk and snatches the newspaper from his hands.*)

MRS. CRITCHFIELD: Yes, to you it's a matter of complete indifference!

OLIVER: What the Sam Hill—!

MRS. CRITCHFIELD: No, Oliver, I shouldn't annoy you! I should go right on bearing the whole intolerable burden just as I've done the past twenty-three or four years.

LILA: Why don't you let him digest his dinner?

MRS. CRITCHFIELD: There are some things more important than digestion.

LILA: That's a matter of opinion.

MRS. CRITCHFIELD: You probably wouldn't think so. But I'm not willing nor able to bury my head in the sand like an ostrich when my daughter's whole future is at stake!

OLIVER: What's the matter with Heavenly?

MRS. CRITCHFIELD: It's high time you asked that question. Oliver, I've deliberately shouldered the whole thing myself because of your disinclination to accept any responsibility and also because of your health—

LILA: Stop carping on Oliver's health.—He's gone through the Memphis clinic this morning, and there's not a thing wrong with him except nervous stomach.

MRS. CRITCHFIELD: Oh! Well. Is this true?

(*Oliver clears his throat uneasily.*)

You didn't mention it to me? You didn't think it was necessary to relieve my mind of all the anxiety I've had to suffer because of your constant complaints?

LILA: I guess he wanted to break it to you gently. (*She switches on the radio.*)

MRS. CRITCHFIELD: But from what Dr. Gray said—

LILA: Dr. Gray said nothing. He never says anything except, "How's your bowels!"

MRS. CRITCHFIELD: Please! Will you turn that radio off?— There's something I've got to discuss seriously with Oliver, something that— (*Her voice breaks.*)

LILA (*rising*): Mind if I take the comics? (*She winks at him and crosses offstage.*)

MRS. CRITCHFIELD (*with extreme acidity as Lila closes the door*): It is sometimes difficult to believe that your sister comes of a genteel family. I suppose Heavenly's lack of principles is not entirely her fault.

OLIVER: If you mean she's a Critchfield, Ezzie, that's nothing to her discredit.—Whatever the girl has done or hasn't, I'm pretty sure it can't be as serious as your hysteria would make a person suppose.

MRS. CRITCHFIELD: Oh, no, it's nothing serious when a girl is being talked about by the whole town!

OLIVER (*a little anxious*): Talked about, eh? I should consider it much more serious if she wasn't being talked about. (*There is a pause while he goes about filling his pipe.*)

MRS. CRITCHFIELD: Leave that pipe alone and listen to what I'm saying!—You've adopted that humorous tone too often in dealing with your child's problems.—This time it won't do.

OLIVER: All right, Esmeralda! When you've told me the cause of Heavenly's disgrace I'll be in a much better position to adopt a suitable tone of voice. What's she done this time?

MRS. CRITCHFIELD: For quite a while I've heard rumors—little insinuations—about Heavenly and that trifling boy she's been going with.

OLIVER: Richard Miles?

MRS. CRITCHFIELD: Yes! I chose to ignore it because I thought my daughter was above such things. Well, now I've discovered that I was mistaken.

OLIVER: Discovered what?

MRS. CRITCHFIELD: This afternoon right here in this room she came to me with the horrible, disgusting confession that— Oh. I don't know how I've managed to keep my senses.

OLIVER (*alarmed*): What in tarnation are you driving at? What confession? Esmeralda!

(*The sound of a car stopping is heard.*)

MRS. CRITCHFIELD (*in a sudden flurry*): Get those things out of here, those papers, your coat, your shoes! It's Arthur Shannon!—We'll finish this talk upstairs!

OLIVER: Good Lord!

(*He belches and rubs his stomach. He crosses the room. Mrs. Critchfield hastily snatches up various articles, arranges sofa pillows and changes the position of her antique chair. She switches on the little museum light over Colonel Wayne's portrait and then rushes out. Arthur enters first. His manner is markedly different from the first scene. His continental poise is lost, and he is awkward as an adolescent. He goes to the radio on which the roses are placed. Heavenly enters.*)

HEAVENLY (*removing her hat*): Lord, I'm glad to get this off! Arthur, I have a marvelous idea for a new spring hat. I'm going to pin a couple of roses on Aunt Lila's purple silk parasol. (*She crosses to Arthur.*) Oh, aren't they lovely! How did you know that talisman roses are my favorite flowers?

ARTHUR: Are they? I thought all girls preferred orchids.

HEAVENLY: I hate orchids.

ARTHUR: Hate them! Why?

HEAVENLY: Oh, I've seen 'em at debuts in Memphis and the girls that wear 'em are always those money-snobs who give you a look that peels the gilt off your slippers and puts ten years on your formal.

ARTHUR: Possibly if you wore one yourself you might overcome that aversion.

HEAVENLY: Yes. Possibly. Orchids are seen around here about as often as Haley's Comet. Gosh, me with an orchid! I wouldn't know what to do with it! I'd probably go parading up and down Front Street, holding it over my head and singing "The Star-spangled Banner"! (*She seats herself on the sofa.*)

ARTHUR: Or you might wear it to Lamphrey's tomorrow night.

HEAVENLY (*springing up breathlessly*): Ahthuh!

ARTHUR: It was just an impulse. They weren't available at Mr. Cutrere's so I ordered one from Memphis.

HEAVENLY: You dahling! (*She hugs him.*) I'm—I'm completely flabbergasted! I'm so excited I could bust!

ARTHUR: I guess I should've surprised you with it, but when you said you hated orchids I was afraid you might be really allergic to them or something and so I—

HEAVENLY: Oh, no—no! I *love* orchids, I'm *crazy* about them! Gosh, me with an orchid! From Memphis? Won't that create a sensation! Oh, I can just see it in the society column— "Miss Heavenly Critchfield lived up to her name last night in a divine white creation with a regal orchid pinned to her shoulder!"

ARTHUR: What's a "divine white creation"?

HEAVENLY: Oh, that's my white organdy— Mrs. Dowd, the society reporter, thinks it's divine because it's so damned everlasting. I graduated in it about five years ago, and it's been getting more divine ever since till now it's about fit to be worn as a nightshirt by Jesus! Wait a minute, will you? (*She flies out of the room and is heard on the stairs—*) Mothuh! Aunt Lila! What do you think?

(*The upstairs door slams on her exuberant voice. Arthur goes hastily to the mantle mirror where he adjusts his tie and combs his hair; in a moment, Heavenly re-enters with two Coke bottles.*)

Mothuh was just tickled silly and so was Aunt Lila. I thought maybe I could get a new pahty dress to go with it but nothing doing. I've got to wear God's nightie. You'll have a Coke with me, won't you? (*She exits through the rear door.*)

ARTHUR: A what?

HEAVENLY (*from offstage*): A Coca-Cola. Don't you know? It's a new kind of drink.

ARTHUR: No, thank you.

HEAVENLY (*re-entering*): Why not?

ARTHUR: I never touch stimulants after six-thirty, especially when I'm not sleeping well.

HEAVENLY (*drinking rapidly from the bottle*): Haven't you been sleeping well?

ARTHUR: No. Not lately.

HEAVENLY: Oh, that's a shame. (*She returns to sofa, finishes one bottle and starts on the second.*) What shall we talk about?

ARTHUR (*uncomfortably*): Well, I—don't know!

HEAVENLY (*giggling*): You know what mother said to me before we went out? She said, "Heavenly, you must try to choose intelligent subjects of conversation so that Arthuh won't get bored!" What do you think of that, Arthur? (*She takes another long gulp.*)

ARTHUR: I think it was quite unnecessary.

HEAVENLY: Yes. So do I. Because I really don't know any intelligent subjects of conversation. (*She laughs.*) I asked Mothuh what she meant and she said, "Oh, books and things!" I said, "Well, I know what books are but what's things?" And that made her furious, she turned as red as a lobster, and Aunt Lila and I both nearly died laughing— She called me an ignoramus! Which is perfectly true . . .

ARTHUR: I don't think it is.

HEAVENLY: Ah! That's terribly chivalrous of you. (*She finishes the second bottle, then leans back on the sofa.*) I feel like music tonight. Music and dancing. I hope we'll have fun at the Lamphrey's, don't you?

ARTHUR: Yes.

(*There is a constrained pause.*)

HEAVENLY: What are you thinking about?

ARTHUR: Pardon?

HEAVENLY: I said what are you thinking about.

ARTHUR (*very uncomfortable*): Oh—things.

HEAVENLY (*with a slightly derisive smile*): Books and things?

ARTHUR: No.

HEAVENLY: Just books?

ARTHUR: No.

HEAVENLY: Oh! Just *things*. That's nice. I wish I could think about things.

ARTHUR: Can't you? (*Heavenly shakes her head.*) Why not? (*Heavenly shrugs.*)

HEAVENLY: It's a wasted effort. It's a lot easier just to feel things and it's a lot more fun.

ARTHUR: Feeling some things isn't fun.

HEAVENLY: No, of cou'se not. But thinking about them doesn't help them any.

ARTHUR: Seems to me we're getting a little metaphysical here.

HEAVENLY (*wide-eyed*): What's that?

ARTHUR: Metaphysical?

HEAVENLY: Yes.

ARTHUR: It's sort of— dealing with insubstantial matters.

HEAVENLY: Oh. Like books and things. (*She laughs.*)

ARTHUR: I always have a rather uncomfortable feeling when you laugh that way.

HEAVENLY: Why?

ARTHUR: I suppose you'd call it a sort of—atavistic emotion.

HEAVENLY: A what?

ARTHUR (*confused*): Nothing.

HEAVENLY: Oh—nothing. (*She smiles almost mockingly and lowers her eyes.*) Look. It's a bunny-rabbit. (*She has twisted her white handkerchief into the semblance of a long-eared rabbit's head.*) It's wiggling its ears at you. It says "Shame on Ahthuh fo' usin' such long words!" (*She laughs.*) It says, "If I went to school at Oxfo'd I'd be sma't too an' use big words, but I'm just a dumb little bunny that doesn't know anything but how to wiggle its ears an' eat grass!" (*Slowly, dreamily she shakes the handkerchief out—she smiles sadly and shakes her head.*) Poor bunny! He's all disappeared —he's just a little white hankie now. But he still smells nice. (*She lifts it delicately to her nostrils, glancing provocatively at Arthur from under her dark lashes.*) He smells like dead rose leaves. Mmmm. Aunt Lila makes your talisman roses into sachets when they're withered an' puts 'em in our handkerchief boxes—gives 'em such a sad, sweet smell. (*She smiles.*) Like old maids' memories, that's what it reminds me of! (*She sniffs the cloth delicately once more, and then smooths it thoughtfully on her lap. Suddenly she raises her face to Arthur's with a look of startling intensity.*) I'd rather die than be an old maid! (*Pause for emphasis.*)

ARTHUR: Surely that's not a possibility!

HEAVENLY (*intensely*): Oh, yes it is. All the boys go No'th or East to make a livin' unless they've got plantations. And that leaves a lot of girls sitting out on the front porch waitin' fo' the afte'noon mail. Sometimes it stops comin'. And they're still sitting out there on the swing in their best white dresses, smilin' so hard it's a wonder they don't crack their faces—so people across the street won't know what's happened! "Isn't it marvelous weather? The sky's so perfectly blue! Mother and I put up six quarts of blackberry jam last night!"—*Oh, God!*— (*She rises quickly and walks over to the French window.*) That's why girls like me act so silly, Ahthuh, like music an' dancing instead of books and things, because we're scared inside, so scared it makes us feel sick at the stomach—

ARTHUR: Scared of what?

HEAVENLY: Of sitting out there forever on the front porch in our best dresses!

ARTHUR: That's quite understandable in the case of some girls.

HEAVENLY: But not in mine?

ARTHUR: Certainly not.

HEAVENLY: Thanks. But you don't know.

ARTHUR: Know what?

HEAVENLY: I made a mistake.

ARTHUR: In what way?

HEAVENLY: I—I loved the wrong boy.

ARTHUR: Oh.—You still do?

HEAVENLY: Yes. And now—

ARTHUR: Now?

HEAVENLY (*desperate fear showing in her face*): Now he's trying to break away—he wants to work on the river! He'd like to get rid of me now!

ARTHUR: Has he said so?

HEAVENLY: No, but I can feel it coming. (*She smiles bitterly.*) Oh, my! (*She turns to the window, parts the curtains, and looks out with her back to Arthur. He looks at her, troubled, confused, his hands clenched.*) —I don't know why I should bother you with all this! (*She laughs.*) It's not your affair! (*She turns slowly back to him.*) It's starting to rain again— it makes such a sleepy sound I can hardly keep my eyes open. . . . (*She has returned to the sofa, draws her feet under her, and leans back provocatively. She looks at Arthur from under her lashes with a very slight smile.*) I hope that Mothuh doesn't come in. I'm not in what you would call a very ladylike position. However I'm too comfortable to care. (*She allows one arm to slip languidly from the sofa, fingers trailing the floor.*)

ARTHUR (*clears his throat and rises*): Heavenly, I—

HEAVENLY: What?

(*He has started toward her and then, as if frightened, draws back. He mechanically removes a small book from his pocket.*)

ARTHUR: I wanted to give you this.

HEAVENLY: What is it?

ARTHUR: A book of modern verse.

HEAVENLY (*in a tone of final despair*): Oh.

ARTHUR: It's an autographed first edition of Humphrey Hard-castle.

HEAVENLY: Oh.

ARTHUR: There's just a short passage I marked last night.

HEAVENLY: Oh.

ARTHUR (*fumbling in an agony of embarrassment through the pages*): Here it is.

HEAVENLY (*sadly*): Please commence the reading.

ARTHUR: It's called "Apostrophe to a Dead Lover!"

HEAVENLY: It sounds so 't of spooky.

(*Arthur springs up violently and flings the book to the floor.*)

HEAVENLY: What's the matter?

ARTHUR (*choked*): Nothing! I don't know. I'm in a state of confusion! (*He crosses the room a few steps.*) I guess you think I'm a pretty queer sort of person. I am. I was brought up in a school for problem children, I've never had any normal relations with people. I want what I'm afraid of and I'm afraid of what I want so that I'm like a storm inside that can't break loose! Do you see?

HEAVENLY: No, not quite. (*She smiles at his back.*)

ARTHUR (*sharply*): Why are you laughing at me?

HEAVENLY: I wasn't.

ARTHUR: You were—I could see you in the mirror!

HEAVENLY: I was only smiling a little.

ARTHUR: You smile like that a great deal. You used to smile that way when I knew you in grade school.

HEAVENLY: Can you remember me that long ago?

ARTHUR: Yes. Very clearly. Especially the way that you smiled.

HEAVENLY: I didn't know my smile was that hard to forget.

ARTHUR: Ordinarily it might not be. But I was sensitive.

HEAVENLY: You mean you thought I was making fun of you?

ARTHUR: I knew that you were.

HEAVENLY: I don't remember.

ARTHUR: Don't you remember that afternoon when a bunch of them cornered me in the recess yard and kept yelling "sissy" at me until I cried? You stood there laughing at me. I never forgot that afternoon. That was something I never got over. It wasn't the boys yelling sissy that hurt me so much. It was you—you standing there laughing at me the way you were laughing a minute ago when I caught your face in the mirror. That laugh, that was why I couldn't go back to school anymore—so they had to send me to Europe and say that I'd had a nervous breakdown.

HEAVENLY: You mean that was all on my account?

ARTHUR: Yes. On account of you.

HEAVENLY: Then I should think you would hate me.

ARTHUR: I did. I hated you.

HEAVENLY: You still do? Now?

ARTHUR: Yes. You don't get over things like that. When I saw you again this spring for the first time in thirteen years it was exactly the same. It started all over again.

HEAVENLY: You mean that afternoon at your mother's reception?

ARTHUR: Yes. When I came downstairs and saw you standing in the hall looking up at me with that politely contemptuous smile of yours—it was the same exactly—all you needed was a white hair ribbon and a handful of jacks!

HEAVENLY: You turned and went back upstairs.

ARTHUR: You must've been awfully amused.

HEAVENLY: I was. At Mothuh's disappointment.

ARTHUR: The next morning I called Cutrere's. Had them send you a dozen roses without any name.

HEAVENLY: What did you do that for?

ARTHUR: I don't know. Everything that I've done since then has been done by compulsion. If you only knew the heroic effort it took for me to ask you to the country club that first time.

HEAVENLY: Your voice sounded funny over the phone.

ARTHUR: I had butterflies in my throat. At lunch I kept dropping the silver.

HEAVENLY: I thought you were sick.

ARTHUR: I was.

HEAVENLY: But if I made you so miserable why did you want to be with me?

ARTHUR: You don't know much about psychology.

HEAVENLY: No.

ARTHUR: The reason I hated you was that I loved you.

HEAVENLY: *Loved* me?

ARTHUR: Yes.

HEAVENLY: I don't see how that's possible. You couldn't love anybody that you hated.

ARTHUR: Oh, yes, you could. Very easily. Strindberg says "It's called love-hatred and it hails from the pit!"

HEAVENLY: I don't know anything about Strindberg, but it doesn't sound practical to me. How could you be in love at that age?

ARTHUR: Thirteen's old enough. Of course, there wasn't anything consciously sexual about it.

HEAVENLY: I should hope not.

ARTHUR: I think you can love more at that age than any time afterwards. At least it's the hardest to get over.

HEAVENLY: But you *have* gotten over it *now*?

ARTHUR: Of course I haven't.

HEAVENLY: You mean you still—?

ARTHUR: Yes. More than ever.

HEAVENLY (*crossing to the sofa*): I don't believe you. What you want is to have your revenge. Once you got me you wouldn't want me anymore. You'd leave me cold.

ARTHUR: No!

HEAVENLY: Yes, that's it. Whether you know it or not that's how it would be. No. Thanks! I'd rather take a chance on Dick. At least he's honest. It's none of your psychological business—we're really in love!

ARTHUR: Heavenly— (*He moves uncertainly toward her.*)

HEAVENLY: You'd better go now. I've got another engagement.

ARTHUR: Who with? Richard Miles?

HEAVENLY: Yes.

ARTHUR (*with childish cruelty*): I've heard about you and him.

HEAVENLY (*stiffening*): Have you?

ARTHUR: Yes. People have told me.

HEAVENLY: Who's told you what? That long-nosed mother of yours?

ARTHUR: You don't have to insult my mother.

HEAVENLY: I don't like having people gossip about my business.

ARTHUR: My mother's never mentioned your name.

HEAVENLY: Oh, hasn't she? I've heard different.

ARTHUR: You've heard that she gossips about you?

HEAVENLY: Yes. (*Her voice breaks.*) They all do.

ARTHUR: If he was the right kind he wouldn't expose you to that sort of thing. He'd respect you too much.

HEAVENLY: He didn't seduce me if that's what you mean. He didn't have to. I wanted him as much as he wanted me.

ARTHUR (*pausing*): We're being childish, both of us. Deliberately hurting each other. It doesn't matter about you and that boy. I've had an affair myself with a girl in London.

HEAVENLY: One of those intellectual affairs?

ARTHUR: No. Quite the opposite.

HEAVENLY: That's sort of hard to imagine.

ARTHUR: Why is it hard to imagine?

HEAVENLY (*smiling cruelly*): Why? I can't explain why.

ARTHUR: STOP IT! (*He raises his hands to his ears, then lowers them slowly.*) Don't smile at me that way!

HEAVENLY: Why did you cover your ears?

ARTHUR: I could hear them—yelling sissy at me—in the yard . . .

HEAVENLY: Oh.

MRS. CRITCHFIELD (*in the hall*): Heavenly, dear!

HEAVENLY (*sotto voce*): It's Mother. Please go now. She'll keep us forever and I've got to meet Dick.

(*Arthur doesn't move.*)

Will you please go?

MRS. CRITCHFIELD (*appearing in the hall with pitcher of lemonade*): Heavenly, I'm going to drop these glasses! Ahthuh, how are you? Mmmm. (*She purrs dotingly as she extends her hand.*) I thought you young people might enjoy a little refreshment. It's just lemonade. (*She giggles foolishly and then notices the empty Coca-Cola bottles.*) Oh, dear, you've already had drinks?

HEAVENLY: I had a Coke. Ahthuh didn't want any.

MRS. CRITCHFIELD: Of course Ahthuh didn't. He's got too much sense to poison himself with that stuff. I've heard it's habit-forming. (*She sets down the pitcher.*). Heavenly, there's a little plate of Aunt Lila's gingerbread cookies on the kitchen table. And you might bring in a few napkins, dear.

HEAVENLY: Yes, mother. (*She crosses quickly out of the room.*)

MRS. CRITCHFIELD (*sitting with a benign purr*): How is Mrs. Shannon?

ARTHUR (*also sitting*): Quite well, thank you.

MRS. CRITCHFIELD: That's good!—Mmmm—I suppose she must have told you about the honor that she received last week?

ARTHUR: An honor?

MRS. CRITCHFIELD: Oh, my *yes*—yes, *indeed*! She was elected Vice-Regent of the D.A. *Ahhh!* I was so pleased when her papers went through. We need women of your mother's caliber so badly in our patriotic societies. I happen to be serving as Regent this year. I've served twice before in that capacity and once as Advisory Regent and once as Sergeant-at-Arms! Mmmm. Club-work is so absorbing. It makes one neglect other things. Such as books. What do you think of the works of James Fenimore Cooper?

ARTHUR (*absently*): Pardon?

MRS. CRITCHFIELD: James Fenimore Cooper—what do you think of his works?

ARTHUR: Oh, yes—yes, indeed!

MRS. CRITCHFIELD (*brightly*): Do you? I wondered if you did!

ARTHUR: Yes. . . .

MRS. CRITCHFIELD: Yes. . . .

(*There is a constrained silence. Mrs. Critchfield clears her throat and looks uneasily toward the rear door.*)

MRS. CRITCHFIELD: Pardon me a moment. I think Heavenly must be having some trouble in the kitchen.

(*Arthur rises as she goes out.*)

MRS. CRITCHFIELD (*from offstage*): Heavenly, dear! Where *are* you, dear?

(*A terrible silence. She is heard running upstairs calling her daughter's name above. Arthur stands waiting in nervous*

misery till Mrs. Critchfield re-enters the room. She is com-
pletely unstrung by Heavenly's shocking flight, but with the
invincible spirit of Colonel Wayne she resolves to carry it off as
bravely as she is able, giving Arthur her most brilliant smile,
a little tremulous at the corners.)

Oh, dear, I'm afraid that Heavenly won't be able to come
back in. The poor child is just prostrated and so I told her
to go right on up to her bed and let me give you her ex-
cuses, Arthur. She didn't want to but when I saw how ill
she was looking I—I just insisted! I told her that I was sure
you would excuse her since she was feeling so badly.

ARTHUR (*embarrassed*): Certainly, I—I'm dreadfully sorry.
(*He moves toward the door.*) I hope it's nothing serious.

MRS. CRITCHFIELD: Oh, no, nothing serious, Arthur. She has
such a nervous stomach, poor child. We call it the curse of
the Critchfields.

ARTHUR: Oh. Please give her my sympathy. And tell her I
hope she'll be well enough to go to the lawn party tomorrow.

MRS. CRITCHFIELD: Oh, she will! Arthur, I'm sure she will.
Her nerves are just a little unstrung you know. She needs
rest—I'll tell her that you excused her, Arthur.

ARTHUR: Thank you, Mrs. Critchfield.—Good night.

(*Arthur turns and goes into the hall. Mrs. Critchfield follows*
him.)

MRS. CRITCHFIELD: Good night, Arthur. Give your mother
my love. Tell her I do hope she'll be at the meeting tomorrow. Good night, Arthur. Good night—

(*The door is heard closing. Mrs. Critchfield comes slowly back*
into the living room with the brilliant, artificial smile still set
on her face, her hand still raised in a parting gesture. The
hand slowly falls and clasps her bosom. She simpers foolishly to
herself, then gazes helplessly about the room. She lifts her hands
to her lips with a breathless gasp, then her face puckers
grotesquely and she begins to cry like a child as—)

The Curtain Falls.

SCENE THREE

It is later that night. The stage is dark. Moonlight shines inter-
mittently through the French window. Heavenly enters from the
hall in pajamas. She walks slowly up to Colonel Wayne's portrait
and speaks to it in a low voice.

HEAVENLY: Colonel Wayne! I'm sorry for what I said. I didn't
mean it. I want you to forgive me! Please excuse me for dis-
gracing your name!—If that's what I've done. I don't want
to disgrace it—not any more than I have to. You know that
as well as I do, Colonel Wayne! So please don't blame me
too much! . . . I'm in an awful fix. I don't know what to
do! . . . So why don't you come down off your horse and
tell me instead of lookin' so big and important up there?

(*A light goes on in the hall. Mr. Critchfield enters in his dress-*
ing robe.)

MR. CRITCHFIELD: Who's in there? Chicken?
HEAVENLY: Yes.
MR. CRITCHFIELD: What are you doing down here at three
o'clock in the morning? I thought I heard you talking to
somebody.
HEAVENLY: I was.
MR. CRITCHFIELD: Who was it? Who did you have in here at
this hour? (*He turns on a table lamp.*)
HEAVENLY: Colonel Wayne.
MR. CRITCHFIELD: What?
HEAVENLY: Colonel Wayne! I was apologizing to him.
MR. CRITCHFIELD: Good Lord! (*He smiles a little.*) It's a long
time since I heard you do that.
HEAVENLY: It's a long time since I told him to go back to
Gettysburg.
MR. CRITCHFIELD: Did you?
HEAVENLY: Yes. Mother and I had a fight this afternoon.
Didn't she tell you?
MR. CRITCHFIELD: Yes. We had a long talk tonight.
HEAVENLY: About—me?
MR. CRITCHFIELD: Yes. About you.
HEAVENLY: Dad, I— What's that you're drinking?
MR. CRITCHFIELD: Whiskey and soda. For my nerves.

HEAVENLY: I'd like to have one, too.

MR. CRITCHFIELD: Well—Heavenly, I—

HEAVENLY: Where is it? Behind the flour bin?

MR. CRITCHFIELD: You're psychic. (*She goes out to the kitchen; he calls to her.*) The soda's in the Frigidaire.

HEAVENLY (*calling*): Yes, I know. (*In a moment she returns with a drink.*) You know, Daddy, this is the first drink we've ever had together.

MR. CRITCHFIELD: Yes, so it is. (*She sits on the sofa beside him.*)

HEAVENLY: It's stopped raining. The moon is coming out. (*She draws up her feet and leans against him.*) Daddy, are you very worried about me?

MR. CRITCHFIELD: Naturally I'm a little disturbed. But I'm not going to cross-examine you about your love affairs. I guess your mother's done plenty of that.

HEAVENLY: Everything's going to turn out all right. Dick's going to work for Mr. Kramer, and we're going to get married this summer. So there's nothing to worry about.

MR. CRITCHFIELD (*ruefully shaking his head*): Chicken, chicken! Are you absolutely sure that you aren't talking through your little spring bonnet?

HEAVENLY (*hiding her face on his shoulder*): No! I'm not!

MR. CRITCHFIELD (*stroking her head*): Not even a little bit?

HEAVENLY (*abruptly straightening*): Daddy! (*She looks at him with desperate pleading.*) Why is everything so crazy, so mixed up!? Why can't people be happy together? Why can't they want the same things, instead of—fighting and torturing and—hating each other—even when they're in love?!!

(*Mr. Critchfield gazes sadly, reflectively at the glittering ice in his glass.*)

MR. CRITCHFIELD: I guess those things are sort of natural phenomena. Like these spring storms we've been having. They do lots of damage. Bust the levees, wash out the bridges, destroy property and even kill people. What for? I don't know. (*He drains his glass and puts it on the table.*) I s'pose they're just the natural necessary parts of the changing season. . . . I'm getting sleepy.

HEAVENLY: Me, too. Let's tell Colonel Wayne good night!

(*Mr. Critchfield switches off the table lamp.*)

MR. CRITCHFIELD (*with grave humor*): Honey, the Colonel and I haven't been on speakin' terms for about twenty years!

(*He puts his arm about her as they go out.*)

Slow lights down—end of Act Two

ACT THREE

SCENE ONE

This scene should follow the dramaturgic pattern of Act One, starting lightly and rising through an emotional crescendo that culminates in the fight between Dick and Arthur and the outbreak of the storm.

The scene is the Lamphrey's lawn party. We are shown a secluded corner of the big lawn—a summer house or an arbor. Japanese lanterns are strung overhead and the set is backed by a trellis covered with flowering vines. In a prominent place is a small fountain with a little statue of Eros. Beside it is a stone bench, and at the right a punch stand with a cut-glass bowl and cups. For a touch of humor, the white-coated Negro servant is asleep, seated directly beneath the statue of Eros. The stringed orchestra from Memphis is playing. It stops—there is laughter and applause. In a moment Mrs. Lamphrey and three chaperones appear from the right.

MRS. DOWD: What do they call it? The Bag?

MRS. BUFORD: No, the Shag! I think it's horrid, don't you?

MRS. DOWD: I fail to see anything graceful about it. Now the old-fashioned cakewalk required some real skill in dancing—

MRS. LAMPHREY: Jackson! Wake up!

JACKSON: Yes'm, Mizz Lamphrey! Did I miss de contes'?

MRS. LAMPHREY: Yes, it's just over.

JACKSON: Doggone.

MRS. LAMPHREY: Pour the ladies some punch.

MRS. BUFORD: Oh, your moonvines are out.

MRS. LAMPHREY: Yes, everything's early this spring.

MRS. DOWD: So early.

MRS. ADAMS: Even Heavenly Critchfield's white organdy has come out a little earlier than usual this year.

MRS. BUFORD: It's fortunate that Esmeralda's so clever with the needle.

MRS. ADAMS: I don't believe they've bought a stitch of new clothes in five years.

MRS. BUFORD: What *are* their circumstances?

MRS. ADAMS: Desperate! Walter's been forced to discontinue their account.

MRS. BUFORD: Goodness!

MRS. LAMPHREY: They've been blacklisted for years by the Merchants' Credit Association.—It's a miracle to me how they're able to keep going. Mrs. Dowd— (*She offers her a glass.*)

MRS. DOWD: Thank you.

MRS. BUFORD: I pity Esmeralda but I've got no sympathy for Heavenly Critchfield.

MRS. ADAMS: She made a disgusting exhibition of herself.

MRS. LAMPHREY: Extremely!—Jackson, don't fill the glasses so full, they splash over.

MRS. ADAMS: Kicking up her skirts like a carnival dancer!

MRS. DOWD: Of course she's quite young—

MRS. ADAMS: Young nothing! She's twenty-three or four.

MRS. DOWD: And with such a fine old family as the Waynes and the Critchfields—

MRS. ADAMS: She'll be ostracized, mark my word! Not a decent boy in town'll be seen with her. She'll end up sitting on a front porch.

MRS. BUFORD: Or going with drummers!

MRS. DOWD: Well, at present the Shannon boy seems to be quite devoted.

MRS. LAMPHREY: I wonder how Mrs. Shannon feels about that?

MRS. ADAMS: Strongly opposed, of course. (*Sotto voce.*) Have you heard what Tom Newby told his mother this morning about what he saw at Moon Lake?

MRS. LAMPHREY: Goodness, no! What?

MRS. ADAMS: Heavenly and the Miles boy were seen coming out of a tourist cabin—

MRS. LAMPHREY: Tourist cabin!

MRS. ADAMS: Yes, at about two o'clock this morning!

MRS. LAMPHREY: Why didn't you tell me before? Oh, my Lord!

MRS. DOWD: I think it's unfair to repeat that kind of gossip.

MRS. ADAMS: It's been substantiated. And of course I've thought right along—

MRS. LAMPHREY: Oh, I did, *too.* But after *this*!

MRS. ADAMS: I think some definite measures should be taken to express our feelings. After all she's associating with our sons and daughters.

MRS. LAMPHREY: Oh, my goodness, yes! Susan has very little to do with her but *still*—

MRS. ADAMS: I've warned Henry.

MRS. BUFORD: Annabelle and John Dudley dropped her in high school. They say she's so uppity and independent that—

MRS. DOWD: Mrs. Lamphrey!

MRS. LAMPHREY: Yes?

MRS. DOWD: Such delicious punch!

MRS. ADAMS: Oh, yes, isn't it though? Are those rain clouds?

MRS. LAMPHREY: If it does rain, we'll simply move the pahty indoors.

MRS. BUFORD: Look! She's coming across the lawn with your son.

MRS. ADAMS (*alarmed*): Henry?

MRS. LAMPHREY: And Arthur Shannon!

MRS. BUFORD: I wouldn't be surprised if—

MRS. LAMPHREY: Shhh!

(*Heavenly enters with Arthur and Henry. The men are in tuxedos. Heavenly is a radiant dream-like vision in her white organdy under the soft-colored lanterns and with the background of poignant string music. She is bearing a frosted, candle-lit cake which she has just won at the dance.*)

HEAVENLY: Oh, I'm still out of breath! Hank, did you get the cake knife?

HENRY: You bet.

HEAVENLY: Thanks. Hello. (*To the ladies in general.*) Can't I offer you a slice, Mrs. Lamphrey? Mrs. Adams—Mrs. Buford—Mrs. Dowd?

(*They decline, Mrs. Dowd politely, but the others with notice-able coolness.*)

Hank, will you?

HENRY: You bet.

MRS. ADAMS (*quickly*): Henry, will you please get me my shawl from the house?

MRS. LAMPHREY: There's a wind coming up. I should have known better than to give an outdoor party at this time of year.

MRS. BUFORD: Such peculiar weather! Torrential rains and days like midsummer! I wonder if the levee's in danger?

MRS. ADAMS: It is north of here. We've moved all our furniture upstairs and the quarters have simply cleared out. (*She turns to her son who has not moved.*) —Henry! Right away, dear!—Mrs. Buford, I want you to meet those Tupelo girls, they're lovely, so nice and *refined*!

(*Mrs. Adams, Mrs. Buford and Mrs. Lamphrey go out right.*)

MRS. DOWD (*to Heavenly*): Congratulations, dear. I enjoyed your dancing so much and your little white dress is divine. I'm going to make a special note of it in my column tomorrow! (*She kisses Heavenly quickly and goes out.*)

HEAVENLY: I don't know which I'd rather be, snubbed or pitied. (*To Jackson.*) Jackson, have you got anything in the punch?

JACKSON: No, Ma'am, Mizz Lamphrey gib me obstructions not to put in a drap.

HEAVENLY: Not even for the gentlemen?

JACKSON: Well, Mr. Lamphrey, he sez, I should keep dis bottle hid unduh de napkin case some ob de *olduh* gennulmens ast for it an'—

HEAVENLY: Give it here!

JACKSON: An' den I was to gib em a small amount an'—

HEAVENLY: Let me have it!

JACKSON: An' no more!

HEAVENLY (*wresting it from him*): I'll do the mixing myself, you might give me too much. Arthur? Oh, I forgot—you never take stimulants after six-thirty.

ARTHUR: Tonight I'll make an exception.

HEAVENLY: Marvelous!—Jackson, if you snitch on me I'll get Dick Miles to skin you alive!—Well, that's *quite* an exception! Are you planning to do some desperate deed tonight?

MRS. LAMPHREY (*offstage*): Jackson!

JACKSON: Yes'm, Mizz Lamphrey?

MRS. LAMPHREY (*appearing, nervous*): Jackson, you'll have to help clear off the table. I'm afraid it's going to rain before long and I want you to get all the linen and silver inside. Heavenly, dear, we'll leave you in chahge of the punch! (*Mrs. Lamphrey exits with Jackson.*)

(*There is a constrained silence between Heavenly and Arthur. He stands by the fountain with his back to her. She seats herself on the stone bench—suddenly laughs.*)

ARTHUR: What are you laughing at?

HEAVENLY: Oh, nothing.—I didn't think I'd ever see you after last night.

ARTHUR: Neither did I.

HEAVENLY: It was sweet of you to fo'give me. In fact it was noble.

ARTHUR: Being noble is one of my worst afflictions.

HEAVENLY: I don't think so.—I know my behavior is awful.

ARTHUR: The worst thing about your behavior is its complete inconsistency.

HEAVENLY: Yes?

ARTHUR: Last night you expressed a desperate fear of being left on a porch swing. And yet right afterwards you do things that are perfectly calculated to bring that about!

HEAVENLY: I know, I know! I'm a fool!—*Look!*

ARTHUR: What?

HEAVENLY (*softly*): It's the first lightnin' bug!

(*Pause. Music is heard.*)

HEAVENLY: Wonder what makes 'em go off and on like that? —Did you take any science courses at Oxfo'd? I took geology my third yeah at high.

ARTHUR (*coldly*): Did you really?

HEAVENLY: Yes. We used to go out on field expeditions they called 'em, collectin' fossils an' things.

ARTHUR: That must've been nice!

HEAVENLY: Yes, an' just think!—Someday we'll be fossils, too. They'll dig us up an' say, "Gosh what long legs that girl had!"—or "Didn't he have nice ears!" —An' that's all they'll know about us, I suppose.

ARTHUR: I suppose so.

HEAVENLY: It won't matter who we got married to or whether we lived to be old or died young. They won't care; it won't make any difference to them. We'll just be little marks on a piece of rock. Or maybe not even that much.— Does it make you feel sad?

ARTHUR: No.—Are you trying to make conversation?

HEAVENLY: Um-hmm.

ARTHUR: What for?

HEAVENLY: It's part of my social training.

ARTHUR: You needn't.

HEAVENLY: You're still mad about last night. I thought you accepted my apologies over the phone.

ARTHUR: I knew you were lying over the phone.

HEAVENLY: You mean about my nervous indigestion?

ARTHUR: Yes, your mother came back to me with that same ridiculous story after calling your name all over the house.

HEAVENLY: Mother's a terrible fool sometimes.

ARTHUR: I felt sorry for her. I could understand your wanting to hurt me—because after all you've done that repeatedly in the past—but it did surprise me a little that you'd be willing to cause your mother such embarrassment.

HEAVENLY: You said I was cruel before.

ARTHUR: I said unconsciously cruel. But what you did last night was on purpose.

HEAVENLY: It really wasn't on purpose. You made me so mad, what you said about Dick an' me, that when mother sent me out for the napkins—well I just kept going till I'd gotten six blocks from the house. An' then it was too late to go back so I went to meet Dick an' he took me out to Moon Lake.

ARTHUR (*coldly*): Oh.

HEAVENLY: But I didn't have any fun. I kept thinking about what I'd done all the time an' I really did feel sorry, Ahthuh. I wasn't lyin' when I told you that over the phone. —Now do you fo'give me?

ARTHUR: I don't think it particularly matters whether I forgive you or not.

HEAVENLY: I think it does. I think I should like you an awful lot if you'd just be a little more human.

ARTHUR: What is being human?

HEAVENLY: You see you don't even know!

(*Henry enters.*)

HENRY: Heavenly, can I speak to you about something?

HEAVENLY: Sure you can, honey.

HENRY: I mean alone, Heavenly.

ARTHUR: Excuse me. (*He exits stage left.*)

HEAVENLY: Gosh, Hank, you look awful serious, honey! What's wrong?

HENRY: I thought you oughta know that Tom Newby's been talking about you to people. He told his mother and she's gone an' told Mizz Lamphrey an' Mizz Lamphrey's told Fanny and—and—

HEAVENLY: Told what?

HENRY: Tom Newby said—he said he saw you an' Dick Miles comin' out of a tourist cabin last night.

HEAVENLY: Oh.

HENRY: At Moon Lake, he said, and it was two o'clock in the morning! Of cou'se I know he's lyin' but—

HEAVENLY: What if it's true? (*She speaks violently.*) Whose business is it anyhow? What right have they got to—!

HENRY: I know but some of the old ladies, I heard 'em talking when I brought Mother's shawl— Mrs. Adams, she said she thought you ought to be—ostracized! What's that?

HEAVENLY: Ostracized? Did she say that?

HENRY: Yes. Is that what they did to that—you know—that girl across the Sunflower River?

HEAVENLY: No. Honey, you run back to the dance.

HENRY: That stinkin' polecat, Newby, I'm gonna push his face in! But I thought you oughta know first.

HEAVENLY: Thanks, honey.

HENRY (*blurting this out*): Heavenly, you're—you're beautiful! I wish that I was Dick Miles! (*He goes quickly out right.*)

(*Heavenly laughs wildly.*)

ARTHUR (*returning*): What's so hilariously funny?

HEAVENLY: He wished he was Dick Miles! Oh, God, it's beautiful, isn't it? (*Then she speaks furiously.*) I'm going to tell those bitches where to head in!

ARTHUR (*catching her wrist*): Heavenly!

HEAVENLY (*quietly after a moment*): Thanks. It's good you did that. Sometimes I don't think what I'm doing.

ARTHUR: You never do. You've got the instinct for self-destruction.

HEAVENLY: Is that what it is?

ARTHUR: Yes.

HEAVENLY: I probably got it from Colonel Wayne. You know he led the charge up Cemetery Hill.

ARTHUR: And you want to do the same thing?

HEAVENLY: If I have to.

ARTHUR: Right in the teeth of their guns with the odds all against you?

HEAVENLY: Why not? I wish I was ten years younger, I'd like to kick Tom Newby so hard he couldn't sit down for a month. I did that once about ten years ago and it's given me satisfaction ever since.

ARTHUR: What's he done?

HEAVENLY: Snitched on me, same as he did last time!

ARTHUR: About what?

HEAVENLY: Oh, you'll hear soon enough. The whole town will.—(*She continues, frightened.*) Mrs. Adams said I ought to be ostracized. Do you know what that means?

ARTHUR: Yes. It's what happens to rebels.

HEAVENLY: I don't give a damn.—It's the Pink Lady Waltz! Let's dance!

ARTHUR: No.

HEAVENLY: Why not?

ARTHUR: I'm not a good dancer.

HEAVENLY: You're good enough. Come on! (*She takes his arm.*)

ARTHUR: I'd rather not dance.

HEAVENLY: Oh, you're ashamed to dance with me? It might damage your good reputation.

ARTHUR: You know it's not that.

HEAVENLY: What is it then?

ARTHUR: I'm very uncomfortable when we're dancing together.

HEAVENLY: Why are you?

ARTHUR: Sometimes it hurts a man to be close to a woman—just so close and not any closer than that.

HEAVENLY: Oh! (*Pause.*) I wouldn't expect you to say a thing like that.

ARTHUR: Why not? Isn't that part of what you call being human?

HEAVENLY: Yes. That's why it surprised me so much.

(*There is a murmur of wind and a glimmer of lighting on the cyclorama.*)

Lightning. It's going to storm.

ARTHUR: Yes. I guess that's why the Little God's so excited. —He likes spring storms.

HEAVENLY: Does he?

ARTHUR: Yes. They've so much in common, you know. They're both so damn cruel—reckless and destructive!

HEAVENLY: Like me. Is that what you mean?

ARTHUR: Yes. I believe the Greeks were laughing when they made him the Little God. Eros is really the biggest god of them all. He's the one that's got thunderbolts!

HEAVENLY: What did you call him?

ARTHUR: Pardon me! I thought that you knew each other!—This is Eros, the Little God of Love, Miss Heavenly Critchfield!

HEAVENLY: How do you do? (*She laughs.*) I've always called him Cupid.

ARTHUR: Yes, that's the usual misconception. People think he's a cute, chubby little fellow with dimples and curly locks—but they're fooling themselves because he's really a monster!

HEAVENLY: Is he?

(*The scene plays very fast from here to Dick's entrance.*)

ARTHUR: Yes. Can't you feel him breathing fire in your face?

(*The wind rises. The orchestra is playing a fast waltz.*)

HEAVENLY: No. Not in mine.

ARTHUR: You're lucky, Miss Critchfield— Luckier than I.— What're you laughing at?

HEAVENLY: At you! You make such fancy speeches!

ARTHUR: You think I'm ludicrous, don't you?

HEAVENLY: No. I think you're a fake! (*Pause.*)

ARTHUR (*quietly*): A fake?

HEAVENLY: Yes, an absolute fake!

ARTHUR: You're right. I *am* a fake. I haven't got a real bone in my body.

HEAVENLY: I know you haven't.

ARTHUR: You know it surprises me sometimes to see that I even make a shadow in the light. It's a wonder the light doesn't shine right through me like it does through a cloud of dust in the road.

HEAVENLY: That's funny—I have the same feeling about you.

ARTHUR: I know that you do. (*He crosses to her.*) But just once I'd like to touch you and make you feel I'm alive.

HEAVENLY (*away*): What?

ARTHUR: Because then maybe I *would* be alive. You could give me back what you took away from me—that afternoon when you laughed at me in the recess yard!

HEAVENLY: What I took away from you? Then?

ARTHUR: Yes! You took away everything!

HEAVENLY: Arthur—

ARTHUR: After that I wasn't real anymore.

HEAVENLY: You're drunk.

ARTHUR: No, I was just the shadow of something and that's all I've been ever since.

HEAVENLY: What could I do about that?

ARTHUR: You could—you could *love* me—make me sure again I'm alive!

HEAVENLY: Oh, I see. (*She laughs.*) You mean what Henry meant when he said he wished that he was Dick Miles— Only you dress it up in prettier speeches, don't you? Here. Take the rest of the whiskey. Go cross the Sunflower River and get yourself one of those bright-skinned women they've got over there. They're marvelous at—at proving you're alive, if that's what you're worried about!

ARTHUR: You don't understand.

HEAVENLY: Oh, yes I do.

ARTHUR: I want you to marry me, Heavenly!

HEAVENLY: What?—You didn't say that! (*Pause.*)

ARTHUR: Will you? Will you, Heavenly?

HEAVENLY (*very softly*): I don't know. I don't see how I could.

ARTHUR: You couldn't love me?

HEAVENLY: How should I know? You've never even kissed me.

ARTHUR (*importunately*): May I? Will you let me?

HEAVENLY: Oh, you're so funny, Arthur! (*She laughs.*) I gave you every chance last night an' you started to read mode'n verse.

ARTHUR: I couldn't help it!—I've always run away from things that I wanted.

HEAVENLY: I don't know what to think, what to say! Everything's going so fast!—You know I can feel the earth moving! It's going a thousand miles a minute, it's spinning round and round!

ARTHUR: That's the wind!

HEAVENLY: I know, I know, but it's making me dizzy! (*She sinks down.*)

FANNY (*offstage*): Oh, Heavenly! Heavenly!

HEAVENLY: You see how fast it's going? We can't be still for a minute! (*She answers Fanny.*) Yes?

(*Fanny enters followed by Dick Miles.*)

FANNY: Oh, here you are, still having a *tête-à-tête* with the guest of honor!—There's another gentleman to see you!

HEAVENLY: Dick!

DICK: Scuse me for bustin' in, but I got something important to talk to you about.

HEAVENLY: How could you come here like this? You look like you've been having a mud-fight!

DICK: I have! I've been rasseling the river.

FANNY: Oh, we'll excuse your appearance. (*To Heavenly.*) We all know that Dick Miles is too big for social conventions.

DICK: That's right.

FANNY (*to Arthur*): Have you all met each othuh?

ARTHUR (*coldly*): I've had the pleasure quite some time ago.

DICK: Sure. (*He grins*) Do you still read *The Wizard of Oz*?

ARTHUR (*furiously*): No. Do you still enjoy taking advantage of your—your physical superiority? Do you still—

HEAVENLY: Arthur!

FANNY: Arthur, that's my favorite piece they're playing!

ARTHUR: Excuse me. (*He goes off with Fanny.*)

HEAVENLY: Now are you satisfied? You've made a beautiful scene!

DICK: Sorry. I had to see you. This is important, honey.

HEAVENLY: Important? You couldn't tell me tomorrow?

DICK: No. I'm not going to be here tomorrow.

HEAVENLY: —What?

DICK: We're leaving town.

HEAVENLY: We? —Thanks for telling me.

DICK: I mean it this time. Absolutely no doggin'. I been to Friar's Point—that's where I picked up this mud I got on me. (*He places his hands on her shoulders.*) Heavenly, I've got a job on the Government levee project.

HEAVENLY: No!

DICK: I've already signed the papers. I can show 'em to you.

HEAVENLY (*desperately*): No, Dick!

DICK: Huh?

HEAVENLY: You can't do a thing like that to me!

DICK: A thing like what?

HEAVENLY: You can't walk out on me, Dick!

DICK: I'm not walking out on you, honey. I'm takin' you with me.

HEAVENLY: Me? On a government levee project?

DICK: Sure, a man's allowed to be married.

HEAVENLY: Is he? I didn't know that. I thought those levee workers lived with niggers.

DICK: Heavenly—

HEAVENLY: That's what I heard. I heard they kept colored women in their shacks with them.

DICK (*disgustedly*): I knew you'd take it like that.

HEAVENLY: Dick, you've got a job here.

DICK: In the drugstore.

HEAVENLY: No. In Mr. Kramer's cotton office.

DICK: That's absolutely out. I won't take it.

HEAVENLY: Dad's made him promise. It's a sure thing.

DICK: No! I won't take it! (*He catches her shoulders.*) Honey, it takes a pair of boots and a flannel shirt to make me feel like a man. I'm sick of bath salts and spirits of ammonia. An' I wouldn't like cotton much better. Cotton's soft. It's fuzzy stuff that sticks to your fingers. I wouldn't like that. I want to get my hands on something hard and tough that fights back, like the river. When you're fighting a river you're fighting something your size. Don't you see? They've put out flood warnings up at Friar's Point. She's rose six feet since morning. Fifty-nine, that's flood stage, and God only knows when she'll stop. They're fighting like crazy to hold her back but she keeps on coming, big an' yellow an' daring 'em all to try an' make her stay put. She'll win this time maybe. Push right through their sandbags an' run 'em out of the county, tearin' down sharecroppers' houses an' drownin' the stock. If the people are lucky they'll climb on top of their roofs an' we'll take 'em off in boats. But some of 'em won't be lucky. Ole Mammies with breakbone fever ain't good at roof climbing. The river'll catch 'em at night an' they won't have a chance. But maybe next time we'll win. We'll catch her an' tame her an' make her stay in her place. That's a big job, honey, the kind of job that I want! (*Pause.*)

HEAVENLY: More than you want me? That much?

DICK: I want you and the job both.

HEAVENLY: You can't have both. I can't live like that, in a shack on the river— You can't ask me to.

DICK: Well, that's what I'm asking. You'll have to go with me or—

HEAVENLY: Oh, it's an ultimatum.

DICK: You can call it that.

HEAVENLY: In other words you're tired of me, you've had enough!

DICK: Come off your high horse!

HEAVENLY: I've still got some pride, some self-respect!

DICK: You've still got your ancestry, your marvelous ancestry! You can't forget about that!

HEAVENLY: I can't forget that I'm decent!

DICK: But you can forget Moon Lake last night, or yesterday up on the hill? You can forget those things in about twenty minutes and throw it up to me that I'm not good enough for you?

HEAVENLY: It's you that's forgetting, not me. Every spring it's the same. You get a spell like this an' later you come to your senses.

DICK: You got around me last spring. Made me stay.

HEAVENLY: Don't you remember *how* I made you stay?

DICK: Yes, I remember how.

HEAVENLY: It wasn't easy for me to do that. I thought it meant something.

DICK: It did.

HEAVENLY: Not to you or you wouldn't be throwing me over.

DICK: Honey, I'm *not* throwing you over.

HEAVENLY: You are. You're throwing me over—you want me to be like Agnes Peabody next door—a front porch girl! She sits on the front porch in her best dress and the men walk by in the evening and tip their hats and keep right on walking. People remember how she went out all the time with a boy that's left town. Now she just sits on the front porch waiting!—waiting for nothing, getting to be an old maid!—That's what you want to happen to me!

DICK: No, honey, you know better than that.

HEAVENLY: How should I know any better?

DICK: I asked you to go with me.

HEAVENLY: Yes, you asked me to go with you! And you knew damn well that I couldn't!

DICK: I knew you loved me. I mean I thought I knew you loved me.

HEAVENLY: Oh. And now you think different. You think that I've done what I've done because I'm just naturally rotten. Is that what you think?

DICK: No. Let it go.

HEAVENLY: I won't. We'll have this out now.

DICK: All right. You can do what you please but I'm goin'.

HEAVENLY (*her voice breaking*): Then it's all finished then. You can go, you don't have to come back. I'd rather sit out on a front porch the rest of my life than ever see you again. —But I won't be sitting on the front porch! I'll take Arthur! He told me he wanted me just now, before you came butting in!

DICK: Heavenly!—

HEAVENLY: Go away!

DICK: You don't want me to! Lissen, Heavenly!

HEAVENLY: No!

DICK: Have you ever spent a night on the river, honey?

HEAVENLY: Let go of me!

(*He forces her down on the bench and holds her against him.*)

DICK: Have you ever spent a night on a river barge, honey? That clean wet smell of the woods and maybe a hole in the roof you can see the stars through? Katydids hummin' an' bullfrogs off in the shallows. That dark warm smell of the water real close an' the sound that it makes that's so quiet it's sca'cely a sound, just a big, big blackness movin' around you, an' up on the deck a nigger pickin' a fiddle an' singin' an ole river song, an' that lazy soft rise an' fall of the water under the boat an' the lightnin' bugs blinkin' way off over there on the flat cotton fields or down in the cypress break an' that wild coon laughter all of a sudden comin' up out of the dark where they're makin' love on the levee— like cryin' almost—an' then not a thing anymore but that slow slappin'-slap of the water . . .

HEAVENLY: Dick—

DICK: I've spent nights like that on the river! By myself or with a bunch of fellows—but never with a girl I loved!

HEAVENLY (*breaking away*): Dick, it's impossible!

(*The wind has risen. They have to shout above it.*)

DICK (*trying to kiss her again*): No, it isn't!

HEAVENLY: Stop it!

DICK (*slowly*): You mean you won't go?

HEAVENLY (*brokenly*): You know that I couldn't stand it.

DICK: You could if you loved me.

HEAVENLY: If I loved you, if I loved you!—All that you think of is self, self, self!

DICK: It's you that don't think of anything but self!

HEAVENLY: Oh, Dick! Don't say any more tonight, please don't!

DICK: I got nothing more to say.

HEAVENLY: They're all going in the house, it's going to storm.—I can't stay out here any longer, Dick.

DICK: I'm not keeping you.

HEAVENLY (*catching his arm*): Oh, Dick—don't, don't! *Please* don't!

(*Arthur enters right.*)

ARTHUR (*drunkenly*): Heavenly, where are you, Heavenly?

DICK: What do *you* want?

ARTHUR: I want to take her inside!

DICK: You take her nowhere, Sonny. She's going with me.

HEAVENLY: Dick, don't make another scene!

ARTHUR: Why don't you leave her alone? You can't marry her, all you can do is make her talked about. (*He's in a drunken rage.*) You know what they say about the two of you—do you know?

HEAVENLY (*screaming*): Arthur! Go 'way! Go back to the house!

ARTHUR: They say she's your mistress! They say—

(*Dick knocks him down—then jerks him up, shakes him, and flings him down again—Heavenly tries to stop him.*)

HEAVENLY: Dick! You'll kill him—he's drunk!

DICK: —I didn't hurt him.

HEAVENLY (*bends over Arthur*): You did.

DICK: All right. You stay here with him. Wrap him up in tissue paper and send him back to Mama with my regards!

(*He starts off.*)

HEAVENLY (*rising*): Dick!—

DICK: Good-bye!

HEAVENLY: Call me tomorrow! You'll call me, won't you?

DICK: Good-bye, Heavenly! (*He exits.*)

(*She runs after him a short distance, calling his name wildly. She stops, sobbing aloud. As the storm breaks, she turns and runs toward the house.*

(*The Japanese lanterns flicker and sway in the wind. The cable that supports them snaps and they are blown tumbling across the stage. There is the sound of branches thrashing, a cacophony of noises from the suddenly disrupted lawn party, and, through it all, expressing the frenzied spirit of the scene, are heard the distant strains of the waltz, fast and feverishly gay. There is a crash of thunder.—Arthur rises, staggering. He goes over to the statue of Eros. He stands unsteadily before it, laughing louder and louder as the storm's fury increases— There is a vivid flash of lightning and then complete darkness.*)

The Curtain Falls

SCENE TWO

The scene is the Carnegie Public Library of Port Tyler. The set is furnished with a yellow oak desk, a table, a chair, and a newspaper and magazine rack. A green-shaded bulb is suspended over the librarian's desk and a small lamp rests on the table. Against the back wall or on the bulletin board are travel posters of "Beautiful Switzerland" and "Romantic Italy." A sign on the desk says "Quiet Please" In the middle of the back wall is an opaque glass-paned door marked "Stacks." Hertha is seated at the desk in a prim gray smock and glasses. She looks tired and strained. Enter Mrs. Kramer, a prim-looking matron.

MRS. KRAMER (*marching to the desk*): I found this book in my daughter's bedroom!

HERTHA: Yes?

MRS. KRAMER: I don't think books like this should be exposed on the shelves.

HERTHA: It happens to be a private copy of my own.

MRS. KRAMER: Well, how did she get it?

HERTHA: She saw me reading it and asked to read it herself.

MRS. KRAMER: Oh. It may be fit reading for an older person, but Dorothea's sixteen. So far I've managed to keep her mind entirely free of—of sordid things such as—

HERTHA: This book? There's nothing sordid about this book, Mrs. Kramer—nothing whatsoever!

MRS. KRAMER: Oh, isn't there? I always consult Reverend Hooker about my child's reading matter— When I showed him this book he turned directly to this passage and asked me if it was the sort of thing I wanted my child's mind infected with—here it is— (*She reads a verse of love poetry.*)

> What lips my lips have kissed, and where and why,
> I have forgotten, and what arms have lain
> Under my head till morning—

HERTHA (*snatching the book*): You can't read it like that, Mrs. Kramer!

MRS. KRAMER: No?

HERTHA (*repeating the passage with feeling*):

> What lips my lips have kissed, and where and why,
> I have forgotten, and what arms have lain
> Under my head till morning; but the rain
> Is full of ghosts tonight, that tap and sigh
> Upon the glass and listen for reply:
>
> And in my heart there stirs a quiet pain
> For unremembered lads that not again
> Will turn to me at midnight with a cry.

(*She fixes her eyes on Mrs. Kramer and recites the rest of the poem from memory.*)

> Thus in the winter stands the lonely tree,
> Nor knows what birds have vanished one by one,
> Yet knows its boughs more silent than before:
> I cannot say what loves have come and gone;
> I only know that summer sang in me
> A little while, that in me sings no more.

Now don't you like it better?

MRS. KRAMER: No. I think it's outrageous. Next time Dorothea wants a book, please give her one of the Alcott series.

HERTHA: Isn't Dorothea rather old for the Alcott series?

MRS. KRAMER (*furiously*): She's not too old for innocence, thank heavens, and she's not too young for common sense— Good night, Miss Neilson. (*She marches out.*)

(*Hertha opens the book— Music comes through the opened windows from the Lamphrey's party. Hertha closes the book, rises quickly and shuts the window. She returns slowly to the desk. After a moment, Miss Schlagmann comes out of the door marked "Stacks."*)

MISS SCHLAGMANN: Oh, it's so close in here. Why did you close that window?

HERTHA: It's going to storm.

MISS SCHLAGMANN: We might as well leave it open till it rains in. (*She goes over and raises the window. Music enters again and there is the glimmer of lightning outside.*) Listen! You can hear the music from the Lamphrey's lawn party!

HERTHA: Yes.

MISS SCHLAGMANN: They've got Japanese lanterns strung all over the place.—It looks like fairyland.

HERTHA: Yes.

MISS SCHLAGMANN: Oh, dear—young people have such a good time, don't they? How would you like to go to the movies with me next Saturday night, Hertha?

HERTHA: Thank you, but—

MISS SCHLAGMANN: It'll be my treat this time!—They have that Tyrone Power picture. And they always have the Tarzan serial.

HERTHA: Do they?

MISS SCHLAGMANN (*laughing sharply*): They're so absurd! But they *are* exciting! At the end of the last one he and the girl were locked in a dungeon with lions!— (*She laughs.*) But I suppose they'll manage to get out somehow.

HERTHA: Yes. (*She smiles slightly.*)

MISS SCHLAGMANN: They're obliged to get out. That's only the sixteenth chapter and there's supposed to be thirty-two— If they killed 'em off now they wouldn't have anything to put in the other sixteen.

HERTHA: No. Not unless they had a very elaborate funeral.

MISS SCHLAGMANN: You don't like the movies?

HERTHA: Sometimes. I liked that last one of Greta Garbo's.

MISS SCHLAGMANN: Her things are always so morbid or sordid or something!

HERTHA (*laughing*): That's twice this evening that I've been accused of having sordid predilections.

MISS SCHLAGMANN (*starting back to the "Stacks," she pauses at the desk*): Here's something *I* like—jonquils!—They're so fresh looking! (*She sniffs them delicately, then exits through the rear door.*)

(*Hertha reopens the book of poems. The muted strains of the Strauss waltz from the Lamphrey's are heard. Suddenly she throws down the book. She rushes to the window and slams it shut. She raises one hand to her lips in an almost terrified gesture, then touches her forehead and returns slowly to the desk. She clears her throat and straightens things on the desk with a furious but aimless haste— A young couple enters—Mabel and Ralph.*)

MABEL: It would have to rain.

RALPH: Jeez, what a wind's comin' up.

MABEL: I'm scared sick a' storms. Specially when it thunders. Ralph! (*She clings to him.*)

RALPH: Aw, honey, thunder can't hurtcha.

MABEL (*giggling*): She's lookin' at us.

RALPH: What do we care, huh?

HERTHA (*rising and approaching them stiffly*): This room is for reading purposes only.

RALPH: What're we doin'?

HERTHA: You're creating a disturbance.

RALPH: A disturbance, huh?

HERTHA: Yes!

RALPH: Can't we even carry on a little conversation in here?

HERTHA: Conversation, yes, but not disorderly behavior.

MABEL (*rising indignantly*): He's my fiancé!—Ralph, let's get out of this place! (*She crosses to the door.*) I'd rather get pneumonia than be bawled out by that cranky old maid!

(*As they go out Ralph laughs rudely. Hertha stands erect till they have gone—then suddenly covers her face— She quickly lowers her hands as the inner door opens and Miss Schlagmann comes back out with an armful of books.*)

MISS SCHLAGMANN: I thought I heard some loud talk in here.

HERTHA: That boy and girl were in here again. The ones that were necking in here last week.

MISS SCHLAGMANN: Oh!

HERTHA: I asked them to please be quiet and they were horribly rude to me.

MISS SCHLAGMANN: I'm going to speak to Mr. Gillam. She works there, at the hosiery counter. I think—being a vestryman of St. George's—he'd like to know how one of his salesgirls spends her free time, making a public show of herself and her common affairs.

HERTHA: No. Don't.—He might discharge her.

MISS SCHLAGMANN: He should.

HERTHA: No. It wasn't anything at all. I haven't been feeling well and they made me nervous.—They called me a—

MISS SCHLAGMANN: Called you what?

HERTHA (*averting her face*): A—cranky old maid.

MISS SCHLAGMANN (*furious*): Well, what preposterous—!

HERTHA: No, they were right! That's what I am now!

MISS SCHLAGMANN (*shocked*): Hertha! What's wrong with you child?

HERTHA (*crossing behind the desk*): Nothing. I'm nervous.

MISS SCHLAGMANN: I'm going to report this to Mr. Gillam.

HERTHA: Please don't. (*She takes a handkerchief from a drawer and turns her back.*)

MISS SCHLAGMANN: Hertha, I'm afraid you're getting run down again this spring. You'd better take a week off.

HERTHA: I'm all right. It's just nervousness. (*She turns and sits down rigidly at the desk.*) —Maybe I'm losing my mind.

MISS SCHLAGMANN: Don't be absurd!

HERTHA: Lots of girls do at my age. Twenty-eight. Lots of them get *dementia praecox* at about that age, especially when they're not married. I've read about it. They get morbid and everything excites them and they think they're being persecuted by people. I'm getting like that.

MISS SCHLAGMANN: You are not! (*She speaks gently.*) I know what's wrong with you, Hertha. It's that Shannon boy— Isn't it now?

HERTHA (*with effort*): —Yes.

MISS SCHLAGMANN: I knew that was it. You took him too seriously. I could have told you right at the start he wouldn't do anything but make you unhappy. I had him spotted. Attractive and intelligent and all that but selfish right to the core. One of these spoiled millionaire's children. They're all the same way. They think the whole earth was created for their entertainment. (*She returns several books to a shelf.*) You get him out of your mind.

HERTHA: I can't. (*She looks almost wildly about the room.*) He's the first man that ever looked at me twice. And I can't stop thinking about him. Even at night. I haven't been sleeping.

MISS SCHLAGMANN: I know you haven't. You need a change of scene.

HERTHA: Oh, no, I can't stop working!

MISS SCHLAGMANN: You can if it's necessary to stop a nervous breakdown.

HERTHA: It wouldn't help. I've got to keep busy. You see when I'm not busy I— (*She presses her hands to her temples.*) Why doesn't God have a little mercy on people like me? You go to church, Miss Schlagmann, you teach Sunday school. You ought to know. Why doesn't God have a little mercy on people like me? Ask Him that the next time you go to St. George's. Tell Him He shouldn't give homely girls the same feelings that He gives the pretty ones. Tell Him that. Tell Him it isn't fair to let the homely girls fall in love with men that don't care!

(*Miss Schlagmann makes a gesture of shocked pity; she bites her lips and fumbles at the silver cross suspended over her flat bosom.*)

MISS SCHLAGMANN (*hesitantly*): Hertha, I wish you would go with me to some of the Lenten services next week at St. George's. It's going to be Holy Week. Our Lord's Passion, you know.—Don't you suppose He went through moments like these that you're going through—when He suffered and doubted and—prepared His soul for climbing up that hill and being nailed on a cross between two thieves!

HERTHA (*slowly*): Well, if He did, He ought to know what it's like and He ought to have some pity! I can't go on living much longer in this kind of vacuum. It isn't fair to make me, it isn't fair!

MISS SCHLAGMANN: Lots of things aren't fair, but we've got to put up with them just the same. That's life.

HERTHA (*fiercely*): I'm tired of hearing people say, "That's life!"

MISS SCHLAGMANN: I know. I've been through the same thing. It's a sort of an emotional crisis that all of us have to go through that don't get married and haven't the courage for anything else. After a while it gets better. You find out that you can put those feelings into other things.

HERTHA (*bitterly*): Yes. Sublimation. Choir singing and raising petunias. I don't want that.

MISS SCHLAGMANN: Hertha!

HERTHA: There ought to be something else! (*She speaks almost to herself.*) A straight line upwards to someplace nobody's ever been yet. I told him that and he laughed, Arthur did. He said I meant 'Paradise'—but I didn't. I don't know what I meant.—Why doesn't your fashionable Episcopal minister at St. George's try to figure that out instead of worrying about how he's going to finance the new pipe organ?

MISS SCHLAGMANN: Don't talk like that!

HERTHA: I know, I know. I ought to keep my mouth shut. That's what's expected of me. But I can't anymore. I'm sick of it.

(*Agnes Peabody enters.*)

MISS SCHLAGMANN: It's Agnes Peabody. You'd better go in the back room.

HERTHA (*turning to the shelves*): No. I'll be all right.

(*Miss Peabody closes the door and shakes her umbrella and comes briskly up to the desk.*)

MISS PEABODY: I know it's closing time, Birdie, but I've just got to see the new *Vogue*. I bought some of that silk print at Gillam's. They had the most marvelous sale, and—

MISS SCHLAGMANN: The new *Vogue*'s out.

MISS PEABODY (*disappointed*): Oh, is it?

MISS SCHLAGMANN: Yes. Mrs. Critchfield has it. She's using one of those patterns, too.

MISS PEABODY: Oh. Something for Heavenly, I guess. Hmmmm. I guess she's planning to sew on a trousseau this spring.

MISS SCHLAGMANN: Trousseau?

MISS PEABODY: Yes. Haven't you heard? (*Glances sharply at Hertha's back.*) I hope I'm not letting the cat out of the bag. That Arthur Shannon created such an excitement when he came back to town— I'm afraid there'll be quite a few disappointed young ladies when they make the announcement! (*She giggles shrilly.*) Did you ever see such a rain? Forty-eight hours without a let up. But that's April for you. OHH! I have a run in my stocking! Hello, Hertha.

HERTHA (*barely turning*): Good evening.

MISS PEABODY (*simpering*): You were so quiet I didn't know you were there. I've got to be running. I'm going to Memphis tomorrow. Did you see the *Commercial-Appeal*? Fifty percent reduction on furs at Hess and Williamson! Isn't that marvelous? That's where I got the muskrat cape I'm wearing with my brown tweed suit. Oh, heavens it's nearly nine! You'll save the new *Vogue* for me? —Good night!

MISS SCHLAGMANN: Good night.

MISS PEABODY (*with marvelous gaiety*): Good night, Hertha!

(*She laughs and snatches up her umbrella and darts out the door. All of her actions have that brilliant, exaggerated animation which is characteristic of some southern spinsters. Miss Schlagmann glances uneasily at Hertha's back. Hertha slowly raises another book and places it on the shelf. As she does so the clock strikes nine in a slow, gentle tone.*)

MISS SCHLAGMANN: We're half an hour late. Hertha, you go on home, you don't need to wait for me.

HERTHA (*turning slowly*): No. I'll wait till you're ready.

MISS SCHLAGMANN: All right! We'll stop in Greenbaum's and have a hot chocolate! It will help you sleep.

HERTHA (*dully*): Yes.

(*Miss Schlagmann retires to the back room and closes the door. Hertha sits down mechanically at the desk and stares in front of her. Her face has a dead expressionless look. After a moment, the outer door is pushed open and Arthur enters—he is drunk, disheveled, his flannel coat and trousers bedraggled with rain and his hair hanging over his forehead. He leans against the door and grins satirically at Hertha.*)

ARTHUR: Good evening, Miss Neilson!

HERTHA: Arthur! (*She touches her hair.*) I wasn't expecting you. You didn't call last night. (*She notices his strange appearance.*) Arthur, what's wrong with you, Arthur?

ARTHUR (*laughing*): Excuse my experience!—I've come here to show you that southern chivalry is still in flower.

HERTHA: I'm afraid you've been drinking.

ARTHUR: She's afraid I've been drinking.—You put it so tactfully, Miss Neilson. Yes, I'm drunk. You ought to try it sometime yourself. It's exciting. Makes everything look different. Even you, Miss Neilson, you look almost human tonight!

HERTHA: What have you done this for? Arthur, why have you gotten yourself in such a condition?

ARTHUR: Haven't you ever seen a drunk man before? Sure you have. Your father, the Terrible Swede, as they call him. He comes home polluted on Saturday nights, so I hear. Makes a big scene, throws things, calls you names. So what are you getting so puritanical for?

HERTHA (*stiffening*): Is that amusing to you? Are you laughing because of that?

ARTHUR (*a bit ashamed*): Sure. Everything's funny tonight. (*He rubs his forehead confusedly.*) Excuse me. Heavenly gave me some liquor and told me to go out and get drunk—so I did.

HERTHA: Heavenly Critchfield—?

ARTHUR: Yes. I told her that I was in love with her, and she said that I should go out and get drunk because that was the only thing that would do me any good. So I got drunk. It's the first time I ever got drunk in my life and it was swell. Till I started thinking about her again making love to Dick Miles.

HERTHA: Arthur! I'm sorry, I— (*She extends her hand towards him in a slight, pitying gesture.*)

ARTHUR: I can forget all that with you, can't I? You're a girl, too. You could make love as well as she could. But not with Dick Miles. With me. (*He moves toward her. Hertha steps back.*) What are you backing away for? Are you scared? That's flattering. Nobody's ever been scared of me before. I was like you, Hertha. I hid behind books all the time because they used to call me a sissy when I was a kid in school. I never got over that. Not till tonight when I got drunk. God! I never knew it could be so good to get drunk and feel like a man inside. Literature and the arts. Stravinsky, Beethoven, Brahms. Concerts, matinees, recitals —what's all that? If I told you you'd blush. You don't like that kind of language. Sure, I sat through all of that stuff and thought it was great. Got my stuff published in those little magazines with the big cultural movements. Art for art's sake. Give America back to the Indians. I thought I was being highbrow. Intellectual. The hell with that stuff. Dick Miles's got the right idea. He was the one that she gave herself to, not me, not me. The one that got drunk and had himself a good time, he was the one that got Heavenly, and me with my intellectual pretensions, my fancy education, and my father's money—what did I get? Pushed in the face! Thrown over for a boy that clerks in a drugstore because he knows how to make love and I don't! Well now I can, too. I can get drunk and act like the rest of them. How about it, Miss Neilson? Why don't you come out from behind those tortoise-shell glasses of yours? (*He reaches across the table and plucks them off.*)

HERTHA: Arthur, please go home. (*She crosses in front of the desk.*) Don't touch me!

ARTHUR (*laughing*): Don't touch you? Yes. That's it—purity! The Carnegie Vestal! (*He crosses toward her.*)

HERTHA: No! Don't touch me!

ARTHUR: Why not? It would do you some good. You with your books, your anthologies, your metaphysical poets. William Blake and John Donne. They're dead, Hertha. All your lovers are dead and bound up in books. They can't touch you. They can't make love to you tonight. They've been in the ground too long. Don't you know that? (*He turns out the suspended light above.*) This is life and you're scared of it. You've never come up against it before. You haven't found it in any of your alphabetical files. It's taken you by surprise, Hertha, the way it took me when I came back from Europe and saw Heavenly Critchfield again, laughing at me the way that she used to. It hurts you. It's big and awful and crazy and makes you want to run and hide from it. But you can't, Hertha. Hiding doesn't do any good. (*He catches one of her hands which she holds before her in a defensive gesture.*) You've got little hands—they're little candle-wax hands.

HERTHA (*faintly*): Let go of me, Arthur.

ARTHUR: No. I won't let go.

HERTHA: Please do.

ARTHUR: No.

HERTHA: If you don't I'll have to call Miss Schlagmann.

ARTHUR: Go ahead. Call her.—Haven't you ever been kissed? No. Only in books. By William Blake and John Donne. "Go, and catch a falling star,/Get with child a mandrake root."—Those are your lovers but they've got cold lips. They've been in the ground so long not even April can make them warm, again, Hertha. But I'm not cold. Heavenly thinks I am but she's mistaken. The whiskey's made me warm for a change. I'm hot inside. If I touched you with my lips you'd think you'd been scorched by fire. You'd crumple up like a little white moth that's flown into the candle flame, Hertha. That's what you'd do. (*He pulls her against him.*)

HERTHA (*breathlessly*): No, no, please let me go.

(*He kisses her. She struggles and then is limp in his arms. After a moment he thrusts her away from him. There is a long pause. The stunned expression recedes from her face and she moves a step toward him.*)

You kissed me, Arthur. (*She touches her lips wonderingly.*)

ARTHUR (*hoarsely*): Excuse me. I was drunk. (*He averts his face in distaste.*)

HERTHA: You kissed me.—It isn't Heavenly Critchfield you're in love with, it's me! Isn't it, Arthur? It's me! (*She smiles raptly like a child.*)

(*Arthur is shocked out of his drunkenness and repelled by his own action and by Hertha's unexpected reaction to it.*)

ARTHUR (*in confusion*): I didn't know what I was doing. I'm sorry. (*He goes back a few steps.*) I'd better be going.

HERTHA (*blind with inner brightness*): Arthur! Now I can tell you!—I love you! I love you. So much that I've nearly gone mad! Oh, God, why didn't you know, why didn't you know? (*Slowly she extends her hand toward the shaded light on the table.*) Arthur! Take me out of here, Arthur, some place where we can be together. (*She turns the light off.*)

ARTHUR (*moving away from her*): No, I don't want you Hertha.

HERTHA: Arthur!

ARTHUR: Don't you understand? I don't want you! (*Pause.*) I didn't know you were like that. I thought you were different.

HERTHA (*agonized*): Arthur!

ARTHUR: You—you *disgust* me!

(*His shadow can be seen moving uncertainly toward the door —it closes and he is gone. A wild cry breaks from Hertha's lips and she falls to her knees. After a moment Miss Schlagmann comes out of the stacks, running.*)

MISS SCHLAGMANN: Hertha! What's happened, child? (*She turns the light on.*)

HERTHA (*vaguely*): There was a man. He scared me. I fainted —please get me some water.

MISS SCHLAGMANN: Hertha! I'll call the police!

HERTHA: No, no! Nothing happened! (*She sobs like a child.*) I want to go home, I want to go home!

MISS SCHLAGMANN: Hertha, poor Hertha!—I'll get you a glass of water!

(*She rushes into the other room. With a choked cry Hertha darts out the front door. When Miss Schlagmann returns with the glass of water, she has disappeared.*)

Hertha! Where are you child? Good heavens, she's gone!

(*Miss Schlagmann rushes out the front door and can be heard calling Hertha's name several times. She returns, frustrated —still holding glass of water. She continues, vaguely.*)

She's gone. . . .

(*She looks helplessly at the glass of water and then slowly, mechanically, pours it into the bowl of yellow jonquils on the desk—*)

Slow Curtain

SCENE THREE

It is the next evening in the Critchfield living room. Aunt Lila is sewing in her rocker. Heavenly enters slowly in a white cellophane rain cape.

LILA: Still raining?

HEAVENLY (*looking stunned*): Oh. Yes.

LILA: What's the matter with you?

HEAVENLY: He's gone.

LILA: Richard?

HEAVENLY: Yes.

LILA: Left town, you mean?

HEAVENLY: Yes.—I don't want to talk about it.

LILA: Don't be so tragic. Sit down here and let's get this thing straightened out.

HEAVENLY: Some things can't be straightened out, Auntie.

LILA: I've never known anything yet didn't straighten itself out if you gave it time enough.

HEAVENLY: Time! Yes! A couple of centuries—

LILA: That's how it looks when you're young.

HEAVENLY (*suddenly angry*): You don't know how it feels!

LILA: Yes, I do know! And I know it's hard to be young! Almost as hard as it is to be old! Sometimes it's even harder because when you're old—you get so you appreciate a good cup of coffee! But the young ones, the kids like you, they think the sun won't rise tomorrow unless they get what they want.

HEAVENLY (*coming down a bit from her anger and despair*): Have you got a cigarette?

LILA (*brightly*): A whole pack of 'em. My dividend came in from the compress stock!

HEAVENLY: Thanks.

LILA: By the way, I'm making you a new dress out of some goods I bought at Power's.

HEAVENLY: Thanks, Auntie.

LILA: It's got a lot of red in it. Your mother thinks it's tacky. But I always say that spring's a damn good excuse for wearing bright colors.

HEAVENLY: It's no use, Auntie. I don't feel like being bucked up. (*Her voice catches.*)

LILA: That's right. Go on and do a little crying—and then go upstairs and get dressed for your dinner date.

HEAVENLY (*sobbing.*): Do you think I'm going out?

LILA: Of course you are. You aren't the sort of girl that gives up going to parties. I was, and look where it got me. (*She offers Heavenly a light.*) Here. Smoke your cigarette. Cigarettes were made for moments like these. Girls didn't smoke 'em back in the days when I had my big romantic catastrophes. I used to go out in the hayloft and stuff my mouth full of straw which wasn't nearly so nice. They had rats in the hayloft. I remember once when I was right on the point of deciding to kill myself when one of those big gray monsters trotted over my ankle and gave me such a fit of the shudders that I completely forgot about my broken heart.

HEAVENLY (*rising impatiently*): Oh, I haven't got any broken heart.

LILA: No. They're out of style. Where's he gone to?

HEAVENLY: To work on the levee. That was his big ambition, that's what he wanted to do. He said it took a flannel shirt and pair of boots to make him feel like a man.—He wanted me to go with him. Me! Live like a nigger on a lousy river barge. He expected me to do that.

LILA: Doesn't he give you credit for having a lick of sense?

HEAVENLY: Oh, I don't know. I might do it if he hadn't been so casual about it. He didn't call me all day so I went down to the drugstore, and the soda jerk told me he'd quit his job and gone to Friar's Point and left a note for me in an empty Alka-Seltzer bottle.

LILA: Huh! What did the note say?

HEAVENLY: If I wanted him, I could meet him in Friar's Point tonight. And get married.

LILA: You wouldn't do a fool thing like that.

HEAVENLY: I don't know.

LILA: He's the restless kind. He's never stuck at anything very long.

HEAVENLY: No, he goes from one thing to another.

LILA: One of these drifters.

HEAVENLY: It isn't just that. He isn't satisfied with the things that other people are satisfied with.

LILA: No. You can't blame him for that. But that isn't a very good reason for marrying him. He wanted to get away from the drugstore and the town. Maybe he'd be wanting to get away from you next.

HEAVENLY: I know. I can't be sure.

LILA: You could never be sure.

HEAVENLY: If I thought I could hold him I'd take a chance on the rest. I'd live like a nigger for him on a lousy river barge. I'd even do that, if I thought he wouldn't decide in the end that I was just another thing that he wanted to break away from.

LILA: When they've got the itch in them shoes there's nothing but six feet of dirt can ever make 'em stay put.

HEAVENLY: Tell me what to do.

LILA: You've got a date with Arthur Shannon tonight. Go upstairs and get dressed for it.

HEAVENLY: No!

LILA: I know that sounds like an awful anticlimax to a broken heart or whatever you call it nowadays, but so was the rat that ran over my ankle in the hayloft, and it was the rat that brought me back to my senses and made me see what a sentimental fool I was being! You're better off than I was. You've got another to fall back on.

HEAVENLY: Arthur? I don't think I could ever care much for him.

LILA: Why not?

HEAVENLY: He doesn't seem quite human. All he does is talk and talk.

LILA: He'll get over that.

HEAVENLY: Oh, God, I don't know what to do!

VOICE OF MESSENGER BOY: Cutrere's!

MRS. CRITCHFIELD: Flowers? How lovely! (*She enters with an open box.*) Look at this! Just look! It's talisman roses! Heavenly! Arthur's sent you a corsage! To wear to the Country Club tonight.

HEAVENLY: Oh, I know, I know.

MRS. CRITCHFIELD (*turning to Lila*): What's the matter with her? What's she crying about?

LILA: Richard Miles left town.

MRS. CRITCHFIELD: Well. Good riddance! I told you how much you could depend on a boy of that kind.— (*She decides to take no further notice of Heavenly's grief.*) Look at this! Did you ever see anything more exquisite? (*She holds the corsage up to Heavenly's shoulder.*) It's going to look lovely on your blue knitted suit.

HEAVENLY (*pushing the corsage aside*): Let go of me! Leave me alone!

MRS. CRITCHFIELD: Well, that's gratitude for you!

LILA: Leave her alone, Esmeralda.

MRS. CRITCHFIELD: Oh, I know that you were fond of him, Heavenly, but I can't help feeling that his leaving town's the most fortunate thing that *could* have happened.

HEAVENLY: Fond of him. (*She laughs wildly.*) I was crazy about him. You ought to know that.

MRS. CRITCHFIELD: I won't hear any more about that disgusting business.

HEAVENLY (*practically shouting*): Crazy about him, do you hear?

MRS. CRITCHFIELD: That horrible—

LILA: Esmeralda!

HEAVENLY: Do you think I'm going to give him up?

MRS. CRITCHFIELD: Of course you're going to give him up. You're going to forget all about him.

HEAVENLY: I won't!

MRS. CRITCHFIELD: You're going to be sensible now.

HEAVENLY: That's what you think!

MRS. CRITCHFIELD: You're going upstairs and get dressed!

HEAVENLY: I'm going upstairs and pack my grip!

MRS. CRITCHFIELD: Do what?

HEAVENLY: I'm going to Friar's Point. Dick's going to meet me there. We're going to get married!

MRS. CRITCHFIELD (*aghast*): No!

HEAVENLY: Yes. By a colored preacher. And we're going to live on a river barge.

MRS. CRITCHFIELD: You wouldn't dare—!

HEAVENLY: I thought you'd know by now how much I'd dare to do. Didn't I open your eyes when I told you what had been going on between him and me? Yes, an affair! The gossips were right this time, you can chalk it up in their favor. But I'm not as immoral as you are, I'm not as indecent as you want to make me. I'm not going to give myself to one man and then go marry another that I don't even like. No, hell, no! I'm gonna take the nine o'clock train to Friar's Point and marry Dick and you can't stop me! (*She flies out of the room.*)

MRS. CRITCHFIELD (*she is nearly prostrate*): Oh! Call her father!

LILA: No. Leave this to me, Esmeralda.

MRS. CRITCHFIELD: Get Oliver this instant! We've got to stop her!

LILA: Now don't go all to pieces. Is it true what she said about her and the boy having had an affair?

MRS. CRITCHFIELD (*choked*): Yes, it's true.

LILA: When did she tell you?

MRS. CRITCHFIELD: Don't stand there and ask me questions!

LILA: If it's true then maybe she'd better go and marry the boy.

MRS. CRITCHFIELD: No! I'd never permit it! She can marry Arthur Shannon.

LILA: Does he know about her and Richard?

MRS. CRITCHFIELD: No, of course he doesn't. Do you think we want it published in all the papers?

LILA: Why didn't you get Oliver to go and see the boy and get it straightened out?

MRS. CRITCHFIELD: Oliver would have shot him! Wouldn't that have created a nice scandal!

LILA: Oliver wouldn't have done any such thing.

MRS. CRITCHFIELD: Then you don't think family honor means anything to your brother?

LILA: Family honor hasn't got anything to do with normal young people's emotions.

MRS. CRITCHFIELD: Normal! Emotions. It's easy to see what side of the family she gets her indecency from.

LILA: Indecency nothing! She's human that's all. Maybe a little too human. And if she gets that from the Critchfields I'm not ashamed of it.

MRS. CRITCHFIELD: No! You're all shameless.

LILA: Maybe so, but that's beside the point. Did Heavenly tell you anything else?

MRS. CRITCHFIELD: No. There haven't been any serious consequences.

LILA: Well, I'm going upstairs.

MRS. CRITCHFIELD (*desperately hopeful*): You're going to talk
her out of it?

LILA: I'm not going to talk her in or out of anything. I'm going to help her decide for herself.

MRS. CRITCHFIELD: Lila!

LILA: It's the only thing to do.

MRS. CRITCHFIELD: I understand your attitude. You're doing
this because you hate the Shannons.

LILA: I don't hate the Shannons. (*She goes out.*)

MRS. CRITCHFIELD (*shouting after her*): Yes, you do. You're
holding a grudge! (*The doorbell rings.*) Oh, that's Arthur.

(*She pulls herself desperately together and scurries about the
shabby room putting things straight. Her actions show a pathetic inability to rise above trivialities, even in a time of
crisis. She switches on the light above Colonel Wayne's portrait; then she rushes into the hall and can be heard ad-
mitting Arthur in her best social manner. She ushers him
into the living room talking a mile a minute to cover up
her nervousness. This should be played for comedy but not
farce.*)

Oh, my dear boy, it's started raining again! Your lovely
white panama hat, did it get very damp? (*She enters the
room followed by Arthur whose manner is very constrained.*)
Oh, I think it was such a dreadful shame about last night.
Susan Lamphrey'd been planning that lawn party for weeks
and then the rains came along and spoiled all the nice
preparations. But that's April for you! I suppose they just
had to move everything indoors. Fortunately they have a
very spacious downstairs—

ARTHUR (*politely disinterested*): Oh, they have.

MRS. CRITCHFIELD: Yes, that's the mahvelous thing about
those old ante-bellum houses, they knew absolutely *nothing* about the economy of space. It's awfully hard to keep
them warm in winter but in spring and summer I think
they're simply delightful.

ARTHUR: Yes. Yes, I suppose so.

MRS. CRITCHFIELD: Oh, I often wish we hadn't given up the old Wayne plantation. The house was nearly two hundred years old. It was the most historic place in the Delta. That's Colonel Wayne's picture there on the wall.

ARTHUR: Oh, is it?

MRS. CRITCHFIELD: Yes. He led the charge up Cemetery Hill. If we'd won the war he would've been president of the Confederacy. He was a great friend of Jefferson Davis. Upstairs we have the very bed that Mr. Davis slept in when he visited our plantation. It's in Heavenly's room.

ARTHUR: Oh, is it?

MRS. CRITCHFIELD: Yes, that chair is hers, too. Mr. Critchfield's always nagging me to have things upholstered, but you know I just can't bear to change them when they're so rich in tradition and all. Sometime I'm going to have you look through our family papers, Arthur. Writers are always so interested in things like that. With your literary gifts I'm quite sure you could write some things up for me. For instance that very dramatic little episode that took place on Colonel Wayne's plantation the second year of the war when it was rumored that Sherman had crossed the border—

(*A loud crash is heard upstairs.*)

Oh, heavens, what's that? (*She pauses nervously, recovers and smiles.*) Heavenly must be romping with the dog! What were we talking about? Oh, yes of course, books! I have a cousin who writes them. Had one published. I forget just what the name of it was. (*Another loud noise is heard above.*) Oh, yes, *The Stroke of Doom*, that was it! A mystery novel based on the most remarkable coincidence that actually took place. (*The noise continues.*) Seems to me the setting was somewhere in Europe. Or was it Africa? Oh, no, it was Australia! And just think, Cousin Alfred was an invalid— he'd never been out of Mississippi in all his life! He got his information, every bit of it, out of the *Encyclopedia Britannica*.

HEAVENLY'S VOICE (*upstairs*): I won't, I tell you, I won't.

(*A door slams violently.*)

MRS. CRITCHFIELD (*in extreme agitation*): Perhaps I'd better go up and tell Heavenly that you're here— If you'll excuse me for just a moment.

ARTHUR (*rising*): Certainly, Mrs. Critchfield.

(*Mrs. Critchfield rushes out. Arthur looks keenly distressed and puzzled. After a brief interval Aunt Lila enters.*)

LILA: Good evening, young man.

ARTHUR: Oh, good evening, Miss Critchfield.

(*Lila adjusts her glasses and looks at him sharply; she touches her forehead with a handkerchief.*)

LILA: Eau de cologne—it's very refreshing when you've been through a nervous ordeal! (*She smiles.*) I've been trying to talk some sense into my niece's head. You probably wondered about that racket up there. Sit down and I'll tell you.

ARTHUR: Uh—thanks.

LILA: I haven't had much chance to get acquainted with Gale Shannon's boy. Tell me about yourself. What are you going to do, what are you planning to be? A young nincompoop all your life? (*She laughs kindly.*) No, you look too much like your father for that. I used to go out with Gale Shannon when I was a girl. He threw me over for your mother, God bless him, but he's still aces with me. (*Then she continues quite seriously and gently.*) Are you in love with Heavenly?

ARTHUR (*rising gravely*): Yes, Ma'am. I do have that misfortune.

LILA: Misfortune? I wouldn't say that!

ARTHUR: Neither would I, Ma'am, if I thought I had a chance in the world.

LILA: I think you have got a chance if you take it. But it's absolutely your last.

ARTHUR: Yes, Ma'am? What's that?

LILA: She's planning to run off with a young jackanapes that's gone to work on the river.

ARTHUR: Richard Miles?

LILA: Yes. There's nothing wrong with that boy and there's nothing wrong with Heavenly, but the two of 'em can't team together, they'd never run the same way— So if you're sure you love her and you want her there's just one thing for you to do.

ARTHUR: What's that?

LILA: Grab her and don't let her go!

ARTHUR: Grab her?

LILA: Certainly. The main reason Nature's provided you with arms, is so you can grab what you want, and by the Eternal, young man, if you don't grab things in this world you don't have a coon's chance of ever getting 'em. Do you think a drink would do you any good?

ARTHUR: Yes, Ma'am, I think it might.

LILA (*producing a bottle from the bookcase*): Take a swig of this. It's Oliver's.

ARTHUR (*taking the bottle*): That's funny.

LILA: What?

ARTHUR: Nothing much. Just a little coincidence.

LILA: Take a good one. She'll be flying down those steps in a minute—pretendin' like she's going to the Country Club. But she isn't. I know what she's got up her sleeve. She's going to ask you to drive her over to Friar's Point where that boy's gone. Don't do it. Just grab her and make her stay here. And make her like it. Heavenly's no angel, in fact she's a regular little hussy. I think she likes you better'n you think if you treat her like she needs to be treated— Here she's coming! Let me get out of here quick!

(*Aunt Lila flies out the rear door as Heavenly enters. Her eyes have a hectic brilliance. She is like some beautiful wild animal at the point of flight.*)

ARTHUR (*starting forward*): Heavenly—

HEAVENLY: What?

ARTHUR: I thought you weren't going to the Country Club.

HEAVENLY: How did you know? Did Auntie tell you?

ARTHUR (*tensely*): I thought you were going to Friar's Point—

HEAVENLY: Shhh! Mother doesn't know. So be quiet till we get outside. (*She crosses to him.*) I want you to do me a big favor, Arthur. I want you to drive me over to Friar's Point tonight— Will you?

ARTHUR: Heavenly, I— Heavenly. (*He suddenly grabs her in his arms.*)

HEAVENLY (*struggling*): What do you think you're doing?

(*Arthur kisses her wildly. She struggles to free herself, strikes at him with her fists, but he doesn't release her.*)

Stop, Arthur. You're hurting me! Don't!

(*He slightly relaxes his grip. She continues aghast.*)

You must be out of your senses, Arthur Shannon!

ARTHUR: Yes, I'm crazy. (*He kisses her again.*)

HEAVENLY: Don't Arthur. I won't stand for this!

ARTHUR: You won't?

HEAVENLY: No, I *won't*.

(*Arthur kisses her repeatedly: on the lips, throat, shoulders. Heavenly gasps for breath, stops resisting. She leans passively against him. There is a long pause.*)

ARTHUR (*in a soft anxious voice*): Heavenly, have I—hurt you, Heavenly?

HEAVENLY: No, I— I guess it doesn't matter. (*She smiles slightly.*) I really didn't think you were capable of doing anything like this.

ARTHUR: I didn't mean to do it. I was—out of my senses. (*He starts to release her.*)

HEAVENLY: No, don't let go of me. Don't let me go.

ARTHUR: You don't want me to?

HEAVENLY: No. I want to rest like this for awhile. I'm so tired. I was going to do something crazy Arthur. Going someplace where I wasn't wanted. But now I guess I don't have to. Maybe this is the answer.

ARTHUR: Heavenly, what do you mean?

HEAVENLY: I don't know yet. Give me a cigarette, please. (*He does.*) Thanks. I'll take a few drags and then I'll be able to tell you.

(*She sinks on the sofa and leans back.*)

ARTHUR: I'm sorry, Heavenly. I can't tell you how I despise myself.

HEAVENLY: Sorry, for what?

ARTHUR: For acting like an animal.

HEAVENLY: Needn't be sorry for that. That's the first thing you've done to convince me that you're a human being. I didn't think you were alive till just now. I thought you were just a sort of walking dictionary or something. I didn't think you could use your lips for anything but putting long words together. And now—well, I'm glad to find out that I was mistaken!

ARTHUR: What were you going to Friar's Point for?

HEAVENLY: I was going to marry Dick. He's gone there. We've been in love for a long time, ever since sophomore cotillion at high school about seven years ago. And you can't expect people to go on loving each other all that time without something happenin' between them.

ARTHUR: You don't need to—

HEAVENLY: Repeat the horrible confession? That's what mother called it. I told her the other day about Dick and me, but she was still anxious for me to give him up and take you. She approves of you, Arthur, and she thinks dishonesty's the best policy in love affairs— She didn't want me to tell you the awful truth.

ARTHUR: I'm glad that you did.

HEAVENLY: Why? Does it make it easier for you to forget me?

ARTHUR: No. I'd never try to do that.

HEAVENLY: Then do you still want me? Even secondhand?

ARTHUR: Yes. Anyway I can have you.

HEAVENLY: All right. (*She puts out her cigarette.*) It's all settled. Instead of marrying Dick and living on a lousy river barge, I'm going to marry Arthur Shannon and live in the biggest house in town!

ARTHUR: Heavenly, is that how you feel about it?

HEAVENLY (*gently*): No, not really—if you hadn't made love to me I would have gone to Friar's Point.

ARTHUR: But you aren't going now?

HEAVENLY: No, I'm not going now. Can you reach the light? (*He extinguishes the table lamp.*) Thanks. It's so much nicer in the dark, especially when there's rain and lightnin' outside. (*He sits beside her.*) What kind of talcum powder do you use? I like the smell of it. (*She leans on his shoulder.*) Mmmm. I like your flannel coat sleeve too. It feels nice. It's astonishing how many nice things I've found out about you, Arthur Shannon, in the last few minutes.—For God's sake, don't start talking!—When you're making love to a girl you should always be quiet because there aren't any words that are good enough to say what you mean anyhow . . .

(*The phone rings in the hall. Heavenly continues, a slight catch in her voice.*)

That's Dick calling from Friar's Point to find out whether or not I'm coming.

ARTHUR: Don't get up. Don't answer it.

HEAVENLY: Why not?

ARTHUR: Because if you do you'll never come back.

HEAVENLY: All right. I'll stay here with you. I won't move.

(*Aunt Lila can be heard answering the phone in the hall. Her voice comes indistinctly through the closed door. After a few moments she opens it and stands in the doorway. She turns on the light.*)

LILA (*with constraint*): I beg your pardon.

HEAVENLY (*laughing*): Auntie, don't be so formal. You know I've been kissed before.

LILA: I wasn't thinking of that.

HEAVENLY: Oh. What were you thinking of?

LILA: Someone just called.

HEAVENLY: For me?

LILA: No.

HEAVENLY (*sharply*): Don't be so mysterious, Auntie! What's happened?

(*Lila turns slowly to Arthur.*)

LILA: Arthur. You haven't heard about Hertha Neilson?

ARTHUR (*anxiously*): Heard *what* about her?

LILA (*after a slight pause*): She was killed last night. They found her body in the freight yards.

(*Arthur is stunned.*)

HEAVENLY: The freight yards!

LILA: Yes. It wasn't identified till an hour ago.

HEAVENLY (*looking at Arthur*): Auntie, why did you have to come in here and tell him like this?

LILA: Because that isn't all. Miss Schlagmann told me that Hertha Neilson and a young man had a violent scene of some kind in the library before it happened.

HEAVENLY: What young man? What did Miss Schlagmann say what man it was?

LILA: She didn't see him and Hertha Neilson didn't say. But maybe Arthur could tell you.

HEAVENLY: No. Leave Arthur alone. Whatever happened I'm sure it wasn't his fault.

LILA: Maybe not. But I think he ought to be prepared for what people are likely to say.

HEAVENLY: What can they say? Everybody knows the poor girl was out of her mind.

(*Arthur rises slowly and goes blindly across the room toward the French doors. Lightning glimmers through them.*)

Arthur, I know it's dreadful. But it wasn't your fault. (*She turns to Lila.*) Auntie, what are you standing there for? Please get out!

LILA: I think Arthur ought to leave now.

HEAVENLY: No. Why should he?

ARTHUR: She's right. I'll have to go.

HEAVENLY: Please, Auntie! Get out!

(*Lila exits.*)

Tell me, Arthur—was it you?

ARTHUR: Yes.

HEAVENLY: What happened?

ARTHUR: I took your advice, I got drunk. After I left you and your lover at the party, I got drunk, but I didn't go across the Sunflower like you suggested. I went to the library instead.

HEAVENLY: What happened? You'd better tell me.

ARTHUR: Oh, God. I can't. The freight yards.

HEAVENLY: Don't think about that.

ARTHUR (*verging on hysteria*): I wonder how many boxcars there were last night? Sometimes they're terribly long. Once I counted fifty-seven.

HEAVENLY: Don't, Arthur! Hold on to yourself!

ARTHUR: No wonder she was dead when they found her. Not identified till just now. How did they ever find out? Because she wasn't down at the library this morning? The Story-book Lady—the dark-haired princess in the Magic Tower. And I called her—The Carnegie Vestal—I called her that. And kissed her. And then she came alive in my arms and begged me to take her. Because she was like I was, lonely and hungry, and I—I lost my desire. I told her that she was disgusting—

HEAVENLY: You didn't do that!

ARTHUR: Yes.

HEAVENLY: That was cruel.

ARTHUR: Yes. And after that she screamed. And I ran out the door and all I could hear for blocks and blocks was that screaming. And then it was quiet. Nothing but rain on my face. I was glad that I'd gotten away. And then a funny thing happened. (*He turns slowly toward Heavenly.*) I came to an alley. It was in back of your house. It was filled with the fresh smell of roses. I went sort of crazy. Covered my face with those flowers and whispered your name. (*He turns away.*) And I guess about that time Hertha was standing out in the freight yards with the rain on her face, too—and the engine's light in her eyes, screaming— We were driving that engine last night, Heavenly, you and me.

HEAVENLY: No.

ARTHUR: We were inside those boxcars, we were the ones that killed her.

HEAVENLY: No. Arthur. You couldn't help it that you loved me instead of her.

ARTHUR: Loved you—yes—I told her that. She climbed up the hill and stood between the two dead trees and said she was one of them now. I was too full of myself to know what she meant or to care.

HEAVENLY: That's natural. We're all of us full of ourselves. (*She kisses him.*)

ARTHUR: How can you stand to do that?

HEAVENLY: Because I want to. It's funny how I feel toward you now. So much diff'rent. (*She clings to him.*) You've done me a favor tonight. You've taught me something very

important about the nature of love. It's our bodies we love
with mostly. When you kissed me just now, I could have
believed it was him, Dick— It gave me the same sensation,
exactly the same— You've made me love you, Arthur.

ARTHUR: How can you talk about *us* after what's happened?

HEAVENLY: Because I was bo'n twice as old as you are an'
you'll never catch up.

(*She goes over to the sofa and switches off the small light above
Colonel Wayne's portrait. Her voice is low.*)

Come over here and be quiet.

ARTHUR: No. Your aunt was right. I've got to leave here.

HEAVENLY: Why should you leave?

ARTHUR: Don't you see why? There'll be an investigation and
they'll find things out. I'll be disgraced. I'll have to leave
town.

HEAVENLY: You're afraid of people?

ARTHUR: Not so much as I'm afraid of myself. I've commit-
ted murder and I can't stay here at the scene of the crime.
It would hound me.

HEAVENLY: Then take me away with you. I don't want to stay
here either.

ARTHUR: I can't take you with me. I've got to be off by myself for awhile. With strangers, Heavenly. They're—they're
a sort of—catharsis. Like cold water on your face and
hands. They make you feel clean. Whenever I touched you
now it would be like dipping my hands in her blood.

HEAVENLY: Arthur. Don't say that.

ARTHUR: It would.—I'm sorry, Heavenly. I'll come back later
if you still want me.

HEAVENLY: No. If you leave me now I'll hate you. I'll never
want to see you again.

ARTHUR: Maybe that would be a good thing. (*He moves toward the hall.*)

HEAVENLY (*desperately*): You're a coward. You're running
away.

ARTHUR (*dully*): Yes. That's a habit of mine.

HEAVENLY: You can't leave me now! (*She follows him to the
hall door.*)

ARTHUR: Good-bye, Heavenly.

HEAVENLY (*wildly*): You can't say that, too! *Arthur!*

(*The door is heard closing. Heavenly is in bewildered agony.*)

Oh—

(*Heavenly wanders back to the middle of the room, her eyes dull and exhausted. After a moment Lila comes quietly in.*)

LILA: He's gone?

HEAVENLY: Yes. They've both gone.

LILA: Are you going to Richard?

HEAVENLY: No, he doesn't want me either. He's got what he wanted. But maybe someday he'll want me again. Or maybe Arthur will. I don't know. I'll have to wait and see.

(*She moves slowly toward the hall.*)

LILA: Where are you going?

(*Heavenly turns in the doorway and stares vacantly into space.*)

HEAVENLY: I'm going out and sit on the front porch till one of them comes back.

Curtain

NOT ABOUT NIGHTINGALES

This play is dedicated to the memory
of Clarence Darrow, The Great Defender,
whose mental frontiers were the
four corners of the sky.

OPENING

The action takes place in a large American prison during the summer of 1938. The conditions which the play presents are those of no particular prison but a composite picture of many.

LOUD-SPEAKER: Yeah, this is the Lorelei excursion steamer, All-day trip around Sandy Point. Leave 8 A.M., return at Midnight. Sight-seeing, dancing, entertainment with Lorelei Lou and her eight Lorelights! Got your ticket, lady? Got your ticket? Okay, that's all. We're shoving off now. Now we're leaving the boat dock, folks. We're out in the harbor. Magnificent skyline of the city against the early morning sunlight. It's still a little misty around the tops of the big towers downtown. Hear those bells ringing? That's St. Patrick's Cathedral. Finest chimes in America. It's eight o'clock sharp. Sun's bright as a dollar, swell day, bright, warm, makes you mighty proud to be alive, yes, Ma'am! There it is! You can see it now, folks. That's the Island. Sort of misty still. See them big stone walls. Dynamite-proof, escape-proof! Thirty-five hundred men in there, folks, and lots of 'em 'll never get out! Boy, oh, boy, I wonder how it feels t' be locked up in a place like that till doomsday? Oh, oh!! There goes the band, folks! Dancing on the Upper Deck! Dancing, folks! Lorelei Lou and her eight Lorelights! Dancing on the Upper Deck—dancing!—Dancing!—Dancing . . . (*Fade.*)

(*Flash forward to end of play. Light fades except for a spot on Eva, clutching Jim's shoes.*)

LOUD-SPEAKER: Aw, there it is! You can see it now, folks. That's the Island! Sort of misty tonight. You'd see it better if there was a moon. Those walls are dynamite-proof, escape-proof— Thirty-five hundred men in there—some won't get out till Doomsday.—There's the band!—Dancing on the Upper Deck, folks! Lorelei Lou and her eight Lorelights! Dancing—dancing—dancing . . . (*Fade.*)

(*Music comes up. The shoes fall from Eva's hands, and she covers her face.*)

Blackout

ACT ONE

Announcer: "Miss Crane Applies for a Job"

A spot lights the bench outside the Warden's office where Mrs. Bristol is sitting. Mrs. B is a worn matron in black, holding a napkin-covered basket on her lap. Eva enters the spot from the right and sits on the bench, nervously. She grips her pocketbook tensely and stares straight ahead.

MRS. B: Your hat!

EVA: My hat?

MRS. B: Yes, look!

EVA: Oh, dear!

MRS. B: Here.

EVA: Thanks!

(*Mrs. Bristol removes a spot from Eva's hat with tissue paper from her basket.*)

MRS. B: It's those pigeons, the little rascals!

EVA: Yes, they're much too casual about such things.

MRS. B: It's such a nice hat, too.

EVA: Oh, it's quite old. (*She puts the hat back on and drops her purse.*)

MRS. B: You're nervous.

EVA: So nervous I could scream!

MRS. B: Is it your husband?

EVA: Who?

MRS. B: That you're coming to see about?

EVA: Oh, no. No I'm coming to see about a job.

MRS. B: A job? Here?

EVA: Yes, here. I've heard there's a vacancy.

MRS. B: But wouldn't you find it an awfully depressing sort of place to work in?

EVA: I don't think so. It's not an ordinary prison.

MRS. B: Isn't it?

EVA: No, it's supposed to be a model institution.

MRS. B: A model institution!

EVA: Yes, everything's done scientifically they say. They've got experts—in psychology and sociology and things like that, you know!

MRS. B: Well!

EVA: The old idea used to be punishment of crime but nowadays it's—social rehabilitation!

MRS. B: Now just imagine! How did you come to know?

EVA: I read all about it in the *Sunday Supplement*!

(*Jim passes across the spot.*)

EVA (*jumping up*): May I see the Warden?

JIM: Sorry. He's not back yet. (*He crosses into the door of the office.*)

EVA: Oh.

MRS. B: I've got a son in here. He used to be a sailor. Jack's his name.

EVA: A sailor?

MRS. B: Yes, he was one of Uncle Sam's Navy-boys. Till he got in trouble with some kind of woman.

EVA: What a shame!

MRS. B: Yes, wasn't it though—the common slut!—Excuse me but that's what she was. My Scott! (*She clutches her bosom.*)

EVA: What?

MRS. B: I've got the most awful palpitations!

EVA (*jumping up*): You're sick? Let me get you some water!

MRS. B: No, thanks, dear. I'll just take one of my phenobarbital tablets, and I'll be all right in a jiffy. (*Stage business.*) I've been under such a strain lately with Jack on my mind all the time.

EVA: You shouldn't be worried. My landlady's brother-in-law is one of the guards—it was through him that I heard about this vacancy—and he says they have less serious trouble here than any penitentiary in the country. Mr. Whalen, the Warden, is very highly respected.

MRS. B: Well, I do hope you're right for Jack's sake. But I haven't gotten much comfort out of his letters. Especially the last one. It was that one which upset me so. It wasn't at all like those long marvelous letters that he used to write me when he was at sea. It was scribbled in such a bad hand

and—well—it sounded sort of—*feverish* to me!—What is Klondike?

EVA: Klondike? Part of Alaska!

MRS. B: That's what I thought. But in Jack's letter he said he'd been sent down there and it was as hot as—well, I won't say it!

EVA: Possibly it's one of those colonization schemes.

MRS. B: No, I don't think so. In fact I'm positive it isn't. He said they wouldn't let him write me about it if they knew, so he was sneakin' the letter out by one of the boys.

EVA: How long does he have to stay here?

MRS. B: Five years!

EVA: Oh, that's not so long.

MRS. B: It seems like forever to me.

EVA: He'll probably come out a better and stronger boy than before he went in.

MRS. B: Oh no. They couldn't make a better and stronger boy than Jack was. I don't understand all about it, but I know one thing—whatever happened it wasn't my boy's fault!— And that's what I'm going to say to the Warden soon as I get in to see him—I've been waiting here two days—he never has time!

EVA (*rising*): I can't stand waiting. It makes me too nervous. I'm going right in and make that young fellow tell me when Mr. Whalen will be here.

MRS. B: Yes, do! Tell him how long I've been waiting! And ask him if Jack—

(*Eva has already entered office—Mrs. B sinks slowly down, clutching her bosom.*)

Oh, dear . . .

(*The spot moves from the bench to the interior of the office.*)

EVA (*at the door*): I beg your pardon.

JIM (*giving her a long look*): For what?

EVA: For intruding like this. But I couldn't sit still any longer. When can I see Mr. Whalen?

JIM: What about?

EVA: A job.

(*Jim is filing papers in a cabinet. He continues all the while.*)

JIM: He's out right now. Inspecting the grounds.

EVA: Oh. Will it take him long?

JIM: That depends on how much grounds he feels like inspecting.

EVA: Oh.

JIM: Sometimes inspecting the grounds doesn't mean inspecting the grounds. (*He gives her a brief smile.*)

EVA: Doesn't it?

JIM: No. (*He crumples a paper.*) Sometimes it's an idiomatic expression for having a couple of beers in the back room at Tony's which is a sort of unofficial clubhouse for the prison staff— Would you like to sit down?

EVA: About how long do you suppose I'd have to wait?

JIM: It's a hot afternoon. He might do a lot of ground-inspection and then again he might not. His actions are pretty unpredictable. That's a good word.

EVA: What?

JIM: Unpredictable. Anything with five syllables is a good word.

EVA: You like long words?

JIM: They're my stock-in-trade. I'm supposed to use a lot of 'em to impress you with my erudition. There's another one right there!

EVA: Erudition?

JIM: Yes, only four but it's unusual. I get 'em all out of this big book.

EVA: Dictionary?

JIM: *Webster's Unabridged.* (*He slams the file cabinet shut and leans against it.*) Y'see I'm one of the exhibition pieces.

EVA: Are you really?

JIM: I'm supposed to tell you that when I came in here I was just an ordinary grifter. But look at me now. I'm reading Spengler's *Decline of the West* and I'm editor of the prison monthly. Ask me what is an archaeopteryx.

EVA: What is it?

JIM: An extinct species of reptile-bird. Here's our latest issue.

EVA (*more and more confused*): Of—what?

JIM: *The Archaeopteryx.* Our monthly publication.

EVA: Why do you call it that?

JIM: It sounds impressive. Do you know what an amaranth is?

EVA: No. What is it?

JIM: A flower that never dies. (*He lifts a book.*) I came across it in here. One of the classical poets compares it to love. What's your opinion of that.

EVA: Well, I—what's yours?

JIM: I wouldn't know. I started my present career at the age of sixteen.

EVA: That early.

JIM: Yes, the usual case of bad influences. And at that age of course—love is something you dream about and blush when you look at yourself in the mirror next morning! (*He laughs. Eva looks away in slight confusion.*) Say, d'you know that song?

EVA: What song?

JIM (*giving a sour imitation*): "Ah, tis love and love alone the world is seeking!" A guy sang it in chapel last night— Is that on the level?

EVA: Well, I—not exactly.

JIM: You're inclined to admit a few qualifications?

EVA: Yes. For instance what I'm seeking is a job. And a new pair of stockings.

JIM: Those look good to me.

EVA: They're worn to shreds!

JIM: Well, perhaps I'm prejudiced.

(*Eva clears her throat. Jim clears his.*)

EVA (*picking up the newspaper*): "Prison: the door to Opportunity!"

JIM: Yes, that's one of my best editorials. It's been reproduced all over the country—I got ten years of copper for writing that.

EVA: Copper?

JIM: Not what they make pennies out of. In here copper means good time. Time off your sentence for good behavior. I've got about ten years of copper stashed away in the files and most of it's for extolling the inspirational quality of prison life—

(*Mrs. Bristol enters timidly, clutching her basket.*)

JIM: Hello.

MRS. B: How do you do. Is Mr. Whalen in yet?

JIM: No, he's still out inspecting the grounds.

MRS. B: Oh, I do so want to see him this afternoon. I'm—I'm Jack Bristol's mother.

JIM: Sailor Jack?

MRS. B (*advancing a few steps*): Yes—yes! You—know him?

JIM: Slightly.

MRS. B (*struggling to speak*): How is my boy?

JIM: Sorry. I'm not allowed to give out information.

MRS. B: Oh.

JIM: You'd better talk to Mr. Whalen tomorrow morning.

MRS. B: What time, please?

JIM: Ten o'clock.

MRS. B: Ten o'clock. Could you give him these now? (*She places the basket carefully on the table.*) I'm afraid they'll get stale if they're kept any longer. They're for my boy. (*She turns slowly and goes out.*)

EVA: Couldn't you tell her something to relieve her mind?

JIM: Not about Sailor Jack!

EVA: Why not?

JIM: He's gone—stir bugs.

EVA: You mean?

JIM (*touching his forehead*): Cracked up in here. It's sort of an occupational disease among convicts.

EVA: But they said in the *Sunday Supplement*—

JIM: I know. They interviewed me and the Warden.

EVA: You didn't tell them the truth?

JIM: What is it that Plato said about truth? Truth is—truth is— Funny I can't remember! Was it the *Sunday Supplement* that gave you the idea of getting a job in here?

EVA: That and my landlady. Her brother-in-law is Mr. McBurney, one of the prison guards.

JIM: Mac's a pretty good screw.

EVA: What?

JIM: That means a guard in here. Here's one of our sample menus. It shows what a connie gets to eat every day. You can see that it compares quite favorably with the bill-of-fare at any well-known boarding school. Everything's done scientifically here. We have an expert dietitian. Weighs everything by calories. Units of body heat— Hello, Mr. Whalen!

(*Whalen enters. He is a powerful man, rather stout, but with coarse good looks.*)

WARDEN: Hello, hello there! (*He removes his coat and tosses it to Jim.*) Breezy day, hot breezy day! (*He winks at Jim, then belches.*) Too much ground-inspection! (*He loosens his collar and tie.*) Excuse me, lady, I'm going to do a striptease! Yep, it's a mighty wind—feels like it comes out of an oven! Reminds me of those—(*He wipes his forehead.*)—those beautiful golden-brown biscuits my mother used to bake! What's this? (*He removes the cover from the basket.*) Speak of biscuits and what turns up but a nice batch of homemade cookies! Have one, young lady—Jimmy boy!

(*Jim takes two.*)

Uh-h, you've got an awful big paw, Jimmy! (*He laughs.*) Show the new Arky-what's-it to Miss *Daily News*—or is it the *Morning Star*? Have a chair! I'll be right with you— (*He vanishes for a moment into the inner room.*) Sweat, sweat, sweat's all I do these hot breezy days!

JIM (*sotto voce*): He thinks you're a newspaper woman.

WARDEN (*emerging*): Turn on that fan. Well, now, let's see—

EVA: To begin with I'm not—

WARDEN: You've probably come here to question me about that ex-convict's story in that damned yellow sheet down there in Wilkes County— That stuff about getting pellagra in here— Jimmy, hand me that sample menu!

JIM: She's not a reporter.

WARDEN: Aw.—What *is* your business, young lady?

EVA (*in breathless haste*): I understand that there's a vacancy here. Mr. McBurney, my landlady's brother-in-law, told her that you were needing a new stenographer, and I'm sure that I can qualify for the position. I'm a college graduate, Mr. Whalen. I've had three years of business experience— references with me—but, oh—I've—I've had such abominable luck these last six months—the last place I worked—the business recession set in—they had to cut down on their salesforce—they gave me a wonderful letter— I've got it with me— (*She opens her purse and spills its contents on the floor.*) Oh, goodness! I've—broken my glasses!

WARDEN: (*coldly*): Yeah?

EVA (*rising slowly*): Could you give me a job?—Please, I'm—terribly nervous, I—if I don't get a job soon I'll—

WARDEN: What? Go off the deep end?

EVA: Yes, something like that! (*She smiles desperately.*)

WARDEN: Well, Miss—uh—

EVA (*eagerly*): Crane! Eva Crane!

WARDEN: They call that window the "Quick Way Out"! It's the only one in the house without bars. I don't need bars. It's right over the bay. So if it's suicide you got in mind that window is at your disposal. No, Miss Crane. Next time you apply for a job don't pull a sob story. What your business executive is interested in is your potential value, not your—your personal misfortunes! (*He takes a cigar.*)

EVA (*turning away*): I see. Then I—

WARDEN: Hold on a minute.

EVA: Yes?

WARDEN (*biting and spitting out the end of the cigar*): There's just one prerequisite for a job in this office. Jimmy will explain that to you.

EVA (*turning to Jim*): Yes?

JIM: The ability to keep your mouth shut except when you're given specific instructions to speak!

WARDEN: Think you could do that?

EVA: Yes.

JIM: The motorboat leaves the dock at seven forty-five in the morning.

EVA: Thanks— Yes, *thanks!* (*She turns quickly and goes out, blind with joy.*)

WARDEN: What do you think of her, Jimmy boy? Okay, huh?

JIM: Yes, Sir.

WARDEN: Yes, Siree! Dizzy as hell— But she's got a shape on her that would knock the bricks out of a Federal Pen! (*He erupts in sudden booming laughter.*)

Dim Out

EPISODE TWO

Announcer: "Sailor Jack."

Musical theme up: "Auprès de ma Blonde." Fade.

There is a spot on a cell. Electric lights from the corridor throw the shadow of bars across floor. The cell is empty except for the figure of Sailor Jack, slumped on a stool with the shadow of bars thrown across him. His face has the vacant look of the schizophrenic, and he is mumbling inaudibly to himself. His voice rises—

SAILOR JACK: Where? Port Said!—And not one of 'em but woulda done it 'emselves if they'd 'ad ha'f a chance. (*He begins to sing hoarsely.*)

> *Auprès de ma blonde*
> *Il fait bon, fait bon, fait bon!*
> *Auprès de ma blonde*
> *qu'il fait bon dormir!*

No chance for advancement, huh? What would you say if I told you that I was Admiral of the whole bitchin' navy? (*He laughs.*)

> *Je donnerai Versailles,*
> *Paris et Saint Denis—*

(*Sounds are heard: a shrill whistle in hall and the shuffle of feet: the door of the cell clangs open and Joe, Butch, and the Queen enter.*)

SCHULTZ: Lights out in five minutes.

BUTCH: Ahh, yuh fruit, go toot yuh goddam horn outa here. Mus' think they runnin' a stinkin' sweatshop, this workin' overtime stuff. Git yuh task done or come back after supper. Goddam machine got stuck. Delib'rate sabotage, he calls it. I'd like to sabotage his guts. (*To Queen.*): What happened to you this mornin'?

QUEEN (*in a high tenor voice*): I got an awful pain in the back of my neck and flipped out. When I come to I was in the

hospital. They was stickin' a needle in my arm— Say! What
does plus four mean?

JOE: Christ! It means—

BUTCH: Pocket yuh marbles!

QUEEN: Naw. Is it bad?

JOE: We're in swell sassiety, Butch. A lunatic an' a case of the
syph!

QUEEN: The syph?

(*A whistle is heard: the lights dim in the corridor.*)

QUEEN: Naw! (*He tries to laugh.*) It don't mean that!

SAILOR: *Auprès de ma blonde*
      Il fait bon, fait bon, fait bon!
      Auprès de ma blonde—

SCHULTZ: Cut the cackle in there! It's after lights.

BUTCH: God damn it, can't you see he's blown his top?

JOE: Yeah, get him out of here!

SCHULTZ: He's putting on an act.

SAILOR: *Je donnerai Versailles,*
      Paris et Saint Denis—

SCHULTZ: You take another trip to Klondike, Sailor, it won't
be on a round-trip ticket!

BUTCH: It's Klondike that got him like this. He's been ravin'
ever since you brung him upstairs. You must've cooked the
brains out of him down there, Schultz.

SAILOR: *La Tour d'Eiffel aussi!*

SCHULTZ (*rapping the bars*): Dummy up, the lot of you! One
more squawk an' I'll call the strong-arm squad!

QUEEN: Mr. Schultz!

SCHULTZ: Yeah?

QUEEN: What does plus four mean?

(*Schultz laughs and moves off.*)

BUTCH: If I wasn't scared of losin' all my copper I'd reach
through and grab that bastard. I'd rattle them pea-pod
brains of his 'n roll 'em out on the floor like a pair of dice.
The trouble is in here you gotta pick your man. If I rubbed
out a screw I'd never git a chance at the boss.—What time
is it?

JOE: Ten-thirty.

BUTCH: Mac comes on duty now.

JOE: You think he'll take the Sailor out?

BUTCH: I'll tell him to.

QUEEN: Naw. It's nothin' that serious or they woulda kept me in the hospital. It's just indigestion. That's what I told 'em, I said the food is no good. It don't set good on my stomach. Spaghetti, spaghetti, spaghetti! I said I'm sicka spaghetti!

SAILOR: *Auprès de ma blonde*
Il fait bon, fait bon, fait bon!
Auprès de ma blonde
qu'il fait bon dormir!

(*Butch clips him with a fist.*)

JOE: What did you do that for?

BUTCH: You wanta tangle with the strong-arm squadron on account of him?

(*A whistle is heard: doors clang.*)

They're changin' now. (*He goes to the bars.*) Who's 'at? McBurney?

MAC: What do you want, Butch?

BUTCH: For Chrissakes git this kid outta here.

MAC: Which kid?

BUTCH: Sailor Jack. He's been stir-bugs since they brung him upstairs a week ago Tuesday.

MAC (*at the door*): What's he doing?

BUTCH: He's out right now. I had to conk him one.

MAC: What did they tell you about roughin' up the boys?

BUTCH: Roughin'? ME? Lissen!—Ask Joe, ask anybody, ask the Canary—the kid had blown his top—Schultz was gonna call the strong-arm squad an' have us all thrown in Klondike cause he wouldn't quit singin' them dirty French songs! Ain't that right, Joe?

JOE: Sure, Mac.

(*Whistle.*)

MAC: Where's his stuff?

BUTCH: Here. I got it tied up nice.

MAC: Well, it's no put-in of mine. He should've done his task in the shop.

BUTCH: He done his task pretty good.

JOE: That boy worked hard.

MAC: Not hard enough to suit the Boss.

(*Enter guards.*)

Awright, git him outta here. Put him in isolation tonight an' have him looked after tomorrow.

QUEEN: Mr. McBurney, what does plus four mean? Mr. McBurney—

(*Mac goes out with guards carrying Sailor. Bird calls are heard in the hall.*)

VOICE (*in hall*): Goodnight, Mac.

MAC: G'night, Jim.

BUTCH: Who's 'at? Allison?

JOE: Yeah. It's the Canary.

SAILOR (*from down the hall*): "*Auprès de ma blonde Il fait bon, fait bon, fait bon!*"

(*The sound fades.*)

BUTCH: Hey, Canary! Allison!

(*The spot shifts to include Allison's cell.*)

JIM: What do you want, Butch? (*He is shown removing his shirt and shoes.*)

BUTCH: Next time you're in a huddle with the boss tell him the Angels in Hall C have put another black mark on his name for Sailor Jack.

JIM: I'll tell him that.

BUTCH: Tell him some day we're going to appoint a special committee of one to come down there an' settle up the score.—You hear me, Stool?

JIM: I hear you.

BUTCH: Just think—I used to be cell-mates with him. I lie awake at night regrettin' all the times I had a chance to split his guts—but didn't!

JOE: Why didn'tcha?

BUTCH: That was before he started workin' for the boss. But now he's number three on the Angel's Records. First Whalen, then Schultz, and then the Stool! You hear that, Stool?

JIM: Yes, I hear you, Butch. (*He rolls and lights a cigarette.*)

BUTCH: That's good. I'm glad you do.

JIM: I know you're glad.

JOE: What's he say?

BUTCH: He says he knows I'm glad.

JOE: He oughta know. Wonder he don't go stir-bugs, too. Nobody have nothin' to do with him but Ollie.

BUTCH: He'll blow his top sometime, if I don't git him first. You hear that, Stool? I said you'll blow your top sometime like Sailor Jack—I'm lookin' forward to it.

JOE: What's he say?

BUTCH: Nothin'. He's smokin' in there.

JOE: We oughta tip 'em off.

BUTCH: Naw, I never ratted on nobody. Not even that Stool.

QUEEN: Allison! Hey! Jim! What does plus four mean?

JIM: Who's got plus four?

QUEEN: I have. What does it mean, Jim?

JIM: It means your physical condition is four points above perfect.

QUEEN (*relieved*): Aw. These bastards had me worried.

BUTCH (*climbing on a stool by the window*): Foghorns. It's thick as soup outside— Lissen!

JOE: What?

BUTCH: Excursion steamer.

JOE: Which one?

BUTCH: The Lorelei.

JOE: Lookit them lights on her, will yuh. Red, white, green, yellow!

BUTCH: Hear that orchester?

JOE: What're they playin'?

BUTCH: "Roses a Picardy!"

JOE: That's an old one.

BUTCH: It come up the year I got sent up. Why, I remember dancin' to that piece. At the Princess Ballroom. With Goldie. She requested that number ev'ry time I took her out on the floor. We danced there the night they pinched me. On the way out—right at the turn-stile—them six bulls met me—six of 'em—that's how many it took—they had the wagon waitin' at the curb.

JOE: Last time it was four bulls. You're gettin' less conservative, Butch.

BUTCH: "Roses a Picardy." I'd like to dance that number one more time. With Goldie.

JOE: Maybe it was her that put the finger on you.

BUTCH: Naw. Not Goldie. I bet that girl's still holdin' the torch for me.

JOE: Keep your illusions, Butch, if they're a comfort to yuh. But I bet if Goldie was still holdin' all the torches that she's held before an' after you got put in the stir she'd throw more light across the water than a third-alarm fire!

QUEEN: Where's my manicure set?

BUTCH: I wonder if a guy is any good at sixty?

JOE: What do you mean?

BUTCH: You know. With women.

JOE: I guess it depends on the guy.

BUTCH: I'll still be good. But twenty years is a lot of time to wait.

QUEEN: Has anybody seen my manicure set?

BUTCH: You know there's a window in Boss Whalen's office from which a guy could jump right into the Bay.

JOE: Yeah. The Quick Way Out.

BUTCH: I was thinkin' that it would be a good way to kill two birds with a stone. Rub him out an' jump through that window for the getaway. Providin' you could swim. But me I can't swim a goddam stroke. I wish that I'd learned how before I come in here.

JOE: Wouldn't do you no good. Nobody's ever swum it yet.

BUTCH: I'd like to try.—They say some people swim instinctive like a duck.

JOE: You'd take a chance on that?

BUTCH: Naw. I'm scared a water.

QUEEN (*excitedly*): I put it here last night. Butch, did you see it?

BUTCH: What?

QUEEN: My manicure set.

BUTCH: It's gone out wit' the slop-bucket.

QUEEN: What did you do that for?

BUTCH: It stunk up the place. Smelt like rotten bananas—
What's this on Sailor Jack's bunk?

JOE: A package a letters from his ole lady.

BUTCH: Aw.

JOE: She said she was comin' from Wisconsin to see him in
the last one.

QUEEN: All my life I've been persecuted by people because
I'm refined.

BUTCH: Somebody oughta told her how the Sailor is.

JOE: Well, she'll find out.

QUEEN: Because I'm sensitive I been persecuted all my life!

BUTCH: Yeah, she'll find out.

QUEEN: Sometimes I wish I was dead. Oh, Lord, Lord, Lord!
I wish I was dead!

(*Musical theme up. Fade.*)

Blackout

EPISODE THREE

Announcer: "The Prognosis"

*A spot comes up on the Warden's office. He's looking at a racing
form-sheet when Eva Crane, his secretary, enters.*

WARDEN (*lifting the phone and dialing*): How's the track,
Bert? Fast? Okay. I want twenty bucks on Windy Blue to
show. (*He hangs up.*) Anybody outside?

EVA: Yes. That woman.

WARDEN: What woman?

EVA: The one from Wisconsin. She's still waiting—

WARDEN: I told you I— (*Sailor Jack's mother has quietly entered. She carries a neatly wrapped bundle in brown paper—
she smiles diffidently at the Warden.*)

MRS. B: I beg your pardon, I—I took the liberty of coming
in. I hope you won't mind. You see I'm Jack Bristol's

mother and I've been wanting to have a talk with you so long about—about my boy!

WARDEN: Set down. I'm pretty short on time.

MRS. B: I won't take much. To begin with, Mr. Whalen, I never felt the jury did exactly right in giving Jack three years. But that's done now. I've got to look to the future.

WARDEN: Yes, the future—that's right.

MRS. B: I haven't heard from Jack lately. He'd been writing me once a week till just lately.

WARDEN: Lots of boys get careless about their correspondence.

MRS. B: For two years not a week passed without a letter. Then suddenly just a month ago they stopped coming. Naturally I felt rather anxious.

WARDEN: Jim!

JIM: Yes, sir?

WARDEN: Check on a boy named Bristol.

MRS. B: Thank you, I—I came all the way from Wisconsin.

WARDEN: Long trip, huh? Wisconsin's where they make all that fine cheese.

MRS. B: Yes, we're very proud of our dairy products up there. (*She looks anxiously after Jim who has gone slowly to the file-case as though stalling for time.*)

WARDEN: They manufacture the best cheese this side of Switzerland. Yes, Siree!

MRS. B: Jack's last letter was strange. I—I have it with me. It's not at all like Jack. He wasn't transferred to any other prison, was he? Because he kept complaining all through his letter about how terribly hot it was in a place called Klondike. His penmanship has always been quite irregular but this was so bad I could scarcely read it at all—I thought possibly he wasn't well when he wrote it—feverish, you know—he's very subject to colds especially this time of year. I—I brought this wool comforter with me. For Jack. I know it's not easy, Mr. Whalen, to make exceptions in an institution like this. But in Jack's case where there are so many, *many* considerations—so much that I regret *myself* when I look back at things— Mistakes that I made—

WARDEN: Mistakes, yes, we all make mistakes.

MRS. B: Such *grave* mistakes, Mr. Whalen. Our household was not an altogether happy one, you see. Jack's father—well, he was a Methodist minister and his views naturally differed quite a bit from most young boys'—

WARDEN (*with a cynical smile.*): A preacher's son?

MRS. B: Yes! But there was a disagreement among the congregation not long ago and my husband was forced to retire.

WARDEN (*impatiently*): I see. I'm very busy, I— (*To Jim.*): Have you found that card?

JIM (*stalling*): Not yet.

MRS. B: He was so—so uncompromising, even with poor Jack. So Jack left home. Of course it was against my wishes but— (*She opens her bag and produces sheaf of letters.*) Oh, those long marvelous letters that he wrote! If you would only read them you'd see for yourself what an exceptional boy Jack was. Port Said, Marseilles, Cairo, Shanghai, Bombay! "Oh, mother, it's so big, so terribly, terribly big," he kept on writing. As though he'd tried to squeeze it in his heart until the bigness of it made this heart crack open! Look! These envelopes! You see they're packed so full that he could hardly close them! Pictures of places, too! Elephants in India. They're used like pack-horses, he said, for common labor. Little Chinese junkets have square sails. They scoot about like dragonflies on top of the water. The bay at Rangoon. Here's where the sun comes up like thunder, he wrote on the back of this one! Kipling, you know— I wrote him constantly—"Jack, there's no advancement in it. A sailor's always a sailor. Get out of it, son. Get into the Civil Service!" He wrote me back—"I kept the middle watch last night. You see more stars down here than in the northern water. The Southern Cross is right above me now, but won't be long—because our course is changing—" I stopped opposing then, I thought that anything he loved as much as that would surely keep him safe. And then he didn't write a while— until this came. I still can't understand it! He mentioned a girl— He said it wasn't his fault, I know that it wasn't— If I could convince you of that—!

WARDEN: It's no use ma'am! You might as well be talking to the moon. He's had his chance.

MRS. B: But in Jack's case—!

WARDEN: I know, I know. I've heard all that before. Jim, have you found that card?

JIM (*coming slowly forward with a card from files*): You'd better look at it yourself.

WARDEN: Read it, read it! We running a social service bureau?

(*Jim looks uncertainly at Mrs. Bristol who raises a clenched hand to her breast.*)

MRS. B (*softly*): If anything's gone wrong I'd like to know.

JIM (*reading huskily*): "Jack Bristol. Larceny. Convicted May, 1936. Sentenced three years." (*Looks up.*) He slacked his work. Spent three days in Klondike.

WARDEN (*sharply*): Is that on the card?

JIM: No, but I wanted to explain to this lady what happened.

MRS. B: (*rising slowly*): What happened?

JIM: You see, ma'am—

WARDEN (*sharply*): Read what's on the card, that's all!

JIM: "Came up before the lunacy commission, May 1938, transferred to the psychopathic ward. Violent. Delusions. Prognosis—Dementia Praecox"—

(*Pause.*)

MRS. B: That isn't—Jack—my boy!

WARDEN: Now see here—I— (*He motions to Jim to get her out.*) I know how you feel about this. I got all the sympathy in the world for you women that come in here, but this is a penal institution and we simply can't be taking time out from our routine business for things like this.

MRS. B: My boy, Jack, my boy! Not what you said! Anything but that! Say he's dead, say you killed him, killed him! But don't tell me that. I know, I know. I know how it was in here. He wrote me letters. The food not decent. I tried to send him food—he didn't get it—no, even that you took from him. That place you sent him three days. Klondike. I know— You tortured him there, that's what you did, you tortured him until you drove him— (*She turns slowly to*

Jim.) —Crazy? Is that what you said?—Oh, my precious Jesus, oh, my God! (*She breaks down, sobbing wildly.*)

WARDEN: Get that woman out!

(*Jim assists her to the door.*)

Whew! (*He lights a cigar and picks up the form-sheet.*)

Blackout

EPISODE FOUR

Announcer: "Conversations at Midnight!"

The spot lights the two cells with a partition between. Ollie kneels praying by his bunk. Butch lounges, covertly smoking, on a bench along the wall. The others sit on their bunks.

OLLIE (*in an audible whisper*): Oh, Lawd, de proteckter an preserbation ob all, remebuh dis nigguh. Remebuh his wife Susie an his six chillun, Rachel, Rebekah, Solomon, Moses, Ecclesiastics an' Deuteronomy Jackson. You look out fo' dem while Ise in jail. An ah'd git out fo de cole weathuh sets in cause Susie's gonna have another baby, Lawd, an' she can't git aroun't' gatherin' kindlin' wood. God bless my ole woman an' daddy an' Presiden' Roosevelt an' de W.P.A. in Jesus Chris' name—Amen. (*He rises stiffly.*)

BUTCH (*grinning*): Hey, Ollie, yuh better have 'em reverse the charges on that one!

OLLIE: It don' cos' nothin'.

BUTCH: It ain't worth nothin'.

OLLIE: De Lawd remembuhs who remembuhs Him.

BUTCH: Hawshit!

(*Ollie sits dejectedly on the edge of his bunk. There are derisive whistles and bird-calls in the hall as Jim enters.*)

JIM: Whatsamatter, Ollie?

OLLIE (*jerking his thumb at Butch's cell*): He says there ain't no God.

JIM: How's he know?

OLLIE: That's what I say.

(*Jim removes his shirt and swabs sweat off his face and chest with it, then pitches it into the corner. He picks up a naked art magazine and fans himself with it.*)

OLLIE: You think they is, don't you, Jim?

JIM: Somebody upstairs?—I dunno. I guess I'm what they call an agnostic.

OLLIE: You mean a Piscopalian?

JIM: Yeah. Rub my back for me, Ollie. I'm tired.

OLLIE: Awright. Liniment aw bacon grease?

JIM: Gimme the liniment.

BUTCH: Haven't you started seein' 'em yet, Canary?

JIM (*as Ollie starts to rub*): Gawd, it burns good.

BUTCH: Them little blue devils, they're the first symptom.

JIM: It makes the air feel cool.

BUTCH: They crawl in through the bars an' sit on the end of yuh bunk an' make faces at yuh.

JIM: Rub harder on the left shoulder.

BUTCH: Yuh'd better start sleepin' with one eye open, Canary. Can yuh do that?

JIM: Never tried it, Butch.—Ah, that's good.

BUTCH: Well, yuh better, cause if they catch you off guard, Canary, they'll climb down yuh throat an' tie knots in yuh gizzard! (*He laughs delightedly at the prospect.*)

JIM: That's good, ah that's—swell.

OLLIE: How'd you get them purple scars, Jim?

JIM: From Dr. Jones.

OLLIE: Who's Dr. Jones?

BUTCH: Dr. Jones is the guy that gave Canary his singin' lessons! Remembuh when I found out that you'd grown feathers?

JIM (*to Ollie*): That's enough. Thanks. (*He produces cigarettes.*) Have one?

OLLIE: Thanks, Jim.

BUTCH: It's lucky for you that I was interrupted—or you'd be readin' books witcha fingers instead of yer eyes! It's listed on th' record as unfinished business, to be took care of at some future date— I figure that ev'ry dog has his day an' mine's comin' pretty soon now.

OLLIE: Don't pay him no mind.

JIM: Naw. There's a wall between him an' me.

BUTCH: You bet there is. Or you'd be a dead Canary. There'd be yellow feathers floating all over Hall C!

JIM (*exhaling smoke as he speaks—à la Jules Garfield*): There's a wall like that around ev'ry man in here an' outside of here, Ollie.

OLLIE: Outside? Naw!

JIM: Sure there is. Ev'ry man living is walking around in a cage. He carries it with him wherever he goes and don't let it go till he's dead. Then the walls come to pieces and he stops being lonesome—

(*Butch grins delightedly and nudges Joe; he describes a circle with his finger and points at Jim's cell. They both crouch grinning, listening, on the bench by the wall.*)

—Cause he's part of something bigger than him.

OLLIE: Bigger than him?

JIM: Yes.

OLLIE: What's that?

JIM (*blowing an enormous smoke ring and piercing it with his finger*): The Universe!

(*Butch erupts in hoarse derisive laughter.*)

JIM (*ignoring Butch's outburst*): But, sometimes, I think, Ollie, a guy don't have to wait till he's dead to get outside of his cage.

OLLIE: Yuh mean he should bump himself off?

JIM: No. A guy can use his brain two ways. He can make it a wall to shut him in from the world or a great big door to let him out. (*He continues musingly.*) Intellectual emancipation!

OLLIE: Huh?

(*Butch gives a long whistle.*)

OLLIE: What's that?

JIM: Couple of words I came across in a book.

OLLIE: Sound like big words.

JIM: They *are* big words. So big that the *world* hangs on 'em. They can tell us what to read, what to say, what to do—

But they can't tell us what to *think*! And as long as man can think as he pleases he's never exactly locked up anywhere. He can think himself outside of all their walls and boundaries and make the world his place to live in— It's a swell feeling, Ollie, when you've done that. It's like being alone on the top of a mountain at night with nothing around you but stars. Only you're not alone, though, cause you know that you're part of everything living and everything living is part of you. Then you get an idea of what God is. Not Mr. Santie Claus, Ollie, dropping answers to prayers down chimneys—

OLLIE: Naw?

JIM: No, not that. But something big and terrible as night is, and yet—

OLLIE: Huh?

JIM: And yet—as soft as a woman. Y'see what I mean?

BUTCH: I see whatcha mean—it's kind of a—*balmy* feeling! (*Butch and Joe laugh. Jim looks resentfully at wall.*)

JIM: You guys don't get what I'm talking about.

OLLIE (*musingly*): Naw, but I do. Thinkin's like prayin', excep' that prayin' yuh feel like yuh've got some one on the other end a th' line . . .

JIM (*smiling*): Yeah.

(*The spot fades on Jim's cell and focuses on Butch's.*)

QUEEN: Be quiet, you *all*. I'm sick. I need my sleep. (*He mutters to himself.*)

(*A searchlight from river shines on the window.*)

JOE: Where's that light from?

BUTCH (*at the window*): Anudder boat load a goddam jitterbugs. Dey're trowin th' glims on us. Whaddaya think this is? Th' Municipal Zoo or something? Go to hell, yuh sons-a-bitches, yuh lousy—

SCHULTZ (*rapping at the bars with a stick*): After lights in there!

BUTCH: Someday it's gonna be permanuntly 'after lights' for that old screw.

JOE (*twisting on bed*): Oooooo!

BUTCH: Bellyache?

JOE: Yeah, from them stinkin' meatballs. By God I'm gonna quit eatin' if they don't start puttin' in more digestable food.

BUTCH (*reflectively*): Quit eating, huh?—I think yuh got something there.

JOE: Oooooo—*Christ!* (*He draws his knees up to his chin.*)

BUTCH: You ever heard of a hunger-strike, Joe?

JOE: Uh.

BUTCH: Sometimes it works. Gits in the papers. Starts investigations. They git better food.

JOE: *Oooooo!* We'd git—*uh!*—*Klondike!*

BUTCH: Klondike won't hold thirty-five hundred men.

JOE: No. But Hall C would go first on account of our reputation.

BUTCH: Okay. We'll beat Klondike.

JOE: You talk too big sometimes. You ever been in Klondike?

BUTCH: Yeah. Once.

JOE: What's it like?

BUTCH: It's a little suburb of hell.

JOE: That's what I thought.

BUTCH: They got radiators all aroun' the walls an' there ain't no windows.

JOE: Christ Almighty!

BUTCH: Steam hisses outa the valves like this. (*He imitates the sound.*) Till it gits so thick you can't see nothing around you. It's like breathin' fire in yer lungs. The floor is so hot you can't stand on it, but there's no place else to stand—

JOE: How do yuh live?

BUTCH: There's an air hole about this size at the bottom of the wall. But when there's a bunch in Klondike they git panicky an' fight over the air hole an' the ones that ain't strong don't make it.

JOE: It kills 'em?

BUTCH: Sure. Unless the Boss takes 'em out. And when you beat Klondike you beat everything they've got to offer in here. It's their Ace of Spades!

QUEEN (*rising sleepily on his bunk*): What's that about Klondike, Butch?

JOE: Nothing. He's talking in his sleep.

QUEEN: I dreamed about Klondike one night.

JOE: Did ja?

QUEEN: Sure. That was the night I woke up screaming. Remember?

JOE: Sure. I remember.—Oooooo! Uhhhhhh! Ahhhhhh! Jesus! (*He springs out of bed and crouches on the floor, clasping his stomach.*)

Blackout

EPISODE FIVE

Announcer: "Band Music!"

Theme up: Tchaikovsky, "1812 Overture," 2nd Theme. Fade.

A spot comes up on the office. Jim is settled comfortably in a chair by the window, writing. Eva enters.

EVA (*brightly*): Good morning.

JIM: Hi.

EVA (*removing her hat, etc.*): I believe you spend more time here than the boss does.

JIM: I like it here. Especially when I'm alone.

EVA: Oh—well, excuse my intrusion.

JIM: I don't mean you. You don't bother me. (*His immediate tension at her entrance belies this.*)

EVA: Thanks.

JIM (*watching her as she removes the cover from the machine*): As a matter of fact it's a rare and enviable privilege for a connie to get close to a member of the opposite sex.

EVA: Really?

JIM: Yes. Really and truly. I have to blink my eyes a couple of times to be sure you're not just one of them—visual and auditory hallucinations—that some fellows develop in stir.

EVA (*inserting a form-sheet in the typewriter*): Wasn't there a girl working here before me?

JIM: There was. But she wasn't nearly such a strain upon one's—credulity.

EVA: How do you mean?

JIM: She was sort of a cow.

EVA: Oh.

JIM: Whalen's wife's second cousin. But he's a remarkable man.

EVA (*whose typing obscured the last phrase*): He is or she is?

JIM: They both were. (*He laughs.*) Now you know why I'm called the Canary. I talk too much.

EVA: No. In what way?

JIM (*thumbing toward the inner room*): He had her in there the first week.

EVA: What's in there?

JIM: He goes in there to relax after ground-inspection. She would go in there with him.—She died of an operation and Whalen bought his wife a mink coat. How do you like your new job?

EVA: Well!—Not so good now.

JIM: There's some features of life on the grounds that aren't mentioned in the *Sunday Supplement*.

EVA: Yes. I didn't sleep last night.

JIM: No?

EVA: From thinking about that boy's mother.

JIM: You'll get used to things like that.

EVA: I don't want to get used to them.

JIM: Why don't you quit, then?

EVA: Say! You don't know much about the unemployment situation.

JIM: No. I got here before the Depression.

EVA: You're lucky.

JIM: Think so?

EVA: There was a case in the paper where a man busted a plate-glass window so he could go to jail and get something to eat.

JIM: I bet he regretted it afterwards. Especially if he came here.

EVA: I don't know. The sample menu's okay.

JIM: Huh! We spill that stuff on everybody comes in the office to cover up what's actually going on.

EVA (*removing the form-sheet*): What's that?

JIM: Starvation.

EVA: You're crazy!

JIM: Sure I am, crazy as a bedbug! But I've still got sense enough to recognize beans an' hamburger an' spaghetti—when I see them six or seven times a week in slightly variegated combinations! You wonder why we make such a fuss about eating? Well, I'll tell you why. It's because eating's all we got. We got nothing else, no women to sleep with, no hammers, no shovels, no papers to write on, no automobiles, no golf—nothin' to do but eat—so eating's important to us. And when they make that so darned monotonous that you feel like puking at the sight of it—then they're putting the match to a keg of powder! (*He lights his cigarette.*) Ask me what is a pyrotechnical display!

EVA: I think I know.

JIM: You'll know better if you stick around. We're going to have the loveliest Fourth o'July you ever laid eyes on. Only it's going to come, maybe in the middle of August. Y'see I've got my ear to the ground—in here and in Hall C—This place, lady, is the practical equivalent of Mt. Vesuvius. Maybe a hundred years from now little woolly white lambs will be grazing peacefully on the slopes of an extinct volcano. But down at the bottom tourist guides will be pointing out the bones of people who didn't get out of Pompeii!

EVA: Too bad you won't be one of the guides. You make such good speeches.

JIM: Okay. Be funny about it.

(*The sound of a brass band playing a martial air in the assembly hall is heard.*)

EVA (*her face brightening*): Band music!

JIM: Yes. They're practicing for the Commissioner's banquet.

EVA (*rising*): Sounds very gay!

JIM: Uh-huh. If you believed in brass bands you'd think the millennium was going to arrive at exactly 6 A.M. tomorrow.

EVA (*facing him with desperate gaiety*): Why not? Maybe it will!—A brass band can sell me *anything*, Jim!

JIM: Can it sell you this? (*He catches her against him in a hard impulsive embrace.*)

EVA (*breaking away*): Yes, it could even sell me that! (*Then she laughs.*)—But not in the Warden's office! (*She goes quickly*

*back to her typing— Jim stands motionless looking at her
back—his arms raised slowly—the hands clench into fists—
they vibrate, outstretched, with a terrific intensity—then
slowly fall to his sides. Eva whistles gaily to the band music.)*

Dim Out

EPISODE SIX

Announcer: "Mister Olympics!"

A spot comes up on the cell. Men have just returned from supper.

JOE: Did you eat yours?

BUTCH: Eat that stuff? Naw. It made me sick to look at it.

JOE: Spaghetti four times a week!

BUTCH: That's nutten. I useta work in a spaghetti factory.

QUEEN: Really?

BUTCH: Yeah. I remember one time the spaghetti machines
got out of control. We couldn't stop 'em. The whole place
was full of spaghetti. It was spaghetti ev'rywhere, oozin'
out of the floor an' the walls, an' the ceilin', spaghetti,
spaghetti, blockin' up the windows an' the doors, a big suf-
focatin' mass of spaghetti.

QUEEN: Please!

BUTCH: So I says to the foreman, "For Chrissakes, how we
gonna git outa this place wit' all this spaghetti sloppin'
aroun' ev'rywhere?"—An' the boss says, "Boys—there's
only one way to git out of here now!"—"How's that?" I ast
him.—"Here!" he says—an' he han's me a big knife an'
fork—"Yuh got to *EAT* yuh way out!"

QUEEN: Oh, for the love of nasturtiums!

(*The steel doors clang.*)

VOICE: Hello, new boy! (*Other greetings are given.*)

BUTCH: They're bringin' a new boy in.

(*Schultz stops in front of the cell with Swifty.*)

SCHULTZ: Here's yer boudoir, Sonny.

SWIFTY: Here?

SCHULTZ: Yeah. Here. (*He shoves him roughly in and slams the door.*)

SWIFTY: What did he do that for? Shove me! I was going in, wasn't I?

JOE: Sure you was going in. He just wanted to help you.

SWIFTY: I don't like being pushed around like that.

JOE: I'd complain to the Governor.

SWIFTY (*pausing as he looks about*): I've got an appeal coming before the Governor.

JOE: Have you now?

SWIFTY: Yes, I didn't get a fair trial. I was railroaded up here. My lawyer said so.

JOE: Your lawyer said so.

SWIFTY: Yes, he said— Hey, do we all stay in here together like this? Jeez, it's too small!

JOE: What's that your lawyer said?

SWIFTY: He said— What's that? A cockroach! Gosh—I don't like being cooped up like this!

JOE: What did your lawyer say?

SWIFTY: He said for me to sit tight. He'd have me out of here in two weeks, a month at the most.

JOE: A month at the most! What do you think of that, Butch?

BUTCH: I think it's a lot of what they use shovels to clean off the stable floor! (*He rises.*)—That's your new bunk, new boy. Get up there an' lissen to what I tell yuh.—Go on!

SWIFTY: Quit shoving!

BUTCH: Huh?

SWIFTY: I told you I don't like being pushed around!

BUTCH (*exhibiting his fists*): When you talk back to me you're talking back to this!—Now git up there an' pay attention to what I say.

SWIFTY: Why should I take orders from you? You're not one of the officials around here.

BUTCH: Ain't I?

SWIFTY: No!

BUTCH: Lissen, buddy. In Spain, it's Mussolini.

JOE: You mean Italy it's Mussolini.

BUTCH: I mean wherever there's wops! An' in Germany it's that monkey wit' the trick mustache!—But in here it's

Butch O'Fallon! And Butch O'Fallon is me! So now that we've been properly introduced I would like to repeat my polite invitation to remove your butt from my bunk an' git up in your own! (*Butch jerks Swifty up by the collar and hoists him by the seat of his pants to the upper bunk.*) What's yuh name?

SWIFTY: Jeremy Trout.

BUTCH: This yuh first stretch?

SWIFTY: Yes. What of it?

BUTCH: What's yuh rap?

SWIFTY: I was indicted for—stealing—money.

BUTCH: What from?

SWIFTY: Cash register in a chain store. I was cashier. But I didn't do it. I was framed by a couple of clerks.

BUTCH: I believe you. You don't look like you'd have gumption enough to crack a till. How much you got?

SWIFTY: On me? Nothing. They even took my cigarettes.

BUTCH: I mean your stretch. How long?

SWIFTY: Judge Eggleston gave me five years. But my lawyer says—

BUTCH: You'll *do* five years.

SWIFTY: In here? Why, I'd go crazy locked in here that long!

BUTCH: Pocket yuh marbles!

SWIFTY: I—I feel sick. The air in here's no good.

BUTCH: No?

SWIFTY: It smells. It's making me sick at the stomach.

BUTCH: There's the slop bucket.

SWIFTY: No!

BUTCH: It ain't been emptied yet. That's your job. The new man always empties.

SWIFTY: No— (*He sinks into his bunk.*) —Five years? I couldn't stand being cooped up that long. I got to have space around me. I get restless. That's why I didn't like working in the chain store. Kept me behind a counter all day, felt like I was tied up there.—At high school I was a runner.

BUTCH: A runner, huh?

QUEEN: That's what I said to myself. He looks athletic.

SWIFTY: Yes. I held the 220 state record for three years.

BUTCH: Fancy that.

SWIFTY: I like anything that's moving, that don't stay put. It's not an ordinary thing with me, it's kind of an obsession. I like to kill distance. See a straight track—get to the other end of it first, before anyone else— That's what I was made for—running—look at my legs!

JOE: Pips, huh?

SWIFTY: That's from training. If this hadn't happened I'd be on my way to the Olympics right now. I could still have a chance at the New York eliminations if my lawyer can spring me before the fifteenth. (*He flexes his legs.*) —But look at that! Getting loose already!—If I could get permission to run around the yard a few times—say, before breakfast or supper—why, I could keep in pretty good shape even in here. Even if I had to stay in here a year—that way I could keep in condition!

JOE: He'll go like Sailor Jack.

BUTCH: Pocket yuh marbles!—Buddy, I ain't sentimental—but I feel sorry for you.

SWIFTY: Why? Don't you think he'll let me?

BUTCH: Naw.

SWIFTY: Why not?

BUTCH: Because you're a con.

SWIFTY: But a con's a human being. He's got to be treated like one.

BUTCH: A con ain't a human being. A con's a con. (*The lights fade on the others and concentrate on Butch.*) He's stuck in here and the world's forgot him. As far as the world is concerned he don't exist anymore. What happens to him in here—them people outside don't know, they don't care. He's entrusted to the care of the State. The State? Hell! The State turns him over to a guy called a Warden and a bunch of other guys called guards. Who're they? Men who like to boss other men. Maybe they could've been truck-drivers or street cleaners or circus clowns. But they didn't wanta be none a them. Why? Cause they've got a natural instinck for swinging a shelailee! They like to crack heads, make sausage out of human flesh! And so they get to be guards. That sounds like 'gods'—which ain't so much a coincidence either, because the only diff'rence between

'guards' an' 'gods' is that 'guards' has an 'r' in it an' the 'r'
stands for 'rat'!—That's what a guard is accordin' to my
definition—'A rat who thinks that he's GOD!'—You better
not forget that. Because, Sonny, you're not in high school
no more. You ain't in the chain store, you're not at the
Olympics— That's Part One of your education. Part Two
is stay away from stool pigeons. Hey, Canary!—He ain't in
yet but we got a little songbird in the next cage who sings
real sweetly sometimes for the boss.—So don't be buddies
wit him. Give 'im a cigarette, Joe.

JOE: Here, mister Olympics.

BUTCH: Keep it covered.—How's yuh stomach now?

SWIFTY: Some better.

BUTCH: Hungry?

SWIFTY: No.

BUTCH: That's good. Because we might quit eating.

QUEEN: Quit eating?

BUTCH: Yep. I been thinkin' over what we talked about las'
night, Joe, an' I'm just about sold on it.

JOE: I'm still on the fence about that.

BUTCH: There ain't any fence to be on, Joe. When I say
hunger strike in here it's going to be hunger strike.

QUEEN: Hunger strike!

SWIFTY: What's that?

BUTCH: Pocket yuh marbles. The Canary's comin' to roost.

(*Derisive whistles are heard in the hall.*)

Help me off wit' these shoes, Queenie. That's right. Here,
hang up my shirt. Joe—

JOE: What the hell?

BUTCH: You fold my pants up nice an' lay 'em over the
chair.—Hello, moon. (*He stands in a shaft of moonlight
through the barred window.*)

JOE: You're going like Sailor Jack, saying hello to the moon!

BUTCH: She's big an' yellow tonight. Y'know me an' God
have got something in common, Joe.

JOE: Yeah, what's that?

BUTCH: A weakness for blondes!

Blackout

EPISODE SEVEN

Announcer: "A Rubber Duck for the Baby!"

A spot comes up on the Warden's office. The Boss is seated at his desk inflating a rubber duck.

WARDEN (*to Eva who lays papers on his desk*): Look at this.

EVA: Yes.

WARDEN: It's a rubber duck for the baby.

EVA: I didn't know you had one.

WARDEN: You bet I got one. Cutest little baby doll you ever set eyes on!

EVA: Boy or girl?

WARDEN: Girl! Wouldn't have nothing else. Will she be tickled when she sees this! (*Eva starts to leave.*) Wait! I'm gonna git her on the phone now! You wanta hear this, Eva? (*He dials.*) Hello, Mama? How's tricks? Yeah? Well, put the baby on, will yuh? (*To Eva*): Now lissen to this! Puddikins? Popsy dust wanted to know if oo was bein' a dood little durl! Oo are? Dat's dood. Popsy'd dot somefin fo dood little durls! No. Not a stick-candies. Oo see when Popsy dets home, 'es oo will! Bye-bye now! Bye-bye!— (*He hangs up with a chuckle.*) Cute 's the dickens—looks just like Shirley Temple—don't she though? (*He shows a picture to Eva.*)

EVA: Yes, there is a resemblance.

(*Jim enters.*)

WARDEN (*heartily*): Hello, Jimmy boy! What's new?

JIM: Nothing new. Just the same old complaints about food. Only they're getting louder all the time, Boss.

WARDEN: What do they want? Caviar? Cream puffs? Charlotte Russes? Do they want us to have printed menus so they can order their meals *à la carte*? Stick these medical reports in the file case, Eva.

JIM: If you look those reports over you'll see there was seven cases of ptomaine poisoning after the Wednesday night supper. Those meatballs were worse on the stomach than they were on the nose!

WARDEN: What do you mean? They weren't good?

JIM: I think they were meant for the buzzards out at the zoo. Got mixed up at the market or something and came over here by mistake.

WARDEN: Look here, Jim. You're talking too uppity. Showing off for Miss Crane, I guess—'s at it?

JIM: No, Sir. If I didn't give you my honest opinion what good would I be?

WARDEN (*slowly, studying Jim's face*): Okay. Yeah, you're a good boy, Jim.

JIM: Thanks.

WARDEN (*leaning back*): I like you, Jim. Why? Cause you got a face that looks like it was cut outa rock. Turn sideways, Jim— Eva?

EVA (*at the files*): Yes, Sir?

WARDEN: Ever seen a cleaner-cut profile than that? Like it was carved in stone, huh? Them jaws, the nose, the mouth? I tried to break that when Jim first come in here. Never did. It stayed like it is—stone face! Never got it to change, not even when I give him fifty stripes with a rubber hose ev'ry morning for fourteen days.—Remember that, Jim?

JIM (*his face barely tightening*): Yes, Sir.

WARDEN: When I seen I couldn't break him I said to myself, "Hey, Bert, here's a man you could use!" So I did. Jim's a trusty, now, a stool pigeon—Canary Jim—that's what the other cons all call him. Ain't that so, Jim?

JIM: Yes, Sir.

WARDEN: Keeps me posted on conditions among the men. He don't come gum-shoeing, whispering like the other stool pigeons I got in here—he comes straight out and says what he thinks!—That's what makes him valuable to me!—But the men don't like him. They hate your guts, don't they, Jim?

JIM: Yes, Sir. (*He speaks in almost a whisper.*)

WARDEN: Jim's on my side, all right. I couldn't break him so I made him useful. Take off your shirt, Jim—show Eva your back.

JIM: Yes, Sir. (*He obeys with curious, machine-like precision. Diagonally across his shoulder down to the waist are long scars which ten years could not obliterate.*)

WARDEN: See them scars, Eva? He got them ten years ago. Pretty sight he was then. Raw meat. The skin hung down from his back like pieces of red tissue paper! The flesh was all pulpy, beat up, the blood squirted out like juice from a ripe tomato ev'ry time I brung the whip down on him. "Had enough, Jim? Ready to go back to that embossing machine?"—"Naw," says Jim,—"Not till it's fixed!"—He defied me like that for fourteen days.—I seen I'd either have to kill him or I'd have to admit that he had me licked.—I says to him, "Jim, you win! You don't go back to that embossing machine, you stay right here in the office an' work for me because you're a man that's made out of stuff that I like!" Stone face! Huh, Jim?

JIM: Yes, Sir. (*The papers have already slipped from Eva's hands. She utters a slight breathless cry and grips the edge of the desk.*)

WARDEN: Thunderation! What's wrong?

JIM: I think she's fainting. (*He catches Eva.*)

WARDEN: Let go of that girl—get your shirt on and get out.—Tell the boys in Hall C I'm tired a complaints about food.—Well, young lady?

EVA: I'm all right now.

WARDEN: Awright, I've got her.—Get your shirt back on, Jim—I want you to have a little talk with Butch O'Fallon tonight.—Tell him I'm tired a complaints in Hall C, and if he wants trouble I'm the baby that can dish it out!—Go on, get on out!

JIM: Yes, Sir. (*He exits slowly.*)

WARDEN (*to Eva who has sunk in her chair*): Well, young lady?

EVA: I'm all right now.

WARDEN: Sorry. I didn't mean to make it that strong. Jim's a good boy, but it don't hurt to remind him once in a while of his old friend Dr. Jones.

(*Eva averts her face.*)

You think I'm brutal, dontcha? You got to realize the position I'm in. I got thirty-five hundred men here, men that would knife their own mothers for the price of a beer. It takes a mighty firm hand.—Yes, Siree! (*He picks up the rubber duck—inflates it some more.*) Cute, huh?—She'll make a fuss over this!

Dim Out

EPISODE EIGHT

Announcer: "Explosion!"

The spot comes up on the cell. We should feel a definite increase of tension over the preceding cell scenes. Butch paces restlessly. The others sit sullenly on their bunks, the Queen with an old movie magazine, Swifty anxiously flexing his legs.

JOE (*entering from the hall and removing the jacket*): Save your shoe leather.

BUTCH: What for?

JOE: You might want to eat it tonight instead of cold beans.

BUTCH: Beans, huh?

SWIFTY (*with a letter*): It's from my lawyer.

QUEEN: What's he say, honey?

SWIFTY: He says for me to sit tight.

QUEEN: Goodness!—My nails are in awful condition.

SWIFTY: Sit tight! What does he think I've been doing since I got here? Sit tight—sit tight! Don't he know I've got to be moving around?

BUTCH: Take it easy, Mister Olympics!—Who toleja cold beans?

JOE: Boy that works in the kitchen.

SWIFTY: I don't trust that lawyer. This time he says six months.

QUEEN: I don't trust no man, honey. No further'n I could kick Grant's Tomb with a fractured toe! (*He giggles.*)

BUTCH: He oughta know.

SWIFTY: My lawyer?

BUTCH: Your lawyer! Naw—the kitchen boy.

JOE: Maybe our friend the Canary forgot to spill.

BUTCH: He'd never forget to spill anything.

JOE: Then maybe the Boss don't care how we feel about cold beans for supper.

BUTCH: He wants to call our hand.

JOE: Sure. He's got an ace in the hole.—Klondike!

BUTCH: We've got one, too.

JOE: Hunger strike?

BUTCH: You named it, Brother.

JOE: Two guys can't hold the ace of spades.

BUTCH: Once I sat in a game where that was the situation.

JOE: How didja solve it?

BUTCH (*producing his razor*): Wit' this.

JOE: You better quit flashin' that thing.

BUTCH: Ev'rybody knows I got tough whiskers. (*He laughs and replaces razor in his belt.*) "Fawchun's always hid-ing—/ I looked ev'rywhere!"

(*Bird calls are heard from the hall.*)

Here it comes, it's th' Canary. (*He gives a shrill whistle.*) Hello, Canary. How's them solo flights you been makin? You know—out there on the mountain tops wit' nothing around ja but the stars? (*He and Joe laugh.*)

OLLIE (*from next cell*): Don't pay 'em no mind, Jim.

JIM: Never mind about that. I got something to tell you.

BUTCH: Tell us about Goldilocks and the bears.

JOE: I like Goody-Two-Shoes.

JIM: Come outside for a minute.

BUTCH: You wanta fight?

JIM: No, I wanta talk.

BUTCH: You allus wanta talk, that's your trouble. If you got something to spill come in here.

JIM: I know what happened last time I got in a cage with you, Butch.

BUTCH: I'm glad I made that good an impression.

JIM: Are you coming out?

BUTCH: Naw. Are you coming in?

JIM: Yeah. I will. Soon as they douse the glims.

QUEEN: Better not, honey. Butch has got tough whiskers.

JIM: Yeah, I know what he cuts 'em with.

BUTCH: Why dontcha spill it, then?

JIM: I never deliberately ratted on nobody, Butch.

(*A whistle sounds. The lights dim.*)

Okay. I'm coming in now. (*He unlocks the cell and enters.*)

QUEEN: Now, Butch—

JOE: Watch, yourself. It's not worth getting jerked to Jesus for.

BUTCH: Naw, Canary, my respect for you is increased two hundred percent. I never thought you'd have what it takes to step inside here.

JIM: It's like what I was telling Ollie last night. We've all got walls around ourselves, Butch, that we can't see through—that's why we make so many mistakes about each other. Have a smoke?

BUTCH: Naw. Just say what you got to say and then take a double powder. I don't wanta lose control.

JIM: I know what you've got in mind.

BUTCH: What?

JIM: Hunger strike.

BUTCH: What of it?

JIM: I don't recommend it, Butch.

BUTCH: Did Whalen tell you to say that?

JIM: Naw, this is on the level, Butch.

BUTCH: Yeah, about as level as the Adirondacks.

JIM: I'll admit I've made myself useful to him. But I haven't forgotten two weeks we spent in the Hole together, and those visits he paid every morning to inquire about our health. He was even more solicitous about mine than yours, Butch. Things like that can make a common bond between men that nothing afterwards can ever—

BUTCH: Come to the point!

JIM: All right. I'm coming up for parole next month.

BUTCH (*rising*): You are, huh?

JIM: There's a chance I might get it. And if I do I'm going to justify my reputation as a brilliant vocalist, Butch. I'm going to sing so loud and so high that the echo will knock these walls down! I know plenty from working in the office. I know all the pet grafts. I know all about the intimidation of employees and torture of convicts; I know about the Hole, about the water cure, about the overcoat—about Klondike!—And I know about the kind of food—or slop, rather!—that we been eating! You wait a month! That's all! When I get through Whalen will be where he belongs—in the psychopathic ward with Sailor Jack! And I promise you things will change in here—look—here's an article about the Industrial Reformatory in Chillicothe!—that's the kind of a place this'll be!

BUTCH (*throwing the paper aside*): I don't want no articles!—Allison, you're full of shit.

JOE: Take it easy, Butch. (*To Jim.*) So you don't want us to go on hunger strike?

JIM: No. It won't do any good. The Boss'll throw the bunch of you in Klondike. Do yourself a favor. Work with me. We can case this jug. But not if we keep on going opposite ways.—Give me your hand on it, Butch.

BUTCH: Fuck you!

JIM: It's no dice, huh? What do you say, Joe? Swifty?

BUTCH: They say what I say! Now git out before I lose my last ounce a restriction!

JIM: Okay. (*He goes out.*)

JOE: Maybe he *was* on the level.

BUTCH: He will be on the level when he's laid out straight under ground. (*He slaps Swifty's rump.*) Git up! It's supper time!

SWIFTY (*his face buried in the pillow*): Leave me alone. I'm sick. I'm not hungry.

BUTCH: You're coming along anyhow. We need you to help make some noise in case the kitchen boy was right about supper.

JOE: Noise?

BUTCH: Yep, *plenty* of noise!

(*The bell rings in the hall.*)

BUTCH: Come along, youse! (*He shoves Queen and jerks Swifty to his feet.*) Hell's bells are ringin'! Come on, boys! Before them biscuits git cold! T-bone steaks for supper! Smothered in mushrooms! Come and git it!

(*A whistle is heard and the lights dim out. Theme up: "1812 Overture." Fade.*)

Blackout

EPISODE NINE

Announcer: "Hunger Strike!"

A spot comes up on the office. Eva enters.

WARDEN: Had your supper?

EVA: Yes.

WARDEN (*watching her as she crosses downstage*): Hate to keep you overtime like this—but with the boys in Hall C kicking up such a rumpus, we got to have all our books in perfect shape—just in case the professional snoopers git on our tails about something!

EVA: Yes Sir. (*She removes the cover from the typewriter.*)

WARDEN (*watching her closely*): Hope working nights don't interfere too much with your social life.

EVA (*tiredly*): I don't have any social life right now.

WARDEN: How come?

EVA: I've been so busy job hunting since I moved here that I haven't had much time to cultivate friends.

WARDEN: No boyfriends, huh?

EVA: Oh, I have a few that I correspond with.

WARDEN: Yeah, but there's a limit to what can be put in an envelope, huh?

EVA: I suppose there is.—Mr. Whalen, there seem to be quite a number of bad discrepancies in the commissary report.

WARDEN: You mean it don't add up right?

EVA: I failed to account for about six hundred dollars.

(*The Warden whistles.*)

What shall I do about it?

WARDEN: I'll git Jim to check it over with you. You know a lot can be done about things like that by a little manipulation of figures. Jim'll explain that to you.

EVA: I see.

WARDEN: How long have you been working here?

EVA: Two weeks.

WARDEN: Gin'rally I git shut of a girl in less time'n that if she don't measure up to the job.

EVA (*tensely*): I hope that I've shown my efficiency.

WARDEN: Aw, efficiency! I don't look for efficiency in my girls.

EVA: What do you look for, Mr. Whalen?

WARDEN: Personality! You're in a position where you got to meet the public. Big men politically come in this office— you give 'em a smile, they feel good—what do they care

about the tax-payers' money?—Those boobs that go aroun'
checkin' over accounts, where did this nickel go, what's
done with that dime—jitney bums, I call 'em!—No, Siree,
I got no respect for a man that wants a job where he's got
to make note of ev'ry red copper that happens to slip
through his hands!—Well—policy, that's what I'm after!—
Being political about certain matters, it don't hurt *ever*,
yuh see?

EVA: Yes, I think so.

WARDEN (*pausing*): What color's that blouse you got on?

EVA (*nervously sensing his approach*): Chartreuse.

WARDEN (*half-extending his hand*): It's right Frenchy-looking.

EVA: Thank you. (*She types rapidly.*)

WARDEN (*opening the inner door and coughing uncertainly*):
Look here.

EVA: Yes?

WARDEN: Why don't you drop that formality stuff? (*He crosses
to her.*) How do I look to you? Unromantic? Not so much
like one of the movie stars?—Well, it might surprise you to
know how well I go over with some of the girls! (*He seats
himself on corner of the desk.*)—I had a date not so long
ago—girl works over at the Cattle and Grain Market—
'bout your age, build, ev'rything—(*He licks his lips.*)—
When I got through loving her up she says to me—"Do it
again, Papa do it again!"—(*He roars with laughter and slaps
the desk.*)—Why? Because she *loved* it, that why! (*He rises
and goes to the inner door.*) You ever been in here?

EVA: No.

WARDEN (*heartily*): Come on in. I wanta show you how nice
I got it fixed up.

EVA: No.

WARDEN: Why not?

EVA (*rising stiffly*): You're married, Mr. Whalen. I'm not that
kind of girl.

WARDEN: Aw, that act's been off the stage for years!

EVA: It's not an act, Mr. Whalen!

WARDEN: Naw, neither was *Uncle Tom's Cabin* when little Eva
goes up to heaven in Act III on a bunch of steel wires! (*He
slams the inner door angrily, then laughs.*) You're okay, sister. You keep right on pitching in there.

EVA: Now that you know me better, do I still have a job?

WARDEN: Why, you betcha life you still got a job! (*He laughs and grips her in a fumbling embrace which she rigidly endures. Jim enters.*)

JIM: Excuse me.

WARDEN (*still laughing*): Come on in, Jimmy boy. Want you to check over this commissary report with Miss Crane. She says there's a few—what you call 'em? Discrepancies! You know how to fix that up!

JIM: Yes, Sir.

WARDEN: How's things in Hall C? Pretty quiet?

JIM: Too quiet.

WARDEN: How's that?

JIM: When they make a noise you know what's going on.

WARDEN: They're scared to let a peep out since I put that bunch in the Hole.

JIM: I don't think so. I got an idea they might quit eating tonight.

WARDEN: Quit eating? You mean—*hunger strike*? (*The word scares him a little.*)

JIM: Yes. They're tired of spaghetti.

WARDEN: Maybe a change of climate would improve their appetites!

JIM: Klondike?

WARDEN: Yeah.

JIM: Klondike won't hold thirty-five hundred men.

WARDEN: It would hold Hall C.

JIM: Yes, but Butch is in Hall C.

WARDEN: What of it?

JIM: He's got a lot of influence with the men.

WARDEN: He's a troublemaker an' I'm gonna sweat it out of him.

JIM: I wouldn't try that, Boss. Hunger makes men pretty desperate and if you tortured them on top of that there's no telling what might happen.

WARDEN: Hunger strike's something I won't put up with in here. Creates a sensation all over the country. Then what? Cranks of ev'ry description start bitching about the brutal treatment of those goddamn mugs that would knife their own mothers for the price of a beer!

JIM: The easiest way to avoid it would be to improve the food.

WARDEN: Avoid it, hell. I'll bust it to pieces! Wait'll they see that gang we've got in the Hole—if that don't make sufficient impression I'll give 'em the heat! (*He leaves the office.*)

JIM: The man's a lunatic. Ask him who he is, he'd say, "Benito Mussolini!"

EVA: You're right about him. I suspected it last week when he made you show me those scars on your back. Just now— before you came in—he convinced me of it.

JIM: What happened?

EVA: He wanted me to go in that room with him.

JIM: You didn't?

EVA: No. I was sure he'd fire me but he only laughed and squeezed my arm— Look!

JIM: What?

EVA: I've got a blue mark on my arm where he pinched me.

JIM: When he was a boy I bet he got lots of fun drowning kittens and pulling the wings off butterflies.—Were you scared?

EVA: Terribly scared—and at the same time—something else.

JIM: What?

EVA: If I told you, you'd be disgusted with me.

JIM: Attracted?

EVA: Yes, in a way. I knew that if he touched me I wouldn't be able to move.

JIM: In the pulps they call it fascinated horror.

EVA: Yes. Or a horrible fascination.

JIM: So you're convinced it's no place for a lady?

EVA: I'm not going to quit. Not yet.

JIM: No? If you wait for a third alarm it might be too late.

EVA: I'm going to stay. I've got a favorite nightmare, Jim, about finding myself alone in a big empty house. And knowing that something or somebody was hidden behind one of the doors, waiting to grab me— But instead of running out of the house I always go searching through it; opening all of the closed doors— Even when I come to the last one, I don't stop, Jim—I open that one, too.

JIM: And what do you find?

EVA: I don't know. I always wake up just then.

JIM: So you're going to try the same thing here?

EVA: Something like that.

JIM: I guarantee you won't be disappointed. Gimme the commissary report— No, take that sheet out, we'll start over again— See how much spaghetti we can make out of a Packard Six. Ten pounds of sodium fluoride. No, you better make it sixteen.

EVA: Sixteen pounds of sodium fluoride.

JIM: Sixteen pounds of—sodium fluoride.

EVA: You just gave me that.

JIM: Aw. Twenty bushels of—

EVA: Jim.

JIM: Yeah?

EVA: Why don't you ever open the door *you're* hiding behind?

JIM: What makes you think I'm hiding behind anything?

EVA: Your eyes, the way your hands shake sometimes.

JIM: Oh. That.

EVA: It would help to let go. I mean with the right person.

JIM: Who is that right person?

EVA: Me.

JIM: How do I know?

EVA: Because I tell you.

JIM: Lots of people tell lots of things and most of them are lies.

EVA: I'm not lying, Jim—I want you to trust me.

JIM: Okay.

EVA: Then tell me—what is it?

JIM: What?

EVA: Your hands—why do they shake like this?

JIM: I thought I gave you a clear demonstration once.

EVA: When?

JIM: That morning we heard the band music.

EVA: You mean it's—repression.

JIM: That's it. Something that's locked up and keeps getting more and more all the time. There's lots of men in here with fingers that shake like this. It's power. Outside it runs dynamos, lights up big cities. But in here the power's all gone to waste. It just feeds on itself, gets bigger, does nothing. Till something sets it off like a match does a keg of powder—and then you got an explosion!

EVA: Explosions are such a—waste—of power!

JIM: Yeah. But what's the alternative here?

EVA: Your writing!

JIM: Editorials for *The Archaeopteryx*?

EVA: No! You've got next month to think of, Jim.

JIM: Next month is still on the lap of the gods. Which is a complimentary way of referring to the Board of Pardons and Paroles.

EVA: I don't know why, but I feel so sure of it, Jim. These ten years of—of waiting— They've made you stronger than other men are— You've stored up so much in you that when you get it out, there's nothing could stand in your way— You'll push down all the ordinary walls and walk right over them, Jim— People will say, "Who is this man? Where did he come from?"—and I'll smile proudly because I'll know.—He's a man from another country, I'll say— He's a giant— He's got lightning in his right hand and thunder in his left— But I'll know— I'll know secrets about you—all the sweet, strange things that only a woman can know—and I can tell you— (*Whalen enters.*) How many pounds was that—of sodium fluoride?

JIM: Sixteen.

WARDEN: How you getting along with that report?

JIM: We haven't done much yet. We got to talking.

WARDEN: About what?

JIM: Fireworks.

WARDEN: Very appropriate. Schultz is bringing the Hole gang up for inspection. Get them chairs out of the way.

JIM: Yes, Sir.

WARDEN: You stand over by the window and look sharp! Eva—you wanta stay in here or go in the next room?

EVA: I'll stay.

(*A buzzer sounds.*)

WARDEN: Okay. March 'em in! (*A file of haggard, ghostly figures shuffles into the room, their eyes blinking against the light, barely able to stand—some with heads bloody, others with clotted, shredded shirts. The Warden whistles.*)

SCHULTZ: Stand up against that wall!

WARDEN: Nice-lookin' bunch. Oughta make quite an impression when they go back to Hall C! (*To Swifty*): How long have you been in the hole, Son?

(*Swifty cannot speak. His lips move and he staggers forward with a pleading gesture. The Warden raises the "billy" and continues.*)

Stand back there! Why don't you speak?

JIM: He can't talk.

WARDEN: Dumb?

EVA: No. Sick. He's had five days in a strait jacket.

WARDEN: I think he needs five more.

(*Swiftly falls to his knees.*)

JIM: I think Swifty's had enough, boss.

WARDEN: Who asked you?

JIM: Nobody.

WARDEN: Just volunteered the information?

JIM: Yes, Sir.

WARDEN: Maybe you'd like to take his place down there?

JIM: No, Sir.

WARDEN: Then you'd better cut the cackle. Ollie?

OLLIE (*faintly*): Yes, Sir.

WARDEN: You look kind of all in.

OLLIE (*his voice shaking*): I is, suh. I neahly checked out las' night. Boss, ah didn' think ad'd live t' see day!

WARDEN: Think another night would just about fix you up?

OLLIE: Couldn't make it, Boss.

WARDEN: What do you think, Schultz?

SCHULTZ: I think another night would do that boy a world of good, Mr. Whalen.

OLLIE (*wildly*): Please, God, Boss, ah cain't make it! Ah cain't *make* it!

WARDEN: Two nights!—One extra for squawking!

OLLIE: Oh, Laws, a mussy, please, oh, Jesus, please, a mussy— (*He continues this prayer in a sort of chant as they are led out the door.*)

WARDEN: Get 'em out! I'll check 'em over again tomorrow morning.

(*They shuffle out slowly, Ollie chanting his prayer. Jim follows.*)

Ever heard such a squawk?

(*Eva sinks wearily into a chair.*)

You going to flip out again?

EVA: No. I'm all right. They looked so awful it made me a little sick.

WARDEN: Sure they looked awful. Maybe they'll appreciate good treatment after this— I'll wager there'll be no more kick about food.

(*From the hall comes the sound of a disturbance—Jim enters.*)

WARDEN: What's going on out there?

JIM: Ollie just—

WARDEN: Took a dive?

JIM: Yes. Butted his head against a wall and broke it.

WARDEN: Head or wall?

JIM: Head.

WARDEN: All right. Cart him over to the sick-house.

JIM: Not the sick-house.

WARDEN: Dead?

JIM: Yes.

WARDEN: Why dontcha watch out? You coulda prevented that— Give Eva one of them cards— Naw, outa the top drawer. Fill that out. Name— What was that smoke's name?

JIM: Oliver. Oliver Jackson.

WARDEN: Special friend of yours?

JIM: All of the men liked Ollie.

WARDEN: Huh. How old?

JIM: Twenty-six.

WARDEN: Color—black! Sentence—

JIM: Three years.

WARDEN: Charge?

JIM (*slowly*): Stole a crate of canned goods off a truck to feed his family.

WARDEN: Larceny!—Cause of death?—What's his Wasserman?

JIM: Negative.

WARDEN: Hmmm. Put this down, Eva. Stomach Ulcers. Severe hemorrhages.

JIM: That's what you gave the boy last week.

WARDEN: Well, make it a bad cold—complications—pneumonia!

(*The sounds of yammering begin to penetrate the office.*)

(*The Warden is unnerved for a moment but continues.*)
What's that?

JIM: They're making a noise.

WARDEN (*instinctively seizing his whip*): Where's it from?
Hall C?

JIM: Naw. Halls A, B, C, D, E, and F!

WARDEN (*shakily*): What are they bitching about now?

JIM: They must have heard about Ollie. They like him pretty
good.

WARDEN: Aw— (*He looks frightened.*) —Schultz! (*He seizes the
phone.*) Schultz? How's the pipes in Klondike? Git them radiators tested an' ready for action.

(*There is a sudden complete darkness on stage.*)

WHISPERS (*gradually rising in volume and pitch*): Somebody
got hurt downstairs— Who was it?—Ollie!—Ollie?—Yeah,
they killed Ollie—Ollie's dead.—They killed Ollie—Ollie's
dead— They KILLED OLLIE—THEY KILLED OLLIE
—OLLIE'S DEAD!

(*A spot comes up on the cell. Butch is bending to the wall. He
suddenly rises.*)

BUTCH: Ollie's dead— THEY KILLED OLLIE! (*He shouts
through the bars.*)

CHORUS: Ollie's dead! They killed Ollie!

JOE: What are we going to do about it?

BUTCH: Quit eating! (*He shouts through the bars*) QUIT
EATING!

CHORUS: Quit eating! Quit eating!

(*Blackout.*)

WHISPERS: What does Butch say?—Butch says quit eating—
hunger strike?—Yeah, hunger strike!—Butch says HUN-
GER STRIKE!—Hunger strike—quit eating—Quit eating
—HUNGER STRIKE!

VOICE: The men in Hall C have quit eating!

SECOND VOICE: Hunger strike in Hall C!

NEWSBOY: *Morning Star!* Paper! *Morning Star!* Paper! Read about the big hunger strike!

WOMAN'S VOICE: It is reported that some of the men in the state prison have gone on a hunger strike!

(*The click of a telegraph is heard.*)

VOICE: Associated Press Bulletin— Hunger strike at Monroe City Penitentiary! Men rebel against monotonous diet!

VOICE: United Press!

VOICE: Columbia Broadcasting System!

VOICE: Commissioners promise an investigation of alleged starvation in state penitentiary!

VOICE: Warden denies hunger strike!

VOICE: Hunger strike reported!

VOICE: Hunger strike denied!

VOICE: Hunger strike! HUNGER STRIKE!

(*Traffic noises, sirens, bells are heard. Theme up: "1812 Overture" theme reprise. Blackout. Fade.*)

End of Act One

ACT TWO

EPISODE ONE

Announcer: "Not About Nightingales!"

A spot comes up on the office. The hunger strike has been in effect for several days and a tense, electric atmosphere prevails as everyone waits for the inevitable explosion when nerves are stretched beyond the point of endurance. Eva is seated alone as the scene opens. Her movements are jittery. The phone rings.

EVA: Warden's office. *The Morning Star?* No, Mr. Whalen is not seeing any reporters. No, there is no serious trouble. No, you can't get on the Island without a special permit from Mr. Whalen. The rule has been in effect for about six days. No, not on account of a hunger strike! Yes, good-bye.

(*During this the Chaplain has entered. Eva is startled, then continues.*)

Oh!

CHAPLAIN: Nervous, young lady?

EVA: Terribly—terribly!

CHAPLAIN: I don't blame you. So am I. This thing has got to be stopped before something serious happens.

EVA: Oh, if it only could be!

CHAPLAIN: That's what I want to see Mr. Whalen about. It does no good trying to suppress all news of what's going on. We might as well face the music—and do something constructive to put a stop to it!

EVA: Yes. Something constructive.

CHAPLAIN: But in the meantime—couldn't you take a little vacation?

EVA: You think there's real—danger?

CHAPLAIN: Certainly there's danger. And it's aggravated by the fact that Mr. Whalen apparently won't recognize it. I wish that I could reason with that man, but— Well— (*He glances at his watch.*) —I'll visit some boys in the hospital and be back here for a talk with the Boss in about twenty minutes.

EVA: All right.

(*Jim enters.*)

CHAPLAIN: Hello, Jim. How are things upstairs?

JIM (*showing a bloody arm in a torn sleeve*): That's the answer!

EVA (*springing up*): Jim!

JIM (*laughing grimly*): I walked too close to one of the cages.

CHAPLAIN: Who did that?

JIM (*slowly shaking his head*): I don't know.

CHAPLAIN (*patting his back*): You've had ten bad years, Jim. I hope next month will be the end of it for you.

JIM: Thanks, Reverend. (*The Chaplain goes out.*)

EVA: Jim, I'll—I'll fix that up for you.

(*He sits down by desk.*)

JIM: They gave me this stuff to put on it down at the sick-house. They were sore as hell because I wouldn't tell them who done it.

EVA (*painting his arm and applying a bandage*): You shouldn't stay up there. It's not safe for you.

JIM: No place is safe in here. Aren't you finally convinced of that?

EVA: Why are you so anxious to get rid of me?

JIM: You know a lot you could tell.

EVA: Yes. I suppose I do.

JIM: Why don't you then?

EVA: I want to stay here a while longer. Maybe next month I'll go—we'll both go then.

JIM: They've been on a hunger strike six days and the Warden only gave them seven. Tonight may be the deadline. Tomorrow night at the latest.

EVA: Then what?

JIM: The boiler room is in perfect condition. The pipes have been reinforced.

EVA: I can't imagine anything as brutal as that—I don't believe it!

JIM: Well—I ought to spill it myself—but if I did it would cost my ticket-of-leave!—It's funny.

EVA: What?

JIM: Nothing has quite so much value as the skin our own guts are wrapped in. (*He takes a book and sits down at the window.*)

(*Eva resumes typing. Jim suddenly tears a page out and throws it on the floor in disgust.*)

Christ!

EVA: What did you do that for?

JIM: I didn't like it.

EVA: What was it?

JIM: A little piece of verbal embroidery by a guy named Keats.

EVA: What's wrong with it?

JIM: It's sissy stuff—"Ode to a Nightingale!" Don't those literary punks know there's something more important to write about than that? They ought to spend a few years in stir before they select their subjects!

EVA: Why don't you show them, then?

JIM: I'd give my right arm for the chance.

EVA: You have the chance!

JIM: Not in here I don't. If I wrote what I wanted to write, I'd stay in here till Klondike becomes an ice-plant!—But maybe next month—

EVA: Yes. Next month—

JIM: Maybe then I'll start writing—but not about nightingales!

EVA: John Keats didn't have a very good time of it, Jim.

JIM: No?

EVA: No. He died at the age of twenty-six.

JIM: Smothered himself in lilies, I guess.

EVA: No. He wanted to live. Terribly. He was like you, he had a lot of things he wanted to say but no chance to say them. He wrote another poem, Jim. A poem you'd like. Give me the book—here it is! (*She reads the sonnet "When I have fears that I may cease to be"*):

> When I have fears that I may cease to be
> Before my pen has gleaned my teeming brain,
> Before high pilèd books, in charactry,
> Hold like rich garners the full-ripened grain;
> When I behold, upon the night's starred face,
> Huge cloudy symbols of high romance,
> And think that I may never live to trace
> Their shadows, with the magic hand of chance;
> And when I feel, fair creature of an hour!
> That I shall never look upon thee more,
> Never have relish in the faery power
> Of unreflecting love!—then on the shore
> Of the wide world I stand alone, and think
> Till Love and Fame to nothingness do sink.

You see he was like you, Jim. He got out of his prison by looking at the stars. He wrote about beauty as a form of escape.

JIM: Escape, huh? That's not my kind of escape.

EVA: What is your form of escape?

JIM: Blowing things wide open!

EVA: Destruction, you mean?

JIM: Yes! Destruction!

EVA: I'm sorry to hear you say that.

JIM: Would you rather hear me warbling about nightingales?

EVA: No. But there are other things.

JIM: For instance?

EVA: There must be some things you love.

JIM: Love?

EVA: Yes.

JIM: Love is something nasty that's done in dark corners around this place.

EVA: I'm sorry you're so bitter.

JIM: Why should you be sorry about anything except the possible loss of your job?

EVA: Why should I? Because I like you, Jim.

JIM: Even after—after the last time we were in here together?

EVA: More than ever.

JIM: When you've been without women as long as I have, there's something mythological about them. You can't believe they're real, not even when you place your hands on them like this and—

EVA: Jim! (*She breaks away as Whalen enters.*)

WARDEN: What's the matter Jim?

JIM: Why?

WARDEN: You got a funny look on your face.

JIM: I'm just concentrating.

WARDEN: On what?

JIM: The new *Archaeopteryx*.

WARDEN: Aw, what are you going to write about, Jim?

JIM (*quietly*): Not about—nightingales.

WARDEN: Huh? (*Absently fiddles with his papers.*) Aw, Jim—

JIM: Yes, Sir?

WARDEN: You might want to drop a word to the boys on hunger strike about the radiator test we made in Klondike. We got the temperature up to 150 degrees— You might mention that. You know a word to the wise is sufficient.

JIM: I'm afraid there's not much wisdom in Hall C. Good night.

(*Jim goes out. The Chaplain enters.*)

WARDEN (*lighting cigar*): What do yuh want, Reverend?

CHAPLAIN: I want to talk to you about the death of Oliver Jackson.

WARDEN: What about it?

CHAPLAIN: I think it could have been avoided.

WARDEN: Sure it could. Nobody made that fool nigger take a dive.

CHAPLAIN: He was goaded to desperation.

WARDEN: Oh, you think so?

CHAPLAIN: There have been too many suicides, several drownings, hangings, so-called accidents, since I've been here. Now it appears that we're in danger of having a mass suicide in Hall C. The men have gone on hunger strike which I think is fully justified by the quality of food they've been getting.

WARDEN: Aw. Now I'm beginning to suspect who's responsible for the wild stories that have been leaking out to the public about things here. I'm afraid you're what the boys call a—stool pigeon, Reverend.

CHAPLAIN: I'm a conscientious steward of Christ, and as such I protest against the inhuman treatment of convicts in this prison!

WARDEN (*jumping up*): Who's running this prison, you or me?

CHAPLAIN: Mr. Whalen, the universe is like a set of blocks. The kind you had in kindergarten. A little one that fits into a big one, a bigger one over that, till you get on up to the very biggest of them all that fits on top of all the rest—

WARDEN: Yes?

CHAPLAIN: Yes, and that biggest block is the one I'm representing—the Kingdom of God. (*He rises with dignity.*)

WARDEN: Well, I'm afraid your work here has begun to interfere with your—your higher duties—I want you to climb up there on top of that great big block you're talkin' about an' stay up there. That's your place. You leave me alone down here on the little block— There's your notice, Reverend— You're free to go now.

CHAPLAIN: I could leave here gladly if it wasn't for what I have to take with me.

WARDEN: You're taking nothing with you but the clothes on your back.

CHAPLAIN: I'm taking much more than that.

WARDEN: Aw. Maybe I'd better have you frisked on the way out.

CHAPLAIN: You could strip me naked and I'd still have these.

WARDEN: These what?

CHAPLAIN: Memories—shadows—ghosts!

WARDEN: Ahhhh? (*He lifts phone.*) Git me Atwater 2770.

CHAPLAIN: Things I've seen that I can't forget. Men, tortured, twisted, driven mad. Death's the least of it. It's the *life* in here that's going to stay with me like an incurable sickness. And by God, Whalen, that's not profanity—by God, I won't rest easy till I've seen these walls torn down, stone by stone, and others put up in their place that let the air in! Good night!— (*He goes out quickly.*)

WARDEN: Hello. Reverend? This is Warden Whalen. Our chaplain's just resigned. I want you to come over and talk to me—might be a steady job in it for you. Yes, Siree! You be over here in time for Sunday service— (*He hangs up.*) Memories, shadows, ghosts! What a screwball! (*He pours himself a drink.*)

Dim Out

EPISODE TWO

Announcer: "Sunday Morning in Hall C!"

A spot comes up on the cell. Joe, Queen, and Swifty are reading sections of a Sunday paper. From down the corridor comes Butch's voice—

BUTCH (*approaching*): "I'm forever BLOW-ing BUB-BLES!" (*He enters the cell with a straight razor, towel, and soap.*) Who gave you that paper?

JOE: Allison. The Canary.

BUTCH: Git it out of here!

JOE: What for?

BUTCH: It's contaminated.

JOE: Aw, take a look at t' comics.

BUTCH: Naw, gimme 'at pitcher section. Hey! Look at 'is!

JOE: What?

BUTCH: "A bow-ket of buds!"

JOE: Yeah. They're comin' out in sassiety.

BUTCH: "Miss Hortense Maxine Schultz, daughter of Mr. and Mrs. Max W. Schultz, 79 Willow Drive, will make her bow to society early this Fall. She is one of a group of young women who traveled through Europe this summer with Mrs. J. Mortimer Finchwell—"

JOE: So what?

BUTCH: "On her fadder's side Miss Schultz is directly descendant from William th' Conq'ror an' on her mudders from Ponce de Leon, Sir Isaac Newton an' George Washington's Aunt!"

JOE: Gosh, de're pikers! Why don't they throw in Benito Mussolini for good measure?

BUTCH: "Her grandfather was duh late Benjamin F. Schultz, President and founder of th' Shultz Bottling Works."

JOE: Lotsa mazooma, huh?

BUTCH: "In addition to her many udder accomplishments—!" Hey, listen to this!

JOE: Huh?

BUTCH: Down here at th' bottom they come right out an' admit that she ain't even human!

JOE: How's that?

BUTCH: It says here "In addition to her many udder accomplishments, Miss Schultz is an excellent *horse*-woman!"

JOE: Hell, you could tell that by lookin' at her pitcher.

Blackout

EPISODE THREE

Announcer: "Mr. Whalen Interviews the New Chaplain!"

A spot comes up on the office. Whalen and the Reverend Hooker have just returned from Sunday dinner. The Reverend Hooker is a nervous, precise little man with a prodigious anxiety to please.

WARDEN: I got you up here on pretty short notice. You see
   me an' the old chaplain had a little disagreement last night,
   which resulted in him handing in his resignation right off
   the bat!—He made one fatal mistake, Reverend— He kind
   of forgot who was in charge of this institution.

REVEREND: I don't think I shall make that error, Mr. Whalen.

WARDEN: Naw, neither do I. First time I seen you I said to
   myself "Here's a man who looks like he could adjust himself to conditions."

REVEREND: I pride myself on being—adjustable!

WARDEN: Good. You'll find that's an asset around this place,
   a definite asset. What's your idea of the universe, Reverend?

REVEREND: I beg your pardon?

WARDEN: Suppose you give me a little word-picture of how
   you conceive of this great mysterious— (*He makes a sweeping gesture.*)

REVEREND: Cosmos?

WARDEN: Yes! In which we humans are little fluttering
   motes, so to speak. (*He makes a derisive fluttering gesture
   with hands.*)

REVEREND: Well—uh—of course there's the orthodox conception of the universe as consisting of three elements—

WARDEN: Yep?

REVEREND: Heaven, earth and the— uh—regions below.

WARDEN: We call that Klondike in here.

REVEREND: I beg your pardon?

WARDEN: Skip it, Reverend.

REVEREND: Hmmm. Of course there is some question as to
   the *material* existence of those—uh—nether regions—

WARDEN: There's no doubt about 'em here. Naw, Sir. But
   what I wanted to know, Reverend, is if you've got any the-
   ories about a set of blocks—with you occupying the one on
   top and me way down at the bottom—that's what got the
   last preacher in trouble with me.

REVEREND: Blocks? Oh, dear, no! That strikes me as rather—
   elementary to say the least!

WARDEN: Yeah, kindergarten stuff. Well, you'll do, Reverend.
   (*He glances at his ponderous gold watch.*) We got about five
   minutes till church takes up. Are you good at makin' up ex-
   temporaneous speeches?

REVEREND: Oh, yes, indeed, yes, indeed! I think I may safely say that I have never lacked words for any occasion, Mr. Whalen.

WARDEN: Well, your job depends on this one. I haven't got time to go into details, Reverend. But I want you to touch on three particular subjects. I don't care how you bring 'em in, just so you *do* and so you give 'em the right emphasis!

REVEREND: Three subjects!

WARDEN: Yes, Siree. You mark 'em down, Reverend—food!

REVEREND: Food?

WARDEN: That's the first one. Then—heat!

REVEREND: Heat?

WARDEN: Yep. And then—Klondike! (*A bell sounds.*) There goes the bell. I'm two minutes slow. Remember, now, food, heat, and Klondike!

REVEREND: What was the last one? Klondike? You mean— uh—missionary work in the far north? Among the Eskimos? I'm afraid the association of ideas is going to be a little difficult for me to grasp, Mr. Whalen—but—

(*Dim out; a spot comes up on the Reverend Hooker behind a small lectern.*)

REVEREND: Yes—uh—very good afternoon to you all. (*He clears his throat: then beams at the convicts.*) I hope that you enjoyed your dinner as much as I did mine—

VOICE: Hamburgers and spaghetti! (*There is a chorus of boo-ing. A warning whistle sounds, then silence.*)

REVEREND: Food is such a familiar blessing that—uh we sometimes forget to be properly grateful for it. But when I read about the horrible conditions in famine-stricken por-tions of Europe and Asia—tch, tch!—I feel that I am in-deed very fortunate to have a full stomach!

(*Booing is heard; someone whistles.*)

When one thinks of food—uh—one also thinks by a natural association of ideas—about—uh—the marvelous blessing of—uh— *Heat!* Heat—uh—that makes food possible— wonderful *heat!* Heat of all kinds! The heat of the sun that warms the earth's atmosphere and permits the growth of the vegetables and the grains and the—uh—fruits—uh—

the heat of the—uh—body—uh— (*He wipes his forehead.*) heat, universal heat— At this time of the year some of us find heat oppressive—uh—but that is ungrateful of us, extremely ungrateful—

(*There is a slow stomping of feet.*)

(*The preacher continues, raising his voice.*) For all living matter depends on the presence of heat—northward and southward from the Equator to the twin poles—even to far Alaska—even in *Klondike*—

(*The stomping grows louder.*)

What would Klondike be without heat? A frozen wasteland! (*He scrubs his forehead and glances nervously about.*) In Klondike our brave missionaries, risking their lives among savage tribes of war—painted Indians—

(*A hymnal is hurled: there is furious stomping.*)

Goodness!—As I was saying—in Klondike—!

(*He is bombarded with hymnals. A whistle blows; there is shouting; a siren sounds. Dim out. A mocking jazz interlude plays. A spot comes up on the office. The Reverend rushes in clasping his handkerchief to his forehead.*)

REVEREND: Oh, mercy upon us!
WARDEN (*at the phone*): Schultz? All guards on duty! Find out who conked the Reverend with that song book. Whew! I give you my word, Reverend, I wasn't expecting no such a reaction as this! It come as a complete surprise!
REVEREND: Ohhhh! I'm afraid I shall have to receive some medical attention.
WARDEN: Yeah, well, I want you to take this fin, Reverend.
REVEREND: And the nervous shock, you know! Tch, Tch!
WARDEN: Yeah? Well—
REVEREND: Terrific, terrific! A shocking experience!
WARDEN: Here's another two bucks.

(*Theme up: jazz*)

Blackout

EPISODE FOUR

Announcer: "Zero Hour!"

A spot comes up on the warden's office. Eva is typing nervously. Jim enters. His chronic tension has now risen to the point of breaking. Even his movements are stiff like those of a mechanical man: his eyes are smoldering.

EVA (*jumping up as he enters*): Jim, you're not—?
JIM: Naw, I'm not locked up in Hall C.
EVA: I hadn't seen you. I was afraid—
JIM: You must have forgotten what a special value there is attached to my hide.
EVA: You look awfully tired, Jim.
JIM: Yes. How do *you* sleep at night?
EVA: Not well lately.
JIM: How do you sleep at all knowing what you know and keeping still?
EVA: What else can I do but keep still?
JIM: You could talk. You could tell the State Humane Society that thirty-five hundred animals are being starved to death and threatened with torture.
EVA: And lose my job?
JIM: Aw. Excuse me for being so impractical.
EVA: You don't understand. I was out of work six months before I got this job.
JIM: You told me that.
EVA: I got down to my last dime. Once a man followed along the street and I stood still, waiting for him to catch up with me. Yes, I'd gotten down that low, I was going to ask him for money—
JIM: Did you?
EVA: No. At the last moment I couldn't. I went hungry instead.

(*Jim looks at her.*)

Now you want me to go back to that? Times haven't improved. Now maybe I'd have more courage, or less decency, or maybe I'd be hungrier than I was before.

JIM: You'd better hold on to your job, Miss Crane—even if it does mean participating in a massacre!

EVA: It's not that bad.

JIM: It's going to be that bad. I'm going to talk myself now. Even if it means giving up my chance of parole.

EVA: No, you can't do that. Wait a while and see how things turn out.

JIM: This is the zero hour. Whalen has given instructions to put Hall C in Klondike tonight if they don't eat supper.

EVA: I know. I heard him.

(*Jim lifts the telephone receiver*)

What are you going to do?

JIM: Blow the lid off this stinking hole!

EVA (*grabbing the phone*): No, Jim! I'll do it, myself! I'll talk!

JIM: When?

EVA (*lowering her voice*): Now. Tonight. I'll visit the newspaper on my way home.

JIM: You will, huh?

EVA: Yes!

JIM: No. Wait till tomorrow. We'll have more definite evidence then. With Hall C in Klondike.

(*Whalen enters.*)

WARDEN: Well, Jim. What do the boys in Hall C think about the change in climate that I've arranged for them?

JIM: They haven't heard yet. Wilson is going to tell them when he brings the men up from the Hole.

WARDEN: They'll be eating supper tonight.

JIM: What have they got for supper?

WARDEN: The old perennial favorites, hamburger and spaghetti. I'm not going to mollycoddle those bastards.— Excuse me, Eva.

JIM: I don't think they'll eat.

WARDEN: You don't, huh? Well, I do! Eva—

EVA (*who has gotten her hat*): Yes, Sir?

WARDEN: I'll want you back after supper. We've got to have things in perfect order in case the snoopers get busy.

EVA: All right.

WARDEN: You'd better catch the ferry at seven-fifteen.

EVA: Yes, Sir. (*She exits.*)

JIM: About my parole, Mr. Whalen—

WARDEN: Yes? What about it?

JIM: It's coming up next month.

WARDEN (*grunting*): Humph.

JIM: I guess it pretty much hangs on your decision.

WARDEN: You've got a lot of brass.

JIM: Why do you say that?

WARDEN: Bothering me about your goddamn parole at a time like this!

JIM: It's important to me. I've been in here ten years and I've got ten years of copper. I'm due for a ticket-of-leave.

WARDEN: You'll get a ticket to Klondike if you got any more to say on that subject!

JIM (*starting forward*): By God, I—

WARDEN: What?

JIM (*with desperate control*): Nothing.

WARDEN (*uneasily*): I'm going out for supper. Be back about eight or eight-thirty. You watch things here.

JIM: Yes, Sir.

(*Whalen exits. Jim covers his face, strangling a sob.*)

Blackout

EPISODE FIVE

Musical theme up: "I'm Forever Blowing Bubbles."

Announcer: "Hall C!" Musical theme fade.

A spot comes up on the cell. The dialogue is fairly light, but an undercurrent of desperation should be felt.

BUTCH (*hoarsely*): "I'm forever blow-ing BUBBLES!"

JOE: Quit croakin' that corny number. Why dontcha learn something new?

BUTCH: That was new last I heard it.

JOE: Before you got in stir?

BUTCH: It had just come out.

JOE: It's had time to grow whiskers since then.

BUTCH: It was Goldie's fav'rite.

JOE: I thought you said she liked *Dardanella*.

BUTCH: She liked that one, too.

JOE: What's become of her?

BUTCH: How should I know? She quit writing ten years ago.

JOE: Christ. She's probably died of the syph by now.

BUTCH: Naw, not Goldie.

QUEEN: I wish I was dead. I used to have nice fingernails. Look at 'em now. My teeth was nice, too. I had nice hair. Now when I look at myself I wish I was dead.

BUTCH: "Faw'chun's always hi-ding! I looked ev'ry where!"

(*A mimic down the hall echoes the refrain.*)

BUTCH (*jumping to the bars*): Who was that? You, Krause?— Anytime I want you small-time grifters to muscle in on my singin' I'll send you a special request.

QUEEN: Yes, I wish I was dead. I hope that I starve to death. And I will. I can feel myself dying already.

BUTCH: "They fly so high, nearly reach the sky—" They used to turn out the light on that number. There was a sort of silver glass ball at the top of the ceilin' that would turn round and round an' throw little rainbow-colored reflections all over the floor an' the walls— God, it was lovely!

QUEEN (*rising*): Honest to God, I can't hold out much longer, Butch!

BUTCH: Naw?

QUEEN: Naw, I got a weak constitution. I was in a nervous run-down condition before I got sent up here. Hell, it was a bum rap. I didn't sell any weeds. I used to smoke 'em but I never sold any!—Persecution, all my life, persecution! Now maybe they'll kill me down there in Klondike, I'll never git out, never—never git out!

BUTCH: Dummy up!

QUEEN: You ever been in Klondike, Joe?

JOE: Naw. Butch has.

QUEEN: What's it like, Butch?

BUTCH (*rising slowly and going to stage front*): "Then like my dreams they fade an' die—"

QUEEN: They say it ain't the heat so much.

JOE: What is it? The humidity?

QUEEN: Naw, you can't breathe good. It's kind of—suffocating! (*He fingers his collar.*)

BUTCH: Fortune's always hiding—I looked ev'rywhere! I'm forever blow-ing BUBBLES! (*He stops short.*)

(*A door clangs—the men rise simultaneously, tense. There is the sound of a wracking cough and delirious sobbing.*)

(*Butch continues softly.*) They're bringin' 'em up from the Hole.

SCHULTZ: Gwan, git a move on, it ain't no funeral march yet awhile!

(*The dull shuffling of feet is heard accompanied by coughing, sobbing. The heads of the men in the cells move slowly from left to right, mouths open, as though watching some awful procession.*)

Halt! Face your cells!—You, too, Shapiro, do I have to speak Yiddish to make you understand?

(*A low yammering commences. Butch seizes his tin cup and holds it poised. A whistle sounds; the cell door opens.*)

March in! Git in there, Trout—Shapiro!

(*Swifty stumbles into the cell, unshaven, ghastly, sobbing.*)

Awright! Take a good look at 'em. An' remember this! The Hole is just a small dose compared to Klondike! Klondike's the big medicine and the Boss is all set to pour it out in double doses for any of you wise bastards that don't feel like eating supper tonight!

VOICE (*slowly and emphatically*): Where's Ollie?

ANOTHER (*staccato*): Yeah, where's Ollie?

CHORUS: Where's Ollie, where's Ollie, what did you do with Ollie?

(*Slight pause.*)

SCHULTZ: Who's responsible if some fool nigger takes a notion to butt his own brains out? (*There is a slight whine of fear in his voice.*)

(*Butch suddenly hammers the cell bar with his cup. Yammering commences. During the preceding speeches, from the point of his entrance, Swifty has stood dazed; then he sags slowly to his knees beside the bunk. The Queen comforts him awkwardly. Joe and Butch stand with attention fixed on Schultz. A whistle sounds. The yammering subsides a little.*)

(*Schultz, standing directly outside the open cell door, continues*): You see this here thermometer? (*He extracts a large one from his pocket.*) See that little red mark there? That says Blood Heat. Now see this one up here twenty degrees more? It says Fever Heat. You think it's going to stop there? Not a chance! It's going to keep right on rising till it busts clean out of the top of the little doojigit! It's going to break all records. It's going to be the biggest heat wave in history. Now if you don't think I'm a good weather prophet, just one of you finicky lads leave a little spaghetti on his plate tonight an' see what happens!

VOICE: Spaghetti?

(*There is complete tense silence for a moment.*)

SCHULTZ: Yeah, spaghetti!

BUTCH: Spaghetti, huh?—We ain't gonna eat it tonight or no other time—not till Whalen cuts out the graft and feeds us something besides hog-slop!

SCHULTZ: Is 'at what you want me to tell him?

BUTCH: Yeah, tell him that, an' if he don't like it—

(*Yammering; a whistle; the door clangs shut; the yammering subsides.*)

VOICE: Klondike?

ANOTHER: Tonight?

ANOTHER: Yeah, if we don't eat!

VOICE: Klondike? No?

ANOTHER: Not if we go to Klondike!

VOICE (*shrill and despairing*): We can't make it!!

(*A wracking cough and delirious sobbing are heard. Mex prays in a hoarse strangled voice.*)

MEX: *Santa María—Madre de Dios*—etc.

(*Butch advances to the bars and raps commandingly.*)

VOICE: It's Butch!

ANOTHER: What does Butch say?

MEX: *Jésus—muerto por nuestros pecados!*

BUTCH: Cut the cackle all of yuz! That goes for you too, Mex. You got plenty of time for talking to Jesus when you git there! Lissen here now!—Anybody in Hall C that eats is gonna pay for his supper in Kangaroo Court. I'll assess the maximum fine, you know what!—You're scared of Klondike? I say let 'em throw us in Klondike!—Maybe some of you weak sisters will be melted down to grease-chunks. But not all twenty-five of us! Some of us are gonna beat Klondike! And Klondike's dere las' trump card, when you got that licked, you've licked everything they've got to offer in here! You got 'em over the barrel for good! So then what happens? They come up to us and they say, "You win! What is it you want?" We say, "Boss Whalen is out! Git us a new Warden! Git us decent livin' conditions! No more overcrowdin', no more bunkin' up wit' contajus diseasus; fresh air in the cell-blocks, fumigation, an' most of all—WE WANT SOME FOOD THAT'S FIT TO PUT IN OUR BELLIES! (*Applause.*) No more hamburger an' spaghetti an' beans, and beans an' hamburger an' spaghetti till you feel like the whole fucking world was made of nothin' else but hamburger an' beans an' spaghetti— (*Applause.*)—Maybe when we git through housecleaning this place'll be like the Industrial Reformatory they got at Chillicothe! A place where guys are learnt how to make a livin' after they git outa stir! Where they teach 'em trades an' improve their ejication! Not just lock 'em up in dirty holes an' hope to God they'll die so as to save the State some money!! (*Fierce yammering.*) Tonight we go to Klondike!—Dere's three compartments! One of 'em's little hell, one of 'em's middle-sized hell an' one of 'em's BIG HELL!—You know which one Butch O'Fallon is gonna be in!—So if I ain't yellow, boys, don't you be neither! That's all I got to say.

VOICE: Okay, Butch.

ANOTHER: We're witcha!

CHORUS: We'll beat Klondike!—You bet we'll bet it!—Put Whalen over a barrel— (*There is nervous laughter and applause.*)

(*Their voices die abruptly under a shadow of fear.*)

MEX (*chanting*): *Muerto—por nuestros pecados—rojo—de sangre es—el Sol!*

Blackout

EPISODE SIX

Announcer: "Definition of Life!"

A spot comes up on the office. Jim, facing downstage, leans against the desk, smoking. Eva enters.

EVA: Hello, Jim.
JIM: Yeah.
EVA: Nice out. A little bit cooler.—What's wrong with you?
JIM (*grinning wryly*): Ask me what life is, Eva.

(*Eva looks at him and crosses downstage.*)

Ask me what it is and I'll tell you.
EVA (*removing her hat*): No, darling.
JIM: Why not?
EVA: It smells like a bad epigram.
JIM (*tossing away his cigarette*): It's a gradual process of dying, that's what it is!
EVA: Worse than I expected.
JIM: That's what it is in here. Maybe it's something else on your side of the fence. I'd like to find out, but I guess I won't have the chance!
EVA (*seriously*): Your parole?

(*Jim strikes a match, watches it burn.*)

Turned down?
JIM: Not yet but it will be. I was talking about it to Whalen.

EVA: Oh. You shouldn't have mentioned it now when he's all steamed up about the hunger strike.

JIM: I didn't mean to. It just popped somehow. I'm getting out of control—Butch named me for the right kind of bird. Canaries never get out of their cages, do they, Eva?

EVA: Jim! Don't be a fool.

JIM: Naw, they die in 'em—singin' sweetly till doomsday! God damn!

EVA (*brushing her hat*): Speaking of birds—I wish the pigeons would be a little more careful! Don't you think it's a nice hat, Jim?

JIM (*without looking*): Yes, colossal.

EVA: I bought it on the way home. I felt sort of gay and irresponsible—knowing tomorrow was the last day, I suppose! Jim! (*She catches his arm: he averts his face.*)

JIM (*his fear visible*): If I get turned down again this time, I'll never get another chance.

EVA: Why not?

JIM: Because I'll blow-up!—Crack to pieces! I'm drawn as tight as I can get right now!

EVA: Don't be a damn fool, Jim.

JIM: You know what it's been like. Hated like poison for ten years by everybody but him. Working for him and all the time hating him so that it made me sick at the guts to look at him even! Ten years of being his stooge. Jimmy boy, do this, do that! Yes, Sir. Yes, Mr. Whalen!—My hands aching to catch that beefy red neck of his and choke the breath out of it! That's one reason why they shake so much—and here's another. Standing here at this window, looking out, seeing the streets, the buildings, the traffic moving, the lights going off and on, and me being pent up here, in these walls, locked in 'em so tight it's like I was buried under the earth in a coffin with a glass lid that I could see the world through! While I felt the worms crawling inside me . . .

EVA: No. Don't be a fool. (*She crosses upstage to the window.*) It's nice out. Gotten cooler.

JIM: You said that before.

EVA (*smiling desperately*): Well, it's still true. There's a carnival on South Bay. I ran in like a kid and took a ride on the zebra!

JIM: Yes?

EVA: There's two seats on the zebra, Jim. One in front, one in back— Next month we'll ride him together!

JIM (*suddenly breaking*): Eva! Eva! (*He covers his face.*)

EVA (*running to him*): I love you!

(*Pause.*)

JIM (*his voice choking*): What is this place? What's it for? Why, why! The judges say guilty. But what is guilty? What does that word mean, anyhow? It's funny, but I don't know. (*He picks up the dictionary.*) Look it up in *Webster's Dictionary*. What's it say? "Responsible for the commission of crime." But why responsible? What's responsible mean? Who's ever been given a choice? When they mix up all the little molecules we're made out of, do they ask each one politely which he will be—rich man, poor man, beggar man, thief? God, no! It's all accidental. And yet the Judge says, "Jim, you're guilty!" (*He tosses the dictionary to the floor.*) This book's no good anymore. We need a new one with a brand new set of definitions.

EVA: Don't say any more—I won't let you! (*She kisses him.*)

JIM: How did this happen between you and me?

EVA: I don't know.

JIM: It's the dirtiest trick they've played on us yet.

EVA: Don't say that!

JIM: We can't have each other. We never can, Eva.

EVA: We can!

JIM: Where?

EVA: Somewhere.

JIM: How?

EVA: I don't know how.

JIM: Neither do I.

EVA: But next month—

JIM: There won't be any next month!

EVA: There will, oh, there will, there must be!

JIM: Why?—Why?

EVA: Because I love you so much that it's got to happen the way I want it to happen!

JIM: Why do you love me?

EVA: Why is anything on earth? I don't know why.

JIM: Neither do I—

(*They cling together in tortured ecstasy. Blackout. The lights come up as the phone rings.*)

JIM: Yes? I'll tell him. (*He hangs up.*)

EVA: What is it?

JIM: Schultz. They won't eat.

EVA: What's he going to do?

JIM: He's already got his instructions from Whalen. They'll be in Klondike at seven.

EVA (*pausing*): I won't be down here tomorrow.

JIM: No?

EVA: I'll be in the newspaper offices. And at City Hall. Any place where people will listen!

JIM: You think they'll listen anywhere, Eva?

EVA: I'll make them listen!

JIM: And afterwards what will you do? With no job?

EVA: I'll only have to wait three weeks. And then I'll be *your* responsibility, Jim!

JIM: I hope to God you're right.

EVA: I am! I know I am!

(*Whalen enters.*)

WARDEN: Hello! Still here, Jim?

JIM: Yes, Sir. Schultz called. They wouldn't eat supper.

WARDEN: Well—he's got his instructions.

JIM: Yes, he said that he had.

WARDEN (*scribbling on a piece of paper*): Take this down to the switchboard and have it posted there and sent to all stations.

JIM: Does this mean—?

WARDEN: Never mind what it means. Just take it down there. And step lively!

JIM: Yes, Sir.

(*Jim goes out.*)

WARDEN (*to Eva*): Back on the job, huh?

EVA: Yes.

WARDEN (*belching and removing his coat*): I should have told you to bring some things with you.

EVA: What things?

WARDEN: Your little silk nightie and stuff.

EVA: What do you mean?

WARDEN: Quarantine! A bad epidemic's broken out! Twenty-five cases are going to be running a pretty high fever tonight so I've put this place under quarantine restrictions —nobody's gonna leave the grounds till the epidemic is over.

EVA: I can't stay here.

WARDEN (*busy with papers*): Sure you can. My wife'll fix a room for you. You'll be very comfortable here.

EVA: No, I won't do it.

WARDEN: You've got no choice in the matter.

EVA: Haven't I?

WARDEN: Naw, I'm not running a risk on any outside interference while this trouble is going on. It's my business, I'm going to keep it my business. So just as a routine precaution I've ordered the boats to take no passengers on or off the island without my special permission.

EVA: I think you're exceeding your authority.

WARDEN: Naw, you're wrong there. Times of emergency I can do what I damn please. Say—what are you worried about?

EVA (*frightened*): I—

WARDEN: I know. It's a nervous strain we've all been under these last few days. I got gas on the stomach myself. Here. (*He pours a shot of whiskey.*)

EVA: No, you've been drinking too much. I'm afraid it's affected your sense of judgment. You ought to know you can't get away with a thing like this!

WARDEN: Hey, now—look here!

EVA (*excitedly*): I'm not a prisoner—I'm free to go and do as I please—you can't stop me!

WARDEN: Look here, now!

(*She grasps the phone.*)

EVA: Riverside 3854 W! Riverside 3–8— (*She realizes the phone is cut off.*)

WARDEN: No out-going calls can get through. You're wasting your time.

EVA: Then I—I *am* a prisoner here!

WARDEN: You're temporarily detained on the island—might as well make the best of it! (*He pours another drink.*)

EVA: Oh!

WARDEN: Here, now, what's wrong with you?

EVA: I don't know why, but I'm terribly frightened.

WARDEN (*soothingly*): You've gone and worked yourself up. There's nothing for you to be nervous about.

EVA: You! I'm afraid of you! (*She backs away from him.*)

WARDEN: Me? Why should you be scared of me?

EVA: I am, though. I'm scared to death of you. You've got to let me go, I can't stay with you any longer, Mr. Whalen.

WARDEN: Now, now.

EVA: No, don't touch me! Please don't.

WARDEN: You're hysterical, Eva.

EVA: Yes!

WARDEN (*purring*): My wife gets spells like that, too—that "don't touch me" stuff!

EVA (*retreating*): Yes!

WARDEN: I know a good treatment for it that always works. There, now little girl you just take it easy. Relax. You're all worked up over nothing. You're stiff, see? Your nerves and your muscles are all drawn up real tight.

EVA: Yes . . . (*She has nearly collapsed with nervous exhaustion—his purring voice has a hypnotic effect.*)

WARDEN: Mmm. Now when my wife gets like this, I—I rub my fingers along her throat—real, real gently—till all the stiffness goes out . . .

EVA (*her eyes falling shut*): Yes . . .

WARDEN (*gazes at her lasciviously*): . . . and then I—

(*Eva sighs as though asleep.*)

WARDEN: Eva?—Eva? (*He rises and opens the inner door, then hesitates—*)

(*The phone rings.*)

For Chrissakes, what is it now? Yeah? What? I'm coming right down there now!— (*He hangs up—purring drunkenly.*) You wait, li'l girl, I'll be right back in here! Yes, Siree . . . (*He fumbles into his coat and goes out.*)

(*Eva gasps as the door slams shut—she slowly rises. The outer door opens— Eva screams— Jim enters.*)

EVA: Jim! Jim!

(*Jim catches her in his arms.*)

Get me out of here, oh, please, *please*, get me out of here! (*She sobs wildly.*)

JIM: Hold on to yourself! (*He shakes her.*) Hold on to yourself!

EVA: I'm trying to, Jim.

JIM: Take a deep breath. Here—at the window.

EVA: Yes!

JIM: See those lights over there?

EVA: Yes!

JIM: That's the Lorelei on her way out. Be real quiet and you can hear the music. (*She leans against him—faint music is heard.*) Better now?

EVA: Yes. Thanks, Jim.

JIM: What happened? Just tell me real quietly and don't get excited about it.

EVA: He told me I—I'm a prisoner here! I can't leave! I don't know why, but it made me terribly frightened all of a sudden. His eyes, the way he looked at me, Jim—I had a feeling that something awful was going to happen—

JIM: Easy, now!

EVA: Yes. I guess I'm an awful sissy.

JIM: No, you've got more guts than me.

EVA: He—he came real close to me—and his voice—sort of put me to sleep.

JIM: Did he—?

EVA: No! He only opened that door. And then a bell rang—I could hear it like it was a thousand miles off!

JIM: A bell?

EVA: They called him upstairs, I guess. He left the room and I—I would have jumped out the window if you hadn't come just then!

JIM: There's nothing but water out there.

EVA: I didn't care. I just wanted to get away somehow.

JIM: You'll get away.

EVA: With you, Jim? You'll take me?

JIM: Yes. In a while. Don't you feel the walls shaking? They can't hold up much longer. There's too much boiling inside them—hate, torture, madness, fury! They'll blow wide open in a little while and we'll be loose!

EVA: I want to be with you when that happens! I want you to hold me like this—so that when the walls start falling I won't be crushed down under them, Jim.

JIM: We'll be together.

EVA: Where?

JIM: Meet me tonight in the southwest corner of the yard.

EVA: Will we be safe there?

JIM (*in a whisper*): It's dark. Nobody could see us.

Blackout—End of Act Two

ACT THREE

EPISODE ONE

Announcer: "Morning of August 15!"

A spot comes up on the office. The warden is at the phone. During the following episodes the theater is filled almost constantly with the soft hiss of live steam from the radiators—

WARDEN: Schultz? How hot is it down there now? 125? What's the matter? Git it up to 130! You got Butch O'Fallon in No. 3 aintcha? Okay, give No. 3 135 and don't let up on it till you git instructions from me. Hey! Got them windows in the hall shut? Good. Keep 'em shut an' let 'em squawk their goddamn heads off!

(*Blackout. A spot comes up on Klondike. The torture cell is seen through a scrim to give a misty or steam-clouded effect to the atmosphere. The men are sprawled on the floor, breathing heavily, their shirts off, skin shiny with sweat. A ceiling light glares relentlessly down on them. The walls are bare and glistening wet. Along them are radiators from which rise hissing clouds of live steam.*)

JOE (*coughing*): W'at time is it?

BUTCH: How in hell would I know?

SWIFTY (*whimpering*): Water—water.

JOE: I wonder if we been in here all night.

BUTCH: Sure we have. I can see daylight through the hole.

JOE: How long was you in that time?

BUTCH: Thirty-six hours.

JOE: Christ!

BUTCH: Yeah. And we've just done about eight.

SWIFTY: Water!

BUTCH: Hey! Y'know what—what the old maid said to the burglar when she—she found him trying to jimmy th' lock on th'—

JOE: Yeah. (*He coughs.*)

QUEEN: Swifty's sick. I am, too. Why don't somebody come here?

BUTCH: Aw, you heard that one?

JOE: Yeah. A long time ago, Butch. (*He coughs.*)

BUTCH: You oughta know some new ones.

JOE: Naw. Not any new ones, Butch.

BUTCH: Then tell some old ones, goddamn it!! Dontcha all lie there like you was ready to be laid under! Let's have some life in this party— Sing! Sing! You know some good songs, Queenie, you got a voice! C'mon you sons-of-guns! Put some pep in it! Sing it out, sing it out loud, boys! (*He sings wildly, hoarsely.*)

> Pack up your troubles in yuhr ole kit bag an'
> Smile, smile, smile!

(*The others join in feebly—*)

Sing it out! Goddamit, sing it out loud!

> What's the use of worrying
> It never was worthwhile!

(*Joe tries to sing—he is suddenly bent double in a paroxysm of coughing.*)

174 NOT ABOUT NIGHTINGALES

SWIFTY (*in a loud anguished cry*): Water! Water! Water! (*He sobs.*)

(*There is a loud shrill hiss of steam from the radiators as more pressure is turned on.*)

QUEEN (*in frantic horror*): They're givin' us more! Oh, my God, why don't they stop now! Why don't they let us out! Oh, Jesus, Jesus, please, please, please! (*He sobs wildly and falls on the floor.*)

SWIFTY (*weakly*): Water—water . . .

BUTCH: Yeah. They're givin' us more heat. Sure, they're givin' us more heat. Dontcha know you're in Klondike? Aw, w'at's a use, yer crybabies. Yuh wanta go on suckin' a sugar-tit all yer life? Gwan, sing it out—

I'm forever blowing BUBBLES!
Pretty bubbles in the—AIR!

SHAPIRO: There is nothing to be done about it, nothing at all. I come of a people that are used to suffer. It is not a new thing. I have it in my blood to suffer persecution, misery, starvation, death.

SWIFTY: Water.

SHAPIRO (*mumbles in Yiddish, then*): My head is full, full. Aching in here. Broken already, perhaps. Rose? Rose? You know the property on South Maple Street—it's all in your name, my darling—be careful—don't make bad investments—

JOE (*coughing*): Lemme at the air hole.

QUEEN: You're hoggin' it!

JOE: Cantcha see I'm choking to death? (*He coughs.*)

(*The steam hisses louder.*)

BUTCH (*rising*): We got to systematize this business. Quit fightin' over the air hole. The only air that's fit to breathe is comin' through there. We gotta take turns breathin' it. We done sixteen hours about. Maybe we'll do ten more, twenty more, thirty more.

JOE: Christ!

QUEEN: We can't make it!

BUTCH: We can if we organize. Keep close to the floor. Stay in a circle round the wall. Each guy take his turn. Fifteen seconds. Maybe later ten seconds or five seconds. I do the counting. And when a guy flips out—he's finished—he's through—push him outa the line— This ain't a first-aid station—this is Klondike—and by God—some of us are gonna beat it—Okay? Okay, Joe?

JOE: Yeah.

BUTCH: Well, git started then.

SWIFTY: Water!

BUTCH: Push the kid up here first.

(*They shove Swifty's inert body to the air hole.*)

Breathe! Breathe! Breathe, goddamn you, breathe! (*He jerks Swifty up by the collar—stares at his face.*) Naw, it's no use. I guess he's beating a cinder track around the stars now!

QUEEN: He ain't dead! Not yet! He's unconscious, Butch! Give him a chance!

BUTCH (*inexorably*): Push him outa the line. (*As the lights dim . . .*) Okay—Shapiro—Joe—

(*Theme up: "I'm Forever Blowing Bubbles." Fade.*)

Dim Out

EPISODE TWO

Announcer: "Evening of August 15!"

A spot comes up on the office. Whalen is at the phone.

WARDEN: You heard 'em what? Singin! Well, give 'em something to sing about! 140? Git it up to 145 in Butch's compartment! You bet I want 'em left in there all night! Naw, keep the windows shut. Water? Let 'em make their own water!

(*Blackout. A spot comes up on Klondike. Swifty lies dead in center, a shirt over his face. The voices are hoarse, breathing more labored. Joe coughs wrackingly. The radiators hiss loudly.*)

BUTCH: Here comes more! Keep down! Keep down!

(*Queen sobs wildly. Shapiro mumbles in Yiddish.*)

Joe! Look! I got it with me! (*He extracts a razor from his belt.*)

JOE: That's one way out.

BUTCH: Maybe the boss will come down here to look us over.

JOE (*coughing*): Naw, he wouldn't.

BUTCH: Maybe Schultz will. Or the Canary. (*He rises.*) Schultz! Schultz! Naw, it's no dice, he's too yellow to stick his puss in here! But if he does ever—

(*A whistle sounds.*)

Hear that? It's the lock-up bell! We've done twenty-four hours, Joe. We only got twelve more to go!

JOE: How d'you know how long it will be?

BUTCH: They don't want to kill us!

JOE: Why don't they? (*He coughs.*)—Your turn, Butch.

BUTCH: Yeah, git moving, Queenie!

QUEEN: Naw! Lemme breathe!

(*Butch tears him away from air hole. Shapiro shouts something in Yiddish. Queen continues rising and staggering.*)

I got to get out of here! Lemme out, lemme out! (*He pounds at the wall, then staggers blindly towards the radiators.*)

BUTCH: Stay away from the radiators!

(*Queen staggers directly into the cloud of steam—screams—falls to the floor.*)

He's scalded himself.

(*Queen screams and sobs.*)

Stop it! Goddamn yuh— (*He grasps Queen's collar and cracks his head against floor.*) There now!

JOE: Butch—you killed him.

BUTCH: Somebody shoulda done him that favor a long time ago.

(*Shapiro mumbles in Yiddish.*)

You heard that one about—the niggers in church? "—Rastus, she says— Naw, he says—Mandy—Mandy how long does the Preacher—"

(*Dim out. A spot comes up on the office. Whalen is on the phone.*)

WARDEN: Schultz? How hot is it down there now in Butch's compartment? 150? Good! Keep it there till I give you further instructions— I'll be in my office till about midnight and if anything comes up—

(*Fade out. A spot comes up on Klondike. Shapiro, Queen, and Swifty are dead and lie in the center. Butch and Joe, gasping, crouch together by the air hole.*)

JOE: Butch—
BUTCH: Yeah.
JOE: Y'know that razor—
BUTCH: What about it?
JOE: Use it on me! Quick! I wanta get done with this!
BUTCH: Keep hold of yourself, Joe. You can make it.
JOE: Naw, I can't, Butch. I'm chokin' t' death. I can't stand it.
BUTCH: Breathe!
JOE: There ain't no air coming in now, Butch.
BUTCH: There's air—breathe it, Joe.
JOE: Naw . . .

(*Butch raises his face and shakes him.*)

BUTCH (*hoarsely*): Goddamn yuh, don't chicken out! Stay with me, Joe! We can beat Klondike!

(*Joe laughs deliriously. Butch continues, springing up.*)

Turn off them fucking radiators!! Turn the heat off, goddamn yuh, turn it off! (*He staggers toward the radiators.*) Stop it, y'hear me? Quit that SSSS! SSSS! (*He imitates the hissing sound.*) I'll turn yuh off, yuh suns-a-bitches! (*He springs on the radiators and grapples with them as though with a human adversary—he tries to throttle steam with his hands—he's scalded—screams with agony—backs away, his*

face contorted, wringing his hands.) SSSSS! SSSSS! SSSSS!
(*He is crazily imitating their noise.*)

JOE: Christ, Butch, it ain't no good that way. You've blown
your top. What's the percentage? (*Butch staggers back to the
air hole.*)

BUTCH: Joe! Hey, Joe! Swifty! You, Queen! Shapiro! (*He tugs
at one of the bodies.*) Let's sing! Let's all sing something!
Sing it out! Loud!

　　　For-tune's always hid-ing!

Why don't you bastards sing something! Come on—sing!
Sing!

　　　I looked ev'rywhere—!

(*The lights dim as the music completes the final lines of
"Bubbles."*)

Dim Out

EPISODE THREE

Announcer: "The Southwest Corner of the Yard!"

Dark stage and complete silence for several moments. Then—

EVA: Jim!

JIM: Here!

EVA: I'm late. I couldn't help it.

JIM: Shhh!

EVA (*lowering her voice*): His wife's not on the Island. She left
this afternoon. I can't stay there in that place with him,
Jim, I can't do it!

JIM: Shhh. Don't talk.

EVA: What am I going to do, Jim? What am I going to do?

JIM: *Don't talk!* It's not safe. They might hear us. Eva—

(*Pause. The beam of a searchlight moves over them.*)

EVA: Jim! They're moving the light!

JIM: Shhh! Keep it down!

(*The light disappears.*)

EVA: Oh. Thank God.
JIM: Now!
EVA: You've never even said that you loved me.
JIM: I love you. Now!
EVA: Oh, Jim—Jim! (*A longer pause.*)
JIM: The light again!

(*It circles lower this time and pauses directly above them.*)

Christ! Keep down low!
EVA: Jim!
JIM: Crawl! No, that way! Quick!

(*The light suddenly moves down and shines full upon Eva's face. Eva screams. A siren sounds. Blackout. A spot comes up on the office. Jim and Eva are there with a Guard. Whalen enters.*)

WARDEN: What *is* this?
GUARD: It looks like the Canary's turned into a lovebird, Mr. Whalen.
WARDEN: Aw!
GUARD: I heard a noise in the southwest corner of the yard. Sounded like a girl's voice. I dropped the light on—there they was!
WARDEN: Aw! Doing what?
GUARD: Well, they weren't picking daisies.
WARDEN: Aw! (*To Eva.*): You a while ago. Got hysterical in here. Objected because there wasn't no chaperone in the house. Then you run out there like a bitch in heat and—
JIM (*starting forward*): Stop it!
WARDEN: Aw!
JIM: It's easy to say things like that when you've got a gun stuck in my back.
WARDEN: Put the gun down. (*He takes a rubber hose from the hall.*) It's disillusioning what happens when you put too much confidence in the wrong people. Take your coat off.
EVA: No, you can't do that to him. I won't stand for it. It wasn't his fault. I asked him to meet me out there. Because I was scared. Scared of you! Scared of this awful place

you've got us locked up in! And now you let us out! You let us both out of here now! Before I scream! I'll let the whole world know what's going on here!

WARDEN: Take hold of that girl!

JIM (*springing toward them*): Let her go!

(*Whalen flails at Jim with the hose. Jim staggers to the floor, covering his face. Eva screams and struggles.*)

WARDEN: Take him out of here!

GUARD: Where to?

WARDEN: Klondike! Throw him in there with Butch O'Fallon! They're real good friends! (*He laughs.*)

(*The guard goes out dragging Jim.*)

Well, Eva—

(*Eva turns her face sharply away.*)

I'm sorry about this whole thing. I mean it sincerely. What I just said—forget that! You probably don't stop to realize what a strain I've been under. It's not easy to be the head of an institution like this. I've handled it like I would handle anything else. The best I knew how. Sometimes—I'm telling you the truth, girl—I've been so sick at heart at things I've had to do and see done—that it hurt me to look into my own little girl's face and hear her call me—Daddy! (*He pours himself a drink.*) Here. You take one, too. (*He is breathing heavily and for the moment is perfectly in earnest.*) Maybe it's done something to me in here. (*He touches his head.*) Sometimes I don't feel quite the same anymore. Awful, awful! Men down there now being subjected to awful torture! But what can I do about it? I got to keep discipline—dealing with criminals—there's no other way— Take your drink.

EVA: Thank you. (*She takes it.*)

WARDEN: There's two ways I could look at this. It could be a serious business. By your own confession you—you remember what you said, you—had Jim meet you out in the yard— Now I'm inclined to be broad-minded about such things—these discrepancies in the commissary report—

(*He shrugs and smiles.*)—things like that—serious sometimes—at least they can look that way—

EVA: What do you mean, Mr. Whalen? You mean you
would—try to accuse me of—!

WARDEN: No, no, no! (*He smiles engagingly.*) Not unless you
forced me to.

EVA: What do you want?

WARDEN: What does any man want? What did Jim want, what
did you give him?—Sympathy!

EVA: Oh.

WARDEN: That way it could be very simple. We're all of
us nervous, strained, overwrought!—Sympathy! All of us
need it!

EVA: Oh. What will you do to Jim now?

WARDEN: Well—

EVA: I love him! You probably don't understand how it
happened between us— He's coming up for parole next
month.

WARDEN: Yes, I have the letter in my desk now.

EVA: What letter?

WARDEN: Recommending Jim's—release! Of course after
this—

EVA: You won't send it?

WARDEN: Well—

EVA: Suppose I—I did sympathize—as you say—and—and
kept my mouth shut and anything else that you want!
Would you send the letter? Would Jim get his parole?

WARDEN (*smiling*): Why not? (*He laughs gently.*) You see how
easy it is to straighten things out!

EVA: Now? Would you send it now?

WARDEN: Now? It's—pretty late now—

EVA: The mailboat leaves at eleven-forty-five. You could have
it sent over by that. Don't worry. I won't back out. I'm not
afraid of you now. I like you—I'd like to show you how
much!

(*The Warden removes the letter from the drawer and rings the
bell. A guard enters.*)

WARDEN: Put this in the mail.

GUARD: Yes, Sir. (*He goes out.*)

WARDEN: My head aches, aches all the time—my wife's left me—the little girl, too— (*He opens the inner door.*) We're all of us nervous and tired, overwrought! Aren't we? Yes— (*He ushers Eva in as the light fades.*)

Dim Out

EPISODE FOUR

Announcer: "The Showdown"

A spot comes up on Klondike. Butch lies by the air hole. The bodies of the others are heaped in the center—Butch is apparently unconscious. Voices are heard in the hall. Butch slowly raises his head, becomes tense.

SCHULTZ (*as the door opens*): —makin' love to the Boss's secretary out in the yard—fancy that!

(*Butch rolls over quickly and feigns unconsciousness.*)

Whew! What a stink! Hey—Chick! C'mere! Steam's s' goddamn thick I can't see nothin'. Gimme that flash—

CHICK: Looks t' me like—Jeez! They're *stiffs*!

SCHULTZ: Stiffs! Y'mean—

CHICK: Roasted! Roasted alive! God Almighty! I didn't know nothin' like this was going on in here.

SCHULTZ: Shut up! How many are there?

(*During this Butch has slowly risen and poised himself for attack.*)

Gimme the flash! Shapiro, Joe—Swifty—The Queen—Where's Butch?

BUTCH (*springing*): Here! Here! (*He clutches Schultz by the throat.*)

(*Jim attacks Chick. A shot is fired; Jim wrests the revolver from the guard.*)

JIM: Toss your mittens!

BUTCH (*slowly releasing Schultz*): Aw! You! The Canary!

SCHULTZ (*uncertainly*): Good work, Jim!

JIM: I mean you, Schultz! Reach high! Butch—get them keys off him!

BUTCH (*slowly grinning*): Aw—aw! (*He snatches the keys.*)

SCHULTZ: What is this?

JIM: Butch—let the boys out! We're going upstairs!

BUTCH: Yeah!

SCHULTZ: You'll get the hot seat for this! Every mother's bastard of you will! What are you going to do, Jim?

JIM: Get into something comfortable, Schultz! You're going to SWEAT!

(*Jim backs out and slams the door. Schultz rushes to it, pounds and screams. Blackout. The stage is dark for a moment. There is the long wail of a siren. A spot comes up in the Warden's office. Whalen steps out of the inner room—he listens, tense with alarm.—The office door is thrown open—Jim enters.*)

WARDEN: Jim!

JIM (*his clothes torn and bloody from the earlier beating*): Yeah! Sometimes even hell breaks open and the damned get loose!

WARDEN: What's happened—downstairs? (*He edges back—pushes a buzzer.*)

JIM: No use pushing that. There's nobody on the other end of it.

WARDEN: They've broken out of—Klondike?

JIM: Yes. All of 'em but four. Four didn't break out cause they're dead—but they sent their regards to you, Boss, they want to be remembered!

WARDEN: How did you get that? (*He points to the revolver.*)

JIM: Raided the munitions!

WARDEN: What happened to Schultz?

JIM: He got in trouble downstairs, he's locked in Klondike, keeping the dead boys company down there— The other screws are locked up in the cellblock. Stand outa the way. (*He removes a revolver from the desk.*) Where's the girl?

WARDEN: She—left.

JIM: You're sure of that.

WARDEN: Yes— Why?

JIM: This ain't a safe place to be right now.

WARDEN: Look here, Jim—

JIM: What's the matter? You don't look good.

WARDEN: I'll make a deal with you—where are the—boys?

JIM (*jerking his thumb toward the door*): Waiting out there at the gate. I wanted to make sure the girl wasn't here before I let 'em come in.

WARDEN: Naw! You can't do that!

JIM: Sure. I'm the reception committee. I've got the keys.

(*Men are heard shouting outside. Eva appears at the inner door.*)

JIM: Eva!

EVA: Jim, don't do it, Jim! It's no use— He's written a letter asking for your parole, he sent it already!

WARDEN: Yes, Jim. I done it just now, because she—

JIM: Because she—what? (*He looks at them both.*) Aw! Get back inside there, Eva.

(*The boss starts to follow. Jim jerks him back.*)

Naw, you stay out here!

EVA: Jim! (*He forces her inside and locks the door.*)

WARDEN: Jim, you wouldn't give up your parole for the chair?

JIM: Sure. It's worth it. I haven't forgotten.

WARDEN: Forgotten—what?

JIM: Twenty-one days in the Hole. Dr. Jones.

WARDEN (*following him to door*): Afterwards I was your friend!

JIM: I wasn't yours!

WARDEN (*nearly screaming*): I was good to you afterwards, Jim!

JIM: I still had your signature on my back! Now we've got a new whipping-boss waiting out there—Butch O'Fallon!

WARDEN: Naw! Jim! Jim!

(*Jim has gone out—the roar of the men rises as doors are opened. The Warden gasps and darts behind the desk— Men enter like a pack of wolves and circle about the walls.*)

BUTCH (*lunging through*): Where is he?

WARDEN: Butch!

BUTCH (*his eyes blinded*): There! I've caught the smell of him now!

(*The two rulers face each other for the first time. Outside there is scattered gunfire, and a flickering light is thrown through the windows like the reflection of flames.*)

It's been you an' me a long time—you in here—me out there— But now it's—together at last— It's a pleasure, pig face, to make your acquaintance!

WARDEN: Look here now, boys—O'Fallon—Jim—I'll make a deal with you all— You've got to remember now—I've got the United States army in back of me!

BUTCH (*laughing and coming toward him*): You've got that wall in back of you— Where's the Doctor?

CONVICT: Here! (*He snatches the rubber hose from the wall and hands it to Butch.*)

BUTCH: Yeah!

WARDEN: Naw! Think of the consequences! Don't be fools!

(*Butch strikes him with the hose.*)

WARDEN (*cowering to the floor*): Stop! I'm a family man! I've got a wife! A daughter! A little—*girrrrl!* (*The final word turns into a scream of anguish as Butch crouches over him with the whip beating him with demoniacal fury till he is senseless.*)

(*The siren of an approaching boat is heard.*)

CONVICT: What is it?

ANOTHER: Gunboat!

ANOTHER: Troopers!

ANOTHER: They're landing!

ANOTHER: Douse the glims!

(*The room is plunged into total darkness except for the weird flickering of flame shadows on the walls— Men begin a panicky exodus from the room.*)

VOICES: Git down there— Fight 'em off— Troopers!—Not a chance— No chance anyhow!—You wanta go back to Klondike?—Fight!—Sure, fight!—We got nothing to lose!

(*Names are shouted—gates clang—machine gun fire is heard.*)

(*The noise becomes remote and dream-like—the room is almost quiet except for the distant, sad wail of the siren which continues endlessly [like the voice of damnation at the palace gates].*)

JIM: What have you done to him?

BUTCH: Thrown his blubbering carcass out the window.

JIM: Into the water?

BUTCH: Yeah. Straight down.

JIM: Butch—we've got a chance that way.

BUTCH: Swim for it? Naw, not me. I don't know how to swim. Besides it's half a mile to shore and rough as hell.

JIM: What will you do?

BUTCH: Stay here and fight it out.

JIM: I think I'll take my chances with the water.

BUTCH (*slowly extending his hand*): Good luck, I had you figured wrong.

JIM: Thanks.

BUTCH (*pulling off ring*): Here. There used to be a girl named Goldie at the Paradise Dance Hall on Brook Street west of the Ferry. If you should ever meet her, give her this— And tell her that I—kept it—all this time.

JIM: Sure, Butch—I will if I make—

BUTCH (*going to the door*): So long.

(*Rapid gunfire and distant shouting heard outside. Jim unlocks the inner door.*)

JIM: Eva.

(*Eva comes out slowly—she falls sobbing on his shoulder.*)

JIM: Don't cry!

EVA: No. I won't. There'd be no use in that. Jim, you were right about the pyrotechnical display!

JIM: Stand back from the window!

EVA (*hysterically gay*): It's lovely, isn't it, Jim!

JIM: Yes, lovely as hell!

EVA: What did they do to him?—Whalen?

JIM (*thumb to window*): The fish will have indigestion.

EVA: Jim! Have you thought what you'll get for this?

JIM: Nothing. They won't have a chance.

EVA: What are you going to do?

(*Sound cue: faint music.*)

JIM: There's water out that window. I can swim.

EVA: No, Jim, there's not a chance that way.

JIM: A chance? What's that? I never heard of it! (*On this speech he slowly approaches the window over the sea.*) Hear that? That music! It's—

EVA: The Lorelei!

JIM: The Lorelei— (*He tears off his coat.*) Now I retract those unkind things I said!

EVA: What will you do?

JIM: Swim out and catch a ride!

EVA: You couldn't, Jim— They'd bring you back— They wouldn't let you go!

JIM: They'll never see me.

EVA: Why?

JIM: Don't ask me why! There'll be a rope or something hanging over the side. Or if she doesn't ride too high I'll grab the rail! How! Don't ask me how! Now is the time for unexpected things, for miracles, for wild adventures like the storybooks!

EVA: Oh, Jim, there's not a chance that way!

JIM: Almost a chance! I've heard of people winning on a long shot. And if I don't— At least I'll be outside!

EVA: Oh, Jim I would have liked to live with you outside. We might have found a place where searchlights couldn't point their fingers at us when we kissed. I would have given you so much you've never had. Quick love is hard. It gives so little pleasure. We should have had long nights together with no walls. Or no *stone* walls— I know the place! A tourist camp beside a highway, Jim, with all night long the great trucks rumbling by—but only making shadows through the blinds! I'd touch the stone you're made of, Jim, and make you warm, so warm, so terribly warm your love would burn a scar upon my body that no length of time could heal!—Oh, Jim. If we could meet like that, at some appointed time, some place decided now, where we could love in secret and be warm, protected, not afraid of things— We could forget all this as something dreamed!—Where shall it be? When, Jim? Tell me before you go!

JIM: Quick! It's almost close enough! Get that shoe off!

EVA (*pulling off his shoes*): Yes Jim! But tell me where?

JIM (*climbing to the sill*): Watch the personal columns!

EVA: Jim!—Good-bye! (*He plunges from the window.*) — Good-bye . . .

(*Music from the Lorelei swells. Flame-shadows brighten on the walls. Shouting and footsteps are heard. Troopers rush in.*)

ONE (*switching on light.*): A girl—

TWO: The Warden's Secretary!

THREE (*crossing to her*): You're all right, sister. (*To others*): She's dazed, can't talk— Get her a drink, somebody.

ONE: What's that she's got?

THREE: A pair of—shoes!

ONE: Whose are they? What's she doing with them?

EVA (*facing the window with a faint smile*): I picked them up somewhere. I can't remember.

(*Light fades except for a spot on Eva, clutching Jim's shoes. Music from the Lorelei rises to a crescendo as a string of colored lights slides past the window. Dim out.*)

LOUD-SPEAKER: Aw there, it is! Y'can see it now, folks. That's the Island! Sort of misty tonight on account of the moon's gone under. Them walls are *escape-proof*, folks. Thirty-five hundred men locked in there an' some of them gonna stay there till Doomsday—(*Music.*)—Ah, music again! Dancing on the upper deck, folks, dancing,— dancing . . .

(*Musical theme up.*)

The End

BATTLE OF ANGELS

PROLOGUE

THE SCENE: *A "mercantile" store in a very small and old-fashioned town in the Deep South. It has large windows facing a tired dirt road, across which is a gasoline pump, a broken down wagon and cotton fields which extend to a cypress brake and the levee. The windows are shielded from sunlight by a tin portico so that the interior is rather dusky. The ceiling is very high and has two or three ceiling fans and old-fashioned lighting fixtures. There are a good many vertical lines which contribute to a dramatic atmosphere in the setting. In the back wall of the store is a steep flight of stairs leading up to the living quarters above. Left of this stairway is an open arch revealing a further room, the store's confectionery department.*

At the time this Prologue takes place—a Sunday afternoon about a year after the culmination of the tragedy—the store is no longer being run as a store, but has been converted into a museum exhibiting souvenirs of the sensational events which had taken place there. Various articles connected with the tragedy are on display, such as the snakeskin jacket, which is suspended in a conspicuous position. All these articles are labeled with crude handlettered signs.

An ancient Negro, The Conjure Man, is dozing in a chair in the archway. There is an awesome dignity in his appearance, despite the grotesque touches of his costume. He is small and cadaverous, a wizard-like figure, with a double strand of bleached chicken or hawk bones strung about his neck, tiny bells sewn to the sleeves of his garments so that he makes a slight tinkling sound when he moves, and various other odd tokens or charms scattered about his garments, which he sells to the superstitious.

(There is a knock at the door.)

WOMAN'S VOICE: Uncle! Uncle! *(The old Negro starts up. He rises and shuffles leisurely across to the door, unbolts it and draws it open on the mellow afternoon sunlight. Eva and Blanch Temple step inside.)*

EVA: Goodness . . .

BLANCH: Gracious sakes alive! It takes you forever to move a couple of inches. Come on in, folks! This is the famous Torrance Mercantile Store of Two Rivers, Mississippi. (*They are followed by a pair of middle-aged tourists.*)

EVA: Some people think it's sort of commercial of us to turn it into what the newspapers refer to as a Tragic Museum— but after all . . .

BLANCH: There's nothing else we can do to pay the taxes. Nobody would use this building for any other purpose, knowing what all happened in here once.

EVA: Not that it's haunted, but . . .

BLANCH: It's full of shadows. Electric power's cut off. Needless expense.

EVA: Electric power was off at the time it happened.

BLANCH: The power always goes off when it rains real hard and that Good Friday was one of the heaviest rains we've had in Two Rivers County.

EVA: Miss Harkaway called it a cataclysm of nature.

BLANCH: She was that wonderful Memphis newspaper-woman who wrote it all up in the *Commercial Appeal.*

EVA: Everything's just as it was.

BLANCH: Except of course the merchandise was removed.

EVA: Nothing has been took out that had a connection.

BLANCH: Everything in the museum has a label on it. You all can just browse around and we'll explain everything.

EVA: How can they ask any questions, you talking so fast?

BLANCH: You get me all balled up with your interruptions! Now that over there is the famous Jesus picture!

EVA: Don't call it *that.*

BLANCH: That's what *everyone* calls it. He *was* good-looking.

EVA: I never noticed he was.

BLANCH: Don't be ridiculous. *Everyone* noticed he was.

EVA: Now that dress there is the dress that Myra was wearing. Beulah said to her, "What do they call that color?"

BLANCH: She smiled an' she said, "They call it ecstasy blue!" Then didn't Myra . . . ?

EVA: Myra went back upstairs. Jabe knocked on the ceiling. That was when Vee . . .

BLANCH: Never mind about that. We'll tell that later. There is the phone . . .

EVA: The receiver is still off the hook.

BLANCH: The cash-box drawer's still open.

EVA: The money has been removed.

BLANCH: (*regretfully*) There *wasn't* much.

EVA: Frightfully, frightfully *little*. We are the only surviving relations, of course.

BLANCH: (*She points to the floor.*) You see those stains?

EVA: They're fading out. We'll have to touch them up.

BLANCH: Across the floor? Toward the confectionery?

EVA: Let's go in there! (*She rushes eagerly forward.*) Uncle, the *lamp*!

BLANCH: You probably wonder why we put up with such a peculiar old man as the caretaker here. Well, it's like this . . .

EVA: He's part of the exhibition!

BLANCH: Don't call it that!

EVA: Oh, the memorial then! What's the difference? This Conjure Man, as they call him . . .

BLANCH: Comes from Blue Mountain. Myra gave him odd jobs.

EVA: He was on the place when everything happened that happened.

BLANCH: He claims he knows some things that he isn't telling.

EVA: He's kind of daft. Now this room here is the Torrance Confectionery. Myra had it all done over for spring.

BLANCH: Yes, re-decorated. Somebody made a remark how lovely it was. "Yes," said Myra, "It's supposed to resemble the orchard across from Moon Lake!" Notice those imitations . . .

EVA: Dogwood blossoms. And that big Japanese lantern. It's dingy now but you all can just imagine how lovely it was.

BLANCH: Miss Harkaway put it in such a beautiful way. The mercantile store, she said, was reality, harsh and drab, but Myra's confectionery . . .

EVA: That was where she kept her dreams. Uncle, turn up that lamp. I want these people to see the place where she kept her dreams. (*The lamp is turned up higher. The confectionery blooms into a nostalgic radiance, as dim and soft as memory itself.*) Remind me, Blanch, to sprinkle a little roach powder on this floor.

EVA: Let's go upstairs.

BLANCH: I think we've left out something.

EVA: You can talk so fast I didn't keep track of it all.

BLANCH: It's you with your interruptions that ball things up. Watch out for these stairs, they're terrible, terrible steep.

EVA: We can't be responsible for an accident on them.

BLANCH: Goodness sakes alive, *no!* These terrible taxes . . .

EVA: Keep us poor as church mice! (*They lead the way up the stairs.*)

BLANCH: You keep awake, Uncle.

EVA: If anyone else stops in, just ring the bell.

BLANCH: (*She opens the door on the landing.*) Now these are the living quarters.

EVA: Myra's bedroom's on the right an' Jabe's on the left. (*The light fades out as the door closes. The Conjure Man laughs to himself as the curtain falls.*)

ACT ONE

THE SCENE: *The same as for the Prologue, except that it is now a year earlier—in early February—and the store is in operation, stocked with merchandise. There are great bolts of pepperell and percale which stand upright on the counters. The black skeleton of a dressmaker's dummy stands meaninglessly in front of a thin white column. Along the wall at the left is the shoe department, with a ladder that slides along the shelves and two or three shoe-fitting chairs. Racks of dresses, marked "Spring Styles," line the right wall.*

Dolly and Beulah are arranging candles and setting a buffet table in the general store. They are wives of small planters, about thirty and over-dressed. Dolly's husband, Pee Wee, and the town sheriff are in the confectionery shooting pin-ball. A train whistles in the distance.

DOLLY: Pee Wee! That's the Cannonball!

PEE WEE: (*from the confectionery*) Okay, Mama! (*Pee Wee enters. He is a heavy man. His vest comes mid-way down the white-shirted bulge of his belly; his laced boots are caked with mud.*) Ninety-five nickels an' no pay-off! What would you call that, Mama?

DOLLY: Outrageous! Not the machine, but you poor suckers that play it.

BEULAH: This meringue turned out real good.

SHERIFF: (*He enters from the confectionery, laughing.*) You got to mid-aisle it three times straight's the only way to crack that goddam pot.

PEE WEE: I'm gonna tell Jabe about it. Ninety-five nickels an' no pay-off. (*They go out.*)

DOLLY: I guess Jabe Torrance has got more to think about than that ole pin-ball game in the confectionery. Huh?

BEULAH: He ought to have. That meringue *is* nice and light. I put in two drops of almond. Yesterday I was talking to Dr. Bob. You know, young Dr. Bob?

DOLLY: Uh-huh. What did he say?

BEULAH: I ast him how Jabe was, what kind of condition he really seemed to be in. He's seen them X-ray pictures they took in the Memphis Hospital after the operation. Well . . .

DOLLY: What did he say, Beulah?

BEULAH: He said the worst that a doctor can ever say.

DOLLY: What's that?

BEULAH: Nothing at all, not a spoken word did he utter; he simply looked at me with those big dark eyes and shook his haid—like this!

DOLLY: (*She speaks with doleful optimism.*) I guess he signed Jabe Torrance's death-warrant with just that single motion of his haid.

BEULAH: Exackly what I thought. I understand that they cut him open . . .

DOLLY: An' sewed him right back up?

BEULAH: (*struggling to speak and strangling on an olive*) Mmm. Mmm. (*She points at her stuffed mouth.*) I didn't know these olives had seeds in them.

DOLLY: You thought they was stuffed?

BEULAH: Uh-huh.

DOLLY: Where's the Temple Sisters?

BEULAH: Snooping around upstairs.

DOLLY: Let Myra catch 'em at it, she'll lay 'em both out good. She never did invite nobody up there.

BEULAH: Well, I was surprised when I went up myself.

DOLLY: I know it.

BEULAH: Two separate bedrooms, too! Maybe it's just since Jabe's been sick.

DOLLY: Naw, it's permanent, honey. As a girl in Tupelo she certainly wasn't cold-blooded. We used to go double together me an' Pee Wee an' her and that Anderson boy. All of one spring we would go to the orchard across from Moon Lake ev'ry night. We was engaged, but they wasn't. Boll weevil and army-worm struck his cotton awful three times straight. He married into the Delta Planters' Bank and Myra married Jabe. Myra was Myra then. Since then she's just a woman that works in a mercantile store.

(*Cassandra Whiteside enters at the door on the right. She is dark and strikingly beautiful, of a type rather peculiar to the South—physically delicate with clear translucent skin and luminous eyes as though burnt thin by her intensity of feeling. With people she has a rather disdainful ease, not deliberate or conscious, but rooted in her class origin and the cynical candor with which she recognizes herself and the social contradictions and tragic falsity of the world she lives in. Sandra is the only woman of aristocratic extraction in the group. Her family is the oldest in this part of the Delta and was once the richest, but their plantation has dwindled with each successive generation. Sandra has been "going out" for ten years and is still unmarried, which is enough in itself to destroy a girl's reputation.*)

DOLLY: Sandra Whiteside! How are you?

SANDRA: Oh, I seem to be still living. God knows why. Where's Myra?

DOLLY: Gone to Memphis to bring Jabe back from the hospital.

BEULAH: The men folks just now went to the depot to meet them.

SANDRA: Oh. . . . I want some cartridges for this pistol of mine. (*She removes it from her bag.*) I thought I better carry one with me. I'm on the road so much you'd think I was making a political campaign tour, the number of places I've got to visit this weekend. Memphis, Jackson— Is this the hardware section? (*approaching the counter*) Aw, here's cartridges! (*She helps herself.*) Then on down to New Awleuns for the start of the carnival season. Tell Myra to charge these to me. I ought to buy an airplane. They say that you only crack up once in the air.

DOLLY: Well, you'd better stay out of airplanes, honey.

BEULAH: How many times have you cracked up on the highway?

SANDRA: Today was the seventh since New Year's.

DOLLY: No!

SANDRA: I fell asleep at the wheel an' ran into a fence.

BEULAH: Goodness!

DOLLY: Gracious!

BEULAH: Last week she had a collision with a mule.

DOLLY: My Lawd!

SANDRA: And just to show you the absolute lack of justice, the mule was killed and I was completely uninjured!

DOLLY: (*with false concern*) Darling, you'd better be careful!

SANDRA: Oh, I don't know. What else can you do when you live in Two River County but drive like hell! (*There is the sound of a car out in front.*)

BEULAH: 'S 'at them?

DOLLY: (*sarcastically*) Naw, it's the Sheriff's little fireside companion.

BEULAH: Vee Talbot! Who is that with her? A *man*! (*This word creates a visible stir among the three women.*)

DOLLY: Uh-huh! Yes, it is!

BEULAH: Who could it be I wonder?

DOLLY: I can't make out. Oh, my goodness! What an outfit he's got on! It looks like a snakeskin jacket.

BEULAH: *Wha-at*? Do you know him?

DOLLY: Naw, I don't know him a-tall. He looks like an absolute stranger. Poor Vee has got her skirt caught in the car door or something, it's hitched up over her knees and she's simply *frantic* about it! (*She utters a sharp laugh.*)

BEULAH: She's such a big clumsy thing. Who do you think the man is?

DOLLY: I told you I never have seen him, don't know him from Adam, darling. Maybe he's one of the Twelve Apostles that she's been painting on.

SANDRA: Is Vee painting the Twelve Apostles?

DOLLY: She's been painting them for twelve years, one each year. She says that she sees them in visions. But every one of them looks like some man around Two River County. She told Birdie Wilson that she was hoping she'd have a vision of Jesus next Passion Week so she could paint Him, too.

BEULAH: You better quit staring.

DOLLY: She's finally got her skirt loose. Oh, God, the hem's ripped out, it's trailing the ground! (*She laughs and crosses from the window.*)

(*Vee enters from the street. She is a heavy, middle-aged woman, about forty, whose personality, frustrated in its contact with externals, has turned deeply inward. She has found refuge in religion and primitive art and has become known as an eccentric. Although a religious fanatic, a mystic, she should not be made ridiculous. Her portrayal will contain certain incidents of humor, but not be devoid of all dignity or pathos. She wanders slowly about with a vague dreamy smile on her face. Her expression is often bewildered.*)

BEULAH: (*with loud, false cordiality*) Hello, Vee honey, how are you?

DOLLY: Hello, Vee.

VEE: (*faintly*) Hello. I got m' skirt caught in the lock of the Chevrolet door an' I think it's torn loose a little. I can't see behind me good. Does it look like it's torn to you? (*She peers awkwardly, ponderously, behind her at the hem which dangles across the floor, like a big heavy dog trying to catch its tail.*)

BEULAH: Just a little bit, honey.

DOLLY: Yes, it's scarcely noticeable even. (*She giggles.*)

VEE: I feel like something was dragging. Oh, it *has* been torn, the young man told me it wasn't!

DOLLY: Say, who is he?

VEE: I don't know who he is, but I think he's all right, though. He told me he'd been saved, doesn't smoke, doesn't drink. His parents are dead, both of them, but he's got an uncle who's a Catholic priest and he says that he stayed six years—I mean his uncle—in some leper colony on a South Sea Island without ever catching any sign of disease. Isn't that wonderful, though?

DOLLY: Huh.

BEULAH: What's he doing here?

VEE: Says he's exploring the world an' ev'rything in it.

DOLLY: Laudamighty!

VEE: He come to the lock-up las' night an' ast for a bed, but he couldn't stay in it, though, the bars made him nervous.

DOLLY: So what did you do with him then?

VEE: What do you mean? I was alone in the house so I give him a blanket, he went out to sleep in his car.

DOLLY: Sounds like a peculiar person.

BEULAH: Yeah.

VEE: Oh, no, he just isn't a type that you are used to seeing. I'm going to speak a good word for him to Myra, she said she might be needing some help around here. (*Val appears in the front door. He is about twenty-five years old. He has a fresh and primitive quality, a virile grace and freedom of body, and a strong physical appeal.*) Come right on in, Mr. Xavier.

VAL: What shall I do with this here?

VEE: Jus' give me the sherbet. I thought Mr. Torrance might need somethin' light an' digestible so I brought sherbet.

BEULAH: What flavuh is it? Pineapple?

VEE: Pineapple.

BEULAH: Oh, goody, I love pineapple. Don't you-all? (*She hands Vee the napkin-wrapped bowl.*)

VEE: Mr. Xavier, I was just telling these ladies about your uncle that went to live with the lepers. Some people are doubtful about the power of faith but there's an example I think should convince anybody.

BEULAH: Isn't it, though? Let's put this right in the frigidaire before it stahts t' melt.

DOLLY: (*She lifts the napkin.*) I'm afraid you're locking the stable after the hause is gone.

BEULAH: Wh-at? Is it melted awready?

DOLLY: Reduced to juice!

BEULAH: Oh foot!—Well, let's put it in anyhow, it might thicken up.

VEE: Where is the frigidaire?

BEULAH: It's in the confectionery. (*The three women go back through the archway. Sandra is left with Val. She laughs in her throat and leans provocatively back. Val stares at her with a touch of antagonism. This challenging silence continues for a marked pause. Then Sandra laughs again, somewhat louder.*)

VAL: (*sharply*) Is something amusing you, lady?

SANDRA: (*drawling*) Yes. Very much. I think it's that jacket you're wearing. What stuff is it made of?

VAL: Snakeskin.

SANDRA: (*with a disgusted grimace*) Ouuu!

VAL: I didn't ask your opinion.

SANDRA: I didn't express one, did I?

VAL: Yeah. You said "Ouuu!" (*He mocks her grimace.*)

SANDRA: You know what that was? It was fascinated revulsion. (*She goes into the confectionery and starts the juke box. It plays "Custro Vidas."*) Would you like to dance?

VAL: I don't know how to dance.

SANDRA: I'd love to teach you. We'll go out jooking some night.

VAL: Jooking? What's that?

SANDRA: That's where you get in a car and drink a little and drive a little and dance a little. Then you drink a little more and drive a little more and dance a little more. Then you stop dancing and just drink and drive. Then you stop driving and you just drink. And then, finally, you stop drinking.

VAL: Then what do you do?

SANDRA: That depends entirely on who you happen to be out jooking with. If you're out with me, and you're sufficiently attractive, you nearly always wind up on Cypress Hill.

VAL: What's that?

SANDRA: That's the graveyard, honey. It's situated, appropriately enough, on the highest point of land in Two River County, a beautiful windy bluff just west of the Sunflower River.

VAL: Why do you go out there?

SANDRA: Because dead people give such good advice.

VAL: What advice do they give?

SANDRA: Just one word—*live!* (*Beulah rushes in with a bowl of something.*)

BEULAH: You're going to stay fo' the pahty, Mr. . . . ?

VAL: Xavier.

BEULAH: I know some Seviers in Blue Mountain. Any relation?

VAL: Spelt with an "S" or an "X"?

BEULAH: An "S," I believe.

VAL: No relation.

BEULAH: (*sympathetically*) Awwww. (*She rushes back out.*)

SANDRA: I have a great aunt who's laid away on Cypress Hill. Her name was Cassandra, the same as mine is, so I always empty my bottles on her grave. She loved to drink. She finally got so she just lay on the bed and drank and drank all night and all day. They asked her if she didn't get tired of it. She said, "No, I never get bored. I have moving pictures on my ceiling. They go on all the time, continuous performance. I'm the main actress," she said, "and I do the most mah-velous things!" That was Cassandra the second. I'm the third. The first was a little Greek girl who slept in the shrine of Apollo. Her ears were snake-bitten, like mine, so that she could understand the secret language of the birds. You know what they told her, Snakeskin? They contradicted everything that she'd been told before. They said it was all stuff an' nonsense, a pack of lies. They advised her to drive her car as fast as she wanted to drive it, to dance like she wanted to dance. Get drunk, they said, raise hell at Moon Lake casina, do bumps an' wiggle your fanny! (*Vee Talbot enters; she stops short with an outraged look. Sandra laughs and extends a pack of cigarettes toward Val.*)

VEE: Mr. Xavier, don't smoke. (*She sets the potato chips down and goes out.*)

DOLLY: (*rushing through*) Mr. Xavier, if you're looking for work, you might drop in on my husband, Pee Wee Bland. He runs that cotton gin right over the road there.

BEULAH: The Marguerites! I smell them burning! (*She runs out.*)

SANDRA: How did you happen to come to this dark, wild river country of ours?

VAL: A broken axle stopped me here last night.

SANDRA: You'd better mend it quick and move along.

VAL: Why's that?

SANDRA: Why? Why? Don't you know what those women are suffering from? Sexual malnutrition! They look at you with eyes that scream "Eureka!" (*She laughs and saunters casually to the door. She raises her revolver and fires two shots into the sky.*)

VAL: For God's sake! (*The three women scream and come rushing back in. The Temple Sisters shriek upstairs and come scuttling down, Blanch losing her footing and sliding down the last three steps. There is babble and confusion.*)

DOLLY: What are you *doing*? Oh, God, in my condition! I . . .

BEULAH: Sandra, for the love of . . .

BLANCH: (*moaning*) I've broke my laig in two!

EVA: (*screaming*) She's broken her laig! (*Vee goes over to her.*)

DOLLY: Oh, she has *not*! Sandra, what on earth did you fire that damn thing faw?

SANDRA: (*She laughs and comes unsteadily back into the store.*) I took a pot shot at a buzzard!

BEULAH: A what? (*Sandra laughs wildly and looks at Val who crosses to her and takes the pistol roughly from her grasp. Myra enters. Myra is a slight, fair woman, about thirty-four years old. She is a woman who met emotional disaster in her girlhood and whose personality bears traces of the resulting trauma. Frequently sharp and suspicious, she verges on hysteria under slight strain. Her voice is often shrill and her body tense. But when in repose, a girlish softness emerges—evidence of her capacity for great tenderness.*)

MYRA: What in God's holy name has been going on here? Who fired those shots out the door? (*She sees Val with the revolver in his hand; she gasps and starts toward the door.*) You! (*They stare at each other for a brief moment.*)

VAL: (*slowly smiling*) No Ma'am, it wasn't me. It was this young lady here.

SANDRA: Yes, I fired it, darling.

MYRA: What at?

SANDRA: A bird of ill-omen was circling over the store.

MYRA: Yea? One of those imaginary things that people see in a certain condition. Hello, Beulah, Dolly. (*She flings off her hat.*) I'm evermore tired. I've never had such a trip. Jabe took a bad spell on the train. They carried him up the back way. How are yuh, Vee. Blanch Temple, what are you sitting on the floor faw?

EVA: She took a spill on the stairs when Sandra Whiteside fired the shots!

MYRA: On the stairs? You two were upstairs, were you?

EVA: Yes, we were straightening things up a little . . .

MYRA: (*quickly*) I see. An investigation?

EVA: Yes. I mean . . .

BLANCH: No, no, no! We wanted to see that ev'rything was in order. I've got such awful weak ankles, I'm always tripping and falling. An' I've got to march in church with the choir if I got to go on crutches. (*She rises painfully with Beulah's and Eva's assistance.*)

MYRA: Oh, look what you all have done, that beautiful table! Candles an' ev'rything sweet that goes to make a nice party! Some of your lovely floating-island, Beulah? Sweet! The spirit is willing but the flesh is completely exhausted. (*A Negro enters, crosses to Myra carrying a tower of pastel-colored hat-boxes and a big gay placard reading "Welcome Sweet Springtime."*) Oh, Joe, bring me those cards. Welcome sweet springtime! I've bought a pile of spring hats. (*She extricates one of the cards.*) This one here is the nicest— "In the spring, a young maid's fancy lightly turns to new chapeaux."

BEULAH: (*reading the rest of it*) "Mary Lou and Jane and Frances wear new hats to please their beaux!"

DOLLY: Oh, that's perfectly dahling. It seems so eahly, though, to think about spring.

EVA: I don't know. Somebody tole me that carps have been seen in Yazoo Pass. That always indicates that flood season's 'bout to start.

BLANCH: Myra . . . .

MYRA: Yes?

BLANCH: I don't suppose you feel like talkin' about it right now, but I do hope Jabe's operation was completely successful.

MYRA: No.

BLANCH: It wasn't? (*All the women stare greedily at Myra.*)

MYRA: No. It *wasn't.*

BLANCH: Oh!

EVA: My! My!

BEULAH: I'm so sorry to hear it.

DOLLY: If there's anything I can do . . . I—? (*Jabe is heard knocking on the ceiling from his room above. Myra's face becomes suddenly listless and tired.*)

EVA: What's that knocking upstairs?

MYRA: Jabe.

SHERIFF: Myra, Jabe wants you.

MYRA: Excuse me, I'll have to go up. (*She crosses wearily toward the stairs, her hat dangling from one hand, pauses before the "Welcome Sweet Springtime" sign, with its bluebirds, flutes and gilded scrolls and cherubim, gravely lifts it and places it in a higher position.*) Dolly, look at this hat! I think it must have been created just for you! (*She smiles and goes on upstairs.*)

SANDRA: (*who has engaged Val in low conversation since Myra's entrance*) Speaking of knocks, I've got one in my engine. A very mysterious noise. I can't decide whether I'm in communication with one of my dead ancestors or whether the carburetor or something is just about to drop out an' leave me stranded, probably at midnight in the middle of some lonesome black forest! (*She smiles at Val.*) I don't suppose you'd have any knowledge of mechanics?

VAL: I dunno. I might. (*Dolly is trying on the hat but is watchful of this exchange—also the other women who are opening hat-boxes.*)

SANDRA: Would you be willing to undertake a kind of exploratory operation on it?

VAL: Well, I might if it didn't take too long.

SANDRA: (*drawling*) Oh, with your expert knowledge it shouldn't take lo-ong at-all! (*Dolly giggles.*)

BEULAH: (*pointedly*) What are you laughin' at?

DOLLY: This hat! Isn't it the strangest thing?

BEULAH: Them things on the brim—what are they—carrots an' peas? I think they'd be much better *creamed*—with chicken croquettes! (*Val has slid slowly off the counter. He moves past Sandra and the secret looks of the women, toward the door.*)

VEE: Mr. Xavier . . . (*She crosses as if to stop him but they have already disappeared.*) Oh. I was going to ask Myra if she would give him a job.

BEULAH: Well . . .

DOLLY: It looks like he's got one now!

EVA: What did she say? A knock . . . ?

BLANCH: In her engine! (*innocently*) Whatever that is.

DOLLY: (*with a peal of laughter*) Did you *evuh* see such a puhfaum-ance! *Nevuh* in all my . . .

BEULAH: Bawn days? *Neither* did I! You see how she looked at the boy? An' the tone of huh voice. Corrupt? Absolutely —de-*grad-ed*!

DOLLY: Hank says her father got drunk one time at the Elks an' told him that she was kicked out of both of those girls' schools. Had to send her out East where morals don't matter. She's got two degrees or something in *lit*-era-*chure.*

BEULAH: Six degrees of fever if you ask me!

VEE: (*who has been silently brooding over the situation*) I certainly hope she doesn't get him to drink.

DOLLY: Vee, honey, you might as well face it, this is one candidate fo' salvation that you have *lost* to the opposition!

VEE: I don't believe it. He told me that he'd been saved already. (*She fixes her resentment on Dolly.*) If some of the older women in Two River County would set a better example there'd be more justice in their talk about girls!

DOLLY: (*with asperity*) What do you mean by that remark?

VEE: I mean that people who give drinkin' pahties an' get so drunk they don't know which is *their husband* an' which is somebody elses' an' people who serve on the altar guild an' still play cards on Sundays . . .

DOLLY: Just stop right there! Now I've discovered the source of that dirty gossip!

VEE: I'm only repeating what I've been told by others! I certainly never have been entertained at such affairs as that!

DOLLY: No, an' you never will be, you're a public kill-joy, a professional hypocrite!

BEULAH: Dolly!

DOLLY: She spends her time re-fauming tramps that her husband puts in the *lock-up*! Brings them here in Myra's store an' tries to get them jobs here when God knows what kind of vicious ideas they've probably got in their heads!

VEE: I try to build up characters! You an' your drinkin' pahties are only concerned with tearin' characters down! I'm goin' upstairs with Myra. (*She goes out.*)

DOLLY: Well, you know what brought on that tantrum? She's jealous of Sandra Whiteside's running off with that strange boy. She hasn't lived as a natural wife for ten years or more (*to Eva*) so her husband has got to pick up with some bright-skinned nigger.

BEULAH: Oh, Dolly, you're awful. Sometimes I think you ought to wear a back-house on your haid instead of a hat.

DOLLY: I've got no earthly patience with that sort of hypocriticism. Beulah, let's put all this perishable stuff in the Frigidaire and get out of here. I've never been so thoroughly disgusted.

BEULAH: Oh, my Lawd! (*They go into the confectionery.*)

EVA: Both of those two women are as common as dirt.

BLANCH: Dolly's folks in Blue Mountain are nothin' at all but the poorest kind of white trash. Why, Lollie Tucker told me the old man sits on the porch with his shoes off drinkin' beer out of a bucket! Nobody wants these Marguerites. (*She goes to the hardware counter and gets her bag.*) Let's take 'em, huh?

EVA: (*looking at the flowers*) I was just wondering what we'd use to decorate the altar with tomorrow. The Bishop Adjutant's comin'. As far's I know nobody's offered flowers. We can give Myra credit in the Parish notes.

BLANCH: Put the olive-nut sandwiches in here with the Marguerites. Be careful you tote them so they won't get squashed.

EVA: They'll come in very nicely for the Bishop's tea. (*Dolly and Beulah re-enter from the confectionery.*)

DOLLY: We still have time to make the second show.

BEULAH: Dolly, you still have on that awful hat!

DOLLY: Oh, Lawd! (*She tosses it on the counter. Dolly and Beulah go out quickly together.*)

EVA: (*when they are out*) Sits on the po'ch with his shoes off?

BLANCH: Yes! Drinkin' *beer* from a *bucket!* (*Eva and Blanch go out. The Sheriff comes downstairs, grunting and puffing, followed by Pee Wee.*)

PEE WEE: Took one dose at noon. When that didn't work, I took a double one about five o'clock. Jabe sure looks bad.

SHERIFF: Looks no better 'n no worse 'n he always looked, but if what they say is correct, he'll more'n likely go under before the cotton comes up! See that there? (*He indicates his bandaged knuckle.*) Broke my knuckle! Never hit a bucktooth nigger in the mouf! That's *the moral of it.* (*Pee Wee laughs.*) Oh, Vee! . . . . Them fool wimmin got in a ruckus down here, I don't know what it's about. (*Vee comes downstairs.*)

VEE: Hush that bawling will yuh? I wanted to speak with Myra about that young man who needs work but I couldn't in front of Jabe. He thinks he's gonna be able to go back to work himself.

SHERIFF: Well, come awn here, quit foolin'!

VEE: I think I ought to wait 'till that young man gets back.

SHERIFF: Mama, you come awn. Aw else stay here, an' *walk* when you git ready. (*He strides out after Pee Wee. The car engine roars. Vee looks troubled and follows them slowly out. There is a slight pause. The Negro enters from the confectionery. He looks about him and laughs with a gentle, quiet laughter at something secret, opens the soft drink cooler and takes a coke out. He laughs again, softly, secretly, and goes out the front door of the store, leaving the door open. A hound bays in the distance. After a moment Val comes back in, and shuts the door behind him. He goes to the table, picks up a paper napkin and scrubs lipstick off his mouth. He settles himself on the counter. After a moment or two Myra comes downstairs bearing an oil lamp. She has on a cheap Japanese kimona of shiny black satin with large scarlet poppies on it. She appears to be very distraught and doesn't notice Val. She crosses directly to the phone and turns the crank.*)

MYRA: Get me the drug-store, please. Mr. Dubinsky? This is Myra Torrance. Were you asleep? I'm sorry. I'm in a bad situation. I left my luminal tablets in the Memphis hotel and I can't sleep without them. . . . I know your store's closed up. So's mine. I know the lights are out, they're out over here. But you don't need a thousand watt bulb to put a few luminal tablets in a little card-board box or paper bag. . . . Now look here, Mr. Dubinsky, if you want to keep my trade, you send your nigger right over with that box of tablets. Gone? Then bring 'em yourself! I'm absolutely desperate from lack of sleep. My nerves are all on edge. If I don't get a good sleep tonight, I'll go all to pieces. I've got a sick man to take care of. . . . Yes, I just brought him home from the Memphis hospital. The operation was not at all successful. Will you do that? I'll be very much obliged. Thank you, Mr. Dubinsky. Excuse me for speaking so sharply. Thank you, Mr. Dubinsky. I appreciate that, Mr. Dubinsky. Goodbye, Mr. Dubinsky. (*She hangs up the phone and leans exhaustedly against the wall.*) Oh, oh, oh, I wish I was dead—dead—dead.

VAL: (*quietly*) No, you don't Mrs. Torrance.

MYRA: My God! (*She gasps and clutches her wrapper about her throat.*)

VAL: I didn't mean to scare you.

MYRA: *What is this?* What are you still doing here? Who *are* you? My God, you got eyes that shine in the dark like a dog's. Get out or I'll call for the Sheriff!

VAL: Lady. . . .

MYRA: Well?

VAL: I've been to the Sheriff's already.

MYRA: Aw. Escaped from the lock-up?

VAL: Naw. The Sheriff's wife took me in there last night.

MYRA: She did, uh?

VAL: She give me a night's flop there but I didn't stay.

MYRA: Naw?

VAL: It made me uneasy being locked up. I got to have space around me.

MYRA: Look here, that's interesting, but this store's closed and I'll thank you to please get out. I've got a sick man upstairs that requires a lot of attention. If you're hungry. . . .

VAL: I'm not.

MYRA: There's lots of fancy stuff they put in the frigidaire, you might as well eat it, I can't.

VAL: No, thanks, but I'd be mighty obliged if you would give me a job.

MYRA: There's no work here.

VAL: Excuse the contradiction but there is. Mizz Talbot told me so.

MYRA: Vee Talbott? I'll thank her to let me decide such things for myself. I'm in the mercantile business, she's a painter of very peculiar pictures she calls the Apostles but look like men around town. She took you in, did she? Well!

VAL: Whatever it is you're suggesting is incorrect. I've met one bitch in this town but it wasn't her.

MYRA: (*furiously*) How—how—*dare* you say that!

VAL: It wasn't you neither, Ma'am! It was one that picked me up in here before you come in. Said she had engine trouble and would I fix it. She took me for a stud—and I slapped her face!

MYRA: You *what*?

VAL: I said I slapped her face. She wasn't a bad piece neither but I didn't like the way she went about it, like she was something special and I was trash!

MYRA: You . . . Cassandra Whiteside? *Slapped*? (*She bursts into wild laughter.*) I've never heard anything so beautiful in all my life! Have a drink and get out; I've got to go up.

VAL: (*stubbornly*) You'll need help here with your husband sick upstairs.

MYRA: You think so, uh? Well, if I do it'll have to be local help. I couldn't hire no stranger. 'Specially one that slapped the face of one of the richest girls in the Mississippi Delta. (*She laughs again.*) You had sales experience?

VAL: I've had all kinds of experience.

MYRA: That's not what I ast you. I ast you if you've had experience in the mercantile line. I want to know if you would be able to sell?

VAL: Sell?

MYRA: Yes!

VAL: Lots in hell to preachers!

MYRA: (*She utters again that sharp startled laugh, her fingers tightly clutching a magazine and nervously turning through it.*) I guess you got character ref'rence?

VAL: Sure.

MYRA: Where was the last place you worked?

VAL: Garage in Oakley.

MYRA: Tennessee?

VAL: Yeah.

MYRA: Grease-monkey, was you?

VAL: (*stiffly*) I wouldn't call myself that.

MYRA: Excuse me. Why did you quit that job?

VAL: If I told you, you'd think I was crazy.

MYRA: I think ev'rybody is crazy, including myself. Why did you quit it?

VAL: The place next door burnt down.

MYRA: What's that got to do with it?

VAL: I don't like fire. I dreamed about it three nights straight so I quit. I was burnt as a kid and ever since then it's been something I can't forget. (*He offers her a paper.*) Here's a letter he wrote.

MYRA: Who?

VAL: Garage manager.

MYRA: (*She reads aloud.*) "This here boy's peculiar but he sure does work real hard and he's honest as daylight." What does he mean "peculiar"?

VAL: Unusual is what he means.

MYRA: Why don't he say unusual?

VAL: He's not exactly an expert in the use of the language.

MYRA: Oh, but you are?

VAL: (*He removes a small book from his pocket.*) See this?

MYRA: Funk and Wagnall's Pocket Dictionary.

VAL: I carry that along with me wherever I go.

MYRA: What for?

VAL: You ever seen a coal-miner's cap? (*Myra shakes her head.*) I wore one once when I was mining in the Red Hills of Alabama. It had a little lamp in front so you could see what your pick was digging into. Well—I'm still digging.

MYRA: Digging?

VAL: I don't claim to know very much, but I am writing a *book*.

MYRA: Well—you don't have to spit in my face to convince me of it!

VAL: (*grinning*) Excuse me.

MYRA: What's your book about?

VAL: Life.

MYRA: Sorry but I can't use you.

VAL: Why not?

MYRA: Other people ain't as charitable as that garage-manager is. They wouldn't say "peculiar," they'd say "nuts!" Also your appearance is much against you.

VAL: What's wrong with that.

MYRA: I don't know exactly. If you're hungry, eat. But other-wise . . . (*She is interrupted by knocking on the ceiling.*) Otherwise . . . get out. I'm too bone-tired to carry on conversation.

VAL: If you'll excuse me for telling you so, you're just about the rudest talking woman I've ever met.

MYRA: Yes, I'm mean inside. You heard me cussing when I come downstairs? Inside I cuss like that all the time. I hate ev'rybody; I wish this town would be bombarded tomor-row and everyone daid. Because—

VAL: Because?

MYRA: I got to live in it when I'd rather be daid in it—an' buried. (*She takes a drink of wine.*) What I meant about your appearance is you're too good-looking. Can you read shoe sizes?

VAL: Yeah.

MYRA: What does 75 David mean? (*Val is stymied.*) You see how you lie? You lie like a dawg in summer! (*She laughs, not unkindly.*) 75 means 7½ in length and David means D wide. For flat-footed wimmin. You would either scare trade out of this store completely or else you'd bring it in so thick the floor would collapse. I can't decide which it would be.

VAL: I'd bring it in, lady.

MYRA: Gosh— (*There is a knock at the front door. Myra crosses to it.*) A new floor would be an awful expense! (*She opens the door and steps outside.*) Thank you Mr. Dubinsky. (*com-ing back in*) That was the Sand Man with my luminal tablets. Suppose you— (*She opens the box and places a tablet on her tongue, washing it down with wine.*)

VAL: Huh?

MYRA: Suppose you try to sell me a pair of white kid pumps out of that new stock there. Imagine me a customer hard to please and you the clerk. Go on . . . Naw, them over there is Red Goose shoes for kiddies. Them're men's shoes.

Growing girls', Misses'. Them on the end of the shelves are Women's; sizes range down from the top. (*He pulls out a pair.*) You call them kid? That's suede, young man; 'snot a pump, neither, 's a blucher oxford; I don't believe you've ever tried to sell a thing in your life. Go on, roll your hoop, you're worse than useless to me! (*as he moves slowly toward the door, Myra says softly*) Sure you're not hungry? You're walking kind of unsteady.

VAL: What's that to you? I've got dog's eyes—you don't like me!

MYRA: I didn't say that.

VAL: I can't read shoe sizes. I don't know suede from kid. You can't use me; I'm worse than useless! What does it matter whether I'm hungry or not? (*He shakes with fury.*)

MYRA: (*very softly, gently, with a slight mournful, tender shake of her head*) Lawd, child, come back in the mawning and I'll give you a job. (*She moves slowly over to the candles and blows them out. Val stares at her dumbly.*)

VAL: God, I—! Lady, you—!

MYRA: (*laughing a little*) God you an' lady me, huh. I think you are kind of exaggerating a little in both cases. (*They laugh. She blows out more of the candles leaving two lighted.*) You never have any trouble getting to sleep?

VAL: No. I know how to relax.

MYRA: How do you relax?

VAL: Imagine yourself a loose piece of string.

MYRA: A loose piece of string. That's lovely! I'm a loose piece of string. (*There is a knock on the ceiling.*)

VAL: What's that knocking upstairs?

MYRA: Jabe. (*She averts her face.*)

VAL: Who?

MYRA: My husband.

VAL: It scared me for a minute.

MYRA: Why?

VAL: Clump. Clump. Clump. Sounds like a skeleton walking around upstairs.

MYRA: Maybe you're gifted with too much imagination. (*She bends over to blow out the last candle.*)

VAL: Uh-huh. That's always been one of my biggest troubles. (*The candles gutter out. A dog is heard baying in the distance; the sound has a peculiar, passionate clarity.*)

MYRA: (*softly*) Hear that houn' dawg? . . . He's bayin' at th' moon. . . . Sky's cleared off? Yes, it's clean as a whistle. . . . Isn't that nice?

VAL: (*hoarsely*) Yes, Ma'am.

MYRA: Well. . . . (*It grows rapidly darker as they stand hesitantly apart, looking at each other. Myra turns slowly back toward the stairs.*) Well . . . The door locks itself when you slam it. Good night.

VAL: (*He speaks in a low, hoarse whisper.*) G'night. (*She starts up the stairs, slowly. He opens the door. Once more the dog is heard baying. They both stop short as though caught by the magic of the sound and face each other again from the stairway and the door. Val speaks again, still more hoarsely.*) G'night.

MYRA: (*in a whisper*) Good night.

Curtain

ACT TWO

SCENE I: *It is about a week later. Val is seated on the counter of the store leaning dreamily against a shelf. In his hand is a pencil and a shoe-box lid. He is raptly composing an idyllic passage in his book. The juke box is playing as he speaks aloud. Myra appears in the confectionery archway with a couple of boxes. She overhears his soliloquy and stops short to listen.*

VAL: Day used to come up slow through the long white curtains.

MYRA: Val! (*Val starts.*) Who are you talking to?

VAL: Myself, I suppose.

MYRA: Isn't that kind of peculiar, talking to yourself?

VAL: No, Ma'am. That's just a habit that lonesome people get into.

MYRA: Please don't do it when anyone's in the store. I don't want it spread around town that a lunatic's been employed here. That sunshine's *terrific*—you better let down the awnings. (*Val moves slowly from the counter.*) Slew-foot!

VAL: Huh?

MYRA: Slew-foot, slew-foot! You walk like you're on fly papers! Pick up your feet when you walk and get a *move* on!
(*Val laughs and saunters leisurely out the door.*) Talks to himself, writing poems on shoe-boxes! What a mess. (*She stares
through the window as Val lowers the awning. Three young
girls follow Val as he comes back in.*)

A GIRL: Hello!

VAL: (*amiably*) Hello there.

THE GIRL: Jane wants to look at some kickies.

SECOND GIRL: (*She giggles.*) No—you do.

THIRD GIRL: I'd like to try on some. Can you dance in kickies?

VAL: Sure you can dance in kickies. Sit down there. Let's measure your little foot.

THE GIRL: (*She beats her to the chair.*) Me first, me first.

VAL: Okay. First come, first serve. (*He pulls her shoe off. She
giggles spasmodically.*)

VAL: Five and one half, Bennie. (*He goes to the shelf.*)

THE GIRL: Isn't he *cute*?

SECOND GIRL: Say, do you dance?

THIRD GIRL: Would you like to go out jooking?

MYRA: Val! I'll wait on these girls. You take these empty
boxes out of here. (*As soon as Val leaves, the girls giggle and
run out of the store. Myra looks very annoyed as Eva Temple
enters.*)

EVA: Mr. Xa-*vier*?

MYRA: (*sharply*) Our popular young shoe-clerk is in the basement. What do you want?

EVA: A pair of bedroom slippers.

MYRA: Sit down and I'll show you some.

EVA: I'll wait till Mr. Xavier comes back upstairs. He seems
to understand my feet so well. How's Cousin Jabe this
mawning?

MYRA: Just the same.

EVA: Dear me. (*Val reappears.*) Mr. Xa-*vier*!

VAL: How are you this mawning?

EVA: I seem to be comin' down with th' most abominable
ear-ache.

MYRA: (*sympathetically*) Aww! Let me give you a little lau-
danum faw it.

EVA: No, thanks. I put some in already. I think Birdie Wilson was partially responsible faw it.

VAL: Why? Is ear-ache contagious?

EVA: No, but Birdie was singing right next to me at choir practice, which did it absolutely no good. (*She titters a little.*) What'm I sittin' here faw?

VAL: T' look at some shoes.

EVA: Aw. Well, I guess I might. Haven't you all noticed about Birdie? Her voice always cracks on that *Te Deum*. She can hit "A" pretty good but she always flats on "B." You'd think she'd have better sense than to even attempt to make "C" because it's completely out of her range, but I'll say this for Birdie, she's got the courage of her convictions.

VAL: These are the new wine shades.

EVA: Oh! Pretty! Yes, she goes right on up there and I'm telling you all, it's a perfect imitation of the Cannonball Express. (*She giggles.*) Oh, my goodness, these *pinch*!

VAL: Do they?

EVA: They certainly do. (*She giggles archly.*)

VAL: Well, let's try a David on that.

EVA: What's David?

VAL: Next size broader!

EVA: Oh, my goodness, no! There must be some mistake!

VAL: (*He climbs the shelf ladder.*) Don't you know what a broad foot's a sign of, Miss Temple? Imagination! And also of . . .

EVA: Of *what*? (*Cassandra Whiteside enters the front door.*)

MYRA: Hello, Sandra!

SANDRA: Hello, Myra. I just drove home from New Awleuns fo' the Delta Planters' Cotillion. And do you know I neglected to bring a single decent pair of evenin' slippers back with me.

MYRA: Oh, honey, we don't keep evenin' slippers in stock, we don't get any calls fo' them here.

SANDRA: (*She notices Val.*) I didn't suppose you would.

MYRA: Oh, wait! Val, reach me down that old Queen Quality box up there! (*Dolly and Beulah enter.*)

BEULAH: Well, it is exasperating to have your table broke up at the very last . . . *Sandra!*

DOLLY: Sandra Whiteside! I thought you were gonna stay in New Awleuns till after Mardi Gras.

SANDRA: I just drove home for the Delta Planters' Cotillion.

MYRA: (*wistfully*) How is Mardi Gras this yeah?

SANDRA: As mahvelously mad as usual. If I were refawming the world I'd make it last forever.

MYRA: I went to it once a long, long time ago. I remembuh they danced in the streets.

SANDRA: They do ev'rything in the streets!

MYRA: I was just fourteen, I had on my first long dress an' a marcel wave an' some perfume called "Baiser d'Amour" (that I bought at the Maison Blanche). Something wonderful happened.

SANDRA: What was it?

MYRA: A boy in a Pierrot suit.

SANDRA: How lovely! What did he do?

MYRA: Caught me around the waist, whirled me till I was dizzy—then kissed me and—*disappeared!*

SANDRA: Disappeared?

MYRA: Completely. In the crowd. The music stopped. I ran straight back to my room and lay on the bed an' stared an' stared at a big yellow spot on the ceiling.

SANDRA: Oh, my Lawd, how tragic.

MYRA: It *was.* (*She smiles.*) I still can feel it whenever the carnival's mentioned.

SANDRA: Your first heart-break!

MYRA: Uh-huh. (*She laughs.*)

VAL: (*He brings a shoe box.*) This one?

MYRA: Yes, that's it. (*to Sandra*) I hope you're not superstitious!

SANDRA: (*She lights a cigarette.*) Why?

MYRA: Because this box contains some silver and white satin slippers that were intended for Rosemary Wildberger . . .

DOLLY: Rosemary!

BEULAH: Wildberger!

MYRA: . . . to wear at her wedding exactly three years ago this Valentine's Day. (*She lifts one of the slippers.*) She had such a tiny foot.

BEULAH: Such a tiny, delicate girl. Rosemary . . .

DOLLY: Wildberger!

SANDRA: (*She laughs lightly.*) Well, what happened? Did she fall dead at the altar?

BEULAH: Oh, no.

DOLLY: Worse than that!

BEULAH: Much worse. The man stood her up.

MYRA: Where did Rosemary go, does anyone know?

BEULAH: Some people say she went crazy an' some people say she went to Cincinnati to study voice.

SANDRA: (*carelessly*) Which was it?

EVA: (*She pipes up resentfully, having been ignored.*) Neither. She went into Chinese missionary work.

DOLLY: (*sarcastically*) Trust Eva Temple to have complete information.

BEULAH: Oh, yes.

SANDRA: And these are the fabulous Rosemary's little silver and white wedding slippers. How lovely.

MYRA: I ordered 'em from St. Louis for her but, of course, I never had the heart to mention them to her parents after she disappeared. What size do you wear, honey?

SANDRA: Four, triple A.

MYRA: Gracious. These are four B. Val, see how they fit Miss Whiteside. (*She turns to Dolly.*) Oh, Dolly, I wanted you to see this; soon as I unpacked it I had a vision of you! (*She removes an outlandish red dress with brass trimming from the racks; it looks like a bareback rider's outfit.*)

DOLLY: (*She rushes to it.*) Oh, my God, ain't it lovely! But you know, honey, I won't be able to wear anything one piece this spring.

MYRA: Really?

DOLLY: Oh, for the usual reason. Y'know there's absolutely no justice in nature. I mean the way she ties some women down while others can run hog wild. Look at Myra, for instance. Not one kid an' me turning out the seventh.

MYRA: (*She averts her face.*) Bring your measurements—I'll order you some maternity garments from Memphis.

DOLLY: Measurements? Fifteen square yards. How long'll it take?

MYRA: Probably two or three weeks. (*Dolly shrieks and throws up her hands.*) Can't you wait that long?

DOLLY: I can, but my figure can't. (*Blanch Temple enters, and trips over the rubber mat at the door. She utters a shrill cry.*)

EVA: (*She jumps up.*) Blanch, that might have *thrown* you!

MYRA: Val, you must tack that down.

VAL: Get the nigger to do it.

BLANCH: My ankle is twisted. I can't even step on that foot.

EVA: Oh, my Lawd, she'll have to have it treated again. Cost us five or six dollars. I simply can't pay for these shoes.

MYRA: All right, you don't have to, Eva, we'll just call it square. Val! Wrap these up for Miss Temple. (*She turns to Sandra.*) How did they fit? (*Val picks up the shoes and goes to the cash register.*)

SANDRA: I couldn't wear them. Let me see a pair of plain, white pumps.

MYRA: Surely.

DOLLY: We must be goin', Beulah, bye, bye, you all. (*Dolly and Beulah go out.*)

BEULAH: (*Her voice is heard off stage.*) I just been thinkin'. Lulu Belle don't play contract at all. She just plays auction.

MYRA: Hurry back! (*She gets some other shoes down; sits on the stool; opens the box for Sandra.*)

BLANCH: (*She is peeking among the Valentines on the counter.*) Here's where she must've bought it 'cause here's another just like it.

VAL: What's that?

BLANCH: Somebody sent us a comic Valentine. It wasn't funny at all, it was simply malicious. Old Maids. There's no such thing as an old maid anymore.

EVA: No, they're bachelor girls.

VAL: (*He suppresses a smile.*) Here's your shoes, Miss Temple.

EVA: Oh, thanks, aw'fly. Miss DeQuincy was telling me you'd been to Yellowstone Park.

VAL: I've travelled all over, not only Yellowstone Park, but Yosemite, Gran' Canyon . . .

BLANCH: How marvelous. Why don't we get him to give us a little descriptive talk at our next auxiliary meeting?

EVA: Oh, would you do that, Mr. . . .

VAL: Xavier.

EVA: Mr. Xavier. You won't fo'get the meeting?

BLANCH: It's Saturday at four-fifteen.

MYRA: Val couldn't take the time off. We're too rushed on Saturday afternoon.

EVA: Aw, what a shame. I meant to ask you, how's Cousin Jabe?

MYRA: No better.

EVA: Aw. What exactly resulted from the operation in Memphis?

BLANCH: Is it true that . . .

EVA: It was too late for surgical interference?

MYRA: Yes, it is true.

BLANCH: Goodness gracious.

EVA: They cut him open and sewed him right back up?

MYRA: (*She turns away in distaste.*) Excuse me.

BLANCH: Eva.

EVA: What did I say?

BLANCH: Good-bye, Mr. Xavier. (*They go out.*)

SANDRA: Aren't they delightful. The little white doves of the Lord. (*with a sidelong glance at Val*) Do you suppose I'll get like that if I remain a virgin?

MYRA: Well, I don't believe I'd worry about it, Sandra. (*Jabe knocks overhead.*)

SANDRA: Ouuu! What's that noise?

MYRA: Jabe's knocking. (*Her face darkens.*)

SANDRA: Oh.

MYRA: I'll have to run up for a minute. (*She goes quickly upstairs.*)

SANDRA: (*She lights a cigarette, with a quizzical look at Val.*) I didn't come in here for evening slippers.

VAL: No. I figured you didn't.

SANDRA: I didn't come home for the Delta Planters' Cotillion. I came back here to see you. I haven't been able to get you off my mind. I woke up thinking about you last night in the Hotel Monteleone. I went downstairs to the bar at three o'clock in the morning. I thought I might forget if I got drunk. They must've poured my whiskey out of the wrong bottle, though. At half past three I was on the highway, headed back to Two Rivers—seventy, eighty, ninety miles an hour—scared that you'd be gone before I got here. What do you think about that?

VAL: I think you'd better go back to the Mardi Gras.

SANDRA: You don't like me very much, do you?

VAL: I want to keep this job. Every place I've gone to it's been some woman I finally had to leave on account of.

SANDRA: I believe that. You're the center of much discussion in Two River County—among the women. That snakeskin jacket, those eyes; that special technique you use in fitting on shoes.

VAL: I don't use any special technique.

SANDRA: Maybe they just imagine that you do. I can understand why. You're beautiful, you're wild. I have a feeling we'll come together some night.

VAL: Yeah?

SANDRA: (*rhapsodically*) In the dark of the moon, beside a broken fence rail in some big rolling meadow. (*Val turns away.*) We won't even say hello.

VAL: Let's quit this!

SANDRA: This what?

VAL: Double talk.

SANDRA: All right. (*She removes her dark glasses and arches her body in a provocative pose. She speaks childishly.*) Why did you slap me, Val?

VAL: Because.

SANDRA: Just because?

VAL: I didn't want to be interfered with by you. You think I've got a sign "Male at Stud" hung on me?

SANDRA: Yes, I think you have. Nobody could possibly make a mistake about it.

VAL: You made a mistake about it. I'm not in your class. I'm the kind of fellow you get to wash your car or chop the cotton. That night you drove me up to Cypress Hill, I wasn't nothing to you. It was like you had hired me to give you a little amusement.

SANDRA: That's what you thought? You were wrong about that. I felt a resemblance between us.

VAL: There's none that I know of, lady.

SANDRA: You must be blind. You—savage. And me—aristocrat. Both of us things whose license has been revoked in the civilized world. Both of us equally damned and for the same good reason. Because we both want freedom. Of course, I knew you were really better than me. A whole lot better. I'm rotten. Neurotic. Our blood's gone bad from too much inter-breeding. They've set up the guillotine, not in the Place de Concorde, but here, inside our own bodies!

VAL: Double talk, smart double talk.

SANDRA: No. Look at my wrists. They're too thin. You could snap them like twigs. You can see through my skin. It's transparent like tissue paper. I'm lovely, aren't I? But I'm not any good. I wear dark glasses over my eyes because I've got secrets in them. Too much of something that makes me rather disgusting. Yes, you were right when you slapped me, Val. You should have killed me, before I kill myself. I will some day. I have an instinct for self-destruction. I'm running away from it all the time. Too fast. New Orleans, Vicksburg, Mobile. All over the God damn country with something after me every inch of the way! But the poison I've got in my blood isn't the kind that makes me fatal to kiss! Why don't you kiss me, Val? (*Val moves away from her but she follows him.*) Scaredy cat! Scaredy cat! (*Val catches his breath and starts to embrace her. She suddenly jabs him in the middle with her knee and bites his hand. She laughs wildly.*) There! There now! That's what I came back for! Nobody's ever slapped me and gotten away with it, Snakeskin! Goodbye! (*She runs out the door.*)

VAL: God damn little bitch! (*Myra appears on the stairway.*)

MYRA: What did she do?

VAL: She dared me to kiss her.

MYRA: Did you oblige her this time or did you slap her again?

VAL: I would've done it if she hadn't kicked me.

MYRA: Well, I'm glad that she kicked you. You can find some other place to do your carrying on.

VAL: I wasn't carrying on.

MYRA: You just admitted you would have if she'd let you. (*She goes to the shelves.*) Oh, lights of delirium, look where you put the kids!

VAL: You didn't say where to put them.

MYRA: In six days time I thought you might've caught on to where some things belong in this store.

VAL: Look here, if I was a mind reader, lady, I'd put up a tent on the commons and tell your fate by the stars at fifty cents a disaster!

MYRA: Disaster is right! I wish you'd use your noggin for something beside sweet looks at the women! Anybody with the brain of a new-born calf should know better'n to put a bunch of kids in here with—look at that, will you?

(*She tosses a box furiously to the floor.*) Those Queen Quality evening slippers stuck in here, too. Why don't you fill up the rest of the space with cigar boxes and candy bars? Why do you wanta show so little imagination that you don't put nothing but shoes in the Shoe Department? You're writing a book? Surely you can think of some fancy new ideas like hanging dresses from the ceiling fans!

VAL: Look here, Myra.

MYRA: Since when am I Myra to you? My name is Mrs. Torrance!

VAL: You call me Val.

MYRA: That's different. I'm the employer here, you work in my store!

VAL: You mean I *worked* in your goddam store! (*He tears off his white clerk's jacket and flings it to the floor. There is a shocked silence.*)

MYRA: I was going to give you your notice tonight, anyhow.

VAL: You don't have to give it to me, I've already took it.

MYRA: Well, you can't walk out in the middle of the day like this.

VAL: Why not? I'm no help to you.

MYRA: I didn't say that . . .

VAL: Oh, no? Actions speak louder than words, Mrs. Torrance! (*Myra looks at him, stunned, as he puts on his snakeskin jacket. A Negro huckster passes along the street singing his wares.*) You are a very difficult, hard-headed woman—and much as I wanted a job I got to admit that working for you is no pleasure. When you tell me to do things, how can I understand you, the way you talk?

MYRA: The way I talk?

VAL: You talk to the *wall*. You talk to the *ceiling*. You never talk straight to *me*! You never even look in my face when you say something to me! I just have to guess what you said 'cause you talk so fast an' hard an' keep your face turned away . . . I've had the feeling ever since I come here that everything I do has displeased you!

MYRA: (*She averts her face.*) I didn't mean to give you that impression. As a matter of fact I was pretty well satisfied with the way you were coming along.

VAL: You certainly kept your satisfaction a secret.

MYRA: I know, I know. I'm nervous, I'm cross, I'm jumpy. (*pathetically*) I thought that you understood my nervous condition and made some allowance for it!

VAL: Being nervous is no excuse for acting like a nine-tailed catawampus!

MYRA: What is a nine-tailed catawampus?

VAL: I don't know. But I sure would hate to meet one.

MYRA: (*She is hurt.*) Oh! (*She raises a handkerchief to her eyes.*) How should I act with you—you carrying on with people like Sandra Whiteside—right here in the store!

VAL: So that's why you flew off the handle.

MYRA: Not just that. You know why those high school girls keep flocking in here?

VAL: Sure. To buy spring shoes.

MYRA: Spring shoes nothing! They come in here for a *thrill*!

VAL: A *what*?

MYRA: A *thrill.* You know know what that is, don't you?

VAL: (*He laughs.*) Can I help it?

MYRA: Yes! You don't have to *give* them one.

VAL: How do I give them a thrill?

MYRA: Don't ask *me* how. You don't have to manipulate their knees to get shoes on them.

VAL: Manipulate their . . . I never *touch* their knees!

MYRA: I've got eyes in my head!

HUCKSTER: (*chanting out in the street*) Ahhhhh ahhhhh. Turnip greens, new potatoes, rutibagas. Ahhh-ahhh. Carrots, string beans, onions!

MYRA: Also your attitude is very suggestive.

VAL: Suggestive of what, Mrs. Torrance?

MYRA: Bedrooms, if you want to know.

VAL: Bedrooms!

MYRA: Yes!

VAL: That sure is peculiar. How do I do *that*?

MYRA: Everything that you do. The way you talk, the way you walk, every single motion of you. Slew-footing this way and that way like one of those awful, disgustin', carnival dancers! (*The huckster is heard calling further away. Val stares at Myra with a long troubled look.*)

MYRA: Quit looking at me like that! (*She sobs.*) I know how awful I look.

VAL: (*gently*) You don't look awful, Myra.

MYRA: Yes, I do—my hair all stringing down—my face always turns so red when I get worked up. (*She sobs and turns away.*)

VAL: (*very gently*) Myra—I mean, Mrs. Torrance. I wanted to keep this job. I was tired of moving around and being lonesome and only meeting with strangers. I wanted to feel like I belonged somewhere and lived like regular people. Instead of like a fox that's chased by hounds!

MYRA: Maybe I haven't understood you exactly.

VAL: No. You haven't.

MYRA: How could I though? You're still a stranger to me.

VAL: My name is Val Xavier.

MYRA: And mine is Myra Torrance. Now do you feel like you know me any better?

VAL: No.

MYRA: (*She is still sobbing a little.*) Well, I don't feel much better acquainted with *you*. Give me one of them tissue paper things. (*She blows her nose.*)

VAL: How do you get to know people? I used to think you did it by touching them with your hands. But later I found out that only made you more of a stranger than ever. Now I know that *nobody* ever gets to *know* anybody.

MYRA: Nobody ever gets to *know* anybody?

VAL: No. Don't you see how it is? We're all of us locked up tight inside our own bodies. Sentenced—you might say—to solitary confinement inside our own skins.

MYRA: (*She gives him a long, puzzled look.*) Is that something out of The Book?

VAL: (*grinning*) No. That goes into The Book.

MYRA: You're a queer one. A lot of people have dropped in off the road since I've been here, but nobody quite like you. I can't figure out what you *belong* to, exactly.

VAL: Me? Belong to? Nothing.

MYRA: Don't you have folks anywhere?

VAL: I used to.

MYRA: What become of them?

VAL: I lost track of 'em after they lost their land.

MYRA: They worked on shares?

VAL: No, not shares—but leavings, scraps, tid-bits! They never owned a single inch of the earth, but all their lives they

gave to working on it. The land got poor, it wouldn't produce no more, and so my folks were thrown off it.

MYRA: Where did they go?

VAL: I don't know where. They were loose chicken feathers
blown around by the wind.

MYRA: You didn't go with 'em?

VAL: No. No, I made up my mind about something and I've
stuck to it ever since.

MYRA: What's that?

VAL: To live by myself. So when the others left, I stayed on
Witches' Bayou. It was a good place to hide in. Big cypress
trees all covered with long grey moss the sun couldn't
hardly shine through. Not in chinks, though, not in squares
but all spread out . . .

MYRA: Misty-like.

VAL: Yeah.

MYRA: How old were you? How did you live?

VAL: Fourteen. I lived like a fox. I hunted and fished but most
of the time I was hungry. I guess it must've made me a
little lightheaded, because I know I had some peculiar
notions . . . I used to lay out naked in a flat-boat with the
sun on me.

MYRA: What did you do that for?

VAL: I had a feeling that something *important* was going to
come *in* to me.

MYRA: In? Through your skin?

VAL: Kind of. Most people don't expect nothing important to
come *in* to them. They just expect to get up early—plow—
rest—go turtle-eggin' an' then back to bed. They never
look up at the sky, dark—or with stars—or blazing yellow
with sunlight—and ask it "Why? why? why?"

MYRA: Did you ask it "Why"?

VAL: That was the first word I learned to spell out at school.
And I expected some answer. I felt there was something secret that I would find out and then it would all make sense.

MYRA: How would you find it out?

VAL: It would come *in* to me. Through my eyes—see?
Through my ears, through my skin. Like a net—see? If
you don't spread it out, you won't catch nothing in it.
But if you do, you *might*. Mine I used to spread it out,

wide-open, those afternoons on the bayous—ears pricked, eyes peeled—watchin', waitin', listenin' for it to come!

MYRA: Did it ever?

VAL: No. Never quite. It would of though, if I hadn't gotten thrown off the track by the girl.

MYRA: There was a girl. What girl?

VAL: A girl I met on the bayou.

MYRA: Oh, what about her?

VAL: She was the first one, yeah. That day I was real excited. I had a feeling that if I just kept polin' on a little bit further I'd come bang on whatever it was I was after!

MYRA: And she was it?

VAL: (*violently*) Naw, she *wasn't*. But she made me *think* she was.

MYRA: How did she do that?

VAL: How? By standin' naked on the dog-trot, in the door of the cabin, without a stitch on.

MYRA: What was she like?

VAL: J'ya ever notice the inside of a shell? How white that is?

MYRA: She was young I suppose. Very young?

VAL: Her shape up here, it wasn't no bigger than this (*slightly cupping his palm*) I hadn't noticed before the special dif-f'rence in women.

MYRA: But you did then?

VAL: Yes, I did then.

MYRA: Was she . . . ?

VAL: What?

MYRA: More attractive than—anyone since?

VAL: She was—th' first.

MYRA: What did you do? What happened?

VAL: I poled th' boat up closer. An' she came out on the dog-trot an' stood there a while with the daylight burnin' around her as bright as heaven as far as I could see! Oh, God, I remember a bird flown out of the moss and its wings made a shadow on her! (*He bows his head.*) An' then it sang a single high clear note. An' as though she was waitin' for that as a kind of a signal—to *trap* me—she turned and smiled an' walked on back in the cabin!

MYRA: And you followed, of course? What was it like inside?

VAL: Inside it was—empty inside.

MYRA: It couldn't have been!

VAL: Well, maybe it wasn't, but all I remember's the bed.

MYRA: Only the bed?

VAL: Made out of cypress an' covered with heaps of moss.

MYRA: Doesn't sound nice.

VAL: Well, it was. She'd been lonesome.

MYRA: How did you know? Did she tell you?

VAL: She didn't have to. She had it carved in her body.

MYRA: Carved? Is lonesomeness carved in people's bodies? (*She unconsciously touches her own.*)

VAL: Kind of. Anyhow you can see it.

MYRA: Could you see it in anybody's?

VAL: Sure. You could see it. Or feel it.

MYRA: (*softly*) What did she say to you?

VAL: She couldn't talk much except in some cajun language. I taught her some words.

MYRA: Such as what?

VAL: Such as *love*.

MYRA: You taught her that?

VAL: It was then I thought I discovered what it was that I'd been hankerin' after all those times I used to go off on the bayou.

MYRA: You thought it was that? (*She turns to the shelves.*) You mean she answered "me"?

VAL: Her! Me! Us together! Then afterwards—afterwards I thought that wasn't it. I couldn't make up my mind. When I was with her, I quit thinking because I was satisfied with just that; that sweetness between us, them long afternoons on the moss. But when I'd left her, the satisfaction would leave me an' I'd be . . . like this. (*He clenches his fist.*) Right on the edge of something tremendous. It wasn't her. She was just a woman, not even a woman quite, and what I wanted was . . .

MYRA: Was *what*?

VAL: Christ I don't know. I gotta find out!

MYRA: I guess your love for her didn't amount to so much after all. What did you do after that?

VAL: I made some money cane-grindin', sold a bunch of 'gator an' diamond-back skins. And bought myself a jalopy. I took to moving around. I thought I might track it down, whatever it was I was after. It always kept one jump ahead of me. That went on for ten years. Then I settled down for a spell in Texas. Seemed like the restlessness had worn off and I might get connected with something. But things went wrong. Something happened.

MYRA: What?

VAL: Never mind what. But everything was different after that. I wasn't free anymore. I was followed by something I couldn't get off my mind. Till I came here . . .

MYRA: Well, now that you've come here and got a good job, you can live a regular life and forget all of that.

VAL: I don't forget as easy as you, Mrs. Torrance. You don't even remember that I've lost my job.

MYRA: You haven't lost your job.

VAL: I'm not fired, huh?

MYRA: (*She smiles and shakes her head.*) We both got a little upset but that's over.

VAL: God, I . . .

MYRA: God you and lady me? (*She laughs.*) What is this place, a funeral parlor. Let's have some lights, some music. Put something on the victrola.

VAL: What would you like?

MYRA: I like that Hawaiian number with the steel guitars.

VAL: Yeah, that one! (*He crosses to the confectionery and starts the music; then he comes back.*) Myra, you know the earth turns.

MYRA: Yes.

VAL: It's turning that way. East. And if a man turned West, no matter how fast, he'd still be going the other way, really, because the earth turns so much faster. It's no use to struggle, to try to move against it. You go the way the earth pulls you whether you want to or not. I don't want to touch you, Myra.

MYRA: No, I don't want you to.

VAL: It wouldn't be right for me to.

MYRA: (*half questioning*) On account of Jabe?

VAL: No, on account of you. You been good to me. I don't want nothing to hurt you. Let's shake hands with each other, huh?

MYRA: That's not necessary! (*Without knowing why, she is suddenly angry. She crosses to the foot of the stairs.*) Take off that horrible jacket and get back to work. I have to fix Jabe's lunch. (*He follows her to the stairs.*)

VAL: Why wouldn't you shake hands with me? You're not still afraid of me, are you? (*Myra starts quickly upstairs.*) Mrs. Torrance! Myra! (*Myra pauses a moment on the landing, looking down at him with nervous hesitation.*)

VAL: (*in an intense whisper*) Myra! (*She disappears through the door and slams it shut. Val stares in bewilderment.*)

Slow Curtain

SCENE II: *It is several hours later on the same day. The mellow afternoon sunlight is muted. There is the puff-puff of the cotton gin. Val stands in the confectionery archway with his back to the audience. He is staring intently up at a large Coca-Cola ad through the arch. In conjunction with the beverage, this ad force-fully expounds the charms of a "Petty Girl" in a one-piece lemon-yellow bathing suit. She and Val appear to be experiencing a long and silent spiritual communion. In his hand Val has a "coke." Slowly, dreamily, he elevates the bottle to his mouth. Outside, at some distance, a rooster crows longingly at the sun. A man enters the front door in boots and riding breeches, bearing a shot gun. He coughs twice to divert Val's attention from the seductive picture.*

VAL: (*turning*) Sorry I was dreaming. Beautiful afternoon, huh?

MAN: I'd like to see Mrs. Torrance.

VAL: She's gone upstairs with her husband. He's not so well.

MAN: Tell her that David Anderson is here.

VAL: Just press that buzzer on the counter and she'll be down.

ANDERSON: Thank you. (*Hesitantly he follows this suggestion. The buzzer is heard above. After a moment, the door on the landing opens and Myra appears. She descends a few steps. Then seeing Anderson, she stops short.*)

MYRA: (*sharply, involuntarily*) David! (*They exchange a long, wordless stare. Then Myra recovers herself and comes down.*)

MYRA: (*to Val*) Will you go to the drug store for me?

VAL: What do you want?

MYRA: Nothing. I mean some ice cream.

VAL: A pint of vanilla? (*Myra says nothing. Val looks curiously at them both and goes out.*)

MYRA: Well.

DAVID: How are you, Myra?

MYRA: Very well, thanks. How are you?

DAVID: (*staring at her*) All right. (*There is an awkward pause.*)

MYRA: You came in here once before and I ordered you out.

DAVID: That was six years ago.

MYRA: No. Eight.

DAVID: Right after your marriage.

MYRA: Not so long after yours.

DAVID: You can't hold a grudge that long.

MYRA: Oh yes I can. I think I can hold one forever. What do you want?

DAVID: Cartridges.

MYRA: You're going out shooting wild birds? I don't have to wish you luck. I haven't forgotten what a good marksman you were. Here's your cartridges. Is there anything else?

DAVID: It seems odd to see you in here, like this.

MYRA: Waiting on trade? Does that seem *common* to you?

DAVID: No. You never were practical, though. You were always such a . . .

MYRA: *Fool?* Yes! But I've changed since then.

DAVID: You haven't changed in appearance.

MYRA: Some women are like green things. They're kept on ice. I guess I'm one of that kind. You've changed a good deal. I wouldn't have known you at all except for your walk. You still move around like you were the lord of creation. I should think you might have found out by this time that your ten thousand acres don't make up the whole universe. Other people have got some property, too. I have this store, for instance. I don't have to *clerk* in it either. I *have* a clerk. (*Her voice trembles.*) I haven't come down so terribly far in the world.

DAVID: (*embarrassed*) Of course you haven't.

MYRA: No, I've gone *up*. And I'm going to go up still *higher*.

DAVID: I'm glad of that, Myra. People have told me about your husband's sickness. I . . .

MYRA: (*feverishly*) Yes. He's dying. After his death I'm planning to sell the store. Thirty or thirty-five thousand it ought to be worth. I'm planning to leave Two River and travel around. Florida, California, New York. I've been an object for pity for a little too long around here. "Poor Myra, she's hopeless, she's crushed!" That isn't exactly the truth and I'm tired of having it whispered behind my back. My life isn't over, my life is only *commencing*. A dollar ten for the cartridges, please.

DAVID: (*extending the money*) Here, Myra.

MYRA: Just put it down on the counter. Now get out. Don't ever come back here again.

DAVID: (*quietly*) All right, Myra. (*He goes slowly out. Myra looks after him. A rooster crows mournfully in the distance. Myra raises her hand to her lips. She looks stunned. Val enters. He grins at her.*)

VAL: Finished your talk?

MYRA: (*vaguely*) Yes, David.

VAL: David?

MYRA: (*starting*) Excuse me, I mean "Val." (*bitterly*) I made a fool of myself.

VAL: Huh?

MYRA: (*evasively*) That rooster always crows about sundown. Sounds like he's remembering something. (*Jabe knocks on the ceiling.*) I wonder if he is. (*She goes back upstairs. Val opens the ice cream, dips it out with his fingers. Vee Talbott enters, stops short in the doorway as though dazed. The rooster crows.*)

VAL: Oh, hello, Mrs. Talbott.

VEE: Something's gone wrong with my eyes. I can't see nothing.

VAL: Here, let me help you. You probably drove up here with that setting sun in your face.

VEE: What? Yes. That must be it.

VAL: There now. Sit down right here.

VEE: Oh, thank you so much.

VAL: I haven't seen you since that night you let me sleep in the lock-up.

VEE: Has the minister called on you yet? Reverend Tooker? I made him promise he would. I told him that you were new in the community and that you weren't affiliated with any church yet. I want you to visit ours.

VAL: Well, that's mighty gracious of you, Mrs. Talbott.

VEE: The Church of the Resurrection! Episcopal, you know. Some people, especially Catholics, think our church was founded by Henry the Eighth, that horrible, lecherous old man who had as many wives as a cat has lives! There's not a word of truth in it. We have direct Apostolic Succession through St. Paul, who converted the early Angles. Angles is what they called the original English.

VAL: Angles, huh?

VEE: Yes, Angles. Our church is sometimes known as the Anglican Church.

VAL: Well, now, that's right int'restin', Mrs. Talbott. What's that picture you got? Something to put on display?

VEE: I thought that Myra might put it up with the Easter decorations.

VAL: I tell you what. We'll put it on display in the confectionery. Myra is going to do it over for spring. What's this picture of?

VEE: The Church of the Resurrection!

VAL: I didn't recognize it.

VEE: Well, I give it a sort of imaginative treatment.

VAL: Aw. What's this?

VEE: The steeple.

VAL: Is the church steeple red?

VEE: Naw.

VAL: Why did you paint it red then?

VEE: I felt it that way. I always paint a thing the way that it strikes me instead of always the way that it actually is. That's why the New Awleuns artists took an in'rest in my work. They say that it shows a lot of imagination. Primitive is what they call it an' one of my pictures they've hung on *ex*-hibition in the Audubon Park museum! (*Her voice shakes with pride as she states this.*)

VAL: Aw. (*He crouches slowly in front of her with a faint smile.*) You need some new shoes.

VEE: Do I?

VAL: Yes. I'll sell you a pair of beautiful wine-colored slippers. (*He clambers quickly up the ladder and jerks out a box.*)

VEE: I don't know.

VAL: Come on. Sit down there. Give me your foot. (*He grasps it roughly and jerks the shoe off. He clasps her foot in both hands and rubs it.*) You got a bad circulation.

VEE: What?

VAL: Your feet are cold. Know why? These here elastic garters are too tight on you. Why don't you leave 'em off and roll your stockings like the other girls do?

VEE: Uh?

VAL: Skittish?

VEE: It's late; I got to be going!

VAL: With one shoe off and one shoe on? "Hey diddle, diddle, my son Tom!" Here, I'll put it back on for you. Just lean on my shoulder a minute!

VEE: No, I . . . (*She sways precariously.*)

VAL: Watch out. (*He clutches her about the thighs and looks up at her, grinning.*) *There* now! Got your balance?

VEE: (*She catches her breath sharply.*) Oh, I got to be going!

VAL: (*He jumps away from her, clambers up the ladder and places the picture on the shelf.*) How's that, Mrs. Talbott? Okay? (*Vee, still too startled to speak, turns vaguely and barges out of the door. Val looks after her, then suddenly breaks into light-hearted laughter. Myra comes back downstairs slowly with a tense, concentrated expression. Val smiles.*)

VAL: Myra, did you ever see a red church steeple?

MYRA: (*absently*) No.

VAL: (*chuckling*) Neither did I.

MYRA: Jabe's took a turn for the worse. I had to give him morphine.

VAL: So?

MYRA: He must be out of his mind; he says such awful things to me. Accuses me of wanting him to die.

VAL: Don't you?

MYRA: No! Death's terrible, Val. You're alive and everything's open and free, and you can go this way or that way, whichever direction you choose. And then all at once the doors start closing on you, the walls creep in, till finally there's just one way you can go—the dark way. Everything else is shut off.

VAL: Yes . . . (*then abruptly*) You got the sun at the back of your head. It brings the gold out in your hair!

MYRA: (*diverted*) Does it?

VAL: Yes, it looks pretty, Myra. (*They stand close together. She moves suddenly away with a slight, nervous smile.*)

MYRA: It's closing time.

VAL: Uh-huh. I'll put these back on the shelves. (*He picks up the wedding slippers.*) She had a small foot.

MYRA: Rosemary Wildberger?

VAL: Naw, Naw, that Whiteside bitch.

MYRA: I could wear these slippers.

VAL: They'd be too small.

MYRA: You want to bet? Try them on me.

VAL: (*laughing*) Okay! (*He slips the shoes on her feet.*) Pinch, don't they?

MYRA: No, they feel marvelous on me!

VAL: (*doubting*) Aw!

MYRA: They do! (*She looks down at them.*) Silver and white. Why isn't everything made out of silver and white?

VAL: Wouldn't be practical, Myra.

MYRA: Practical? What's that? I never heard of practical before. I wasn't cut out for the mercantile business, Val.

VAL: What was you cut out for? (*A derelict Negro, Loon, stops outside the door and begins to play his guitar in the fading warmth of the afternoon sun. At first the music is uncertain and sad; then it lifts suddenly into a gay waltz.*) What was you cut out for, Myra?

MYRA: (*She is enrapt with the music.*) Me cut out for? Silver and white! Music! Dancing! The orchard across from Moon Lake! You don't believe me, do you? Well, look at this. You know where I am? I'm on the Peabody Roof! I'm dancing to music! My dress is made out of mousseline de soie! Yes, with silver stars on it! And in my hair I've got lovely Cape Jasmine blossoms! I'm whirling; I'm dancing faster and faster! A Hollywood talent scout, a Broadway producer: "Isn't she lovely!" Photographers taking my pictures for the *Commercial Appeal* and for the *Times-Picayune*, for all the society columns and for the rotogravure! I'm surrounded by people. Autograph seekers, they want me to sign my name! But I keep on laughing and dancing and scattering stars and lovely Cape Jasmine blossoms! (*Her rhapsodic speech is suddenly interrupted by Jabe's furious knocking on the ceiling. Her elation is instantly crushed out. She stops dancing.*) I thought he had enough to go to sleep . . .

VAL: Why don't you give him enough to . . . ?

MYRA: Val! I'm a decent woman.

VAL: What's decent? I never heard of that word. I've written a book full of words but I never used that one. Why? Because it's disgusting. Decent is something that's scared like a little white rabbit. I'll give you a better word, Myra.

MYRA: What word is that? (*The guitar changes back to its original slow melody.*)

VAL: Love, Myra. The one I taught the little girl on the bayou.

MYRA: That's an old one.

VAL: You've never heard it before.

MYRA: You're wrong about that, my dear. I heard it mentioned quite often the spring before I got married.

VAL: Who was it mentioned by—Jabe?

MYRA: No! By a boy named David.

VAL: Oh. David.

MYRA: We used to go every night to the orchard across from Moon Lake. He used to say, "Love! Love! Love!" And so did I, and both of us meant it, I thought. But he quit me that summer for some aristocratic girl, a girl like Cassandra Whiteside! I seen a picture of them dancing together on the Peabody Roof in Memphis. Prominent planter's son and the debutante daughter of . . . Of course, after that, what I really wanted was death. But Jabe was the next best thing. A man who could take care of me, although there wasn't much talk about love between us.

VAL: No. There was nothing but hate.

MYRA: No!

VAL: Nothing but hate. Like the cancer, you wish you could kill him.

MYRA: Don't! You scare me. Don't talk that way. (*She crosses slowly to the door and Loon sings as the scene dims out.*)

SCENE III: *Immediately following without break in the music. As Loon stops playing Sheriff Talbott enters the store.*

SHERIFF: Hey, Loon! Didn't I see you on Front Street this mawnin' an' tell you to clear out of town?

LOON: I thought you was jokin', Cap'n.

SHERIFF: Well, you made a big mistake. We don't allow no unemployed white transients in this town an' I'll be dogged if I'm gonna put up with colored ones.

LOON: I ain't transient, Cap'n.

SHERIFF: Where you livin'?

LOON: Nowhere, right this minute. Slep' on the levee las' night.

SHERIFF: Where you workin'?

LOON: Nowhere, Cap'n. I'se dispossessed.

SHERIFF: Aw, you'se dispossessed! Where'd you pick up all that fancy langwidge? You mean that Mr. Henley got fed up with your no-'countness an' turned you offen his property?

LOON: He turned me off but not fo' no-'countness. I wukked hard.

SHERIFF: If you work hard, you oughta make the state a good road-hand. Come on, you're under arrest.

LOON: What fo', Cap'n.

SHERIFF: Vagrancy. Ten dollar fine or thirty days hard labor.

LOON: Cap'n Talbot, I likes nine-fifty of bein' able to pay that fine.

SHERIFF: Come along.

VAL: Just a minute. I owe this boy ten dollars on his guitar.

SHERIFF: Huh?

VAL: I just bought his musical instrument off him. Here's the money. (*Loon starts to turn it over to the Sheriff.*) Just a minute. Put that in your pocket. You can't fine a man for vagrancy when he's got ten dollars, can you, Sheriff? Not if I'm acquainted with the law.

SHERIFF: Huh?

VAL: He's also got a job. Hey, Loon, you drop back in tonight an' give me a *lesson* on this thing. Okay?

LOON: Yes, suh! Okay! (*He shuffles hurriedly out. The Sheriff stares hard and silently at Val. Val casually strums a chord on the guitar. Deputy Sheriff Pee Wee Bland wobbles ponderously into the doorway laughing heartily, having just delivered some witticism to the men on the porch. He notices the tension and beckons the others to enter. They have all been drinking.*)

MYRA: (*nervously*) Val, take these boxes . . .

SHERIFF: (*interrupting*) Just a minute. (*He catches Val's arm as Val starts to move past him. Val jerks his arm free. All this happens very rapidly.*) You beat the county out of a good road-hand.

VAL: I thought he might be better as a musician.

SHERIFF: Musician, hell! That worthless no'count nigger?

VAL: A man's not worthless because he's dispossessed.

PEE WEE: Hear, hear! *Dispossessed!*

FIRST MAN: Where'd he pick up that Nawthun radical lingo?

SECOND MAN: Who's he talkin' about?

FIRST MAN: That nigger, Loon.

SECOND MAN: Come down here to organize our niggers?

FIRST MAN: Make them bosses, huh? Us chop their cotton for 'em?

PEE WEE: It's talk like that that's back of all our colored tenant trouble. (*He wobbles up to Val.*) Dispossessed? Did you say *dispossessed*?

VAL: Yes, I *did*.

PEE WEE: How yuh figure a man can be dispossessed from somethin' that never was his'n.

VAL: The land belongs to the man that works the land!

PEE WEE: Hear, hear!

FIRST MAN: That's red talk!

SECOND MAN: Yeah, go back to Rooshuh!

FIRST MAN: Anybody don't like this guvement oughta go back to Rooshuh!

SECOND MAN: Pack 'em all off togethuh, Jews, and radicals, and niggers! Ship 'em all back to *Rooshuh*!

FIRST MAN: Back to Africa with 'em!

MYRA: (*frightened*) Sheriff, stop this disturbance! My husband is sick upstairs!

SHERIFF: Quiet down you boys!

PEE WEE: (*Very drunk and sententious, he talks like a Southern orator of the old school.*) Yeh, you all hush up. I'm talkin' to this young fellow. Now, looky here: a nigger works on a white man's property, don't he? White man houses him an' feeds him an' pays him livin' wages as long as he *produces*. But when he *don't*, it's like my daddy said, he's gotta be blasted out a th' ground like a *daid tree stump* befo' you can run a *plow* th'ough it! (*A third man enters; he is a huge lout.*)

THIRD MAN: What's this here?

FIRST MAN: Some red-neck peckerwood with a nawthun edji-cation's tellin' us how we oughta run our niggers!

MYRA: Sheriff, make them stop right now!

PEE WEE: That nigger, Loon, got dispossessed from nothin'. The land wasn't his.

VAL: No, nothin' was his. Nothin' but his own black skin and that was his damnation!

FIRST MAN: Listen to that!

SECOND MAN: The carpet-baggers are comin' back agin!

THIRD MAN: (*He goes up to Val.*) You know what I do when I see a snake?

VAL: No, what?

MYRA: Val!

THIRD MAN: I get me a good fork stick to pin it down with. Then I scotch it under the heel of my boot—I scotch its goddam yellow gizzards out!

SECOND MAN: Go *on*!

FIRST MAN: *Show* him, Pinkie.

MYRA: Sheriff! Please!

(*The Third Man spits at Val's shoe.*)

VAL: You spit on my shoe! Wipe it off! (*He spits again. Val knocks him down. The men close in about Val like a pack of hounds. There is a near riot for a few moments. Then the Sheriff disperses them.*)

SHERIFF: Come on, you all! Clear out! *Clear* out! Pee Wee, you're Deputy. Git these men out of here! (*The men are shoved out, grumbling.*)

MYRA: Those drunken stave-mill workers make nothing but trouble!

SHERIFF: (*to Val*) Who are you? What's your name?

VAL: Val Xavier.

MYRA: Val didn't mean anything; he's just a talker.

SHERIFF: Where do you come from?

VAL: Any number of places! (*He picks up the guitar again.*)

MYRA: Down state—Witches' Bayou.

SHERIFF: Let him answer for himself, Mizz Torrance.

MYRA: Well, don't snap questions at him like he was up on trial. I know everything about this boy.

SHERIFF: You do, huh?

MYRA: Yes, I do. He come to me with the highest recommendations.

SHERIFF: Who from?

MYRA: Friends, relatives. He likes to talk. He's done some writing, but he's no more a radical than you or me! I give you my trusted word on it.

SHERIFF: It ain't a question of doubtin' your word, Mizz Torrance.

MYRA: All right. Goodbye. I'm closin' up the store.

SHERIFF: Just one more question, please. What's your draft number, buddy? (*Val stares at him and strikes a chord on the guitar.*) *What's your draft number?*

MYRA: (*quickly*) Eight thousand an' something. Val, take those empty shoe-boxes out to the incinerator! (*Val goes out with the boxes.*)

SHERIFF: How do you happen to know his draft number?

MYRA: He happened to tell me this mawning. Is there anything else that I can do for you, Sheriff?

SHERIFF: Yes, ma'am. You can do yourself a favor an' get a new clerk. That impudent young peckerwood won't bring yuh nothin' but trouble. G'night. (*The Sheriff goes out. Myra leans exhaustedly against the door. Val re-enters slowly.*)

MYRA: Oh, Val, Val, Val, why didn't you keep your head. Why didn't you hold your tongue?

VAL: A man has got to stick up for his own kind of people.

MYRA: Your kind of people? That old colored beggar, Loon?

VAL: We're both of us dispossessed. Just give me my wages an' I'll be moving along.

MYRA: Where?

VAL: Where I was headed when I broke that axle. (*Myra stares at him speechlessly.*)

MYRA: Val, I don't want you to go.

VAL: I'd ruin your business for you.

MYRA: Never mind that.

VAL: Besides I'm under suspicion now, and it wouldn't be safe.

MYRA: Just wait. This'll all blow over.

VAL: No. There's something I didn't mention about me this mawning.

MYRA: What happened in Texas?

VAL: Yes. I'm *wanted*, Myra.

MYRA: Wanted You're *wanted*? (*Val gravely picks up the guitar, without looking at Myra, and strikes a slow chord on it.*) What are you *wanted* for, Val?

VAL: (*quietly, without looking up*) For rape.

MYRA: What?

VAL: Rape!

MYRA: Shhh! I don't believe it. That's something *nigguhs* are lynched for—not *you*, Val.

VAL: Yes, me. (*He strikes a chord on the guitar.*)

MYRA: When did it happen?

VAL: About two years ago.

MYRA: Who was the woman? (*Val punctuates his speech with strumming on the guitar which he never puts down till the end of the scene. He avoids Myra's eyes.*)

VAL: A woman from Waco, Texas. Wife of an oil-field superintendent. I boarded with them while I was working down there. A plain sort of woman; I never noticed her much. One night her husband got drunk. Passed out in the car. This woman from Waco come to my room that night. Well, I was drunk. What happened was accidental. Afterwards, I was disgusted with her and with me, I said to her, "Listen, I don't want nothing like this; I'm getting away!" "I'm goin' with yuh," she said. "Oh, no you're not," I told her, "I travel alone." She started to scream. She run to the phone and screamed that she'd been raped. I lost my head for a minute and struck her in the mouth. Then I left. I drove clean out of Texas before daybreak. But not long afterwards, though, I begun to see my name and my description in public buildings—"Wanted for Rape in Texas."

MYRA: You've changed your name.

VAL: Yes, but not my description.

MYRA: That's why you're quitting this job. You're scared she'll track you down?

VAL: Not just for that reason. I have another reason.

MYRA: What's that?

VAL: *You.* Like I told you this morning, I oughtn't to touch you, but I keep *wanting* to, Myra.

MYRA: Oh.

VAL: You don't get rid of something by holding it in. It gathers, it grows, it gets to be *enormous.*

MYRA: Yes.

VAL: You said this morning I touched the women too much when I tried shoes on them. Maybe I do. My hands—I'm afraid of my hands. I hold them in so hard the muscles ache. (*He strikes a chord sharply.*) You know what it's like? A herd of elephants, straining at a rope. How do I know the rope won't break sometime? With you or with somebody else?

MYRA: (*She goes slowly to the door.*) You don't have to leave on account of a reason like that. (*She touches her forehead.*) My head's still whirling from all that excitement in here. I don't seem able to *think.* The cotton gin bothers me, too. It makes a sound like your heart was pounding a lot too fast.

VAL: Mine does sometimes. (*strumming*)

MYRA: Everyone's does sometimes.

VAL: Your belt's untied in the back.

MYRA: Is it? Fix it for me.

VAL: (*Slowly he sets down the guitar on the counter. Crossing slowly to her, he touches her waist.*) You come way in at the middle.

MYRA: I haven't let go of my figure like some women do. I've kept it.

VAL: For what?

MYRA: What for? Maybe because I don't feel everything's done for me yet.

VAL: Why should you?

MYRA: Some women do about my age. They have babies.

VAL: You never?

MYRA: No. I lived in a state of—what do they call it?—artificial respiration. Something that pumps the breath in and out of your body when otherwise you'd be dead. Dead as a rock is, Val! (*She turns abruptly to him.*) Oh, Val, I don't want you to go. I'll make it all right. I'll fix things up so nobody's going to suspicion. I'll make up all kinds of stories if you'll stay here! Huh? Huh, Val?

VAL: (*hoarsely*) Myra. . . .

MYRA: Yes?

VAL: Let's—let's—go in the back room a minute. (*The cotton gin can be heard in the distance.*)

MYRA: That room's locked, Val.

VAL: Where's the key?

MYRA: I took it an' thrown it away.

VAL: What did you do that for?

MYRA: Because I known you would ask me to go in there sometime an' I was scared I might be weak enough to do it. So I took the key and I thrown it away so far I don't think you could find it. (*He releases her and goes quickly out through the confectionery. The gin seems to pump even louder. After a moment Val returns to the room.*)

VAL: (*in a hoarse whisper*) That lock was no good, Myra.

MYRA: You broke it open?

VAL: Yes.

MYRA: Christ! I was scared that you would. (*For a long moment they stare at each other, then rush together in a convulsive embrace.*)

Curtain

ACT THREE

THE SCENE: *The same, but the room in the rear through the arch has been re-decorated. The walls have been painted pale blue and have been copiously hung with imitation dogwood blossoms to achieve a striking effect of an orchard in full bloom. The room is almost subjective, a mood or a haunting memory beyond the drab actuality of the drygoods department. Its lighting fixtures have been covered with Japanese lanterns so that, when lighted, they give the room a soft, rosy glow. It is a rainy spring afternoon about two months after the preceding scene. The old-fashioned lights of the store cannot entirely dispel the silvery gloom. The Gothic features of the room are accentuated by this shadowy effect. Val is alone in the store. He is working on his book, the loose pages of which he keeps in a battered old tin box.*

He writes with a stub pencil which he chews reflectively; then scribbles with rapt expression. The juke-box is playing a number with steel guitars. He looks very simple and lonely, a little faun-like, seated on one of the low shoe-fitting stools, absorbed in his creative labor. There is a faint whisper of rain, and of wind. Myra enters from the street in a transparent white raincoat, very glowing and warm and happy. Val quickly stuffs the script back in the box and pushes it out of sight.

MYRA: Hello, hello, hello! What are you hiding from me? Is it the book? Ah, the mysterious book. I never was quite sure that it existed.

VAL: What d'ja think it was?

MYRA: Something you dreamed those afternoons on the bayou! Let me look at it.

VAL: No.

MYRA: Let me just hold it.

VAL: Don't be silly.

MYRA: Please! (*He surrenders the bundle of papers grudgingly.*) It's like holding a baby! Such a big book, too; so good an' solid.

VAL: It's got life in it, Myra. When people read it, they're going to be frightened. They'll say it's crazy because it tells the truth! Now, give it back to me, Myra. It's not finished yet.

MYRA: I wish that I had something to do with it, too. Wouldn't it make it kind of more legitimate like if it had two parents, Val? (*She laughs tenderly, and hands it back to him.*) I had a wonderful time this afternoon. After I got Jabe's new prescription, I drove over to Tunica to get my hair done. I knew it would be my last chance before Easter. How does it look, Val?

VAL: Swell.

MYRA: How're things going?

VAL: Slow. I haven't rung up a single cash-sale since noon.

MYRA: Rain, rain. You certainly kill our trade. I was stuck on th' road coming home for nearly an hour before I got pulled out. (*She takes off her raincape and puts on a bright smock.*) I kind of enjoyed it, though. The air was so fresh, an' when the bells started ringing . . .

VAL: What're they ringing for?

MYRA: Good Friday church service. Dr. Hector is preaching the Seven Last Words from the Cross. Just as they started to ring, a big white moth flew in the car window. Val, I hate most bugs, but this one I felt a kind of a sympathy for. He was terribly young.

VAL: How do you know he was young? Did you ask him his age?

MYRA: No, but he had that surprised, inexperienced look about him that young things have. It was easy to see he had just come from the cocoon, and was *sooo* disappointed. Of cou'se he expected th' world t' be bright an' gold, but what he found was a nasty, cold spring rain. His two long whiskers were covered with strings of pearls. He sat on the steering wheel an' shook them off. I asked him, "Why?" An' he said, "Don'tcha know? It's in bad taste to put on pearls before dark!"

VAL: You're talking foolishness, Myra.

MYRA: Am I? Fo'give me, da'ling. I'm in that kind of a humor. My God, you got eyes that shine in th' dark like a dawg's. (*She starts humming a tune.*) Remember that? Such a long time ago. Before Columbus discovered America even. Oh, beautiful fo' spacious skies, for amber fields of grain. . . . Greta Garbo is at the Delta Brilliant. . . . Fo' purple mountain majesties, above the fruited . . . Lemme up on that ladder. I want to be on a high, high place in the sun! What's these here?

VAL: Women's soft sole slippers. They just come in. (*Impulsively she gathers them up like an armful of plushy red flowers and tosses them into the air.*)

MYRA: (*ecstatically*) Wake me early, Mother, fo' I shall be Queen of the May!

VAL: For Chrissakes, Myra, what did'ja do that for?

MYRA: Oh, soft sole slippers. Women's soft sole slippers! They seem t' be so damned unnecessary!

VAL: What's the matter with you this afternoon?

MYRA: When people have dreams, unusually good dreams, they get up singing, they go to the beauty parlor, and act like fools all day! When serious-minded people who write big books say, "What's th' matter with you?" they simply smile an' say, "We have our secrets." (*Val opens the door.*) The rain's slacked up?

VAL: Yeah, a little.

MYRA: That's good. Maybe we'll have a nice bright Easter, Val. We'll go to church an' look so lovely the Lawd will have to fo'give us for all our sins!

VAL: (*in the doorway*) River's way up over flood-stage at Friar's Point Landing. They say sometimes this place is cut off by water.

MYRA: They say! They say! What of it? Ten thousand years from today we'll just be little tell-tale marks on the sides of rocks which people refer to as fossils. (*There is the sound of slow tolling bells across the wide, rainy fields.*) That's all will be left of our big tremendous adventures! (*She smiles with amazement at this thought.*) Teeny-weeny little pencil-scratches, things like pigeon tracks will be what's left of Myra—what's left of Val! Then old Mr. Important Scientific Professor will pick up his microscope—"Humph!" he'll say, "This girl had remarkable legs." Or, "Goodness, this young man lost a rib somewhere." That will be all they'll ever find out about us! Were we in love? Were we happy? Did white moths fly in our windows? How do they know? They can't tell. History isn't written about *little* people. All that little people ever get to be is marks on rocks called *fossils.*

VAL: Yes, unless they write books or something.

MYRA: Oh, yes, of course, unless they write books or something! Then they're remembered *always!* (*She jumps down from the ladder and hugs him tenderly against her.*) You will be, da'ling! Don't worry!

VAL: Sarcasm?

MYRA: No, not a bit! (*She laughs gently.*) You're such a wonderful, wonderful baby! When I'm a fossil, even if it makes Mr. Science Professor blush, I hope he discovers my scratches are all scrambled up with yours. (*She laughs gaily. A small Negro boy enters the store.*) Wipe yo' feet off, Sonny, don't track th' floor.

BOY: Yes, Ma'am.

MYRA: What do you want? Peanuts?

BOY: I wan' peanuts, but granny wan' a nickel's worth a snuff.

MYRA: Aw. Well, Granny's got to have her snuff, now, don't she? How is Granny feelin'?

BOY: She been laid up in bed with break-bone fever.

MYRA: Aw, now, that's a shame. You tell 'er Mizz Torrance say to get well quick, quick, quick, cause we can't do without 'er. (*A young Negro enters in overalls.*)

BOY: Yes, Ma'am.

NEGRO: Howdy, Mizz Torr'nce.

MYRA: Hello, Bennie. Val, give the little boy a bag full a goobers, will yuh? They're on th' house.

NEGRO: (*admiringly*) You sho' are gracious, Ma'am. I wunder if you would take my note for somethin'?

MYRA: Bennie, I've got enough notes from you to paper th' store with already. What do you want?

NEGRO: A little plug tobacco.

MYRA: Well, put your cross on this.

NEGRO: Thanks, Ma'am. (*The Negro boy comes back out with the peanuts and goes out the front door. There is a sound of shouting.*)

MYRA: Oh, they're shouting up over there at the big Lent meeting. Sounds like they might be hitting the sawdust trail.

NEGRO: Will be before sundown.

MYRA: How 'bout you, Bennie?

NEGRO: Me hit it? Naw, I guess I glories too much in the flesh for that. Good afternoon, Mizz Torrance.

MYRA: (*to the Negro*) Good afternoon. Where you takin' that load of sand-bags to?

NEGRO: Down river t' Mr. Sikeses.

MYRA: You think there's a chance the levee might go out?

NEGRO: Ah reckon not unless th' Lawd intends it to. G'by, Ma'am.

MYRA: Goodbye. (*The Negro starts the mules. His wagon wheels are heard.*) Val? (*There is no answer. She switches on the lights in the confectionery. Spring blooms with a soft radiance for an instant and then dies out as she releases the switch.*) Val! (*She turns smiling slightly, her lips moving as she whispers, excitedly, to herself. With a sudden, rapturous awareness she draws her hands up the front of her body and clasps them over her breasts.*) Oh . . . (*In the archway there is suspended a string of Chinese glass pendants with a tiny gong. With an impulse of childish gaiety, she sets the pendants tinkling, softly, musically, in the store's greenish gloom and she laughs to herself with a child's quick, delicate laughter. While her back is turned, The Conjure Man glides noiselessly into the store. Now, for the first time, there is a low muttering of thunder. The lights in the confectionery flicker a little. Still unaware of The Conjure Man's presence, Myra shivers slightly and a bewildered, uncertain look appears on her face and she raises a hand to touch her cheek and her forehead. As though with a disturbing prescience of something unnatural, she turns about slowly and meets the Negro's gaze. She catches her breath in a sudden, sharp gasp. The Conjure Man smiles and makes a slight obeisance. He stretches out his small claw-like hand, in the hollow of which he is presenting some object.)*

MYRA: (*breathlessly*) What—what do you want? (*The Conjure man mumbles something which cannot be heard.*) What? No! No, I don't want it. (*then, smiling defiantly*) I don't need holy stones to bring me luck. (*The Conjure Man makes another slight bow, then starts to turn away.*) If you want to make an honest dollar, though, you can go out back and wash the Mississippi Delta off my car. You'll find a sponge, a bucket, and a bunch of old chamoises hanging in the garage. (*The Conjure Man mumbles some eager words of thanks and starts to the confectionery. Myra looks after him, troubled, not knowing why. In the archway he stops and looks back over his shoulder to meet her gaze. There is a moment of curiously tense stillness. Then he grins and makes another slight bow and disappears. There is the sound of low thunder again. The front door opens and Dolly comes in.*)

DOLLY: Has he gone?

MYRA: Who?

DOLLY: That *awful* lookin' ole darky.

MYRA: He's gone out back. Who is he?

DOLLY: They call him The Conjure Man—from Blue Mountain. When I first caught a sight of him out there, I swear to goodness I neahly had a conniption! I was scared to death that he would *mark* my *baby*! Which reminds me to ask you! Have those maternity garments got here yet?

MYRA: No, they haven't come yet.

DOLLY: What? I ordered 'em two months ago.

MYRA: I know, and I can't understand what's causin' the delay.

DOLLY: Neither can I. My God, what am I going to do?

MYRA: I'm sorry.

DOLLY: I guess I'll have to hang out a sign, "Excuse me people." (*Myra turns away in distaste. Beulah rushes in.*)

BEULAH: Excitement! Cassandra Whiteside's come in town drunk as a lord.

DOLLY: No.

BEULAH: I just seen her on Front Street. Wearin' a white satin evenin' dress. She's been in another wreck; the side of the car's bashed in.

DOLLY: I thought they revoked her license.

BEULAH: She's got her a nigger chauffeur. At least I *hope* he's a chauffeur.

DOLLY: Beulah.

BEULAH: Well, there has been a great deal of speculation about 'em that's not very pleasant. They say that she's been ostracized in Memphis, asked to leave sev'ral parties; and her father has actually received a warning note from the Klan.

DOLLY: Goodness. She'll be worse than ostracized if she keeps up at this rate.

BEULAH: Myra, what will you do if she comes in here and starts to make a disturbance?

MYRA: (*shortly*) Put her out.

BEULAH: You think you could? They say she fights like a tiger.

MYRA: (*as Val enters*) I think Val would be able to handle her for me.

VAL: (*He sets the boxes down.*) What did you call me for, Myra?

MYRA: (*confused*) Call you? Oh, yes, I—I can't remember just now.

BEULAH: That sounds extremely suspicious. (*She winks.*)

DOLLY: Don't it, though? Look, they're blushing.

BEULAH: Both of them. Oh, I think it's marvelous to see a man who can blush.

MYRA: (*with nervous haste*) Val, are those the new Keds?

VAL: No, women's rubbers.

MYRA: Just in time for the rain; how very lucky.

DOLLY: (*meaningfully*) How's Jabe?

MYRA: (*still confused*) Jabe?

DOLLY: Yes, your husband, honey. Jabe Torrance.

MYRA: Jabe's no better.

DOLLY: Ain't that turr'ble!

BEULAH: I don't guess you *could* look for much improvement.

MYRA: No. All we can do is try to relieve the pain. Val, bring up the rest of those boxes and stack them up there. (*Val is glad to get out.*)

DOLLY: Myra, that green is your color!

BEULAH: Don't it look sweet on her, though? I had my eye on that dress; it's the nices' thing you had in stock, Myra Torrance.

MYRA: It's more of a blue than a green.

BEULAH: What do they call it?

MYRA: (*with a slight, suppressed smile*) They call it "ecstasy blue."

DOLLY: I swan. (*She exchanges a significant look with Beulah.*)

BEULAH: But don't it become her, though? It brings the gold out in her hair.

DOLLY: *It does.*

MYRA: I just had it washed. That always brightens the color.

DOLLY: What with? Goldenfoam?

MYRA: No, with a few drops of lemon. That's all I use.

DOLLY: Honestly? Well, she's took on more *sparkle* this spring.

BEULAH: I think it's wonderful that you can be so brave.

MYRA: What do you mean?

BEULAH: Why, I mean about Jabe's condition.

MYRA: Oh, excuse me a minute. I gotta take Jabe his medicine. He's been so restless today. (*She goes back upstairs. Beulah looks at Dolly and giggles. Dolly looks at Beulah and giggles an octave higher. They both cover their mouths as the Temple sisters enter.*)

BLANCH: I want you to know . . .

EVA: Dr. Hector had just finished preaching the Seven Last Words from the Cross . . .

BLANCH: When who should we run into . . .

EVA: Yes! on Front Street.

BEULAH: Sandra Whiteside?

EVA AND BLANCH: Yes!

DOLLY: I know. We just been talking.

EVA: (*She catches her breath.*) Did you know she was just put out of the Cross Roads Inn?

BLANCH: Literally thrown out. They tried to get her father on the phone. Useless!

EVA: He's drunker than she is. We passed her just now up there on the Sunflower Bridge. She seemed to be having D.T.'s. What's that she was shouting, Blanch?

BLANCH: "Behold Cassandra! Shouting doom at the gates!"

EVA: Yes. An' some bright-skin nigger was in the car with her. It's really created a perfeckly terrible stir.

BLANCH: Imagine—on Good Friday!

EVA: Utterly shameless! Where's that nice-lookin' young man?

BLANCH: I got to return those shoes. I went to a very expensive obstetrician in Memphis. He said they'd ruined my feet. Why, Palm Sunday mawning I couldn't hardly march in church with the choir. (*She calls out.*) Mr. Xavier? Oh, they've closed the confectionery.

EVA: Yes. The noise was disturbing to Jabe.

BLANCH: She's had it re-decorated.

EVA: All done over. She says it's supposed to resemble the orchard across from Moon Lake. (*Vee enters. She wears black, nun-like garments for Good Friday, and her look is exalted.*) Vee! How are you, honey?

VEE: (*almost sobbing*) I've waited and prayed so long. Now it's finally come.

BEULAH: *What's* come?

VEE: The vision. I seen him early this mawning. I painted the picture.

BEULAH: Picture of what?

VEE: Of Jesus!

DOLLY: I thought you said you'd never paint the Lawd until you'd actually seen Him face to face.

VEE: (*simply*) I have. This mawning. On the way to church, by the cottonwood tree, where the road branches off toward the levee. I been on a fast since Ash Wednesday to clear my sight. Veils seemed to drop off my eyes. Light— light! I never have seen such brilliance. Like needles it was in my eyes; they actually ached when I stepped out in it.

BEULAH: In what?

VEE: The sun this mawning, before the Passion began.

DOLLY: Weakness from fasting. You're such an excitable nature.

VEE: No, no. I've had other signs. Look at my palms.

BEULAH: What about them?

VEE: Can't you see the red marks?

BEULAH: They do look so't of inflamed.

BLANCH: Ain't that remarkable, though?

BEULAH: What happened?

VEE: I been tormented. He took all the torment off me.

DOLLY: Tormented by what?

VEE: Evil thoughts. Those men in the lock-up, they write nasty words on the walls. At night I can see them. They keep coming up in my mind. He took that cross off me when he touched me.

BEULAH: Touched you?

DOLLY: Where? (*Vee lifts her hand reverently and touches her bosom.*) Aw. (*She giggles.*) He made a pass at you? (*She giggles.*) He made a pass at you?

BEULAH: Dolly, you're awful!

DOLLY: I couldn't help it; it just popped out of my mouth.

BEULAH: Vee, can't we see the picture?

BLANCH: Yes, let's see it.

VEE: I brung it here for Myra t' put on display. (*She starts to unwrap the canvas. There is the sound of an angry outburst and the simultaneous crash of glass on the floor above.*)

BEULAH: What's that? (*The women congregate quickly at the foot of the stairs in listening attitudes.*)

VEE: No, I've had other manifestations. (*at the right of Dolly*) When I was seven years old, my little sister, Rose, got typhoid fever.

MYRA: (*upstairs*) Jabe.

BEULAH: What's that?

DOLLY: Can you make it out?

MYRA: Jabe!

BEULAH: (*She goes to the foot of the steps.*) What's that shouting upstairs?

VEE: She hadn't been baptized yet an' the doctor said she was dyin'. So Reverend Dabney come over at midnight.

JABE: No, I won't take it.

MYRA: The doctor prescribed it for you. It helps the pain.

JABE: I know what you're trying to do. You're trying to kill me.

DOLLY: What?

BEULAH: What?

MYRA: You're out of your head.

DOLLY: What's that?

BLANCH: Sssh.

EVA: Sssh.

VEE: Afterwards, he give me the bowl of Holy water an' told me to empty it outside on the bare ground. But I didn't. I poured it out in the kitchen sink.

MYRA: Jabe, you don't know what you're saying. (*The door bangs open.*) I'll call for the doctor.

BLANCH: Delirious!

EVA: Yes, out of his haid!

VEE: (*slowly*) The kitchen sink turned *black. Black*—absolutely *black!* (*The door above is suddenly thrown open and Myra calls out wildly.*)

MYRA: Val! Val!

DOLLY: I'll get him for yuh, Myra! Mr. Xavier! (*There is great excitement. Val comes in.*)

VAL: What's the matter?

BLANCH: Oh, something's goin' on, I don't know what . . .

EVA: But it's awful! (*Myra appears above.*)

MYRA: *Val?*

VAL: Yeah?

MYRA: Phone Dr. Bob, and tell him to come right over! (*She slams the door.*)

EVA: Where's Dr. Bob?

BLANCH: Ain't he in Jackson Springs?

VAL: Howdy, Mizz Talbott.

EVA: I'm very much afraid the wires are down! (*As Val crosses in front of Vee, she slowly rises, following him with her eyes, her lower jaw sagging open slowly with a stricken expression.*)

VAL: (*He lifts the phone.*) Get me Jackson Springs. (*Vee utters a stifled cry. Val is struck by her shocked gaze.*) What's the matter, Mizz Talbott? (*into the phone*) Jackson Springs?

VEE: No, no!

DOLLY: What's the matter with Vee? She's white as goat's milk.

BEULAH: Seems to me like she's tooken some kind of a spell.

DOLLY: (*She grasps her shoulders roughly.*) Vee!

VEE: Le' me go! Leave me be!

BLANCH: That vision she had has probably got her wrought up.

EVA: Passion Week always upsets her. Get a wet cloth, some-body!

VAL: The wires are down.

BEULAH: Don't Myra keep some kind of a stimulant on the place?

VAL: There's some rum in the back. I'll get it.

VEE: (*She struggles up, panting.*) Naw, I can't stay, le' me go!

DOLLY: Nobody's holding you, honey.

VEE: (*Her eyes follow Val as he crosses to the confectionery.*) Where's he going to?

BEULAH: Get you a little something to pull you together. (*Dolly picks up the picture.*)

VEE: (*She cries out wildly.*) You take your hands off my pic-ture! (*She wrests it from Dolly before she can see it.*)

BEULAH: Well!

VEE: It's not t' be touched by you, you foul-minded thing!

DOLLY: I thought that you brung it here to put on dis-*play*.

VEE: I never.

DOLLY: Just let me take one look!

VEE: No! (*Dolly makes a move toward the canvas. Beulah crosses to the right of the steps. Vee cries out and thrusts her away. Myra appears on the stairs.*)

MYRA: Oh, for God's sake, will you all please hush up? I've got to get in touch with Dr. Bob! (*Her hair is disarranged, and her dress torn open as though she had been in a struggle.*) Jabe's delirious. He wouldn't take the morphine. Did you hear him? He said I was trying to kill him! (*She picks up the receiver, jiggles it.*)

EVA: Val tried to phone.

BLANCH: They told him the wires were down.

MYRA: Then I'll just have to drive over.

BLANCH: Oh, but they say there's danger of the bridge col-lapsing.

MYRA: What else can I do?

EVA: Blanch, if you were married and your husband was des-perately ill, wouldn't you take a chance on the bridge collapsing?

BLANCH: No, I certainly wouldn't. No, I certainly. . . . Oh, before you go, Myra—about these shoes . . .

MYRA: (*She snatches a raincoat from the closet.*) Oh, I'm distracted, I—Val, tell the nigger to put the chains on the tires!

VAL: I can't do six things at once. Miss Eva here wants some money back on a pair of shoes.

MYRA: Money back? What money? You got the shoes for nothing!

BLANCH: Oh, horrors, don't you remember how I tripped over that rubber mat an' practickly broke my ankle?

EVA: Two trips to the doctor it cost us!

BLANCH: Six dollars!

EVA: But we'll take five since Myra has been so . . .

MYRA: Thanks. Val, give the ladies five dollars out of the cashbox. Now if you'll excuse me . . .

BEULAH: Myra, if there's anything I can do.

DOLLY: Don't hesitate to call on me if they is. (*Myra has already disappeared through the confectionery.*)

BLANCH: Gracious . . .

EVA: Sakes alive! What excitement! Blanch, you go up an' sit with Cousin Jabe.

BLANCH: Oh, I couldn't. I'm having palpitations!

VEE: I . . . I . . . have to leave, too. (*She retreats toward the door.*)

DOLLY: Not without showin' the picture!

VEE: Dolly, get out of my way!

BEULAH: (*She snatches the picture held behind her back and tears the paper wrapping off. She gasps and shrieks with laughter.*) Mr. Xavier!

DOLLY: Mr. *Xavier?*

VAL: What?

BEULAH: Vee Talbott here has just conferred a wonderful honor on you.

DOLLY: Oh, so it *is*, I *suspected!*

BEULAH: You're going to sit at the head of the table with all of the Twelve Apostles sitting around'ja!

DOLLY: You even have a silver dish-pan sort of on top of your haid! (*They both shriek with laughter.*)

VEE: (*wildly*) No, no, no! Let go of my picture!

BEULAH: Ain't it a wonderful likeness?

DOLLY: From memory, too. Or did you pose for it, Val?

BEULAH: He didn't *have to*. She seen him in the cottonwood tree. The *lynching* tree, as they call it!

DOLLY: I hope that don't make you *nervous*, Val!

VEE: No! You're all of you cooking up something without no excuse!

DOLLY: No? No excuse? That's why you nearly collapsed when Mr. Xavier came up an' said hello to yuh!

BEULAH: Your spiritual nature an' all, what a big joke it is!

DOLLY: Carping at other people, criticizing their morals . . .

BEULAH: Stirring up all that card-playing rumpus here in the congregation.

DOLLY: Declaring in public that I wasn't fit to associate with because I had drinking parties.

BLANCH: Dolly!

EVA: Don't you all go on like this!

DOLLY: She's got to have her eyes opened, now, once an' for all. A vision of Jesus? No, but of Val Xavier, the shoe-clerk who sold 'er them shoes.

VAL: Mrs. Bland!

DOLLY: And where did she have this vision? Where? Under the cottonwood tree where the road turns off toward the levee. Exactly where time an' time again you see couples parked in cars with all of the shades pulled down! And what did he do? He stretched out his hand and *touched* yuh! (*She thrusts her hand against Vee's bosom. Vee cries aloud as though the hand were a knife thrust into her, and, turning awkwardly, runs out of the store.*)

VAL: You all better go or you'll get bogged down on th' road.

BLANCH: Dolly, you shouldn't have done that.

EVA: So unnecessary!

BEULAH: I don't know. She's always held herself so high.

DOLLY: Yes, superior to us all. I guess after this she won't have so much to say on the subjeck of bridge during Lent! Come on Beulah, let's go! Blanch, you an' Eva comin'?

BLANCH: Yes, just a minute! What happened to those old shoes? You see 'em, Mr. Xavier?

VAL: I thrown 'em in the trash-bin. You want 'em back?

BLANCH: Please.

EVA: We couldn't wear 'em, of course, but it's no use throwin' 'em away.

BLANCH: No. Wilful waste makes woeful want, they say. (*She giggles as they back skittishly out of the door.*) Don't you feel it? The atmosphere is simply charged with electric disturbance! (*Val is left alone. He picks up the canvas Vee left, places it on the counter and stares at it for several seconds. The Conjure Man comes back into the archway, gliding noiselessly as before. He stares inscrutably at Val's back. Val turns, as Myra had turned, with the same air of troubled presentiment, and catches the Negro's gaze. Unconsciously he raises his hands to draw his shirt closer about his throat as though the air had turned colder.*)

VAL: What—what do you want? (*The Conjure Man mumbles almost indistinguishably.*) Oh. Sure. You can stay back there all night, if it don't stop raining! (*The Conjure Man grins and bows, then extends his palm with the lucky token.*) Huh? Naw, naw, naw, I don't want it! Sorry but I don't truck with that conjure stuff. (*The Conjure Man bows once more and disappears as noiselessly as he came. There is a low muttering of thunder. Val looks uneasy. He takes off his working jacket. There is a wild burst of drunken laughter outside. The door is thrown open and Sandra enters, a flash of lightning behind her. Her hair hangs loose and she wears a rain-spattered, grass-stained white satin evening gown.*)

SANDRA: Behold Cassandra, shouting doom at the gates!

VAL: What do you want?

SANDRA: Oh. It's you. Snakeskin. Remember we're even now.

VAL: What do you want in here?

SANDRA: Protection. I'm in danger.

VAL: Danger of what?

SANDRA: Immolation at the hands of the outraged citizens of Two Rivers County. They've confiscated the nigger that drove my car and ordered me out of Two Rivers.

VAL: You must've given 'em some provocation.

SANDRA: Plenty of provocation. They say that I run around wild and stir up trouble—and neither parental nor civil law is able to restrain me. Why, only this afternoon I was on Cypress Hill with that bright-skinned nigger. They suspect me of having improper relations with him.

VAL: Did you?

SANDRA: No. I poured a libation of rum on my great-aunt's grave. But they don't believe me. The Vigilantes decided that I was persona non grata and warned me to leave before something bad happened to me. How about you?

VAL: Huh?

SANDRA: Why don't you come along with me? You an' me, we belong to the fugitive kind. We live on motion. Think of it, Val. Nothing but motion, motion, mile after mile, keeping up with the wind, or even faster! Doesn't that make you hungry for what you live on? (*Val shakes his head.*) Maybe we'll find something new, something never discovered. We'll stake out our claim before the others get to it. What do you say? (*Val turns away.*) Where's Myra?

VAL: She's gone to Jackson Springs to get a doctor.

SANDRA: Good! We're alone together.

VAL: What's good about it?

SANDRA: Why do you hate me, Val?

VAL: I don't want trouble.

SANDRA: Am I trouble?

VAL: Yeah. As fine a piece of trouble as ever I've seen.

SANDRA: Is Myra trouble?

VAL: Leave her out of it.

SANDRA: Don't you think I know what's going on?

VAL: What are you talking about?

SANDRA: I saw her in Tupelo this morning, having her hair fixed up! What radiance! What joy!

VAL: Shut up about Myra.

SANDRA: Oh, you'd better watch out. It isn't kiss and good-bye with a woman like that! She'll want to keep you forever. I'm not like that.

VAL: Aw, leave me alone. (*He takes his jacket from a hook.*)

SANDRA: Women will never leave you alone. Not as long as you wear that marvelous jacket.

VAL: I want to close up.

SANDRA: I'll go in a minute.

VAL: Make it *this* minute, will you? (*Sandra crosses to him. She loosens her red velvet cape and drops it to the floor at her feet. The white evening gown clings nakedly to her body.*)

VAL: Don't stand there in front of me like that!

SANDRA: Why not? I'm just looking at you. You know what I feel when I look at you, Val? Always the weight of your body bearing me down.

VAL: *Christ!*

SANDRA: You think I ought to be ashamed to say that? Well, I'm not. I think that passion is something to be proud of. It's the only one of the little alphabet blocks they give us to play with that seems to stand for anything of importance. Val . . . (*She touches his shoulder. He shoves her roughly away. The door opens and Myra enters.*)

MYRA: Oh!

SANDRA: (*casually*) Hello, there. I thought you'd gone for the doctor.

MYRA: I couldn't get over the river. The bridge is out. What are *you* doing here?

SANDRA: I came here to give you a warning.

MYRA: A warning? Warning of what?

SANDRA: They've passed a law against passion. Our license has been revoked. We have to give it up or else be ostracized by Memphis society. Jackson and Vicksburg, too. Whoever has too much passion, we're going to be burned like witches because we know too much.

MYRA: What are you talking about?

SANDRA: Damnation! You see my lips have been touched by prophetic fire.

MYRA: I think they've also been touched by too much liquor. The store is closed.

SANDRA: I want to talk to you, Myra.

MYRA: Come back in the morning.

SANDRA: What morning? There isn't going to be any.

MYRA: I think there is.

SANDRA: That's just a case of unwarranted optimism. I have it on the very best of authority that Time is all used up. There's no more time. Can't you see it? Feel it? (*with drunken exultation*) The atmosphere is pregnant with disaster! (*She laughs and suddenly clasps the palms of her hands to her ears.*) Now, I can even *hear* it!

VAL: What?

SANDRA: A battle in heaven. A battle of *angels* above us! And *thunder!* And *storm!* (*She laughs wildly.*)

MYRA: Sandra, I've had too much. I can't stand anything more. You go home now before I do something I shouldn't.

SANDRA: I believe you *would*. You'd fight like a *tiger* for him.

MYRA: Be careful, Sandra.

SANDRA: Yes, I can tell by looking at you in that mad dress with your eyes spitting fire like the Devil's, you've learned what I've learned, that there's nothing on earth you can do. No, nothing! But catch at whatever comes near you with both your hands, until your fingers are broken! (*Sandra flings herself upon Val and kisses him with abandon. Myra springs at her like a tiger and slaps her fiercely across the face.*)

MYRA: Leave him be, damn you, or I'll . . . (*Sandra whimpers and staggers to the counter. Her head lolls forward and the dark hair slides over her face; she slips to her knees on the floor.*) Take her upstairs to my room. When dogs go mad, they ought to be locked and chained. (*Val picks Sandra up and carries her up the stairs. The storm increases in violence; rain beats loud on the tin portico outside. There is a terribly loud thunder clap. Myra gasps. The electric current is disrupted and the lights dim out. Someone bangs at the door. Myra calls—*) The store's closed up!

MAN: It's me, Mrs. Torrance. Jim Talbott!

MYRA: Oh, Sheriff Talbott. (*She opens the door.*) Is something the matter?

SHERIFF: Yes. (*He enters, followed by a woman. There is something remarkably sinister about the woman's appearance. She is a hard, dyed blond in a dark suit. Her body is short and heavy but her face appears to have been burned thin by some consuming fever accentuated by the mask-like makeup she wears and the falsely glittering gems on her fingers which are knotted tight around her purse.*) This is Mrs. Regan from Waco, Texas.

WOMAN: Never mind about that. Where is the man that clerks here?

MYRA: Val?

WOMAN: Is that what he calls himself? In Waco he was known as Jonathan West.

MYRA: (*to the Sheriff*) What does this woman want here?

WOMAN: I want that man.

SHERIFF: That clerk of yours is wanted for rape in Texas.

MYRA: I'm sure you're mistaken.

WOMAN: Oh, no, I don't think I am. I've sent out descriptions of him to every town in the country. Canada, Mexico, even. The minute I got news of this shoe-clerk I hopped a plane out of Waco. I feel pretty sure that I've finally tracked him down. Where is he? Where does he keep himself?

MYRA: I don't know.

WOMAN: Surely you . . .

MYRA: I don't have any idea!

WOMAN: You—you *must*, Mrs. Torrance!

MYRA: *No!* No, I don't. Oh, yes, he—he drove into Memphis.

WOMAN: Two days before Easter? He suddenly drove into Memphis and left you without any help? That certainly does sound peculiar.

MYRA: I gave him his notice. He's gone.

WOMAN: I don't believe you.

MYRA: (*to the Sheriff*) This woman has got a pistol in her purse.

WOMAN: What if I have? You don't go hunting a dangerous animal down without any weapons. (*She suddenly starts forward.*) Wait! Look here! This picture! (*She crosses to Vee's portrait.*)

SHERIFF: It's one of my wife's.

WOMAN: Now I'm convinced. It's *him*. I'd recognize it hanging on the moon. Come along, Sheriff, we're wasting time with this woman. She's telling us lies to protect him. The place to look is them sporting houses on Front Street. (*She rushes from the store.*)

SHERIFF: Don't play with fire, Mrs. Torrance. (*He follows her out. Myra gasps and crosses to the door, bolting it shut. Val steps noiselessly out upon the upstairs landing and stares down at Myra. He descends a few steps with caution.*)

VAL: (*on the stairs*) Who was it?

MYRA: Sheriff Talbott.

VAL: (*descending two steps*) Who was the woman? (*Myra stares up at him dumbly.*) *Who was the woman with him?*

MYRA: Val, don't act so excited.

VAL: Oh. It was her then.

MYRA: Yes. The woman from Waco.

VAL: Christ! I heard her voice but I thought I must be dreaming. (*He suddenly catches his breath and darts down the stairs and toward the front door.*)

MYRA: Where do you think you're goin'?

VAL: *Out!*

MYRA: Don't be a fool. You can't leave now. Those drunken stave-mill workers are on the street.

VAL: They know, already? She's *told* 'em?

MYRA: Val, will you please . . .

VAL: Lock up that door!

MYRA: It's locked.

VAL: The door in the confectionery?

MYRA: That's locked, too.

VAL: What happened to the lights?

MYRA: Went out in the storm. I'll turn on a lamp . . .

VAL: No. *Don't!*

MYRA: In the confectionery. They can't see in.

VAL: What did you tell her?

MYRA: That you'd gone into Memphis.

VAL: Did she believe you?

MYRA: No.

VAL: Where did they go to look for me?

MYRA: Sporting houses on Front Street.

VAL: Yeah. She'd think of that. Oh, God, Myra, I've washed myself in melted snow on mountains trying to get the touch of her off my body. It's no good.

MYRA: Keep *hold* of yourself.

VAL: You can't understand what it is to be hounded by somebody's hate.

MYRA: I looked in her face. What I saw wasn't hate.

VAL: What was it then?

MYRA: A terrible, hopeless, twisted kind of *love*.

VAL: That's worse than hate.

MYRA: I *know*. (*She picks up a lamp.*) Dry as a bone. Give me the other one, Val. (*Val stares at nothing.*) Never mind, I'll get it. You're safe in here. They looked here once; they won't come back until morning.

VAL: *Safe?* She mentioned it in her description.

MYRA: Mentioned what?

VAL: Scars from burns on his legs. Afraid of fire. She'll have them *burn* me, Myra.

MYRA: Oh, Val, darling, don't act like a scared little boy.

VAL: I'm not so scared. I'm sick.

MYRA: I know how you feel.

VAL: Like something was crawling on me. Something that crawled up out of the basement of my brain. How did she look?

MYRA: A vicious, pitiful, artificial blond.

VAL: She had on black?

MYRA: Yes.

VAL: All loaded down with imitation diamonds. That's how I see her. Leaning against a wall and screaming, "You can't get away! Anywhere that yuh go I'll track yuh down!" And now she has— She's *here!*

MYRA: (*pityingly*) Oh, Val, stay there on the stairs. I'm going to fix you a drink. The rain has made the air colder. Don't you feel it?

VAL: No.

MYRA: I do. I seem to be shaking a little. I guess my blood's too thin. Of course, you'll have to get away from Two River.

VAL: Get away? Yes, if I'm lucky!

MYRA: Oh, you'll be lucky, darling. I was just thinking, thinking about *myself*. Val . . .

VAL: What?

MYRA: I haven't traveled much. I've never been west of the Mississippi. Never much east of it either. I think it's time I took a trip somewhere.

VAL: What are you talking about?

MYRA: I'm leaving here with you tonight!

VAL: No.

MYRA: Oh, yes, I *am*. I've *got* to. We'll run off *together* as soon as the storm slacks up.

VAL: (*He rises.*) Myra . . .

MYRA: Give me a nickel; I want to play the victrola.

VAL: Myra, you're . . .

MYRA: No. Never mind. I've got some change in my pocket. Wait just a minute. (*She goes to the juke box and starts the music.*)

VAL: Myra, you've got to . . .

MYRA: *Shhh!* (*She comes back in.*) When I was a girl, I was always expecting something tremendous to happen. Maybe not this time but next time. I used to dance all night, come home drunk at daybreak and tiptoe barefooted up the back stairs. The sky used to be so white in the early mornings. You know it's been a long time since I've even noticed what color the sky is at daybreak. Traveling on a lonely road all night in an open car I guess you'd notice such things. I'd enjoy that. I could point them out to you while you were driving the car. I'd say, "Look, Val, here's something to put in the book!" "What is it?" I'd say, "It's white!" "What is?" "The sky is!" "Oh," you'd say, "is it?" "Yes, I'd say, "it is, it is, it *is*!" And you would have to believe me! (*She clings to him; Val breaks away from her.*)

VAL: I got to go by myself. I couldn't take anyone with me.

MYRA: That's where you're mistaken. You're dreadfully mistaken if you think that I'm going to stay on here by myself in a store full of bottles and boxes while you go traipsing around through all the world's dark corners without me having a forwarding address even.

VAL: I'll give you a forwarding address.

MYRA: That's not enough. What could I do with a forwarding address, Val? Take it into the backroom with me at night? Oh, my darling, darling forwarding address! A wonderful companion *that* would be. So sweet. And satisfying!

VAL: Myra! Don't talk so loud!

MYRA: (*breathlessly*) Excuse me. I'll get your drink. (*She goes to the confectionery and comes back out with a bottle.*) How much do you want? Three fingers? What was I . . . ? Oh, Oh, yes, I wanted to tell you (*She pours the rum.*) we had a fig tree in the back of our yard that never bore any fruit. We thought that it never would. I'd always pitied it so because they said it was barren. But it surprised us one spring. I was the one that discovered the first little fig. Oh, my God, I was so excited. I ran in the house; I was screaming! "Daddy, daddy, it isn't barren, it isn't barren, daddy! The little fig tree . . ." I told him, "It's going to have figs this year!" It seemed such a marvelous thing, it needed a big celebration, so I took out Christmas ornaments. Yes, little colored glass bells and tinsel and artificial snow! (*She laughs breathlessly.*) And I put them all over the fig tree, there, in the middle of April, because it was going to bear fruit! Here, Val, step up to the bar and take your drink! (*Val crosses to her.*) Oh, darling, haven't we any Christmas ornaments to hang on me? (*Val stops short.*)

VAL: (*sharply*) What do you mean?

MYRA: I mean that I'm not barren. Not anymore!

VAL: You're making this up!

MYRA: No, Val! You see, being clever, Val, isn't enough when you're up against something as big as life is. Sure, you can make keys for a door. That's clever, Val, but somebody comes along and breaks the door down. That's life! And that's what happened to me. Oh, God, I knew that I wouldn't be barren when we went together that first time. I felt it already, stirring up inside me, beginning to live! The first little fig on the tree they said wouldn't bear! What a mistake they made! Here. Here's your drink. (*He stares at her dumbly.*) Take it! (*She thrusts it into his hand.*) So now you see we can't be separated! We're bound together, Val!

VAL: Bound? No! I'm not bound to nothing! Never could be, Myra!

MYRA: Oh, yes, you could!

VAL: What do you mean by that?

MYRA: In one respect I'm like that woman from Waco. I'll never let you get away from me, Val. I want you to understand that.

VAL: There's one thing you don't understand good, Myra.

MYRA: No? What's that?

VAL: I travel by myself. I don't take anything with me but my skin.

MYRA: Then I'm your skin. Skin yourself and you'll be rid of me!

VAL: Listen, Myra, there's one thing safe for me to do. Go back to New Mexico and live by myself.

MYRA: On the desert?

VAL: Yes.

MYRA: Would I make the desert crowded?

VAL: Yes, you would. You'd make it crowded, Myra.

MYRA: Oh, my God, I thought a desert was *big*.

VAL: It is big, Myra. It stretches clean out 'til tomorrow. Over here is the Labos mountains, and over there, that's Sangre de Cristo. And way up there, that's the sky! And there ain't nothing else in between, not you, not anybody, or nothing.

MYRA: I see.

VAL: Why, my God, it seems like sometimes when you're out there alone by yourself (not with nobody else!) that your brain is stretched out so far, it's pushing right up against the edges of the stars!

MYRA: Uh, huh! Maybe, that's what happened! (*She laughs harshly.*) That's why you act so peculiar; you scrambled your brains on the stars so you can't think straight!

VAL: Shut up, God damn you!

MYRA: Val! (*Rain falls in a gust on the tin portico. There is a silence between them.*)

VAL: I'm sorry, Myra.

MYRA: So what are you planning to do? Drive west by yourself?

VAL: Yes. (*He moves to the wall and takes his book out.*)

MYRA: You can't leave yet. Those stave-mill workers are still across the street.

VAL: In two or three more years she may forget . . .

MYRA: The woman from Waco?

VAL: Yes.

MYRA: I don't think so. I don't think she ever will.

VAL: Well, anyway, when I've finished this book I'm going to send for you.

MYRA: Are you? Why?

VAL: Because I do love you, Myra.

MYRA: Love? You're too selfish for love. You're just like a well full of water without any rope, without any bucket, without any tin cup even. God pity the fool that comes to you with a dry tongue!

VAL: I promise I'll send for you, Myra.

MYRA: Thanks. Thanks. And what'll I do in the meantime? Stay on here with our lucky little . . . What shall I call it? Myra's little Miracle from Heaven? (*She laughs wildly. Jabe knocks on the ceiling.*)

VAL: Jabe's knocking.

MYRA: Don't you think that I hear him? Knock, knock, knock! It sounds like bones, like death, and that's what it is. Ask me how it feels to be coupled with death up there. His face was always so thin, so yellow, so drawn. I swear to you, Val, his face on the pillow at night, it resembled a skull. He wore a night shirt like a shroud, and when he got up in the dark, you know what I said to myself? "It's walking," I said to myself, "the ghost is walking!" And I—I had to endure him! Ahh, my flesh always crawled when he touched me. Yes, but I stood it, though. I guess I knew in my heart that it wouldn't go on forever, the way I suppose the fig tree knew in spite of those ten useless springs it wouldn't be barren always. When you come in off the road and asked for a job, I said to myself "This is it, this is what you been waiting for, Myra!" So I said with my eyes, "Stay here, stay here, for the love of God, stay here." And you did, you stayed. And just about at that time, as though for that special purpose, he started dying upstairs, when I started coming to life. It was like a battle had gone on between us those ten years, and I, the living, had beaten, him the dead one, back to the grave he climbed out of! Oh, for a while I tried to fight myself but it was no use. It was like I was standing down there at the foot of the levee and watched it break and known it was no use running. I tried to get rid of the key but that didn't work. Since then all decency's left me, I've stood like a woman naked with nothing but love—love, love. (*She clings to him fiercely.*)

VAL: Let go of me, Myra. (*He shoves her roughly away.*) You're like the woman from Waco. The way you . . .

MYRA: (*slowly*) You know what I've done? I've smashed myself against a rock. (*She crosses to the door.*) If you try to leave here without me, I'll call for the Sheriff!

VAL: That's what she did.

MYRA: *I'll* do it, *too.* Strike me in the face so I can scream. (*She catches at him again, he breaks loose, she utters a choked cry. The door slams open on the landing. At this instant a flickering matchlight appears on the stairs and spills down them across the floor. Heavy dragging footsteps and hoarse breathing are heard.*)

MYRA: (*whispering*) Christ in Heaven, what's that? (*The ghastly, phantom-like effect of this entrance is dramatically underlined. Jabe's shadow precedes him down the stairs and his approach has the slow, clumping fatality of the traditional spook's. He is a living symbol of death, as Myra has described him. He wears a purple bathrobe which hangs shroud-like about his figure and his face is a virtual death-mask. Just as he appears in full-view in the stairwall, the match which he holds under his face flickers out and disappears from view, swallowed in darkness like a vanished apparition.*)

MYRA: (*horrified, incredulous*) Jabe.

JABE: (*hoarsely*) Yes, it's me! (*He strikes another match and this time his face wears a grotesque, grinning expression.*) I didn't have much luck at knocking on the floor.

MYRA: (*dazed*) I didn't hear you.

JABE: Naw?

MYRA: The storm made too much noise.

JABE: Aw, absorbed in the storm.

MYRA: Yes.

JABE: Lamp-light, huh?

MYRA: Yes, the lights went out when that awful lightning struck.

JABE: Your dress is torn open.

MYRA: You did that, Jabe, when I tried to give you morphine.

JABE: I thought you might give me too much.

MYRA: How did you get out of bed?

JABE: The usual way. Why? Does that seem remarkable to you?

MYRA: Yes. I didn't know you was able to.

JABE: You always been too optimistic about my condition. (*Myra gasps involuntarily with loathing. Jabe laughs hoarsely.*) I'm okay now. I'm not going to cash my checks in yet for a while. (*Val coughs uneasily and clears his throat.*)

MYRA: Jabe—Jabe, this is Val Xavier.

JABE: You don't need to introduce me. I know him; I'm payin' his wages. (*to Val*) Myra here seems to think I had a tumor on the brain and they cut the brain out an' left the tumor. (*He laughs again and Myra repeats her involuntary gasp of loathing.*) Gimme that lamp; I wanta look at the stock.

MYRA: Here. We finished straightening up.

JABE: Aw, is that what you was doing?

MYRA: Yes. Val couldn't go home in the storm so we took advantage of the extra time.

JABE: Uh-huh. (*He takes the candle and goes unsteadily toward the confectionery. He passes through the archway, the pale walls hung with artificial blossoms have an eery effect in candle-light. The confectionery has a misty, flickering unreal pallor like a region of death, and Jabe, in his long, dark robe, stands at the entrance like the very Prince of Darkness. He hesitates as though he senses that death-like quality himself.*) Hell. It looks like a goddam honky-tonk since you done it over! (*He moves resolutely on into the room.*)

MYRA: (*under her breath*) Oh, God, I can't stand it, Val. I'm going to scream! Say something to him. Don't stand there doing nothing!

VAL: What should I say to him?

MYRA: Oh, I don't know—anything! (*She speaks in a loud, false tone.*) It seems miraculous, don't it, to see him downstairs?

VAL: (*uncertainly*) Yes. (*Jabe laughs mockingly in the next room.*) (*very softly*) Death's in the orchard, Myra!

MYRA: Val.

JABE: How about a little pinball game? Would you like to play one, Mr. Whatsit?

MYRA: Answer him!

VAL: (*inaudibly*) No.

JABE: Huh? Can't you talk out loud in there?

VAL: (*shouting*) No! No!

MYRA: Shhh!

JABE: I think I'll shoot a few.

VAL: Give me my wages. Let me get out. (*Val moves towards the counter, but Myra blocks him.*)

MYRA: You can't leave me alone with him, would you?

JABE: Hot damn. I clicked on three.

MYRA: You couldn't be such a coward.

VAL: Let go of my arm.

JABE: Twenty-five hundred, Myra.

VAL: This place is shrinking; the walls are closing in!

JABE: Thirty-five. Forty-five.

MYRA: Give me time, darling. A little more time. (*Val tears loose.*)

JABE: Fifty!

MYRA: I swear to God, I won't let you.

JABE: Right down the middle aisle, twice straight.

VAL: Let go!

JABE: Sixty-five, seventy.

MYRA: You've got to stick with me, Val.

VAL: Don't have to do nothing. I'm going!

JABE: Buzzards! Buzzards!!!! I hear you croaking in there. You think you've got a corpse to feed on, but you ain't! I'm going to live, Myra (*Myra's hysteria is released. She laughs wildly and rushes to the doorway.*)

MYRA: Oh, no, you're not; no, you're not! You're going to die, Jabe. You're rotten with death already!

JABE: (*shouting*) Die, am I?

MYRA: Yes, and I'm glad, I'm *glad*, I'm planning a celebration! I'm going to wear Christmas ornaments in my hair! Why? Because I'm not barren. I've gotten death out of me and now I've taken life in! Yes, oh, yes, I've got *life* in me— in *here*! (*She clasps her hands over her stomach.*) Do you see what I've got my hands on? Well, that's where it *is*, you see! I'm way, way, way up *high*! And you can't drag me *down*! Not any more, *Mr. Death*! We're through with each other. (*She laughs in wild exultance; then suddenly covers her face and runs sobbing back to Val. She is terrified.*) Val! (*She clutches his arm. He breaks away and crosses toward the front door of the store.*)

VAL: It's finished! (*He goes to the cash register, rings it open. Jabe creeps in with the lantern, unseen by them, and steals towards the hardware counter.*)

MYRA: (*She screams at him wildly, completely distracted.*) What are you doing? You're robbing the store!

VAL: I'm taking my wages out.

MYRA: You're robbing the store; I won't let you! (*She rushes to the phone and shouts into it. Jabe is loading a revolver.*) Give me the Sheriff's house. The store's being robbed!

VAL: Go on, you little bitch.

MYRA: The store's being robbed, the clerk is robbing the store. He's running off with the money; you got to stop him! (*Jabe's face is livid with hatred and he holds the revolver which he levels carefully at Myra, holding the candle above him to give a light.*)

JABE: Buzzards! (*He fires. The first shot strikes Myra. She utters a smothered cry and clutches at the wall. Val springs at him and wrests the revolver from his grasp.*)

VAL: You shot her.

JABE: (*slowly, panting*) Naw. You shot her. Didn't'ja hear her shouting your name on the phone? She said you was robbing the store! They'll come here an' burn you for it! Buzzards! (*He turns slowly and staggers out the front door. His voice is heard shouting wildly against the wind. Val gasps, slams the door, and bolts it, the revolver still in his grasp. Myra moves out from the shadow of the wall with a slight, sobbing breath.*)

VAL: Myra! You're hurt!

MYRA: Yes.

VAL: How bad?

MYRA: I don't know. I don't feel nothing at all. It struck me here, where I would have carried the child. There's nothing but death in me now.

VAL: I'll call for the doctor!

MYRA: There's no way to get any doctor. Go on, look out for yourself, get away! I don't need anyone now . . . (*She staggers out from the wall.*) Isn't it funny that I should just now remember what happened to the fig tree? It was struck down in a storm, the very spring that I hung those ornaments on it. Why? Why? For what reason? Because some things are enemies of light and there is a battle between them in which some fall! (*The confectionery suddenly blooms into soft spring-like radiance as the electric current resumes.*) Oh, look! The lights have come on in the confectionery! (*She staggers through the archway.*) That's what I wanted! Not death, but David—the orchard across from Moon Lake! (*She advances a few more steps and disappears from sight. Her body is heard falling. Val crosses to the archway.*)

VAL: Myra! Myra! (*The lights flicker and go out. Now the clamor of the crowd is heard distantly. Under his breath.*) Fire! (*He looks frenziedly about him for a moment, then plunges out through the confectionery. A door opens at the top of the stairs and Sandra appears, aroused by the clamor. At first she descends the steps fearfully, then with a sort of exulta-*

tion, appearing like a priestess in her long, sculptural white dress. When she has reached the bottom of the stairs, the front door is opened and The Woman from Waco enters, the crowd crying out behind her and the pine torches glaring through the windows.)

WOMAN: (*to Sandra*) You—where is he?

SHERIFF: Watch out, Mrs. Regan! He's armed!

MRS. REGAN: So am I! Where is he?

SHERIFF: (*He advances not too bravely.*) Xavier! (*A flickering light appears in the confectionery.*)

MAN: In back!

VOICES: In the confectionery! Get him! Git him outta there! Kill him! Burn the son of a bitch! Burn him!

WOMAN FROM WACO: What are you waiting fo'? Scared— scared? (*She plunges toward the archway with drawn revolver. The Conjure Man suddenly appears bearing a lantern. The shocking apparitional effect of his entrance stuns them for a second. The woman from Waco stops short with a stifled cry.*)

VOICE: Christ! Who's that? The Conjure Man! The Conjure Man from Blue Mountain!

WOMAN: Git out of my way! Make him git outta my way!

SHERIFF: (*He steps up beside her.*) Where is Xavier, you niggah? (*Slowly, tremblingly, the Negro elevates something in his hand. He holds it above his head. There is a momentary hush as all eyes are centered upon this lividly mottled object, which, though inanimate, still keeps about it the hard, immaculate challenge of things untamed.*)

A VOICE: His jacket!

ANOTHER: *The Snakeskin Jacket!* (*The Woman from Waco screams and covers her face. A gong is struck and the stage is drowned in instant and utter blackness.*)

Curtain

EPILOGUE

THE SCENE: *After a few seconds the curtain is raised again, and we are returned to the Sunday afternoon a year later. The scene is the same as for The Prologue. The stage is empty and sinister with its testimony of past violence. Faintly, as from some distance, there comes the sound of chanting from a Negro church. The store itself is like a pillaged temple with the late afternoon sunlight thrown obliquely through the high Gothic windows in the wall at the left. The Conjure Man sits with immobile dignity upon his stool near the archway like The Spirit of the Dead Watching. The door at the top of the stairs opens and the Temple Sisters emerge with their customers.*

BLANCH: Watch out for these stairs; they're awful, awful steep! Eva, you better go first with the lamp.

EVA: (*She descends first.*) Uncle! Uncle!

BLANCH: He's deaf as a post! (*The Conjure Man rises.*)

EVA: Oh, there you are, Uncle. Bring us Cassandra's things from that shelf over there. (*The Conjure Man complies with slow dignity.*)

BLANCH: We only have two things that belonged to Cassandra Whiteside on display in the Museum.

EVA: (*She displays the articles.*) This pair of dark sun-glasses and this bright red cape.

BLANCH: Cassandra's body was never recovered from the Sunflower River.

EVA: Some people say that she didn't know the bridge was washed out.

BLANCH: But we know better, however. She deliberately drove her car into the river and drowned because she knew that *decent* people were done with her.

EVA: Absolutely. The Vigilantes had warned her to get out of town.

BLANCH: Now, Uncle, the *Snakeskin Jacket.*

EVA: He's already got it.

BLANCH: That is one article in the Museum that me an' Eva won't lay our bare hands on.

EVA: I don't know what, but it simply terrifies me.

BLANCH: Uncle, hold it up there in the archway like you did when you reported his capture. (*The Conjure Man unfolds the jacket which he had held in his lap and elevates it above his head as he did at the end of the preceding scene.*)

EVA: It's marvelous how fresh and clean it stays.

BLANCH: Other things get dusty. But not the jacket. What was it that Memphis newspaper-woman called it? "A souvenir of the jungle!"

EVA: "A shameless, flaunting symbol of the Beast Untamed!"

BLANCH: Put it down, Uncle. Uncle was washing the car in back of the store when the murderer tried to escape by that back door.

EVA: He fell right in the hands of the stave-mill workers.

BLANCH: They torn off his clothes an' thrown him into a car.

EVA: Drove him right down the road to the lynching tree . . .

BLANCH: That big cottonwood where the road turned off toward th' levee.

EVA: Exackly where Vee Talbott seen him that day in her vision.

BLANCH: We showed you the Jesus picture? That was the last thing she painted before she lost her mind.

EVA: Which makes five lives, as they said in one of the papers . . .

BLANCH: "Tied together in one fatal knot of passion."

EVA: Not counting the Woman from Waco, who disappeared.

BLANCH: Nobody knows what ever become of her. (*She crosses to the wall and takes something down.*)

EVA: (*with relish*) Oh, the blow-tawch!

BLANCH: It's not the original one but it's one just like it. Look! (*She presses a valve and a fierce blue jet of flame stabs into the dark atmosphere. A woman tourist utters a sharp, involuntary cry and sways slightly forward, covering her eyes.*)

WOMAN: Oliver, take me out! (*A man hastily assists her to the door.*)

BLANCH: (*to Eva*) They haven't paid yet!

EVA: *Fifty cents, please! That will be fifty cents!*

BLANCH: To keep up the museum!

EVA: Yes, to preserve the memorial—twenty-five cents each. (*They go out, following the tourists. The door remains open. Sunlight flows serenely, warmly, through it, a golden contradiction of all that is past. The Conjure Man glides toward the door. His face assumes a venomous, mocking look. He crouches forward, and spits out the open door with dry crackling laughter, then turns, and, unfolding the brilliant snakeskin jacket once more, he goes to the back wall and hangs it above his head in the shaft of sunlight through the door. He seems to make a slight obeisance before it. The religious chant from across the wide cotton fields now swells in exaltation as the curtain falls.)*

THE HISTORY OF A PLAY
(WITH PARENTHESES)

Battle of Angels was not my first play. I had previously written four others, long tragedies, innocent of structure. These earlier works were little more than preliminary exercises. Inept as the *Battle* is in certain respects, it was a huge advance over its predecessors, written before I knew what a proscenium arch is. Probably no man has ever written for the theatre with less foreknowledge of it. I had never been back-stage. I had not seen more than two or three professional productions: touring companies that passed through the South and Middle West. My conversion to the theatre arrived as mysteriously as those impulses that enter the flesh at puberty. Suddenly I found that I had a stage inside me: actors appeared out of nowhere; shaggy, undisciplined mummers trooped out of the shadowy wings and took the stage over. This cry of players had a gift for improvisation: they carried with them a greasy bundle of old scripts, crumpled and wadded into the bottom of the brass-bound trunk, beneath the tarnished helmets and rhinestone tiaras, the twisted candelabra and moth-eaten velvet capes and scarlet dominoes of traditional mummery. Now and then they would toss me a sheaf of papers like an old bone: only the title and theme were still apparent: the script illegible. "Write this over!" I was commanded. The work was mainly the actors' improvisations. But how I loved it!—this abuse of Cothurnus—is that her name? And the actors loved it, too. They could not wait for the lines to be set down. What thrilling disorder!

I took to the theatre with the impetus of compulsion. Writing since I was a child, I had begun to feel a frustrating lack of vitality in words alone. I wanted a plastic medium. I conceived things visually, in sound and color and movement. The writing of prose was just their description, not their essential being: or so I felt it to be. I was impatient of sentences. Tricks of style, polish, urbanity, all of those things that belong to the successful practitioner of letters seemed all the world removed from what I wanted and what I was writing for. The turbulent business of my nerves demanded something more animate than written language could be. It seemed to me that even the giants of literature, such as Chekhov, when writing narratives were only describing dramas. And they were altogether dependent upon the sensitivity of their readers. Nothing lived of what they had created unless the reader had the stage inside him, or the screen, on which their images could be visibly projected. However with a play, a play on a stage—let any fool come to it! It is there, it is really and truly there—whether the audience understands it or not! This may be a childish distinction: however, I felt it that way.

It seemed to me that all good writing is not just writing but is something organic. I say that as though it was a startling discovery of my own. Excuse me. But that is how it came to me, as a personal revelation. It should have come earlier, for I had been writing since twelve and was already wrapped up in literary style like the bandages of a mummy—and I am still struggling to break out of it. Lately the word "professional" has become odious to me because it seems removed from the flesh and blood business of my vocation. The best avenue away from professionalism in writing is really the stage, because the stage is ideally the most plastic, the most objective exercise for the writer. For me there was no other medium that was even relatively satisfactory. I am speaking for myself, not anyone else. If this sounds like a rejection of poetry—kick my face in! I don't mean any such thing. But poetry is also potentially a plastic medium. Nothing goes more naturally onto the ideal stage.

Later on I became sick and furious, unreasonably so, when I learned that people who feel as I do about the theatre cannot possess it. It doesn't belong to us. It belongs to Money. Then, after that, I felt more reasonably about it, for I saw that works for the ideal theatre can live on paper until the emancipated theatre is ready for them: just as a race of slaves can survive their period of bondage and eventually come into the sun as free individuals to realize their destiny. All that we really need is to believe, to work, and to survive with honesty. Virgo intacta.

That is Parenthesis One!

Battle of Angels was the first of these plays to release and purify the emotional storms of my earlier youth. The stage or setting of this drama was the country of my childhood. Onto it I projected the violent symbols of my adolescence. It was a synthesis of the two parts of my life already passed through. And so the history of the play begins anterior to the impulse to write it. It begins as far back as I remember, in the mysterious landscape of the Delta country, the smoky quality of light in the late afternoons when I, as a child, accompanied my grandfather, an Episcopal clergyman, on seemingly endless rounds of rural parishioners about such villages as Columbus, Canton, Clarksdale, and Lyons in Mississippi. Wherever my grandfather went, I tagged along. I remember a sympathetic old lady saying, "Tom looks tired," and my grandfather answering, "Tom is strong as an ox." It seems to me those afternoons were always spent in tremendously tall interiors to which memory gives a Gothic architecture, and that the light was always rather dustily golden. I remember a lady named Laura Young. She was dressed in checkered silk. She had a high, clear voice: a cataract of water. Something about her made me think of cherries and she was very beautiful. She was something cool and green in a sulphurous landscape. But there was a shadow upon her. There was something the matter with her. For that reason we called upon her more frequently than anyone else. She loved me. I adored her. She lived in a white house near an orchard and in an arch between two rooms were hung some pendants of glass that were a thousand colors. "That is a prism," she said. She lifted me and told me to shake them. When I did they made a delicate music.

This prism became a play.

When we stopped going there, I learned that the lady was dead. It was the death of a lady and the beginning of a personal myth. For this bright, misty lady was the beginning of Myra Torrance—even that long ago!

But these childish recollections provided me only with the country and with characters of phantom dimensions. I had to animate them with the turbulent stuff of later experience. The opportunity for this came after I had knocked about the States for five years, much as the character Val, with some such shadowy design as his mysterious "Book" as a fleeting objective. I retreated to the family home, which was then in Clayton, Missouri, and because I was stopped and temporarily worn out, it seemed like a final retreat. I hated Saint Louis, of which this town was the suburb—hated it quite unreasonably, associating it with certain personal disasters which had taken place there—so I immured myself in the attic of our home and wrote the tortured first draft of *Battle of Angels*, never at any time regarding it as more than a katharsis for myself. By this time, however, I had acquired from the distance a few contacts with the professional theatre. They were the Group Theatre and Audrey Wood, the agent. All of a sudden they worked a marvelous change in my situation. They had submitted earlier works of mine to the Rockefeller Foundation, which was at that time distributing fellowships of a thousand dollars each to promising playwrights. I received one of these about a week after completing *Battle of Angels* and so I came with the manuscript to New York and began to explore for the first time the world of the professional theatre.

The absurd though tragic dilemma of that little microcosmos is something that I am not at all prepared to write about. That the most exalted of the arts should have fallen into the receivership of business men and gamblers is a situation parallel in absurdity to the conduct of worship becoming the responsibility of a herd of water-buffalos. It is one of those things that a man of reason had rather not think about until the means of redemption is more apparent. That in spite of this situation small islands of idealism still remain in the American theatre is all the more miraculous and to be praised. Men and women of unquestionable integrity still operate in the American theatre, many in eminent positions. They only wait for the release of the money octopus to create out of their own high designs a theatre where truth can resume its exploration of our spiritual night. But as for the theatre as it now exists, I will only say that I feel a person desiring to write fine plays could make a much worse mistake than never visiting a Broadway playhouse.

By the end of this first season in New York my fellowship money had dangerously dwindled. I had already received enough disturbing impressions of the theatre capital to feel an impulse to travel. Summarily and with little enough warning to anybody concerned, I packed my property, mostly paper, and departed for Mexico. I had left behind me the first draft of *Battle of Angels*. The Theatre Guild, one of those small islands alluded to, had taken an option on it. No one, least of all myself, thought they would do more than finger it a little before passing it back to the tangent stream that poetic properties follow. When the monthly advances no longer reached me in Acapulco, where I was spending the summer, I assumed without any surprise that this release had already occurred. The fact that I had traveled too rapidly for mail to catch up with me was the true explanation, and the one I didn't think of. My life was an approximate paradise at this tropical port. I called it "La Vie Horizontale." I wrote in a hammock all morning, swam all afternoon in the warm waters of a land-locked bay, spent the evenings talking lazily to another American writer, Andrew Gun, and drinking rum-cocos on the verandah of hammocks. I would have been content to pursue this life for the rest of my days, but, toward the end of summer, too much Mexican grease or unwashed greens resulted in gastric disturbances in both myself and Mr. Gun. Mr. Gun was a war refugee from Tahiti and he had spent nearly all our evenings telling me about that island and a little French girl who was waiting for him there. Fearing to be immured there for the duration of the war due to the cancellation of passenger shipping, he had fled on the last boat out—now he regretted the action. He had learned of a means of returning and had covinced me that I also was a spiritual native of Tahiti. We were all set to go there, when shortly after we had again entered the States, I got hold of a copy of *The New York Times* and was startled to read in the dramatic columns that the Theatre Guild was doing *Battle of Angels* as their initial play of the season and that Miss Miriam Hopkins had already flown from Hollywood to take the starring role.

Well, I returned post-haste to New York and dived unwittingly into the little maelstrom my play had provoked. I was delighted with the selection of Miss Hopkins for the role of Myra, but I was alarmed that things had gone ahead so rapidly, that casting was already in progress when the script was really only a first draft. I knew that the ending of the play, as it then stood, was a melodramatic *tour-de-force*. Conceptually it was fine—the store was set afire and everything went up in the fiery purgation. Yes, very exciting. "A Wagnerian experience," as someone put it in the Guild office! "But how in hell are you going to stage it?" asked Margaret Webster, who had been engaged as director. This question and others were held in abeyance while the production went rocketing ahead. I realized that I had fooled these people. Because certain qualities in my writing had startled them, they took it for granted that I was an accomplished playwright and that some afternoon when I was not busy with interviews, casting, rehearsals, I would quietly withdraw for an hour or two and work out the dramaturgic problems as deftly as such things were done by men like Barry and Kaufmann and Behrmann. They had no idea how dazed and stymied I was by the rush of events into which my dreamy self was precipitated. Meantime Peggy Webster and I caught a plane to the Mississippi Delta. We spent two days down there, introducing Peggy to the South—visiting country stores and talking to Delta people. Peggy absorbed the South in twenty-four hours. It was a bit too much for her. She began to look a little punch-drunk, seeing just enough of this extraordinary country and its people to make them more mysterious than they were before. On a plane returning to New York, I recall a talk that we had. We had been reciting verse to each other, mostly lyrics of Shakespeare. I repeated the one containing the lines "Nothing of him that doth fade but doth suffer a sea-change into something rich and strange." "That," said Peggy, "is what they should say about *Battle of Angels*."—"Perhaps," I answered, "but there are so many other things they may say about it."—Peggy assented gravely. Neither of us, however, had at this moment any intimation of the line of attack that really would be taken.

During all this time and the weeks that followed it had somehow occurred to none of us working on the production that we were dealing with a play that might be attacked on grounds of morality. If it was in the minds of others, certainly this suspicion was never communicated to me. Was I totally amoral? Was I too innocent or too evil—that I remained unprepared for what the audiences, censors and magistracy of

Boston were going to find in my play? I knew, of course, that I had written a play that touched upon human longings, about the sometimes conflicting desires of the flesh and the spirit. This struggle was thematic; implicit in the title of the play. Why had I never dreamed that such struggles could strike many people as filthy and seem to them unfit for articulation? Oh, if I had written a play full of licentious wiggling in filmy costumes, replete with allusions to the latrine, a play that was built about some titillating and vulgarly ribald predicament in a bedroom—why, then I would feel apprehensive about its moral valuation. However, it seemed to me that if *Battle of Angels* was nothing else, it was certainly clean, it was certainly idealistic. The very experience of writing it was like taking a bath in snow. Its purity seemed beyond question. But then—the dogma of the moral censor!—there again is something I cannot cope with and will have to pass over.

As rehearsals progressed it became more and more apparent that if nothing else needed fixing, the ending of the play certainly did. The store did not burn down convincingly nor were we, in the crucial parts of Cassandra and Val, able to find actors who seemed anything better than arbitrarily thrust into the parts. Three different leading men were unsuccessfully tried out in the five weeks of rehearsal before Wesley Addy was removed from *Twelfth Night* to play opposite Miss Hopkins. Though he did not have the physical quality the part demanded, Mr. Addy understood the play and certainly had talent enough to do a creative job. Miss Doris Dudley in the role of Cassandra was cruelly miscast. One of the most beautiful women in the theatre and also one of the sweetest, the terrifying demands of this part only increased her embarrassment. It was she who had to stand on the stairs of the burning store and lift the tragedy into a state of purgation with a set of lines—nowhere now present in the text—which she and all of us felt were quite impossible to integrate with the rest of the play as they seemed to come out of an altogether different script.

Toward the end of rehearsals, a series of frenzied conferences were held. Miss Hopkins, who played her part with heartbreaking beauty and something that only a woman of poetic understanding and deep experience could give—

whenever the confusion lifted sufficiently to give her a chance
to do so—was now becoming definitely frightened. She
looked to me for salvation. After all, I—poor captive thing—
was the author. How it wrung my heart that I could do nothing for her! She had staked so much on this play. It was to
mark her triumphal return to the stage, where her talent as a
dramatic actress could operate without the bonds that bad
screen vehicles had recently put on her. One could easily see
why she regarded the production almost as a matter of life
and death. Oh, if only my head would clear up a little—if I
could only find some lucid interval in this dervish frenzy that
was sweeping us all unprepared into Boston and disaster! But
all the conferences only added to my feeling of impotence.
Miss Hopkins' pleas and protestations—"For heaven's sake,
do something, something!"—only made it more impossible
for me to do anything at all. At last I went to Peggy and told
her exactly how unable I was to cope with the emergency. "It
is too late," I said, "I can't do anything more! If I could get
away from all of you for a month—I could return with a new
script. But that is not possible, so you will just have to take
what there is and do what you can with it!"

"Very well," said Peggy, "the store will burn down! Now
you stop worrying about it."

To insert another parenthesis: it seems to me that directly
behind capital investment as a menace to good theatre is the
fact that everything is done with such a machine-like haste.
Five weeks is not long enough to prepare a complex play.
Ideally it should have three months. Why wasn't that done
with the Federal Theatre Project? Why didn't they put on
one great play a season, instead of imitating the scrambling
rush of Broadway? No wonder nearly all players have a ten-
dency to chatter rather than speak on the stage! A play has
become something like a feat of legerdemain. I will allow
that rapid execution is the best policy with most Broadway
plays, but when now and then something comes along that
deserves a more leisurely gestation—why does it have to
hop, skip and jump across the schedule as briskly as something that hinges upon the loss of a G-string or getting
somebody's garter?

Answer: Money.

So after five weeks, only about three of which were conducted with a final cast, the company entrained for its opening engagement in the city of Boston. Only Miss Helburn and Mr. Langner appeared unshaken by any rumors of premonition. This I set down to their seniority, the fact that they had out-ridden so many previous storms. It was encouraging to observe their Olympian calm, but it made one all the more conscious of his own callow emotionalism.

In Boston we had but one night of rehearsal before we opened, in the Christmas season of 1940.

That night was about as black as any I'd experienced. Everything that had gone well, or passably well, at previous rehearsals went about as badly as possible. All the meaning seemed to have gone from the lines: nothing fitted together: the effect was kaleidoscopic. When it came time for the store to burn down—the little trickles of smoke under the wings, the flickering red lights, the bawling voices—against these had to be played the all-important scene that lifted the play to katharsis. Never had it seemed so impossible to combine the two actions. Either you heard only the mob's demonstration or you heard only the interior scene. Also it was suddenly discovered at this rehearsal that the musical score composed for the play could not be used. In my frank opinion, it was terrible. Miss Hopkins felt the same way about it. Almost tearfully she cried out, "How can I dance to that music?" No doubt it was a fine composition technically; but for the play, it was terrible. All of it went out, and at the last moment recorded selections were substituted: banal and make-shift they were but we were devoutly thankful—at least Miriam Hopkins and I—when the high-brow composition released its depressing grip. Suitable music could have done a great deal for the production, but this was really a solo composition—the sort of thing you would expect to hear at a modern dance recital where it could be accorded the proper deference.

I remember that Peggy jumped off the stage at one point and caught her ankle in a folding seat. She uttered a slight cry of pain—Miriam Hopkins screamed as if the sky had fallen— such was the state of our nerves.

I went home too exhausted to think or to sleep. Toward morning I wrote a new final scene. Dreadful it probably was!

Nobody paid any attention to it, but I remember saying dramatically that I would crawl on my belly through brimstone if they would only put off the opening and give me a few more days to contrive something else. Mr. Langner smiled at me fondly. A very kind man, he gave me what comfort and reassurance he could. Miss Helburn sent me a telegram—"Saint Michael and all Good Angels be with you!"—signed "Connecticut Updyke" (her married name, with the territorial appellation she had adapted in imitation of mine).

Opening night. Things started rolling peacefully enough. The elegant first night audience entered the theatre with an air of nobility and refinement which boded little of what was to come in our next three hours of communion with them. They looked on the first scenes with bland satisfaction. Gowned by Bergdorf-Goodman, Miss Hopkins was as radiantly beautiful as any of their debutante daughters. The character women upset the dowagers a little from time to time, but the general attitude toward the earthy humor they brought to the script was still indulgent. It was not till the action concerning Vee's visionary portrait of Val—not until that revelation—that the peculiar attitude which this audience brought to the theatre began to make itself seen, heard, and felt. Up and down the aisles the ladies and gentlemen began to converse with each other in sibilant whispers. Subdued hissings and clucking were punctuated now and then by the banging up of a seat and the regal swish of silken garments drawn hurriedly over projecting knees as here and there it became impossible for some spectator to countenance further infractions of standards.

The nature of this phenomenon, the fashionable first night audience, became shockingly plain to me all at once. What interests them is themselves, their dignity, their prestige and pretenses. What they want is a flattering mirror, a picture that does the opposite of Dorian Gray's, one that takes off all their blemishes in its reflection. After the play had closed a Brookline dowager wrote the Theatre Guild—I saw this letter—to say that when she went to the theatre she wanted to see cultivated people, people who talked, acted and dressed as she and her friends. Pictures of other *milieux* were not acceptable to her. I am afraid that she expressed a fairly widespread attitude among what is known as the "carriage trade" on which our theatre is still financially dependent. Hence the failure of the theatre really to explore the many levels of society except in the superficial and sensational way of *Tobacco Road* and its prototypes, which pleases the carriage trade inversely to polite drawing-room comedy by representing their social inferiors as laughable grotesques.

Returning to the performance. It was not until the point of the conflagration that the Boston audience was in a strategic position to vent its full displeasure. At the final dress-rehearsal there had not been enough smoke to make the fire convincing. Obviously this deficiency had been thoroughly impressed upon the gentlemen operating the smoke-pots, for on opening night when it came time for the store to burn down it was like the burning of Rome. Great sulphurous billows rolled chokingly onto the stage and coiled over the foot-lights. To an already antagonistic audience this was sufficient to excite something in the way of pandemonium. Outraged squawks, gabbling, spluttering spread through all the front rows of the theatre. Nothing that happened on the stage from then on was of any importance. Indeed the scene was nearly eclipsed by the fumes. Voices were lost in the banging up of seats as the front rows were evacuated.

When the curtain at last came down, as curtains eventually must, I had come to that point where one must laugh or go crazy. I laughed. There was little joy in it, but knowing I had to laugh, I found that I could. Miriam Hopkins accepted the same necessity. I see her coming out to face her audience. The stage is still full of smoke. Before her smiling face she is waving a small white hand, to clear the fumes away. She is coughing a little, apologetically touching her throat and chest. Their backs are turned to her, these elegant first-nighters, as they push up the aisles like heavy, heedless cattle. But she is still gallantly smiling and waving away the smoke with her delicate hand. The curtain bobs foolishly up and down to a patter of hands in the balcony that goes on after the lower floor is emptied.

The failure of a play!

The Boston reviewers tried to judge what they had seen as fairly and calmly as possible. In the reviewers there was none of the downright cruelty that the first-night audience had exhibited. Under the circumstances, the reviewers were as good as could be hoped for. Obviously that is not saying that they were good. References were made, however, to the reality of the atmosphere in the earlier scenes of the play and one lady reviewer went so far as to say that there were occasional lines of beauty in the script. Another reviewer made guarded allusions to good character touches in the lesser figures. There was an atmosphere of wariness and bated breath in all these printed reactions.

The magistracy of Boston did not step in till after the play had run for about a week. Then it was that the censors sat out front and demanded excision from the script of practically all that made it intelligible, let alone moving. Fortunately I had already left Boston at that time and did not take part in this really posthumous disturbance.

The play as you now read it was written many months later.

Some day it will be done again. For that occasion I will probably prepare still another version, omitting the present prologue and epilogue. They were a defensive gesture which I wouldn't have made if it were not for the appalling memory of Boston. But I have never written a play that I thought was completed and I don't think I ever will. There is too much to say and not enough time to say it. Nor is there power enough. I am not a good writer. Sometimes I am a very bad writer indeed. There is hardly a successful writer in the field who cannot write circles around me and I am the first to admit it. But I think of writing as something more organic than words, something closer to being and action. I want to work more and more with a more plastic theatre than the one that I have so far. I have never for one moment doubted that there are people—millions!—to say things to. We come to each other, gradually, but with love. It is the short reach of my arms that hinders, not the length and multiplicity of theirs. With love and with honesty, the embrace is inevitable.

TENNESSEE WILLIAMS

Manhattan, March, 1944.

I RISE IN FLAME,
CRIED THE PHŒNIX

The action of this play, which is imaginary, takes place in the French Riviera where D. H. Lawrence died.

Not long before Lawrence's death an exhibition of his paintings was held in London. Primitive in technique and boldly sensual in matter, this exhibition created a little tempest. The pictures were seized by the police and would have been burned if the authorities had not been restrained by an injunction. At this time Lawrence's great study of sexual passion, Lady Chatterly's Lover, *was likewise under the censor's ban, as much of his work had been in the past.*

Lawrence felt the mystery and power of sex, as the primal life urge, and was the lifelong adversary of those who wanted to keep the subject locked away in the cellars of prudery. Much of his work is chaotic and distorted by tangent obsessions, such as his insistence upon the woman's subservience to the male, but all in all his work is probably the greatest modern monument to the dark roots of creation.

—T. W.

New Orleans, September, 1941

A NOTE BY FRIEDA LAWRENCE

This book has a beautiful title. When I read this short play, I forgot that it was supposed to be Lawrence and me; it happens in that other world where creation takes place. The theme of it is the eternal antagonism and attraction between man and woman. This was between Lawrence and me too. But the greater reality was something else. I wish I could say in convincing words what it was—it is difficult. What was it? It was so different from the ordinary everyday being-in-love, that has its limits so very soon. It was life in its freedom, its limitless possibilities, that bound us together. In our poverty the whole world with everything in it was ours. It was living every moment, not only existing day by day. All that happened was a new experience. Because of the background of death, every happening was more vivid. Die we must, and no "Forest Lawn" can wipe death out.

Lawrence infused new meaning into the written word, by going deeper than the surface. We have had a lot of surface. We have become bored. Lawrence faced his own dying a death with clear courage, he lived it right through. When finally it was over for him and he lay dead on his bed, I felt a triumph in him. He was dead, but he had died with an unbroken spirit, he had lived in superb honesty and the pride of a man.

When I think of him now after all these years, it is as if a kind wind blew on my flame of life to make it burn brighter. He will do the same for others, if they give him a chance.

—Frieda Lawrence

The characters in this play are Lawrence, Frieda, and Bertha. The scene is at Vence, France, in the Alpes-Maritimes. It is late afternoon.

Lawrence is seated on a sunporch, the right wall of which is a window that faces the sun. A door in this wall opens out on the high seacliff. It is windy: the surf can be heard. Lawrence looks out that way. Behind him, on the left wall, woven in silver and scarlet and gold, is a large banner that bears the design of the Phœnix in a nest of flames—Lawrence's favorite symbol.

He sits quite still. His beard is fiercely red and his face is immobile, the color of baked clay with tints of purple in it. The hands that gripped the terrible stuff of life and made it plastic are folded on the black and white checked surface of an invalid's blanket. The long fingers of the Welsh coalminers, with their fine blond hairs and their knobby knuckles, made for rending the black heart out of the earth, are knotted together with a tightness that betrays the inner lack of repose. His slightly distended nostrils draw the breath in and out as tenderly as if it were an invisible silk thread that any unusual tension might snap in two. Born for contention, he is contending with something he can't get his hands on. He has to control his fury. And so he is seated motionless in the sunlight—wrapped in a checkered blanket and lavender wool shawl . . . The tiger in him is trapped, but not destroyed yet.

Frieda comes in, a large handsome woman of fifty, rather like a Valkyrie. She holds up a fancily wrapped little package.

LAWRENCE: (*without even turning his head*) What is it?
FRIEDA: Something left on the doorstep.
LAWRENCE: Give it here.
FRIEDA: The donor is anonymous. I only caught a glimpse of her through the window.
LAWRENCE: A woman?
FRIEDA: Yes . . .
LAWRENCE: Yes . . .

FRIEDA: Some breathless little spinster in a blue pea-jacket. She stuck it on the porch and scuttled back down the hill before I could answer the doorbell.

LAWRENCE: (*his voice rising, querulously shrill*) It's for me, isn't it?

FRIEDA: Ja, es ist für dich.

LAWRENCE: Well, give it here, damn you, you—!

FRIEDA: Tch! I thought that the sun had put you in a good humor.

LAWRENCE: It's put me in a vile humor. We've sat here making faces at each other the whole afternoon. I say to the sun, Make me well, you old bitch, give me strength, take hold of my hands and pull me up out of this chair! But the sun is a stingy Hausfrau. She goes about sweeping the steps and pretends not to hear me begging. Ah, well, I don't blame her. I never did care for beggars myself very much. A man shouldn't beg. A man should seize what he wants and tear it out of the hands of the adversary. And if he can't get it, if he can't tear it away, then he should let it go and give up and be contented with nothing. Look. (*He has unwrapped the package.*) A little jar of orange marmalade. (*He smiles with childish pleasure.*) This is the month of August put in a bottle.

FRIEDA: Ja! Sehr gut. You can have it for breakfast.

LAWRENCE: (*drawing tenderly on the fine gold thread*) Uh-huh. I can have it for breakfast as long as I live, huh, Frieda? It's just the right size for that.

FRIEDA: Shut up. (*She starts to take the jar from him. Quick as a cat, he snatches her wrist in a steel grip.*)

LAWRENCE: Leave go of it, damn you!

FRIEDA: (*laughing*) My God, but you still are strong!

LAWRENCE: You didn't think so?

FRIEDA: I had forgotten. You've been so gentle lately.

LAWRENCE: Thought you'd tamed me?

FRIEDA: Yes, but I should have known better. I should have suspected what you've been doing inside you, lapping that yellow cream up, you sly old fox, sucking the fierce red sun in your body all day and turning it into venom to spew in my face!

LAWRENCE: No . . . I've been making a trap. I've been mak-

ing a shiny steel trap to catch you in, you vixen! Now break
away if you can!

FRIEDA: (*grinning and wincing*) Oh, God, how you hurt!

LAWRENCE: (*slowly releasing her*) . . . Don't lie . . . You with
that great life in you . . . Why did God give you so much
and me so little? You could take my arm and snap it like a dry
stick.

FRIEDA: No . . . You were always the stronger one. Big as I
am, I never could beat you, could I?

LAWRENCE: (*with satisfaction*) No. You couldn't. (*His breath
rasps hoarsely.*) Put the jar down on the sill.

FRIEDA: (*complying*) Ah, there's a card stuck on it. "From
one of your devoted readers." And on the other side it says:
"I worship you, Mr. Lawrence, because I know that only a
god could know so much about Life!"

LAWRENCE: (*dryly*) In looking for God so unsuccessfully myself, it seems that I have accidentally managed to create one
for an anonymous spinster in a blue pea-jacket. Upon the
altar of her pagan deity she places a dainty jar of orange
marmalade! What a *cynical* little woman she is! Only the little ones of the earth, who scuttle downhill like pebbles dis-
lodged by the rain, are really capable of such monumental
disbelief. They find their god and they give him marmalade.
If I find mine . . . ever . . . If I found mine, I'd tear the
heart out of my body and burn it before him.

FRIEDA: Your health is returning.

LAWRENCE: What makes you think so?

FRIEDA: You are getting so sentimental about yourself and so
unappreciated and so misunderstood . . . You can't stand
Jesus Christ because he beat you to it. Oh, how you would
have loved to suffer the *original* crucifixion!

LAWRENCE: If only I had your throat between my fingers.

FRIEDA: (*crouching beside him*) Here is my throat . . . . Now
choke me.

LAWRENCE: (*gently touching her throat with the tips of his fingers*) Frieda . . . do you think I will ever get back to New
Mexico?

FRIEDA: You will do what you want to do, Lawrence. There
has never been any kind of resistance you couldn't jump
over or crawl under or squeeze through.

LAWRENCE: Do you think I will ever get back on a strong white horse and go off like the wind across the glittering desert? I'm not a literary man, I'm tired of books. Nobody knows what an ugly joke it is that a life like mine should only come out in books.

FRIEDA: What else should it come out in?

LAWRENCE: In some kind of violent action. But all that I ever do is go packing around the world with women and manuscripts and a vile disposition. I pretend to be waging a war with bourgeois conceptions of morality, with prudery, with intellectuality, with all kinds of external forces that aren't external at all. What I'm fighting with really's the little old maid in myself, the breathless little spinster who scuttles back down the hill before God can answer the doorbell. Now I want to get back on the desert and try all over again to become a savage. I want to stand up on the Lobos and watch a rainstorm coming ten miles off like a silver-helmeted legion of marching giants. And that's what I'm going to do, damn you!

FRIEDA: Whoever said that you wouldn't?

LAWRENCE: You! . . You know that I won't. You know that the male savage part of me's dead and all that's left is the old pusillanimous squaw. Women have such a fine intuition of death. They smell it coming before it's started even. I think it's women that actually let death in. They whisper and beckon and slip it the dark latchkey from under their aprons . . . Don't they?

FRIEDA: No . . . It's women that pay the price of admission for life. And all of their lives they make of their arms a crossbar at the door that death wants to come in by. Men love death . . . Women don't. Men cut wounds in each other and women stop the bleeding.

LAWRENCE: Yes. By drinking the blood. Don't touch me so much! (*She releases his fingers.*) Your fingers, they make me feel weaker, they drain the strength out of my body.

FRIEDA: Oh, no, no, no, they put it back *in*, mein Liebchen.

LAWRENCE: I want you to promise me something. If I should die, Frieda . . . the moment I'm dying, please to leave me alone! . . Don't touch me, don't put your hands on me, and don't let anyone else . . . . I have a nightmarish feeling that while I'm dying I'll be surrounded by women. They'll burst in the door and the windows the moment I lose the strength to push them away. They'll moan and they'll flutter like doves around the burnt-out Phœnix. They'll cover my face and my hands with filmy kisses and little trickling tears. Alma the nymphomaniac and the virginal Bertha—all of the under- and over-sexed women I've known, who think me the oracle of their messed-up libidos—they'll all return with their suffocating devotion. I don't want that. I want to die as a lonely old animal does. I want to die fiercely and cleanly with nothing but anger and fear and other hard things like that to deal with at the finish. You understand, Frieda? I've still got a bit of the male left in me and that's the part that I'm going to meet death with. When the last bleeding comes, and it *will* in a little while now, I won't be put into bed and huddled over by women. I won't stay in the house, Frieda. I'll open this door and go outside on the cliff. And I don't wish to be followed. That's the important point, Frieda. I'm going to do it alone. With the rocks and the water. Sunlight . . . starlight on me. No hands, no lips, no women! Nothing but . . . pitiless nature . . .

FRIEDA: I don't believe you. I don't think people want nothing but "pitiless nature" when they're . . .

LAWRENCE: Frieda! You mean you refuse?

FRIEDA: No. I consent absolutely.

LAWRENCE: You give me your promise?

FRIEDA: Ja doch! Ganz durch die Ewigkeit! Now think about something else. I'll go fix tea. (*She starts to go out.*)

LAWRENCE: (*suddenly noticing something*) Ah, my God.

FRIEDA: What's the matter?

LAWRENCE: Put the aquarium on the windowsill.

FRIEDA: Why?

LAWRENCE: So I can keep an eye on it. That detestable cat has attacked the goldfish again.

FRIEDA: How do you know?

LAWRENCE: How do I know? There used to be *four*, now there's *three*! *Beau Soleil!*

FRIEDA: She's gone outside.

LAWRENCE: To lick her chops, God damn her! Set the goldfish bowl on the windowsill.

FRIEDA: You can't keep them there in the sun. The sun will kill them.

LAWRENCE: (*furiously*) Don't answer me back, put 'em *there*!

FRIEDA: Wie du willst! (*She hastens to place the aquarium on the sill.*)

LAWRENCE: You know what I think? I think you *fed* her the fish. It's like you to do such a thing. You're both so fat, so rapacious, so viciously healthy and hungry!

FRIEDA: Such a fuss over a goldfish!

LAWRENCE: It isn't just a goldfish.

FRIEDA: What is it then?

LAWRENCE: Now that my strength's used up I can't help thinking how much of it's been thrown away in squabbling with you.

FRIEDA: (*suddenly covering her face*) Oh, Lawrence.

LAWRENCE: What are you doing? Crying? Stop it. I can't stand crying. It makes me worse.

FRIEDA: I think you *hate* me, Lawrence.

(*After a moment he shyly touches her arm.*)

LAWRENCE: Don't believe me . . . I love you. Ich liebe dich, Frieda. Put some rum in the tea. I'm getting much stronger, so why should I feel so weak?

FRIEDA: (*touching his forehead*) I wish you would go back to bed.

LAWRENCE: The bed's an old tarbaby. I'd get stuck. How do I know that I'd get loose again? Is my forehead hot? (*Frieda places her hand tenderly over his eyes. He recites in a childish treble:*)

> "Ladybug, ladybug, fly away home,
>   thine house is on fire, thy children will burn!"

(*He smiles slightly.*) My mother used to sing that whenever she saw one . . . Simple . . . Most people are so damned complicated and yet there is nothing much to them.

FRIEDA: (*She starts out, then pauses before the banner.*) Ah, you old Phœnix . . . you brave and angry old bird in your nest of flames! I think you are just a little bit sentimental.

LAWRENCE: (*leaning suddenly forward*) Tea for three!

FRIEDA: Who is it?

LAWRENCE: Bertha! . . Back from London with news of the exhibition. (*He pulls himself out of the chair.*)

FRIEDA: What are you doing?

LAWRENCE: I'm going outside to meet her.

FRIEDA: Sit down, you fool! I'll meet her. And don't you dare to ask her to stay in this house . . . If you do, I'll leave! (*She goes out.*)

LAWRENCE: Cluck-cluck-cluck-cluck! . . You think I'm anxious to have more hens around me? (*He wriggles fretfully in the chair for a moment, then throws off the blanket and pushes himself to his feet. Stumbling with dizziness and breathing heavily, he moves to the inside rear door of the porch. He reaches it and pauses with a fit of coughing. He looks anxiously back toward the chair.*) No, no, damn you . . . I won't! (*He looks up at the Phœnix, straightens himself heroically and goes out.*)

(*After a few moments Frieda returns with Bertha, a small, sprightly person, an English gentlewoman with the quick voice and eyes of a child.*)

FRIEDA: My God, he's got up!

BERTHA: He shouldn't?

FRIEDA: Another hemorrhage will kill him. The least exertion is likely to bring one on. Lorenzo, where are you?

LAWRENCE: (*from the rear*) Quit clucking, you old wet hen. I'm fetching the tea.

BERTHA: Go back to him, make him stop!

FRIEDA: He wouldn't.

BERTHA: Does he want to die?

FRIEDA: Oh, no, no, no! He has no lungs and yet he goes on breathing. The heart's worn out and yet the heart keeps beating. It's awful to watch, this struggle. I wish he would stop, I wish that he'd give it up and just let go!

BERTHA: Frieda!

FRIEDA: His body's a house that's made out of tissuepaper and caught on fire. The walls are transparent, they're all lit up with the flame! When people are dying the spirit ought to go out, it ought to die out slowly before the flesh. You shouldn't be able to see it so terribly brightly consuming the walls that give it a place to inhabit!

BERTHA: I never have believed that Lorenzo could die. I don't think he will even now.

FRIEDA: But can he do it? Live without a body, I mean, be just a flame with nothing to feed itself on?

BERTHA: The Phœnix could do it.

FRIEDA: The Phœnix was legendary. Lorenzo's a man.

BERTHA: He's more than a man.

FRIEDA: I know you always thought so. But you're mistaken.

BERTHA: You'd never admit that Lorenzo was a god.

FRIEDA: Having slept with him . . . No, I wouldn't.

BERTHA: There's more to be known of a person than carnal knowledge.

FRIEDA: But carnal knowledge comes first.

BERTHA: I disagree with you.

FRIEDA: And also with Lawrence, then. He always insisted you couldn't know women until you had known their bodies.

BERTHA: Frieda, I think it is you who kept him so much in his body!

FRIEDA: Well, if I did he's got that to thank me for.

BERTHA: I'm not so sure it's something to be thankful for.

FRIEDA: What would you have done with him if ever you got your claws on him?

BERTHA: Claws? . . Frieda!

FRIEDA: You would have plucked him out of his body. Where would he be? . . In the air? Ah, your deep understanding and my stupidity always!

BERTHA: Frieda!

FRIEDA: You just don't know. The meaning of Lawrence escapes you. In all of his work he celebrates the body. How he despises the prudery of people that want to hide it!

BERTHA: Oh, Frieda, the same old quarrel!

FRIEDA: Yes, let's stop it. What's left of Lorenzo, let's not try to divide it!

BERTHA: What's left of Lorenzo is something that can't be divided!

FRIEDA: Sh! . . He's coming.

BERTHA: (*advancing a few steps to the door*) Lorenzo!

LAWRENCE: (*He is out of sight as he speaks.*) "Pussycat, pussycat, where have you been?"

BERTHA: (*gaily*) "I've been to London to look at the Queen!"

LAWRENCE: (*coming nearer*) "Pussycat, pussycat, what did you there?"

BERTHA: (*her voice catching slightly*) "I chased a little mouse . . . under a chair!"

(*Laughing, Lawrence appears in the doorway, pushing a small tea-cart. Bertha stares aghast.*)

LAWRENCE: Yes, I know . . . I know . . . I look an amateur's job of embalming, don't I?

BERTHA: (*bravely*) Lorenzo, you look very well.

LAWRENCE: It isn't rouge, it's the fever! I'm burning, burning, and still I never burn out. The doctors are all astonished. And disappointed. As for that expectant widow of mine, she's almost given up hope. (*Bertha moves to assist him with the table.*) Don't bother me. I can manage.

FRIEDA: He won't be still, he won't rest!

LAWRENCE: Cluck-cluck-cluck-cluck! You better watch out for the rooster, you old wet hen!

FRIEDA: A wonderful Chanticleer you make in that lavender shawl!

LAWRENCE: Who put it on me? *You*, you bitch! (*He flings it off.*) Rest was never any good for me, Brett.

BERTHA: Rest for a little while. Then we go sailing again!

LAWRENCE: We three go sailing again!

> "Rub-a-dub-dub!
>   Three fools in a tub!
>   The Brett, the Frieda,
>   the old Fire-eater!"

BERTHA: (*tugging at his beard*) The old Fire-eater!

LAWRENCE: Watch out! Now I'll have to comb it. (*He takes out a little mirror and comb.*)

FRIEDA: So vain of his awful red whiskers!

LAWRENCE: (*combing*) She envies me my beard. All women resent men's whiskers. They can't stand anything, Brett, that distinguishes men from women.

FRIEDA: Quite the contrary. (*She pours the tea.*)

LAWRENCE: They take the male in their bodies . . . but only because they secretly hope that he won't be able to get back out again, that he'll be captured for good.

FRIEDA: What kind of talk for a maiden lady to hear!

LAWRENCE: There she goes again, Brett . . . obscene old creature! Gloating over your celibacy!

FRIEDA: Gloating over it? Never! I think how lucky she is that she doesn't have to be told a hundred times every day that a man is life and that woman is just a passive hunk of protoplasm.

LAWRENCE: I never said passive. I always said malignant. (*He puts the comb away and stares in the mirror.*) Ain't I the devil to look at?

FRIEDA: I tell you, Brett, his ideas of sex are becoming downright cosmic! When the sun comes up in the morning . . . you know what he says? No, I won't repeat it! And when the sun's going down . . . Oh, well, you will hear him yourself.

LAWRENCE: (*chuckling*) Yes, I always make the same remark. You'll hear me yourself in just a few more minutes . . . (*He puts the mirror away.*) Well, Brett!

BERTHA: Well, Lorenzo?

LAWRENCE: You haven't said anything yet.

BERTHA: Anything? About what?

LAWRENCE: What do you think that I sent you to London for?

BERTHA: To get me out of the way!

LAWRENCE: What else? . . Out with it, damn you! The show! How did they like my pictures?

BERTHA: Well . . .

FRIEDA: Go on, Brett, tell him the truth. The monster will not be satisfied till he hears it!

BERTHA: Well . . .

FRIEDA: The exhibition was a complete fiasco! Just as I said it would be!

LAWRENCE: You mean that they *liked* my pictures?

FRIEDA: *Liked* your pictures? They called your pictures *disgusting*!

LAWRENCE: Ah! . . *Success!* They said that I couldn't paint? That I draw like a child? They called my figures grotesque? Lumpy, obscene, misshapen, monstrous, deformed?

BERTHA: You must have seen the reviews, you've read them yourself!

LAWRENCE: Why? Am I quoting exactly?

FRIEDA: Yes, you are quoting exactly!

LAWRENCE: And what did the public think? And what of the people?

FRIEDA: The people laughed!

LAWRENCE: They laughed?

FRIEDA: Of course they laughed! Lorenzo, you're not a painter, you're a writer! Why, you can't even draw a straight line!

LAWRENCE: No! But I can draw a *crooked* line, Frieda. And that is the reason that I can put *life* in my pictures! How was the attendance? How many came to look?

BERTHA: After the disturbance, the entrance had to be roped off to hold back the crowds.

LAWRENCE: Disturbance? What disturbance?

FRIEDA: Just look. The monster's exulting!

LAWRENCE: Go on, tell me what happened!

BERTHA: A group of ladies' club members attempted to slash the picture of Adam and Eve.

(*Lawrence shakes with laughter.*)

FRIEDA: Lorenzo! Stop that!

BERTHA: That was what called the attention of the police.

LAWRENCE: The police? (*He rises.*) What did they do to my pictures? Burn them? *Destroy them?*

BERTHA: No. We got out an injunction to keep them from burning the pictures.

LAWRENCE: The pictures are safe?

BERTHA: The pictures are safe, Lorenzo.

FRIEDA: Sit down in that chair or I'll have to put you to bed!

(*She tries to push him down. He slaps her fiercely.*)

BERTHA: Lorenzo!

LAWRENCE: Vaunting her power, gloating over my weakness! Put me to bed? Just try it . . . I dare you to touch me!

FRIEDA: Lawrence, sit down in that chair or you'll start the bleeding again.

(*He stares at her for a moment and then obeys slowly.*)

LAWRENCE: (*weakly*) Give me back that shawl. The sun's getting weaker. The young blond god is beginning to be seduced by the harlot of darkness . . .

FRIEDA: Now he's going to make his classic remarks on the sunset. (*She puts the shawl about him.*)

LAWRENCE: Yes . . . the pictures . . . they weren't very good but they had a fierce life in them.

BERTHA: They had *you* in them. But why did you want to *paint*, Lorenzo?

LAWRENCE: Why did I want to write? Because I'm an artist . . . What is an artist? . . A man who loves life too intensely, a man who loves life till he hates her and has to strike out with his fist as I struck out at Frieda . . . To show her he knows her tricks, and he's still the master! (*The smoky yellow light is beginning to dim.*) Oh, Brett, oh, Frieda . . . I wanted to stretch out the long, sweet arms of my art and embrace the whole world! But it isn't enough to go out to the world with love. And so I doubled my fist and I struck and I struck. Words weren't enough . . . I had to have color, too. I took to paint and I painted the way that I wrote! Fiercely, without any shame! *This* is life, I told them, life is like *this*! Wonderful! Dark! Terrific! They banned my books and they wanted to burn my pictures! That's how it is . . . When first you look at the sun it strikes you blind. Life's . . . blinding . . . (*He stirs and leans forward.*) The sun's . . . going down. He's seduced by the harlot of darkness.

FRIEDA: Now he is going to say it . . . Stop up your ears!

LAWRENCE: Now she has got him, they're copulating together! The sun is exhausted, the harlot has taken his strength and now she will start to destroy him. She's eating him up . . . Oh, but he won't stay down. He'll climb back out of her belly and there will be light. In the end there will always be light . . . And I am the prophet of it! (*He rises with difficulty.*)

BERTHA: Lorenzo!

FRIEDA: Lawrence, be careful!

LAWRENCE: Shut up! Don't touch me! (*He staggers to the great window.*) In the end there is going to be light . . . light, light! (*His voice rises and he stretches his arms out like a Biblical prophet.*) Great light! . . Great, blinding, universal *light*! And *I* . . . I'm the *prophet* of it! (*He staggers and clutches his mouth.*)

FRIEDA: *Lawrence!*

BERTHA: (*terrified*) What *is* it?

FRIEDA: The *bleeding!*

BERTHA: *Lorenzo!* (*She tries to rush to him but Frieda clutches her arm.*)

LAWRENCE: Don't touch me, you women. I want to do it alone . . . Don't move till it's finished. (*Gradually, as though forced down to the earth by invisible arms, he begins to collapse, but still he clings to the wall and shuffles along it, gasping for breath, until he has reached the door. He opens the door.*) Don't follow. (*He goes out.*)

BERTHA: (*struggling fiercely with Frieda*) Let me go, let me go, I want to go to him.

FRIEDA: I promised "no women"!

BERTHA: You go!

FRIEDA: Nobody, nobody goes to him! Not you, not me, no woman!

BERTHA: He can't die alone, I won't let him! No human being would let him!

FRIEDA: (*agonized*) I will, I promised, I'll let him!

(*The wind blows open the door to the terrace. There is the sound of waves breaking. The silk banner of the Phœnix billows out from the wall. Bertha almost breaks away, but Frieda violently restrains her again. In the struggle the lamp is upset and goes out. Bertha cries* Monster! *and collapses sobbing to the floor. For a few moments, stillness: then faintly, as if from a distance, Lawrence's voice:*)

LAWRENCE: *Frieda!*

(*All in one instant Frieda thrusts the sobbing woman violently away from her and sweeps out upon the terrace like a great winged bird.*)

FRIEDA: (*wildly, with infinite tenderness*) Ich komm', Ich komm', mein Liebchen!

FROM

27 WAGONS FULL OF COTTON
AND OTHER ONE-ACT PLAYS
(1946)

27 *Wagons Full of Cotton*

A Mississippi Delta Comedy

> 'Now Eros shakes my soul, a wind on the
> mountain, falling on the oaks.'
>
> SAPPHO

CHARACTERS

JAKE MEIGHAN, *a cotton-gin owner.*
FLORA MEIGHAN, *his wife.*
SILVA VICARRO, *superintendent*
of the Syndicate Plantation.

All of the action takes place on the front porch of the Meighans'
residence near Blue Mountain, Mississippi.

SCENE: *The front porch of the Meighans' cottage near Blue*
Mountain, Mississippi. The porch is narrow and rises into a sin-
gle narrow gable. There are spindling white pillars on either side
supporting the porch roof and a door of Gothic design and two
Gothic windows on either side of it. The peaked door has an oval
of richly stained glass, azure, crimson, emerald and gold. At the
windows are fluffy white curtains gathered coquettishly in the
middle by baby-blue satin bows. The effect is not unlike a doll's
house.

SCENE I

It is early evening and there is a faint rosy dusk in the sky.
Shortly after the curtain rises, Jake Meighan, a fat man of sixty,
scrambles out the front door and races around the corner of the
house carrying a gallon can of coal-oil. A dog barks at him. A
car is heard starting and receding rapidly in the distance. A
moment later Flora calls from inside the house.

FLORA: Jake! I've lost m' white kid purse! (*closer to the door*)
Jake? Look'n see 'f uh laid it on th' swing. (*There is a*

307

pause.) Guess I could've left it in th' Chevy? (*She comes up to screen door.*) Jake. Look'n see if uh left it in th' Chevy. Jake? (*She steps outside in the fading rosy dusk. She switches on the porch light and stares about, slapping at gnats attracted by the light. Locusts provide the only answering voice. Flora gives a long nasal call.*) Ja-ay—a-a-ake! (*A cow moos in the distance with the same inflection. There is a muffled explosion somewhere about half a mile away. A strange flickering glow appears, the reflection of a burst of flame. Distant voices are heard exclaiming.*)

VOICES: (*shrill, cackling like hens*)
You heah that noise?
Yeah! Sound like a bomb went off!
Oh, look!
Why, it's a fire!
Where's it at? You tell?
Th' Syndicate Plantation!
Oh, my God! Let's go! (*A fire whistle sounds in the distance.*)
Henry! Start th' car! You all wanta go with us?
Yeah, we'll be right out!
Hurry, honey! (*A car can be heard starting up.*)
Be right there!
Well, hurry.

VOICE: (*just across the dirt road*) Missus Meighan?

FLORA: Ye-ah?

VOICE: Ahn't you goin' th' fire?

FLORA: I wish I could but Jake's gone off in th' Chevy.

VOICE: Come awn an' go with us, honey!

FLORA: Oh, I cain't an' leave th' house wide open! Jake's gone off with th' keys. What do you all think it is on fire?

VOICE: Th' Syndicate Plantation!

FLORA: Th' Syndicate Plan-*ta*-tion? (*The car starts off and recedes.*) Oh, my Go-od! (*She climbs laboriously back up on the porch and sits on the swing which faces the front. She speaks tragically to herself.*) Nobody! Nobody! Never! Never! Nobody! (*Locusts can be heard. A car is heard approaching and stopping at a distance back of house. After a moment Jake ambles casually up around the side of the house.*)

FLORA: (*in a petulant babyish tone*) Well!

JAKE: Whatsamatter, Baby?

FLORA: I never known a human being could be that mean an' thoughtless!

JAKE: Aw, now, that's a mighty broad statement fo' you to make, Mrs. Meighan. What's the complaint this time?

FLORA: Just flew out of the house without even sayin' a word!

JAKE: What's so bad about that?

FLORA: I told you I had a headache comin' on an' had to have a dope, there wassen a single bottle lef' in th' house, an' you said, Yeah, get into yuh things 'n' we'll drive in town right away! So I get into m' things an' I cain't find m' white kid purse. Then I remember I left it on th' front seat of th' Chevy. I come out here t' git it. Where are you? Gone off! Without a word! Then there's a big explosion! Feel my heart!

JAKE: Feel my baby's heart? (*He puts a hand on her huge bosom.*)

FLORA: Yeah, just you feel it, poundin' like a hammer! How'd I know what happened? You not here, just disappeared somewhere!

JAKE: (*sharply*) Shut up! (*He pushes her head roughly.*)

FLORA: Jake! What did you do that fo'?

JAKE: I don't like how you holler! Holler ev'ry thing you say!

FLORA: What's the matter with you?

JAKE: Nothing's the matter with me.

FLORA: Well, why did you go off?

JAKE: I didn' go off!

FLORA: You certainly *did* go off! Try an' tell me that you never went off when I just now seen an' heard you drivin' back in th' car? What uh you take me faw? No sense a-tall?

JAKE: If you got sense you keep your big mouth shut!

FLORA: Don't talk to me like that!

JAKE: Come on inside.

FLORA: I won't. Selfish an' inconsiderate, that's what you are! I told you at supper, There's not a bottle of Coca-Cola left on th' place. You said, Okay, right after supper we'll drive on over to th' White Star drugstore an' lay in a good supply. When I come out of th' house—

JAKE: (*He stands in front of her and grips her neck with both hands.*) Look here! Listen to what I tell you!

FLORA: *Jake!*

JAKE: Shhh! Just listen, Baby.

FLORA: Lemme go! G'damn you, le' go my throat!

JAKE: Jus' try an' concentrate on what I tell yuh!

FLORA: Tell me what?

JAKE: I ain't been off th' po'ch.

FLORA: Huh!

JAKE: I ain't been off th' front po'ch! Not since supper! Understand that, now?

FLORA: Jake, honey, you've gone out of you' mind!

JAKE: Maybe so. Never you mind. Just get that straight an' keep it in your haid. I ain't been off the porch of this house since supper.

FLORA: But you sure as God *was* off it! (*He twists her wrist.*) Ouuuu! Stop it, stop it, stop it!

JAKE: Where have I been since supper?

FLORA: Here, here! On th' porch! Fo' God's sake, quit that twistin'!

JAKE: Where have I been?

FLORA: Porch! Porch! Here!

JAKE: Doin' what?

FLORA: *Jake!*

JAKE: Doin' what?

FLORA: Lemme go! Christ, Jake! Let loose! Quit twisting, you'll break my wrist!

JAKE: (*laughing between his teeth*) Doin' what? What doin'? Since supper?

FLORA: (*crying out*) How in hell do I know!

JAKE: 'Cause you was right here with me, all the time, for every second! You an' me, sweetheart, was sittin' here together on th' swing, just swingin' back an' forth every minute since supper! You got that in your haid good now?

FLORA: (*whimpering*) Le'-go!

JAKE: Got it? In your haid good now?

FLORA: Yeh, yeh, yeh—leggo!

JAKE: What was I doin', then?

FLORA: Swinging! For Christ's sake—swingin'! (*He releases her. She whimpers and rubs her wrist but the impression is that the experience was not without pleasure for both parties. She groans and whimpers. He grips her loose curls in his hand and bends her head back. He plants a long wet kiss on her mouth.*)

FLORA: (*whimpering*) Mmmm-hmmmm! Mmmm! Mmmm!

JAKE: (*huskily*) Tha's my swee' baby girl.

FLORA: Mmmmm! Hurt! Hurt!

JAKE: Hurt?

FLORA: Mmmm! Hurt!

JAKE: Kiss?

FLORA: Mmmm!

JAKE: Good?

FLORA: Mmmm . . .

JAKE: Good! Make little room.

FLORA: Too hot!

JAKE: Go on, make little room.

FLORA: Mmmmm . . .

JAKE: Cross patch?

FLORA: Mmmmmm.

JAKE: Whose baby? Big? Sweet?

FLORA: Mmmmm! Hurt!

JAKE: Kiss! (*He lifts her wrist to his lips and makes gobbling sounds.*)

FLORA: (*giggling*) Stop! Silly! Mmmm!

JAKE: What would I do if you was a big piece of cake?

FLORA: Silly.

JAKE: Gobble! Gobble!

FLORA: Oh, you—

JAKE: What would I do if you was angel food cake? Big white piece with lots of nice thick icin'?

FLORA: (*giggling*) Quit!

JAKE: Gobble, gobble, gobble!

FLORA: (*squealing*) Jake!

JAKE: Huh?

FLORA: You *tick*-le!

JAKE: Answer little question!

FLORA: Wh-at?

JAKE: Where I been since supper?

FLORA: Off in the Chevy! (*He instantly seizes the wrist again. She shrieks.*)

JAKE: Where've I been since supper?

FLORA: Po'ch! Swing!

JAKE: Doin' what?

FLORA: *Swingin'!* Oh, Christ, Jake, let loose!

JAKE: Hurt?

FLORA: Mmmmm . . .

JAKE: Good?

FLORA: (*whimpering*) Mmmmm . . .

JAKE: Now you know where I been an' what I been doin' since supper?

FLORA: Yeah . . .

JAKE: Case anybody should ask?

FLORA: Who's going to ast?

JAKE: Never mind who's goin' t' ast, just you know the answers! Uh-huh?

FLORA: Uh-huh. (*lisping babyishly*) This is where you been. Settin' on th' swing since we had supper. Swingin'—back an' fo'th—back an' fo'th. . . . You didn' go off in th' Chevy. (*slowly*) An' you was awf'ly surprised w'en th' syndicate fire broke out! (*Jake slaps her.*) Jake!

JAKE: Everything you said is awright. But don't you get ideas.

FLORA: Ideas?

JAKE: A woman like you's not made to have ideas. Made to be hugged an' squeezed!

FLORA: (*babyishly*) Mmmm. . . .

JAKE: But not for ideas. So don't you have ideas. (*He rises.*) Go out an' get in th' Chevy.

FLORA: We goin to th' fire?

JAKE: No. We ain' goin' no fire. We goin in town an' get us a case a dopes because we're hot an' thirsty.

FLORA: (*vaguely, as she rises*) I lost m' white—kid—purse . . .

JAKE: It's on the seat of th' Chevy whe' you left it.

FLORA: Whe' *you* goin'?

JAKE: I'm goin in t' th' toilet. I'll be right out. (*He goes inside, letting the screen door slam. Flora shuffles to the edge of the steps and stands there with a slight idiotic smile. She begins to descend, letting herself down each time with the same foot, like a child just learning to walk. She stops at the bottom of the steps and stares at the sky, vacantly and raptly, her fingers closing gently around the bruised wrist. Jake can be heard singing inside.*)

> 'My baby don' care fo' rings
> or other expensive things—
> My baby just cares—fo'—me!'

Curtain

Scene II

It is just after noon. The sky is the color of the satin bows on the window curtains—a translucent, innocent blue. Heat devils are shimmering over the flat Delta country and the peaked white front of the house is like a shrill exclamation. Jake's gin is busy; heard like a steady pulse across the road. A delicate lint of cotton is drifting about in the atmosphere.

Jake appears, a large and purposeful man with arms like hams covered with a fuzz of fine blond hair. He is followed by Silva Vicarro who is the Superintendent of the Syndicate Plantation where the fire occurred last night. Vicarro is a rather small and wiry man of dark Latin looks and nature. He wears whipcord breeches, laced boots, and a white undershirt. He has a Roman Catholic medallion on a chain about his neck.

JAKE: (*with the good-natured condescension of a very large man for a small one*) Well, suh, all I got to say is you're a mighty lucky little fellow.

VICARRO: Lucky? In what way?

JAKE: That I can take on a job like this right now! Twenty-seven wagons full of cotton 's a pretty big piece of bus'ness, Mr. Vicarro. (*stopping at the steps*) Baby! (*He bites off a piece of tobacco plug.*) What's yuh firs' name?

VICARRO: Silva.

JAKE: How do you spell it?

VICARRO: S-I-L-V-A.

JAKE: Silva! Like a silver lining! Ev'ry cloud has got a silver lining. What does that come from? The Bible?

VICARRO: (*sitting on the steps*) No. The Mother Goose Book.

JAKE: Well, suh, you sure are lucky that I can do it. If I'd been busy like I was two weeks ago I would 've turned it down. *BABY! COME OUT HERE A MINUTE!* (*There is a vague response from inside.*)

VICARRO: Lucky. Very lucky. (*He lights a cigarette. Flora pushes open the screen door and comes out. She has on her watermelon pink silk dress and is clutching against her body the big white kid purse with her initials on it in big nickel plate.*)

JAKE: (*proudly*) Mr. Vicarro—I want you to meet Mrs. Meighan. Baby, this is a very down-at-the-mouth young fellow I want you to cheer up fo' me. He thinks he's out of luck because his cotton gin burnt down. He's got twenty-seven wagons full of cotton to be ginned out on a hurry-up order from his most impo'tant customers in Mobile. Well, suh, I said to him, Mr. Vicarro, you're to be congratulated —not because it burnt down, but because I happen to be in a situation to take the business over. Now you tell him just how lucky he is!

FLORA: (*nervously*) Well, I guess he don't see how it was lucky to have his gin burned down.

VICARRO: (*acidly*) No, ma'am.

JAKE: (*quickly*) Mr. Vicarro. Some fellows marry a girl when she's little an' tiny. They like a small figure. See? Then, when the girl gets comfo'tably settled down—what does she do? Puts on flesh—of cou'se!

FLORA: (*bashfully*) Jake!

JAKE: Now then! How do they react? Accept it as a matter of cou'se, as something which 'as been ordained by nature? Nope! No, suh, not a bit! They sta't to feeling abused. They think that fate must have a grudge against them because the little woman is not so little as she used to be. Because she's gone an' put on a matronly figure. Well, suh, that's at the root of a lot of domestic trouble. However, Mr. Vicarro, I never made that mistake. When I fell in love with this baby-doll I've got here, she was just the same size then that you see her today.

FLORA: (*crossing shyly to porch rail*) Jake . . .

JAKE: (*grinning*) A woman not large but tremendous! That's how I liked her—tremendous! I told her right off, when I slipped th' ring on her finger, one Satiddy night in a boathouse on Moon Lake—I said to her, Honey, if you take off one single pound of that body—I'm going to quit yuh! I'm going to quit yuh, I said, the minute I notice you've started to take off weight!

FLORA: Aw, Jake—please!

JAKE: I don't want nothing little, not in a woman. I'm not after nothing *petite*, as the Frenchmen call it. This is what I wanted—and what I *got!* Look at her, Mr. Vicarro. Look at her blush! (*He grips the back of Flora's neck and tries to turn her around.*)

FLORA: Aw, quit, Jake! Quit, will yuh?

JAKE: See what a doll she is? (*Flora turns suddenly and spanks him with the kid purse. He cackles and runs down the steps. At the corner of the house, he stops and turns.*) Baby, you keep Mr. Vicarro comfo'table while I'm ginnin' out that twenty-seven wagons full of cotton. Th' good-neighbor policy, Mr. Vicarro. You do me a good turn an' I'll do you a good one! Be see'n' yuh! So long, Baby! (*He walks away with an energetic stride.*)

VICARRO: The good-neighbor policy! (*He sits on the porch steps.*)

FLORA: (*sitting on the swing*) Izzen he out-*ray*-juss! (*She laughs foolishly and puts the purse in her lap. Vicarro stares gloomily across the dancing brilliance of the fields. His lip sticks out like a pouting child's. A rooster crows in the distance.*)

FLORA: I would'n' dare to expose myself like that.

VICARRO: Expose? To what?

FLORA: The sun. I take a terrible burn. I'll never forget the burn I took one time. It was on Moon Lake one Sunday before I was married. I never did like t' go fishin' but this young fellow, one of the Peterson boys, insisted that we go fishin'. Well, he didn't catch nothin' but jus' kep' fishin' an' fishin' an' I set there in th' boat with all that hot sun on me. I said, Stay under the willows. But he would'n' lissen to me, an' sure enough I took such an awful burn I had t' sleep on m' stummick th' nex' three nights.

VICARRO: (*absently*) What did you say? You got sun-burned?

FLORA: Yes. One time on Moon Lake.

VICARRO: That's too bad. You got over it all right?

FLORA: Oh, yes. Finally. Yes.

VICARRO: That must 've been pretty bad.

FLORA: I fell in the lake once, too. Also with one of the Peterson boys. On another fishing trip. That was a wild bunch of boys, those Peterson boys. I never went out with 'em but something happened which made me wish I hadn't. One time, sun-burned. One time, nearly drowned. One time—poison ivy! Well, lookin' back on it, now, we had a good deal of fun in spite of it, though.

VICARRO: The good-neighbor policy, huh? (*He slaps his boot with the riding crop. Then he rises from steps.*)

FLORA: You might as well come up on th' po'ch an' make
you'self as comfo'table as you can.

VICARRO: Uh-huh.

FLORA: I'm not much good at—makin' conversation.

VICARRO: (*finally noticing her*) Now don't you bother to
make conversation for my benefit, Mrs. Meighan. I'm the
type that prefers a quiet understanding. (*Flora laughs uncertainly.*) One thing I always notice about you ladies . . .

FLORA: What's that, Mr. Vicarro?

VICARRO: You always have something in your hands—to hold
onto. Now that kid purse . . .

FLORA: My purse?

VICARRO: You have no reason to keep that purse in your
hands. You're certainly not afraid that I'm going to
snatch it!

FLORA: Oh, God, no! I wassen afraid of that!

VICARRO: That wouldn't be the good-neighbor policy, would
it? But you hold onto that purse because it gives you something to get a grip on. Isn't that right?

FLORA: Yes. I always like to have something in my hands.

VICARRO: Sure you do. You feel what a lot of uncertain things
there are. Gins burn down. The volunteer fire department
don't have decent equipment. Nothing is any protection.
The afternoon sun is hot. It's no protection. The trees are
back of the house. They're no protection. The goods that
dress is made of—is no protection. So what do you do,
Mrs. Meighan? You pick up the white kid purse. It's solid.
It's sure. It's certain. It's something to hold *on* to. You get
what I mean?

FLORA: Yeah. I think I do.

VICARRO: It gives you a feeling of being attached to something. The mother protects the baby? No, no, no—the
baby protects the mother! From being lost and empty and
having nothing but lifeless things in her hands! Maybe you
think there isn't much connection!

FLORA: You'll have to excuse me from thinking. I'm too lazy.

VICARRO: What's your name, Mrs. Meighan?

FLORA: Flora.

VICARRO: Mine is Silva. Something not gold but—Silva!

FLORA: Like a silver dollar?

VICARRO: No, like a silver dime! It's an Italian name. I'm a native of New Orleans.

FLORA: Then it's not sun-burn. You're natcherally dark.

VICARRO: (*raising his undershirt from his belly*) Look at this!

FLORA: Mr. Vicarro!

VICARRO: Just as dark as my arm is!

FLORA: You don't have to show me! I'm not from Missouri!

VICARRO: (*grinning*) Excuse me.

FLORA: (*She laughs nervously.*) Whew! I'm sorry to say we don't have a coke in the house. We meant to get a case of cokes las' night, but what with all the excitement going on—

VICARRO: What excitement was that?

FLORA: Oh, the fire and all.

VICARRO: (*lighting a cigarette*) I shouldn't think you all would of been excited about the fire.

FLORA: A fire is always exciting. After a fire, dogs an' chickens don't sleep. I don't think our chickens got to sleep all night.

VICARRO: No?

FLORA: They cackled an' fussed an' flopped around on the roost—took on something awful! Myself, I couldn't sleep neither. I jus' lay there an' sweated all night long.

VICARRO: On account of th' fire?

FLORA: An' the heat an' mosquitoes. And I was mad at Jake.

VICARRO: Mad at Mr. Meighan? What about?

FLORA: Oh, he went off an' left me settin' here on this ole po'ch last night without a Coca-Cola on the place.

VICARRO: Went off an' left you, did he?

FLORA: Yep. Right after supper. An' when he got back the fire 'd already broke out an' instead of drivin' in to town like he said, he decided to go an' take a look at your burnt-down cotton gin. I got smoke in my eyes an' my nose an' throat. It hurt my sinus an' I was in such a wo'n out, nervous condition, it made me cry. I cried like a baby. Finally took two teaspoons of paregoric. Enough to put an elephant to sleep. But still I stayed awake an' heard them chickens carryin' on out there!

VICARRO: It sounds like you passed a very uncomfortable night.

FLORA: Sounds like? Well, it *was*.

VICARRO: So Mr. Meighan—you say—disappeared after supper? (*There is a pause while Flora looks at him blankly.*)

FLORA: Huh?

VICARRO: You say Mr. Meighan was out of the house for a while after supper? (*Something in his tone makes her aware of her indiscretion.*)

FLORA: Oh—uh—just for a moment.

VICARRO: Just for a moment, huh? How long a moment? (*He stares at her very hard.*)

FLORA: What are you driving at, Mr. Vicarro?

VICARRO: Driving at? Nothing.

FLORA: You're looking at me so funny.

VICARRO: He disappeared for a moment! Is that what he did? How long a moment did he disappear for? Can you remember, Mrs. Meighan?

FLORA: What difference does that make? What's it to you, anyhow?

VICARRO: Why should you mind me asking?

FLORA: You make this sound like I was on trial for something!

VICARRO: Don't you like to pretend like you're a witness?

FLORA: Witness of what, Mr. Vicarro?

VICARRO: Why—for instance—say—a case of arson!

FLORA: (*wetting her lips*) Case of—? What is—arson?

VICARRO: The willful destruction of property by fire. (*He slaps his boots sharply with the riding crop.*)

FLORA: (*startled*) Oh! (*She nervously fingers the purse.*) Well, now, don't you go and be getting any—funny ideas.

VICARRO: Ideas about what, Mrs. Meighan?

FLORA: My husband's disappearin'—after supper. I can explain that.

VICARRO: Can you?

FLORA: Sure I can.

VICARRO: Good! How do you explain it? (*He stares at her. She looks down.*) What's the matter? Can't you collect your thoughts, Mrs. Meighan?

FLORA: No, but—

VICARRO: Your mind's a blank on the subject?

FLORA: Look here, now— (*She squirms on the swing.*)

VICARRO: You find it impossible to remember just what your husband disappeared for after supper? You can't imagine what kind of errand it was that he went out on, can you?

FLORA: No! No, I can't!

VICARRO: But when he returned—let's see . . . The fire had just broken out at the Syndicate Plantation?

FLORA: Mr. Vicarro, I don't have the slightest idear what you could be driving at.

VICARRO: You're a very unsatisfactory witness, Mrs. Meighan.

FLORA: I never can think when people—stare straight at me.

VICARRO: Okay. I'll look away, then. (*He turns his back to her.*) Now does that improve your memory any? Now are you able to concentrate on the question?

FLORA: Huh . . .

VICARRO: No? You're not? (*He turns around again, grinning evilly.*) Well . . . shall we drop the subject?

FLORA: I sure do wish you would.

VICARRO: It's no use crying over a burnt-down gin. This world is built on the principle of tit for tat.

FLORA: What do you mean?

VICARRO: Nothing at all specific. Mind if I . . . ?

FLORA: What?

VICARRO: You want to move over a little an' make some room? (*Flora edges aside on the swing. He sits down with her.*) I like a swing. I've always liked to sit an' rock on a swing. Relaxes you . . . You relaxed?

FLORA: Sure.

VICARRO: No, you're not. Your nerves are all tied up.

FLORA: Well, you made me feel kind of nervous. All of them questions you ast me about the fire.

VICARRO: I didn' ask you questions about the fire. I only asked you about your husband's leaving the house after supper.

FLORA: I explained that to you.

VICARRO: Sure. That's right. You did. The good-neighbor policy. That was a lovely remark your husband made about the good-neighbor policy. I see what he means by that now.

FLORA: He was thinking about President Roosevelt's speech. We sat up an' lissened to it one night last week.

VICARRO: No, I think that he was talking about something closer to home, Mrs. Meighan. You do me a good turn and I'll do you one, that was the way that he put it. You have a piece of cotton on your face. Hold still—I'll pick it off. (*He delicately removes the lint.*) There now.

FLORA: (*nervously*) Thanks.

VICARRO: There's a lot of fine cotton lint floating round in the air.

FLORA: I know there is. It irritates my nose. I think it gets up in my sinus.

VICARRO: Well, you're a delicate woman.

FLORA: Delicate? Me? Oh, no. I'm too big for that.

VICARRO: Your size is part of your delicacy, Mrs. Meighan.

FLORA: How do you mean?

VICARRO: There's a lot of you, but every bit of you is delicate. Choice. Delectable, I might say.

FLORA: Huh?

VICARRO: I mean you're altogether lacking in any—coarseness. You're soft. Fine-fibered. And smooth.

FLORA: Our talk is certainly taking a personal turn.

VICARRO: Yes. You make me think of cotton.

FLORA: Huh?

VICARRO: Cotton!

FLORA: Well! Should I say thanks or something?

VICARRO: No, just smile, Mrs. Meighan. You have an attractive smile. Dimples!

FLORA: No . . .

VICARRO: Yes, you have! Smile, Mrs. Meighan! Come on—smile! (*Flora averts her face, smiling helplessly.*) There now. See? You've got them! (*He delicately touches one of the dimples.*)

FLORA: Please don't touch me. I don't like to be touched.

VICARRO: Then why do you giggle?

FLORA: Can't help it. You make me feel kind of hysterical, Mr. Vicarro. Mr. Vicarro—

VICARRO: Yes?

FLORA: I hope you don't think that Jake was mixed up in that fire. I swear to goodness he never left the front porch. I remember it perfeckly now. We just set here on the swing till the fire broke out and then we drove in town.

VICARRO: To celebrate?

FLORA: No, no, no.

VICARRO: Twenty-seven wagons full of cotton's a pretty big piece of business to fall in your lap like a gift from the gods, Mrs. Meighan.

FLORA: I thought you said that we would drop the subjeck.

VICARRO: You brought it up that time.

FLORA: Well, please don't try to mix me up any more. I swear to goodness the fire had already broke out when he got back.

VICARRO: That's not what you told me a moment ago.

FLORA: You got me all twisted up. We went in town. The fire broke out an' we didn't know about it.

VICARRO: I thought you said it irritated your sinus.

FLORA: Oh, my God, you sure put words in my mouth. Maybe I'd better make us some lemonade.

VICARRO: Don't go to the trouble.

FLORA: I'll go in an' fix it direckly, but right at this moment I'm too weak to get up. I don't know why, but I can't hardly hold my eyes open. They keep falling shut. . . . I think it's a little too crowded, two on a swing. Will you do me a favor an' set back down over there?

VICARRO: Why do you want me to move?

FLORA: It makes too much body heat when we're crowded together.

VICARRO: One body can borrow coolness from another.

FLORA: I always heard that bodies borrowed heat.

VICARRO: Not in this case. I'm cool.

FLORA: You don't seem like it to me.

VICARRO: I'm just as cool as a cucumber. If you don't believe it, touch me.

FLORA: Where?

VICARRO: Anywhere.

FLORA: (*rising with great effort*) Excuse me. I got to go in. (*He pulls her back down.*) What did you do that for?

VICARRO: I don't want to be deprived of your company yet.

FLORA: Mr. Vicarro, you're getting awf'ly familiar.

VICARRO: Haven't you got any fun-loving spirit about you?

FLORA: This isn't fun.

VICARRO: Then why do you giggle?

FLORA: I'm ticklish! Quit switching me, will yuh?

VICARRO: I'm just shooing the flies off.

FLORA: Leave 'em be, then, please. They don't hurt nothin'.

VICARRO: I think you like to be switched.

FLORA: I don't. I wish you'd quit.

VICARRO: You'd like to be switched harder.

FLORA: No, I wouldn't.

VICARRO: That blue mark on your wrist—

FLORA: What about it?

VICARRO: I've got a suspicion.

FLORA: Of what?

VICARRO: It was twisted. By your husband.

FLORA: You're crazy.

VICARRO: Yes, it was. And you liked it.

FLORA: I certainly didn't. Would you mind moving your arm?

VICARRO: Don't be so skittish.

FLORA: Awright. I'll get up then.

VICARRO: Go on.

FLORA: I feel so weak.

VICARRO: Dizzy?

FLORA: A little bit. Yeah. My head's spinning round. I wish you would stop the swing.

VICARRO: It's not swinging much.

FLORA: But even a little's too much.

VICARRO: You're a delicate woman. A pretty big woman, too.

FLORA: So is America. Big.

VICARRO: That's a funny remark.

FLORA: Yeah. I don't know why I made it. My head's so buzzy.

VICARRO: Fuzzy?

FLORA: Fuzzy an'—buzzy . . . Is something on my arm?

VICARRO: No.

FLORA: Then what 're you brushing?

VICARRO: Sweat off.

FLORA: Leave it alone.

VICARRO: Let me wipe it. (*He brushes her arm with a handkerchief.*)

FLORA: (*laughing weakly*) No, please, don't. It feels funny.

VICARRO: How does it feel?

FLORA: It tickles me. All up an' down. You cut it out now. If you don't cut it out I'm going to call.

VICARRO: Call who?

FLORA: I'm going to call that nigger. The nigger that's cutting the grass across the road.

VICARRO: Go on. Call, then.

FLORA: (*weakly*) Hey! Hey, boy!

VICARRO: Can't you call any louder?

FLORA: I feel so funny. What is the matter with me?

VICARRO: You're just relaxing. You're big. A big type of woman. I like you. Don't get so excited.

FLORA: I'm not, but you—

VICARRO: What am I doing?

FLORA: Suspicions. About my husband and ideas you have about me.

VICARRO: Such as what?

FLORA: He burnt your gin down. He didn't. And I'm not a big piece of cotton. (*She pulls herself up.*) I'm going inside.

VICARRO: (*rising*) I think that's a good idea.

FLORA: I said I was. Not you.

VICARRO: Why not me?

FLORA: Inside it might be crowded, with you an' me.

VICARRO: Three's a crowd. We're two.

FLORA: You stay out. Wait here.

VICARRO: What'll you do?

FLORA: I'll make us a pitcher of nice cold lemonade.

VICARRO: Okay. You go on in.

FLORA: What'll you do?

VICARRO: I'll follow.

FLORA: That's what I figured you might be aiming to do. We'll both stay out.

VICARRO: In the sun?

FLORA: We'll sit back down in th' shade. (*He blocks her.*) Don't stand in my way.

VICARRO: You're standing in mine.

FLORA: I'm dizzy.

VICARRO: You ought to lie down.

FLORA: How can I?

VICARRO: Go in.

FLORA: You'd follow me.

VICARRO: What if I did?

FLORA: I'm afraid.

VICARRO: You're starting to cry.

FLORA: I'm afraid!

VICARRO: What of?

FLORA: Of you.

VICARRO: I'm little.

FLORA: I'm dizzy. My knees are so weak they're like water. I've got to sit down.

VICARRO: Go in.

FLORA: I can't.

VICARRO: Why not?

FLORA: You'd follow.

VICARRO: Would that be so awful?

FLORA: You've got a mean look in your eyes and I don't like the whip. Honest to God he never. He didn't, I swear!

VICARRO: Do what?

FLORA: The fire . . .

VICARRO: Go on.

FLORA: Please don't!

VICARRO: Don't what?

FLORA: Put it down. The whip, please put it down. Leave it out here on the porch.

VICARRO: What are you scared of?

FLORA: You.

VICARRO: Go on. (*She turns helplessly and moves to the screen. He pulls it open.*)

FLORA: Don't follow. Please don't follow! (*She sways uncertainly. He presses his hand against her. She moves inside. He follows. The door is shut quietly. The gin pumps slowly and steadily across the road. From inside the house there is a wild and despairing cry. A door is slammed. The cry is repeated more faintly.*)

Curtain

Scene III

It is about nine o'clock the same evening. Although the sky behind the house is a dusky rose color, a full September moon of almost garish intensity gives the front of the house a ghostly brilliance. Dogs are howling like demons across the prostrate fields of the Delta.

The front porch of the Meighans is empty.

After a moment the screen door is pushed slowly open and Flora Meighan emerges gradually. Her appearance is ravaged. Her eyes have a vacant limpidity in the moonlight, her lips are slightly apart. She moves with her hands stretched gropingly before her till she has reached a pillar of the porch. There she stops and stands moaning a little. Her hair hangs loose and disordered. The upper part of her body is unclothed except for a torn pink band about her breasts. Dark streaks are visible on the bare shoulders and arms and there is a large discoloration along one cheek. A dark trickle, now congealed, descends from one corner of her mouth. These more apparent tokens she covers with one hand when Jake comes up on the porch. He is now heard approaching, singing to himself.

JAKE: By the light—by the light—by the light—Of the silvery mo-o-on! (*Instinctively Flora draws back into the sharply etched shadow from the porch roof. Jake is too tired and triumphant to notice her appearance.*) How's a baby? (*Flora utters a moaning grunt.*) Tired? Too tired t' talk? Well, that's how I feel. Too tired t' talk. Too goddam tired t' speak a friggin' word! (*He lets himself down on the steps, groaning and without giving Flora more than a glance.*) Twenty-seven wagons full of cotton. That's how much I've ginned since ten this mawnin'. A man-size job.

FLORA: (*huskily*) Uh-huh. . . . A man-size—job. . . .

JAKE: *Twen*-ty *sev*-en *wa*-gons *full* of *cot*-ton!

FLORA: (*senselessly repeating*) *Twen*-ty *sev*-en *wa*-gons *full* of *cot*-ton (*A dog howls. Flora utters a breathless laugh.*)

JAKE: What're you laughin' at, honey? Not at me, I hope.

FLORA: No. . . .

JAKE: That's good. The job that I've turned out is nothing to laugh at. I drove that pack of niggers like a mule-skinner. They don't have a brain in their bodies. All they got is bodies. You got to drive, drive, drive. I don't even see how niggers eat without somebody to tell them to put the food in their moufs! (*She laughs again, like water spilling out of her mouth.*) Huh! You got a laugh like a— Christ. A terrific day's work I finished.

FLORA: (*slowly*) I would'n' brag—about it. . . .

JAKE: I'm not braggin' about it, I'm just sayin' I done a big day's work, I'm all wo'n out an' I want a little appreciation, not cross speeches. Honey. . . .

FLORA: I'm not—(*She laughs again.*)—makin' cross speeches.

JAKE: To take on a big piece of work an' finish it up an' mention the fack that it's finished I wouldn't call braggin'.

FLORA: You're not the only one's—done a big day's—work.

JAKE: Who else that you know of? (*There is a pause.*)

FLORA: Maybe you think that I had an easy time. (*Her laughter spills out again.*)

JAKE: You're laughin' like you been on a goddam jag. (*Flora laughs.*) What did you get pissed on? Roach poison or citronella? I think I make it pretty easy for you, workin' like a mule-skinner so you can hire you a nigger to do the wash an' take the house-work on. An elephant woman who acks as frail as a kitten, that's the kind of a woman I got on m' hands.

FLORA: Sure. . . . (*She laughs.*) You make it easy!

JAKE: I've yet t' see you lift a little finger. Even gotten too lazy t' put you' things on. Round the house ha'f naked all th' time. Y' live in a cloud. All you can think of is "Give me a Coca-Cola!" Well, you better look out. They got a new bureau in the guvamint files. It's called U.W. Stands for Useless Wimmen. Tha's secret plans on foot t' have 'em shot! (*He laughs at his joke.*)

FLORA: Secret—plans—on foot?

JAKE: T' have 'em *shot.*

FLORA: That's good. I'm glad t' hear it. (*She laughs again.*)

JAKE: I come home tired an' you cain't wait t' peck at me. What 're you cross about now?

FLORA: I think it was a mistake.

JAKE: What was a mistake?

FLORA: Fo' you t' fool with th' Syndicate—Plantation. . . .

JAKE: I don't know about that. We wuh kind of up-against it, honey. Th' Syndicate buyin' up all th' lan' aroun' here an' turnin' the ole croppers off it without their wages—mighty near busted ev'ry mercantile store in Two Rivers County! An' then they build their own gin to gin their own cotton. It looked for a while like I was stuck up high an' dry. But when the gin burnt down an' Mr. Vicarro decided he'd better throw a little bus'ness my way—I'd say the situation was much improved!

FLORA: (*She laughs weakly.*) Then maybe you don't understand th' good-neighbor—policy.

JAKE: Don't understand it? Why, I'm the boy that invented it.

FLORA: Huh-huh! What an—*invention!* All I can say is—I hope you're satisfied now that you've ginned out—twenty-seven wagons full of—cotton.

JAKE: Vicarro was pretty well pleased w'en he dropped over.

FLORA: Yeah. He was—pretty well—pleased.

JAKE: How did you all get along?

FLORA: We got along jus' fine. Jus' fine an'—dandy.

JAKE: He didn't seem like a such a bad little guy. He takes a sensible attitude.

FLORA: (*laughing helplessly*) He—sure—does!

JAKE: I hope you made him comfo'table in the house?

FLORA: (*giggling*) I made him a pitcher—of nice cold—lemonade!

JAKE: With a little gin in it, huh? That's how you got pissed. A nice cool drink don't sound bad to me right now. Got any left?

FLORA: Not a bit, Mr. Meighan. We drank it *a-a-ll* up! (*She flops onto the swing.*)

JAKE: So you didn't have such a tiresome time after all?

FLORA: No. Not tiresome a bit. I had a nice conversation with Mistuh—Vicarro. . . .

JAKE: What did you all talk about?

FLORA: Th' good-neighbor policy.

JAKE: (*chuckling*) How does he feel about th' good-neighbor policy?

FLORA: Oh—(*She giggles.*)—He thinks it's a—good idea! He says—

JAKE: Huh? (*Flora laughs weakly.*) Says what?

FLORA: Says— (*She goes off into another spasm of laughter.*)

JAKE: What ever he said must've been a panic!

FLORA: He says—(*controlling her spasm*)—he don't think he'll build him a new cotton gin any more. He's gonna let you do a-a-lll his ginnin'—fo' him!

JAKE: I told you he'd take a sensible attitude.

FLORA: Yeah. Tomorrow he plans t' come back—with lots more cotton. Maybe another twenty-seven wagons.

JAKE: Yeah?

FLORA: An' while you're ginnin' it out—he'll have me entertain him with—nice lemonade! (*She has another fit of giggles.*)

JAKE: The more I hear about that lemonade the better I like it. Lemonade highballs, huh? Mr. Thomas Collins?

FLORA: I guess it's—gonna go on fo'—th' rest of th'—summer. . . .

JAKE: (*rising and stretching happily*) Well, it'll . . . it'll soon be fall. Cooler nights comin' on.

FLORA: I don't know that that will put a—stop to it—though. . . .

JAKE: (*obliviously*) The air feels cooler already. You shouldn't be settin' out here without you' shirt on, honey. A change in the air can give you a mighty bad cold.

FLORA: I couldn't stan' nothin' on me—nex' to my—skin.

JAKE: It ain't the heat that gives you all them hives, it's too much liquor. Grog-blossoms, that's what you got! I'm goin' inside to the toilet. When I come out— (*He opens the screen door and goes in.*)—We'll drive in town an' see what's at th' movies. You go hop in the Chevy! (*Flora laughs to herself. She slowly opens the huge kid purse and removes a wad of Kleenex. She touches herself tenderly here and there, giggling breathlessly.*)

FLORA: (*aloud*) I really oughtn' t' have a white kid purse. It's wadded full of—Kleenex—to make it big—like a baby! Big—in my arms—like a baby!

JAKE: (*from inside*) What did you say, Baby?

FLORA: (*dragging herself up by the chain of the swing*) I'm not—Baby. Mama! Ma! That's—me. . . . (*Cradling the big white purse in her arms, she advances slowly and tenderly to the edge of the porch. The moon shines full on her smiling and ravaged face. She begins to rock and sway gently, rocking the purse in her arms and crooning.*)

> Rock-a-bye Baby—in uh tree-tops!
> If a wind blows—a cradle will rock! (*She descends a step.*)
> If a bough bends—a baby will fall! (*She descends another step.*)
> Down will come Baby—cradle—an'—all! (*She laughs and stares raptly and vacantly up at the moon.*)

Curtain

The Lady of Larkspur Lotion *

CHARACTERS

MRS. HARDWICKE-MOORE.
MRS. WIRE.
THE WRITER.

SCENE: *A wretchedly furnished room in the French Quarter of New Orleans. There are no windows, the room being a cubicle partitioned off from several others by imitation walls. A small slanting skylight admits the late and unencouraging day. There is a tall, black armoire, whose doors contain cracked mirrors, a swinging electric bulb, a black and graceless dresser, an awful picture of a Roman Saint and over the bed a coat-of-arms in a frame.*

Mrs. Hardwicke-Moore, a dyed-blonde woman of forty, is seated passively on the edge of the bed as though she could think of nothing better to do.

There is a rap at the door.

MRS. HARDWICKE-MOORE: (*in a sharp, affected tone*) Who is at the door, please?

MRS. WIRE: (*from outside, bluntly*) Me! (*Her face expressing a momentary panic, Mrs. Hardwicke-Moore rises stiffly.*)

MRS. HARDWICKE-MOORE: Oh. . . . Mrs. Wire. Come in. (*The landlady enters, a heavy, slovenly woman of fifty.*) I was just going to drop in your room to speak to you about something.

MRS. WIRE: Yeah? What about?

MRS. HARDWICKE-MOORE: (*humorously, but rather painfully smiling*) Mrs. Wire, I'm sorry to say that I just don't consider these cockroaches to be the most desirable kind of room-mates—do you?

MRS. WIRE: Cockroaches, huh?

MRS. HARDWICKE-MOORE: Yes. Precisely. Now I have had very little experience with cockroaches in my life but the

---

*Larkspur Lotion is a common treatment for body vermin.

329

few that I've seen before have been the pedestrian kind, the kind that *walk*. These, Mrs. Wire, appear to be *flying* cockroaches! I was shocked, in fact I was literally stunned, when one of them took off the floor and started to whiz through the air, around and around in a circle, just missing my face by barely a couple of inches. Mrs. Wire, I sat down on the edge of this bed and *wept*, I was just so shocked and disgusted! Imagine! Flying cockroaches, something I never dreamed to be in existence, whizzing around and around and around in front of my face! Why, Mrs. Wire, I want you to know—

MRS. WIRE: (*interrupting*) Flying cockroaches are nothing to be surprised at. They have them all over, even uptown they have them. But that ain't what I wanted to—

MRS. HARDWICKE-MOORE: (*interrupting*) That may be true, Mrs. Wire, but I may as well tell you that I have a horror of roaches, even the plain old-fashioned, pedestrian kind, and as for this type that flies—! If I'm going to stay on here these flying cockroaches have got to be gotten rid of and gotten rid of at *once!*

MRS. WIRE: Now how'm I going to stop them flying cockroaches from coming in through the windows? But that, however, is not what I—

MRS. HARDWICKE-MOORE: (*interrupting*) I don't know *how*, Mrs. Wire, but there certainly must be a method. All I know is they must be gotten rid of before I will sleep here one more night, Mrs. Wire. Why, if I woke up in the night and found one on my bed, I'd have a convulsion, I swear to goodness I'd simply *die* of convulsions!

MRS. WIRE: If you'll excuse me for sayin' so, Mrs. Hardshell-Moore, you're much more likely to die from over-drinkin' than cockroach convulsions! (*She seizes a bottle from the dresser.*) What's this here? Larkspur Lotion! *Well!*

MRS. HARDWICKE-MOORE: (*flushing*) I use it to take the old polish off my nails.

MRS. WIRE: Very fastidious, yes!

MRS. HARDWICKE-MOORE: What do you mean?

MRS. WIRE: There ain't an old house in the Quarter that don't have roaches.

MRS. HARDWICKE-MOORE: But not in such enormous quantities, do they? I tell you this place is actually crawling with them!

MRS. WIRE: It ain't as bad as all that. And by the way, you ain't yet paid me the rest of this week's rent. I don't want to get you off the subjeck of roaches, but, nevertheless, I want to colleck that money.

MRS. HARDWICKE-MOORE: I'll pay you the rest of the rent as soon as you've exterminated these roaches!

MRS. WIRE: You'll have to pay me the rent right away or get out.

MRS. HARDWICKE-MOORE: I intend to get out unless these *roaches* get out!

MRS. WIRE: Then get out then and quit just talking about it!

MRS. HARDWICKE-MOORE: You must be out of your mind, I can't get out right now!

MRS. WIRE: Then what did you mean about roaches?

MRS. HARDWICKE-MOORE: I meant what I said about roaches, they are not, in my opinion, the most desirable room-mates!

MRS. WIRE: Okay! Don't room with them! Pack your stuff and move where they don't have roaches!

MRS. HARDWICKE-MOORE: You mean that you *insist* upon having the roaches?

MRS. WIRE: No, I mean I insist upon having the rent you owe me.

MRS. HARDWICKE-MOORE: Right at the moment that is out of the question.

MRS. WIRE: Out of the question, is it?

MRS. HARDWICKE-MOORE: Yes, and I'll tell you why! The quarterly payments I receive from the man who is taking care of the rubber plantation have not been forwarded yet. I've been expecting them to come in for several weeks now but in the letter that I received this morning it seems there has been some little misunderstanding about the last year's taxes and—

MRS. WIRE: Oh, now stop it, I've heard enough of that goddam rubber plantation! The Brazilian rubber plantation! You think I've been in this business seventeen years without learning nothing about your kind of women?

MRS. HARDWICKE-MOORE: (*stiffly*) What is the implication in
that remark?

MRS. WIRE: I suppose the men that you have in here nights
come in to discuss the Brazilian rubber plantation?

MRS. HARDWICKE-MOORE: You must be crazy to say such a
thing as that!

MRS. WIRE: I hear what I hear an' I know what's going on!

MRS. HARDWICKE-MOORE: I know you spy, I know you listen
at doors!

MRS. WIRE: I never spy and I never listen at doors! The first
thing a landlady in the French Quarter learns is not to *see*
and not to *hear* but only collect your *money!* As long as that
comes in—okay, I'm blind, I'm deaf, I'm dumb! But soon
as it stops, I recover my hearing and also my sight and also
the use of my voice. If necessary I go to the phone and call
up the chief of police who happens to be an in-law of my
sister's! I heard last night that argument over money.

MRS. HARDWICKE-MOORE: What argument? What money?

MRS. WIRE: He shouted so loud I had to shut the front
window to keep the noise from carrying out on the
streets! I heard no mention of any Brazilian plantation! But
plenty of other things were plainly referred to in that little
midnight conversation you had! Larkspur Lotion—to take
the polish off nails! Am I in my infancy, am I? That's on
a par with the wonderful *rubber* plantation! (*The door is
thrown open. The Writer, wearing an ancient purple bathrobe,
enters.*)

WRITER: Stop!

MRS. WIRE: *Oh!* It's *you!*

WRITER: Stop persecuting this woman!

MRS. WIRE: The second Mr. Shakespeare enters the scene!

WRITER: I heard your demon howling in my sleep!

MRS. WIRE: *Sleep?* Ho-*ho!* I think that what you *mean* is your
drunken stupor!

WRITER: I rest because of my illness! Have I no right—

MRS. WIRE: (*interrupting*) Illness—*alcoholic!* Don't try to pull
that beautiful wool over my eyes. I'm glad you come in
now. Now I repeat for your benefit what I just said to this
woman. I'm *done* with *dead beats!* Now is that plain to yuh?
Completely fed-up with all you Quarter rats, half-breeds,

drunkards, degenerates, who try to get by on promises, lies, delusions!

MRS. HARDWICKE-MOORE: (*covering her ears*) *Oh, please, please, please stop shrieking!* It's not necessary!

MRS. WIRE: (*turning on Mrs. Hardwicke-Moore*) You with your Brazilian rubber plantation. That coat-of-arms on the wall that you got from the junk-shop—the woman who sold it *told* me! One of the Hapsburgs! Yes! A titled lady! *The Lady of Larkspur Lotion! There's* your *title!* (*Mrs. Hardwicke-Moore cries out wildly and flings herself face down on the sagging bed.*)

WRITER: (*with a pitying gesture*) Stop badgering this unfortunate little woman! Is there no mercy left in the world anymore? What has become of compassion and understanding? Where have they all gone to? Where's God? Where's Christ? (*He leans trembling against the armoire.*) What if there *is* no Brazilian rubber plantation?

MRS. HARDWICKE-MOORE: (*sitting passionately erect*) I tell you there is, there *is!* (*Her throat is taut with conviction, her head thrown back.*)

WRITER: What if there *is* no rubber king in her life! There *ought* to be rubber kings in her life! Is she to be blamed because it is necessary for her to compensate for the cruel deficiencies of reality by the exercise of a little—what shall I say?—God-given—imagination?

MRS. HARDWICKE-MOORE: (*throwing herself face down on the bed once more*) No, no, no, no, it *isn't*—imagination!

MRS. WIRE: I'll ask you to please stop spitting me in the face those high-flown speeches! You with your 780-page masterpiece—right on a par with the Lady of Larkspur Lotion as far as the use of imagination's concerned!

WRITER: (*in a tired voice*) Ah, well, now, what if I am? Suppose there *is* no 780-page masterpiece in existence. (*He closes his eyes and touches his forehead.*) Supposing there is in existence no masterpiece whatsoever! What of that, Mrs. Wire? But only a few, a very few—vain scribblings—in my old trunk-bottom. . . . Suppose I wanted to be a great artist but lacked the force and the power! Suppose my books fell short of the final chapter, even my verses languished uncompleted! Suppose the curtains of my exalted fancy rose on magnificent dramas—but the house-lights darkened before the curtain fell! Suppose all of these unfortunate things are true! And suppose that I—stumbling from bar to bar, from drink to drink, till I sprawl at last on the lice-infested mattress of this brothel—suppose that I, to make this nightmare bearable for as long as I must continue to be the helpless protagonist of it—suppose that I ornament, illuminate—glorify it! With dreams and fictions and fancies! Such as the existence of a 780-page masterpiece—impending Broadway productions—marvelous volumes of verse in the hands of publishers only waiting for signatures to release them! Suppose that I live in this world of pitiful fiction! What satisfaction can it give you, good woman, to tear it to pieces, to crush it—call it a *lie?* I tell you this—now listen! There are no lies but the lies that are stuffed in the mouth by the hard-knuckled hand of need, the cold iron fist of necessity, Mrs. Wire! So I am a liar, yes! But your world is built on a lie, your world is a hideous fabrication of lies! Lies! Lies! . . . Now I'm tired and I've said my say and I have no money to give you so get away and leave this woman in peace! Leave her alone. Go on, get out, get away! (*He shoves her firmly out the door.*)

MRS. WIRE: (*shouting from the other side*) Tomorrow morning! Money or out you go! Both of you. Both together! 780-page masterpiece and Brazilian rubber plantation! *BALONEY!* (*Slowly the derelict Writer and the derelict woman turn to face each other. The daylight is waning grayly through the skylight. The Writer slowly and stiffly extends his arms in a gesture of helplessness.*)

MRS. HARDWICKE-MOORE: (*turning to avoid his look*) Roaches! Everywhere! Walls, ceiling, floor! The place is infested with them.

WRITER: (*gently*) I know. I suppose there weren't any roaches on the Brazilian rubber plantation.

MRS. HARDWICKE-MOORE: (*warming*) No, of course there weren't. Everything was immaculate always—always. *Immaculate!* The floors were so bright and clean they used to shine like—mirrors!

WRITER: I know. And the windows—I suppose they commanded a very lovely view!

MRS. HARDWICKE-MOORE: Indescribably lovely!

WRITER: How far was it from the Mediterranean?

MRS. HARDWICKE-MOORE: (*dimly*) The Mediterranean? Only a mile or two!

WRITER: On a very clear morning I daresay it was possible to distinguish the white chalk cliffs of Dover? . . . Across the channel?

MRS. HARDWICKE-MOORE: Yes—in very clear weather it *was*. (*The Writer silently passes her a pint bottle of whisky.*) Thank you, Mr.—?

WRITER: Chekhov! Anton Pavlovitch Chekhov!

MRS. HARDWICKE-MOORE: (*smiling with the remnants of coquetry*) Thank you, Mr.—Chekhov.

Curtain

The Last of My Solid Gold Watches

Ce ne peut être que la fin du monde, en avançant.
RIMBAUD

CHARACTERS

MR. CHARLIE COLTON.
A NEGRO, *a porter in the hotel.*
HARPER, *a traveling salesman.*

SCENE: *A hotel room in a Mississippi Delta town. The room has looked the same, with some deterioration, for thirty or forty years. The walls are mustard-colored. There are two windows with dull green blinds, torn slightly, a ceiling-fan, a white iron bed with a pink counterpane, a washstand with rose-buds painted on the pitcher and bowl, and on the wall a colored lithograph of blind-folded Hope with her broken lyre.*

The door opens and Mr. Charlie Colton comes in. He is a legendary character, seventy-eight years old but still "going strong." He is lavish of flesh, superbly massive and with a kingly dignity of bearing. Once he moved with a tidal ease and power. Now he puffs and rumbles; when no one is looking he clasps his hand to his chest and cocks his head to the warning heart inside him. His huge expanse of chest and belly is criss-crossed by multiple gold chains with various little fobs and trinkets suspended from them. On the back of his head is a derby and in his mouth a cigar. This is "Mistuh Charlie"—who sadly but proudly refers to himself as "the last of the Delta drummers." He is followed into the room by a Negro porter, as old as he is—thin and toothless and grizzled. He totes the long orange leather sample cases containing the shoes which Mr. Charlie is selling. He sets them down at the foot of the bed as Mr. Charlie fishes in his pocket for a quarter.

MR. CHARLIE: (*handing the coin to the Negro*) Hyunh!
NEGRO: (*breathlessly*) Thankyseh!

This play is inscribed to Mr. Sidney Greenstreet, for whom the principal character was hopefully conceived.

MR. CHARLIE: Huh! You're too old a darkey to tote them big heavy cases.

NEGRO: (*grinning sadly*) Don't say that, Mistuh Charlie.

MR. CHARLIE: I reckon you'll keep right at it until yuh drop some day.

NEGRO: That's right, Mistuh Charlie. (*Mr. Charlie fishes in his pocket for another quarter and tosses it to the Negro, who crouches and cackles as he receives it.*)

MR. CHARLIE: Hyunh!

NEGRO: Thankyseh, thankyseh!

MR. CHARLIE: Now set that fan in motion an' bring me in some ice-water by an' by!

NEGRO: De fan don' work, Mistuh Charlie.

MR. CHARLIE: Huh! Deterioration! Everything's going down-hill around here lately!

NEGRO: Yes, suh, dat's de troof, Mistuh Charlie, ev'ything's goin' down-hill.

MR. CHARLIE: Who all's registered here of my acquaintance? Any ole-timers in town?

NEGRO: Naw, suh, Mistuh Charlie.

MR. CHARLIE: "Naw-suh-Mistuh-Charlie" 's all I get any more! You mean to say I won't be able to scare up a poker-game?

NEGRO: (*chuckling sadly*) Mistuh Charlie, you's de bes' judge about dat!

MR. CHARLIE: Well, it's mighty slim pickin's these days. Ev'ry time I come in a town there's less of the old and more of the new and by God, nigguh, this new stand of cotton I see around the Delta's not worth pickin' off th' ground! Go down there an' tell that young fellow, Mr. Bob Harper, to drop up here for a drink!

NEGRO: (*withdrawing*) Yes, suh.

MR. CHARLIE: It looks like otherwise I'd be playin' solitaire!

(*The Negro closes the door. Mr. Charlie crosses to the window and raises the blind. The evening is turning faintly blue. He sighs and opens his valise to remove a quart of whisky and some decks of cards which he slaps down on the table. He pauses and clasps his hand over his chest.*)

MR. CHARLIE: (*ominously to himself*) Boom-boom-boom-boom-boom! Here comes th' parade! (*After some moments there comes a rap at the door.*) Come awn in! (*Harper, a salesman of thirty-five, enters. He has never known the "great days of the road" and there is no vestige of grandeur in his manner. He is lean and sallow and has a book of colored comics stuffed in his coat pocket.*)

HARPER: How is the ole war-horse?

MR. CHARLIE: (*heartily*) Mighty fine an' dandy! How's the young squirrel?

HARPER: Okay.

MR. CHARLIE: That's the right answer! Step on in an' pour you'self a drink! Cigar?

HARPER: (*accepting both*) Thanks, Charlie.

MR. CHARLIE: (*staring at his back with distaste*) Why do you carry them comic sheets around with yuh?

HARPER: Gives me a couple of laughs ev'ry once and a while.

MR. CHARLIE: Poverty of imagination! (*Harper laughs a little resentfully.*) You can't tell me there's any real amusement in them things. (*He pulls it out of Harper's coat pocket.*) "Superman," "The Adventures of Tom Tyler!" Huh! None of it's half as fantastic as life itself! When you arrive at my age—which is seventy-eight—you have a perspective of time on earth that astounds you! Literally astounds you! Naw, you say it's not true, all of that couldn't have happened! And for what *reason?* Naw! You begin to wonder. . . . Well . . . You're with Schultz and Werner?

HARPER: That's right, Charlie.

MR. CHARLIE: That concern's comparatively a new one.

HARPER: I don't know about that. They been in th' bus'ness fo' goin' on twenty-five years now, Charlie.

MR. CHARLIE: Infancy! Infancy! You heard this one, Bob? A child in its infancy don't have half as much fun as adults— in their adultery! (*He roars with laughter. Harper grins. Mr. Charlie falls silent abruptly. He would have appreciated a more profound response. He remembers the time when a joke of his would precipitate a tornado. He fills up Harper's glass with whisky.*)

HARPER: Ain't you drinkin'?

MR. CHARLIE: Naw, suh. Quit!

HARPER: How come?

MR. CHARLIE: Stomach! Perforated!

HARPER: Ulcers? (*Mr. Charlie grunts. He bends with difficulty and heaves a sample case onto the bed.*) I had ulcers once.

MR. CHARLIE: *Ev'ry* drinkin' man has ulcers once. Some *twice.*

HARPER: You've fallen off some, ain't you?

MR. CHARLIE: (*opening the sample case*) Twenty-seven pounds I lost since August. (*Harper whistles. Mr. Charlie is fishing among his samples.*) Yay-*ep!* Twenty-seven pounds I lost since August. (*He pulls out an oxford which he regards disdainfully.*) Hmmm. . . . A waste of cow-hide! (*He throws it back in and continues fishing.*) A man of my age an' constitution, Bob—he oughtn't to carry so much of that— adipose tissue! It's— (*He straightens up, red in the face and puffing.*) —a terrible strain—on the *heart!* Hand me that other sample—over yonder. I wan' t' show you a little eyeful of queenly footwear in our new spring line! Some people say that the Cosmopolitan's not abreast of the times! That is an allegation which I deny and which I intend to disprove by the simple display of one little calf-skin slipper! (*opening up the second case*) Here we are, Son! (*fishing among the samples*) You knew ole "Marblehead" Langner in Friar's Point, Mississippi.

HARPER: Ole "Marblehead" Langner? Sure.

MR. CHARLIE: They found him dead in his bath-tub a week ago Satiddy night. *Here's* what I'm lookin' faw!

HARPER: "Marblehead"? Dead?

MR. CHARLIE: *Buried!* Had a Masonic funeral. I helped carry th' casket. Bob, I want you t' look at this Cuban-heel, shawl-tongue, perforated toe, calf-skin Misses' sport-oxford! (*He elevates it worshipfully.*) I want you to look at this shoe —and tell me what you think of it in plain language! (*Harper whistles and bugs his eyes.*) Ain't that a piece of *real* merchandise, you squirrel? Well, suh, I want you t' know—!

HARPER: Charlie, that certainly is a piece of merchandise there!

MR. CHARLIE: Bob, that piece of merchandise is only a small indication—of what our spring line consists of! You don't have to pick up a piece of merchandise like that—with I.S.C. branded on it!—and examine it with the microscope t' find out if it's quality stuff as well as quality *looks!* This ain't a shoe that Mrs. Jones of Hattiesburg, Mississippi, is going to throw back in your face a couple or three weeks later because it come to pieces like *card*-board in th' first *rain!* No, suh—I want you to know! We got some pretty fast-movers in our spring line—I'm layin' my samples out down there in th' lobby first thing in th' mornin'—I'll pack 'em up an' be gone out of town by *noon*— But by the Almighty Jehovah I bet you I'll have to *wire* the office to mail me a bunch of *brand*-new order-books at my next stopping-*off* place, Bob! *Hot* cakes! *That's* what I'm sellin'! (*He returns exhaustedly to the sample case and tosses the shoe back in, somewhat disheartened by Harper's vaguely benevolent contemplation of the brass light-fixture. He remembers a time when people's attention could be more securely riveted by talk. He slams the case shut and glances irritably at Harper who is staring very sadly at the brown carpet.*) Well, suh— (*He pours a shot of whisky.*) It was a mighty shocking piece of news I received this afternoon.

HARPER: (*blowing a smoke ring*) What piece of news was that?

MR. CHARLIE: The news about ole Gus Hamma—one of the old war-horses from *way* back, Bob. He and me an' this boy's daddy, C.C., used t' play poker ev'ry time we hit town together in this here self-same room! Well, suh, I want you t' know—

HARPER: (*screwing up his forehead*) I think I heard about that. Didn't he have a stroke or something a few months ago?

MR. CHARLIE: He *did*. An' partly *recovered*.

HARPER: Yeah? Last I heard he had t' be fed with a spoon.

MR. CHARLIE: (*quickly*) He did an' he partly recovered! He's been goin' round, y'know, in one of them chairs with a 'lectric motor on it. Goes chug-chug-chuggin' along th' road with th' butt of a cigar in his mouth. Well, suh, yestuddy in Blue Mountain, as I go out the Elks' Club door I pass him comin' in, bein' helped by th' nigguh— "Hello! Hiyuh, Gus!" That was at six-fifteen. Just half an hour later Carter Bowman stepped inside the hotel lobby where I was packin' up my sample cases an' give me the information that ole Gus Hamma had just now burnt himself to death in the Elks' Club lounge!

HARPER: (*involuntarily grinning*) What uh yuh talkin' about?

MR. CHARLIE: Yes, suh, the ole war-horse had fallen asleep with that nickel cigar in his mouth—set his clothes on fire—and burnt himself right up like a piece of paper!

HARPER: I don't believe yuh!

MR. CHARLIE: Now, why on earth would I be lyin' to yuh about a thing like that? He burnt himself right up like a piece of paper!

HARPER: Well, ain't that a bitch of a way for a man to go?

MR. CHARLIE: *One* way—*another* way—! (*gravely*) Maybe you don't *know* it—but all of us ole-timers, Bob, are disappearin' *fast!* We all gotta quit th' road one time or another. Me, I reckon I'm pretty nearly the last of th' Delta drummers!

HARPER: (*restively squirming and glancing at his watch*) The last—of th' Delta drummers! How long you been on th' road?

MR. CHARLIE: Fawty-six yeahs in Mahch!

HARPER: I don't believe yuh.

MR. CHARLIE: Why would I tell you a lie about something like that? No, suh, I want you t' know— I want you t' know— Hmmm. . . . I lost a mighty good customer this week.

HARPER: (*with total disinterest, adjusting the crotch of his trousers*) How's that, Charlie?

MR. CHARLIE: (*grimly*) Ole Ben Summers—Friar's Point, Mississippi . . . Fell over dead like a bolt of lightning had struck him just as he went to pour himself a drink at the Cotton Planters' Cotillion!

HARPER: Ain't that terrible, though! What was the trouble?

MR. CHARLIE: Mortality, that was the trouble! Some people think that millions now living are never going to *die*. I don't think that—I think it's a misapprehension not borne out by the facts! We go like flies when we come to the end of the summer . . . And who is going to prevent it? (*He becomes depressed.*) Who—is going—to prevent it! (*He nods gravely.*) The road is changed. The shoe industry is changed. These times are—revolution! (*He rises and moves to the window.*) I don't like the way that it looks. You can take it from me—the world that I used to know—the world

that this boy's father used t' know—the world we belonged
to, us old time war-horses!—is slipping and sliding away
from under our shoes. Who is going to prevent it? The ALL
LEATHER slogan don't sell shoes any more. The stuff that
a shoe's made of is not what's going to sell it any more!
No! STYLE! SMARTNESS! APPEARANCE! That's what
counts with the modern shoe-purchaser, Bob! But try an'
tell your style department that. Why, I remember the time
when all I had to do was lay out my samples down there in
the lobby. Open up my order-book an' write out orders
until my fingers *ached!* A *sales*-talk was not *necessary.* A store
was a place where people sold merchandise and to sell merchandise the retail-dealer had to obtain it from the wholesale manufacturer, Bob! Where they get merchandise now I
do not pretend to know. But it don't look like they buy it
from wholesale dealers! Out of the air—I guess it materializes! Or maybe stores don't *sell* stuff any more! Maybe I'm
living in a world of illusion! I recognize that possibility, too!

HARPER: (*casually, removing the comic paper from his pocket*)
Yep—yep. You must have witnessed some changes.

MR. CHARLIE: Changes? A mild expression. Young man—I
have witnessed—a REVOLUTION! (*Harper has opened his
comic paper but Mr. Charlie doesn't notice, for now his per-
oration is really addressed to himself.*) Yes, a *revolution!* The
atmosphere that I *breathe* is not the same! Ah, well—I'm an
old war-horse. (*He opens his coat and lifts the multiple
golden chains from his vest. An amazing number of watches
rise into view. Softly, proudly he speaks.*) Looky here, young
fellow! You ever seen a man with this many watches? How
did I *acquire* this many time-pieces? (*Harper has seen them
before. He glances above the comic sheet with affected amazement.*) At every one of the annual sales conventions of the
Cosmopolitan Shoe Company in St. Louis a seventeen-
jewel, solid-gold, Swiss-movement Hamilton watch is presented to the ranking salesman of the year! Fifteen of those
watches have been awarded to me! I think that represents
something! I think that's *something* in the way of achievement! . . . Don't *you?*

HARPER: Yes, *siree!* You bet I *do,* Mistuh Charlie! (*He chuckles at a remark in the comic sheet. Mr. Charlie sticks out his*

lips with a grunt of disgust and snatches the comic sheet from the young man's hands.)

MR. CHARLIE: Young man—I'm talkin' to *you*, I'm talkin' for your *benefit*. And I expect the courtesy of your attention until I am through! I may be an old war-horse. I may have received—the last of my solid gold watches . . . But just the same—good manners are still a part of the road's tradition. And part of the *South's* tradition. Only a young peckerwood would look at the comics when old Charlie Colton is talking.

HARPER: (*taking another drink*) Excuse me, Charlie. I got a lot on my mind. I got some business to attend to directly.

MR. CHARLIE: And directly you shall attend to it! I just want you to know what I think of this new world of yours! I'm not one of those that go howling about a Communist being stuck in the White House now! I don't say that Washington's been took over by Reds! I don't say all of the wealth of the country is in the hands of the Jews! I like the Jews and I'm a friend to the niggers! I *do* say *this*—however. . . . The world I knew is gone—gone—gone with the wind! My pockets are full of watches which tell me that my time's just about over! (*A look of great trouble and bewilderment appears on his massive face. The rather noble tone of his speech slackens into a senile complaint.*) All of them— pigs that was slaughtered—carcasses dumped in the river! Farmers receivin' payment *not* t' grow wheat an' corn an' *not* t' plant cotton! All of these alphabet letters that's sprung up all about me! Meaning—unknown—to men of my generation! The rudeness—the lack of respect—the newspapers full of strange items! The terrible—fast—dark— rush of events in the world! Toward what and where and why! . . . I don't pretend to have any knowledge of now! I only say—and I say this very humbly—I don't understand—what's happened. . . . I'm one of them monsters you see reproduced in museums—out of the dark old ages—the giant *rep*-tiles, and the dino-whatever-you-callems. BUT—I *do* know *this*! And I state it without any shame! Initiative—self-reliance—independence of character! The old sterling qualities that distinguished one man from another—the clay from the potters—the potters from the clay—are— (*kneading the air with his hands*) How is it the old song goes? . . . Gone with the roses of *yesterday!* Yes—with the *wind!*

HARPER: (*whose boredom has increased by leaps and bounds*) You old-timers make one mistake. You only read one side of the vital statistics.

MR. CHARLIE: (*stung*) What do you mean by that?

HARPER: In the papers they print people *dead* in one corner and people *born* in the next and usually *one* just about levels *off* with the *other.*

MR. CHARLIE: Thank you for that information. I happen to be the godfather of several new infants in various points on the road. However, I think you have missed the whole point of what I was saying.

HARPER: I don't think so, Mr. Charlie.

MR. CHARLIE: Oh, yes, you have, young fellow. My point is this: the ALL-LEATHER slogan is not what sells any more—not in shoes and not in humanity, neither! The emphasis isn't on quality. Production, production, yes! But out of inferior goods! *Ersatz*—that's what they're making 'em out of!

HARPER: (*getting up*) That's your opinion because you belong to the past.

MR. CHARLIE: (*furiously*) A piece of impertinence, young man! I expect to be accorded a certain amount of respect by whipper-snappers like you!

HARPER: Hold on, Charlie.

MR. CHARLIE: I belong to—tradition. I am a *legend*. Known from one end of the Delta to the other. From the Peabody hotel in Memphis to Cat-Fish Row in Vicksburg. Mistuh Charlie—*Mistuh Charlie!* Who knows *you?* What do *you* represent? A line of goods of doubtful value, some kike concern in the East! Get out of my room! I'd rather play solitaire, than poker with men who're no more solid characters than the jacks in the deck! (*He opens the door for the young salesman who shrugs and steps out with alacrity. Then he slams the door shut and breathes heavily. The Negro enters with a pitcher of ice water.*)

NEGRO: (*grinning*) What you shoutin' about, Mistuh Charlie?

MR. CHARLIE: I lose my patience sometimes. Nigger—

NEGRO: Yes, suh?

MR. CHARLIE: You remember the way it used to be.

NEGRO: (*gently*) Yes, suh.

MR. CHARLIE: I used to come in town like a conquering hero! Why, my God, nigger—they all but laid red carpets at my feet! Isn't that so?

NEGRO: That's so, Mistuh Charlie.

MR. CHARLIE: This room was like a *throne*-room. My samples laid out over there on green velvet cloth! The ceiling-fan ~~going~~—now *broken!* And over here—the wash-bowl an' pitcher removed and the table-top *loaded* with *liquor!* In and out from the time I arrived till the time I left, the men of the road who knew me, to whom I stood for things commanding respect! Poker—continuous! Shouting, laughing—hilarity! Where have they all gone to?

NEGRO: (*solemnly nodding*) The graveyard is crowded with folks we knew, Mistuh Charlie. It's mighty late in the day!

MR. CHARLIE: Huh! (*He crosses to the window.*) Nigguh, it ain't even late in the day any more— (*He throws up the blind.*) It's NIGHT! (*The space of the window is black.*)

NEGRO: (*softly, with a wise old smile*) Yes, suh . . . *Night*, Mistuh Charlie!

Curtain

Portrait of a Madonna

Respectfully dedicated to the talent and charm of Miss Lillian Gish.

CHARACTERS

MISS LUCRETIA COLLINS.
THE PORTER.
THE ELEVATOR BOY.
THE DOCTOR.
THE NURSE.
MR. ABRAMS.

SCENE: *The living room of a moderate-priced city apartment. The furnishings are old-fashioned and everything is in a state of neglect and disorder. There is a door in the back wall to a bedroom, and on the right to the outside hall.*

MISS COLLINS: Richard! (*The door bursts open and Miss Collins rushes out, distractedly. She is a middle-aged spinster, very slight and hunched of figure with a desiccated face that is flushed with excitement. Her hair is arranged in curls that would become a young girl and she wears a frilly negligee which might have come from an old hope chest of a period considerably earlier.*) No, no, no, no! I don't care if the whole church hears about it! (*She frenziedly snatches up the phone.*) Manager, I've got to speak to the manager! Hurry, oh, please hurry, there's a *man*—! (*wildly aside as if to an invisible figure*) Lost all respect, absolutely no respect! . . . Mr. Abrams? (*in a tense hushed voice*) I don't want any reporters to hear about this but something awful has been going on upstairs. Yes, this is Miss Collins' apartment on the top floor. I've refrained from making any complaint because of my connections with the church. I used to be assistant to the Sunday School superintendent and I once had the primary class. I helped them put on the Christmas pageant. I made the dress for the Virgin and Mother, made robes for the Wise Men. Yes, and now this has happened,

346

I'm not responsible for it, but night after night after night this man has been coming into my apartment and—indulging his senses! Do you understand? Not once but repeatedly, Mr. Abrams! I don't know whether he comes in the door or the window or up the fire-escape or whether there's some secret entrance they know about at the church, but he's here now, in my bedroom, and I can't force him to leave, I'll have to have some assistance! No, he isn't a thief, Mr. Abrams, he comes of a very fine family in Webb, Mississippi, but this woman has ruined his character, she's destroyed his respect for ladies! Mr. Abrams? Mr. Abrams! Oh, goodness! (*She slams up the receiver and looks distractedly about for a moment; then rushes back into the bedroom.*) Richard! (*The door slams shut. After a few moments an old porter enters in drab gray cover-alls. He looks about with a sorrowfully humorous curiosity, then timidly calls.*)

PORTER: Miss Collins? (*The elevator door slams open in hall and the Elevator Boy, wearing a uniform, comes in.*)

ELEVATOR BOY: Where is she?

PORTER: Gone in 'er bedroom.

ELEVATOR BOY: (*grinning*) She got him in there with her?

PORTER: Sounds like it. (*Miss Collins' voice can be heard faintly protesting with the mysterious intruder.*)

ELEVATOR BOY: What'd Abrams tell yuh to do?

PORTER: Stay here an' keep a watch on 'er till they git here.

ELEVATOR BOY: Jesus.

PORTER: Close 'at door.

ELEVATOR BOY: I gotta leave it open a little so I can hear the buzzer. Ain't this place a holy sight though?

PORTER: Don't look like it's had a good cleaning in fifteen or twenty years. I bet it ain't either. Abrams'll bust a blood-vessel when he takes a lookit them walls.

ELEVATOR BOY: How comes it's in this condition?

PORTER: She wouldn't let no one in.

ELEVATOR BOY: Not even the paper-hangers?

PORTER: Naw. Not even the plumbers. The plaster washed down in the bathroom underneath hers an' she admitted her plumbin' had been stopped up. Mr. Abrams had to let the plumber in with this here pass-key when she went out for a while.

ELEVATOR BOY: Holy Jeez. I wunner if she's got money stashed around here. A lotta freaks do stick away big sums of money in ole mattresses an' things.

PORTER: She ain't. She got a monthly pension check or something she always turned over to Mr. Abrams to dole it out to 'er. She tole him that Southern ladies was never brought up to manage finanshul affairs. Lately the checks quit comin'.

ELEVATOR BOY: Yeah?

PORTER: The pension give out or somethin'. Abrams says he got a contribution from the church to keep 'er on here without 'er knowin' about it. She's proud as a peacock's tail in spite of 'er awful appearance.

ELEVATOR BOY: Lissen to 'er in there!

PORTER: What's she sayin'?

ELEVATOR BOY: Apologizin' to him! For callin' the *police!*

PORTER: She thinks police 're comin'?

MISS COLLINS: (*from bedroom*) Stop it, it's got to stop!

ELEVATOR BOY: Fightin' to protect her honor again! What a commotion, no wunner folks are complainin'!

PORTER: (*lighting his pipe*) This here'll be the last time.

ELEVATOR BOY: She's goin' out, huh?

PORTER: (*blowing out the match*) Tonight.

ELEVATOR BOY: Where'll she go?

PORTER: (*slowly moving to the old gramophone*) She'll go to the state asylum.

ELEVATOR BOY: Holy G!

PORTER: Remember this ole number? (*He puts on a record of "I'm Forever Blowing Bubbles."*)

ELEVATOR BOY: Naw. When did that come out?

PORTER: Before your time, sonny boy. Machine needs oilin'. (*He takes out small oil-can and applies oil about the crank and other parts of gramophone.*)

ELEVATOR BOY: How long is the old girl been here?

PORTER: Abrams says she's been livin' here twenty-five, thirty years, since before he got to be manager even.

ELEVATOR BOY: Livin' alone all that time?

PORTER: She had an old mother died of an operation about fifteen years ago. Since then she ain't gone out of the place excep' on Sundays to church or Friday nights to some kind of religious meeting.

ELEVATOR BOY: Got an awful lot of ol' magazines piled aroun' here.

PORTER: She used to collect 'em. She'd go out in back and fish 'em out of the incinerator.

ELEVATOR BOY: What'n hell for?

PORTER: Mr. Abrams says she used to cut out the Campbell soup kids. Them red-tomato-headed kewpie dolls that go with the soup advertisements. You seen 'em, ain'tcha?

ELEVATOR BOY: Uh-huh.

PORTER: She made a collection of 'em. Filled a big lot of scrapbooks with them paper kiddies an' took 'em down to the Children's Hospitals on Xmas Eve an' Easter Sunday, exactly twicet a year. Sounds better, don't it? (*referring to gramophone, which resumes its faint, wheedling music*) Eliminated some a that crankin' noise . . .

ELEVATOR BOY: I didn't know that she'd been nuts *that* long.

PORTER: Who's nuts an' who ain't? If you ask me the world is populated with people that's just as peculiar as she is.

ELEVATOR BOY: Hell. She don't have brain *one*.

PORTER: There's important people in Europe got less'n she's got. Tonight they're takin' her off 'n' lockin' her up. They'd do a lot better to leave 'er go an' lock up some a them maniacs over there. She's harmless; they ain't. They kill millions of people an' go scot free!

ELEVATOR BOY: An ole woman like her is disgusting, though, imaginin' somebody's raped her.

PORTER: Pitiful, not disgusting. Watch out for them cigarette ashes.

ELEVATOR BOY: What's uh diff'rence? So much dust you can't see it. All a this here goes out in the morning, don't it?

PORTER: Uh-huh.

ELEVATOR BOY: I think I'll take a couple a those ole records as curiosities for my girl friend. She's got a portable in 'er bedroom, she says it's better with music!

PORTER: Leave 'em alone. She's still got 'er property rights.

ELEVATOR BOY: Aw, she's got all she wants with them dream-lovers of hers!

PORTER: *Hush up!* (*He makes a warning gesture as Miss Collins enters from bedroom. Her appearance is that of a ravaged woman. She leans exhaustedly in the doorway, hands clasped over her flat, virginal bosom.*)

MISS COLLINS: (*breathlessly*) Oh, Richard—Richard . . .

PORTER: (*coughing*) Miss—Collins.

ELEVATOR BOY: Hello, Miss Collins.

MISS COLLINS: (*just noticing the men*) Goodness! You've arrived already! Mother didn't tell me you were here! (*Self-consciously she touches her ridiculous corkscrew curls with the faded pink ribbon tied through them. Her manner becomes that of a slightly coquettish but prim little Southern belle.*) I must ask you gentlemen to excuse the terrible disorder.

PORTER: That's all right, Miss Collins.

MISS COLLINS: It's the maid's day off. Your No'thern girls receive such excellent domestic training, but in the South it was never considered essential for a girl to have anything but prettiness and charm! (*She laughs girlishly.*) Please do sit down. Is it too close? Would you like a window open?

PORTER: No, Miss Collins.

MISS COLLINS: (*advancing with delicate grace to the sofa*) Mother will bring in something cool after while. . . . Oh, my! (*She touches her forehead.*)

PORTER: (*kindly*) Is anything wrong, Miss Collins?

MISS COLLINS: Oh, no, no, thank you, nothing! My head is a little bit heavy. I'm always a little bit—malarial—this time of year! (*She sways dizzily as she starts to sink down on the sofa.*)

PORTER: (*helping her*) Careful there, Miss Collins.

MISS COLLINS: (*vaguely*) Yes, it is, I hadn't noticed before. (*She peers at them near-sightedly with a hesitant smile.*) You gentlemen have come from the church?

PORTER: No, ma'am. I'm Nick, the porter, Miss Collins, and this boy here is Frank that runs the elevator.

MISS COLLINS: (*stiffening a little*) Oh? . . . I don't understand.

PORTER: (*gently*) Mr. Abrams just asked me to drop in here an' see if you was getting along all right.

MISS COLLINS: Oh! Then he must have informed you of what's been going on in here!

PORTER: He mentioned some kind of—disturbance.

MISS COLLINS: Yes! Isn't it outrageous? But it mustn't go any further, you understand. I mean you mustn't repeat it to other people.

PORTER: No, I wouldn't say nothing.

MISS COLLINS: Not a word of it, please!

ELEVATOR BOY: Is the man still here, Miss Collins?

MISS COLLINS: Oh, no. No, he's gone now.

ELEVATOR BOY: How did he go, out the bedroom window, Miss Collins?

MISS COLLINS: (*vaguely*) Yes. . . .

ELEVATOR BOY: I seen a guy that could do that once. He crawled straight up the side of the building. They called him The Human Fly! Gosh, that's a wonderful publicity angle, Miss Collins—"Beautiful Young Society Lady Raped by The Human Fly!"

PORTER: (*nudging him sharply*) Git back in your cracker box!

MISS COLLINS: Publicity? No! It would be so humiliating! Mr. Abrams surely hasn't reported it to the papers!

PORTER: No, ma'am. Don't listen to this smarty pants.

MISS COLLINS: (*touching her curls*) Will pictures be taken, you think? There's one of him on the mantel.

ELEVATOR BOY: (*going to the mantel*) This one here, Miss Collins?

MISS COLLINS: Yes. Of the Sunday School faculty picnic. I had the little kindergarteners that year and he had the older boys. We rode in the cab of a railroad locomotive from Webb to Crystal Springs. (*She covers her ears with a girlish grimace and toss of her curls.*) Oh, how the steam-whistle blew! Blew! (*giggling*) Blewwwwww! It frightened me so, he put his arm round my shoulders! But she was there, too, though she had no business being. She grabbed his hat and stuck it on the back of her head and they—they *rassled* for it, they actually *rassled* together! Everyone said it was *shameless!* Don't you think that it was?

PORTER: Yes, Miss Collins.

MISS COLLINS: That's the picture, the one in the silver frame up there on the mantel. We cooled the watermelon in the springs and afterwards played games. She hid somewhere and he took ages to find her. It got to be dark and he hadn't found her yet and everyone whispered and giggled about it and finally they came back together—her hangin' on to his arm like a common little strumpet—and Daisy Belle Huston shrieked out, "Look, everybody, the seat of Evelyn's skirt!" It was—covered with—grass-stains! Did you ever hear of anything as outrageous? It didn't faze her, though, she laughed like it was something very, very amusing! Rather *triumphant* she was!

ELEVATOR BOY: Which one is him, Miss Collins?

MISS COLLINS: The tall one in the blue shirt holding onto one of my curls. He loved to play with them.

ELEVATOR BOY: Quite a Romeo—1910 model, huh?

MISS COLLINS: (*vaguely*) Do you? It's nothing, really, but I like the lace on the collar. I said to Mother, "Even if I don't wear it, Mother, it will be *so* nice for my hope-chest!"

ELEVATOR BOY: How was he dressed tonight when he climbed into your balcony, Miss Collins?

MISS COLLINS: Pardon?

ELEVATOR BOY: Did he still wear that nifty little stick-candy-striped blue shirt with the celluloid collar?

MISS COLLINS: He hasn't changed.

ELEVATOR BOY: Oughta be easy to pick him up in that. What color pants did he wear?

MISS COLLINS: (*vaguely*) I don't remember.

ELEVATOR BOY: Maybe he didn't wear any. Shimmied out of 'em on the way up the wall! You could get him on grounds of indecent exposure, Miss Collins!

PORTER: (*grasping his arm*) Cut that or git back in your cage! Understand?

ELEVATOR BOY: (*snickering*) Take it easy. She don't hear a thing.

PORTER: Well, you keep a decent tongue or get to hell out. Miss Collins here is a lady. You understand that?

ELEVATOR BOY: Okay. She's Shoiley Temple.

PORTER: She's a *lady*!

ELEVATOR BOY: Yeah! (*He returns to the gramophone and looks through the records.*)

MISS COLLINS: I really shouldn't have created this disturbance. When the officers come I'll have to explain that to them. But you can understand my feelings, can't you?

PORTER: Sure, Miss Collins.

MISS COLLINS: When men take advantage of common white-trash women who smoke in public there is probably some excuse for it, but when it occurs to a lady who is single and always com-*pletely* above reproach in her moral behavior, there's really nothing to do but call for police protection! Unless of course the girl is fortunate enough to have a father and brothers who can take care of the matter privately without any scandal.

PORTER: Sure. That's right, Miss Collins.

MISS COLLINS: Of course it's bound to cause a great deal of very disagreeable talk. Especially 'round the *church!* Are you gentlemen Episcopalian?

PORTER: No, ma'am. Catholic, Miss Collins.

MISS COLLINS: Oh. Well, I suppose you know in England we're known as the English Catholic church. We have direct Apostolic succession through St. Paul who christened the Early Angles—which is what the original English people were called—and established the English branch of the Catholic church over there. So when you hear ignorant people claim that our church was founded by—by Henry the *Eighth*—that horrible, *lech*erous old man who had so many wives—as many as *Blue*-beard they say!—you can see how ridiculous it *is* and how thoroughly ob*nox*-ious to anybody who really *knows* and under*stands* Church *His*tory!

PORTER: (*comfortingly*) Sure, Miss Collins. Everybody knows that.

MISS COLLINS: I wish they *did*, but they need to be in-*struc*ted! Before he died, my father was Rector at the Church of St. Michael and St. George at Glorious Hill, Mississippi. . . . I've literally grown up right in the very *shad*ow of the Episcopal church. At Pass Christian and Natchez, Biloxi, Gulfport, Port Gibson, Columbus and Glorious Hill! (*with gentle, bewildered sadness*) But you know I sometimes suspect that there has been some kind of spiritual schism in the modern church. These northern dioceses have completely departed from the good old church traditions. For instance our Rector at the Church of the Holy Communion has never darkened my door. It's a fashionable church and he's terribly busy, but even so you'd think he might have time to make a stranger in the congregation feel at home. But he doesn't though! Nobody seems to have the time any more. . . . (*She grows more excited as her mind sinks back into illusion.*) I ought not to mention this, but do you know they actually take a malicious de-*light* over there at the Holy Communion—where I've recently transferred my letter—in what's been going on here at night in this apartment? *Yes!!* (*She laughs wildly and throws up her hands.*) They take a malicious de*LIGHT* in it!! (*She catches her breath and gropes vaguely about her wrapper.*)

PORTER: You lookin' for somethin', Miss Collins?

MISS COLLINS: My—handkerchief . . . (*She is blinking her eyes against tears.*)

PORTER: (*removing a rag from his pocket*) Here. Use this, Miss Collins. It's just a rag but it's clean, except along that edge where I wiped off the phonograph handle.

MISS COLLINS: Thanks. You gentlemen are very kind. Mother will bring in something cool after while. . . .

ELEVATOR BOY: (*placing a record on machine*) This one is got some kind of foreign title. (*The record begins to play Tschaikowsky's "None But the Lonely Heart."*)

MISS COLLINS: (*stuffing the rag daintily in her bosom*) Excuse me, please. Is the weather nice outside?

PORTER: (*huskily*) Yes, it's nice, Miss Collins.

MISS COLLINS: (*dreamily*) So wa'm for this time of year. I wore my little astrakhan cape to service but had to *carry* it *home*, as the weight of it actually seemed *oppres*sive to me. (*Her eyes fall shut.*) The sidewalks seem so dreadfully long in summer. . . .

ELEVATOR BOY: This ain't summer, Miss Collins.

MISS COLLINS: (*dreamily*) I used to think I'd never get to the end of that last block. And that's the block where all the trees went down in the big tornado. The walk is simply *glit*-tering with sunlight. (*pressing her eyelids*) Impossible to shade your face and I *do* perspire so freely! (*She touches her forehead daintily with the rag.*) Not a branch, not a leaf to give you a little protection! You simply *have* to en-*dure* it. Turn your hideous red face away from all the front-porches and walk as fast as you decently *can* till you get *by* them!

Oh, dear, dear Savior, sometimes you're not so lucky and you *meet* people and have to *smile!* You can't *avoid* them unless you cut *across* and that's so *ob*-vious, you know. . . . People would say you're pe*cul*iar. . . . His house is right in the middle of that awful leafless block, *their* house, his and *hers*, and they have an automobile and always get home early and sit on the porch and *watch* me walking by—Oh, Father in Heaven—with a ma*li*cious de*light!* (*She averts her face in remembered torture.*) She has such *penetrating* eyes, they look straight through me. She sees that terrible choking thing in my throat and the pain I have in *here*—(*touching her chest*)—and she points it out and laughs and whispers to him, "There she goes with her shiny big red nose, the poor old maid—that *loves* you!" (*She chokes and hides her face in the rag.*)

PORTER: Maybe you better forget all that, Miss Collins.

MISS COLLINS: Never, never forget it! Never, never! I left my parasol once—the one with long white fringe that belonged to Mother—I left it behind in the cloak-room at the church so I didn't have anything to cover my face with when I walked by, and I couldn't turn back either, with all those people behind me—giggling back of me, poking fun at my clothes! Oh, dear, dear! I had to walk straight forward—past the last elm tree and into that *merciless* sunlight. Oh! It beat down on me, *scorching* me! *Whips!* . . . Oh, Jesus! . . . Over my face and my body! . . . I tried to walk on fast but was dizzy and they kept closer behind me—! I stumbled, I nearly fell, and all of them burst out laughing! My face turned so *horribly* red, it got so red and wet, I knew how ugly it was in all that merciless glare—not a single shadow to hide in! And then—(*Her face contorts with fear.*)—their automobile drove up in front of their house, right where I had to pass by it, and *she* stepped out, in white, so fresh and easy, her stomach round with a baby, the first of the *six*. Oh, God! . . . And he stood smiling behind her, white and easy and cool, and they stood there waiting for me. *Waiting!* I had to keep on. What else could I do? I couldn't turn *back*, could I? *No!* I said dear *God*, strike me *dead!* He didn't, though. I put my head way down like I couldn't see them! You know what she did? She stretched out her hand to *stop* me! And *he*—he stepped up straight in front of me, *smiling*, blocking the walk with his terrible big white body! "*Lucretia*," he said, "Lucretia *Collins!*" I—I tried to speak but I couldn't, the breath went out of my body! I covered my face and—ran! . . . Ran! . . . *Ran!* (*beating the arm of the sofa*) Till I reached the end of the block—and the elm trees—*started* again. . . . Oh, Merciful Christ in Heaven, how *kind* they were! (*She leans back exhaustedly, her hand relaxed on sofa. She pauses and the music ends.*) I said to Mother, "Mother, we've got to leave town!" We *did* after that. And now after all these years he's finally remembered and come *back!* Moved away from that house and the woman and come *here*—I saw him in the back of the church one day. I wasn't sure—but it *was.* The night after that was the night that he first broke in—and indulged his senses with me. . . . He doesn't realize that I've changed, that I can't feel again the way that I used to feel, now that he's got six children by that Cincinnati girl—three in high-school already! Six! Think of that? Six children! I don't know what he'll say when he knows another one's coming! He'll probably blame *me* for it because a man always *does!* In spite of the fact that he *forced* me!

ELEVATOR BOY: (*grinning*) Did you say—a *baby*, Miss Collins?

MISS COLLINS: (*lowering her eyes but speaking with tenderness and pride*) Yes—I'm expecting a *child.*

ELEVATOR BOY: *Jeez!* (*He claps his hand over his mouth and turns away quickly.*)

MISS COLLINS: Even if it's not legitimate, I think it has a perfect right to its father's name—don't you?

PORTER: Yes. Sure, Miss Collins.

MISS COLLINS: A child is innocent and pure. No matter how it's conceived. And it must *not* be made to suffer! So I intend to dispose of the little property Cousin Ethel left me and give the child a private education where it won't come under the evil influence of the Christian church! I want to make sure that it doesn't grow up in the shadow of the cross and then have to walk along blocks that scorch you with terrible sunlight! (*The elevator buzzer sounds from the hall.*)

PORTER: Frank! Somebody wants to come up. (*The Elevator Boy goes out. The elevator door bangs shut. The Porter clears his throat.*) Yes, it'd be better—to go off some place else.

MISS COLLINS: If only I had the courage—but I don't. I've grown so used to it here, and people outside—it's always so *hard* to *face* them!

PORTER: Maybe you won't—have to face nobody, Miss Collins. (*The elevator door clangs open.*)

MISS COLLINS: (*rising fearfully*) Is someone coming—here?

PORTER: You just take it easy, Miss Collins.

MISS COLLINS: If that's the officers coming for Richard, tell them to go away. I've decided not to prosecute Mr. Martin. (*Mr. Abrams enters with the Doctor and the Nurse. The Elevator Boy gawks from the doorway. The Doctor is the weary, professional type, the Nurse hard and efficient. Mr. Abrams is a small, kindly person, sincerely troubled by the situation.*)

MISS COLLINS: (*shrinking back, her voice faltering*) I've decided not to—prosecute Mr. Martin . . .

DOCTOR: Miss Collins?

MR. ABRAMS: (*with attempted heartiness*) Yes, this is the lady you wanted to meet, Dr. White.

DOCTOR: Hmmm. (*briskly to the Nurse*) Go in her bedroom and get a few things together.

NURSE: Yes, sir. (*She goes quickly across to the bedroom.*)

MISS COLLINS: (*fearfully shrinking*) Things?

DOCTOR: Yes, Miss Tyler will help you pack up an overnight bag. (*smiling mechanically*) A strange place always seems more homelike the first few days when we have a few of our little personal articles around us.

MISS COLLINS: A strange—place?

DOCTOR: (*carelessly, making a memorandum*) Don't be disturbed, Miss Collins.

MISS COLLINS: I know! (*excitedly*) You've come from the Holy Communion to place me under arrest! On moral charges!

MR. ABRAMS: Oh, no, Miss Collins, you got the wrong idea. This is a doctor who—

DOCTOR: (*impatiently*) Now, now, you're just going away for a while till things get straightened out. (*He glances at his watch.*) Two-twenty-five! Miss Tyler?

NURSE: Coming!

MISS COLLINS: (*with slow and sad comprehension*) Oh. . . . I'm going away. . . .

MR. ABRAMS: She was always a lady, Doctor, such a perfect lady.

DOCTOR: Yes. No doubt.

MR. ABRAMS: It seems too bad!

MISS COLLINS: Let me—write him a note. A pencil? Please?

MR. ABRAMS: Here, Miss Collins. (*She takes the pencil and crouches over the table. The Nurse comes out with a hard, forced smile, carrying a suitcase.*)

DOCTOR: Ready, Miss Tyler?

NURSE: All ready, Dr. White. (*She goes up to Miss Collins.*) Come along, dear, we can tend to that later!

MR. ABRAMS: (*sharply*) Let her finish the note!

MISS COLLINS: (*straightening with a frightened smile*) It's— finished.

NURSE: All right, dear, come along. (*She propels her firmly toward the door.*)

MISS COLLINS: (*turning suddenly back*) Oh, Mr. Abrams!

MR. ABRAMS: Yes, Miss Collins?

MISS COLLINS: If he should come again—and find me gone— I'd rather you didn't tell him—about the baby. . . . I think its better for *me* to tell him *that*. (*gently smiling*) You know how men *are*, don't you?

MR. ABRAMS: Yes, Miss Collins.

PORTER: Goodbye, Miss Collins. (*The Nurse pulls firmly at her arm. She smiles over her shoulder with a slight apologetic gesture.*)

MISS COLLINS: Mother will bring in—something cool—after while . . . (*She disappears down the hall with the Nurse. The elevator door clangs shut with the metallic sound of a locked cage. The wires hum.*)

MR. ABRAMS: She wrote him a note.

PORTER: What did she write, Mr. Abrams?

MR. ABRAMS: "Dear—Richard. I'm going away for a while. But don't worry, I'll be back. I have a secret to tell you. Love—Lucretia." (*He coughs.*) We got to clear out this stuff an' pile it down in the basement till I find out where it goes.

PORTER: (*dully*) Tonight, Mr. Abrams?

MR. ABRAMS: (*roughly to hide his feeling*) No, no, not tonight, you old fool. Enough has happened tonight! (*then gently*) We can do it tomorrow. Turn out that bedroom light— and close the window. (*Music playing softly becomes audible as the men go out slowly, closing the door, and the light fades out.*)

Curtain

Auto-Da-Fé

A Tragedy in One Act

CHARACTERS

MME. DUVENET
ELOI,* *her son.*

SCENE: *The front porch of an old frame cottage in the Vieux Carré of New Orleans. There are palm or banana trees, one on either side of the porch steps: pots of geraniums and other vivid flowers along the low balustrade. There is an effect of sinister antiquity in the setting, even the flowers suggesting the richness of decay. Not far off on Bourbon Street the lurid procession of bars and hot-spots throws out distance-muted strains of the juke-organs and occasional shouts of laughter. Mme. Duvenet, a frail woman of sixty-seven, is rocking on the porch in the faint, sad glow of an August sunset. Eloi, her son, comes out the screen-door. He is a frail man in his late thirties, a gaunt, ascetic type with feverish dark eyes.*

Mother and son are both fanatics and their speech has something of the quality of poetic or religious incantation.

MME. DUVENET: Why did you speak so crossly to Miss Bordelon?
ELOI: (*standing against the column*) She gets on my nerves.
MME. DUVENET: You take a dislike to every boarder we get.
ELOI: She's not to be trusted. I think she goes in my room.
MME. DUVENET: What makes you think that?
ELOI: I've found some evidence of it.
MME. DUVENET: Well, I can assure you she doesn't go in your room.
ELOI: Somebody goes in my room and roots through my things.

*Pronounced Ell-wah. The part is created for Mr. John Abbott.

360

MME. DUVENET: Nobody ever touches a thing in your room.

ELOI: My room is my own. I don't want anyone in it.

MME. DUVENET: You know very well that I have to go in to clean it.

ELOI: I don't want it cleaned.

MME. DUVENET: You want the room to be filthy?

ELOI: Just don't go in it to clean it or anything else.

MME. DUVENET: How could you live in a room that was never cleaned?

ELOI: I'll clean it myself when cleaning is necessary.

MME. DUVENET: A person would think that you were concealing something.

ELOI: What would I have to conceal?

MME. DUVENET: Nothing that I can imagine. That's why it's so strange that you have such a strong objection to even your mother going into your room.

ELOI: Everyone wants a little privacy, Mother.

MME. DUVENET: (*stiffly*) Your privacy, Eloi, shall be regarded as sacred.

ELOI: Huh.

MME. DUVENET: I'll just allow the filth to accumulate there.

ELOI: (*sharply*) What do you mean by "the filth"?

MME. DUVENET: (*sadly*) The dust and disorder that you would rather live in than have your mother come in to clean it up.

ELOI: Your broom and your dust-pan wouldn't accomplish much. Even the air in this neighborhood is unclean.

MME. DUVENET: It is not as clean as it might be. I love clean window-curtains, I love white linen, I want immaculate, spotless things in a house.

ELOI: Then why don't we move to the new part of town where it's cleaner?

MME. DUVENET: The property in this block has lost all value. We couldn't sell our place for what it would cost us to put new paint on the walls.

ELOI: I don't understand you, Mother. You harp on purity, purity all the time, and yet you're willing to stay in the midst of corruption.

MME. DUVENET: I harp on nothing. I stay here because I have to. And as for corruption, I've never allowed it to touch me.

ELOI: It does, it does. We can't help breathing it here. It gets
in our nostrils and even goes in our blood.

MME. DUVENET: I think you're the one that harps on things
around here. You won't talk quietly. You always fly off on
some tangent and raise your voice and get us all stirred up
for no good reason.

ELOI: I've had about all that I can put up with, Mother.

MME. DUVENET: Then what do you want to do?

ELOI: Move, move. This asthma of mine, in a pure atmosphere uptown where the air is fresher, I know that I
wouldn't have it nearly so often.

MME. DUVENET: I leave it entirely to you. If you can find
someone to make an acceptable offer, I'm willing to move.

ELOI: You don't have the power to move or the will to break
from anything that you're used to. You don't know how
much we've been affected already!

MME. DUVENET: By what, Eloi?

ELOI: This fetid old swamp we live in, the Vieux Carré! Every
imaginable kind of degeneracy springs up here, not at arm's
length, even, but right in our presence!

MME. DUVENET: Now I think you're exaggerating a little.

ELOI: You read the papers, you hear people talk, you walk
past open windows. You can't be entirely unconscious of
what goes on! A woman was horribly mutilated last night.
A man smashed a bottle and twisted the jagged end of it in
her face.

MME. DUVENET: They bring such things on themselves by
their loose behavior.

ELOI: Night after night there are crimes taking place in the
parks.

MME. DUVENET: The parks aren't all in the Quarter.

ELOI: The parks aren't all in the Quarter but decadence is.
This is the primary lesion, the—focal infection, the—chan-
cre! In medical language, it spreads by—metastasis! It
creeps through the capillaries and into the main blood vessels. From there it is spread all through the surrounding tissue! Finally nothing is left outside the decay!

MME. DUVENET: Eloi, you are being unnecessarily violent in
your speech.

ELOI: I feel that strongly about it.

MME. DUVENET: You mustn't allow yourself to sound like a fanatic.

ELOI: You take no stand against it?

MME. DUVENET: You know the stand that I take.

ELOI: I know what ought to be done.

MME. DUVENET: There ought to be legislation to make for reforms.

ELOI: Not only reforms but action really drastic!

MME. DUVENET: I favor that, too, within all practical bounds.

ELOI: Practical, practical. You can't be practical, Mother, and wipe out evil! The town should be razed.

MME. DUVENET: You mean this old section torn down?

ELOI: Condemned and demolished!

MME. DUVENET: That's not a reasonable stand.

ELOI: It's the stand I take.

MME. DUVENET: Then I'm afraid you're not a reasonable person.

ELOI: I have good precedence for it.

MME. DUVENET: What do you mean?

ELOI: All through the Scriptures are cases of cities destroyed by the justice of fire when they got to be nests of foulness!

MME. DUVENET: Eloi, Eloi.

ELOI: Condemn it, I say, and purify it with fire!

MME. DUVENET: You're breathing hoarsely. That's what brings on asthma, over-excitement, not just breathing bad air!

ELOI: (*after a thoughtful pause*) I *am* breathing hoarsely.

MME. DUVENET: Sit down and try to relax.

ELOI: I can't any more.

MME. DUVENET: You'd better go in and take an amytal tablet.

ELOI: I don't want to get to depending too much on drugs. I'm not very well, I'm never well any more.

MME. DUVENET: You never will take the proper care of yourself.

ELOI: I can hardly remember the time when I really felt good.

MME. DUVENET: You've never been quite as strong as I'd like you to be.

ELOI: I seem to have chronic fatigue.

MME. DUVENET: The Duvenet trouble has always been mostly with nerves.

ELOI: Look! I had a sinus infection! You call that nerves?

MME. DUVENET: No, but—

ELOI: Look! This asthma, this choking, this suffocation I have, do you call that nerves?

MME. DUVENET: I never agreed with the doctor about that condition.

ELOI: You hate all doctors, you're rabid on the subject!

MME. DUVENET: I think all healing begins with faith in the spirit.

ELOI: How can I keep on going when I don't sleep?

MME. DUVENET: I think your insomnia's caused by eating at night.

ELOI: It soothes my stomach.

MME. DUVENET: Liquids would serve that purpose!

ELOI: Liquids don't satisfy me.

MME. DUVENET: Well, something digestible, then. A little hot cereal maybe with cocoa or Postum.

ELOI: All that kind of slop is nauseating to look at!

MME. DUVENET: I notice at night you won't keep the covers on you.

ELOI: I can't stand covers in summer.

MME. DUVENET: You've got to have something over your body at night.

ELOI: Oh, Lord, oh, Lord.

MME. DUVENET: Your body perspires and when it's exposed, you catch cold!

ELOI: You're rabid upon the subject of catching cold.

MME. DUVENET: Only because you're unusually prone to colds.

ELOI: (*with curious intensity*) It isn't a cold! It is a sinus infection!

MME. DUVENET: Sinus infection and all catarrhal conditions are caused by the same things as colds!

ELOI: At ten every morning, as regular as clock-work, a headache commences and doesn't let up till late in the afternoon.

MME. DUVENET: Nasal congestion is often the cause of headache.

ELOI: Nasal congestion has nothing to do with this one!

MME. DUVENET: How do you know?

ELOI: It isn't in that location!

MME. DUVENET: Where is it, then?

ELOI: It's here at the base of the skull. And it runs around here.

MME. DUVENET: Around where?

ELOI: Around here!

MME. DUVENET: (*touching his forehead*) Oh! There!

ELOI: No, no, are you blind? I said *here!*

MME. DUVENET: Oh, here!

ELOI: *Yes! Here!*

MME. DUVENET: Well, that could be eye-strain.

ELOI: When I've just changed my glasses?

MME. DUVENET: You read consistently in the wrong kind of light.

ELOI: You seem to think I'm a saboteur of myself.

MME. DUVENET: You actually are.

ELOI: You just don't know. (*darkly*) There's lots of things that you don't know about, Mother.

MME. DUVENET: I've never pretended nor wished to know a great deal. (*They fall into a silence, and Mme. Duvenet rocks slowly back and forth. The light is nearly gone. A distant juke-box can be heard playing "The New San Antonio Rose." She speaks, finally, in a gentle, liturgical tone.*) There are three simple rules I wish that you would observe. One: you should wear under-shirts whenever there's changeable weather! Two: don't sleep without covers, don't kick them off in the night! Three: chew your food, don't gulp it. Eat like a human being and not like a dog! In addition to those three very simple rules of common hygiene, all that you need is faith in spiritual healing! (*Eloi looks at her for a moment in weary desperation. Then he groans aloud and rises from the steps.*) Why that look, and the groan?

ELOI: (*intensely*) You—just—don't—*know!*

MME. DUVENET: Know what?

ELOI: Your world is so simple, you live in a fool's paradise!

MME. DUVENET: Do I indeed!

ELOI: Yes, Mother, you do indeed! I stand in your presence a stranger, a person unknown! I live in a house where nobody knows my name!

MME. DUVENET: You tire me, Eloi, when you become so excited!

ELOI: You just don't know. You rock on the porch and talk about clean white curtains! While I'm all flame, all burning, and no bell rings, nobody gives an alarm!

MME. DUVENET: What are you talking about?

ELOI: Intolerable burden! The conscience of all dirty men!

MME. DUVENET: I don't understand you.

ELOI: How can I speak any plainer?

MME. DUVENET: You go to confession!

ELOI: The priest is a cripple in skirts!

MME. DUVENET: How can you say that!

ELOI: Because I have seen his skirts and his crutches and heard his meaningless mumble through the wall!

MME. DUVENET: Don't speak like that in my presence!

ELOI: It's worn-out magic, it doesn't burn any more!

MME. DUVENET: Burn any more? Why should it!

ELOI: Because there needs to be burning!

MME. DUVENET: For what?

ELOI: (*leaning against the column*) For the sake of burning, for God, for the purification! Oh, God, oh, God. I can't go back in the house, and I can't stay out on the porch! I can't even breathe very freely, I don't know what is about to happen to me!

MME. DUVENET: You're going to bring on an attack. Sit down! Now tell me quietly and calmly what is the matter? What have you had on your mind for the last ten days?

ELOI: How do you know that I've had something on my mind?

MME. DUVENET: You've had something on your mind since a week ago Tuesday.

ELOI: Yes, that's true. I have. I didn't suppose you'd noticed . . .

MME. DUVENET: What happened at the post-office?

ELOI: How did you guess it was there?

MME. DUVENET: Because there is nothing at home to explain your condition.

ELOI: (*leaning back exhaustedly*) No.

MME. DUVENET: Then obviously it was something where you work.

ELOI: Yes . . .

MME. DUVENET: What was it, Eloi? (*Far down the street a tamale vendor cries out in his curiously rich haunting voice: "Re-ed ho-ot, re-ed ho-ot, re-e-ed!" He moves in the other direction and fades from hearing.*) What *was* it, Eloi?

ELOI: A letter.

MME. DUVENET: You got a letter from someone? And that upset you?

ELOI: I didn't get any letter.

MME. DUVENET: Then what did you mean by "a letter"?

ELOI: A letter came into my hands by accident, Mother.

MME. DUVENET: While you were sorting the mail?

ELOI: Yes.

MME. DUVENET: What was there about it to prey on your mind so much?

ELOI: The letter was mailed unsealed, and something fell out.

MME. DUVENET: Something fell out of the unsealed envelope?

ELOI: Yes!

MME. DUVENET: What was it fell out?

ELOI: A picture.

MME. DUVENET: A what?

ELOI: A picture!

MME. DUVENET: What kind of a picture? (*He does not answer. The juke-box starts playing again the same tune with its idiotic gaiety in the distance.*) Eloi, what kind of a picture fell out of the envelope?

ELOI: (*gently and sadly*) Miss Bordelon is standing in the hall and overhearing every word I say.

MME. DUVENET: (*turning sharply*) She's not in the hall.

ELOI: Her ear is clapped to the door!

MME. DUVENET: She's in her bedroom reading.

ELOI: Reading what?

MME. DUVENET: How do I know what she's reading? What difference does it make what she is reading!

ELOI: She keeps a journal of everything said in the house. I feel her taking short-hand notes at the table!

MME. DUVENET: Why, for what purpose, would she take short-hand notes on our conversation?

ELOI: Haven't you heard of hired investigators?

MME. DUVENET: Eloi, you're talking and saying such horrible things!

ELOI: (*gently*) I may be wrong. I may be wrong.

MME. DUVENET: Eloi, of course you're mistaken! Now go on and tell me what you started to say about the picture.

ELOI: A lewd photograph fell out of the envelope.

MME. DUVENET: A what?

ELOI: An indecent picture.

MME. DUVENET: Of whom?

ELOI: Of two naked figures.

MME. DUVENET: Oh! . . . That's all it was?

ELOI: You haven't looked at the picture.

MME. DUVENET: Was it so bad?

ELOI: It passes beyond all description!

MME. DUVENET: As bad as all that?

ELOI: No. Worse. I felt as though something exploded, blew up in my hands, and scalded my face with acid!

MME. DUVENET: Who sent this horrible photograph to you, Eloi?

ELOI: It wasn't to me.

MME. DUVENET: Who was it addressed to?

ELOI: One of those—opulent—antique dealers on—Royal . . .

MME. DUVENET: And who was the sender?

ELOI: A university student.

MME. DUVENET: Isn't the sender liable to prosecution?

ELOI: Of course. And to years in prison.

MME. DUVENET: I see no reason for clemency in such a case.

ELOI: Neither did I.

MME. DUVENET: Then what did you do about it?

ELOI: I haven't done anything yet.

MME. DUVENET: Eloi! You haven't reported it to the authorities yet?

ELOI: I haven't reported it to the authorities yet.

MME. DUVENET: I can't imagine one reason to hesitate!

ELOI: I couldn't proceed without some investigation.

MME. DUVENET: Investigation? Of what?

ELOI: Of all the circumstances around the case.

MME. DUVENET: What circumstances are there to think of but the fact that somebody used the mails for that purpose!

ELOI: The youth of the sender has something to do with the case.

MME. DUVENET: The sender was young?

ELOI: The sender was only nineteen.

MME. DUVENET: And are the sender's parents still alive?

ELOI: Both of them still living and in the city. The sender happens to be an only child.

MME. DUVENET: How do you know these facts about the sender?

ELOI: Because I've conducted a private investigation.

MME. DUVENET: How did you go about that?

ELOI: I called on the sender, I went to the dormitory. We talked in private and everything was discussed. The attitude taken was that I had come for money. That I was intending to hold the letter for blackmail.

MME. DUVENET: How perfectly awful.

ELOI: Of course I had to explain that I was a federal employee who had some obligation to his employers, and that it was really excessively fair on my part to even delay the action that ought to be taken.

MME. DUVENET: The action that has to be taken!

ELOI: And then the sender began to be ugly. Abusive. I can't repeat the charges, the evil suggestions! I ran from the room. I left my hat in the room. I couldn't even go back to pick it up!

MME. DUVENET: Eloi, Eloi. Oh, my dear Eloi. When did this happen, the interview with the sender?

ELOI: The interview was on Friday.

MME. DUVENET: Three days ago. And you haven't done anything yet?

ELOI: I thought and I thought and I couldn't take any action!

MME. DUVENET: Now it's too late.

ELOI: Why do you say it's too late?

MME. DUVENET: You've held the letter too long to take any action.

ELOI: Oh, no, I haven't. I'm not paralyzed any longer.

MME. DUVENET: But if you report on the letter now they will ask why you haven't reported on it sooner!

ELOI: I can explain the responsibility of it!

MME. DUVENET: No, no, it's much better not to do anything now!

ELOI: I've got to do something.

MME. DUVENET: You'd better destroy the letter.

ELOI: And let the offenders go scot free?

MME. DUVENET: What else can you do since you've hesitated so long!

ELOI: There's got to be punishment for it!

MME. DUVENET: Where is the letter?

ELOI: I have it here in my pocket.

MME. DUVENET: You have that thing on your person?

ELOI: My inside pocket.

MME. DUVENET: Oh, Eloi, how stupid, how foolish! Suppose something happened and something like that was found on you while you were unconscious and couldn't explain how you got it.

ELOI: Lower your voice! That woman is listening to us!

MME. DUVENET: Miss Bordelon? No!

ELOI: She is, she is. She's hired as investigator. She claps her ear to the wall when I talk in my sleep!

MME. DUVENET: Eloi, Eloi.

ELOI: They've hired her to spy, to poke and pry in the house!

MME. DUVENET: Who do you mean?

ELOI: The sender, the antique-dealer!

MME. DUVENET: You're talking so wildly you scare me. Eloi, you've got to destroy that letter at once!

ELOI: Destroy it?

MME. DUVENET: Yes!

ELOI: How?

MME. DUVENET: Burn it! (*Eloi rises unsteadily. For a third time the distant juke-organ begins to grind out "The New San Antonio Rose," with its polka rhythm and cries of insane exultation.*)

ELOI: (*faintly*) Yes, yes—burn it!

MME. DUVENET: Burn it this very instant!

ELOI: I'll take it inside to burn it.

MME. DUVENET: No, burn it right here in my presence.

ELOI: You can't look at it.

MME. DUVENET: My God, my God, I would pluck out my eyes before they would look at that picture!

ELOI: (*hoarsely*) I think it is better to go in the kitchen or
  basement.

MME. DUVENET: No, no, Eloi, burn it here! On the porch!

ELOI: Somebody might see.

MME. DUVENET: What of it?

ELOI: It might be thought that it was something of mine.

MME. DUVENET: Eloi, Eloi, take it out and burn it! Do you
  hear me? Burn it now! This instant!

ELOI: Turn your back. I'll take it out of my pocket.

MME. DUVENET: (*turning*) Have you matches, Eloi?

ELOI: (*sadly*) Yes, I have them, Mother.

MME. DUVENET: Very well, then. Burn the letter and burn the
  terrible picture. (*Eloi fumblingly removes some papers from
  his inside pocket. His hand is shaking so that the picture falls
  from his grasp to the porch-steps. Eloi groans as he stoops slowly
  to pick it up.*) Eloi! What is the matter?

ELOI: I—dropped the picture.

MME. DUVENET: Pick it up and set fire to it quickly!

ELOI: Yes . . . (*He strikes a match. His face is livid in the glow
  of the flame and as he stares at the slip of paper, his eyes seem
  to start from his head. He is breathing hoarsely. He draws the
  flame and the paper within one inch of each other but seems
  unable to move them any closer. All at once he utters a strangled cry and lets the match fall.*)

MME. DUVENET: (*turning*) Eloi, you've burned your fingers!

ELOI: Yes!

MME. DUVENET: Oh, come in the kitchen and let me put soda
  on it! (*Eloi turns and goes quickly into the house. She starts to
  follow.*) Go right in the kitchen! We'll put on baking soda!
  (*She reaches for the handle of the screen door. Eloi slips the
  latch into place. Madame Duvenet pulls the door and finds it
  locked.*) Eloi! (*He stares at her through the screen. A note of
  terror comes into her voice.*) Eloi! You've latched the door!
  What are you thinking of, Eloi? (*Eloi backs slowly away and
  out of sight.*) Eloi, Eloi! Come back here and open this
  door! (*A door slams inside the house, and the boarder's voice
  is raised in surprise and anger. Mme. Duvenet is now calling
  frantically.*) Eloi, Eloi! Why have you locked me out? What
  are you doing in there? Open the screen-door, please!
  (*Eloi's voice is raised violently. The woman inside cries out*

with fear. There is a metallic clatter as though a tin object were hurled against a wall. The woman screams; then there is a muffled explosion. Mme. Duvenet claws and beats at the screen door.) Eloi! Eloi! Oh, answer me, Eloi! *(There is a sudden burst of fiery light from the interior of the cottage. It spills through the screen door and out upon the clawing, witch-like figure of the old woman. She screams in panic and turns dizzily about. With stiff, grotesque movements and gestures, she staggers down the porch-steps, and begins to shout hoarsely and despairingly.)* Fire! Fire! The house is on fire, on fire, the house is on fire!

Curtain

Lord Byron's Love Letter

CHARACTERS

THE SPINSTER.
THE OLD WOMAN.
THE MATRON.
THE HUSBAND.

SCENE: *The parlor of a faded old residence in the French Quarter of New Orleans in the late nineteenth century. The shuttered doors of the room open directly upon the sidewalk and the noise of the Mardi Gras festivities can be faintly distinguished. The interior is very dusky. Beside a rose-shaded lamp, the Spinster, a woman of forty, is sewing. In the opposite corner, completely motionless, the Old Woman sits in a black silk dress. The doorbell tinkles.*

SPINSTER: (*rising*) It's probably someone coming to look at the letter.

OLD WOMAN: (*rising on her cane*) Give me time to get out. (*She withdraws gradually behind the curtains. One of her claw-like hands remains visible, holding a curtain slightly open so that she can watch the visitors. The Spinster opens the door and the Matron, a middle-aged woman, walks into the room.*)

SPINSTER: Won't you come in?

MATRON: Thank you.

SPINSTER: You're from out of town?

MATRON: Oh, yes, we're all the way from Milwaukee. We've come for Mardi Gras, my husband and I. (*She suddenly notices a stuffed canary in its tiny pink and ivory cage.*) Oh, this poor little bird in such a tiny cage! It's much too small to keep a canary in!

SPINSTER: It isn't a live canary.

OLD WOMAN: (*from behind the curtains*) No. It's stuffed.

MATRON: Oh. (*She self-consciously touches a stuffed bird on her hat.*) Winston is out there dilly-dallying on the street, afraid he'll miss the parade. The parade comes by here, don't it?

373

SPINSTER: Yes, unfortunately it does.

MATRON: I noticed your sign at the door. Is it true that you have one of Lord Byron's love letters?

SPINSTER: Yes.

MATRON: How very interesting! How did you get it?

SPINSTER: It was written to my grandmother, Irénée Marguerite de Poitevent.

MATRON: How very interesting! Where did she meet Lord Byron?

SPINSTER: On the steps of the Acropolis in Athens.

MATRON: How very, *very* interesting! I didn't know that Lord Byron was ever in Greece.

SPINSTER: Lord Byron spent the final years of his turbulent life in Greece.

OLD WOMAN: (*still behind the curtains*) He was exiled from England!

SPINSTER: Yes, he went into voluntary exile from England.

OLD WOMAN: Because of scandalous gossip in the Regent's court.

SPINSTER: Yes, involving his half-sister!

OLD WOMAN: It was false—completely.

SPINSTER: It was never confirmed.

OLD WOMAN: He was a passionate man but not an evil man.

SPINSTER: Morals are such ambiguous matters, I think.

MATRON: Won't the lady behind the curtains come in?

SPINSTER: You'll have to excuse her. She prefers to stay out.

MATRON: (*stiffly*) Oh. I see. What was Lord Byron doing in Greece, may I ask?

OLD WOMAN: (*proudly*) *Fighting for freedom!*

SPINSTER: Yes, Lord Byron went to Greece to join the forces that fought against the infidels.

OLD WOMAN: He gave his life in defense of the universal cause of freedom!

MATRON: What was that, did she say?

SPINSTER: (*repeating automatically*) He gave his life in defense of the universal cause of freedom.

MATRON: Oh, how very interesting!

OLD WOMAN: Also he swam the Hellespont.

SPINSTER: Yes.

OLD WOMAN: And burned the body of the poet Shelley who was drowned in a storm on the Mediterranean with a volume of Keats in his pocket!

MATRON: (*incredulously*) Pardon?

SPINSTER: (*repeating*) And burned the body of the poet Shelley who was drowned in a storm on the Mediterranean with a volume of Keats in his pocket.

MATRON: Oh. How very, very interesting! Indeed. I'd like so much to have my husband hear it. Do you mind if I just step out for a moment to call him in?

SPINSTER: Please do. (*The Matron steps out quickly, calling, "Winston! Winston!"*)

OLD WOMAN: (*poking her head out for a moment*) Watch them carefully! Keep a sharp eye on them!

SPINSTER: Yes. Be still. (*The Matron returns with her husband who has been drinking and wears a paper cap sprinkled with confetti.*)

MATRON: Winston, remove that cap. Sit down on the sofa. These ladies are going to show us Lord Byron's love letter.

SPINSTER: Shall I proceed?

MATRON: Oh, yes. This—uh—is my husband—Mr. Tutwiler.

SPINSTER: (*coldly*) How do you do.

MATRON: I am *Mrs.* Tutwiler.

SPINSTER: Of course. Please keep your seat.

MATRON: (*nervously*) He's been—celebrating a little.

OLD WOMAN: (*shaking the curtain that conceals her*) Ask him please to be careful with his cigar.

SPINSTER: Oh, that's all right, you may use this bowl for your ashes.

OLD WOMAN: Smoking is such an unnecessary habit!

HUSBAND: Uh?

MATRON: This lady was telling us how her Grandmother happened to meet Lord Byron. In Italy, wasn't it?

SPINSTER: No.

OLD WOMAN: (*firmly*) In Greece, in Athens, on the steps of the Acropolis! We've mentioned that *twice*, I believe. Ariadne, you may read them a passage from the journal first.

SPINSTER: Yes.

OLD WOMAN: But please be careful what you choose to read! (*The Spinster has removed from the secretary a volume wrapped in tissue and tied with a ribbon.*)

SPINSTER: Like many other young American girls of that day and this, my Grandmother went to Europe.

OLD WOMAN: The year before she was going to be presented to society!

MATRON: How old was she?

OLD WOMAN: Sixteen! Barely sixteen! She was very beautiful, too! Please show her the picture, show these people the picture! It's in the front of the journal. (*The Spinster removes the picture from the book and hands it to the Matron.*)

MATRON: (*taking a look*) What a lovely young girl. (*passing it to the Husband*) Don't you think it resembles Agnes a little?

HUSBAND: Uh.

OLD WOMAN: Watch out! Ariadne, you'll have to *watch* that man. I believe he's been drinking. I *do* believe that he's been—

HUSBAND: (*truculently*) Yeah? What is she saying back there?

MATRON: (*touching his arm warningly*) Winston! Be *quiet.*

HUSBAND: Uh!

SPINSTER: (*quickly*) Near the end of her tour, my Grandmother and her Aunt went to Greece, to study the classic remains of the oldest civilization.

OLD WOMAN: (*correcting*) The oldest *European* civilization.

SPINSTER: It was an early morning in April of the year eighteen hundred and—

OLD WOMAN: Twenty-seven!

SPINSTER: Yes. In my Grandmother's journal she mentions—

OLD WOMAN: Read it, read it, *read* it.

MATRON: Yes, *please* read it to us.

SPINSTER: I'm trying to find the place, if you'll just be patient.

MATRON: Certainly, excuse me. (*She punches her Husband who is nodding.*) Winston!

SPINSTER: Ah, here it is.

OLD WOMAN: Be *careful!* Remember where to *stop* at, Ariadne!

SPINSTER: Shhh! (*She adjusts her glasses and seats herself by the lamp.*) "We set out early that morning to inspect the ruins of the Acropolis. I know I shall never forget how extraordinarily pure the atmosphere was that morning. It seemed as though the world were not very old but very, very young, almost as though the world had been newly created. There was a taste of earliness in the air, a feeling of fresh-ness, exhilarating my senses, exalting my spirit. How shall I tell you, dear Diary, the way the sky looked? It was almost as though I had moistened the tip of my pen in a shallow bowl full of milk, so delicate was the blue in the dome of the heavens. The sun was barely up yet, a tentative breeze disturbed the ends of my scarf, the plumes of the marvelous hat which I had bought in Paris and thrilled me with pride whenever I saw them reflected! The papers that morning, we read them over our coffee before we left the hotel, had spoken of possible war, but it seemed unlikely, unreal: noth-ing was real, indeed, but the spell of golden antiquity and rose-colored romance that breathed from this fabulous city."

OLD WOMAN: Skip that part! Get on to where she meets him!

SPINSTER: Yes. . . . (*She turns several pages and continues.*) "Out of the tongues of ancients, the lyrical voices of many long-ago poets who dreamed of the world of ideals, who had in their hearts the pure and absolute image—"

OLD WOMAN: *Skip* that part! Slip down to where—

SPINSTER: Yes! *Here! Do* let us manage without any more *in-terruptions!* "The carriage came to a halt at the foot of the hill and my Aunt, not being too well—"

OLD WOMAN: She had a sore throat that morning.

SPINSTER: "—preferred to remain with the driver while I un-dertook the rather steep climb on foot. As I ascended the long and crumbling flight of old stone steps—"

OLD WOMAN: Yes, yes, that's the place! (*The Spinster looks up in annoyance. The Old Woman's cane taps impatiently be-hind the curtains.*) Go *on*, Ariadne!

SPINSTER: "I could not help observing continually above me a man who walked with a barely perceptible limp—"

OLD WOMAN: (*in hushed wonder*) Yes—Lord Byron!

SPINSTER: "—and as he turned now and then to observe be-neath him the lovely panorama—"

OLD WOMAN: Actually he was watching the girl behind him!

SPINSTER: (*sharply*) Will you *please* let me finish? (*There is no answer from behind the curtains, and she continues to read.*)

"I was irresistibly impressed by the unusual nobility and re-finement of his features!" (*She turns a page.*)

OLD WOMAN: The handsomest man that ever walked the earth! (*She emphasizes the speech with three slow but loud taps of her cane.*)

SPINSTER: (*flurriedly*) "The strength and grace of his throat, like that of a statue, the classic outlines of his profile, the sensitive lips and the slightly dilated nostrils, the dark lock of hair that fell down over his forehead in such a way that—"

OLD WOMAN: (*tapping her cane rapidly*) Skip that, it goes on for pages!

SPINSTER: ". . . When he had reached the very summit of the Acropolis he spread out his arms in a great, magnificent gesture like a young god. Now, thought I to myself, Apollo has come to earth in modern dress."

OLD WOMAN: Go on, skip that, get on to where she *meets* him!

SPINSTER: "Fearing to interrupt his poetic trance, I slackened my pace and pretended to watch the view. I kept my look thus carefully averted until the narrowness of the steps compelled me to move close by him."

OLD WOMAN: Of course he pretended not to see she was coming!

SPINSTER: "Then finally I faced him."

OLD WOMAN: Yes!

SPINSTER: "Our eyes came together!"

OLD WOMAN: Yes! Yes! That's the part!

SPINSTER: "A thing which I don't understand had occurred between us, a flush as of recognition swept through my whole being! Suffused my—"

OLD WOMAN: Yes . . . Yes, that's the part!

SPINSTER: " 'Pardon me,' he exclaimed, 'you have dropped your glove!' And indeed to my surprise I found that I had, and as he returned it to me, his fingers ever so slightly pressed the cups of my palm."

OLD WOMAN: (*hoarsely*) Yes! (*Her bony fingers clutch higher up on the curtain, the other hand also appears, slightly widening the aperture.*)

SPINSTER: "Believe me, dear Diary, I became quite faint and breathless, I almost wondered if I could continue my lonely walk through the ruins. Perhaps I stumbled, perhaps I swayed a little. I leaned for a moment against the side of a column. The sun seemed terribly brilliant, it hurt my eyes. Close behind me I heard that voice again, almost it seemed I could feel his breath on my—"

OLD WOMAN: Stop *there!* That will be quite enough! (*The Spinster closes the journal.*)

MATRON: Oh, is that all?

OLD WOMAN: There's a great deal more that's not to be read to people.

MATRON: Oh.

SPINSTER: I'm sorry. I'll show you the letter.

MATRON: How nice! I'm dying to see it! Winston? *Do* sit *up!*

(*He has nearly fallen asleep. The Spinster produces from the cabinet another small packet which she unfolds. It contains the letter. She hands it to the Matron, who starts to open it.*)

OLD WOMAN: Watch out, watch *out*, that woman can't *open* the letter!

SPINSTER: No, no, please, you mustn't. The contents of the letter are strictly private. I'll hold it over here at a little distance so you can see the writing.

OLD WOMAN: Not too close, she's holding up her glasses! (*The Matron quickly lowers her lorgnette.*)

SPINSTER: Only a short while later Byron was killed.

MATRON: How did he die?

OLD WOMAN: He was killed in action, defending the cause of freedom! (*This is uttered so strongly the husband starts.*)

SPINSTER: When my Grandmother received the news of Lord Byron's death in battle, she retired from the world and remained in complete seclusion for the rest of her life.

MATRON: Tch-tch-tch! How dreadful! I think that was foolish of her. (*The cane taps furiously behind the curtains.*)

SPINSTER: You don't understand. When a life is completed, it ought to be put away. It's like a sonnet. When you've written the final couplet, why go on any further? You only destroy the part that's already written!

OLD WOMAN: Read them the poem, the sonnet your Grandmother wrote to the memory of Lord Byron.

SPINSTER: Would you be interested?

MATRON: We'd adore it—truly!

SPINSTER: It's called *Enchantment.*

MATRON: (*She assumes a rapt expression.*) *Aahhh!*

SPINSTER: (*reciting*)

> "*Un saison enchanté!* I mused. Beguiled
> Seemed Time herself, her erstwhile errant ways
> Briefly forgotten, she stayed here and smiled,
> Caught in a net of blue and golden days."

OLD WOMAN: Not blue and golden—gold and *azure* days!

SPINSTER:

> "Caught in a net—of gold and azure days!
>
> But I lacked wit to see how lightly shoon
> Were Time and you, to vagrancy so used—"

(*The Old Woman begins to accompany in a hoarse undertone. Faint band music can be heard.*)

> "That by the touch of one October moon
> From summer's tranquil spell you might be loosed!"

OLD WOMAN: (*rising stridently with intense feeling above the Spinster's voice*)

> "Think you love is writ on my soul with chalk,
> To be washed off by a few parting tears?
> Then you know not with what slow step I walk
> The barren way of those hibernal years—
>
> My life a vanished interlude, a shell
> Whose walls are your first kiss—and last farewell!"

(*The band, leading the parade, has started down the street, growing rapidly louder. It passes by like the heedless, turbulent years. The Husband, roused from his stupor, lunges to the door.*)

MATRON: What's that, what's that? The *parade?* (*The Husband slaps the paper cap on his head and rushes for the door.*)

HUSBAND: (*at the door*) Come on, Mama, you'll miss it!

SPINSTER: (*quickly*) We usually accept—you understand?—a small sum of money, just anything that you happen to think you can spare.

OLD WOMAN: Stop him! He's gone outside! (*The Husband has escaped to the street. The band blares through the door.*)

SPINSTER: (*extending her hand*) Please—a *dollar* . . .

OLD WOMAN: *Fifty cents!*

SPINSTER: Or a *quarter!*

MATRON: (*paying no attention to them*) Oh, my goodness—
Winston! He's *disappeared* in the *crowd!* Winston—*Winston!*
Excuse me! (*She rushes out onto the door sill.*) *Winston!* Oh,
my goodness gracious, he's off again!

SPINSTER: (*quickly*) We usually accept a little money for the
display of the letter. Whatever you feel that you are able to
give. As a matter of fact it's all that we have to *live* on!

OLD WOMAN: (*loudly*) One dollar!

SPINSTER: Fifty cents—or a quarter!

MATRON: (*oblivious, at the door*) Winston! *Winston!* Heavenly
days. *Goodbye!* (*She rushes out on the street. The Spinster follows to the door, and shields her eyes from the light as she looks
after the Matron. A stream of confetti is tossed through the
doorway into her face. Trumpets blare. She slams the door shut
and bolts it.*)

SPINSTER: *Canaille!* . . . *Canaille!*

OLD WOMAN: Gone? Without paying? *Cheated* us? (*She parts
the curtains.*)

SPINSTER: Yes—the *canaille!* (*She fastidiously plucks the thread
of confetti from her shoulder. The Old Woman steps from behind the curtains, rigid with anger.*)

OLD WOMAN: Ariadne, my letter! You've dropped my letter!
Your Grandfather's letter is lying on the floor!

Curtain

This Property Is Condemned

CHARACTERS

WILLIE, *a young girl.*
TOM, *a boy.*

SCENE: *A railroad embankment on the outskirts of a small Mississippi town on one of those milky white winter mornings peculiar to that part of the country. The air is moist and chill. Behind the low embankment of the tracks is a large yellow frame house which has a look of tragic vacancy. Some of the upper windows are boarded, a portion of the roof has fallen away. The land is utterly flat. In the left background is a billboard that says "GIN WITH JAKE" and there are some telephone poles and a few bare winter trees. The sky is a great milky whiteness: crows occasionally make a sound of roughly torn cloth.*

The girl Willie is advancing precariously along the railroad track, balancing herself with both arms outstretched, one clutching a banana, the other an extraordinarily dilapidated doll with a frowsy blond wig.

She is a remarkable apparition—thin as a beanpole and dressed in outrageous cast-off finery. She wears a long blue velvet party dress with a filthy cream lace collar and sparkling rhinestone beads. On her feet are battered silver kid slippers with large ornamental buckles. Her wrists and her fingers are resplendent with dimestore jewelry. She has applied rouge to her childish face in artless crimson daubs and her lips are made up in a preposterous Cupid's bow. She is about thirteen and there is something ineluctably childlike and innocent in her appearance despite the makeup. She laughs frequently and wildly and with a sort of precocious, tragic abandon.

The boy Tom, slightly older, watches her from below the embankment. He wears corduroy pants, blue shirt and a sweater and carries a kite of red tissue paper with a gaudily ribboned tail.

TOM: Hello. Who are you?
WILLIE: Don't talk to me till I fall off. (*She proceeds dizzily.*

Tom watches with mute fascination. Her gyrations grow wider and wider. She speaks breathlessly.) Take my—crazy doll —will you?

TOM: (*scrambling up the bank*) Yeh.

WILLIE: I don't wanta—break her when—I fall! I don't think I can—stay on much—longer—do you?

TOM: Naw.

WILLIE: I'm practically—off—right now! (*Tom offers to assist her.*) No, don't touch me. It's no fair helping. You've got to do it—all—by yourself! God, I'm wobbling! I don't know what's made me so nervous! You see that water-tank way back yonder?

TOM: Yeah?

WILLIE: That's where I—started—from! This is the furthest— I ever gone—without once—falling off. I mean it will be— if I can manage to stick on—to the next—telephone—pole! Oh! Here I go! (*She becomes completely unbalanced and rolls down the bank.*)

TOM: (*standing above her now*) Hurtcha self?

WILLIE: Skinned my knee a little. Glad I didn't put my silk stockings on.

TOM: (*coming down the bank*) Spit on it. That takes the sting away.

WILLIE: Okay.

TOM: That's animal's medicine, you know. They always lick their wounds.

WILLIE: I know. The principal damage was done to my bracelet, I guess. I knocked out one of the diamonds. Where did it go?

TOM: You never could find it in all them cinders.

WILLIE: I don't know. It had a lot of shine.

TOM: It wasn't a genuine diamond.

WILLIE: How do you know?

TOM: I just imagine it wasn't. Because if it was you wouldn't be walking along a railroad track with a banged-up doll and a piece of a rotten banana.

WILLIE: Oh, I wouldn't be so sure. I might be peculiar or something. You never can tell. What's your name?

TOM: Tom.

WILLIE: Mine's Willie. We've both got boy's names.

TOM: How did that happen?

WILLIE: I was expected to be a boy but I wasn't. They had one girl already. Alva. She was my sister. Why ain't you at school?

TOM: I thought it was going to be windy so I could fly my kite.

WILLIE: What made you think that?

TOM: Because the sky was so white.

WILLIE: Is that a sign?

TOM: Yeah.

WILLIE: I know. It looks like everything had been swept off with a broom. Don't it?

TOM: Yeah.

WILLIE: It's perfectly white. It's white as a clean piece of paper.

TOM: Uh-huh.

WILLIE: But there isn't a wind.

TOM: Naw.

WILLIE: It's up too high for us to feel it. It's way, way up in the attic sweeping the dust off the furniture up there!

TOM: Uh-huh. Why ain't you at school?

WILLIE: I quituated. Two years ago this winter.

TOM: What grade was you in?

WILLIE: Five A.

TOM: Miss Preston.

WILLIE: Yep. She used to think my hands was dirty until I explained that it was cinders from falling off the railroad tracks so much.

TOM: She's pretty strict.

WILLIE: Oh, no, she's just disappointed because she didn't get married. Probably never had an opportunity, poor thing. So she has to teach Five A for the rest of her natural life. They started teaching algebra an' I didn't give a goddam what X stood for so I quit.

TOM: You'll never get an education walking the railroad tracks.

WILLIE: You won't get one flying a red kite neither. Besides . . .

TOM: What?

WILLIE: What a girl needs to get along is social training. I learned all of that from my sister Alva. She had a wonderful popularity with the railroad men.

TOM: Train engineers?

WILLIE: Engineers, firemen, conductors. Even the freight sup'rintendent. We run a boarding-house for railroad men. She was I guess you might say The Main Attraction. Beautiful? Jesus, she looked like a movie star!

TOM: Your sister?

WILLIE: Yeah. One of 'em used to bring her regular after each run a great big heart-shaped red-silk box of assorted chocolates and nuts and hard candies. Marvelous?

TOM: Yeah. (*The cawing of crows sounds through the chilly air.*)

WILLIE: You know where Alva is now?

TOM: Memphis?

WILLIE: Naw.

TOM: New Awleuns?

WILLIE: Naw.

TOM: St. Louis?

WILLIE: You'll never guess.

TOM: Where is she then? (*Willie does not answer at once.*)

WILLIE: (*very solemnly*) She's in the bone-orchard.

TOM: What?

WILLIE: (*violently*) Bone-orchard, cemetery, graveyard! Don't you understand English?

TOM: Sure. That's pretty tough.

WILLIE: You don't know the half of it, buddy. We used to have some high old times in that big yellow house.

TOM: I bet you did.

WILLIE: Musical instruments going all of the time.

TOM: Instruments? What kind?

WILLIE: Piano, victrola, Hawaiian steel guitar. Everyone played on something. But now it's—awful quiet. You don't hear a sound from there, do you?

TOM: Naw. Is it empty?

WILLIE: Except for me. They got a big sign stuck up.

TOM: What does it say?

WILLIE: (*loudly but with a slight catch*) "THIS PROPERTY IS CONDEMNED!"

TOM: You ain't still living there?

WILLIE: Uh-huh.

TOM: What happened? Where did everyone go?

WILLIE: Mama run off with a brakeman on the C.&E.I. After that everything went to pieces. (*A train whistles far off.*) You hear that whistle? That's the Cannonball Express. The fastest thing on wheels between St. Louis, New Awleuns an' Memphis. My old man got to drinking.

TOM: Where is he now?

WILLIE: Disappeared. I guess I ought to refer his case to the Bureau of Missing Persons. The same as he done with Mama when she disappeared. Then there was me and Alva. Till Alva's lungs got affected. Did you see Greta Garbo in *Camille*? It played at the Delta Brilliant one time las' spring. She had the same what Alva died of. Lung affection.

TOM: Yeah?

WILLIE: Only it was—very beautiful the way she had it. You know. Violins playing. And loads and loads of white flowers. All of her lovers come back in a beautiful scene!

TOM: Yeah?

WILLIE: But Alva's all disappeared.

TOM: Yeah?

WILLIE: Like rats from a sinking ship! That's how she used to describe it. Oh, it—wasn't like death in the movies.

TOM: Naw?

WILLIE: She says, "Where is Albert? Where's Clemence?" None of them was around. I used to lie to her, I says, "They send their regards. They're coming to see you tomorrow." "Where's Mr. Johnson?" she asked me. He was the freight sup'rintendent, the most important character we ever had in our rooming-house. "He's been transferred to Grenada," I told her. "But wishes to be remembered." She known I was lying.

TOM: Yeah?

WILLIE: "This here is the pay-off!" she says. "They all run out on me like rats from a sinking ship!" Except Sidney.

TOM: Who was Sidney?

WILLIE: The one that used to give her the great big enormous red-silk box of American Beauty choc'lates.

TOM: Oh.

WILLIE: He remained faithful to her.

TOM: That's good.

WILLIE: But she never did care for Sidney. She said his teeth was decayed so he didn't smell good.

TOM: Aw!

WILLIE: It wasn't like death in the movies. When somebody dies in the movies they play violins.

TOM: But they didn't for Alva.

WILLIE: Naw. Not even a goddam victrola. They said it didn't agree with the hospital regulations. Always singing around the house.

TOM: Who? Alva?

WILLIE: Throwing enormous parties. This was her favorite number. (*She closes her eyes and stretches out her arms in the simulated rapture of the professional blues singer. Her voice is extraordinarily high and pure with a precocious emotional timbre.*)

You're the only star
In my blue hea-ven
And you're shining just
For me!

This is her clothes I got on. Inherited from her. Everything Alva's is mine. Except her solid gold beads.

TOM: What happened to them?

WILLIE: Them? She never took 'em off.

TOM: Oh!

WILLIE: I've also inherited all of my sister's beaux. Albert and Clemence and even the freight sup'rintendent.

TOM: Yeah?

WILLIE: They all disappeared. Afraid that they might get stuck for expenses I guess. But now they turn up again, all of 'em, like a bunch of bad pennies. They take me out places at night. I've got to be popular now. To parties an' dances an' all of the railroad affairs. Lookit here!

TOM: What?

WILLIE: I can do bumps! (*She stands in front of him and shoves her stomach toward him in a series of spasmodic jerks.*)

TOM: Frank Waters said that . . .

WILLIE: What?

TOM: You know.

WILLIE: Know what?

TOM: You took him inside and danced for him with your clothes off.

WILLIE: Oh. Crazy Doll's hair needs washing. I'm scared to wash it though 'cause her head might come unglued where she had that compound fracture of the skull. I think that most of her brains spilled out. She's been acting silly ever since. Saying an' doing the most outrageous things.

TOM: Why don't you do that for me?

WILLIE: What? Put glue on your compound fracture?

TOM: Naw. What you did for Frank Waters.

WILLIE: Because I was lonesome then an' I'm not lonesome now. You can tell Frank Waters that. Tell him that I've inherited all of my sister's beaux. I go out steady with men in responsible jobs. The sky sure is white. Ain't it? White as a clean piece of paper. In Five A we used to draw pictures. Miss Preston would give us a piece of white foolscap an' tell us to draw what we pleased.

TOM: What did you draw?

WILLIE: I remember I drawn her a picture one time of my old man getting conked with a bottle. She thought it was good, Miss Preston, she said, "Look here. Here's a picture of Charlie Chaplin with his hat on the side of his head!" I said, "Aw, naw, that's not Charlie Chaplin, that's my father, an' that's not his hat, it's a bottle!"

TOM: What did she say?

WILLIE: Oh, well. You can't make a school-teacher laugh.

You're the only star
In my blue hea-VEN . . .

The principal used to say there must've been something wrong with my home atmosphere because of the fact that we took in railroad men an' some of 'em slept with my sister.

TOM: Did they?

WILLIE: She was The Main Attraction. The house is sure empty now.

TOM: You ain't still living there, are you?

WILLIE: Sure.

TOM: By yourself?

WILLIE: Uh-huh. I'm not supposed to be but I am. The property is condemned but there's nothing wrong with it.

Some county investigator come snooping around yesterday. I recognized her by the shape of her hat. It wasn't exactly what I would call stylish-looking.

TOM: Naw?

WILLIE: It looked like something she took off the lid of the stove. Alva knew lots about style. She had ambitions to be a designer for big wholesale firms in Chicago. She used to submit her pictures. It never worked out.

> You're the only star
> In my blue hea-ven . . .

TOM: What did you do? About the investigators?

WILLIE: Laid low upstairs. Pretended like no one was home.

TOM: Well, how do you manage to keep on eating?

WILLIE: Oh, I don't know. You keep a sharp look-out you see things lying around. This banana, perfectly good, for instance. Thrown in a garbage pail in back of the Blue Bird Café. (*She finishes the banana and tosses away the peel.*)

TOM: (*grinning*) Yeh. Miss Preston for instance.

WILLIE: Naw, not her. She gives you a white piece of paper, says "Draw what you please!" One time I drawn her a picture of— Oh, but I told you that, huh? Will you give Frank Waters a message?

TOM: What?

WILLIE: Tell him the freight sup'rintendent has bought me a pair of kid slippers. Patent. The same as the old ones of Alva's. I'm going to dances with them at Moon Lake Casino. All night I'll be dancing an' come home drunk in the morning! We'll have serenades with all kinds of musical instruments. Trumpets an' trombones. An' Hawaiian steel guitars. Yeh! Yeh! (*She rises excitedly.*) The sky will be white like this.

TOM: (*impressed*) Will it?

WILLIE: Uh-huh. (*She smiles vaguely and turns slowly toward him.*) White—as a clean—piece of paper . . . (*then excitedly*) I'll draw—pictures on it!

TOM: Will you?

WILLIE: Sure!

TOM: Pictures of what?

WILLIE: Me dancing! With the freight sup'rintendent! In a pair of patent kid shoes! Yeh! Yeh! With French heels on them as high as telegraph poles! An' they'll play my favorite music!

TOM: Your favorite?

WILLIE: Yeh. The same as Alva's. (*breathlessly, passionately*)
　　　You're the only STAR—
　　　In my blue HEA-VEN . . .
I'll—

TOM: What?

WILLIE: I'll—wear a corsage!

TOM: What's that?

WILLIE: Flowers to pin on your dress at a formal affair! Rosebuds! Violets! And lilies-of-the-valley! When you come home it's withered but you stick 'em in a bowl of water to freshen 'em up.

TOM: Uh-huh.

WILLIE: That's what Alva done. (*She pauses, and in the silence the train whistles.*) The Cannonball Express . . .

TOM: You think a lot about Alva. Don't you?

WILLIE: Oh, not so much. Now an' then. It wasn't like death in the movies. Her beaux disappeared. An' they didn't have violins playing. I'm going back now.

TOM: Where to, Willie?

WILLIE: The water-tank.

TOM: Yeah?

WILLIE: An' start all over again. Maybe I'll break some kind of continuous record. Alva did once. At a dance marathon in Mobile. Across the state line. Alabama. You can tell Frank Waters everything that I told you. I don't have time for inexperienced people. I'm going out now with popular railroad men, men with good salaries, too. Don't you believe me?

TOM: No. I think you're drawing an awful lot on your imagination.

WILLIE: Well, if I wanted to I could prove it. But you wouldn't be worth convincing. (*She smooths out Crazy Doll's hair.*) I'm going to live for a long, long time like my sister. An' when my lungs get affected I'm going to die like she did— maybe not like in the movies, with violins playing—but with my pearl earrings on an' my solid gold beads from Memphis. . . .

TOM: Yes?

WILLIE: (*examining Crazy Doll very critically*) An' then I guess—

TOM: What?

WILLIE: (*gaily but with a slight catch*) Somebody else will inherit all of my beaux! The sky sure is white.

TOM: It sure is.

WILLIE: White as a clean piece of paper. I'm going back now.

TOM: So long.

WILLIE: Yeh. So long. (*She starts back along the railroad track, weaving grotesquely to keep her balance. She disappears. Tom wets his finger and holds it up to test the wind. Willie is heard singing from a distance.*)

You're the only star
In my blue heaven—

(*There is a brief pause. The stage begins to darken.*)

An' you're shining just—
For me!

Curtain

THE GLASS MENAGERIE

Nobody, not even the rain, has such small hands.
E. E. CUMMINGS

THE CHARACTERS

AMANDA WINGFIELD (*the mother*) ....Laurette Taylor

A little woman of great but confused vitality clinging frantically to another time and place. Her characterization must be carefully created, not copied from type. She is not paranoiac, but her life is paranoia. There is much to admire in Amanda, and as much to love and pity as there is to laugh at. Certainly she has endurance and a kind of heroism, and though her foolishness makes her unwittingly cruel at times, there is tenderness in her slight person.

LAURA WINGFIELD (*her daughter*) ....Julie Haydon

Amanda, having failed to establish contact with reality, continues to live vitally in her illusions, but Laura's situation is even graver. A childhood illness has left her crippled, one leg slightly shorter than the other, and held in a brace. This defect need not be more than suggested on the stage. Stemming from this, Laura's separation increases till she is like a piece of her own glass collection, too exquisitely fragile to move from the shelf.

TOM WINGFIELD (*her son*) ....Eddie Dowling

And the narrator of the play. A poet with a job in a warehouse. His nature is not remorseless, but to escape from a trap he has to act without pity.

JIM O'CONNOR (*the gentleman caller*).........................Anthony Ross

A nice, ordinary, young man.

SCENE

AN ALLEY IN ST. LOUIS
PART I. Preparation for a Gentleman Caller.
PART II. The Gentleman calls.

Time: Now and the Past.

PRODUCTION NOTES

Being a "memory play," *The Glass Menagerie* can be presented with unusual freedom of convention. Because of its considerably delicate or tenuous material, atmospheric touches and subtleties of direction play a particularly important part. Expressionism and all other unconventional techniques in drama have only one valid aim, and that is a closer approach to truth. When a play employs unconventional techniques, it is not, or certainly shouldn't be, trying to escape its responsibility of dealing with reality, or interpreting experience, but is actually or should be attempting to find a closer approach, a more penetrating and vivid expression of things as they are. The straight realistic play with its genuine frigidaire and authentic ice-cubes, its characters that speak exactly as its audience speaks, corresponds to the academic landscape and has the same virtue of a photographic likeness. Everyone should know nowadays the unimportance of the photographic in art: that truth, life, or reality is an organic thing which the poetic imagination can represent or suggest, in essence, only through transformation, through changing into other forms than those which were merely present in appearance.

These remarks are not meant as a preface only to this particular play. They have to do with a conception of a new, plastic theatre which must take the place of the exhausted theatre of realistic conventions if the theatre is to resume vitality as a part of our culture.

THE SCREEN DEVICE

There is *only one important difference between the original and acting version of the play* and that is the *omission* in the latter of the device which I tentatively included in my *original* script. This device was the use of a screen on which were projected magic-lantern slides bearing images or titles. I do not regret the omission of this device from the present Broadway production. The extraordinary power of Miss Taylor's performance made it suitable to have the utmost simplicity in the physical production. But I think it may be interesting to some readers to see how this device was conceived.

So I am putting it into the published manuscript. These images and legends, projected from behind, were cast on a section of wall between the front-room and dining-room areas, which should be indistinguishable from the rest when not in use.

The purpose of this will probably be apparent. It is to give accent to certain values in each scene. Each scene contains a particular point (or several) which is structurally the most important. In an episodic play, such as this, the basic structure or narrative line may be obscured from the audience; the effect may seem fragmentary rather than architectural. This may not be the fault of the play so much as a lack of attention in the audience. The legend or image upon the screen will strengthen the effect of what is merely allusion in the writing and allow the primary point to be made more simply and lightly than if the entire responsibility were on the spoken lines. Aside from this structural value, I think the screen will have a definite emotional appeal, less definable but just as important. An imaginative producer or director may invent many other uses for this device than those indicated in the present script. In fact the possibilities of the device seem much larger to me than the instance of this play can possibly utilize.

THE MUSIC

Another extra-literary accent in this play is provided by the use of music. A single recurring tune, "The Glass Menagerie," is used to give emotional emphasis to suitable passages. This tune is like circus music, not when you are on the grounds or in the immediate vicinity of the parade, but when you are at some distance and very likely thinking of something else. It seems under those circumstances to continue almost interminably and it weaves in and out of your preoccupied consciousness; then it is the lightest, most delicate music in the world and perhaps the saddest. It expresses the surface vivacity of life with the underlying strain of immutable and inexpressible sorrow. When you look at a piece of delicately spun glass you think of two things: how beautiful it is and how easily it can be broken. Both of those ideas should be woven into the recurring tune, which dips in and out of the play as if it were carried on a wind that changes. It serves as a thread of connection and allusion between the narrator with his separate point in time and space and the subject of his story. Between each episode it returns as reference to the emotion, nostalgia, which is the first condition of the play. It is primarily Laura's music and therefore comes out most clearly when the play focuses upon her and the lovely fragility of glass which is her image.

THE LIGHTING

The lighting in the play is not realistic. In keeping with the atmosphere of memory, the stage is dim. Shafts of light are focused on selected areas or actors, sometimes in contradistinction to what is the apparent center. For instance, in the quarrel scene between Tom and Amanda, in which Laura has no active part, the clearest pool of light is on her figure. This is also true of the supper scene, when her silent figure on the sofa should remain the visual center. The light upon Laura should be distinct from the others, having a peculiar pristine clarity such as light used in early religious portraits of female saints or madonnas. A certain correspondence to light in religious paintings, such as El Greco's, where the figures are radiant in atmosphere that is relatively dusky, could be effectively used throughout the play. (It will also permit a more effective use of the screen.) A free, imaginative use of light can be of enormous value in giving a mobile, plastic quality to plays of a more or less static nature.

T. W.

SCENE I

The Wingfield apartment is in the rear of the building, one of those vast hive-like conglomerations of cellular living-units that flower as warty growths in overcrowded urban centers of lower middle-class population and are symptomatic of the impulse of this largest and fundamentally enslaved section of American society to avoid fluidity and differentiation and to exist and function as one interfused mass of automatism.

The apartment faces an alley and is entered by a fire-escape, a structure whose name is a touch of accidental poetic truth, for all of these huge buildings are always burning with the slow and implacable fires of human desperation. The fire-escape is included in the set—that is, the landing of it and steps descending from it.

The scene is memory and is therefore nonrealistic. Memory takes a lot of poetic license. It omits some details; others are exaggerated, according to the emotional value of the articles it touches, for memory is seated predominantly in the heart. The interior is therefore rather dim and poetic.

At the rise of the curtain, the audience is faced with the dark, grim rear wall of the Wingfield tenement. This building, which runs parallel to the footlights, is flanked on both sides by dark, narrow alleys which run into murky canyons of tangled clothes-lines, garbage cans and the sinister lattice-work of neighboring fire-escapes. It is up and down these side alleys that exterior entrances and exits are made, during the play. At the end of Tom's opening commentary, the dark tenement wall slowly reveals (by means of a transparency) the interior of the ground floor Wingfield apartment.

Downstage is the living room, which also serves as a sleeping room for Laura, the sofa unfolding to make her bed. Upstage, center, and divided by a wide arch or second proscenium with transparent faded portieres (or second curtain), is the dining room. In an old-fashioned what-not in the living room are seen scores of transparent glass animals. A blown-up photograph of the father hangs on the wall of the living room, facing the audience, to the left of the archway. It is the face of a very handsome young man in a doughboy's First World War cap. He is

399

gallantly smiling, ineluctably smiling, as if to say, "I will be smiling forever."

The audience hears and sees the opening scene in the dining room through both the transparent fourth wall of the building and the transparent gauze portieres of the dining-room arch. It is during this revealing scene that the fourth wall slowly ascends, out of sight. This transparent exterior wall is not brought down again until the very end of the play, during Tom's final speech.

The narrator is an undisguised convention of the play. He takes whatever license with dramatic convention as is convenient to his purposes.

Tom enters dressed as a merchant sailor from alley, stage left, and strolls across the front of the stage to the fire-escape. There he stops and lights a cigarette. He addresses the audience.

TOM: Yes, I have tricks in my pocket, I have things up my sleeve. But I am the opposite of a stage magician. He gives you illusion that has the appearance of truth. I give you truth in the pleasant disguise of illusion.

To begin with, I turn back time. I reverse it to that quaint period, the thirties, when the huge middle class of America was matriculating in a school for the blind. Their eyes had failed them, or they had failed their eyes, and so they were having their fingers pressed forcibly down on the fiery Braille alphabet of a dissolving economy.

In Spain there was revolution. Here there was only shouting and confusion.

In Spain there was Guernica. Here there were disturbances of labor, sometimes pretty violent, in otherwise peaceful cities such as Chicago, Cleveland, Saint Louis . . .

This is the social background of the play.

(MUSIC.)

The play is memory.

Being a memory play, it is dimly lighted, it is sentimental, it is not realistic.

In memory everything seems to happen to music. That explains the fiddle in the wings.

I am the narrator of the play, and also a character in it.

The other characters are my mother, Amanda, my sister, Laura, and a gentleman caller who appears in the final scenes.

He is the most realistic character in the play, being an emissary from a world of reality that we were somehow set apart from.

But since I have a poet's weakness for symbols, I am using this character also as a symbol; he is the long delayed but always expected something that we live for.

There is a fifth character in the play who doesn't appear except in this larger-than-life-size photograph over the mantel.

This is our father who left us a long time ago.

He was a telephone man who fell in love with long distances; he gave up his job with the telephone company and skipped the light fantastic out of town . . .

The last we heard of him was a picture post-card from Mazatlan, on the Pacific coast of Mexico, containing a message of two words—

"Hello— Good-bye!" and no address.

I think the rest of the play will explain itself. . . .

(*Amanda's voice becomes audible through the portieres.*)

(LEGEND ON SCREEN: "OU SONT LES NEIGES.")

(*He divides the portieres and enters the upstage area.*)

(*Amanda and Laura are seated at a drop-leaf table. Eating is indicated by gestures without food or utensils. Amanda faces the audience. Tom and Laura are seated in profile.*)

(*The interior has lit up softly and through the scrim we see Amanda and Laura seated at the table in the upstage area.*)

AMANDA: (*Calling*) Tom?

TOM: Yes, Mother.

AMANDA: We can't say grace until you come to the table!

TOM: Coming, Mother. (*He bows slightly and withdraws, reappearing a few moments later in his place at the table.*)

AMANDA: (*To her son*) Honey, don't *push* with your *fingers*. If you have to push with something, the thing to push with is a crust of bread. And chew—chew! Animals have sections in their stomachs which enable them to digest food without mastication, but human beings are supposed to chew their food before they swallow it down. Eat food leisurely, son, and really enjoy it. A well-cooked meal has lots of delicate flavors that have to be held in the mouth for appreciation. So chew your food and give your salivary glands a chance to function!

(*Tom deliberately lays his imaginary fork down and pushes his chair back from the table.*)

TOM: I haven't enjoyed one bite of this dinner because of your constant directions on how to eat it. It's you that make me rush through meals with your hawk-like attention to every bite I take. Sickening—spoils my appetite—all this discussion of—animals' secretion—salivary glands—mastication!

AMANDA: (*Lightly*) Temperament like a Metropolitan star! (*He rises and crosses downstage*) You're not excused from the table.

TOM: I'm getting a cigarette.

AMANDA: You smoke too much.

(*Laura rises.*)

LAURA: I'll bring in the blanc mange.

(*He remains standing with his cigarette by the portieres during the following.*)

AMANDA: (*Rising*) No, sister, no, sister—you be the lady this time and I'll be the darky.

LAURA: I'm already up.

AMANDA: Resume your seat, little sister—I want you to stay fresh and pretty—for gentlemen callers!

LAURA: I'm not expecting any gentlemen callers.

AMANDA: (*Crossing out to kitchenette. Airily*) Sometimes they come when they are least expected! Why, I remember one Sunday afternoon in Blue Mountain— (*Enters kitchenette.*)

TOM: I know what's coming!

LAURA: Yes. But let her tell it.

TOM: Again?

LAURA: She loves to tell it.

(*Amanda returns with bowl of dessert.*)

AMANDA: One Sunday afternoon in Blue Mountain—your mother received—*seventeen!*—gentlemen callers! Why, sometimes there weren't chairs enough to accommodate them all. We had to send the nigger over to bring in folding chairs from the parish house.

TOM: (*Remaining at portieres*) How did you entertain those gentlemen callers?

AMANDA: I understood the art of conversation!

TOM: I bet you could talk.

AMANDA: Girls in those days *knew* how to talk, I can tell you.

TOM: Yes?

(IMAGE: AMANDA AS A GIRL ON A PORCH, GREETING CALLERS.)

AMANDA: They knew how to entertain their gentlemen callers. It wasn't enough for a girl to be possessed of a pretty face and a graceful figure—although I wasn't slighted in either respect. She also needed to have a nimble wit and a tongue to meet all occasions.

TOM: What did you talk about?

AMANDA: Things of importance going on in the world! Never anything coarse or common or vulgar. (*She addresses Tom as though he were seated in the vacant chair at the table though he remains by portieres. He plays this scene as though he held the book*) My callers were gentlemen—all! Among my callers were some of the most prominent young planters of the Mississippi Delta—planters and sons of planters!

(*Tom motions for music and a spot of light on Amanda.*)

(*Her eyes lift, her face glows, her voice becomes rich and elegiac.*)

(SCREEN LEGEND: "OU SONT LES NEIGES.")

There was young Champ Laughlin who later became vice-president of the Delta Planters Bank.

Hadley Stevenson who was drowned in Moon Lake and left his widow one hundred and fifty thousand in Government bonds.

There were the Cutrere brothers, Wesley and Bates. Bates was one of my bright particular beaux! He got in a quarrel with that wild Wainwright boy. They shot it out on the floor of Moon Lake Casino. Bates was shot through the stomach. Died in the ambulance on his way to Memphis. His widow was also well-provided for, came into eight or ten thousand acres, that's all. She married him on the rebound—never loved her—carried my picture on him the night he died!

And there was that boy that every girl in the Delta had set her cap for! That beautiful, brilliant young Fitzhugh boy from Greene County!

TOM: What did he leave his widow?

AMANDA: He never married! Gracious, you talk as though all of my old admirers had turned up their toes to the daisies!

TOM: Isn't this the first you've mentioned that still survives?

AMANDA: That Fitzhugh boy went North and made a fortune—came to be known as the Wolf of Wall Street! He had the Midas touch, whatever he touched turned to gold!

And I could have been Mrs. Duncan J. Fitzhugh, mind you! But—I picked your *father*!

LAURA: (*Rising*) Mother, let me clear the table.

AMANDA: No, dear, you go in front and study your typewriter chart. Or practice your shorthand a little. Stay fresh and pretty!—It's almost time for our gentlemen callers to start arriving. (*She flounces girlishly toward the kitchenette*) How many do you suppose we're going to entertain this afternoon?

(*Tom throws down the paper and jumps up with a groan.*)

LAURA: (*Alone in the dining room*) I don't believe we're going to receive any, Mother.

AMANDA: (*Reappearing, airily*) What? No one—not one? You must be joking! (*Laura nervously echoes her laugh. She slips in a fugitive manner through the half-open portieres and draws them gently behind her. A shaft of very clear light is thrown on her face against the faded tapestry of the curtains.* MUSIC: "THE GLASS MENAGERIE" UNDER FAINTLY. *Lightly*) Not one gentleman caller? It can't be true! There must be a flood, there must have been a tornado!

LAURA: It isn't a flood, it's not a tornado, Mother. I'm just not popular like you were in Blue Mountain. . . . (*Tom utters another groan. Laura glances at him with a faint,*

apologetic smile. Her voice catching a little) Mother's afraid
I'm going to be an old maid.

THE SCENE DIMS OUT WITH "GLASS MENAGERIE" MUSIC

SCENE II

"Laura, Haven't You Ever Liked Some Boy?"
On the dark stage the screen is lighted with the image of blue roses.
Gradually Laura's figure becomes apparent and the screen goes out.
The music subsides.
Laura is seated in the delicate ivory chair at the small claw-foot table.
She wears a dress of soft violet material for a kimono—her hair tied back from her forehead with a ribbon.
She is washing and polishing her collection of glass.
Amanda appears on the fire-escape steps. At the sound of her ascent, Laura catches her breath, thrusts the bowl of ornaments away and seats herself stiffly before the diagram of the typewriter keyboard as though it held her spellbound.
Something has happened to Amanda. It is written in her face as she climbs to the landing: a look that is grim and hopeless and a little absurd.
She has on one of those cheap or imitation velvety-looking cloth coats with imitation fur collar. Her hat is five or six years old, one of those dreadful cloche hats that were worn in the late twenties and she is clasping an enormous black patent-leather pocket-book with nickel clasps and initials. This is her full-dress outfit, the one she usually wears to the D.A.R.
Before entering she looks through the door.
She purses her lips, opens her eyes very wide, rolls them upward and shakes her head.
Then she slowly lets herself in the door. Seeing her mother's expression Laura touches her lips with a nervous gesture.

LAURA: Hello, Mother, I was— (*She makes a nervous gesture toward the chart on the wall. Amanda leans against the shut door and stares at Laura with a martyred look.*)

AMANDA: Deception? Deception? (*She slowly removes her hat and gloves, continuing the sweet suffering stare. She lets the hat and gloves fall on the floor—a bit of acting.*)

LAURA: (*Shakily*) How was the D.A.R. meeting? (*Amanda slowly opens her purse and removes a dainty white handkerchief which she shakes out delicately and delicately touches to her lips and nostrils*) Didn't you go to the D.A.R. meeting, Mother?

AMANDA: (*Faintly, almost inaudibly*) —No.—No. (*Then more forcibly*) I did not have the strength—to go to the D.A.R. In fact, I did not have the courage! I wanted to find a hole in the ground and hide myself in it forever! (*She crosses slowly to the wall and removes the diagram of the typewriter keyboard. She holds it in front of her for a second, staring at it sweetly and sorrowfully—then bites her lips and tears it in two pieces.*)

LAURA: (*Faintly*) Why did you do that, Mother? (*Amanda repeats the same procedure with the chart of the Gregg Alphabet*) Why are you—

AMANDA: Why? Why? How old are you, Laura?

LAURA: Mother, you know my age.

AMANDA: I thought that you were an adult; it seems that I was mistaken. (*She crosses slowly to the sofa and sinks down and stares at Laura.*)

LAURA: Please don't stare at me, Mother.

(*Amanda closes her eyes and lowers her head. Count ten.*)

AMANDA: What are we going to do, what is going to become of us, what is the future?

(*Count ten.*)

LAURA: Has something happened, Mother? (*Amanda draws a long breath and takes out the handkerchief again. Dabbing process*) Mother, has—something happened?

AMANDA: I'll be all right in a minute, I'm just bewildered— (*Count five*)—by life. . . .

LAURA: Mother, I wish that you would tell me what's happened!

AMANDA: As you know, I was supposed to be inducted into my office at the D.A.R. this afternoon. (IMAGE: A SWARM

OF TYPEWRITERS) But I stopped off at Rubicam's business college to speak to your teachers about your having a cold and ask them what progress they thought you were making down there.

LAURA: Oh. . . .

AMANDA: I went to the typing instructor and introduced myself as your mother. She didn't know who you were. Wingfield, she said. We don't have any such student enrolled at the school!

I assured her she did, that you had been going to classes since early in January.

"I wonder," she said, "if you could be talking about that terribly shy little girl who dropped out of school after only a few days' attendance?"

"No," I said, "Laura, my daughter, has been going to school every day for the past six weeks!"

"Excuse me," she said. She took the attendance book out and there was your name, unmistakably printed, and all the dates you were absent until they decided that you had dropped out of school.

I still said, "No, there must have been some mistake! There must have been some mix-up in the records!"

And she said, "No—I remember her perfectly now. Her hands shook so that she couldn't hit the right keys! The first time we gave a speed-test, she broke down completely —was sick at the stomach and almost had to be carried into the wash-room! After that morning she never showed up any more. We phoned the house but never got any answer—" while I was working at Famous and Barr, I suppose, demonstrating those— Oh!

I felt so weak I could barely keep on my feet!

I had to sit down while they got me a glass of water!

Fifty dollars' tuition, all of our plans—my hopes and ambitions for you—just gone up the spout, just gone up the spout like that.

(*Laura draws a long breath and gets awkwardly to her feet. She crosses to the victrola and winds it up.*)

What are you doing?

LAURA: Oh! (*She releases the handle and returns to her seat.*)

AMANDA: Laura, where have you been going when you've gone out pretending that you were going to business college?

LAURA: I've just been going out walking.

AMANDA: That's not true.

LAURA: It is. I just went walking.

AMANDA: Walking? Walking? In winter? Deliberately courting pneumonia in that light coat? Where did you walk to, Laura?

LAURA: All sorts of places—mostly in the park.

AMANDA: Even after you'd started catching that cold?

LAURA: It was the lesser of two evils, Mother. (IMAGE: WINTER SCENE IN PARK) I couldn't go back up. I—threw up—on the floor!

AMANDA: From half past seven till after five every day you mean to tell me you walked around in the park, because you wanted to make me think that you were still going to Rubicam's Business College?

LAURA: It wasn't as bad as it sounds. I went inside places to get warmed up.

AMANDA: Inside where?

LAURA: I went in the art museum and the bird-houses at the Zoo. I visited the penguins every day! Sometimes I did without lunch and went to the movies. Lately I've been spending most of my afternoons in the Jewel-box, that big glass house where they raise the tropical flowers.

AMANDA: You did all this to deceive me, just for deception? (*Laura looks down*) Why?

LAURA: Mother, when you're disappointed, you get that awful suffering look on your face, like the picture of Jesus' mother in the museum!

AMANDA: Hush!

LAURA: I couldn't face it.

(*Pause. A whisper of strings.*)

(LEGEND: "THE CRUST OF HUMILITY.")

AMANDA: (*Hopelessly fingering the huge pocketbook*) So what are we going to do the rest of our lives? Stay home and watch the parades go by? Amuse ourselves with the glass menagerie, darling? Eternally play those worn-out phono-graph records your father left as a painful reminder of him?

We won't have a business career—we've given that up because it gave us nervous indigestion! (*Laughs wearily*) What is there left but dependency all our lives? I know so well what becomes of unmarried women who aren't pre-pared to occupy a position. I've seen such pitiful cases in the South—barely tolerated spinsters living upon the grudging patronage of sister's husband or brother's wife!—stuck away in some little mouse-trap of a room—encour-aged by one in-law to visit another—little birdlike women without any nest—eating the crust of humility all their life!

Is that the future that we've mapped out for ourselves?

I swear it's the only alternative I can think of!

It isn't a very pleasant alternative, is it?

Of course—some girls *do marry.*

(*Laura twists her hands nervously.*)

Haven't you ever liked some boy?

LAURA: Yes. I liked one once. (*Rises*) I came across his picture a while ago.

AMANDA: (*With some interest*) He gave you his picture?

LAURA: No, it's in the year-book.

AMANDA: (*Disappointed*) Oh—a high-school boy.

(SCREEN IMAGE: JIM AS HIGH-SCHOOL HERO BEARING A SILVER CUP.)

LAURA: Yes. His name was Jim. (*Laura lifts the heavy annual from the claw-foot table*) Here he is in *The Pirates of Penzance.*

AMANDA: (*Absently*) The what?

LAURA: The operetta the senior class put on. He had a won-derful voice and we sat across the aisle from each other Mondays, Wednesdays and Fridays in the Aud. Here he is with the silver cup for debating! See his grin?

AMANDA: (*Absently*) He must have had a jolly disposition.

LAURA: He used to call me—Blue Roses.

(IMAGE: BLUE ROSES.)

AMANDA: Why did he call you such a name as that?

LAURA: When I had that attack of pleurosis—he asked me what was the matter when I came back. I said pleurosis—he thought that I said Blue Roses! So that's what he always called me after that. Whenever he saw me, he'd holler, "Hello, Blue Roses!" I didn't care for the girl that he went out with. Emily Meisenbach. Emily was the best-dressed girl at Soldan. She never struck me, though, as being sincere . . . It says in the Personal Section—they're engaged. That's—six years ago! They must be married by now.

AMANDA: Girls that aren't cut out for business careers usually wind up married to some nice man. (*Gets up with a spark of revival*) Sister, that's what you'll do!

(*Laura utters a startled, doubtful laugh. She reaches quickly for a piece of glass.*)

LAURA: But, Mother—
AMANDA: Yes? (*Crossing to photograph.*)
LAURA: (*In a tone of frightened apology*) I'm—crippled!

(IMAGE: SCREEN.)

AMANDA: Nonsense! Laura, I've told you never, never to use that word. Why, you're not crippled, you just have a little defect—hardly noticeable, even! When people have some slight disadvantage like that, they cultivate other things to make up for it—develop charm—and vivacity—and—*charm!* That's all you have to do! (*She turns again to the photograph*) One thing your father had *plenty of*—was *charm!*

(*Tom motions to the fiddle in the wings.*)

THE SCENE FADES OUT WITH MUSIC

SCENE III

LEGEND ON SCREEN: "AFTER THE FIASCO—"

Tom speaks from the fire-escape landing.

TOM: After the fiasco at Rubicam's Business College, the idea of getting a gentleman caller for Laura began to play a more and more important part in Mother's calculations.

It became an obsession. Like some archetype of the universal unconscious, the image of the gentleman caller haunted our small apartment. . . .

(IMAGE: YOUNG MAN AT DOOR WITH FLOWERS.)

An evening at home rarely passed without some allusion to this image, this spectre, this hope. . . .

Even when he wasn't mentioned, his presence hung in Mother's preoccupied look and in my sister's frightened, apologetic manner—hung like a sentence passed upon the Wingfields!

Mother was a woman of action as well as words.

She began to take logical steps in the planned direction.

Late that winter and in the early spring—realizing that extra money would be needed to properly feather the nest and plume the bird—she conducted a vigorous campaign on the telephone, roping in subscribers to one of those magazines for matrons called *The Home-maker's Companion*, the type of journal that features the serialized sublimations of ladies of letters who think in terms of delicate cup-like breasts, slim, tapering waists, rich, creamy thighs, eyes like wood-smoke in autumn, fingers that soothe and caress like strains of music, bodies as powerful as Etruscan sculpture.

(SCREEN IMAGE: GLAMOR MAGAZINE COVER.)

(*Amanda enters with phone on long extension cord. She is spotted in the dim stage.*)

AMANDA: Ida Scott? This is Amanda Wingfield!

We *missed* you at the D.A.R. last Monday!

I said to myself: She's probably suffering with that sinus condition! How is that sinus condition?

Horrors! Heaven have mercy!—You're a Christian martyr, yes, that's what you are, a Christian martyr!

Well, I just now happened to notice that your subscription to the *Companion*'s about to expire! Yes, it expires with the next issue, honey!—just when that wonderful new serial by Bessie Mae Hopper is getting off to such an exciting start. Oh, honey, it's something that you can't miss!

You remember how *Gone With the Wind* took everybody by
storm? You simply couldn't go out if you hadn't read it. All
everybody *talked* was Scarlett O'Hara. Well, this is a book
that critics already compare to *Gone With the Wind*. It's the
Gone With the Wind of the post-World War generation!—
What?—Burning?—Oh, honey, don't let them burn, go
take a look in the oven and I'll hold the wire! Heavens—I
think she's hung up!

DIM OUT

(LEGEND ON SCREEN: "YOU THINK I'M IN LOVE WITH CON-
TINENTAL SHOEMAKERS?")

(*Before the stage is lighted, the violent voices of Tom and
Amanda are heard.*)

(*They are quarreling behind the portieres. In front of them
stands Laura with clenched hands and panicky expression.*)

(*A clear pool of light on her figure throughout this scene.*)

TOM: What in Christ's name am I—

AMANDA: (*Shrilly*) Don't you use that—

TOM: Supposed to do!

AMANDA: Expression! Not in my—

TOM: Ohhh!

AMANDA: Presence! Have you gone out of your senses?

TOM: I have, that's true, *driven* out!

AMANDA: What is the matter with you, you—big—big—
IDIOT!

TOM: Look!—I've got *no thing*, no single thing—

AMANDA: Lower your voice!

TOM: In my life here that I can call my OWN! Everything is—

AMANDA: Stop that shouting!

TOM: Yesterday you confiscated my books! You had the
nerve to—

AMANDA: I took that horrible novel back to the library—yes!
That hideous book by that insane Mr. Lawrence. (*Tom
laughs wildly*) I cannot control the output of diseased
minds or people who cater to them— (*Tom laughs still more
wildly*) BUT I WON'T ALLOW SUCH FILTH BROUGHT INTO
MY HOUSE! No, no, no, no, no!

TOM: House, house! Who pays rent on it, who makes a slave of himself to—

AMANDA: (*Fairly screeching*) Don't you DARE to—

TOM: No, no, *I* mustn't say things! *I've* got to just—

AMANDA: Let me tell you—

TOM: I don't want to hear any more! (*He tears the portieres open. The upstage area is lit with a turgid smoky red glow.*)

(*Amanda's hair is in metal curlers and she wears a very old bathrobe, much too large for her slight figure, a relic of the faithless Mr. Wingfield.*)

(*An upright typewriter and a wild disarray of manuscripts is on the drop-leaf table. The quarrel was probably precipitated by Amanda's interruption of his creative labor. A chair lying overthrown on the floor.*)

(*Their gesticulating shadows are cast on the ceiling by the fiery glow.*)

AMANDA: You *will* hear more, you—

TOM: No, I won't hear more, I'm going out!

AMANDA: You come right back in—

TOM: Out, out, out! Because I'm—

AMANDA: Come back here, Tom Wingfield! I'm not through talking to you!

TOM: Oh, go—

LAURA: (*Desperately*)— Tom!

AMANDA: You're going to listen, and no more insolence from you! I'm at the end of my patience!

(*He comes back toward her.*)

TOM: What do you think I'm at? Aren't I supposed to have any patience to reach the end of, Mother? I know, I know. It seems unimportant to you, what I'm *doing*—what I *want* to do—having a little *difference* between them! You don't think that—

AMANDA: I think you've been doing things that you're ashamed of. That's why you act like this. I don't believe that you go every night to the movies. Nobody goes to the movies night after night. Nobody in their right minds goes to the movies as often as you pretend to. People don't go to the movies at nearly midnight, and movies don't let out at two A.M. Come in stumbling. Muttering to yourself like a maniac! You get three hours' sleep and then go to work. Oh, I can picture the way you're doing down there. Moping, doping, because you're in no condition.

TOM: (*Wildly*) No, I'm in no condition!

AMANDA: What right have you got to jeopardize your job? Jeopardize the security of us all? How do you think we'd manage if you were—

TOM: Listen! You think I'm crazy *about* the *warehouse*? (*He bends fiercely toward her slight figure*) You think I'm in love with the Continental Shoemakers? You think I want to spend fifty-five *years* down there in that—*celotex interior!* with—*fluorescent—tubes!* Look! I'd rather somebody picked up a crowbar and battered out my brains—than go back mornings! I *go!* Every time you come in yelling that God damn *"Rise and Shine!" "Rise and Shine!"* I say to myself, "How *lucky dead* people are!" But I get up. I *go!* For sixty-five dollars a month I give up all that I dream of doing and being *ever!* And you say self—*self's* all I ever think of. Why, listen, if self is what I thought of, Mother, I'd be where he is—GONE! (*Pointing to father's picture*) As far as the system of transportation reaches! (*He starts past her. She grabs his arm*) Don't grab at me, Mother!

AMANDA: Where are you going?

TOM: I'm going to the *movies*!

AMANDA: I don't believe that lie!

TOM: (*Crouching toward her, overtowering her tiny figure. She backs away, gasping*) I'm going to opium dens! Yes, opium dens, dens of vice and criminals' hang-outs, Mother. I've joined the Hogan gang, I'm a hired assassin, I carry a tommy-gun in a violin case! I run a string of cat-houses in the Valley! They call me Killer, Killer Wingfield, I'm leading a double-life, a simple, honest warehouse worker by day, by night a dynamic *czar* of the *underworld, Mother.* I go to gambling casinos, I spin away fortunes on the roulette table! I wear a patch over one eye and a false mustache, sometimes I put on green whiskers. On those occasions they call me—*El Diablo!* Oh, I could tell you things to make you sleepless! My enemies plan to dynamite this

place. They're going to blow us all sky-high some night!
I'll be glad, very happy, and so will you! You'll go up, up
on a broomstick, over Blue Mountain with seventeen gentlemen callers! You ugly—babbling old—*witch.* . . . (*He
goes through a series of violent, clumsy movements, seizing his
overcoat, lunging to the door, pulling it fiercely open. The
women watch him, aghast. His arm catches in the sleeve of the
coat as he struggles to pull it on. For a moment he is pinioned
by the bulky garment. With an outraged groan he tears the
coat off again, splitting the shoulder of it, and hurls it across
the room. It strikes against the shelf of Laura's glass collection,
there is a tinkle of shattering glass. Laura cries out as if
wounded.*)

(MUSIC. LEGEND: "THE GLASS MENAGERIE.")

LAURA: (*Shrilly*) *My glass!*—menagerie. . . . (*She covers her
face and turns away.*)

(*But Amanda is still stunned and stupefied by the "ugly
witch" so that she barely notices this occurrence. Now she recovers her speech.*)

AMANDA: (*In an awful voice*) I won't speak to you—until you
apologize! (*She crosses through portieres and draws them together behind her. Tom is left with Laura. Laura clings
weakly to the mantel with her face averted. Tom stares at her
stupidly for a moment. Then he crosses to shelf. Drops awkwardly on his knees to collect the fallen glass, glancing at
Laura as if he would speak but couldn't.*)
      "*The Glass Menagerie*" steals in as

                THE SCENE DIMS OUT

                    SCENE IV

The interior is dark. Faint light in the alley.
*A deep-voiced bell in a church is tolling the hour of five as the
scene commences.*
*Tom appears at the top of the alley. After each solemn boom of
the bell in the tower, he shakes a little noise-maker or rattle as if*

to express the tiny spasm of man in contrast to the sustained power and dignity of the Almighty. This and the unsteadiness of his advance make it evident that he has been drinking.

As he climbs the few steps to the fire-escape landing light steals up inside. Laura appears in night-dress, observing Tom's empty bed in the front room.

Tom fishes in his pockets for door-key, removing a motley assortment of articles in the search, including a perfect shower of movie-ticket stubs and an empty bottle. At last he finds the key, but just as he is about to insert it, it slips from his fingers. He strikes a match and crouches below the door.

TOM: (*Bitterly*) One crack—and it falls through!

(*Laura opens the door.*)

LAURA: Tom! Tom, what are you doing?
TOM: Looking for a door-key.
LAURA: Where have you been all this time?
TOM: I have been to the movies.
LAURA: All this time at the movies?
TOM: There was a very long program. There was a Garbo picture and a Mickey Mouse and a travelogue and a newsreel and a preview of coming attractions. And there was an organ solo and a collection for the milk-fund—simultaneously—which ended up in a terrible fight between a fat lady and an usher!
LAURA: (*Innocently*) Did you have to stay through everything?
TOM: Of course! And, oh, I forgot! There was a big stage show! The headliner on this stage show was Malvolio the Magician. He performed wonderful tricks, many of them, such as pouring water back and forth between pitchers. First it turned to wine and then it turned to beer and then it turned to whiskey. I know it was whiskey it finally turned into because he needed somebody to come up out of the audience to help him, and I came up—both shows! It was Kentucky Straight Bourbon. A very generous fellow, he gave souvenirs. (*He pulls from his back pocket a shimmering rainbow-colored scarf*) He gave me this. This is his magic scarf. You can have it, Laura. You wave it over a canary cage and you get a bowl of gold-fish. You wave it over the

gold-fish bowl and they fly away canaries. . . . But the wonderfullest trick of all was the coffin trick. We nailed him into a coffin and he got out of the coffin without removing one nail. (*He has come inside*) There is a trick that would come in handy for me—get me out of this 2 by 4 situation! (*Flops onto bed and starts removing shoes.*)

LAURA: Tom—Shhh!

TOM: What're you shushing me for?

LAURA: You'll wake up Mother.

TOM: Goody, goody! Pay 'er back for all those "Rise an' Shines." (*Lies down, groaning*) You know it don't take much intelligence to get yourself into a nailed-up coffin, Laura. But who in hell ever got himself out of one without removing one nail?

(*As if in answer, the father's grinning photograph lights up.*)

SCENE DIMS OUT

(*Immediately following: The church bell is heard striking six. At the sixth stroke the alarm clock goes off in Amanda's room, and after a few moments we hear her calling: "Rise and Shine! Rise and Shine! Laura, go tell your brother to rise and shine!"*)

TOM: (*Sitting up slowly*) I'll rise—but I won't shine. (*The light increases.*)

AMANDA: Laura, tell your brother his coffee is ready.

(*Laura slips into front room.*)

LAURA: Tom!—It's nearly seven. Don't make Mother nervous. (*He stares at her stupidly. Beseechingly*) Tom, speak to Mother this morning. Make up with her, apologize, speak to her!

TOM: She won't to me. It's her that started not speaking.

LAURA: If you just say you're sorry she'll start speaking.

TOM: Her not speaking—is that such a tragedy?

LAURA: Please—please!

AMANDA: (*Calling from kitchenette*) Laura, are you going to do what I asked you to do, or do I have to get dressed and go out myself?

LAURA: Going, going—soon as I get on my coat! (*She pulls on a shapeless felt hat with nervous, jerky movement, pleadingly glancing at Tom. Rushes awkwardly for coat. The coat is one of Amanda's, inaccurately made-over, the sleeves too short for Laura*) Butter and what else?

AMANDA: (*Entering upstage*) Just butter. Tell them to charge it.

LAURA: Mother, they make such faces when I do that.

AMANDA: Sticks and stones can break our bones, but the expression on Mr. Garfinkel's face won't harm us! Tell your brother his coffee is getting cold.

LAURA: (*At door*) Do what I asked you, will you, will you, Tom? (*He looks sullenly away.*)

AMANDA: Laura, go now or just don't go at all!

LAURA: (*Rushing out*) Going—going! (*A second later she cries out. Tom springs up and crosses to door. Amanda rushes anxiously in. Tom opens the door.*)

TOM: Laura?

LAURA: I'm all right. I slipped, but I'm all right.

AMANDA: (*Peering anxiously after her*) If anyone breaks a leg on those fire-escape steps, the landlord ought to be sued for every cent he possesses! (*She shuts door. Remembers she isn't speaking and returns to other room.*)

(*As Tom enters listlessly for his coffee, she turns her back to him and stands rigidly facing the window on the gloomy gray vault of the areaway. Its light on her face with its aged but childish features is cruelly sharp, satirical as a Daumier print.*)

(MUSIC UNDER: "AVE MARIA.")

(*Tom glances sheepishly but sullenly at her averted figure and slumps at the table. The coffee is scalding hot; he sips it and gasps and spits it back in the cup. At his gasp, Amanda catches her breath and half turns. Then catches herself and turns back to window.*)

(*Tom blows on his coffee, glancing sidewise at his mother. She clears her throat. Tom clears his. He starts to rise. Sinks back down again, scratches his head, clears his throat again. Amanda coughs. Tom raises his cup in both hands to blow on it, his eyes staring over the rim of it at his mother for several moments. Then he slowly sets the cup down and awkwardly and hesitantly rises from the chair.*)

TOM: (*Hoarsely*) Mother. I—I apologize, Mother. (*Amanda draws a quick, shuddering breath. Her face works grotesquely. She breaks into childlike tears*) I'm sorry for what I said, for everything that I said, I didn't mean it.

AMANDA: (*Sobbingly.*) My devotion has made me a witch and so I make myself hateful to my children!

TOM: *No*, you *don't*.

AMANDA: I worry so much, don't sleep, it makes me nervous!

TOM: (*Gently*) I understand that.

AMANDA: I've had to put up a solitary battle all these years. But you're my right-hand bower! Don't fall down, don't fail!

TOM: (*Gently*) I try, Mother.

AMANDA: (*With great enthusiasm*) Try and you will SUCCEED! (*The notion makes her breathless.*) Why, you—you're just *full* of natural endowments! Both of my children—they're *unusual* children! Don't you think I know it? I'm so—*proud!* Happy and—feel I've—so much to be thankful for but— Promise me one thing, Son!

TOM: What, Mother?

AMANDA: Promise, son, you'll—never be a drunkard!

TOM: (*Turns to her grinning*) I will never be a drunkard, Mother.

AMANDA: That's what frightened me so, that you'd be drinking! Eat a bowl of Purina!

TOM: Just coffee, Mother.

AMANDA: Shredded wheat biscuit?

TOM: No. No, Mother, just coffee.

AMANDA: You can't put in a day's work on an empty stomach. You've got ten minutes—don't gulp! Drinking too-hot liquids makes cancer of the stomach. . . . Put cream in.

TOM: No, thank you.

AMANDA: To cool it.

TOM: No! No, thank you, I want it black.

AMANDA: I know, but it's not good for you. We have to do all that we can to build ourselves up. In these trying times we live in, all that we have to cling to is—each other. . . . That's why it's so important to— Tom, I—I sent out your sister so I could discuss something with you. If you hadn't spoken I would have spoken to you. (*Sits down.*)

TOM: (*Gently*) What is it, Mother, that you want to discuss?
AMANDA: *Laura!*

(*Tom puts his cup down slowly.*)

(LEGEND ON SCREEN: "LAURA.")

(MUSIC: "THE GLASS MENAGERIE.")

TOM: —Oh.—Laura . . .
AMANDA: (*Touching his sleeve*) You know how Laura is. So quiet but—still water runs deep! She notices things and I think she—broods about them. (*Tom looks up*) A few days ago I came in and she was crying.
TOM: What about?
AMANDA: You.
TOM: Me?
AMANDA: She has an idea that you're not happy here.
TOM: What gave her that idea?
AMANDA: What gives her any idea? However, you do act strangely. I—I'm not criticizing, understand *that!* I know your ambitions do not lie in the warehouse, that like everybody in the whole wide world—you've had to—make sacrifices, but—Tom—Tom—life's not easy, it calls for—Spartan endurance! There's so many things in my heart that I cannot describe to you! I've never told you but I—*loved* your father. . . .
TOM: (*Gently*) I know that, Mother.
AMANDA: And you—when I see you taking after his ways! Staying out late—and—well, you *had* been drinking the night you were in that—terrifying condition! Laura says that you hate the apartment and that you go out nights to get away from it! Is that true, Tom?
TOM: No. You say there's so much in your heart that you can't describe to me. That's true of me, too. There's so much in my heart that I can't describe to *you!* So let's respect each other's—
AMANDA: But, why—*why*, Tom—are you always so *restless?* Where do you *go* to, nights?
TOM: I—go to the movies.
AMANDA: Why do you go to the movies so much, Tom?

TOM: I go to the movies because—I like adventure. Adventure is something I don't have much of at work, so I go to the movies.

AMANDA: But, Tom, you go to the movies *entirely* too *much*!

TOM: I like a lot of adventure.

(*Amanda looks baffled, then hurt. As the familiar inquisition resumes he becomes hard and impatient again. Amanda slips back into her querulous attitude toward him.*)

(IMAGE ON SCREEN: SAILING VESSEL WITH JOLLY ROGER.)

AMANDA: Most young men find adventure in their careers.

TOM: Then most young men are not employed in a warehouse.

AMANDA: The world is full of young men employed in warehouses and offices and factories.

TOM: Do all of them find adventure in their careers?

AMANDA: They do or they do without it! Not everybody has a craze for adventure.

TOM: Man is by instinct a lover, a hunter, a fighter, and none of those instincts are given much play at the warehouse!

AMANDA: Man is by instinct! Don't quote instinct to me! Instinct is something that people have got away from! It belongs to animals! Christian adults don't want it!

TOM: What do Christian adults want, then, Mother?

AMANDA: Superior things! Things of the mind and the spirit! Only animals have to satisfy instincts! Surely your aims are somewhat higher than theirs! Than monkeys—pigs—

TOM: I reckon they're not.

AMANDA: You're joking. However, that isn't what I wanted to discuss.

TOM: (*Rising*) I haven't much time.

AMANDA: (*Pushing his shoulders*) Sit down.

TOM: You want me to punch in red at the warehouse, Mother?

AMANDA: You have five minutes. I want to talk about Laura.

(LEGEND: "PLANS AND PROVISIONS.")

TOM: All right! What about Laura?

AMANDA: We have to be making some plans and provisions for her. She's older than you, two years, and nothing has happened. She just drifts along doing nothing. It frightens me terribly how she just drifts along.

TOM: I guess she's the type that people call home girls.

AMANDA: There's no such type, and if there is, it's a pity! That is unless the home is hers, with a husband!

TOM: What?

AMANDA: Oh, I can see the handwriting on the wall as plain as I see the nose in front of my face! It's terrifying!

More and more you remind me of your father! He was out all hours without explanation!—Then *left! Good-bye!*

And me with the bag to hold. I saw that letter you got from the Merchant Marine. I know what you're dreaming of. I'm not standing here blindfolded.

Very well, then. Then *do* it!

But not till there's somebody to take your place.

TOM: What do you mean?

AMANDA: I mean that as soon as Laura has got somebody to take care of her, married, a home of her own, independent—why, then you'll be free to go wherever you please, on land, on sea, whichever way the wind blows you!

But until that time you've got to look out for your sister. I don't say me because I'm old and don't matter! I say for your sister because she's young and dependent.

I put her in business college—a dismal failure! Frightened her so it made her sick at the stomach.

I took her over to the Young People's League at the church. Another fiasco. She spoke to nobody, nobody spoke to her. Now all she does is fool with those pieces of glass and play those worn-out records. What kind of a life is that for a girl to lead?

TOM: What can I do about it?

AMANDA: Overcome selfishness!

Self, self, self is all that you ever think of!

(*Tom springs up and crosses to get his coat. It is ugly and bulky. He pulls on a cap with earmuffs.*)

Where is your muffler? Put your wool muffler on!

(*He snatches it angrily from the closet and tosses it around his neck and pulls both ends tight.*)

Tom! I haven't said what I had in mind to ask you.

TOM: I'm too late to—

AMANDA: (*Catching his arm—very importunately. Then shyly*) Down at the warehouse, aren't there some—nice young men?

TOM: No!

AMANDA: There *must* be—*some . . .*

TOM: Mother— (*Gesture.*)

AMANDA: Find out one that's clean-living—doesn't drink and —ask him out for sister!

TOM: What?

AMANDA: For *sister!* To *meet!* Get *acquainted!*

TOM: (*Stamping to door*) Oh, my *go-osh!*

AMANDA: Will you? (*He opens door. Imploringly*) Will you? (*He starts down*) Will you? *Will* you, dear?

TOM: (*Calling back*) YES!

(*Amanda closes the door hesitantly and with a troubled but faintly hopeful expression.*)

SCREEN IMAGE: GLAMOR MAGAZINE COVER.

Spot Amanda at phone.

AMANDA: Ella Cartwright? This is Amanda Wingfield!
How are you, honey?
How is that kidney condition?

(*Count five.*)

Horrors!

(*Count five.*)

You're a Christian martyr, yes, honey, that's what you are, a Christian martyr!

Well, I just now happened to notice in my little red book that your subscription to the *Companion* has just run out! I knew that you wouldn't want to miss out on the wonderful serial starting in this new issue. It's by Bessie Mae Hopper, the first thing she's written since *Honeymoon for Three.*

Wasn't that a strange and interesting story? Well, this one is even lovelier, I believe. It has a sophisticated, society background. It's all about the horsey set on Long Island!

FADE OUT

SCENE V

LEGEND ON SCREEN: "ANNUNCIATION." *Fade with music.*

It is early dusk of a spring evening. Supper has just been finished in the Wingfield apartment. Amanda and Laura in light-colored dresses are removing dishes from the table, in the upstage area, which is shadowy, their movements formalized almost as a dance or ritual, their moving forms as pale and silent as moths.

Tom, in white shirt and trousers, rises from the table and crosses toward the fire-escape.

AMANDA: (*As he passes her*) Son, will you do me a favor?

TOM: What?

AMANDA: Comb your hair! You look so pretty when your hair is combed! (*Tom slouches on sofa with evening paper. Enormous caption "Franco Triumphs"*) There is only one respect in which I would like you to emulate your father.

TOM: What respect is that?

AMANDA: The care he always took of his appearance. He never allowed himself to look untidy. (*He throws down the paper and crosses to fire-escape*) Where are you going?

TOM: I'm going out to smoke.

AMANDA: You smoke too much. A pack a day at fifteen cents a pack. How much would that amount to in a month? Thirty times fifteen is how much, Tom? Figure it out and you will be astounded at what you could save. Enough to give you a night-school course in accounting at Washington U! Just think what a wonderful thing that would be for you, Son!

(*Tom is unmoved by the thought.*)

TOM: I'd rather smoke. (*He steps out on landing, letting the screen door slam.*)

AMANDA: (*Sharply*) I know! That's the tragedy of it. . . .
(*Alone, she turns to look at her husband's picture.*)

(DANCE MUSIC: "ALL THE WORLD IS WAITING FOR THE
SUNRISE!")

TOM: (*To the audience*) Across the alley from us was the
Paradise Dance Hall. On evenings in spring the windows
and doors were open and the music came outdoors.
Sometimes the lights were turned out except for a large
glass sphere that hung from the ceiling. It would turn
slowly about and filter the dusk with delicate rainbow colors. Then the orchestra played a waltz or a tango, something that had a slow and sensuous rhythm. Couples would
come outside, to the relative privacy of the alley. You could
see them kissing behind ash-pits and telephone poles.
This was the compensation for lives that passed like
mine, without any change or adventure.
Adventure and change were imminent in this year. They
were waiting around the corner for all these kids.
Suspended in the mist over Berchtesgaden, caught in the
folds of Chamberlain's umbrella—
In Spain there was Guernica!
But here there was only hot swing music and liquor,
dance halls, bars, and movies, and sex that hung in the
gloom like a chandelier and flooded the world with brief,
deceptive rainbows. . . .
All the world was waiting for bombardments!

(*Amanda turns from the picture and comes outside.*)

AMANDA: (*Sighing*) A fire-escape landing's a poor excuse for a
porch. (*She spreads a newspaper on a step and sits down,
gracefully and demurely as if she were settling into a swing on
a Mississippi veranda*) What are you looking at?
TOM: The moon.
AMANDA: Is there a moon this evening?
TOM: It's rising over Garfinkel's Delicatessen.
AMANDA: So it is! A little silver slipper of a moon. Have you
made a wish on it yet?
TOM: Um-hum.
AMANDA: What did you wish for?

TOM: That's a secret.

AMANDA: A secret, huh? Well, I won't tell mine either. I will be just as mysterious as you.

TOM: I bet I can guess what yours is.

AMANDA: Is my head so transparent?

TOM: You're not a sphinx.

AMANDA: No, I don't have secrets. I'll tell you what I wished for on the moon. Success and happiness for my precious children! I wish for that whenever there's a moon, and when there isn't a moon, I wish for it, too.

TOM: I thought perhaps you wished for a gentleman caller.

AMANDA: Why do you say that?

TOM: Don't you remember asking me to fetch one?

AMANDA: I remember suggesting that it would be nice for your sister if you brought home some nice young man from the warehouse. I think that I've made that suggestion more than once.

TOM: Yes, you have made it repeatedly.

AMANDA: Well?

TOM: We are going to have one.

AMANDA: *What?*

TOM: A gentleman caller!

(THE ANNUNCIATION IS CELEBRATED WITH MUSIC.)

(*Amanda rises.*)

(IMAGE ON SCREEN: CALLER WITH BOUQUET.)

AMANDA: You mean you have asked some nice young man to come over?

TOM: Yep. I've asked him to dinner.

AMANDA: You really did?

TOM: I did!

AMANDA: You did, and did he—*accept?*

TOM: He did!

AMANDA: Well, well—well, well! That's—lovely!

TOM: I thought that you would be pleased.

AMANDA: It's definite, then?

TOM: Very definite.

AMANDA: Soon?

TOM: Very soon.

AMANDA: For heaven's sake, stop putting on and tell me some things, will you?

TOM: What things do you want me to tell you?

AMANDA: *Naturally* I would like to know when he's *coming*!

TOM: He's coming tomorrow.

AMANDA: *Tomorrow?*

TOM: Yep. Tomorrow.

AMANDA: But, Tom!

TOM: Yes, Mother?

AMANDA: Tomorrow gives me no time!

TOM: Time for what?

AMANDA: Preparations! Why didn't you phone me at once, as soon as you asked him, the minute that he accepted? Then, don't you see, I could have been getting ready!

TOM: You don't have to make any fuss.

AMANDA: Oh, Tom, Tom, Tom, of course I have to make a fuss! I want things nice, not sloppy! Not thrown together. I'll certainly have to do some fast thinking, won't I?

TOM: I don't see why you have to think at all.

AMANDA: You just don't know. We can't have a gentleman caller in a pig-sty! All my wedding silver has to be polished, the monogrammed table linen ought to be laundered! The windows have to be washed and fresh curtains put up. And how about clothes? We have to *wear* something, don't we?

TOM: Mother, this boy is no one to make a fuss over!

AMANDA: Do you realize he's the first young man we've introduced to your sister?

It's terrible, dreadful, disgraceful that poor little sister has never received a single gentleman caller! Tom, come inside! (*She opens the screen door.*)

TOM: What for?

AMANDA: I want to ask you some things.

TOM: If you're going to make such a fuss, I'll call it off, I'll tell him not to come!

AMANDA: You certainly won't do anything of the kind. Nothing offends people worse than broken engagements. It simply means I'll have to work like a Turk! We won't be brilliant, but we will pass inspection. Come on inside. (*Tom follows, groaning*) Sit down.

TOM: Any particular place you would like me to sit?

AMANDA: Thank heavens I've got that new sofa! I'm also making payments on a floor lamp I'll have sent out! And put the chintz covers on, they'll brighten things up! Of course I'd hoped to have these walls re-papered. . . . What is the young man's name?

TOM: His name is O'Connor.

AMANDA: That, of course, means fish—tomorrow is Friday! I'll have that salmon loaf—with Durkee's dressing! What does he do? He works at the warehouse?

TOM: Of course! How else would I—

AMANDA: Tom, he—doesn't drink?

TOM: Why do you ask me that?

AMANDA: Your father *did!*

TOM: Don't get started on that!

AMANDA: He *does* drink, then?

TOM: Not that I know of!

AMANDA: Make sure, be certain! The last thing I want for my daughter's a boy who drinks!

TOM: Aren't you being a little bit premature? Mr. O'Connor has not yet appeared on the scene!

AMANDA: But will tomorrow. To meet your sister, and what do I know about his character? Nothing! Old maids are better off than wives of drunkards!

TOM: Oh, my God!

AMANDA: Be still!

TOM: (*Leaning forward to whisper*) Lots of fellows meet girls whom they don't marry!

AMANDA: Oh, talk sensibly, Tom—and don't be sarcastic! (*She has gotten a hairbrush.*)

TOM: What are you doing?

AMANDA: I'm brushing that cow-lick down!

What is this young man's position at the warehouse?

TOM: (*Submitting grimly to the brush and the interrogation*) This young man's position is that of a shipping clerk, Mother.

AMANDA: Sounds to me like a fairly responsible job, the sort of a job *you* would be in if you just had more *get-up.*

What is his salary? Have you any idea?

TOM: I would judge it to be approximately eighty-five dollars a month.

AMANDA: Well—not princely, but—

TOM: Twenty more than I make.

AMANDA: Yes, how well I know! But for a family man, eighty-five dollars a month is not much more than you can just get by on. . . .

TOM: Yes, but Mr. O'Connor is not a family man.

AMANDA: He might be, mightn't he? Some time in the future?

TOM: I see. Plans and provisions.

AMANDA: You are the only young man that I know of who ignores the fact that the future becomes the present, the present the past, and the past turns into everlasting regret if you don't plan for it!

TOM: I will think that over and see what I can make of it.

AMANDA: Don't be supercilious with your mother! Tell me some more about this—what do you call him?

TOM: James D. O'Connor. The D. is for Delaney.

AMANDA: Irish on *both* sides! *Gracious!* And doesn't drink?

TOM: Shall I call him up and ask him right this minute?

AMANDA: The only way to find out about those things is to make discreet inquiries at the proper moment. When I was a girl in Blue Mountain and it was suspected that a young man drank, the girl whose attentions he had been receiving, if any girl *was*, would sometimes speak to the minister of his church, or rather her father would if her father was living, and sort of feel him out on the young man's character. That is the way such things are discreetly handled to keep a young woman from making a tragic mistake! ← her mistake

TOM: Then how did you happen to make a tragic mistake?

AMANDA: That innocent look of your father's had everyone fooled!

He *smiled*—the world was *enchanted!*

No girl can do worse than put herself at the mercy of a handsome appearance!

I hope that Mr. O'Connor is not too good-looking.

TOM: No, he's not too good-looking. He's covered with freckles and hasn't too much of a nose.

AMANDA: He's not right-down homely, though?

TOM: Not right-down homely. Just medium homely, I'd say.

AMANDA: Character's what to look for in a man.

TOM: That's what I've always said, Mother.

AMANDA: You've never said anything of the kind and I suspect you would never give it a thought.

TOM: Don't be so suspicious of me.

AMANDA: At least I hope he's the type that's up and coming.

TOM: I think he really goes in for self-improvement.

AMANDA: What reason have you to think so?

TOM: He goes to night school.

AMANDA: (*Beaming*) Splendid! What does he do, I mean study?

TOM: Radio engineering and public speaking!

AMANDA: Then he has visions of being advanced in the world! Any young man who studies public speaking is aiming to have an executive job some day!

And radio engineering? A thing for the future!

Both of these facts are very illuminating. Those are the sort of things that a mother should know concerning any young man who comes to call on her daughter. Seriously or—not.

TOM: One little warning. He doesn't know about Laura. I didn't let on that we had dark ulterior motives. I just said, why don't you come and have dinner with us? He said okay and that was the whole conversation.

AMANDA: I bet it was! You're eloquent as an oyster.

However, he'll know about Laura when he gets here. When he sees how lovely and sweet and pretty she is, he'll thank his lucky stars he was asked to dinner.

TOM: Mother, you mustn't expect too much of Laura.

AMANDA: What do you mean?

TOM: Laura seems all those things to you and me because she's ours and we love her. We don't even notice she's crippled any more.

AMANDA: Don't say crippled! You know that I never allow that word to be used!

TOM: But face facts, Mother. She is and—that's not all—

AMANDA: What do you mean "not all"?

TOM: Laura is very different from other girls.

AMANDA: I think the difference is all to her advantage.

TOM: Not quite all—in the eyes of others—strangers—she's terribly shy and lives in a world of her own and those things make her seem a little peculiar to people outside the house.

AMANDA: Don't say peculiar.

TOM: Face the facts. She is.

(THE DANCE-HALL MUSIC CHANGES TO A TANGO THAT HAS
A MINOR AND SOMEWHAT OMINOUS TONE.)

AMANDA: In what way is she peculiar—may I ask?

TOM: (*Gently*) She lives in a world of her own—a world of—
little glass ornaments, Mother. . . . (*Gets up. Amanda remains holding brush, looking at him, troubled*) She plays old
phonograph records and—that's about all— (*He glances at
himself in the mirror and crosses to door.*)

AMANDA: (*Sharply*) Where are you going?

TOM: I'm going to the movies. (*Out screen door.*)

AMANDA: Not to the movies, every night to the movies!
(*Follows quickly to screen door*) I don't believe you always go
to the movies! (*He is gone. Amanda looks worriedly after
him for a moment. Then vitality and optimism return and
she turns from the door. Crossing to portieres*) Laura! Laura!
(*Laura answers from kitchenette.*)

LAURA: Yes, Mother.

AMANDA: Let those dishes go and come in front! (*Laura appears with dish towel. Gaily*) Laura, come here and make a
wish on the moon!

(SCREEN IMAGE: MOON.)

LAURA: (*Entering*) Moon—moon?

AMANDA: A little silver slipper of a moon.
Look over your left shoulder, Laura, and make a wish!

(*Laura looks faintly puzzled as if called out of sleep.
Amanda seizes her shoulders and turns her at an angle by
the door.*)

Now!
Now, darling, *wish!*

LAURA: What shall I wish for, Mother?

AMANDA: (*Her voice trembling and her eyes suddenly filling
with tears*) Happiness! Good fortune! (*The violin rises and
the stage dims out.*)

CURTAIN

SCENE VI

IMAGE: HIGH SCHOOL HERO.

And so the following evening I brought Jim home to dinner. I had known Jim slightly in high school. In high school Jim was a hero. He had tremendous Irish good nature and vitality with the scrubbed and polished look of white chinaware. He seemed to move in a continual spotlight. He was a star in basketball, captain of the debating club, president of the senior class and the glee club and he sang the male lead in the annual light operas. He was always running or bounding, never just walking. He seemed always at the point of defeating the law of gravity. He was shooting with such velocity through his adolescence that you would logically expect him to arrive at nothing short of the White House by the time he was thirty. But Jim apparently ran into more interference after his graduation from Soldan. His speed had definitely slowed. Six years after he left high school he was holding a job that wasn't much better than mine.

(IMAGE: CLERK.)

He was the only one at the warehouse with whom I was on friendly terms. I was valuable to him as someone who could remember his former glory, who had seen him win basketball games and the silver cup in debating. He knew of my secret practice of retiring to a cabinet of the wash-room to work on poems when business was slack in the warehouse. He called me Shakespeare. And while the other boys in the warehouse regarded me with suspicious hostility, Jim took a humorous attitude toward me. Gradually his attitude affected the others, their hostility wore off and they also began to smile at me as people smile at an oddly fashioned dog who trots across their path at some distance.

I knew that Jim and Laura had known each other at Soldan, and I had heard Laura speak admiringly of his voice. I didn't know if Jim remembered her or not. In high school Laura had been as unobtrusive as Jim had been astonishing. If he did remember Laura, it was not as my sister, for when I asked him to dinner, he grinned and said, "You know, Shakespeare, I never thought of you as having folks!"

He was about to discover that I did. . . .

(LIGHT UP STAGE.)

(LEGEND ON SCREEN: "THE ACCENT OF A COMING FOOT.")

(*Friday evening. It is about five o'clock of a late spring evening which comes "scattering poems in the sky."*)

(*A delicate lemony light is in the Wingfield apartment.*)

(*Amanda has worked like a Turk in preparation for the gentleman caller. The results are astonishing. The new floor lamp with its rose-silk shade is in place, a colored paper lantern conceals the broken light fixture in the ceiling, new billowing white curtains are at the windows, chintz covers are on chairs and sofa, a pair of new sofa pillows make their initial appearance.*)

(*Open boxes and tissue paper are scattered on the floor.*)

(*Laura stands in the middle with lifted arms while Amanda crouches before her, adjusting the hem of the new dress, devout and ritualistic. The dress is colored and designed by memory. The arrangement of Laura's hair is changed; it is softer and more becoming. A fragile, unearthly prettiness has come out in Laura: she is like a piece of translucent glass touched by light, given a momentary radiance, not actual, not lasting.*)

AMANDA: (*Impatiently*) Why are you trembling?
LAURA: Mother, you've made me so nervous!
AMANDA: How have I made you nervous?
LAURA: By all this fuss! You make it seem so important!
AMANDA: I don't understand you, Laura. You couldn't be satisfied with just sitting home, and yet whenever I try to arrange something for you, you seem to resist it. (*She gets up.*)
   Now take a look at yourself.
   No, wait! Wait just a moment—I have an idea!
LAURA: What is it now?

(*Amanda produces two powder puffs which she wraps in handkerchiefs and stuffs in Laura's bosom.*)

LAURA: Mother, what are you doing?

AMANDA: They call them "Gay Deceivers"!

LAURA: I won't wear them!

AMANDA: You will!

LAURA: Why should I?

AMANDA: Because, to be painfully honest, your chest is flat.

LAURA: You make it seem like we were setting a trap.

AMANDA: All pretty girls are a trap, a pretty trap, and men expect them to be.

(LEGEND: "A PRETTY TRAP.")

Now look at yourself, young lady. This is the prettiest you will ever be!

I've got to fix myself now! You're going to be surprised by your mother's appearance! (*She crosses through portieres, humming gaily.*)

(*Laura moves slowly to the long mirror and stares solemnly at herself.*)

(*A wind blows the white curtains inward in a slow, graceful motion and with a faint, sorrowful sighing.*)

AMANDA: (*Off stage*) It isn't dark enough yet. (*She turns slowly before the mirror with a troubled look.*)

(LEGEND ON SCREEN: "THIS IS MY SISTER: CELEBRATE HER WITH STRINGS!" MUSIC.)

AMANDA: (*Laughing, off*) I'm going to show you something. I'm going to make a spectacular appearance!

LAURA: What is it, Mother?

AMANDA: Possess your soul in patience—you will see!

Something I've resurrected from that old trunk! Styles haven't changed so terribly much after all. . . . (*She parts the portieres.*)

Now just look at your mother! (*She wears a girlish frock of yellowed voile with a blue silk sash. She carries a bunch of jonquils—the legend of her youth is nearly revived. Feverishly.*)

This is the dress in which I led the cotillion. Won the cakewalk twice at Sunset Hill, wore one spring to the Governor's ball in Jackson!

See how I sashayed around the ballroom, Laura? (*She raises her skirt and does a mincing step around the room.*)

I wore it on Sundays for my gentlemen callers! I had it on the day I met your father—

I had malaria fever all that spring. The change of climate from East Tennessee to the Delta—weakened resistance—I had a little temperature all the time—not enough to be serious—just enough to make me restless and giddy!—Invitations poured in—parties all over the Delta!—"Stay in bed," said Mother, "you have fever!"—but I just wouldn't.—I took quinine but kept on going, going!—Evenings, dances!—Afternoons, long, long rides! Picnics—lovely!—So lovely, that country in May.—All lacy with dogwood, literally flooded with jonquils!—That was the spring I had the craze for jonquils. Jonquils became an absolute obsession. Mother said, "Honey, there's no more room for jonquils." And still I kept on bringing in more jonquils. Whenever, wherever I saw them, I'd say, "Stop! Stop! I see jonquils!" I made the young men help me gather the jonquils! It was a joke, Amanda and her jonquils! Finally there were no more vases to hold them, every available space was filled with jonquils. No vases to hold them? All right, I'll hold them myself! And then I— (*She stops in front of the picture.* MUSIC) met your father!

Malaria fever and jonquils and then—this—boy. . . . (*She switches on the rose-colored lamp.*)

I hope they get here before it starts to rain. (*She crosses upstage and places the jonquils in bowl on table.*)

I gave your brother a little extra change so he and Mr. O'Connor could take the service car home.

LAURA: (*With altered look*) What did you say his name was?

AMANDA: O'Connor.

LAURA: What is his first name?

AMANDA: I don't remember. Oh, yes, I do. It was—Jim!

(*Laura sways slightly and catches hold of a chair.*)

(LEGEND ON SCREEN: "NOT JIM!")

LAURA: (*Faintly*) Not—Jim!

AMANDA: Yes, that was it, it was Jim! I've never known a Jim that wasn't nice!

(MUSIC: OMINOUS.)

LAURA: Are you sure his name is Jim O'Connor?

AMANDA: Yes. Why?

LAURA: Is he the one that Tom used to know in high school?

AMANDA: He didn't say so. I think he just got to know him at the warehouse.

LAURA: There was a Jim O'Connor we both knew in high school— (*Then, with effort*) If that is the one that Tom is bringing to dinner—you'll have to excuse me, I won't come to the table.

AMANDA: What sort of nonsense is this?

LAURA: You asked me once if I'd ever liked a boy. Don't you remember I showed you this boy's picture?

AMANDA: You mean the boy you showed me in the year book?

LAURA: Yes, that boy.

AMANDA: Laura, Laura, were you in love with that boy?

LAURA: I don't know, Mother. All I know is I couldn't sit at the table if it was him!

AMANDA: It won't be him! It isn't the least bit likely. But whether it is or not, you will come to the table. You will not be excused.

LAURA: I'll have to be, Mother.

AMANDA: I don't intend to humor your silliness, Laura. I've had too much from you and your brother, both!

So just sit down and compose yourself till they come. Tom has forgotten his key so you'll have to let them in, when they arrive.

LAURA: (*Panicky*) Oh, Mother—*you* answer the door!

AMANDA: (*Lightly*) I'll be in the kitchen—busy!

LAURA: Oh, Mother, please answer the door, don't make me do it!

AMANDA: (*Crossing into kitchenette*) I've got to fix the dressing for the salmon. Fuss, fuss—silliness!—over a gentleman caller!

(*Door swings shut. Laura is left alone.*)

(LEGEND: "TERROR!")

(*She utters a low moan and turns off the lamp—sits stiffly on the edge of the sofa, knotting her fingers together.*)

(LEGEND ON SCREEN: "THE OPENING OF A DOOR!")

(*Tom and Jim appear on the fire-escape steps and climb to landing. Hearing their approach, Laura rises with a panicky gesture. She retreats to the portieres.*)

(*The doorbell. Laura catches her breath and touches her throat. Low drums.*)

AMANDA: (*Calling*) Laura, sweetheart! The door!

(*Laura stares at it without moving.*)

JIM: I think we just beat the rain.
TOM: Uh-huh. (*He rings again, nervously. Jim whistles and fishes for a cigarette.*)
AMANDA: (*Very, very gaily*) Laura, that is your brother and Mr. O'Connor! Will you let them in, darling?

(*Laura crosses toward kitchenette door.*)

LAURA: (*Breathlessly*) Mother—you go to the door!

(*Amanda steps out of kitchenette and stares furiously at Laura. She points imperiously at the door.*)

LAURA: Please, please!
AMANDA: (*In a fierce whisper*) What is the matter with you, you silly thing?
LAURA: (*Desperately*) Please, you answer it, *please!*
AMANDA: I told you I wasn't going to humor you, Laura. Why have you chosen this moment to lose your mind?
LAURA: Please, please, please, you go!
AMANDA: You'll have to go to the door because I can't!
LAURA: (*Despairingly*) I can't either!
AMANDA: *Why?*
LAURA: I'm *sick!*
AMANDA: I'm sick, too—of your nonsense! Why can't you and your brother be normal people? Fantastic whims and behavior!

(*Tom gives a long ring.*)

Preposterous goings on! Can you give me one reason— (*Calls out lyrically*) COMING! JUST ONE SECOND!—why you should be afraid to open a door? Now you answer it, Laura!

LAURA: Oh, oh, oh . . . (*She returns through the portieres. Darts to the victrola and winds it frantically and turns it on.*)

AMANDA: Laura Wingfield, you march right to that door!

LAURA: Yes—yes, Mother! (*A faraway, scratchy rendition of "Dardanella" softens the air and gives her strength to move through it. She slips to the door and draws it cautiously open.*)

(*Tom enters with the caller, Jim O'Connor.*)

TOM: Laura, this is Jim. Jim, this is my sister, Laura.

JIM: (*Stepping inside*) I didn't know that Shakespeare had a sister!

LAURA: (*Retreating stiff and trembling from the door*) How—how do you do?

JIM: (*Heartily extending his hand*) Okay!

(*Laura touches it hesitantly with hers.*)

JIM: Your hand's *cold*, Laura!

LAURA: Yes, well—I've been playing the victrola. . . .

JIM: Must have been playing classical music on it! You ought to play a little hot swing music to warm you up!

LAURA: Excuse me—I haven't finished playing the victrola. . . . (*She turns awkwardly and hurries into the front room. She pauses a second by the victrola. Then catches her breath and darts through the portieres like a frightened deer.*)

JIM: (*Grinning*) What was the matter?

TOM: Oh—with Laura? Laura is—terribly shy.

JIM: Shy, huh? It's unusual to meet a shy girl nowadays. I don't believe you ever mentioned you had a sister.

TOM: Well, now you know. I have one. Here is the *Post Dispatch*. You want a piece of it?

JIM: Uh-huh.

TOM: What piece? The comics?

JIM: Sports! (*Glances at it*) Ole Dizzy Dean is on his bad behavior.

TOM: (*Disinterest*) Yeah? (*Lights cigarette and crosses back to fire-escape door.*)

JIM: Where are *you* going?

TOM: I'm going out on the terrace.

JIM: (*Goes after him*) You know, Shakespeare—I'm going to sell you a bill of goods!

TOM: What goods?

JIM: A course I'm taking.

TOM: Huh?

JIM: In public speaking! You and me, we're not the warehouse type.

TOM: Thanks—that's good news. But what has public speaking got to do with it?

JIM: It fits you for—executive positions!

TOM: Awww.

JIM: I tell you it's done a helluva lot for me.

(IMAGE: EXECUTIVE AT DESK.)

TOM: In what respect?

JIM: In every! Ask yourself what is the difference between you an' me and men in the office down front? Brains?—No!—Ability?—No! Then what? Just one little thing—

TOM: What is that one little thing?

JIM: Primarily it amounts to—social poise! Being able to square up to people and hold your own on any social level!

AMANDA: (*Off stage*) Tom?

TOM: Yes, Mother?

AMANDA: Is that you and Mr. O'Connor?

TOM: Yes, Mother.

AMANDA: Well, you just make yourselves comfortable in there.

TOM: Yes, Mother.

AMANDA: Ask Mr. O'Connor if he would like to wash his hands.

JIM: Aw, no—no—thank you—I took care of that at the warehouse. Tom—

TOM: Yes?

JIM: Mr. Mendoza was speaking to me about you.

TOM: Favorably?

JIM: What do you think?

TOM: Well—

JIM: You're going to be out of a job if you don't wake up.

TOM: I am waking up—

JIM: You show no signs.

TOM: The signs are interior.

(IMAGE ON SCREEN: THE SAILING VESSEL WITH JOLLY ROGER AGAIN.)

TOM: I'm planning to change. (*He leans over the rail speaking with quiet exhilaration. The incandescent marquees and signs of the first-run movie houses light his face from across the alley. He looks like a voyager*) I'm right at the point of committing myself to a future that doesn't include the warehouse and Mr. Mendoza or even a night-school course in public speaking.

JIM: What are you gassing about?

TOM: I'm tired of the movies.

JIM: Movies!

TOM: Yes, movies! Look at them— (*A wave toward the marvels of Grand Avenue*) All of those glamorous people—having adventures—hogging it all, gobbling the whole thing up! You know what happens? People go to the *movies* instead of *moving!* Hollywood characters are supposed to have all the adventures for everybody in America, while everybody in America sits in a dark room and watches them have them! Yes, until there's a war. That's when adventure becomes available to the masses! *Everyone's* dish, not only Gable's! Then the people in the dark room come out of the dark room to have some adventures themselves—Goody, goody!—It's our turn now, to go to the South Sea Island—to make a safari—to be exotic, far-off!—But I'm not patient. I don't want to wait till then. I'm tired of the *movies* and I am *about* to *move!*

JIM: (*Incredulously*) Move?

TOM: Yes.

JIM: When?

TOM: Soon!

JIM: Where? Where?

(THEME THREE MUSIC SEEMS TO ANSWER THE QUESTION, WHILE TOM THINKS IT OVER. HE SEARCHES AMONG HIS POCKETS.)

TOM: I'm starting to boil inside. I know I seem dreamy, but inside—well, I'm boiling!—Whenever I pick up a shoe, I

shudder a little thinking how short life is and what I am doing!—Whatever that means, I know it doesn't mean shoes
—except as something to wear on a traveler's feet! (*Finds
paper*) Look—

JIM: What?

TOM: I'm a member.

JIM: (*Reading*) The Union of Merchant Seamen.

TOM: I paid my dues this month, instead of the light bill.

JIM: You will regret it when they turn the lights off.

TOM: I won't be here.

JIM: How about your mother?

TOM: I'm like my father. The bastard son of a bastard! See
how he grins? And he's been absent going on sixteen years!

JIM: You're just talking, you drip. How does your mother feel
about it?

TOM: Shhh!—Here comes Mother! Mother is not acquainted
with my plans!

AMANDA: (*Enters portieres*) Where are you all?

TOM: On the terrace, Mother.

(*They start inside. She advances to them. Tom is distinctly
shocked at her appearance. Even Jim blinks a little. He is
making his first contact with girlish Southern vivacity and in
spite of the night-school course in public speaking is somewhat
thrown off the beam by the unexpected outlay of social charm.*)

(*Certain responses are attempted by Jim but are swept aside
by Amanda's gay laughter and chatter. Tom is embarrassed
but after the first shock Jim reacts very warmly. Grins and
chuckles, is altogether won over.*)

(IMAGE: AMANDA IS A GIRL.)

AMANDA: (*Coyly smiling, shaking her girlish ringlets*) Well,
well, well, so this is Mr. O'Connor. Introductions entirely
unnecessary. I've heard so much about you from my boy. I
finally said to him, Tom—good gracious!—why don't you
bring this paragon to supper? I'd like to meet this nice
young man at the warehouse!—Instead of just hearing him
sing your praises so much!

I don't know why my son is so stand-offish—that's not
Southern behavior!

Let's sit down and— I think we could stand a little more air in here! Tom, leave the door open. I felt a nice fresh breeze a moment ago. Where has it gone to?

Mmm, so warm already! And not quite summer, even. We're going to burn up when summer really gets started.

However, we're having—we're having a very light supper. I think light things are better fo' this time of year. The same as light clothes are. Light clothes an' light food are what warm weather calls fo'. You know our blood gets so thick during th' winter—it takes a while fo' us to *adjust* ou'selves!—when the season changes . . .

It's come so quick this year. I wasn't prepared. All of a sudden—heavens! Already summer!—I ran to the trunk an' pulled out this light dress— Terribly old! Historical almost! But feels so good—so good an' co-ol, y' know. . . .

TOM: Mother—

AMANDA: Yes, honey?

TOM: How about—supper?

AMANDA: Honey, you go ask Sister if supper is ready! You know that Sister is in full charge of supper!

Tell her you hungry boys are waiting for it. (*To Jim.*) Have you met Laura?

JIM: She—

AMANDA: Let you in? Oh, good, you've met already! It's rare for a girl as sweet an' pretty as Laura to be domestic! But Laura is, thank heavens, not only pretty but also very domestic. I'm not at all. I never was a bit. I never could make a thing but angel-food cake. Well, in the South we had so many servants. Gone, gone, gone. All vestige of gracious living! Gone completely! I wasn't prepared for what the future brought me. All of my gentlemen callers were sons of planters and so of course I assumed that I would be married to one and raise my family on a large piece of land with plenty of servants. But man proposes—and woman accepts the proposal!—To vary that old, old saying a little bit— I married no planter! I married a man who worked for the telephone company!—That gallantly smiling gentleman over there! (*Points to the picture*) A telephone man who— fell in love with long-distance!—Now he travels and I don't even know where!—But what am I going on for about my—tribulations?

Tell me yours—I hope you don't have any!

Tom?

TOM: (*Returning*) Yes, Mother?

AMANDA: Is supper nearly ready?

TOM: It looks to me like supper is on the table.

AMANDA: Let me look— (*She rises prettily and looks through portieres*) Oh, lovely!—But where is Sister?

TOM: Laura is not feeling well and she says that she thinks she'd better not come to the table.

AMANDA: What?—Nonsense!—Laura? Oh, Laura!

LAURA: (*Off stage, faintly*) Yes, Mother.

AMANDA: You really must come to the table. We won't be seated until you come to the table!

Come in, Mr. O'Connor. You sit over there, and I'll— Laura? Laura Wingfield!

You're keeping us waiting, honey! We can't say grace until you come to the table!

(*The back door is pushed weakly open and Laura comes in. She is obviously quite faint, her lips trembling, her eyes wide and staring. She moves unsteadily toward the table.*)

(LEGEND: "TERROR!")

(*Outside a summer storm is coming abruptly. The white curtains billow inward at the windows and there is a sorrowful murmur and deep blue dusk.*)

(*Laura suddenly stumbles—she catches at a chair with a faint moan.*)

TOM: Laura!

AMANDA: Laura!

(*There is a clap of thunder.*)

(LEGEND: "AH!")

(*Despairingly*)

Why, Laura, you *are* sick, darling! Tom, help your sister into the living room, dear!

Sit in the living room, Laura—rest on the sofa.
Well!
(*To the gentleman caller.*) Standing over the hot stove made her ill!—I told her that it was just too warm this evening, but—

(*Tom comes back in. Laura is on the sofa.*)

Is Laura all right now?

TOM: Yes.

AMANDA: What *is* that? Rain? A nice cool rain has come up! (*She gives the gentleman caller a frightened look.*) I think we may—have grace—now . . . (*Tom looks at her stupidly.*) Tom, honey—you say grace!

TOM: Oh . . .

"For these and all thy mercies—" (*They bow their heads, Amanda stealing a nervous glance at Jim. In the living room Laura, stretched on the sofa, clenches her hand to her lips, to hold back a shuddering sob.*) God's Holy Name be praised—

THE SCENE DIMS OUT

SCENE VII

A Souvenir.

Half an hour later. Dinner is just being finished in the up-stage area which is concealed by the drawn portieres.

As the curtain rises Laura is still huddled upon the sofa, her feet drawn under her, her head resting on a pale blue pillow, her eyes wide and mysteriously watchful. The new floor lamp with its shade of rose-colored silk gives a soft, becoming light to her face, bringing out the fragile, unearthly prettiness which usually escapes attention. There is a steady murmur of rain, but it is slackening and stops soon after the scene begins; the air outside becomes pale and luminous as the moon breaks out.

A moment after the curtain rises, the lights in both rooms flicker and go out.

JIM: Hey, there, Mr. Light Bulb!

(*Amanda laughs nervously.*)

(LEGEND: "SUSPENSION OF A PUBLIC SERVICE.")

AMANDA: Where was Moses when the lights went out? Ha-ha. Do you know the answer to that one, Mr. O'Connor?

JIM: No, Ma'am, what's the answer?

AMANDA: In the dark! (*Jim laughs appreciatively.*) Everybody sit still. I'll light the candles. Isn't it lucky we have them on the table? Where's a match? Which of you gentlemen can provide a match?

JIM: Here.

AMANDA: Thank you, sir.

JIM: Not at all, Ma'am!

AMANDA: I guess the fuse has burnt out. Mr. O'Connor, can you tell a burnt-out fuse? I know I can't and Tom is a total loss when it comes to mechanics.

(SOUND: GETTING UP: VOICES RECEDE A LITTLE TO KITCH-ENETTE.)

Oh, be careful you don't bump into something. We don't want our gentleman caller to break his neck. Now wouldn't that be a fine howdy-do?

JIM: Ha-ha! Where is the fuse-box?

AMANDA: Right here next to the stove. Can you see anything?

JIM: Just a minute.

AMANDA: Isn't electricity a mysterious thing? Wasn't it Benjamin Franklin who tied a key to a kite? We live in such a mysterious universe, don't we? Some people say that science clears up all the mysteries for us. In my opinion it only creates more!

Have you found it yet?

JIM: No, Ma'am. All these fuses look okay to me.

AMANDA: Tom!

TOM: Yes, Mother?

AMANDA: That light bill I gave you several days ago. The one I told you we got the notices about?

(LEGEND: "HA!")

TOM: Oh.—Yeah.

AMANDA: You didn't neglect to pay it by any chance?

TOM: Why, I—

AMANDA: Didn't! I might have known it!

JIM: Shakespeare probably wrote a poem on that light bill, Mrs. Wingfield.

AMANDA: I might have known better than to trust him with it! There's such a high price for negligence in this world!

JIM: Maybe the poem will win a ten-dollar prize.

AMANDA: We'll just have to spend the remainder of the evening in the nineteenth century, before Mr. Edison made the Mazda lamp!

JIM: Candlelight is my favorite kind of light.

AMANDA: That shows you're romantic! But that's no excuse for Tom.

Well, we got through dinner. Very considerate of them to let us get through dinner before they plunged us into everlasting darkness, wasn't it, Mr. O'Connor?

JIM: Ha-ha!

AMANDA: Tom, as a penalty for your carelessness you can help me with the dishes.

JIM: Let me give you a hand.

AMANDA: Indeed you will not!

JIM: I ought to be good for something.

AMANDA: Good for something? (*Her tone is rhapsodic.*) *You?* Why, Mr. O'Connor, nobody, *nobody's* given me this much entertainment in years—as you have!

JIM: Aw, now, Mrs. Wingfield!

AMANDA: I'm not exaggerating, not one bit! But Sister is all by her lonesome. You go keep her company in the parlor!

I'll give you this lovely old candelabrum that used to be on the altar at the church of the Heavenly Rest. It was melted a little out of shape when the church burnt down. Lightning struck it one spring. Gypsy Jones was holding a revival at the time and he intimated that the church was destroyed because the Episcopalians gave card parties.

JIM: Ha-ha.

AMANDA: And how about you coaxing Sister to drink a little wine? I think it would be good for her! Can you carry both at once?

JIM: Sure. I'm Superman!

AMANDA: Now, Thomas, get into this apron!

(*The door of kitchenette swings closed on Amanda's gay laughter; the flickering light approaches the portieres.*)

(*Laura sits up nervously as he enters. Her speech at first is low and breathless from the almost intolerable strain of being alone with a stranger.*)

(THE LEGEND: "I DON'T SUPPOSE YOU REMEMBER ME AT ALL!")

(*In her first speeches in this scene, before Jim's warmth overcomes her paralyzing shyness, Laura's voice is thin and breathless as though she has just run up a steep flight of stairs.*)

(*Jim's attitude is gently humorous. In playing this scene it should be stressed that while the incident is apparently unimportant, it is to Laura the climax of her secret life.*)

JIM: Hello, there, Laura.

LAURA: (*Faintly*) Hello. (*She clears her throat.*)

JIM: How are you feeling now? Better?

LAURA: Yes. Yes, thank you.

JIM: This is for you. A little dandelion wine. (*He extends it toward her with extravagant gallantry.*)

LAURA: Thank you.

JIM: Drink it—but don't get drunk! (*He laughs heartily. Laura takes the glass uncertainly; laughs shyly.*) Where shall I set the candles?

LAURA: Oh—oh, anywhere . . .

JIM: How about here on the floor? Any objections?

LAURA: No.

JIM: I'll spread a newspaper under to catch the drippings. I like to sit on the floor. Mind if I do?

LAURA: Oh, no.

JIM: Give me a pillow?

LAURA: What?

JIM: A pillow!

LAURA: Oh . . . (*Hands him one quickly.*)

JIM: How about you? Don't you like to sit on the floor?

LAURA: Oh—yes.

JIM: Why don't you, then?

LAURA: I—will.

JIM: Take a pillow! (*Laura does. Sits on the other side of the candelabrum. Jim crosses his legs and smiles engagingly at her*) I can't hardly see you sitting way over there.

LAURA: I can—see you.

JIM: I know, but that's not fair, I'm in the limelight. (*Laura moves her pillow closer*) Good! Now I can see you! Comfortable?

LAURA: Yes.

JIM: So am I. Comfortable as a cow! Will you have some gum?

LAURA: No, thank you.

JIM: I think that I will indulge, with your permission. (*Musingly unwraps it and holds it up*) Think of the fortune made by the guy that invented the first piece of chewing gum. Amazing, huh? The Wrigley Building is one of the sights of Chicago. —I saw it summer before last when I went up to the Century of Progress. Did you take in the Century of Progress?

LAURA: No, I didn't.

JIM: Well, it was quite a wonderful exposition. What impressed me most was the Hall of Science. Gives you an idea of what the future will be in America, even more wonderful than the present time is! (*Pause. Smiling at her*) Your brother tells me you're shy. Is that right, Laura?

LAURA: I—don't know.

JIM: I judge you to be an old-fashioned type of girl. Well, I think that's a pretty good type to be. Hope you don't think I'm being too personal—do you?

LAURA: (*Hastily, out of embarrassment*) I believe I *will* take a piece of gum, if you—don't mind. (*Clearing her throat*) Mr. O'Connor, have you—kept up with your singing?

JIM: Singing? Me?

LAURA: Yes. I remember what a beautiful voice you had.

JIM: When did you hear me sing?

(VOICE OFF STAGE IN THE PAUSE.)

VOICE: (*Off stage*)
    O blow, ye winds, heigh-ho,
    A-roving I will go!
     I'm off to my love
     With a boxing glove—
    Ten thousand miles away!

JIM: You say you've heard me sing?

LAURA: Oh, yes! Yes, very often . . . . I—don't suppose—you remember me—at all?

JIM: (*Smiling doubtfully*) You know I have an idea I've seen you before. I had that idea soon as you opened the door. It seemed almost like I was about to remember your name. But the name that I started to call you—wasn't a name! And so I stopped myself before I said it.

LAURA: Wasn't it—Blue Roses?

JIM: (*Springs up. Grinning*) Blue Roses!—My gosh, yes— Blue Roses! That's what I had on my tongue when you opened the door! Isn't it funny what tricks your memory plays? I didn't connect you with high school somehow or other. But that's where it was; it was high school. I didn't even know you were Shakespeare's sister! Gosh, I'm sorry.

LAURA: I didn't expect you to. You—barely knew me!

JIM: But we did have a speaking acquaintance, huh?

LAURA: Yes, we—spoke to each other.

JIM: When did you recognize me?

LAURA: Oh, right away!

JIM: Soon as I came in the door?

LAURA: When I heard your name I thought it was probably you. I knew that Tom used to know you a little in high school. So when you came in the door— Well, then I was— sure.

JIM: Why didn't you *say* something, then?

LAURA: (*Breathlessly*) I didn't know what to say, I was—too surprised!

JIM: For goodness' sakes! You know, this sure is funny!

LAURA: Yes! Yes, isn't it, though . . .

JIM: Didn't we have a class in something together?

LAURA: Yes, we did.

JIM: What class was that?

LAURA: It was—singing—Chorus!

JIM: Aw!

LAURA: I sat across the aisle from you in the Aud.

JIM: Aw.

LAURA: Mondays, Wednesdays and Fridays.

JIM: Now I remember—you always came in late.

LAURA: Yes, it was so hard for me, getting upstairs. I had that brace on my leg—it clumped so loud!

JIM: I never heard any clumping.

LAURA: (*Wincing at the recollection*) To me it sounded like—thunder!

JIM: Well, well, well, I never even noticed.

LAURA: And everybody was seated before I came in. I had to walk in front of all those people. My seat was in the back row. I had to go clumping all the way up the aisle with everyone watching!

JIM: You shouldn't have been self-conscious.

LAURA: I know, but I was. It was always such a relief when the singing started.

JIM: Aw, yes, I've placed you now! I used to call you Blue Roses. How was it that I got started calling you that?

LAURA: I was out of school a little while with pleurosis. When I came back you asked me what was the matter. I said I had pleurosis—you thought I said Blue Roses. That's what you always called me after that!

JIM: I hope you didn't mind.

LAURA: Oh, no—I liked it. You see, I wasn't acquainted with many—people. . . .

JIM: As I remember you sort of stuck by yourself.

LAURA: I—I—never have had much luck at—making friends.

JIM: I don't see why you wouldn't.

LAURA: Well, I—started out badly.

JIM: You mean being—

LAURA: Yes, it sort of—stood between me—

JIM: You shouldn't have let it!

LAURA: I know, but it did, and—

JIM: You were shy with people!

LAURA: I tried not to be but never could—

JIM: Overcome it?

LAURA: No, I—I never could!

JIM: I guess being shy is something you have to work out of kind of gradually.

LAURA: (*Sorrowfully*) Yes—I guess it—

JIM: Takes time!

LAURA: Yes—

JIM: People are not so dreadful when you know them. That's what you have to remember! And everybody has problems, not just you, but practically everybody has got some problems. You think of yourself as having the only problems, as being the only one who is disappointed. But just look around you and you will see lots of people as disappointed as you are. For instance, I hoped when I was going to high school that I would be further along at this time, six years later, than I am now— You remember that wonderful write-up I had in *The Torch*?

LAURA: Yes! (*She rises and crosses to table.*)

JIM: It said I was bound to succeed in anything I went into! (*Laura returns with the annual*) Holy Jeez! *The Torch!* (*He accepts it reverently. They smile across it with mutual wonder. Laura crouches beside him and they begin to turn through it. Laura's shyness is dissolving in his warmth.*)

LAURA: Here you are in *The Pirates of Penzance*!

JIM: (*Wistfully*) I sang the baritone lead in that operetta.

LAURA: (*Raptly*) So—*beautifully*!

JIM: (*Protesting*) Aw—

LAURA: Yes, yes—beautifully—beautifully!

JIM: You heard me?

LAURA: All three times!

JIM: No!

LAURA: Yes!

JIM: All three performances?

LAURA: (*Looking down*) Yes.

JIM: Why?

LAURA: I—wanted to ask you to—autograph my program.

JIM: Why didn't you ask me to?

LAURA: You were always surrounded by your own friends so much that I never had a chance to.

JIM: You should have just—

LAURA: Well, I—thought you might think I was—

JIM: Thought I might think you was—what?

LAURA: Oh—

JIM: (*With reflective relish*) I was beleaguered by females in those days.

LAURA: You were terribly popular!

JIM: Yeah—

LAURA: You had such a—friendly way—

JIM: I was spoiled in high school.

LAURA: Everybody—liked you!

JIM: Including you?

LAURA: I—yes, I—I did, too— (*She gently closes the book in her lap.*)

JIM: Well, well, well!—Give me that program, Laura. (*She hands it to him. He signs it with a flourish*) There you are—better late than never!

LAURA: Oh, I—what a—surprise!

JIM: My signature isn't worth very much right now. But some day—maybe—it will increase in value! Being disappointed is one thing and being discouraged is something else. I am disappointed but I am not discouraged. I'm twenty-three years old. How old are you?

LAURA: I'll be twenty-four in June.

JIM: That's not old age!

LAURA: No, but—

JIM: You finished high school?

LAURA: (*With difficulty*) I didn't go back.

JIM: You mean you dropped out?

LAURA: I made bad grades in my final examinations. (*She rises and replaces the book and the program. Her voice strained*) How is—Emily Meisenbach getting along?

JIM: Oh, that kraut-head!

LAURA: Why do you call her that?

JIM: That's what she was.

LAURA: You're not still—going with her?

JIM: I never see her.

LAURA: It said in the Personal Section that you were—engaged!

JIM: I know, but I wasn't impressed by that—propaganda!

LAURA: It wasn't—the truth?

JIM: Only in Emily's optimistic opinion!

LAURA: Oh—

(LEGEND: "WHAT HAVE YOU DONE SINCE HIGH SCHOOL?")

(*Jim lights a cigarette and leans indolently back on his elbows smiling at Laura with a warmth and charm which lights her inwardly with altar candles. She remains by the table and turns in her hands a piece of glass to cover her tumult.*)

JIM: (*After several reflective puffs on a cigarette*) What have you done since high school? (*She seems not to hear him*) Huh? (*Laura looks up*) I said what have you done since high school, Laura?

LAURA: Nothing much.

JIM: You must have been doing something these six long years.

LAURA: Yes.

JIM: Well, then, such as what?

LAURA: I took a business course at business college—

JIM: How did that work out?

LAURA: Well, not very—well—I had to drop out, it gave me— indigestion— (*Jim laughs gently.*)

JIM: What are you doing now?

LAURA: I don't do anything—much. Oh, please don't think I sit around doing nothing! My glass collection takes up a good deal of time. Glass is something you have to take good care of.

JIM: What did you say—about glass?

LAURA: Collection I said—I have one— (*She clears her throat and turns away again, acutely shy.*)

JIM: (*Abruptly*) You know what I judge to be the trouble with you? Inferiority complex! Know what that is? That's what they call it when someone low-rates himself! I understand it because I had it, too. Although my case was not so aggravated as yours seems to be. I had it until I took up public speaking, developed my voice, and learned that I had an aptitude for science. Before that time I never thought of myself as being outstanding in any way whatsoever!

   Now I've never made a regular study of it, but I have a friend who says I can analyze people better than doctors that make a profession of it. I don't claim that to be necessarily true, but I can sure guess a person's psychology, Laura! (*Takes out his gum*) Excuse me, Laura. I always take it out when the flavor is gone. I'll use this scrap of paper to wrap it in. I know how it is to get it stuck on a shoe.

   Yep—that's what I judge to be your principal trouble. A lack of confidence in yourself as a person. You don't have the proper amount of faith in yourself. I'm basing that fact on a number of your remarks and also on certain observations I've made. For instance that clumping you thought was so awful in high school. You say that you even dreaded to walk into class. You see what you did? You dropped out of school, you gave up an education because of a clump, which as far as I know was practically non-existent! A little physical defect is what you have. Hardly noticeable even! Magnified thousands of times by imagination!

You know what my strong advice to you is? Think of yourself as *superior* in some way!

LAURA: In what way would I think?

JIM: Why, man alive, Laura! Just look about you a little. What do you see? A world full of common people! All of 'em born and all of 'em going to die! Which of them has one-tenth of your good points! Or mine! Or anyone else's, as far as that goes— Gosh! Everybody excels in some one thing. Some in many! (*Unconsciously glances at himself in the mirror.*) All you've got to do is discover in *what!* Take me, for instance. (*He adjusts his tie at the mirror.*) My interest happens to lie in electro-dynamics. I'm taking a course in radio engineering at night school, Laura, on top of a fairly responsible job at the warehouse. I'm taking that course and studying public speaking.

LAURA: Ohhhh.

JIM: Because I believe in the future of television! (*Turning back to her.*) I wish to be ready to go up right along with it. Therefore I'm planning to get in on the ground floor. In fact I've already made the right connections and all that remains is for the industry itself to get under way! Full steam— (*His eyes are starry.*) *Knowledge*—Zzzzzp! *Money*—Zzzzzzp!—*Power!* That's the cycle democracy is built on! (*His attitude is convincingly dynamic. Laura stares at him, even her shyness eclipsed in her absolute wonder. He suddenly grins.*) I guess you think I think a lot of myself!

LAURA: No—o-o-o, I—

JIM: Now how about you? Isn't there something you take more interest in than anything else?

LAURA: Well, I do—as I said—have my—glass collection— (*A peal of girlish laughter from the kitchen.*)

JIM: I'm not right sure I know what you're talking about. What kind of glass is it?

LAURA: Little articles of it, they're ornaments mostly! Most of them are little animals made out of glass, the tiniest little animals in the world. Mother calls them a glass menagerie! Here's an example of one, if you'd like to see it! This one is one of the oldest. It's nearly thirteen.

(MUSIC: "THE GLASS MENAGERIE.")

(*He stretches out his hand.*)

Oh, be careful—if you breathe, it breaks!

JIM: I'd better not take it. I'm pretty clumsy with things.

LAURA: Go on, I trust you with him! (*Places it in his palm*) There now—you're holding him gently! Hold him over the light, he loves the light! You see how the light shines through him?

JIM: It sure does shine!

LAURA: I shouldn't be partial, but he is my favorite one.

JIM: What kind of a thing is this one supposed to be?

LAURA: Haven't you noticed the single horn on his forehead?

JIM: A unicorn, huh?

LAURA: Mmm-hmmm!

JIM: Unicorns, aren't they extinct in the modern world?

LAURA: I know!

JIM: Poor little fellow, he must feel sort of lonesome.

LAURA: (*Smiling*) Well, if he does he doesn't complain about it. He stays on a shelf with some horses that don't have horns and all of them seem to get along nicely together.

JIM: How do you know?

LAURA: (*Lightly*) I haven't heard any arguments among them!

JIM: (*Grinning*) No arguments, huh? Well, that's a pretty good sign! Where shall I set him?

LAURA: Put him on the table. They all like a change of scenery once in a while!

JIM: (*Stretching*) Well, well, well, well— Look how big my shadow is when I stretch!

LAURA: Oh, oh, yes—it stretches across the ceiling!

JIM: (*Crossing to door*) I think it's stopped raining. (*Opens fire-escape door*) Where does the music come from?

LAURA: From the Paradise Dance Hall across the alley.

JIM: How about cutting the rug a little, Miss Wingfield?

LAURA: Oh, I—

JIM: Or is your program filled up? Let me have a look at it. (*Grasps imaginary card*) Why, every dance is taken! I'll just have to scratch some out. (WALTZ MUSIC: "LA GOLOND-RINA") Ahhh, a waltz! (*He executes some sweeping turns by himself then holds his arms toward Laura.*)

LAURA: (*Breathlessly*) I—can't dance!

JIM: There you go, that inferiority stuff!

LAURA: I've never danced in my life!

JIM: Come on, try!

LAURA: Oh, but I'd step on you!

JIM: I'm not made out of glass.

LAURA: How—how—how do we start?

JIM: Just leave it to me. You hold your arms out a little.

LAURA: Like this?

JIM: A little bit higher. Right. Now don't tighten up, that's that's the main thing about it—relax.

LAURA: (*Laughing breathlessly*) It's hard not to.

JIM: Okay.

LAURA: I'm afraid you can't budge me.

JIM: What do you bet I can't? (*He swings her into motion.*)

LAURA: Goodness, yes, you can!

JIM: Let yourself go, now, Laura, just let yourself go.

LAURA: I'm—

JIM: Come on!

LAURA: Trying!

JIM: Not so stiff— Easy does it!

LAURA: I know but I'm—

JIM: Loosen th' backbone! There now, that's a lot better.

LAURA: Am I?

JIM: Lots, lots better! (*He moves her about the room in a clumsy waltz.*)

LAURA: Oh, my!

JIM: Ha-ha!

LAURA: Oh, my goodness!

JIM: Ha-ha-ha! (*They suddenly bump into the table. Jim stops*) What did we hit on?

LAURA: Table.

JIM: Did something fall off it? I think—

LAURA: Yes.

JIM: I hope that it wasn't the little glass horse with the horn!

LAURA: Yes.

JIM: Aw, aw, aw. Is it broken?

LAURA: Now it is just like all the other horses.

JIM: It's lost its—

LAURA: Horn! It doesn't matter. Maybe it's a blessing in disguise.

JIM: You'll never forgive me. I bet that that was your favorite piece of glass.

LAURA: I don't have favorites much. It's no tragedy, Freckles. Glass breaks so easily. No matter how careful you are. The traffic jars the shelves and things fall off them.

JIM: Still I'm awfully sorry that I was the cause.

LAURA: (*Smiling*) I'll just imagine he had an operation. The horn was removed to make him feel less—freakish! (*They both laugh.*) Now he will feel more at home with the other horses, the ones that don't have horns . . .

JIM: Ha-ha, that's very funny! (*Suddenly serious.*) I'm glad to see that you have a sense of humor. You know—you're—well—very different! Surprisingly different from anyone else I know! (*His voice becomes soft and hesitant with a genuine feeling.*) Do you mind me telling you that? (*Laura is abashed beyond speech.*) I mean it in a nice way . . . (*Laura nods shyly, looking away.*) You make me feel sort of—I don't know how to put it! I'm usually pretty good at expressing things, but— This is something that I don't know how to say! (*Laura touches her throat and clears it—turns the broken unicorn in her hands.*) (*Even softer.*) Has anyone ever told you that you were pretty? (PAUSE: MUSIC.) (*Laura looks up slowly, with wonder, and shakes her head.*) Well, you are! In a very different way from anyone else. And all the nicer because of the difference, too. (*His voice becomes low and husky. Laura turns away, nearly faint with the novelty of her emotions.*) I wish that you were my sister. I'd teach you to have some confidence in yourself. The different people are not like other people, but being different is nothing to be ashamed of. Because other people are not such wonderful people. They're one hundred times one thousand. You're one times one! They walk all over the earth. You just stay here. They're common as—weeds, but—you—well, you're—*Blue Roses!*

(IMAGE ON SCREEN: BLUE ROSES.)

(MUSIC CHANGES.)

LAURA: But blue is wrong for—roses . . .

JIM: It's right for you!—You're—pretty!

LAURA: In what respect am I pretty?

JIM: In all respects—believe me! Your eyes—your hair—are pretty! (*He catches hold of her hand.*) You think I'm making this up because I'm invited to dinner and have to be nice. Oh, I could do that! I could put on an act for you, Laura, and say lots of things without being very sincere. But this time I am. I'm talking to you sincerely. I happened to notice you had this inferiority complex that keeps you from feeling comfortable with people. Somebody needs to build your confidence up and make you proud instead of shy and turning away and—blushing— Somebody—ought to— Ought to—*kiss* you, Laura!

(*His hand slips slowly up her arm to her shoulder.*)

(MUSIC SWELLS TUMULTUOUSLY.)

(*He suddenly turns her about and kisses her on the lips.*)

(*When he releases her, Laura sinks on the sofa with a bright, dazed look.*)

(*Jim backs away and fishes in his pocket for a cigarette.*)

(LEGEND ON SCREEN: "SOUVENIR.")

Stumble-john!

(*He lights the cigarette, avoiding her look.*)

(*There is a peal of girlish laughter from Amanda in the kitchen.*)

(*Laura slowly raises and opens her hand. It still contains the little broken glass animal. She looks at it with a tender, bewildered expression.*)

Stumble-john! I shouldn't have done that— That was way off the beam. You don't smoke, do you?

(*She looks up, smiling, not hearing the question.*)

(*He sits beside her a little gingerly. She looks at him speech-lessly—waiting.*)

(*He coughs decorously and moves a little farther aside as he considers the situation and senses her feelings, dimly, with perturbation.*)

(*Gently.*)

Would you—care for a—mint?

(*She doesn't seem to hear him but her look grows brighter even.*)

Peppermint—Life-Saver? My pocket's a regular drug store—wherever I go . . . (*He pops a mint in his mouth. Then gulps and decides to make a clean breast of it. He speaks slowly and gingerly.*) Laura, you know, if I had a sister like you, I'd do the same thing as Tom. I'd bring out fellows and—introduce her to them. The right type of boys of a type to—appreciate her. Only—well—he made a mistake about me. Maybe I've got no call to be saying this. That may not have been the idea in having me over. But what if it was? There's nothing wrong about that. The only trouble is that in my case—I'm not in a situation to—do the right thing. I can't take down your number and say I'll phone. I can't call up next week and—ask for a date. I thought I had better explain the situation in case you—misunderstood it and—hurt your feelings. . . .

(*Pause.*)

(*Slowly, very slowly, Laura's look changes, her eyes returning slowly from his to the ornament in her palm.*)

(*Amanda utters another gay laugh in the kitchen.*)

LAURA: (*Faintly*) You—won't—call again?

JIM: No, Laura, I can't. (*He rises from the sofa.*) As I was just explaining, I've—got strings on me. Laura, I've—been going steady! I go out all of the time with a girl named Betty. She's a home-girl like you, and Catholic, and Irish, and in a great many ways we—get along fine. I met her last summer on a moonlight boat trip up the river to Alton, on the *Majestic*. Well—right away from the start it was—love!

(LEGEND: LOVE!)

(*Laura sways slightly forward and grips the arm of the sofa. He fails to notice, now enrapt in his own comfortable being.*)

Being in love has made a new man of me!

(*Leaning stiffly forward, clutching the arm of the sofa, Laura struggles visibly with her storm. But Jim is oblivious, she is a long way off.*)

The power of love is really pretty tremendous! Love is something that—changes the whole world, Laura! (*The storm abates a little and Laura leans back. He notices her again.*) It happened that Betty's aunt took sick, she got a wire and had to go to Centralia. So Tom—when he asked me to dinner—I naturally just accepted the invitation, not knowing that you—that he—that I— (*He stops awkwardly.*) Huh—I'm a stumble-john! (*He flops back on the sofa.*)

(*The holy candles in the altar of Laura's face have been snuffed out. There is a look of almost infinite desolation.*)

(*Jim glances at her uneasily.*)

I wish that you would—say something. (*She bites her lip which was trembling and then bravely smiles. She opens her hand again on the broken glass ornament. Then she gently takes his hand and raises it level with her own. She carefully places the unicorn in the palm of his hand, then pushes his fingers closed upon it*) What are you—doing that for? You want me to have him?—Laura? (*She nods*) What for?

LAURA: A—souvenir . . .

(*She rises unsteadily and crouches beside the victrola to wind it up.*)

(LEGEND ON SCREEN: "THINGS HAVE A WAY OF TURNING OUT SO BADLY!")

(OR IMAGE: "GENTLEMAN CALLER WAVING GOOD-BYE!— GAILY.")

(*At this moment Amanda rushes brightly back in the front room. She bears a pitcher of fruit punch in an old-fashioned cut-glass pitcher and a plate of macaroons. The plate has a gold border and poppies painted on it.*)

AMANDA: Well, well, well! Isn't the air delightful after the shower? I've made you children a little liquid refreshment. (*Turns gaily to the gentleman caller*) Jim, do you know that song about lemonade?

> "Lemonade, lemonade
> Made in the shade and stirred with a spade—
> Good enough for any old maid!"

JIM: (*Uneasily*) Ha-ha! No—I never heard it.

AMANDA: Why, Laura! You look so serious!

JIM: We were having a serious conversation.

AMANDA: Good! Now you're better acquainted!

JIM: (*Uncertainly*) Ha-ha! Yes.

AMANDA: You modern young people are much more serious-minded than my generation. I was so gay as a girl!

JIM: You haven't changed, Mrs. Wingfield.

AMANDA: Tonight I'm rejuvenated! The gaiety of the occasion, Mr. O'Connor! (*She tosses her head with a pearl of laughter. Spills lemonade.*) Oooo! I'm baptizing myself!

JIM: Here—let me—

AMANDA: (*Setting the pitcher down*) There now. I discovered we had some maraschino cherries. I dumped them in, juice and all!

JIM: You shouldn't have gone to that trouble, Mrs. Wingfield.

AMANDA: Trouble, trouble? Why, it was loads of fun! Didn't you hear me cutting up in the kitchen? I bet your ears were burning! I told Tom how outdone with him I was for keeping you to himself so long a time! He should have brought you over much, much sooner! Well, now that you've found your way, I want you to be a very frequent caller! Not just occasional but all the time.

Oh, we're going to have a lot of gay times together! I see them coming!

Mmm, just breathe that air! So fresh, and the moon's so pretty!

I'll skip back out—I know where my place is when young folks are having a—serious conversation!

JIM: Oh, don't go out, Mrs. Wingfield. The fact of the matter is I've got to be going.

AMANDA: Going, now? You're joking! Why, it's only the shank of the evening, Mr. O'Connor!

JIM: Well, you know how it is.

AMANDA: You mean you're a young workingman and have to keep workingmen's hours. We'll let you off early tonight. But only on the condition that next time you stay later. What's the best night for you? Isn't Saturday night the best night for you workingmen?

JIM: I have a couple of time-clocks to punch, Mrs. Wingfield. One at morning, another one at night!

AMANDA: My, but you *are* ambitious! You work at night, too?

JIM: No, Ma'am, not work but—Betty! (*He crosses deliberately to pick up his hat. The band at the Paradise Dance Hall goes into a tender waltz.*)

AMANDA: Betty? Betty? Who's—Betty! (*There is an ominous cracking sound in the sky.*)

JIM: Oh, just a girl. The girl I go steady with! (*He smiles charmingly. The sky falls.*)

(LEGEND: "THE SKY FALLS.")

AMANDA: (*A long-drawn exhalation*) Ohhhh . . . Is it a serious romance, Mr. O'Connor?

JIM: We're going to be married the second Sunday in June.

AMANDA: Ohhhh—how nice! Tom didn't mention that you were engaged to be married.

JIM: The cat's not out of the bag at the warehouse yet. You know how they are. They call you Romeo and stuff like that. (*He stops at the oval mirror to put on his hat. He carefully shapes the brim and the crown to give a discreetly dashing effect.*) It's been a wonderful evening, Mrs. Wingfield. I guess this is what they mean by Southern hospitality.

AMANDA: It really wasn't anything at all.

JIM: I hope it don't seem like I'm rushing off. But I promised Betty I'd pick her up at the Wabash depot, an' by the time I get my jalopy down there her train'll be in. Some women are pretty upset if you keep 'em waiting.

AMANDA: Yes, I know— The tyranny of women! (*Extends her hand.*) Good-bye, Mr. O'Connor. I wish you luck—and happiness—and success! All three of them, and so does Laura!—Don't you, Laura?

LAURA: Yes!

JIM: (*Taking her hand*) Good-bye, Laura. I'm certainly going to treasure that souvenir. And don't you forget the good advice I gave you. (*Raises his voice to a cheery shout.*) So long, Shakespeare! Thanks again, ladies— Good night! (*He grins and ducks jauntily out.*)

(*Still bravely grimacing, Amanda closes the door on the gentleman caller. Then she turns back to the room with a puzzled expression. She and Laura don't dare to face each other. Laura crouches beside the victrola to wind it.*)

AMANDA: (*Faintly*) Things have a way of turning out so badly. I don't believe that I would play the victrola. Well, well— well— Our gentleman caller was engaged to be married! Tom!

TOM: (*From back*) Yes, Mother?

AMANDA: Come in here a minute. I want to tell you something awfully funny.

TOM: (*Enters with macaroon and a glass of the lemonade*) Has the gentleman caller gotten away already?

AMANDA: The gentleman caller has made an early departure. What a wonderful joke you played on us!

TOM: How do you mean?

AMANDA: You didn't mention that he was engaged to be married.

TOM: Jim? Engaged?

AMANDA: That's what he just informed us.

TOM: I'll be jiggered! I didn't know about that.

AMANDA: That seems very peculiar.

TOM: What's peculiar about it?

AMANDA: Didn't you call him your best friend down at the warehouse?

TOM: He is, but how did I know?

AMANDA: It seems extremely peculiar that you wouldn't know your best friend was going to be married!

TOM: The warehouse is where I work, not where I know things about people!

AMANDA: You don't know things anywhere! You live in a dream; you manufacture illusions! (*He crosses to door.*) Where are you going?

TOM: I'm going to the movies.

AMANDA: That's right, now that you've had us make such fools of ourselves. The effort, the preparations, all the expense! The new floor lamp, the rug, the clothes for Laura! All for what? To entertain some other girl's fiancé!

Go to the movies, go! Don't think about us, a mother deserted, an unmarried sister who's crippled and has no job! Don't let anything interfere with your selfish pleasure! Just go, go, go—to the movies!

TOM: All right, I will! The more you shout about my selfishness to me the quicker I'll go, and I won't go to the movies!

AMANDA: Go, then! Then go to the moon—you selfish dreamer!

(*Tom smashes his glass on the floor. He plunges out on the fire-escape, slamming the door. Laura screams—cut by door.*)

(*Dance-hall music up. Tom goes to the rail and grips it desperately, lifting his face in the chill white moonlight penetrating the narrow abyss of the alley.*)

(LEGEND ON SCREEN: "AND SO GOOD-BYE . . .")

(*Tom's closing speech is timed with the interior pantomime. The interior scene is played as though viewed through sound-proof glass. Amanda appears to be making a comforting speech to Laura who is huddled upon the sofa. Now that we cannot hear the mother's speech, her silliness is gone and she has dignity and tragic beauty. Laura's dark hair hides her face until at the end of the speech she lifts it to smile at her mother. Amanda's gestures are slow and graceful, almost dance-like, as she comforts the daughter. At the end of her speech she glances a moment at the father's picture—then withdraws through the portieres. At close of Tom's speech, Laura blows out the candles, ending the play.*)

TOM: I didn't go to the moon, I went much further—for time is the longest distance between two places—

Not long after that I was fired for writing a poem on the lid of a shoe-box.

I left Saint Louis. I descended the steps of this fire-escape for a last time and followed, from then on, in my father's footsteps, attempting to find in motion what was lost in space—

I traveled around a great deal. The cities swept about me like dead leaves, leaves that were brightly colored but torn away from the branches.

I would have stopped, but I was pursued by something.

It always came upon me unawares, taking me altogether by surprise. Perhaps it was a familiar bit of music. Perhaps it was only a piece of transparent glass—

Perhaps I am walking along a street at night, in some strange city, before I have found companions. I pass the lighted window of a shop where perfume is sold. The window is filled with pieces of colored glass, tiny transparent bottles in delicate colors, like bits of a shattered rainbow.

Then all at once my sister touches my shoulder. I turn around and look into her eyes . . .

Oh, Laura, Laura, I tried to leave you behind me, but I am more faithful than I intended to be!

I reach for a cigarette, I cross the street, I run into the movies or a bar, I buy a drink, I speak to the nearest stranger—anything that can blow your candles out!

(*Laura bends over the candles.*)

—for nowadays the world is lit by lightning! Blow out your candles, Laura—and so good-bye. . . .

(*She blows the candles out.*)

THE SCENE DISSOLVES

A STREETCAR NAMED DESIRE

And so it was I entered the broken world
To trace the visionary company of love, its voice
An instant in the wind (I know not whither hurled)
But not for long to hold each desperate choice.

"The Broken Tower" by Hart Crane

THE CHARACTERS

BLANCHE
STELLA
STANLEY
MITCH
EUNICE
STEVE
PABLO
A NEGRO WOMAN
A DOCTOR
A NURSE
A YOUNG COLLECTOR
A MEXICAN WOMAN
A TAMALE VENDOR

SCENE ONE

The exterior of a two-story corner building on a street in New Orleans which is named Elysian Fields and runs between the L&N tracks and the river. The section is poor but, unlike corresponding sections in other American cities, it has a raffish charm. The houses are mostly white frame, weathered grey, with rickety outside stairs and galleries and quaintly ornamented gables. This building contains two flats, upstairs and down. Faded white stairs ascend to the entrances of both.

It is first dark of an evening early in May. The sky that shows around the dim white building is a peculiarly tender blue, almost a turquoise, which invests the scene with a kind of lyricism and gracefully attenuates the atmosphere of decay. You can almost feel the warm breath of the brown river beyond the river warehouses with their faint redolences of bananas and coffee. A corresponding air is evoked by the music of Negro entertainers at a barroom around the corner. In this part of New Orleans you are practically always just around the corner, or a few doors down the street, from a tinny piano being played with the infatuated fluency of brown fingers. This "Blue Piano" expresses the spirit of the life which goes on here.

Two women, one white and one colored, are taking the air on the steps of the building. The white woman is Eunice, who occupies the upstairs flat; the colored woman a neighbor, for New Orleans is a cosmopolitan city where there is a relatively warm and easy intermingling of races in the old part of town.

Above the music of the "Blue Piano" the voices of people on the street can be heard overlapping.

NEGRO WOMAN (*to Eunice*): . . . she says St. Barnabas would send out his dog to lick her and when he did she'd feel an icy cold wave all up an' down her. Well, that night when—

A MAN (*to a Sailor*): You keep right on going and you'll find it. You'll hear them tapping on the shutters.

SAILOR (*to Negro Woman and Eunice*): Where's the Four Deuces?

VENDOR: Red hot! Red hots!

NEGRO WOMAN: Don't waste your money in that clip joint!

SAILOR: I've got a date there.

VENDOR: Re-e-ed h-o-o-t!

NEGRO WOMAN: Don't let them sell you a Blue Moon cocktail or you won't go out on your own feet!

(*Two men come around the corner, Stanley Kowalski and Mitch. They are about twenty-eight or thirty years old, roughly dressed in blue denim work clothes. Stanley carries his bowling jacket and a red-stained package from a butcher's.*)

STANLEY (*to Mitch*): Well, what did he say?

MITCH: He said he'd give us even money.

STANLEY: Naw! We gotta have odds!

(*They stop at the foot of the steps.*)

STANLEY (*bellowing*): Hey, there! Stella, Baby!

(*Stella comes out on the first floor landing, a gentle young woman, about twenty-five, and of a background obviously quite different from her husband's.*)

STELLA (*mildly*): Don't holler at me like that. Hi, Mitch.

STANLEY: Catch!

STELLA: What?

STANLEY: Meat!

(*He heaves the package at her. She cries out in protest but manages to catch it: then she laughs breathlessly. Her husband and his companion have already started back around the corner.*)

STELLA (*calling after him*): Stanley! Where are you going?

STANLEY: Bowling!

STELLA: Can I come watch?

STANLEY: Come on. (*He goes out.*)

STELLA: Be over soon. (*To the white woman*) Hello, Eunice. How are you?

EUNICE: I'm all right. Tell Steve to get him a poor boy's sandwich 'cause nothing's left here.

(*They all laugh; the colored woman does not stop. Stella goes out.*)

COLORED WOMAN: What was that package he th'ew at 'er? (*She rises from steps, laughing louder.*)

EUNICE: You hush, now!

NEGRO WOMAN: Catch *what!*

(*She continues to laugh. Blanche comes around the corner, carrying a valise. She looks at a slip of paper, then at the building, then again at the slip and again at the building. Her expression is one of shocked disbelief. Her appearance is incongruous to this setting. She is daintily dressed in a white suit with a fluffy bodice, necklace and earrings of pearl, white gloves and hat, looking as if she were arriving at a summer tea or cocktail party in the garden district. She is about five years older than Stella. Her delicate beauty must avoid a strong light. There is something about her uncertain manner, as well as her white clothes, that suggests a moth.*)

EUNICE (*finally*): What's the matter, honey? Are you lost?

BLANCHE (*with faintly hysterical humor*): They told me to take a street-car named Desire, and then transfer to one called Cemeteries and ride six blocks and get off at— Elysian Fields!

EUNICE: That's where you are now.

BLANCHE: At Elysian Fields?

EUNICE: This here is Elysian Fields.

BLANCHE: They mustn't have—understood—what number I wanted . . .

EUNICE: What number you lookin' for?

(*Blanche wearily refers to the slip of paper.*)

BLANCHE: Six thirty-two.

EUNICE: You don't have to look no further.

BLANCHE (*uncomprehendingly*): I'm looking for my sister, Stella DuBois. I mean—Mrs. Stanley Kowalski.

EUNICE: That's the party.—You just did miss her, though.

BLANCHE: This—can this be—her home?

EUNICE: She's got the downstairs here and I got the up.

BLANCHE: Oh. She's—out?

EUNICE: You noticed that bowling alley around the corner?

BLANCHE: I'm—not sure I did.

EUNICE: Well, that's where she's at, watchin' her husband bowl. (*There is a pause*) You want to leave your suitcase here an' go find her?

BLANCHE: No.

NEGRO WOMAN: I'll go tell her you come.

BLANCHE: Thanks.

NEGRO WOMAN: You welcome. (*She goes out.*)

EUNICE: She wasn't expecting you?

BLANCHE: No. No, not tonight.

EUNICE: Well, why don't you just go in and make yourself at home till they get back.

BLANCHE: How could I—do that?

EUNICE: We own this place so I can let you in.

> (*She gets up and opens the downstairs door. A light goes on behind the blind, turning it light blue. Blanche slowly follows her into the downstairs flat. The surrounding areas dim out as the interior is lighted.*
>
> (*Two rooms can be seen, not too clearly defined. The one first entered is primarily a kitchen but contains a folding bed to be used by Blanche. The room beyond this is a bedroom. Off this room is a narrow door to a bathroom.*)

EUNICE (*defensively, noticing Blanche's look*): It's sort of messed up right now but when it's clean it's real sweet.

BLANCHE: Is it?

EUNICE: Uh-huh, I think so. So you're Stella's sister?

BLANCHE: Yes. (*Wanting to get rid of her*) Thanks for letting me in.

EUNICE: *Por nada*, as the Mexicans say, *por nada!* Stella spoke of you.

BLANCHE: Yes?

EUNICE: I think she said you taught school.

BLANCHE: Yes.

EUNICE: And you're from Mississippi, huh?

BLANCHE: Yes.

EUNICE: She showed me a picture of your home-place, the plantation.

BLANCHE: Belle Reve?

EUNICE: A great big place with white columns.

BLANCHE: Yes . . .

EUNICE: A place like that must be awful hard to keep up.

BLANCHE: If you will excuse me, I'm just about to drop.

EUNICE: Sure, honey. Why don't you set down?

BLANCHE: What I meant was I'd like to be left alone.

EUNICE (*offended*): Aw. I'll make myself scarce, in that case.

BLANCHE: I didn't mean to be rude, but—

EUNICE: I'll drop by the bowling alley an' hustle her up. (*She goes out the door.*)

(*Blanche sits in a chair very stiffly with her shoulders slightly hunched and her legs pressed close together and her hands tightly clutching her purse as if she were quite cold. After a while the blind look goes out of her eyes and she begins to look slowly around. A cat screeches. She catches her breath with a startled gesture. Suddenly she notices something in a half opened closet. She springs up and crosses to it, and removes a whiskey bottle. She pours a half tumbler of whiskey and tosses it down. She carefully replaces the bottle and washes out the tumbler at the sink. Then she resumes her seat in front of the table.*)

BLANCHE (*faintly to herself*): I've got to keep hold of myself!

(*Stella comes quickly around the corner of the building and runs to the door of the downstairs flat.*)

STELLA (*calling out joyfully*): Blanche!

(*For a moment they stare at each other. Then Blanche springs up and runs to her with a wild cry.*)

BLANCHE: Stella, oh, Stella, Stella! Stella for Star!

(*She begins to speak with feverish vivacity as if she feared for either of them to stop and think. They catch each other in a spasmodic embrace.*)

BLANCHE: Now, then, let me look at you. But don't you look at me, Stella, no, no, no, not till later, not till I've bathed and rested! And turn that over-light off! Turn that off! I won't be looked at in this merciless glare! (*Stella laughs and complies*) Come back here now! Oh, my baby! Stella! Stella for Star! (*She embraces her again*) I thought you would never come back to this horrible place! What am I saying? I didn't mean to say that. I meant to be nice about it and say—Oh, what a convenient location and such— Ha-a-ha! Precious lamb! You haven't said a *word* to me.

STELLA: You haven't given me a chance to, honey! (*She laughs, but her glance at Blanche is a little anxious.*)

BLANCHE: Well, now you talk. Open your pretty mouth and talk while I look around for some liquor! I know you must have some liquor on the place! Where could it be, I wonder? Oh, I spy, I spy!

(*She rushes to the closet and removes the bottle; she is shaking all over and panting for breath as she tries to laugh. The bottle nearly slips from her grasp.*)

STELLA (*noticing*): Blanche, you sit down and let me pour the drinks. I don't know what we've got to mix with. Maybe a coke's in the icebox. Look'n see, honey, while I'm—

BLANCHE: No coke, honey, not with my nerves tonight! Where—where—where is—?

STELLA: Stanley? Bowling! He loves it. They're having a— found some soda!—tournament . . .

BLANCHE: Just water, baby, to chase it! Now don't get worried, your sister hasn't turned into a drunkard, she's just all shaken up and hot and tired and dirty! You sit down, now, and explain this place to me! What are you doing in a place like this?

STELLA: Now, Blanche—

BLANCHE: Oh, I'm not going to be hypocritical, I'm going to be honestly critical about it! Never, never, never in my worst dreams could I picture— Only Poe! Only Mr. Edgar Allan Poe!—could do it justice! Out there I suppose is the ghoul-haunted woodland of Weir! (*She laughs.*)

STELLA: No, honey, those are the L&N tracks.

BLANCHE: No, now seriously, putting joking aside. Why didn't you tell me, why didn't you write me, honey, why didn't you let me know?

STELLA (*carefully, pouring herself a drink*): Tell you what, Blanche?

BLANCHE: Why, that you had to live in these conditions!

STELLA: Aren't you being a little intense about it? It's not that bad at all! New Orleans isn't like other cities.

BLANCHE: This has got nothing to do with New Orleans. You might as well say—forgive me, blessed baby! (*She suddenly stops short*) The subject is closed!

STELLA (*a little drily*): Thanks.

(*During the pause, Blanche stares at her. She smiles at Blanche.*)

BLANCHE (*looking down at her glass, which shakes in her hand*): You're all I've got in the world, and you're not glad to see me!

STELLA (*sincerely*): Why, Blanche, you know that's not true.

BLANCHE: No?—I'd forgotten how quiet you were.

STELLA: You never did give me a chance to say much, Blanche. So I just got in the habit of being quiet around you.

BLANCHE (*vaguely*): A good habit to get into . . . (*then, abruptly*) You haven't asked me how I happened to get away from the school before the spring term ended.

STELLA: Well, I thought you'd volunteer that information—if you wanted to tell me.

BLANCHE: You thought I'd been fired?

STELLA: No, I—thought you might have—resigned . . .

BLANCHE: I was so exhausted by all I'd been through my—nerves broke. (*Nervously tamping cigarette*) I was on the verge of—lunacy, almost! So Mr. Graves—Mr. Graves is the high school superintendent—he suggested I take a leave of absence. I couldn't put all of those details into the wire . . . (*She drinks quickly*) Oh, this buzzes right through me and feels so *good!*

STELLA: Won't you have another?

BLANCHE: No, one's my limit.

STELLA: Sure?

BLANCHE: You haven't said a word about my appearance.

STELLA: You look just fine.

BLANCHE: God love you for a liar! Daylight never exposed so total a ruin! But you—you've put on some weight, yes, you're just as plump as a little partridge! And it's so becoming to you!

STELLA: Now, Blanche—

BLANCHE: Yes, it is, it is or I wouldn't say it! You just have to watch around the hips a little. Stand up.

STELLA: Not now.

BLANCHE: You hear me? I said stand up! (*Stella complies reluctantly*) You messy child, you, you've spilt something on that pretty white lace collar! About your hair—you ought to have it cut in a feather bob with your dainty features. Stella, you have a maid, don't you?

STELLA: No. With only two rooms it's—

BLANCHE: What? *Two* rooms, did you say?

STELLA: This one and— (*She is embarrassed.*)

BLANCHE: The other one? (*She laughs sharply. There is an embarrassed silence*) How quiet you are, you're so peaceful. Look how you sit there with your little hands folded like a cherub in choir!

STELLA (*uncomfortably*): I never had anything like your energy, Blanche.

BLANCHE: Well, I never had your beautiful self-control. I am going to take just one little tiny nip more, sort of to put the stopper on, so to speak. . . . Then put the bottle away so I won't be tempted. (*She rises*) I want you to look at *my* figure! (*She turns around*) You know I haven't put on one ounce in ten years, Stella? I weigh what I weighed the summer you left Belle Reve. The summer Dad died and you left us . . .

STELLA (*a little wearily*): It's just incredible, Blanche, how well you're looking.

BLANCHE: You see I still have that awful vanity about my looks even now that my looks are slipping! (*She laughs nervously and glances at Stella for reassurance.*)

STELLA (*dutifully*): They haven't slipped one particle.

BLANCHE: After all I've been through? You think I believe that story? Blessed child! (*She touches her forehead shakily*) Stella, there's—only two rooms?

STELLA: And a bathroom.

BLANCHE: Oh, you do have a bathroom! First door to the right at the top of the stairs? (*They both laugh uncomfortably*) But, Stella, I don't see where you're going to put me!

STELLA: We're going to put you in here.

BLANCHE: What kind of bed's this—one of those collapsible things?

(*She sits on it.*)

STELLA: Does it feel all right?

BLANCHE (*dubiously*): Wonderful, honey. I don't like a bed that gives much. But there's no door between the two rooms, and Stanley—will it be decent?

STELLA: Stanley is Polish, you know.

BLANCHE: Oh, yes. They're something like Irish, aren't they?

STELLA: Well—

BLANCHE: Only not so—highbrow? (*They both laugh again in the same way*) I brought some nice clothes to meet all your lovely friends in.

STELLA: I'm afraid you won't think they are lovely.

BLANCHE: What are they like?

STELLA: They're Stanley's friends.

BLANCHE: Polacks?

STELLA: They're a mixed lot, Blanche.

BLANCHE: Heterogeneous—types?

STELLA: Oh, yes. Yes, types is right!

BLANCHE: Well—anyhow—I brought nice clothes and I'll wear them. I guess you're hoping I'll say I'll put up at a hotel, but I'm not going to put up at a hotel. I want to be *near* you, got to be *with* somebody, I *can't* be *alone!* Because—as you must have noticed—I'm—*not* very *well* . . . (*Her voice drops and her look is frightened.*)

STELLA: You seem a little bit nervous or overwrought or something.

BLANCHE: Will Stanley like me, or will I be just a visiting in-law, Stella? I couldn't stand that.

STELLA: You'll get along fine together, if you'll just try not to—well—compare him with men that we went out with at home.

BLANCHE: Is he so—different?

STELLA: Yes. A different species.

BLANCHE: In what way; what's he like?

STELLA: Oh, you can't describe someone you're in love with! Here's a picture of him! (*She hands a photograph to Blanche.*)

BLANCHE: An officer?

STELLA: A Master Sergeant in the Engineers' Corps. Those are decorations!

BLANCHE: He had those on when you met him?

STELLA: I assure you I wasn't just blinded by all the brass.

BLANCHE: That's not what I—

STELLA: But of course there were things to adjust myself to later on.

BLANCHE: Such as his civilian background! (*Stella laughs uncertainly*) How did he take it when you said I was coming?

STELLA: Oh, Stanley doesn't know yet.

BLANCHE (*frightened*): You—haven't told him?

STELLA: He's on the road a good deal.

BLANCHE: Oh. Travels?

STELLA: Yes.

BLANCHE: Good. I mean—isn't it?

STELLA (*half to herself*): I can hardly stand it when he is away for a night . . .

BLANCHE: Why, Stella!

STELLA: When he's away for a week I nearly go wild!

BLANCHE: Gracious!

STELLA: And when he comes back I cry on his lap like a baby . . .

(*She smiles to herself.*)

BLANCHE: I guess that is what is meant by being in love . . . (*Stella looks up with a radiant smile.*) Stella—

STELLA: What?

BLANCHE (*in an uneasy rush*): I haven't asked you the things you probably thought I was going to ask. And so I'll expect you to be understanding about what *I* have to tell *you.*

STELLA: What, Blanche? (*Her face turns anxious.*)

BLANCHE: Well, Stella—you're going to reproach me, I know that you're bound to reproach me—but before you do— take into consideration—you left! I stayed and struggled! You came to New Orleans and looked out for yourself! *I* stayed at *Belle Reve* and tried to hold it together! I'm not meaning this in any reproachful way, but *all* the burden descended on *my* shoulders.

STELLA: The best I could do was make my own living, Blanche.

(*Blanche begins to shake again with intensity.*)

BLANCHE: I know, I know. But you are the one that abandoned Belle Reve, not I! I stayed and fought for it, bled for it, almost died for it!

STELLA: Stop this hysterical outburst and tell me what's happened? What do you mean fought and bled? What kind of—

BLANCHE: I knew you would, Stella. I knew you would take this attitude about it!

STELLA: About—what?—please!

BLANCHE (*slowly*): The loss—the loss . . .

STELLA: Belle Reve? Lost, is it? No!

BLANCHE: Yes, Stella.

(*They stare at each other across the yellow-checked linoleum of the table. Blanche slowly nods her head and Stella looks slowly down at her hands folded on the table. The music of the "blue piano" grows louder. Blanche touches her handkerchief to her forehead.*)

STELLA: But how did it go? What happened?

BLANCHE (*springing up*): You're a fine one to ask me how it went!

STELLA: Blanche!

BLANCHE: You're a fine one to sit there *accusing me* of it!

STELLA: *Blanche!*

BLANCHE: I, I, *I* took the blows in my face and my body! All of those deaths! The long parade to the graveyard! Father, mother! Margaret, that dreadful way! So big with it, it couldn't be put in a coffin! But had to be burned like rubbish! You just came home in time for the funerals, Stella. And funerals are pretty compared to deaths. Funerals are quiet, but deaths—not always. Sometimes their breathing is hoarse, and sometimes it rattles, and sometimes they even cry out to you, "Don't let me go!" Even the old, sometimes, say, "Don't let me go." As if you were able to stop them! But funerals are quiet, with pretty flowers. And, oh, what gorgeous boxes they pack them away in! Unless you were there at the bed when they cried out, "Hold me!" you'd never suspect there was the struggle for breath and bleeding. You didn't dream, but I saw! *Saw! Saw!* And now you sit there telling me with your eyes that I let the place go! How in hell do you think all that sickness and dying was paid for? Death is expensive, Miss Stella! And old Cousin Jessie's right after Margaret's, hers! Why, the Grim Reaper had put up his tent on our doorstep! . . . Stella. Belle Reve was his headquarters! Honey—that's how it slipped through my fingers! Which of them left us a fortune? Which of them left a cent of insurance even? Only poor Jessie—one hundred to pay for her coffin. That was all, Stella! And I with my pitiful salary at the school. Yes, accuse me! Sit there and stare at me, thinking I let the place go! *I* let the place go? Where were *you!* In bed with your—Polack!

STELLA (*springing*): Blanche! You be still! That's enough! (*She starts out.*)

BLANCHE: Where are you going?

STELLA: I'm going into the bathroom to wash my face.

BLANCHE: Oh, Stella, Stella, you're crying!

STELLA: Does that surprise you?

(*Stella goes into the bathroom.*
(*Outside is the sound of men's voices. Stanley, Steve and Mitch cross to the foot of the steps.*)

STEVE: And the old lady is on her way to Mass and she's late and there's a cop standin' in front of th' church an' she comes runnin' up an' says, "Officer—is Mass out yet?" He looks her over and says, "No, Lady, y'r ass ain't out but y'r hat's on crooked!" (*They give a hoarse bellow of laughter.*)

STEVE: Playing poker tomorrow night?

STANLEY: Yeah—at Mitch's.

MITCH: Not at my place. My mother's still sick. (*He starts off.*)

STANLEY (*calling after him*): All right, we'll play at my place . . . but you bring the beer.

EUNICE (*hollering down from above*): Break it up down there! I made the spaghetti dish and ate it myself.

STEVE (*going upstairs*): I told you and phoned you we was playing. (*To the men*) Jax beer!

EUNICE: You never phoned me once.

STEVE: I told you at breakfast—and phoned you at lunch . . .

EUNICE: Well, never mind about that. You just get yourself home here once in a while.

STEVE: You want it in the papers?

(*More laughter and shouts of parting come from the men. Stanley throws the screen door of the kitchen open and comes in. He is of medium height, about five feet eight or nine, and strongly, compactly built. Animal joy in his being is implicit in all his movements and attitudes. Since earliest manhood the center of his life has been pleasure with women, the giving and taking of it, not with weak indulgence, dependently, but with the power and pride of a richly feathered male bird among hens. Branching out from this complete and satisfying center are all the auxiliary channels of his life, such as his heartiness with men, his appreciation of rough humor, his love of good drink and food and games, his car, his radio, everything that is his, that bears his emblem of the gaudy seed-bearer. He sizes women up at a glance, with sexual classifications, crude images flashing into his mind and determining the way he smiles at them.*)

BLANCHE (*drawing involuntarily back from his stare*): You must be Stanley. I'm Blanche.

STANLEY: Stella's sister?

BLANCHE: Yes.

STANLEY: H'lo. Where's the little woman?

BLANCHE: In the bathroom.

STANLEY: Oh. Didn't know you were coming in town.

BLANCHE: I—uh—

STANLEY: Where you from, Blanche?

BLANCHE: Why, I—live in Laurel.

(*He has crossed to the closet and removed the whiskey bottle.*)

STANLEY: In Laurel, huh? Oh, yeah. Yeah, in Laurel, that's right. Not in my territory. Liquor goes fast in hot weather. (*He holds the bottle to the light to observe its depletion.*) Have a shot?

BLANCHE: No, I—rarely touch it.

STANLEY: Some people rarely touch it, but it touches them often.

BLANCHE (*faintly*): Ha-ha.

STANLEY: My clothes're stickin' to me. Do you mind if I make myself comfortable? (*He starts to remove his shirt.*)

BLANCHE: Please, please do.

STANLEY: Be comfortable is my motto.

BLANCHE: It's mine, too. It's hard to stay looking fresh. I haven't washed or even powdered my face and—here you are!

STANLEY: You know you can catch cold sitting around in damp things, especially when you been exercising hard like bowling is. You're a teacher, aren't you?

BLANCHE: Yes.

STANLEY: What do you teach, Blanche?

BLANCHE: English.

STANLEY: I never was a very good English student. How long you here for, Blanche?

BLANCHE: I—don't know yet.

STANLEY: You going to shack up here?

BLANCHE: I thought I would if it's not inconvenient for you all.

STANLEY: Good.

BLANCHE: Traveling wears me out.

STANLEY: Well, take it easy.

(*A cat screeches near the window. Blanche springs up.*)

BLANCHE: What's that?

STANLEY: Cats . . . Hey, Stella!

STELLA (*faintly, from the bathroom*): Yes, Stanley.

STANLEY: Haven't fallen in, have you? (*He grins at Blanche. She tries unsuccessfully to smile back. There is a silence*) I'm afraid I'll strike you as being the unrefined type. Stella's spoke of you a good deal. You were married once, weren't you?

(*The music of the polka rises up, faint in the distance.*)

BLANCHE: Yes. When I was quite young.

STANLEY: What happened?

BLANCHE: The boy—the boy died. (*She sinks back down*) I'm afraid I'm—going to be sick!

(*Her head falls on her arms.*)

SCENE TWO

It is six o'clock the following evening. Blanche is bathing. Stella is completing her toilette. Blanche's dress, a flowered print, is laid out on Stella's bed.

Stanley enters the kitchen from outside, leaving the door open on the perpetual "blue piano" around the corner.

STANLEY: What's all this monkey doings?

STELLA: Oh, Stan! (*She jumps up and kisses him which he accepts with lordly composure*) I'm taking Blanche to Galatoire's for supper and then to a show, because it's your poker night.

STANLEY: How about my supper, huh? I'm not going to no Galatoire's for supper!

STELLA: I put you a cold plate on ice.

STANLEY: Well, isn't that just dandy!

STELLA: I'm going to try to keep Blanche out till the party breaks up because I don't know how she would take it. So we'll go to one of the little places in the Quarter afterwards and you'd better give me some money.

STANLEY: Where is she?

STELLA: She's soaking in a hot tub to quiet her nerves. She's terribly upset.

STANLEY: Over what?

STELLA: She's been through such an ordeal.

STANLEY: Yeah?

STELLA: Stan, we've—lost Belle Reve!

STANLEY: The place in the country?

STELLA: Yes.

STANLEY: How?

STELLA (*vaguely*): Oh, it had to be—sacrificed or something. (*There is a pause while Stanley considers. Stella is changing into her dress*) When she comes in be sure to say something nice about her appearance. And, oh! Don't mention the baby. I haven't said anything yet, I'm waiting until she gets in a quieter condition.

STANLEY (*ominously*): So?

STELLA: And try to understand her and be nice to her, Stan.

BLANCHE (*singing in the bathroom*):

"From the land of the sky blue water,
    They brought a captive maid!"

STELLA: She wasn't expecting to find us in such a small place. You see I'd tried to gloss things over a little in my letters.

STANLEY: So?

STELLA: And admire her dress and tell her she's looking wonderful. That's important with Blanche. Her little weakness!

STANLEY: Yeah. I get the idea. Now let's skip back a little to where you said the country place was disposed of.

STELLA: Oh!—yes . . .

STANLEY: How about that? Let's have a few more details on that subjeck.

STELLA: It's best not to talk much about it until she's calmed down.

STANLEY: So that's the deal, huh? Sister Blanche cannot be annoyed with business details right now!

STELLA: You saw how she was last night.

STANLEY: Uh-hum, I saw how she was. Now let's have a gander at the bill of sale.

STELLA: I haven't seen any.

STANLEY: She didn't show you no papers, no deed of sale or nothing like that, huh?

STELLA: It seems like it wasn't sold.

STANLEY: Well, what in hell was it then, give away? To charity?

STELLA: Shhh! She'll hear you.

STANLEY: I don't care if she hears me. Let's see the papers!

STELLA: There weren't any papers, she didn't show any papers, I don't care about papers.

STANLEY: Have you ever heard of the Napoleonic code?

STELLA: No, Stanley, I haven't heard of the Napoleonic code and if I have, I don't see what it—

STANLEY: Let me enlighten you on a point or two, baby.

STELLA: Yes?

STANLEY: In the state of Louisiana we have the Napoleonic code according to which what belongs to the wife belongs to the husband and vice versa. For instance if I had a piece of property, or you had a piece of property—

STELLA: My head is swimming!

STANLEY: All right. I'll wait till she gets through soaking in a hot tub and then I'll inquire if *she* is acquainted with the Napoleonic code. It looks to me like you have been swindled, baby, and when you're swindled under the

Napoleonic code I'm swindled *too*. And I don't like to be *swindled*.

STELLA: There's plenty of time to ask her questions later but if you do now she'll go to pieces again. I don't understand what happened to Belle Reve but you don't know how ridiculous you are being when you suggest that my sister or I or anyone of our family could have perpetrated a swindle on anyone else.

STANLEY: Then where's the money if the place was sold?

STELLA: Not sold—*lost, lost!*

(*He stalks into bedroom, and she follows him.*)

Stanley!

(*He pulls open the wardrobe trunk standing in middle of room and jerks out an armful of dresses.*)

STANLEY: Open your eyes to this stuff! You think she got them out of a teacher's pay?

STELLA: Hush!

STANLEY: Look at these feathers and furs that she come here to preen herself in! What's this here? A solid-gold dress, I believe! And this one! What is these here? Fox-pieces! (*He blows on them*) Genuine fox fur-pieces, a half a mile long! Where are your fox-pieces, Stella? Bushy snow-white ones, no less! Where are your white fox-pieces?

STELLA: Those are inexpensive summer furs that Blanche has had a long time.

STANLEY: I got an acquaintance who deals in this sort of merchandise. I'll have him in here to appraise it. I'm willing to bet you there's thousands of dollars invested in this stuff here!

STELLA: Don't be such an idiot, Stanley!

(*He hurls the furs to the daybed. Then he jerks open small drawer in the trunk and pulls up a fist-full of costume jewelry.*)

STANLEY: And what have we here? The treasure chest of a pirate!

STELLA: Oh, Stanley!

STANLEY: Pearls! Ropes of them! What is this sister of yours, a deep-sea diver who brings up sunken treasures? Or is she the champion safe-cracker of all time! Bracelets of solid gold, too! Where are your pearls and gold bracelets?

STELLA: Shhh! Be still, Stanley!

STANLEY: And diamonds! A crown for an empress!

STELLA: A rhinestone tiara she wore to a costume hall.

STANLEY: What's rhinestone?

STELLA: Next door to glass.

STANLEY: Are you kidding? I have an acquaintance that works in a jewelry store. I'll have him in here to make an appraisal of this. Here's your plantation, or what was left of it, here!

STELLA: You have no idea how stupid and horrid you're being! Now close that trunk before she comes out of the bathroom!

(*He kicks the trunk partly closed and sits on the kitchen table.*)

STANLEY: The Kowalskis and the DuBois have different notions.

STELLA (*angrily*): Indeed they have, thank heavens!—*I'm* going outside. (*She snatches up her white hat and gloves and crosses to the outside door*) You come out with me while Blanche is getting dressed.

STANLEY: Since when do you give me orders?

STELLA: Are you going to stay here and insult her?

STANLEY: You're damn tootin' I'm going to stay here.

(*Stella goes out to the porch. Blanche comes out of the bathroom in a red satin robe.*)

BLANCHE (*airily*): Hello, Stanley! Here I am, all freshly bathed and scented, and feeling like a brand new human being!

(*He lights a cigarette.*)

STANLEY: That's good.

BLANCHE (*drawing the curtains at the windows*): Excuse me while I slip on my pretty new dress!

STANLEY: Go right ahead, Blanche.

(*She closes the drapes between the rooms.*)

BLANCHE: I understand there's to be a little card party to which we ladies are cordially *not* invited!

STANLEY (*ominously*): Yeah?

(*Blanche throws off her robe and slips into a flowered print dress.*)

BLANCHE: Where's Stella?

STANLEY: Out on the porch.

BLANCHE: I'm going to ask a favor of you in a moment.

STANLEY: What could that be, I wonder?

BLANCHE: Some buttons in back! You may enter!

(*He crosses through drapes with a smoldering look.*)

How do I look?

STANLEY: You look all right.

BLANCHE: Many thanks! Now the buttons!

STANLEY: I can't do nothing with them.

BLANCHE: You men with your big clumsy fingers. May I have a drag on your cig?

STANLEY: Have one for yourself.

BLANCHE: Why, thanks! . . . It looks like my trunk has exploded.

STANLEY: Me an' Stella were helping you unpack.

BLANCHE: Well, you certainly did a fast and thorough job of it!

STANLEY: It looks like you raided some stylish shops in Paris.

BLANCHE: Ha-ha! Yes—clothes are my passion!

STANLEY: What does it cost for a string of fur-pieces like that?

BLANCHE: Why, those were a tribute from an admirer of mine!

STANLEY: He must have had a lot of—admiration!

BLANCHE: Oh, in my youth I excited some admiration. But look at me now! (*She smiles at him radiantly*) Would you think it possible that I was once considered to be—attractive?

STANLEY: Your looks are okay.

BLANCHE: I was fishing for a compliment, Stanley.

STANLEY: I don't go in for that stuff.

BLANCHE: What—stuff?

STANLEY: Compliments to women about their looks. I never met a woman that didn't know if she was good-looking or not without being told, and some of them give themselves credit for more than they've got. I once went out with a doll who said to me, "I am the glamorous type, I am the glamorous type!" I said, "So what?"

BLANCHE: And what did she say then?

STANLEY: She didn't say nothing. That shut her up like a clam.

BLANCHE: Did it end the romance?

STANLEY: It ended the conversation—that was all. Some men are took in by this Hollywood glamor stuff and some men are not.

BLANCHE: I'm sure you belong in the second category.

STANLEY: That's right.

BLANCHE: I cannot imagine any witch of a woman casting a spell over you.

STANLEY: That's—right.

BLANCHE: You're simple, straightforward and honest, a little bit on the primitive side I should think. To interest you a woman would have to— (*She pauses with an indefinite gesture.*)

STANLEY (*slowly*): Lay . . . her cards on the table.

BLANCHE (*smiling*): Yes—yes—cards on the table. . . . Well, life is too full of evasions and ambiguities, I think. I like an artist who paints in strong, bold colors, primary colors. I don't like pinks and creams and I never cared for wishy-washy people. That was why, when you walked in here last night, I said to myself—"My sister has married a man!" —Of course that was all that I could tell about you.

STANLEY (*booming*): Now let's cut the re-bop!

BLANCHE (*pressing hands to her ears*): Ouuuuu!

STELLA (*calling from the steps*): Stanley! You come out here and let Blanche finish dressing!

BLANCHE: I'm through dressing, honey.

STELLA: Well, you come out, then.

STANLEY: Your sister and I are having a little talk.

BLANCHE (*lightly*): Honey, do me a favor. Run to the drug-store and get me a lemon-coke with plenty of chipped ice in it!—Will you do that for me, Sweetie?

STELLA (*uncertainly*): Yes. (*She goes around the corner of the building.*)

BLANCHE: The poor little thing was out there listening to us, and I have an idea she doesn't understand you as well as I do. . . . All right; now, Mr. Kowalski, let us proceed without any more double-talk. I'm ready to answer all questions. I've nothing to hide. What is it?

STANLEY: There is such a thing in this State of Louisiana as the Napoleonic code, according to which whatever belongs to my wife is also mine—and vice versa.

BLANCHE: My, but you have an impressive judicial air!

(*She sprays herself with her atomizer; then playfully sprays him with it. He seizes the atomizer and slams it down on the dresser. She throws back her head and laughs.*)

STANLEY: If I didn't know that you was my wife's sister I'd get ideas about you!

BLANCHE: Such as what!

STANLEY: Don't play so dumb. You know what!—Where's the papers?

BLANCHE: Papers?

STANLEY: Papers! That stuff people write on!

BLANCHE: Oh, papers, papers! Ha-ha! The first anniversary gift, all kinds of papers!

STANLEY: I'm talking of legal papers. Connected with the plantation.

BLANCHE: There *were* some papers.

STANLEY: You mean they're no longer existing?

BLANCHE: They probably are, somewhere.

STANLEY: But not in the trunk.

BLANCHE: Everything that I own is in that trunk.

STANLEY: Then why don't we have a look for them? (*He crosses to the trunk, shoves it roughly open and begins to open compartments.*)

BLANCHE: What in the name of heaven are you thinking of! What's in the back of that little boy's mind of yours? That I am absconding with something, attempting some kind of treachery on my sister?—Let me do that! It will be faster and simpler . . . (*She crosses to the trunk and takes out a box*) I keep my papers mostly in this tin box. (*She opens it.*)

STANLEY: What's them underneath? (*He indicates another sheaf of paper.*)

BLANCHE: These are love-letters, yellowing with antiquity, all from one boy. (*He snatches them up. She speaks fiercely*) Give those back to me!

STANLEY: I'll have a look at them first!

BLANCHE: The touch of your hands insults them!

STANLEY: Don't pull that stuff!

(*He rips off the ribbon and starts to examine them. Blanche snatches them from him, and they cascade to the floor.*)

BLANCHE: Now that you've touched them I'll burn them!

STANLEY (*staring, baffled*): What in hell are they?

BLANCHE (*on the floor gathering them up*): Poems a dead boy wrote. I hurt him the way that you would like to hurt me, but you can't! I'm not young and vulnerable any more. But my young husband was and I—never mind about that! Just give them back to me!

STANLEY: What do you mean by saying you'll have to burn them?

BLANCHE: I'm sorry, I must have lost my head for a moment. Everyone has something he won't let others touch because of their—intimate nature . . .

(*She now seems faint with exhaustion and she sits down with the strong box and puts on a pair of glasses and goes methodically through a large stack of papers.*)

Ambler & Ambler. Hmmmmm. . . . Crabtree. . . . More Ambler & Ambler.

STANLEY: What is Ambler & Ambler?

BLANCHE: A firm that made loans on the place.

STANLEY: Then it *was* lost on a mortgage?

BLANCHE (*touching her forehead*): That must've been what happened.

STANLEY: I don't want no ifs, ands or buts! What's all the rest of them papers?

(*She hands him the entire box. He carries it to the table and starts to examine the papers.*)

BLANCHE (*picking up a large envelope containing more papers*): There are thousands of papers, stretching back over hundreds of years, affecting Belle Reve as, piece by piece, our improvident grandfathers and father and uncles and brothers exchanged the land for their epic fornications—to put it plainly! (*She removes her glasses with an exhausted laugh*)

The four-letter word deprived us of our plantation, till finally all that was left—and Stella can verify that!—was the house itself and about twenty acres of ground, including a graveyard, to which now all but Stella and I have retreated. (*She pours the contents of the envelope on the table*) Here all of them are, all papers! I hereby endow you with them! Take them, peruse them—commit them to memory, even! I think it's wonderfully fitting that Belle Reve should finally be this bunch of old papers in your big, capable hands! . . . I wonder if Stella's come back with my lemon-coke . . . (*She leans back and closes her eyes.*)

STANLEY: I have a lawyer acquaintance who will study these out.

BLANCHE: Present them to him with a box of aspirin tablets.

STANLEY (*becoming somewhat sheepish*): You see, under the Napoleonic code—a man has to take an interest in his wife's affairs—especially now that she's going to have a baby.

(*Blanche opens her eyes. The "blue piano" sounds louder.*)

BLANCHE: Stella? Stella going to have a baby? (*dreamily*) I didn't know she was going to have a baby!

(*She gets up and crosses to the outside door. Stella appears around the corner with a carton from the drug-store.*
(*Stanley goes into the bedroom with the envelope and the box.*
(*The inner rooms fade to darkness and the outside wall of the house is visible. Blanche meets Stella at the foot of the steps to the sidewalk.*)

BLANCHE: Stella, Stella for Star! How lovely to have a baby! (*She embraces her sister. Stella returns the embrace with a convulsive sob. Blanche speaks softly*) Everything is all right; we thrashed it out. I feel a bit shaky, but I think I handled it nicely. I laughed and treated it all as a joke, called him a little boy and laughed—and flirted! Yes—I was flirting with your husband, Stella!

(*Steve and Pablo appear carrying a case of beer.*)

The guests are gathering for the poker party.

(*The two men pass between them, and with a short, curious stare at Blanche, they enter the house.*)

STELLA: I'm sorry he did that to you.

BLANCHE: He's just not the sort that goes for jasmine perfume! But maybe he's what we need to mix with our blood now that we've lost Belle Reve and have to go on without Belle Reve to protect us . . . How pretty the sky is! I ought to go there on a rocket that never comes down.

(*A tamale Vendor calls out as he rounds the corner.*)

VENDOR: Red hot! Red hots!

(*Blanche utters a sharp, frightened cry and shrinks away; then she laughs breathlessly again.*)

BLANCHE: Which way do we—go now—Stella?

VENDOR: Re-e-d ho-o-ot!

BLANCHE: The blind are—leading the blind!

(*They disappear around the corner, Blanche's desperate laughter ringing out once more.*

(*Then there is a bellowing laugh from the interior of the flat.*

(*Then the "blue piano" and the hot trumpet sound louder.*)

SCENE THREE

THE POKER NIGHT

There is a picture of Van Gogh's of a billiard-parlor at night. The kitchen now suggests that sort of lurid nocturnal brilliance, the raw colors of childhood's spectrum. Over the yellow linoleum of the kitchen table hangs an electric bulb with a vivid green glass shade. The poker players—Stanley, Steve, Mitch and Pablo— wear colored shirts, solid blues, a purple, a red-and-white check, a light green, and they are men at the peak of their physical manhood, as coarse and direct and powerful as the primary colors. There are vivid slices of watermelon on the table, whiskey bottles and glasses. The bedroom is relatively dim with only the light that spills between the portieres and through the wide window on the street.

For a moment, there is absorbed silence as a hand is dealt.

STEVE: Anything wild this deal?

PABLO: One-eyed jacks are wild.

STEVE: Give me two cards.

PABLO: You, Mitch?

MITCH: I'm out.

PABLO: One.

MITCH: Anyone want a shot?

STANLEY: Yeah. Me.

PABLO: Why don't somebody go to the Chinaman's and bring back a load of chop suey?

STANLEY: When I'm losing you want to eat! Ante up! Openers? Openers! Get y'r ass off the table, Mitch. Nothing belongs on a poker table but cards, chips and whiskey.

(*He lurches up and tosses some watermelon rinds to the floor.*)

MITCH: Kind of on your high horse, ain't you?

STANLEY: How many?

STEVE: Give me three.

STANLEY: One.

MITCH: I'm out again. I oughta go home pretty soon.

STANLEY: Shut up.

MITCH: I gotta sick mother. She don't go to sleep until I come in at night.

STANLEY: Then why don't you stay home with her?

MITCH: She says to go out, so I go, but I don't enjoy it. All the while I keep wondering how she is.

STANLEY: Aw, for the sake of Jesus, go home, then!

PABLO: What've you got?

STEVE: Spade flush.

MITCH: You all are married. But I'll be alone when she goes.—I'm going to the bathroom.

STANLEY: Hurry back and we'll fix you a sugar-tit.

MITCH: Aw, go rut. (*He crosses through the bedroom into the bathroom.*)

STEVE (*dealing a hand*): Seven card stud. (*Telling his joke as he deals*) This ole nigger is out in back of his house sittin' down th'owing corn to the chickens when all at once he hears a loud cackle and this young hen comes lickety split around the side of the house with the rooster right behind her and gaining on her fast.

STANLEY (*impatient with the story*): Deal!

STEVE: But when the rooster catches sight of the nigger th'owing the corn he puts on the brakes and lets the hen get away and starts pecking corn. And the old nigger says, "Lord God, I hopes I never gits *that* hongry!"

(*Steve and Pablo laugh. The sisters appear around the corner of the building.*)

STELLA: The game is still going on.

BLANCHE: How do I look?

STELLA: Lovely, Blanche.

BLANCHE: I feel so hot and frazzled. Wait till I powder before you open the door. Do I look done in?

STELLA: Why no. You are as fresh as a daisy.

BLANCHE: One that's been picked a few days.

(*Stella opens the door and they enter.*)

STELLA: Well, well, well. I see you boys are still at it!

STANLEY: Where you been?

STELLA: Blanche and I took in a show. Blanche, this is Mr. Gonzales and Mr. Hubbell.

BLANCHE: Please don't get up.

STANLEY: Nobody's going to get up, so don't be worried.

STELLA: How much longer is this game going to continue?

STANLEY: Till we get ready to quit.

BLANCHE: Poker is so fascinating. Could I kibitz?

STANLEY: You could not. Why don't you women go up and sit with Eunice?

STELLA: Because it is nearly two-thirty. (*Blanche crosses into the bedroom and partially closes the portieres*) Couldn't you call it quits after one more hand?

(*A chair scrapes. Stanley gives a loud whack of his hand on her thigh.*)

STELLA (*sharply*): That's not fun, Stanley.

(*The men laugh. Stella goes into the bedroom.*)

STELLA: It makes me so mad when he does that in front of people.

BLANCHE: I think I will bathe.

STELLA: Again?

BLANCHE: My nerves are in knots. Is the bathroom occupied?

STELLA: I don't know.

(*Blanche knocks. Mitch opens the door and comes out, still wiping his hands on a towel.*)

BLANCHE: Oh!—good evening.

MITCH: Hello. (*He stares at her.*)

STELLA: Blanche, this is Harold Mitchell. My sister, Blanche DuBois.

MITCH (*with awkward courtesy*): How do you do, Miss DuBois.

STELLA: How is your mother now, Mitch?

MITCH: About the same, thanks. She appreciated your sending over that custard.—Excuse me, please.

(*He crosses slowly back into the kitchen, glancing back at Blanche and coughing a little shyly. He realizes he still has the towel in his hands and with an embarrassed laugh hands it to Stella. Blanche looks after him with a certain interest.*)

BLANCHE: That one seems—superior to the others.

STELLA: Yes, he is.

BLANCHE: I thought he had a sort of sensitive look.

STELLA: His mother is sick.

BLANCHE: Is he married?

STELLA: No.

BLANCHE: Is he a wolf?

STELLA: Why, Blanche! (*Blanche laughs.*) I don't think he would be.

BLANCHE: What does—what does he do?

(*She is unbuttoning her blouse.*)

STELLA: He's on the precision bench in the spare parts department. At the plant Stanley travels for.

BLANCHE: Is that something much?

STELLA: No. Stanley's the only one of his crowd that's likely to get anywhere.

BLANCHE: What makes you think Stanley will?

STELLA: Look at him.

BLANCHE: I've looked at him.

STELLA: Then you should know.

BLANCHE: I'm sorry, but I haven't noticed the stamp of genius even on Stanley's forehead.

(*She takes off the blouse and stands in her pink silk brassiere and white skirt in the light through the portieres. The game has continued in undertones.*)

STELLA: It isn't on his forehead and it isn't genius.

BLANCHE: Oh. Well, what is it, and where? I would like to know.

STELLA: It's a drive that he has. You're standing in the light, Blanche!

BLANCHE: Oh, am I!

(*She moves out of the yellow streak of light. Stella has removed her dress and put on a light blue satin kimona.*)

STELLA (*with girlish laughter*): You ought to see their wives.

BLANCHE (*laughingly*): I can imagine. Big, beefy things, I suppose.

STELLA: You know that one upstairs? (*More laughter*) One time (*laughing*) the plaster—(*laughing*) cracked—

STANLEY: You hens cut out that conversation in there!

STELLA: You can't hear us.

STANLEY: Well, you can hear me and I said to hush up!

STELLA: This is my house and I'll talk as much as I want to!

BLANCHE: Stella, don't start a row.

STELLA: He's half drunk!—I'll be out in a minute.

(*She goes into the bathroom. Blanche rises and crosses leisurely to a small white radio and turns it on.*)

STANLEY: Awright, Mitch, you in?

MITCH: What? Oh!—No, I'm out!

(*Blanche moves back into the streak of light. She raises her arms and stretches, as she moves indolently back to the chair.*
(*Rhumba music comes over the radio. Mitch rises at the table.*)

STANLEY: Who turned that on in there?

BLANCHE: I did. Do you mind?

STANLEY: Turn it off!

STEVE: Aw, let the girls have their music.

PABLO: Sure, that's good, leave it on!

STEVE: Sounds like Xavier Cugat!

(*Stanley jumps up and, crossing to the radio, turns it off. He stops short at the sight of Blanche in the chair. She returns his look without flinching. Then he sits again at the poker table.* (*Two of the men have started arguing hotly.*)

STEVE: I didn't hear you name it.

PABLO: Didn't I name it, Mitch?

MITCH: I wasn't listenin'.

PABLO: What were you doing, then?

STANLEY: He was looking through them drapes. (*He jumps up and jerks roughly at curtains to close them*) Now deal the hand over again and let's play cards or quit. Some people get ants when they win.

(*Mitch rises as Stanley returns to his seat.*)

STANLEY (*yelling*): Sit down!

MITCH: I'm going to the "head." Deal me out.

PABLO: Sure he's got ants now. Seven five-dollar bills in his pants pocket folded up tight as spitballs.

STEVE: Tomorrow you'll see him at the cashier's window getting them changed into quarters.

STANLEY: And when he goes home he'll deposit them one by one in a piggy bank his mother give him for Christmas. (*Dealing*) This game is Spit in the Ocean.

(*Mitch laughs uncomfortably and continues through the portieres. He stops just inside.*)

BLANCHE (*softly*): Hello! The Little Boys' Room is busy right now.

MITCH: We've—been drinking beer.

BLANCHE: I hate beer.

MITCH: It's—a hot weather drink.

BLANCHE: Oh, I don't think so; it always makes me warmer. Have you got any cigs? (*She has slipped on the dark red satin wrapper.*)

MITCH: Sure.

BLANCHE: What kind are they?

MITCH: Luckies.

BLANCHE: Oh, good. What a pretty case. Silver?

MITCH: Yes. Yes; read the inscription.

BLANCHE: Oh, is there an inscription? I can't make it out. (*He strikes a match and moves closer*) Oh! (*reading with feigned difficulty*):

> "And if God choose,
>   I shall but love thee better—after—death!"

Why, that's from my favorite sonnet by Mrs. Browning!

MITCH: You know it?

BLANCHE: Certainly I do!

MITCH: There's a story connected with that inscription.

BLANCHE: It sounds like a romance.

MITCH: A pretty sad one.

BLANCHE: Oh?

MITCH: The girl's dead now.

BLANCHE (*in a tone of deep sympathy*): *Oh!*

MITCH: She knew she was dying when she give me this. A very strange girl, very sweet—very!

BLANCHE: She must have been fond of you. Sick people have such deep, sincere attachments.

MITCH: That's right, they certainly do.

BLANCHE: Sorrow makes for sincerity, I think.

MITCH: It sure brings it out in people.

BLANCHE: The little there is belongs to people who have experienced some sorrow.

MITCH: I believe you are right about that.

BLANCHE: I'm positive that I am. Show me a person who hasn't known any sorrow and I'll show you a shuperficial— Listen to me! My tongue is a little—thick! You boys are responsible for it. The show let out at eleven and we couldn't come home on account of the poker game so we had to go somewhere and drink. I'm not accustomed to having more than one drink. Two is the limit—and *three!* (*She laughs*) Tonight I had three.

STANLEY: Mitch!

MITCH: Deal me out. I'm talking to Miss—

BLANCHE: DuBois.

MITCH: Miss DuBois?

BLANCHE: It's a French name. It means woods and Blanche means white, so the two together mean white woods. Like an orchard in spring! You can remember it by that.

MITCH: You're French?

BLANCHE: We are French by extraction. Our first American ancestors were French Huguenots.

MITCH: You are Stella's sister, are you not?

BLANCHE: Yes, Stella is my precious little sister. I call her little in spite of the fact she's somewhat older than I. Just slightly. Less than a year. Will you do something for me?

MITCH: Sure. What?

BLANCHE: I bought this adorable little colored paper lantern at a Chinese shop on Bourbon. Put it over the light bulb! Will you, please?

MITCH: Be glad to.

BLANCHE: I can't stand a naked light bulb, any more than I can a rude remark or a vulgar action.

MITCH (*adjusting the lantern*): I guess we strike you as being a pretty rough bunch.

BLANCHE: I'm very adaptable—to circumstances.

MITCH: Well, that's a good thing to be. You are visiting Stanley and Stella?

BLANCHE: Stella hasn't been so well lately, and I came down to help her for a while. She's very run down.

MITCH: You're not—?

BLANCHE: Married? No, no. I'm an old maid schoolteacher!

MITCH: You may teach school but you're certainly not an old maid.

BLANCHE: Thank you, sir! I appreciate your gallantry!

MITCH: So you are in the teaching profession?

BLANCHE: Yes. Ah, yes . . .

MITCH: Grade school or high school or—

STANLEY (*bellowing*): Mitch!

MITCH: *Coming!*

BLANCHE: Gracious, what lung-power! . . . I teach high school. In Laurel.

MITCH: What do you teach? What subject?

BLANCHE: Guess!

MITCH: I bet you teach art or music? (*Blanche laughs delicately*) Of course I could be wrong. You might teach arithmetic.

BLANCHE: Never arithmetic, sir; never arithmetic! (*with a laugh*) I don't even know my multiplication tables! No, I have the misfortune of being an English instructor. I attempt to instill a bunch of bobby-soxers and drug-store Romeos with reverence for Hawthorne and Whitman and Poe!

MITCH: I guess that some of them are more interested in other things.

BLANCHE: How very right you are! Their literary heritage is not what most of them treasure above all else! But they're sweet things! And in the spring, it's touching to notice them making their first discovery of love! As if nobody had ever known it before!

(*The bathroom door opens and Stella comes out. Blanche continues talking to Mitch.*)

Oh! Have you finished? Wait—I'll turn on the radio.

(*She turns the knobs on the radio and it begins to play "Wien, Wien, nur du allein." Blanche waltzes to the music with romantic gestures. Mitch is delighted and moves in awkward imitation like a dancing bear.*

(*Stanley stalks fiercely through the portieres into the bedroom. He crosses to the small white radio and snatches it off the table. With a shouted oath, he tosses the instrument out the window.*)

STELLA: *Drunk—drunk—animal thing, you!* (*She rushes through to the poker table*) All of you—please go home! If any of you have one spark of decency in you—

BLANCHE (*wildly*): Stella, watch out, he's—

(*Stanley charges after Stella.*)

MEN (*feebly*): Take it easy, Stanley. Easy, fellow.—Let's all—

STELLA: You lay your hands on me and I'll—

(*She backs out of sight. He advances and disappears. There is the sound of a blow. Stella cries out. Blanche screams and runs into the kitchen. The men rush forward and there is grappling and cursing. Something is overturned with a crash.*)

BLANCHE (*shrilly*): My sister is going to have a baby!

MITCH: This is terrible.

BLANCHE: Lunacy, absolute lunacy!

MITCH: Get him in here, men.

(*Stanley is forced, pinioned by the two men, into the bedroom. He nearly throws them off. Then all at once he subsides and is limp in their grasp.*

(*They speak quietly and lovingly to him and he leans his face on one of their shoulders.*)

STELLA (*in a high, unnatural voice, out of sight*): I want to go away, I want to go away!

MITCH: Poker shouldn't be played in a house with women.

(*Blanche rushes into the bedroom*)

BLANCHE: I want my sister's clothes! We'll go to that woman's upstairs!

MITCH: Where is the clothes?

BLANCHE (*opening the closet*): I've got them! (*She rushes through to Stella*) Stella, Stella, precious! Dear, dear little sister, don't be afraid!

(*With her arms around Stella, Blanche guides her to the outside door and upstairs.*)

STANLEY (*dully*): What's the matter; what's happened?

MITCH: You just blew your top, Stan.

PABLO: He's okay, now.

STEVE: Sure, my boy's okay!

MITCH: Put him on the bed and get a wet towel.

PABLO: I think coffee would do him a world of good, now.

STANLEY (*thickly*): I want water.

MITCH: Put him under the shower!

(*The men talk quietly as they lead him to the bathroom.*)

STANLEY: Let the rut go of me, you sons of bitches!

(*Sounds of blows are heard. The water goes on full tilt.*)

STEVE: Let's get quick out of here!

(*They rush to the poker table and sweep up their winnings on their way out.*)

MITCH (*sadly but firmly*): Poker should not be played in a house with women.

(*The door closes on them and the place is still. The Negro entertainers in the bar around the corner play "Paper Doll" slow and blue. After a moment Stanley comes out of the bathroom dripping water and still in his clinging wet polka dot drawers.*)

STANLEY: Stella! (*There is a pause*) My baby doll's left me! (*He breaks into sobs. Then he goes to the phone and dials, still shuddering with sobs.*) Eunice? I want my baby! (*He waits a moment; then he hangs up and dials again*) Eunice! I'll keep on ringin' until I talk with my baby!

(*An indistinguishable shrill voice is heard. He hurls phone to floor. Dissonant brass and piano sounds as the rooms dim out to darkness and the outer walls appear in the night light. The "blue piano" plays for a brief interval.*

(*Finally, Stanley stumbles half-dressed out to the porch and down the wooden steps to the pavement before the building. There he throws back his head like a baying hound and bellows his wife's name: "Stella! Stella, sweetheart! Stella!"*)

STANLEY: Stell-*lahhhhh!*

EUNICE (*calling down from the door of her upper apartment*): Quit that howling out there an' go back to bed!

STANLEY: I want my baby down here. Stella, Stella!

EUNICE: She ain't comin' down so you quit! Or you'll git th' law on you!

STANLEY: Stella!

EUNICE: You can't beat on a woman an' then call 'er back! She won't come! And her goin' t' have a baby! . . . You stinker! You whelp of a Polack, you! I hope they do haul you in and turn the fire hose on you, same as the last time!

STANLEY (*humbly*): Eunice, I want my girl to come down with me!

EUNICE: Hah! (*She slams her door.*)

STANLEY (*with heaven-splitting violence*): STELL-LAHHHHH!

(*The low-tone clarinet moans. The door upstairs opens again. Stella slips down the rickety stairs in her robe. Her eyes are glistening with tears and her hair loose about her throat and shoulders. They stare at each other. Then they come together with low, animal moans. He falls to his knees on the steps and presses his face to her belly, curving a little with maternity. Her eyes go blind with tenderness as she catches his head and raises him level with her. He snatches the screen door open and lifts her off her feet and bears her into the dark flat.*

(*Blanche comes out on the upper landing in her robe and slips fearfully down the steps.*)

BLANCHE: Where is my little sister? Stella? Stella?

(*She stops before the dark entrance of her sister's flat. Then catches her breath as if struck. She rushes down to the walk before the house. She looks right and left as if for a sanctuary.*)

(*The music fades away. Mitch appears from around the corner.*)

MITCH: Miss DuBois?

BLANCHE: Oh!

MITCH: All quiet on the Potomac now?

BLANCHE: She ran downstairs and went back in there with him.

MITCH: Sure she did.

BLANCHE: I'm terrified!

MITCH: Ho-ho! There's nothing to be scared of. They're crazy about each other.

BLANCHE: I'm not used to such—

MITCH: Naw, it's a shame this had to happen when you just got here. But don't take it serious.

BLANCHE: Violence! Is so—

MITCH: Set down on the steps and have a cigarette with me.

BLANCHE: I'm not properly dressed.

MITCH: That don't make no difference in the Quarter.

BLANCHE: Such a pretty silver case.

MITCH: I showed you the inscription, didn't I?

BLANCHE: Yes. (*During the pause, she looks up at the sky*) There's so much—so much confusion in the world . . . (*He coughs diffidently*) Thank you for being so kind! I need kindness now.

SCENE FOUR

It is early the following morning. There is a confusion of street cries like a choral chant.

Stella is lying down in the bedroom. Her face is serene in the early morning sunlight. One hand rests on her belly, rounding slightly with new maternity. From the other dangles a book of colored comics. Her eyes and lips have that almost narcotized tranquility that is in the faces of Eastern idols.

The table is sloppy with remains of breakfast and the debris of the preceding night, and Stanley's gaudy pyjamas lie across the threshold of the bathroom. The outside door is slightly ajar on a sky of summer brilliance.

Blanche appears at this door. She has spent a sleepless night and her appearance entirely contrasts with Stella's. She presses her knuckles nervously to her lips as she looks through the door, before entering.

BLANCHE: Stella?
STELLA (*stirring lazily*): Hmmh?

(*Blanche utters a moaning cry and runs into the bedroom, throwing herself down beside Stella in a rush of hysterical tenderness.*)

BLANCHE: Baby, my baby sister!
STELLA (*drawing away from her*): Blanche, what is the matter with you?

(*Blanche straightens up slowly and stands beside the bed looking down at her sister with knuckles pressed to her lips.*)

BLANCHE: He's left?
STELLA: Stan? Yes.
BLANCHE: Will he be back?
STELLA: He's gone to get the car greased. Why?
BLANCHE: Why! I've been half crazy, Stella! When I found out you'd been insane enough to come back in here after what happened—I started to rush in after you!
STELLA: I'm glad you didn't.
BLANCHE: What were you thinking of? (*Stella makes an indefinite gesture*) Answer me! What? What?

STELLA: Please, Blanche! Sit down and stop yelling.

BLANCHE: All right, Stella. I will repeat the question quietly now. How could you come back in this place last night? Why, you must have slept with him!

(*Stella gets up in a calm and leisurely way.*)

STELLA: Blanche, I'd forgotten how excitable you are. You're making much too much fuss about this.

BLANCHE: Am I?

STELLA: Yes, you are, Blanche. I know how it must have seemed to you and I'm awful sorry it had to happen, but it wasn't anything as serious as you seem to take it. In the first place, when men are drinking and playing poker anything can happen. It's always a powder-keg. He didn't know what he was doing. . . . He was as good as a lamb when I came back and he's really very, very ashamed of himself.

BLANCHE: And that—that makes it all right?

STELLA: No, it isn't all right for anybody to make such a terrible row, but—people do sometimes. Stanley's always smashed things. Why, on our wedding night—soon as we came in here—he snatched off one of my slippers and rushed about the place smashing the light-bulbs with it.

BLANCHE: He did—*what*?

STELLA: He smashed all the light-bulbs with the heel of my slipper! (*She laughs.*)

BLANCHE: And you—you *let* him? Didn't *run*, didn't *scream*?

STELLA: I was—sort of—thrilled by it. (*She waits for a moment*) Eunice and you had breakfast?

BLANCHE: Do you suppose I wanted any breakfast?

STELLA: There's some coffee left on the stove.

BLANCHE: You're so—matter of fact about it, Stella.

STELLA: What other can I be? He's taken the radio to get it fixed. It didn't land on the pavement so only one tube was smashed.

BLANCHE: And you are standing there smiling!

STELLA: What do you want me to do?

BLANCHE: Pull yourself together and face the facts.

STELLA: What are they, in your opinion?

BLANCHE: In my opinion? You're married to a madman!

STELLA: No!

BLANCHE: Yes, you are, your fix is worse than mine is! Only you're not being sensible about it. I'm going to *do* something. Get hold of myself and make myself a new life!

STELLA: Yes?

BLANCHE: But you've given in. And that isn't right, you're not old! You can get out.

STELLA (*slowly and emphatically*): I'm not in anything I want to get out of.

BLANCHE (*incredulously*): What—Stella?

STELLA: I said I am not in anything that I have a desire to get out of. Look at the mess in this room! And those empty bottles! They went through two cases last night! He promised this morning that he was going to quit having these poker parties, but you know how long such a promise is going to keep. Oh, well, it's his pleasure, like mine is movies and bridge. People have got to tolerate each other's habits, I guess.

BLANCHE: I don't understand you. (*Stella turns toward her*) I don't understand your indifference. Is this a Chinese philosophy you've—cultivated?

STELLA: Is what—what?

BLANCHE: This—shuffling about and mumbling—'One tube smashed—beer-bottles—mess in the kitchen!'—as if nothing out of the ordinary has happened! (*Stella laughs uncertainly and picking up the broom, twirls it in her hands.*)

BLANCHE: Are you deliberately shaking that thing in my face?

STELLA: No.

BLANCHE: Stop it. Let go of that broom. I won't have you cleaning up for him!

STELLA: Then who's going to do it? Are you?

BLANCHE: I? I!

STELLA: No, I didn't think so.

BLANCHE: Oh, let me think, if only my mind would function! We've got to get hold of some money, that's the way out!

STELLA: I guess that money is always nice to get hold of.

BLANCHE: Listen to me. I have an idea of some kind. (*Shakily she twists a cigarette into her holder*) Do you remember Shep Huntleigh? (*Stella shakes her head*) Of course you remember Shep Huntleigh. I went out with him at college and wore his pin for a while. Well—

STELLA: Well?

BLANCHE: I ran into him last winter. You know I went to Miami during the Christmas holidays?

STELLA: No.

BLANCHE: Well, I did. I took the trip as an investment, thinking I'd meet someone with a million dollars.

STELLA: Did you?

BLANCHE: Yes. I ran into Shep Huntleigh—I ran into him on Biscayne Boulevard, on Christmas Eve, about dusk . . . getting into his car—Cadillac convertible; must have been a block long!

STELLA: I should think it would have been—inconvenient in traffic!

BLANCHE: You've heard of oil-wells?

STELLA: Yes—remotely.

BLANCHE: He has them, all over Texas. Texas is literally spouting gold in his pockets.

STELLA: My, my.

BLANCHE: Y'know how indifferent I am to money. I think of money in terms of what it does for you. But he could do it, he could certainly do it!

STELLA: Do what, Blanche?

BLANCHE: Why—set us up in a—shop!

STELLA: What kind of a shop?

BLANCHE: Oh, a—shop of some kind! He could do it with half what his wife throws away at the races.

STELLA: He's married?

BLANCHE: Honey, would I be here if the man weren't married? (*Stella laughs a little. Blanche suddenly springs up and crosses to phone. She speaks shrilly*) How do I get Western Union?—Operator! Western Union!

STELLA: That's a dial phone, honey.

BLANCHE: I can't dial, I'm too—

STELLA: Just dial O.

BLANCHE: O?

STELLA: Yes, "O" for Operator! (*Blanche considers a moment; then she puts the phone down.*)

BLANCHE: Give me a pencil. Where is a slip of paper? I've got to write it down first—the message, I mean . . .

(*She goes to the dressing table, and grabs up a sheet of Kleenex and an eyebrow pencil for writing equipment.*)

Let me see now . . . (*She bites the pencil*) 'Darling Shep. Sister and I in desperate situation.'

STELLA: I beg your pardon!

BLANCHE: 'Sister and I in desperate situation. Will explain details later. Would you be interested in—?' (*She bites the pencil again*) 'Would you be—interested—in . . .' (*She smashes the pencil on the table and springs up*) You never get anywhere with direct appeals!

STELLA (*with a laugh*): Don't be so ridiculous, darling!

BLANCHE: But I'll think of something, I've *got* to think of—*some*thing! Don't, don't laugh at me, Stella! Please, please don't—I—I want you to look at the contents of my purse! Here's what's in it! (*She snatches her purse open*) Sixty-five measly cents in coin of the realm!

STELLA (*crossing to bureau*): Stanley doesn't give me a regular allowance, he likes to pay bills himself, but—this morning he gave me ten dollars to smooth things over. You take five of it, Blanche, and I'll keep the rest.

BLANCHE: Oh, no. No, Stella.

STELLA (*insisting*): I know how it helps your morale just having a little pocket-money on you.

BLANCHE: No, thank you—I'll take to the streets!

STELLA: Talk sense! How did you happen to get so low on funds?

BLANCHE: Money just goes—it goes places. (*She rubs her forehead*) Sometime today I've got to get hold of a bromo!

STELLA: I'll fix you one now.

BLANCHE: Not yet—I've got to keep thinking!

STELLA: I wish you'd just let things go, at least for a—while . . .

BLANCHE: Stella, I can't live with him! You can, he's your husband. But how could I stay here with him, after last night, with just those curtains between us?

STELLA: Blanche, you saw him at his worst last night.

BLANCHE: On the contrary, I saw him at his best! What such a man has to offer is animal force and he gave a wonderful

exhibition of that! But the on[ly]
is to—go to bed with him! And tha[t]

STELLA: After you've rested a little, you'll
work out. You don't have to worry about an[y]
you're here. I mean—expenses . . .

BLANCHE: I have to plan for us both, to get us both—out!

STELLA: You take it for granted that I am in something that I
want to get out of.

BLANCHE: I take it for granted that you still have sufficient
memory of Belle Reve to find this place and these poker
players impossible to live with.

STELLA: Well, you're taking entirely too much for granted.

BLANCHE: I can't believe you're in earnest.

STELLA: No?

BLANCHE: I understand how it happened—a little. You saw
him in uniform, an officer, not here but—

STELLA: I'm not sure it would have made any difference
where I saw him.

BLANCHE: Now don't say it was one of those mysterious electric things between people! If you do I'll laugh in your face.

STELLA: I am not going to say anything more at all about it!

BLANCHE: All right, then, don't!

STELLA: But there are things that happen between a man and
a woman in the dark—that sort of make everything else
seem—unimportant. (*Pause.*)

BLANCHE: What you are talking about is brutal desire—just—
Desire!—the name of that rattle-trap street-car that bangs
through the Quarter, up one old narrow street and down
another . . .

STELLA: Haven't you ever ridden on that street-car?

BLANCHE: It brought me here.—Where I'm not wanted and
where I'm ashamed to be . . .

STELLA: Then don't you think your superior attitude is a bit
out of place?

BLANCHE: I am not being or feeling at all superior, Stella.
Believe me I'm not! It's just this. This is how I look at it.
A man like that is someone to go out with—once—twice—
three times when the devil is in you. But live with? Have a
child by?

STELLA: I have told you I love him.

ast—tremble for

ı insist on trembling!

ainly as you want to.

hes. They are silent till the noise
he bedroom.
rain's noise Stanley enters from out-
by the women, holding some packages
in ,. erhears their following conversation. He
wears w. rt and grease-stained seersucker pants.)

BLANCHE: Well —if you'll forgive me—he's *common!*

STELLA: Why, yes, I suppose he is.

BLANCHE: Suppose! You can't have forgotten that much of our bringing up, Stella, that you just *suppose* that any part of a gentleman's in his nature! *Not one particle, no!* Oh, if he was just—*ordinary!* Just *plain*—but good and wholesome, but—*no*. There's something downright—*bestial*—about him! You're hating me saying this, aren't you?

STELLA (*coldly*): Go on and say it all, Blanche.

BLANCHE: He acts like an animal, has an animal's habits! Eats like one, moves like one, talks like one! There's even something—sub-human—something not quite to the stage of humanity yet! Yes, something—ape-like about him, like one of those pictures I've seen in—anthropological studies! Thousands and thousands of years have passed him right by, and there he is—Stanley Kowalski—survivor of the stone age! Bearing the raw meat home from the kill in the jungle! And you—*you* here—*waiting* for him! Maybe he'll strike you or maybe grunt and kiss you! That is, if kisses have been discovered yet! Night falls and the other apes gather! There in the front of the cave, all grunting like him, and swilling and gnawing and hulking! His poker night!— you call it—this party of apes! Somebody growls—some creature snatches at something—the fight is on! *God!* Maybe we are a long way from being made in God's image, but Stella—my sister—there has been *some* progress since

then! Such things as art—as poetry and music—such kinds
of new light have come into the world since then! In some
kinds of people some tenderer feelings have had some little
beginning! That we have got to make *grow*! And *cling* to,
and hold as our flag! In this dark march toward whatever it
is we're approaching. . . . *Don't—don't hang back with the
brutes!*

(*Another train passes outside. Stanley hesitates, licking his
lips. Then suddenly he turns stealthily about and withdraws
through front door. The women are still unaware of his presence. When the train has passed he calls through the closed
front door.*)

STANLEY: Hey! Hey, Stella!
STELLA (*who has listened gravely to Blanche*): Stanley!
BLANCHE: Stell, I—

(*But Stella has gone to the front door. Stanley enters casually
with his packages.*)

STANLEY: Hiyuh, Stella. Blanche back?
STELLA: Yes, she's back.
STANLEY: Hiyuh, Blanche. (*He grins at her.*)
STELLA: You must've got under the car.
STANLEY: Them darn mechanics at Fritz's don't know their
ass fr'm— *Hey!*

(*Stella has embraced him with both arms, fiercely, and full
in the view of Blanche. He laughs and clasps her head to him.
Over her head he grins through the curtains at Blanche.*
(*As the lights fade away, with a lingering brightness on
their embrace, the music of the "blue piano" and trumpet
and drums is heard.*)

SCENE FIVE

*Blanche is seated in the bedroom fanning herself with a palm
leaf as she reads over a just completed letter. Suddenly she bursts
into a peal of laughter. Stella is dressing in the bedroom.*

STELLA: What are you laughing at, honey?

BLANCHE: Myself, myself, for being such a liar! I'm writing a letter to Shep. (*She picks up the letter*) "Darling Shep. I am spending the summer on the wing, making flying visits here and there. And who knows, perhaps I shall take a sudden notion to *swoop* down on *Dallas!* How would you feel about that? Ha-ha! (*She laughs nervously and brightly, touching her throat as if actually talking to Shep*) Forewarned is forearmed, as they say!"—How does that sound?

STELLA: Uh-huh . . .

BLANCHE (*going on nervously*): "Most of my sister's friends go north in the summer but some have homes on the Gulf and there has been a continued round of entertainments, teas, cocktails, and luncheons—"

(*A disturbance is heard upstairs at the Hubbell's apartment.*)

STELLA (*crossing to the door*): Eunice seems to be having some trouble with Steve.

(*Eunice's voice shouts in terrible wrath.*)

EUNICE: I heard about you and that blonde!

STEVE: That's a damn lie!

EUNICE: You ain't pulling the wool over my eyes! I wouldn't mind if you'd stay down at the Four Deuces, but you always going up.

STEVE: Who ever seen me up?

EUNICE: I seen you chasing her 'round the balcony—I'm gonna call the vice squad!

STEVE: Don't you throw that at me!

EUNICE (*shrieking*): You hit me! I'm gonna call the police!

(*A clatter of aluminum striking a wall is heard, followed by a man's angry roar, shouts and overturned furniture. There is a crash; then a relative hush.*)

BLANCHE (*brightly*): Did he *kill* her?

(*Eunice appears on the steps in daemonic disorder.*)

STELLA: No! She's coming downstairs.

EUNICE: Call the police, I'm going to call the police! (*She rushes around the corner.*)

STELLA (*returning from the door*): Some of your sister's friends have stayed in the city.

(*They laugh lightly. Stanley comes around the corner in his green and scarlet silk bowling shirt. He trots up the steps and bangs into the kitchen. Blanche registers his entrance with nervous gestures.*)

STANLEY: What's a matter with Eun-uss?

STELLA: She and Steve had a row. Has she got the police?

STANLEY: Naw. She's gettin' a drink.

STELLA: That's much more practical!

(*Steve comes down nursing a bruise on his forehead and looks in the door.*)

STEVE: *She here?*

STANLEY: Naw, naw. At the Four Deuces.

STEVE: That rutting hunk! (*He looks around the corner a bit timidly, then turns with affected boldness and runs after her.*)

BLANCHE: I must jot that down in my notebook. Ha-ha! I'm compiling a notebook of quaint little words and phrases I've picked up here.

STANLEY: You won't pick up nothing here you ain't heard before.

BLANCHE: Can I count on that?

STANLEY: You can count on it up to five hundred.

BLANCHE: That's a mighty high number. (*He jerks open the bureau drawer, slams it shut and throws shoes in a corner. At each noise Blanche winces slightly. Finally she speaks*) What sign were you born under?

STANLEY (*while he is dressing*): Sign?

BLANCHE: Astrological sign. I bet you were born under Aries. Aries people are forceful and dynamic. They dote on noise! They love to bang things around! You must have had lots of banging around in the army and now that you're out, you make up for it by treating inanimate objects with such a fury!

(*Stella has been going in and out of closet during this scene. Now she pops her head out of the closet.*)

STELLA: Stanley was born just five minutes after Christmas.

BLANCHE: Capricorn—the Goat!

STANLEY: What sign were *you* born under?

BLANCHE: Oh, my birthday's next month, the fifteenth of September; that's under Virgo.

STANLEY: What's Virgo?

STANLEY: Virgo is the Virgin.

STANLEY (*contemptuously*): *Hah!* (*He advances a little as he knots his tie*) Say, do you happen to know somebody named Shaw?

(*Her face expresses a faint shock. She reaches for the cologne bottle and dampens her handkerchief as she answers carefully.*)

BLANCHE: Why, everybody knows somebody named Shaw!

STANLEY: Well, this somebody named Shaw is under the impression he met you in Laurel, but I figure he must have got you mixed up with some other party because this other party is someone he met at a hotel called the Flamingo.

(*Blanche laughs breathlessly as she touches the cologne-dampened handkerchief to her temples.*)

BLANCHE: I'm afraid he does have me mixed up with this "other party." The Hotel Flamingo is not the sort of establishment I would dare to be seen in!

STANLEY: You know of it?

BLANCHE: Yes, I've seen it and smelled it.

STANLEY: You must've got pretty close if you could smell it.

BLANCHE: The odor of cheap perfume is penetrating.

STANLEY: That stuff you use is expensive?

BLANCHE: Twenty-five dollars an ounce! I'm nearly out. That's just a hint if you want to remember my birthday! (*She speaks lightly but her voice has a note of fear.*)

STANLEY: Shaw must've got you mixed up. He goes in and out of Laurel all the time so he can check on it and clear up any mistake.

(*He turns away and crosses to the portieres. Blanche closes her eyes as if faint. Her hand trembles as she lifts the handkerchief again to her forehead.*

(*Steve and Eunice come around corner. Steve's arm is around Eunice's shoulder and she is sobbing luxuriously and*

he is cooing love-words. There is a murmur of thu
go slowly upstairs in a tight embrace.)

STANLEY (*to Stella*): I'll wait for you at the Four Deuces!
STELLA: Hey! Don't I rate one kiss?
STANLEY: Not in front of your sister.

(*He goes out. Blanche rises from her chair. She seems faint;
looks about her with an expression of almost panic.*)

BLANCHE: Stella! What have you heard about me?
STELLA: Huh?
BLANCHE: What have people been telling you about me?
STELLA: Telling?
BLANCHE: You haven't heard any—unkind—gossip about me?
STELLA: Why, no, Blanche, of course not!
BLANCHE: Honey, there was—a good deal of talk in Laurel.
STELLA: About *you*, Blanche?
BLANCHE: I wasn't so good the last two years or so, after
Belle Reve had started to slip through my fingers.
STELLA: All of us do things we—
BLANCHE: I never was hard or self-sufficient enough. When
people are soft—soft people have got to court the favor of
hard ones, Stella. Have got to be seductive—put on soft
colors, the colors of butterfly wings, and glow—make a little—temporary magic just in order to pay for—one night's
shelter! That's why I've been—not so awf'ly good lately.
I've run for protection, Stella, from under one leaky roof to
another leaky roof—because it was storm—all storm, and I
was—caught in the center. . . . People don't see you—
men don't—don't even admit your existence unless they are
making love to you. And you've got to have your existence
admitted by someone, if you're going to have someone's
protection. And so the soft people have got to—shimmer
and glow—put a—paper lantern over the light. . . . But
I'm scared now—awf'ly scared. I don't know how much
longer I can turn the trick. It isn't enough to be soft. You've
got to be soft *and attractive*. And I—I'm fading now!

(*The afternoon has faded to dusk. Stella goes into the bedroom
and turns on the light under the paper lantern. She holds a
bottled soft drink in her hand.*)

BLANCHE: Have you been listening to me?

STELLA: I don't listen to you when you are being morbid!
 (*She advances with the bottled coke.*)

BLANCHE (*with abrupt change to gaiety*): Is that coke for me?

STELLA: Not for anyone else!

BLANCHE: Why, you precious thing, you! Is it just coke?

STELLA (*turning*): You mean you want a shot in it!

BLANCHE: Well, honey, a shot never does a coke any harm!
 Let me! You mustn't wait on me!

STELLA: I like to wait on you, Blanche. It makes it seem more
 like home. (*She goes into the kitchen, finds a glass and pours
 a shot of whiskey into it.*)

BLANCHE: I have to admit I love to be waited on . . .

(*She rushes into the bedroom. Stella goes to her with the glass.
Blanche suddenly clutches Stella's free hand with a moaning
sound and presses the hand to her lips. Stella is embarrassed by
her show of emotion. Blanche speaks in a choked voice.*)

You're—you're—so *good* to me! And I—

STELLA: Blanche.

BLANCHE: I know, I won't! You hate me to talk sentimental!
 But honey, *believe* I feel things more than I *tell* you! I *won't*
 stay long! I won't, I *promise* I—

STELLA: Blanche!

BLANCHE (*hysterically*): I won't, I promise, *I'll* go! Go *soon!*
 I will *really!* I *won't* hang around until he—throws me
 out . . .

STELLA: Now will you stop talking foolish?

BLANCHE: Yes, honey. Watch how you pour—that fizzy stuff
 foams over!

(*Blanche laughs shrilly and grabs the glass, but her hand
shakes so it almost slips from her grasp. Stella pours the coke
into the glass. It foams over and spills. Blanche gives a piercing cry.*)

STELLA (*shocked by the cry*): Heavens!

BLANCHE: Right on my pretty white skirt!

STELLA: Oh . . . Use my hanky. Blot gently.

BLANCHE (*slowly recovering*): I know—gently—gently . . .

STELLA: Did it stain?

BLANCHE: Not a bit. Ha-ha! Isn't that lucky? (*She sits down shakily, taking a grateful drink. She holds the glass in both hands and continues to laugh a little.*)

STELLA: Why did you scream like that?

BLANCHE: I don't know why I screamed! (*continuing nervously*) Mitch—Mitch is coming at seven. I guess I am just feeling nervous about our relations. (*She begins to talk rapidly and breathlessly*) He hasn't gotten a thing but a goodnight kiss, that's all I have given him, Stella. I want his respect. And men don't want anything they get too easy. But on the other hand men lose interest quickly. Especially when the girl is over—thirty. They think a girl over thirty ought to—the vulgar term is—"put out." . . . And I—I'm not "putting out." Of course he—he doesn't know—I mean I haven't informed him—of my real age!

STELLA: Why are you sensitive about your age?

BLANCHE: Because of hard knocks my vanity's been given. What I mean is—he thinks I'm sort of—prim and proper, you know! (*She laughs out sharply*) I want to *deceive* him enough to make him—want me . . .

STELLA: Blanche, do you want *him*?

BLANCHE: I want to *rest*! I want to breathe quietly again! Yes—I *want* Mitch . . . *very badly!* Just think! If it happens! I can leave here and not be anyone's problem . . .

(*Stanley comes around the corner with a drink under his belt.*)

STANLEY (*bawling*): Hey, Steve! Hey, Eunice! Hey, Stella!

(*There are joyous calls from above. Trumpet and drums are heard from around the corner.*)

STELLA (*kissing Blanche impulsively*): It *will* happen!

BLANCHE (*doubtfully*): It will?

STELLA: It *will*! (*She goes across into the kitchen, looking back at Blanche.*) It will, honey, it will. . . . But don't take another drink! (*Her voice catches as she goes out the door to meet her husband.*

(*Blanche sinks faintly back in her chair with her drink. Eunice shrieks with laughter and runs down the steps. Steve bounds after her with goat-like screeches and chases her around corner. Stanley and Stella twine arms as they follow, laughing.*

(Dusk settles deeper. The music from the Four Deuces is slow and blue.)

BLANCHE: Ah, me, ah, me, ah, me . . .

(Her eyes fall shut and the palm leaf fan drops from her fingers. She slaps her hand on the chair arm a couple of times; then she raises herself wearily to her feet and picks up the hand mirror. There is a little glimmer of lightning about the building.

(The Negro Woman, cackling hysterically, swaying drunkenly, comes around the corner from the Four Deuces. At the same time, a Young Man enters from the opposite direction. The Negro Woman snaps her fingers before his belt.)

NEGRO WOMAN: Hey! Sugar!

(She says something indistinguishable. The Young Man shakes his head violently and edges hastily up the steps. He rings the bell. Blanche puts down the mirror. The Negro Woman has wandered down the street.)

BLANCHE: Come in.

(The Young Man appears through the portieres. She regards him with interest.)

BLANCHE: Well, well! What can I do for *you?*
YOUNG MAN: I'm collecting for *The Evening Star.*
BLANCHE: I didn't know that stars took up collections.
YOUNG MAN: It's the paper.
BLANCHE: I know, I was joking—feebly! Will you—have a drink?
YOUNG MAN: No, ma'am. No, thank you. I can't drink on the job.
BLANCHE: Oh, well, now, let's see. . . . No, I don't have a dime! I'm not the lady of the house. I'm her sister from Mississippi. I'm one of those poor relations you've heard about.
YOUNG MAN: That's all right. I'll drop by later. *(He starts to go out. She approaches a little.)*

BLANCHE: Hey! (*He turns back shyly. She puts a cigarette in a long holder*) Could you give me a light? (*She crosses toward him. They meet at the door between the two rooms.*)

YOUNG MAN: Sure. (*He takes out a lighter*) This doesn't always work.

BLANCHE: It's temperamental? (*It flares*) Ah!—thank you. (*He starts away again*) Hey! (*He turns again, still more uncertainly. She goes close to him*) Uh—what time is it?

YOUNG MAN: Fifteen of seven.

BLANCHE: That late, and still not dark! It just goes to show. . . . Do I seem intoxicated? (*The Young Man laughs uncomfortably*) I sure hope not because I'm expecting a caller bye and bye.

YOUNG MAN (*starting off*): Well, I—

BLANCHE: I bet you're going to college! And you work after school?

YOUNG MAN: That's right.

BLANCHE: What do you study?

YOUNG MAN: Pre-Med.

BLANCHE: Going to be a doctor! What's your name?

YOUNG MAN: Romano.

BLANCHE: Give me all three of them; I believe in numerology! (*She sways a little.*)

YOUNG MAN: Lucio Francesco Romano.

BLANCHE: My, my, my! I don't know what a numerologist would make out of that! (*The Young Man looks embarrassed*) Forgive me. (*She makes a gentle gesture*) I'm not a conventional person, and I'm so—restless today. . . . Don't you love these long, rainy afternoons in New Orleans when an hour isn't just an hour but a little piece of eternity dropped in our hands?—And who knows what to do with it!

(*In the ensuing pause, the "blue piano" is heard. It continues through the rest of this scene and the opening of the next. The young man clears his throat and looks yearningly at the door.*)

Young man! Young, young, young man! Has anyone ever told you that you look like a young Prince out of the Arabian Nights?

(*The Young Man laughs uncomfortably and stands like a bashful kid. Blanche speaks softly to him.*)

Well, you do, honey lamb! Come here. I want to kiss you, just once, softly and sweetly on your mouth!

(*Without waiting for him to accept, she crosses quickly to him and presses her lips to his.*)

Now run along, now, quickly! It would be nice to keep you, but I've got to be good—and keep my hands off children.

(*He stares at her a moment. She opens the door for him and blows a kiss at him as he goes down the steps with a dazed look. She stands there a little dreamily after he has disappeared. Then Mitch appears around the corner with a bunch of roses.*)

BLANCHE (*gaily*): Look who's coming! My Rosenkavalier! Bow to me first . . . now present them! *Ahhhh—Merciiii!*

(*She looks at him over them, coquettishly pressing them to her lips. He beams at her selfconsciously.*)

SCENE SIX

It is about two A.M. on the same evening. The outer wall of the building is visible. Blanche and Mitch come in. The utter exhaustion which only a neurasthenic personality can know is evident in Blanche's voice and manner. Mitch is stolid but depressed. They have probably been out to the amusement park on Lake Pontchartrain, for Mitch is bearing, upside down, a plaster statuette of Mae West, the sort of prize won at shooting-galleries and carnival games of chance.

BLANCHE (*stopping lifelessly at the steps*): Well—

(*Mitch laughs uneasily.*)

Well . . .

MITCH: I guess it must be pretty late—and you're tired.

BLANCHE: Even the hot tamale man has deserted the street, and he hangs on till the end. (*Mitch laughs uneasily again*) How will you get home?

MITCH: I'll walk over to Bourbon and catch an owl-car.

BLANCHE (*laughing grimly*): Is that street-car named Desire still grinding along the tracks at this hour?

MITCH (*heavily*): I'm afraid you haven't gotten much fun out of this evening, Blanche.

BLANCHE: I spoiled it for *you*.

MITCH: No, you didn't, but I felt all the time that I wasn't giving you much—entertainment.

BLANCHE: I simply couldn't rise to the occasion. That was all. I don't think I've ever tried so hard to be gay and made such a dismal mess of it. I get ten points for trying! —I *did* try.

MITCH: Why did you try if you didn't feel like it, Blanche?

BLANCHE: I was just obeying the law of nature.

MITCH: Which law is that?

BLANCHE: The one that says the lady must entertain the gentleman—or no dice! See if you can locate my door-key in this purse. When I'm so tired my fingers are all thumbs!

MITCH (*rooting in her purse*): This it?

BLANCHE: No, honey, that's the key to my trunk which I must soon be packing.

MITCH: You mean you are leaving here soon?

BLANCHE: I've outstayed my welcome.

MITCH: This it?

(*The music fades away.*)

BLANCHE: Eureka! Honey, you open the door while I take a last look at the sky. (*She leans on the porch rail. He opens the door and stands awkwardly behind her.*) I'm looking for the Pleiades, the Seven Sisters, but these girls are not out tonight. Oh, yes they are, there they are! God bless them! All in a bunch going home from their little bridge party. . . . Y' get the door open? Good boy! I guess you—want to go now . . .

(*He shuffles and coughs a little.*)

MITCH: Can I—uh—kiss you—goodnight?

BLANCHE: Why do you always ask me if you may?

MITCH: I don't know whether you want me to or not.

BLANCHE: Why should you be so doubtful?

MITCH: That night when we parked by the lake and I kissed you, you—

BLANCHE: Honey, it wasn't the kiss I objected to. I liked the kiss very much. It was the other little—familiarity—that I felt obliged to—discourage. . . . I didn't resent it! Not a bit in the world! In fact, I was somewhat flattered that you—desired me! But, honey, you know as well as I do that a single girl, a girl alone in the world, has got to keep a firm hold on her emotions or she'll be lost!

MITCH (*solemnly*): Lost?

BLANCHE: I guess you are used to girls that like to be lost. The kind that get lost immediately, on the first date!

MITCH: I like you to be exactly the way that you are, because in all my—experience—I have never known anyone like you.

(*Blanche looks at him gravely; then she bursts into laughter and then claps a hand to her mouth.*)

MITCH: Are you laughing at me?

BLANCHE: No, honey. The lord and lady of the house have not yet returned, so come in. We'll have a night-cap. Let's leave the lights off. Shall we?

MITCH: You just—do what you want to.

(*Blanche precedes him into the kitchen. The outer wall of the building disappears and the interiors of the two rooms can be dimly seen.*)

BLANCHE (*remaining in the first room*): The other room's more comfortable—go on in. This crashing around in the dark is my search for some liquor.

MITCH: You want a drink?

BLANCHE: I want *you* to have a drink! You have been so anxious and solemn all evening, and so have I; we have both been anxious and solemn and now for these few last remaining moments of our lives together—I want to create— *joie de vivre!* I'm lighting a candle.

MITCH: That's good.

BLANCHE: We are going to be very Bohemian. We are going to pretend that we are sitting in a little artists' cafe on the Left Bank in Paris! (*She lights a candle stub and puts it in a bottle.*) *Je suis la Dame aux Camellias! Vous êtes—Armand!* Understand French?

MITCH (*heavily*): Naw. Naw, I—

BLANCHE: *Voulez-vous couchez avec moi ce soir? Vous ne comprenez pas? Ah, quelle dommage!*—I mean it's a damned good thing. . . . I've found some liquor! Just enough for two shots without any dividends, honey . . .

MITCH (*heavily*): That's—good.

(*She enters the bedroom with the drinks and the candle.*)

BLANCHE: Sit down! Why don't you take off your coat and loosen your collar?

MITCH: I better leave it on.

BLANCHE: No. I want you to be comfortable.

MITCH: I am ashamed of the way I perspire. My shirt is sticking to me.

BLANCHE: Perspiration is healthy. If people didn't perspire they would die in five minutes. (*She takes his coat from him*) This is a nice coat. What kind of material is it?

MITCH: They call that stuff alpaca.

BLANCHE: Oh. Alpaca.

MITCH: It's very light weight alpaca.

BLANCHE: Oh. Light weight alpaca.

MITCH: I don't like to wear a wash-coat even in summer because I sweat through it.

BLANCHE: Oh.

MITCH: And it don't look neat on me. A man with a heavy build has got to be careful of what he puts on him so he don't look too clumsy.

BLANCHE: You are not too heavy.

MITCH: You don't think I am?

BLANCHE: You are not the delicate type. You have a massive bone-structure and a very imposing physique.

MITCH: Thank you. Last Christmas I was given a membership to the New Orleans Athletic Club.

BLANCHE: Oh, good.

MITCH: It was the finest present I ever was given. I work out there with the weights and I swim and I keep myself fit. When I started there, I was getting soft in the belly but now my belly is hard. It is so hard now that a man can punch me in the belly and it don't hurt me. Punch me! Go on! See? (*She pokes lightly at him.*)

BLANCHE: Gracious. (*Her hand touches her chest.*)

MITCH: Guess how much I weigh, Blanche?

BLANCHE: Oh, I'd say in the vicinity of—one hundred and eighty?

MITCH: Guess again.

BLANCHE: Not that much?

MITCH: No. More.

BLANCHE: Well, you're a tall man and you can carry a good deal of weight without looking awkward.

MITCH: I weigh two hundred and seven pounds and I'm six feet one and one half inches tall in my bare feet—without shoes on. And that is what I weigh stripped.

BLANCHE: Oh, my goodness, me! It's awe-inspiring.

MITCH (*embarrassed*): My weight is not a very interesting subject to talk about. (*He hesitates for a moment*) What's yours?

BLANCHE: My weight?

MITCH: Yes.

BLANCHE: Guess!

MITCH: Let me lift you.

BLANCHE: Samson! Go on, lift me. (*He comes behind her and puts his hands on her waist and raises her lightly off the ground*) Well?

MITCH: You are light as a feather.

BLANCHE: Ha-ha! (*He lowers her but keeps his hands on her waist. Blanche speaks with an affectation of demureness*) You may release me now.

MITCH: Huh?

BLANCHE (*gaily*): I said unhand me, sir. (*He fumblingly embraces her. Her voice sounds gently reproving*) Now, Mitch. Just because Stanley and Stella aren't at home is no reason why you shouldn't behave like a gentleman.

MITCH: Just give me a slap whenever I step out of bounds.

BLANCHE: That won't be necessary. You're a natural gentleman, one of the very few that are left in the world. I don't want you to think that I am severe and old maid schoolteacherish or anything like that. It's just—well—

MITCH: Huh?

BLANCHE: I guess it is just that I have—old-fashioned ideals! (*She rolls her eyes, knowing he cannot see her face. Mitch goes to the front door. There is a considerable silence between them. Blanche sighs and Mitch coughs selfconsciously.*)

MITCH (*finally*): Where's Stanley and Stella tonight?

BLANCHE: They have gone out. With Mr. and Mrs. Hubbell upstairs.

MITCH: Where did they go?

BLANCHE: I think they were planning to go to a midnight preview at Loew's State.

MITCH: We should all go out together some night.

BLANCHE: No. That wouldn't be a good plan.

MITCH: Why not?

BLANCHE: You are an old friend of Stanley's?

MITCH: We was together in the Two-forty-first.

BLANCHE: I guess he talks to you frankly?

MITCH: Sure.

BLANCHE: Has he talked to you about me?

MITCH: Oh—not very much.

BLANCHE: The way you say that, I suspect that he has.

MITCH: No, he hasn't said much.

BLANCHE: But what he *has* said. What would you say his attitude toward me was?

MITCH: Why do you want to ask that?

BLANCHE: Well—

MITCH: Don't you get along with him?

BLANCHE: What do you think?

MITCH: I don't think he understands you.

BLANCHE: That is putting it mildly. If it weren't for Stella about to have a baby, I wouldn't be able to endure things here.

MITCH: He isn't—nice to you?

BLANCHE: He is insufferably rude. Goes out of his way to offend me.

MITCH: In what way, Blanche?

BLANCHE: Why, in every conceivable way.

MITCH: I'm surprised to hear that.

BLANCHE: Are you?

MITCH: Well, I—don't see how anybody could be rude to you.

BLANCHE: It's really a pretty frightful situation. You see, there's no privacy here. There's just these portieres between the two rooms at night. He stalks through the rooms in his underwear at night. And I have to ask him to close the bathroom door. That sort of commonness isn't necessary. You probably wonder why I don't move out. Well, I'll tell you frankly. A teacher's salary is barely sufficient for her living-expenses. I didn't save a penny last year and so I had to come here for the summer. That's why I have to put up with my sister's husband. And he has to put up with me, apparently so much against his wishes. . . . Surely he must have told you how much he hates me!

MITCH: I don't think he hates you.

BLANCHE: He hates me. Or why would he insult me? Of course there is such a thing as the hostility of—perhaps in some perverse kind of way he— No! To think of it makes me . . . (*She makes a gesture of revulsion. Then she finishes her drink. A pause follows.*)

MITCH: Blanche—

BLANCHE: Yes, honey?

MITCH: Can I ask you a question?

BLANCHE: Yes. What?

MITCH: How old are you?

(*She makes a nervous gesture.*)

BLANCHE: Why do you want to know?

MITCH: I talked to my mother about you and she said, "How old is Blanche?" And I wasn't able to tell her. (*There is another pause.*)

BLANCHE: You talked to your mother about me?

MITCH: Yes.

BLANCHE: Why?

MITCH: I told my mother how nice you were, and I liked you.

BLANCHE: Were you sincere about that?

MITCH: You know I was.

BLANCHE: Why did your mother want to know my age?

MITCH: Mother is sick.

BLANCHE: I'm sorry to hear it. Bad,

MITCH: She won't live long. Maybe jus

BLANCHE: Oh.

MITCH: She worries because I'm not settled.

BLANCHE: Oh.

MITCH: She wants me to be settled down before *voice is hoarse and he clears his throat twice, shuffl vously around with his hands in and out of his pockets.)*

BLANCHE: You love her very much, don't you?

MITCH: Yes.

BLANCHE: I think you have a great capacity for devotion. You will be lonely when she passes on, won't you? (*Mitch clears his throat and nods.*) I understand what that is.

MITCH: To be lonely?

BLANCHE: I loved someone, too, and the person I loved I lost.

MITCH: Dead? (*She crosses to the window and sits on the sill, looking out. She pours herself another drink.*) A man?

BLANCHE: He was a boy, just a boy, when I was a very young girl. When I was sixteen, I made the discovery—love. All at once and much, much too completely. It was like you suddenly turned a blinding light on something that had always been half in shadow, that's how it struck the world for me. But I was unlucky. Deluded. There was something different about the boy, a nervousness, a softness and tenderness which wasn't like a man's, although he wasn't the least bit effeminate looking—still—that thing was there. . . . He came to me for help. I didn't know that. I didn't find out anything till after our marriage when we'd run away and come back and all I knew was I'd failed him in some mysterious way and wasn't able to give the help he needed but couldn't speak of! He was in the quicksands and clutching at me—but I wasn't holding him out, I was slipping in with him! I didn't know that. I didn't know anything except I loved him unendurably but without being able to help him or help myself. Then I found out. In the worst of all possible ways. By coming suddenly into a room that I thought was empty—which wasn't empty, but had two people in it . . . the boy I had married and an older man who had been his friend for years . . .

motive is heard approaching outside. She claps her hands to her ears and crouches over. The headlight of the locomotive glares into the room as it thunders past. As the noise recedes she straightens slowly and continues speaking.)

Afterwards we pretended that nothing had been discovered. Yes, the three of us drove out to Moon Lake Casino, very drunk and laughing all the way.

(*Polka music sounds, in a minor key faint with distance.*)

We danced the Varsouviana! Suddenly in the middle of the dance the boy I had married broke away from me and ran out of the casino. A few moments later—a shot!

(*The Polka stops abruptly.*
(*Blanche rises stiffly. Then, the Polka resumes in a major key.*)

I ran out—all did!—all ran and gathered about the terrible thing at the edge of the lake! I couldn't get near for the crowding. Then somebody caught my arm. "Don't go any closer! Come back! You don't want to see!" See? See what! Then I heard voices say—Allan! Allan! The Grey boy! He'd stuck the revolver into his mouth, and fired—so that the back of his head had been—blown away!

(*She sways and covers her face.*)

It was because—on the dance-floor—unable to stop myself —I'd suddenly said—"I saw! I know! You disgust me . . ." And then the searchlight which had been turned on the world was turned off again and never for one moment since has there been any light that's stronger than this— kitchen—candle . . .

(*Mitch gets up awkwardly and moves toward her a little. The Polka music increases. Mitch stands beside her.*)

MITCH (*drawing her slowly into his arms*): You need somebody. And I need somebody, too. Could it be—you and me, Blanche?

(*She stares at him vacantly for a moment. Then with a soft cry huddles in his embrace. She makes a sobbing effort to speak*

*but the words won't come. He kisses her forehead and her eyes
and finally her lips. The Polka tune fades out. Her breath is
drawn and released in long, grateful sobs.)*

BLANCHE: Sometimes—there's God—so quickly!

SCENE SEVEN

It is late afternoon in mid-September.
*The portieres are open and a table is set for a birthday supper,
with cake and flowers.*
Stella is completing the decorations as Stanley comes in.

STANLEY: What's all this stuff for?

STELLA: Honey, it's Blanche's birthday.

STANLEY: She here?

STELLA: In the bathroom.

STANLEY (*mimicking*): "Washing out some things"?

STELLA: I reckon so.

STANLEY: How long she been in there?

STELLA: All afternoon.

STANLEY (*mimicking*): "Soaking in a hot tub"?

STELLA: Yes.

STANLEY: Temperature 100 on the nose, and she soaks herself
in a hot tub.

STELLA: She says it cools her off for the evening.

STANLEY: And you run out an' get her cokes, I suppose? And
serve 'em to Her Majesty in the tub? (*Stella shrugs*) Set
down here a minute.

STELLA: Stanley, I've got things to do.

STANLEY: Set down! I've got th' dope on your big sister, Stella.

STELLA: Stanley, stop picking on Blanche.

STANLEY: That girl calls *me* common!

STELLA: Lately you been doing all you can think of to rub her
the wrong way, Stanley, and Blanche is sensitive and you've
got to realize that Blanche and I grew up under very different circumstances than you did.

STANLEY: So I been told. And told and told and told! You
know she's been feeding us a pack of lies here?

STELLA: No, I don't, and—

STANLEY: Well, she has, however. But now the cat's out of the bag! I found out some things!

STELLA: What—things?

STANLEY: Things I already suspected. But now I got proof from the most reliable sources—which I have checked on!

(*Blanche is singing in the bathroom a saccharine popular ballad which is used contrapuntally with Stanley's speech.*)

STELLA (*to Stanley*): Lower your voice!

STANLEY: Some canary-bird, huh!

STELLA: Now please tell me quietly what you think you've found out about my sister.

STANLEY: Lie Number One: All this squeamishness she puts on! You should just know the line she's been feeding to Mitch. He thought she had never been more than kissed by a fellow! But Sister Blanche is no lily! Ha-ha! Some lily she is!

STELLA: What have you heard and who from?

STANLEY: Our supply-man down at the plant has been going through Laurel for years and he knows all about her and everybody else in the town of Laurel knows all about her. She is as famous in Laurel as if she was the President of the United States, only she is not respected by any party! This supply-man stops at a hotel called the Flamingo.

BLANCHE (*singing blithely*):
"Say, it's only a paper moon, Sailing over a cardboard sea
—But it wouldn't be make-believe If you believed in me!"

STELLA: What about the—Flamingo?

STANLEY: She stayed there, too.

STELLA: My sister lived at Belle Reve.

STANLEY: This is after the home-place had slipped through her lily-white fingers! She moved to the Flamingo! A second-class hotel which has the advantage of not interfering in the private social life of the personalities there! The Flamingo is used to all kinds of goings-on. But even the management of the Flamingo was impressed by Dame Blanche! In fact they was so impressed by Dame Blanche

that they requested her to turn in her room-key—for permanently! This happened a couple of weeks before she
showed here.

BLANCHE (*singing*):

> "It's a Barnum and Bailey world, Just as phony as it
> can be—
>
> But it wouldn't be make-believe If you believed in me!"

STELLA: What—contemptible—lies!

STANLEY: Sure, I can see how you would be upset by this. She
pulled the wool over your eyes as much as Mitch's!

STELLA: It's pure invention! There's not a word of truth in it
and if I were a man and this creature had dared to invent
such things in my presence—

BLANCHE (*singing*):

> "Without your love,
>   It's a honky-tonk parade!
> Without your love,
>   It's a melody played In a penny arcade . . ."

STANLEY: Honey, I told you I thoroughly checked on these
stories! Now wait till I'm finished. The trouble with Dame
Blanche was that she couldn't put on her act any more in
Laurel! They got wised up after two or three dates with her
and then they quit, and she goes on to another, the same
old line, same old act, same old hooey! But the town was
too small for this to go on forever! And as time went by she
became a town character. Regarded as not just different but
downright loco—nuts.

(*Stella draws back.*)

And for the last year or two she has been washed up like
poison. That's why she's here this summer, visiting royalty,
putting on all this act—because she's practically told by the
mayor to get out of town! Yes, did you know there was an
army camp near Laurel and your sister's was one of the
places called "Out-of-Bounds"?

BLANCHE:

> "It's only a paper moon, Just as phony as it can be—
>   But it wouldn't be make-believe If you believed in me!"

STANLEY: Well, so much for her being such a refined and particular type of girl. Which brings us to Lie Number Two.

STELLA: I don't want to hear any more!

STANLEY: She's not going back to teach school! In fact I am willing to bet you that she never had no idea of returning to Laurel! She didn't resign temporarily from the high school because of her nerves! No, siree, Bob! She didn't. They kicked her out of that high school before the spring term ended—and I hate to tell you the reason that step was taken! A seventeen-year-old boy—she'd gotten mixed up with!

BLANCHE:

"It's a Barnum and Bailey world, Just as phony as it can be—"

(*In the bathroom the water goes on loud; little breathless cries and peals of laughter are heard as if a child were frolicking in the tub.*)

STELLA: This is making me—sick!

STANLEY: The boy's dad learned about it and got in touch with the high school superintendent. Boy, oh, boy, I'd like to have been in that office when Dame Blanche was called on the carpet! I'd like to have seen her trying to squirm out of that one! But they had her on the hook good and proper that time and she knew that the jig was all up! They told her she better move on to some fresh territory. Yep, it was practickly a town ordinance passed against her!

(*The bathroom door is opened and Blanche thrusts her head out, holding a towel about her hair.*)

BLANCHE: Stella!

STELLA (*faintly*): Yes, Blanche?

BLANCHE: Give me another bath-towel to dry my hair with. I've just washed it.

STELLA: Yes, Blanche. (*She crosses in a dazed way from the kitchen to the bathroom door with a towel.*)

BLANCHE: What's the matter, honey?

STELLA: Matter? Why?

BLANCHE: You have such a strange expression on your face!

STELLA: Oh— (*She tries to laugh*) I guess I'm a little tired!

BLANCHE: Why don't you bathe, too, soon as I get out?

STANLEY (*calling from the kitchen*): How soon is that going to be?

BLANCHE: Not so terribly long! Possess your soul in patience!

STANLEY: It's not my soul, it's my kidneys I'm worried about!

(*Blanche slams the door. Stanley laughs harshly. Stella comes slowly back into the kitchen.*)

STANLEY: Well, what do you think of it?

STELLA: I don't believe all of those stories and I think your supply-man was mean and rotten to tell them. It's possible that some of the things he said are partly true. There are things about my sister I don't approve of—things that caused sorrow at home. She was always—flighty!

STANLEY: Flighty is some word for it!

STELLA: But when she was young, very young, she had an experience that—killed her illusions!

STANLEY: What experience was that?

STELLA: I mean her marriage, when she was—almost a child! She married a boy who wrote poetry. . . . He was extremely good-looking. I think Blanche didn't just love him but worshipped the ground he walked on! Adored him and thought him almost too fine to be human! But then she found out—

STANLEY: What?

STELLA: This beautiful and talented young man was a degenerate. Didn't your supply-man give you that information?

STANLEY: All we discussed was recent history. That must have been a pretty long time ago.

STELLA: Yes, it was—a pretty long time ago . . .

(*Stanley comes up and takes her by the shoulders rather gently. She gently withdraws from him. Automatically she starts sticking little pink candles in the birthday cake.*)

STANLEY: How many candles you putting in that cake?

STELLA: I'll stop at twenty-five.

STANLEY: Is company expected?

STELLA: We asked Mitch to come over for cake and ice-cream.

(*Stanley looks a little uncomfortable. He lights a cigarette from the one he has just finished.*)

STANLEY: I wouldn't be expecting Mitch over tonight.

(Stella pauses in her occupation with candles and looks slowly around at Stanley.)

STELLA: *Why?*

STANLEY: Mitch is a buddy of mine. We were in the same outfit together—Two-forty-first Engineers. We work in the same plant and now on the same bowling team. You think I could face him if—

STELLA: Stanley Kowalski, did you—did you repeat what that—?

STANLEY: You're goddam right I told him! I'd have that on my conscience the rest of my life if I knew all that stuff and let my best friend get caught!

STELLA: Is Mitch through with her?

STANLEY: Wouldn't you be if—?

STELLA: I said, *Is Mitch through with her?*

(Blanche's voice is lifted again, serenely as a bell. She sings "But it wouldn't be make believe if you believed in me.")

STANLEY: No, I don't think he's necessarily through with her—just wised up!

STELLA: Stanley, she thought Mitch was—going to—going to marry her. I was hoping so, too.

STANLEY: Well, he's not going to marry her. Maybe he *was,* but he's not going to jump in a tank with a school of sharks —now! *(He rises)* Blanche! Oh, Blanche! Can I please get in my bathroom? *(There is a pause.)*

BLANCHE: Yes, indeed, sir! Can you wait one second while I dry?

STANLEY: Having waited one hour I guess one second ought to pass in a hurry.

STELLA: And she hasn't got her job? Well, what will she do!

STANLEY: She's not stayin' here after Tuesday. You know that, don't you? Just to make sure I bought her ticket myself. A bus-ticket!

STELLA: In the first place, Blanche wouldn't go on a bus.

STANLEY: She'll go on a bus and like it.

STELLA: No, she won't, no, she won't, Stanley!

STANLEY: *She'll go!* Period. P.S. She'll go *Tuesday!*

STELLA *(slowly)*: What'll—she—do? What on earth will she —do!

STANLEY: Her future is mapped out for her.
STELLA: What do you mean?

(*Blanche sings.*)

STANLEY: Hey, canary bird! Toots! Get *OUT* of the *BATH-ROOM!* Must I speak more plainly?

(*The bathroom door flies open and Blanche emerges with a gay peal of laughter, but as Stanley crosses past her, a fright-ened look appears in her face, almost a look of panic. He doesn't look at her but slams the bathroom door shut as he goes in.*)

BLANCHE (*snatching up a hair-brush*): Oh, I feel so good af-ter my long, hot bath, I feel so good and cool and—rested!
STELLA (*sadly and doubtfully from the kitchen*): Do you, Blanche?
BLANCHE (*brushing her hair vigorously*): Yes, I do, so re-freshed! (*She tinkles her highball glass.*) A hot bath and a long, cold drink always give me a brand new outlook on life! (*She looks through the portieres at Stella, standing be-tween them, and slowly stops brushing*) Something has hap-pened!—What is it?
STELLA (*turning away quickly*): Why, nothing has happened, Blanche.
BLANCHE: You're lying! Something has!

(*She stares fearfully at Stella, who pretends to be busy at the table. The distant piano goes into a hectic breakdown.*)

SCENE EIGHT

Three-quarters of an hour later.
The view through the big windows is fading gradually into a still-golden dusk. A torch of sunlight blazes on the side of a big water-tank or oil-drum across the empty lot toward the business district which is now pierced by pinpoints of lighted windows or windows reflecting the sunset.
The three people are completing a dismal birthday supper. Stanley looks sullen. Stella is embarrassed and sad.

Blanche has a tight, artificial smile on her drawn face. There is a fourth place at the table which is left vacant.

BLANCHE (*suddenly*): Stanley, tell us a joke, tell us a funny story to make us all laugh. I don't know what's the matter, we're all so solemn. Is it because I've been stood up by my beau?

(*Stella laughs feebly.*)

It's the first time in my entire experience with men, and I've had a good deal of all sorts, that I've actually been stood up by anybody! Ha-ha! I don't know how to take it. . . . Tell us a funny little story, Stanley! Something to help us out.

STANLEY: I didn't think you liked my stories, Blanche.

BLANCHE: I like them when they're amusing but not indecent.

STANLEY: I don't know any refined enough for your taste.

BLANCHE: Then let me tell one.

STELLA: Yes, you tell one, Blanche. You used to know lots of good stories.

(*The music fades.*)

BLANCHE: Let me see, now. . . . I must run through my repertoire! Oh, yes—I love parrot stories! Do you all like parrot stories? Well, this one's about the old maid and the parrot. This old maid, she had a parrot that cursed a blue streak and knew more vulgar expressions than Mr. Kowalski!

STANLEY: Huh.

BLANCHE: And the only way to hush the parrot up was to put the cover back on its cage so it would think it was night and go back to sleep. Well, one morning the old maid had just uncovered the parrot for the day—when who should she see coming up the front walk but the preacher! Well, she rushed back to the parrot and slipped the cover back on the cage and then she let in the preacher. And the parrot was perfectly still, just as quiet as a mouse, but just as she was asking the preacher how much sugar he wanted in his cof-fee—the parrot broke the silence with a loud—(*She whistles*)—and said—"God *damn*, but that was a short day!"

(*She throws back her head and laughs. Stella also makes an ineffectual effort to seem amused. Stanley pays no attention to the story but reaches way over the table to spear his fork into the remaining chop which he eats with his fingers.*)

BLANCHE: Apparently Mr. Kowalski was not amused.

STELLA: Mr. Kowalski is too busy making a pig of himself to think of anything else!

STANLEY: That's right, baby.

STELLA: Your face and your fingers are disgustingly greasy. Go and wash up and then help me clear the table.

(*He hurls a plate to the floor.*)

STANLEY: That's how I'll clear the table! (*He seizes her arm*) Don't ever talk that way to me! "Pig—Polack—disgusting —vulgar—greasy!"—them kind of words have been on your tongue and your sister's too much around here! What do you two think you are? A pair of queens? Remember what Huey Long said—"Every Man is a King!" And I am the king around here, so don't forget it! (*He hurls a cup and saucer to the floor*) My place is cleared! You want me to clear your places?

(*Stella begins to cry weakly. Stanley stalks out on the porch and lights a cigarette.*
(*The Negro entertainers around the corner are heard.*)

BLANCHE: What happened while I was bathing? What did he tell you, Stella?

STELLA: Nothing, nothing, nothing!

BLANCHE: I think he told you something about Mitch and me! You know why Mitch didn't come but you won't tell me! (*Stella shakes her head helplessly*) I'm going to call him!

STELLA: I wouldn't call him, Blanche.

BLANCHE: I am, I'm going to call him on the phone.

STELLA (*miserably*): I wish you wouldn't.

BLANCHE: I intend to be given some explanation from someone!

(*She rushes to the phone in the bedroom. Stella goes out on the porch and stares reproachfully at her husband. He grunts and turns away from her.*)

STELLA: I hope you're pleased with your doings. I never had so much trouble swallowing food in my life, looking at that girl's face and the empty chair! (*She cries quietly.*)

BLANCHE (*at the phone*): Hello. Mr. Mitchell, please. . . . Oh. . . . I would like to leave a number if I may. Magnolia 9047. And say it's important to call. . . . Yes, very important. . . . Thank you. (*She remains by the phone with a lost, frightened look.*)

(*Stanley turns slowly back toward his wife and takes her clumsily in his arms.*)

STANLEY: Stell, it's gonna be all right after she goes and after you've had the baby. It's gonna be all right again between you and me the way that it was. You remember that way that it was? Them nights we had together? God, honey, it's gonna be sweet when we can make noise in the night the way that we used to and get the colored lights going with nobody's sister behind the curtains to hear us!

(*Their upstairs neighbors are heard in bellowing laughter at something. Stanley chuckles.*)

Steve an' Eunice . . .

STELLA: Come on back in. (*She returns to the kitchen and starts lighting the candles on the white cake.*) Blanche?

BLANCHE: Yes. (*She returns from the bedroom to the table in the kitchen.*) Oh, those pretty, pretty little candles! Oh, don't burn them, Stella.

STELLA: I certainly will.

(*Stanley comes back in.*)

BLANCHE: You ought to save them for baby's birthdays. Oh, I hope candles are going to glow in his life and I hope that his eyes are going to be like candles, like two blue candles lighted in a white cake!

STANLEY (*sitting down*): What poetry!

BLANCHE: His Auntie knows candles aren't safe, that candles burn out in little boys' and girls' eyes, or wind blows them out and after that happens, electric light bulbs go on and you see too plainly . . . (*She pauses reflectively for a moment*) I shouldn't have called him.

STELLA: There's lots of things could have happened.

BLANCHE: There's no excuse for it, Stella. I don't have to put up with insults. I won't be taken for granted.

STANLEY: Goddamn, it's hot in here with the steam from the bathroom.

BLANCHE: I've said I was sorry three times. (*The piano fades out.*) I take hot baths for my nerves. Hydro-therapy, they call it. You healthy Polack, without a nerve in your body, of course you don't know what anxiety feels like!

STANLEY: I am not a Polack. People from Poland are Poles, not Polacks. But what I am is a one hundred percent American, born and raised in the greatest country on earth and proud as hell of it, so don't ever call me a Polack.

(*The phone rings. Blanche rises expectantly.*)

BLANCHE: Oh, that's for me, I'm sure.

STANLEY: *I'm* not sure. Keep your seat. (*He crosses leisurely to phone.*) H'lo. Aw, yeh, hello, Mac.

(*He leans against wall, staring insultingly in at Blanche. She sinks back in her chair with a frightened look. Stella leans over and touches her shoulder.*)

BLANCHE: Oh, keep your hands off me, Stella. What is the matter with you? Why do you look at me with that pitying look?

STANLEY (*bawling*): QUIET IN THERE!—We've got a noisy woman on the place.—Go on, Mac. At Riley's? No, I don't wanta bowl at Riley's. I had a little trouble with Riley last week. I'm the team-captain, ain't I? All right, then, we're not gonna bowl at Riley's, we're gonna bowl at the West Side or the Gala! All right, Mac. See you!

(*He hangs up and returns to the table. Blanche fiercely controls herself, drinking quickly from her tumbler of water. He doesn't look at her but reaches in a pocket. Then he speaks slowly and with false amiability.*)

Sister Blanche, I've got a little birthday remembrance for you.

BLANCHE: Oh, have you, Stanley? I wasn't expecting any, I— I don't know why Stella wants to observe my birthday! I'd

much rather forget it—when you—reach twenty-seven!
Well—age is a subject that you'd prefer to—ignore!

STANLEY: Twenty-seven?

BLANCHE (*quickly*): What is it? Is it for *me*?

(*He is holding a little envelope toward her.*)

STANLEY: Yes, I hope you like it!

BLANCHE: Why, why— Why, it's a—

STANLEY: Ticket! Back to Laurel! On the Greyhound!
Tuesday!

(*The Varsouviana music steals in softly and continues playing. Stella rises abruptly and turns her back. Blanche tries to
smile. Then she tries to laugh. Then she gives both up and
springs from the table and runs into the next room. She
clutches her throat and then runs into the bathroom.
Coughing, gagging sounds are heard.*)

Well!

STELLA: You didn't need to do that.

STANLEY: Don't forget all that I took off her.

STELLA: You needn't have been so cruel to someone alone as
she is.

STANLEY: Delicate piece she is.

STELLA: She is. She was. You didn't know Blanche as a girl.
Nobody, nobody, was tender and trusting as she was. But
people like you abused her, and forced her to change.

(*He crosses into the bedroom, ripping off his shirt, and changes
into a brilliant silk bowling shirt. She follows him.*)

Do you think you're going bowling now?

STANLEY: Sure.

STELLA: You're not going bowling. (*She catches hold of his
shirt*) Why did you do this to her?

STANLEY: I done nothing to no one. Let go of my shirt.
You've torn it.

STELLA: I want to know why. Tell me why.

STANLEY: When we first met, me and you, you thought I was
common. How right you was, baby. I was common as dirt.
You showed me the snapshot of the place with the
columns. I pulled you down off them columns and how

you loved it, having them colored lights going! And wasn't we happy together, wasn't it all okay till she showed here?

(*Stella makes a slight movement. Her look goes suddenly inward as if some interior voice had called her name. She begins a slow, shuffling progress from the bedroom to the kitchen, leaning and resting on the back of the chair and then on the edge of a table with a blind look and listening expression. Stanley, finishing with his shirt, is unaware of her reaction.*)

And wasn't we happy together? Wasn't it all okay? Till she showed here. Hoity-toity, describing me as an ape. (*He suddenly notices the change in Stella*) Hey, what is it, Stel? (*He crosses to her.*)

STELLA (*quietly*): Take me to the hospital.

(*He is with her now, supporting her with his arm, murmuring indistinguishably as they go outside. The "Varsouviana" is heard, its music rising with sinister rapidity as the bathroom door opens slightly. Blanche comes out twisting a washcloth. She begins to whisper the words as the light fades slowly.*)

BLANCHE:

> *El pan de mais, el pan de mais,*
> *El pan de mais sin sal.*
> *El pan de mais, el pan de mais,*
> *El pan de mais sin sal . . .*

SCENE NINE

A while later that evening. Blanche is seated in a tense hunched position in a bedroom chair that she has recovered with diagonal green and white stripes. She has on her scarlet satin robe. On the table beside chair is a bottle of liquor and a glass. The rapid, feverish polka tune, the "Varsouviana," is heard. The music is in her mind; she is drinking to escape it and the sense of disaster closing in on her, and she seems to whisper the words of the song. An electric fan is turning back and forth across her.

Mitch comes around the corner in work clothes: blue denim shirt and pants. He is unshaven. He climbs the steps to the door and rings. Blanche is startled.

BLANCHE: Who is it, please?
MITCH (*hoarsely*): Me. Mitch.

(*The polka tune stops.*)

BLANCHE: Mitch!—Just a minute.

(*She rushes about frantically, hiding the bottle in a closet, crouching at the mirror and dabbing her face with cologne and powder. She is so excited that her breath is audible as she dashes about. At last she rushes to the door in the kitchen and lets him in.*)

Mitch!—Y'know, I really shouldn't let you in after the treatment I have received from you this evening! So utterly uncavalier! But hello, beautiful!

(*She offers him her lips. He ignores it and pushes past her into the flat. She looks fearfully after him as he stalks into the bedroom.*)

My, my, what a cold shoulder! And a face like a thundercloud! And such uncouth apparel! Why, you haven't even shaved! The unforgivable insult to a lady! But I forgive you. I forgive you because it's such a relief to see you. You've stopped that polka tune that I had caught in my head. Have you ever had anything caught in your head? Some words, a piece of music? That goes relentlessly on and on in your head? No, of course you haven't, you dumb angel-puss, you'd never get anything awful caught in your head!

(*He stares at her while she follows him while she talks. It is obvious that he has had a few drinks on the way over.*)

MITCH: Do we have to have that fan on?
BLANCHE: No!
MITCH: I don't like fans.
BLANCHE: Then let's turn it off, honey. I'm not partial to them!

(*She presses the switch and the fan nods slowly off. She clears her throat uneasily as Mitch plumps himself down on the bed in the bedroom and lights a cigarette.*)

I don't know what there is to drink. I—haven't investigated.

MITCH: I don't want Stan's liquor.

BLANCHE: It isn't Stan's. Everything here isn't Stan's. Some things on the premises are actually mine! How is your mother? Isn't your mother well?

MITCH: Why?

BLANCHE: Something's the matter tonight, but never mind. I won't cross-examine the witness. I'll just—(*She touches her forehead vaguely. The polka tune starts up again.*)—pretend I don't notice anything different about you! That—music again . . .

MITCH: What music?

BLANCHE: The "Varsouviana"! The polka tune they were playing when Allan— Wait!

(*A distant revolver shot is heard. Blanche seems relieved.*)

There now, the shot! It always stops after that.

(*The polka music dies out again.*)

Yes, now it's stopped.

MITCH: Are you boxed out of your mind?

BLANCHE: I'll go and see what I can find in the way of— (*She crosses into the closet, pretending to search for the bottle.*) Oh, by the way, excuse me for not being dressed. But I'd practically given you up! Had you forgotten your invitation to supper?

MITCH: I wasn't going to see you any more.

BLANCHE: Wait a minute. I can't hear what you're saying and you talk so little that when you do say something, I don't want to miss a single syllable of it. . . . What am I looking around here for? Oh, yes—liquor! We've had so much excitement around here this evening that I *am* boxed out of my mind! (*She pretends suddenly to find the bottle. He draws his foot up on the bed and stares at her contemptuously.*) Here's something. Southern Comfort! What is that, I wonder?

MITCH: If you don't know, it must belong to Stan.

BLANCHE: Take your foot off the bed. It has a light cover on it. Of course you boys don't notice things like that. I've done so much with this place since I've been here.

MITCH: I bet you have.

BLANCHE: You saw it before I came. Well, look at it now! This room is almost—dainty! I want to keep it that way. I wonder if this stuff ought to be mixed with something? Ummm, it's sweet, so sweet! It's terribly, terribly sweet! Why, it's a *liqueur*, I believe! Yes, that's what it *is*, a liqueur! (*Mitch grunts.*) I'm afraid you won't like it, but try it, and maybe you will.

MITCH: I told you already I don't want none of his liquor and I mean it. You ought to lay off his liquor. He says you been lapping it up all summer like a wild-cat!

BLANCHE: What a fantastic statement! Fantastic of him to say it, fantastic of you to repeat it! I won't descend to the level of such cheap accusations to answer them, even!

MITCH: Huh.

BLANCHE: What's in your mind? I see something in your eyes!

MITCH (*getting up*): It's dark in here.

BLANCHE: I like it dark. The dark is comforting to me.

MITCH: I don't think I ever seen you in the light. (*Blanche laughs breathlessly*) That's a fact!

BLANCHE: Is it?

MITCH: I've never seen you in the afternoon.

BLANCHE: Whose fault is that?

MITCH: You never want to go out in the afternoon.

BLANCHE: Why, Mitch, you're at the plant in the afternoon!

MITCH: Not Sunday afternoon. I've asked you to go out with me sometimes on Sundays but you always make an excuse. You never want to go out till after six and then it's always some place that's not lighted much.

BLANCHE: There is some obscure meaning in this but I fail to catch it.

MITCH: What it means is I've never had a real good look at you, Blanche.

BLANCHE: What are you leading up to?

MITCH: Let's turn the light on here.

BLANCHE (*fearfully*): Light? Which light? What for?

MITCH: This one with the paper thing on it. (*He tears the paper lantern off the light bulb. She utters a frightened gasp.*)

BLANCHE: What did you do that for?

MITCH: So I can take a look at you good and plain!

BLANCHE: Of course you don't really mean to be insulting!

MITCH: No, just realistic.

BLANCHE: I don't want realism.

MITCH: Naw, I guess not.

BLANCHE: I'll tell you what I want. Magic! (*Mitch laughs*) Yes, yes, magic! I try to give that to people. I misrepresent things to them. I don't tell truth, I tell what *ought* to be truth. And if that is sinful, then let me be damned for it!— *Don't turn the light on!*

(*Mitch crosses to the switch. He turns the light on and stares at her. She cries out and covers her face. He turns the light off again.*)

MITCH (*slowly and bitterly*): I don't mind you being older than what I thought. But all the rest of it—Christ! That pitch about your ideals being so old-fashioned and all the malarkey that you've dished out all summer. Oh, I knew you weren't sixteen any more. But I was a fool enough to believe you was straight.

BLANCHE: Who told you I wasn't—'straight'? My loving brother-in-law. And you believed him.

MITCH: I called him a liar at first. And then I checked on the story. First I asked our supply-man who travels through Laurel. And then I talked directly over long-distance to this merchant.

BLANCHE: Who is this merchant?

MITCH: Kiefaber.

BLANCHE: The merchant Kiefaber of Laurel! I know the man. He whistled at me. I put him in his place. So now for revenge he makes up stories about me.

MITCH: Three people, Kiefaber, Stanley and Shaw, swore to them!

BLANCHE: Rub-a-dub-dub, three men in a tub! And such a filthy tub!

MITCH: Didn't you stay at a hotel called The Flamingo?

BLANCHE: Flamingo? No! Tarantula was the name of it! I stayed at a hotel called The Tarantula Arms!

MITCH (*stupidly*): Tarantula?

BLANCHE: Yes, a big spider! That's where I brought my victims. (*She pours herself another drink*) Yes, I had many intimacies with strangers. After the death of Allan—intimacies with strangers was all I seemed able to fill my empty heart with. . . . I think it was panic, just panic, that drove me from one to another, hunting for some protection—here and there, in the most—unlikely places—even, at last, in a seventeen-year-old boy but—somebody wrote the superintendent about it—"This woman is morally unfit for her position!"

(*She throws back her head with convulsive, sobbing laughter. Then she repeats the statement, gasps, and drinks.*)

True? Yes, I suppose—unfit somehow—anyway. . . . So I came here. There was nowhere else I could go. I was played out. You know what played out is? My youth was suddenly gone up the water-spout, and—I met you. You said you needed somebody. Well, I needed somebody, too. I thanked God for you, because you seemed to be gentle—a cleft in the rock of the world that I could hide in! The poor man's Paradise—is a little peace. . . . But I guess I was asking, hoping—too much! Kiefaber, Stanley and Shaw have tied an old tin can to the tail of the kite.

(*There is a pause. Mitch stares at her dumbly.*)

MITCH: You lied to me, Blanche.
BLANCHE: Don't say I lied to you.
MITCH: Lies, lies, inside and out, all lies.
BLANCHE: Never inside, I didn't lie in my heart . . .

(*A Vendor comes around the corner. She is a blind Mexican woman in a dark shawl, carrying bunches of those gaudy tin flowers that lower class Mexicans display at funerals and other festive occasions. She is calling barely audibly. Her figure is only faintly visible outside the building.*)

MEXICAN WOMAN: *Flores. Flores. Flores para los muertos. Flores. Flores.*
BLANCHE: What? Oh! Somebody outside. . . . I—I lived in a house where dying old women remembered their dead men . . .
MEXICAN WOMAN: *Flores. Flores para los muertos . . .*

(*The polka tune fades in.*)

BLANCHE (*as if to herself*): Crumble and fade and—regrets—recriminations . . . 'If you'd done this, it wouldn't've cost me that!'

MEXICAN WOMAN: *Corones para los muertos. Corones . . .*

BLANCHE: Legacies! Huh. . . . And other things such as bloodstained pillow-slips—'Her linen needs changing'—'Yes Mother. But couldn't we get a colored girl to do it?' No, we couldn't of course. Everything gone but the—

MEXICAN WOMAN: *Flores.*

BLANCHE: Death—I used to sit here and she used to sit over there and death was as close as you are. . . . We didn't dare even admit we had ever heard of it!

MEXICAN WOMAN: *Flores para los muertos, flores—flores . . .*

BLANCHE: The opposite is desire. So do you wonder? How could you possibly wonder! Not far from Belle Reve, before we had lost Belle Reve, was a camp where they trained young soldiers. On Saturday nights they would go in town to get drunk—

MEXICAN WOMAN (*softly*): *Corones . . .*

BLANCHE: —and on the way back they would stagger onto my lawn and call—'Blanche! Blanche!'—The deaf old lady remaining suspected nothing. But sometimes I slipped outside to answer their calls. . . . Later the paddy-wagon would gather them up like daisies . . . the long way home . . .

(*The Mexican Woman turns slowly and drifts back off with her soft mournful cries. Blanche goes to the dresser and leans forward on it. After a moment, Mitch rises and follows her purposefully. The polka music fades away. He places his hands on her waist and tries to turn her about.*)

BLANCHE: What do you want?

MITCH (*fumbling to embrace her*): What I been missing all summer.

BLANCHE: Then marry me, Mitch!

MITCH: I don't think I want to marry you any more.

BLANCHE: No?

MITCH (*dropping his hands from her waist*): You're not clean enough to bring in the house with my mother.

BLANCHE: Go away, then. (*He stares at her*) Get out of here quick before I start screaming fire! (*Her throat is tightening with hysteria*) Get out of here quick before I start screaming fire.

(*He still remains staring. She suddenly rushes to the big window with its pale blue square of the soft summer light and cries wildly.*)

Fire! Fire! Fire!

(*With a startled gasp, Mitch turns and goes out the outer door, clatters awkwardly down the steps and around the corner of the building. Blanche staggers back from the window and falls to her knees. The distant piano is slow and blue.*)

SCENE TEN

It is a few hours later that night.

Blanche has been drinking fairly steadily since Mitch left. She has dragged her wardrobe trunk into the center of the bedroom. It hangs open with flowery dresses thrown across it. As the drinking and packing went on, a mood of hysterical exhilaration came into her and she has decked herself out in a somewhat soiled and crumpled white satin evening gown and a pair of scuffed silver slippers with brilliants set in their heels.

Now she is placing the rhinestone tiara on her head before the mirror of the dressing-table and murmuring excitedly as if to a group of spectral admirers.

BLANCHE: How about taking a swim, a moonlight swim at the old rock-quarry? If anyone's sober enough to drive a car! Ha-ha! Best way in the world to stop your head buzzing! Only you've got to be careful to dive where the deep pool is—if you hit a rock you don't come up till tomorrow . . .

(*Tremblingly she lifts the hand mirror for a closer inspection. She catches her breath and slams the mirror face down with such violence that the glass cracks. She moans a little and attempts to rise.*

(*Stanley appears around the corner of the building. He still has on the vivid green silk bowling shirt. As he rounds the corner the honky-tonk music is heard. It continues softly throughout the scene.*

(*He enters the kitchen, slamming the door. As he peers in at Blanche, he gives a low whistle. He has had a few drinks on the way and has brought some quart beer bottles home with him.*)

BLANCHE: How is my sister?

STANLEY: She is doing okay.

BLANCHE: And how is the baby?

STANLEY (*grinning amiably*): The baby won't come before morning so they told me to go home and get a little shut-eye.

BLANCHE: Does that mean we are to be alone in here?

STANLEY: Yep. Just me and you, Blanche. Unless you got somebody hid under the bed. What've you got on those fine feathers for?

BLANCHE: Oh, that's right. You left before my wire came.

STANLEY: You got a wire?

BLANCHE: I received a telegram from an old admirer of mine.

STANLEY: Anything good?

BLANCHE: I think so. An invitation.

STANLEY: What to? A fireman's ball?

BLANCHE (*throwing back her head*): A cruise of the Caribbean on a yacht!

STANLEY: Well, well. What do you know?

BLANCHE: I have never been so surprised in my life.

STANLEY: I guess not.

BLANCHE: It came like a bolt from the blue!

STANLEY: Who did you say it was from?

BLANCHE: An old beau of mine.

STANLEY: The one that give you the white fox-pieces?

BLANCHE: Mr. Shep Huntleigh. I wore his ATO pin my last year at college. I hadn't seen him again until last Christmas. I ran in to him on Biscayne Boulevard. Then—just now— this wire—inviting me on a cruise of the Caribbean! The problem is clothes. I tore into my trunk to see what I have that's suitable for the tropics!

STANLEY: And come up with that—gorgeous—diamond—tiara?

BLANCHE: This old relic? Ha-ha! It's only rhinestones.

STANLEY: Gosh. I thought it was Tiffany diamonds. (*He unbuttons his shirt.*)

BLANCHE: Well, anyhow, I shall be entertained in style.

STANLEY: Uh-huh. It goes to show, you never know what is coming.

BLANCHE: Just when I thought my luck had begun to fail me—

STANLEY: Into the picture pops this Miami millionaire.

BLANCHE: This man is not from Miami. This man is from Dallas.

STANLEY: This man is from Dallas?

BLANCHE: Yes, this man is from Dallas where gold spouts out of the ground!

STANLEY: Well, just so he's from somewhere! (*He starts removing his shirt.*)

BLANCHE: Close the curtains before you undress any further.

STANLEY (*amiably*): This is all I'm going to undress right now. (*He rips the sack off a quart beer-bottle*) Seen a bottle-opener?

(*She moves slowly toward the dresser, where she stands with her hands knotted together.*)

I used to have a cousin who could open a beer-bottle with his teeth. (*Pounding the bottle cap on the corner of table*) That was his only accomplishment, all he could do—he was just a human bottle-opener. And then one time, at a wedding party, he broke his front teeth off! After that he was so ashamed of himself he used t' sneak out of the house when company came . . .

(*The bottle cap pops off and a geyser of foam shoots up. Stanley laughs happily, holding up the bottle over his head.*)

Ha-ha! Rain from heaven! (*He extends the bottle toward her*) Shall we bury the hatchet and make it a loving-cup? Huh?

BLANCHE: No, thank you.

STANLEY: Well, it's a red letter night for us both. You having an oil-millionaire and me having a baby.

(*He goes to the bureau in the bedroom and crouches to remove something from the bottom drawer.*)

BLANCHE (*drawing back*): What are you doing in here?

STANLEY: Here's something I always break out on special occasions like this. The silk pyjamas I wore on my wedding night!

BLANCHE: Oh.

STANLEY: When the telephone rings and they say, "You've got a son!" I'll tear this off and wave it like a flag! (*He shakes out a brilliant pyjama coat*) I guess we are both entitled to put on the dog. (*He goes back to the kitchen with the coat over his arm.*)

BLANCHE: When I think of how divine it is going to be to have such a thing as privacy once more—I could weep with joy!

STANLEY: This millionaire from Dallas is not going to interfere with your privacy any?

BLANCHE: It won't be the sort of thing you have in mind. This man is a gentleman and he respects me. (*Improvising feverishly*) What he wants is my companionship. Having great wealth sometimes makes people lonely!

STANLEY: I wouldn't know about that.

BLANCHE: A cultivated woman, a woman of intelligence and breeding, can enrich a man's life—immeasurably! I have those things to offer, and this doesn't take them away. Physical beauty is passing. A transitory possession. But beauty of the mind and richness of the spirit and tenderness of the heart—and I have all of those things—aren't taken away, but grow! Increase with the years! How strange that I should be called a destitute woman! When I have all of these treasures locked in my heart. (*A choked sob comes from her*) I think of myself as a very, very rich woman! But I have been foolish—casting my pearls before swine!

STANLEY: Swine, huh?

BLANCHE: Yes, swine! Swine! And I'm thinking not only of you but of your friend, Mr. Mitchell. He came to see me tonight. He dared to come here in his work-clothes! And to repeat slander to me, vicious stories that he had gotten from you! I gave him his walking papers . . .

STANLEY: You did, huh?

BLANCHE: But then he came back. He returned with a box of roses to beg my forgiveness! He implored my forgiveness. But some things are not forgivable. Deliberate cruelty is not forgivable. It is the one unforgivable thing in my opinion and it is the one thing of which I have never, never been guilty. And so I told him, I said to him, "Thank you," but it was foolish of me to think that we could ever adapt ourselves to each other. Our ways of life are too different. Our attitudes and our backgrounds are incompatible. We have to be realistic about such things. So farewell, my friend! And let there be no hard feelings . . .

STANLEY: Was this before or after the telegram came from the Texas oil millionaire?

BLANCHE: What telegram? No! No, after! As a matter of fact, the wire came just as—

STANLEY: As a matter of fact there wasn't no wire at all!

BLANCHE: Oh, oh!

STANLEY: There isn't no millionaire! And Mitch didn't come back with roses 'cause I know where he is—

BLANCHE: Oh!

STANLEY: There isn't a goddam thing but imagination!

BLANCHE: Oh!

STANLEY: And lies and conceit and tricks!

BLANCHE: Oh!

STANLEY: And look at yourself! Take a look at yourself in that worn-out Mardi Gras outfit, rented for fifty cents from some rag-picker! And with the crazy crown on! What queen do you think you are?

BLANCHE: Oh—God . . .

STANLEY: I've been on to you from the start! Not once did you pull any wool over this boy's eyes! You come in here and sprinkle the place with powder and spray perfume and cover the light-bulb with a paper lantern, and lo and behold the place has turned into Egypt and you are the Queen of the Nile! Sitting on your throne and swilling down my liquor! I say—*Ha!*—*Ha!* Do you hear me? *Ha—ha—ha!* (*He walks into the bedroom.*)

BLANCHE: Don't come in here!

(*Lurid reflections appear on the walls around Blanche. The shadows are of a grotesque and menacing form. She catches her breath, crosses to the phone and jiggles the hook. Stanley goes into the bathroom and closes the door.*)

Operator, operator! Give me long-distance, please. . . . I want to get in touch with Mr. Shep Huntleigh of Dallas. He's so well-known he doesn't require any address. Just ask anybody who— Wait!!—No, I couldn't find it right now. . . . Please understand, I— No! No, wait! . . . One moment! Someone is— Nothing! Hold on, please!

(*She sets the phone down and crosses warily into the kitchen. The night is filled with inhuman voices like cries in a jungle.*

(*The shadows and lurid reflections move sinuously as flames along the wall spaces.*

(*Through the back wall of the rooms, which have become transparent, can be seen the sidewalk. A prostitute has rolled a drunkard. He pursues her along the walk, overtakes her and there is a struggle. A policeman's whistle breaks it up. The figures disappear.*

(*Some moments later the Negro Woman appears around the corner with a sequined bag which the prostitute had dropped on the walk. She is rooting excitedly through it.*

(*Blanche presses her knuckles to her lips and returns slowly to the phone. She speaks in a hoarse whisper.*)

BLANCHE: Operator! Operator! Never mind long-distance. Get Western Union. There isn't time to be— Western— Western Union!

(*She waits anxiously.*)

Western Union? Yes! I—want to—Take down this message! "In desperate, desperate circumstances! Help me! Caught in a trap. Caught in—" *Oh!*

(*The bathroom door is thrown open and Stanley comes out in the brilliant silk pyjamas. He grins at her as he knots the tasseled sash about his waist. She gasps and backs away from the phone. He stares at her for a count of ten. Then a clicking becomes audible from the telephone, steady and rasping.*)

STANLEY: You left th' phone off th' hook.

(*He crosses to it deliberately and sets it back on the hook. After he has replaced it, he stares at her again, his mouth slowly curving into a grin, as he waves between Blanche and the outer door.*

The barely audible "blue piano" begins to drum up louder. The sound of it turns into the roar of an approaching locomotive. Blanche crouches, pressing her fists to her ears until it has gone by.)

BLANCHE (*finally straightening*): Let me—let me get by you!

STANLEY: Get by me? Sure. Go ahead. (*He moves back a pace in the doorway.*)

BLANCHE: You—you stand over there! (*She indicates a further position.*)

STANLEY (*grinning*): You got plenty of room to walk by me now.

BLANCHE: Not with you there! But I've got to get out somehow!

STANLEY: You think I'll interfere with you? Ha-ha!

(*The "blue piano" goes softly. She turns confusedly and makes a faint gesture. The inhuman jungle voices rise up. He takes a step toward her, biting his tongue which protrudes between his lips.*)

STANLEY (*softly*): Come to think of it—maybe you wouldn't be bad to—interfere with . . .

(*Blanche moves backward through the door into the bedroom.*)

BLANCHE: Stay back! Don't you come toward me another step or I'll—

STANLEY: What?

BLANCHE: Some awful thing will happen! It will!

STANLEY: What are you putting on now?

(*They are now both inside the bedroom.*)

BLANCHE: I warn you, don't, I'm in danger!

(*He takes another step. She smashes a bottle on the table and faces him, clutching the broken top.*)

STANLEY: What did you do that for?

BLANCHE: So I could twist the broken end in your face!

STANLEY: I bet you would do that!

BLANCHE: I would! I will if you—

STANLEY: Oh! So you want some rough-house! All right, let's have some rough-house!

(*He springs toward her, overturning the table. She cries out and strikes at him with the bottle top but he catches her wrist.*)

Tiger—tiger! Drop the bottle-top! Drop it! We've had this date with each other from the beginning!

(*She moans. The bottle-top falls. She sinks to her knees. He picks up her inert figure and carries her to the bed. The hot trumpet and drums from the Four Deuces sound loudly.*)

SCENE ELEVEN

It is some weeks later. Stella is packing Blanche's things. Sound of water can be heard running in the bathroom.

The portieres are partly open on the poker players—Stanley, Steve, Mitch and Pablo—who sit around the table in the kitchen. The atmosphere of the kitchen is now the same raw, lurid one of the disastrous poker night.

The building is framed by the sky of turquoise. Stella has been crying as she arranges the flowery dresses in the open trunk.

Eunice comes down the steps from her flat above and enters the kitchen. There is an outburst from the poker table.

STANLEY: Drew to an inside straight and made it, by God.

PABLO: *Maldita sea tu suerto!*

STANLEY: Put it in English, greaseball.

PABLO: I am cursing your rutting luck.

STANLEY (*prodigiously elated*): You know what luck is? Luck is believing you're lucky. Take at Salerno. I believed I was lucky. I figured that 4 out of 5 would not come through but I would . . . and I did. I put that down as a rule. To hold front position in this rat-race you've got to believe you are lucky.

MITCH: You . . . you . . . you. . . . Brag . . . brag . . . bull . . . bull.

(*Stella goes into the bedroom and starts folding a dress.*)

STANLEY: What's the matter with him?

EUNICE (*walking past the table*): I always did say that men are callous things with no feelings, but this does beat anything. Making pigs of yourselves. (*She comes through the portieres into the bedroom.*)

STANLEY: What's the matter with her?

STELLA: How is my baby?

EUNICE: Sleeping like a little angel. Brought you some grapes. (*She puts them on a stool and lowers her voice.*) Blanche?

STELLA: Bathing.

EUNICE: How is she?

STELLA: She wouldn't eat anything but asked for a drink.

EUNICE: What did you tell her?

STELLA: I—just told her that—we'd made arrangements for her to rest in the country. She's got it mixed in her mind with Shep Huntleigh.

(*Blanche opens the bathroom door slightly.*)

BLANCHE: Stella.

STELLA: Yes, Blanche?

BLANCHE: If anyone calls while I'm bathing take the number and tell them I'll call right back.

STELLA: Yes.

BLANCHE: That cool yellow silk—the bouclé. See if it's crushed. If it's not too crushed I'll wear it and on the lapel that silver and turquoise pin in the shape of a seahorse. You will find them in the heart-shaped box I keep my accessories in. And Stella . . . Try and locate a bunch of artificial violets in that box, too, to pin with the seahorse on the lapel of the jacket.

(*She closes the door. Stella turns to Eunice.*)

STELLA: I don't know if I did the right thing.

EUNICE: What else could you do?

STELLA: I couldn't believe her story and go on living with Stanley.

EUNICE: Don't ever believe it. Life has got to go on. No matter what happens, you've got to keep on going.

(*The bathroom door opens a little.*)

BLANCHE (*looking out*): Is the coast clear?
STELLA: Yes, Blanche. (*To Eunice*) Tell her how well she's looking.
BLANCHE: Please close the curtains before I come out.
STELLA: They're closed.
STANLEY: —How many for you?
PABLO: —Two.
STEVE: —Three.

(*Blanche appears in the amber light of the door. She has a tragic radiance in her red satin robe following the sculptural lines of her body. The "Varsouviana" rises audibly as Blanche enters the bedroom.*)

BLANCHE (*with faintly hysterical vivacity*): I have just washed my hair.
STELLA: Did you?
BLANCHE: I'm not sure I got the soap out.
EUNICE: Such fine hair!
BLANCHE: (*accepting the compliment*): It's a problem. Didn't I get a call?
STELLA: Who from, Blanche?
BLANCHE: Shep Huntleigh . . .
STELLA: Why, not yet, honey!
BLANCHE: How strange! I—

(*At the sound of Blanche's voice Mitch's arm supporting his cards has sagged and his gaze is dissolved into space. Stanley slaps him on the shoulder.*)

STANLEY: Hey, Mitch, come to!

(*The sound of this new voice shocks Blanche. She makes a shocked gesture, forming his name with her lips. Stella nods and looks quickly away. Blanche stands quite still for some moments—the silverbacked mirror in her hand and a look of sorrowful perplexity as though all human experience shows on her face. Blanche finally speaks but with sudden hysteria.*)

BLANCHE: What's going on here?

(*She turns from Stella to Eunice and back to Stella. Her rising voice penetrates the concentration of the game. Mitch ducks his head lower but Stanley shoves back his chair as if about to rise. Steve places a restraining hand on his arm.*)

BLANCHE (*continuing*): What's happened here? I want an explanation of what's happened here.

STELLA (*agonizingly*): Hush! Hush!

EUNICE: Hush! Hush! Honey.

STELLA: Please, Blanche.

BLANCHE: Why are you looking at me like that? Is something wrong with me?

EUNICE: You look wonderful, Blanche. Don't she look wonderful?

STELLA: Yes.

EUNICE: I understand you are going on a trip.

STELLA: Yes, Blanche *is*. She's going on a vacation.

EUNICE: I'm green with envy.

BLANCHE: Help me, help me get dressed!

STELLA (*handing her dress*): Is this what you—

BLANCHE: Yes, it will do! I'm anxious to get out of here—this place is a trap!

EUNICE: What a pretty blue jacket.

STELLA: It's lilac colored.

BLANCHE: You're both mistaken. It's Della Robbia blue. The blue of the robe in the old Madonna pictures. Are these grapes washed?

(*She fingers the bunch of grapes which Eunice had brought in.*)

EUNICE: Huh?

BLANCHE: Washed, I said. Are they washed?

EUNICE: They're from the French Market.

BLANCHE: That doesn't mean they've been washed. (*The cathedral bells chime*) Those cathedral bells—they're the only clean thing in the Quarter. Well, I'm going now. I'm ready to go.

EUNICE (*whispering*): She's going to walk out before they get here.

STELLA: Wait, Blanche.

BLANCHE: I don't want to pass in front of those men.

EUNICE: Then wait'll the game breaks up.

STELLA: Sit down and . . .

(*Blanche turns weakly, hesitantly about. She lets them push her into a chair.*)

BLANCHE: I can smell the sea air. The rest of my time I'm going to spend on the sea. And when I die, I'm going to die on the sea. You know what I shall die of? (*She plucks a grape*) I shall die of eating an unwashed grape one day out on the ocean. I will die—with my hand in the hand of some nice-looking ship's doctor, a very young one with a small blond mustache and a big silver watch. "Poor lady," they'll say, "the quinine did her no good. That unwashed grape has transported her soul to heaven." (*The cathedral chimes are heard*) And I'll be buried at sea sewn up in a clean white sack and dropped overboard—at noon—in the blaze of summer—and into an ocean as blue as (*Chimes again*) my first lover's eyes!

(*A Doctor and a Matron have appeared around the corner of the building and climbed the steps to the porch. The gravity of their profession is exaggerated—the unmistakable aura of the state institution with its cynical detachment. The Doctor rings the doorbell. The murmur of the game is interrupted.*)

EUNICE (*whispering to Stella*): That must be them.

(*Stella presses her fists to her lips.*)

BLANCHE (*rising slowly*): What is it?

EUNICE (*affectedly casual*): Excuse me while I see who's at the door.

STELLA: Yes.

(*Eunice goes into the kitchen.*)

BLANCHE (*tensely*): I wonder if it's for me.

(*A whispered colloquy takes place at the door.*)

EUNICE (*returning, brightly*): Someone is calling for Blanche.

BLANCHE: It *is* for me, then! (*She looks fearfully from one to the other and then to the portieres. The "Varsouviana" faintly plays*) Is it the gentleman I was expecting from Dallas?

EUNICE: I think it is, Blanche.

BLANCHE: I'm not quite ready.

STELLA: Ask him to wait outside.

BLANCHE: I . . .

(*Eunice goes back to the portieres. Drums sound very softly.*)

STELLA: Everything packed?

BLANCHE: My silver toilet articles are still out.

STELLA: Ah!

EUNICE (*returning*): They're waiting in front of the house.

BLANCHE: They! Who's "they"?

EUNICE: There's a lady with him.

BLANCHE: I cannot imagine who this "lady" could be! How is she dressed?

EUNICE: Just—just a sort of a—plain-tailored outfit.

BLANCHE: Possibly she's— (*Her voice dies out nervously.*)

STELLA: Shall we go, Blanche?

BLANCHE: Must we go through that room?

STELLA: I will go with you.

BLANCHE: How do I look?

STELLA: Lovely.

EUNICE (*echoing*): Lovely.

(*Blanche moves fearfully to the portieres. Eunice draws them open for her. Blanche goes into the kitchen.*)

BLANCHE (*to the men*): Please don't get up. I'm only passing through.

(*She crosses quickly to outside door. Stella and Eunice follow. The poker players stand awkwardly at the table—all except Mitch, who remains seated, looking down at the table. Blanche steps out on a small porch at the side of the door. She stops short and catches her breath.*)

DOCTOR: How do you do?

BLANCHE: You are not the gentleman I was expecting. (*She suddenly gasps and starts back up the steps. She stops by Stella, who stands just outside the door, and speaks in a frightening whisper*) That man isn't Shep Huntleigh.

(*The "Varsouviana" is playing distantly.*

(*Stella stares back at Blanche. Eunice is holding Stella's arm. There is a moment of silence—no sound but that of Stanley steadily shuffling the cards.*

(*Blanche catches her breath again and slips back into the flat. She enters the flat with a peculiar smile, her eyes wide and brilliant. As soon as her sister goes past her, Stella closes her eyes and clenches her hands. Eunice throws her arms comfortingly about her. Then she starts up to her flat. Blanche stops just inside the door. Mitch keeps staring down at his hands on the table, but the other men look at her curiously. At last she starts around the table toward the bedroom. As she does, Stanley suddenly pushes back his chair and rises as if to block her way. The Matron follows her into the flat.*)

STANLEY: Did you forget something?
BLANCHE (*shrilly*): Yes! Yes, I forgot something!

(*She rushes past him into the bedroom. Lurid reflections appear on the walls in odd, sinuous shapes. The "Varsouviana" is filtered into a weird distortion, accompanied by the cries and noises of the jungle. Blanche seizes the back of a chair as if to defend herself.*)

STANLEY: Doc, you better go in.
DOCTOR (*motioning to the Matron*): Nurse, bring her out.

(*The Matron advances on one side, Stanley on the other. Divested of all the softer properties of womanhood, the Matron is a peculiarly sinister figure in her severe dress. Her voice is bold and toneless as a firebell.*)

MATRON: Hello, Blanche.

(*The greeting is echoed and re-echoed by other mysterious voices behind the walls, as if reverberated through a canyon of rock.*)

STANLEY: She says that she forgot something.

(*The echo sounds in threatening whispers.*)

MATRON: That's all right.

STANLEY: What did you forget, Blanche?

BLANCHE: I— I—

MATRON: It don't matter. We can pick it up later.

STANLEY: Sure. We can send it along with the trunk.

BLANCHE (*retreating in panic*): I don't know you—I don't know you. I want to be—left alone—please!

MATRON: Now, Blanche!

ECHOES (*rising and falling*): Now, Blanche—now, Blanche—now, Blanche!

STANLEY: You left nothing here but spilt talcum and old empty perfume bottles—unless it's the paper lantern you want to take with you. You want the lantern?

(*He crosses to dressing table and seizes the paper lantern, tearing it off the light bulb, and extends it toward her. She cries out as if the lantern was herself. The Matron steps boldly toward her. She screams and tries to break past the Matron. All the men spring to their feet. Stella runs out to the porch, with Eunice following to comfort her, simultaneously with the confused voices of the men in the kitchen. Stella rushes into Eunice's embrace on the porch.*)

STELLA: Oh, my God, Eunice help me! Don't let them do that to her, don't let them hurt her! Oh, God, oh, please God, don't hurt her! What are they doing to her? What are they doing? (*She tries to break from Eunice's arms.*)

EUNICE: No, honey, no, no, honey. Stay here. Don't go back in there. Stay with me and don't look.

STELLA: What have I done to my sister? Oh, God, what have I done to my sister?

EUNICE: You done the right thing, the only thing you could do. She couldn't stay here; there wasn't no other place for her to go.

(*While Stella and Eunice are speaking on the porch the voices of the men in the kitchen overlap them.*)

STANLEY (*running in from the bedroom*): Hey! Hey! Doctor! Doctor, you better go in!

DOCTOR: Too bad, too bad. I always like to avoid it.

PABLO: This is a very bad thing.

STEVE: This is no way to do it. She should've been told.

PABLO: *Madre de Dios! Cosa mala, muy, muy mala!*

(*Mitch has started toward the bedroom. Stanley crosses to block him.*)

MITCH (*wildly*): You! You done this, all o' your God damn rutting with things you—

STANLEY: Quit the blubber! (*He pushes him aside.*)

MITCH: I'll kill you! (*He lunges and strikes at Stanley.*)

STANLEY: Hold this bone-headed cry-baby!

STEVE (*grasping Mitch*): Stop it, Mitch.

PABLO: Yeah, yeah, take it easy!

(*Mitch collapses at the table, sobbing.*
(*During the preceding scenes, the Matron catches hold of Blanche's arm and prevents her flight. Blanche turns wildly and scratches at the Matron. The heavy woman pinions her arms. Blanche cries out hoarsely and slips to her knees.*

MATRON: These fingernails have to be trimmed. (*The Doctor comes into the room and she looks at him.*) Jacket, Doctor?

DOCTOR: Not unless necessary.

(*He takes off his hat and now he becomes personalized. The unhuman quality goes. His voice is gentle and reassuring as he crosses to Blanche and crouches in front of her. As he speaks her name, her terror subsides a little. The lurid reflections fade from the walls, the inhuman cries and noises die out and her own hoarse crying is calmed.*)

DOCTOR: Miss DuBois.

(*She turns her face to him and stares at him with desperate pleading. He smiles; then he speaks to the Matron.*)

It won't be necessary.

BLANCHE (*faintly*): Ask her to let go of me.

DOCTOR (*to the Matron*): Let go.

(*The Matron releases her. Blanche extends her hands toward the Doctor. He draws her up gently and supports her with his arm and leads her through the portieres.*)

BLANCHE (*holding tight to his arm*): Whoever you are—I have always depended on the kindness of strangers.

(*The poker players stand back as Blanche and the Doctor cross the kitchen to the front door. She allows him to lead her as if she were blind. As they go out on the porch, Stella cries out her sister's name from where she is crouched a few steps up on the stairs.*)

STELLA: Blanche! Blanche, Blanche!

(*Blanche walks on without turning, followed by the Doctor and the Matron. They go around the corner of the building.*
(*Eunice descends to Stella and places the child in her arms. It is wrapped in a pale blue blanket. Stella accepts the child, sobbingly. Eunice continues downstairs and enters the kitchen where the men, except for Stanley, are returning silently to their places about the table. Stanley has gone out on the porch and stands at the foot of the steps looking at Stella.*)

STANLEY (*a bit uncertainly*): Stella?

(*She sobs with inhuman abandon. There is something luxurious in her complete surrender to crying now that her sister is gone.*)

STANLEY (*voluptuously, soothingly*): Now, honey. Now, love. Now, now, love. (*He kneels beside her and his fingers find the opening of her blouse*) Now, now, love. Now, love. . . .

(*The luxurious sobbing, the sensual murmur fade away under the swelling music of the "blue piano" and the muted trumpet.*)

STEVE: This game is seven-card stud.

Curtain

SUMMER AND SMOKE

*Who, if I were to cry out, would hear me
among the angelic orders?*

RILKE

CHARACTERS

ALMA *as a child*
JOHN *as a child*
REV. WINEMILLER, *her father*
MRS. WINEMILLER, *her mother*
ALMA WINEMILLER
JOHN BUCHANAN, JR.
DR. BUCHANAN, *his father*
ROSA GONZALES
PAPA GONZALES, *her father*
NELLIE EWELL
MRS. BASSETT
ROGER DOREMUS
MR. KRAMER
ROSEMARY
VERNON
DUSTY

SCENES

PART ONE

A SUMMER

PART TWO

A WINTER

*The entire action of the play takes place in Glorious Hill, Mississippi.
The time is the turn of the Century through 1916.*

AUTHOR'S PRODUCTION NOTES

As the concept of a design grows out of reading a play I will not do more than indicate what I think are the most essential points.

First of all—*The Sky*.

There must be a great expanse of sky so that the entire action of the play takes place against it. This is true of interior as well as exterior scenes. But in fact there are no really interior scenes, for the walls are omitted or just barely suggested by certain necessary fragments such as might be needed to hang a picture or to contain a door-frame.

During the day scenes the sky should be a pure and intense blue (like the sky of Italy as it is so faithfully represented in the religious paintings of the Renaissance) and costumes should be selected to form dramatic color contrasts to this intense blue which the figures stand against. (Color harmonies and other visual effects are tremendously important.)

In the night scenes, the more familiar constellations, such as Orion and the Great Bear and the Pleiades, are clearly projected on the night sky, and above them, splashed across the top of the cyclorama, is the nebulous radiance of the Milky Way. Fleecy cloud forms may also be projected on this cyclorama and made to drift across it.

So much for *The Sky*.

Now we descend to the so-called interior sets of the play. There are two of these "interior" sets, one being the parlor of an Episcopal Rectory and the other the home of a doctor next door to the Rectory. The architecture of these houses is barely suggested but is of an American Gothic design of the Victorian era. There are no actual doors or windows or walls. Doors and windows are represented by delicate frameworks of Gothic design. These frames have strings of ivy clinging to them, the leaves of emerald and amber. Sections of wall are used only where they are functionally required. There should be a fragment of wall in back of the Rectory sofa, supporting a romantic landscape in a gilt frame. In the doctor's house there should be a section of wall to support the chart of anatomy. Chirico has used fragmentary walls and interiors in a very evocative way in his painting called "Conversation among the Ruins." We will deal more specifically with these interiors as we come to them in the course of the play.

Now we come to the main exterior set which is a promontory in a park or public square in the town of Glorious Hill. Situated on this promontory is a fountain in the form of a stone angel, in a gracefully crouching position with wings lifted and her hands held together to form a cup from which water flows, a public drinking fountain. The stone angel of the fountain should probably be elevated so that it appears in the background of the interior scenes as a symbolic figure (Eternity) brooding over the course of the play. *This entire exterior set may be on an upper level, above that of the two fragmentary interiors.* I would like all three units to form an harmonious whole like one complete picture rather than three separate ones. An imaginative designer may solve these plastic problems in a variety of ways and should not feel bound by any of my specific suggestions.

There is one more set, a very small exterior representing an arbor, which we will describe when we reach it.

Everything possible should be done to give an unbroken fluid quality to the sequence of scenes.

There should be no curtain except for the intermission. The other divisions of the play should be accomplished by changes of lighting.

Finally, the matter of music. One basic theme should recur and the points of recurrence have been indicated here and there in the stage directions.

Rome, March, 1948.

PART ONE
A Summer

PROLOGUE

In the park near the angel of the fountain. At dusk of an evening in May, in the first few years of this Century.

Alma, as a child of ten, comes into the scene. She wears a middy blouse and has ribboned braids. She already has the dignity of an adult; there is a quality of extraordinary delicacy and tenderness or spirituality in her, which must set her distinctly apart from other children. She has a habit of holding her hands, one cupped under the other in a way similar to that of receiving the wafer at Holy Communion. This is a habit that will remain with her as an adult. She stands like that in front of the stone angel for a few moments; then bends to drink at the fountain.

While she is bent at the fountain, John, as a child, enters. He shoots a pea-shooter at Alma's bent-over back. She utters a startled cry and whirls about. He laughs.

JOHN: Hi, Preacher's daughter. (*He advances toward her.*) I been looking for you.

ALMA (*hopefully*): You have?

JOHN: Was it you that put them handkerchiefs on my desk? (*Alma smiles uncertainly.*) Answer up!

ALMA: I put a box of handkerchiefs on your desk.

JOHN: I figured it was you. What was the idea, Miss Priss?

ALMA: You needed them.

JOHN: Trying to make a fool of me?

ALMA: Oh, no!

JOHN: Then what was the idea?

ALMA: You have a bad cold and your nose has been running all week. It spoils your appearance.

JOHN: You don't have to look at me if you don't like my appearance.

ALMA: I like your appearance.

JOHN (*coming closer*): Is that why you look at me all the time?

ALMA: I—don't!

571

JOHN: Oh, yeh, you do. You been keeping your eyes on me all the time. Every time I look around I see them cat eyes of yours looking at me. That was the trouble today when Miss Blanchard asked you where the river Amazon was. She asked you twice and you still didn't answer because you w' lookin' at me. What's the idea? What've'y' got on y' mind anyhow? Answer up!

ALMA: I was only thinking how handsome you'd be if your face wasn't dirty. You know why your face is dirty? Because you don't use a handkerchief and you wipe your nose on the sleeve of that dirty old sweater.

JOHN (*indignantly*): Hah!

ALMA: That's why I put the handkerchiefs on your desk and I wrapped them up so nobody would know what they were. It isn't my fault that you opened the box in front of everybody!

JOHN: What did you think I'd do with a strange box on my desk? Just leave it there till it exploded or something? Sure I opened it up. I didn't expect to find no—*handkerchiefs!*—in it . . .

ALMA (*in a shy trembling voice*): I'm sorry that you were embarrassed. I honestly am awfully sorry that you were embarrassed. Because I wouldn't embarrass you for the world!

JOHN: Don't flatter yourself that I was embarrassed. I don't embarrass that easy.

ALMA: It was stupid and cruel of those girls to laugh.

JOHN: Hah!

ALMA: They should all realize that you don't have a mother to take care of such things for you. It was a pleasure to me to be able to do something for you, only I didn't want you to know it was me who did it.

JOHN: Hee-haw! Ho-hum! Take 'em back! (*He snatches out the box and thrusts it toward her.*)

ALMA: *Please* keep them.

JOHN: What do I want with them?

(*She stares at him helplessly. He tosses the box to the ground and goes up to the fountain and drinks. Something in her face mollifies him and he sits down at the base of the fountain with a manner that does not preclude a more friendly relation. The dusk gathers deeper.*)

ALMA: Do you know the name of the angel?

JOHN: Does she have a name?

ALMA: Yes, I found out she does. It's carved in the base, but it's all worn away so you can't make it out with your eyes.

JOHN: Then how do you know it?

ALMA: You have to read it with your fingers. I did and it gave me cold shivers! *You* read it and see if it doesn't give *you* cold shivers! Go on! Read it with your fingers!

JOHN: Why don't you tell me and save me the trouble?

ALMA: I'm not going to tell you.

(*John grins indulgently and turns to the pediment, crouching before it and running his fingers along the worn inscription.*)

JOHN: E?

ALMA: Yes, E is the first letter!

JOHN: T?

ALMA: Yes!

JOHN: E?

ALMA: E!

JOHN: K?

ALMA: No, no, not K!—R! (*He slowly straightens up.*)

JOHN: Eternity?

ALMA: *Eternity!*—Didn't it give you the cold shivers?

JOHN: Nahh.

ALMA: Well, it did me!

JOHN: Because you're a preacher's daughter. Eternity. What is eternity?

ALMA (*in a hushed wondering voice*): It's something that goes on and on when life and death and time and everything else is all through with.

JOHN: There's no such thing.

ALMA: There is. It's what people's souls live in when they have left their bodies. My name is Alma and Alma is Spanish for soul. Did you know that?

JOHN: Hee-haw! Ho-hum! Have you ever seen a dead person?

ALMA: No.

JOHN: I have. They made me go in the room when my mother was dying and she caught hold of my hand and wouldn't let me go—and so I screamed and hit her.

ALMA: Oh, you didn't do that.

JOHN (*somberly*): Uh-huh. She didn't look like my mother. Her face was all ugly and yellow and—terrible—bad-smelling! And so I hit her to make her let go of my hand. They told me that I was a devil!

ALMA: You didn't know what you were doing.

JOHN: My dad is a doctor.

ALMA: I know.

JOHN: He wants to send me to college to study to be a doctor but I wouldn't be a doctor for the world. And have to go in a room and watch people dying! . . . Jesus!

ALMA: You'll change your mind about that.

JOHN: Oh, no, I won't. I'd rather *be* a devil, like they called me and go to South America on a boat! . . . Give me one of them handkerchiefs. (*She brings them eagerly and humbly to the fountain. He takes one out and wets it at the fountain and scrubs his face with it.*) Is my face clean enough to suit you now?

ALMA: Yes!—Beautiful!

JOHN: *What!*

ALMA: I said "Beautiful"!

JOHN: Well—let's—kiss each other.

(*Alma turns away.*)

JOHN: Come on, let's just try it!

(*He seizes her shoulders and gives her a quick rough kiss. She stands amazed with one hand cupping the other.*

(*The voice of a child in the distance calls "Johnny! Johnny!"*

(*He suddenly snatches at her hair-ribbon, jerks it loose and then runs off with a mocking laugh.*

(*Hurt and bewildered, Alma turns back to the stone angel, for comfort. She crouches at the pediment and touches the inscription with her fingers. The scene dims out with music.*)

SCENE ONE

Before the curtain rises a band is heard playing a patriotic anthem, punctuated with the crackle of fireworks.

The scene is the same as for the Prologue. It is the evening of July 4th in a year shortly before the first World War. There is a band concert and a display of fireworks in the park. During the scene the light changes from faded sunlight to dusk. Sections of roof, steeples, weather-vanes, should have a metallic surface that catches the mellow light on the backdrop; when dusk has fallen the stars should be visible.

As the curtain rises, the Rev. and Mrs. Winemiller come in and sit on the bench near the fountain. Mrs. Winemiller was a spoiled and selfish girl who evaded the responsibilities of later life by slipping into a state of perverse childishness. She is known as Mr. Winemiller's "Cross."

MR. WINEMILLER (*suddenly rising*): There is Alma, getting on the bandstand! (*Mrs. Winemiller is dreamily munching popcorn.*)

AN ANNOUNCER'S VOICE (*at a distance*): The Glorious Hill Orchestra brings you Miss Alma Winemiller, The Nightingale of the Delta, singing . . . "La Golondrina."

MR. WINEMILLER (*sitting back down again*): This is going to provoke a lot of criticism.

(*The song commences. The voice is not particularly strong, but it has great purity and emotion. John Buchanan comes along. He is now a Promethean figure, brilliantly and restlessly alive in a stagnant society. The excess of his power has not yet found a channel. If it remains without one, it will burn him up. At present he is unmarked by the dissipations in which he relieves his demoniac unrest; he has the fresh and shining look of an epic hero. He walks leisurely before the Winemillers' bench, negligently touching the crown of his hat but not glancing at them; climbs the steps to the base of the fountain, then turns and looks in the direction of the singer. A look of interest touched with irony appears on his face. A couple, strolling in the park, pass behind the fountain.*)

THE GIRL: Look who's by the fountain!
THE MAN: Bright as a new silver dollar!

JOHN: Hi, Dusty! Hi, Pearl!

THE MAN: How'd you make out in that floating crap game?

JOHN: I floated with it as far as Vicksburg, then sank.

THE GIRL: Everybody's been calling: "Johnny, Johnny—where's Johnny?"

(*John's father, Dr. Buchanan, comes on from the right, as Rev. and Mrs. Winemiller move off the scene to the left, toward the band music. Dr. Buchanan is an elderly man whose age shows in his slow and stiff movements. He walks with a cane. John sees him coming, but pretends not to and starts to walk off.*)

DR. BUCHANAN: John!

JOHN (*slowly turning around, as the couple move off*): Oh! Hi, Dad. . . . (*They exchange a long look.*) I—uh—meant to wire you but I must've forgot. I got tied up in Vicksburg Friday night and just now got back to town. Haven't been to the house yet. Is everything . . . going okay? (*He takes a drink of water at the fountain.*)

DR. BUCHANAN (*slowly, in a voice hoarse with emotion*): There isn't any room in the medical profession for wasters, drunkards and lechers. And there isn't any room in my house for wasters—drunkards—lechers! (*A child is heard calling "I sp-yyyyyy!" in the distance.*) I married late in life. I brought over five hundred children into this world before I had one of my own. And by God it looks like I've given myself the rottenest one of the lot. . . . (*John laughs uncertainly.*) You will find your things at the Alhambra Hotel.

JOHN: Okay. If that's how you want it.

(*There is a pause. The singing comes through on the music. John tips his hat diffidently and starts away from the fountain. He goes a few feet and his father suddenly calls after him.*)

DR. BUCHANAN: John! (*John pauses and looks back.*) Come here.

JOHN: Yes, Sir? (*He walks back to his father and stands before him.*)

DR. BUCHANAN (*hoarsely*): Go to the Alhambra Hotel and pick up your things and—bring them back to the house.

JOHN (*gently*): Yes, Sir. If that's how you want it. (*He diffidently extends a hand to touch his father's shoulder.*)

DR. BUCHANAN (*brushing the hand roughly off*): You! . . . You infernal *whelp*, you!

(*Dr. Buchanan turns and goes hurriedly away. John looks after him with a faint, affectionate smile, then sits down on the steps with an air of relief, handkerchief to forehead, and a whistle of relief. Just then the singing at the bandstand ends and there is the sound of applause. Mrs. Winemiller comes in from the left, followed by her husband.*)

MRS. WINEMILLER: Where is the ice cream man?

MR. WINEMILLER: Mother, hush! (*He sees his daughter approaching.*) Here we are, Alma!

(*The song ends. There is applause. Then the band strikes up the Santiago Waltz.*

(*Alma Winemiller enters. Alma had an adult quality as a child and now, in her middle twenties, there is something prematurely spinsterish about her. An excessive propriety and self-consciousness is apparent in her nervous laughter; her voice and gestures belong to years of church entertainments, to the position of hostess in a rectory. People her own age regard her as rather quaintly and humorously affected. She has grown up mostly in the company of her elders. Her true nature is still hidden even from herself. She is dressed in pale yellow and carries a yellow silk parasol.*

(*As Alma passes in front of the fountain, John slaps his hands resoundingly together a few times. She catches her breath in a slight laughing sound, makes as if to retreat, with a startled "Oh!", but then goes quickly to her parents. The applause from the crowd continues.*)

MR. WINEMILLER: They seem to want to hear you sing again, Alma.

(*She turns nervously about, touching her throat and her chest. John grins, applauding by the fountain. When the applause dies out, Alma sinks faintly on the bench.*)

ALMA: Open my bag, Father. My fingers have frozen stiff! (*She draws a deep labored breath.*) I don't know what came

SUMMER AND SMOKE

over me—absolute panic! Never, never again, it isn't worth
it—the tortures that I go through!

MR. WINEMILLER (*anxiously*): You're having one of your nervous attacks?

ALMA: My heart's beating so! It seemed to be in my *throat*
the whole time I was singing! (*John laughs audibly from the
fountain.*) Was it noticeable, Father?

MR. WINEMILLER: You sang extremely well, Alma. But you
know how I feel about this, it was contrary to my wishes
and I cannot imagine why you wanted to do it, especially
since it seemed to upset you so.

ALMA: I don't see how anyone could object to my singing at
a patriotic occasion. If I had just sung well! But I barely got
through it. At one point I thought that I wouldn't. The
words flew out of my mind. Did you notice the pause?
Blind panic! They really never came back, but I went on
singing—I think I must have been improvising the lyric!
Whew! Is there a handkerchief in it?

MRS. WINEMILLER (*suddenly*): Where is the ice cream man?

ALMA (*rubbing her fingers together*): Circulation is slowly coming back . . .

MR. WINEMILLER: Sit back quietly and take a deep breath,
Alma.

ALMA: Yes, my handkerchief—now . . .

MRS. WINEMILLER: Where is the ice cream man?

MR. WINEMILLER: Mother, there isn't any ice cream man.

ALMA: No, there isn't any ice cream man, Mother. But on the
way home Mr. Doremus and I will stop by the drug store
and pick up a pint of ice cream.

MR. WINEMILLER: Are you intending to stay here?

ALMA: Until the concert is over. I promised Roger I'd wait for
him.

MR. WINEMILLER: I suppose you have noticed who is by the
fountain?

ALMA: *Shhh!*

MR. WINEMILLER: Hadn't you better wait on a different
bench?

ALMA: This is where Roger will meet me.

MR. WINEMILLER: Well, Mother, we'll run along now. (*Mrs.
Winemiller has started vaguely toward the fountain, Mr.*

Winemiller firmly restraining her.) This way, this way, Mother! (*He takes her arm and leads her off.*)

MRS. WINEMILLER (*calling back, in a high, childish voice*): Strawberry, Alma. Chocolate, chocolate and strawberry mixed! Not vanilla!

ALMA (*faintly*): Yes, yes, Mother—vanilla . . .

MRS. WINEMILLER (*furiously*): I said *not* vanilla. (*shouting*) Strawberry!

MR. WINEMILLER (*fiercely*): Mother! We're attracting attention. (*He propels her forcibly away.*)

(*John laughs by the fountain. Alma moves her parasol so that it shields her face from him. She leans back closing her eyes. John notices a firecracker by the fountain. He leans over negligently to pick it up. He grins and lights it and tosses it toward Alma's bench. When it goes off she springs up with a shocked cry, letting the parasol drop.*)

JOHN (*jumping up as if outraged*): Hey! Hey, you! (*He looks off to the right. Alma sinks back weakly on the bench. John solicitously advances.*) Are you all right?

ALMA: I can't seem to—catch my breath! Who threw it?

JOHN: Some little rascal.

ALMA: Where?

JOHN: He ran away quick when I hollered!

ALMA: There ought to be an ordinance passed in this town forbidding firecrackers.

JOHN: Dad and I treated fifteen kids for burns the last couple of days. I think you need a little restorative, don't you? (*He takes out a flask.*) Here!

ALMA: What is it?

JOHN: Apple-jack brandy.

ALMA: No thank you.

JOHN: Liquid dynamite.

ALMA: I'm sure.

(*John laughs and returns it to his pocket. He remains looking down at her with one foot on the end of her bench. His steady, smiling look into her face is disconcerting her.*

(*In Alma's voice and manner there is a delicacy and elegance, a kind of "airiness," which is really natural to her as it is, in a less marked degree, to many Southern girls. Her gestures and mannerisms are a bit exaggerated but in a graceful way. It is understandable that she might be accused of "putting on airs" and of being "affected" by the other young people of the town. She seems to belong to a more elegant age, such as the Eighteenth Century in France. Out of nervousness and self-consciousness she has a habit of prefacing and concluding her remarks with a little breathless laugh. This will be indicated at points, but should be used more freely than indicated; however, the characterization must never be stressed to the point of making her at all ludicrous in a less than sympathetic way.)*

ALMA: You're—home for the summer? (*John gives an affirmative grunt.*) Summer is not the pleasantest time of year to renew an acquaintance with Glorious Hill—is it? (*John gives an indefinite grunt. Alma laughs airily.*) The Gulf wind has failed us this year, disappointed us dreadfully this summer. We used to be able to rely on the Gulf wind to cool the nights off for us, but this summer has been an exceptional season. (*He continues to grin disconcertingly down at her; she shows her discomfiture in flurried gestures.*)

JOHN (*slowly*): Are you—disturbed about something?

ALMA: That firecracker was a shock.

JOHN: You should be over that shock by now.

ALMA: I don't get over shocks quickly.

JOHN: I see you don't.

ALMA: You're planning to stay here and take over some of your father's medical practice?

JOHN: I haven't made up my mind about anything yet.

ALMA: I hope so, we all hope so. Your father was telling me that you have succeeded in isolating the germ of that fever epidemic that's broken out at Lyon.

JOHN: Finding something to kill it is more of a trick.

ALMA: You'll do that! He's so positive that you will. He says that you made a special study of bacter—bacter . . .

JOHN: Bacteriology!

ALMA: Yes! At Johns Hopkins! That's in Boston, isn't it?

JOHN: No. Baltimore.

ALMA: Oh, Baltimore. Baltimore, Maryland. Such a beautiful combination of names. And bacteriology—isn't that something you do with a microscope?

JOHN: Well—partly. . . .

ALMA: I've looked through a telescope, but never a microscope. What . . . what do you—see?

JOHN: A—universe, Miss Alma.

ALMA: What kind of a universe?

JOHN: Pretty much the same kind that you saw through the lens of a telescope—a mysterious one. . . .

ALMA: Oh, yes. . . .

JOHN: Part anarchy—and part order!

ALMA: The footprints of God!

JOHN: But not God.

ALMA (*ecstatically*): To be a doctor! And deal with these mysteries under the microscope lens . . . I think it is more religious than being a priest! There is so much suffering in the world it actually makes one sick to think about it, and most of us are so helpless to relieve it. . . . But a physician! Oh, my! With his magnificent gifts and training what a joy it must be to know that he is equipped and appointed to bring relief to all of this fearful suffering—and fear! And it's an expanding profession, it's a profession that is continually widening its horizons. So many diseases have already come under scientific control but the commencement is just—beginning! I mean there is so much more that is yet to be done, such as mental afflictions to be brought under control. . . . And with your father's example to inspire you! Oh, my!

JOHN: I didn't know you had so many ideas about the medical profession.

ALMA: Well, I am a great admirer of your father, as well as a patient. It's such a comfort knowing that he's right next door, within arm's reach as it were!

JOHN: Why? Do you have fits? . . .

ALMA: Fits? (*She throws back her head with a peal of gay laughter.*) Why no, but I do have attacks!—of nervous heart trouble. Which can be so alarming that I run straight to your father!

JOHN: At two or three in the morning?

ALMA: Yes, as late as that, even . . . occasionally. He's very patient with me.

JOHN: But does you no good?

ALMA: He always reassures me.

JOHN: Temporarily?

ALMA: Yes . . .

JOHN: Don't you want more than that?

ALMA: What?

JOHN: It's none of my business.

ALMA: What were you going to say?

JOHN: You're Dad's patient. But I have an idea . . .

ALMA: Please go on! (*John laughs a little.*) Now you have to go on! You can't leave me up in the air! What were you going to tell me?

JOHN: Only that I suspect you need something more than a little temporary reassurance.

ALMA: *Why?* Why? You think it's more serious than . . . ?

JOHN: You're swallowing air.

ALMA: I'm what?

JOHN: You're swallowing air, Miss Alma.

ALMA: I'm swallowing air?

JOHN: Yes, you swallow air when you laugh or talk. It's a little trick that hysterical women get into.

ALMA (*uncertainly*): Ha-ha . . . !

JOHN: You swallow air and it presses on your heart and gives you palpitations. That isn't serious in itself but it's a symptom of something that is. Shall I tell you frankly?

ALMA: Yes!

JOHN: Well, what I think you have is a *doppelganger*! You have a *doppelganger* and the *doppelganger* is badly irritated.

ALMA: Oh, my goodness! I have an irritated *doppelganger*! (*She tries to laugh, but is definitely uneasy.*) How awful that sounds! What exactly *is* it?

JOHN: It's none of *my* business. You are not *my* patient.

ALMA: But that's downright wicked of you! To tell me I have something awful-sounding as that, and then refuse to let me know what it is! (*She tries to laugh again, unsuccessfully.*)

JOHN: I shouldn't have said anything! I'm not your doctor. . . .

ALMA: Just how did you arrive at this—diagnosis of my case? (*She laughs.*) But of course you're teasing me. Aren't you? . . . There, the Gulf wind is stirring! He's actually moving the leaves of the palmetto! And listen to them complaining. . . .

(*As if brought in by this courier from the tropics, Rosa Gonzales enters and crosses to the fountain. Her indolent walk produces a sound and an atmosphere like the Gulf wind on the palmettos, a whispering of silk and a slight rattle of metallic ornaments. She is dressed in an almost outrageous finery, with lustrous feathers on her hat, greenish blue, a cascade of them, also diamond and emerald earrings.*)

JOHN (*sharply*): Who is that?

ALMA: I'm surprised that you don't know.

JOHN: I've been away quite a while.

ALMA: That's the Gonzales girl. . . . Her father's the owner of the gambling casino on Moon Lake. (*Rosa drinks at the fountain and wanders leisurely off.*) She smiled at you, didn't she?

JOHN: I thought she did.

ALMA: I hope that you have a strong character. (*He places a foot on the end of the bench.*)

JOHN: Solid rock.

ALMA (*nervously*): The pyrotechnical display is going to be brilliant.

JOHN: The what?

ALMA: The fireworks.

JOHN: Aw!

ALMA: I suppose you've lost touch with most of your *old* friends here.

JOHN (*laconically*): Yeah.

ALMA: You must make some *new* ones! I belong to a little group that meets every ten days. I think you'd enjoy them, too. They're young people with—intellectual and artistic interests. . . .

JOHN (*sadly*): Aw, I see . . . intellectual. . . .

ALMA: You must come!—sometime—I'm going to remind you of it. . . .

JOHN: Thanks. Do you mind if I sit down?

ALMA: Why, certainly not, there's room enough for two! Neither of us are—terribly large in diameter! (*She laughs shrilly.*)

(*A girl's voice is heard calling: "Goodbye, Nellie!" and another answers: "Goodbye!" Nellie Ewell enters—a girl of sixteen with a radiantly fresh healthy quality.*)

ALMA: Here comes someone much nicer! One of my adorable little vocal pupils, the youngest and prettiest one with the least gift for music.

JOHN: I know that one.

ALMA: Hello, there, Nellie dear!

NELLIE: Oh, Miss Alma, your singing was so beautiful it made me cry.

ALMA: It's sweet of you to fib so. I sang terribly.

NELLIE: You're just being modest, Miss Alma. Hello, Dr. John! Dr. John?

JOHN: Yeah?

NELLIE: That book you gave me is too full of long words.

JOHN: Look 'em up in the dictionary, Nellie.

NELLIE: I did, but you know how dictionaries are. You look up one long word and it gives you another and you look up that one and it gives you the long word you looked up in the first place. (*John laughs.*) I'm coming over tomorrow for you to explain it all to me. (*She laughs and goes off.*)

ALMA: What book is she talking about?

JOHN: A book I gave her about the facts of nature. She came over to the office and told me her mother wouldn't tell her anything and she had to know because she'd fallen in love.

ALMA: Why the precocious little—imp! (*She laughs.*)

JOHN: What sort of a mother has she?

ALMA: Mrs. Ewell's the merry widow of Glorious Hill. They say that she goes to the depot to meet every train in order to make the acquaintance of traveling salesmen. Of course she is ostracized by all but a few of her own type of women in town, which is terribly hard for Nellie. It isn't fair to the child. Father didn't want me to take her as a pupil because of her mother's reputation, but I feel that one has a duty to perform toward children in such—circumstances. . . . And I always say that life is such a mysteriously complicated thing that no one should really presume to judge and condemn the behavior of anyone else!

(*There is a faraway "puff" and a burst of golden light over their heads. Both look up. There is a long-drawn "Ahhh . . ." from the invisible crowd. This is an effect that will be repeated at intervals during the scene.*)

There goes the first sky-rocket! Oh, look at it burst into a million stars!

(*John leans way back to look up and allows his knees to spread wide apart so that one of them is in contact with Alma's. The effect upon her is curiously disturbing.*)

JOHN (*after a moment*): Do you have a chill?

ALMA: Why, no!—no. Why?

JOHN: You're shaking.

ALMA: Am I?

JOHN: Don't you feel it?

ALMA: I have a touch of malaria lingering on.

JOHN: You have malaria?

ALMA: Never severely, never really severely. I just have touches of it that come and go. (*She laughs airily.*)

JOHN (*with a gentle grin*): Why do you laugh that way?

ALMA: What way?

(*John imitates her laugh. Alma laughs again in embarrassment.*)

JOHN: Yeah. That way.

ALMA: I do declare, you haven't changed in the slightest. It used to delight you to embarrass me and it still does!

JOHN: I guess I shouldn't tell you this, but I heard an imitation of you at a party.

ALMA: Imitation? Of what?

JOHN: You.

ALMA: I?—I? Why, *what* did they imitate?

JOHN: You singing at a wedding.

ALMA: My voice?

JOHN: Your gestures and facial expression!

ALMA: How mystifying!

JOHN: No, I shouldn't have told you. You're upset about it.

ALMA: I'm not in the least upset, I am just mystified.

JOHN: Don't you know that you have a reputation for putting on airs a little—for gilding the lily a bit?

ALMA: I have no idea what you are talking about.

JOHN: Well, some people seem to have gotten the idea that you are just a little bit—affected!

ALMA: Well, well, well, well. (*She tries to conceal her hurt.*) That may be so, it may seem so to some people. But since I am innocent of any attempt at affectation, I really don't know what I can do about it.

JOHN: You have a rather fancy way of talking.

ALMA: Have I?

JOHN: Pyrotechnical display instead of fireworks, and that sort of thing.

ALMA: So?

JOHN: And how about that accent?

ALMA: Accent? This leaves me quite speechless! I have sometimes been accused of having a put-on accent by people who disapprove of good diction. My father was a Rhodes scholar at Oxford, and while over there he fell into the natural habit of using the long A where it is correct to use it. I suppose I must have picked it up from him, but it's entirely unconscious. Who gave this imitation at this party you spoke of?

JOHN (*grinning*): I don't think she'd want that told.

ALMA: Oh, it was a *she* then?

JOHN: You don't think a man could do it?

ALMA: No, and I don't think a lady would do it either!

JOHN: I didn't think it would have made you so mad, or I wouldn't have brought it up.

ALMA: Oh, I'm not mad. I'm just mystified and amazed as I always am by unprovoked malice in people. I don't understand it when it's directed at me and I don't understand it when it is directed at anybody else. I just don't understand it, and perhaps it is better not to understand it. These people who call me affected and give these unkind imitations of me—I wonder if they stop to think that I have had certain difficulties and disadvantages to cope with—which may be partly the cause of these peculiarities of mine—which they find so offensive!

JOHN: Now, Miss Alma, you're making a mountain out of a mole-hill!

ALMA: I wonder if they stop to think that my circumstances

are somewhat different from theirs? My father and I have a certain—cross—to bear!

JOHN: What cross?

ALMA: Living next door to us, you should know what cross.

JOHN: Mrs. Winemiller?

ALMA: She had her breakdown while I was still in high school. And from that time on I have had to manage the Rectory and take over the social and household duties that would ordinarily belong to a minister's wife, not his daughter. And that may have made me seem strange to some of my more critical contemporaries. In a way it may have—deprived me of—my youth. . . .

(*Another rocket goes up. Another "Ahhh . . ." from the crowd.*)

JOHN: You ought to go out with young people.

ALMA: I am not a recluse. I don't fly around here and there giving imitations of other people at parties. But I am not a recluse by any manner of means. Being a minister's daughter I have to be more selective than most girls about the—society I keep. But I do go out now and then. . . .

JOHN: I have seen you in the public library and the park, but only two or three times I have seen you out with a boy and it was always someone like this Roger Doremus.

ALMA: I'm afraid that you and I move in different circles. If I wished to be as outspoken as you are, which is sometimes just an excuse for being rude—I might say that I've yet to see you in the company of a—well, a—reputable young woman. You've heard unfavorable talk about me in your circle of acquaintances and I've heard equally unpleasant things about you in mine. And the pity of it is that you are preparing to be a doctor. You're intending to practice your father's profession here in Glorious Hill. (*She catches her breath in a sob.*) Most of us have no choice but to lead useless lives! But you have a gift for scientific research! You have a chance to serve humanity. Not just to go on enduring for the sake of endurance, but to serve a noble, humanitarian cause, to relieve human suffering. And what do you do about it? Everything that you can to alienate the confidence of nice people who love and respect your father.

While he is devoting himself to the fever at Lyon you drive your automobile at a reckless pace from one disorderly roadhouse to another! You say you have seen two things through the microscope, anarchy and order? Well, obviously *order* is not the thing that impressed you . . . conducting yourself like some overgrown schoolboy who wants to be known as the wildest fellow in town! And you—a gifted young doctor—*Magna cum Laude!* (*She turns aside, touching her eyelids with a handkerchief.*) You know what I call it? I call it a *desecration!* (*She sobs uncontrollably. Then she springs up from the bench. John catches her hand.*)

JOHN: You're not going to run off, are you?

ALMA: Singing in public always—always upsets me!—Let go of my hand. (*He holds on to it, grinning up at her in the deepening dusk. The stars are coming out in the cyclorama with its leisurely floating cloud-forms. In the distance the band is playing "La Golondrina."*) Please let go of my hand.

JOHN: Don't run off mad.

ALMA: Let's not make a spectacle of ourselves.

JOHN: Then sit back down.

(*A skyrocket goes up. The crowd "Ahhh . . . s."*)

ALMA: You threw that firecracker and started a conversation just in order to tease me as you did as a child. You came to this bench in order to embarrass me and to hurt my feelings with the report of that vicious—imitation! No, let go of my hand so I can leave, now. You've succeeded in your purpose. I *was* hurt, I *did* make a fool of myself as you intended! So let me go now!

JOHN: You're attracting attention! Don't you know that I really *like* you, Miss Alma?

ALMA: No, you don't.

(*Another skyrocket.*)

JOHN: Sure I do. A lot. Sometimes when I come home late at night I look over at the Rectory. I see something white at the window. Could that be you, Miss Alma? Or, is it your *doppelganger*, looking out of the window that faces my way?

ALMA: Enough about *doppelganger*—whatever that is!

JOHN: There goes a nice one, Roman candle they call it!

(*This time the explosion is in back of them. A Roman candle shoots up puffs of rainbow-colored light in back of the stone angel of the fountain. They turn in profile to watch it.*)

JOHN (*counting the puffs of light*): Four—five—six—that's all? No—seven! (*There is a pause. Alma sits down slowly.*)
ALMA (*vaguely*): Dear me . . . (*She fans herself.*)
JOHN: How about going riding?
ALMA (*too eagerly*): When . . . now?

(*Rosa Gonzales has wandered up to the fountain again. John's attention drifts steadily toward her and away from Alma.*)

JOHN (*too carelessly*): Oh . . . some afternoon.
ALMA: Would you observe the speed limit?
ALMA: Strictly with you, Miss Alma.
ALMA: Why then, I'd be glad to—John.

(*John has risen from the bench and crosses to the fountain.*)

JOHN: And wear a hat with a plume!
ALMA: I don't have a hat with a plume!
JOHN: Get one!

(*Another skyrocket goes up, and there is another long "Ahhh . . ." from the crowd. John saunters up to the fountain. Rosa has lingered beside it. As he passes her he whispers something. She laughs and moves leisurely off. John takes a quick drink at the fountain, then follows Rosa, calling back "Good night" to Alma. There is a sound of laughter in the distance. Alma sits motionless for a moment, then touches a small white handkerchief to her lips and nostrils. Mr. Doremus comes in, carrying a French horn case. He is a small man, somewhat like a sparrow.*)

ROGER: *Whew!* Golly! Moses!—Well, how did it go, Miss Alma?
ALMA: How did—what—go?
ROGER (*annoyed*): My solo on the French horn.
ALMA (*slowly, without thinking*): I paid no attention to it. (*She rises slowly and takes his arm.*) I'll have to hang on your arm—I'm feeling so dizzy!

(*The scene dims out. There is a final skyrocket and a last
"Ahhh . . ." from the crowd in the distance. Music is heard,
and there is light on the angel.*)

SCENE TWO

*Inside the Rectory, which is lighted. Mrs. Winemiller comes in
and makes her way stealthily to the love seat, where she seats herself. Opening her parasol, she takes out a fancy white-plumed
hat which she had concealed there. Rising, she turns to the mirror on the wall over the love seat and tries on the hat. She draws
a long, ecstatic breath as she places it squarely on her head. At
that moment the telephone rings. Startled, she snatches off the
hat, hides it behind the center table and quickly resumes her seat.
The telephone goes on ringing. Alma comes in to answer it.*

ALMA: Hello. . . . Yes, Mr. Gillam. . . . She did? . . . Are
you sure? . . . How shocking! . . . (*Mrs. Winemiller now
retrieves the hat, seats herself in front of Alma and puts the
hat on.*) Thank you, Mr. Gillam . . . the hat is here.

(*Mr. Winemiller comes in. He is distracted.*)

MR. WINEMILLER: Alma! Alma, your mother . . . !
ALMA (*coming in*): I know, Father, Mr. Gillam just phoned.
He told me she picked up a white plumed hat and he pre-
tended not to notice in order to save you the embarrass-
ment, so I—I told him to just charge it to us.
MR. WINEMILLER: That hat looks much too expensive.
ALMA: It's fourteen dollars. You pay six of it, Father, and I'll
pay eight. (*She gives him the parasol.*)
MR. WINEMILLER: What an insufferable cross we have to bear.
(*He retires despairingly from the room.*)

(*Alma goes over to her mother and seats her in a chair at the
table.*)

ALMA: I have a thousand and one things to do before my club
meeting tonight, so you work quietly on your picture puzzle or I shall take the hat back, plume and all.

MRS. WINEMILLER (*throwing a piece of the puzzle on the floor*): The pieces don't fit! (*Alma picks up the piece and puts it on the table.*) The pieces don't fit!

(*Alma stands for a moment in indecision. She reaches for the phone, then puts it down. Then she takes it up again, and gives a number. The telephone across the way in the doctor's office rings and that part of the scene lights up. John comes in.*)

JOHN (*answering the phone*): Hello?

ALMA: John! (*She fans herself rapidly with a palm leaf clutched in her free hand and puts on a brilliant, strained smile as if she were actually in his presence.*)

JOHN: Miss Alma?

ALMA: You recognized my voice?

JOHN: I recognized your laugh.

ALMA: Ha-ha! How are you, you stranger you?

JOHN: I'm pretty well, Miss Alma. How're you doing?

ALMA: Surviving, just surviving! Isn't it fearful?

JOHN: Uh-huh.

ALMA: You seem unusually laconic. Or perhaps I should say more than usually laconic.

JOHN: I had a big night and I'm just recovering from it.

ALMA: Well, sir, I have a bone to pick with you!

JOHN: What's that, Miss Alma? (*He drains a glass of bromo.*)

ALMA: The time of our last conversation on the Fourth of July, you said you were going to take me riding in your automobile.

JOHN: Aw. Did I say that?

ALMA: Yes indeed you did, sir! And all these hot afternoons I've been breathlessly waiting and hoping that you would remember that promise. But now I know how insincere you are. Ha-ha! Time and again the four-wheeled phenomenon flashes by the Rectory and I have yet to put my—my quaking foot in it!

(*Mrs. Winemiller begins to mock Alma's speech and laughter.*)

JOHN: What was that, Miss Alma? I didn't understand you.

ALMA: I was just reprimanding you, sir! Castigating you verbally! Ha-ha!

MRS. WINEMILLER (*grimacing*): Ha-ha.

JOHN: What about, Miss Alma? (*He leans back and puts his feet on table.*)

ALMA: Never mind. I know how busy you are! (*She whispers.*) Mother, *hush!*

JOHN: I'm afraid we have a bad connection.

ALMA: I hate telephones. I don't know why but they always make me laugh as if someone were poking me in the ribs! I swear to goodness they do!

JOHN: Why don't you just go to your window and I'll go to mine and we can holler across?

ALMA: The yard's so wide I'm afraid it would crack my voice! And I've got to sing at somebody's wedding tomorrow.

JOHN: You're going to sing at a wedding?

ALMA: Yes. "The Voice That Breathed O'er Eden!" And I'm as hoarse as a frog! (*Another gale of laughter almost shakes her off her feet.*)

JOHN: Better come over and let me give you a gargle.

ALMA: Nasty gargles—I hate them!

MRS. WINEMILLER (*mockingly*): Nasty gargles—I hate them!

ALMA: Mother, shhh!—please! As you no doubt have gathered, there is some interference at this end of the line! What I wanted to say is—you remember my mentioning that little club I belong to?

JOHN: Aw! Aw, yes! Those intellectual meetings!

ALMA: Oh, now, don't call it that. It's just a little informal gathering every Wednesday and we talk about the new books and read things out loud to each other!

JOHN: Serve any refreshments?

ALMA: Yes, we serve refreshments!

JOHN: Any liquid refreshments?

ALMA: Both liquid and solid refreshments.

JOHN: Is this an invitation?

ALMA: Didn't I promise I'd ask you? It's going to be tonight! —at eight at my house, at the Rectory, so all you'll have to do is cross the yard!

JOHN: I'll try to make it, Miss Alma.

ALMA: Don't say try as if it required some Herculean effort! All you have to do is . . .

JOHN: Cross the yard! Uh-huh—reserve me a seat by the punch bowl.

ALMA: That gives me an idea! We *will* have punch, fruit punch, with claret in it. Do you like claret?

JOHN: I just dote on claret.

ALMA: Now you're being sarcastic! Ha-ha-ha!

JOHN: Excuse me, Miss Alma, but Dad's got to use this phone.

ALMA: I won't hang up till you've said you'll come without fail!

JOHN: I'll be there, Miss Alma. You can count on it.

ALMA: Au revoir, then! Until eight.

JOHN: G'bye, Miss Alma.

(*John hangs up with an incredulous grin. Alma remains holding the phone with a dazed smile until the office interior has dimmed slowly out.*)

MRS. WINEMILLER: Alma's in love—in love. (*She waltzes mockingly.*)

ALMA (*sharply*): Mother, you are wearing out my patience! Now I am expecting another music pupil and I have to make preparations for the club meeting so I suggest that you . . . (*Nellie rings the bell.*) Will you go up to your room? (*Then she calls sweetly.*) Yes, Nellie, coming, Nellie. All right, stay down here then. But keep your attention on your picture puzzle or there will be no ice cream for you after supper!

(*She admits Nellie, who is wildly excited over something. This scene should be played lightly and quickly.*)

NELLIE: Oh, Miss Alma! (*She rushes past Alma in a distracted manner, throws herself on the sofa and hugs herself with excited glee.*)

ALMA: What is it, Nellie? Has something happened at home? (*Nellie continues her exhilaration.*) Oh, now, Nellie, stop that! Whatever it is, it can't be *that* important!

NELLIE (*blurting out suddenly*): Miss Alma, haven't you ever had—*crushes?*

ALMA: What?

NELLIE: Crushes?

ALMA: Yes—I suppose I have. (*She sits down.*)

NELLIE: Did you know that I used to have a crush on *you*, Miss Alma?

ALMA: No, Nellie.

NELLIE: Why do you think that I took singing lessons?

ALMA: I supposed it was because you wished to develop your voice.

NELLIE (*cutting in*): Oh, you know, and I know, I never had any voice. I had a crush on you though. Those were the days when I had crushes on girls. Those days are all over, and now I have crushes on boys. Oh, Miss Alma, you know about Mother, how I was brought up so nobody nice except you would have anything to do with us—Mother meeting the trains to pick up the traveling salesmen and bringing them home to drink and play poker—all of them acting like pigs, pigs, pigs!

MRS. WINEMILLER (*mimicking*): Pigs, pigs, pigs!

NELLIE: Well, I thought I'd always hate men. Loathe and despise them. But last night— Oh!

ALMA: Hadn't we better run over some scales until you are feeling calmer?

NELLIE (*cutting in*): I'd heard them downstairs for hours but didn't know who it was—I'd fallen asleep—when all of a sudden my door banged open. He'd thought it was the bathroom!

ALMA (*nervously*): Nellie, I'm not sure I want to hear any more of this story.

NELLIE (*interrupting*): Guess who it was?

ALMA: I couldn't possibly guess.

NELLIE: Someone you know. Someone I've seen you with.

ALMA: Who?

NELLIE: The wonderfullest person in all the big wide world! When he saw it was me he came and sat down on the bed and held my hand and we talked and talked until Mother came up to see what had happened to him. You should have heard him bawl her out. Oh, he laid the law down! He said she ought to send me off to a girl's school because she wasn't fit to bring up a daughter! Then she started to bawl him out. You're a fine one to talk, she said, you're not fit to call yourself a doctor. (*Alma rises abruptly.*)

ALMA: John Buchanan?

NELLIE: Yes, of course, Dr. Johnny.

ALMA: Was—with—your—mother?

NELLIE: Oh, he wasn't her beau! He had a girl with him, and Mother had somebody else!

ALMA: Who—did—he—have?

NELLIE: Oh, some loud tacky thing with a Z in her name!

ALMA: Gonzales? Rosa Gonzales?

NELLIE: Yes, that was it! (*Alma sits slowly back down.*) But him! Oh, Miss Alma! He's the *wonderfullest* person that I . . .

ALMA (*interrupting*): Your mother was right! He isn't fit to call himself a doctor! I hate to disillusion you, but this wonderfullest person is pitiably weak.

(*Someone calls "Johnny" outside.*)

NELLIE (*in hushed excitement*): Someone is calling him now!

ALMA: Yes, these people who shout his name in front of his house are of such a character that the old doctor cannot permit them to come inside the door. And when they have brought him home at night, left him sprawling on the front steps, sometimes at daybreak—it takes two people, his father and the old cook, one pushing and one pulling, to get him upstairs. (*She sits down.*) All the gifts of the gods were showered on him. . . . (*The call of "Johnny" is repeated.*) But all he cares about is indulging his senses! (*Another call of "Johnny."*)

NELLIE: Here he comes down the steps! (*Alma crosses toward the window.*) Look at him jump!

ALMA: Oh.

NELLIE: Over the banisters. Ha-ha!

ALMA: Nellie, don't lean out the window and have us caught spying.

MRS. WINEMILLER (*suddenly*): Show Nellie how *you* spy on him! Oh, she's a good one at spying. She stands behind the curtain and *peeks* around it, and . . .

ALMA (*frantically*): Mother!

MRS. WINEMILLER: She spies on him. Whenever he comes in at night she rushes downstairs to watch him out of this window!

ALMA (*interrupting her*): Be still!

MRS. WINEMILLER (*going right on*): She called him just now and had a fit on the telephone! (*The old lady cackles derisively.*

Alma snatches her cigarette from her and crushes it under her foot.) Alma's in love! Alma's in love!

ALMA (*interrupting*): Nellie, Nellie, please go.

NELLIE (*with a startled giggle*): All right, Miss Alma, I'm going. (*She crosses quickly to the door, looking back once with a grin.*) Good night, Mrs. Winemiller!

(*Nellie goes out gaily, leaving the door slightly open. Alma rushes to it and slams it shut. She returns swiftly to Mrs. Winemiller, her hands clenched with anger.*)

ALMA: If ever I hear you say such a thing again, if ever you dare to repeat such a thing in my presence or anybody else's—then it will be the last straw! You understand me? Yes, you understand me! You act like a child, but you have the devil in you. And God will punish you—yes! I'll punish you too. I'll take your cigarettes from you and give you no more. I'll give you no ice cream either. Because I'm tired of your malice. Yes, I'm tired of your malice and your self-indulgence. People wonder why I'm tied down here! They pity me—think of me as an old maid already! In spite of I'm young. Still young! It's you—it's you, you've taken my youth away from me! I wouldn't say that—I'd try not even to think it—if you were just kind, just simple! But I could spread my life out like a rug for you to step on and you'd step on it, and not even say "Thank you, Alma!" Which is what you've done always—and now you dare to tell a disgusting lie about me—in front of that girl!

MRS. WINEMILLER: Don't you think I hear you go to the window at night to watch him come in and . . .

ALMA: Give me that plumed hat, Mother! It goes back now, it goes back!

MRS. WINEMILLER: *Fight! Fight!*

(*Alma snatches at the plumed hat. Mrs. Winemiller snatches too. The hat is torn between them. Mrs. Winemiller retains the hat. The plume comes loose in Alma's hand. She stares at it a moment with a shocked expression.*)

ALMA (*sincerely*): Heaven have mercy upon us!

SCENE THREE

Inside the Rectory.

The meeting is in progress, having just opened with the reading of the minutes by Alma. She stands before the green plush sofa and the others. This group includes Mr. Doremus, Vernon, a willowy younger man with an open collar and Byronic locks, the widow Bassett, and a wistful older girl with a long neck and thick-lensed glasses.

ALMA (*reading*): Our last meeting which fell on July fourteenth . . .

MRS. BASSETT: Bastille Day!

ALMA: Pardon me?

MRS. BASSETT: It fell on Bastille Day! But, honey, that was the meeting before last.

ALMA: You're perfectly right. I seem to be on the wrong page. . . . (*She drops the papers.*)

MRS. BASSETT: Butterfingers!

ALMA: Here we are! July twenty-fifth! Correct?

MRS. BASSETT: Correct! (*A little ripple of laughter goes about the circle.*)

ALMA (*continuing*): It was debated whether or not we ought to suspend operations for the remainder of the summer as the departure of several members engaged in the teaching profession for their summer vacations . . .

MRS. BASSETT: Lucky people!

ALMA: . . . had substantially contracted our little circle.

MRS. BASSETT: Decimated our ranks! (*There is another ripple of laughter.*)

(*John appears outside the door-frame and rings the bell.*)

ALMA (*with agitation*): Is that—is that—the doorbell?

MRS. BASSETT: It sure did sound like it to me.

ALMA: Excuse me a moment. I think it may be . . .

(*She crosses to the door-frame and makes the gesture of opening the door. John steps in, immaculately groomed and shining, his white linen coat over his arm and a white Panama hat in his hand. He is a startling contrast to the other male*

*company, who seem to be outcasts of a state in which he is a
prominent citizen.*)

ALMA (*shrilly*): Yes, it is—our guest of honor! Everybody, this
is Dr. John Buchanan, Jr.

JOHN (*easily glancing about the assemblage*): Hello, everybody.

MRS. BASSETT: I never thought he'd show up. Congratulations, Miss Alma.

JOHN: Did I miss much?

ALMA: Not a thing! Just the minutes—I'll put you on the
sofa. Next to me. (*She laughs breathlessly and makes an uncertain gesture. He settles gingerly on the sofa. They all stare
at him with a curious sort of greediness.*) Well, now! we are
completely assembled!

MRS. BASSETT (*eagerly*): Vernon has his verse play with him
tonight!

ALMA (*uneasily*): Is that right, Vernon? (*Obviously, it is.
Vernon has a pile of papers eight inches thick on his knees. He
raises them timidly with downcast eyes.*)

ROGER (*quickly*): We decided to put that off till cooler
weather. Miss Rosemary is supposed to read us a paper
tonight on William Blake.

MRS. BASSETT: Those dead poets can keep!

(*John laughs.*)

ALMA (*excitedly jumping up*): Mrs. Bassett, everybody! This is
the way I feel about the verse play. It's too important a
thing to read under any but ideal circumstances. Not only
atmospheric—on some cool evening with music planned to
go with it!—but everyone present so that nobody will miss
it! Why don't we . . .

ROGER: Why don't we take a standing vote on the matter?

ALMA: Good, good, perfect!

ROGER: All in favor of putting the verse play off till cooler
weather, stand up!

(*Everybody rises but Rosemary and Mrs. Bassett. Rosemary
starts vaguely to rise, but Mrs. Bassett jerks her arm.*)

ROSEMARY: Was this a vote?

ROGER: Now, Mrs. Bassett, no rough tactics, please!

ALMA: Has everybody got fans? John, you haven't got one!

(*She looks about for a fan for him. Not seeing one, she takes Roger's out of his hand and gives it to John. Roger is non-plussed. Rosemary gets up with her paper.*)

ROSEMARY: The poet—William Blake.

MRS. BASSETT: Insane, insane, that man was a mad fanatic! (*She squints her eyes tight shut and thrusts her thumbs into her ears. The reactions range from indignant to conciliatory.*)

ROGER: Now, Mrs. Bassett!

MRS. BASSETT: This is a free country. I can speak my opinion. And I have *read up* on him. Go on, Rosemary. I wasn't criticizing your paper. (*But Rosemary sits down, hurt.*)

ALMA: Mrs. Bassett is only joking, Rosemary.

ROSEMARY: No, I don't want to read it if she feels that strongly about it.

MRS. BASSETT: Not a bit, don't be silly! I just don't see why we should encourage the writings of people like that who have already gone into a drunkard's grave!

VARIOUS VOICES (*exclaiming*): Did he? I never heard that about him. Is that true?

ALMA: Mrs. Bassett is mistaken about that. Mrs. Bassett, you have confused Blake with someone else.

MRS. BASSETT (*positively*): Oh, no, don't tell me. I've read up on him and know what I'm talking about. He traveled around with that Frenchman who took a shot at him and landed them both in jail! Brussels, Brussels!

ROGER (*gaily*): Brussels sprouts!

MRS. BASSETT: That's where it happened, fired a gun at him in a drunken stupor, and later one of them died of T.B. in the gutter! All right. I'm finished. I won't say anything more. Go on with your paper, Rosemary. There's nothing like contact with culture!

(*Alma gets up.*)

ALMA: Before Rosemary reads her paper on Blake, I think it would be a good idea, since some of us aren't acquainted with his work, to preface the critical and biographical comments with a reading of one of his loveliest lyric poems.

ROSEMARY: I'm not going to read anything at all! Not I!

ALMA: Then let me read it then. (*She takes a paper from Rosemary.*) . . . This is called "Love's Secret."

(*She clears her throat and waits for a hush to settle. Rosemary looks stonily at the carpet. Mrs. Bassett looks at the ceiling. John coughs.*)

> Never seek to tell thy love,
> Love that never told can be,
> For the gentle wind doth move
> Silently, invisibly.
> I told my love, I told my love,
> I told him all my heart.
> Trembling, cold in ghastly fear
> Did my love depart.
>
> No sooner had he gone from me
> Than a stranger passing by,
> Silently, invisibly,
> Took him with a sigh!

(*There are various effusions and enthusiastic applause.*)

MRS. BASSETT: Honey, you're right. That isn't the man I meant. I was thinking about the one who wrote about "the bought red lips." Who was it that wrote about the "bought red lips"?

(*John has risen abruptly. He signals to Alma and points to his watch. He starts to leave.*)

ALMA (*springing up*): John!

JOHN (*calling back*): I have to call on a patient!

ALMA: Oh, John!

(*She calls after him so sharply that the group is startled into silence.*)

ROSEMARY (*interpreting this as a cue to read her paper*): "The poet, William Blake, was born in 1757 . . ."

(*Alma suddenly rushes to the door and goes out after John.*)

ROGER: Of poor but honest parents.

MRS. BASSETT: No supercilious comments out of you, sir. Go on Rosemary. (*She speaks loudly.*) She has such a beautiful *voice!*

(*Alma returns inside, looking stunned.*)

ALMA: Please excuse the interruption, Rosemary. Dr. Buchanan had to call on a patient.

MRS. BASSETT (*archly*): I bet I know who the patient was. Ha-ha! That Gonzales girl whose father owns Moon Lake Casino and goes everywhere with two pistols strapped on his belt. Johnny Buchanan will get himself shot in that crowd!

ALMA: Why, Mrs. Bassett, what gave you such an idea? I don't think that John even knows that Gonzales girl!

MRS. BASSETT: He knows her, all right. In the Biblical sense of the word, if you'll excuse me!

ALMA: No, I will not excuse you! A thing like that is inexcusable!

MRS. BASSETT: Have you fallen for him, Miss Alma? Miss Alma has fallen for the young doctor! They tell me he has lots of new lady patients!

ALMA: Stop it! (*She stamps her foot furiously and crushes the palm leaf fan between her clenched hands.*) I won't have malicious talk here! You drove him away from the meeting after I'd bragged so much about how bright and interesting you all were! You put your worst foot forward and simpered and chattered and carried on like idiots, idiots! What am I saying? I—I—please excuse me!

(*She rushes out the inner door.*)

ROGER: I move that the meeting adjourn.
MRS. BASSETT: I second the motion.
ROSEMARY: I don't understand. What happened?
MRS. BASSETT: Poor Miss Alma!
ROGER: She hasn't been herself lately. . . .

(*They all go out. After a moment Alma reenters with a tray of refreshments, looks about the deserted interior and bursts into hysterical laughter. The light dims out.*)

SCENE FOUR

In the doctor's office.
John has a wound on his arm which he is bandaging with Rosa's assistance.

JOHN: Hold that end. Wrap it around. Pull it tight.

(*There is a knock at the door. They look up silently. The knock is repeated.*)

I better answer before they wake up the old man.

(*He goes out. A few moments later he returns followed by Alma. He is rolling down his sleeve to conceal the bandage. Alma stops short at the sight of Rosa.*)

Wait outside, Rosa. In the hall. But be quiet!

(*Rosa gives Alma a challenging look as she withdraws from the lighted area. John explains about Rosa.*)

A little emergency case.

ALMA: The patient you had to call on. (*John grins.*) I want to see your father.

JOHN: He's asleep. Anything I can do?

ALMA: No, I think not. I have to see your father.

JOHN: It's 2 A.M., Miss Alma.

ALMA: I know, I'm afraid I'll have to see him.

JOHN: What's the trouble?

(*The voice of John's father is heard, calling from above.*)

DR. BUCHANAN: John! What's going on down there?

JOHN (*at the door*): Nothing much, Dad. Somebody got cut in a fight.

DR. BUCHANAN: I'm coming down.

JOHN: No. Don't! Stay in bed! (*He rolls up his sleeve to show Alma the bandaged wound. She gasps and touches her lips.*) I've patched him up, Dad. You sleep!

(*John executes the gesture of closing a door quietly on the hall.*)

ALMA: You've been in a brawl with that—woman! (*John nods and rolls the sleeve back down. Alma sinks faintly into a chair.*)

JOHN: Is your *doppelganger* cutting up again?

ALMA: It's your father I want to talk to.

JOHN: Be reasonable, Miss Alma. You're not that sick.

ALMA: Do you suppose I would come here at two o'clock in the morning if I were not seriously ill?

JOHN: It's no telling what you would do in a state of hysteria. (*He puts some powders in a glass of water.*) Toss that down, Miss Alma.

ALMA: What is it?

JOHN: A couple of little white tablets dissolved in water.

ALMA: What kind of tablets?

JOHN: You don't trust me?

ALMA: You are not in any condition to inspire much confidence. (*John laughs softly. She looks at him helplessly for a moment, then bursts into tears. He draws up a chair beside hers and puts his arm gently about her shoulders.*) I seem to be all to pieces.

JOHN: The intellectual meeting wore you out.

ALMA: You made a quick escape from it.

JOHN: I don't like meetings. The only meetings I like are between two people.

ALMA: Such as between yourself and the lady outside?

JOHN: Or between you and me.

ALMA (*nervously*): Where is the . . . ?

JOHN: Oh. You've decided to take it?

ALMA: Yes, if you . . .

(*She sips and chokes. He gives her his handkerchief. She touches her lips with it.*)

JOHN: Bitter?

ALMA: Awfully bitter.

JOHN: It'll make you sleepy.

ALMA: I do hope so. I wasn't able to sleep.

JOHN: And you felt panicky?

ALMA: Yes. I felt walled in.

JOHN: You started hearing your heart?

ALMA: Yes, like a drum!

JOHN: It scared you?

ALMA: It always does.

JOHN: Sure. I know.

ALMA: I don't think I will be able to get through the summer.

JOHN: You'll get through it, Miss Alma.

ALMA: How?

JOHN: One day will come after another and one night will come after another till sooner or later the summer will be all through with and then it will be fall, and you will be saying, I don't see how I'm going to get through the fall.

ALMA: Oh . . .

JOHN: That's right. Draw a deep breath!

ALMA: Ah . . .

JOHN: Good. Now draw another!

ALMA: Ah . . .

JOHN: Better? Better?

ALMA: A little.

JOHN: Soon you'll be much better. (*He takes out a big silver watch and holds her wrist.*) Did y' know that time is one side of the four-dimensional continuum we're caught in?

ALMA: What?

JOHN: Did you know space is curved, that it turns back onto itself like a soap-bubble, adrift in something that's even less than space. (*He laughs a little as he replaces the watch.*)

ROSA (*faintly from outside*): Johnny!

JOHN (*looking up as if the cry came from there*): Did you know that the Magellanic clouds are a hundred thousand light years away from the earth? No? (*Alma shakes her head slightly.*) That's something to think about when you worry over your heart, that little red fist that's got to keep knocking, knocking against the big black door.

ROSA (*more distinctly*): Johnny!

(*She opens the door a crack.*)

JOHN: Calla de la boca! (*The door closes and he speaks to Alma.*) There's nothing wrong with your heart but a little functional disturbance, like I told you before. You want me to check it? (*Alma nods mutely. John picks up his stethoscope.*)

ALMA: The lady outside, I hate to keep her waiting.

JOHN: Rosa doesn't mind waiting. Unbutton your blouse.

ALMA: Unbutton . . . ?

JOHN: The blouse.

ALMA: Hadn't I better—better come back in the morning, when your father will be able to . . . ?

JOHN: Just as you please, Miss Alma. (*She hesitates. Then begins to unbutton her blouse. Her fingers fumble.*) Fingers won't work?

ALMA (*breathlessly*): They are just as if frozen!

JOHN (*smiling*): Let me. (*He leans over her.*) Little pearl buttons . . .

ALMA: If your father discovered that woman in the house . . .

JOHN: He won't discover it.

ALMA: It would distress him terribly.

JOHN: Are you going to tell him?

ALMA: Certainly not! (*He laughs and applies the stethoscope to her chest.*)

JOHN: Breathe! . . . Out! . . . Breathe! . . . Out!

ALMA: Ah . . .

JOHN: Um-hmmm . . .

ALMA: What do you hear?

JOHN: Just a little voice saying—"Miss Alma is lonesome!" (*She rises and turns her back to him.*)

ALMA: If your idea of helping a patient is to ridicule and insult . . .

JOHN: My idea of helping you is to tell you the truth. (*Alma looks up at him. He lifts her hand from the chair arm.*) What is this stone?

ALMA: A topaz.

JOHN: Beautiful stone. . . . Fingers still frozen?

ALMA: A little. (*He lifts her hand to his mouth and blows his breath on her fingers.*)

JOHN: I'm a poor excuse for a doctor, I'm much too selfish. But let's try to think about you.

ALMA: Why should you bother about me? (*She sits down.*)

JOHN: You know I like you and I think you're worth a lot of consideration.

ALMA: Why?

JOHN: Because you have a lot of feeling in your heart, and that's a rare thing. It makes you too easily hurt. Did I hurt you tonight?

ALMA: You hurt me when you sprang up from the sofa and rushed from the Rectory in such—in such mad haste that you left your coat behind you!

JOHN: I'll pick up the coat sometime.

ALMA: The time of our last conversation you said you would take me riding in your automobile sometime, but you forgot to.

JOHN: I didn't forget. Many's the time I've looked across at the Rectory and wondered if it would be worth trying, you and me. . . .

ALMA: You decided it wasn't?

JOHN: I went there tonight, but it wasn't you and me. . . . Fingers warm now?

ALMA: Those tablets work quickly. I'm already feeling drowsy. (*She leans back with her eyes nearly shut.*) I'm beginning to feel almost like a water lily. A water lily on a Chinese lagoon.

(*A heavy iron bell strikes three.*)

ROSA: *Johnny?*

(*Alma starts to rise.*)

ALMA: I *must* go.

JOHN: I will call for you Saturday night at eight o'clock.

ALMA: What?

JOHN: I'll give you this box of tablets but watch how you take them. Never more than one or two at a time.

ALMA: Didn't you say something else a moment ago?

JOHN: I said I would call for you at the Rectory Saturday night.

ALMA: Oh . . .

JOHN: Is that all right? (*Alma nods speechlessly. She remains with the box resting in the palm of her hand as if not knowing it was there. John gently closes her fingers on the box.*)

ALMA: Oh! (*She laughs faintly.*)

ROSA (*outside*): *Johnny!*

JOHN: Do you think you can find your way home, Miss Alma?

(*Rosa steps back into the office with a challenging look. Alma catches her breath sharply and goes out the side door.*

(*John reaches above him and turns out the light. He crosses to Rosa by the anatomy chart and takes her roughly in his arms. The light lingers on the chart as the interior dims out.*)

SCENE FIVE

In the Rectory.
Before the light comes up a soprano voice is heard singing "From the Land of the Sky Blue Waters."
As the curtain rises, Alma gets up from the piano. Mr. and Mrs. Winemiller, also, are in the lighted room.

ALMA: What time is it, Father? (*He goes on writing. She raises her voice.*) What time is it, Father?

MR. WINEMILLER: Five of eight. I'm working on my sermon.

ALMA: Why don't you work in the study?

MR. WINEMILLER: The study is suffocating. So don't disturb me.

ALMA: Would there be any chance of getting Mother upstairs if someone should call?

MR. WINEMILLER: Are you expecting a caller?

ALMA: Not expecting. There is just a chance of it.

MR. WINEMILLER: Whom are you expecting?

ALMA: I said I wasn't expecting anyone, that there was just a possibility . . .

MR. WINEMILLER: Mr. Doremus? I thought that this was his evening with his mother?

ALMA: Yes, it is his evening with his mother.

MR. WINEMILLER: Then who is coming here, Alma?

ALMA: Probably no one. Probably no one at all.

MR. WINEMILLER: This is all very mysterious.

MRS. WINEMILLER: That tall boy next door is coming to see her, that's who's coming to see her.

ALMA: If you will go upstairs, Mother, I'll call the drug store and ask them to deliver a pint of fresh peach ice cream.

MRS. WINEMILLER: I'll go upstairs when I'm ready—good and ready, and you can put that in your pipe and smoke it, Miss Winemiller!

(*She lights a cigarette. Mr. Winemiller turns slowly away with a profound sigh.*)

ALMA: I may as well tell you who might call, so that if he calls there will not be any unpleasantness about it. Young Dr. John Buchanan said he might call.

MRS. WINEMILLER: See!

MR. WINEMILLER: You can't be serious.

MRS. WINEMILLER: Didn't I tell you?

ALMA: Well, I am.

MR. WINEMILLER: That young man might come here?

ALMA: He asked me if he might and I said, yes, if he wished to. But it is now after eight so it doesn't look like he's coming.

MR. WINEMILLER: If he does come you will go upstairs to your room and I will receive him.

ALMA: If he does come I'll do no such thing, Father.

MR. WINEMILLER: You must be out of your mind.

ALMA: I'll receive him myself. You may retire to your study and Mother upstairs. But if he comes I'll receive him. I don't judge people by the tongues of gossips. I happen to know that he has been grossly misjudged and misrepresented by old busybodies who're envious of his youth and brilliance and charm!

MR. WINEMILLER: If you're not out of your senses, then I'm out of mine.

ALMA: I daresay we're all a bit peculiar, Father. . . .

MR. WINEMILLER: Well, I have had one almost insufferable cross to bear and perhaps I can bear another. But if you think I'm retiring into my study when this young man comes, probably with a whiskey bottle in one hand and a pair of dice in the other, you have another think coming. I'll sit right here and look at him until he leaves. (*He turns back to his sermon.*)

(*A whistle is heard outside the open door.*)

ALMA (*speaking quickly*): As a matter of fact I think I'll walk down to the drug store and call for the ice cream myself. (*She crosses to the door, snatching up her hat, gloves and veil.*)

MRS. WINEMILLER: There she goes to him! Ha-ha! (*Alma rushes out.*)

MR. WINEMILLER (*looking up*): Alma! Alma!

MRS. WINEMILLER: Ha-ha-haaaaa!

MR. WINEMILLER: Where is Alma?—Alma! (*He rushes through the door.*) Alma!

MRS. WINEMILLER: Ha-ha! Who got fooled? Who got fooled! Ha-haaaa! Insufferable cross yourself, you old—windbag. . . .

(*The curtain comes down.*)

SCENE SIX

A delicately suggested arbor, enclosing a table and two chairs. Over the table is suspended a torn paper lantern. This tiny set may be placed way downstage in front of the two interiors, which should be darkened out, as in the fountain scenes. In the background, as it is throughout the play, the angel of the fountain is dimly visible.

Music from the nearby pavilion of the Casino can be used when suitable for background.

John's voice is audible before he and Alma enter.

JOHN (*from the darkness*): I don't understand why we can't go in the casino.

ALMA: You do understand. You're just pretending not to.

JOHN: Give me one reason.

ALMA (*coming into the arbor*): I am a minister's daughter.

JOHN: That's no reason. (*He follows her in. He wears a white linen suit, carrying the coat over his arm.*)

ALMA: You're a doctor. That's a better reason. You can't any more afford to be seen in such places than I can—less!

JOHN (*bellowing*): Dusty!

DUSTY (*from the darkness*): Coming!

JOHN: What are you fishing in that pocketbook for?

ALMA: Nothing.

JOHN: What have you got there?

ALMA: Let go!

JOHN: Those sleeping tablets I gave you?

ALMA: Yes.

JOHN: What for?

ALMA: I need one.

JOHN: *Now?*

ALMA: Yes.

JOHN: Why?

ALMA: Why? Because I nearly died of heart failure in your automobile. What possessed you to drive like that? A demon?

(*Dusty enters.*)

JOHN: A bottle of vino rosso.

DUSTY: Sure. (*He withdraws.*)

JOHN: Hey! Tell Shorty I want to hear the "Yellow Dog Blues."

ALMA: Please give me back my tablets.

JOHN: You want to turn into a dope-fiend taking this stuff? I said take one when you need one.

ALMA: I need one now.

JOHN: Sit down and stop swallowing air. (*Dusty returns with a tall wine bottle and two thin-stemmed glasses.*) When does the cock-fight start?

DUSTY: 'Bout ten o'clock, Dr. Johnny.

ALMA: When does *what start?*

JOHN: They have a cock-fight here every Saturday night. Ever seen one?

ALMA: Perhaps in some earlier incarnation of mine.

JOHN: When you wore a brass ring in your nose?

ALMA: Then maybe I went to exhibitions like that.

JOHN: You're going to see one tonight.

ALMA: Oh, no, I'm not.

JOHN: That's what we came here for.

ALMA: I didn't think such exhibitions were legal.

JOHN: This is Moon Lake Casino where anything goes.

ALMA: And you're a frequent patron?

JOHN: I'd say constant.

ALMA: Then I'm afraid you must be serious about giving up your medical career.

JOHN: You bet I am! A doctor's life is walled in by sickness and misery and death.

ALMA: May I be so presumptuous as to inquire what you'll do when you quit?

JOHN: You may be so presumptuous as to inquire.

ALMA: But you won't tell me?

JOHN: I haven't made up my mind, but I've been thinking of South America lately.

ALMA (*sadly*): Oh . . .

JOHN: I've heard that cantinas are lots more fun than saloons, and senoritas are caviar among females.

ALMA: Dorothy Sykes' brother went to South America and was never heard of again. It takes a strong character to survive in the tropics. Otherwise it's a quagmire.

JOHN: You think my character's weak?

ALMA: I think you're confused, just awfully, awfully confused, as confused as I am—but in a different way. . . .

JOHN (*stretching out his legs*): Hee-haw, ho-hum.

ALMA: You used to say that as a child—to signify your disgust!

JOHN (*grinning*): Did I?

ALMA (*sharply*): Don't sit like that!

JOHN: Why not?

ALMA: You look so indolent and worthless.

JOHN: Maybe I am.

ALMA: If you must go somewhere, why don't you choose a place with a bracing climate?

JOHN: Parts of South America are as cool as a cucumber.

ALMA: I never knew that.

JOHN: Well, now you do.

ALMA: Those Latins all dream in the sun—and indulge their senses.

JOHN: Well, it's yet to be proven that anyone on this earth is crowned with so much glory as the one that uses his senses to get all he can in the way of—satisfaction.

ALMA: Self-satisfaction?

JOHN: What other kind is there?

ALMA: I will answer that question by asking you one. Have you ever seen, or looked at a picture, of a Gothic cathedral?

JOHN: Gothic cathedrals? What about them?

ALMA: How everything reaches up, how everything seems to be straining for something out of the reach of stone—or human—fingers? . . . The immense stained windows, the great arched doors that are five or six times the height of the tallest man—the vaulted ceiling and all the delicate spires—all reaching up to something beyond attainment! To me—well, that is the secret, the principle back of existence—the everlasting struggle and aspiration for more than our human limits have placed in our reach. . . . Who was that said that—oh, so beautiful thing!—"All of us are in the gutter, but some of us are looking at the stars!"

JOHN: Mr. Oscar Wilde.

ALMA (*somewhat taken aback*): Well, regardless of who said it, it's still true. Some of us are looking at the stars! (*She looks up raptly and places her hand over his.*)

JOHN: It's no fun holding hands with gloves on, Miss Alma.

ALMA: That's easily remedied. I'll just take the gloves off. (*Music is heard.*)

JOHN: Christ! (*He rises abruptly and lights a cigarette.*) Rosa Gonzales is dancing in the Casino.

ALMA: You *are* unhappy. You hate me for depriving you of the company inside. Well, you'll escape by and by. You'll drive me home and come back out by yourself. . . . I've only gone out with three young men at all seriously, and with each one there was a desert between us.

JOHN: What do you mean by a desert?

ALMA: Oh—wide, wide stretches of uninhabitable ground.

JOHN: Maybe you made it that way by being stand-offish.

ALMA: I made quite an effort with one or two of them.

JOHN: What kind of an effort?

ALMA: Oh, I—tried to entertain them the first few times. I would play and sing for them in the Rectory parlor.

JOHN: With your father in the next room and the door half open?

ALMA: I don't think that was the trouble.

JOHN: What was the trouble?

ALMA: I—I didn't have my heart in it. (*She laughs uncertainly.*) A silence would fall between us. You know, a silence?

JOHN: Yes, I know a silence.

ALMA: I'd try to talk and he'd try to talk and neither would make a go of it.

JOHN: The silence would fall?

ALMA: Yes, the enormous silence.

JOHN: Then you'd go back to the piano?

ALMA: I'd twist my ring. Sometimes I twisted it so hard that the band cut my finger! He'd glance at his watch and we'd both know that the useless undertaking had come to a close. . . .

JOHN: You'd call it quits?

ALMA: Quits is—what we'd call it. . . . One or two times I was rather sorry about it.

JOHN: But you didn't have your heart in it?

ALMA: None of them really engaged my serious feelings.

JOHN: You do have serious feelings—of that kind?

ALMA: Doesn't everyone—sometimes?

JOHN: Some women are cold. Some women are what is called frigid.

ALMA: Do I give that impression?

JOHN: Under the surface you have a lot of excitement, a great deal more than any other woman I have met. So much that you have to carry these sleeping pills with you. The question is why? (*He leans over and lifts her veil.*)

ALMA: What are you doing that for?

JOHN: So that I won't get your veil in my mouth when I kiss you.

ALMA (*faintly*): Do you want to do that?

JOHN (*gently*): Miss Alma. (*He takes her arms and draws her to her feet.*) Oh, Miss Alma, Miss Alma! (*He kisses her.*)

ALMA (*in a low, shaken voice*): Not "Miss" any more. Just Alma.

JOHN (*grinning gently*): "Miss" suits you better, Miss Alma. (*He kisses her again. She hesitantly touches his shoulders, but not quite to push him away. John speaks softly to her.*) Is it so hard to forget you're a preacher's daughter?

ALMA: There is no reason for me to forget that I am a minister's daughter. A minister's daughter's no different from any other young lady who tries to remember that she *is* a lady.

JOHN: This lady stuff, is that so important?

ALMA: Not to the sort of girls that you may be used to bringing to Moon Lake Casino. But suppose that some day . . . (*She crosses out of the arbor and faces away from him.*) suppose that some day you—*married*. . . . The woman that you selected to be your wife, and not only your wife but—

the mother of your children! (*She catches her breath at the thought.*) Wouldn't you want that woman to be a lady? Wouldn't you want her to be somebody that you, as her husband, and they as her precious children—could look up to with very deep respect? (*There is a pause.*)

JOHN: There's other things between a man and a woman besides respect. Did you know that, Miss Alma?

ALMA: Yes. . . .

JOHN: There's such a thing as intimate relations.

ALMA: Thank you for telling me that. So plainly.

JOHN: It may strike you as unpleasant. But it does have a good deal to do with—connubial felicity, as you'd call it. There are some women that just give in to a man as a sort of obligation imposed on them by the—cruelty of nature! (*He finishes his glass and pours another.*) And there you are.

ALMA: There *I* am?

JOHN: I'm speaking generally.

ALMA: Oh.

(*Hoarse shouts go up from the Casino.*)

JOHN: The cock-fight has started!

ALMA: Since you have spoken so plainly, I'll speak plainly, too. There are some women who turn a possibly beautiful thing into something no better than the coupling of beasts!—but love is what you bring to it.

JOHN: You're right about that.

ALMA: Some people bring just their bodies. But there are some people, there are some women, John—who can bring their hearts to it, also—who can bring their souls to it!

JOHN (*derisively*): Souls again, huh?—those Gothic cathedrals you dream of!

(*There is another hoarse prolonged shout from the Casino.*)

Your name is Alma and Alma is Spanish for soul. Some time I'd like to show you a chart of the human anatomy that I have in the office. It shows what our insides are like, and maybe you can show me where the beautiful soul is located on the chart. (*He drains the wine bottle.*) Let's go watch the cock-fight.

ALMA: No! (*There is a pause.*)

JOHN: I know something else we could do. There are rooms above the Casino. . . .

ALMA (*her back stiffening*): I'd heard that you made suggestions like that to girls that you go out with, but I refused to believe such stories were true. What made you think I might be amenable to such a suggestion?

JOHN: I counted your pulse in the office the night you ran out because you weren't able to sleep.

ALMA: The night I was ill and went to your father for help.

JOHN: It was me you went to.

ALMA: It was your father, and you wouldn't call your father.

JOHN: Fingers frozen stiff when I . . .

ALMA (*rising*): Oh! I want to go home. But I won't go with you. I will go in a taxi! (*She wheels about hysterically.*) Boy! Boy! Call a taxi!

JOHN: I'll call one for you, Miss Alma.—Taxi! (*He goes out of the arbor.*)

ALMA (*wildly*): *You're not a gentleman!*

JOHN (*from the darkness*): Taxi!

ALMA: *You're not a gentleman!*

(*As he disappears she makes a sound in her throat like a hurt animal. The light fades out of the arbor and comes up more distinctly on the stone angel of the fountain.*)

PART TWO
A Winter

SCENE SEVEN

The sky and the southern constellations, almost imperceptibly moving with the earth's motion, appear on the great cyclorama. The Rectory interior is lighted first, disclosing Alma and Roger Doremus seated on the green plush sofa under the romantic landscape in its heavy gilt frame. On a tiny table beside them is a cut glass pitcher of lemonade with cherries and orange slices in it, like a little aquarium of tropical fish. Roger is entertaining Alma with a collection of photographs and postcards, mementoes of his mother's trip to the Orient. He is enthusiastic about them and describes them in phrases his mother must have assimilated from a sedulous study of literature provided by Cook's Tours. Alma is less enthusiastic; she is preoccupied with the sounds of a wild party going on next door at the doctor's home. At present there is Mexican music with shouts and stamping.

Only the immediate area of the sofa is clearly lighted; the fountain is faintly etched in light and the night sky walls the interior.

ROGER: And this is Ceylon, The Pearl of the Orient!

ALMA: And who is this fat young lady?

ROGER: That is Mother in a hunting costume.

ALMA: The hunting costume makes her figure seem bulky. What was your mother hunting?

ROGER (*gaily*): Heaven knows what she was hunting! But she found Papa.

ALMA: Oh, she met your father on this Oriental tour?

ROGER: Ha-ha!—yes. . . . He was returning from India with dysentery and they met on the boat.

ALMA (*distastefully*): Oh . . .

ROGER: And here she is on top of a ruined temple!

ALMA: How did she get up there?

ROGER: Climbed up, I suppose.

ALMA: What an active woman.

ROGER: Oh, yes, active—is no word for it! Here she is on an elephant's back in Burma.

ALMA: Ah!

ROGER: You're looking at it upside down, Miss Alma!

ALMA: Deliberately—to tease you. (*The doorbell rings.*) Perhaps that's your mother coming to fetch you home.

ROGER: It's only ten-fifteen. I never leave till ten-thirty.

(*Mrs. Bassett comes in.*)

ALMA: Mrs. Bassett!

MRS. BASSETT: I was just wondering who I could turn to when I saw the Rectory light and I thought to myself, Grace Bassett, you trot yourself right over there and talk to Mr. Winemiller!

ALMA: Father has retired.

MRS. BASSETT: Oh, what a pity. (*She sees Roger.*) Hello, Roger! . . . I saw that fall your mother took this morning. I saw her come skipping out of the Delta Planters' Bank and I thought to myself, now isn't that remarkable, a woman of her age and weight so light on her feet? And just at that very moment—*down she went!* I swear to goodness I thought she had broken her hip! Was she bruised much?

ROGER: Just shaken up, Mrs. Bassett.

MRS. BASSETT: Oh, how lucky! She certainly must be made out of India rubber! (*She turns to Alma.*) Alma—Alma, if it is not too late for human intervention, your father's the one right person to call up old Dr. Buchanan at the fever clinic at Lyon and let him know!

ALMA: About—what?

MRS. BASSETT: You must be stone-deaf if you haven't noticed what's been going on next door since the old doctor left to fight the epidemic. One continual orgy! Well, not five minutes ago a friend of mine who works at the County Courthouse called to inform me that young Dr. John and Rosa Gonzales have taken a license out and are going to be married tomorrow!

ALMA: Are you—quite certain?

MRS. BASSETT: Certain? I'm always certain before I speak!

ALMA: Why would he—do such a thing?

MRS. BASSETT: August madness! They say it has something to do with the falling stars. Of course it might also have something to do with the fact that he lost two or three thousand dollars at the Casino which he can't pay except by giving himself to Gonzales' daughter. (*She turns to Alma.*) Alma, what are you doing with that picture puzzle?

ALMA (*with a faint, hysterical laugh*): The pieces don't fit!

MRS. BASSETT (*to Roger*): I shouldn't have opened my mouth.

ALMA: Will both of you please go!

(*Roger goes out.*)

MRS. BASSETT: I knew this was going to upset you. Good night, Alma. (*She leaves. Alma suddenly springs up and seizes the telephone.*)

ALMA: Long distance. . . . Please get me the fever clinic at Lyon. . . . I want to speak to Dr. Buchanan.

(*The light in the Rectory dims out and light comes on in the doctor's office. Rosa's voice is heard calling.*)

ROSA: *Johnny!*

(*The offstage calling of John's name is used throughout the play as a cue for theme music.*

(*John enters the office interior. He is dressed, as always, in a white linen suit. His face has a look of satiety and confusion. He throws himself down in a swivel chair at the desk.*

(*Rosa Gonzales comes in. She is dressed in a Flamenco costume and has been dancing. She crosses and stands before the anatomy chart and clicks her castanets to catch his attention, but he remains looking up at the roofless dark. She approaches him.*)

ROSA: You have blood on your face!

JOHN: You bit my ear.

ROSA: Ohhh . . . (*She approaches him with exaggerated concern.*)

JOHN: You never make love without scratching or biting or something. Whenever I leave you I have a little blood on me. Why is that?

ROSA: Because I know I can't hold you.

JOHN: I think you're doing a pretty good job of it. Better than anyone else. Tomorrow we leave here together and Father or somebody else can tell old Mrs. Arbuckle her eighty-five years are enough and she's got to go now on the wings of carcinoma. Dance, Rosa! (*Accordion music is heard. She performs a slow and joyless dance around his chair. John continues while she dances.*) Tomorrow we leave here together. We sail out of Galveston, don't we?

ROSA: You say it but I don't believe it.

JOHN: I have the tickets.

ROSA: Two pieces of paper that you can tear in two.

JOHN: We'll go all right, and live on fat remittances from your Papa! Ha-ha!

ROSA: Ha-ha-ha!

JOHN: Not long ago the idea would have disgusted me, but not now. (*He catches her by the wrist.*) Rosa! Rosa Gonzales! Did anyone ever slide downhill as fast as I have this summer? Ha-ha! Like a greased pig. And yet every evening I put on a clean white suit. I have a dozen. Six in the closet and six in the wash. And there isn't a sign of depravity in my face. And yet all summer I've sat around here like *this*, remembering last night, anticipating the next one! The trouble with me is, I should have been *castrated*! (*He flings his wine glass at the anatomy chart. She stops dancing.*) Dance, Rosa! Why don't you dance? (*Rosa shakes her head dumbly.*) What is the matter, Rosa? Why don't you go on dancing? (*The accordion continues; he thrusts her arm savagely over her head in the Flamenco position.*)

ROSA (*suddenly weeping*): I can't dance any more! (*She throws herself to the floor, pressing her weeping face to his knees. The voice of her father is heard, bellowing, in the next room.*)

GONZALES: *The sky is the limit!*

(*John is sobered.*)

JOHN: Why does your father want me for a son-in-law?

ROSA (*sobbing*): I want you—I, I want you!

JOHN (*raising her from the floor*): Why do you?

ROSA (*clinging to him*): Maybe because—I was born in Piedras Negras, and grew up in a one room house with a dirt floor, and all of us had to sleep in that one room, five Mexicans and three geese and a little game-cock named Pepe! Ha-ha! (*She laughs hysterically.*) Pepe was a good fighter! That's how Papa began to make money, winning bets on Pepe! Ha-ha! We all slept in the one room. And in the night, I would hear the love-making. Papa would grunt like a pig to show his passion. I thought to myself, how dirty it was, love-making, and how dirty it was to be Mexicans and all have to sleep in one room with a dirt floor and not smell good because there was not any bathtub! (*The accordion continues.*)

JOHN: What has that got to do with . . . ?

ROSA: Me wanting you? You're tall! You smell good! And, oh, I'm so glad that you never grunt like a pig to show your passion! (*She embraces him convulsively.*) Ah, but *quien sabe!* Something might happen tonight, and I'll wind up with some dark little friend of Papa's.

GONZALES (*imperiously*): Rosa! Rosa!

ROSA: Si, si, Papa, aqui estoy!

GONZALES (*entering unsteadily*): The gold beads . . . (*He fingers a necklace of gold beads that Rosa is wearing.*) Johnny . . . (*He staggers up to John and catches him in a drunken embrace.*) Listen! When my girl Rosa was little she see a string a gold bead and she want those gold bead so bad that she cry all night for it. I don' have money to buy a string a gold bead so next day I go for a ride up to Eagle Pass and I walk in a dry good store and I say to the man: "Please give me a string a gold bead." He say: "Show me the money," and I say: "Here is the money!" And I reach down to my belt and I pull out—not the money—but this! (*He pulls out a revolver.*) Now—now I have money, but I still have this! (*laughing*) She got the gold bead. Anything that she want I get for her with this (*He pulls out a roll of bills.*) or this! (*He waves the revolver.*)

JOHN (*pushing Gonzales away*): Keep your stinking breath out of my face, Gonzales!

ROSA: Dejalo, dejalo, Papa!

GONZALES (*moving unsteadily to the couch, with Rosa supporting him*): Le doy la tierra y si la tierra no basta—le doy el cielo! (*He collapses onto the couch.*) The sky is the limit!

ROSA (*to John*): Let him stay there. Come on back to the party.

(*Rosa leaves the room. John goes over to the window facing the Rectory and looks across. The light comes up in the Rectory living room as Alma enters, dressed in a robe. She goes to the window and looks across at the doctor's house. As Alma and John stand at the windows looking toward each other through the darkness music is heard. Slowly, as if drawn by the music, John walks out of his house and crosses over to the Rectory. Alma remains motionless at the window until John enters the room, behind her. The music dies away and there is a murmur of wind. She slowly turns to face John.*)

JOHN: I took the open door for an invitation. The Gulf wind is blowing tonight . . . cools things off a little. But my head's on fire. . . . (*Alma says nothing. John moves a few steps toward her.*) The silence? (*Alma sinks onto the love seat, closing her eyes.*) Yes, the enormous silence. (*He goes over to her.*) I will go in a minute, but first I want you to put your

hands on my face. . . . (*He crouches beside her.*) Eternity
and Miss Alma have such cool hands. (*He buries his face in
her lap. The attitude suggests a stone* Pieta. *Alma's eyes remain closed.*)

(*On the other side of the stage Dr. Buchanan enters his house
and the light builds a little as he looks around in the door of
his office. The love theme music fades out and the Mexican
music comes up strongly, with a definitely ominous quality, as
Rosa enters the office from the other side.*)

ROSA: Johnny! (*She catches sight of Dr. Buchanan and checks
herself in surprise.*) Oh! I thought you were Johnny! . . .
But you are Johnny's father. . . . I'm Rosa Gonzales!

DR. BUCHANAN: I know who you are. What's going on in my
house?

ROSA (*nervously*): John's giving a party because we're leaving
tomorrow. (*defiantly*) Yes! Together! I hope you like the
idea, but if you don't, it don't matter, because *we* like the
idea and my father likes the idea.

GONZALES (*drunkenly, sitting up on the couch*): The sky is the
limit!

(*Dr. Buchanan slowly raises his silver-headed cane in a
threatening gesture.*)

DR. BUCHANAN: Get your—swine out of—my house! (*He
strikes Gonzales with his cane.*)

GONZALES (*staggering up from the couch in pain and surprise*):
Aieeeee!

ROSA (*breathlessly, backing against the chart of anatomy*): No!
No, Papa!

DR. BUCHANAN (*striking at the chest of the bull-like man with
his cane*): Get your swine out, I said! Get them out of my
house!

(*He repeats the blow. The drunken Mexican roars with pain
and surprise. He backs up and reaches under his coat.*)

ROSA (*wildly and despairingly*): No, no, no, no, no, no!

(*She covers her face against the chart of anatomy. A revolver
is fired. There is a burst of light. The cane drops. The music*

stops short. Everything dims out but a spot of light on Rosa standing against the chart of anatomy with closed eyes and her face twisted like that of a tragic mask.)

ROSA (*senselessly*): Aaaaaahhhhhh . . . Aaaaaahhhhhh . . .

(*The theme music is started faintly and light disappears from everything but the wings of the stone angel.*)

SCENE EIGHT

The doctor's office.
The stone angel is dimly visible above.
John is seated in a hunched position at the table. Alma enters with a coffee tray. The sounds of a prayer come through the inner door.

JOHN: What is that mumbo-jumbo your father is spouting in there?

ALMA: A prayer.

JOHN: Tell him to quit. We don't want that worn-out magic.

ALMA: You may not want it, but it's not a question of what you want any more. I've made you some coffee.

JOHN: I don't want any.

ALMA: Lean back and let me wash your face off, John. (*She presses a towel to the red marks on his face.*) It's such a fine face, a fine and sensitive face, a face that has power in it that shouldn't be wasted.

JOHN: Never mind that. (*He pushes her hand away.*)

ALMA: You have to go in to see him.

JOHN: I couldn't. He wouldn't want me.

ALMA: This happened because of his devotion to you.

JOHN: It happened because some meddlesome Mattie called him back here tonight. Who was it did that?

ALMA: I did.

JOHN: It *was* you then!

ALMA: I phoned him at the fever clinic in Lyon as soon as I learned what you were planning to do. I wired him to come here and stop it.

JOHN: You brought him here to be shot.

ALMA: You can't put the blame on anything but your weakness.

JOHN: *You* call me weak?

ALMA: Sometimes it takes a tragedy like this to make a weak person strong.

JOHN: You—white-blooded spinster! You so right people, pious pompous mumblers, preachers and preacher's daughter, all muffled up in a lot of worn-out magic! And I was supposed to minister to your neurosis, give you tablets for sleeping and tonics to give you the strength to go on mumbling your worn-out mumbo-jumbo!

ALMA: Call me whatever you want, but don't let your father hear your drunken shouting. (*She tries to break away from him.*)

JOHN: Stay here! I want you to look at something. (*He turns her about.*) This chart of anatomy, look!

ALMA: I've seen it before. (*She turns away.*)

JOHN: You've never dared to look at it.

ALMA: Why should I?

JOHN: You're scared to.

ALMA: You must be out of your senses.

JOHN: You talk about weakness but can't even look at a picture of human insides.

ALMA: They're not important.

JOHN: That's your mistake. You think you're stuffed with rose-leaves. Turn around and look at it, it may do you good!

ALMA: How can you behave like this with your father dying and you so . . .

JOHN: Hold still!

ALMA: . . . so much to blame for it!

JOHN: No more than you are!

ALMA: At least for this little while . . .

JOHN: Look here!

ALMA: . . . you could feel some shame!

JOHN (*with crazy, grinning intensity*): Now listen here to the anatomy lecture! This upper story's the brain which is hungry for something called truth and doesn't get much but keeps on feeling hungry! This middle's the belly which is hungry for food. This part down here is the sex which is hungry for love because it is sometimes lonesome. I've fed all three, as much of all three as I could or as much as I wanted— You've fed none—nothing. Well—maybe your belly a little—watery subsistence— But love or truth, nothing but—nothing but hand-me-down notions!—attitudes! —poses! (*He releases her.*) Now you can go. The anatomy lecture is over.

ALMA: So that is your high conception of human desires. What you have here is not the anatomy of a beast, but a man. And I—I reject your opinion of where love is, and the kind of truth you believe the brain to be seeking!—There is something not shown on the chart.

JOHN: You mean the part that Alma is Spanish for, do you?

ALMA: Yes, that's not shown on the anatomy chart! But it's there, just the same, yes, there! Somewhere, not seen, but there. And it's *that* that I loved you with—that! Not what you mention!—Yes, did love you with, John, did nearly *die* of when you hurt me! (*He turns slowly to her and speaks gently.*)

JOHN: I wouldn't have made love to you.

ALMA (*uncomprehendingly*): What?

JOHN: The night at the Casino—I wouldn't have made love to you. Even if you had consented to go upstairs. I couldn't have made love to you. (*She stares at him as if anticipating some unbearable hurt.*) Yes, yes! Isn't that funny? I'm more afraid of your soul than you're afraid of my body. You'd have been as safe as the angel of the fountain—because I wouldn't feel *decent* enough to touch you. . . .

(*Mr. Winemiller comes in.*)

MR. WINEMILLER: He's resting more easily now.

ALMA: Oh . . . (*She nods her head. John reaches for his coffee cup.*) It's cold. I'll heat it.

JOHN: It's all right.

MR. WINEMILLER: Alma, Dr. John wants you.

ALMA: I . . .

MR. WINEMILLER: He asked if you would sing for him.

ALMA: I—couldn't—now.

JOHN: Go in and sing to him, Miss Alma!

(*Mr. Winemiller withdraws through the outer door. Alma looks back at John hunched over the coffee cup. He doesn't*

return her look. She passes into the blurred orange space be-
yond the inner door, leaving it slightly open. After a few min-
utes her voice rises softly within, singing. John suddenly rises.
He crosses to the door, shoves it slowly open and enters.)

JOHN (*softly and with deep tenderness*): Father?

(*The light dims out in the house, but lingers on the stone angel.*)

SCENE NINE

The cyclorama is the faint blue of a late afternoon in au-
tumn. There is band-music—a Sousa march, in the distance. As
it grows somewhat louder, Alma enters the Rectory interior in a
dressing gown and with her hair hanging loose. She looks as if she
had been through a long illness, the intensity drained, her pale
face listless. She crosses to the window frame but the parade is not
in sight so she returns weakly to the sofa and sits down closing
her eyes with exhaustion.

The Rev. and Mrs. Winemiller enter the outer door frame of
the Rectory, a grotesque-looking couple. Mrs. Winemiller has on
her plumed hat, at a rakish angle, and a brilliant scarf about
her throat. Her face wears a roguish smile that suggests a musi-
cal comedy pirate. One hand holds the minister's arm and with
the other she is holding an ice cream cone.

MR. WINEMILLER: Now you may let go of my arm, if you
please! She was on her worst behavior. Stopped in front of
the White Star Pharmacy on Front Street and stood there
like a mule; wouldn't budge till I bought her an ice cream
cone. I had it wrapped in tissue paper because she had
promised me that she wouldn't eat it until we got home.
The moment I gave it to her she tore off the paper and
walked home licking it every step of the way!—just—just to
humiliate me! (*Mrs. Winemiller offers him the half-eaten*
cone, saying "Lick?")
MR. WINEMILLER: No, thank you!
ALMA: Now, now, children.

(*Mr. Winemiller's irritation shifts to Alma.*)

MR. WINEMILLER: Alma! Why don't you get dressed? It hurts me to see you sitting around like this, day in, day out, like an invalid when there is nothing particularly wrong with you. I can't read your mind. You may have had some kind of disappointment, but you must not make it an excuse for acting as if the world had come to an end.

ALMA: I have made the beds and washed the breakfast dishes and phoned the market and sent the laundry out and peeled the potatoes and shelled the peas and set the table for lunch. What more do you want?

MR. WINEMILLER (*sharply*): I want you to either get dressed or stay in your room. (*Alma rises indifferently, then her father speaks suddenly.*) At night you get dressed. Don't you? Yes, I heard you slipping out of the house at two in the morning. And that was not the first time.

ALMA: I don't sleep well. Sometimes I have to get up and walk for a while before I am able to sleep.

MR. WINEMILLER: What am I going to tell people who ask about you?

ALMA: Tell them I've changed and you're waiting to see in what way.

(*The band music becomes a little louder.*)

MR. WINEMILLER: Are you going to stay like this indefinitely?

ALMA: Not indefinitely, but you may wish that I had.

MR. WINEMILLER: Stop twisting that ring! Whenever I look at you you're twisting that ring. Give me that ring! I'm going to take that ring off your finger! (*He catches her wrist. She breaks roughly away from him.*)

MRS. WINEMILLER (*joyfully*): Fight! Fight!

MR. WINEMILLER: Oh, I give up!

ALMA: That's better. (*She suddenly crosses to the window as the band music gets louder.*) Is there a parade in town?

MRS. WINEMILLER: Ha-ha—yes! They met him at the station with a great big silver loving-cup!

ALMA: Who? Who did they . . . ?

MRS. WINEMILLER: That boy next door, the one you watched all the time!

ALMA: Is that true, Father?

MR. WINEMILLER (*unfolding his newspaper*): Haven't you looked at the papers?

ALMA: No, not lately.

MR. WINEMILLER (*wiping his eyeglasses*): These people are grasshoppers, just as likely to jump one way as another. He's finished the work his father started, stamped out the fever and gotten all of the glory. Well, that's how it is in this world. Years of devotion and sacrifice are overlooked an' forgotten while someone young an' lucky walks off with the honors!

(*Alma has crossed slowly to the window. The sun brightens and falls in a shaft through the frame.*)

ALMA (*suddenly crying out*): *There he is!* (*She staggers away from the window. There is a roll of drums and then silence. Alma now speaks faintly.*) What . . . happened? Something . . . struck me! (*Mr. Winemiller catches her arm to support her.*)

MR. WINEMILLER: Alma . . . I'll call a doctor.

ALMA: No, no, don't. Don't call anybody to help me. I want to die! (*She collapses on the sofa.*)

(*The band strikes up again and recedes down the street. The Rectory interior dims out. Then the light is brought up in the doctor's office. John enters, with his loving-cup. He is sprucely dressed and his whole manner suggests a new-found responsibility. While he is setting the award on the table, removing his coat and starched collar, Nellie Ewell appears in the door behind him. She stands by the anatomy chart and watches him until he discovers her presence. Nellie has abruptly grown up, and wears very adult clothes, but has lost none of her childish impudence and brightness. John gives a startled whistle as he sees her. Nellie giggles.*)

JOHN: High heels, feathers . . . and paint!

NELLIE: Not paint!

JOHN: Natural color?

NELLIE: Excitement.

JOHN: Over what?

NELLIE: Everything! You! You here! Didn't you see me at the depot? I shouted and waved my arm off! I'm home for Thanksgiving.

JOHN: From where?

NELLIE: Sophie Newcomb's. (*He remains staring at her, unbelieving. At last she draws a book from under her arm.*) Here is that nasty book you gave me last summer when I was pretending such ignorance of things!

JOHN: Only pretending?

NELLIE: Yes. (*He ignores the book. She tosses it on the table.*) . . . Well? (*John laughs uneasily and sits on the table.*) Shall I go now, or will you look at my tongue? (*She crosses to him, sticking out her tongue.*)

JOHN: Red as a berry!

NELLIE: Peppermint drops! Will you have one? (*She holds out a sack.*)

JOHN: Thanks. (*Nellie giggles as he takes one.*) What's the joke, Nellie?

NELLIE: They make your mouth so sweet!

JOHN: So?

NELLIE: I always take one when I hope to be kissed.

JOHN (*after a pause*): Suppose I took you up on that?

NELLIE: I'm not scared. Are you?

(*He gives her a quick kiss. She clings to him, raising her hand to press his head against her own. He breaks free after a moment and turns the light back on.*)

JOHN (*considerably impressed*): Where did you learn such tricks?

NELLIE: I've been away to school. But they didn't teach me to love.

JOHN: Who are you to be using that long word?

NELLIE: That isn't a long word!

JOHN: No? (*He turns away from her.*) Run along Nellie before we get into trouble.

NELLIE: Who's afraid of trouble, you or me?

JOHN: I am. Run along! Hear me?

NELLIE: Oh, I'll go. But I'll be back for Christmas!

(*She laughs and runs out. He whistles and wipes his forehead with a handkerchief.*)

SCENE TEN

An afternoon in December. At the fountain in the park. It is very windy.

Alma enters. She seems to move with an effort against the wind. She sinks down on the bench.

A widow with a flowing black veil passes across the stage and pauses by Alma's bench. It is Mrs. Bassett.

MRS. BASSETT: Hello Alma.

ALMA: Good afternoon, Mrs. Bassett.

MRS. BASSETT: Such wind, such wind!

ALMA: Yes, it nearly swept me off my feet. I had to sit down to catch my breath for a moment.

MRS. BASSETT: I wouldn't sit too long if I were you.

ALMA: No, not long.

MRS. BASSETT: It's good to see you out again after your illness.

ALMA: Thank you.

MRS. BASSETT: Our poor little group broke up after you dropped out.

ALMA (*insincerely*): What a pity.

MRS. BASSETT: You should have come to the last meeting.

ALMA: Why, what happened?

MRS. BASSETT: Vernon read his verse play!

ALMA: Ah, how was it received?

MRS. BASSETT: Maliciously, spitefully and vindictively torn to pieces, the way children tear the wings of butterflies. I think next Spring we might reorganize. (*She throws up her black-gloved hands in a deploring gesture.*)

(*Nellie Ewell appears. She is dressed very fashionably and carrying a fancy basket of Christmas packages.*)

NELLIE: Miss Alma!

MRS. BASSETT (*rushing off*): Goodbye!

NELLIE: Oh, there you are!

ALMA: Why Nellie . . . Nellie Ewell!

NELLIE: I was by the Rectory. Just popped in for a second; the holidays are so short that every minute is precious. They told me you'd gone to the park.

ALMA: This is the first walk I've taken in quite a while.

NELLIE: You've been ill!

ALMA: Not ill, just not very well. How you've grown up, Nellie.

NELLIE: It's just my clothes. Since I went off to Sophie Newcombe I've picked out my own clothes, Miss Alma. When Mother had jurisdiction over my wardrobe, she tried to keep me looking like a child!

ALMA: Your voice is grown-up, too.

NELLIE: They're teaching me diction, Miss Alma. I'm learning to talk like you, long A's and everything, such as "cahn't" and "bahth" and "lahf" instead of "laugh." Yesterday I slipped. I said I "lahfed and lahfed till I nearly died laughing." Johnny was so amused at me!

ALMA: Johnny?

NELLIE: Your nextdoor neighbor!

ALMA: Oh! I'm sure it must be a very fashionable school.

NELLIE: Oh yes, they're preparing us to be young ladies in society. What a pity there's no society here to be a young lady in . . . at least not for me, with Mother's reputation!

ALMA: You'll find other fields to conquer.

NELLIE: What's this I hear about *you*?

ALMA: I have no idea, Nellie.

NELLIE: That you've quit teaching singing and gone into retirement.

ALMA: Naturally I had to stop teaching while I was ill and as for retiring from the world . . . it's more a case of the world retiring from me.

NELLIE: I know somebody whose feelings you've hurt badly.

ALMA: Why, who could that be, Nellie?

NELLIE: Somebody who regards you as an angel!

ALMA: I can't think who might hold me in such esteem.

NELLIE: Somebody who says that you refused to see him.

ALMA: I saw nobody. For several months. The long summer wore me out so.

NELLIE: Well, anyhow, I'm going to give you your present. (*She hands her a small package from the basket.*)

ALMA: Nellie, you shouldn't have given me anything.

NELLIE: I'd like to know why not!

ALMA: I didn't expect it.

NELLIE: After the trouble you took with my horrible voice?

ALMA: It's very sweet of you, Nellie.

NELLIE: Open it!

ALMA: Now?

NELLIE: Why, sure.

ALMA: It's so prettily wrapped I hate to undo it.

NELLIE: I love to wrap presents and since it was for you, I did a specially dainty job of it.

ALMA (*winding the ribbon about her fingers*): I'm going to save this ribbon. I'm going to keep this lovely paper too, with the silver stars on it. And the sprig of holly . . .

NELLIE: Let me pin it on your jacket, Alma.

ALMA: Yes, do. I hardly realized that Christmas was coming. . . . (*She unfolds the paper, revealing a lace handkerchief and a card.*) What an exquisite handkerchief.

NELLIE: I hate to give people handkerchiefs, it's so unimaginative.

ALMA: I love to get them.

NELLIE: It comes from Maison Blanche!

ALMA: Oh, does it really?

NELLIE: Smell it!

ALMA: Sachet *Roses!* Well, I'm just more touched and pleased than I can possibly tell you!

NELLIE: The card!

ALMA: Card?

NELLIE: You dropped it. (*She snatches up the card and hands it to Alma.*)

ALMA: Oh, how clumsy of me! Thank you, Nellie. "Joyeux Noel . . . to Alma . . . from Nellie and . . . (*She looks up slowly.*) *John?*"

NELLIE: He helped me wrap presents last night and when we came to yours we started talking about you. Your ears must have burned!

(*The wind blows loudly. Alma bends stiffly forward.*)

ALMA: You mean you—spoke well of me?

NELLIE: "Well of"! We raved, simply raved! Oh, he told me the influence you'd had on him!

ALMA: Influence?

NELLIE: He told me about the wonderful talks he'd had with you last summer when he was so mixed up and how you inspired him and you more than anyone else was responsible for his pulling himself together, after his father was killed, and he told me about . . . (*Alma rises stiffly from the bench.*) Where are you going, Miss Alma?

ALMA: To drink at the fountain.

NELLIE: He told me about how you came in the house that night like an angel of mercy!

ALMA (*laughing harshly by the fountain*): This is the only angel in Glorious Hill. (*She bends to drink.*) Her body is stone and her blood is mineral water.

(*The wind is louder.*)

NELLIE: How penetrating the wind is!

ALMA: I'm going home, Nellie. You run along and deliver your presents now. . . . (*She starts away.*)

NELLIE: But wait till I've told you the wonderfullest thing I . . .

ALMA: I'm going home now. Goodbye.

NELLIE: Oh— Goodbye, Miss Alma.

(*She snatches up her festive basket and rushes in the other direction with a shrill giggle as the wind pulls at her skirts. The lights dim out.*)

SCENE ELEVEN

An hour later. In John's office.

The interior is framed by the traceries of Victorian architecture and there is one irregular section of wall supporting the anatomy chart. Otherwise the stage is open to the cyclorama.

In the background mellow golden light touches the vane of a steeple (a gilded weathercock). Also the wings of the stone angel. A singing wind rises and falls throughout scene.

John is seated at a white enameled table examining a slide through a microscope.

(*A bell tolls the hour of five as Alma comes hesitantly in. She wears a russet suit and a matching hat with a plume. The light changes, the sun disappearing behind a cloud, fading from the steeple and the stone angel till the bell stops tolling. Then it brightens again.*)

ALMA: No greetings? No greetings at all?

JOHN: Hello, Miss Alma.

ALMA (*speaking with animation to control her panic*): How white it is here, such glacial brilliance! (*She covers her eyes, laughing.*)

JOHN: New equipment.

ALMA: Everything new but the chart.

JOHN: The human anatomy's always the same old thing.

ALMA: And such a tiresome one! I've been plagued with sore throats.

JOHN: Everyone has here lately. These Southern homes are all improperly heated. Open grates aren't enough.

ALMA: They burn the front of you while your back is freezing!

JOHN: Then you go into another room and get chilled off.

ALMA: Yes, yes, chilled to the bone.

JOHN: But it never gets quite cold enough to convince the damn fools that a furnace is necessary so they go on building without them.

(*There is the sound of wind.*)

ALMA: Such a strange afternoon.

JOHN: Is it? I haven't been out.

ALMA: The Gulf wind is blowing big, white—what do they call them? cumulus?—clouds over! Ha-ha! It seemed determined to take the plume off my hat, like that fox terrier we had once named Jacob, snatched the plume off a hat and dashed around and around the back yard with it like a trophy!

JOHN: I remember Jacob. What happened to him?

ALMA: Oh, Jacob. Jacob was such a mischievous thief. We had to send him out to some friends in the country. Yes, he ended his days as—a country squire! The tales of his exploits . . .

JOHN: Sit down, Miss Alma.

ALMA: If I'm disturbing you . . . ?

JOHN: No—I called the Rectory when I heard you were sick. Your father told me you wouldn't see a doctor.

ALMA: I needed a rest, that was all. . . . You were out of town mostly. . . .

JOHN: I was mostly in Lyon, finishing up Dad's work in the fever clinic.

ALMA: Covering yourself with sudden glory!

JOHN: Redeeming myself with good works.

ALMA: It's rather late to tell you how happy I am, and also how proud. I almost feel as your father might have felt— if . . . And—are you—happy now, John?

JOHN (*uncomfortably, not looking at her*): I've settled with life on fairly acceptable terms. Isn't that all a reasonable person can ask for?

ALMA: He can ask for much more than that. He can ask for the coming true of his most improbable dreams.

JOHN: It's best not to ask for too much.

ALMA: I disagree with you. I say, ask for all, but be prepared to get nothing! (*She springs up and crosses to the window. She continues.*) No, I haven't been well. I've thought many times of something you told me last summer, that I have a *doppelganger.* I looked that up and I found that it means another person inside me, another self, and I don't know whether to thank you or not for making me conscious of it!—I haven't been well. . . . For a while I thought I was dying, that that was the change that was coming.

JOHN: When did you have that feeling?

ALMA: August. September. But now the Gulf wind has blown that feeling away like a cloud of smoke, and I know now I'm not dying, that it isn't going to turn out to be that simple. . . .

JOHN: Have you been anxious about your heart again? (*He retreats to a professional manner and takes out a silver watch, putting his fingers on her wrist.*)

ALMA: And now the stethoscope? (*He removes the stethoscope from the table and starts to loosen her jacket. She looks down at his bent head. Slowly, involuntarily, her gloved hands lift and descend on the crown of his head. He gets up awkwardly. She suddenly leans toward him and presses her mouth to his.*) Why don't you say something? Has the cat got your tongue?

JOHN: Miss Alma, what can I say?

ALMA: You've gone back to calling me "Miss Alma" again.

JOHN: We never really got past that point with each other.

ALMA: Oh, yes, we did. We were so close that we almost breathed together!

JOHN (*with embarrassment*): I didn't know that.

ALMA: No? Well, I did, I knew it. (*Her hand touches his face tenderly.*) You shave more carefully now? You don't have those little razor cuts on your chin that you dusted with gardenia talcum. . . .

JOHN: I shave more carefully now.

ALMA: So that explains it! (*Her fingers remain on his face, moving gently up and down it like a blind person reading Braille. He is intensely embarrassed and gently removes her hands from him.*) Is it—impossible now?

JOHN: I don't think I know what you mean.

ALMA: You know what I mean, all right! So be honest with me. One time I said "no" to something. You may remember the time, and all that demented howling from the cock-fight? But now I have changed my mind, or the girl who said "no," she doesn't exist any more, she died last summer—suffocated in smoke from something on fire inside her. No, she doesn't live now, but she left me her ring—You see? This one you admired, the topaz ring set in pearls. . . . And she said to me when she slipped this ring on my finger—"Remember I died empty-handed, and so make sure that your hands have *something in them!*" (*She drops her gloves. She clasps his head again in her hands.*) I said, "But what about pride?"—She said, "Forget about pride whenever it stands between you and what you must have!" (*He takes hold of her wrists.*) And then I said, "But what if he doesn't want me?" I don't know what she said then. I'm not sure whether she said anything or not—her lips stopped moving—yes, I think she stopped breathing! (*He gently removes her craving hands from his face.*) No? (*He shakes his head in dumb suffering.*) Then the answer is "no"!

JOHN (*forcing himself to speak*): I have a respect for the truth, and I have a respect for you—so I'd better speak honestly if you want me to speak. (*Alma nods slightly.*) You've won the argument that we had between us.

ALMA: What—argument?

JOHN: The one about the chart.

ALMA: Oh—the chart!

(*She turns from him and wanders across to the chart. She gazes up at it with closed eyes, and her hands clasped in front of her.*)

JOHN: It shows that we're not a package of rose leaves, that every interior inch of us is taken up with something ugly and functional and no room seems to be left for anything else in there.

ALMA: No . . .

JOHN: But I've come around to your way of thinking, that something else is in there, an immaterial something—as thin as smoke—which all of those ugly machines combine to produce and that's their whole reason for being. It can't be seen so it can't be shown on the chart. But it's there, just the same, and knowing it's there—why, then the whole thing—this—this unfathomable experience of ours—takes on a new value, like some—some wildly romantic work in a laboratory! Don't you see?

(*The wind comes up very loud, almost like a choir of voices. Both of them turn slightly, Alma raising a hand to her plumed head as if she were outdoors.*)

ALMA: Yes, I see! Now that you no longer want it to be otherwise you're willing to believe that a spiritual bond can exist between us two!

JOHN: Can't you believe that I am sincere about it?

ALMA: Maybe you are. But I don't want to be talked to like some incurably sick patient you have to comfort. (*A harsh and strong note comes into her voice.*) Oh, I suppose I am sick, one of those weak and divided people who slip like shadows among you solid strong ones. But sometimes, out of necessity, we shadowy people take on a strength of our own. I have that now. You needn't try to deceive me.

JOHN: I wasn't.

ALMA: You needn't try to comfort me. I haven't come here on any but equal terms. You said, let's talk truthfully. Well, let's do! Unsparingly, truthfully, even shamelessly, then! It's no longer a secret that I love you. It never was. I loved you as long ago as the time I asked you to read the stone angel's name with your fingers. Yes, I remember the long afternoons of our childhood, when I had to stay indoors to practice my music—and heard your playmates calling you, "Johnny, Johnny!" How it went through me, just to hear your name called! And how I—rushed to the window to watch you jump the porch railing! I stood at a distance, halfway down the block, only to keep in sight of your torn red sweater, racing about the vacant lot you played in. Yes, it had begun that early, this affliction of love, and has never let go of me since, but kept on growing. I've lived next door to you all the days of my life, a weak and divided person who stood in adoring awe of your singleness, of your strength. And that is my story! Now I wish *you* would tell *me*—why didn't it happen between us? Why did I fail? Why did you come almost close enough—and no closer?

JOHN: Whenever we've gotten together, the three or four times that we have . . .

ALMA: As few as that?

JOHN: It's only been three or four times that we've—come face to face. And each of those times—we seemed to be trying to find something in each other without knowing what it was that we wanted to find. It wasn't a body hunger although—I acted as if I thought it might be the night I wasn't a gentleman—at the Casino—it wasn't the physical you that I really wanted!

ALMA: I know, you've already . . .

JOHN: You didn't have that to give me.

ALMA: Not at that time.

JOHN: You had something else to give.

ALMA: What did I have?

(*John strikes a match. Unconsciously he holds his curved palm over the flame of the match to warm it. It is a long kitchen match and it makes a good flame. They both stare at it with a sorrowful understanding that is still perplexed. It is about to burn his fingers. She leans forward and blows it out, then she puts on her gloves.*)

JOHN: You couldn't name it and I couldn't recognize it. I thought it was just a Puritanical ice that glittered like flame. But now I believe it *was* flame, mistaken for ice. I still don't understand it, but I know it was there, just as I know that

your eyes and your voice are the two most beautiful things
I've ever known—and also the warmest, although they
don't seem to be set in your body at all. . . .

ALMA: You talk as if my body had ceased to exist for you,
John, in spite of the fact that you've just counted my pulse.
Yes, that's it! You tried to avoid it, but you've told me
plainly. The tables have turned, yes, the tables have turned
with a vengeance! You've come around to my old way of
thinking and I to yours like two people exchanging a call
on each other at the same time, and each one finding the
other one gone out, the door locked against him and no
one to answer the bell! (*She laughs.*) I came here to tell you
that being a gentleman, doesn't seem so important to me
any more, but you're telling me I've got to remain a lady.
(*She laughs rather violently.*) The tables have turned with a
vengeance!—The air in here smells of ether— It's making
me dizzy . . .

JOHN: I'll open a window.

ALMA: Please.

JOHN: There now.

ALMA: Thank you, that's better. Do you remember those little white tablets you gave me? I've used them all up and I'd
like to have some more.

JOHN: I'll write the prescription for you. (*He bends to write.*)

(*Nellie is in the waiting room. They hear her voice.*)

ALMA: Someone is waiting in the waiting room, John. One of
my vocal pupils. The youngest and prettiest one with the
least gift for music. The one that you helped wrap up this
handkerchief for me. (*She takes it out and touches her eyes
with it.*)

(*The door opens, first a crack. Nellie peers in and giggles.
Then she throws the door wide open with a peal of merry
laughter. She has holly pinned on her jacket. She rushes up to
John and hugs him with childish squeals.*)

NELLIE: I've been all over town just shouting, shouting!

JOHN: Shouting what?

NELLIE: Glad tidings!

(*John looks at Alma over Nellie's shoulder.*)

JOHN: I thought we weren't going to tell anyone for a while.

NELLIE: I couldn't stop myself. (*She wheels about.*) Oh, Alma, has he told *you?*

ALMA (*quietly*): He didn't need to, Nellie. I guessed . . . from the Christmas card with your two names written on it!

(*Nellie rushes over to Alma and hugs her. Over Nellie's shoulder Alma looks at John. He makes a thwarted gesture as if he wanted to speak. She smiles desperately and shakes her head. She closes her eyes and bites her lips for a moment. Then she releases Nellie with a laugh of exaggerated gaiety.*)

NELLIE: So, Alma, you were really the first to know!

ALMA: I'm proud of that, Nellie.

NELLIE: See on my finger! This was the present I couldn't tell you about!

ALMA: Oh, what a lovely, lovely solitaire! But solitaire is such a wrong name for it. Solitaire means single and this means *two!* It's blinding, Nellie! Why it . . . hurts my eyes!

(*John catches Nellie's arm and pulls her to him. Almost violently Alma lifts her face; it is bathed in tears. She nods gratefully to John for releasing her from Nellie's attention. She picks up her gloves and purse.*)

JOHN: Excuse her, Miss Alma. Nellie's still such a child.

ALMA (*with a breathless laugh*): I've got to run along now.

JOHN: Don't leave your prescription.

ALMA: Oh, yes, where's my prescription?

JOHN: On the table.

ALMA: I'll take it to the drug store right away!

(*Nellie struggles to free herself from John's embrace which keeps her from turning to Alma.*)

NELLIE: Alma, don't go! Johnny, let go of me, Johnny! You're hugging me so tight I can't breathe!

ALMA: Goodbye.

NELLIE: Alma! Alma, you know you're going to sing at the wedding! The very first Sunday in Spring!—which will be Palm Sunday! "The Voice that Breathed o'er Eden."

(*Alma has closed the door. John shuts his eyes tight with a look of torment. He rains kisses on Nellie's forehead and throat and lips. The scene dims out with music.*)

SCENE TWELVE

In the park near the angel of the fountain. About dusk.

Alma enters the lighted area and goes slowly up to the fountain and bends to drink. Then she removes a small white package from her pocketbook and starts to unwrap it. While she is doing this, a Young Man comes along. He is dressed in a checked suit and a derby. He pauses by the bench. They glance at each other.

A train whistles in the distance. The Young Man clears his throat. The train whistle is repeated. The Young Man crosses toward the fountain, his eyes on Alma. She hesitates, with the unwrapped package in her hand. Then she crosses toward the bench and stands hesitantly in front of it. He stuffs his hands in his pockets and whistles. He glances with an effect of unconcern back over his shoulder.

Alma pushes her veil back with an uncertain gesture. His whistle dies out. He sways back and forth on his heels as the train whistles again. He suddenly turns to the fountain and bends to drink. Alma slips the package back into her purse. As the young man straightens up, she speaks in a barely audible voice.

ALMA: The water—is—cool.
THE YOUNG MAN (*eagerly*): Did you say something?
ALMA: I said, the water is cool.
THE YOUNG MAN: Yes, it sure is, it's nice and cool!
ALMA: It's always cool.
THE YOUNG MAN: Is it?
ALMA: Yes. Yes, even in summer. It comes from deep underground.
THE YOUNG MAN: That's what keeps it cool.
ALMA: Glorious Hill is famous for its artesian springs.
THE YOUNG MAN: I didn't know that.

(*The Young Man jerkily removes his hands from his pockets. She gathers confidence before the awkwardness of his youth.*)

ALMA: Are you a stranger in town?

THE YOUNG MAN: I'm a traveling salesman.

ALMA: Ah, you're a salesman who travels! (*She laughs gently.*) But you're younger than most of them are, and not so fat!

THE YOUNG MAN: I'm just starting out. I travel for Red Goose shoes.

ALMA: Ah! The Delt's your territory?

THE YOUNG MAN: From the Peabody Lobby to Cat-Fish Row in Vicksburg.

(*Alma leans back and looks at him under half-closed lids, perhaps a little suggestively.*)

ALMA: The life of a traveling salesman is interesting . . . but lonely.

THE YOUNG MAN: You're right about that. Hotel bedrooms are lonely.

(*There is a pause. Far away the train whistles again.*)

ALMA: All rooms are lonely where there is only one person. (*Her eyes fall shut.*)

THE YOUNG MAN (*gently*): You're tired, aren't you?

ALMA: I? Tired? (*She starts to deny it; then laughs faintly and confesses the truth.*) Yes . . . a little. . . . But I shall rest now. I've just now taken one of my sleeping tablets.

THE YOUNG MAN: So early?

ALMA: Oh, it won't put me to sleep. It will just quiet my nerves.

THE YOUNG MAN: What are you nervous about?

ALMA: I won an argument this afternoon.

THE YOUNG MAN: That's nothing to be nervous over. You ought to be nervous if you *lost* one.

ALMA: It wasn't the argument that I wanted to win. . . .

THE YOUNG MAN: Well, I'm nervous too.

ALMA: What over?

THE YOUNG MAN: It's my first job and I'm scared of not making good.

(*That mysteriously sudden intimacy that sometimes occurs between strangers more completely than old friends or lovers moves them both. Alma hands the package of tablets to him.*)

ALMA: Then you must take one of my tablets.

THE YOUNG MAN: Shall I?

ALMA: Please take one!

THE YOUNG MAN: Yes, I shall.

ALMA: You'll be surprised how infinitely merciful they are. The prescription number is 96814. I think of it as the telephone number of God! (*They both laugh. He places one of the tablets on his tongue and crosses to the fountain to wash it down.*)

THE YOUNG MAN (*to the stone figure*): Thanks, angel. (*He gives her a little salute, and crosses back to Alma.*)

ALMA: Life is full of little mercies like that, not *big* mercies but comfortable *little* mercies. And so we are able to keep on going. . . . (*She has leaned back with half-closed eyes.*)

THE YOUNG MAN (*returning*): You're falling asleep.

ALMA: Oh no, I'm not. I'm just closing my eyes. You know what I feel like now? I feel like a water-lily.

THE YOUNG MAN: A water-lily?

ALMA: Yes, I feel like a water-lily on a Chinese lagoon. Won't you sit down? (*The Young Man does.*) My name is Alma. Spanish for soul! What's yours?

THE YOUNG MAN: Ha-ha! Mine's Archie Kramer. Mucho gusto, as they say in Spain.

ALMA: Usted habla Espanol, senor?

THE YOUNG MAN: Un poquito! Usted habla Espanol, senorita?

ALMA: Me tambien. Un poquito!

THE YOUNG MAN (*delightedly*): Ha . . . ha . . . ha! Sometimes un poquito is plenty! (*Alma laughs . . . in a different way than she has ever laughed before, a little wearily, but quite naturally. The Young Man leans toward her confidentially.*) What's there to do in this town after dark?

ALMA: There's not much to do in this town after dark, but there are resorts on the lake that offer all kinds of after-dark entertainment. There's one called Moon Lake Casino. It's under new management, now, but I don't suppose its character has changed.

THE YOUNG MAN: What was its character?

ALMA: Gay, very gay, Mr. Kramer. . . .

THE YOUNG MAN: Then what in hell are we sitting here for? Vamonos!

ALMA: Como no, senor!

THE YOUNG MAN: Ha-ha-ha! (*He jumps up.*) I'll call a taxi. (*He goes off shouting "Taxi."*)

(*Alma rises from the bench. As she crosses to the fountain the grave mood of the play is reinstated with a phrase of music. She faces the stone angel and raises her gloved hand in a sort of valedictory salute. Then she turns slowly about toward the audience with her hand still raised in a gesture of wonder and finality as . . . the curtain falls.*)

THE ROSE TATTOO

TO FRANK
in return for Sicily

THE TIMELESS WORLD OF A PLAY

CARSON MCCULLERS concludes one of her lyric poems with the line: "Time, the endless idiot, runs screaming 'round the world." It is this continual rush of time, so violent that it appears to be screaming, that deprives our actual lives of so much dignity and meaning, and it is, perhaps more than anything else, the *arrest of time* which has taken place in a completed work of art that gives to certain plays their feeling of depth and significance. In the London notices of *Death of a Salesman* a certain notoriously skeptical critic made the remark that Willy Loman was the sort of man that almost any member of the audience would have kicked out of an office had he applied for a job or detained one for conversation about his troubles. The remark itself possibly holds some truth. But the implication that Willy Loman is consequently a character with whom we have no reason to concern ourselves in drama, reveals a strikingly false conception of what plays are. Contemplation is something that exists outside of time, and so is the tragic sense. Even in the actual world of commerce, there exists in some persons a sensibility to the unfortunate situations of others, a capacity for concern and compassion, surviving from a more tender period of life outside the present whirling wire-cage of business activity. Facing Willy Loman across an office desk, meeting his nervous glance and hearing his querulous voice, we would be very likely to glance at our wrist watch and our schedule of other appointments. We would not kick him out of the office, no, but we would certainly *ease* him out with more expedition than Willy had feebly hoped for. But suppose there had been no wrist watch or office clock and suppose there had *not* been the schedule of pressing appointments, and suppose that we were not actually facing Willy across a desk—and facing a person is *not* the best way to *see* him!—suppose, in other words, that the meeting with Willy Loman had somehow occurred in a world *outside* of time. Then I think we would receive him with concern and kindness and even with respect. If the world of a play did not offer us this occasion to view its characters under that special condition of a *world without time*, then, indeed, the characters and occurrences of drama would become equally pointless, equally trivial, as corresponding meetings and happenings in life.

The classic tragedies of Greece had tremendous nobility. The actors wore great masks, movements were formal, dance-like, and the speeches had an epic quality which doubtless were as removed from the normal conversation of their contemporary society as they seem today. Yet they did not seem false to the Greek audiences: the magnitude of the events and the passions aroused by them did not seem ridiculously out of proportion to common experience. And I wonder if this was not because the Greek audiences knew, instinctively or by training, that the created world of a play is removed from that element which makes people *little* and their emotions fairly inconsequential.

Great sculpture often follows the lines of the human body: yet the repose of great sculpture suddenly transmutes those human lines to something that has an absoluteness, a purity, a beauty, which would not be possible in a living mobile form.

A play may be violent, full of motion: yet it has that special kind of repose which allows contemplation and produces the climate in which tragic importance is a possible thing, provided that certain modern conditions are met.

In actual existence the moments of love are succeeded by the moments of satiety and sleep. The sincere remark is followed by a cynical distrust. Truth is fragmentary, at best: we love and betray each other not in quite the same breath but in two breaths that occur in fairly close sequence. But the fact that passion occurred in *passing*, that it then declined into a more familiar sense of indifference, should not be regarded as proof of its inconsequence. And this is the very truth that drama wishes to bring us . . .

Whether or not we admit it to ourselves, we are all haunted by a truly awful sense of impermanence. I have always had a particularly keen sense of this at New York cocktail parties, and perhaps that is why I drink the martinis almost as fast as I can snatch them from the tray. This sense is the febrile thing that hangs in the air. Horror of insincerity, of *not meaning*, overhangs these affairs like the cloud of cigarette smoke and the hectic chatter. This horror is the only thing, almost, that is left unsaid at such functions. All social functions involving a group of people not intimately known to each other are always under this shadow. They are almost always (in an unconscious way) like that last dinner of the condemned: where steak or turkey, whatever the doomed man wants, is served in his cell as a mockingly cruel reminder of what the great-big-little-transitory world had to offer.

In a play, time is arrested in the sense of being confined. By a sort of legerdemain, events are made to remain *events*, rather than being reduced so quickly to mere *occurrences*. The audience can sit back in a comforting dusk to watch a world which is flooded with light and in which emotion and action have a dimension and dignity that they would likewise have in real existence, if only the shattering intrusion of time could be locked out.

About their lives people ought to remember that when they are finished, everything in them will be contained in a marvelous state of repose which is the same as that which they unconsciously admired in drama. The rush is temporary. The great and only possible dignity of man lies in his power deliberately to choose certain moral values by which to live as steadfastly as if he, too, like a character in a play, were immured against the corrupting rush of time. Snatching the eternal out of the desperately fleeting is the great magic trick of human existence. As far as we know, as far as there exists any kind of empiric evidence, there is no way to beat the game of *being* against *non-being*, in which non-being is the predestined victor on realistic levels.

Yet plays in the tragic tradition offer us a view of certain moral values in violent juxtaposition. Because we do not participate, except as spectators, we can view them clearly, within the limits of our emotional equipment. These people on the stage do not return our looks. We do not have to answer their questions nor make any sign of being in company with them, nor do we have to compete with their virtues nor resist their offenses. All at once, for this reason, we are able to *see* them! Our hearts are wrung by recognition and pity, so that the dusky shell of the auditorium where we are gathered anonymously together is flooded with an almost liquid warmth of unchecked human sympathies, relieved of self-consciousness, allowed to function . . .

Men pity and love each other more deeply than they permit themselves to know. The moment after the phone has been hung up, the hand reaches for a scratch pad and scrawls a notation: "Funeral Tuesday at five, Church of the Holy Redeemer, don't forget flowers." And the same hand is only a little shakier than usual as it reaches, some minutes later, for a highball glass that will pour a stupefaction over the kindled nerves. Fear and evasion are the two little beasts that chase each other's tails in the revolving wire-cage of our nervous world. They distract us from feeling too much about things. Time rushes toward us with its hospital tray of infinitely varied narcotics, even while it is preparing us for its inevitably fatal operation . . .

So successfully have we disguised from ourselves the intensity of our own feelings, the sensibility of our own hearts, that plays in the tragic tradition have begun to seem untrue. For a couple of hours we may surrender ourselves to a world of fiercely illuminated values in conflict, but when the stage is covered and the auditorium lighted, almost immediately there is a recoil of disbelief. "Well, well!" we say as we shuffle back up the aisle, while the play dwindles behind us with the sudden perspective of an early Chirico painting. By the time we have arrived at Sardi's, if not as soon as we pass beneath the marquee, we have convinced ourselves once more that life has as little resemblance to the curiously stirring and meaningful occurrences on the stage as a jingle has to an elegy of Rilke.

This modern condition of his theater audience is something that an author must know in advance. The diminishing influence of life's destroyer, time, must be somehow worked into the context of his play. Perhaps it is a certain foolery, a certain distortion toward the grotesque, which will solve the problem for him. Perhaps it is only restraint, putting a mute on the strings that would like to break all bounds. But almost surely, unless he contrives in some way to relate the dimensions of his tragedy to the dimensions of a world in which time is *included*—he will be left among his magnificent debris on a dark stage, muttering to himself: "Those fools . . ."

And if they could hear him above the clatter of tongues, glasses, chinaware and silver, they would give him this answer: "But you have shown us a world not ravaged by time. We admire your innocence. But we have seen our photographs, past and present. Yesterday evening we passed our first wife on the street. We smiled as we spoke but we didn't really see her! It's too bad, but we know what is true and not true, and at 3 A.M. your disgrace will be in print!"

—Tennessee Williams

SCENES

ACT ONE

ACT TWO

ACT THREE

AUTHOR'S PRODUCTION NOTES

The locale of the play is a village populated mostly by Sicilians somewhere along the Gulf Coast between New Orleans and Mobile. The time is the present.

As the curtain rises we hear a Sicilian folk-singer with a guitar. He is singing. At each major division of the play this song is resumed and it is completed at the final curtain.

The first lighting is extremely romantic. We see a frame cottage, in a rather poor state of repair, with a palm tree leaning dreamily over one end of it and a flimsy little entrance porch, with spindling pillars, sagging steps and broken rails, at the other end. The setting seems almost tropical, for, in addition to the palm trees, there are tall canes with feathery fronds and a fairly thick growth of pampas grass. These are growing on the slope of an embankment along which runs a highway, which is not visible, but the cars passing on it can occasionally be heard. The house has a rear door which cannot be seen. The facing wall of the cottage is either a transparency that lifts for the interior scenes, or is cut away to reveal the interior.

The romantic first lighting is that of late dusk, the sky a delicate blue with an opalescent shimmer more like water than air. Delicate points of light appear and disappear like lights reflected in a twilight harbor. The curtain rises well above the low tin roof of the cottage.

We see an interior that is as colorful as a booth at a carnival. There are many religious articles and pictures of ruby and gilt, the brass cage of a gaudy parrot, a large bowl of goldfish, cutglass decanters and vases, rose-patterned wallpaper and a rose-colored carpet; everything is exclamatory in its brightness like the projection of a woman's heart passionately in love. There is a small shrine against the wall between the rooms, consisting of a prie-dieu and a little statue of the Madonna in a starry blue robe and gold crown. Before this burns always a vigil light in its ruby glass cup. Our purpose is to show these gaudy, childlike mysteries with sentiment and humor in equal measure, without ridicule and with respect for the religious yearnings they symbolize.

An outdoor sign indicates that Serafina, whose home the cottage is, does "SEWING." The interior furnishings give evidence of this vocation. The most salient feature is a collection of dress-maker's dummies. There are at least seven of these life-size man-nequins, in various shapes and attitudes. (They will have to be made especially for the play as their purpose is not realistic. They have pliable joints so that their positions can be changed. Their arms terminate at the wrist. In all their attitudes there is an air of drama, somewhat like the poses of declamatory actresses of the old school.) Principal among them are a widow and a bride who face each other in violent attitudes, as though having a shrill argument, in the parlor. The widow's costume is complete from black-veiled hat to black slippers. The bride's featureless head wears a chaplet of orange blossoms from which is depended a flowing veil of white marquisette, and her net gown is trimmed in white satin—lustrous, immaculate.

Most of the dummies and sewing equipment are confined to the dining room which is also Serafina's work room. In that room there is a tall cupboard on top of which are several dusty bottles of imported Sicilian Spumanti.

O slinger! crack the nut of my eye! my heart twittered with joy under the splendour of the quicklime, the bird sings O Senectus! . . . the streams are in their beds like the cries of women and this world has more beauty than a ram's skin painted red!

St. John Perse: *Anabasis*
T. S. ELIOT TRANSLATION

ACT ONE

It is the hour that the Italians call "prima sera," the begin-
ning of dusk. Between the house and the palm tree burns the fe-
male star with an almost emerald lustre.

The mothers of the neighborhood are beginning to call their
children home to supper, in voices near and distant, urgent and
tender, like the variable notes of wind and water. There are three
children: Bruno, Salvatore, and Vivi, ranged in front of the
house, one with a red paper kite, one with a hoop, and the little
girl with a doll dressed as a clown. They are in attitudes of mo-
mentary repose, all looking up at something—a bird or a plane
passing over—as the mothers' voices call them.

BRUNO: The white flags are flying at the Coast Guard station.
SALVATORE: That means fair weather.
VIVI: I love fair weather.
GIUSEPPINA: Vivi! Vieni mangiare!
PEPPINA: Salvatore! Come home!
VIOLETTA: Bruno! Come home to supper!

(The calls are repeated tenderly, musically.

(The interior of the house begins to be visible. Serafina delle
Rose is seen on the parlor sofa, waiting for her husband
Rosario's return. Between the curtains is a table set lovingly
for supper; there is wine in a silver ice-bucket and a great
bowl of roses.

(Serafina looks like a plump little Italian opera singer in
the role of Madame Butterfly. Her black hair is done in a
high pompadour that glitters like wet coal. A rose is held in
place by glittering jet hairpins. Her voluptuous figure is
sheathed in pale rose silk. On her feet are dainty slippers with
glittering buckles and French heels. It is apparent from the
way she sits, with such plump dignity, that she is wearing a
tight girdle. She sits very erect, in an attitude of forced com-
posure, her ankles daintily crossed and her plump little hands
holding a yellow paper fan on which is painted a rose. Jewels
gleam on her fingers, her wrists and her ears and about her
throat. Expectancy shines in her eyes. For a few moments she
seems to be posing for a picture.

(*Rosa delle Rose appears at the side of the house, near the palm tree. Rosa, the daughter of the house, is a young girl of twelve. She is pretty and vivacious, and has about her a particular intensity in every gesture.*)

SERAFINA: Rosa, where are you?
ROSA: Here, Mama.
SERAFINA: What are you doing, cara?
ROSA: I've caught twelve lightning bugs.

(*The cracked voice of Assunta is heard, approaching.*)

SERAFINA: I hear Assunta! Assunta!

(*Assunta appears and goes into the house, Rosa following her in. Assunta is an old woman in a gray shawl, bearing a basket of herbs, for she is a fattuchiere, a woman who practises a simple sort of medicine. As she enters the children scatter.*)

ASSUNTA: Vengo, vengo. Buona sera. Buona sera. There is something wild in the air, no wind but everything's moving.
SERAFINA: I don't see nothing moving and neither do you.
ASSUNTA: Nothing is moving so you can see it moving, but everything is moving, and I can hear the star-noises. Hear them? Hear the star-noises?
SERAFINA: Naw, them ain't the star-noises. They're termites, eating the house up. What are you peddling, old woman, in those little white bags?
ASSUNTA: Powder, wonderful powder. You drop a pinch of it in your husband's coffee.
SERAFINA: What is it good for?
ASSUNTA: What is a husband good for! I make it out of the dry blood of a goat.
SERAFINA: Davero!
ASSUNTA: Wonderful stuff! But be sure you put it in his coffee at supper, not in his breakfast coffee.
SERAFINA: My husband don't need no powder!
ASSUNTA: Excuse me, Baronessa. Maybe he needs the opposite kind of a powder, I got that, too.
SERAFINA: Naw, naw, *no* kind of powder at all, old woman.
(*She lifts her head with a proud smile.*)

(*Outside the sound of a truck is heard approaching up on the highway.*)

ROSA (*joyfully*): Papa's truck!

(*They stand listening for a moment, but the truck goes by without stopping.*)

SERAFINA (*to Assunta*): That wasn't him. It wasn't no 10-ton truck. It didn't rattle the shutters! Assunta, Assunta, undo a couple of hooks, the dress is tight on me!

ASSUNTA: Is it true what I told you?

SERAFINA: Yes, it is true, but nobody needed to tell me. Assunta, I'll tell you something which maybe you won't believe.

ASSUNTA: It is impossible to tell me anything that I don't believe.

SERAFINA: Va bene! Senti, Assunta!—I knew that I had conceived on the very night of conception! (*There is a phrase of music as she says this.*)

ASSUNTA: Ahhhh?

SERAFINA: Senti! That night I woke up with a burning pain on me, here, on my left breast! A pain like a needle, quick, quick, hot little stitches. I turned on the light, I uncovered my breast!—On it I saw the rose tattoo of my husband!

ASSUNTA: Rosario's tattoo?

SERAFINA: On me, on my breast, his tattoo! And when I saw it I knew that I had conceived . . .

(*Serafina throws her head back, smiling proudly, and opens her paper fan. Assunta stares at her gravely, then rises and hands her basket to Serafina.*)

ASSUNTA: Ecco! *You* sell the powders! (*She starts toward the door.*)

SERAFINA: You don't believe that I saw it?

ASSUNTA (*stopping*): Did Rosario see it?

SERAFINA: I screamed. But when he woke up, it was gone. It only lasted a moment. But I *did* see it, and I *did* know, when I seen it, that I had conceived, that in my body another rose was growing!

ASSUNTA: Did he believe that you saw it?

SERAFINA: No. He laughed.—He laughed and I cried . . .

ASSUNTA: And he took you into his arms, and you stopped crying!

SERAFINA: Si!

ASSUNTA: Serafina, for you everything has got to be different. A sign, a miracle, a wonder of some kind. You speak to Our Lady. You say that She answers your questions. She nods or shakes Her head at you. Look, Serafina, underneath Our Lady you have a candle. The wind through the shutters makes the candle flicker. The shadows move. Our Lady seems to be nodding!

SERAFINA: She gives me signs.

ASSUNTA: Only to you? Because you are more important? The wife of a barone? Serafina! In Sicily they called his uncle a baron, but in Sicily everybody's a baron that owns a piece of the land and a separate house for the goats!

SERAFINA: They said to his uncle "Voscenza!" and they kissed their hands to him! (*She kisses the back of her hand repeatedly, with vehemence.*)

ASSUNTA: His uncle in Sicily!—Si—But *here* what's he do? Drives a truck of bananas?

SERAFINA (*blurting out*): No! *Not* bananas!

ASSUNTA: Not bananas?

SERAFINA: Stai zitta! (*She makes a warning gesture.*)—No—Vieni qui, Assunta! (*She beckons her mysteriously. Assunta approaches.*)

ASSUNTA: Cosa dici?

SERAFINA: On top of the truck is bananas! But underneath—something else!

ASSUNTA: Che altre cose?

SERAFINA: Whatever it is that the Brothers Romano want hauled out of the state, he hauls it for them, underneath the bananas! (*She nods her head importantly.*) And money, he gets so much it spills from his pockets! Soon I don't have to make dresses!

ASSUNTA (*turning away*): Soon I think you will have to make a black veil!

SERAFINA: Tonight is the last time he does it! Tomorrow he quits hauling stuff for the Brothers Romano! He pays for the 10-ton truck and works for himself. We live with dignity in America, then! Own truck! Own house! And in the house will be everything electric! Stove—deep-freeze—*tutto!*—But tonight, stay with me . . . I can't swallow my heart!—Not till I hear the truck stop in front of the house and his key in the lock of the door!—When I call him, and him shouting back, *"Si, sono qui!"* In his hair, Assunta, he has—oil of roses. And when I wake up at night—the air, the dark room's—full of—roses . . . Each time is the first time with him. Time doesn't pass . . .

(*Assunta picks up a small clock on the cupboard and holds it to her ear.*)

ASSUNTA: Tick, tick, tick, tick.—You say the clock is a liar.

SERAFINA: No, the clock is a fool. I don't listen to it. My clock is my heart and my heart don't say tick-tick, it says love-love! And now I have two hearts in me, both of them saying love-love!

(*A truck is heard approaching, then passes. Serafina drops her fan. Assunta opens a bottle of spumanti with a loud pop. Serafina cries out.*)

ASSUNTA: Stai tranquilla! Calmati! (*She pours her a glass of wine.*) Drink this wine and before the glass is empty he'll be in your arms!

SERAFINA: I can't—swallow my heart!

ASSUNTA: A woman must not have a heart that is too big to swallow! (*She crosses to the door.*)

SERAFINA: Stay with me!

ASSUNTA: I have to visit a woman who drank rat poison because of a heart too big for her to swallow.

(*Assunta leaves. Serafina returns indolently to the sofa. She lifts her hands to her great swelling breasts and murmurs aloud:*)

SERAFINA: Oh, it's so wonderful, having *two* lives in the body, not *one* but two! (*Her hands slide down to her belly, luxuriously.*) I am heavy with life, I am big, big, big with life! (*She picks up a bowl of roses and goes into the back room.*)

(*Estelle Hohengarten appears in front of the house. She is a thin blonde woman in a dress of Egyptian design, and her*)

blonde hair has an unnatural gloss in the clear, greenish dusk.
Rosa appears from behind the house, calling out:)

ROSA: Twenty lightning bugs, Mama!

ESTELLE: Little girl? Little girl?

ROSA (*resentfully*): Are you talking to me? (*There is a pause.*)

ESTELLE: Come here. (*She looks Rosa over curiously.*) You're a
twig off the old rose-bush.—Is the lady that does the
sewing in the house?

ROSA: Mama's at home.

ESTELLE: I'd like to see her.

ROSA: Mama?

SERAFINA: Dimi?

ROSA: There's a lady to see you.

SERAFINA: Oh. Tell her to wait in the parlor. (*Estelle enters and
stares curiously about. She picks up a small framed picture on
the cupboard. She is looking at it as Serafina enters with a bowl
of roses. Serafina speaks sharply.*) That is my husband's picture.

ESTELLA: Oh!—I thought it was Valentino.—With a mustache.

SERAFINA (*putting the bowl down on the table*): You want
something?

ESTELLE: Yes. I heard you do sewing.

SERAFINA: Yes, I do sewing.

ESTELLE: How fast can you make a shirt for me?

SERAFINA: That all depends. (*She takes the picture from Estelle
and puts it back on the cupboard.*)

ESTELLE: I got the piece of silk with me. I want it made into
a shirt for a man I'm in love with. Tomorrow's the anniversary of the day we met . . . (*She unwraps a piece of
rose-colored silk which she holds up like a banner.*)

SERAFINA (*involuntarily*): Che bella stoffa!—Oh, that would
be wonderful stuff for a lady's blouse or for a pair of
pyjamas!

ESTELLE: I want a man's shirt made with it.

SERAFINA: Silk this color for a shirt for a *man*?

ESTELLE: This man is wild like a Gypsy.

SERAFINA: A woman should not encourage a man to be wild.

ESTELLE: A man that's wild is hard for a woman to hold, huh?
But if he was tame—would the woman want to hold him?
Huh?

SERAFINA: I am a married woman in business. I don't know nothing about wild men and wild women and I don't have much time—so . . .

ESTELLE: I'll pay you twice what you ask me.

(*Outside there is the sound of the goat bleating and the jingle of its harness; then the crash of wood splintering.*)

ROSA (*suddenly appearing at the door*): Mama, the black goat is loose! (*She runs down the steps and stands watching the goat. Serafina crosses to the door.*)

THE STREGA (*in the distance*): Hyeh, Billy, hyeh, hyeh, Billy!

ESTELLE: I'll pay you three times the price that you ask me for it.

SERAFINA (*shouting*): Watch the goat! Don't let him get in our yard! (*to Estelle*)—If I ask you five dollars?

ESTELLE: I will pay you fifteen. Make it twenty; money is not the object. But it's got to be ready tomorrow.

SERAFINA: Tomorrow?

ESTELLE: Twenty-five dollars! (*Serafina nods slowly with a stunned look. Estelle smiles.*) I've got the measurements with me.

SERAFINA: Pin the measurements and your name on the silk and the shirt will be ready tomorrow.

ESTELLE: My name is Estelle Hohengarten.

(*A little boy races excitedly into the yard.*)

THE BOY: Rosa, Rosa, the black goat's in your yard!

ROSA (*calling*): Mama, the goat's in the yard!

SERAFINA (*furiously, forgetting her visitor*): Il becco della strega!—Scusi! (*She runs out onto the porch.*) Catch him, catch him before he gets at the vines!

(*Rosa dances gleefully. The Strega runs into the yard. She has a mop of wild grey hair and is holding her black skirts up from her bare hairy legs. The sound of the goat's bleating and the jingling of his harness is heard in the windy blue dusk.*

(*Serafina descends the porch steps. The high-heeled slippers, the tight silk skirt and the dignity of a baronessa make the descent a little gingerly. Arrived in the yard, she directs the goat-chase imperiously with her yellow paper fan, pointing this way and that, exclaiming in Italian.*

(She fans herself rapidly and crosses back of the house. The goat evidently makes a sudden charge. Screaming, Serafina rushes back to the front of the house, all out of breath, the glittering pompadour beginning to tumble down over her forehead.)

SERAFINA: Rosa! You go in the house! Don't look at the Strega!

(Alone in the parlor, Estelle takes the picture of Rosario. Impetuously, she thrusts it in her purse and runs from the house, just as Serafina returns to the front yard.)

ROSA *(refusing to move)*: Why do you call her a witch?

(Serafina seizes her daughter's arm and propels her into the house.)

SERAFINA: She has a white eye and every finger is crooked.
(She pulls Rosa's arm.)
ROSA: She has a cataract, Mama, and her fingers are crooked because she has rheumatism!
SERAFINA: Malocchio—the evil eye—*that's* what she's got! And her fingers are crooked because she shook hands with the devil. Go in the house and wash your face with salt water and throw the salt water away! *Go in! Quick!* She's coming!

(The boy utters a cry of triumph.

(Serafina crosses abruptly to the porch. At the same moment the boy runs triumphantly around the house leading the captured goat by its bell harness. It is a middle-sized black goat with great yellow eyes. The Strega runs behind with the broken rope. As the grotesque little procession runs before her—the Strega, the goat and the children—Serafina cries out shrilly. She crouches over and covers her face. The Strega looks back at her with a derisive cackle.)

SERAFINA: Malocchio! Malocchio!

(Shielding her face with one hand, Serafina makes the sign of the horns with the other to ward off the evil eye. And the scene dims out.)

SCENE TWO

It is just before dawn the next day. Father De Leo, a priest, and several black-shawled women, including Assunta, are standing outside the house. The interior of the house is very dim.

GIUSEPPINA: There is a light in the house.

PEPPINA: I hear the sewing machine!

VIOLETTA: There's Serafina! She's working. She's holding up a piece of rose-colored silk.

ASSUNTA: She hears our voices.

VIOLETTA: She's dropped the silk to the floor and she's . . .

GIUSEPPINA: Holding her throat! I think she . . .

PEPPINA: Who's going to tell her?

VIOLETTA: Father De Leo will tell her.

FATHER DE LEO: I think a woman should tell her. I think Assunta must tell her that Rosario is dead.

ASSUNTA: It will not be necessary to tell her. She will know when she sees us.

(*It grows lighter inside the house. Serafina is standing in a frozen attitude with her hand clutching her throat and her eyes staring fearfully toward the sound of voices.*)

ASSUNTA: I think she already knows what we have come to tell her!

FATHER DE LEO: Andiamo, Signore! We must go to the door.

(*They climb the porch steps. Assunta opens the door.*)

SERAFINA (*gasping*): Don't speak!

(*She retreats from the group, stumbling blindly backwards among the dressmaker's dummies. With a gasp she turns and runs out the back door. In a few moments we see her staggering about outside near the palm tree. She comes down in front of the house, and stares blindly off into the distance.*)

SERAFINA (*wildly*): Don't speak!

(*The voices of the women begin keening in the house. Assunta comes out and approaches Serafina with her arms extended. Serafina slumps to her knees, whispering hoarsely: "Don't speak!" Assunta envelopes her in the grey shawl of pity as the scene dims out.*)

SCENE THREE

It is noon of the same day. Assunta is removing a funeral wreath on the door of the house. A doctor and Father De Leo are on the porch.

THE DOCTOR: She's lost the baby. (*Assunta utters a low moan of pity and crosses herself.*) Serafina's a very strong woman and that won't kill her. But she is trying not to breathe. She's got to be watched and not allowed out of the bed. (*He removes a hypodermic and a small package from his bag and hands them to Assunta.*)—This is morphia. In the arm with the needle if she screams or struggles to get up again.

ASSUNTA: Capisco!

FATHER DE LEO: One thing I want to make plain. The body of Rosario must not be burned.

THE DOCTOR: Have you seen the "body of Rosario?"

FATHER DE LEO: Yes, I have seen his body.

THE DOCTOR: Wouldn't you say it was burned?

FATHER DE LEO: Of course the body was burned. When he was shot at the wheel of the truck, it crashed and caught fire. But deliberate cremation is not the same thing. It's an abomination in the sight of God.

THE DOCTOR: Abominations are something I don't know about.

FATHER DE LEO: The Church has set down certain laws.

THE DOCTOR: But the instructions of a widow have to be carried out.

FATHER DE LEO: Don't you know why she wants the body cremated? So she can keep the ashes here in the house.

THE DOCTOR: Well, why not, if that's any comfort to her?

FATHER DE LEO: Pagan idolatry is what I call it!

THE DOCTOR: Father De Leo, you love your people but you don't understand them. They find God in each other. And when they lose each other, they lose God and they're lost. And it's hard to help them.—Who is that woman?

(*Estelle Hohengarten has appeared before the house. She is black-veiled, and bearing a bouquet of roses.*)

ESTELLE: I am Estelle Hohengarten.

(*Instantly there is a great hubbub in the house. The women mourners flock out to the porch, whispering and gesticulating excitedly.*)

FATHER DE LEO: What have you come here for?

ESTELLE: To say good-bye to the body.

FATHER DE LEO: The casket is closed; the body cannot be seen. And you must never come here. The widow knows nothing about you. Nothing at all.

GIUSEPPINA: *We* know about you!

PEPPINA: Va via! Sporcacciona!

VIOLETTA: Puttana!

MARIELLA: Assassina!

TERESA: You sent him to the Romanos.

FATHER DE LEO: Shhh!

(*Suddenly the women swarm down the steps like a cloud of attacking birds, all crying out in Sicilian. Estelle crouches and bows her head defensively before their savage assault. The bouquet of roses is snatched from her black-gloved hands and she is flailed with them about the head and shoulders. The thorns catch her veil and tear it away from her head. She covers her white sobbing face with her hands.*)

FATHER DE LEO: Ferme! Ferme! Signore, fermate vi nel nome di Dio!—Have a little respect!

(*The women fall back from Estelle, who huddles weeping on the walk.*)

ESTELLE: See him, see him, just see him . . .

FATHER DE LEO: The body is crushed and burned. Nobody can see it. Now go away and don't ever come here again, Estelle Hohengarten!

THE WOMEN (*in both languages, wildly*): Va via, va via, go way.

(*Rosa comes around the house. Estelle turns and retreats. One of the mourners spits and kicks at the tangled veil and roses. Father De Leo leaves. The others return inside, except Rosa.*

(*After a few moments the child goes over to the roses. She picks them up and carefully untangles the veil from the thorns.*

(*She sits on the sagging steps and puts the black veil over her head. Then for the first time she begins to weep, wildly, histrionically. The little boy appears and gazes at her, momentarily impressed by her performance. Then he picks up a rubber ball and begins to bounce it.*

(Rosa is outraged. She jumps up, tears off the veil and runs to the little boy, giving him a sound smack and snatching the ball away from him.)

ROSA: Go home! My papa is dead!

(The scene dims out, as the music is heard again.)

SCENE FOUR

A June day, three years later. It is morning and the light is bright. A group of local mothers are storming Serafina's house, indignant over her delay in delivering the graduation dresses for their daughters. Most of the women are chattering continually in Sicilian, racing about the house and banging the doors and shutters. The scene moves swiftly and violently until the moment when Rosa finally comes out in her graduation dress.

GIUSEPPINA: Serafina! Serafina delle Rose!

PEPPINA: Maybe if you call her "Baronessa" she will answer the door. *(with a mocking laugh)* Call her "Baronessa" and kiss your hand to her when she opens the door.

GIUSEPPINA *(tauntingly)*: Baronessa! *(She kisses her hand toward the door.)*

VIOLETTA: When did she promise your dress?

PEPPINA: All week she say, "Domani—domani—domani." But yestiddy I told her . . .

VIOLETTA: Yeah?

PEPPINA: Oh yeah. I says to her, "Serafina, domani's the high school graduation. I got to try the dress on my daughter *today*." "Domani," she says, "Sicuro! sicuro! sicuro!" So I start to go away. Then I hear a voice call, "Signora! Signora!" So I turn round and I see Serafina's daughter at the window.

VIOLETTA: Rosa?

PEPPINA: Yeah, Rosa. An' you know how?

VIOLETTA: How?

PEPPINA: *Naked!* Nuda, nuda! (*She crosses herself and repeats a prayer.*) In nominis padri et figlio et spiritus sancti. Aaahh!

VIOLETTA: What did she do?

PEPPINA: Do? She say, "Signora! Please, you call this numero and ask for Jack and tell Jack my clothes are lock up so I can't get out from the house." Then Serafina come and she grab-a the girl by the hair and she pull her way from the window and she slam the shutters right in my face!

GIUSEPPINA: Whatsa the matter the daughter?

VIOLETTA: Who is this boy? Where did she meet him?

PEPPINA: Boy! What boy? He's a sailor. (*At the word "sailor" the women say "Ahhh!"*) She met him at the high school dance and somebody tell Serafina. That's why she lock up the girl's clothes so she can't leave the house. She can't even go to the high school to take the examinations. Imagine!

VIOLETTA: Peppina, this time *you* go to the door, yeah?

PEPPINA: Oh yeah, I go. Now I'm getting nervous. (*The women all crowd to the door.*) Sera-feee-na!

VIOLETTA: Louder, louder!

PEPPINA: Apri la porta! Come on, come on!

THE WOMEN (*together*): Yeah, apri la porta! . . . Come on, hurry up! . . . Open up!

GIUSEPPINA: I go get-a police.

VIOLETTA: Whatsa matta? You want more trouble?

GIUSEPPINA: Listen, I pay in advance five dollars and get no dress. Now what she wear, my daughter, to graduate in? A couple of towels and a rose in the hair? (*There is a noise inside: a shout and running footsteps.*)

THE WOMEN: Something is going on in the house! I hear someone! Don't I? Don't you?

(*A scream and running footsteps are heard. The front door opens and Serafina staggers out onto the porch. She is wearing a soiled pink slip and her hair is wild.*)

SERAFINA: Aiuto! Aiuto! (*She plunges back into the house.*)

(*Miss Yorke, a spinsterish high school teacher, walks quickly up to the house. The Sicilian women, now all chattering at once like a cloud of birds, sweep about her as she approaches.*)

MISS YORKE: You ladies know I don't understand Italian! So, please . . .

(*She goes directly into the house. There are more outcries inside. The Strega comes and stands at the edge of the yard, cackling derisively.*)

THE STREGA (*calling back to someone*): The Wops are at it again!—She got the daughter lock up naked in there all week. Ho, ho, ho! She lock up all week—naked—shouting out the window tell people to call a number and give a message to Jack. Ho, ho, ho! I guess she's in trouble already, and only fifteen!—They ain't civilized, these Sicilians. In the old country they live in caves in the hills and the country's run by bandits. Ho, ho, ho! More of them coming over on the boats all the time. (*The door is thrown open again and Serafina reappears on the porch. She is acting wildly, as if demented.*)

SERAFINA (*gasping in a hoarse whisper*): She cut her wrist, my daughter, she cut her wrist! (*She runs out into the yard.*) Aiiii-eeee! Aiutatemi, aiutatemi! Call the dottore! (*Assunta rushes up to Serafina and supports her as she is about to fall to her knees in the yard.*) Get the knife away from her! Get the knife, please! Get the knife away from—she cut her wrist with—Madonna! Madonna mia . . .

ASSUNTA: Smettila, smettila, Serafina.

MISS YORKE (*coming out of the back room*): Mrs. Delle Rose, your daughter has not cut her wrist. Now come back into the house.

SERAFINA (*panting*): Che dice, che dice? Che cosa? Che cosa dice?

MISS YORKE: Your daughter's all right. Come back into the house. And you ladies please go away!

ASSUNTA: Vieni, Serafina. Andiamo a casa. (*She supports the heavy, sagging bulk of Serafina to the steps. As they climb the steps one of the Sicilian mothers advances from the whispering group.*)

GIUSEPPINA (*boldly*): Serafina, we don't go away until we get our dresses.

PEPPINA: The graduation begins and the girls ain't dressed.

(*Serafina's reply to this ill-timed request is a long, animal howl of misery as she is supported into the house. Miss Yorke follows and firmly closes the door upon the women, who then go around back of the house. The interior of the house is lighted up.*)

MISS YORKE (*to Serafina*): No, no, no, she's not bleeding. Rosa? Rosa, come here and show your mother that you are not bleeding to death.

(*Rosa appears silently and sullenly between the curtains that separate the two rooms. She has a small white handkerchief tied around one wrist. Serafina points at the wrist and cries out: "Aiieee!"*)

MISS YORKE (*severely*): Now *stop* that, Mrs. Delle Rose!

(*Serafina rushes to Rosa, who thrusts her roughly away.*)

ROSA: Lasciami stare, Mama!—I'm so ashamed I could die. This is the way she goes around all the time. She hasn't put on clothes since my father was killed. For three years she sits at the sewing machine and never puts a dress on or goes out of the house, and now she has locked my clothes up so *I* can't go out. She wants me to be like her, a freak of the neighborhood, the way she is! Next time, next time, I won't cut my wrist but my throat! I don't want to live locked up with a bottle of ashes! (*She points to the shrine.*)

ASSUNTA: Figlia, figlia, figlia, non devi parlare cosí!

MISS YORKE: Mrs. Delle Rose, please give me the key to the closet so that your daughter can dress for the graduation!

SERAFINA (*surrendering the key*): Ecco la—chiave . . . (*Rosa snatches the key and runs back through the curtains.*)

MISS YORKE: Now why did you lock her clothes up, Mrs. Delle Rose?

SERAFINA: The wrist is still bleeding!

MISS YORKE: No, the wrist is not bleeding. It's just a skin cut, a scratch. But the child is exhausted from all this excitement and hasn't eaten a thing in two or three days.

ROSA (*running into the dining room*): Four days! I only asked her one favor. Not to let me go out but to let Jack come to the house so she could meet him!—Then she locked my clothes up!

MISS YORKE: Your daughter missed her final examinations at the high school, but her grades have been so good that she will be allowed to graduate with her class and take the examinations later.—You understand me, Mrs. Delle Rose!

(*Rosa goes into the back of the house.*)

SERAFINA (*standing at the curtains*): See the way she looks at me? I've got a wild thing in the house, and her wrist is still bleeding!

MISS YORKE: Let's not have any more outbursts of emotion!

SERAFINA: Outbursts of—you make me sick! Sick! Sick at my stomach you make me! Your school, you make all this trouble! You give-a this dance where she gets mixed up with a sailor.

MISS YORKE: You are talking about the Hunter girl's brother, a sailor named Jack, who attended the dance with his sister?

SERAFINA: "Attended with sister!—Attended with *sister!*—My daughter, she's nobody's sister!

(*Rosa comes out of the back room. She is radiantly beautiful in her graduation gown.*)

ROSA: Don't listen to her, don't pay any attention to her, Miss Yorke.—I'm ready to go to the high school.

SERAFINA (*stunned by her daughter's beauty, and speaking with a wheedling tone and gestures, as she crouches a little*) O tesoro, tesoro! Vieni qua, Rosa, cara!—Come here and kiss Mama one minute!—Don't go like that, now!

ROSA: Lasciami stare!

(*She rushes out on the porch. Serafina gazes after her with arms slowly drooping from their imploring gesture and jaw dropping open in a look of almost comic desolation.*)

SERAFINA: Ho solo te, solo te—in questo mondo!

MISS YORKE: Now, now, Mrs. Delle Rose, no more excitement, please!

SERAFINA (*suddenly plunging after them in a burst of fury*): Senti, senti, per favore!

ROSA: Don't you dare come out on the street like that!—
Mama!

(*She crouches and covers her face in shame, as Serafina heed-
lessly plunges out into the front yard in her shocking desha-
bille, making wild gestures.*)

SERAFINA: You give this dance where she gets mixed up with
a sailor. What do you think you want to do at this high
school? (*In weeping despair, Rosa runs to the porch.*) How
high is this high school? Listen, how high is this high
school? Look, look, look, I will show you! It's high as that
horse's dirt out there in the street! (*Serafina points violently
out in front of the house.*) Si! 'Sta fetentissima scuola! Scuola
maledetta!

(*Rosa cries out and rushes over to the palm tree, leaning
against it, with tears of mortification.*)

MISS YORKE: Mrs. Delle Rose, you are talking and behaving
extremely badly. I don't understand how a woman that acts
like you could have such a sweet and refined young girl for
a daughter!—You don't deserve it!—Really . . . (*She crosses
to the palm tree.*)

SERAFINA: Oh, you want me to talk refined to you, do you?
Then do me one thing! Stop ruining the girls at the high
school! (*As Serafina paces about, she swings her hips in the
exaggeratedly belligerent style of a parading matador.*)

ASSUNTA: Piantala, Serafina! Andiamo a casa!

SERAFINA: No, no, I ain't through talking to this here
teacher!

ASSUNTA: Serafina, look at yourself, you're not dressed!

SERAFINA: I'm dressed okay; I'm not naked! (*She glares savagely at the teacher by the palm tree. The Sicilian mothers return to the front yard.*)

ASSUNTA: Serafina, cara? Andiamo a casa, adesso!—Basta!
Basta!

SERAFINA: Aspetta!

ROSA: I'm so ashamed I could die, I'm so ashamed. Oh, you
don't know, Miss Yorke, the way that we live. She never
puts on a dress; she stays all the time in that dirty old pink
slip!—And talks to my father's ashes like he was living.

SERAFINA: Teacher! Teacher, senti! What do you think you want to do at this high school? Sentite! per favore! You give this a dance! What kind of a spring dance is it? Answer this question, please, for me! What kind of a spring dance is it? She meet this boy there who don't even go to no high school. What kind of a boy? Guardate! *A sailor that wears a gold earring!* That kind of a boy is the kind of boy she meets there!—That's why I lock her clothes up so she can't go back to the high school! (*suddenly to Assunta*) She cut her wrist! It's still bleeding! (*She strikes her forehead three times with her fist.*)

ROSA: Mama, you look disgusting! (*She rushes away.*)

(*Miss Yorke rushes after her. Serafina shades her eyes with one hand to watch them departing down the street in the brilliant spring light.*)

SERAFINA: Did you hear what my daughter said to me?— "You look—disgusting."—She calls me . . .

ASSUNTA: Now, Serafina, we must go in the house. (*She leads her gently to the porch of the little house.*)

SERAFINA (*proudly*): How pretty she look, my daughter, in the white dress, like a bride! (*to all*) Excuse me! Excuse me, please! Go away! Get out of my yard!

GIUSEPPINA (*taking the bull by the horns*): No, we ain't going to go without the dresses!

ASSUNTA: Give the ladies the dresses so the girls can get dressed for the graduation.

SERAFINA: That one there, she only paid for the goods. I charge for the work.

GIUSEPPINA: Ecco! I got the money!

THE WOMEN: We *got* the money!

SERAFINA: The names are pinned on the dresses. Go in and get them. (*She turns to Assunta.*) Did you hear what my daughter called me? She called me "disgusting!"

(*Serafina enters the house, slamming the door. After a moment the mothers come out, cradling the white voile dresses tenderly in their arms, murmuring "carino!" and "bellissimo!"*)

(*As they disappear the inside light is brought up and we see Serafina standing before a glazed mirror, looking at herself and repeating the daughter's word.*)

SERAFINA: Disgusting!

(*The music is briefly resumed to mark a division.*)

SCENE FIVE

Immediately following. Serafina's movements gather momentum. She snatches a long-neglected girdle out of a bureau drawer and holds it experimentally about her waist. She shakes her head doubtfully, drops the girdle and suddenly snatches the $8.98 hat off the millinery dummy and plants it on her head. She turns around distractedly, not remembering where the mirror is. She gasps with astonishment when she catches sight of herself, snatches the hat off and hastily restores it to the blank head of the dummy. She makes another confused revolution or two, then gasps with fresh inspiration and snatches a girlish frock off a dummy—an Alice blue gown with daisies crocheted on it. The dress sticks on the dummy. Serafina mutters savagely in Sicilian. She finally overcomes this difficulty but in her exasperation she knocks the dummy over. She throws off the robe and steps hopefully into the gown. But she discovers it won't fit over her hips. She seizes the girdle again; then hurls it angrily away. The parrot calls to her; she yells angrily back at the parrot: "Zitto!"

In the distance the high school band starts playing. Serafina gets panicky that she will miss the graduation ceremonies, and hammers her forehead with her fist, sobbing a little. She wriggles despairingly out of the blue dress and runs out back in her rayon slip just as Flora and Bessie appear outside the house. Flora and Bessie are two female clowns of middle years and juvenile temperament. Flora is tall and angular; Bessie is rather stubby. They are dressed for a gala. Flora runs up the steps and bangs at the cottage door.

BESSIE: I fail to understand why it's so important to pick up a polka-dot blouse when it's likely to make us miss the twelve o'clock train.

FLORA: Serafina! Serafina!

BESSIE: We only got fifteen minutes to get to the depot and I'll get faint on the train if I don't have m' coffee . . .

FLORA: Git a coke on th' train, Bessie.

BESSIE: Git nothing on the train if we don't git the train!

(*Serafina runs back out of the bedroom, quite breathless, in a purple silk dress. As she passes the millinery dummy she snatches the hat off again and plants it back on her head.*)

SERAFINA: Wrist-watch! Wrist-watch! Where'd I put th' wrist-watch? (*She hears Flora shouting and banging and rushes to the door.*)

BESSIE: Try the door if it ain't open.

FLORA (*pushing in*): Just tell me, is it ready or not?

SERAFINA: Oh! You. Don't bother me. I'm late for the graduation of my daughter and now I can't find her graduation present.

FLORA: You got plenty of time.

SERAFINA: Don't you hear the band playing?

FLORA: They're just warming up. Now, Serafina, where is my blouse?

SERAFINA: Blouse? Not ready! I had to make fourteen graduation dresses!

FLORA: A promise is a promise and an excuse is just an excuse!

SERAFINA: I got to get to the high school!

FLORA: I got to get to the depot in that blouse!

BESSIE: We're going to the American Legion parade in New Orleans.

FLORA: There, there, there, there it is! (*She grabs the blouse from the machine.*) Get started, woman, stitch them bandanas together! If you don't do it, I'm a-gonna report you to the Chamber of Commerce and git your license revoked!

SERAFINA (*anxiously*): What license you talking about? I got no license!

FLORA: You hear that, Bessie? *She hasn't got no license!*

BESSIE: *She ain't even got a license?*

SERAFINA (*crossing quickly to the machine*): I—I'll stitch them together! But if you make me late to my daughter's graduation, I'll make you sorry some way . . .

(*She works with furious rapidity. A train whistle is heard.*)

BESSIE (*wildly and striking at Flora with her purse*): Train's pullin' out! Oh, God, you made us miss it!

FLORA: Bessie, you know there's another at 12:45!

BESSIE: It's the selfish—principle of it that makes me sick! (*She walks rapidly up and down.*)

FLORA: Set down, Bessie. Don't wear out your feet before we git to th' city . . .

BESSIE: Molly tole me the town was full of excitement. They're dropping paper sacks full of water out of hotel windows.

FLORA: Which hotel are they dropping paper sacks out of?

BESSIE: What a fool question! The Monteleone Hotel.

FLORA: That's an old-fashioned hotel.

BESSIE: It might be old-fashioned but you'd be surprised at some of the modern, up-to-date things that go on there.

FLORA: I heard, I heard that the Legionnaires caught a girl on Canal Street! They tore the clothes off her and sent her home in a taxi!

BESSIE: I double dog dare anybody to try that on me!

FLORA: You?! Huh! You never need any assistance gittin' undressed!

SERAFINA (*ominously*): You two ladies watch how you talk in there. This here is a Catholic house. You are sitting in the same room with Our Lady and with the blessed ashes of my husband!

FLORA (*acidly*): Well, ex-cuse *me*! (*She whispers maliciously to Bessie.*) It sure is a pleasant surprise to see you wearing a dress, Serafina, but the surprise would be twice as pleasant if it was more the right size. (*to Bessie, loudly*) She used to have a sweet figure, a little bit plump but attractive, but setting there at that sewing machine for three years in a kimona and not stepping out of the house has naturally given her hips!

SERAFINA: If I didn't have hips I would be a very uncomfortable woman when I set down.

(*The parrot squawks. Serafina imitates its squawk.*)

FLORA: Polly want a cracker?

SERAFINA: No. He don't want a cracker! What is she doing over there at that window?

BESSIE: Some Legionnaires are on the highway!

FLORA: A Legionnaire? No kidding?

(*She springs up and joins her girl friend at the window. They both laugh fatuously, bobbing their heads out the window.*)

BESSIE: He's looking this way; yell something!

FLORA (*leaning out the window*): Mademoiselle from Armentieres, parley-voo!

BESSIE (*chiming in rapturously*): Mademoiselle from Armentieres, parley-voo!

A VOICE OUTSIDE (*gallantly returning the salute*): Mademoiselle from Armentieres, hadn't been kissed for forty years!

BOTH GIRLS (*together; very gaily*): Hinky-dinky parley-voooo!

(*They laugh and applaud at the window. The Legionnaires are heard laughing. A car horn is heard as the Legionnaires drive away. Serafina springs up and rushes over to the window, jerks them away from it and slams the shutters in their faces.*)

SERAFINA (*furiously*): I told you wimmen that you was not in a honky-tonk! Now take your blouse and git out! Get out on the streets where you kind a wimmen belong.—This is the house of Rosario delle Rose and those are his ashes in that marble urn and I won't have—unproper things going on here or dirty talk, neither!

FLORA: Who's talking dirty?

BESSIE: What a helluva nerve.

FLORA: I want you to listen!

SERAFINA: You are, you are, dirty talk, all the time men, men, men! You men-crazy things, you!

FLORA: Sour grapes—sour grapes is your trouble! You're wild with envy!

BESSIE: Isn't she green with jealousy? Huh!

SERAFINA (*suddenly and religiously*): When I think of men I think about my husband. My husband was a Sicilian. We had love together every night of the week, we never skipped one, from the night we was married till the night he was killed in his fruit truck on that road there! (*She catches her breath in a sob.*) And maybe that is the reason I'm not man-crazy and don't like hearing the talk of women that are. But I am interested, now, in the happiness of my daughter who's graduating this morning out of high school. And now I'm going to be late, the band is playing! And I have lost her wrist watch!—her graduation present! (*She whirls about distractedly.*)

BESSIE: Flora, let's go!—The hell with that goddam blouse!

FLORA: Oh, no, just wait a minute! I don't accept insults from no one!

SERAFINA: Go on, go on to New Orleans, you two man-crazy things, you! And pick up a man on Canal Street but not in my house, at my window, in front of my dead husband's ashes! (*The high school band is playing a martial air in the distance. Serafina's chest is heaving violently; she touches her heart and momentarily seems to forget that she must go.*) I am not at all interested, I am not interested in men getting fat and bald in soldier-boy play suits, tearing the clothes off girls on Canal Street and dropping paper sacks out of hotel windows. I'm just not interested in that sort of man-crazy business. I remember my husband with a body like a young boy and hair on his head as thick and black as mine is and skin on him smooth and sweet as a yellow rose petal.

FLORA: Oh, a *rose*, was he?

SERAFINA: Yes, yes, a rose, a rose!

FLORA: Yes, a rose of a Wop!—of a gangster!—shot smuggling dope under a load of bananas!

BESSIE: Flora, Flora, let's go!

SERAFINA: My folks was peasants, contadini, but he—he come from *land*-owners! *Signorile*, my husband!—At night I sit here and I'm satisfied to remember, because I had the best.—Not the third best and not the second best, but the *first* best, the *only* best!—So now I stay here and am satisfied now to remember, . . .

BESSIE: Come on, come out! To the depot!

FLORA: Just wait, I wanta hear this, it's too good to miss!

SERAFINA: I count up the nights I held him all night in my arms, and I can tell you how many. Each night for twelve years. Four thousand—three hundred—and eighty. The number of nights I held him all night in my arms. Sometimes I didn't sleep, just held him all night in my arms. And I am satisfied with it. I grieve for him. Yes, my pillow at night's never dry—but I'm satisfied to remember. And I would feel cheap and degraded and not fit to live with my daughter or under the roof with the urn of his blessed ashes, those—ashes of a rose—if after that memory, after knowing that man, I went to some other, some middle-aged man, not young, not full of young passion, but getting a pot belly on him and losing his hair and smelling of sweat and liquor—and trying to fool myself that *that* was love-making! I *know* what love-making was. And I'm satisfied just to remember . . . (*She is panting as though she had run upstairs.*) Go on, you do it, you go on the streets and let them drop their sacks of dirty water on you!—I'm satisfied to remember the love of a man that was mine—*only mine*! Never touched by the hand of *nobody*! *Nobody* but *me*!—Just me! (*She gasps and runs out to the porch. The sun floods her figure. It seems to astonish her. She finds herself sobbing. She digs in her purse for her handkerchief.*)

FLORA (*crossing to the open door*): Never touched by nobody?

SERAFINA (*with fierce pride*): Never nobody but me!

FLORA: *I* know somebody that could a tale unfold! And not so far from here neither. Not no further than the Square Roof is, that place on Esplanade!

BESSIE: Estelle Hohengarten!

FLORA: Estelle Hohengarten!—the blackjack dealer from Texas!

BESSIE: Get into your blouse and let's go!

FLORA: Everybody's known it but Serafina. I'm just telling the facts that come out at the inquest while she was in bed with her eyes shut tight and the sheet pulled over her head like a female ostrich! Tie this damn thing on me! It was a romance, not just a fly-by-night thing, but a steady affair that went on for more than a year.

(*Serafina has been standing on the porch with the door open behind her. She is in the full glare of the sun. She appears to have been struck senseless by the words shouted inside. She turns slowly about. We see that her dress is unfastened down the back, the pink slip showing. She reaches out gropingly with one hand and finds the porch column which she clings to while the terrible words strike constantly deeper. The high school band continues as a merciless counterpoint.*)

BESSIE: Leave her in ignorance. Ignorance is bliss.

FLORA: He had a rose tattoo on his chest, the stuck-up thing, and Estelle was so gone on him she went down to Bourbon Street and had one put on her. (*Serafina comes onto the porch and Flora turns to her, viciously.*) Yeah, a rose tattoo on her chest same as the Wop's!

SERAFINA (*very softly*): Liar . . . (*She comes inside; the word seems to give her strength.*)

BESSIE (*nervously*): Flora, let's go, let's go!

SERAFINA (*in a terrible voice*): Liar!—*Lie*-arrrr!

(*She slams the wooden door shut with a violence that shakes the walls.*)

BESSIE (*shocked into terror*): Let's get outa here, Flora!

FLORA: Let her howl her head off. I don't care.

(*Serafina has snatched up a broom.*)

BESSIE: What's she up to?

FLORA: I don't care what she's up to!

BESSIE: I'm a-scared of these Wops.

FLORA: I'm not afraid of nobody!

BESSIE: She's gonna hit you.

FLORA: She'd better not hit me!

(*But both of the clowns are in retreat to the door. Serafina suddenly rushes at them with the broom. She flails Flora about the hips and shoulders. Bessie gets out. But Flora is trapped in a corner. A table is turned over. Bessie, outside, screams for the police and cries:* "Murder! Murder!" *The high school band is playing* The Stars and Stripes Forever. *Flora breaks wildly past the flailing broom and escapes out of the house. She also takes up the cry for help. Serafina follows them out. She is flailing the brilliant noon air with the broom. The two women run off, screaming.*)

FLORA (*calling back*): I'm going to have her arrested! Police, police! I'm going to have you arrested!

SERAFINA: *Have* me arrested, *have* me, you dirt, you devil, you *liar*! Li-i-arrr!

(*She comes back inside the house and leans on the work table for a moment, panting heavily. Then she rushes back to the door, slams it and bolts it. Then she rushes to the windows, slams the shutters and fastens them. The house is now dark except for the vigil light in the ruby glass cup before the Madonna, and the delicate beams admitted through the shutter slats.)*

SERAFINA (*in a crazed manner*): Have me—have me—arrested—dirty slut—bitch—liar! (*She moves about helplessly, not knowing what to do with her big, stricken body. Panting for breath, she repeats the word "liar" monotonously and helplessly as she thrashes about. It is necessary for her, vitally necessary for her, to believe that the woman's story is a malicious invention. But the words of it stick in her mind and she mumbles them aloud as she thrashes crazily around the small confines of the parlor.*) Woman—Estelle— (*The sound of band music is heard.*) Band, band, already—started.— Going to miss—graduation. Oh! (*She retreats toward the Madonna.*) Estelle, Estelle Hohengarten?—"A shirt for a man I'm in love with! This man—is—wild like a gypsy."— Oh, oh, Lady—The—rose-colored—silk. (*She starts toward the dining room, then draws back in terror.*) No, no, no, no, no! I don't remember! It wasn't that name, I don't remember the name! (*The band music grows louder.*) High school—graduation—late! I'll be—late for it.—Oh, Lady, give me a—*sign*! (*She cocks her head toward the statue in a fearful listening attitude.*) Che? Che dice, Signora? *Oh, Lady! Give me a sign!*

(*The scene dims out.*)

SCENE SIX

It is two hours later. The interior of the house is in complete darkness except for the vigil light. With the shutters closed, the interior is so dark that we do not know Serafina is present. All that we see clearly is the starry blue robe of Our Lady above the flickering candle of the ruby glass cup. After a few moments we hear Serafina's voice, very softly, in the weak, breathless tone of a person near death.

SERAFINA (*very softly*): Oh, Lady, give me a sign . . .

(*Gay, laughing voices are heard outside the house. Rosa and Jack appear, bearing roses and gifts. They are shouting back to others in a car.*)

JACK: Where do we go for the picnic?

A GIRL'S VOICE (*from the highway*): We're going in three sail-boats to Diamond Key.

A MAN'S VOICE: Be at Municipal Pier in half an hour.

ROSA: Pick us up here! (*She races up the steps.*) Oh, the door's locked! Mama's gone *out*! There's a key in that bird bath.

(*Jack opens the door. The parlor lights up faintly as they enter.*)

JACK: It's dark in here.

ROSA: Yes, Mama's gone out!

JACK: How do you know she's out?

ROSA: The door was locked and all the shutters are closed! Put down those roses.

JACK: Where shall I . . .

ROSA: Somewhere, anywhere!—Come here! (*He approaches her rather diffidently.*) I want to teach you a little Dago word. The word is "bacio."

JACK: What does this word mean?

ROSA: This and this and this! (*She rains kisses upon him till he forcibly removes her face from his.*) Just think. A week ago Friday—I didn't know boys existed!—Did you know girls existed before the dance?

JACK: Yes, I knew they existed . . .

ROSA (*holding him*): Do you remember what you said to me on the dance floor? "Honey, you're dancing too close?"

JACK: Well, it was—hot in the Gym and the—floor was crowded.

ROSA: When my girl friend was teaching me how to dance, I asked her, "How do you know which way the boy's going to move?" And she said, "You've got to feel how he's go-ing to move with your body!" I said, "How do you feel with your body?" And she said, "By pressing up close!"—That's why I pressed up close! I didn't realize that I was—Ha, ha! Now you're blushing! Don't go *away*!—And a few minutes later you said to me, "Gee, you're beautiful!" I said, "Excuse me," and ran to the ladies' room. Do you know why? To look at myself in the mirror! And I saw that I was! For the first time in my life I was beautiful! You'd made me beautiful when you *said* that I was!

JACK (*humbly*): You *are* beautiful, Rosa! So much, I . . .

ROSA: *You've* changed, *too.* You've stopped laughing and joking. Why have you gotten so old and serious, Jack?

JACK: Well, honey, you're sort of . . .

ROSA: What am I "sort of?"

JACK (*finding the exact word*): Wild! (*She laughs. He seizes the bandaged wrist.*) I didn't know nothing like this was going to happen.

ROSA: Oh, that, that's nothing! I'll take the handkerchief off and you can forget it.

JACK: How could you do a thing like that over me? I'm—nothing!

ROSA: Everybody is nothing until you love them!

JACK: Give me that handkerchief. I want to show it to my shipmates. I'll say, "This is the blood of a beautiful girl who cut her wrist with a knife because she loved me!"

ROSA: Don't be so pleased with yourself. It's mostly Mercurochrome!

SERAFINA (*violently, from the dark room adjoining*): Stai zitta!—Cretina!

(*Rosa and Jack draw abruptly apart.*)

JACK (*fearfully*): I knew somebody was here!

ROSA (*sweetly and delicately*): Mama? Are you in there, Mama?

SERAFINA: No, no, no, I'm not, I'm dead and buried!

ROSA: Yes, Mama's in there!

JACK: Well, I—better go and—wait outside for a—while . . .

ROSA: You stay right here!—Mama?—Jack is with me.—Are you dressed up nicely? (*There is no response.*) Why's it so dark in here?—Jack, open the shutters!—I want to introduce you to my mother . . .

JACK: Hadn't I better go and . . .

ROSA: No. Open the shutters!

(*The shutters are opened and Rosa draws apart the curtains between the two rooms. Sunlight floods the scene. Serafina is*

*revealed slumped in a chair at her work table in the dining
room near the Singer sewing machine. She is grotesquely surrounded by the dummies, as though she had been holding a
silent conference with them. Her appearance, in slovenly des-
habille, is both comic and shocking.*)

ROSA (*terribly embarrassed*): Mama, Mama, you said you were
dressed up pretty! Jack, stay out for a minute! What's happened, Mama?

(*Jack remains in the parlor. Rosa pulls the curtains, snatches
a robe and flings it over Serafina. She brushes Serafina's hair
back from her sweat-gleaming face, rubs her face with a
handkerchief and dusts it with powder. Serafina submits to
this cosmetic enterprise with a dazed look.*)

ROSA (*gesturing vertically*): Su, su, su, su, su, su, su, su, su!

(*Serafina sits up slightly in her chair, but she is still looking
stupefied. Rosa returns to the parlor and opens the curtains
again.*)

ROSA: Come in, Jack! Mama is ready to meet you!

(*Rosa trembles with eagerness as Jack advances nervously
from the parlor. But before he enters Serafina collapses again
into her slumped position, with a low moan.*)

ROSA (*violently*): Mama, Mama, su, Mama! (*Serafina sits half
erect.*) She didn't sleep good last night.—Mama, this is Jack
Hunter!

JACK: Hello, Mrs. Delle Rose. It sure is a pleasure to meet you.

(*There is a pause. Serafina stares indifferently at the boy.*)

ROSA: Mama, Mama, say something!

JACK: Maybe your Mama wants me to . . . (*He makes an
awkward gesture toward the door.*)

ROSA: No, no, Mama's just tired. Mama makes dresses; she
made a whole lot of dresses for the graduation! How many,
Mama, how many graduation dresses did you have to make?

SERAFINA (*dully*): Fa niente . . .

JACK: I was hoping to see you at the graduation, Mrs. Delle
Rose.

THE ROSE TATTOO

ROSA: I guess that Mama was too worn out to go.

SERAFINA: Rosa, shut the front door, shut it and lock it. There was a—policeman . . . (*There is a pause.*) What?—What?

JACK: My sister was graduating. My mother was there and my aunt was there—a whole bunch of cousins—I was hoping that you could—all—get together . . .

ROSA: Jack brought you some flowers.

JACK: I hope you are partial to roses as much as I am. (*He hands her the bouquet. She takes them absently.*)

ROSA: Mama, say something, say something simple like "Thanks."

SERAFINA: Thanks.

ROSA: Jack, tell Mama about the graduation; describe it to her.

JACK: My mother said it was just like fairyland.

ROSA: Tell her what the boys wore!

JACK: What did—what did they wear?

ROSA: Oh, you know what they wore. They wore blue coats and white pants and each one had a carnation! And there were three couples that did an old-fashioned dance, a minuet, Mother, to Mendelssohn's *Spring Song*! Wasn't it lovely, Jack? But one girl slipped; she wasn't used to long dresses! She slipped and fell on her—ho, ho! Wasn't it funny, Jack, wasn't it, wasn't it, Jack?

JACK (*worriedly*): I think that your Mama . . .

ROSA: Oh, my prize, my prize, I have forgotten my prize!

JACK: Where is it?

ROSA: You set them down by the sewing sign when you looked for the key.

JACK: Aw, excuse me, I'll get them. (*He goes out through the parlor. Rosa runs to her mother and kneels by her chair.*)

ROSA (*in a terrified whisper*): Mama, something has happened! What has happened, Mama? Can't you tell me, Mama? Is it because of this morning? Look. I took the bandage off, it was only a scratch! So, Mama, forget it! Think it was just a bad dream that never happened! Oh, Mama! (*She gives her several quick kisses on the forehead. Jack returns with two big books tied in white satin ribbon.*)

JACK: Here they are.

ROSA: Look what I got, Mama.

SERAFINA (*dully*): What?

ROSA: The Digest of Knowledge!

JACK: Everything's in them, from Abracadabra to Zoo! My sister was jealous. She just got a diploma!

SERAFINA (*rousing a bit*): Diploma, where is it? Didn't you get no diploma?

ROSA: Si, si, Mama! Eccolo! Guarda, guarda! (*She holds up the diploma tied in ribbon.*)

SERAFINA: Va bene.—Put it in the drawer with your father's clothes.

JACK: Mrs. Delle Rose, you should be very, very proud of your daughter. She stood in front of the crowd and recited a poem.

ROSA: Yes, I did. Oh, I was so excited!

JACK: And Mrs. Delle Rose, your daughter, Rosa, was so pretty when she walked on the stage—that people went "Ooooooooooo!"—like that! Y'know what I mean? They all went—"Ooooooooo!" Like a—like a—*wind* had—blown over! Because your daughter, Rosa, was so—*lovely* looking! (*He has crouched over to Serafina to deliver this description close to her face. Now he straightens up and smiles proudly at Rosa.*) How does it feel to be the mother of the prettiest girl in the world?

ROSA (*suddenly bursting into pure delight*): Ha, ha, ha, ha, ha, ha! (*She throws her head back in rapture.*)

SERAFINA (*rousing*): Hush!

ROSA: Ha, ha, ha, ha, ha, ha, ha, ha, ha, ha! (*She cannot control her ecstatic laughter. She presses her hand to her mouth but the laughter still bubbles out.*)

SERAFINA (*suddenly rising in anger*): Pazza, pazza, pazza! Finiscila! Basta, via! (*Rosa whirls around to hide her convulsions of joy. To Jack:*) Put the prize books in the parlor, and shut the front door; there was a policeman come here because of—some trouble . . . (*Jack takes the books.*)

ROSA: Mama, I've never seen you like this! What will Jack think, Mama?

SERAFINA: Why do I care what Jack thinks?—You wild, wild crazy thing, you—with the eyes of your—father . . .

JACK (*returning*): Yes, ma'am, Mrs. Delle Rose, you certainly got a right to be very proud of your daughter.

SERAFINA (*after a pause*): I am proud of the—memory of her—father.—He was a baron . . . (*Rosa takes Jack's arm.*) And who are *you*? What are you?—per piacere!

ROSA: Mama, I just introduced him; his name is Jack Hunter.

SERAFINA: Hunt-er?

JACK: Yes, ma'am, Hunter. Jack Hunter.

SERAFINA: What are you hunting?—Jack?

ROSA: Mama!

SERAFINA: What all of 'em are hunting? To have a good time, and the Devil cares who pays for it? I'm sick of men, I'm almost as sick of men as I am of wimmen.—Rosa, get out while I talk to this boy!

ROSA: I didn't bring Jack here to be insulted!

JACK: Go on, honey, and let your Mama talk to me. I think your Mama has just got a slight wrong—impression . . .

SERAFINA (*ominously*): Yes, I got an impression!

ROSA: I'll get dressed! Oh, Mama, don't spoil it for me!—the happiest day of my life! (*She goes into the back of the house.*)

JACK (*after an awkward pause*): Mrs. Delle Rose . . .

SERAFINA (*correcting his pronunciation*): Delle Rose!

JACK: Mrs. Delle Rose, I'm sorry about all this. Believe me, Mrs. Delle Rose, the last thing I had in mind was getting mixed up in a family situation. I come home after three months to sea, I docked at New Orleans, and come here to see my folks. My sister was going to a high school dance. She took me with her, and there I met your daughter.

SERAFINA: What did you do?

JACK: At the high school dance? We danced! My sister had told me that Rosa had a very strict mother and wasn't allowed to go on dates with boys so when it was over, I said, "I'm sorry you're not allowed to go out." And she said, "Oh! What gave you the idea I *wasn't!*" So then I thought my sister had made a mistake and I made a date with her for the next night.

SERAFINA: What did you do the next night?

JACK: The next night we went to the movies.

SERAFINA: And what did you do—that night?

JACK: At the movies? We ate a bag of popcorn and watched the movie!

SERAFINA: She come home at midnight and said she had been with a girl-friend studying "civics."

JACK: Whatever story she told you, it ain't my fault!

SERAFINA: And the night after that?

JACK: Last Tuesday? We went roller skating!

SERAFINA: And afterwards?

JACK: After the skating? We went to a drug store and had an ice cream soda!

SERAFINA: Alone?

JACK: At the drug store? No. It was crowded. And the skating rink was full of people skating!

SERAFINA: You mean that you haven't been alone with my Rosa?

JACK: Alone or not alone, what's the point of that question? I still don't see the point of it.

SERAFINA: We are Sicilians. We don't leave the girls with the boys they're not engaged to!

JACK: Mrs. Delle Rose, this is the United States.

SERAFINA: But we are Sicilians, and we are not cold-blooded. —My girl is a *virgin*! She *is*—or she *was*—I would like to know—*which*!

JACK: Mrs. Delle Rose! I got to tell you something. You might not believe it. It is a hard thing to say. But I am— *also* a—*virgin* . . .

SERAFINA: *What? No.* I do not believe it.

JACK: Well, it's true, though. This is the first time—I . . .

SERAFINA: First time you *what*?

JACK: The first time I really wanted to . . .

SERAFINA: Wanted to what?

JACK: Make—love . . .

SERAFINA: You? A sailor?

JACK (*sighing deeply*): Yes, ma'am. I had opportunities to!— But I—always thought of my mother . . . I always asked myself, would she or would she not—think—this or that person was—decent!

SERAFINA: But with my daughter, my Rosa, your mother tells you *okay*?—go ahead, son!

JACK: Mrs. Delle Rose! (*with embarrassment*)—Mrs. Delle Rose, I . . .

SERAFINA: Two weeks ago I was slapping her hands for scratching mosquito bites. She rode a bicycle to school. Now all at once—I've got a wild thing in the house. She says she's in love. And you? Do you say *you're* in love?

JACK (*solemnly*): Yes, ma'am, I do, I'm in love!—very much . . .

SERAFINA: Bambini, tutti due, bambini!

(*Rosa comes out, dressed for the picnic.*)

ROSA: I'm ready for Diamond Key!

SERAFINA: Go out on the porch. Diamond Key!

ROSA (*with a sarcastic curtsy*): Yes, Mama!

SERAFINA: What are you? Catholic?

JACK: Me? Yes, ma'am, Catholic.

SERAFINA: You don't look Catholic to me!

ROSA (*shouting, from the door*): Oh, God, Mama, how do Catholics look? How do they look different from anyone else?

SERAFINA: Stay out till I call you! (*Rosa crosses to the bird bath and prays. Serafina turns to Jack.*) Turn around, will you?

JACK: Do what, ma'am?

SERAFINA: I said, *turn around!* (*Jack awkwardly turns around.*) Why do they make them Navy pants so tight?

ROSA (*listening in the yard*): Oh, my God . . .

JACK (*flushing*): That's a question you'll have to ask the Navy, Mrs. Delle Rose.

SERAFINA: And that gold earring, what's the gold earring for?

ROSA (*yelling from the door*): For crossing the equator, Mama; he crossed it three times. He was initiated into the court of Neptune and gets to wear a gold earring! He's a shellback!

(*Serafina springs up and crosses to slam the porch door. Rosa runs despairingly around the side of the house and leans, exhausted with closed eyes, against the trunk of a palm tree. The Strega creeps into the yard, listening.*)

SERAFINA: You see what I got. A wild thing in the house!

JACK: Mrs. Delle Rose, I guess that Sicilians are very emotional people . . .

SERAFINA: I want nobody to take advantage of that!

JACK: You got the wrong idea about me, Mrs. Delle Rose.

SERAFINA: I know what men want—not to eat popcorn with girls or to slide on ice! And boys are the same, only younger.—Come here. Come here!

(*Rosa hears her mother's passionate voice. She rushes from the palm tree to the back door and pounds on it with both fists.*)

ROSA: Mama! Mama! Let me in the door, Jack!
JACK: Mrs. Delle Rose, your daughter is calling you.
SERAFINA: Let her call!—Come here. (*She crosses to the shrine of Our Lady.*) Come here!

(*Despairing of the back door, Rosa rushes around to the front. A few moments later she pushes open the shutters of the window in the wall and climbs half in. Jack crosses apprehensively to Serafina before the Madonna.*)

SERAFINA: You said you're Catholic, ain't you?
JACK: Yes, ma'am.
SERAFINA: Then kneel down in front of Our Lady!
JACK: Do—do what, did you say?
SERAFINA: I said to get down on your knees in front of Our Lady!

(*Rosa groans despairingly in the window. Jack kneels awkwardly upon the hassock.*)

ROSA: Mama, Mama, *now* what?!

(*Serafina rushes to the window, pushes Rosa out and slams the shutters.*)

SERAFINA (*returning to Jack*): Now say after me what I say!
JACK: Yes, ma'am.

(*Rosa pushes the shutters open again.*)

SERAFINA: I promise the Holy Mother that I will respect the innocence of the daughter of . . .
ROSA (*in anguish*): Ma-*maaa!*
SERAFINA: Get back out of that window!—Well? Are you gonna say it?
JACK: Yes, ma'am. What was it, again?
SERAFINA: I promise the Holy Mother . . .
JACK: I promise the Holy Mother . . .

SERAFINA: As I hope to be saved by the Blessed Blood of Jesus . . .

JACK: As I hope to be saved by the . . .

SERAFINA: Blessed Blood of . . .

JACK: Jesus . . .

SERAFINA: That I will respect the innocence of the daughter, Rosa, of Rosario delle Rose.

JACK: That I will respect the innocence—of—Rosa . . .

SERAFINA: Cross yourself! (*He crosses himself.*) Now get up, get up, get up! I am satisfied now . . .

(*Rosa jumps through the window and rushes to Serafina with arms outflung and wild cries of joy.*)

SERAFINA: Let me go, let me breathe! (*Outside the Strega cackles derisively.*)

ROSA: Oh, wonderful Mama, don't breathe! Oh, Jack! *Kiss* Mama! *Kiss Mama!* Mama, please kiss Jack!

SERAFINA: Kiss? Me? No, no, no, no!—Kiss my *hand* . . .

(*She offers her hand, shyly, and Jack kisses it with a loud smack. Rosa seizes the wine bottle.*)

ROSA: Mama, get some wine glasses!

(*Serafina goes for the glasses, and Rosa suddenly turns to Jack. Out of her mother's sight, she passionately grabs hold of his hand and presses it, first to her throat, then to her lips and finally to her breast. Jack snatches her hand away as Serafina returns with the glasses. Voices are heard calling from the highway.*)

VOICES OUTSIDE: Ro-osa!—Ro-osa!—Ro-osa!

(*A car horn is heard blowing.*)

SERAFINA: Oh, I forgot the graduation present.

(*She crouches down before the bureau and removes a fancily wrapped package from its bottom drawer. The car horn is honking, and the voices are calling.*)

ROSA: They're calling for us! *Coming!* Jack! (*She flies out the door, calling back to her mother.*) G'bye, Mama!

JACK (*following Rosa*): Good-bye, Mrs. Delle Rose!

SERAFINA (*vaguely*): It's a Bulova wrist watch with seventeen jewels in it . . . (*She realizes that she is alone.*) Rosa! (*She goes to the door, still holding out the present. Outside the car motor roars, and the voices shout as the car goes off. Serafina stumbles outside, shielding her eyes with one hand, extending the gift with the other.*) Rosa, Rosa, your present! Regalo, regalo—tesoro!

(*But the car has started off, with a medley of voices shouting farewells, which fade quickly out of hearing. Serafina turns about vaguely in the confusing sunlight and gropes for the door. There is a derisive cackle from the witch next door. Serafina absently opens the package and removes the little gold watch. She winds it and then holds it against her ear. She shakes it and holds it again to her ear. Then she holds it away from her and glares at it fiercely.*)

SERAFINA (*pounding her chest three times*): Tick—tick—tick! (*She goes to the Madonna and faces it.*) Speak to me, Lady! Oh, Lady, give me a sign!

(*The scene dims out.*)

ACT TWO

It is two hours later the same day.

Serafina comes out onto the porch, barefooted, wearing a rayon slip. Great shadows have appeared beneath her eyes; her face and throat gleam with sweat. There are dark stains of wine on the rayon slip. It is difficult for her to stand, yet she cannot sit still. She makes a sick moaning sound in her throat almost continually.

A hot wind rattles the cane-brake. Vivi, the little girl, comes up to the porch to stare at Serafina as at a strange beast in a cage. Vivi is chewing a licorice stick which stains her mouth and her fingers. She stands chewing and staring. Serafina evades her stare. She wearily drags a broken grey wicker chair down off the porch, all the way out in front of the house, and sags heavily into it. It sits awry on a broken leg.

Vivi sneaks toward her. Serafina lurches about to face her angrily. The child giggles and scampers back to the porch.

SERAFINA (*sinking back into the chair*): Oh, Lady, Lady, Lady,
give me a—sign . . . (*She looks up at the white glare of
the sky.*)

(*Father De Leo approaches the house. Serafina crouches low in
the chair to escape his attention. He knocks at the door.
Receiving no answer, he looks out into the yard, sees her, and
approaches her chair. He comes close to address her with a gentle severity.*)

FATHER DE LEO: Buon giorno, Serafina.

SERAFINA (*faintly, with a sort of disgust*): Giorno . . .

FATHER DE LEO: I'm surprised to see you sitting outdoors like
this. What is that thing you're wearing?—I think it's an un-
dergarment!—It's hanging off one shoulder, and your
head, Serafina, looks as if you had stuck it in a bucket of oil.
Oh, I see now why the other ladies of the neighborhood
aren't taking their afternoon naps! They find it more entertaining to sit on the porches and watch the spectacle you
are putting on for them!—Are you listening to me?—I
must tell you that the change in your appearance and
behavior since Rosario's death is shocking—shocking! A
woman can be dignified in her grief but when it's carried
too far it becomes a sort of self-indulgence. Oh, I knew this
was going to happen when you broke the Church law and
had your husband cremated! (*Serafina lurches up from the
chair and shuffles back to the porch. Father De Leo follows
her.*)—Set up a little idolatrous shrine in your house and
give worship to a bottle of ashes. (*She sinks down upon the
steps.*)—Are you listening to me?

(*Two women have appeared on the embankment and descend
toward the house. Serafina lurches heavily up to meet them,
like a weary bull turning to face another attack.*)

SERAFINA: You ladies, what you want? I don't do sewing!
Look, I quit doing sewing. (*She pulls down the "*SEWING*"
sign and hurls it away.*) Now you got places to go, you
ladies, go places! Don't hang around front of my house!

FATHER DE LEO: The ladies want to be friendly.

SERAFINA: Naw, they don't come to be friendly. They think
they know something that Serafina don't know; they think

I got *these* on my head! (*She holds her fingers like horns at either side of her forehead.*) Well, I ain't got them! (*She goes padding back out in front of the house. Father De Leo follows.*)

FATHER DE LEO: You called me this morning in distress over something.

SERAFINA: I called you this morning but now it is afternoon.

FATHER DE LEO: I had to christen the grandson of the Mayor.

SERAFINA: The Mayor's important people, not Serafina!

FATHER DE LEO: You don't come to confession.

SERAFINA (*starting back toward the porch*): No, I don't come, I don't go, I—Ohhh! (*She pulls up one foot and hops on the other.*)

FATHER DE LEO: You stepped on something?

SERAFINA (*dropping down on the steps*): No, no, no, no, no, I don't step on—noth'n . . .

FATHER DE LEO: Come in the house. We'll wash it with antiseptic. (*She lurches up and limps back toward the house.*) Walking barefooted you will get it infected.

SERAFINA: Fa niente . . .

(*At the top of the embankment a little boy runs out with a red kite and flourishes it in the air with rigid gestures, as though he were giving a distant signal. Serafina shades her eyes with a palm to watch the kite, and then, as though its motions conveyed a shocking message, she utters a startled soft cry and staggers back to the porch. She leans against a pillar, running her hand rapidly and repeatedly through her hair. Father De Leo approaches her again, somewhat timidly.*)

FATHER DE LEO: Serafina?

SERAFINA: Che, che, che cosa vuole?

FATHER DE LEO: I am thirsty. Will you go in the house and get me some water?

SERAFINA: Go in. Get you some water. The faucet is working.—I can't go in the house.

FATHER DE LEO: Why can't you go in the house?

SERAFINA: The house has a tin roof on it. I got to breathe.

FATHER DE LEO: You can breathe in the house.

SERAFINA: No, I can't breathe in the house. The house has a tin roof on it and I . . .

(*The Strega has been creeping through the cane-brake pretending to search for a chicken.*)

THE STREGA: Chick, chick, chick, chick, chick? (*She crouches to peer under the house.*)

SERAFINA: What's that? Is that the . . . ? Yes, the Strega! (*She picks up a flower pot containing a dead plant and crosses the yard.*) Strega! Strega! (*The Strega looks up, retreating a little.*) Yes, you, I mean you! You ain't look for no chick! Getta hell out of my yard! (*The Strega retreats, viciously muttering, back into the cane-brake. Serafina makes the protective sign of the horns with her fingers. The goat bleats.*)

FATHER DE LEO: You have no friends, Serafina.

SERAFINA: I don't want friends.

FATHER DE LEO: You are still a young woman. Eligible for—loving and—bearing again! I remember you dressed in pale blue silk at Mass one Easter morning, yes, like a lady wearing a—piece of the—weather! Oh, how proudly you walked, *too* proudly!—But now you crouch and shuffle about barefooted; you live like a convict, dressed in the rags of a convict. You have no companions; women you don't mix with. You . . .

SERAFINA: No, I don't mix with them women. (*glaring at the women on the embankment*) The dummies I got in my house, I mix with them better because they don't make up no lies!—What kind of women are them? (*mimicking fiercely*) "Eee, Papa, eeee, baby, eee, me, me, me! At thirty years old they got no more use for the letto matrimoniale, no. The big bed goes to the basement! They get little beds from Sears Roebuck and sleep on their bellies!

FATHER DE LEO: Attenzione!

SERAFINA: They make the life without glory. Instead of the heart they got the deep-freeze in the house. The men, they don't feel no glory, not in the house with them women; they go to the bars, fight in them, get drunk, get fat, put horns on the women because the women don't give them the love which is glory.—I did, I give him the glory. To me the big bed was beautiful like a religion. Now I lie on it with dreams, with memories only! But it is still beautiful to me and I don't believe that the man in my heart gave me horns! (*The women whisper.*) What, what are they saying? Does ev'rybody know something that I don't know?—No, all I want is a sign, a sign from Our Lady, to tell me the lie is a lie! And then I . . . (*The women laugh on the embankment. Serafina starts fiercely toward them. They scatter.*) Squeak, squeak, squawk, squawk! Hens—like water thrown on them! (*There is the sound of mocking laughter.*)

FATHER DE LEO: People are laughing at you on all the porches.

SERAFINA: I'm laughing, too. Listen to me, I'm laughing! (*She breaks into loud, false laughter, first from the porch, then from the foot of the embankment, then crossing in front of the house.*) Ha, ha, ha, ha, ha, ha, ha! Now ev'rybody is laughing. Ha, ha, ha, ha, ha, ha!

FATHER DE LEO: Zitta ora!—Think of your daughter.

SERAFINA (*understanding the word "daughter"*): You, *you* think of my daughter! Today you give out the diplomas, today at the high school you give out the prizes, diplomas! You give to my daughter a set of books call the Digest of Knowledge! What does she know? How to be cheap already?—Oh, yes, that is what to learn, how to be cheap and to cheat!—You know what they do at this high school? They ruin the girls there! They give the spring dance because the girls are man-crazy. And there at that dance my daughter goes with a sailor that has in his ear a gold ring! And pants so tight that a woman ought not to look at him! This morning, this morning she cuts with a knife her wrist if I don't let her go!—Now all of them gone to some island, they call it a picnic, all of them, gone in a—boat!

FATHER DE LEO: There *was* a school picnic, chaperoned by the teachers.

SERAFINA: Oh, lo so, lo so! The man-crazy old-maid teachers! —They all run wild on the island!

FATHER DE LEO: Serafina delle Rose! (*He picks up the chair by the back and hauls it to the porch when she starts to resume her seat.*)—I *command* you to go in the house.

SERAFINA: Go in the house? I will. I will go in the house if you will answer one question.—Will you answer one question?

FATHER DE LEO: I will if I know the answer.

SERAFINA: Aw, you know the answer!—You used to hear the confessions of my husband. (*She turns to face the priest.*)

FATHER DE LEO: Yes, I heard his confessions . . .

SERAFINA (*with difficulty*): Did he ever speak to you of a *woman*?

(*A child cries out and races across in front of the house. Father De Leo picks up his panama hat. Serafina paces slowly toward him. He starts away from the house.*)

SERAFINA (*rushing after him*): Aspettate! Aspettate un momento!

FATHER DE LEO (*fearfully, not looking at her*): Che volete?

SERAFINA: Rispondetemi! (*She strikes her breast.*) Did he speak of a woman to you?

FATHER DE LEO: You know better than to ask me such a question. I don't break the Church laws. The secrets of the confessional are sacred to me. (*He walks away.*)

SERAFINA (*pursuing and clutching his arm*): I got to know. You could tell me.

FATHER DE LEO: Let go of me, Serafina!

SERAFINA: Not till you tell me, Father. Father, you tell me, please tell me! Or I will go mad! (*in a fierce whisper*) I will go back in the house and smash the urn with the ashes—if you don't tell me! I will go mad with the doubt in my heart and I will smash the urn and scatter the ashes—of my husband's body!

FATHER DE LEO: What could I tell you? If you would not believe the known facts about him . . .

SERAFINA: Known facts, who knows the known facts?

(*The neighbor women have heard the argument and begin to crowd around, muttering in shocked whispers at Serafina's lack of respect.*)

FATHER DE LEO (*frightened*): Lasciatemi, lasciatemi stare!— Oh, Serafina, I am too old for this—please!—Everybody is . . .

SERAFINA (*in a fierce, hissing whisper*): Nobody knew my rose of the world but me and now they can lie because the rose ain't living. They want the marble urn broken; they want me to smash it. They want the rose ashes scattered because

I had too much glory. They don't want glory like *that* in nobody's heart. They want—mouse-squeaking!—known facts.—Who knows the known facts? You—padres—wear black because of the fact that the facts are known by nobody!

FATHER DE LEO: Oh, Serafina! There are people watching!

SERAFINA: Let them watch something. That will be a change for them.—It's been a long time I wanted to break out like this and now I . . .

FATHER DE LEO: I am too old a man; I am not strong enough. I am sixty-seven years old! Must I call for help, now?

SERAFINA: Yes, call! Call for help, but I won't let you go till you tell me!

FATHER DE LEO: You're not a respectable woman.

SERAFINA: No, I'm not a respectable; I'm a woman.

FATHER DE LEO: No, you are not a woman. You are an animal!

SERAFINA: Si, si, animale! Sono animale! Animale. Tell them all, shout it all to them, up and down the whole block! The widow Delle Rose is not respectable, she is not even a woman, she is an animal! She is attacking the priest! She will tear the black suit off him unless he tells her the whores in this town are lying to her!

(*The neighbor women have been drawing closer as the argument progresses, and now they come to Father De Leo's rescue and assist him to get away from Serafina, who is on the point of attacking him bodily. He cries out, "Officer! Officer!" but the women drag Serafina from him and lead him away with comforting murmurs.*)

SERAFINA (*striking her wrists together*): Yes, it's me, it's me!! Lock me up, lock me, lock me up! Or I will—*smash!*—the marble . . . (*She throws her head far back and presses her fists to her eyes. Then she rushes crazily to the steps and falls across them.*)

ASSUNTA: Serafina! Figlia! Figlia! Andiamo a casa!

SERAFINA: Leave me alone, old woman.

(*She returns slowly to the porch steps and sinks down on them, sitting like a tired man, her knees spread apart and her head cupped in her hands. The children steal back around the house. A little boy shoots a bean-shooter at her. She starts up with a cry. The children scatter, shrieking. She sinks back down on the steps, then leans back, staring up at the sky, her body rocking.*)

SERAFINA: Oh, Lady, Lady, Lady, give me a sign!

(*As if in mocking answer, a novelty salesman appears and approaches the porch. He is a fat man in a seersucker suit and a straw hat with a yellow, red and purple band. His face is beetred and great moons of sweat have soaked through the armpits of his jacket. His shirt is lavender, and his tie, pale blue with great yellow polka dots, is a butterfly bow. His entrance is accompanied by a brief, satiric strain of music.*)

THE SALESMAN: Good afternoon, lady. (*She looks up slowly. The salesman talks sweetly, as if reciting a prayer.*) I got a little novelty here which I am offering to just a few lucky people at what we call an introductory price. Know what I mean? Not a regular price but a price which is less than what it costs to manufacture the article, a price we are making for the sake of introducing the product in the Gulf Coast territory. Lady, this thing here that I'm droppin' right in youah lap is bigger than television; it's going to revolutionize the domestic life of America.—Now I don't do house to house canvassing. I sell directly to merchants but when I stopped over there to have my car serviced, I seen you taking the air on the steps and I thought I would just drop over and . . .

(*There is the sound of a big truck stopping on the highway, and a man's voice, Alvaro's, is heard, shouting.*)

ALVARO: Hey! Hey, you road hog!

THE SALESMAN (*taking a sample out of his bag*): Now, lady, this little article has a deceptive appearance. First of all, I want you to notice how *compact* it is. It takes up no more space than . . .

(*Alvaro comes down from the embankment. He is about twenty-five years old, dark and very goodlooking. He is one of those Mediterranean types that resemble glossy young bulls. He is short in stature, has a massively sculptural torso and bluish-black curls. His face and manner are clownish; he has a charming awkwardness. There is a startling, improvised air about him; he frequently seems surprised at his own speeches and actions, as though he had not at all anticipated them. At the moment when we first hear his voice the sound of a tim-pani begins, at first very pianissimo, but building up as he ap-proaches, till it reaches a vibrant climax with his appearance to Serafina beside the house.)*

ALVARO: Hey.

THE SALESMAN (*without glancing at him*): Hay is for horses! —Now, madam, you see what happens when I press this button?

(*The article explodes in Serafina's face. She slaps it away with an angry cry. At the same time Alvaro advances, trembling with rage, to the porch steps. He is sweating and stammering with pent-up fury at a world of frustrations which are tem-porarily localized in the gross figure of this salesman.*)

ALVARO: Hey, you! Come here! What the hell's the idea, back there at that curve? You make me drive off the highway!

THE SALESMAN (*to Serafina*): Excuse me for just one minute. (*He wheels menacingly about to face Alvaro.*) Is something giving you gas pains, Maccaroni?

ALVARO: My name is not Maccaroni.

THE SALESMAN: All right. Spaghetti.

ALVARO (*almost sobbing with passion*): I am not maccaroni. I am not spaghetti. I am a human being that drives a truck of bananas. I drive a truck of bananas for the Southern Fruit Company for a living, not to play cowboys and Indians on no highway with no rotten road hog. You got a 4-lane high-way between Pass Christian and here. I give you the sign to pass me. You tail me and give me the horn. You yell "Wop" at me and "Dago." "Move over, Wop, move over, Dago." Then at the goddam curve, you go pass me and make me drive off the highway and yell back "Son of a bitch of a Dago!" I don't like that, no, no! And I am glad you stop here. Take the cigar from your mouth, take out the cigar!

THE SALESMAN: Take it out for me, greaseball.

ALVARO: If I take it out I will push it down your throat. I got three dependents! If I fight, I get fired, but I will fight and get fired. Take out the cigar!

(*Spectators begin to gather at the edge of the scene. Serafina stares at the truck driver, her eyes like a somnambule's. All at once she utters a low cry and seems about to fall.*)

ALVARO: Take out the cigar, take out, take out the cigar!

(*He snatches the cigar from the salesman's mouth and the salesman brings his knee up violently into Alvaro's groin. Bending double and retching with pain, Alvaro staggers over to the porch.*)

THE SALESMAN (*shouting, as he goes off*): I got your license number, Maccaroni! I know your boss!

ALVARO (*howling*): Drop dead! (*He suddenly staggers up the steps.*) Lady, lady, I got to go in the house!

(*As soon as he enters, he bursts into rending sobs, leaning against a wall and shaking convulsively. The spectators outside laugh as they scatter. Serafina slowly enters the house. The screen door rasps loudly on its rusty springs as she lets it swing gradually shut behind her, her eyes remaining fixed with a look of stupefied wonder upon the sobbing figure of the truck driver. We must understand her profound unconscious response to this sudden contact with distress as acute as her own. There is a long pause as the screen door makes its whining, catlike noise swinging shut by degrees.*)

SERAFINA: Somebody's—in my house? (*finally, in a hoarse, tremulous whisper*) What are you—doing in here? Why have you—come in my house?

ALVARO: Oh, lady—leave me alone!—Please—now!

SERAFINA: You—got no business—in here . . .

ALVARO: I got to cry after a fight. I'm sorry, lady. I . . . (*The sobs still shake him. He leans on a dummy.*)

SERAFINA: Don't lean on my dummy. Sit down if you can't stand up.—What is the matter with you?

ALVARO: I always cry after a fight. But I don't want people to see me. It's not like a man. (*There is a long pause; Serafina's attitude seems to warm toward the man.*)

SERAFINA: A man is not no different from no one else . . .
(*All at once her face puckers up, and for the first time in the play Serafina begins to weep, at first soundlessly, then audibly. Soon she is sobbing as loudly as Alvaro. She speaks between sobs.*)—I always cry—when somebody else is crying . . .

ALVARO: No, no, lady, *don't* cry! Why should *you* cry? I will stop. I will stop in a minute. This is not like a man. I am ashame of myself. I will stop now; please, lady . . .

(*Still crouching a little with pain, a hand clasped to his abdomen, Alvaro turns away from the wall. He blows his nose between two fingers. Serafina picks up a scrap of white voile and gives it to him to wipe his fingers.*)

SERAFINA: Your jacket is torn.

ALVARO (*sobbing*): My company jacket is torn?

SERAFINA: Yes . . .

ALVARO: Where is it torn?

SERAFINA (*sobbing*): Down the—back.

ALVARO: Oh, Dio!

SERAFINA: Take it off. I will sew it up for you. I do—sewing.

ALVARO: Oh, Dio! (*sobbing*) I got three dependents! (*He holds up three fingers and shakes them violently at Serafina.*)

SERAFINA: Give me—give me your jacket.

ALVARO: He took down my license number!

SERAFINA: People are always taking down license numbers and telephone numbers and numbers that don't mean nothing—all them numbers . . .

ALVARO: Three, three dependents! Not citizens, even! No relief checks, no nothing! (*Serafina sobs.*) He is going to complain to the boss.

SERAFINA: I wanted to cry all day.

ALVARO: He said he would fire me if I don't stop fighting!

SERAFINA: Stop crying so I can stop crying.

ALVARO: I am a sissy. Excuse me. I am ashame.

SERAFINA: Don't be ashame of nothing, the world is too crazy for people to be ashame in it. I'm not ashame and I had two fights on the street and my daughter called me "disgusting." I got to sew this by hand; the machine is broke in a fight with two women.

ALVARO: That's what—they call a cat fight . . . (*He blows his nose.*)

SERAFINA: Open the shutters, please, for me. I can't see to work. (*She has crossed to her work table. He goes over to the window. As he opens the shutters, the light falls across his fine torso, the undershirt clinging wetly to his dark olive skin. Serafina is struck and murmurs: "Ohhh . . ." There is the sound of music.*)

ALVARO: What, lady?

SERAFINA (*in a strange voice*): The light on the body was like a man that lived here . . .

ALVARO: Che dice?

SERAFINA: Niente.—Ma com'è strano!—Lei è Napoletano? (*She is threading a needle.*)

ALVARO: Io sono Siciliano! (*Serafina sticks her finger with her needle and cries out.*) Che fa?

SERAFINA: I—stuck myself with the—needle!—You had—better wash up . . .

ALVARO: Dov'è il gabinetto?

SERAFINA (*almost inaudibly*): Dietro. (*She points vaguely back.*)

ALVARO: Con permesso! (*He moves past her. As he does so, she picks up a pair of broken spectacles on the work table. Holding them up by the single remaining side piece, like a lorgnette, she inspects his passing figure with an air of stupefaction. As he goes out, he says:*) A kick like that can have serious consequences! (*He goes into the back of the house.*)

SERAFINA (*after a pause*): Madonna Santa!—My *husband's body*, with the head of a *clown*! (*She crosses to the Madonna.*) O Lady, O Lady! (*She makes an imploring gesture.*) Speak to me!—What are you saying?—Please, Lady, I can't hear you! Is it a sign? Is it a sign of something? What does it mean? Oh, *speak to me*, Lady!—Everything is too strange!

(*She gives up the useless entreaty to the impassive statue. Then she rushes to the cupboard, clambers up on a chair and seizes a bottle of wine from the top shelf. But she finds it impossible to descend from the chair. Clasping the dusty bottle to her breast, she crouches there, helplessly whimpering like a child, as Alvaro comes back in.*)

ALVARO: Ciao!

SERAFINA: I can't get up.

ALVARO: You mean you can't get down?

SERAFINA: I mean I—can't get down . . .

ALVARO: Con permesso, Signora! (*He lifts her down from the chair.*)

SERAFINA: Grazie.

ALVARO: I am ashame of what happen. Crying is not like a man. Did anyone see me?

SERAFINA: Nobody saw you but me. To me it don't matter.

ALVARO: You are simpatica, molto!—It was not just the fight that makes me break down. I was like this all today! (*He shakes his clenched fists in the air.*)

SERAFINA: You and—me, too!—What was the trouble today?

ALVARO: My name is Mangiacavallo which means "Eat-a-horse." It's a comical name, I know. Maybe two thousand and seventy years ago one of my grandfathers got so hungry that he ate up a horse! That ain't my fault. Well, today at the Southern Fruit Company I find on the pay envelope not "Mangiacavallo" but "EAT A HORSE" in big print! Ha, ha, ha, very funny!—I open the pay envelope! In it I find a notice.—The wages have been *garnishee*! You know what garnishee is? (*Serafina nods gravely.*) Garnishee!—Eat a horse!—Road hog!—All in one day is too much! I go crazy, I boil, I cry, and I am ashame but I am not able to help it!—Even a Wop truck driver's a human being! And human beings must cry . . .

SERAFINA: Yes, they must cry. I couldn't cry all day but now I have cried and I am feeling much better.—I will sew up the jacket . . .

ALVARO (*licking his lips*): What is that in your hand? A bottle of vino?

SERAFINA: This is Spumanti. It comes from the house of the family of my husband. The Delle Rose! A very great family. I was a peasant, but I married a baron!—No, I still don't believe it! I married a baron when I didn't have shoes!

ALVARO: Excuse me for asking—but where is the Baron, now? (*Serafina points gravely to the marble urn.*) Where did you say?

SERAFINA: Them're his ashes in that marble urn.

ALVARO: Ma! Scusatemi! Scusatemi! (*crossing himself*)—I hope he is resting in peace.

SERAFINA: It's him you reminded me of—when you opened the shutters. Not the face but the body.—Please get me some ice from the icebox in the kitchen. I had a—very bad day . . .

ALVARO: Oh, ice! Yes—ice—I'll get some . . . (*As he goes out, she looks again through the broken spectacles at him.*)

SERAFINA: *Non posso crederlo!*—A clown of a face like that with my husband's body!

(*There is the sound of ice being chopped in the kitchen. She inserts a corkscrew in the bottle but her efforts to open it are clumsily unsuccessful. Alvaro returns with a little bowl of ice. He sets it down so hard on the table that a piece flies out. He scrambles after it, retrieves it and wipes it off on his sweaty undershirt.*)

SERAFINA: I think the floor would be cleaner!

ALVARO: Scusatemi!—I wash it again?

SERAFINA: Fa niente!

ALVARO: I am a—clean!—I . . .

SERAFINA: Fa niente, niente!—The bottle should be in the ice but the next best thing is to pour the wine over the bottle.

ALVARO: You mean over the ice?

SERAFINA: I mean over the . . .

ALVARO: Let me open the bottle. Your hands are not used to rough work. (*She surrenders the bottle to him and regards him through the broken spectacles again.*)

SERAFINA: These little bits of white voile on the floor are not from a snowstorm. I been making voile dresses for high school graduation.—One for my daughter and for thirteen other girls.—All of the work I'm not sure didn't kill me!

ALVARO: The wine will make you feel better.

(*There is a youthful cry from outside.*)

SERAFINA: There is a wild bunch of boys and girls in this town. In Sicily the boys would dance with the boys because a girl and a boy could not dance together unless they was going to be married. But here they run wild on islands!— boys, girls, man-crazy teachers . . .

ALVARO: Ecco! (*The cork comes off with a loud pop. Serafina cries out and staggers against the table. He laughs. She laughs with him, helplessly, unable to stop, unable to catch her breath.*)—I like a woman that laughs with all her heart.

SERAFINA: And a woman that cries with her heart?

ALVARO: I like everything that a woman does with her heart.

(*Both are suddenly embarrassed and their laughter dies out. Serafina smooths down her rayon slip. He hands her a glass of the sparkling wine with ice in it. She murmurs "Grazie."*)

(*Unconsciously the injured finger is lifted again to her lip and she wanders away from the table with the glass held shakily.*)

ALVARO (*continuing nervously*): I see you had a bad day.

SERAFINA: Sono così—stanca . . .

ALVARO (*suddenly springing to the window and shouting*): Hey, you kids, git down off that truck! Keep your hands off them bananas! (*At the words "truck" and "bananas" Serafina gasps again and spills some wine on her slip.*) Little buggers!—Scusatemi . . .

SERAFINA: You haul—you haul bananas?

ALVARO: Si, Signora.

SERAFINA: Is it a 10-ton truck?

ALVARO: An 8-ton truck.

SERAFINA: My husband hauled bananas in a 10-ton truck.

ALVARO: Well, he was a baron.

SERAFINA: Do you haul just bananas?

ALVARO: Just bananas. What else would I haul?

SERAFINA: My husband hauled bananas, but underneath the bananas was something else. He was—wild like a—Gypsy. —"Wild—like a—Gypsy?" Who said that?—I hate to start to remember, and then not remember . . .

(*The dialogue between them is full of odd hesitations, broken sentences and tentative gestures. Both are nervously exhausted after their respective ordeals. Their fumbling communication has a curious intimacy and sweetness, like the meeting of two lonely children for the first time. It is oddly luxurious to them both, luxurious as the first cool wind of evening after a scorching day. Serafina idly picks up a little Sicilian souvenir cart from a table.*)

SERAFINA: The priest was against it.

ALVARO: What was the priest against?

SERAFINA: Me keeping the ashes. It was against the Church law. But I had to have something and that was all I could have. (*She sets down the cart.*)

ALVARO: I don't see nothing wrong with it.

SERAFINA: You don't?

ALVARO: No! Niente!—The body would've decayed, but ashes always stay clean.

SERAFINA (*eagerly*): Si, si, bodies decay, but ashes always stay clean! Come here. I show you this picture—my wedding. (*She removes a picture tenderly from the wall.*) Here's me a bride of fourteen, and this—this—*this!* (*drumming the picture with her finger and turning her face to Alvaro with great lustrous eyes*) My *husband!* (*There is a pause. He takes the picture from her hand and holds it first close to his eyes, then far back, then again close with suspirations of appropriate awe.*) Annnh?—Annnnh?—Che dice!

ALVARO (*slowly, with great emphasis*): Che bell' uomo! Che bell' uomo!

SERAFINA (*replacing the picture*): A rose of a man. On his chest he had the tattoo of a rose. (*then, quite suddenly*)— Do you believe strange things, or do you doubt them?

ALVARO: If strange things didn't happen, I wouldn't be here. You wouldn't be here. We wouldn't be talking together.

SERAFINA: Davvero! I'll tell you something about the tattoo of my husband. My husband, he had this rose tattoo on his chest. One night I woke up with a burning pain on me here. I turn on the light. I look at my naked breast and on it I see the rose tattoo of my husband, on me, on *my* breast, *his* tattoo.

ALVARO: Strano!

SERAFINA: And that was the night that—I got to speak frankly to tell you . . .

ALVARO: Speak frankly! We're grown-up people.

SERAFINA: That was the night I conceived my son—the little boy that was lost when I lost my husband . . .

ALVARO: Che cosa—strana!—Would you be willing to show me the rose tattoo?

SERAFINA: Oh, it's gone now, it only lasted a moment. But I did see it. I saw it clearly.—Do you believe me?

ALVARO: Lo credo!

SERAFINA: I don't know why I told you. But I like what you said. That bodies decay but ashes always stay clean—immacolate!—But, you know, there are some people that want to make everything dirty. Two of them kind of people come in the house today and told me a terrible lie in front of the ashes.—So awful a lie that if I thought it was true—I would smash the urn—and throw the ashes away! (*She hurls her glass suddenly to the floor.*) Smash it, *smash it like that!*

ALVARO: Ma!—Baronessa!

(*Serafina seizes a broom and sweeps the fragments of glass away.*)

SERAFINA: And take this broom and sweep them out the back door like so much trash!

ALVARO (*impressed by her violence and a little awed*): What lie did they tell you?

SERAFINA: No, no, no! I don't want to talk about it! (*She throws down the broom.*) I just want to forget it; it wasn't true, it was false, false, false!—as the hearts of the bitches that told it . . .

ALVARO: Yes. I would forget anything that makes you unhappy.

SERAFINA: The memory of a love don't make you unhappy unless you believe a lie that makes it dirty. I don't believe in the lie. The ashes are clean. The memory of the rose in my heart is perfect!—Your glass is weeping . . .

ALVARO: *Your* glass is weeping too.

(*While she fills his glass, he moves about the room, looking here and there. She follows him. Each time he picks up an article for inspection she gently takes it from him and examines it herself with fresh interest.*)

ALVARO: Cozy little homelike place you got here.

SERAFINA: Oh, it's—molto modesto.—You got a nice place too?

ALVARO: I got a place with three dependents in it.

SERAFINA: What—dependents?

ALVARO (*counting them on his fingers*): One old maid sister, one feeble-minded grandmother, one lush of a pop that's not worth the powder it takes to blow him to hell.—They got the parchesi habit. They play the game of parchesi, morning, night, noon. Passing a bucket of beer around the table . . .

SERAFINA: They got the beer habit, too?

ALVARO: Oh, yes. And the numbers habit. This spring the old maid sister gets female trouble—mostly mental, I think—she turns the housekeeping over to the feeble-minded grandmother, a very sweet old lady who don't think it is necessary to pay the grocery bill so long as there's money to play the numbers. She plays the numbers. She has a perfect system except it don't ever work. And the grocery bill goes up, up, up, up, up!—so high you can't even see it!—Today the Ideal Grocery Company garnishees my wages . . . There, now! I've told you my life . . . (*The parrot squawks. He goes over to the cage.*) Hello, Polly, how's tricks?

SERAFINA: The name ain't Polly. It ain't a she; it's a he.

ALVARO: How can you tell with all them tail feathers? (*He sticks his finger in the cage, pokes at the parrot and gets bitten.*) Owww!

SERAFINA (*vicariously*): Ouuu . . . (*Alvaro sticks his injured finger in his mouth. Serafina puts her corresponding finger in her mouth. He crosses to the telephone.*) I told you watch out.—What are you calling, a doctor?

ALVARO: I am calling my boss in Biloxi to explain why I'm late.

SERAFINA: The call to Biloxi is a ten-cent call.

ALVARO: Don't worry about it.

SERAFINA: I'm not worried about it. You will pay it.

ALVARO: You got a sensible attitude toward life . . . Give me the Southern Fruit Company in Biloxi—seven-eight-seven!

SERAFINA: You are a bachelor. With three dependents? (*She glances below his belt.*)

ALVARO: I'll tell you my hopes and dreams!

SERAFINA: Who? Me?

ALVARO: I am hoping to meet some sensible older lady. Maybe a lady a little bit older than me.—I don't care if she's a little too plump or not such a stylish dresser! (*Serafina self-consciously pulls up a dangling strap.*) The important thing in a lady is understanding. Good sense. And I want her to have a well-furnished house and a profitable little business of some kind . . . (*He looks about him significantly.*)

SERAFINA: And such a lady, with a well-furnished house and business, what does she want with a man with three dependents with the parchesi and the beer habit, playing the numbers!

ALVARO: Love and affection!—in a world that is lonely—and cold!

SERAFINA: It might be lonely but I would not say "cold" on this particular day!

ALVARO: Love and affection is what I got to offer on hot or cold days in this lonely old world and is what I am looking for. I got nothing else. Mangiacavallo has nothing. In fact, he is the grandson of the village idiot of Ribera!

SERAFINA (*uneasily*): I see you like to make—jokes!

ALVARO: No, no joke!—Davvero!—He chased my grandmother in a flooded rice field. She slip on a wet rock.—Ecco! Here I am.

SERAFINA: You ought to be more respectful.

ALVARO: What have I got to respect? The rock my grandmother slips on?

SERAFINA: Yourself at least! Don't you work for a living?

ALVARO: If I *don't* work for a living I would respect myself *more*. Baronessa, I am a healthy young man, existing without no love life. I look at the magazine pictures. Them girls in the advertisement—you know what I mean? A little bitty thing here? A little bitty thing there?

(*He touches two portions of his anatomy. The latter portion embarrasses Serafina, who quietly announces:*)

SERAFINA: The call is ten cents for three minutes. Is the line busy?

ALVARO: Not the line, but the boss.

SERAFINA: And the charge for the call goes higher. That ain't the phone of a millionaire you're using!

ALVARO: I think you talk a poor mouth. (*He picks up the piggy bank and shakes it.*) This pig sounds well-fed to me.

SERAFINA: Dimes and quarters.

ALVARO: Dimes and quarters're better than nickels and dimes. (*Serafina rises severely and removes the piggy bank from his grasp.*) Ha, ha, ha! You think I'm a bank robber?

SERAFINA: I think you are maleducato! Just get your boss on the phone or hang the phone up.

ALVARO: What, what! Mr. Siccardi? How tricks at the Southern Fruit Comp'ny this hot afternoon? Ha, ha, ha!—Mangiacavallo!—What? You got the complaint already? Sentite, per favore! This road hog was—Mr. Siccardi? (*He jiggles the hook; then slowly hangs up.*) A man with three dependents!—out of a job . . . (*There is a pause.*)

SERAFINA: Well, you better ask the operator the charges.

ALVARO: Oofla! A man with three dependents—out of a job!

SERAFINA: I can't see to work no more. I got a suggestion to make. Open the bottom drawer of that there bureau and you will find a shirt in white tissue paper and you can wear that one while I am fixing this. And call for it later. (*He crosses to the bureau.*)—It was made for somebody that never called for it. (*He removes the package.*) Is there a name pinned to it?

ALVARO: Yes, it's . . .

SERAFINA (*fiercely, but with no physical movement*): Don't tell me the name! Throw it away, out the window!

ALVARO: Perchè?

SERAFINA: Throw it, throw it away!

ALVARO (*crumpling the paper and throwing it through the window*): Ecco fatto! (*There is a distant cry of children as he unwraps the package and holds up the rose silk shirt, exclaiming in Latin delight at the luxury of it.*) Colore di rose! Seta! Seta pura!—Oh, this shirt is too good for Mangiacavallo! Everything here is too good for Mangiacavallo!

SERAFINA: Nothing's too good for a man if the man is good.

ALVARO: The grandson of a village idiot is not that good.

SERAFINA: No matter whose grandson you are, put it on; you are welcome to wear it.

ALVARO (*slipping voluptuously into the shirt*): Sssssssss!

SERAFINA: How does it feel, the silk, on you?

ALVARO: It feels like a girl's hands on me! (*There is a pause, while he shows her the whiteness of his teeth.*)

SERAFINA (*holding up her broken spectacles*): It will make you less trouble.

ALVARO: There is nothing more beautiful than a gift between people!—Now you are smiling!—You like me a little bit better?

SERAFINA (*slowly and tenderly*): You know what they should of done when you was a baby? They should of put tape on your ears to hold them back so when you grow up they wouldn't stick out like the wings of a little kewpie! (*She touches his ear, a very slight touch, betraying too much of her heart. Both laugh a little and she turns away, embarrassed.*)

(*Outside the goat bleats and there is the sound of splintering timber. One of the children races into the front yard, crying out.*)

SALVATORE: Mizz' Dell' Rose! The black goat's in your yard!

SERAFINA: Il becco della strega!

(*Serafina dashes to the window, throws the shutters violently open and leans way out. This time, she almost feels relief in this distraction. The interlude of the goat chase has a quality of crazed exaltation. Outside is heard the wild bleating of the goat and the jingling of his harness.*)

SERAFINA: Miei pomodori! Guarda i miei pomodori!

THE STREGA (*entering the front yard with a broken length of rope, calling out*): Heyeh, Billy! Heyeh. Heyeh, Billy!

SERAFINA (*making the sign of horns with her fingers*): There is the Strega! She lets the goat in my yard to eat my tomatoes! (*backing from the window*) She has the eye; she has the malocchio, and so does the goat! The goat has the evil eye, too. He got in my yard the night that I lost Rosario and my boy! Madonna, Madonna mia! Get that goat out of my yard! (*She retreats to the Madonna, making the sign of the horns with her fingers, while the goat chase continues outside.*)

ALVARO: Now take it easy! I will catch the black goat and give him a kick that he will never forget!

(*Alvaro runs out the front door and joins in the chase. The little boy is clapping together a pair of tin pan lids which sound like cymbals. The effect is weird and beautiful with the wild cries of the children and the goat's bleating. Serafina*) *remains anxiously half way between the shutters and the protecting Madonna. She gives a furious imitation of the bleating goat, contorting her face with loathing. It is the fury of woman at the desire she suffers. At last the goat is captured.*)

BRUNO: Got him, got him, got him!

ALVARO: Vieni presto, Diavolo!

(*Alvaro appears around the side of the house with a tight hold on the broken rope around the goat's neck. The boy follows behind, gleefully clapping the tin lids together, and further back follows the Strega, holding her broken length of rope, her grey hair hanging into her face and her black skirts caught up in one hand, revealing bare feet and hairy legs. Serafina comes out on the porch as the grotesque little procession passes before it, and she raises her hand with the fingers making horns as the goat and the Strega pass her. Alvaro turns the goat over to the Strega and comes panting back to the house.*)

ALVARO: Niente paura!—I got to go now.—You have been troppo gentile, Mrs. . . .

SERAFINA: I am the widow of the Baron Delle Rose.—Excuse the way I'm—not dressed . . . (*He keeps hold of her hand as he stands on the porch steps. She continues very shyly, panting a little.*) I am not always like this.—Sometimes I fix myself up!—When my husband was living, when my husband comes home, when he was living—I had a clean dress on! And sometimes even, I—put a rose in my hair . . .

ALVARO: A rose in your hair would be pretty!

SERAFINA: But for a widow—it ain't the time of roses . . .

(*The sound of music is heard, of a mandolin playing.*)

ALVARO: Naw, you make a mistake! It's always for everybody the time of roses! The rose is the heart of the world like the heart is the—heart of the—body! But you, Baronessa—you know what I think you have done?

SERAFINA: What—what have I—done?

ALVARO: You have put your heart in the marble urn with the ashes. (*Now singing is heard along with the music, which continues to the end of the scene.*) And if in a storm sometime, or sometime when a 10-ton truck goes down the highway—the marble urn was to *break!* (*He suddenly points up at the sky.*) Look! Look, Baronessa!

SERAFINA (*startled*): Look? Look? I don't see!

ALVARO: I was pointing at your heart, broken out of the urn and away from the ashes!—*Rondinella felice!* (*He makes an airy gesture toward the fading sky.*)

SERAFINA: Oh! (*He whistles like a bird and makes graceful winglike motions with his hands.*) Buffone, buffone—piantatela! I take you serious—then you make it a joke . . . (*She smiles involuntarily at his antics.*)

ALVARO: When can I bring the shirt back?

SERAFINA: When do you pass by again?

ALVARO: I will pass by tonight for supper. Volete?

SERAFINA: Then look at the window tonight. If the shutters are open and there is a light in the window, you can stop by for your—jacket—but if the shutters are closed, you better not stop because my Rosa will be home. Rosa's my daughter. She has gone to a picnic—maybe—home early— but you know how picnics are. They—wait for the moon to—start singing.—Not that there's nothing wrong in two grown-up people having a quiet conversation!—but Rosa's fifteen—I got to be careful to set her a perfect example.

ALVARO: I will look at the window.—I will look at the win-dooow! (*He imitates a bird flying off with gay whistles.*)

SERAFINA: Buffone!

ALVARO (*shouting from outside*): Hey, you little buggers, climb down off that truck! Lay offa them bananas!

(*His truck is heard starting and pulling away. Serafina stands motionless on the porch, searching the sky with her eyes.*)

SERAFINA: Rosario, forgive me! Forgive me for thinking the awful lie could be true!

(*The light in the house dims out. A little boy races into the yard holding triumphantly aloft a great golden bunch of bananas. A little girl pursues him with shrill cries. He eludes her. They dash around the house. The light fades and the curtain falls.*)

ACT THREE

It is the evening of the same day. The neighborhood children are playing games around the house. One of them is counting by fives to a hundred, calling out the numbers, as he leans against the palm tree.

Serafina is in the parlor, sitting on the sofa. She is seated stiffly and formally, wearing a gown that she has not worn since the death of her husband, and with a rose in her hair. It becomes obvious from her movements that she is wearing a girdle that constricts her unendurably.

(There is the sound of a truck approaching up on the highway. Serafina rises to an odd, crouching position. But the truck passes by without stopping. The girdle is becoming quite intolerable to Serafina and she decides to take it off, going behind the sofa to do so. With much grunting, she has gotten it down as far as her knees, when there is the sound outside of another truck approaching. This time the truck stops up on the highway, with a sound of screeching brakes. She realizes that Alvaro is coming, and her efforts to get out of the girdle, which is now pinioning her legs, become frantic. She hobbles from behind the sofa as Alvaro appears in front of the house.)

ALVARO (*gaily*): Rondinella felice! I will look at win-dooooo! Signora delle Rose!

(Serafina's response to this salutation is a groan of anguish. She hobbles and totters desperately to the curtains between the rooms and reaches them just in time to hide herself as Alvaro comes into the parlor from the porch through the screen door. He is carrying a package and a candy box.)

ALVARO: C'è nessuno?

SERAFINA (*at first inaudibly*): Si, si, sono qui. (*then loudly and hoarsely, as she finally gets the girdle off her legs*) Si, si, sono qui! (*To cover her embarrassment, she busies herself with fixing wine glasses on a tray.*)

ALVARO: I hear the rattle of glasses! Let me help you! (*He goes eagerly through the curtain but stops short, astonished.*)

SERAFINA: Is—something the—matter?

ALVARO: I didn't expect to see you looking so pretty! You are a *young* little widow!

SERAFINA: You are—fix yourself up . . .

ALVARO: I been to The Ideal Barber's! I got the whole works!

SERAFINA (*faintly, retreating from him a little*): You got—rose oil—in your hair . . .

ALVARO: Olio di rose! You like the smell of it? (*Outside there is a wild, distant cry of children, and inside a pause. Serafina shakes her head slowly with the infinite wound of a recollection.*)—You—*don't*—like—the smell of it? Oh, then I wash the smell *out*, I go and . . . (*He starts toward the back. She raises her hand to stop him.*)

SERAFINA: No, no, no, fa—niente.—I—*like* the smell of it . . .

(*A little boy races into the yard, ducks some invisible missile, sticks out his tongue and yells: "Yahhhhh!" Then he dashes behind the house.*)

SERAFINA: Shall we—set down in the parlor?

ALVARO: I guess that's better than standing up in the dining room. (*He enters formally.*)—Shall we set down on the sofa?

SERAFINA: You take the sofa. I will set down on this chair.

ALVARO (*disappointed*): You don't like to set on a sofa?

SERAFINA: I lean back too far on that sofa. I like a straight back behind me . . .

ALVARO: That chair looks not comfortable to me.

SERAFINA: This chair is a comfortable chair.

ALVARO: But it's more easy to talk with two on a sofa!

SERAFINA: I talk just as good on a chair as I talk on a sofa . . .
(*There is a pause. Alvaro nervously hitches his shoulder.*) Why do you hitch your shoulders like that?

ALVARO: Oh, that!—That's a—nervous—habit . . .

SERAFINA: I thought maybe the suit don't fit you good . . .

ALVARO: I bought this suit to get married in four years ago.

SERAFINA: But didn't get married?

ALVARO: I give her, the girl, a zircon instead of a diamond. She had it examined. The door was slammed in my face.

SERAFINA: I think that maybe I'd do the same thing myself.

ALVARO: Buy the zircon?

SERAFINA: No, slam the door.

ALVARO: Her eyes were not sincere looking. You've got sincere looking eyes. Give me your hand so I can tell your fortune! (*She pushes her chair back from him.*) I see two men in your life. One very handsome. One not handsome. His ears are too big but not as big as his heart! He has three dependents.—In fact he has four dependents! Ha, ha, ha!

SERAFINA: What is the fourth dependent?

ALVARO: The one that every man's got, his biggest expense, worst troublemaker and chief liability! Ha, ha, ha!

SERAFINA: I hope you are not talking vulgar. (*She rises and turns her back to him. Then she discovers the candy box.*) What's that fancy red box?

ALVARO: A present I bought for a nervous but nice little lady!

SERAFINA: Chocolates? Grazie! Grazie! But I'm too fat.

ALVARO: You are not fat, you are just pleasing and plump. (*He reaches way over to pinch the creamy flesh of her upper arm.*)

SERAFINA: No, please. Don't make me nervous. If I get nervous again I will start to cry . . .

ALVARO: Let's talk about something to take your mind off your troubles. You say you got a young daughter?

SERAFINA (*in a choked voice*): Yes. I got a young daughter. Her name is Rosa.

ALVARO: Rosa, Rosa! She's pretty?

SERAFINA: She has the eyes of her father, and his wild, stubborn blood! Today was the day of her graduation from high school. She looked so pretty in a white voile dress with a great big bunch of—roses . . .

ALVARO: Not no prettier than her Mama, I bet—with that rose in your hair!

SERAFINA: She's only fifteen.

ALVARO: Fifteen?

SERAFINA (*smoothing her blue silk lap with a hesitant hand*): Yes, only fifteen . . .

ALVARO: But has a boyfriend, does she?

SERAFINA: She met a sailor.

ALVARO: Oh, Dio! No wonder you seem to be nervous.

SERAFINA: I didn't want to let her go out with this sailor. He had a gold ring in his ear.

ALVARO: Madonna Santa!

SERAFINA: This morning she cut her wrist—not much but enough to bleed—with a kitchen knife!

ALVARO: Tch, tch! A very wild girl!

SERAFINA: I had to give in and let her bring him to see me. He said he was Catholic. I made him kneel down in front of Our Lady there and give Her his promise that he would respect the innocence of my Rosa!—But how do I know that he was a Catholic, *really*?

ALVARO (*taking her hand*): Poor little worried lady! But you got to face facts. Sooner or later the innocence of your daughter cannot be respected.—Did he—have a—tattoo?

SERAFINA (*startled*): Did who have—what?

ALVARO: The sailor friend of your daughter, did he have a tattoo?

SERAFINA: Why do you ask me that?

ALVARO: Just because most sailors have a tattoo.

SERAFINA: How do I know if he had a tattoo or not!

ALVARO: *I* got a tattoo!

SERAFINA: *You* got a tattoo?

ALVARO: Si, si, veramente!

SERAFINA: What kind of tattoo you got?

ALVARO: What kind you think?

SERAFINA: Oh, I think—you have got—a South Sea girl without clothes on . . .

ALVARO: No South Sea girl.

SERAFINA: Well, maybe a big red heart with MAMA written across it.

ALVARO: Wrong again, Baronessa.

(*He takes off his tie and slowly unbuttons his shirt, gazing at her with an intensely warm smile. He divides the unbuttoned shirt, turning toward her his bare chest. She utters a gasp and rises.*)

SERAFINA: No, no, no!—*Not a rose!* (*She says it as if she were evading her feelings.*)

ALVARO: Si, si, una rosa!

SERAFINA: I—don't feel good! The air is . . .

ALVARO: Che fate, che fate, che dite?

SERAFINA: The house has a tin roof on it!—The air is—I got to go outside the house to breathe! Scu—scusatemi! (*She goes out onto the porch and clings to one of the spindling porch columns for support, breathing hoarsely with a hand to her throat. He comes out slowly.*)

ALVARO (*gently*): I didn't mean to surprise you!—Mi dispiace molto!

SERAFINA (*with enforced calm*): Don't—talk about it! Anybody could have a rose tattoo.—It don't mean nothing.—You know how a tin roof is. It catches the heat all day and it don't cool off until—midnight . . .

ALVARO: No, no, not until midnight. (*She makes a faint laughing sound, is quite breathless and leans her forehead against the porch column. He places his fingers delicately against the small of her back.*) It makes it hot in the bedroom—so that you got to sleep without nothing on you . . .

SERAFINA: No, you—can't stand the covers . . .

ALVARO: You can't even stand a—*nightgown!* (*His fingers press her back.*)

SERAFINA: Please. There is a strega next door; she's always watching!

ALVARO: It's been so long since I felt the soft touch of a woman! (*She gasps loudly and turns to the door.*) Where are you going?

SERAFINA: I'm going back in the house! (*She enters the parlor again, still with forced calm.*)

ALVARO (*following her inside*): Now, now, what is the matter?

SERAFINA: I got a feeling like I have—forgotten something.

ALVARO: What?

SERAFINA: I can't remember.

ALVARO: It couldn't be nothing important if you can't remember. Let's open the chocolate box and have some candy.

SERAFINA (*eager for any distraction*): Yes! Yes, open the box!

(*Alvaro places a chocolate in her hand. She stares at it blankly.*)

ALVARO: Eat it, eat the chocolate. If you don't eat it, it will melt in your hand and make your fingers all gooey!

SERAFINA: Please, I . . .

ALVARO: Eat it!

SERAFINA (*weakly and gagging*): I can't, I can't, I would choke! Here, you eat it.

ALVARO: Put it in my mouth! (*She puts the chocolate in his mouth.*) Now, look. Your fingers are gooey!

SERAFINA: Oh!—I better go wash them! (*She rises unsteadily. He seizes her hands and licks her fingers.*)

ALVARO: Mmmm! Mmmmm! Good, very good!

SERAFINA: Stop that, stop that, stop that! That—ain't— nice . . .

ALVARO: I'll lick off the chocolate for you.

SERAFINA: No, no, no!—I am the mother of a fifteen-year-old girl!

ALVARO: You're as old as your arteries, Baronessa. Now set back down. The fingers are now white as snow!

SERAFINA: You don't—understand—how I feel . . .

ALVARO: You don't understand how *I* feel.

SERAFINA (*doubtfully*): How do you—feel? (*In answer, he stretches the palms of his hands out toward her as if she were a fireplace in a freezing-cold room.*)—What does—that— mean?

ALVARO: The night is warm but I feel like my hands are— freezing!

SERAFINA: Bad—circulation . . .

ALVARO: No, too *much* circulation! (*Alvaro becomes tremulously pleading, shuffling forward a little, slightly crouched like a beggar.*) Across the room I feel the sweet warmth of a lady!

SERAFINA (*retreating, doubtfully*): Oh, you talk a sweet mouth. I think you talk a sweet mouth to fool a woman.

ALVARO: No, no, I know—I know that's what warms the world, that is what makes it the summer! (*He seizes the hand she hold defensively before her and presses it to his own breast in a crushing grip.*) Without it, the rose—the rose would not grow on the bush; the fruit would not grow on the tree!

SERAFINA: I know, and the truck—the truck would not haul the bananas! But, Mr. Mangiacavallo, that is my hand, not a sponge. I got bones in it. Bones break!

ALVARO: Scusatemi, Baronessa! (*He returns her hand to her with a bow.*) For me it is winter, because I don't have in my life the sweet warmth of a lady. I live with my hands in my pockets! (*He stuffs his hands violently into his pants' pockets, then jerks them out again. A small cellophane-wrapped disk falls on the floor, escaping his notice, but not Serafina's.*)—You don't like the poetry!—How can a man talk to you?

SERAFINA (*ominously*): I like the poetry good. Is that a piece of the poetry that you dropped out of your pocket? (*He looks down.*)—No, no, right by your foot!

ALVARO (*aghast as he realizes what it is that she has seen*): Oh, that's—that's nothing! (*He kicks it under the sofa.*)

SERAFINA (*fiercely*): You talk a sweet mouth about women. Then drop such a thing from your pocket?—Va via, vigliacco! (*She marches grandly out of the room, pulling the curtains together behind her. He hangs his head despairingly between his hands. Then he approaches the curtains timidly.*)

ALVARO (*in a small voice*): Baronessa?

SERAFINA: Pick up what you dropped on the floor and go to the Square Roof with it. Buona notte!

ALVARO: Baronessa! (*He parts the curtains and peeks through them.*)

SERAFINA: I told you good night. Here is no casa privata. Io, non sono puttana!

ALVARO: Understanding is—very—necessary!

SERAFINA: I understand plenty. You think you got a good thing, a thing that is cheap!

ALVARO: You make a mistake, Baronessa! (*He comes in and drops to his knees beside her, pressing his cheek to her flank. He speaks rhapsodically.*) So soft is a lady! So, so, so, so, so soft—is a lady!

SERAFINA: Andate via, sporcaccione, andate a casa! Lasciatemi! Lasciatemi stare!

(*She springs up and runs into the parlor. He pursues. The chase is grotesquely violent and comic. A floor lamp is overturned. She seizes the chocolate box and threatens to slam it into his face if he continues toward her. He drops to his knees, crouched way over, and pounds the floor with his fists, sobbing.*)

ALVARO: Everything in my life turns out like this!

SERAFINA: Git up, git up, git up!—you village idiot's grand-son! There is people watching you through that window, the—strega next door . . . (*He rises slowly.*) And where is the shirt that I loaned you? (*He shuffles abjectly across the room, then hands her a neatly wrapped package.*)

ALVARO: My sister wrapped it up for you.—My sister was very happy I met this *nice* lady!

SERAFINA: Maybe she thinks I will pay the grocery bill while she plays the numbers!

ALVARO: She don't think nothing like that. She is an old maid, my sister. She wants—nephews—nieces . . .

SERAFINA: You tell her for me I don't give nephews and nieces!

(*Alvaro hitches his shoulders violently in his embarrassment and shuffles over to where he had left his hat. He blows the dust off it and rubs the crown on his sleeve. Serafina presses a knuckle to her lips as she watches his awkward gestures. She is a little abashed by his humility. She speaks next with the great dignity of a widow whose respectability has stood the test.*)

SERAFINA: Now, Mr. Mangiacavallo, please tell me the truth about something. *When* did you get the tattoo put on your chest?

ALVARO (*shyly and sadly, looking down at his hat*): I got it tonight—after supper . . .

SERAFINA: That's what I thought. You had it put on because I told you about my husband's tattoo.

ALVARO: I wanted to be—close to you . . . to make you—happy . . .

SERAFINA: Tell it to the marines! (*He puts on his hat with an apologetic gesture.*) You got the tattoo and the chocolate box after supper, and then you come here to fool me!

ALVARO: I got the chocolate box a long time ago.

SERAFINA: How long ago? If that is not too much a personal question!

ALVARO: I got it the night the door was slammed in my face by the girl that I give—the zircon . . .

SERAFINA: Let that be a lesson. Don't try to fool women. You are not smart enough!—Now take the shirt back. You can keep it.

ALVARO: Huh?

SERAFINA: Keep it. I don't want it back.

ALVARO: You just now said that you did.

SERAFINA: It's a man's shirt, ain't it?

ALVARO: You just now accused me of trying to steal it off you.

SERAFINA: Well, you been making me nervous!

ALVARO: Is it my fault you been a widow too long?

SERAFINA: You make a mistake!

ALVARO: *You* make a mistake!

SERAFINA: Both of us make a mistake!

(*There is a pause. They both sigh profoundly.*)

ALVARO: We should of have been friends, but I think we meet the wrong day.—Suppose I go out and come in the door again and we start all over?

SERAFINA: No, I think it's no use. The day was wrong to begin with, because of two women. Two women, they told me today that my husband had put on my head the nanny-goat's horns!

ALVARO: How is it possible to put horns on a widow?

SERAFINA: That was before, before! They told me my husband was having a steady affair with a woman at the Square Roof. What was the name on the shirt, on the slip of paper? Do you remember the name?

ALVARO: You told me to . . .

SERAFINA: Tell me! Do you remember?

ALVARO: I remember the name because I know the woman. The name was Estelle Hohengarten.

SERAFINA: Take me there! Take me to the Square Roof!—Wait, wait!

(*She plunges into the dining room, snatches a knife out of the sideboard drawer and thrusts it in her purse. Then she rushes back, with the blade of the knife protruding from the purse.*)

ALVARO (*noticing the knife*): They—got a cover charge there . . .

SERAFINA: I will charge them a cover! Take me there now, this minute!

ALVARO: The fun don't start till midnight.

SERAFINA: I will start the fun sooner.

ALVARO: The floor show commences at midnight.

SERAFINA: I will commence it! (*She rushes to the phone.*) Yellow Cab, please, Yellow Cab. I want to go to the Square Roof out of my house! Yes, you come to my house and take me to the Square Roof right this minute! My number is— what is my number? Oh my God, what is my number?—64 is my number on Front Street! Subito, subito—quick!

(*The goat bleats outside.*)

ALVARO: Baronessa, the knife's sticking out of your purse. (*He grabs the purse.*) What do you want with this weapon?

SERAFINA: To cut the lying tongue out of a woman's mouth! Saying she has on her breast the tattoo of my husband because he had put on me the horns of a goat! I cut the heart out of that woman, she cut the heart out of me!

ALVARO: Nobody's going to cut the heart out of nobody!

(*A car is heard outside, and Serafina rushes to the porch.*)

SERAFINA (*shouting*): Hey, Yellow Cab, Yellow Cab, Yellow— Cab . . . (*The car passes by without stopping. With a sick moan she wanders into the yard. He follows her with a glass of wine.*)—Something hurts—in my heart . . .

ALVARO (*leading her gently back to the house*): Baronessa, drink this wine on the porch and keep your eyes on that star. (*He leads her to a porch pillar and places the glass in her trembling hand. She is now submissive.*) You know the name of that star? That star is Venus. She is the only female star in the sky. Who put her up there? Mr. Siccardi, the transportation manager of the Southern Fruit Company? No. She was put there by God. (*He enters the house and removes the knife from her purse.*) And yet there's some people that don't believe in nothing. (*He picks up the telephone.*) Esplanade 9-7-0.

SERAFINA: What are you doing?

ALVARO: Drink that wine and I'll settle this whole problem for you. (*on the telephone*) I want to speak to the blackjack dealer, please, Miss Estelle Hohengarten . . .

SERAFINA: Don't talk to that woman, she'll lie!

ALVARO: Not Estelle Hohengarten. She deals a straight game of cards.—Estelle? This is Mangiacavallo. I got a question to ask you which is a personal question. It has to do with a very goodlooking truckdriver, not living now but once on a time thought to have been a very well-known character at the Square Roof. His name was . . . (*He turns questioningly to the door where Serafina is standing.*) What was his name, Baronessa?

SERAFINA (*hardly breathing*): Rosario delle Rose!

ALVARO: Rosario delle Rose was the name. (*There is a pause.*) —È vero?—Mah! Che peccato . . .

(*Serafina drops her glass and springs into the parlor with a savage outcry. She snatches the phone from Alvaro and screams into it.*)

SERAFINA (*wildly*): This is the wife that's speaking! What do you know of my husband, what is the lie?

(*A strident voice sounds over the wire.*)

THE VOICE (*loud and clear*): Don't you remember? I brought you the rose-colored silk to make him a shirt. You said, "For a man?" and I said, "Yes, for a man that's wild like a Gypsy!" But if you think I'm a liar, come here and let me show you his rose tattooed on my chest!

(*Serafina holds the phone away from her as though it had burst into flame. Then, with a terrible cry, she hurls it to the floor. She staggers dizzily toward the Madonna. Alvaro seizes her arm and pushes her gently onto the sofa.*)

ALVARO: Piano, piano, Baronessa! This will be gone, this will pass in a moment. (*He puts a pillow behind her, then replaces the telephone.*)

SERAFINA (*staggering up from the sofa*): The room's—going round . . .

ALVARO: You ought to stay lying down a little while longer. I know, I know what you need! A towel with some ice in it to put on your forehead—Baronessa.—You stay right there while I fix it! (*He goes into the kitchen, and calls back.*) Torno subito, Baronessa!

(*The little boy runs into the yard. He leans against the bending trunk of the palm, counting loudly.*)

THE LITTLE BOY: Five, ten, fifteen, twenty, twenty-five, thirty . . .

(*There is the sound of ice being chopped in the kitchen.*)

SERAFINA: Dove siete, dove siete?
ALVARO: In cucina!—Ghiaccio . . .
SERAFINA: Venite qui!
ALVARO: Subito, subito . . .
SERAFINA (*turning to the shrine, with fists knotted*): Non voglio, non voglio farlo!

(*But she crosses slowly, compulsively toward the shrine, with a trembling arm stretched out.*)

THE LITTLE BOY: Seventy-five, eighty, eighty-five, ninety, ninety-five, one hundred! (*then, wildly*) *Ready or not you shall be caught!*

(*At this cry, Serafina seizes the marble urn and hurls it violently into the furthest corner of the room. Then, instantly, she covers her face. Outside the mothers are heard calling their children home. Their voices are tender as music, fading in and out. The children appear slowly at the side of the house, exhausted from their wild play.*)

GIUSEPPINA: Vivi! Vi-vi!
PEPINA: Salvatore!
VIOLETTA: Bruno! Come home, come home!

(*The children scatter. Alvaro comes in with the ice-pick.*)

ALVARO: I broke the point of the ice-pick.
SERAFINA (*removing her hands from her face*): I don't want ice . . . (*She looks about her, seeming to gather a fierce strength in her body. Her voice is hoarse, her body trembling with violence, eyes narrow and flashing, her fists clenched.*) Now I show you how wild and strong like a man a woman can be! (*She crosses to the screen door, opens it and shouts.*) Buona notte, Mr. Mangiacavallo!
ALVARO: You—you make me go *home*, now?
SERAFINA: No, no; senti, cretino! (*in a strident whisper*) You make out like you are going. You drive the truck out of sight where the witch can't see it. Then you come back and

I leave the back door open for you to come in. Now, tell me good-bye so all the neighbors can hear you! (*She shouts.*) Arrivederci!

ALVARO: Ha, ha! Capish! (*He shouts too.*) Arrivederci! (*He runs to the foot of the embankment steps.*)

SERAFINA (*still more loudly*): Buona notte!

ALVARO: Buona notte, Baronessa!

SERAFINA (*in a choked voice*): Give them my love; give everybody—my love . . . Arrivederci!

ALVARO: Ciao!

(*Alvaro scrambles on down the steps and goes off. Serafina comes down into the yard. The goat bleats. She mutters savagely to herself.*)

SERAFINA: Sono una bestia, una bestia feroce!

(*She crosses quickly around to the back of the house. As she disappears, the truck is heard driving off; the lights sweep across the house. Serafina comes in through the back door. She is moving with great violence, gasping and panting. She rushes up to the Madonna and addresses her passionately with explosive gestures, leaning over so that her face is level with the statue's.*)

SERAFINA: Ora, ascolta, Signora! You hold in the cup of your hand this little house and you smash it! You break this little house like the shell of a bird in your hand, because you have hate Serafina?—Serafina that *loved* you!—No, no, no, you don't speak! I don't believe in you, Lady! You're just a poor little doll with the paint peeling off, and now I blow out the light and I forget you the way you forget Serafina! (*She blows out the vigil light.*) Ecco—fatto!

(*But now she is suddenly frightened; the vehemence and boldness have run out. She gasps a little and backs away from the shrine, her eyes rolling apprehensively this way and that. The parrot squawks at her. The goat bleats. The night is full of sinister noises, harsh bird cries, the sudden flapping of wings in the cane-brake, a distant shriek of Negro laughter. Serafina retreats to the window and opens the shutters wider to admit the moonlight. She stands panting by the window with a fist pressed to her mouth. In the back of the house a door slams open. Serafina catches her breath and moves as though for protection*) *behind the dummy of the bride. Alvaro enters through the back door, calling out softly and hoarsely, with great excitement.*)

ALVARO: Dove? Dove sei, cara?

SERAFINA (*faintly*): Sono qui . . .

ALVARO: You have turn out the light!

SERAFINA: The moon is enough . . . (*He advances toward her. His white teeth glitter as he grins. Serafina retreats a few steps from him. She speaks tremulously, making an awkward gesture toward the sofa.*) Now we can go on with our— conversation . . . (*She catches her breath sharply.*)

(*The curtain comes down.*)

SCENE TWO

It is just before daybreak of the next day. Rosa and Jack appear at the top of the embankment steps.

ROSA: I thought they would never leave. (*She comes down the steps and out in front of the house, then calls back to him.*) Let's go down there.

(*He obeys hesitatingly. Both are very grave. The scene is played as close as possible to the audience. She sits very straight. He stands behind her with his hands on her shoulders.*)

ROSA (*leaning her head back against him*): This was the happiest day of my life, and this is the saddest night . . . (*He crouches in front of her.*)

SERAFINA (*from inside the house*): Aaaaaahhhhhhhh!

JACK (*springing up, startled*): What's that?

ROSA (*resentfully*): Oh! That's Mama dreaming about my father.

JACK: I—feel like a—*heel!* I feel like a rotten heel!

ROSA: Why?

JACK: That promise I made your mother.

ROSA: I hate her for it.

JACK: Honey—Rosa, she—wanted to protect you.

(*There is a long-drawn cry from the back of the house: "Ohhhh—Rosario!"*)

ROSA: She wanted me not to have what she's dreaming about . . .

JACK: Naw, naw, honey, she—wanted to—protect you . . .

(*The cry from within is repeated softly.*)

ROSA: Listen to her making love in her sleep! Is that what she wants *me* to do, just—*dream* about it?

JACK (*humbly*): She knows that her Rosa *is* a rose. And she wants her rose to have someone—better than *me* . . .

ROSA: *Better* than—*you*! (*She speaks as if the possibility were too preposterous to think of.*)

JACK: You see me through—rose-colored—glasses . . .

ROSA: I see you with love!

JACK: Yes, but your Mama sees me with—common sense . . . (*Serafina cries out again.*) I got to be going! (*She keeps a tight hold on him. A rooster crows.*) Honey, it's so late the roosters are crowing!

ROSA: They're fools, they're fools, it's early!

JACK: Honey, on that island I almost forgot my promise. Almost, but not quite. Do you understand, honey?

ROSA: Forget the promise!

JACK: I made it on my knees in front of Our Lady. I've got to leave now, honey.

ROSA (*clasping him fiercely*): You'd have to break my arms to!

JACK: Rosa, Rosa! You want to drive me crazy?

ROSA: I want you not to remember.

JACK: You're a very young girl! Fifteen—fifteen is too young!

ROSA: Caro, caro, carissimo!

JACK: You got to save some of those feelings for when you're grown up!

ROSA: Carissimo!

JACK: Hold some of it back until you're grown!

ROSA: I have been grown for two years!

JACK: No, no, that ain't what I . . .

ROSA: Grown enough to be married, and have a—baby!

JACK (*springing up*): Oh, good—Lord! (*He circles around her, pounding his palm repeatedly with his fist and champing his teeth together with a grimace. Suddenly he speaks.*) I got to be going!

ROSA: You want me to scream? (*He groans and turns away from her to resume his desperate circle. Rosa is blocking the way with her body.*)—I know, I know! You don't want me! (*Jack groans through his gritting teeth.*) No, no, you don't want me . . .

JACK: Now you listen to me! You almost got into trouble to-day on that island! You almost did, but not quite!—But it didn't quite happen and no harm is done and you can just—forget it . . .

ROSA: It is the only thing in my life that I want to remember! —When are you going back to New Orleans?

JACK: Tomorrow.

ROSA: When does your—ship sail?

JACK: Tomorrow.

ROSA: Where to?

JACK: Guatemala.

SERAFINA (*from the house*): Aahh!

ROSA: Is that a long trip?

JACK: After Guatemala, Buenos Aires. After Buenos Aires, Rio. Then around the Straits of Magellan and back up the west coast of South America, putting in at three ports be-fore we dock at San Francisco.

ROSA: I don't think I will—ever see you again . . .

JACK: The ship won't sink!

ROSA (*faintly and forlornly*): No, but—I think it could just happen once, and if it don't happen that time, it never can —later . . . (*A rooster crows. They face each other sadly and quietly.*) You don't need to be very old to understand how it works out. One time, one time, only once, it could be— God!—to remember.—Other times? Yes—they'd be some-thing.—But only once, God—to remember . . . (*With a little sigh she crosses to pick up his white cap and hand it gravely to him.*)—I'm sorry to you it didn't—mean—that much . . .

JACK (*taking the cap and hurling it to the ground*): Look! Look at my knuckles! You see them scabs on my knuckles? You know how them scabs got there? They got there because I banged my knuckles that hard on the deck of the sailboat!

ROSA: Because it—didn't quite happen? (*Jack jerks his head up and down in grotesquely violent assent to her question. Rosa picks up his cap and returns it to him again.*)—Because of the promise to Mama! I'll never forgive her . . . (*There is a pause.*) What time in the afternoon must you be on the boat?

JACK: Why?

ROSA: Just tell me what time.

JACK: Five!—Why?

ROSA: What will you be doing till five?

JACK: Well, I could be a goddam liar and tell you I was going to—pick me a hatful of daisies in—Audubon Park.—Is that what you want me to tell you?

ROSA: No, tell me the truth.

JACK: All right, I'll tell you the truth. I'm going to check in at some flea-bag hotel on North Rampart Street. Then I'm going to get loaded! And then I'm going to get . . . (*He doesn't complete the sentence but she understands him. She places the hat more becomingly on his blond head.*)

ROSA: Do me a little favor. (*Her hand slides down to his cheek and then to his mouth.*) Before you get loaded and before you—before you—

JACK: Huh?

ROSA: Look in the waiting room at the Greyhound bus station, please. At twelve o'clock, noon!

JACK: Why?

ROSA: You might find me there, waiting for you . . .

JACK: What—what good would that do?

ROSA: I never been to a hotel but I know they have numbers on doors and sometimes—numbers are—lucky.—Aren't they?—Sometimes?—Lucky?

JACK: You want to buy me a ten-year stretch in the brig?

ROSA: I want you to give me that little gold ring on your ear to put on my finger.—I want to give you my heart to keep forever! And ever! And ever! (*Slowly and with a barely audible sigh she leans her face against him.*) Look for me! I will be there!

JACK (*breathlessly*): In all of my life, I never felt nothing so sweet as the feel of your little warm body in my arms . . .

(*He breaks away and runs toward the road. From the foot of the steps he glares fiercely back at her like a tiger through the bars of a cage. She clings to the two porch pillars, her body leaning way out.)*

ROSA: Look for me! I will be there!

(Jack runs away from the house. Rosa returns inside. Listlessly she removes her dress and falls on the couch in her slip, kicking off her shoes. Then she begins to cry, as one cries only once in a lifetime, and the scene dims out.)

SCENE THREE

The time is three hours later.
We see first the exterior view of the small frame building against a night sky which is like the starry blue robe of Our Lady. It is growing slightly paler.

(The faint light discloses Rosa asleep on the couch. The covers are thrown back for it has been a warm night, and on the concave surface of the white cloth, which is like the dimly lustrous hollow of a shell, is the body of the sleeping girl which is clad only in a sheer white slip.

(A cock crows. A gentle wind stirs the white curtains inward and the tendrils of vine at the windows, and the sky lightens enough to distinguish the purple trumpets of the morning glory against the very dim blue of the sky in which the planet Venus remains still undimmed.

(In the back of the cottage someone is heard coughing hoarsely and groaning in the way a man does who has drunk very heavily the night before. Bedsprings creak as a heavy figure rises. Light spills dimly through the curtains, now closed, between the two front rooms.

(There are heavy, padding footsteps and Alvaro comes stumbling rapidly into the dining room with the last bottle of Spumanti in the crook of an arm, his eyes barely open, legs rubbery, saying, "Wuh-wuh-wuh-wuh-wuh-wuh . . ." like the breathing of an old dog. The scene should be played with the pantomimic lightness, almost fantasy, of an early Chaplin comedy. He is wearing only his trousers and his chest is bare. As he enters he collides with the widow dummy, staggers

back, pats her inflated bosom in a timid, apologetic way, remarking:)

ALVARO: Scusami, Signora, I am the grandson of the village idiot of Ribera!

(*Alvaro backs into the table and is propelled by the impact all the way to the curtained entrance to the parlor. He draws the curtains apart and hangs onto them, peering into the room. Seeing the sleeping girl, he blinks several times, suddenly makes a snoring sound in his nostrils and waves one hand violently in front of his eyes as if to dispel a vision. Outside the goat utters a long "Baaaaaaaaaaa!" As if in response, Alvaro whispers, in the same basso key, "Che bella!" The first vowel of "bella" is enormously prolonged like the "baaa" of the goat. On his rubbery legs he shuffles forward a few steps and leans over to peer more intently at the vision. The goat bleats again. Alvaro whispers more loudly: "Che* bel-*la!" He drains the Spumanti, then staggers to his knees, the empty bottle rolling over the floor. He crawls on his knees to the foot of the bed, then leans against it like a child peering into a candy shop window, repeating: "Che* bel-*la, che* bel-*la!" with antiphonal responses from the goat outside. Slowly, with tremendous effort, as if it were the sheer side of a precipice, he clambers upon the couch and crouches over the sleeping girl in a leap-frog position, saying "Che* bel-*la!" quite loudly, this time, in a tone of innocently joyous surprise. All at once Rosa wakens. She screams, even before she is quite awake, and springs from the couch so violently that Alvaro topples over to the floor.*

(*Serafina cries out almost instantly after Rosa. She lunges through the dining room in her torn and disordered nightgown. At the sight of the man crouched by the couch a momentary stupefaction turns into a burst of savage fury. She flies at him like a great bird, tearing and clawing at his stupefied figure. With one arm Alvaro wards off her blows, plunging to the floor and crawling into the dining room. She seizes a broom with which she flails him about the head, buttocks and shoulders while he scrambles awkwardly away. The assault is nearly wordless. Each time she strikes at him she hisses: "Sporcaccione!" He continually groans: "Dough, dough,*

dough!" At last he catches hold of the widow dummy which he holds as a shield before him while he entreats the two women.)

ALVARO: Senti, Baronessa! Signorina! I didn't know what I was doin', I was dreamin', I was just dreamin'! I got turn around in the house; I got all twisted! I thought that you was your Mama!—Sono ubriaco! Per favore!

ROSA (*seizing the broom*): That's enough, Mama!

SERAFINA (*rushing to the phone*): Police!

ROSA (*seizing the phone*): No, no, no, no, no, no!—You want everybody to know?

SERAFINA (*weakly*): Know?—Know *what*, cara?

ROSA: Just give him his clothes, now, Mama, and let him get out! (*She is clutching a bedsheet about herself.*)

ALVARO: Signorina—young lady! I swear I was *dreaming!*

SERAFINA: Don't speak to my daughter! (*then, turning to Rosa*)—Who is this man? How did this man get here?

ROSA (*coldly*): Mama, don't say any more. Just give him his clothes in the bedroom so he can get out!

ALVARO (*still crouching*): I am so sorry, so sorry! I don't remember a thing but that I was dreaming!

SERAFINA (*shoving him toward the back of the room with her broom*): Go on, go get your clothes on, you—idiot's grandson, you!—Svelto, svelto, più svelto! (*Alvaro continues his apologetic mumbling in the back room.*) Don't talk to me, don't say nothing! Or I will kill you!

(*A few moments later Alvaro rushes around the side of the house, his clothes half buttoned and his shirt-tails out.*)

ALVARO: But, Baronessa, I *love* you! (*A tea kettle sails over his head from behind the house. The Strega bursts into laughter. Despairingly Alvaro retreats, tucking his shirt-tails in and shaking his head.*) Baronessa, Baronessa, I love you!

(*As Alvaro runs off, the Strega is heard cackling:*)

THE STREGA'S VOICE: The Wops are at it again. Had a truck-driver in the house all night!

(*Rosa is feverishly dressing. From the bureau she has snatched a shimmering white satin slip, disappearing for a moment behind a screen to put it on as Serafina comes padding sheepishly back into the room, her nightgown now covered by a black rayon kimona sprinkled with poppies, her voice tremulous with fear, shame and apology.*)

ROSA (*behind the screen*): Has the man gone?

SERAFINA: That—man?

ROSA: Yes, "that man!"

SERAFINA (*inventing desperately*): I don't know how he got in. Maybe the back door was open.

ROSA: Oh, yes, maybe it was!

SERAFINA: Maybe he—climbed in a window . . .

ROSA: Or fell down the chimney, maybe! (*She comes from behind the screen, wearing the white bridal slip.*)

SERAFINA: Why you put on the white things I save for your wedding?

ROSA: Because I want to. That's a good enough reason. (*She combs her hair savagely.*)

SERAFINA: I want you to understand about that man. That was a man that—that was—that was a man that . . .

ROSA: You can't think of a lie?

SERAFINA: He was a—truckdriver, cara. He got in a fight, he was chase by—policemen!

ROSA: They chased him into your bedroom?

SERAFINA: I took pity on him, I give him first aid, I let him sleep on the floor. He give me his promise—he . . .

ROSA: Did he kneel in front of Our Lady? Did he promise that he would respect your innocence?

SERAFINA: Oh, cara, cara! (*abandoning all pretense*) He was Sicilian; he had rose oil in his hair and the rose tattoo of your father. In the dark room I couldn't see his clown face. I closed my eyes and dreamed that he was your father! I closed my eyes! I dreamed that he was your father . . .

ROSA: Basta, basta, non voglio sentire più niente! The only thing worse than a liar is a liar that's also a hypocrite!

SERAFINA: Senti, per favore! (*Rosa wheels about from the mirror and fixes her mother with a long and withering stare. Serafina cringes before it.*) Don't look at me like that with the eyes of your father! (*She shields her face as from a terrible glare.*)

ROSA: Yes, I am looking at you with the eyes of my father. I see you the way *he* saw you. (*She runs to the table and seizes the piggy bank.*) Like this, this *pig!* (*Serafina utters a long, shuddering cry like a cry of childbirth.*) I need five dollars. I'll take it out of this! (*Rosa smashes the piggy bank to the floor and rakes some coins into her purse. Serafina stoops to the floor. There is the sound of a train whistle. Rosa is now fully dressed, but she hesitates, a little ashamed of her cruelty—but only a little. Serafina cannot meet her daughter's eyes. At last the girl speaks.*)

SERAFINA: How beautiful—is my daughter! Go to the boy!

ROSA (*as if she might be about to apologize*): Mama? He didn't touch me—he just said—"Che bella!"

(*Serafina turns slowly, shamefully, to face her. She is like a peasant in the presence of a young princess. Rosa stares at her a moment longer, then suddenly catches her breath and runs out of the house. As the girl leaves, Serafina calls:*)

SERAFINA: Rosa, Rosa, the—wrist watch! (*Serafina snatches up the little gift box and runs out onto the porch with it. She starts to call her daughter again, holding the gift out toward her, but her breath fails her.*) Rosa, Rosa, the—wrist watch . . . (*Her arms fall to her side. She turns, the gift still ungiven. Senselessly, absently, she holds the watch to her ear again. She shakes it a little, then utters a faint, startled laugh.*)

(*Assunta appears beside the house and walks directly in, as though Serafina had called her.*)

SERAFINA: Assunta, the urn is broken. The ashes are spilt on the floor and I can't touch them.

(*Assunta stoops to pick up the pieces of the shattered urn. Serafina has crossed to the shrine and relights the candle before the Madonna.*)

ASSUNTA: There are no ashes.

SERAFINA: Where—where are they? Where have the ashes gone?

ASSUNTA (*crossing to the shrine*): The wind has blown them away.

(*Assunta places what remains of the broken urn in Serafina's hands. Serafina turns it tenderly in her hands and then re-places it on the top of the prie-dieu before the Madonna.*)

SERAFINA: A man, when he burns, leaves only a handful of ashes. No woman can hold him. The wind must blow him away.

(*Alvaro's voice is heard, calling from the top of the highway embankment.*)

ALVARO'S VOICE: Rondinella felice!

(*The neighborhood women hear Alvaro calling, and there is a burst of mocking laughter from some of them. Then they all converge on the house from different directions and gather before the porch.*)

PEPPINA: Serafina delle Rose!
GIUSEPPINA: Baronessa! Baronessa delle Rose!
PEPPINA: There is a man on the road without the shirt!
GIUSEPPINA (*with delight*): Si, si! Senza camicia!
PEPPINA: All he got on his chest is a rose tattoo! (*to the women*) She lock up his shirt so he can't go to the high school?

(*The women shriek with laughter. In the house Serafina snatches up the package containing the silk shirt, while Assunta closes the shutters of the parlor windows.*)

SERAFINA: Un momento! (*She tears the paper off the shirt and rushes out onto the porch, holding the shirt above her head defiantly.*) Ecco la camicia!

(*With a soft cry, Serafina drops the shirt, which is immediately snatched up by Peppina. At this point the music begins again, with a crash of percussion, and continues to the end of the play. Peppina flourishes the shirt in the air like a banner and tosses it to Giuseppina, who is now on the embankment. Giuseppina tosses it on to Mariella, and she in her turn to Violetta, who is above her, so that the brilliantly colored shirt moves in a zig-zag course through the pampas grass to the very top of the embankment, like a streak of flame shooting up a dry hill. The women call out as they pass the shirt along:*)

PEPPINA: Guardate questa camicia! Coloro di rose!
MARIELLA (*shouting up to Alvaro*): Corragio, signor!
GIUSEPPINA: Avanti, avanti, signor!

VIOLETTA (*at the top of the embankment, giving the shirt a final flourish above her*): Corragio, corragio! The Baronessa is waiting!

(*Bursts of laughter are mingled with the cries of the women. Then they sweep away like a flock of screaming birds, and Serafina is left upon the porch, her eyes closed, a hand clasped to her breast. In the meanwhile, inside the house, Assunta has poured out a glass of wine. Now she comes to the porch, offering the wine to Serafina and murmuring:*)

ASSUNTA: Stai tranquilla.

SERAFINA (*breathlessly*): Assunta, I'll tell you something that maybe you won't believe.

ASSUNTA (*with tender humor*): It is impossible to tell me anything that I don't believe.

SERAFINA: Just now I felt on my breast the burning again of the rose. I know what it means. It means that I have conceived! (*She lifts the glass to her lips for a moment and then returns it to Assunta.*) Two lives again in the body! Two, two lives again, two!

ALVARO'S VOICE (*nearer now, and sweetly urgent*): Rondinella felice!

(*Alvaro is not visible on the embankment but Serafina begins to move slowly toward his voice.*)

ASSUNTA: Dove vai, Serafina?

SERAFINA (*shouting now, to Alvaro*): Vengo, vengo, amore!

(*She starts up the embankment toward Alvaro and the curtain falls as the music rises with her in great glissandi of sound.*)

CAMINO REAL

*"In the middle of the journey of our life I came to myself
in a dark wood where the straight way was lost."*

CANTO I, DANTE'S Inferno

FOR ELIA KAZAN

FOREWORD *

It is amazing and frightening how completely one's whole being becomes absorbed in the making of a play. It is almost as if you were frantically constructing another world while the world that you live in dissolves beneath your feet, and that your survival depends on completing this construction at least one second before the old habitation collapses.

More than any other work that I have done, this play has seemed to me like the construction of another world, a separate existence. Of course, it is nothing more nor less than my conception of the time and world that I live in, and its people are mostly archetypes of certain basic attitudes and qualities with those mutations that would occur if they had continued along the road to this hypothetical terminal point in it.

A convention of the play is existence outside of time in a place of no specific locality. If you regard it that way, I suppose it becomes an elaborate allegory, but in New Haven we opened directly across the street from a movie theatre that was showing *Peter Pan* in Technicolor and it did not seem altogether inappropriate to me. Fairy tales nearly always have some simple moral lesson of good and evil, but that is not the secret of their fascination any more, I hope, than the philosophical import that might be distilled from the fantasies of *Camino Real* is the principal element of its appeal.

To me the appeal of this work is its unusual degree of freedom. When it began to get under way I felt a new sensation of release, as if I could "ride out" like a tenor sax taking the breaks in a Dixieland combo or a piano in a bop session. You may call it self-indulgence, but I was not doing it merely for myself. I could not have felt a purely private thrill of release unless I had hope of sharing this experience with lots and lots of audiences to come.

My desire was to give these audiences my own sense of something wild and unrestricted that ran like water in the mountains, or clouds changing shape in a gale, or the con-

---

*Written prior to the Broadway premiere of *Camino Real* and published in the New York *Times* on Sunday, March 15, 1953.

743

tinually dissolving and transforming images of a dream. This sort of freedom is not chaos nor anarchy. On the contrary, it is the result of painstaking design, and in this work I have given more conscious attention to form and construction than I have in any work before. Freedom is not achieved simply by working freely.

Elia Kazan was attracted to this work mainly, I believe, for the same reason—its freedom and mobility of form. I know that we have kept saying the word "flight" to each other as if the play were merely an abstraction of the impulse to fly, and most of the work out of town, his in staging, mine in cutting and revising, has been with this impulse in mind: the achievement of a continual flow. Speech after speech and bit after bit that were nice in themselves have been remorselessly blasted out of the script and its staging wherever they seemed to obstruct or divert this flow.

There have been plenty of indications already that this play will exasperate and confuse a certain number of people which we hope is not so large as the number it is likely to please. At each performance a number of people have stamped out of the auditorium, with little regard for those whom they have had to crawl over, almost as if the building had caught on fire, and there have been sibilant noises on the way out and demands for money back if the cashier was foolish enough to remain in his box.

I am at a loss to explain this phenomenon, and if I am being facetious about one thing, I am being quite serious about another when I say that I had never for one minute supposed that the play would seem obscure and confusing to anyone who was willing to meet it even less than halfway. It was a costly production, and for this reason I had to read it aloud, together with a few of the actors on one occasion, before large groups of prospective backers, before the funds to produce it were in the till. It was only then that I came up against the disconcerting surprise that some people would think that the play needed clarification.

My attitude is intransigent. I still don't agree that it needs any explanation. Some poet has said that a poem should not mean but be. Of course, a play is not a poem, not even a poetic play has quite the same license as a poem. But to go to

Camino Real with the inflexible demands of a logician is un-fair to both parties.

In Philadelphia a young man from a literary periodical saw the play and then cross-examined me about all its dream-like images. He had made a list of them while he watched the play, and afterward at my hotel he brought out the list and asked me to explain the meaning of each one. I can't deny that I use a lot of those things called symbols but being a self-defensive creature, I say that symbols are nothing but the nat-ural speech of drama.

We all have in our conscious and unconscious minds a great vocabulary of images, and I think all human communication is based on these images as are our dreams; and a symbol in a play has only one legitimate purpose which is to say a thing more directly and simply and beautifully than it could be said in words.

I hate writing that is a parade of images for the sake of im-ages; I hate it so much that I close a book in disgust when it keeps on saying one thing is like another; I even get disgusted with poems that make nothing but comparisons between one thing and another. But I repeat that symbols, when used re-spectfully, are the purest language of plays. Sometimes it would take page after tedious page of exposition to put across an idea that can be said with an object or a gesture on the lighted stage.

To take one case in point: the battered portmanteau of Jacques Casanova is hurled from the balcony of a luxury ho-tel when his remittance check fails to come through. While the portmanteau is still in the air, he shouts: "Careful, I have—"—and when it has crashed to the street he continues —"fragile—mementoes . . ." I suppose that is a symbol, at least it is an object used to express as directly and vividly as possible certain things which could be said in pages of dull talk.

As for those patrons who departed before the final scene, I offer myself this tentative bit of solace: that these theatre-goers may be a little domesticated in their theatrical tastes. A cage represents security as well as confinement to a bird that has grown used to being in it; and when a theatrical work kicks over the traces with such apparent insouciance, security seems challenged and, instead of participating in its sense of freedom, one out of a certain number of playgoers will rush back out to the more accustomed implausibility of the street he lives on.

To modify this effect of complaisance I would like to admit to you quite frankly that I can't say with any personal conviction that I have written a good play, I only know that I have felt a release in this work which I wanted you to feel with me.

Tennessee Williams

AFTERWORD

Once in a while someone will say to me that he would rather wait for a play to come out as a book than see a live performance of it, where he would be distracted from its true values, if it has any, by so much that is mere spectacle and sensation and consequently must be meretricious and vulgar. There are plays meant for reading. I have read them. I have read the works of "thinking playwrights" as distinguished from us who are permitted only to feel, and probably read them earlier and appreciated them as much as those who invoke their names nowadays like the incantation of Aristophanes' frogs. But the incontinent blaze of a live theatre, a theatre meant for seeing and for feeling, has never been and never will be extinguished by a bucket brigade of critics, new or old, bearing vessels that range from cut-glass punch bowl to Haviland teacup. And in my dissident opinion, a play in a book is only the shadow of a play and not even a clear shadow of it. Those who did not like *Camino Real* on the stage will not be likely to form a higher opinion of it in print, for of all the works I have written, this one was meant most for the vulgarity of performance. The printed script of a play is hardly more than an architect's blueprint of a house not yet built or built and destroyed.

The color, the grace and levitation, the structural pattern in motion, the quick interplay of live beings, suspended like fitful lightning in a cloud, these things are the play, not words on paper, nor thoughts and ideas of an author, those shabby things snatched off basement counters at Gimbel's.

My own creed as a playwright is fairly close to that expressed by the painter in Shaw's play *The Doctor's Dilemma*: "I believe in Michelangelo, Velasquez and Rembrandt; in the might of design, the mystery of color, the redemption of all things by beauty everlasting and the message of art that has made these hands blessed. Amen."

How much art his hands were blessed with or how much mine are, I don't know, but that art is a blessing is certain and that it contains its message is also certain, and I feel, as the painter did, that the message lies in those abstract beauties of form and color and line, to which I would add light and motion.

In these following pages are only the formula by which a play could exist.

Dynamic is a word in disrepute at the moment, and so, I suppose, is the word *organic,* but those terms still define the dramatic values that I value most and which I value more as they are more deprecated by the ones self-appointed to save what they have never known.

Tennessee Williams

June 1, 1953

PROLOGUE

As the curtain rises, on an almost lightless stage, there is a loud singing of wind, accompanied by distant, measured reverberations like pounding surf or distant shellfire. Above the ancient wall that backs the set and the perimeter of mountains visible above the wall, are flickers of a white radiance as though daybreak were a white bird caught in a net and struggling to rise.

The plaza is seen fitfully by this light. It belongs to a tropical seaport that bears a confusing, but somehow harmonious, resemblance to such widely scattered ports as Tangiers, Havana, Vera Cruz, Casablanca, Shanghai, New Orleans.

On stage left is the luxury side of the street, containing the façade of the Siete Mares hotel and its low terrace on which are a number of glass-topped white iron tables and chairs. In the downstairs there is a great bay window in which are seen a pair of elegant "dummies," one seated, one standing behind, looking out into the plaza with painted smiles. Upstairs is a small balcony and behind it a large window exposing a wall on which is hung a phoenix painted on silk: this should be softly lighted now and then in the play, since resurrections are so much a part of its meaning.

Opposite the hotel is Skid Row which contains the Gypsy's gaudy stall, the Loan Shark's establishment with a window containing a variety of pawned articles, and the "Ritz Men Only" which is a flea-bag hotel or flophouse and which has a practical window above its downstairs entrance, in which a bum will appear from time to time to deliver appropriate or contrapuntal song titles.

Upstage is a great flight of stairs that mount the ancient wall to a sort of archway that leads out into "Terra Incognita," as it is called in the play, a wasteland between the walled town and the distant perimeter of snow-topped mountains.

Downstage right and left are a pair of arches which give entrance to dead-end streets.

Immediately after the curtain rises a shaft of blue light is thrown down a central aisle of the theatre, and in this light, advancing from the back of the house, appears Don Quixote de la Mancha, dressed like an old "desert rat." As he enters the aisle he shouts, "Hola!", in a cracked old voice which is still full of energy and is answered by another voice which is impatient and tired, that of his squire, Sancho Panza. Stumbling with a fatigue which is only physical, the old knight comes down the aisle, and Sancho follows a couple of yards behind him, loaded down with equipment that ranges from a medieval shield to a military canteen or Thermos bottle. Shouts are exchanged between them.

QUIXOTE (*ranting above the wind in a voice which is nearly as old*): Blue is the color of distance!

SANCHO (*wearily behind him*): Yes, distance is blue.

QUIXOTE: Blue is also the color of nobility.

SANCHO: Yes, nobility's blue.

QUIXOTE: Blue is the color of distance and nobility, and that's why an old knight should always have somewhere about him a bit of blue ribbon . . .

(*He jostles the elbow of an aisle-sitter as he staggers with fatigue; he mumbles an apology.*)

SANCHO: Yes, a bit of blue ribbon.

QUIXOTE: A bit of faded blue ribbon, tucked away in whatever remains of his armor, or borne on the tip of his lance, his—unconquerable lance! It serves to remind an old knight of distance that he has gone and distance he has yet to go . . .

(*Sancho mutters the Spanish word for excrement as several pieces of rusty armor fall into the aisle.*

(*Quixote has now arrived at the foot of the steps onto the forestage. He pauses there as if wandering out of or into a dream. Sancho draws up clanking behind him.*

(*Mr. Gutman, a lordly fat man wearing a linen suit and a pith helmet, appears dimly on the balcony of the Siete Mares, a white cockatoo on his wrist. The bird cries out harshly.*)

GUTMAN: Hush, Aurora.

QUIXOTE: It also reminds an old knight of that green country he lived in which was the youth of his heart, before such singing words as *Truth!*

SANCHO (*panting*): — Truth.

QUIXOTE: *Valor!*

SANCHO: —Valor.

QUIXOTE (*elevating his lance*): *Devoir!*

SANCHO: —Devoir . . .

QUIXOTE: —turned into the meaningless mumble of some old monk hunched over cold mutton at supper!

(*Gutman alerts a pair of Guards in the plaza, who cross with red lanterns to either side of the proscenium where they lower black and white striped barrier gates as if the proscenium marked a frontier. One of them, with a hand on his holster, advances toward the pair on the steps.*)

GUARD: Vien aquí.

(*Sancho hangs back but Quixote stalks up to the barrier gate. The Guard turns a flashlight on his long and exceedingly grave red face, "frisks" him casually for concealed weapons, examines a rusty old knife and tosses it contemptuously away.*)

Sus papeles! Sus documentos!

(*Quixote fumblingly produces some tattered old papers from the lining of his hat.*)

GUTMAN (*impatiently*): Who is it?

GUARD: An old desert rat named Quixote.

GUTMAN: Oh!—Expected!—Let him in.

(*The Guards raise the barrier gate and one sits down to smoke on the terrace. Sancho hangs back still. A dispute takes place on the forestage and steps into the aisle.*)

QUIXOTE: Forward!

SANCHO: Aw, naw. I know this place. (*He produces a crumpled parchment.*) Here it is on the chart. Look, it says here: "Continue until you come to the square of a walled town which is the end of the Camino Real and the beginning of the Camino Real. Halt there," it says, "and turn back, Traveler, for the spring of humanity has gone dry in this place and—"

QUIXOTE (*He snatches the chart from him and reads the rest of the inscription.*): "—there are no birds in the country except wild birds that are tamed and kept in—" (*He holds the chart close to his nose.*) —Cages!

SANCHO (*urgently*): Let's go back to La Mancha!

QUIXOTE: Forward!

SANCHO: The time has come for retreat!

QUIXOTE: The time for retreat never comes!

SANCHO: *I'm* going back to *La Mancha!* (*He dumps the knightly equipment into the orchestra pit.*)

QUIXOTE: *Without me?*

SANCHO (*bustling up the aisle*): With you or without you, old tireless and tiresome master!

QUIXOTE (*imploringly*): *Saaaaaan-choooooooooo!*

SANCHO (*near the top of the aisle*): I'm going back to La *Maaaaaaaaan-chaaaaaaa . . .*

(*He disappears as the blue light in the aisle dims out. The Guard puts out his cigarette and wanders out of the plaza. The wind moans and Gutman laughs softly as the Ancient Knight enters the plaza with such a desolate air.*)

QUIXOTE (*looking about the plaza*): —Lonely . . .

(*To his surprise the word is echoed softly by almost unseen figures huddled below the stairs and against the wall of the town. Quixote leans upon his lance and observes with a wry smile—*)

—When so many are lonely as seem to be lonely, it would be inexcusably selfish to be lonely alone.

(*He shakes out a dusty blanket. Shadowy arms extend toward him and voices murmur.*)

VOICE: Sleep. Sleep. Sleep.

QUIXOTE (*arranging his blanket*): Yes, I'll sleep for a while, I'll sleep and dream for a while against the wall of this town . . .

(*A mandolin or guitar plays "The Nightingale of France."*)

—And my dream will be a pageant, a masque in which old meanings will be remembered and possibly new ones discovered, and when I wake from this sleep and this disturbing pageant of a dream, I'll choose one among its shadows to take along with me in the place of Sancho . . .

(*He blows his nose between his fingers and wipes them on his shirttail.*)

—For new companions are not as familiar as old ones but all the same—they're old ones with only slight differences of face and figure, which may or may not be improvements, and it would be selfish of me to be lonely alone . . .

(*He stumbles down the incline into the Pit below the stairs where most of the Street People huddle beneath awnings of open stalls.*
(*The white cockatoo squawks.*)

GUTMAN: Hush, Aurora.

QUIXOTE: And tomorrow at this same hour, which we call madrugada, the loveliest of all words, except the word alba, and that word also means daybreak—

—Yes, at daybreak tomorrow I will go on from here with a new companion and this old bit of blue ribbon to keep me in mind of distance that I have gone and distance I have yet to go, and also to keep me in mind of—

(*The cockatoo cries wildly.*
(*Quixote nods as if in agreement with the outcry and folds himself into his blanket below the great stairs.*)

GUTMAN (*stroking the cockatoo's crest*): Be still, Aurora. I know it's morning, Aurora.

(*Daylight turns the plaza silver and slowly gold. Vendors rise beneath white awnings of stalls. The Gypsy's stall opens. A tall, courtly figure, in his late middle years [Jacques Casanova] crosses from the Siete Mares to the Loan Shark's, removing a silver snuff box from his pocket as Gutman speaks. His costume, like that of all the legendary characters in the play [except perhaps Quixote] is generally "modern" but with vestigial touches of the period to which he was actually related. The cane and the snuff box and perhaps a brocaded vest may be sufficient to give this historical suggestion in Casanova's case. He bears his hawklike head with a sort of anxious pride on most occasions, a pride maintained under a steadily mounting pressure.*)

—It's morning and after morning. It's afternoon, ha ha! And now I must go downstairs to announce the beginning of that old wanderer's dream . . .

(*He withdraws from the balcony as old Prudence Duvernoy stumbles out of the hotel, as if not yet quite awake from an afternoon siesta. Chattering with beads and bracelets, she wanders vaguely down into the plaza, raising a faded green silk parasol, damp henna-streaked hair slipping under a monstrous hat of faded silk roses; she is searching for a lost poodle.*)

PRUDENCE: Trique? Trique?

(*Jacques comes out of the Loan Shark's replacing his case angrily in his pocket.*)

JACQUES: Why, I'd rather give it to a street beggar! This case is a Boucheron, I won it at faro at the summer palace, at Tsarskoe Selo in the winter of—

(*The Loan Shark slams the door. Jacques glares, then shrugs and starts across the plaza. Old Prudence is crouched over the filthy gray bundle of a dying mongrel by the fountain.*)

PRUDENCE: Trique, oh, Trique!

(*The Gypsy's son, Abdullah, watches, giggling.*)

JACQUES (*reproving*): It is a terrible thing for an old woman to outlive her dogs.

(*He crosses to Prudence and gently disengages the animal from her grasp.*)

Madam, that is not Trique.

PRUDENCE: —When I woke up she wasn't in her basket . . .

JACQUES: Sometimes we sleep too long in the afternoon and when we wake we find things changed, Signora.

PRUDENCE: Oh, you're Italian!

JACQUES: I am from Venice, Signora.

PRUDENCE: Ah, Venice, city of pearls! I saw you last night on the terrace dining with— Oh, I'm so worried about her! I'm an old friend of hers, perhaps she's mentioned me to you. Prudence Duvernoy? I was her best friend in the old days in Paris, but now she's forgotten so much . . .

I hope you have influence with her!

(*A waltz of Camille's time in Paris is heard.*)

I want you to give her a message from a certain wealthy old gentleman that she met at one of those watering places she used to go to for her health. She resembled his daughter who died of consumption and so he adored Camille, lavished everything on her! What did she do? Took a young lover who hadn't a couple of pennies to rub together, disinherited by his father because of *her!* Oh, you can't do that, not now, not any more, you've got to be realistic on the Camino Real!

(*Gutman has come out on the terrace: he announces quietly—*)

GUTMAN: Block One on the Camino Real.

BLOCK ONE

PRUDENCE (*continuing*): Yes, you've got to be practical on it! Well, give her this message, please, Sir. He wants her back on any terms whatsoever! (*Her speech gathers furious momentum.*) Her evenings will be free. He wants only her mornings, mornings are hard on old men because their hearts beat slowly, and he wants only her mornings! Well, that's how it should be! A sensible arrangement! Elderly gentlemen have to content themselves with a lady's spare time before supper! Isn't that so? Of course so! And so I told him! I told him, Camille isn't well! She requires delicate care! Has many debts, creditors storm her door! "How much does she owe?" he asked me, and, oh, did I do some lightning mathematics! Jewels in pawn, I told him, pearls, rings, necklaces, bracelets, diamond ear-drops are in pawn! Horses put up for sale at a public auction!

JACQUES (*appalled by this torrent*): Signora, Signora, all of these things are—

PRUDENCE: —What?

JACQUES: *Dreams!*

(*Gutman laughs. A woman sings at a distance.*)

PRUDENCE (*continuing with less assurance*): —You're not so
young as I thought when I saw you last night on the terrace by candlelight on the— Oh, but— Ho ho!—I bet
there is *one* old fountain in this plaza that hasn't gone dry!

(*She pokes him obscenely. He recoils. Gutman laughs. Jacques
starts away but she seizes his arm again, and the torrent of
speech continues.*)

PRUDENCE: Wait, wait, listen! Her candle is burning low. But
how can you tell? She might have a lingering end, and charity hospitals? Why, you might as well take a flying leap into
the Streetcleaners' barrel. Oh, I've told her and told her
not to live in a dream! A dream is nothing to live in, why,
it's gone like a—
   Don't let her elegance fool you! That girl has done the
Camino in carriages but she has also done it on foot! She
knows every stone the Camino is paved with! So tell her
this. You tell her, she won't listen to me!—Times and conditions have undergone certain changes since we were
friends in Paris, and now we dismiss young lovers with skins
of silk and eyes like a child's first prayer, we put them away
as lightly as we put away white gloves meant only for
summer, and pick up a pair of black ones, suitable for
winter . . .

(*The singing voice rises: then subsides.*)

JACQUES: Excuse me, Madam.

(*He tears himself from her grasp and rushes into the Siete
Mares.*)

PRUDENCE (*dazed, to Gutman*): —What block is this?
GUTMAN: Block One.
PRUDENCE: I didn't hear the announcement . . .
GUTMAN (*coldly*): Well, now you do.

(*Olympe comes out of the lobby with a pale orange silk parasol like a floating moon.*)

OLYMPE: Oh, there you are, I've looked for you high and
low!—mostly low . . .

(They float vaguely out into the dazzling plaza as though a capricious wind took them, finally drifting through the Moorish arch downstage right.

(The song dies out.)

GUTMAN *(lighting a thin cigar)*: Block Two on the Camino Real.

BLOCK TWO

After Gutman's announcement, a hoarse cry is heard. A figure in rags, skin blackened by the sun, tumbles crazily down the steep alley to the plaza. He turns about blindly, murmuring: "A donde la fuente?" He stumbles against the hideous old prostitute Rosita who grins horribly and whispers something to him, hitching up her ragged, filthy skirt. Then she gives him a jocular push toward the fountain. He falls upon his belly and thrusts his hands into the dried-up basin. Then he staggers to his feet with a despairing cry.

THE SURVIVOR: La fuente está seca!

(Rosita laughs madly but the other Street People moan. A dry gourd rattles.)

ROSITA: The fountain is dry, but there's plenty to drink in the Siete Mares!

(She shoves him toward the hotel. The proprietor, Gutman, steps out, smoking a thin cigar, fanning himself with a palm leaf. As the Survivor advances, Gutman whistles. A man in military dress comes out upon the low terrace.)

OFFICER: Go back!

(The Survivor stumbles forward. The Officer fires at him. He lowers his hands to his stomach, turns slowly about with a lost expression, looking up at the sky, and stumbles toward the fountain. During the scene that follows, until the entrance of La Madrecita and her Son, the Survivor drags himself slowly about the concrete rim of the fountain, almost entirely ignored,

*as a dying pariah dog in a starving country. Jacques Casa-
nova comes out upon the terrace of the Siete Mares. Now he
passes the hotel proprietor's impassive figure, descending a step
beneath and a little in advance of him, and without looking
at him.)*

JACQUES (*with infinite weariness and disgust*): What has
happened?

GUTMAN (*serenely*): We have entered the second in a progress
of sixteen blocks on the Camino Real. It's five o'clock.
That angry old lion, the Sun, looked back once and
growled and then went switching his tail toward the cool
shade of the Sierras. Our guests have taken their afternoon
siestas . . .

*(The Survivor has come out upon the forestage, now, not like
a dying man but like a shy speaker who has forgotten the opening line of his speech. He is only a little crouched over with a
hand obscuring the red stain over his belly. Two or three
Street People wander about calling their wares: "Tacos, tacos,
fritos . . ."—"Lotería, lotería"—Rosita shuffles around,
calling "Love? Love?"—pulling down the filthy décolletage of
her blouse to show more of her sagging bosom. The Survivor
arrives at the top of the stairs descending into the orchestra of
the theatre, and hangs onto it, looking out reflectively as a
man over the rail of a boat coming into a somewhat dis-
turbingly strange harbor.)*

GUTMAN (*continuing*): —They suffer from extreme fatigue,
our guests at the Siete Mares, all of them have a degree or
two of fever. Questions are passed amongst them like something illicit and shameful, like counterfeit money or drugs
or indecent postcards—

(He leans forward and whispers:)

—"What is this place? Where are we? What is the meaning
of—*Shhhh!*"—Ha ha . . .

THE SURVIVOR (*very softly to the audience*): I once had a pony
named Peeto. He caught in his nostrils the scent of thun-
derstorms coming even before the clouds had crossed the
Sierra . . .

VENDOR: Tacos, tacos, fritos . . .

ROSITA: Love? Love?

LADY MULLIGAN (*to waiter on terrace*): Are you sure no one called me? I was expecting a call . . .

GUTMAN (*smiling*): My guests are confused and exhausted but at this hour they pull themselves together, and drift downstairs on the wings of gin and the lift, they drift into the public rooms and exchange notes again on fashionable couturiers and custom tailors, restaurants, vintages of wine, hair-dressers, plastic surgeons, girls and young men susceptible to offers . . .

(*There is a hum of light conversation and laughter within.*)

—Hear them? They're exchanging notes . . .

JACQUES (*striking the terrace with his cane*): I asked you what has happened in the plaza!

GUTMAN: Oh, in the plaza, ha ha!—Happenings in the plaza don't concern us . . .

JACQUES: I heard shots fired.

GUTMAN: Shots were fired to remind you of your good fortune in staying here. The public fountains have gone dry, you know, but the Siete Mares was erected over the only perpetual never-dried-up spring in Tierra Caliente, and of course that advantage has to be—protected—sometimes by—martial law . . .

(*The guitar resumes.*)

THE SURVIVOR: When Peeto, my pony, was born—he stood on his four legs at once, and accepted the world!—He was wiser than I . . .

VENDOR: Fritos, fritos, tacos!

ROSITA: Love!

THE SURVIVOR: —When Peeto was one year old he was wiser than God!

(*A wind sings across the plaza; a dry gourd rattles.*)

"Peeto, Peeto!" the Indian boys call after him, trying to stop him—trying to stop the wind!

(*The Survivor's head sags forward. He sits down as slowly as an old man on a park bench. Jacques strikes the terrace again*

*with his cane and starts toward the Survivor. The Guard
seizes his elbow.*)

JACQUES: Don't put your hand on *me*!
GUARD: *Stay here.*
GUTMAN: Remain on the terrace, please, Signor Casanova.
JACQUES (*fiercely*):— *Cognac!*

(*The Waiter whispers to Gutman. Gutman chuckles.*)

GUTMAN: The Maître D' tells me that your credit has been
discontinued in the restaurant and bar, he says that he has
enough of your tabs to pave the terrace with!
JACQUES: What a piece of impertinence! I told the man that
the letter that I'm expecting has been delayed in the mail.
The postal service in this country is fantastically disorga-
nized, and you know it! You also know that Mlle. Gautier
will guarantee my tabs!
GUTMAN: Then let her pick them up at dinner tonight if
you're hungry!
JACQUES: I'm not accustomed to this kind of treatment on
the Camino Real!
GUTMAN: Oh, you'll be, you'll be, after a single night at the
"Ritz Men Only." That's where you'll have to transfer your
patronage if the letter containing the remittance check
doesn't arrive tonight.
JACQUES: I assure you that I shall do nothing of the sort!—
Tonight or ever!
GUTMAN: Watch out, old hawk, the wind is ruffling your
feathers!

(*Jacques sinks trembling into a chair.*)

—Give him a thimble of brandy before he collapses . . .
Fury is a luxury of the young, their veins are resilient, but
his are brittle . . .
JACQUES: Here I sit, submitting to insult for a thimble of
brandy—while directly in front of me—

(*The singer, La Madrecita, enters the plaza. She is a blind
woman led by a ragged Young Man. The Waiter brings
Jacques a brandy.*)

—a man in the plaza dies like a pariah dog!—I take the brandy! I sip it!—My heart is too tired to break, my heart is too tired to—break . . .

(*La Madrecita chants softly. She slowly raises her arm to point at the Survivor crouched on the steps from the plaza.*)

GUTMAN (*suddenly*): Give me the phone! Connect me with the Palace. Get me the Generalissimo, quick, quick, quick!

(*The Survivor rises feebly and shuffles very slowly toward the extended arms of "The Little Blind One."*)

Generalissimo? Gutman speaking! Hello, sweetheart. There has been a little incident in the plaza. You know that party of young explorers that attempted to cross the desert on foot? Well, one of them's come back. He was very thirsty. He found the fountain dry. He started toward the hotel. He was politely advised to advance no further. But he disregarded this advice. Action had to be taken. And now, and now—that old blind woman they call "La Madrecita"?— She's come into the plaza with the man called "The Dreamer" . . .

SURVIVOR: Donde?

THE DREAMER: Aquí!

GUTMAN (*continuing*): You remember those two! I once mentioned them to you. You said "They're harmless dreamers and they're loved by the people."—"What," I asked you, "is harmless about a dreamer, and what," I asked you, "is harmless about the love of the people?— Revolution only needs good dreamers who remember their dreams, and the love of the people belongs safely only to you—their Generalissimo!"—Yes, now the blind woman has recovered her sight and is extending her arms to the wounded Survivor, and the man with the guitar is leading him to her . . .

(*The described action is being enacted.*)

Wait one moment! There's a possibility that the forbidden word may be spoken! Yes! The forbidden word is about to be spoken!

(*The Dreamer places an arm about the blinded Survivor, and cries out:*)

THE DREAMER: *Hermano!*

(*The cry is repeated like springing fire and a loud murmur sweeps the crowd. They push forward with cupped hands extended and the gasping cries of starving people at the sight of bread. Two Military Guards herd them back under the colonnades with clubs and drawn revolvers. La Madrecita chants softly with her blind eyes lifted. A Guard starts toward her. The People shout "NO!")*

LA MADRECITA (*chanting*): "Rojo está el sol! Rojo está el sol de sangre! Blanca está la luna! Blanca está la luna de miedo!"

(*The crowd makes a turning motion.*)

GUTMAN (*to the waiter*): *Put up the ropes!*

(*Velvet ropes are strung very quickly about the terrace of the Siete Mares. They are like the ropes on decks of steamers in rough waters. Gutman shouts into the phone again:*)

The word was spoken. The crowd is agitated. Hang on!

(*He lays down instrument.*)

JACQUES (*hoarsely, shaken*): He said "Hermano." That's the word for brother.

GUTMAN (*calmly*): Yes, the most dangerous word in any human tongue is the word for brother. It's inflammatory.— I don't suppose it can be struck out of the language altogether but it must be reserved for strictly private usage in back of soundproof walls. Otherwise it disturbs the population . . .

JACQUES: The people need the word. They're thirsty for it!

GUTMAN: What are these creatures? Mendicants. Prostitutes. Thieves and petty vendors in a bazaar where the human heart is a part of the bargain.

JACQUES: Because they need the word and the word is forbidden!

GUTMAN: The word is said in pulpits and at tables of council where its volatile essence can be contained. But on the lips of these creatures, what is it? A wanton incitement to riot, without understanding. For what is a brother to them but someone to get ahead of, to cheat, to lie to, to undersell in the market. Brother, you say to a man whose wife you sleep with!—But now, you see, the word has disturbed the people and made it necessary to invoke martial law!

(*Meanwhile the Dreamer has brought the Survivor to La Madrecita, who is seated on the cement rim of the fountain. She has cradled the dying man in her arms in the attitude of a* Pietà. *The Dreamer is crouched beside them, softly playing a guitar. Now he springs up with a harsh cry:*)

THE DREAMER: *Muerto!*

(*The Streetcleaners' piping commences at a distance. Gutman seizes the phone again.*)

GUTMAN (*into phone*): Generalissimo, the Survivor is no longer surviving. I think we'd better have some public diversion right away. Put the Gypsy on! Have her announce the Fiesta!

LOUDSPEAKER (*responding instantly*): Damas y Caballeros! The next voice you hear will be the voice of—the Gypsy!

GYPSY (*over loudspeaker*): Hoy! Noche de Fiesta! Tonight the moon will restore the virginity of my daughter!

GUTMAN: Bring on the Gypsy's daughter, Esmeralda. Show the virgin-to-be!

(*Esmeralda is led from the Gypsy's stall by a severe duenna, "Nursie," out upon the forestage. She is manacled by the wrist to the duenna. Her costume is vaguely Levantine.*
(*Guards are herding the crowd back again.*)

GUTMAN: Ha ha! Ho ho ho! Music!

(*There is gay music. Rosita dances.*)

Abdullah! You're on!

(*Abdullah skips into the plaza, shouting histrionically.*)

ABDULLAH: Tonight the moon will restore the virginity of my sister, Esmeralda!

GUTMAN: *Dance, boy!*

(*Esmeralda is led back into the stall. Throwing off his burnoose, Abdullah dances with Rosita. Behind their dance, armed Guards force La Madrecita and the Dreamer to retreat from the fountain, leaving the lifeless body of the survivor. All at once there is a discordant blast of brass instruments.*

(*Kilroy comes into the plaza. He is a young American vagrant, about twenty-seven. He wears dungarees and a skivvy shirt, the pants faded nearly white from long wear and much washing, fitting him as closely as the clothes of sculpture. He has a pair of golden boxing gloves slung about his neck and he carries a small duffle bag. His belt is ruby-and-emerald-studded with the word CHAMP in bold letters. He stops before a chalked inscription on a wall downstage which says: "Kilroy Is Coming!" He scratches out "Coming" and over it prints "Here!"*)

GUTMAN: Ho ho!—a clown! The Eternal Punchinella! That's exactly what's needed in a time of crisis!

Block Three on the Camino Real.

BLOCK THREE

KILROY (*genially, to all present*): Ha ha!

(*Then he walks up to the Officer by the terrace of the Siete Mares.*)

Buenas dias, señor.

(*He gets no response—barely even a glance.*)

Habla Inglesia? Usted?

OFFICER: What is it you want?

KILROY: Where is Western Union or Wells-Fargo? I got to send a wire to some friends in the States.

OFFICER: No hay Western Union, no hay Wells-Fargo.

KILROY: That is very peculiar. I never struck a town yet that didn't have one or the other. I just got off a boat. Lousiest frigging tub I ever shipped on, one continual hell it was, all the way up from Rio. And me sick, too. I picked up one of those tropical fevers. No sick-bay on that tub, no doctor, no medicine or nothing, not even one quinine pill, and I was burning up with Christ knows how much fever. I couldn't make them understand I was sick. I got a bad heart, too. I had to retire from the prize ring because of my heart. I was the light heavyweight champion of the West Coast, won these gloves!—before my ticker went bad.— Feel my chest! Go on, feel it! Feel it. I've got a heart in my chest as big as the head of a baby. Ha ha! They stood me in front of a screen that makes you transparent and that's what they seen inside me, a heart in my chest as big as the head of a baby! With something like that you don't need the Gypsy to tell you, "Time is short, Baby—get ready to hitch on wings!" The medics wouldn't okay me for no more fights. They said to give up liquor and smoking and sex!—To give up sex!—I used to believe a man couldn't live without sex—but he can—if he wants to! My real true woman, my wife, she would of stuck with me, but it was all spoiled with her being scared and me, too, that a real hard kiss would kill me!—So one night while she was sleeping I wrote her good-bye . . .

(*He notices a lack of attention in the Officer: he grins.*)

No comprendo the lingo?

OFFICER: What is it you want?

KILROY: Excuse my ignorance, but what place is this? What is this country and what is the name of this town? I know it seems funny of me to ask such a question. Loco! But I was so glad to get off that rotten tub that I didn't ask nothing of no one except my pay—and I got short-changed on that. I have trouble counting these pesos or Whatzit-you-call-'em.

(*He jerks out his wallet.*)

All-a-this-here. In the States that pile of lettuce would make you a plutocrat!—But I bet you this stuff don't add up to fifty dollars American coin. Ha ha!

OFFICER: Ha ha.

KILROY: Ha ha!

OFFICER (*making it sound like a death-rattle*): Ha-ha-ha-ha-ha.

(*He turns and starts into the cantina. Kilroy grabs his arm.*)

KILROY: Hey!

OFFICER: What is it you want?

KILROY: What is the name of this country and this town?

(*The Officer thrusts his elbow in Kilroy's stomach and twists his arm loose with a Spanish curse. He kicks the swinging doors open and enters the cantina.*)

Brass hats are the same everywhere.

(*As soon as the Officer goes, the Street People come forward and crowd about Kilroy with their wheedling cries.*)

STREET PEOPLE: Dulces, dulces! Lotería! Lotería! Pasteles, café con leche!

KILROY: No caree, no caree!

(*The Prostitute creeps up to him and grins.*)

ROSITA: Love? Love?

KILROY: What did you say?

ROSITA: *Love?*

KILROY: Sorry—I don't feature that. (*To audience*) I have ideals.

(*The Gypsy appears on the roof of her establishment with Esmeralda whom she secures by handcuffs to the iron railing.*)

GYPSY: Stay there while I give the pitch!

(*She then advances with a portable microphone.*)

Testing! One, two, three, four!

NURSIE (*from offstage*): You're on the air!

GYPSY'S LOUDSPEAKER: Are you perplexed by something? Are you tired out and confused? Do you have a fever?

(*Kilroy looks around for the source of the voice.*)

Do you feel yourself to be spiritually unprepared for the age of exploding atoms? Do you distrust the newspapers? Are you suspicious of governments? Have you arrived at a point on the Camino Real where the walls converge not in the distance but right in front of your nose? Does further progress appear impossible to you? Are you afraid of anything at all? Afraid of your heartbeat? Or the eyes of strangers! Afraid of breathing? Afraid of not breathing? Do you wish that things could be straight and simple again as they were in your childhood? Would you like to go back to Kindy Garten?

(*Rosita has crept up to Kilroy while he listens. She reaches out to him. At the same time a Pickpocket lifts his wallet.*)

KILROY (*catching the whore's wrist*): Keep y'r hands off me, y' dirty ole bag! No caree putas! No loteria, no dulces, nada—so get away! Vamoose! All of you! Quit picking at me!

(*He reaches in his pocket and jerks out a handful of small copper and silver coins which he flings disgustedly down the street. The grotesque people scramble after it with their inhuman cries. Kilroy goes on a few steps—then stops short—feeling the back pocket of his dungarees. Then he lets out a startled cry.*)

Robbed! My God, I've been robbed!

(*The Street People scatter to the walls.*)

Which of you got my wallet? *Which* of you dirty—? Shh—Uh!

(*They mumble with gestures of incomprehension. He marches back to the entrance to the hotel.*)

Hey! Officer! Official!—General!

(*The Officer finally lounges out of the hotel entrance and glances at Kilroy.*)

Tiende? One of them's got my wallet! Picked it out of my pocket while that old whore there was groping me! Don't you comprendo?

OFFICER: Nobody rob you. You don't have no pesos.

KILROY: Huh?

OFFICER: You just dreaming that you have money. You don't ever have money. Nunca! Nada!

(*He spits between his teeth.*)

Loco . . .

(*The Officer crosses to the fountain. Kilroy stares at him, then bawls out:*)

KILROY (*to the Street People*): We'll see what the American Embassy has to say about this! I'll go to the American Consul. Whichever of you rotten spivs lifted my wallet is going to jail—calaboose! I hope I have made myself plain. If not, I will make myself plainer!

(*There are scattered laughs among the crowd. He crosses to the fountain. He notices the body of the no longer Survivor, kneels beside it, shakes it, turns it over, springs up and shouts:*)

Hey! This guy is dead!

(*There is the sound of the Streetcleaners' piping. They trundle their white barrel into the plaza from one of the downstage arches. The appearance of these men undergoes a progressive alteration through the play. When they first appear they are almost like any such public servants in a tropical country; their white jackets are dirtier than the musicians' and some of the stains are red. They have on white caps with black visors. They are continually exchanging sly jokes and giggling unpleasantly together. Lord Mulligan has come out upon the terrace and as they pass him, they pause for a moment, point at him, snicker. He is extremely discomfited by this impertinence, touches his chest as if he felt a palpitation and turns back inside.*)

(*Kilroy yells to the advancing Streetcleaners.*)

There's a dead man layin' here!

(*They giggle again. Briskly they lift the body and stuff it into the barrel; then trundle it off, looking back at Kilroy, giggling, whispering. They return under the downstage arch through which they entered. Kilroy, in a low, shocked voice:*)

What *is* this place? What kind of a hassle have I got myself into?

LOUDSPEAKER: If anyone on the Camino is bewildered, come to the Gypsy. A poco dinero will tickle the Gypsy's palm and give her visions!

ABDULLAH (*giving Kilroy a card*): If you got a question, ask my mama, the Gypsy!

KILROY: Man, whenever you see those three brass balls on a street, you don't have to look a long ways for a Gypsy. Now le' me think. I am faced with three problems. One: I'm hungry. Two: I'm lonely. Three: I'm in a place where I don't know what it is or how I got there! First action that's indicated is to—cash in on something—Well . . . let's see . . .

(*Honky-tonk music fades in at this point and the Skid Row façade begins to light up for the evening. There is the Gypsy's stall with its cabalistic devices, its sectional cranium and palm, three luminous brass balls overhanging the entrance to the Loan Shark and his window filled with a vast assortment of hocked articles for sale: trumpets, banjos, fur coats, tuxedos, a gown of scarlet sequins, loops of pearls and rhinestones. Dimly behind this display is a neon sign in three pastel colors, pink, green, and blue. It fades softly in and out and it says: "Magic Tricks Jokes." There is also the advertisement of a flea-bag hotel or flophouse called "Ritz Men Only." This sign is also pale neon or luminous paint, and only the entrance is on the street floor, the rooms are above the Loan Shark and Gypsy's stall. One of the windows of this upper story is practical. Figures appear in it sometimes, leaning out as if suffocating or to hawk and spit into the street below. This side of the street should have all the color and animation that are permitted by the resources of the production. There may be moments of dancelike action [a fight, a seduction, sale of narcotics, arrest, etc.].*)

KILROY (*to the audience from the apron*): What've I got to cash in on? My golden gloves? Never! I'll say that once more, never! The silver-framed photo of my One True Woman? Never! Repeat that! Never! What else have I got of a detachable and a negotiable nature? Oh! My ruby-and-emerald-studded belt with the word CHAMP on it.

(*He whips it off his pants.*)

This is not necessary to hold on my pants, but this is a precious reminder of the sweet used-to-be. Oh, well. Sometimes a man has got to hock his sweet used-to-be in order to finance his present situation . . .

(*He enters the Loan Shark's. A Drunken Bum leans out the practical window of the "Ritz Men Only" and shouts:*)

BUM: O Jack o' Diamonds, you robbed my pockets, you robbed my pockets of silver and gold!

(*He jerks the window shade down.*)

GUTMAN (*on the terrace*): Block Four on the Camino Real!

BLOCK FOUR

There is a phrase of light music as the Baron de Charlus, an elderly foppish sybarite in a light silk suit, a carnation in his lapel, crosses from the Siete Mares to the honky-tonk side of the street. On his trail is a wild-looking young man of startling beauty called Lobo. Charlus is aware of the follower and, during his conversation with A. Ratt, he takes out a pocket mirror to inspect him while pretending to comb his hair and point his moustache. As Charlus approaches, the Manager of the flea-bag puts up a vacancy sign and calls out:

A. RATT: Vacancy here! A bed at the "Ritz Men Only"! A little white ship to sail the dangerous night in . . .

THE BARON: Ah, bon soir, Mr. Ratt.

A. RATT: Cruising?

THE BARON: No, just—walking!

A. RATT: That's all you need to do.

THE BARON: I sometimes find it suffices. You have a vacancy, do you?

A. RATT: For you?

THE BARON: And a possible guest. You know the requirements. An iron bed with no mattress and a considerable length of stout knotted rope. No! Chains this evening, metal chains. I've been very bad, I have a lot to atone for . . .

A. RATT: Why don't you take these joy-rides at the Siete Mares?

THE BARON (*with the mirror focused on Lobo*): They don't have Ingreso Libero at the Siete Mares. Oh, I don't like places in the haute saison, the alta staggione, and yet if you go between the fashionable seasons, it's too hot or too damp or appallingly overrun by all the wrong sort of people who rap on the wall if canaries sing in your bed-springs after midnight. I don't know why such people don't stay at home. Surely a Kodak, a Brownie, or even a Leica works just as well in Milwaukee or Sioux City as it does in these places they do on their whirlwind summer tours, and don't look now, but I think I am being followed!

A. RATT: Yep, you've made a pickup!

THE BARON: Attractive?

A. RATT: That depends on who's driving the bicycle, Dad.

THE BARON: Ciao, Caro! Expect me at ten.

(*He crosses elegantly to the fountain.*)

A. RATT: Vacancy here! A little white ship to sail the dangerous night in!

(*The music changes. Kilroy backs out of the Loan Shark's, belt unsold, engaged in a violent dispute. The Loan Shark is haggling for his golden gloves. Charlus lingers, intrigued by the scene.*)

LOAN SHARK: I don't want no belt! I want the gloves! Eight-fifty!

KILROY: No dice.

LOAN SHARK: Nine, nine-fifty!

KILROY: Nah, nah, nah!

LOAN SHARK: Yah, yah, yah.

KILROY: I say nah.

LOAN SHARK: I say yah.

KILROY: The nahs have it.

LOAN SHARK: Don't be a fool. What can you do with a pair of golden gloves?

KILROY: I can remember the battles I fought to win them! I can remember that I used to be—CHAMP!

(*Fade in Band Music: "March of the Gladiators"—ghostly cheers, etc.*)

LOAN SHARK: You can remember that you *used to be*—Champ?

KILROY: Yes! I used to be—CHAMP!

THE BARON: Used to be is the past tense, meaning useless.

KILROY: Not to me, Mister. These are my gloves, these gloves are gold, and I fought a lot of hard fights to win 'em! I broke clean from the clinches. I never hit a low blow, the referee never told me to mix it up! And the fixers never got to me!

LOAN SHARK: In other words, a sucker!

KILROY: Yep, I'm a sucker that won the golden gloves!

LOAN SHARK: Congratulations. My final offer is a piece of green paper with Alexander Hamilton's picture on it. Take it or leave it.

KILROY: I leave it for you to *stuff* it! I'd hustle my heart on this street, I'd peddle my heart's true blood before I'd leave my golden gloves hung up in a loan shark's window between a rusted trombone and some poor lush's long ago mildewed tuxedo!

LOAN SHARK: So you say but I will see you later.

THE BARON: The name of the Camino is not unreal!

(*The Bum sticks his head out the window and shouts:*)

BUM: Pa dam, Pa dam, Pa dam!

THE BARON (*continuing the Bum's song*): Echoes the beat of my heart! Pa dam, Pa dam—*hello!*

(*He has crossed to Kilroy as he sings and extends his hand to him.*)

KILROY (*uncertainly*): Hey, mate. It's wonderful to see you.

THE BARON: Thanks, but why?

KILROY: A normal American. In a clean white suit.

THE BARON: My suit is pale yellow. My nationality is French, and my normality has been often subject to question.

KILROY: I still say your suit is clean.

THE BARON: Thanks. That's more than I can say for your apparel.

KILROY: Don't judge a book by the covers. I'd take a shower if I could locate the "Y."

THE BARON: What's the "Y"?

KILROY: Sort of a Protestant church with a swimmin' pool in it. Sometimes it also has an employment bureau. It does good in the community.

THE BARON: Nothing in this community does much good.

KILROY: I'm getting the same impression. This place is confusing to me. I think it must be the aftereffects of fever. Nothing seems real. Could you give me the scoop?

THE BARON: Serious questions are referred to the Gypsy. Once upon a time. Oh, once upon a time. I used to wonder. Now I simply wander. I stroll about the fountain and hope to be followed. Some people call it corruption. I call it—simplification . . .

BUM (*very softly at the window*): I wonder what's become of Sally, that old gal of mine?

(*He lowers the blind.*)

KILROY: Well, anyhow . . .

THE BARON: Well, anyhow?

KILROY: How about the hot-spots in this town?

THE BARON: Oh, the hot-spots, ho ho! There's the Pink Flamingo, the Yellow Pelican, the Blue Heron, and the Prothonotary Warbler! They call it the Bird Circuit. But I don't care for such places. They stand three-deep at the bar and look at themselves in the mirror and what they see is depressing. One sailor comes in—they faint! My own choice of resorts is the Bucket of Blood downstairs from the "Ritz Men Only."—How about a match?

KILROY: Where's your cigarette?

THE BARON (*gently and sweetly*): Oh, I don't smoke. I just wanted to see your eyes more clearly . . .

KILROY: Why?

THE BARON: The eyes are the windows of the soul, and yours are too gentle for someone who has as much as I have to atone for. (*He starts off.*) Au revoir . . .

KILROY: —A very unusual type character . . .

(*Casanova is on the steps leading to the arch, looking out at the desert beyond. Now he turns and descends a few steps, laughing with a note of tired incredulity. Kilroy crosses to him.*)

Gee, it's wonderful to see you, a normal American in a—

(*There is a strangulated outcry from the arch under which the Baron has disappeared.*)

Excuse me a minute!

(*He rushes toward the source of the outcry. Jacques crosses to the bench before the fountain. Rhubarb is heard through the arch. Jacques shrugs wearily as if it were just a noisy radio. Kilroy comes plummeting out backwards, all the way to Jacques.*)

I tried to interfere, but what's th' use?!
JACQUES: No use at all!

(*The Streetcleaners come through the arch with the Baron doubled up in their barrel. They pause and exchange sibilant whispers, pointing and snickering at Kilroy.*)

KILROY: Who are they pointing at? At me, Kilroy?

(*The Bum laughs from the window. A. Ratt laughs from his shadowy doorway. The Loan Shark laughs from his.*)

Kilroy is here and he's not about to be there!—If he can help it . . .

(*He snatches up a rock and throws it at the Streetcleaners. Everybody laughs louder and the laughter seems to reverberate from the mountains. The light changes, dims a little in the plaza.*)

Sons a whatever you're sons of! Don't look at me, I'm not about to take no ride in the barrel!

(*The Baron, his elegant white shoes protruding from the barrel, is wheeled up the Alleyway Out. Figures in the square resume their dazed attitudes and one or two Guests return to the terrace of the Siete Mares as—*)

GUTMAN: Block Five on the Camino Real!

(*He strolls off.*)

BLOCK FIVE

KILROY (*to Jacques*): Gee, the blocks go fast on this street!

JACQUES: Yes. The blocks go fast.

KILROY: My name's Kilroy. I'm here.

JACQUES: Mine is Casanova. I'm here, too.

KILROY: But you been here longer than me and maybe could brief me on it. For instance, what do they do with a stiff picked up in this town?

(*The Guard stares at them suspiciously from the terrace.*
(*Jacques whistles "La Golondrina" and crosses downstage. Kilroy follows.*)

Did I say something untactful?

JACQUES (*smiling into a sunset glow*): The exchange of serious questions and ideas, especially between persons from opposite sides of the plaza, is regarded unfavorably here. You'll notice I'm talking as if I had acute laryngitis. I'm gazing into the sunset. If I should start to whistle "La Golondrina" it means we're being overheard by the Guards on the terrace. Now you want to know what is done to a body from which the soul has departed on the Camino Real!—Its disposition depends on what the Streetcleaners happen to find in its pockets. If its pockets are empty as the unfortunate Baron's turned out to be, and as mine are at this moment—the "stiff" is wheeled straight off to the Laboratory. And there the individual becomes an undistinguished member of a collectivist state. His chemical components are separated and poured into vats containing the corresponding elements of countless others. If any of his vital organs or parts are at all unique in size or structure, they're placed on exhibition in bottles containing a very foul-smelling solution called formaldehyde. There is a charge of admission to this museum. The proceeds go to the maintenance of the military police.

(*He whistles "La Golondrina" till the Guard turns his back again. He moves toward the front of the stage.*)

KILROY (*following*): —I guess that's—sensible . . .

JACQUES: Yes, but not romantic. And romance is important. Don't you think?

KILROY: Nobody thinks romance is more important than me!

JACQUES: Except possibly me!

KILROY: Maybe that's why fate has brung us together! We're buddies under the skin!

JACQUES: Travelers born?

KILROY: Always looking for something!

JACQUES: Satisfied by nothing!

KILROY: Hopeful?

JACQUES: Always!

OFFICER: Keep moving!

(*They move apart till the Officer exits.*)

KILROY: And when a joker on the Camino gets fed up with one continual hassle—how does he get *off* it?

JACQUES: You see the narrow and very steep stairway that passes under what is described in the travel brochures as a "Magnificent Arch of Triumph"?—Well, that's the Way Out!

KILROY: That's the way out?

(*Kilroy without hesitation plunges right up to almost the top step; then pauses with a sound of squealing brakes. There is a sudden loud wind.*)

JACQUES (*shouting with hand cupped to mouth*): Well, how does the prospect please you, Traveler born?

KILROY (*shouting back in a tone of awe*): It's too unknown for my blood. Man, I seen nothing like it except through a telescope once on the pier on Coney Island. "Ten cents to see the craters and plains of the moon!"—And here's the same view in three dimensions for nothing!

(*The desert wind sings loudly: Kilroy mocks it.*)

JACQUES: Are you—ready to cross it?

KILROY: Maybe sometime with someone but not right now and alone! How about you?

JACQUES: I'm not alone.

KILROY: You're with a party?

JACQUES: No, but I'm sweetly encumbered with a—lady . . .

KILROY: It wouldn't do with a lady. I don't see nothing but nothing—and then more nothing. And then I see some mountains. But the mountains are covered with snow.

JACQUES: Snowshoes would be useful!

(*He observes Gutman approaching through the passage at upper left. He whistles "La Golondrina" for Kilroy's attention and points with his cane as he exits.*)

KILROY (*descending steps disconsolately*): Mush, mush.

(*The Bum comes to his window. A. Ratt enters his doorway. Gutman enters below Kilroy.*)

BUM: It's sleepy time down South!

GUTMAN (*warningly as Kilroy passes him*): Block Six in a progress of sixteen blocks on the Camino Real.

BLOCK SIX

KILROY (*from the stairs*): Man, I could use a bed now.—I'd like to make me a cool pad on this camino now and lie down and sleep and dream of being with someone—friendly . . .

(*He crosses to the "Ritz Men Only."*)

A. RATT (*softly and sleepily*): Vacancy here! I got a single bed at the "Ritz Men Only," a little white ship to sail the dangerous night in.

(*Kilroy crosses down to his doorway.*)

KILROY: —You got a vacancy here?

A. RATT: I got a vacancy here if you got the one-fifty there.

KILROY: Ha ha! I been in countries where money was not legal tender. I mean it was legal but it wasn't tender.

(*There is a loud groan from offstage above.*)

—Somebody dying on you or just drunk?

A. RATT: Who knows or cares in this pad, Dad?

KILROY: I heard once that a man can't die while he's drunk. Is that a fact or a fiction?

A. RATT: Strictly a fiction.

VOICE ABOVE: *Stiff in number seven! Call the Streetcleaners!*

A. RATT (*with absolutely no change in face or voice*): Number seven is vacant.

> (*Streetcleaners' piping is heard.*
> (*The Bum leaves the window.*)

KILROY: Thanks, but tonight I'm going to sleep under the stars.

> (*A. Ratt gestures "Have it your way" and exits.*
> (*Kilroy, left alone, starts downstage. He notices that La Madrecita is crouched near the fountain, holding something up, inconspicuously, in her hand. Coming to her he sees that it's a piece of food. He takes it, puts it in his mouth, tries to thank her but her head is down, muffled in her rebozo and there is no way for him to acknowledge the gift. He starts to cross. Street People raise up their heads in their Pit and motion him invitingly to come in with them. They call softly, "Sleep, sleep . . ."*)

GUTMAN (*from his chair on the terrace*): Hey, Joe.

> (*The Street People duck immediately.*)

KILROY: Who? Me?
GUTMAN: Yes, you, Candy Man. Are you disocupado?
KILROY: —That means—unemployed, don't it?

> (*He sees Officers converging from right.*)

GUTMAN: Jobless. On the bum. Carrying the banner!
KILROY: —Aw, no, aw, no, don't try to hang no vagrancy rap on me! I was robbed on this square and I got plenty of witnesses to prove it.
GUTMAN (*with ironic courtesy*): Oh?

> (*He makes a gesture asking "Where?"*)

KILROY (*coming down to apron left and crossing to the right*): Witnesses! Witness! Witnesses!

> (*He comes to La Madrecita.*)

You were a witness!

> (*A gesture indicates that he realizes her blindness. Opposite the Gypsy's balcony he pauses for a second.*)

Hey, Gypsy's daughter!

(*The balcony is dark. He continues up to the Pit. The Street People duck as he calls down:*)

You were witnesses!

(*An Officer enters with a Patsy outfit. He hands it to Gutman.*)

GUTMAN: Here, Boy! Take these.

(*Gutman displays and then tosses on the ground at Kilroy's feet the Patsy outfit—the red fright wig, the big crimson nose that lights up and has horn rimmed glasses attached, a pair of clown pants that have a huge footprint on the seat.*)

KILROY: What is this outfit?

GUTMAN: The uniform of a Patsy.

KILROY: I know what a Patsy is—he's a clown in the circus who takes prat-falls but *I'm no Patsy!*

GUTMAN: Pick it up.

KILROY: Don't give me orders. Kilroy is a free agent—

GUTMAN (*smoothly*): But a Patsy isn't. Pick it up and put it on, Candy Man. You are now the Patsy.

KILROY: So you say but you are completely mistaken.

(*Four Officers press in on him.*)

And don't crowd me with your torpedoes! I'm a stranger here but I got a clean record in all the places I been, I'm not in the books for nothin' but vagrancy and once when I was hungry I walked by a truck-load of pineapples without picking one, because I was brought up good—

(*Then, with a pathetic attempt at making friends with the Officer to his right.*)

and there was a cop on the corner!

OFFICER: Ponga selo!

KILROY: What'd you say? (*Desperately to audience he asks:*) What did he say?

OFFICER: Ponga selo!

KILROY: What'd you say?

(*The Officer shoves him down roughly to the Patsy outfit. Kilroy picks up the pants, shakes them out carefully as if about to step into them and says very politely:*)

Why, surely. I'd be delighted. My fondest dreams have come true.

(*Suddenly he tosses the Patsy dress into Gutman's face and leaps into the aisle of the theatre.*)

GUTMAN: Stop him! Arrest that vagrant! Don't let him get away!

LOUDSPEAKER: Be on the lookout for a fugitive Patsy. The Patsy has escaped. Stop him, stop that Patsy!

(*A wild chase commences. The two Guards rush madly down either side to intercept him at the back of the house. Kilroy wheels about at the top of the center aisle, and runs back down it, panting, gasping out questions and entreaties to various persons occupying aisle seats, such as:*)

KILROY: How do I git out? Which way do I go, which way do I get out? Where's the Greyhound depot? Hey, do you know where the Greyhound bus depot is? What's the best way out, if there is any way out? I got to find one. I had enough of this place. I had too much of this place. I'm free. I'm a free man with equal rights in this world! You better believe it because that's news for you and you had better believe it! Kilroy's a free man with equal rights in this world! All right, now, help me, somebody, help me find a way out, I got to find one, I don't like this place! It's not for me and I am not buying any! Oh! Over there! I see a sign that says EXIT. That's a sweet word to me, man, that's a lovely word, EXIT! That's the entrance to paradise for Kilroy! Exit, I'm coming, Exit, I'm coming!

(*The Street People have gathered along the forestage to watch the chase. Esmeralda, barefooted, wearing only a slip, bursts out of the Gypsy's establishment like an animal broken out of a cage, darts among the Street People to the front of the Crowd which is shouting like the spectators at the climax of a corrida. Behind her, Nursie appears, a male actor, wigged and dressed austerely as a duenna, crying out in both languages.*)

NURSIE: Esmeralda! Esmeralda!
GYPSY: Police!
NURSIE: Come back here, Esmeralda!
GYPSY: Catch her, idiot!
NURSIE: Where is my lady bird, where is my precious treasure?
GYPSY: Idiot! I told you to keep her door locked!
NURSIE: She jimmied the lock, Esmeralda!

(*These shouts are mostly lost in the general rhubarb of the chase and the shouting Street People. Esmeralda crouches on the forestage, screaming encouragement in Spanish to the fugitive. Abdullah catches sight of her, seizes her wrist, shouting:*)

ABDULLAH: Here she is! I got her!

(*Esmeralda fights savagely. She nearly breaks loose, but Nursie and the Gypsy close upon her, too, and she is overwhelmed and dragged back, fighting all the way, toward the door from which she escaped.*

(Meanwhile—timed with the above action—shots are fired in the air by Kilroy's Pursuers. He dashes, panting, into the boxes of the theatre, darting from one box to another, shouting incoherently, now, sobbing for breath, crying out:)

KILROY: *Mary, help a Christian! Help a Christian, Mary!*
ESMERALDA: *Yankee! Yankee, jump!*

(*The Officers close upon him in the box nearest the stage. A dazzling spot of light is thrown on him. He lifts a little gilded chair to defend himself. The chair is torn from his grasp. He leaps upon the ledge of the box.*)

Jump! Jump, Yankee!

(*The Gypsy is dragging the girl back by her hair.*)

KILROY: *Watch out down there! Geronimo!*

(*He leaps onto the stage and crumples up with a twisted ankle. Esmeralda screams demoniacally, breaks from her mother's grasp and rushes to him, fighting off his pursuers who have leapt after him from the box. Abdullah, Nursie and the Gypsy seize her again, just as Kilroy is seized by his pursuers. The Officers beat him to his knees. Each time he is struck, Esmeralda screams as if she received the blow herself. As his*) *cries subside into sobbing, so do hers, and at the end, when he is quite helpless, she is also overcome by her captors and as they drag her back to the Gypsy's she cries to him:*)

ESMERALDA: *They've got you! They've got me!*

(*Her mother slaps her fiercely.*)

Caught! Caught! We're caught!

(*She is dragged inside. The door is slammed shut on her continuing outcries. For a moment nothing is heard but Kilroy's hoarse panting and sobbing. Gutman takes command of the situation, thrusting his way through the crowd to face Kilroy who is pinioned by two Guards.*)

GUTMAN (*smiling serenely*): Well, well, how do you do! I understand that you're seeking employment here. We need a Patsy and the job is yours for the asking!

KILROY: I don't. Accept. This job. I been. Shanghied!

(*Kilroy dons Patsy outfit.*)

GUTMAN: Hush! The Patsy doesn't talk. He lights his nose, that's all!

GUARD: Press the little button at the end of the cord.

GUTMAN: That's right. Just press the little button at the end of the cord!

(*Kilroy lights his nose. Everybody laughs.*)

GUTMAN: Again, ha ha! Again, ha ha! Again!

(*The nose goes off and on like a firefly as the stage dims out.* (*The curtain falls. There is a short intermission.*)

BLOCK SEVEN

The Dreamer is singing with mandolin, "Noche de Ronde." The Guests murmur, "cool—cool . . ." Gutman stands on the podiumlike elevation downstage right, smoking a long thin cigar, signing an occasional tab from the bar or café. He is standing in an amber spot. The rest of the stage is filled with blue dusk. At the signal the song fades to a whisper and Gutman speaks.

GUTMAN: Block Seven on the Camino Real— I like this hour.

(*He gives the audience a tender gold-toothed smile.*)

The fire's gone out of the day but the light of it lingers . . .
In Rome the continual fountains are bathing stone heroes
with silver, in Copenhagen the Tivoli gardens are lighted,
they're selling the lottery on San Juan de Latrene . . .

(*The Dreamer advances a little, playing the mandolin softly.*)

LA MADRECITA (*holding up glass beads and shell necklaces*):
Recuerdos, recuerdos?

GUTMAN: And these are the moments when we look into ourselves and ask with a wonder which never is lost altogether:
"Can this be all? Is there nothing more? Is this what the
glittering wheels of the heavens turn for?"

(*He leans forward as if conveying a secret.*)

—Ask the Gypsy! Un poco dinero will tickle the Gypsy's
palm and give her visions!

(*Abdullah emerges with a silver tray, calling:*)

ABDULLAH: Letter for Signor Casanova, letter for Signor
Casanova!

(*Jacques springs up but stands rigid.*)

GUTMAN: Casanova, you have received a letter. Perhaps it's
the letter with the remittance check in it!

JACQUES (*in a hoarse, exalted voice*): Yes! It is! The letter!
With the remittance check in it!

GUTMAN: Then why don't you take it so you can maintain
your residence at the Siete Mares and so avoid the more
somber attractions of the "Ritz Men Only"?

JACQUES: My hand is—

GUTMAN: Your hand is paralyzed? . . . By what? *Anxiety?*
Apprehension? . . . Put the letter in Signor Casanova's
pocket so he can open it when he recovers the use of his
digital extremities. Then give him a shot of brandy on the
house before he falls on his face!

(*Jacques has stepped down into the plaza. He looks down at
Kilroy crouched to the right of him and wildly blinking his nose.*)

JACQUES: Yes. I know the Morse code.

(*Kilroy's nose again blinks on and off.*)

Thank you, brother.

(*This is said as if acknowledging a message.*)

I knew without asking the Gypsy that something of this sort would happen to you. You have a spark of anarchy in your spirit and that's not to be tolerated. Nothing wild or honest is tolerated here! It has to be extinguished or used only to light up your nose for Mr. Gutman's amusement . . .

(*Jacques saunters around Kilroy whistling "La Golondrina." Then satisfied that no one is suspicious of this encounter . . .*)

Before the final block we'll find some way out of here! Meanwhile, patience and courage, little brother!

(*Jacques feeling he's been there too long starts away giving Kilroy a reassuring pat on the shoulder and saying:*)

Patience! . . . Courage!

LADY MULLIGAN (*from the Mulligans' table*): Mr. Gutman!

GUTMAN: Lady Mulligan! And how are you this evening, Lord Mulligan?

LADY MULLIGAN (*interrupting Lord Mulligan's rumblings*): He's not at all well. This . . . climate is so enervating!

LORD MULLIGAN: I was so weak this morning . . . I couldn't screw the lid on my tooth paste!

LADY MULLIGAN: Raymond, tell Mr. Gutman about those two impertinent workmen in the square! . . . These two idiots pushing a white barrel! Pop up every time we step outside the hotel!

LORD MULLIGAN: —point and giggle at me!

LADY MULLIGAN: Can't they be discharged?

GUTMAN: They can't be discharged, disciplined nor bribed! All you can do is pretend to ignore them.

LADY MULLIGAN: I can't eat! . . . Raymond, stop stuffing!

LORD MULLIGAN: *Shut up!*

GUTMAN (*to the audience*): When the big wheels crack on this street it's like the fall of a capital city, the destruction of Carthage, the sack of Rome by the white-eyed giants from

the North! I've seen them fall! I've seen the destruction of
them! Adventurer suddenly frightened of a dark room!
Gamblers unable to choose between odd and even! Con
men and pitchmen and plume-hatted cavaliers turned baby-
soft at one note of the Streetcleaners' pipes! When I observe this change, I say to myself: "Could it happen to ME?"
—The answer is "YES!" And that's what curdles my blood
like milk on the doorstep of someone gone for the summer!

(*A Hunchback Mummer somersaults through his hoop of silver bells, springs up and shakes it excitedly toward a downstage arch which begins to flicker with a diamond-blue
radiance; this marks the advent of each legendary character
in the play. The music follows: a waltz from the time of
Camille in Paris.*)

GUTMAN (*downstage to the audience*): Ah, there's the music of
another legend, one that everyone knows, the legend of the
sentimental whore, the courtesan who made the mistake of
love. But now you see her coming into this plaza not as she
was when she burned with a fever that cast a thin light over
Paris, but changed, yes, faded as lanterns and legends fade
when they burn into day!

(*He turns and shouts:*)

Rosita, sell her a flower!

(*Marguerite has entered the plaza. A beautiful woman of
indefinite age. The Street People cluster about her with
wheedling cries, holding up glass beads, shell necklaces and so
forth. She seems confused, lost, half-awake. Jacques has sprung
up at her entrance but has difficulty making his way through
the cluster of vendors. Rosita has snatched up a tray of flowers
and cries out:*)

ROSITA: Camellias, camellias! Pink or white, whichever a lady
finds suitable to the moon!
GUTMAN: That's the ticket!
MARGUERITE: Yes, I would like a camellia.
ROSITA (*in a bad French accent*): Rouge ou blanc ce soir?
MARGUERITE: It's always a white one, now . . . but there
used to be five evenings out of the month when a pink

camellia, instead of the usual white one, let my admirers
know that the moon those nights was unfavorable to pleasure, and so they called me—Camille . . .

JACQUES: Mia cara!

(*Imperiously, very proud to be with her, he pushes the Street
People aside with his cane.*)

Out of the way, make way, let us through, please!

MARGUERITE: Don't push them with your cane.

JACQUES: If they get close enough they'll snatch your purse.

(*Marguerite utters a low, shocked cry.*)

What is it?

MARGUERITE: *My purse is gone! It's lost! My papers were in it!*

JACQUES: Your passport was in it?

MARGUERITE: My passport and my permiso de residencia!

(*She leans faint against the arch during the following scene.
(Abdullah turns to run. Jacques catches him.*)

JACQUES (*seizing Abdullah's wrist*): Where did you take her?

ABDULLAH: Oww!—P'tit Zoco.

JACQUES: The Souks?

ABDULLAH: The Souks!

JACQUES: Which cafés did she go to?

ABDULLAH: Ahmed's, she went to—

JACQUES: Did she smoke at Ahmed's?

ABDULLAH: Two kif pipes!

JACQUES: Who was it took her purse? Was it *you*? We'll see!

(*He strips off the boy's burnoose. He crouches whimpering,
shivering in a ragged slip.*)

MARGUERITE: Jacques, let the boy go, he didn't take it!

JACQUES: He doesn't have it on him but knows who does!

ABDULLAH: No, no, I don't know!

JACQUES: You little son of a Gypsy! Senta! . . . You know
who I am? I am Jacques Casanova! I belong to the Secret
Order of the Rose-colored Cross! . . . Run back to
Ahmed's. Contact the spiv that took the lady's purse. Tell
him to keep it but give her back her papers! There'll be a
large reward.

(*He thumps his cane on the ground to release Abdullah from the spell. The boy dashes off. Jacques laughs and turns triumphantly to Marguerite.*)

LADY MULLIGAN: Waiter! That adventurer and his mistress must not be seated next to Lord Mulligan's table!

JACQUES (*loudly enough for Lady Mulligan to hear*): This hotel has become a mecca for black marketeers and their expensively kept women!

LADY MULLIGAN: Mr. Gutman!

MARGUERITE: Let's have dinner upstairs!

WAITER (*directing them to terrace table*): *This* way, M'sieur.

JACQUES: We'll take our usual table.

(*He indicates one.*)

MARGUERITE: Please!

WAITER (*overlapping Marguerite's "please!"*): This table is reserved for Lord Byron!

JACQUES (*masterfully*): This table is always our table.

MARGUERITE: I'm not hungry.

JACQUES: Hold out the lady's chair, cretino!

GUTMAN (*darting over to Marguerite's chair*): Permit me!

(*Jacques bows with mock gallantry to Lady Mulligan as he turns to his chair during seating of Marguerite.*)

LADY MULLIGAN: We'll move to *that* table!

JACQUES: —You must learn how to carry the banner of Bohemia into the enemy camp.

(*A screen is put up around them.*)

MARGUERITE: Bohemia has no banner. It survives by discretion.

JACQUES: I'm glad that you value discretion. *Wine list!* Was it discretion that led you through the bazaars this afternoon wearing your cabochon sapphire and diamond ear-drops? You were fortunate that you lost only your purse and papers!

MARGUERITE: Take the wine list.

JACQUES: Still or sparkling?

MARGUERITE: Sparkling.

GUTMAN: May I make a suggestion, Signor Casanova?

JACQUES: Please do.

GUTMAN: It's a very cold and dry wine from only ten metres below the snowline in the mountains. The name of the wine is Quando!—meaning when! Such as "When are remittances going to be received?" "When are accounts to be settled?" Ha ha ha! Bring Signor Casanova a bottle of Quando with the compliments of the house!

JACQUES: I'm sorry this had to happen in—your presence . . .

MARGUERITE: That doesn't matter, my dear. But why don't you *tell* me when you are short of money?

JACQUES: I thought the fact was apparent. It is to everyone else.

MARGUERITE: The letter you were expecting, it still hasn't come?

JACQUES (*removing it from his pocket*): It came this afternoon —Here it is!

MARGUERITE: You haven't opened the letter!

JACQUES: I haven't had the nerve to! I've had so many unpleasant surprises that I've lost faith in my luck.

MARGUERITE: Give the letter to me. Let me open it for you.

JACQUES: Later, a little bit later, after the—wine . . .

MARGUERITE: Old hawk, anxious old hawk!

(*She clasps his hand on the table: he leans toward her: she kisses her fingertips and places them on his lips.*)

JACQUES: Do you call that a kiss?

MARGUERITE: I call it the ghost of a kiss. It will have to do for now.

(*She leans back, her blue-tinted eyelids closed.*)

JACQUES: Are you tired? Are you tired, Marguerite? You know you should have rested this afternoon.

MARGUERITE: I looked at silver and rested.

JACQUES: You looked at silver at Ahmed's?

MARGUERITE: No, I rested at Ahmed's, and had mint-tea.

(*The Dreamer accompanies their speech with his guitar. The duologue should have the style of an antiphonal poem, the cues picked up so that there is scarcely a separation between the speeches, and the tempo quick and the voices edged.*)

JACQUES: You had mint-tea downstairs?

MARGUERITE: No, upstairs.

JACQUES: Upstairs where they burn the poppy?

MARGUERITE: Upstairs where it's cool and there's music and the haggling of the bazaar is soft as the murmur of pigeons.

JACQUES: That sounds restful. Reclining among silk pillows on a divan, in a curtained and perfumed alcove above the bazaar?

MARGUERITE: Forgetting for a while where I am, or that I don't know where I am . . .

JACQUES: Forgetting alone or forgetting with some young companion who plays the lute or the flute or who had silver to show you? Yes. That sounds very restful. And yet you do seem tired.

MARGUERITE: If I seem tired, it's your insulting solicitude that I'm tired of!

JACQUES: Is it insulting to feel concern for your safety in this place?

MARGUERITE: Yes, it is. The implication is.

JACQUES: What is the implication?

MARGUERITE: You know what it is: that I am one of those *aging*—*voluptuaries*—who used to be paid for pleasure but now have to pay!—Jacques, I won't be followed, I've gone too far to be followed!—*What is it?*

(*The Waiter has presented an envelope on a salver.*)

WAITER: A letter for the lady.

MARGUERITE: How strange to receive a letter in a place where nobody knows I'm staying! Will you open it for me?

(*The Waiter withdraws. Jacques takes the letter and opens it.*)

Well! What is it?

JACQUES: Nothing important. An illustrated brochure from some resort in the mountains.

MARGUERITE: What is it called?

JACQUES: Bide-a-While.

(*A chafing dish bursts into startling blue flame at the Mulligans' table. Lady Mulligan clasps her hands and exclaims with affected delight, the Waiter and Mr. Gutman laugh agreeably. Marguerite springs up and moves out upon the forestage. Jacques goes to her.*)

Do you know this resort in the mountains?

MARGUERITE: Yes. I stayed there once. It's one of those places with open sleeping verandahs, surrounded by snowy pine woods. It has rows and rows of narrow white iron beds as regular as tombstones. The invalids smile at each other when axes flash across valleys, ring, flash, ring again! Young voices shout across valleys Hola! And mail is delivered. The friend that used to write you ten-page letters contents himself now with a postcard bluebird that tells you to "Get well Quick!"

(*Jacques throws the brochure away.*)

—And when the last bleeding comes, not much later nor earlier than expected, you're wheeled discreetly into a little tent of white gauze, and the last thing you know of this world, of which you've known so little and yet so much, is the smell of an empty ice box.

(*The blue flame expires in the chafing dish. Gutman picks up the brochure and hands it to the Waiter, whispering something.*)

JACQUES: You won't go back to that place.

(*The Waiter places the brochure on the salver again and approaches behind them.*)

MARGUERITE: I wasn't released. I left without permission. They sent me this to remind me.

WAITER (*presenting the salver*): You dropped this.

JACQUES: We threw it away!

WAITER: Excuse me.

JACQUES: Now, from now on, Marguerite, you must take better care of yourself. Do you hear me?

MARGUERITE: I hear you. No more distractions for me? No more entertainers in curtained and perfumed alcoves above the bazaar, no more young men that a pinch of white powder or a puff of gray smoke can almost turn to someone devoutly remembered?

JACQUES: No, from now on—

MARGUERITE: What "from now on," old hawk?

JACQUES: Rest. Peace.

MARGUERITE: Rest in peace is that final bit of advice they carve on gravestones, and I'm not ready for it! Are you? Are *you* ready for it?

(*She returns to the table. He follows her.*)

Oh, Jacques, when are we going to leave here, how are we going to leave here, you've got to tell me!

JACQUES: I've told you all I know.

MARGUERITE: Nothing, you've given up hope!

JACQUES: I haven't, that's not true.

(*Gutman has brought out the white cockatoo which he shows to Lady Mulligan at her table.*)

GUTMAN (*his voice rising above the murmurs*): Her name is Aurora.

LADY MULLIGAN: Why do you call her Aurora?

GUTMAN: She cries at daybreak.

LADY MULLIGAN: Only at daybreak?

GUTMAN: Yes, at daybreak only.

(*Their voices and laughter fade under.*)

MARGUERITE: How long is it since you've been to the travel agencies?

JACQUES: This morning I made the usual round of Cook's, American Express, Wagon-lits Universal, and it was the same story. There are no flights out of here till further orders from someone higher up.

MARGUERITE: Nothing, nothing at all?

JACQUES: Oh, there's a rumor of something called the Fugitivo, but—

MARGUERITE: The What!!!?

JACQUES: The Fugitivo. It's one of those non-scheduled things that—

MARGUERITE: When, when, when?

JACQUES: I told you it was non-scheduled. Non-scheduled means it comes and goes at no predictable—

MARGUERITE: Don't give me the dictionary! I want to know how does one get on it? Did you bribe them? Did you offer them money? No. Of course you didn't! And I know

why! You really don't want to leave here. You *think* you
don't want to go because you're brave as an old hawk. But
the truth of the matter—the real not the royal truth—is
that you're terrified of the Terra Incognita outside that wall.

JACQUES: You've hit upon the truth. I'm terrified of the unknown country inside or outside this wall or any place on
earth without you with me! The only country, known or
unknown that I can breathe in, or care to, is the country in
which we breathe together, as we are now at this table. And
later, a little while later, even closer than this, the sole in-
habitants of a tiny world whose limits are those of the light
from a rose-colored lamp—beside the sweetly, completely
known country of your cool bed!

MARGUERITE: The little comfort of love?

JACQUES: Is that comfort so little?

MARGUERITE: Caged birds accept each other but flight is
what they long for.

JACQUES: I want to stay here with you and love you and
guard you until the time or way comes that we both can
leave with honor.

MARGUERITE: "Leave with honor"? Your vocabulary is almost
as out-of-date as your cape and your cane. How could anyone quit this field with honor, this place where there's
nothing but the gradual wasting away of everything decent
in us . . . the sort of desperation that comes after even desperation has been worn out through long wear! . . . Why
have they put these screens around the table?

(*She springs up and knocks one of them over.*)

LADY MULLIGAN: There! You see? I don't understand why
you let such people stay here.

GUTMAN: They pay the price of admission the same as you.

LADY MULLIGAN: What price is that?

GUTMAN: Desperation!—With cash here!

(*He indicates the Siete Mares.*)

Without cash there!

(*He indicates Skid Row.*)

Block Eight on the Camino Real!

BLOCK EIGHT

There is the sound of loud desert wind and a flamenco cry followed by a dramatic phrase of music.

A flickering diamond blue radiance floods the hotel entrance. The crouching, grimacing Hunchback shakes his hoop of bells which is the convention for the appearance of each legendary figure.

Lord Byron appears in the doorway readied for departure. Gutman raises his hand for silence.

GUTMAN: You're leaving us, Lord Byron?

BYRON: Yes, I'm leaving you, Mr. Gutman.

GUTMAN: What a pity! But this is a port of entry and departure. There are no permanent guests. Possibly you are getting a little restless?

BYRON: The luxuries of this place have made me soft. The metal point's gone from my pen, there's nothing left but the feather.

GUTMAN: That may be true. But what can you do about it?

BYRON: Make a departure!

GUTMAN: From yourself?

BYRON: From my present self to myself as I used to be!

GUTMAN: *That's* the *furthest* departure a man could make! I guess you're sailing to Athens? There's another war there and like all wars since the beginning of time it can be interpreted as a—struggle for *what*?

BYRON: —For *freedom!* You may laugh at it, but it still means something to *me*!

GUTMAN: Of course it does! I'm not laughing a bit, I'm beaming with admiration.

BYRON: I've allowed myself many distractions.

GUTMAN: Yes, indeed!

BYRON: But I've never altogether forgotten my old devotion to the—

GUTMAN: —To the *what*, Lord Byron?

(*Byron passes nervous fingers through his hair.*)

You can't remember the object of your one-time devotion?

(*There is a pause. Byron limps away from the terrace and goes toward the fountain.*)

BYRON: When Shelley's corpse was recovered from the sea . . .

(*Gutman beckons the Dreamer who approaches and accompanies Byron's speech.*)

—It was burned on the beach at Viareggio.—I watched the spectacle from my carriage because the stench was revolting . . . Then it—fascinated me! I got out of my carriage. Went nearer, holding a handkerchief to my nostrils! —I saw that the front of the skull had broken away in the flames, and there—

(*He advances out upon the stage apron, followed by Abdullah with the pine torch or lantern.*)

And there was the brain of Shelley, indistinguishable from a cooking stew!—*boiling, bubbling, hissing!*—in the *blackening—cracked—pot*—of his skull!

(*Marguerite rises abruptly. Jacques supports her.*)

—Trelawney, his friend, Trelawney, threw salt and oil and frankincense in the flames and finally the almost intolerable stench—

(*Abdullah giggles. Gutman slaps him.*)

—was *gone* and the burning was *pure*!—as a man's burning should be . . .
    A man's burning *ought* to be pure!—*not* like mine—(a crepe suzette—burned in brandy . . .)
    Shelley's burning was finally very *pure*!
    But the body, the corpse, split open like a grilled pig!

(*Abdullah giggles irrepressibly again. Gutman grips the back of his neck and he stands up stiff and assumes an expression of exaggerated solemnity.*)

—And then Trelawney—as the ribs of the corpse unlocked —reached into them as a baker reaches quickly into an oven!

(*Abdullah almost goes into another convulsion.*)

—And snatched out—as a baker would a biscuit!—the *heart* of Shelley! Snatched the heart of Shelley out of the blistering corpse!—Out of the purifying—blue-flame . . .

(*Marguerite resumes her seat; Jacques his.*)

—And it was *over*!—I thought—

(*He turns slightly from the audience and crosses upstage from the apron. He faces Jacques and Marguerite.*)

—I thought it was a disgusting thing to do, to snatch a man's heart from his body! What can one man do with another man's heart?

(*Jacques rises and strikes the stage with his cane.*)

JACQUES (*passionately*): He can do this with it!

(*He seizes a loaf of bread on his table, and descends from the terrace.*)

He can twist it like this!

(*He twists the loaf.*)

He can tear it like this!

(*He tears the loaf in two.*)

He can crush it under his foot!

(*He drops the bread and stamps on it.*)

—And kick it away—like this!

(*He kicks the bread off the terrace. Lord Byron turns away from him and limps again out upon the stage apron and speaks to the audience.*)

BYRON: That's very true, Señor. But a poet's vocation, which used to be my vocation, is to influence the heart in a gentler fashion than you have made your mark on that loaf of bread. He ought to purify it and lift it above its ordinary level. For what is the heart but a sort of—

(*He makes a high, groping gesture in the air.*)

—A sort of—*instrument!*—that translates *noise* into *music*, chaos into—*order* . . .

(*Abdullah ducks almost to the earth in an effort to stifle his mirth. Gutman coughs to cover his own amusement.*)

—a *mysterious order!*

(*He raises his voice till it fills the plaza.*)

—That was my vocation once upon a time, before it was obscured by vulgar plaudits!—Little by little it was lost among gondolas and palazzos!—masked balls, glittering salons, huge shadowy courts and torch-lit entrances!— Baroque façades, canopies and carpets, candelabra and gold plate among snowy damask, ladies with throats as slender as flower-stems, bending and breathing toward me their fragrant breath—

—Exposing their breasts to me!

Whispering, half-smiling!—And everywhere marble, the visible grandeur of marble, pink and gray marble, veined and tinted as flayed corrupting flesh,—all these provided agreeable distractions from the rather frightening solitude of a poet. Oh, I wrote many cantos in Venice and Constantinople and in Ravenna and Rome, on all of those Latin and Levantine excursions that my twisted foot led me into—but I wonder about them a little. They seem to improve as the wine in the bottle—dwindles . . . *There is a passion for declivity in this world!*

And lately I've found myself listening to hired musicians behind a row of artificial palm trees—instead of the single —pure-stringed instrument of my heart . . .

Well, then, it's time to leave here!

(*He turns back to the stage.*)

—There is a time for departure even when there's no certain place to go!

I'm going to look for one, now. I'm sailing to Athens. At least I can look up at the Acropolis, I can stand at the foot of it and look up at broken columns on the crest of a hill— if not purity, at least its recollection . . .

I can sit quietly looking for a long, long time in absolute silence, and possibly, yes, *still* possibly—

The old pure music will come to me again. Of course on the other hand I may hear only the little noise of insects in the grass . . .

But I am sailing to Athens! *Make voyages!—Attempt them!* —there's nothing else . . .

MARGUERITE (*excitedly*): *Watch where he goes!*

(*Lord Byron limps across the plaza with his head bowed, making slight, apologetic gestures to the wheedling Beggars who shuffle about him. There is music. He crosses toward the steep Alleyway Out. The following is played with a quiet intensity so it will be in a lower key than the later Fugitivo Scene.*)

Watch him, watch him, see which way he goes. Maybe he knows of a way that we haven't found out.

JACQUES: Yes, I'm watching him, Cara.

(*Lord and Lady Mulligan half rise, staring anxiously through monocle and lorgnon.*)

MARGUERITE: Oh, my God, I believe he's going up that alley.

JACQUES: Yes, he is. He has.

LORD and LADY MULLIGAN: Oh, the fool, the idiot, he's going under the arch!

MARGUERITE: Jacques, run after him, warn him, tell him about the desert he has to cross.

JACQUES: I think he knows what he's doing.

MARGUERITE: I can't look!

(*She turns to the audience, throwing back her head and closing her eyes. The desert wind sings loudly as Byron climbs to the top of the steps.*)

BYRON (*to several porters carrying luggage—which is mainly caged birds*): THIS WAY!

(*He exits.*
(*Kilroy starts to follow. He stops at the steps, cringing and looking at Gutman. Gutman motions him to go ahead. Kilroy rushes up the stairs. He looks out, loses his nerve and sits—blinking his nose. Gutman laughs as he announces—*)

GUTMAN: Block Nine on the Camino Real!

(*He goes into the hotel.*)

BLOCK NINE

Abdullah runs back to the hotel with the billowing flambeau. A faint and far away humming sound becomes audible . . . Marguerite opens her eyes with a startled look. She searches the sky for something. A very low percussion begins with the humming sound, as if excited hearts are beating.

MARGUERITE: Jacques! I hear something in the sky!

JACQUES: I think what you hear is—

MARGUERITE (*with rising excitement*): —No, it's a plane, a great one, I see the lights of it, now!

JACQUES: Some kind of fireworks, Cara.

MARGUERITE: Hush! LISTEN!

(*She blows out the candle to see better above it. She rises, peering into the sky.*)

I see it! I see it! There! It's circling over us!

LADY MULLIGAN: Raymond, Raymond, sit down, your face is flushed!

HOTEL GUESTS (*overlapping*):

—What is it?

—The FUGITIVO!

—THE FUGITIVO! THE FUGITIVO!

—Quick, get my jewelry from the hotel safe!

—Cash a check!

—Throw some things in a bag! I'll wait here!

—Never mind luggage, we have our money and papers!

—Where is it now?

—There, there!

—It's turning to land!

—To go like this?

—Yes, go anyhow, just go anyhow, just go!

—Raymond! Please!

—Oh, it's rising again!

—Oh, it's—*SHH! MR. GUTMAN!*

(*Gutman appears in the doorway. He raises a hand in a commanding gesture.*)

GUTMAN: Signs in the sky should not be mistaken for wonders!

(*The Voices modulate quickly.*)

Ladies, gentlemen, please resume your seats!

(*Places are resumed at tables, and silver is shakily lifted. Glasses are raised to lips, but the noise of concerted panting of excitement fills the stage and a low percussion echoes frantic heart beats.*

(*Gutman descends to the plaza, shouting furiously to the Officer.*)

Why wasn't I told the Fugitivo was coming?

(*Everyone, almost as a man, rushes into the hotel and reappears almost at once with hastily collected possessions. Marguerite rises but appears stunned.*

(*There is a great whistling and screeching sound as the aerial transport halts somewhere close by, accompanied by rainbow splashes of light and cries like children's on a roller-coaster. Some incoming Passengers approach the stage down an aisle of the theatre, preceded by Redcaps with luggage.*)

PASSENGERS:
—What a heavenly trip!
—The scenery was thrilling!
—It's so quick!
—The only way to travel! Etc., etc.

(*A uniformed man, the Pilot, enters the plaza with a megaphone.*)

PILOT (*through the megaphone*): Fugitivo now loading for departure! Fugitivo loading immediately for departure! Northwest corner of the plaza!

MARGUERITE: Jacques, it's the Fugitivo, it's the non-scheduled thing you heard of this afternoon!

PILOT: All out-going passengers on the Fugitivo are requested to present their tickets and papers immediately at this station.

MARGUERITE: He said "out-going passengers"!

PILOT: Out-going passengers on the Fugitivo report immediately at this station for customs inspection.

MARGUERITE (*with a forced smile*): Why are you just standing there?

JACQUES (*with an Italian gesture*): Che cosa possa fare!

MARGUERITE: Move, move, do something!

JACQUES: *What!*

MARGUERITE: Go to them, ask, find out!

JACQUES: I have no idea what the damned thing is!

MARGUERITE: I do, I'll tell you! It's a way to escape from this abominable place!

JACQUES: Forse, forse, non so!

MARGUERITE: It's a way *out* and *I'm* not going to miss it!

PILOT: Ici la Douane! Customs inspection here!

MARGUERITE: Customs. That means luggage. Run to my room! Here! Key! Throw a few things in a bag, my jewels, my furs, but hurry! Vite, vite, vite! I don't believe there's much time! No, everybody is—

(*Outgoing Passengers storm the desk and table.*)

—Clamoring for tickets! There must be limited space! Why don't you do what I tell you?

(*She rushes to a man with a rubber stamp and a roll of tickets.*)

Monsieur! Señor! Pardonnez-moi! I'm going, I'm going out! I want my ticket!

PILOT (*coldly*): Name, please.

MARGUERITE: Mademoiselle—Gautier—but I—

PILOT: Gautier? Gautier? We have no Gautier listed.

MARGUERITE: I'm—*not* listed! I mean I'm—traveling under another name.

TRAVEL AGENT: What name are you traveling under?

(*Prudence and Olympe rush out of the hotel half dressed, dragging their furs. Meanwhile Kilroy is trying to make a fast buck or two as a Redcap. The scene gathers wild momen-*)

tum, is punctuated by crashes of percussion. Grotesque mummers act as demon custom inspectors and immigration authorities, etc. Baggage is tossed about, ripped open, smuggled goods seized, arrests made, all amid the wildest importunities, protests, threats, bribes, entreaties; it is a scene for improvisation.)

PRUDENCE: Thank God I woke up!

OLYMPE: Thank God I wasn't asleep!

PRUDENCE: I knew it was non-scheduled but I *did* think they'd give you time to get in your girdle.

OLYMPE: Look who's trying to crash it! I know damned well *she* don't have a reservation!

PILOT (*to Marguerite*): What name did you say, Mademoiselle? Please! People are waiting, you're holding up the line!

MARGUERITE: I'm so confused! Jacques! What name did you make my reservation under?

OLYMPE: She has no reservation!

PRUDENCE: *I have, I got mine!*

OLYMPE: *I got mine!*

PRUDENCE: *I'm* next!

OLYMPE: Don't push *me*, you old bag!

MARGUERITE: I was here first! I was here before anybody! Jacques, quick! Get my money from the hotel safe!

(*Jacques exits.*)

AGENT: *Stay in line!*

(*There is a loud warning whistle.*)

PILOT: Five minutes. The Fugitivo leaves in five minutes. Five, five minutes only!

(*At this announcement the scene becomes riotous.*)

TRAVEL AGENT: *Four minutes! The Fugitivo leaves in four minutes!*

(*Prudence and Olympe are shrieking at him in French. The warning whistle blasts again.*)

Three minutes, the Fugitivo leaves in three minutes!

MARGUERITE (*topping the turmoil*): Monsieur! Please! I was here first, I was here before anybody! Look!

(*Jacques returns with her money.*)

I have thousands of francs! Take whatever you want! Take all of it, it's yours!

PILOT: Payment is only accepted in pounds sterling or dollars. Next, please.

MARGUERITE: You don't accept francs? They do at the hotel! They accept my francs at the Siete Mares!

PILOT: Lady, don't argue with me, I don't make the rules!

MARGUERITE (*beating her forehead with her fist*): Oh, God, Jacques! Take these back to the cashier!

(*She thrusts the bills at him.*)

Get them changed to dollars or—*Hurry! Tout de suite!* I'm—going to faint . . .

JACQUES: But Marguerite—

MARGUERITE: *Go! Go! Please!*

PILOT: Closing, we're closing now! The Fugitivo leaves in two minutes!

(*Lord and Lady Mulligan rush forward.*)

LADY MULLIGAN: Let Lord Mulligan through.

PILOT (*to Marguerite*): You're standing in the way.

(*Olympe screams as the Customs Inspector dumps her jewels on the ground. She and Prudence butt heads as they dive for the gems: the fight is renewed.*)

MARGUERITE (*detaining the Pilot*): Oh, look, Monsieur! Regardez ça! My diamond, a solitaire—two carats! Take that as security!

PILOT: Let me go. The Loan Shark's across the plaza!

(*There is another warning blast. Prudence and Olympe seize hat boxes and rush toward the whistle.*)

MARGUERITE (*clinging desperately to the Pilot*): You don't understand! Señor Casanova has gone to change money! He'll be here in a second. And I'll pay five, ten, twenty times the price of—*JACQUES! JACQUES! WHERE ARE YOU?*

VOICE (*back of auditorium*): We're closing the gate!

MARGUERITE: You can't close the gate!

PILOT: Move, Madame!

MARGUERITE: I won't move!

LADY MULLIGAN: I tell you, Lord Mulligan is the Iron & Steel man from Cobh! Raymond! They're closing the gate!

LORD MULLIGAN: I can't seem to get through!

GUTMAN: Hold the gate for Lord Mulligan!

PILOT (*to Marguerite*): Madame, stand back or I will have to use force!

MARGUERITE: Jacques! Jacques!

LADY MULLIGAN: Let us through! We're clear!

PILOT: Madame! Stand back and let these passengers through!

MARGUERITE: No, No! I'm first! I'm next!

LORD MULLIGAN: Get her out of our way! That woman's a whore!

LADY MULLIGAN: How dare you stand in our way?

PILOT: Officer, take this woman!

LADY MULLIGAN: Come on, Raymond!

MARGUERITE (*as the Officer pulls her away*): Jacques! Jacques! Jacques!

(*Jacques returns with changed money.*)

Here! Here is the money!

PILOT: All right, give me your papers.

MARGUERITE: —My papers? Did you say my papers?

PILOT: Hurry, hurry, your passport!

MARGUERITE: —Jacques! He wants my papers! Give him my papers, Jacques!

JACQUES: —The lady's papers are lost!

MARGUERITE (*wildly*): No, no, no, THAT IS NOT TRUE! HE WANTS TO KEEP ME HERE! HE'S LYING ABOUT IT!

JACQUES: Have you forgotten that your papers were stolen?

MARGUERITE: I gave you my papers, I gave you my papers to keep, you've got my papers.

(*Screaming, Lady Mulligan breaks past her and descends the stairs.*)

LADY MULLIGAN: Raymond! Hurry!

LORD MULLIGAN (*staggering on the top step*): I'm sick! I'm sick!

(*The Streetcleaners disguised as expensive morticians in swal-
lowtail coats come rapidly up the aisle of the theatre and wait
at the foot of the stairway for the tottering tycoon.*)

LADY MULLIGAN: You cannot be sick till we get on the
Fugitivo!

LORD MULLIGAN: Forward all cables to Guaranty Trust in
Paris.

LADY MULLIGAN: Place de la Concorde.

LORD MULLIGAN: Thank you! All purchases C.O.D. to
Mulligan Iron & Steel Works in Cobh—Thank you!

LADY MULLIGAN: Raymond! Raymond! Who are these men?

LORD MULLIGAN: I know these men! I recognize their faces!

LADY MULLIGAN: Raymond! They're the Streetcleaners!

(*She screams and runs up the aisle screaming repeatedly, stopping half-way to look back. The Two Streetcleaners seize Lord
Mulligan by either arm as he crumples.*)

Pack Lord Mulligan's body in dry ice! Ship Air Express to
Cobh care of Mulligan Iron & Steel Works, in Cobh!

(*She runs sobbing out of the back of the auditorium as the
whistle blows repeatedly and a Voice shouts.*)

I'm coming! I'm coming!

MARGUERITE: Jacques! Jacques! Oh, God!

PILOT: The Fugitivo is leaving, all aboard!

(*He starts toward the steps. Marguerite clutches his arm.*)

Let go of me!

MARGUERITE: You can't go without me!

PILOT: Officer, hold this woman!

JACQUES: Marguerite, let him go!

(*She releases the Pilot's arm and turns savagely on Jacques.
She tears his coat open, seizes a large envelope of papers and
rushes after the Pilot who has started down the steps over the
orchestra pit and into a center aisle of the house. Timpani
build up as she starts down the steps, screaming—*)

MARGUERITE: Here! I have them here! Wait! I have my papers now, I have my papers!

(*The Pilot runs cursing up the center aisle as the Fugitivo whistle gives repeated short, shrill blasts; timpani and dissonant brass are heard.*

(*Outgoing Passengers burst into hysterical song, laughter, shouts of farewell. These can come over a loudspeaker at the back of the house.*)

VOICE IN DISTANCE: Going! Going! Going!

MARGUERITE (*attempting as if half-paralyzed to descend the steps*): NOT WITHOUT ME, NO, NO, NOT WITHOUT ME!

(*Her figure is caught in the dazzling glacial light of the follow-spot. It blinds her. She makes violent, crazed gestures, clinging to the railing of the steps; her breath is loud and hoarse as a dying person's, she holds a blood-stained handkerchief to her lips.*

(*There is a prolonged, gradually fading, rocketlike roar as the Fugitivo takes off. Shrill cries of joy from departing passengers; something radiant passes above the stage and streams of confetti and tinsel fall into the plaza. Then there is a great calm, the ship's receding roar diminished to the hum of an insect.*)

GUTMAN (*somewhat compassionately*): Block Ten on the Camino Real.

BLOCK TEN

There is something about the desolation of the plaza that suggests a city devastated by bombardment. Reddish lights flicker here and there as if ruins were smoldering and wisps of smoke rise from them.

LA MADRECITA (*almost inaudibly*): Donde?
THE DREAMER: Aquí. Aquí, Madrecita.
MARGUERITE: Lost! Lost! Lost! Lost!

(*She is still clinging brokenly to the railing of the steps. Jacques descends to her and helps her back up the steps.*)

JACQUES: Lean against me, Cara. Breathe quietly, now.

MARGUERITE: Lost!

JACQUES: Breathe quietly, quietly, and look up at the sky.

MARGUERITE: Lost . . .

JACQUES: These tropical nights are so clear. There's the Southern Cross. Do you see the Southern Cross, Marguerite?

(*He points through the proscenium. They are now on the bench before the fountain; she is resting in his arms.*)

And there, over there, is Orion, like a fat, golden fish swimming North in the deep clear water, and we are together, breathing quietly together, leaning together, quietly, quietly together, completely, sweetly together, not frightened, now, not alone, but completely quietly together . . .

(*La Madrecita, led into the center of the plaza by her son, has begun to sing very softly; the reddish flares dim out and the smoke disappears.*)

All of us have a desperate bird in our hearts, a memory of— some distant mother with—wings . . .

MARGUERITE: I would have—left—without you . . .

JACQUES: I know, I know!

MARGUERITE: Then how can you—still—?

JACQUES: Hold you?

(*Marguerite nods slightly.*)

Because you've taught me that part of love which is tender. I never knew it before. Oh, I had—mistresses that circled me like moons! I scrambled from one bed-chamber to another bed-chamber with shirttails always aflame, from girl to girl, like buckets of coal-oil poured on a conflagration! But never loved until now with the part of love that's tender . . .

MARGUERITE: —We're used to each other. That's what you think is love . . . You'd better leave me now, you'd better go and let me go because there's a cold wind blowing out of the mountains and over the desert and into my heart, and if you stay with me now, I'll say cruel things, I'll wound your vanity, I'll taunt you with the decline of your male vigor!

JACQUES: Why does disappointment make people unkind to each other?

MARGUERITE: Each of us is very much alone.

JACQUES: Only if we distrust each other.

MARGUERITE: We have to distrust each other. It is our only defense against betrayal.

JACQUES: I think our defense is love.

MARGUERITE: Oh, Jacques, we're used to each other, we're a pair of captive hawks caught in the same cage, and so we've grown used to each other. That's what passes for love at this dim, shadowy end of the Camino Real . . .

What are we sure of? Not even of our existence, dear comforting friend! And whom can we ask the questions that torment us? "What is this place?" "Where are we?"—a fat old man who gives sly hints that only bewilder us more, a fake of a Gypsy squinting at cards and tea-leaves. What else are we offered? The never-broken procession of little events that assure us that we and strangers about us are still going on! Where? Why? and the perch that we hold is unstable! We're threatened with eviction, for this is a port of entry and departure, there are no permanent guests! And where else have we to go when we leave here? Bide-a-While? "Ritz Men Only"? Or under that ominous arch into Terra Incognita? We're lonely. We're frightened. We hear the Streetcleaners' piping not far away. So now and then, although we've wounded each other time and again—we stretch out hands to each other in the dark that we can't escape from—we huddle together for some dim-communal comfort—and that's what passes for love on this terminal stretch of the road that used to be royal. What is it, this feeling between us? When you feel my exhausted weight against your shoulder—when I clasp your anxious old hawk's head to my breast, what is it we feel in whatever is left of our hearts? Something, yes, something—delicate, unreal, bloodless! The sort of violets that could grow on the moon, or in the crevices of those far away mountains, fertilized by the droppings of carrion birds. Those birds are familiar to us. Their shadows inhabit the plaza. I've heard them flapping their wings like old charwomen beating worn-out carpets with gray brooms . . .

But tenderness, the violets in the mountains—can't break
the rocks!

JACQUES: The violets in the mountains can break the rocks if
you believe in them and allow them to grow!

(*The plaza has resumed its usual aspect. Abdullah enters
through one of the downstage arches.*)

ABDULLAH: Get your carnival hats and noisemakers here!
Tonight the moon will restore the virginity of my sister!

MARGUERITE (*almost tenderly touching his face*): Don't you
know that tonight I am going to betray you?

JACQUES: —Why would you do that?

MARGUERITE: Because I've out-lived the tenderness of my
heart. Abdullah, come here! I have an errand for you! Go
to Ahmed's and deliver a message!

ABDULLAH: I'm working for Mama, making the Yankee dollar! Get your carnival hats and—

MARGUERITE: *Here, boy!*

(*She snatches a ring off her finger and offers it to him.*)

JACQUES: —Your cabochon sapphire?

MARGUERITE: Yes, my cabochon sapphire!

JACQUES: Are you mad?

MARGUERITE: Yes, I'm mad, or nearly! The specter of lunacy's at my heels tonight!

(*Jacques drives Abdullah back with his cane.*)

Catch, boy! The other side of the fountain! Quick!

(*The guitar is heard molto vivace. She tosses the ring across the
fountain. Jacques attempts to hold the boy back with his cane.
Abdullah dodges in and out like a little terrier, laughing.
Marguerite shouts encouragement in French. When the boy is
driven back from the ring, she snatches it up and tosses it to
him again, shouting:*)

Catch, boy! Run to Ahmed's! Tell the charming young man
that the French lady's bored with her company tonight! Say
that the French lady missed the Fugitivo and wants to forget she missed it! Oh, and reserve a room with a balcony so

I can watch your sister appear on the roof when the moonrise makes her a virgin!

(*Abdullah skips shouting out of the plaza. Jacques strikes the stage with his cane. She says, without looking at him:*)

Time betrays us and we betray each other.

JACQUES: Wait, Marguerite.

MARGUERITE: No! I can't! The wind from the desert is sweeping me away!

(*A loud singing wind sweeps her toward the terrace, away from him. She looks back once or twice as if for some gesture of leave-taking but he only stares at her fiercely, striking the stage at intervals with his cane, like a death-march. Gutman watches, smiling, from the terrace, bows to Marguerite as she passes into the hotel. The drum of Jacques' cane is taken up by other percussive instruments, and almost unnoticeably at first, weird-looking celebrants or carnival mummers creep into the plaza, silently as spiders descending a wall.*

(*A sheet of scarlet and yellow rice paper bearing some cryptic device is lowered from the center of the plaza. The percussive effects become gradually louder. Jacques is oblivious to the scene behind him, standing in front of the plaza, his eyes closed.*)

GUTMAN: Block Eleven on the Camino Real.

BLOCK ELEVEN

GUTMAN: The Fiesta has started. The first event is the coronation of the King of Cuckolds.

(*Blinding shafts of light are suddenly cast upon Casanova on the forestage. He shields his face, startled, as the crowd closes about him. The blinding shafts of light seem to strike him like savage blows and he falls to his knees as—*

(*The Hunchback scuttles out of the Gypsy's stall with a crown of gilded antlers on a velvet pillow. He places it on Jacques' head. The celebrants form a circle about him chanting.*)

JACQUES: What is this?—a crown—

GUTMAN: A crown of horns!

CROWD: Cornudo! Cornudo! Cornudo! Cornudo! Cornudo!

GUTMAN: Hail, all hail, the King of Cuckolds on the Camino Real!

(*Jacques springs up, first striking out at them with his cane. Then all at once he abandons self-defense, throws off his cape, casts away his cane, and fills the plaza with a roar of defiance and self-derision.*)

JACQUES: Si, si, sono cornudo! Cornudo! Cornudo! Casanova is the King of Cuckolds on the Camino Real! Show me crowned to the world! Announce the honor! Tell the world of the honor bestowed on Casanova, Chevalier de Seingalt! Knight of the Golden Spur by the Grace of His Holiness the Pope . . . Famous adventurer! Con man Extraordinary! Gambler! Pitch-man par excellence! Shill! Pimp! Spiv! *And—great—lover* . . .

(*The Crowd howls with applause and laughter but his voice rises above them with sobbing intensity.*)

Yes, I said GREAT LOVER! The greatest lover wears the longest horns on the Camino! GREAT! LOVER!

GUTMAN: Attention! Silence! The moon is rising! The restoration is about to occur!

(*A white radiance is appearing over the ancient wall of the town. The mountains become luminous. There is music. Everyone, with breathless attention, faces the light.*

(*Kilroy crosses to Jacques and beckons him out behind the crowd. There he snatches off the antlers and returns him his fedora. Jacques reciprocates by removing Kilroy's fright wig and electric nose. They embrace as brothers. In a Chaplinesque dumb-play, Kilroy points to the wildly flickering three brass balls of the Loan Shark and to his golden gloves: then with a terrible grimace he removes the gloves from about his neck, smiles at Jacques and indicates that the two of them together will take flight over the wall. Jacques shakes his head sadly, pointing to his heart and then to the Siete Mares. Kilroy nods with regretful understanding of a human and manly folly. A Guard has been silently approaching them in a*

soft shoe dance. Jacques whistles "La Golondrina." Kilroy as-
sumes a very nonchalant pose. The Guard picks up curiously
the discarded fright wig and electric nose. Then glancing sus-
piciously at the pair, he advances. Kilroy makes a run for it.
He does a baseball slide into the Loan Shark's welcoming
doorway. The door slams. The Cop is about to crash it when a
gong sounds and Gutman shouts:)

GUTMAN: SILENCE! ATTENTION! THE GYPSY!
GYPSY (*appearing on the roof with a gong*): The moon has restored the virginity of my daughter Esmeralda!

(*The gong sounds.*)

STREET PEOPLE: Ahh!
GYPSY: The moon in its plenitude has made her a virgin!

(*The gong sounds.*)

STREET PEOPLE: Ahh!
GYPSY: Praise her, celebrate her, give her suitable homage!

(*The gong sounds.*)

STREET PEOPLE: Ahh!
GYPSY: Summon her to the roof!

(*She shouts:*)

ESMERALDA!

(*Dancers shout the name in rhythm.*)

RISE WITH THE MOON, MY DAUGHTER! CHOOSE
THE HERO!

(*Esmeralda appears on the roof in dazzling light. She seems to*
be dressed in jewels. She raises her jeweled arms with a harsh
flamenco cry.)

ESMERALDA: OLE!
DANCERS: OLE!

(*The details of the Carnival are a problem for director and*
choreographer but it has already been indicated in the script
that the Fiesta is a sort of serio-comic, grotesque-lyric "Rites of
Fertility" with roots in various pagan cultures.)

(*It should not be over-elaborated or allowed to occupy much time. It should not be more than three minutes from the appearance of Esmeralda on the Gypsy's roof till the return of Kilroy from the Loan Shark's.*

(*Kilroy emerges from the Pawn Shop in grotesque disguise, a turban, dark glasses, a burnoose and an umbrella or sunshade.*)

KILROY (*to Jacques*): So long, pal, I wish you could come with me.

(*Jacques clasps his cross in Kilroy's hands.*)

ESMERALDA: Yankee!

KILROY (*to the audience*): So long, everybody. Good luck to you all on the Camino! I hocked my golden gloves to finance this expedition. I'm going. Hasta luega. I'm going. I'm gone!

ESMERALDA: Yankee!

(*He has no sooner entered the plaza than the riotous women strip off everything but the dungarees and skivvy which he first appeared in.*)

KILROY (*to the women*): Let me go. Let go of me! Watch out for my equipment!

ESMERALDA: Yankee! Yankee!

(*He breaks away from them and plunges up the stairs of the ancient wall. He is half-way up them when Gutman shouts out:*)

GUTMAN: Follow-spot on that gringo, light the stairs!

(*The light catches Kilroy. At the same instant Esmeralda cries out to him:*)

ESMERALDA: *Yankee! Yankee!*
GYPSY: What's goin' on down there?

(*She rushes into the plaza.*)

KILROY: Oh, no, I'm on my way out!
ESMERALDA: Espere un momento!

(*The Gypsy calls the police, but is ignored in the crowd.*)

KILROY: Don't tempt me, baby! I hocked my golden gloves to finance this expedition!

ESMERALDA: Querido!

KILROY: Querido means sweetheart, a word which is hard to resist but I must resist it.

ESMERALDA: Champ!

KILROY: I used to be Champ but why remind me of it?

ESMERALDA: Be champ again! Contend in the contest! Compete in the competition!

GYPSY (*shouting*): *Naw, naw, not eligible!*

ESMERALDA: *Pl-eeeeeze!*

GYPSY: Slap her, Nursie, she's flippin'.

(*Esmeralda slaps Nursie instead.*)

ESMERALDA: Hero! Champ!

KILROY: I'm not in condition!

ESMERALDA: You're still the Champ, the undefeated Champ of the golden gloves!

KILROY: Nobody's called me that in a long, long time!

ESMERALDA: Champ!

KILROY: My resistance is crumbling!

ESMERALDA: Champ!

KILROY: It's crumbled!

ESMERALDA: Hero!

KILROY: GERONIMO!

(*He takes a flying leap from the stairs into the center of the plaza. He turns toward Esmeralda and cries:*)

DOLL!!

(*Kilroy surrounded by cheering Street People goes into a triumphant eccentric dance which reviews his history as fighter, traveler and lover.*
(*At finish of the dance, the music is cut off, as Kilroy lunges, arm uplifted towards Esmeralda, and cries:*)

KILROY: *Kilroy the Champ!*

ESMERALDA: *KILROY the Champ!*

(*She snatches a bunch of red roses from the stunned Nursie and tosses them to Kilroy.*)

CROWD (*sharply*): OLE!

(*The Gypsy, at the same instant, hurls her gong down, creating a resounding noise.*
(*Kilroy turns and comes down towards the audience, saying to them:*)

KILROY: *Y'see?*

(*Cheering Street People surge towards him and lift him in the air. The lights fade as the curtain descends.*)

CROWD (*in a sustained yell*): OLE!

(*The curtain falls. There is a short intermission.*)

BLOCK TWELVE

The stage is in darkness except for a spot light which picks out Esmeralda on the Gypsy's roof.

ESMERALDA: Mama, what happened?—Mama, the lights went out!—Mama, where are you? It's so dark I'm scared!—MAMA!

(*The lights are turned on displaying a deserted plaza. The Gypsy is seated at a small table before her stall.*)

GYPSY: Come on downstairs, Doll. The mischief is done. You've chosen your hero!

GUTMAN (*from the balcony of the Siete Mares*): Block Twelve on the Camino Real.

NURSIE (*at the fountain*): Gypsy, the fountain is still dry!

GYPSY: What d'yuh expect? There's nobody left to uphold the old traditions! You raise a girl. She watches television. Plays be-bop. Reads *Screen Secrets*. Comes the Big Fiesta. The moonrise makes her a virgin—which is the neatest trick of the week! And what does she do? Chooses a Fugitive Patsy for the Chosen Hero! Well, show him in! Admit the joker and get the virgin ready!

NURSIE: You're going through with it?

GYPSY: Look, Nursie! I'm operating a legitimate joint! This joker'll get the same treatment he'd get if he breezed down

the Camino in a blizzard of G-notes! Trot, girl! Lubricate
your means of locomotion!

*(Nursie goes into the Gypsy's stall. The Gypsy rubs her hands
together and blows on the crystal ball, spits on it and gives it
the old one-two with a "shammy" rag . . . She mutters
"Crystal ball, tell me all . . . crystal ball tell me all" . . . as:*
*(Kilroy bounds into the plaza from her stall . . . a rose be-
tween his teeth.)*

GYPSY: Siente se, por favor.
KILROY: No comprendo the lingo.
GYPSY: Put it down!
NURSIE (*offstage*): Hey, Gypsy!
GYPSY: Address me as Madam!
NURSIE (*entering*): *Madam!* Winchell has scooped you!
GYPSY: In a pig's eye!
NURSIE: The Fugitivo has *"fftt . . ."*!
GYPSY: In Elizabeth, New Jersey . . . ten fifty seven P.M. . . .
Eastern Standard Time—while you were putting them
kiss-me-quicks in your hair-do! Furthermore, my second
exclusive is that the solar system is drifting towards the con-
stellation of Hercules: *Skiddoo!*

(Nursie exits. Stamping is heard offstage.)

Quiet, back there! God damn it!
NURSIE (*offstage*): She's out of control!
GYPSY: Give her a double-bromide!

(To Kilroy:)

Well, how does it feel to be the Chosen Hero?
KILROY: I better explain something to you.
GYPSY: Save your breath. You'll need it.
KILROY: I want to level with you. Can I level with you?
GYPSY (*rapidly stamping some papers*): How could you help
but level with the Gypsy?
KILROY: I don't know what the hero is chosen for.

(Esmeralda and Nursie shriek offstage.)

GYPSY: Time will brief you . . . Aw, I hate paper work! . . .
NURSEHH!

(*Nursie comes out and stands by the table.*)

This filing system is screwed up six ways from Next Sunday . . . File this crap under crap!—

(*To Kilroy:*)

The smoking lamp is lit. Have a stick on me!

(*She offers him a cigarette.*)

KILROY: No thanks.

GYPSY: Come on, indulge yourself. You got nothing to lose that won't be lost.

KILROY: If that's a professional opinion, I don't respect it.

GYPSY: Resume your seat and give me your full name.

KILROY: Kilroy.

GYPSY (*writing all this down*): Date of birth and place of that disaster?

KILROY: Both unknown.

GYPSY: Address?

KILROY: Traveler.

GYPSY: Parents?

KILROY: Anonymous.

GYPSY: Who brought you up?

KILROY: I was brought up and down by an eccentric old aunt in Dallas.

GYPSY: Raise both hands simultaneously and swear that you have not come here for the purpose of committing an immoral act.

ESMERALDA (*from offstage*): Hey, Chico!

GYPSY: *QUIET!* Childhood diseases?

KILROY: Whooping cough, measles and mumps.

GYPSY: Likes and dislikes?

KILROY: I like situations I can get out of. I don't like cops and—

GYPSY: Immaterial! Here! Signature on this!

(*She hands him a blank.*)

KILROY: What is it?

GYPSY: You always sign something, don't you?

KILROY: Not till I know what it is.

GYPSY: It's just a little formality to give a tone to the establishment and make an impression on our out-of-town trade. Roll up your sleeve.

KILROY: What for?

GYPSY: A shot of some kind.

KILROY: What kind?

GYPSY: Any kind. Don't they always give you some kind of a shot?

KILROY: "They"?

GYPSY: Brass-hats, Americanos!

(*She injects a hypo.*)

KILROY: I am no guinea pig!

GYPSY: Don't kid yourself. We're all of us guinea pigs in the laboratory of God. Humanity is just a work in progress.

KILROY: I don't make it out.

GYPSY: Who does? The Camino Real is a funny paper read backwards!

(*There is weird piping outside. Kilroy shifts on his seat. The Gypsy grins.*)

Tired? The altitude makes you sleepy?

KILROY: It makes me nervous.

GYPSY: I'll show you how to take a slug of tequila! It dilates the capillaries. First you sprinkle salt on the back of your hand. Then lick it off with your tongue. Now then you toss the shot down!

(*She demonstrates.*)

—And then you bite into the lemon. That way it goes down easy, but what a bang!—You're next.

KILROY: No, thanks, I'm on the wagon.

GYPSY: There's an old Chinese proverb that says, "When your goose is cooked you might as well have it cooked with plenty of gravy."

(*She laughs.*)

Get up, baby. Let's have a look at yuh!—You're not a bad-looking boy. Sometimes working for the Yankee dollar isn't a painful profession. Have you ever been attracted by older women?

KILROY: Frankly, no, ma'am.

GYPSY: Well, there's a first time for everything.

KILROY: That is a subject I cannot agree with you on.

GYPSY: You think I'm an old bag?

(*Kilroy laughs awkwardly. The Gypsy slaps his face.*)

Will you take the cards or the crystal?

KILROY: It's immaterial.

GYPSY: All right, we'll begin with the cards.

(*She shuffles and deals.*)

Ask me a question.

KILROY: Has my luck run out?

GYPSY: Baby, your luck ran out the day you were born. Another question.

KILROY: Ought I to leave this town?

GYPSY: It don't look to me like you've got much choice in the matter . . . Take a card.

(*Kilroy takes one.*)

GYPSY: Ace?

KILROY: Yes, ma'am.

GYPSY: What color?

KILROY: Black.

GYPSY: Oh, oh— That does it. How big is your heart?

KILROY: As big as the head of a baby.

GYPSY: It's going to break.

KILROY: That's what I was afraid of.

GYPSY: The Streetcleaners are waiting for you outside the door.

KILROY: Which door, the front one? I'll slip out the back!

GYPSY: Leave us face it frankly, your number is up! You must've known a long time that the name of Kilroy was on the Streetcleaners' list.

KILROY: Sure. But not on top of it!

GYPSY: It's always a bit of a shock. Wait a minute! Here's good news. The Queen of Hearts has turned up in proper position.

KILROY: What's that mean?

GYPSY: Love, Baby!

KILROY: Love?

GYPSY: The Booby Prize!—Esmeralda!

(*She rises and hits a gong. A divan is carried out. The Gypsy's Daughter is seated in a reclining position, like an odalisque, on this low divan. A spangled veil covers her face. From this veil to the girdle below her navel, that supports her diaphanous bifurcated skirt, she is nude except for a pair of glittering emerald snakes coiled over her breasts. Kilroy's head moves in a dizzy circle and a canary warbles inside it.*)

KILROY: WHAT'S—WHAT'S *HER* SPECIALTY?—Tea-leaves?

(*The Gypsy wags a finger.*)

GYPSY: You know what curiosity did to the tom cat!—Nursie, give me my glamour wig and my forty-five. I'm hitting the street! I gotta go down to Walgreen's for change.

KILROY: What change?

GYPSY: The change from that ten-spot you're about to give me.

NURSIE: Don't argue with her. She has a will of iron.

KILROY: I'm not arguing!

(*He reluctantly produces the money.*)

But let's be *fair* about this! I hocked my golden gloves for this saw-buck!

NURSIE: All of them Yankee bastids want something for nothing!

KILROY: I want a receipt for this bill.

NURSIE: No one is gypped at the Gypsy's!

KILROY: That's wonderful! How do I know it?

GYPSY: It's in the cards, it's in the crystal ball, it's in the tea-leaves! Absolutely no one is gypped at the Gypsy's!

(*She snatches the bill. The wind howls.*)

Such changeable weather! I'll slip on my summer furs! Nursie, break out my summer furs!

NURSIE (*leering grotesquely*): *Mink or sable?*

GYPSY: *Ha ha, that's a doll!* Here! Clock him!

(*Nursie tosses her a greasy blanket, and the Gypsy tosses Nursie an alarm clock. The Gypsy rushes through the beaded string curtains.*)

Adios! Ha ha!!

(*She is hardly offstage when two shots ring out. Kilroy starts.*)

ESMERALDA (*plaintively*): Mother has such an awful time on the street.

KILROY: You mean that she is insulted on the street?

ESMERALDA: By strangers.

KILROY (*to the audience*): I shouldn't think acquaintances would do it.

(*She curls up on the low divan. Kilroy licks his lips.*)

—You seem very different from—this afternoon . . .

ESMERALDA: This afternoon?

KILROY: Yes, in the plaza when I was being roughed up by them gorillas and you was being dragged in the house by your Mama!

(*Esmeralda stares at him blankly.*)

You don't remember?

ESMERALDA: I never remember what happened before the moonrise makes me a virgin.

KILROY: —That—comes as a shock to you, huh?

ESMERALDA: Yes. It comes as a shock.

KILROY (*smiling*): You have a little temporary amnesia they call it!

ESMERALDA: Yankee . . .

KILROY: Huh?

ESMERALDA: I'm glad I chose you. I'm glad that you were chosen.

(*Her voice trails off.*)

I'm glad. I'm very glad . . .

NURSIE: Doll!

ESMERALDA: —What is it, Nursie?

NURSIE: How are things progressing?

ESMERALDA: Slowly, Nursie—

(*Nursie comes lumbering in.*)

NURSIE: I want some light reading matter.

ESMERALDA: He's sitting on *Screen Secrets*.

KILROY (*jumping up*): Aw. Here.

(*He hands her the fan magazine. She lumbers back out, coyly.*)

—I—I feel——self-conscious . .

(*He suddenly jerks out a silver-framed photo.*)

—D'you—like pictures?

ESMERALDA: Moving pictures?

KILROY: No, a—motionless—snapshot!

ESMERALDA: Of you?

KILROY: Of my—real—true woman . . . She was a platinum blonde the same as Jean Harlow. Do you remember Jean Harlow? No, you wouldn't remember Jean Harlow. It shows you are getting old when you remember Jean Harlow.

(*He puts the snapshot away.*)

. . . They say that Jean Harlow's ashes are kept in a little private cathedral in Forest Lawn . . . Wouldn't it be wonderful if you could sprinkle them ashes over the ground like seeds, and out of each one would spring another Jean Harlow? And when spring comes you could just walk out and pick them off the bush! . . . You don't talk much.

ESMERALDA: You want me to *talk*?

KILROY: Well, that's the way we do things in the States. A little vino, some records on the victrola, some quiet conversation—and then if both parties are in a mood for romance . . . Romance—

ESMERALDA: Music!

(*She rises and pours some wine from a slender crystal decanter as music is heard.*)

They say that the monetary system has got to be stabilized all over the world.

KILROY (*taking the glass*): Repeat that, please. My radar was not wide open.

ESMERALDA: I said that *they* said that—uh, skip it! But we couldn't care less as long as we keep on getting the Yankee dollar . . . plus federal tax!

KILROY: That's for surely!

ESMERALDA: How do you feel about the class struggle? Do you take sides in that?

KILROY: Not that I—

ESMERALDA: Neither do we because of the dialectics.

KILROY: Who! Which?

ESMERALDA: Languages with accents, I suppose. But Mama don't care as long as they don't bring the Pope over here and put him in the White House.

KILROY: Who would do that?

ESMERALDA: Oh, the Bolsheviskies, those nasty old things with whiskers! *Whiskers scratch!* But little moustaches tickle . . .

(*She giggles.*)

KILROY: I always got a smooth shave . . .

ESMERALDA: And how do you feel about the Mumbo Jumbo? Do you think they've got the Old Man in the bag yet?

KILROY: The Old Man?

ESMERALDA: God. We don't think so. We think there has been so much of the Mumbo Jumbo it's put Him to sleep!

(*Kilroy jumps up impatiently.*)

KILROY: This is not what I mean by a quiet conversation. I mean this is no where! *No where!*

ESMERALDA: What sort of talk do you want?

KILROY: Something more—intimate sort of! You know, like—

ESMERALDA: —Where did you get those eyes?

KILROY: *PERSONAL! Yeah* . . .

ESMERALDA: Well,—where did you get those eyes?

KILROY: Out of a dead cod-fish!

NURSIE (*shouting offstage*): DOLL!

(*Kilroy springs up, pounding his left palm with his right fist.*)

ESMERALDA: What?

NURSIE: Fifteen minutes!

KILROY: I'm no hot-rod mechanic.

(*To the audience:*)

I bet she's out there holding a stop watch to see that I don't over-stay my time in this place!

ESMERALDA (*calling through the string curtains*): *Nursie, go to bed, Nursie!*

KILROY (*in a fierce whisper*): That's right, go to bed, Nursie!!

(*There is a loud crash offstage.*)

ESMERALDA: —Nursie has gone to bed . . .

(*She drops the string curtains and returns to the alcove.*)

KILROY (*with vast relief*): —Ahhhhhhhhhh . . .

ESMERALDA: What've you got your eyes on?

KILROY: Those green snakes on you—what do you wear them for?

ESMERALDA: Supposedly for protection, but really for fun.

(*He crosses to the divan.*)

What are you going to do?

KILROY: I'm about to establish a beach-head on that sofa.

(*He sits down.*)

How about—lifting your veil?

ESMERALDA: I can't lift it.

KILROY: Why not?

ESMERALDA: I promised Mother I wouldn't.

KILROY: I thought your mother was the broadminded type.

ESMERALDA: Oh, she is, but you know how mothers are. You can lift it for me, if you say pretty please.

KILROY: Aww——

ESMERALDA: Go on, say it! Say pretty please!

KILROY: No!!

ESMERALDA: Why not?

KILROY: It's silly.

ESMERALDA: Then you can't lift my veil!

KILROY: Oh, all right. Pretty please.

ESMERALDA: Say it again!

KILROY: Pretty please.

ESMERALDA: Now say it once more like you meant it.

(*He jumps up. She grabs his hand.*)

Don't go away.

KILROY: You're making a fool out of me.

ESMERALDA: I was just teasing a little. Because you're so cute. Sit down again, please—*pretty* please!

(*He falls on the couch.*)

KILROY: What is that wonderful perfume you've got on?

ESMERALDA: Guess!

KILROY: Chanel Number Five?

ESMERALDA: No.

KILROY: Tabu?

ESMERALDA: No.

KILROY: I give up.

ESMERALDA: It's *Noche en Acapulco*! I'm just dying to go to Acapulco. I wish that you would take me to Acapulco.

(*He sits up.*)

What's the matter?

KILROY: You gypsies' daughters are invariably reminded of something without which you cannot do—just when it looks like everything has been fixed.

ESMERALDA: That isn't nice at all. I'm not the gold-digger type. Some girls see themselves in silver foxes. I only see myself in Acapulco!

KILROY: At Todd's Place?

ESMERALDA: Oh, no, at the Mirador! Watching those pretty boys dive off the Quebrada!

KILROY: Look again, Baby. Maybe you'll see yourself in Paramount Pictures or having a Singapore Sling at a Statler bar!

ESMERALDA: You're being sarcastic?

KILROY: Nope. Just realistic. All of you gypsies' daughters have hearts of stone, and I'm not whistling "Dixie"! But just the same, the night before a man dies, he says, "Pretty please—will you let me lift your veil?"—while the Street-cleaners wait for him right outside the door!—Because to be warm for a little longer is life. And love?—that's a four-letter word which is sometimes no better than one you see printed on fences by kids playing hooky from school!—Oh, well—what's the use of complaining? You gypsies' daughters have ears that only catch sounds like the snap of a gold cigarette case! Or, pretty please, Baby,—we're going to Acapulco!

ESMERALDA: *Are* we?

KILROY: See what I mean?

(*To the audience:*)

Didn't I tell you?!

(*To Esmeralda:*)

Yes! In the morning!

ESMERALDA: Ohhhh! I'm dizzy with joy! My little heart is going pitty-pat!

KILROY: My big heart is going boom-boom! Can I lift your veil now?

ESMERALDA: If you will be gentle.

KILROY: I would not hurt a fly unless it had on leather mittens.

(*He touches a corner of her spangled veil.*)

ESMERALDA: Ohhh . . .

KILROY: What?

ESMERALDA: Ohhhhhh!!

KILROY: Why! What's the matter?

ESMERALDA: You are not being gentle!

KILROY: I *am* being gentle.

ESMERALDA: You are *not* being gentle.

KILROY: What was I being, then?

ESMERALDA: Rough!

KILROY: I am *not* being rough.

ESMERALDA: Yes, you *are* being rough. You have to be gentle with me because you're the first.

KILROY: Are you kidding?

ESMERALDA: No.

KILROY: How about all of those other fiestas you've been to?

ESMERALDA: Each one's the first one. That is the wonderful thing about gypsies' daughters!

KILROY: You can say that again!

ESMERALDA: I don't like you when you're like that.

KILROY: Like what?

ESMERALDA: Cynical and sarcastic.

KILROY: I am sincere.

ESMERALDA: Lots of boys aren't sincere.

KILROY: Maybe they aren't but I am.

ESMERALDA: Everyone says he's sincere, but everyone isn't sincere. If everyone was sincere who says he's sincere there wouldn't be half so many insincere ones in the world and there would be lots, lots, lots more really sincere ones!

KILROY: I think you have got something there. But how about gypsies' daughters?

ESMERALDA: Huh?

KILROY: Are they one hundred percent in the really sincere category?

ESMERALDA: Well, yes, and no, mostly no! But some of them are for a while if their sweethearts are gentle.

KILROY: Would you believe I am sincere and gentle?

ESMERALDA: I would believe that you believe that you are . . . For a while . . .

KILROY: Everything's for a while. For a while is the stuff that dreams are made of, Baby! Now?—Now?

ESMERALDA: Yes, now, but be gentle!—*gentle* . . .

(*He delicately lifts a corner of her veil. She utters a soft cry. He lifts it further. She cries out again. A bit further . . . He turns the spangled veil all the way up from her face.*)

KILROY: I am sincere.

ESMERALDA: I am sincere.

KILROY: I am sincere.

ESMERALDA: I am sincere.

KILROY: I am sincere.

ESMERALDA: I am sincere.

KILROY: I am sincere.

ESMERALDA: I am sincere.

(*Kilroy leans back, removing his hand from her veil. She opens her eyes.*)

Is that all?

KILROY: I am tired.

ESMERALDA: —Already?

(*He rises and goes down the steps from the alcove.*)

KILROY: I am tired, and full of regret . . .

ESMERALDA: Oh!

KILROY: It wasn't much to give my golden gloves for.

ESMERALDA: You pity yourself?

KILROY: That's right, I pity myself and everybody that goes to the Gypsy's daughter. I pity the world and I pity the God who made it.

(*He sits down.*)

ESMERALDA: It's always like that as soon as the veil is lifted. They're all so ashamed of having degraded themselves, and their hearts have more regret than a heart can hold!

KILROY: Even a heart that's as big as the head of a baby!

ESMERALDA: You don't even notice how pretty my face is, do you?

KILROY: You look like all gypsies' daughters, no better, no worse. But as long as you get to go to Acapulco, your cup runneth over with ordinary contentment.

ESMERALDA: —I've never been so insulted in all my life!

KILROY: Oh, yes, you have, Baby. And you'll be insulted worse if you stay in this racket. You'll be insulted so much that it will get to be like water off *a duck's back*!

(*The door slams. Curtains are drawn apart on the Gypsy. Esmeralda lowers her veil hastily. Kilroy pretends not to notice the Gypsy's entrance. She picks up a little bell and rings it over his head.*)

Okay, Mamacita! I am aware of your presence!

GYPSY: Ha-ha! I was followed three blocks by some awful man!

KILROY: Then you caught him.

GYPSY: Naw, he ducked into a subway! I waited fifteen minutes outside the men's room and he never came out!

KILROY: Then you went in?

GYPSY: No! I got myself a sailor!—The streets are brilliant! . . . Have you all been good children?

(*Esmeralda makes a whimpering sound.*)

The pussy will play while the old mother cat is away?

KILROY: Your sense of humor is wonderful, but how about my change, Mamacita?

GYPSY: What change are you talking about?

KILROY: Are you boxed out of your mind? The change from that ten-spot you trotted over to Walgreen's?

GYPSY: Ohhhhh—

KILROY: *Oh, what?*

GYPSY (*counting on her fingers*): Five for the works, one dollar luxury tax, two for the house percentage and two more pour la service!—makes ten! Didn't I tell you?

KILROY: —What kind of a deal is this?

GYPSY (*whipping out a revolver*): A rugged one, Baby!

ESMERALDA: Mama, don't be unkind!

GYPSY: Honey, the gentleman's friends are waiting outside the door and it wouldn't be nice to detain him! Come on— Get going— Vamoose!

KILROY: Okay, Mamacita! Me voy!

(*He crosses to the beaded string curtains: turns to look back at the Gypsy and her daughter. The piping of the Streetcleaners is heard outside.*)

Sincere?—Sure! That's the wonderful thing about gypsies' daughters!

(*He goes out. Esmeralda raises a wondering fingertip to one eye. Then she cries out:*)

ESMERALDA: Look, Mama! Look, Mama! A tear!

GYPSY: You have been watching television too much . . .

(*She gathers the cards and turns off the crystal ball as—*)
(*Light fades out on the phony paradise of the Gypsy's.*)

GUTMAN: Block Thirteen on the Camino Real.

(*He exits.*)

BLOCK THIRTEEN

In the blackout the Streetcleaners place a barrel in the center and then hide in the Pit.

Kilroy, who enters from the right, is followed by a spot light. He sees the barrel and the menacing Streetcleaners and then runs to the closed door of the Siete Mares and rings the bell. No one answers. He backs up so he can see the balcony and calls:

KILROY: Mr. Gutman! Just gimme a cot in the lobby. I'll do odd jobs in the morning. I'll be the Patsy again. I'll light my nose sixty times a minute. I'll take prat-falls and assume the position for anybody that drops a dime on the street . . . Have a heart! Have just a LITTLE heart. Please!

(There is no response from Gutman's balcony. Jacques enters. He pounds his cane once on the pavement.)

JACQUES: Gutman! Open the door!—*GUTMAN! GUTMAN!*

(Eva, a beautiful woman, apparently nude, appears on the balcony.)

GUTMAN *(from inside)*: Eva darling, you're exposing yourself!

(He appears on the balcony with a portmanteau.)

JACQUES: What are you doing with my portmanteau?
GUTMAN: Haven't you come for your luggage?
JACQUES: Certainly not! I haven't checked out of here!
GUTMAN: Very few do . . . but residences are frequently terminated.
JACQUES: Open the door!
GUTMAN: Open the letter with the remittance check in it!
JACQUES: In the morning!
GUTMAN: Tonight!
JACQUES: Upstairs in my room!
GUTMAN: Downstairs at the entrance!
JACQUES: I won't be intimidated!
GUTMAN *(raising the portmanteau over his head)*: What?!
JACQUES: Wait!—

(He takes the letter out of his pocket.)

Give me some light.

(Kilroy strikes a match and holds it over Jacques' shoulder.)

Thank you. What does it say?
GUTMAN: —Remittances?

KILROY (*reading the letter over Jacques' shoulder*): —discontinued . . .

(*Gutman raises the portmanteau again.*)

JACQUES: Careful, I have—

(*The portmanteau lands with a crash.*
(*The Bum comes to the window at the crash. A. Ratt comes out to his doorway at the same time.*)

—fragile—mementoes . . .

(*He crosses slowly down to the portmanteau and kneels as . . .*
(*Gutman laughs and slams the balcony door. Jacques turns to Kilroy. He smiles at the young adventurer.*)

—"And so at last it has come, the distinguished thing!"

(*A. Ratt speaks as Jacques touches the portmanteau.*)

A. RATT: Hey, Dad—Vacancy here! A bed at the "Ritz Men Only." A little white ship to sail the dangerous night in.
JACQUES: Single or double?
A. RATT: There's only singles in this pad.
JACQUES (*to Kilroy*): Match you for it.
KILROY: What the hell, we're buddies, we can sleep spoons! If we can't sleep, we'll push the wash stand against the door and sing old popular songs till the crack of dawn! . . . "Heart of my heart, I love that melody!" . . . You bet your life I do.

(*Jacques takes out a pocket handkerchief and starts to grasp the portmanteau handle.*)

—It looks to me like you could use a Redcap and my rates are non-union!

(*He picks up the portmanteau and starts to cross towards the "Ritz Men Only." He stops at right center.*)

Sorry, buddy. Can't make it! The altitude on this block has affected my ticker! And in the distance which is nearer than further, I hear—the Streetcleaners'—piping!

(*Piping is heard.*)

JACQUES: COME ALONG!

(*He lifts the portmanteau and starts on.*)

KILROY: NO. Tonight! I prefer! To sleep! Out! Under! The stars!

JACQUES (*gently*): I understand, Brother!

KILROY (*to Jacques as he continues toward the "Ritz Men Only"*): Bon Voyage! I hope that you sail the dangerous night to the sweet golden port of morning!

JACQUES (*exiting*): Thanks, Brother!

KILROY: Excuse the *corn*! I'm sincere!

BUM: Show me the way to go home! . . .

GUTMAN (*appearing on the balcony with white parakeet*): Block Fourteen on the Camino Real.

BLOCK FOURTEEN

At opening, the Bum is still at the window.

The Streetcleaners' piping continues a little louder. Kilroy climbs, breathing heavily, to the top of the stairs and stands looking out at Terra Incognita as . . .

Marguerite enters the plaza through alleyway at right. She is accompanied by a silent Young Man who wears a domino.

MARGUERITE: Don't come any further with me. I'll have to wake the night porter. Thank you for giving me safe conduct through the Medina.

(*She has offered her hand. He grips it with a tightness that makes her wince.*)

Ohhhh . . . I'm not sure which is more provocative in you, your ominous silence or your glittering smile or—

(*He's looking at her purse.*)

What do you want? . . . Oh!

(*She starts to open the purse. He snatches it. She gasps as he suddenly strips her cloak off her. Then he snatches off her pearl necklace. With each successive despoilment, she gasps and retreats but makes no resistance. Her eyes are closed. He continues to smile. Finally, he rips her dress and runs his hands over her body as if to see if she had anything else of value concealed on her.)*

—What else do I have that you want?

THE YOUNG MAN (*contemptuously*): Nothing.

(The Young Man exits through the cantina, examining his loot. The Bum leans out his window, draws a deep breath and says:)

BUM: Lonely.

MARGUERITE (*to herself*): Lonely . . .

KILROY (*on the steps*): Lonely . . .

> *(The Streetcleaners' piping is heard.)*
> *(Marguerite runs to the Siete Mares and rings the bell. Nobody answers. She crosses to the terrace. Kilroy, meanwhile, has descended the stairs.)*

MARGUERITE: Jacques!

(Piping is heard.)

KILROY: Lady?

MARGUERITE: What?

KILROY: —*I'm—safe* . . .

MARGUERITE: I wasn't expecting that music tonight, were you?

(Piping.)

KILROY: It's them Streetcleaners.

MARGUERITE: I know.

(Piping.)

KILROY: You better go on in, lady.

MARGUERITE: No.

KILROY: GO ON IN!

MARGUERITE: NO! I want to stay out here and I do what I want to do!

(Kilroy looks at her for the first time.)

Sit down with me please.

KILROY: They're coming for me. The Gypsy told me I'm on top of their list. Thanks for. Taking my. Hand.

(*Piping is heard.*)

MARGUERITE: Thanks for taking mine.

(*Piping.*)

KILROY: Do me one more favor. Take out of my pocket a picture. My fingers are. Stiff.

MARGUERITE: This one?

KILROY: My one. True. Woman.

MARGUERITE: A silver-framed photo! Was she really so fair?

KILROY: She was so fair and much fairer than they could tint that picture!

MARGUERITE: Then you have been on the street when the street was royal.

KILROY: Yeah . . . when the street was royal!

(*Piping is heard. Kilroy rises.*)

MARGUERITE: Don't get up, don't leave me!

KILROY: I want to be on my feet when the Streetcleaners come for me!

MARGUERITE: Sit back down again and tell me about your girl.

(*He sits.*)

KILROY: Y'know what it is you miss most? When you're separated. From someone. You lived. With. And loved? It's waking up in the night! With that—warmness beside you!

MARGUERITE: Yes, that *warmness* beside you!

KILROY: Once you get used to that. *Warmness!* It's a hell of a lonely feeling to wake up without it! Specially in some dollar-a-night hotel room on Skid! A hot-water bottle won't do. And a stranger. Won't do. It has to be some one you're used to. And that you. *KNOW LOVES* you!

(*Piping is heard.*)

Can you see them?

MARGUERITE: I see no one but you.

KILROY: I looked at my wife one night when she was sleeping and that was the night that the medics wouldn't okay me for no more fights . . . Well . . . My wife was sleeping with a smile like a child's. I kissed her. She didn't wake up. I took a pencil and paper. I wrote her. Good-bye!

MARGUERITE: That was the night she would have loved you the most!

KILROY: Yeah, *that* night, but what about *after* that night? Oh, Lady . . . Why should a beautiful girl tie up with a broken-down champ?—The earth still turning and her obliged to turn with it, not out—of dark into light but out of light into dark? Naw, naw, naw, naw!—Washed up!—Finished!

(*Piping.*)

. . . that ain't a word that a man can't look at . . . There ain't no words in the language a man can't look at . . . and know just what they mean. and be. And act. And *go*!

(*He turns to the waiting Streetcleaners.*)

Come on! . . . Come on! . . . COME ON, YOU SONS OF BITCHES! KILROY IS HERE! HE'S READY!

(*A gong sounds.*
(*Kilroy swings at the Streetcleaners. They circle about him out of reach, turning him by each of their movements. The swings grow wilder like a boxer. He falls to his knees still swinging and finally collapses flat on his face.*
(*The Streetcleaners pounce but La Madrecita throws herself protectingly over the body and covers it with her shawl.*
(*Blackout.*)

MARGUERITE: Jacques!

GUTMAN (*on balcony*): Block Fifteen on the Camino Real.

BLOCK FIFTEEN

La Madrecita is seated: across her knees is the body of Kilroy. Up center, a low table on wheels bears a sheeted figure. Beside the table stands a Medical Instructor addressing Students and Nurses, all in white surgical outfits.

INSTRUCTOR: This is the body of an unidentified vagrant.

LA MADRECITA: This was thy son, America—and now mine.

INSTRUCTOR: He was found in an alley along the Camino Real.

LA MADRECITA: Think of him, now, as he was before his luck failed him. Remember his time of greatness, when he was not faded, not frightened.

INSTRUCTOR: More light, please!

LA MADRECITA: More light!

INSTRUCTOR: Can everyone see clearly!

LA MADRECITA: Everyone must see clearly!

INSTRUCTOR: There is no external evidence of disease.

LA MADRECITA: He had clear eyes and the body of a champion boxer.

INSTRUCTOR: There are no marks of violence on the body.

LA MADRECITA: He had the soft voice of the South and a pair of golden gloves.

INSTRUCTOR: His death was apparently due to natural causes.

(*The Students make notes. There are keening voices.*)

LA MADRECITA: Yes, blow wind where night thins! He had many admirers!

INSTRUCTOR: There are no legal claimants.

LA MADRECITA: He stood as a planet among the moons of their longing, haughty with youth, a champion of the prize-ring!

INSTRUCTOR: No friends or relatives having identified him—

LA MADRECITA: You should have seen the lovely monogrammed robe in which he strode the aisles of the Colosseums!

INSTRUCTOR: After the elapse of a certain number of days, his body becomes the property of the State—

LA MADRECITA: Yes, blow wind where night thins—for laurel is not everlasting . . .

INSTRUCTOR: And now is transferred to our hands for the nominal sum of five dollars.

LA MADRECITA: This was thy son,—and now mine . . .

INSTRUCTOR: We will now proceed with the dissection. Knife, please!

LA MADRECITA: Blow wind!

(*Keening is heard offstage.*)

Yes, blow wind where night thins! You are his passing bell and his lamentation.

(*More keening is heard.*)

Keen for him, all maimed creatures, deformed and mutilated—his homeless ghost is your own!

INSTRUCTOR: First we will open up the chest cavity and examine the heart for evidence of coronary occlusion.

LA MADRECITA: His heart was pure gold and as big as the head of a baby.

INSTRUCTOR: We will make an incision along the vertical line.

LA MADRECITA: Rise, ghost! Go! Go bird! "Humankind cannot bear very much reality."

(*At the touch of her flowers, Kilroy stirs and pushes himself up slowly from her lap. On his feet again, he rubs his eyes and looks around him.*)

VOICES (*crying offstage*): Olé! Olé! Olé!

KILROY: Hey! Hey, somebody! Where am I?

(*He notices the dissection room and approaches.*)

INSTRUCTOR (*removing a glittering sphere from a dummy corpse*): Look at this heart. It's as big as the head of a baby.

KILROY: My heart!

INSTRUCTOR: Wash it off so we can look for the pathological lesions.

KILROY: Yes, siree, that's my heart!

GUTMAN: Block Sixteen!

(*Kilroy pauses just outside the dissection area as a Student takes the heart and dips it into a basin on the stand beside the table. The Student suddenly cries out and holds aloft a glittering gold sphere.*)

INSTRUCTOR: Look! This heart's solid gold!

BLOCK SIXTEEN

KILROY (*rushing forward*): That's mine, you bastards!

(*He snatches the golden sphere from the Medical Instructor. The autopsy proceeds as if nothing had happened as the spot of light on the table fades out, but for Kilroy a ghostly chase commences, a dreamlike re-enactment of the chase that occurred at the end of Block Six. Gutman shouts from his balcony:*)

GUTMAN: Stop, thief, stop, corpse! That gold heart is the property of the State! Catch him, catch the golden-heart robber!

(*Kilroy dashes offstage into an aisle of the theatre. There is the wail of a siren: the air is filled with calls and whistles, roar of motors, screeching brakes, pistol-shots, thundering footsteps. The dimness of the auditorium is transected by searching rays of light—but there are no visible pursuers.*)

KILROY (*as he runs panting up the aisle*): This is my heart! It don't belong to no State, not even the U.S.A. Which way is out? Where's the Greyhound depot? Nobody's going to put my heart in a bottle in a museum and charge admission to support the rotten police! Where are they? Which way are they going? Or coming? Hey, somebody, help me get out of here! Which way do I—which way—which way do I—*go! go! go! go! go!*

(*He has now arrived in the balcony.*)

Gee, I'm lost! I don't know where I am! I'm all turned around, I'm *confused*, I don't understand—what's—happened, it's like a—*dream*, it's—just like a—dream . . . *Mary! Oh, Mary! Mary!*

(*He has entered the box from which he leapt in Act One.*
(*A clear shaft of light falls on him. He looks up into it, crying:*)

Mary, help a Christian!! Help a Christian, Mary!—It's like a dream . . .

(*Esmeralda appears in a childish nightgown beside her gauze-tented bed on the Gypsy's roof. Her Mother appears with a cup of some sedative drink, cooing . . .*)

GYPSY: Beddy-bye, beddy-bye, darling. It's sleepy-time down South and up North, too, and also East and West!

KILROY (*softly*): Yes, it's—like a—*dream* . . .

(*He leans panting over the ledge of the box, holding his heart like a football, watching Esmeralda.*)

GYPSY: Drink your Ovaltine, Ducks, and the sandman will come on tip-toe with a bag full of dreams . . .

ESMERALDA: I want to dream of the Chosen Hero, Mummy.

GYPSY: Which one, the one that's coming or the one that is gone?

ESMERALDA: The *only* one, *Kilroy! He* was *sincere!*

KILROY: That's *right! I was*, for a while!

GYPSY: How do you know that Kilroy was sincere?

ESMERALDA: He said so.

KILROY: That's the truth, I *was!*

GYPSY: When did he say that?

ESMERALDA: When he lifted my veil.

GYPSY: Baby, they're always sincere when they lift your veil; it's one of those natural reflexes that don't mean a thing.

KILROY (*aside*): What a cynical old bitch that Gypsy mama is!

GYPSY: And there's going to be lots of other fiestas for you, baby doll, and lots of other chosen heroes to lift your little veil when Mamacita and Nursie are out of the room.

ESMERALDA: No, Mummy, never, I mean it!

KILROY: I *believe* she means it!

GYPSY: Finish your Ovaltine and say your Now-I-Lay-Me.

(*Esmeralda sips the drink and hands her the cup.*)

KILROY (*with a catch in his voice*): I had one true woman, which I can't go back to, but now I've found another.

(*He leaps onto the stage from the box.*)

ESMERALDA (*dropping to her knees*): Now I lay me down to sleep, I pray the Lord my soul to keep. If I should die before I wake, I pray the Lord my soul to take.

GYPSY: God bless Mummy!

ESMERALDA: And the crystal ball and the tea-leaves.

KILROY: *Pssst!*

ESMERALDA: What's that?

GYPSY: A tom-cat in the plaza.

ESMERALDA: God bless all cats without pads in the plaza tonight.

KILROY: Amen!

(*He falls to his knees in the empty plaza.*)

ESMERALDA: God bless all con men and hustlers and pitch-men who hawk their hearts on the street, all two-time losers who're likely to lose once more, the courtesan who made the mistake of love, the greatest of lovers crowned with the longest horns, the poet who wandered far from his heart's green country and possibly will and possibly won't be able to find his way back, look down with a smile tonight on the last cavaliers, the ones with the rusty armor and soiled white plumes, and visit with understanding and something that's almost tender those fading legends that come and go in this plaza like songs not clearly remembered, oh, sometime and somewhere, let there be something to mean the word *honor* again!

QUIXOTE (*hoarsely and loudly, stirring slightly among his verminous rags*): Amen!

KILROY: Amen . . .

GYPSY (*disturbed*): —That will do, now.

ESMERALDA: *And, oh, God, let me dream tonight of the Chosen Hero!*

GYPSY: Now, sleep. Fly away on the magic carpet of dreams!

(*Esmeralda crawls into the gauze-tented cot. The Gypsy descends from the roof.*)

KILROY: *Esmeralda! My little Gypsy sweetheart!*

ESMERALDA (*sleepily*): Go away, cat.

(*The light behind the gauze is gradually dimming.*)

KILROY: This is no cat. This is the chosen hero of the big fiesta, Kilroy, the champion of the golden gloves with his gold heart cut from his chest and in his hands to give you!

ESMERALDA: Go away. Let me dream of the Chosen Hero.

KILROY: What a hassle! Mistook for a cat! What can I do to convince this doll I'm real?

(*Three brass balls wink brilliantly.*)

—Another transaction seems to be indicated!

(*He rushes to the Loan Shark's. The entrance immediately lights up.*)

My heart is gold! What will you give me for it?

(*Jewels, furs, sequined gowns, etc., are tossed to his feet. He throws his heart like a basketball to the Loan Shark, snatches up the loot and rushes back to the Gypsy's.*)

Doll! Behold this loot! I gave my golden heart for it!

ESMERALDA: Go away, cat . . .

(*She falls asleep. Kilroy bangs his forehead with his fist, then rushes to the Gypsy's door, pounds it with both fists. The door is thrown open and the sordid contents of a large jar are thrown at him. He falls back gasping, spluttering, retching. He retreats and finally assumes an exaggerated attitude of despair.*)

KILROY: Had for a button! Stewed, screwed and tattooed on the Camino Real! Baptized, finally, with the contents of a slop-jar!—Did anybody say the deal was rugged?!

(*Quixote stirs against the wall of Skid Row. He hawks and spits and staggers to his feet.*)

GUTMAN: Why, the old knight's awake, his dream is over!

QUIXOTE (*to Kilroy*): Hello! Is that a fountain?

KILROY: —Yeah, but—

QUIXOTE: I've got a mouthful of old chicken feathers . . .

(*He approaches the fountain. It begins to flow. Kilroy falls back in amazement as the Old Knight rinses his mouth and drinks and removes his jacket to bathe, handing the tattered garment to Kilroy.*)

QUIXOTE (*as he bathes*): Qué pasa, mi amigo?

KILROY: The deal is rugged. D'you know what I mean?

QUIXOTE: Who knows better than I what a rugged deal is!

(*He produces a tooth brush and brushes his teeth.*)

—Will you take some advice?

KILROY: Brother, at this point on the Camino I will take any-thing which is offered!

QUIXOTE: *Don't! Pity! Your! Self!*

(*He takes out a pocket mirror and grooms his beard and moustache.*)

The wounds of the vanity, the many offenses our egos have to endure, being housed in bodies that age and hearts that grow tired, are better accepted with a tolerant smile—like *this!*—You *see?*

(*He cracks his face in two with an enormous grin.*)

GUTMAN: Follow-spot on the face of the ancient knight!

QUIXOTE: Otherwise what you become is a bag full of curdled cream—*leche mala,* we call it!—attractive to nobody, least of all to yourself!

(*He passes the comb and pocket mirror to Kilroy.*)

Have you got any plans?

KILROY (*a bit uncertainly, wistfully*): Well, I was thinking of—going *on* from—*here!*

QUIXOTE: Good! Come with me.

KILROY (*to the audience*): Crazy old bastard.

(*Then to the Knight:*)

Donde?

QUIXOTE (*starting for the stairs*): Quien sabe!

(*The fountain is now flowing loudly and sweetly. The Street People are moving toward it with murmurs of wonder. Marguerite comes out upon the terrace.*)

KILROY: Hey, there's—!

QUIXOTE: Shhh! Listen!

(*They pause on the stairs.*)

MARGUERITE: Abdullah!

(*Gutman has descended to the terrace.*)

GUTMAN: Mademoiselle, allow me to deliver the message for you. It would be in bad form if I didn't take some final part in the pageant.

(*He crosses the plaza to the opposite façade and shouts "Casanova!" under the window of the "Ritz Men Only."*)

(*Meanwhile Kilroy scratches out the verb "is" and prints the correction "was" in the inscription on the ancient wall.*)

Casanova! Great lover and King of Cuckolds on the Camino Real! The last of your ladies has guaranteed your tabs and is expecting you for breakfast on the terrace!

(*Casanova looks first out of the practical window of the flophouse, then emerges from its scabrous doorway, haggard, unshaven, crumpled in dress but bearing himself as erectly as ever. He blinks and glares fiercely into the brilliant morning light.*)

(*Marguerite cannot return his look, she averts her face with a look for which anguish would not be too strong a term, but at the same time she extends a pleading hand toward him. After some hesitation, he begins to move toward her, striking the pavement in measured cadence with his cane, glancing once, as he crosses, out at the audience with a wry smile that makes admissions that would be embarrassing to a vainer man than Casanova now is. When he reaches Marguerite she gropes for his hand, seizes it with a low cry and presses it spasmodically to her lips while he draws her into his arms and looks above her sobbing, dyed-golden head with the serene, clouded gaze of someone mortally ill as the mercy of a narcotic laps over his pain.*)

(*Quixote raises his lance in a formal gesture and cries out hoarsely, powerfully from the stairs:*)

QUIXOTE: *The violets in the mountains have broken the rocks!*

(*Quixote goes through the arch with Kilroy.*)

GUTMAN (*to the audience*): The Curtain Line has been spoken!

(*To the wings:*)

Bring it down!

(*He bows with a fat man's grace as—*
(*The curtain falls.*)

"SOMETHING WILD . . ."

W<small>HILE</small> I was on the road with *Summer and Smoke* I was entertained one evening by the company of a successful community theater, one of the pioneer outfits of this kind and one of the few that operate on a profitable self-supporting basis. It had been 10 years since I had had a connection with a community theater. I was professionally spawned by one 10 years ago in St. Louis, but like most offspring, once I departed from the maternal shelter, I gave it scarcely a backward glance. Backward glances are a bit impractical, anyhow, in a theatrical career.

Now I felt considerable curiosity about the contact I was about to renew: but the moment I walked in the door I felt something wrong. Not so much something wrong as something missing. It seemed all so respectable. The men in their conservative business suits with their neat hair-cuts and highly polished shoes could have passed for corporation lawyers and the women, mostly their wives, were impeccably lady-like. There was no scratchy phonograph music, there were no dimly lit alcoves where dancing couples stood practically still, no sofas with ruptured upholstery, no garlands of colored crepe paper festooning the ceiling and collapsing onto the floor.

In my opinion art is a kind of anarchy, and the theater is a province of art. What was missing here, was something anarchistic in the air. I must modify that statement about art and anarchy. Art is only anarchy in juxtaposition with organized society. It runs counter to the sort of orderliness on which organized society apparently must be based. It is a benevolent anarchy: it must be that and if it is true art, it is. It is benevolent in the sense of constructing something which is missing, and what it constructs may be merely criticism of things as they exist. I felt in this group no criticism but rather an adaptation which was almost obsequious. And my mind shot back to the St. Louis group I have mentioned, a group called The Mummers.

The Mummers were sort of a long-haired outfit. Now there is no virtue, *per se*, in not going to the barber. And I don't suppose there is any particular virtue in girls having runs in their stockings. Yet one feels a kind of nostalgia for that sort of disorderliness now and then.

Somehow you associate it with things that have no logical connection with it. You associate it with really good times and with intense feelings and with convictions. Most of all with convictions! In the party I have mentioned there was a notable lack of convictions. Nobody was shouting for—or against—anything, there was just a lot of polite chit-chat going on among people who seemed to have known each other long enough to have exhausted all interest in each other's ideas.

While I stood there among them, the sense that something was missing clarified itself into a tremendous wave of longing for something that I had not been conscious of wanting until that moment. The open sky of my youth!—a peculiarly American youth which somehow seems to have slipped a little bit out of our grasp nowadays. . . .

The Mummers of St. Louis were my professional youth. They were the disorderly theater group of St. Louis, standing socially, if not also artistically, opposite to the usual Little Theater group. That opposite group need not be described. They were eminently respectable, predominantly middle-aged, and devoted mainly to the presentation of Broadway hits a season or two after Broadway. Their stage was narrow and notices usually mentioned how well they had overcome their spatial limitations, but it never seemed to me that they produced anything in a manner that needed to overcome limitations of space. The dynamism which is theater was as foreign to their philosophy as the tongue of Chinese.

Dynamism was what The Mummers had, and for about five years—roughly from about 1935 to 1940—they burned like one of Miss Millay's improvident little candles—and then expired. Yes, there was about them that kind of excessive romanticism which is youth and which is the best and purest part of life.

The first time I worked with them was in 1936, when I was a student at Washington University in St. Louis. They were, then, under the leadership of a man named Willard Holland, their organizer and their director. Holland always wore a blue

suit which was not only baggy but shiny. He needed a hair-
cut and he sometimes wore a scarf instead of a shirt. This was
not what made him a great director, but a great director he
was. Everything that he touched he charged with electricity.
Was it my youth that made it seem that way? Possibly, but not
probably. In fact not even possibly: you judge theater, really,
by its effect on audiences, and Holland's work never failed to
deliver, and when I say deliver I mean a sock!

The first thing I worked with them on was *Bury the Dead*,
by Irwin Shaw. That play ran a little bit short of full length
and they needed a curtain-raiser to fill out the program.
Holland called me up. He did not have a prepossessing voice.
It was high-pitched and nervous. He said I hear you go to
college and I hear you can write. I admitted some justice in
both of these charges. Then he asked me: How do you feel
about compulsory military training? I then assured him that I
had left the University of Missouri because I could not get a
passing grade in the ROTC. Swell!, said Holland, you are just
the guy I am looking for. How would you like to write something against militarism?

So I did.

Shaw's play, one of the greatest lyric plays America has produced, was a solid piece of flame. Actors and script, under
Holland's dynamic hand, were one piece of vibrant living-
tissue. Now St. Louis is not a town that is easily impressed.
They love music, they are ardent devotees of the symphony
concerts, but they preserve a fairly rigid decorum when they
are confronted with anything off-beat which they are not
used to. They certainly were not used to the sort of hot lead
which the Mummers pumped into their bellies that night of
Shaw's play. They were not used to it, but it paralyzed them.
There wasn't a cough or creak in the house, and nobody left
the Wednesday Club Auditorium (which the Mummers
rented out for their performances) without a disturbing kink
in their nerves or guts, and I doubt if any of them have forgotten it to this day.

It was The Mummers that I remembered at this polite supper party which I attended last month.

Now let me give you a picture of the Mummers! Most of
them worked at other jobs besides theater. They had to,

because The Mummers were not a paying proposition. There were laborers. There were clerks. There were waitresses. There were students. There were whores and tramps and there was even a post-debutante who was a member of the Junior League of St. Louis. Many of them were fine actors. Many of them were not. Some of them could not act at all, but what they lacked in ability, Holland inspired them with in the way of enthusiasm. I guess it was all run by a kind of beautiful witchcraft! It was like a definition of what I think theater is. Something wild, something exciting, something that you are not used to. Offbeat is the word.

They put on bad shows sometimes, but they never put on a show that didn't deliver a punch to the solar plexus, maybe not in the first act, maybe not in the second, but always at last a good hard punch was delivered, and it made a difference in the lives of the spectators that they had come to that place and seen that show.

The plays I gave them were bad. But the first of these plays was a smash hit. It even got rave notices out of all three papers, and there was a real demonstration on the opening night with shouts and cheers and stamping, and the pink-faced author took his first bow among the grey-faced coal-miners that he had created out of an imagination never stimulated by the sight of an actual coal-mine. The second play that I gave them, *Fugitive Kind*, was a flop. It got one rave notice out of the *Star-Times*, but the *Post-Dispatch* and the *Globe Democrat* gave it hell. Nevertheless it packed a considerable wallop and there are people in St. Louis who still remember it. Bad plays, both of them, amateurish and coarse and juvenile and talky. But Holland and his players put them across the footlights without apology and they put them across with the bang that is theater.

Oh, how long ago that was!

The Mummers lived only five years. Yes, they had something in common with lyric verse of a too romantic nature. From 1935 to 1940 they had their fierce little flame, and then they expired, and now there is not a visible trace of them. Where is Holland? In Hollywood, I think. And where are the players? God knows. . . .

I am here, remembering them wistfully.

Now I shall have to say something to give this recollection a meaning to you.

All right. This is it.

Today we are living in a world which is threatened by totalitarianism. The Fascist and the Communist states have thrown us into a panic of reaction. Reactionary opinion descends like a ton of bricks on the head of any artist who speaks out against the current of prescribed ideas. We are all under wraps of one kind or another, trembling before the spectre of investigating committees and even with Buchenwald in the back of our minds when we consider whether or not we dare to say we were for Henry Wallace. *Yes, it is as bad as that.*

And yet it isn't *really* as bad as that.

America is still America, democracy is still democracy.

In our history books are still the names of Jefferson and Lincoln and Tom Paine. The direction of the Democratic impulse, which is entirely and irresistibly away from the police state and away from any and all forms of controlled thought and feeling—which is entirely and irresistibly in the direction of that which is individual and humane and equitable and free—that direction can be confused but it cannot be lost.

I have a way of jumping from the particular to the abstract, for the particular is sometimes as much as we know of the abstract.

Now let me jump back again: where? To the subject of community theaters and their social function.

It seems to me, as it seems to many artists right now, that an effort is being made to put creative work and workers under wraps.

Nothing could be more dangerous to Democracy, for the irritating grain of sand which is creative work in a society must be kept inside the shell or the pearl of idealistic progress cannot be made. For God's sake let us defend ourselves against whatever is hostile to us without imitating the thing which we are afraid of!

Community theaters have a social function and it is to be that kind of an irritant in the shell of their community. Not to conform, not to wear the conservative business suit of their audience, but to let their hair grow long and even greasy, to make wild gestures, break glasses, fight, shout, and fall downstairs! When you see them acting like this—not respectably, not quite decently, even!—then you will know that something is going to happen in that outfit, something disturbing, something irregular, something brave and honest.

The biologist will tell you that progress is the result of mutations. Mutations are another word for freaks. For God's sake let's have a little more freakish behavior—not less.

Maybe 90 per cent of the freaks will be just freaks, ludicrous and pathetic and getting nowhere but into trouble.

Eliminate them, however—bully them into conformity—and nobody in America will ever be really young any more and we'll be left standing in the dead center of nowhere.

TALK TO ME LIKE THE RAIN
AND LET ME LISTEN . . .

CHARACTERS
MAN
WOMAN
CHILD'S VOICE (off stage)

SCENE: *A furnished room west of Eighth Avenue in midtown Manhattan. On a folding bed lies a Man in crumpled underwear, struggling out of sleep with the sighs of a man who went to bed very drunk. A Woman sits in a straight chair at the room's single window, outlined dimly against a sky heavy with a rain that has not yet begun to fall. The Woman is holding a tumbler of water from which she takes small, jerky sips like a bird drinking. Both of them have ravaged young faces like the faces of children in a famished country. In their speech there is a sort of politeness, a sort of tender formality like that of two lonely children who want to be friends, and yet there is an impression that they have lived in this intimate situation for a long time and that the present scene between them is the repetition of one that has been repeated so often that its plausible emotional contents, such as reproach and contrition, have been completely worn out and there is nothing left but acceptance of something hopelessly inalterable between them.*

MAN: (*hoarsely*) What time is it? (*The Woman murmurs something inaudible.*) What, honey?
WOMAN: Sunday.
MAN: I know it's Sunday. You never wind the clock.

> (*The Woman stretches a thin bare arm out of the ravelled pink rayon sleeve of her kimona and picks up the tumbler of water and the weight of it seems to pull her forward a little. The Man watches solemnly, tenderly from the bed as she sips the water. A thin music begins, hesitantly, repeating a phrase several times as if someone in a next room were trying to*

remember a song on a mandolin. Sometimes a phrase is sung in Spanish. The song could be Estrellita.

(*Rain begins; it comes and goes during the play; there is a drumming flight of pigeons past the window and a child's voice chants outside—*)

CHILD'S VOICE: Rain, rain, go away!
           Come again some other day!

(*The chant is echoed mockingly by another child farther away.*)

MAN: (*finally*) I wonder if I cashed my unemployment. (*The Woman leans forward with the weight of the glass seeming to pull her; sets it down on the window-sill with a small crash that seems to startle her. She laughs breathlessly for a moment. The Man continues, without much hope.*) I hope I didn't cash my unemployment. Where's my clothes? Look in my pockets and see if I got the cheque on me.

WOMAN: You came back while I was out looking for you and picked the cheque up and left a note on the bed that I couldn't make out.

MAN: You couldn't make out the note?

WOMAN: Only a telephone number. I called the number but there was so much noise I couldn't hear.

MAN: Noise? Here?

WOMAN: No, noise there.

MAN: Where was "there"?

WOMAN: I don't know. Somebody said come over and hung up and all I got afterwards was a busy signal . . .

MAN: When I woke up I was in a bathtub full of melting ice-cubes and Miller's High Life beer. My skin was blue. I was gasping for breath in a bathtub full of ice-cubes. It was near a river but I don't know if it was the East or the Hudson. People do terrible things to a person when he's unconscious in this city. I'm sore all over like I'd been kicked downstairs, not like I fell but was kicked. One time I remember all my hair was shaved off. Another time they stuffed me into a trash-can in the alley and I've come to with cuts and burns on my body. Vicious people abuse you when you're unconscious. When I woke up I was naked in a bathtub full of melting ice-cubes. I crawled out and went into the parlor and someone was going out of the other door as I came in and I opened the door and heard the door of an elevator shut and saw the doors of a corridor in a hotel. The TV was on and there was a record playing at the same time; the parlor was full of rolling tables loaded with stuff from Room Service, and whole hams, whole turkeys, three-decker sandwiches cold and turning stiff, and bottles and bottles and bottles of all kinds of liquors that hadn't even been opened and buckets of ice-cubes melting . . . Somebody closed a door as I came in . . . (*The Woman sips water.*) As I came in someone was going out. I heard a door shut and I went to the door and heard the door of an elevator shut . . . (*The Woman sets her glass down.*)—All over the floor of this pad near the river—articles—clothing—scattered . . . (*The Woman gasps as a flight of pigeons sweeps past the open window.*)—Bras!—Panties!—Shirts, ties, socks—and so forth . . .

WOMAN: (*faintly*) Clothes?

MAN: Yes, all kinds of personal belongings and broken glass and furniture turned over as if there'd been a free-for-all fight going on and the pad was—raided . . .

WOMAN: Oh.

MAN: Violence must have—broken out in the—place . . .

WOMAN: You were—?

MAN: —in the bathtub on—ice . . .

WOMAN: Oh . . .

MAN: And I remember picking up the phone to ask what hotel it was but I don't remember if they told me or not . . . Give me a drink of that water. (*Both of them rise and meet in the center of the room. The glass is passed gravely between them. He rinses his mouth, staring at her gravely, and crosses to spit out the window. Then he returns to the center of the room and hands the glass back to her. She takes a sip of the water. He places his fingers tenderly on her long throat.*) Now I've recited the litany of my sorrows! (*Pause: the mandolin is heard.*) And what have you got to tell me? Tell me a little something of what's going on behind your— (*His fingers trail across her forehead and eyes. She closes her eyes and lifts a hand in the air as if about to touch him. He takes the hand and examines it upside down and then he presses its fingers to*

his lips. When he releases her fingers she touches him with them.
She touches his thin smooth chest which is smooth as a child's
and then she touches his lips. He raises his hand and lets his
fingers slide along her throat and into the opening of the ki-
mona as the mandolin gathers assurance. She turns and leans
against him, her throat curving over his shoulder, and he runs
his fingers along the curve of her throat and says—) It's been
so long since we have been together except like a couple of
strangers living together. Let's find each other and maybe
we won't be lost. Talk to me! I've been lost!—I thought of
you often but couldn't call you, honey. Thought of you all
the time but couldn't call. What could I say if I called?
Could I say, I'm lost? Lost in the city? Passed around like a
dirty *post*card among people?—And then hang up . . . I am
lost in this—city . . .

WOMAN: I've had nothing but water since you left! (*She says*
this almost gaily, laughing at the statement. The Man holds
her tight to him with a soft, shocked cry.)—Not a thing but
instant coffee until it was used up, and water! (*She laughs*
convulsively.)

MAN: Can you talk to me, honey? Can you talk to me, now?

WOMAN: Yes!

MAN: Well, talk to me like the rain and—let me listen, let me
lie here and—listen . . . (*He falls back across the bed, rolls*
on his belly, one arm hanging over the side of the bed and
occasionally drumming the floor with his knuckles. The
mandolin continues.) It's been too long a time since—we
levelled with each other. Now tell me things. What have
you been thinking in the silence?—While I've been passed
around like a dirty postcard in this city . . . Tell me, talk
to me! Talk to me like the rain and I will lie here and
listen.

WOMAN: I—

MAN: You've got to, it's necessary! I've got to know, so talk
to me like the rain and I will lie here and listen, I will lie
here and—

WOMAN: I want to go away.

MAN: You do?

WOMAN: *I want to go away!*

MAN: How?

WOMAN: *Alone!* (*She returns to window.*)—I'll register under a made-up name at a little hotel on the coast . . .

MAN: What name?

WOMAN: Anna—Jones . . . The chambermaid will be a little old lady who has a grandson that she talks about . . . . I'll sit in the chair while the old lady makes the bed, my arms will hang over the—sides, and—her voice will be—peaceful . . . She'll tell me what her grandson had for supper!—tapioca and—cream . . . (*The Woman sits by the window and sips the water.*)—The room will be shadowy, cool, and filled with the murmur of—

MAN: Rain?

WOMAN: Yes. Rain.

MAN: And—?

WOMAN: Anxiety will—pass—over!

MAN: Yes . . .

WOMAN: After a while the little old woman will say, Your bed is made up, Miss, and I'll say—Thank you . . . Take a dollar out of my pocketbook. The door will close. And I'll be alone again. The windows will be tall with long blue shutters and it will be a season of rain—rain—rain . . . My life will be like the room, cool—shadowy cool and—filled with the murmur of—

MAN: Rain . . .

WOMAN: I will receive a check in the mail every week that I can count on. The little old lady will cash the checks for me and get me books from a library and pick up—laundry . . . I'll always have clean things!—I'll dress in white. I'll never be very strong or have much energy left, but have enough after a while to walk on the—esplanade—to walk on the beach without effort . . . In the evening I'll walk on the esplanade along the beach. I'll have a certain beach where I go to sit, a little way from the pavillion where the band plays Victor Herbert selections while it gets dark . . . I'll have a big room with shutters on the windows. There will be a season of rain, rain, rain. And I will be so exhausted after my life in the city that I won't mind just listening to the rain. I'll be so quiet. The lines will disappear from my face. My eyes won't be inflamed at all any more. I'll have no friends. I'll have no acquaintances even. When I get sleepy,

I'll walk slowly back to the little hotel. The clerk will say, Good evening, Miss Jones, and I'll just barely smile and take my key. I won't ever look at a newspaper or hear a radio; I won't have any idea of what's going on in the world. I will not be conscious of time passing at all . . . One day I will look in the mirror and I will see that my hair is beginning to turn grey and for the first time I will realize that I have been living in this little hotel under a made-up name without any friends or acquaintances or any kind of connections for twenty-five years. It will surprise me a little but it won't bother me any. I will be glad that time has passed as easily as that. Once in a while I may go out to the movies. I will sit in the back row with all that darkness around me and figures sitting motionless on each side not conscious of me. Watching the screen. Imaginary people. People in stories. I will read long books and the journals of dead writers. I will feel closer to them than I ever felt to people I used to know before I withdrew from the world. It will be sweet and cool this friendship of mine with dead poets, for I won't have to touch them or answer their questions. They will talk to me and not expect me to answer. And I'll get sleepy listening to their voices explaining the mysteries to me. I'll fall asleep with the book still in my fingers, and it will rain. I'll wake up and hear the rain and go back to sleep. A season of rain, rain, rain . . . Then one day, when I have closed a book or come home alone from the movies at eleven o'clock at night—I will look in the mirror and see that my hair has turned white. White, absolutely white. As white as the foam on the waves. (*She gets up and moves about the room as she continues*—) I'll run my hands down my body and feel how amazingly light and thin I have grown. Oh, my, how thin I will be. Almost transparent. Not hardly real any more. Then I will realize, I will know, sort of dimly, that I have been staying on here in this little hotel, without any—social connections, responsibilities, anxieties or disturbances of any kind—for just about fifty years. Half a century. Practically a lifetime. I won't even remember the names of the people I knew before I came here nor how it feels to be someone waiting for someone that—may not come . . . Then I will know—

looking in the mirror—the first time has come for me to walk out alone once more on the esplanade with the strong wind beating on me, the white clean wind that blows from the edge of the world, from even further than that, from the cool outer edges of space, from even beyond whatever there is beyond the edges of space . . . (*She sits down again unsteadily by the window.*)—Then I'll go out and walk on the esplanade. I'll walk alone and be blown thinner and thinner.

MAN: Baby. Come back to bed.

WOMAN: And thinner and thinner and thinner and thinner and thinner! (*He crosses to her and raises her forcibly from the chair.*)—Till finally I won't have any body at all, and the wind picks me up in its cool white arms forever, and takes me away!

MAN: (*presses his mouth to her throat.*) Come on back to bed with me!

WOMAN: *I want to go away, I want to go away!* (*He releases her and she crosses to center of room sobbing uncontrollably. She sits down on the bed. He sighs and leans out the window, the light flickering beyond him, the rain coming down harder. The Woman shivers and crosses her arms against her breasts. Her sobbing dies out but she breathes with effort. Light flickers and wind whines coldly. The Man remains leaning out. At last she says to him softly—*) Come back to bed. Come on back to bed, baby . . . (*He turns his lost face to her as—*)

The Curtain Falls

SOMETHING UNSPOKEN

CHARACTERS
MISS CORNELIA SCOTT
MISS GRACE LANCASTER

SCENE: *Miss Cornelia Scott, 60, a wealthy southern spinster, is seated at a small mahogany table which is set for two. The other place, not yet occupied, has a single rose in a crystal vase before it. Miss Scott's position at the table is flanked by a cradle phone, a silver tray of mail, and an ornate silver coffee urn. An imperial touch is given by purple velvet drapes directly behind her figure at the table. A console phonograph is at the edge of lighted area.*

At rise of the curtain she is dialing a number on the phone.

CORNELIA: Is this Mrs. Horton Reid's residence? I am calling for Miss Cornelia Scott. Miss Scott is sorry that she will not be able to attend the meeting of the Confederate Daughters this afternoon as she woke up this morning with a sore throat and has to remain in bed, and will you kindly give her apologies to Mrs. Reid for not letting her know sooner. Thank you. Oh, wait a moment! I think Miss Scott has another message.

(Grace Lancaster enters the lighted area. Cornelia raises her hand in a warning gesture.)

—What is it, Miss Scott? *(There is a brief pause.)* Oh. Miss Scott would like to leave word for Miss Esmeralda Hawkins to call her as soon as she arrives. Thank you. Goodbye. *(She hangs up.)* You see I am having to impersonate my secretary this morning!

GRACE: The light was so dim it didn't wake me up.

(Grace Lancaster is 40 or 45, faded but still pretty. Her blonde hair, greying slightly, her pale eyes, her thin figure, in a pink silk dressing-gown, give her an insubstantial quality in sharp contrast to Miss Scott's Roman grandeur. There is between the

858

two women a mysterious tension, an atmosphere of something unspoken.)

CORNELIA: I've already opened the mail.

GRACE: Anything of interest?

CORNELIA: A card from Thelma Peterson at Mayo's.

GRACE: Oh, how is Thelma?

CORNELIA: She says she's "progressing nicely," whatever that indicates.

GRACE: Didn't she have something removed?

CORNELIA: Several things, I believe.

GRACE: *Oh, here's the "Fortnightly Review of Current Letters!"*

CORNELIA: Much to my astonishment. I thought I had cancelled my subscription to that publication.

GRACE: Really, Cornelia?

CORNELIA: Surely you remember. I cancelled my subscription immediately after the issue came out with that scurrilous attack on my cousin Cecil Tutwiler Bates, the only dignified novelist the South has produced since Thomas Nelson Page.

GRACE: Oh, yes, I do remember. You wrote a furious letter of protest to the editor of the magazine and you received such a conciliatory reply from an associate editor named Caroline Something or Other that you were completely mollified and cancelled the cancellation!

CORNELIA: I have never been mollified by conciliatory replies, never completely and never even partially, and if I wrote to the editor-in-chief and was answered by an associate editor, my reaction to that piece of impertinence would hardly be what you call "mollified."

GRACE: (*She changes the subject.*) Oh, here's the new catalogue from the Gramophone Shoppe in Atlanta!

CORNELIA: (*She concedes a point.*) Yes, there it is.

GRACE: I see you've checked several items.

CORNELIA: I think we ought to build up our collection of Lieder.

GRACE: You've checked a Sibelius that we already have.

CORNELIA: It's getting a little bit scratchy. (*She inhales deeply and sighs, her look fastened upon the silent phone.*) You'll also notice that I've checked a few operatic selections.

GRACE: (*excitedly*) Where, which ones, I don't see them!

CORNELIA: Why are you so excited over the catalogue, dear?

GRACE: I adore phonograph records!

CORNELIA: I wish you adored them enough to put them back in their proper places in albums.

GRACE: Oh, here's the Vivaldi we wanted!

CORNELIA: Not "we" dear. Just you.

GRACE: Not *you*, Cornelia?

CORNELIA: I think Vivaldi's a very thin shadow of Bach.

GRACE: How strange that I should have the impression you— (*The phone rings.*)—Shall I answer?

CORNELIA: If you will be so kind.

GRACE: (*lifting receiver*) *Miss Scott's* residence! (*This announcement is made in a tone of reverence, as though mentioning a seat of holiness.*) Oh, no, no, this is Grace, but Cornelia is right by my side. (*She passes the phone.*) Esmeralda Hawkins.

CORNELIA: (*grimly*) I've been expecting her call. (*into phone*) Hello, Esmeralda, my dear. I've been expecting your call. Now where are you calling me from? Of course I know that you're calling me from the meeting, ça va sans dire, ma petite! Ha ha! But from which phone in the house, there's two, you know, the one in the downstairs hall and the one in the chatelaine's boudoir where the ladies will probably be removing their wraps. Oh. You're on the downstairs', are you? Well, by this time I presume that practically all the daughters have assembled. Now go upstairs and call me back from there so we can talk with a little more privacy, dear, as I want to make my position very clear before the meeting commences. Thank you, dear. (*She hangs up and looks grimly into space.*)

GRACE: The—Confederate Daughters?

CORNELIA: Yes! They're holding the Annual Election today.

GRACE: Oh, how exciting! Why aren't you at the meeting?

CORNELIA: I preferred not to go.

GRACE: You preferred *not* to go?

CORNELIA: Yes, I preferred not to *go* . . . (*She touches her chest breathing heavily as if she had run upstairs.*)

GRACE: But it's the annual election of officers!

CORNELIA: Yes! I told you it was! (*Grace drops the spoon. Cornelia cries out and jumps a little.*)

GRACE: I'm so sorry! (*She rings the bell for a servant.*)

CORNELIA: Intrigue, intrigue and duplicity, revolt me so that I wouldn't be able to breathe in the same atmosphere! (*Grace rings the bell louder.*) Why are you ringing that bell? You know Lucinda's not here!

GRACE: I'm so sorry. Where has Lucinda gone?

CORNELIA: (*in a hoarse whisper, barely audible*) There's a big colored funeral in town. (*She clears her throat violently and repeats the statement.*)

GRACE: Oh, dear. You have that nervous laryngitis.

CORNELIA: No sleep, no sleep last night.

(*The phone screams at her elbow. She cries out and thrusts it from her as if it were on fire.*)

GRACE: (*She picks up the phone.*) Miss Scott's residence. Oh. Just a moment, please.

CORNELIA: (*snatching phone*) Esmeralda, are you upstairs now?

GRACE: (*in a loud whisper*) It isn't Esmeralda, it's Mrs. C. C. Bright!

CORNELIA: One moment, one moment, one moment! (*She thrusts phone back at Grace with a glare of fury.*) How dare you put me on the line with that woman!

GRACE: Cornelia, I didn't, I was just going to ask you if you—

CORNELIA: *Hush!* (*She springs back from the table, glaring across it.*)—Now give me that phone. (*She takes it, and says coldly:*) What can I do for you, please? No. I'm afraid that my garden will not be open to the Pilgrims this spring. I think the cultivation of gardens is an esthetic hobby and not a competitive sport. Individual visitors will be welcome if they call in advance so that I can arrange for my gardener to show them around, but no bands of Pilgrims, not after the devastation my garden suffered last spring—Pilgrims coming with dogs—picking flowers and— You're entirely welcome, yes, goodbye! (*She returns the phone to Grace.*)

GRACE: I think the election would have been less of a strain if you'd gone to it, Cornelia.

CORNELIA: I don't know what you are talking about.

GRACE: Aren't you up for office?

CORNELIA: "Up for office"? What is "up for office"?

GRACE: Why, ha ha!—*running* for—something?

CORNELIA: Have you ever known me to *"run"* for anything, Grace? Whenever I've held an office in a society or club it's been at the *insistence* of the members because I really have an *aversion* to holding office. But this is a different thing, a different thing altogether. It's a test of something. You see I have known for some time, now, that there is a little group, a *clique*, in the Daughters, which is hostile to me!

GRACE: Oh, Cornelia, I'm sure you must be mistaken.

CORNELIA: No. There is a movement against me.

GRACE: A movement? A movement against you?

CORNELIA: An organized movement to keep me out of any important office.

GRACE: But haven't you always held some important office in the Chapter?

CORNELIA: I have never been *Regent* of it!

GRACE: Oh, you want to be *Regent*?

CORNELIA: No. You misunderstand me. I don't *"want"* to be Regent.

GRACE: Oh?

CORNELIA: I don't "want" to be anything whatsoever. I simply want to break up this movement against me and for that purpose I have rallied my forces.

GRACE: Your—*forces*? (*Her lips twitch slightly as if she had an hysterical impulse to smile.*)

CORNELIA: Yes. I still have some friends in the chapter who have resisted the movement.

GRACE: Oh?

CORNELIA: I have the solid support of all the older Board members.

GRACE: Why, then, I should think you'd have nothing to worry about!

CORNELIA: The Chapter has expanded too rapidly lately. Women have been admitted that couldn't get into a front pew at the Second Baptist Church! And that's the disgraceful truth . . .

GRACE: But since it's really a patriotic society . . .

CORNELIA: My dear Grace, there are two chapters of the Confederate Daughters in the city of Meridian. There is the Forrest chapter, which is for social riff-raff, and there is *this* chapter which was *supposed* to have a *little* bit of *distinction*! I'm not a snob. I'm nothing if not democratic. You know *that*! But—(*The phone rings. Cornelia reaches for it, then pushes it to Grace.*)

GRACE: Miss Scott's residence! Oh, yes, yes, just a moment! (*She passes phone to Cornelia.*) It's Esmeralda Hawkins.

CORNELIA: (*into phone*) Are you upstairs now, dear? Well, I wondered, it took you so long to call back. Oh, but I thought you said the luncheon was over. Well, I'm glad that you fortified yourself with a bite to eat. What did the buffet consist of? Chicken à la king! Wouldn't you know it! That is so characteristic of poor Amelia! With bits of pimiento and tiny mushrooms in it? What did the ladies counting their calories do! Nibbled around the edges? Oh, poor dears!—and afterwards I suppose there was lemon sherbet with lady-fingers? What, lime sherbet! And *no* lady-fingers? *What a departure!* What a *shocking* apostasy! I'm quite stunned! Ho ho ho . . . (*She reaches shakily for her cup.*) Now what's going on? Discussing the Civil Rights Program? Then they won't take the vote for at least half an hour!—Now Esmeralda, I *do* hope that you understand my position clearly. I don't wish to hold any office in the chapter unless it's by acclamation. You know what that means, don't you? It's a parliamentary term. It means when someone is desired for an office so unanimously that no vote has to be taken. In other words, elected automatically, simply by nomination, unopposed. Yes, my dear, it's just as simple as that. I have served as Treasurer for three terms, twice as Secretary, once as Chaplain—and what a dreary office that was with those long-drawn prayers for the Confederate dead!—Altogether I've served on the Board for, let's see, fourteen years!—Well, now, my dear, the point is simply this. If Daughters feel that I have demonstrated my capabilities and loyalty strongly enough that I should simply be named as Regent without a vote being taken—by unanimous acclamation!—why, then, of course I would feel obliged to accept . . . (*Her voice trembles with emotion.*) —But if, on the other hand, the—uh—*clique!*—and you know the ones I mean!—is bold enough to propose someone else for the office—Do you understand my position? In that eventuality, hard as it is to imagine,—I prefer to bow out of the picture entirely!—The moment another nomination is made and seconded, my own must be withdrawn, at once, unconditionally! Is that quite understood, Esmeralda? Then good! Go back downstairs to the meeting. Digest your chicken à la king, my dear, and call me again on the upstairs phone as soon as there's something to tell me. (*She hangs up and stares grimly into space. Grace lifts a section of grapefruit on a tiny silver fork.*)

GRACE: They haven't had it yet?

CORNELIA: Had what, dear?

GRACE: The election!

CORNELIA: No, not yet. It seems to be—imminent, though . . .

GRACE: Cornelia, why don't you think about something else until it's over!

CORNELIA: What makes you think that I am nervous about it?

GRACE: You're—you're *breathing* so fast!

CORNELIA: I didn't sleep well last night. You were prowling about the house with that stitch in your side.

GRACE: I *am* so sorry. You know it's nothing. A muscular contraction that comes from strain.

CORNELIA: What strain does it come from, Grace?

GRACE: What strain? (*She utters a faint, perplexed laugh.*) Why!—I don't know . . .

CORNELIA: The strain of *what?* Would you like *me* to tell you?

GRACE: —Excuse me, I—(*rising*)

CORNELIA: (*sharply*) Where are you going?

GRACE: Upstairs for a moment! I just remembered I should have taken my drops of belladonna!

CORNELIA: It does no good *after* eating.

GRACE: I suppose that's right. It doesn't.

CORNELIA: But you want to escape?

GRACE: Of course not . . .

CORNELIA: Several times lately you've rushed away from me as if I'd suddenly threatened you with a knife.

GRACE: Cornelia!—I've been—jumpy!

CORNELIA: It's always when something is almost—*spoken*—between us!

GRACE: I hate to see you so agitated over the outcome of a silly club-woman's election!

CORNELIA: I'm not talking about the Daughters. I'm not even thinking about them, I'm—

GRACE: I wish you'd dismiss it completely from your mind. Now would be a good time to play some records. Let me put a symphony on the machine!

CORNELIA: No.

GRACE: How about the Bach For Piano and Strings! The one we received for Christmas from Jessie and Gay?

CORNELIA: No, I said, No, I said, No!

GRACE: Something very light and quiet, then, the old French madrigals, maybe?

CORNELIA: Anything to avoid a talk between us? Anything to evade a conversation, especially when the servant is not in the house?

GRACE: Oh, here it is! This is just the thing! (*She has started the phonograph. Landowska is playing a harpsichord selection. The phonograph is at the edge of the lighted area or just outside it.*)

(*Cornelia stares grimly as Grace resumes her seat with an affectation of enchantment, clasping her hands and closing her eyes.*)

(*in an enchanted voice:*) Oh, how it smooths things over, how sweet, and gentle, and—pure . . .

CORNELIA: Yes! And completely dishonest!

GRACE: Music? Dishonest?

CORNELIA: Completely! It "smooths things over" instead of —speaking them out . . .

GRACE: "Music hath charms to soothe the savage breast."

CORNELIA: Yes, oh, yes, if the savage breast permits it.

GRACE: Oh, sublime—sublime . . .

CORNELIA: (*grudgingly*) Landowska is an artist of rare precision.

GRACE: (*ecstatically*) And such a noble face, a profile as fine and strong as Edith Sitwell's. After this we'll play Edith Sitwell's Façade. "Jane, Jane, tall as a crane, the morning light creaks down again . . ."

CORNELIA: Dearest, isn't there something you've failed to notice?

GRACE: Where?

CORNELIA: Right under your nose.

GRACE: Oh! You mean my flower?

CORNELIA: Yes! I mean your rose!

GRACE: Of course I noticed my rose, the moment I came in the room I saw it here!

CORNELIA: You made no allusion to it.

GRACE: I would have, but you were so concerned over the meeting.

CORNELIA: I'm not concerned over the meeting.

GRACE: Whom do I have to thank for this lovely rose? My gracious employer?

CORNELIA: You will find fourteen others on your desk in the library when you go in to take care of the correspondence.

GRACE: Fourteen other roses?

CORNELIA: A total of fifteen!

GRACE: How wonderful!—Why fifteen?

CORNELIA: How long have you been here, dearest? How long have you made this house a house of roses?

GRACE: What a nice way to put it! Why, of course! I've been your secretary for fifteen years!

CORNELIA: Fifteen years my companion! A rose for every year, a year for every rose!

GRACE: What a charming sort of a way to—observe the—occasion . . .

CORNELIA: First I thought "pearls" and then I thought, No, roses, but perhaps I should have given you something golden, ha ha!—Silence is golden they say!

GRACE: Oh, dear, that stupid machine is playing the same record over!

CORNELIA: Let it, let it, I like it!

GRACE: Just let me—

CORNELIA: Sit down!!—It was fifteen years ago this very morning, on the sixth day of November, that someone very sweet and gentle and silent!—a shy, little, quiet little widow!—arrived for the first time at Seven Edgewater Drive. The season was Autumn. I had been raking dead leaves over the rose-bushes to protect them from frost when I heard footsteps on the gravel, light, quick, delicate footsteps like Spring coming in the middle of Autumn, and looked up, and sure enough, there Spring was! A little person so thin that light shone through her as if she were made of the silk of a white parasol! (*Grace utters a short, startled laugh. Wounded, Cornelia says harshly:*) Why did you laugh? Why did you laugh like that?

GRACE: It sounded—ha ha!—it sounded like the first paragraph of a woman's magazine story.

CORNELIA: What a cutting remark!

GRACE: I didn't mean it that way, I—

CORNELIA: What other way could you mean it!

GRACE: Cornelia, you know how I am! I'm always a little embarrassed by sentiment, aren't I?

CORNELIA: Yes, frightened of anything that betrays some feeling!

GRACE: People who don't know you well, nearly all people we know, would be astounded to hear you, Cornelia Scott, that grave and dignified lady, expressing herself in such a lyrical manner!

CORNELIA: People who don't know me well are everybody! Yes, I think even *you*!

GRACE: Cornelia, you must admit that sentiment isn't like you!

CORNELIA: *Is nothing like me but silence? (The clock ticks loudly.) Am I sentenced to silence for a life-time?*

GRACE: It's just not like you to—

CORNELIA: Not like me, not like me, what do you know what's like me or not like me!

GRACE: You may deny it, Cornelia, as much as you please, but it's evident to me that you are completely unstrung by your anxieties over the Confederate Daughters' election!

CORNELIA: Another thinly veiled insult?

GRACE: Oh, Cornelia, please!

CORNELIA: (*imitating her gesture*) "Oh, Cornelia, please!!"

GRACE: If I've said anything wrong, I beg your pardon, I offer my very humble apologies for it.

CORNELIA: I don't want apologies from you. (*There is a strained silence. The clock ticks. Suddenly Grace reaches across to touch the veined jewelled hand of Miss Scott. Cornelia snatches her own hand away as though the touch had burned her.*)

GRACE: Thank you for the roses.

CORNELIA: I don't want thanks from you either. All that I want is a little return of affection, not much, but sometimes a little!

GRACE: You have that always, Cornelia.

CORNELIA: And one thing more: a little outspokenness, too.

GRACE: Outspokenness?

CORNELIA: Yes, outspokenness, if that's not too much to ask from such a proud young lady!

GRACE: (*rising from table*) I am not proud and I am not young, Cornelia.

CORNELIA: Sit down. Don't leave the table.

GRACE: Is that an order?

CORNELIA: I don't give orders to you, I make requests!

GRACE: Sometimes the requests of an employer are hard to distinguish from orders. (*She sits down.*)

CORNELIA: Please turn off the victrola. (*Grace rises and stops the machine.*) Grace!—Don't you feel there's—*something unspoken* between us?

GRACE: No. No, I don't.

CORNELIA: I do. I've felt for a long time something unspoken between us.

GRACE: Don't you think there is always something unspoken between two people?

CORNELIA: I see no reason for it.

GRACE: But don't a great many things exist without reason?

CORNELIA: Let's not turn this into a metaphysical discussion.

GRACE: All right. But you mystify me.

CORNELIA: It's very simple. It's just that I feel that there's something unspoken between us that ought to be spoken. . . . Why are you looking at me like that?

GRACE: How am I looking at you?

CORNELIA: With positive terror!

GRACE: Cornelia!

CORNELIA: You are, you are, but I'm not going to be shut up!

GRACE: Go on, continue, please, do!

CORNELIA: I'm going to, I will, I will, I— (*The phone rings and Grace reaches for it.*) No, no, no, let it ring! (*It goes on ringing.*) Take it off the hook!

GRACE: Do just let me—

CORNELIA: Off the hook, I told you! (*Grace takes the phone off the hook. A voice says: "Hello? Hello? Hello? Hello?"*)

GRACE: (*Suddenly she is sobbing.*) I can't stand it!

CORNELIA: Be STILL! Someone can hear you!

VOICE: Hello? Hello? Cornelia? Cornelia Scott? (*Cornelia seizes phone and slams it back into its cradle.*)

CORNELIA: Now stop that! Stop that silly little female trick!

GRACE: You say there's something unspoken. Maybe there is. I don't know. But I do know some things are better left unspoken. Also I know that when a silence between two people has gone on for a long time it's like a wall that's impenetrable between them! Maybe between us there is such a wall. One that's impenetrable. Or maybe *you* can break it. I know I can't. I can't even attempt to. You're the strong one of us two and surely you know it.—Both of us have turned grey!—But not the same kind of grey. In that velvet dressing-gown you look like the Emperor Tiberius!—In his imperial toga!—Your hair and your eyes are both the color of iron! Iron grey. Invincible looking! People nearby are all somewhat—frightened of you. They feel your force and they admire you for it. They come to you here for opinions on this or that. What plays are good on Broadway this season, what books are worth reading and what books are trash and what—what records are valuable and—what is the proper attitude toward—bills in Congress!—Oh, you're a fountain of wisdom!—And in addition to that, you have your—*wealth!* Yes, you have your—*fortune!*—All of your real-estate holdings, your blue-chip stocks, your—bonds, your—mansion on Edgewater Drive, your—shy little—secretary, your—fabulous gardens that Pilgrims cannot go into . . .

CORNELIA: Oh, yes, now you are speaking, now you are speaking at last! Go on, please go on speaking.

GRACE: I am—very—different!—Also turning grey but my grey is different. Not iron, like yours, not imperial, Cornelia, but grey, yes, grey, the—color of a . . . *cobweb* . . . (*She starts the record again, very softly.*)—Something white getting soiled, the grey of something forgotten. (*The phone rings again. Neither of them seems to notice it.*)—And that being the case, that being the difference between our two kinds of grey, yours and mine— You mustn't expect me to give bold answers to questions that make the house shake with silence! To speak out things that are fifteen years unspoken!—That long a time can make a silence a wall that nothing less than dynamite could break through and— (*She picks up the phone.*) I'm not strong enough, bold enough, I'm not—

CORNELIA: (*fiercely*) You're speaking into the phone!

GRACE: (*into phone*) Hello? Oh, yes, she's here. It's Esmeralda Hawkins. (*Cornelia snatches the phone.*)

CORNELIA: What is it, Esmeralda? What are you saying, is the room full of women? Such a babble of voices! What are you trying to tell me? Have they held the election already? What, what, what? Oh, this is maddening! I can't hear a word that you're saying, it sounds like the Fourth of July, a great celebration! Ha, ha, now try once more with your mouth closer to the phone! What, what? Would I be willing to what? You can't be serious! Are you out of your mind? (*She speaks to Grace in a panicky voice.*) She wants to know if I would be willing to serve as *vice*-Regent! (*into phone*) Esmeralda! Will you listen to me? What's going on? Are there some fresh defections? How does it look? Why did you call me again before the vote? Louder, please speak louder, and cup your mouth to the phone in case they're eavesdropping! Who asked if I would accept the vice-regency, dear? Oh, Mrs. Colby, of course!—that treacherous witch!—*Esmeralda!!* Listen! I—WILL ACCEPT—NO OFFICE—EXCEPT—THE HIGHEST! Did you understand that? I—WILL ACCEPT NO OFFICE EXCEPT— *ESMERALDA!* (*She drops phone into its cradle.*)

GRACE: Have they held the election?

CORNELIA: (*dazed*) What?—No, there's a five-minute recess before the election begins . . .

GRACE: Things are not going well?

CORNELIA: "Would you accept the vice-Regency," she asked me, "if for some reason they don't elect you Regent?"— Then she hung up as if somebody had snatched the phone away from her, or the house had—caught fire!

GRACE: You shouted so I think she must have been frightened.

CORNELIA: Whom can you trust in this world, whom can you ever rely on?

GRACE: I think perhaps you should have gone to the meeting.

CORNELIA: I think my not being there is much more pointed.

GRACE: (*rising again*) May I be excused, now?

CORNELIA: No! Stay here!

GRACE: If that is just a request, I—

CORNELIA: That's an order! (*Grace sits down and closes her eyes.*) When you first came to this house—do you know I didn't expect you?

GRACE: Oh, but, Cornelia, you'd invited me here.

CORNELIA: We hardly knew each other.

GRACE: We'd met the summer before when Ralph was—

CORNELIA: Living! Yes, we met at Sewanee where he was a summer instructor.

GRACE: He was already ill.

CORNELIA: I thought what a pity that lovely, delicate girl hasn't found someone she could lean on, who could protect her! And two months later I heard through Clarabelle Drake that he was dead . . .

GRACE: You wrote me such a sweet letter, saying how lonely you were since the loss of your mother and urging me to rest here till the shock was over. You seemed to understand how badly I needed to withdraw for a while from—old associations. I hesitated to come. I didn't until you wrote me a second letter . . .

CORNELIA: After I received yours. You wanted urging.

GRACE: I wanted to be quite sure I was really wanted! I only came intending to stay a few weeks. I was so afraid that I would outstay my welcome!

CORNELIA: How blind of you not to see how desperately I wanted to keep you here forever!

GRACE: Oh, I did see that you— (*The phone rings.*) Miss Scott's residence!—Yes, she's here.

CORNELIA: (*She snatches it up finally.*) Cornelia Scott speaking! Oh. It's you, Esmeralda! Well, how did it come out?— *I don't believe you! I simply don't believe you . . . (Grace sits down quietly at the table.)*—MRS. HORNSBY ELECTED? Well, there's a dark horse for you! Less than a year in the chapter . . . Did you—nominate—*me?*—Oh—I see! But I told you to withdraw my name if— No, no, no, don't explain, it doesn't matter, I have too much already. You know I am going into the Daughters of the Barons of Runymede! Yes, it's been established, I have a direct line to the Earl of— No, it's been straightened out, a clear line is established, and then of course I am also eligible for the Colonial Dames and for the Huguenot Society, and what with all my other activities and so forth, why, I couldn't *possibly* have taken it on if they'd—*wanted*. . . . Of course I'm going to resign from the local chapter! Oh, yes, I am! My secretary is sitting right here by me. She has her pencil, her notebook! I'm going to dictate my letter of resignation from the local chapter the moment that I hang up on this conversation. Oh, no, no, no, I'm not mad, not outraged, at all. I'm just a little—ha ha!—a little—amused . . . *MRS. HORNSBY?* Nothing succeeds like mediocrity, does it? Thanks and goodbye, Esmeralda. (*She hangs up, stunned. Grace rises.*)

GRACE: Notebook and pencil?

CORNELIA: Yes. Notebook and pencil . . . I have to—dictate a letter . . . (*Grace leaves the table. Just at the edge of the lighted area, she turns to glance at Cornelia's rigid shoulders and a slight, equivocal smile appears momentarily on her face; not quite malicious but not really sympathetic. Then she crosses out of the light. A moment later her voice comes from the outer dark.*)

GRACE: *What lovely roses! One for every year!*

Curtain

CAT ON A HOT TIN ROOF

And you, my father, there on the sad height,
Curse, bless, me now with your fierce tears, I pray.
Do not go gentle into that good night.
Rage, rage against the dying of the light!

DYLAN THOMAS

PERSON—TO—PERSON

OF COURSE it is a pity that so much of all creative work is so closely related to the personality of the one who does it.

It is sad and embarrassing and unattractive that those emotions that stir him deeply enough to demand expression, and to charge their expression with some measure of light and power, are nearly all rooted, however changed in their surface, in the particular and sometimes peculiar concerns of the artist himself, that special world, the passions and images of it that each of us weaves about him from birth to death, a web of monstrous complexity, spun forth at a speed that is incalculable to a length beyond measure, from the spider mouth of his own singular perceptions.

It is a lonely idea, a lonely condition, so terrifying to think of that we usually don't. And so we talk to each other, write and wire each other, call each other short and long distance across land and sea, clasp hands with each other at meeting and at parting, fight each other and even destroy each other because of this always somewhat thwarted effort to break through walls to each other. As a character in a play once said, "We're all of us sentenced to solitary confinement inside our own skins."

Personal lyricism is the outcry of prisoner to prisoner from the cell in solitary where each is confined for the duration of his life.

I once saw a group of little girls on a Mississippi sidewalk, all dolled up in their mothers' and sisters' castoff finery, old raggedy ball gowns and plumed hats and high-heeled slippers, enacting a meeting of ladies in a parlor with a perfect mimicry of polite Southern gush and simper. But one child was not satisfied with the attention paid her enraptured performance by the others, they were too involved in their own performances to suit her, so she stretched out her skinny arms and threw back her skinny neck and shrieked to the deaf heavens and her equally oblivious playmates, "Look at me, look at me, look at me!"

And then her mother's high-heeled slippers threw her off balance and she fell to the sidewalk in a great howling tangle of soiled white satin and torn pink net, and still nobody looked at her.

I wonder if she is not, now, a Southern writer.

Of course it is not only Southern writers, of lyrical bent, who engage in such histrionics and shout, "Look at me!" Perhaps it is a parable of all artists. And not always do we topple over and land in a tangle of trappings that don't fit us. However, it is well to be aware of that peril, and not to content yourself with a demand for attention, to know that out of your personal lyricism, your sidewalk histrionics, something has to be created that will not only attract observers but participants in the performance.

I try very hard to do that.

The fact that I want you to observe what I do for your possible pleasure and to give you knowledge of things that I feel I may know better than you, because my world is different from yours, as different as every man's world is from the world of others, is not enough excuse for a personal lyricism that has not yet mastered its necessary trick of rising above the singular to the plural concern, from personal to general import. But for years and years now, which may have passed like a dream because of this obsession, I have been trying to learn how to perform this trick and make it truthful, and sometimes I feel that I am able to do it. Sometimes, when the enraptured streetcorner performer in me cries out "Look at me!," I feel that my hazardous footwear and fantastic regalia may not quite throw me off balance. Then, suddenly, you fellow-performers in the sidewalk show may turn to give me your attention and allow me to hold it, at least for the interval between 8:40 and 11 something P.M.

Eleven years ago this month of March, when I was far closer than I knew, only nine months away from that long-delayed, but always expected, something that I lived for, the time when I would first catch and hold an audience's attention, I wrote my first preface to a long play. The final paragraph went like this:

"There is too much to say and not enough time to say it. Nor is there power enough. I am not a good writer. Sometimes I am a very bad writer indeed. There is hardly a successful writer in the field who cannot write circles around me . . . but I think of writing as something more organic than words, something closer to being and action. I want to work more and more with a more plastic theatre than the one I have (worked with) before. I have never for one moment doubted that there are people—millions!—to say things to. We come to each other, gradually, but with love. It is the short reach of my arms that hinders, not the length and multiplicity of theirs. With love and with honesty, the embrace is inevitable."

This characteristically emotional, if not rhetorical, statement of mine at that time seems to suggest that I thought of myself as having a highly personal, even intimate relationship with people who go to see plays. I did and I still do. A morbid shyness once prevented me from having much direct communication with people, and possibly that is why I began to write to them plays and stories. But even now when that tongue-locking, face-flushing, silent and crouching timidity has worn off with the passage of the troublesome youth that it sprang from, I still find it somehow easier to "level with" crowds of strangers in the hushed twilight of orchestra and balcony sections of theatres than with individuals across a table from me. Their being strangers somehow makes them more familiar and more approachable, easier to talk to.

Of course I know that I have sometimes presumed too much upon corresponding sympathies and interest in those to whom I talk boldly, and this has led to rejections that were painful and costly enough to inspire more prudence. But when I weigh one thing against another, an easy liking against a hard respect, the balance always tips the same way, and whatever the risk of being turned a cold shoulder, I still don't want to talk to people only about the surface aspects of their lives, the sort of things that acquaintances laugh and chatter about on ordinary social occasions.

I feel that they get plenty of that, and heaven knows so do I, before and after the little interval of time in which I have their attention and say what I have to say to them. The discretion of social conversation, even among friends, is exceeded only by the discretion of "the deep six," that grave wherein nothing is mentioned at all. Emily Dickinson, that lyrical spinster of Amherst, Massachusetts, who wore a strict and savage heart on a taffeta sleeve, commented wryly on that kind of posthumous discourse among friends in these lines:

> *I died for beauty, but was scarce*
> *Adjusted in the tomb,*
> *When one who died for truth was lain*
> *In an adjoining room.*
>
> *He questioned softly why I failed?*
> *"For beauty," I replied.*
> *"And I for truth,—the two are one;*
> *We brethren are," he said.*
>
> *And so, as kinsmen met a night,*
> *We talked between the rooms,*
> *Until the moss had reached our lips,*
> *And covered up our names.*

Meanwhile!—I want to go on talking to you as freely and intimately about what we live and die for as if I knew you better than anyone else whom you know.

Tennessee Williams

CHARACTERS OF THE PLAY

MARGARET

BRICK

MAE, sometimes called Sister Woman

BIG MAMA

DIXIE, a little girl

BIG DADDY

REVEREND TOOKER

GOOPER, sometimes called Brother Man

DOCTOR BAUGH, pronounced "Baw"

LACEY, a Negro servant

SOOKEY, another

Another little girl and two small boys

(The playing script of Act III also includes TRIXIE, another
little girl, also DAISY, BRIGHTIE and SMALL, servants.)

NOTES FOR THE DESIGNER

The set is the bed-sitting-room of a plantation home in the Mississippi Delta. It is along an upstairs gallery which probably runs around the entire house; it has two pairs of very wide doors opening onto the gallery, showing white balustrades against a fair summer sky that fades into dusk and night during the course of the play, which occupies precisely the time of its performance, excepting, of course, the fifteen minutes of intermission.

Perhaps the style of the room is not what you would expect in the home of the Delta's biggest cotton-planter. It is Victorian with a touch of the Far East. It hasn't changed much since it was occupied by the original owners of the place, Jack Straw and Peter Ochello, a pair of old bachelors who shared this room all their lives together. In other words, the room must evoke some ghosts; it is gently and poetically haunted by a relationship that must have involved a tenderness which was uncommon. This may be irrelevant or unnecessary, but I once saw a reproduction of a faded photograph of the verandah of Robert Louis Stevenson's home on that Samoan Island where he spent his last years, and there was a quality of tender light on weathered wood, such as porch furniture made of bamboo and wicker, exposed to tropical suns and tropical rains, which came to mind when I thought about the set for this play, bringing also to mind the grace and comfort of light, the reassurance it gives, on a late and fair afternoon in summer, the way that no matter what, even dread of death, is gently touched and soothed by it. For the set is the background for a play that deals with human extremities of emotion, and it needs that softness behind it.

The bathroom door, showing only pale-blue tile and silver towel racks, is in one side wall; the hall door in the opposite wall. Two articles of furniture need mention: a big double bed which staging should make a functional part of the set as often as suitable, the surface of which should be slightly raked to make figures on it seen more easily; and against the wall space between the two huge double doors upstage: a monumental monstrosity peculiar to our times, a *huge* console combination of radio-phonograph (Hi-Fi with three speakers) TV set *and* liquor cabinet, bearing and containing many glasses and bottles, all in one piece, which is a composition of muted silver tones, and the opalescent tones of reflecting glass, a chromatic link, this thing, between the sepia (tawny gold) tones of the interior and the cool (white and blue) tones of the gallery and sky. This piece of furniture (?!), this monument, is a very complete and compact little shrine to virtually all the comforts and illusions behind which we hide from such things as the characters in the play are faced with. . . .

The set should be far less realistic than I have so far implied in this description of it. I think the walls below the ceiling should dissolve mysteriously into air; the set should be roofed by the sky; stars and moon suggested by traces of milky pallor, as if they were observed through a telescope lens out of focus.

Anything else I can think of? Oh, yes, fanlights (transoms shaped like an open glass fan) above all the doors in the set, with panes of blue and amber, and above all, the designer should take as many pains to give the actors room to move about freely (to show their restlessness, their passion for breaking out) as if it were a set for a ballet.

An evening in summer. The action is continuous, with two intermissions.

ACT ONE

At the rise of the curtain someone is taking a shower in the bath-room, the door of which is half open. A pretty young woman, with anxious lines in her face, enters the bedroom and crosses to the bathroom door.

MARGARET (*shouting above roar of water*): One of those no-neck monsters hit me with a hot buttered biscuit so I have t' change!

(*Margaret's voice is both rapid and drawling. In her long speeches she has the vocal tricks of a priest delivering a litur-gical chant, the lines are almost sung, always continuing a little beyond her breath so she has to gasp for another. Sometimes she intersperses the lines with a little wordless singing, such as "Da-da-daaaa!"*)

(*Water turns off and Brick calls out to her, but is still un-seen. A tone of politely feigned interest, masking indifference, or worse, is characteristic of his speech with Margaret.*)

BRICK: Wha'd you say, Maggie? Water was on s' loud I couldn't hearya. . . .

MARGARET: Well, I!—just remarked that!—one of th' no-neck monsters messed up m' lovely lace dress so I got t'—cha-a-ange. . . .

(*She opens and kicks shut drawers of the dresser.*)

BRICK: Why d'ya call Gooper's kiddies no-neck monsters?

MARGARET: Because they've got no necks! Isn't that a good enough reason?

BRICK: Don't they have any necks?

MARGARET: None visible. Their fat little heads are set on their fat little bodies without a bit of connection.

BRICK: That's too bad.

MARGARET: Yes, it's too bad because you can't wring their necks if they've got no necks to wring! Isn't that right, honey?

(*She steps out of her dress, stands in a slip of ivory satin and lace.*)

Yep, they're no-neck monsters, all no-neck people are monsters . . .

(*Children shriek downstairs.*)

Hear them? Hear them screaming? I don't know where their voice-boxes are located since they don't have necks. I tell you I got so nervous at that table tonight I thought I would throw back my head and utter a scream you could hear across the Arkansas border an' parts of Louisiana an' Tennessee. I said to your charming sister-in-law, Mae, honey, couldn't you feed those precious little things at a separate table with an oilcloth cover? They make such a mess an' the lace cloth looks *so* pretty! She made enormous eyes at me and said, "Ohhh, noooooo! On Big Daddy's birthday? Why, he would never forgive me!" Well, I want you to know, Big Daddy hadn't been at the table two minutes with those five no-neck monsters slobbering and drooling over their food before he threw down his fork an' shouted, "Fo' God's sake, Gooper, why don't you put them pigs at a trough in th' kitchen?"—Well, I swear, I simply could have di-ieed!

Think of it, Brick, they've got five of them and number six is coming. They've brought the whole bunch down here like animals to display at a county fair. Why, they have those children doin' tricks all the time! "Junior, show Big Daddy how you do this, show Big Daddy how you do that, say your little piece fo' Big Daddy, Sister. Show your dimples, Sugar. Brother, show Big Daddy how you stand on your head!"—It goes on all the time, along with constant little remarks and innuendos about the fact that you and I have not produced any children, are totally childless and therefore totally useless!—Of course it's comical but it's also disgusting since it's so obvious what they're up to!

BRICK (*without interest*): What are they up to, Maggie?

MARGARET: Why, you know what they're up to!

BRICK (*appearing*): No, I don't know what they're up to.

(*He stands there in the bathroom doorway drying his hair with a towel and hanging onto the towel rack because one ankle is broken, plastered and bound. He is still slim and firm as a boy. His liquor hasn't started tearing him down outside.*

He has the additional charm of that cool air of detachment that people have who have given up the struggle. But now and then, when disturbed, something flashes behind it, like lightning in a fair sky, which shows that at some deeper level he is far from peaceful. Perhaps in a stronger light he would show some signs of deliquescence, but the fading, still warm, light from the gallery treats him gently.)

MARGARET: I'll tell you what they're up to, boy of mine!— They're up to cutting you out of your father's estate, and—

(*She freezes momentarily before her next remark. Her voice drops as if it were somehow a personally embarrassing admission.*)

—Now we know that Big Daddy's dyin' of—*cancer. . . .*

(*There are voices on the lawn below: long-drawn calls across distance. Margaret raises her lovely bare arms and powders her armpits with a light sigh.*

(*She adjusts the angle of a magnifying mirror to straighten an eyelash, then rises fretfully saying:*)

There's so much light in the room it—
BRICK (*softly but sharply*): Do we?
MARGARET: Do we what?
BRICK: Know Big Daddy's dyin' of cancer?
MARGARET: Got the report today.
BRICK: Oh . . .
MARGARET (*letting down bamboo blinds which cast long, gold-fretted shadows over the room*): Yep, got th' report just now . . . it didn't surprise me, Baby. . . .

(*Her voice has range, and music; sometimes it drops low as a boy's and you have a sudden image of her playing boy's games as a child.*)

I recognized the symptoms soon's we got here last spring and I'm willin' to bet you that Brother Man and his wife were pretty sure of it, too. That more than likely explains why their usual summer migration to the coolness of the Great Smokies was passed up this summer in favor of— hustlin' down here ev'ry whipstitch with their whole screamin' tribe! And why so many allusions have been made to Rainbow Hill lately. You know what Rainbow Hill is? Place that's famous for treatin' alcoholics an' dope fiends in the movies!

BRICK: I'm not in the movies.

MARGARET: No, and you don't take dope. Otherwise you're a perfect candidate for Rainbow Hill, Baby, and that's where they aim to ship you—over my dead body! Yep, over my dead body they'll ship you there, but nothing would please them better. Then Brother Man could get a-hold of the purse strings and dole out remittances to us, maybe get power-of-attorney and sign checks for us and cut off our credit wherever, whenever he wanted! Son-of-a-bitch!— How'd you like that, Baby?—Well, you've been doin' just about ev'rything in your power to bring it about, you've just been doin' ev'rything you can think of to aid and abet them in this scheme of theirs!—Quittin' work, devoting yourself to the occupation of drinkin'!—Breakin' your ankle last night on the high school athletic field: doin' what? Jumpin' hurdles? At two or three in the morning? Just fantastic! Got in the paper. *Clarksdale Register* carried a nice little item about it, human interest story about a well-known former athlete stagin' a one-man track meet on the Glorious Hill High School athletic field last night, but was slightly out of condition and didn't clear the first hurdle! Brother Man Gooper claims he exercised his influence t' keep it from goin' out over AP or UP or every goddam "P."

But, Brick? You still have one big advantage!

(*During the above swift flood of words, Brick has reclined with contrapuntal leisure on the snowy surface of the bed and has rolled over carefully on his side or belly.*)

BRICK (*wryly*): Did you *say* something, Maggie?

MARGARET: Big Daddy dotes on you, honey. And he can't stand Brother Man and Brother Man's wife, that monster of fertility, Mae; she's downright odious to him! Know how I know? By little expressions that flicker over his face when that woman is holding fo'th on one of her choice topics such as—how she refused twilight sleep!—when the twins were delivered! Because she feels motherhood's an experi-

ence that a woman ought to experience fully!—in order to
fully appreciate the wonder and beauty of it! HAH!

(*This loud "HAH!" is accompanied by a violent action such
as slamming a drawer shut.*)

—and how she made Brother Man come in an' stand beside her in the delivery room so he would not miss out on
the "wonder and beauty" of it either!—producin' those no-
neck monsters. . . .

(*A speech of this kind would be antipathetic from almost anybody but Margaret; she makes it oddly funny, because her eyes
constantly twinkle and her voice shakes with laughter which is
basically indulgent.*)

—Big Daddy shares my attitude toward those two! As for
me, well—I give him a laugh now and then and he toler-
ates me. In fact!—I sometimes suspect that Big Daddy har-
bors a little unconscious "lech" fo' me. . . .

BRICK: What makes you think that Big Daddy has a lech for
you, Maggie?

MARGARET: Way he always drops his eyes down my body
when I'm talkin' to him, drops his eyes to my boobs an'
licks his old chops! Ha ha!

BRICK: That kind of talk is disgusting.

MARGARET: Did anyone ever tell you that you're an ass-
aching Puritan, Brick?

I think it's mighty fine that that ole fellow, on the
doorstep of death, still takes in my shape with what I think
is deserved appreciation!

And you wanta know something else? Big Daddy didn't
know how many little Maes and Goopers had been produced! "How many kids have you got?" he asked at the
table, just like Brother Man and his wife were new acquaintances to him! Big Mama said he was jokin', but that
ole boy wasn't jokin', Lord, no!

And when they infawmed him that they had five already
and were turning out number six!—the news seemed to
come as a sort of unpleasant surprise . . .

(*Children yell below.*)

Scream, monsters!

(*Turns to Brick with a sudden, gay, charming smile which fades as she notices that he is not looking at her but into fading gold space with a troubled expression.*
(*It is constant rejection that makes her humor "bitchy."*)

Yes, you should of been at that supper-table, Baby.

(*Whenever she calls him "baby" the word is a soft caress.*)

Y'know, Big Daddy, bless his ole sweet soul, he's the dearest ole thing in the world, but he does hunch over his food as if he preferred not to notice anything else. Well, Mae an' Gooper were side by side at the table, direckly across from Big Daddy, watchin' his face like hawks while they jawed an' jabbered about the cuteness an' brillance of th' no-neck monsters!

(*She giggles with a hand fluttering at her throat and her breast and her long throat arched.*
(*She comes downstage and recreates the scene with voice and gesture.*)

And the no-neck monsters were ranged around the table, some in high chairs and some on th' *Books of Knowledge*, all in fancy little paper caps in honor of Big Daddy's birthday, and all through dinner, well, I want you to know that Brother Man an' his partner never once, for one moment, stopped exchanging pokes an' pinches an' kicks an' signs an' signals!—Why, they were like a couple of cardsharps fleecing a sucker.—Even Big Mama, bless her ole sweet soul, she isn't th' quickest an' brightest thing in the world, she finally noticed, at last, an' said to Gooper, "Gooper, what are you an' Mae makin' all these signs at each other about?"—I swear t' goodness, I nearly choked on my chicken!

(*Margaret, back at the dressing-table, still doesn't see Brick. He is watching her with a look that is not quite definable.— Amused? shocked? contemptuous?—part of those and part of something else.*)

Y'know—your brother Gooper still cherishes the illusion he took a giant step up on the social ladder when he married Miss Mae Flynn of the Memphis Flynns.

(*Margaret moves about the room as she talks, stops before the mirror, moves on.*)

But I have a piece of Spanish news for Gooper. The Flynns never had a thing in this world but money and they lost that, they were nothing at all but fairly successful climbers. Of course, Mae Flynn came out in Memphis eight years before I made my debut in Nashville, but I had friends at Ward-Belmont who came from Memphis and they used to come to see me and I used to go to see them for Christmas and spring vacations, and so I know who rates an' who doesn't rate in Memphis society. Why, y'know ole Papa Flynn, he barely escaped doing time in the Federal pen for shady manipulations on th' stock market when his chain stores crashed, and as for Mae having been a cotton carnival queen, as they remind us so often, lest we forget, well, that's one honor that I don't envy her for!—Sit on a brass throne on a tacky float an' ride down Main Street, smilin', bowin', and blowin' kisses to all the trash on the street—

(*She picks out a pair of jeweled sandals and rushes to the dressing-table.*)

Why, year before last, when Susan McPheeters was singled out fo' that honor, y'know what happened to her? Y'know what happened to poor little Susie McPheeters?

BRICK (*absently*): No. What happened to little Susie McPheeters?

MARGARET: Somebody spit tobacco juice in her face.

BRICK (*dreamily*): Somebody spit tobacco juice in her face?

MARGARET: That's right, some old drunk leaned out of a window in the Hotel Gayoso and yelled, "Hey, Queen, hey, hey, there, Queenie!" Poor Susie looked up and flashed him a radiant smile and he shot out a squirt of tobacco juice right in poor Susie's face.

BRICK: Well, what d'you know about that.

MARGARET (*gaily*): What do I know about it? I was there, I saw it!

BRICK (*absently*): Must have been kind of funny.

MARGARET: Susie didn't think so. Had hysterics. Screamed like a banshee. They had to stop th' parade an' remove her from her throne an' go on with—

(*She catches sight of him in the mirror, gasps slightly, wheels about to face him. Count ten.*)

—Why are you looking at me like that?

BRICK (*whistling softly, now*): Like what, Maggie?

MARGARET (*intensely, fearfully*): The way y' were lookin' at me just now, befo' I caught your eye in the mirror and you started t' whistle! I don't know how t' describe it but it froze my blood!—I've caught you lookin' at me like that so often lately. What are you thinkin' of when you look at me like that?

BRICK: I wasn't conscious of lookin' at you, Maggie.

MARGARET: Well, I was conscious of it! What were you thinkin'?

BRICK: I don't remember thinking of anything, Maggie.

MARGARET: Don't you think I know that—? Don't you—? —Think I know that—?

BRICK (*coolly*): Know *what*, Maggie?

MARGARET (*struggling for expression*): That I've gone through this—*hideous!*—*transformation,* become—*hard! Frantic!*

(*Then she adds, almost tenderly:*)

—*cruel!!*

That's what you've been observing in me lately. How could y' help but observe it? That's all right. I'm not— thin-skinned any more, can't afford t' be thin-skinned any more.

(*She is now recovering her power.*)

—But Brick? Brick?

BRICK: Did you say something?

MARGARET: I was *goin'* t' say something: that I get—lonely. Very!

BRICK: Ev'rybody gets that . . .

MARGARET: Living with someone you love can be lonelier—than living entirely *alone!*—if the one that y' love doesn't love you. . . .

(*There is a pause. Brick hobbles downstage and asks, without looking at her:*)

BRICK: Would you like to live alone, Maggie?

(*Another pause: then—after she has caught a quick, hurt breath:*)

MARGARET: *No!—God!—I wouldn't!*

(*Another gasping breath. She forcibly controls what must have been an impulse to cry out. We see her deliberately, very forcibly, going all the way back to the world in which you can talk about ordinary matters.*)

Did you have a nice shower?

BRICK: Uh-huh.

MARGARET: Was the water cool?

BRICK: No.

MARGARET: But it made y' feel fresh, huh?

BRICK: Fresher. . . .

MARGARET: I know something would make y' feel *much* fresher!

BRICK: What?

MARGARET: An alcohol rub. Or cologne, a rub with cologne!

BRICK: That's good after a workout but I haven't been workin' out, Maggie.

MARGARET: You've kept in good shape, though.

BRICK (*indifferently*): You think so, Maggie?

MARGARET: I always thought drinkin' men lost their looks, but I was plainly mistaken.

BRICK (*wryly*): Why, thanks, Maggie.

MARGARET: You're the only drinkin' man I know that it never seems t' put fat on.

BRICK: I'm gettin' softer, Maggie.

MARGARET: Well, sooner or later it's bound to soften you up. It was just beginning to soften up Skipper when—

(*She stops short.*)

I'm sorry. I never could keep my fingers off a sore—I wish you *would* lose your looks. If you did it would make the martyrdom of Saint Maggie a little more bearable. But no such goddam luck. I actually believe you've gotten better looking since you've gone on the bottle. Yeah, a person who didn't know you would think you'd never had a tense nerve in your body or a strained muscle.

(*There are sounds of croquet on the lawn below: the click of mallets, light voices, near and distant.*)

Of course, you always had that detached quality as if you were playing a game without much concern over whether you won or lost, and now that you've lost the game, not lost but just quit playing, you have that rare sort of charm that usually only happens in very old or hopelessly sick people, the charm of the defeated.—You look so cool, so cool, so enviably cool.

(*Music is heard.*)

They're playing croquet. The moon has appeared and it's white, just beginning to turn a little bit yellow. . . .

You were a wonderful lover. . . .

Such a wonderful person to go to bed with, and I think mostly because you were really indifferent to it. Isn't that right? Never had any anxiety about it, did it naturally, easily, slowly, with absolute confidence and perfect calm, more like opening a door for a lady or seating her at a table than giving expression to any longing for her. Your indifference made you wonderful at lovemaking—*strange?*—but true. . . .

You know, if I thought you would never, never, *never* make love to me again—I would go downstairs to the kitchen and pick out the longest and sharpest knife I could find and stick it straight into my heart, I swear that I would!

But one thing I don't have is the charm of the defeated, my hat is still in the ring, and I am determined to win!

(*There is the sound of croquet mallets hitting croquet balls.*)

—What is the victory of a cat on a hot tin roof?—I wish I knew. . . .

Just staying on it, I guess, as long as she can. . . .

(*More croquet sounds.*)

Later tonight I'm going to tell you I love you an' maybe by that time you'll be drunk enough to believe me. Yes, they're playing croquet. . . .

Big Daddy is dying of cancer. . . .

What were you thinking of when I caught you looking at me like that? Were you thinking of Skipper?

(*Brick takes up his crutch, rises.*)

Oh, excuse me, forgive me, but laws of silence don't work! No, laws of silence don't work. . . .

(*Brick crosses to the bar, takes a quick drink, and rubs his head with a towel.*)

Laws of silence don't work. . . .

When something is festering in your memory or your imagination, laws of silence don't work, it's just like shutting a door and locking it on a house on fire in hope of forgetting that the house is burning. But not facing a fire doesn't put it out. Silence about a thing just magnifies it. It grows and festers in silence, becomes malignant. . . .

Get dressed, Brick.

(*He drops his crutch.*)

BRICK: I've dropped my crutch.

(*He has stopped rubbing his hair dry but still stands hanging onto the towel rack in a white towel-cloth robe.*)

MARGARET: Lean on me.

BRICK: No, just give me my crutch.

MARGARET: Lean on my shoulder.

BRICK: *I don't want to lean on your shoulder, I want my crutch!*

(*This is spoken like sudden lightning.*)

Are you going to give me my crutch or do I have to get down on my knees on the floor and—

MARGARET: *Here, here, take it, take it!*

(*She has thrust the crutch at him.*)

BRICK (*hobbling out*): Thanks . . .

MARGARET: We mustn't scream at each other, the walls in this house have ears. . . .

(*He hobbles directly to liquor cabinet to get a new drink.*)

—but that's the first time I've heard you raise your voice in a long time, Brick. A crack in the wall?—Of composure?
—I think that's a good sign. . . .
A sign of nerves in a player on the defensive!

(*Brick turns and smiles at her coolly over his fresh drink.*)

BRICK: It just hasn't happened yet, Maggie.

MARGARET: What?

BRICK: The click I get in my head when I've had enough of this stuff to make me peaceful. . . .
Will you do me a favor?

MARGARET: Maybe I will. What favor?

BRICK: Just, just keep your voice down!

MARGARET (*in a hoarse whisper*): I'll do you that favor, I'll speak in a whisper, if not shut up completely, if *you* will do *me* a favor and make that drink your last one till after the party.

BRICK: What party?

MARGARET: Big Daddy's birthday party.

BRICK: Is this Big Daddy's birthday?

MARGARET: You know this is Big Daddy's birthday!

BRICK: No, I don't, I forgot it.

MARGARET: Well, I remembered it for you. . . .

(*They are both speaking as breathlessly as a pair of kids after a fight, drawing deep exhausted breaths and looking at each other with faraway eyes, shaking and panting together as if they had broken apart from a violent struggle.*)

BRICK: Good for you, Maggie.

MARGARET: You just have to scribble a few lines on this card.

BRICK: You scribble something, Maggie.

MARGARET: It's got to be your handwriting; it's your present, I've given him my present; it's got to be your handwriting!

(*The tension between them is building again, the voices becoming shrill once more.*)

BRICK: I didn't get him a present.

MARGARET: I got one for you.

BRICK: All right. You write the card, then.

MARGARET: And have him know you didn't remember his birthday?

BRICK: I didn't remember his birthday.

MARGARET: You don't have to prove you didn't!

BRICK: I don't want to fool him about it.

MARGARET: Just write "Love, Brick!" for God's—

BRICK: No.

MARGARET: You've *got* to!

BRICK: I don't have to do anything I don't want to do. You keep forgetting the conditions on which I agreed to stay on living with you.

MARGARET (*out before she knows it*): I'm not living with you. We occupy the same cage.

BRICK: You've got to remember the conditions agreed on.

MARGARET: They're impossible conditions!

BRICK: Then why don't you—?

MARGARET: HUSH! Who is out there? Is somebody at the door?

(*There are footsteps in hall.*)

MAE (*outside*): May I enter a moment?

MARGARET: Oh, *you!* Sure. Come in, Mae.

(*Mae enters bearing aloft the bow of a young lady's archery set.*)

MAE: Brick, is this thing yours?

MARGARET: Why, Sister Woman—that's my Diana Trophy. Won it at the intercollegiate archery contest on the Ole Miss campus.

MAE: It's a mighty dangerous thing to leave exposed round a house full of nawmal rid-blooded children attracted t' weapons.

MARGARET: "Nawmal rid-blooded children attracted t' weapons" ought t' be taught to keep their hands off things that don't belong to them.

MAE: Maggie, honey, if you had children of your own you'd know how funny that is. Will you please lock this up and put the key out of reach?

MARGARET: Sister Woman, nobody is plotting the destruction of your kiddies.—Brick and I still have our special archers' license. We're goin' deer-huntin' on Moon Lake as soon as the season starts. I love to run with dogs through chilly woods, run, run leap over obstructions—

(*She goes into the closet carrying the bow.*)

MAE: How's the injured ankle, Brick?

BRICK: Doesn't hurt. Just itches.

MAE: Oh, my! Brick—Brick, you should've been downstairs after supper! Kiddies put on a show. Polly played the piano, Buster an' Sonny drums, an' then they turned out the lights an' Dixie an' Trixie puhfawmed a toe dance in fairy costume with *spahkluhs!* Big Daddy just beamed! He just beamed!

MARGARET (*from the closet with a sharp laugh*): Oh, I bet. It breaks my heart that we missed it!

(*She reenters.*)

But Mae? Why did y'give dawgs' names to all your kiddies?

MAE: *Dogs'* names?

(*Margaret has made this observation as she goes to raise the bamboo blinds, since the sunset glare has diminished. In crossing she winks at Brick.*)

MARGARET (*sweetly*): Dixie, Trixie, Buster, Sonny, Polly!— Sounds like four dogs and a parrot . . . animal act in a circus!

MAE: Maggie?

(*Margaret turns with a smile.*)

Why are you so catty?

MARGARET: Cause I'm a cat! But why can't *you* take a joke, Sister Woman?

MAE: Nothin' pleases me more than a joke that's funny. You know the real names of our kiddies. Buster's real name is Robert. Sonny's real name is Saunders. Trixie's real name is Marlene and Dixie's—

(*Someone downstairs calls for her. "Hey, Mae!"—She rushes to door, saying:*)

Intermission is over!

MARGARET (*as Mae closes door*): I wonder what Dixie's real name is?

BRICK: Maggie, being catty doesn't help things any . . .

MARGARET: I know! *WHY!*—Am I so catty?—Cause I'm consumed with envy an' eaten up with longing?—Brick, I've laid out your beautiful Shantung silk suit from Rome and one of your monogrammed silk shirts. I'll put your cufflinks in it, those lovely star sapphires I get you to wear so rarely. . . .

BRICK: I can't get trousers on over this plaster cast.

MARGARET: Yes, you can, I'll help you.

BRICK: I'm not going to get dressed, Maggie.

MARGARET: Will you just put on a pair of white silk pajamas?

BRICK: Yes, I'll do that, Maggie.

MARGARET: *Thank* you, thank you so *much!*

BRICK: Don't mention it.

MARGARET: *Oh, Brick!* How long does it have t' go on? This punishment? Haven't I done time enough, haven't I served my term, can't I apply for a—pardon?

BRICK: Maggie, you're spoiling my liquor. Lately your voice always sounds like you'd been running upstairs to warn somebody that the house was on fire!

MARGARET: Well, no wonder, no wonder. Y'know what I feel like, Brick?

(*Children's and grownups' voices are blended, below, in a loud but uncertain rendition of "My Wild Irish Rose."*)

I feel all the time like a cat on a hot tin roof!

BRICK: Then jump off the roof, jump off it, cats can jump off roofs and land on their four feet uninjured!

MARGARET: Oh, yes!

BRICK: Do it!—fo' God's sake, do it . . .

MARGARET: Do what?

BRICK: Take a lover!

MARGARET: I can't see a man but you! Even with my eyes closed, I just see you! Why don't you get ugly, Brick, why don't you please get fat or ugly or something so I could stand it?

(*She rushes to hall door, opens it, listens.*)

The concert is still going on! Bravo, no-necks, bravo!

(*She slams and locks door fiercely.*)

BRICK: What did you lock the door for?
MARGARET: To give us a little privacy for a while.
BRICK: You know better, Maggie.
MARGARET: No, I don't know better. . . .

(*She rushes to gallery doors, draws the rose-silk drapes across them.*)

BRICK: Don't make a fool of yourself.
MARGARET: I don't mind makin' a fool of myself over you!
BRICK: I mind, Maggie. I feel embarrassed for you.
MARGARET: Feel embarrassed! But don't continue my torture. I can't live on and on under these circumstances.
BRICK: You agreed to—
MARGARET: I know but—
BRICK: —Accept that condition!
MARGARET: *I CAN'T! CAN'T! CAN'T!*

(*She seizes his shoulder.*)

BRICK: Let go!

(*He breaks away from her and seizes the small boudoir chair and raises it like a lion-tamer facing a big circus cat.*
(*Count five. She stares at him with her fist pressed to her mouth, then bursts into shrill, almost hysterical laughter. He remains grave for a moment, then grins and puts the chair down.*
(*Big Mama calls through closed door.*)

BIG MAMA: Son? Son? Son?
BRICK: What is it, Big Mama?
BIG MAMA (*outside*): Oh, son! We got the most wonderful news about Big Daddy. I just had t' run up an' tell you right this—

(*She rattles the knob.*)

—What's this door doin', locked, faw? You all think there's robbers in the house?

MARGARET: Big Mama, Brick is dressin', he's not dressed yet.

BIG MAMA: That's all right, it won't be the first time I've seen Brick not dressed. Come on, open this door!

(*Margaret, with a grimace, goes to unlock and open the hall door, as Brick hobbles rapidly to the bathroom and kicks the door shut. Big Mama has disappeared from the hall.*)

MARGARET: Big Mama?

(*Big Mama appears through the opposite gallery doors behind Margaret, huffing and puffing like an old bulldog. She is a short, stout woman; her sixty years and 170 pounds have left her somewhat breathless most of the time; she's always tensed like a boxer, or rather, a Japanese wrestler. Her "family" was maybe a little superior to Big Daddy's, but not much. She wears a black or silver lace dress and at least half a million in flashy gems. She is very sincere.*)

BIG MAMA (*loudly, startling Margaret*): Here—I come through Gooper's and Mae's gall'ry door. Where's Brick? *Brick*— Hurry on out of there, son, I just have a second and want to give you the news about Big Daddy.—I hate locked doors in a house. . . .

MARGARET (*with affected lightness*): I've noticed you do, Big Mama, but people have got to have *some* moments of privacy, don't they?

BIG MAMA: No, ma'am, not in *my* house. (*Without pause*) Whacha took off you' dress faw? I thought that little lace dress was so sweet on yuh, honey.

MARGARET: I thought it looked sweet on me, too, but one of m' cute little table-partners used it for a napkin so—!

BIG MAMA (*picking up stockings on floor*): What?

MARGARET: You know, Big Mama, Mae and Gooper's so touchy about those children—thanks, Big Mama . . .

(*Big Mama has thrust the picked-up stockings in Margaret's hand with a grunt.*)

—that you just don't dare to suggest there's any room for improvement in their—

BIG MAMA: Brick, hurry out!—Shoot, Maggie, you just don't like children.

MARGARET: I do SO like children! Adore them!—well brought up!

BIG MAMA (*gentle—loving*): Well, why don't you have some and bring them up well, then, instead of all the time pickin' on Gooper's an' Mae's?

GOOPER (*shouting up the stairs*): Hey, hey, Big Mama, Betsy an' Hugh got to go, waitin' t' tell yuh g'by!

BIG MAMA: Tell 'em to hold their hawses, I'll be right down in a jiffy!

(*She turns to the bathroom door and calls out.*)

Son? Can you hear me in there?

(*There is a muffled answer.*)

We just got the full report from the laboratory at the Ochsner Clinic, completely negative, son, ev'rything negative, right on down the line! Nothin' a-tall's wrong with him but some little functional thing called a spastic colon. Can you hear me, son?

MARGARET: He can hear you, Big Mama.

BIG MAMA: Then why don't he say something? God Almighty, a piece of news like that should make him shout. It made *me* shout, I can tell you. I shouted and sobbed and fell right down on my knees!—Look!

(*She pulls up her skirt.*)

See the bruises where I hit my kneecaps? Took both doctors to haul me back on my feet!

(*She laughs—she always laughs like hell at herself.*)

Big Daddy was furious with me! But ain't that wonderful news?

(*Facing bathroom again, she continues:*)

After all the anxiety we been through to git a report like that on Big Daddy's birthday? Big Daddy tried to hide how

much of a load that news took off his mind, but didn't fool
me. He was mighty close to crying about it *himself*!

(*Goodbyes are shouted downstairs, and she rushes to door.*)

Hold those people down there, don't let them go!—Now, git
dressed, we're all comin' up to this room fo' Big Daddy's
birthday party because of your ankle.—How's his ankle,
Maggie?

MARGARET: Well, he broke it, Big Mama.

BIG MAMA: I know he broke it.

(*A phone is ringing in hall. A Negro voice answers: "Mistuh
Polly's res'dence."*)

I mean does it hurt him much still.

MARGARET: I'm afraid I can't give you that information, Big
Mama. You'll have to ask Brick if it hurts much still or not.

SOOKEY (*in the hall*): It's Memphis, Mizz Polly, it's Miss Sally
in Memphis.

BIG MAMA: Awright, Sookey.

(*Big Mama rushes into the hall and is heard shouting on the
phone:*)

Hello, Miss Sally. How are you, Miss Sally?—Yes, well, I
was just gonna call you about it. *Shoot!*—

(*She raises her voice to a bellow.*)

*Miss Sally? Don't ever call me from the Gayoso Lobby, too
much talk goes on in that hotel lobby, no wonder you can't
hear me!* Now listen, Miss Sally. They's nothin' serious
wrong with Big Daddy. We got the report just now, they's
nothin' wrong but a thing called a—spastic! *SPASTIC!*—
colon . . .

(*She appears at the hall door and calls to Margaret.*)

—Maggie, come out here and talk to that fool on the
phone. I'm shouted breathless!

MARGARET (*goes out and is heard sweetly at phone*): Miss Sally?
This is Brick's wife, Maggie. So nice to hear your voice.
Can you hear *mine*? Well, *good!*—Big Mama just wanted
you to know that they've got the report from the Ochsner

Clinic and what Big Daddy has is a spastic colon. Yes.
Spastic colon, Miss Sally. That's right, spastic colon. *G'bye,
Miss Sally, hope I'll see you real soon!*

(*Hangs up a little before Miss Sally was probably ready to terminate the talk. She returns through the hall door.*)

She heard me perfectly. I've discovered with deaf people
the thing to do is not shout at them but just enunciate
clearly. My rich old Aunt Cornelia was deaf as the dead but
I could make her hear me just by sayin' each word slowly,
distinctly, close to her ear. I read her the *Commercial
Appeal* ev'ry night, read her the classified ads in it, even,
she never missed a word of it. But was she a mean ole
thing! Know what I got when she died? Her unexpired
subscriptions to five magazines and the Book-of-the-Month
Club and a LIBRARY full of ev'ry dull book ever written!
All else went to her hellcat of a sister . . . meaner than she
was, even!

(*Big Mama has been straightening things up in the room
during this speech.*)

BIG MAMA (*closing closet door on discarded clothes*): *Miss Sally
sure is a case!* Big Daddy says she's always got her hand out
fo' something. He's not mistaken. That poor ole thing always has her hand out fo' somethin'. I don't think Big
Daddy gives her as much as he should.

(*Somebody shouts for her downstairs and she shouts:*)

I'm comin'!

(*She starts out. At the hall door, turns and jerks a forefinger,
first toward the bathroom door, then toward the liquor cabinet,
meaning: "Has Brick been drinking?" Margaret pretends not
to understand, cocks her head and raises her brows as if the
pantomimic performance was completely mystifying to her.*
(*Big Mama rushes back to Margaret:*)

Shoot! Stop playin' so dumb!—I mean has he been drinkin'
that stuff much yet?

MARGARET (*with a little laugh*): Oh! I think he had a highball
after supper.

BIG MAMA: Don't laugh about it!—Some single men stop drinkin' when they git married and others start! Brick never touched liquor before he—!

MARGARET (*crying out*): *THAT'S NOT FAIR!*

BIG MAMA: Fair or not fair I want to ask you a question, one question: D'you make Brick happy in bed?

MARGARET: Why don't you ask if he makes *me* happy in bed?

BIG MAMA: Because I know that—

MARGARET: *It works both ways!*

BIG MAMA: Something's not right! You're childless and my son drinks!

(*Someone has called her downstairs and she has rushed to the door on the line above. She turns at the door and points at the bed.*)

—When a marriage goes on the rocks, the rocks are *there*, right *there!*

MARGARET: *That's—*

(*Big Mama has swept out of the room and slammed the door.*)

—not—*fair . . .*

(*Margaret is alone, completely alone, and she feels it. She draws in, hunches her shoulders, raises her arms with fists clenched, shuts her eyes tight as a child about to be stabbed with a vaccination needle. When she opens her eyes again, what she sees is the long oval mirror and she rushes straight to it, stares into it with a grimace and says: "Who are you?"— Then she crouches a little and answers herself in a different voice which is high, thin, mocking: "I am Maggie the Cat!"— Straightens quickly as bathroom door opens a little and Brick calls out to her.*)

BRICK: Has Big Mama gone?

MARGARET: She's gone.

(*He opens the bathroom door and hobbles out, with his liquor glass now empty, straight to the liquor cabinet. He is whistling softly. Margaret's head pivots on her long, slender throat to watch him.*

(*She raises a hand uncertainly to the base of her throat, as if it was difficult for her to swallow, before she speaks:*)

You know, our sex life didn't just peter out in the usual way, it was cut off short, long before the natural time for it to, and it's going to revive again, just as sudden as that. I'm confident of it. That's what I'm keeping myself attractive for. For the time when you'll see me again like other men see me. Yes, like other men see me. They still see me, Brick, and they like what they see. Uh-huh. Some of them would give their—

Look, Brick!

(*She stands before the long oval mirror, touches her breast and then her hips with her two hands.*)

How high my body stays on me!—Nothing has fallen on me—not a fraction. . . .

(*Her voice is soft and trembling: a pleading child's. At this moment as he turns to glance at her—a look which is like a player passing a ball to another player, third down and goal to go—she has to capture the audience in a grip so tight that she can hold it till the first intermission without any lapse of attention.*)

Other men still want me. My face looks strained, sometimes, but I've kept my figure as well as you've kept yours, and men admire it. I still turn heads on the street. Why, last week in Memphis everywhere that I went men's eyes burned holes in my clothes, at the country club and in restaurants and department stores, there wasn't a man I met or walked by that didn't just eat me up with his eyes and turn around when I passed him and look back at me. Why, at Alice's party for her New York cousins, the best lookin' man in the crowd—followed me upstairs and tried to force his way in the powder room with me, followed me to the door and tried to force his way in!

BRICK: Why didn't you let him, Maggie?

MARGARET: Because I'm not that common, for one thing. Not that I wasn't almost tempted to. You like to know who it was? It was Sonny Boy Maxwell, that's who!

BRICK: Oh, yeah, Sonny Boy Maxwell, he was a good end-runner but had a little injury to his back and had to quit.

MARGARET: He has no injury now and has no wife and still has a lech for me!

BRICK: I see no reason to lock him out of a powder room in that case.

MARGARET: And have someone catch me at it? I'm not that stupid. Oh, I might sometime cheat on you with someone, since you're so insultingly eager to have me do it!—But if I do, you can be damned sure it will be in a place and a time where no one but me and the man could possibly know. Because I'm not going to give you any excuse to divorce me for being unfaithful or anything else. . . .

BRICK: Maggie, I wouldn't divorce you for being unfaithful or anything else. Don't you know that? Hell. I'd be relieved to know that you'd found yourself a lover.

MARGARET: Well, I'm taking no chances. No, I'd rather stay on this hot tin roof.

BRICK: A hot tin roof's 'n uncomfo'table place t' stay on. . . .

(*He starts to whistle softly.*)

MARGARET (*through his whistle*): Yeah, but I can stay on it just as long as I have to.

BRICK: You could leave me, Maggie.

(*He resumes whistle. She wheels about to glare at him.*)

MARGARET: *Don't want to and will not!* Besides if I did, you don't have a cent to pay for it but what you get from Big Daddy and he's dying of cancer!

(*For the first time a realization of Big Daddy's doom seems to penetrate to Brick's consciousness, visibly, and he looks at Margaret.*)

BRICK: Big Mama just said he *wasn't*, that the report was okay.

MARGARET: That's what she thinks because she got the same story that they gave Big Daddy. And was just as taken in by it as he was, poor ole things. . . .

But tonight they're going to tell her the truth about it. When Big Daddy goes to bed, they're going to tell her that he is dying of cancer.

(*She slams the dresser drawer.*)

—It's malignant and it's terminal.

BRICK: Does Big Daddy know it?

MARGARET: Hell, do they *ever* know it? Nobody says, "You're dying." You have to fool them. They have to fool *themselves.*

BRICK: Why?

MARGARET: *Why?* Because human beings dream of life everlasting, that's the reason! But most of them want it on earth and not in heaven.

(*He gives a short, hard laugh at her touch of humor.*)

Well. . . . (*She touches up her mascara.*) That's how it is, anyhow. . . . (*She looks about.*) Where did I put down my cigarette? Don't want to burn up the home-place, at least not with Mae and Gooper and their five monsters in it!

(*She has found it and sucks at it greedily. Blows out smoke and continues:*)

So this is Big Daddy's last birthday. And Mae and Gooper, they know it, oh, *they* know it, all right. They got the first information from the Ochsner Clinic. That's why they rushed down here with their no-neck monsters. Because. Do you know something? Big Daddy's made no will? Big Daddy's never made out any will in his life, and so this campaign's afoot to impress him, forcibly as possible, with the fact that you drink and I've borne no children!

(*He continues to stare at her a moment, then mutters something sharp but not audible and hobbles rather rapidly out onto the long gallery in the fading, much faded, gold light.*)

MARGARET (*continuing her liturgical chant*): Y'know, I'm *fond* of Big Daddy, I am genuinely fond of that old man, I really *am*, you know. . . .

BRICK (*faintly, vaguely*): Yes, I know you are. . . .

MARGARET: I've always sort of admired him in spite of his coarseness, his four-letter words and so forth. Because Big Daddy *is* what he *is,* and he makes no bones about it. He hasn't turned gentleman farmer, he's still a Mississippi red neck, as much of a red neck as he must have been when he was just overseer here on the old Jack Straw and Peter

Ochello place. But he got hold of it an' built it into th' biggest an' finest plantation in the Delta.—I've always *liked* Big Daddy. . . .

(*She crosses to the proscenium.*)

Well, this is Big Daddy's last birthday. I'm sorry about it. But I'm facing the facts. It takes money to take care of a drinker and that's the office that I've been elected to lately.

BRICK: You don't have to take care of me.

MARGARET: Yes, I do. Two people in the same boat have got to take care of each other. At least you want money to buy more Echo Spring when this supply is exhausted, or will you be satisfied with a ten-cent beer?

Mae an' Gooper are plannin' to freeze us out of Big Daddy's estate because you drink and I'm childless. But we can defeat that plan. We're *going* to defeat that plan!

Brick, y'know, I've been so God damn disgustingly poor all my life!—That's the *truth*, Brick!

BRICK: I'm not sayin' it isn't.

MARGARET: Always had to suck up to people I couldn't stand because they had money and I was poor as Job's turkey. You don't know what that's like. Well, I'll tell you, it's like you would feel a thousand miles away from Echo Spring!— And had to get back to it on that broken ankle . . . without a crutch!

That's how it feels to be as poor as Job's turkey and have to suck up to relatives that you hated because they had money and all you had was a bunch of hand-me-down clothes and a few old moldy three per cent government bonds. My daddy loved his liquor, he fell in love with his liquor the way you've fallen in love with Echo Spring!— And my poor Mama, having to maintain some semblance of social position, to keep appearances up, on an income of one hundred and fifty dollars a month on those old government bonds!

When I came out, the year that I made my debut, I had just two evening dresses! One Mother made me from a pattern in *Vogue*, the other a hand-me-down from a snotty rich cousin I hated!

—The dress that I married you in was my grandmother's weddin' gown. . . .

So that's why I'm like a cat on a hot tin roof!

(*Brick is still on the gallery. Someone below calls up to him in a warm Negro voice, "Hiya, Mistuh Brick, how yuh feelin'?" Brick raises his liquor glass as if that answered the question.*)

MARGARET: You can be young without money but you can't be old without it. You've got to be old *with* money because to be old without it is just too awful, you've got to be one or the other, either *young* or *with money,* you can't be old and *without* it.—That's the *truth,* Brick. . . .

(*Brick whistles softly, vaguely.*)

Well, now I'm dressed, I'm all dressed, there's nothing else for me to do.

(*Forlornly, almost fearfully.*)

I'm dressed, all dressed, nothing else for me to do. . . .

(*She moves about restlessly, aimlessly, and speaks, as if to herself.*)

I know when I made my mistake.—What am I—? Oh!—my bracelets. . . .

(*She starts working a collection of bracelets over her hands onto her wrists, about six on each, as she talks.*)

I've thought a whole lot about it and now I know when I made my mistake. Yes, I made my mistake when I told you the truth about that thing with Skipper. Never should have confessed it, a fatal error, tellin' you about that thing with Skipper.

BRICK: Maggie, shut up about Skipper. I mean it, Maggie; you got to shut up about Skipper.

MARGARET: You ought to understand that Skipper and I—

BRICK: You don't think I'm serious, Maggie? You're fooled by the fact that I am saying this quiet? Look, Maggie. What you're doing is a dangerous thing to do. You're—you're—you're—foolin' with something that—nobody ought to fool with.

MARGARET: This time I'm going to finish what I have to say to you. Skipper and I made love, if love you could call it, because it made both of us feel a little bit closer to you. You see, you son of a bitch, you asked too much of people, of me, of him, of all the unlucky poor damned sons of bitches that happen to love you, and there was a whole pack of them, yes, there was a pack of them besides me and Skipper, you asked too goddam much of people that loved you, you—superior creature!—you godlike being!— And so we made love to each other to dream it was you, both of us! Yes, yes, yes! Truth, truth! What's so awful about it? I like it, I think the truth is—yeah! I shouldn't have told you. . . .

BRICK (*holding his head unnaturally still and uptilted a bit*): It was Skipper that told me about it. Not you, Maggie.

MARGARET: I told you!

BRICK: After he told me!

MARGARET: What does it matter who—?

(*Brick turns suddenly out upon the gallery and calls:*)

BRICK: Little girl! Hey, little girl!

LITTLE GIRL (*at a distance*): What, Uncle Brick?

BRICK: Tell the folks to come up!—Bring everybody upstairs!

MARGARET: I can't stop myself! I'd go on telling you this in front of them all, if I had to!

BRICK: Little girl! Go on, go on, will you? Do what I told you, call them!

MARGARET: Because it's got to be told and you, you!—you never let me!

(*She sobs, then controls herself, and continues almost calmly.*)

It was one of those beautiful, ideal things they tell about in the Greek legends, it couldn't be anything else, you being you, and that's what made it so sad, that's what made it so awful, because it was love that never could be carried through to anything satisfying or even talked about plainly. Brick, I tell you, you got to believe me, Brick, I *do* understand all about it! I—I think it was—*noble!* Can't you tell I'm sincere when I say I respect it? My only point, the only point that I'm making, is life has got to be

allowed to continue even after the *dream* of life is—all—
over. . . .

(*Brick is without his crutch. Leaning on furniture, he crosses
to pick it up as she continues as if possessed by a will outside
herself.*)

– Why I remember when we double-dated at college, Gladys
Fitzgerald and I and you and Skipper, it was more like a
date between you and Skipper. Gladys and I were just sort
of tagging along as if it was necessary to chaperone you!—
to make a good public impression—

BRICK (*turns to face her, half lifting his crutch*): Maggie, you
want me to hit you with this crutch? Don't you know I
could kill you with this crutch?

MARGARET: Good Lord, man, d' you think I'd care if you did?

BRICK: One man has one great good true thing in his life.
One great good thing which is true!—I had friendship with
Skipper.—You are naming it dirty!

MARGARET: I'm not naming it dirty! I am naming it clean.

BRICK: Not love with you, Maggie, but friendship with Skipper
was that one great true thing, and you are naming it dirty!

MARGARET: Then you haven't been listenin', not understood
what I'm saying! I'm naming it so damn clean that it killed
poor Skipper!—You two had something that had to be kept
on ice, yes, incorruptible, yes!—and death was the only icebox where you could keep it. . . .

BRICK: I married you, Maggie. Why would I marry you,
Maggie, if I was—?

MARGARET: Brick, don't brain me yet, let me finish!—I know,
believe me I know, that it was only Skipper that harbored
even any *unconscious* desire for anything not perfectly pure
between you two!—Now let me skip a little. You married me
early that summer we graduated out of Ole Miss, and we
were happy, weren't we, we were blissful, yes, hit heaven together ev'ry time that we loved! But that fall you an' Skipper
turned down wonderful offers of jobs in order to keep on
bein' football heroes—pro-football heroes. You organized
the Dixie Stars that fall, so you could keep on bein' team-
mates forever! But somethin' was not right with it!—*Me included!*—between you. Skipper began hittin' the bottle . . .

you got a spinal injury—couldn't play the Thanksgivin' game in Chicago, watched it on TV from a traction bed in Toledo. I joined Skipper. The Dixie Stars lost because poor Skipper was drunk. We drank together that night all night in the bar of the Blackstone and when cold day was comin' up over the Lake an' we were comin' out drunk to take a dizzy look at it, I said, "SKIPPER! STOP LOVIN' MY HUSBAND OR TELL HIM HE'S GOT TO LET YOU ADMIT IT TO HIM!"—one way or another!

HE SLAPPED ME HARD ON THE MOUTH!—then turned and ran without stopping once, I am sure, all the way back into his room at the Blackstone. . . .

—When I came to his room that night, with a little scratch like a shy little mouse at his door, he made that piti-ful, ineffectual little attempt to prove that what I had said wasn't true. . . .

(*Brick strikes at her with crutch, a blow that shatters the gem-like lamp on the table.*)

—In this way, I destroyed him, by telling him truth that he and his world which he was born and raised in, yours and his world, had told him could not be told?

—From then on Skipper was nothing at all but a recep-tacle for liquor and drugs. . . .

—*Who shot cock-robin? I with my*—

(*She throws back her head with tight shut eyes.*)

—*merciful arrow!*

(*Brick strikes at her; misses.*)

Missed me!—Sorry,—I'm not tryin' to whitewash my be-havior, Christ, no! Brick, I'm not good. I don't know why people have to pretend to be good, nobody's good. The rich or the well-to-do can afford to respect moral patterns, conventional moral patterns, but I could never afford to, yeah, but—I'm honest! Give me credit for just that, will you *please*?—Born poor, raised poor, expect to die poor un-less I manage to get us something out of what Big Daddy leaves when he dies of cancer! But Brick?!—*Skipper is dead! I'm alive!* Maggie the cat is—

(*Brick hops awkwardly forward and strikes at her again with his crutch.*)

—alive! I am alive, alive! I am . . .

(*He hurls the crutch at her, across the bed she took refuge behind, and pitches forward on the floor as she completes her speech.*)

—alive!

(*A little girl, Dixie, bursts into the room, wearing an Indian war bonnet and firing a cap pistol at Margaret and shouting: "Bang, bang, bang!"*

(*Laughter downstairs floats through the open hall door. Margaret had crouched gasping to bed at child's entrance. She now rises and says with cool fury:*)

Little girl, your mother or someone should teach you— (*Gasping*)—to knock at a door before you come into a room. Otherwise people might think that you—lack—good breeding. . . .

DIXIE: Yanh, yanh, yanh, what is Uncle Brick doin' on th' floor?

BRICK: I tried to kill your Aunt Maggie, but I failed—and I fell. Little girl, give me my crutch so I can get up off th' floor.

MARGARET: Yes, give your uncle his crutch, he's a cripple, honey, he broke his ankle last night jumping hurdles on the high school athletic field!

DIXIE: What were you jumping hurdles for, Uncle Brick?

BRICK: Because I used to jump them, and people like to do what they used to do, even after they've stopped being able to do it. . . .

MARGARET: That's right, that's your answer, now go away, little girl.

(*Dixie fires cap pistol at Margaret three times.*)

Stop, you stop that, monster! You little no-neck monster!

(*She seizes the cap pistol and hurls it through gallery doors.*)

DIXIE (*with a precocious instinct for the cruelest thing*): You're *jealous!*—You're just jealous because you can't have babies!

(*She sticks out her tongue at Margaret as she sashays past her with her stomach stuck out, to the gallery. Margaret slams the gallery doors and leans panting against them. There is a pause. Brick has replaced his spilt drink and sits, faraway, on the great four-poster bed.*)

MARGARET: You see?—they gloat over us being childless, even in front of their five little no-neck monsters!

(*Pause. Voices approach on the stairs.*)

Brick?—I've been to a doctor in Memphis, a—a gynecologist. . . .

I've been completely examined, and there is no reason why we can't have a child whenever we want one. And this is my time by the calendar to conceive. Are you listening to me? Are you? Are you LISTENING TO ME!

BRICK: Yes. I hear you, Maggie.

(*His attention returns to her inflamed face.*)

—But how in hell on earth do you imagine—that you're going to have a child by a man that can't stand you?

MARGARET: That's a problem that I will have to work out.

(*She wheels about to face the hall door.*)

Here they come!

(*The lights dim.*)

Curtain

ACT TWO

There is no lapse of time. Margaret and Brick are in the same positions they held at the end of Act I.

MARGARET (*at door*): *Here they come!*

(*Big Daddy appears first, a tall man with a fierce, anxious look, moving carefully not to betray his weakness even, or especially, to himself.*)

BIG DADDY: Well, Brick.

BRICK: Hello, Big Daddy.—Congratulations!

BIG DADDY: —Crap. . . .

> (*Some of the people are approaching through the hall, others along the gallery: voices from both directions. Gooper and Reverend Tooker become visible outside gallery doors, and their voices come in clearly.*
> (*They pause outside as Gooper lights a cigar.*)

REVEREND TOOKER (*vivaciously*): Oh, but St. Paul's in Grenada has three memorial windows, and the latest one is a Tiffany stained-glass window that cost twenty-five hundred dollars, a picture of Christ the Good Shepherd with a Lamb in His arms.

GOOPER: Who give that window, Preach?

REVEREND TOOKER: Clyde Fletcher's widow. Also presented St. Paul's with a baptismal font.

GOOPER: Y'know what somebody ought t' give your church is a *coolin'* system, Preach.

REVEREND TOOKER: Yes, siree, Bob! And y'know what Gus Hamma's family gave in his memory to the church at Two Rivers? A complete new stone parish-house with a basketball court in the basement and a—

BIG DADDY (*uttering a loud barking laugh which is far from truly mirthful*): Hey, Preach! What's all this talk about memorials, Preach? Y' think somebody's about t' kick off around here? 'S that it?

> (*Startled by this interjection, Reverend Tooker decides to laugh at the question almost as loud as he can.*
> (*How he would answer the question we'll never know, as he's spared that embarrassment by the voice of Gooper's wife, Mae, rising high and clear as she appears with "Doc" Baugh, the family doctor, through the hall door.*)

MAE (*almost religiously*): —Let's see now, they've had their *tyyy*-phoid shots, and their tetanus shots, their diphtheria shots and their hepatitis shots and their polio shots, they got *those* shots every month from May through September, and—Gooper? Hey! Gooper!—What all have the kiddies been shot faw?

MARGARET (*overlapping a bit*): Turn on the Hi-Fi, Brick! Let's have some music t' start off th' party with!

(*The talk becomes so general that the room sounds like a great aviary of chattering birds. Only Brick remains unengaged, leaning upon the liquor cabinet with his faraway smile, an ice cube in a paper napkin with which he now and then rubs his forehead. He doesn't respond to Margaret's command. She bounds forward and stoops over the instrument panel of the console.*)

GOOPER: We gave 'em that thing for a third anniversary present, got three speakers in it.

(*The room is suddenly blasted by the climax of a Wagnerian opera or a Beethoven symphony.*)

BIG DADDY: *Turn that damn thing off!*

(*Almost instant silence, almost instantly broken by the shouting charge of Big Mama, entering through hall door like a charging rhino.*)

BIG MAMA: *Wha's my Brick, wha's mah precious baby!!*
BIG DADDY: *Sorry! Turn it back on!*

(*Everyone laughs very loud. Big Daddy is famous for his jokes at Big Mama's expense, and nobody laughs louder at these jokes than Big Mama herself, though sometimes they're pretty cruel and Big Mama has to pick up or fuss with something to cover the hurt that the loud laugh doesn't quite cover.*
(*On this occasion, a happy occasion because the dread in her heart has also been lifted by the false report on Big Daddy's condition, she giggles, grotesquely, coyly, in Big Daddy's direction and bears down upon Brick, all very quick and alive.*)

BIG MAMA: Here he is, here's my precious baby! What's that you've got in your hand? You put that liquor down, son, your hand was made fo' holdin' somethin' better than that!
GOOPER: Look at Brick put it down!

(*Brick has obeyed Big Mama by draining the glass and handing it to her. Again everyone laughs, some high, some low.*)

BIG MAMA: Oh, you bad boy, you, you're my bad little boy. Give Big Mama a kiss, you bad boy, you!—Look at him shy away, will you? Brick never liked bein' kissed or made a fuss over, I guess because he's always had too much of it!

Son, you turn that thing off!

(*Brick has switched on the TV set.*)

I can't stand TV, radio was bad enough but TV has gone it one better, I mean—(*Plops wheezing in chair*)—one worse, ha ha! Now what'm I sittin' down here faw? I want t' sit next to my sweetheart on the sofa, hold hands with him and love him up a little!

(*Big Mama has on a black and white figured chiffon. The large irregular patterns, like the markings of some massive animal, the luster of her great diamonds and many pearls, the brilliants set in the silver frames of her glasses, her riotous voice, booming laugh, have dominated the room since she entered. Big Daddy has been regarding her with a steady grimace of chronic annoyance.*)

BIG MAMA (*still louder*): Preacher, Preacher, hey, Preach! Give me you' hand an' help me up from this chair!
REVEREND TOOKER: None of your tricks, Big Mama!
BIG MAMA: What tricks? You give me you' hand so I can get up an'—

(*Reverend Tooker extends her his hand. She grabs it and pulls him into her lap with a shrill laugh that spans an octave in two notes.*)

Ever seen a preacher in a fat lady's lap? Hey, hey, folks! Ever seen a preacher in a fat lady's lap?

(*Big Mama is notorious throughout the Delta for this sort of inelegant horseplay. Margaret looks on with indulgent humor, sipping Dubonnet "on the rocks" and watching Brick, but Mae and Gooper exchange signs of humorless anxiety over these antics, the sort of behavior which Mae thinks may account for their failure to quite get in with the smartest young married set in Memphis, despite all. One of the Negroes, Lacey or Sookey, peeks in, cackling. They are waiting for a sign to bring in the cake and champagne. But Big Daddy's not*) amused. *He doesn't understand why, in spite of the infinite mental relief he's received from the doctor's report, he still has these same old fox teeth in his guts. "This spastic thing sure is something," he says to himself, but aloud he roars at Big Mama:*)

BIG DADDY: *BIG MAMA, WILL YOU QUIT HORSIN'?*—You're too old an' too fat fo' that sort of crazy kid stuff an' besides a woman with your blood-pressure—she had two hundred last spring!—is riskin' a stroke when you mess around like that. . . .

BIG MAMA: *Here comes Big Daddy's birthday!*

(*Negroes in white jackets enter with an enormous birthday cake ablaze with candles and carrying buckets of champagne with satin ribbons about the bottle necks.*

(*Mae and Gooper strike up song, and everybody, including the Negroes and Children, joins in. Only Brick remains aloof.*)

EVERYONE:
> Happy birthday to you.
> Happy birthday to you.
> Happy birthday, Big Daddy—

(*Some sing: "Dear, Big Daddy!"*)

> Happy birthday to you.

(*Some sing: "How old are you?"*)

(*Mae has come down center and is organizing her children like a chorus. She gives them a barely audible: "One, two, three!" and they are off in the new tune.*)

CHILDREN:
> Skinamarinka—dinka—dink
> Skinamarinka—do
> We love you.
> Skinamarinka—dinka—dink
> Skinamarinka—do.

(*All together, they turn to Big Daddy.*)

> Big Daddy, you!

(*They turn back front, like a musical comedy chorus.*)

> We love you in the morning;
> We love you in the night.
> We love you when we're with you,
> And we love you out of sight.
> Skinamarinka—dinka—dink
> Skinamarinka—do.

(*Mae turns to Big Mama.*)

> Big Mama, too!

(*Big Mama bursts into tears. The Negroes leave.*)

BIG DADDY: Now Ida, what the hell is the matter with you?

MAE: She's just so happy.

BIG MAMA: I'm just so happy, Big Daddy, I have to cry or something.

(*Sudden and loud in the hush:*)

> Brick, do you know the wonderful news that Doc Baugh got from the clinic about Big Daddy? Big Daddy's one hundred per cent!

MARGARET: Isn't that wonderful?

BIG MAMA: He's just one hundred per cent. Passed the examination with flying colors. Now that we know there's nothing wrong with Big Daddy but a spastic colon, I can tell you something. I was worried sick, half out of my mind, for fear that Big Daddy might have a thing like—

(*Margaret cuts through this speech, jumping up and exclaiming shrilly:*)

MARGARET: Brick, honey, aren't you going to give Big Daddy his birthday present?

(*Passing by him, she snatches his liquor glass from him.*
(*She picks up a fancily wrapped package.*)

Here it is, Big Daddy, this is from Brick!

BIG MAMA: This is the biggest birthday Big Daddy's ever had, a hundred presents and bushels of telegrams from—

MAE (*at same time*): What is it, Brick?

GOOPER: I bet 500 to 50 that Brick don't *know* what it is.

BIG MAMA: The fun of presents is not knowing what they are till you open the package. Open your present, Big Daddy.

BIG DADDY: Open it you'self. I want to ask Brick somethin! Come here, Brick.

MARGARET: Big Daddy's callin' you, Brick.

(*She is opening the package.*)

BRICK: Tell Big Daddy I'm crippled.

BIG DADDY: I see you're crippled. I want to know how you got crippled.

MARGARET (*making diversionary tactics*): *Oh, look, oh, look, why, it's a cashmere robe!*

(*She holds the robe up for all to see.*)

MAE: You sound surprised, Maggie.

MARGARET: I never saw one before.

MAE: That's funny.—*Hah!*

MARGARET (*turning on her fiercely, with a brilliant smile*): Why is it funny? All my family ever had was family—and luxuries such as cashmere robes still surprise me!

BIG DADDY (*ominously*): Quiet!

MAE (*heedless in her fury*): I don't see how you could be so surprised when you bought it yourself at Loewenstein's in Memphis last Saturday. You know how I know?

BIG DADDY: I said, Quiet!

MAE: —I know because the salesgirl that sold it to you waited on me and said, Oh, Mrs. Pollitt, your sister-in-law just bought a cashmere robe for your husband's father!

MARGARET: Sister Woman! Your talents are wasted as a housewife and mother, you really ought to be with the FBI or—

BIG DADDY: QUIET!

(*Reverend Tooker's reflexes are slower than the others'. He finishes a sentence after the bellow.*)

REVEREND TOOKER (*to Doc Baugh*): —the Stork and the Reaper are running neck and neck!

(*He starts to laugh gaily when he notices the silence and Big Daddy's glare. His laugh dies falsely.*)

BIG DADDY: Preacher, I hope I'm not butting in on more talk about memorial stained-glass windows, am I, Preacher?

(*Reverend Tooker laughs feebly, then coughs dryly in the embarrassed silence.*)

Preacher?

BIG MAMA: Now, Big Daddy, don't you pick on Preacher!

BIG DADDY (*raising his voice*): You ever hear that expression all hawk and no spit? You bring that expression to mind with that little dry cough of yours, all hawk an' no spit. . . .

(*The pause is broken only by a short startled laugh from Margaret, the only one there who is conscious of and amused by the grotesque.*)

MAE (*raising her arms and jangling her bracelets*): I wonder if the mosquitoes are active tonight?

BIG DADDY: What's that, Little Mama? Did you make some remark?

MAE: Yes, I said I wondered if the mosquitoes would eat us alive if we went out on the gallery for a while.

BIG DADDY: Well, if they do, I'll have your bones pulverized for fertilizer!

BIG MAMA (*quickly*): Last week we had an airplane spraying the place and I think it done some good, at least I haven't had a—

BIG DADDY (*cutting her speech*): Brick, they tell me, if what they tell me is true, that you done some jumping last night on the high school athletic field?

BIG MAMA: Brick, Big Daddy is talking to you, son.

BRICK (*smiling vaguely over his drink*): What was that, Big Daddy?

BIG DADDY: They said you done some jumping on the high school track field last night.

BRICK: That's what they told me, too.

BIG DADDY: Was it jumping or humping that you were doing out there? What were you doing out there at three A.M., layin' a woman on that cinder track?

BIG MAMA: Big Daddy, you are off the sick-list, now, and I'm not going to excuse you for talkin' so—

BIG DADDY: Quiet!

BIG MAMA: —*nasty* in front of Preacher and—

BIG DADDY: *QUIET!*—I ast you, Brick, if you was cuttin' you'self a piece o' poon-tang last night on that cinder track? I thought maybe you were chasin' poon-tang on that track an' tripped over something in the heat of the chase— 'sthat it?

(*Gooper laughs, loud and false, others nervously following suit. Big Mama stamps her foot, and purses her lips, crossing to Mae and whispering something to her as Brick meets his father's hard, intent, grinning stare with a slow, vague smile that he offers all situations from behind the screen of his liquor.*)

BRICK: No, sir, I don't think so. . . .

MAE (*at the same time, sweetly*): Reverend Tooker, let's you and I take a stroll on the widow's walk.

(*She and the preacher go out on the gallery as Big Daddy says:*)

BIG DADDY: Then what the hell were you doing out there at three o'clock in the morning?

BRICK: Jumping the hurdles, Big Daddy, runnin' and jumpin' the hurdles, but those high hurdles have gotten too high for me, now.

BIG DADDY: Cause you was drunk?

BRICK (*his vague smile fading a little*): Sober I wouldn't have tried to jump the *low* ones. . . .

BIG MAMA (*quickly*): Big Daddy, blow out the candles on your birthday cake!

MARGARET (*at the same time*): I want to propose a toast to Big Daddy Pollitt on his sixty-fifth birthday, the biggest cotton-planter in—

BIG DADDY (*bellowing with fury and disgust*): *I told you to stop it, now stop it, quit this*—!

BIG MAMA (*coming in front of Big Daddy with the cake*): Big Daddy, I will not allow you to talk that way, not even on your birthday, I—

BIG DADDY: I'll talk like I want to on my birthday, Ida, or any other goddam day of the year and anybody here that don't like it knows what they can do!

BIG MAMA: You don't mean that!

BIG DADDY: What makes you think I don't mean it?

(*Meanwhile various discreet signals have been exchanged and Gooper has also gone out on the gallery.*)

BIG MAMA: I just know you don't mean it.

BIG DADDY: You don't know a goddam thing and you never did!

BIG MAMA: Big Daddy, you don't mean that.

BIG DADDY: Oh, yes, I do, oh, yes, I do, I mean it! I put up with a whole lot of crap around here because I thought I was dying. And you thought I was dying and you started taking over, well, you can stop taking over now, Ida, because I'm not gonna die, you can just stop now this business of taking over because you're not taking over because I'm not dying, I went through the laboratory and the goddam exploratory operation and there's nothing wrong with me but a spastic colon. And I'm not dying of cancer which you thought I was dying of. Ain't that so? Didn't you think that I was dying of cancer, Ida?

(*Almost everybody is out on the gallery but the two old people glaring at each other across the blazing cake.*

(*Big Mama's chest heaves and she presses a fat fist to her mouth.*

(*Big Daddy continues, hoarsely:*)

Ain't that so, Ida? Didn't you have an idea I was dying of cancer and now you could take control of this place and everything on it? I got that impression, I seemed to get that impression. Your loud voice everywhere, your fat old body butting in here and there!

BIG MAMA: Hush! The Preacher!

BIG DADDY: Rut the goddam preacher!

(*Big Mama gasps loudly and sits down on the sofa which is almost too small for her.*)

Did you hear what I said? I said rut the goddam preacher!

(*Somebody closes the gallery doors from outside just as there is a burst of fireworks and excited cries from the children.*)

BIG MAMA: I never seen you act like this before and I can't think what's got in you!

BIG DADDY: I went through all that laboratory and operation and all just so I would know if you or me was boss here! Well, now it turns out that I am and you ain't—and that's my birthday present—and my cake and champagne!—because for three years now you been gradually taking over. Bossing. Talking. Sashaying your fat old body around the place I made! I made this place! I was overseer on it! I was the overseer on the old Straw and Ochello plantation. I quit school at ten! I quit school at ten years old and went to work like a nigger in the fields. And I rose to be overseer of the Straw and Ochello plantation. And old Straw died and I was Ochello's partner and the place got bigger and bigger and bigger and bigger and bigger! I did all that myself with no goddam help from you, and now you think you're just about to take over. Well, I am just about to tell you that you are not just about to take over, you are not just about to take over a God damn thing. Is that clear to you, Ida? Is that very plain to you, now? Is that understood completely? I been through the laboratory from A to Z. I've had the goddam exploratory operation, and nothing is wrong with me but a spastic colon—made spastic, I guess, by *disgust*! By all the goddam lies and liars that I have had to put up with, and all the goddam hypocrisy that I lived with all these forty years that we been livin' together!

Hey! Ida! Blow out the candles on the birthday cake! Purse up your lips and draw a deep breath and blow out the goddam candles on the cake!

BIG MAMA: Oh, Big Daddy, oh, oh, oh, Big Daddy!

BIG DADDY: What's the matter with you?

BIG MAMA: *In all these years you never believed that I loved you??*

BIG DADDY: Huh?

BIG MAMA: *And I did, I did so much, I did love you!*—I even loved your hate and your hardness, Big Daddy!

(*She sobs and rushes awkwardly out onto the gallery.*)

BIG DADDY (*to himself*): *Wouldn't it be funny if that was true. . . .*

(*A pause is followed by a burst of light in the sky from the fireworks.*)

BRICK! HEY, BRICK!

(*He stands over his blazing birthday cake.*

(*After some moments, Brick hobbles in on his crutch, holding his glass.*

(*Margaret follows him with a bright, anxious smile.*)

I didn't call you, Maggie. I called Brick.

MARGARET: I'm just delivering him to you.

(*She kisses Brick on the mouth which he immediately wipes with the back of his hand. She flies girlishly back out. Brick and his father are alone.*)

BIG DADDY: Why did you do that?

BRICK: Do what, Big Daddy?

BIG DADDY: Wipe her kiss off your mouth like she'd spit on you.

BRICK: I don't know. I wasn't conscious of it.

BIG DADDY: That woman of yours has a better shape on her than Gooper's but somehow or other they got the same look about them.

BRICK: What sort of look is that, Big Daddy?

BIG DADDY: I don't know how to describe it but it's the same look.

BRICK: They don't look peaceful, do they?

BIG DADDY: No, they sure in hell don't.

BRICK: They look nervous as cats?

BIG DADDY: That's right, they look nervous as cats.

BRICK: Nervous as a couple of cats on a hot tin roof?

BIG DADDY: That's right, boy, they look like a couple of cats on a hot tin roof. It's funny that you and Gooper being so different would pick out the same type of woman.

BRICK: Both of us married into society, Big Daddy.

BIG DADDY: Crap . . . I wonder what gives them both that look?

BRICK: Well. They're sittin' in the middle of a big piece of land, Big Daddy, twenty-eight thousand acres is a pretty big piece of land and so they're squaring off on it, each determined to knock off a bigger piece of it than the other whenever you let it go.

BIG DADDY: I got a surprise for those women. I'm not gonna let it go for a long time yet if that's what they're waiting for.

BRICK: That's right, Big Daddy. You just sit tight and let them scratch each other's eyes out. . . .

BIG DADDY: You bet your life I'm going to sit tight on it and let those sons of bitches scratch their eyes out, ha ha ha. . . .

But Gooper's wife's a good breeder, you got to admit she's fertile. Hell, at supper tonight she had them all at the table and they had to put a couple of extra leafs in the table to make room for them, she's got five head of them, now, and another one's comin'.

BRICK: Yep, number six is comin'. . . .

BIG DADDY: Brick, you know, I swear to God, I don't know the way it happens?

BRICK: The way what happens, Big Daddy?

BIG DADDY: You git you a piece of land, by hook or crook, an' things start growin' on it, things accumulate on it, and the first thing you know it's completely out of hand, completely out of hand!

BRICK: Well, they say nature hates a vacuum, Big Daddy.

BIG DADDY: That's what they say, but sometimes I think that a vacuum is a hell of a lot better than some of the stuff that nature replaces it with.

Is someone out there by that door?

BRICK: Yep.

BIG DADDY: Who?

(*He has lowered his voice.*)

BRICK: Someone int'rested in what we say to each other.

BIG DADDY: Gooper?——*GOOPER!*

(*After a discreet pause, Mae appears in the gallery door.*)

MAE: Did you call Gooper, Big Daddy?

BIG DADDY: Aw, it was you.

MAE: Do you want Gooper, Big Daddy?

BIG DADDY: No, and I don't want you. I want some privacy here, while I'm having a confidential talk with my son

Brick. Now it's too hot in here to close them doors, but if I have to close those rutten doors in order to have a private talk with my son Brick, just let me know and I'll close 'em. Because I hate eavesdroppers, I don't like any kind of sneakin' an' spyin'.

MAE: Why, Big Daddy—

BIG DADDY: You stood on the wrong side of the moon, it threw your shadow!

MAE: I was just—

BIG DADDY: You was just nothing but *spyin'* an' you *know* it!

MAE (*begins to sniff and sob*): Oh, Big Daddy, you're so un-kind for some reason to those that really love you!

BIG DADDY: Shut up, shut up, shut up! I'm going to move you and Gooper out of that room next to this! It's none of your goddam business what goes on in here at night between Brick an' Maggie. You listen at night like a couple of rutten peek-hole spies and go and give a report on what you hear to Big Mama an' she comes to me and says they say such and such and so and so about what they heard goin' on between Brick an' Maggie, and Jesus, it makes me sick. I'm goin' to move you an' Gooper out of that room, I can't stand sneakin' an' spyin', it makes me sick. . . .

(*Mae throws back her head and rolls her eyes heavenward and extends her arms as if invoking God's pity for this unjust martyrdom; then she presses a handkerchief to her nose and flies from the room with a loud swish of skirts.*)

BRICK (*now at the liquor cabinet*): They listen, do they?

BIG DADDY: Yeah. They listen and give reports to Big Mama on what goes on in here between you and Maggie. They say that—

(*He stops as if embarrassed.*)

—You won't sleep with her, that you sleep on the sofa. Is that true or not true? If you don't like Maggie, get rid of Maggie!—What are you doin' there now?

BRICK: Fresh'nin' up my drink.

BIG DADDY: Son, you know you got a real liquor problem?

BRICK: Yes, sir, yes, I know.

BIG DADDY: Is that why you quit sports-announcing, because of this liquor problem?

BRICK: Yes, sir, yes, sir, I guess so.

(*He smiles vaguely and amiably at his father across his re-plenished drink.*)

BIG DADDY: Son, don't guess about it, it's too important.

BRICK (*vaguely*): Yes, sir.

BIG DADDY: And listen to me, don't look at the damn chandelier. . . .

(*Pause. Big Daddy's voice is husky.*)

—Somethin' else we picked up at th' big fire sale in Europe.

(*Another pause.*)

Life is important. There's nothing else to hold onto. A man that drinks is throwing his life away. Don't do it, hold onto your life. There's nothing else to hold onto. . . .

Sit down over here so we don't have to raise our voices, the walls have ears in this place.

BRICK (*hobbling over to sit on the sofa beside him*): All right, Big Daddy.

BIG DADDY: Quit!—how'd that come about? Some disappointment?

BRICK: I don't know. Do you?

BIG DADDY: I'm askin' you, God damn it! How in hell would I know if you don't?

BRICK: I just got out there and found that I had a mouth full of cotton. I was always two or three beats behind what was goin' on on the field and so I—

BIG DADDY: Quit!

BRICK (*amiably*): Yes, quit.

BIG DADDY: Son?

BRICK: Huh?

BIG DADDY (*inhales loudly and deeply from his cigar; then bends suddenly a little forward, exhaling loudly and raising a hand to his forehead*): —Whew!—ha ha!—I took in too much smoke, it made me a little light-headed. . . .

(*The mantel clock chimes.*)

Why is it so damn hard for people to talk?
BRICK: Yeah. . . .

(*The clock goes on sweetly chiming till it has completed the stroke of ten.*)

—Nice peaceful-soundin' clock, I like to hear it all night. . . .

(*He slides low and comfortable on the sofa; Big Daddy sits up straight and rigid with some unspoken anxiety. All his gestures are tense and jerky as he talks. He wheezes and pants and sniffs through his nervous speech, glancing quickly, shyly, from time to time, at his son.*)

BIG DADDY: We got that clock the summer we wint to Europe, me an' Big Mama on that damn Cook's Tour, never had such an awful time in my life, I'm tellin' you, son, those gooks over there, they gouge your eyeballs out in their grand hotels. And Big Mama bought more stuff than you could haul in a couple of boxcars, that's no crap. Everywhere she wint on this whirlwind tour, she bought, bought, bought. Why, half that stuff she bought is still crated up in the cellar, under water last spring!

(*He laughs.*)

That Europe is nothin' on earth but a great big auction, that's all it is, that bunch of old worn-out places, it's just a big fire-sale, the whole rutten thing, an' Big Mama wint wild in it, why, you couldn't hold that woman with a mule's harness! Bought, bought, bought!—lucky I'm a rich man, yes siree, Bob, an' half that stuff is mildewin' in th' basement. It's lucky I'm a rich man, it sure is lucky, well, I'm a rich man, Brick, yep, I'm a mighty rich man.

(*His eyes light up for a moment.*)

Y'know how much I'm worth? Guess, Brick! Guess how much I'm worth!

(*Brick smiles vaguely over his drink.*)

Close on ten million in cash an' blue chip stocks, outside, mind you, of twenty-eight thousand acres of the richest land this side of the valley Nile!

(*A puff and crackle and the night sky blooms with an eerie greenish glow. Children shriek on the gallery.*)

But a man can't buy his life with it, he can't buy back his life with it when his life has been spent, that's one thing not offered in the Europe fire-sale or in the American markets or any markets on earth, a man can't buy his life with it, he can't buy back his life when his life is finished. . . .

That's a sobering thought, a very sobering thought, and that's a thought that I was turning over in my head, over and over and over—until today. . . .

I'm wiser and sadder, Brick, for this experience which I just gone through. They's one thing else that I remember in Europe.

BRICK: What is that, Big Daddy?

BIG DADDY: The hills around Barcelona in the country of Spain and the children running over those bare hills in their bare skins beggin' like starvin' dogs with howls and screeches, and how fat the priests are on the streets of Barcelona, so many of them and so fat and so pleasant, ha ha!—Y'know I could feed that country? I got money enough to feed that goddam country, but the human animal is a selfish beast and I don't reckon the money I passed out there to those howling children in the hills around Barcelona would more than upholster one of the chairs in this room, I mean pay to put a new cover on this chair!

Hell, I threw them money like you'd scatter feed corn for chickens, I threw money at them just to get rid of them long enough to climb back into th' car and—drive away. . . .

And then in Morocco, them Arabs, why, prostitution begins at four or five, that's no exaggeration, why, I remember one day in Marrakech, that old walled Arab city, I set on a broken-down wall to have a cigar, it was fearful hot there and this Arab woman stood in the road and looked at me till I was embarrassed, she stood stock still in the dusty hot road and looked at me till I was embarrassed. But listen to this. She had a naked child with her, a little naked girl with her, barely able to toddle, and after a while she set this child on the ground and give her a push and whispered something to her.

This child come toward me, barely able t' walk, come toddling up to me and—

Jesus, it makes you sick t' remember a thing like this! It stuck out its hand and tried to unbutton my trousers!

That child was not yet five! Can you believe me? Or do you think that I am making this up? I wint back to the hotel and said to Big Mama, Git packed! We're clearing out of this country. . . .

BRICK: Big Daddy, you're on a talkin' jag tonight.

BIG DADDY (*ignoring this remark*): Yes, sir, that's how it is, the human animal is a beast that dies but the fact that he's dying don't give him pity for others, no, sir, it—

—Did you say something?

BRICK: Yes.

BIG DADDY: What?

BRICK: Hand me over that crutch so I can get up.

BIG DADDY: Where you goin'?

BRICK: I'm takin' a little short trip to Echo Spring.

BIG DADDY: To where?

BRICK: Liquor cabinet. . . .

BIG DADDY: Yes, sir, boy—

(*He hands Brick the crutch.*)

—the human animal is a beast that dies and if he's got money he buys and buys and buys and I think the reason he buys everything he can buy is that in the back of his mind he has the crazy hope that one of his purchases will be life everlasting!—Which it never can be. . . . The human animal is a beast that—

BRICK (*at the liquor cabinet*): Big Daddy, you sure are shootin' th' breeze here tonight.

(*There is a pause and voices are heard outside.*)

BIG DADDY: I been quiet here lately, spoke not a word, just sat and stared into space. I had something heavy weighing on my mind but tonight that load was took off me. That's why I'm talking.—The sky looks diff'rent to me. . . .

BRICK: You know what I like to hear most?

BIG DADDY: What?

BRICK: Solid quiet. Perfect unbroken quiet.

BIG DADDY: Why?

BRICK: Because it's more peaceful.

BIG DADDY: Man, you'll hear a lot of that in the grave.

(*He chuckles agreeably.*)

BRICK: Are you through talkin' to me?

BIG DADDY: Why are you so anxious to shut me up?

BRICK: Well, sir, ever so often you say to me, Brick, I want to have a talk with you, but when we talk, it never materializes. Nothing is said. You sit in a chair and gas about this and that and I look like I listen. I try to look like I listen, but I don't listen, not much. Communication is—awful hard between people an'—somehow between you and me, it just don't—

BIG DADDY: Have you ever been scared? I mean have you ever felt downright terror of something?

(*He gets up.*)

Just one moment. I'm going to close these doors. . . .

(*He closes doors on gallery as if he were going to tell an important secret.*)

BRICK: What?

BIG DADDY: Brick?

BRICK: Huh?

BIG DADDY: Son, I thought I had it!

BRICK: Had what? Had what, Big Daddy?

BIG DADDY: Cancer!

BRICK: Oh . . .

BIG DADDY: I thought the old man made out of bones had laid his cold and heavy hand on my shoulder!

BRICK: Well, Big Daddy, you kept a tight mouth about it.

BIG DADDY: A pig squeals. A man keeps a tight mouth about it, in spite of a man not having a pig's advantage.

BRICK: What advantage is that?

BIG DADDY: Ignorance—of mortality—is a comfort. A man don't have that comfort, he's the only living thing that conceives of death, that knows what it is. The others go without knowing which is the way that anything living should go, go without knowing, without any knowledge of it, and yet a pig squeals, but a man sometimes, he can keep a tight mouth about it. Sometimes he—

(*There is a deep, smoldering ferocity in the old man.*)

—can keep a tight mouth about it. I wonder if—
BRICK: What, Big Daddy?
BIG DADDY: A whiskey highball would injure this spastic condition?
BRICK: No, sir, it might do it good.
BIG DADDY (*grins suddenly, wolfishly*): *Jesus, I can't tell you! The sky is open! Christ, it's open again! It's open, boy, it's open!*

(*Brick looks down at his drink.*)

BRICK: You feel better, Big Daddy?
BIG DADDY: Better? Hell! I can breathe!—All of my life I been like a doubled up fist. . . .

(*He pours a drink.*)

—Poundin', smashin', drivin'!—now I'm going to loosen these doubled up hands and touch things *easy* with them. . . .

(*He spreads his hands as if caressing the air.*)

You know what I'm contemplating?
BRICK (*vaguely*): No, sir. What are you contemplating?
BIG DADDY: Ha ha!—*Pleasure!*—pleasure with *women!*

(*Brick's smile fades a little but lingers.*)

Brick, this stuff burns me!—
—Yes, boy. I'll tell you something that you might not guess. I still have desire for women and this is my sixty-fifth birthday.
BRICK: I think that's mighty remarkable, Big Daddy.
BIG DADDY: Remarkable?

BRICK: *Admirable*, Big Daddy.

BIG DADDY: You're damn right it is, remarkable and admirable both. I realize now that I never had me enough. I let many chances slip by because of scruples about it, scruples, convention—crap. . . . All that stuff is bull, bull, bull!—It took the shadow of death to make me see it. Now that shadow's lifted, I'm going to cut loose and have, what is it they call it, have me a—ball!

BRICK: A ball, huh?

BIG DADDY: That's right, a ball, a ball! Hell!—I slept with Big Mama till, let's see, five years ago, till I was sixty and she was fifty-eight, and never even liked her, never did!

(*The phone has been ringing down the hall. Big Mama enters, exclaiming:*)

BIG MAMA: Don't you men hear that phone ring? I heard it way out on the gall'ry.

BIG DADDY: There's five rooms off this front gall'ry that you could go through. Why do you go through this one?

(*Big Mama makes a playful face as she bustles out the hall door.*)

Hunh!—Why, when Big Mama goes out of a room, I can't remember what that woman looks like, but when Big Mama comes back into the room, boy, then I see what she looks like, and I wish I didn't!

(*Bends over laughing at this joke till it hurts his guts and he straightens with a grimace. The laugh subsides to a chuckle as he puts the liquor glass a little distrustfully down on the table.*
(*Brick has risen and hobbled to the gallery doors.*)

Hey! Where you goin'?

BRICK: Out for a breather.

BIG DADDY: Not yet you ain't. Stay here till this talk is finished, young fellow.

BRICK: I thought it was finished, Big Daddy.

BIG DADDY: It ain't even begun.

BRICK: My mistake. Excuse me. I just wanted to feel that river breeze.

BIG DADDY: Turn on the ceiling fan and set back down in that chair.

(*Big Mama's voice rises, carrying down the hall.*)

BIG MAMA: Miss Sally, you're a case! You're a caution, Miss Sally. Why didn't you give me a chance to explain it to you?

BIG DADDY: Jesus, she's talking to my old maid sister again.

BIG MAMA: Well, goodbye, now, Miss Sally. You come down real soon, Big Daddy's dying to see you! Yaisss, goodbye, Miss Sally. . . .

(*She hangs up and bellows with mirth. Big Daddy groans and covers his ears as she approaches.*
(*Bursting in:*)

Big Daddy, that was Miss Sally callin' from Memphis again! You know what she done, Big Daddy? She called her doctor in Memphis to git him to tell her what that spastic thing is! Ha-*HAAAA!*—And called back to tell me how relieved she was that— Hey! Let me in!

(*Big Daddy has been holding the door half closed against her.*)

BIG DADDY: Naw I ain't. I told you not to come and go through this room. You just back out and go through those five other rooms.

BIG MAMA: Big Daddy? Big Daddy? Oh, big Daddy!—You didn't mean those things you said to me, did you?

(*He shuts door firmly against her but she still calls.*)

Sweetheart? Sweetheart? Big Daddy? You didn't mean those awful things you said to me?—I know you didn't. I know you didn't mean those things in your heart. . . .

(*The childlike voice fades with a sob and her heavy footsteps retreat down the hall. Brick has risen once more on his crutches and starts for the gallery again.*)

BIG DADDY: All I ask of that woman is that she leave me alone. But she can't admit to herself that she makes me sick. That comes of having slept with her too many years. Should of quit much sooner but that old woman she never got enough of it—and I was good in bed . . . I never should of wasted so much of it on her. . . . They say you got just so many and each one is numbered. Well, I got a few left in me, a few, and I'm going to pick me a good one to spend 'em on! I'm going to pick me a choice one, I don't care how much she costs, I'll smother her in—minks! Ha ha! I'll strip her naked and smother her in minks and choke her with diamonds! Ha ha! I'll strip her naked and choke her with diamonds and smother her with minks and hump her from hell to breakfast. *Ha aha ha ha ha!*

MAE (*gaily at door*): Who's that laughin' in there?

GOOPER: Is Big Daddy laughin' in there?

BIG DADDY: Crap!—them two—*drips.* . . .

(*He goes over and touches Brick's shoulder.*)

Yes, son. Brick, boy.—I'm—*happy!* I'm happy, son, I'm happy!

(*He chokes a little and bits his under lip, pressing his head quickly, shyly against his son's head and then, coughing with embarrassment, goes uncertainly back to the table where he set down the glass. He drinks and makes a grimace as it burns his guts. Brick sighs and rises with effort.*)

What makes you so restless? Have you got ants in your britches?

BRICK: Yes, sir . . .

BIG DADDY: Why?

BRICK: —Something—hasn't—happened. . . .

BIG DADDY: Yeah? What is that!

BRICK (*sadly*): —the click. . . .

BIG DADDY: Did you say click?

BRICK: Yes, click.

BIG DADDY: What click?

BRICK: A click that I get in my head that makes me peaceful.

BIG DADDY: I sure in hell don't know what you're talking about, but it disturbs me.

BRICK: It's just a mechanical thing.

BIG DADDY: What is a mechanical thing?

BRICK: This click that I get in my head that makes me peaceful. I got to drink till I get it. It's just a mechanical thing, something like a—like a—like a—

BIG DADDY: Like a—

BRICK: Switch clicking off in my head, turning the hot light off and the cool night on and—

(*He looks up, smiling sadly.*)

—all of a sudden there's—peace!

BIG DADDY (*whistles long and soft with astonishment; he goes back to Brick and clasps his son's two shoulders*): Jesus! I didn't know it had gotten that bad with you. Why, boy, you're—*alcoholic!*

BRICK: That's the truth, Big Daddy. I'm alcoholic.

BIG DADDY: This shows how I—let things go!

BRICK: I have to hear that little click in my head that makes me peaceful. Usually I hear it sooner than this, sometimes as early as—noon, but—

    —Today it's—dilatory. . . .

    —I just haven't got the right level of alcohol in my bloodstream yet!

(*This last statement is made with energy as he freshens his drink.*)

BIG DADDY: Uh—huh. Expecting death made me blind. I didn't have no idea that a son of mine was turning into a drunkard under my nose.

BRICK (*gently*): Well, now you do, Big Daddy, the news has penetrated.

BIG DADDY: UH-huh, yes, now I do, the news has—penetrated. . . .

BRICK: And so if you'll excuse me—

BIG DADDY: No, I won't excuse you.

BRICK: —I'd better sit by myself till I hear that click in my head, it's just a mechanical thing but it don't happen except when I'm alone or talking to no one. . . .

BIG DADDY: You got a long, long time to sit still, boy, and talk to no one, but now you're talkin' to me. At least I'm talking to you. And you set there and listen until I tell you the conversation is over!

BRICK: But this talk is like all the others we've ever had together in our lives! It's nowhere, nowhere!—it's—it's *painful*, Big Daddy. . . .

BIG DADDY: All right, then let it be painful, but don't you move from that chair!—I'm going to remove that crutch. . . .

(*He seizes the crutch and tosses it across room.*)

BRICK: I can hop on one foot, and if I fall, I can crawl!

BIG DADDY: If you ain't careful you're gonna crawl off this plantation and then, by Jesus, you'll have to hustle your drinks along Skid Row!

BRICK: That'll come, Big Daddy.

BIG DADDY: Naw, it won't. You're my son and I'm going to straighten you out; now that *I'm* straightened out, I'm going to straighten out you!

BRICK: Yeah?

BIG DADDY: Today the report come in from Ochsner Clinic. Y'know what they told me?

(*His face glows with triumph.*)

The only thing that they could detect with all the instruments of science in that great hospital is a little spastic condition of the colon! And nerves torn to pieces by all that worry about it.

(*A little girl bursts into room with a sparkler clutched in each fist, hops and shrieks like a monkey gone mad and rushes back out again as Big Daddy strikes at her.*
(*Silence. The two men stare at each other. A woman laughs gaily outside.*)

I want you to know I breathed a sigh of relief almost as powerful as the Vicksburg tornado!

BRICK: You weren't ready to go?

BIG DADDY: GO WHERE?—crap. . . .

—When you are gone from here, boy, you are long gone and no where! The human machine is not no different from the animal machine or the fish machine or the bird machine or the reptile machine or the insect machine! It's just a whole God damn lot more complicated and consequently more trouble to keep together. Yep. I thought I had it. The earth shook under my foot, the sky come down like the black lid of a kettle and I couldn't breathe!—

Today!!—that lid was lifted, I drew my first free breath in—
how many years?—*God!*—*three.* . . .

(*There is laughter outside, running footsteps, the soft, plushy
sound and light of exploding rockets.*

(*Brick stares at him soberly for a long moment; then makes
a sort of startled sound in his nostrils and springs up on one
foot and hops across the room to grab his crutch, swinging on
the furniture for support. He gets the crutch and flees as if in
horror for the gallery. His father seizes him by the sleeve of his
white silk pajamas.*)

Stay here, you son of a bitch!—till I say go!

BRICK: I can't.

BIG DADDY: You sure in hell will, God damn it.

BRICK: No, I can't. We talk, you talk, in—circles! We get no
where, no where! It's always the same, you say you want to
talk to me and don't have a ruttin' thing to say to me!

BIG DADDY: Nothin' to say when I'm tellin' you I'm going to
live when I thought I was dying?!

BRICK: Oh—*that!*—Is that what you have to say to me?

BIG DADDY: Why, you son of a bitch! Ain't that, ain't that—
important?!

BRICK: Well, you said that, that's said, and now I—

BIG DADDY: Now you set back down.

BRICK: You're all balled up, you—

BIG DADDY: I ain't balled up!

BRICK: You are, you're all balled up!

BIG DADDY: Don't tell me what I am, you drunken whelp!
I'm going to tear this coat sleeve off if you don't set
down!

BRICK: Big Daddy—

BIG DADDY: Do what I tell you! I'm the boss here, now! I
want you to know I'm back in the driver's seat now!

(*Big Mama rushes in, clutching her great heaving bosom.*)

What in hell do you want in here, Big Mama?

BIG MAMA: Oh, Big Daddy! Why are you shouting like that?
I just cain't *stainnnnnnnd*—it. . . .

BIG DADDY (*raising the back of his hand above his head*): GIT!
—outa here.

(*She rushes back out, sobbing.*)

BRICK (*softly, sadly*): *Christ.* . . .
BIG DADDY (*fiercely*): Yeah! Christ!—is right . . .

> (*Brick breaks loose and hobbles toward the gallery.*
> (*Big Daddy jerks his crutch from under Brick so he steps with the injured ankle. He utters a hissing cry of anguish, clutches a chair and pulls it over on top of him on the floor.*)

Son of a—tub of—hog fat. . . .
BRICK: Big Daddy! Give me my crutch.

> (*Big Daddy throws the crutch out of reach.*)

Give me that crutch, Big Daddy.
BIG DADDY: Why do you drink?
BRICK: Don't know, give me my crutch!
BIG DADDY: You better think why you drink or give up drinking!
BRICK: Will you please give me my crutch so I can get up off this floor?
BIG DADDY: First you answer my question. Why do you drink? Why are you throwing your life away, boy, like somethin' disgusting you picked up on the street?
BRICK (*getting onto his knees*): Big Daddy, I'm in pain, I stepped on that foot.
BIG DADDY: Good! I'm glad you're not too numb with the liquor in you to feel some pain!
BRICK: You—spilled my—drink . . .
BIG DADDY: I'll make a bargain with you. You tell me why you drink and I'll hand you one. I'll pour you the liquor myself and hand it to you.
BRICK: Why do I drink?
BIG DADDY: Yea! Why?
BRICK: Give me a drink and I'll tell you.
BIG DADDY: Tell me first!
BRICK: I'll tell you in one word.
BIG DADDY: What word?
BRICK: DISGUST!

> (*The clock chimes softly, sweetly. Big Daddy gives it a short, outraged glance.*)

Now how about that drink?

BIG DADDY: What are you disgusted with? You got to tell me that, first. Otherwise being disgusted don't make no sense!

BRICK: Give me my crutch.

BIG DADDY: You heard me, you got to tell me what I asked you first.

BRICK: I told you, I said to kill my disgust!

BIG DADDY: DISGUST WITH WHAT!

BRICK: You strike a hard bargain.

BIG DADDY: What are you disgusted with?—an' I'll pass you the liquor.

BRICK: I can hop on one foot, and if I fall, I can crawl.

BIG DADDY: You want liquor that bad?

BRICK (*dragging himself up, clinging to bedstead*): Yeah, I want it that bad.

BIG DADDY: If I give you a drink, will you tell me what it is you're disgusted with, Brick?

BRICK: Yes, sir, I will try to.

(*The old man pours him a drink and solemnly passes it to him.*

(*There is silence as Brick drinks.*)

Have you ever heard the word "mendacity"?

BIG DADDY: Sure. Mendacity is one of them five dollar words that cheap politicians throw back and forth at each other.

BRICK: You know what it means?

BIG DADDY: Don't it mean lying and liars?

BRICK: Yes, sir, lying and liars.

BIG DADDY: Has someone been lying to you?

CHILDREN (*chanting in chorus offstage*):
    We want Big Dad-dee!
    We want Big Dad-dee!

(*Gooper appears in the gallery door.*)

GOOPER: Big Daddy, the kiddies are shouting for you out there.

BIG DADDY (*fiercely*): Keep out, Gooper!

GOOPER: 'Scuse *me!*

(*Big Daddy slams the doors after Gooper.*)

BIG DADDY: Who's been lying to you, has Margaret been lying to you, has your wife been lying to you about something, Brick?

BRICK: Not her. That wouldn't matter.

BIG DADDY: Then who's been lying to you, and what about?

BRICK: No one single person and no one lie. . . .

BIG DADDY: Then what, what then, for Christ's sake?

BRICK: —The whole, the whole—thing. . . .

BIG DADDY: Why are you rubbing your head? You got a headache?

BRICK: No, I'm tryin' to—

BIG DADDY: —Concentrate, but you can't because your brain's all soaked with liquor, is that the trouble? Wet brain!

(*He snatches the glass from Brick's hand.*)

What do you know about this mendacity thing? Hell! I could write a book on it! Don't you know that? I could write a book on it and still not cover the subject? Well, I could, I could write a goddam book on it and still not cover the subject anywhere near enough!!—Think of all the lies I got to put up with!—Pretenses! Ain't that mendacity? Having to pretend stuff you don't think or feel or have any idea of? Having for instance to act like I care for Big Mama!—I haven't been able to stand the sight, sound, or smell of that woman for forty years now!—even when I *laid* her!—regular as a piston. . . .

Pretend to love that son of a bitch of a Gooper and his wife Mae and those five same screechers out there like parrots in a jungle? Jesus! Can't stand to look at 'em!

Church!—it bores the Bejesus out of me but I go!—I go an' sit there and listen to the fool preacher!

Clubs!—Elks! Masons! Rotary!—*crap!*

(*A spasm of pain makes him clutch his belly. He sinks into a chair and his voice is softer and hoarser.*)

You I *do* like for some reason, did always have some kind of real feeling for—affection—respect—yes, always. . . .

You and being a success as a planter is all I ever had any devotion to in my whole life!—and that's the truth. . . .

I don't know why, but it is!

I've lived with mendacity!—Why can't *you* live with it? Hell, you *got* to live with it, there's nothing *else* to *live* with except mendacity, is there?

BRICK: Yes, sir. Yes, sir there is something else that you can live with!

BIG DADDY: What?

BRICK (*lifting his glass*): This!—Liquor. . . .

BIG DADDY: That's not living, that's dodging away from life.

BRICK: I want to dodge away from it.

BIG DADDY: Then why don't you kill yourself, man?

BRICK: I like to drink. . . .

BIG DADDY: Oh, God, I can't talk to you. . . .

BRICK: I'm sorry, Big Daddy.

BIG DADDY: Not as sorry as I am. I'll tell you something. A little while back when I thought my number was up—

(*This speech should have torrential pace and fury.*)

—before I found out it was just this—spastic—colon. I thought about you. Should I or should I not, if the jig was up, give you this place when I go—since I hate Gooper an' Mae an' know that they hate me, and since all five same monkeys are little Maes an' Goopers.—And I thought, No!—Then I thought, Yes!—I couldn't make up my mind. I hate Gooper and his five same monkeys and that bitch Mae! Why should I turn over twenty-eight thousand acres of the richest land this side of the valley Nile to not my kind?—But why in hell, on the other hand, Brick—should I subsidize a goddam fool on the bottle?—Liked or not liked, well, maybe even—*loved!*—Why should I do that?— Subsidize worthless behavior? Rot? Corruption?

BRICK (*smiling*): I understand.

BIG DADDY: Well, if you do, you're smarter than I am, God damn it, because I don't understand. And this I will tell you frankly. I didn't make up my mind at all on that question and still to this day I ain't made out no will!—Well, now I don't *have* to. The pressure is gone. I can just wait and see if you pull yourself together or if you don't.

BRICK: That's right, Big Daddy.

BIG DADDY: You sound like you thought I was kidding.

BRICK (*rising*): No, sir, I know you're not kidding.

BIG DADDY: But you don't care—?

BRICK (*hobbling toward the gallery door*): No, sir, I don't care. . . .

Now how about taking a look at your birthday fireworks and getting some of that cool breeze off the river?

(*He stands in the gallery doorway as the night sky turns pink and green and gold with successive flashes of light.*)

BIG DADDY: *WAIT!*—Brick. . . .

(*His voice drops. Suddenly there is something shy, almost tender, in his restraining gesture.*)

Don't let's—leave it like this, like them other talks we've had, we've always—talked around things, we've—just talked around things for some rutten reason, I don't know what, it's always like something was left not spoken, something avoided because neither of us was honest enough with the —other. . . .

BRICK: I never lied to you, Big Daddy.

BIG DADDY: Did I ever to *you*?

BRICK: No, sir. . . .

BIG DADDY: Then there is at least two people that never lied to each other.

BRICK: But we've never *talked* to each other.

BIG DADDY: We can *now*.

BRICK: Big Daddy, there don't seem to be anything much to say.

BIG DADDY: You say that you drink to kill your disgust with lying.

BRICK: You said to give you a reason.

BIG DADDY: Is liquor the only thing that'll kill this disgust?

BRICK: Now. Yes.

BIG DADDY: But not once, huh?

BRICK: Not when I was still young an' believing. A drinking man's someone who wants to forget he isn't still young an' believing.

BIG DADDY: Believing what?

BRICK: Believing. . . .

BIG DADDY: Believing *what*?

BRICK (*stubbornly evasive*): Believing. . . .

BIG DADDY: I don't know what the hell you mean by believing and I don't think you know what you mean by believing, but if you still got sports in your blood, go back to sports announcing and—

BRICK: Sit in a glass box watching games I can't play? Describing what I can't do while players do it? Sweating out their disgust and confusion in contests I'm not fit for? Drinkin' a coke, half bourbon, so I can stand it? That's no goddam good any more, no help—time just outran me, Big Daddy—got there first . . .

BIG DADDY: I think you're passing the buck.

BRICK: You know many drinkin' men?

BIG DADDY (*with a slight, charming smile*): I have known a fair number of that species.

BRICK: Could any of them tell you why he drank?

BIG DADDY: Yep, you're passin' the buck to things like time and disgust with "mendacity" and—crap!—if you got to use that kind of language about a thing, it's ninety-proof bull, and I'm not buying any.

BRICK: I had to give you a reason to get a drink!

BIG DADDY: You started drinkin' when your friend Skipper died.

(*Silence for five beats. Then Brick makes a startled movement, reaching for his crutch.*)

BRICK: What are you suggesting?

BIG DADDY: I'm suggesting nothing.

(*The shuffle and clop of Brick's rapid hobble away from his father's steady, grave attention.*)

—But Gooper an' Mae suggested that there was something not right exactly in your—

BRICK (*stopping short downstage as if backed to a wall*): "Not right"?

BIG DADDY: Not, well, exactly *normal* in your friendship with—

BRICK: They suggested that, too? I thought that was Maggie's suggestion.

(Brick's detachment is at last broken through. His heart is accelerated; his forehead sweat-beaded; his breath becomes more rapid and his voice hoarse. The thing they're discussing, timidly and painfully on the side of Big Daddy, fiercely, violently on Brick's side, is the inadmissible thing that Skipper died to disavow between them. The fact that if it existed it had to be disavowed to "keep face" in the world they lived in, may be at the heart of the "mendacity" that Brick drinks to kill his disgust with. It may be the root of his collapse. Or maybe it is only a single manifestation of it, not even the most important. The bird that I hope to catch in the net of this play is not the solution of one man's psychological problem. I'm trying to catch the true quality of experience in a group of people, that cloudy, flickering, evanescent—fiercely charged! —interplay of live human beings in the thundercloud of a common crisis. Some mystery should be left in the revelation of character in a play, just as a great deal of mystery is always left in the revelation of character in life, even in one's own character to himself. This does not absolve the playwright of his duty to observe and probe as clearly and deeply as he legitimately can: but it should steer him away from "pat" conclusions, facile definitions which make a play just a play, not a snare for the truth of human experience.

(The following scene should be played with great concentration, with most of the power leashed but palpable in what is left unspoken.)

Who else's suggestion is it, is it *yours?* How many others thought that Skipper and I were—

BIG DADDY (*gently*): Now, hold on, hold on a minute, son.— I knocked around in my time.

BRICK: What's that got to do with—

BIG DADDY: I said 'Hold on!'—I bummed, I bummed this country till I was—

BRICK: Whose suggestion, who else's suggestion is it?

BIG DADDY: Slept in hobo jungles and railroad Y's and flophouses in all cities before I—

BRICK: Oh, *you* think so, too, you call me your son and a queer. Oh! Maybe that's why you put Maggie and me in this room that was Jack Straw's and Peter Ochello's, in which that pair of old sisters slept in a double bed where both of 'em died!

BIG DADDY: *Now just don't go throwing rocks at—*

(*Suddenly Reverend Tooker appears in the gallery doors, his head slightly, playfully, fatuously cocked, with a practised clergyman's smile, sincere as a bird-call blown on a hunter's whistle, the living embodiment of the pious, conventional lie.*

(*Big Daddy gasps a little at this perfectly timed, but incongruous, apparition.*)

—What're you lookin' for, Preacher?

REVEREND TOOKER: The gentleman's lavatory, ha ha!—heh, heh . . .

BIG DADDY (*with strained courtesy*): —Go back out and walk down to the other end of the gallery, Reverend Tooker, and use the bathroom connected with my bedroom, and if you can't find it, ask them where it is!

REVEREND TOOKER: Ah, thanks.

(*He goes out with a deprecatory chuckle.*)

BIG DADDY: It's hard to talk in this place . . .

BRICK: Son of a—!

BIG DADDY (*leaving a lot unspoken*): —I seen all things and understood a lot of them, till 1910. Christ, the year that— I had worn my shoes through, hocked my— I hopped off a yellow dog freight car half a mile down the road, slept in a wagon of cotton outside the gin— Jack Straw an' Peter Ochello took me in. Hired me to manage this place which grew into this one.—When Jack Straw died—why, old Peter Ochello quit eatin' like a dog does when its master's dead, and died, too!

BRICK: Christ!

BIG DADDY: I'm just saying I understand such—

BRICK (*violently*): Skipper is dead. I have not quit eating!

BIG DADDY: No, but you started drinking.

(*Brick wheels on his crutch and hurls his glass across the room shouting.*)

BRICK: YOU THINK SO, TOO?

BIG DADDY: *Shhh!*

(*Footsteps run on the gallery. There are women's calls.*
(*Big Daddy goes toward the door.*)

Go way!—Just broke a glass. . . .

(*Brick is transformed, as if a quiet mountain blew suddenly up in volcanic flame.*)

BRICK: You think so, too? You think so, too? You think me an' Skipper did, did, did!—*sodomy!*—together?

BIG DADDY: Hold—!

BRICK: That what you—

BIG DADDY: —*ON*—a minute!

BRICK: You think we did dirty things between us, Skipper an'—

BIG DADDY: Why are you shouting like that? Why are you—

BRICK: —Me, is that what you think of Skipper, is that—

BIG DADDY: —so excited? I don't think nothing. I don't know nothing. I'm simply telling you what—

BRICK: You think that Skipper and me were a pair of dirty old men?

BIG DADDY: Now that's—

BRICK: Straw? Ochello? A couple of—

BIG DADDY: Now just—

BRICK: —ducking sissies? Queers? Is that what you—

BIG DADDY: Shhh.

BRICK: —think?

(*He loses his balance and pitches to his knees without noticing the pain. He grabs the bed and drags himself up.*)

BIG DADDY: Jesus!—Whew. . . . Grab my hand!

BRICK: Naw, I don't want your hand. . . .

BIG DADDY: Well, I want yours. Git up!

(*He draws him up, keeps an arm about him with concern and affection.*)

You broken out in a sweat! You're panting like you'd run a race with—

BRICK (*freeing himself from his father's hold*): Big Daddy, you shock me, Big Daddy, you, you—*shock* me! Talkin' so—

(*He turns away from his father.*)

—casually!—about a—thing like that . . .

—Don't you know how people *feel* about things like that? How, how *disgusted* they are by things like that? Why, at Ole Miss when it was discovered a pledge to our fraternity, Skipper's and mine, did a, *attempted* to do a, unnatural thing with—

We not only dropped him like a hot rock!—We told him to git off the campus, and he did, he got!—All the way to—

(*He halts, breathless.*)

BIG DADDY: —Where?

BRICK: —North Africa, last I heard!

BIG DADDY: Well, I have come back from further away than that, I have just now returned from the other side of the moon, death's country, son, and I'm not easy to shock by anything here.

(*He comes downstage and faces out.*)

Always, anyhow, lived with too much space around me to be infected by ideas of other people. One thing you can grow on a big place more important than cotton!—is *tolerance!*—I grown it.

(*He returns toward Brick.*)

BRICK: Why can't exceptional friendship, *real, real, deep, deep friendship!* between two men be respected as something clean and decent without being thought of as—

BIG DADDY: It can, it is, for God's sake.

BRICK: —*Fairies.* . . .

(*In his utterance of this word, we gauge the wide and profound reach of the conventional mores he got from the world that crowned him with early laurel.*)

BIG DADDY: I told Mae an' Gooper—

BRICK: Frig Mae and Gooper, frig all dirty lies and liars!—Skipper and me had a clean, true thing between us!—had a clean friendship, practically all our lives, till Maggie got the idea you're talking about. Normal? No!—It was too rare to be normal, any true thing between two people is too rare

to be normal. Oh, once in a while he put his hand on my
shoulder or I'd put mine on his, oh, maybe even, when
we were touring the country in pro-football an' shared
hotel-rooms we'd reach across the space between the two
beds and shake hands to say goodnight, yeah, one or two
times we—

BIG DADDY: Brick, nobody thinks that that's not normal!

BRICK: Well, they're mistaken, it was! It was a pure an' true
thing an' that's not normal.

(*They both stare straight at each other for a long moment. The
tension breaks and both turn away as if tired.*)

BIG DADDY: Yeah, it's—hard t'—talk. . . .

BRICK: All right, then, let's—let it go. . . .

BIG DADDY: Why did Skipper crack up? Why have you?

(*Brick looks back at his father again. He has already decided,
without knowing that he has made this decision, that he is going to tell his father that he is dying of cancer. Only this could
even the score between them: one inadmissible thing in return
for another.*)

BRICK (*ominously*): All right. You're asking for it, Big Daddy.
We're finally going to have the real true talk you wanted.
It's too late to stop it, now, we got to carry it through and
cover every subject.

(*He hobbles back to the liquor cabinet.*)

Uh-huh.

(*He opens the ice bucket and picks up the silver tongs with slow
admiration of their frosty brightness.*)

Maggie declares that Skipper and I went into pro-football
after we left "Ole Miss" because we were scared to grow
up . . .

(*He moves downstage with the shuffle and clop of a cripple on
a crutch. As Margaret did when her speech became "recita-
tive," he looks out into the house, commanding its attention by
his direct, concentrated gaze—a broken, "tragically elegant"
figure telling simply as much as he knows of "the Truth":*)

—Wanted to— keep on tossing—those long, long!—high, high!—passes that—couldn't be intercepted except by time, the aerial attack that made us famous! And so we did, we did, we kept it up for one season, that aerial attack, we held it high!—Yeah, but—

—that summer, Maggie, she laid the law down to me, said, Now or never, and so I married Maggie. . . .

BIG DADDY: How was Maggie in bed?

BRICK (*wryly*): Great! the greatest!

(*Big Daddy nods as if he thought so.*)

She went on the road that fall with the Dixie Stars. Oh, she made a great show of being the world's best sport. She wore a—wore a—tall bearskin cap! A shako, they call it, a dyed moleskin coat, a moleskin coat dyed red!—Cut up crazy! Rented hotel ballrooms for victory celebrations, wouldn't cancel them when it—turned out—defeat. . . .

MAGGIE THE CAT! Ha ha!

(*Big Daddy nods.*)

—But Skipper, he had some fever which came back on him which doctors couldn't explain and I got that injury— turned out to be just a shadow on the X-ray plate—and a touch of bursitis. . . .

I lay in a hospital bed, watched our games on TV, saw Maggie on the bench next to Skipper when he was hauled out of a game for stumbles, fumbles!—Burned me up the way she hung on his arm!—Y'know, I think that Maggie had always felt sort of left out because she and me never got any closer together than two people just get in bed, which is not much closer than two cats on a—fence humping. . . .

So! She took this time to work on poor dumb Skipper. He was a less than average student at Ole Miss, you know that, don't you?!—Poured in his mind the dirty, false idea that what we were, him and me, was a frustrated case of that ole pair of sisters that lived in this room, Jack Straw and Peter Ochello!—He, poor Skipper, went to bed with Maggie to prove it wasn't true, and when it didn't work out, he thought it *was* true!—Skipper broke in two like a rotten stick—nobody ever turned so fast to a lush—or died of it so quick. . . .

—Now are you satisfied?

(*Big Daddy has listened to this story, dividing the grain from the chaff. Now he looks at his son.*)

BIG DADDY: Are *you* satisfied?

BRICK: With what?

BIG DADDY: That half-ass story!

BRICK: What's half-ass about it?

BIG DADDY: Something's left out of that story. What did you leave out?

(*The phone has started ringing in the hall. As if it reminded him of something, Brick glances suddenly toward the sound and says:*)

BRICK: Yes!—I left out a long-distance call which I had from Skipper,—in which he made a drunken confession to me and on which I hung up!—last time we spoke to each other in our lives. . . .

(*Muted ring stops as someone answers phone in a soft, indistinct voice in hall.*)

BIG DADDY: You hung up?

BRICK: Hung up. Jesus! Well—

BIG DADDY: Anyhow now!—we have tracked down the lie with which you're disgusted and which you are drinking to kill your disgust with, Brick. You been passing the buck. This disgust with mendacity is disgust with yourself.

You!—dug the grave of your friend and kicked him in it! —before you'd face truth with him!

BRICK: *His* truth, not *mine*!

BIG DADDY: His truth, okay! But you wouldn't face it with him!

BRICK: Who *can* face truth? Can *you*?

BIG DADDY: Now don't start passin' the rotten buck again, boy!

BRICK: *How about these birthday congratulations, these many, many happy returns of the day, when ev'rybody but you knows there won't be any!*

(*Whoever has answered the hall phone lets out a high, shrill laugh; the voice becomes audible saying: "no, no, you got it all wrong! Upside down! Are you crazy?"*

(*Brick suddenly catches his breath as he realized that he has made a shocking disclosure. He hobbles a few paces, then freezes, and without looking at his father's shocked face, says:*)

Let's, let's—go out, now, and—

(*Big Daddy moves suddenly forward and grabs hold of the boy's crutch like it was a weapon for which they were fighting for possession.*)

BIG DADDY: Oh, no, no! No one's going out! What did you start to say?

BRICK: I don't remember.

BIG DADDY: "Many happy returns when they know there won't be any"?

BRICK: Aw, hell, Big Daddy, forget it. Come on out on the gallery and look at the fireworks they're shooting off for your birthday. . . .

BIG DADDY: First you finish that remark you were makin' before you cut off. "Many happy returns when they know there won't be any"?—Ain't that what you just said?

BRICK: Look, now. I can get around without that crutch if I have to but it would be a lot easier on the furniture an' glassware if I didn' have to go swinging along like Tarzan of th'—

BIG DADDY: FINISH! WHAT YOU WAS SAYIN'!

(*An eerie green glow shows in sky behind him.*)

BRICK (*sucking the ice in his glass, speech becoming thick*): Leave th' place to Gooper and Mae an' their five little same little monkeys. All I want is—

BIG DADDY: "LEAVE TH' PLACE," did you say?

BRICK (*vaguely*): All twenty-eight thousand acres of the richest land this side of the valley Nile.

BIG DADDY: Who said I was "leaving the place" to Gooper or anybody? This is my sixty-fifth birthday! I got fifteen years or twenty years left in me! I'll outlive *you*! I'll bury you an' have to pay for your coffin!

BRICK: Sure. Many happy returns. Now let's go watch the fireworks, come on, let's—

BIG DADDY: Lying, have they been lying? About the report from th'—clinic? Did they, did they—find something?— *Cancer.* Maybe?

BRICK: Mendacity is a system that we live in. Liquor is one way out an' death's the other. . . .

> (*He takes the crutch from Big Daddy's loose grip and swings out on the gallery leaving the doors open.*
> (*A song, "Pick a Bale of Cotton," is heard.*)

MAE (*appearing in door*): Oh, Big Daddy, the field-hands are singin' fo' you!

BIG DADDY (*shouting hoarsely*): BRICK! BRICK!

MAE: He's outside drinkin', Big Daddy.

BIG DADDY: *BRICK!*

> (*Mae retreats, awed by the passion of his voice. Children call Brick in tones mocking Big Daddy. His face crumbles like broken yellow plaster about to fall into dust.*
> (*There is a glow in the sky. Brick swings back through the doors, slowly, gravely, quite soberly.*)

BRICK: I'm sorry, Big Daddy. My head don't work any more and it's hard for me to understand how anybody could care if he lived or died or was dying or cared about anything but whether or not there was liquor left in the bottle and so I said what I said without thinking. In some ways I'm no better than the others, in some ways worse because I'm less alive. Maybe it's being alive that makes them lie, and being almost *not* alive makes me sort of accidentally truthful—I don't know but—anyway—we've been friends . . .

—And being friends is telling each other the truth. . . .

(*There is a pause.*)

You told *me*! I told *you*!

(*A child rushes into the room and grabs a fistful of firecrackers and runs out again.*)

CHILD (*screaming*): Bang, bang, bang, bang, bang, bang, bang, bang, bang!

BIG DADDY (*slowly and passionately*): CHRIST—DAMN—ALL—LYING SONS OF—LYING BITCHES!

(*He straightens at last and crosses to the inside door. At the door he turns and looks back as if he had some desperate question he couldn't put into words. Then he nods reflectively and says in a hoarse voice:*)

Yes, all liars, all liars, all lying dying liars!

(*This is said slowly, slowly, with a fierce revulsion. He goes on out.*)

—Lying! Dying! Liars!

(*His voice dies out. There is the sound of a child being slapped. It rushes, hideously bawling, through room and out the hall door.*

(*Brick remains motionless as the lights dim out and the curtain falls.*)

Curtain

ACT THREE

There is no lapse of time.
Mae enters with Reverend Tooker.

MAE: Where is Big Daddy! Big Daddy?

BIG MAMA (*entering*): Too much smell of burnt fireworks makes me feel a little bit sick at my stomach.—Where is Big Daddy?

MAE: That's what I want to know, where has Big Daddy gone?

BIG MAMA: He must have turned in, I reckon he went to baid. . . .

(*Gooper enters.*)

GOOPER: Where is Big Daddy?

MAE: We don't know where he is!

BIG MAMA: I reckon he's gone to baid.

GOOPER: Well, then, now we can talk.

BIG MAMA: What *is* this talk, *what* talk?

(*Margaret appears on gallery, talking to Dr. Baugh.*)

MARGARET (*musically*): My family freed their slaves ten years before abolition, my great-great grandfather gave his slaves their freedom five years before the war between the States started!

MAE: Oh, for God's sake! Maggie's climbed back up in her family tree!

MARGARET (*sweetly*): What, Mae?—Oh, where's Big Daddy?!

(*The pace must be very quick. Great Southern animation.*)

BIG MAMA (*addressing them all*): I think Big Daddy was just worn out. He loves his family, he loves to have them around him, but it's a strain on his nerves. He wasn't himself tonight, Big Daddy wasn't himself, I could tell he was all worked up.

REVEREND TOOKER: I think he's remarkable.

BIG MAMA: Yaisss! Just remarkable. Did you all notice the food he ate at that table? Did you all notice the supper he put away? Why, he ate like a hawss!

GOOPER: I hope he doesn't regret it.

BIG MAMA: Why, that man—ate a huge piece of cawn-bread with molasses on it! Helped himself twice to hoppin' john.

MARGARET: Big Daddy loves hoppin' john.—We had a real country dinner.

BIG MAMA (*overlapping Margaret*): Yais, he simply adores it! An' candied yams? That man put away enough food at that table to stuff a nigger *field*-hand!

GOOPER (*with grim relish*): I hope he don't have to pay for it later on. . . .

BIG MAMA (*fiercely*): What's *that*, Gooper?

MAE: Gooper says he hopes Big Daddy doesn't suffer tonight.

BIG MAMA: Oh, shoot, Gooper says, Gooper says! Why should Big Daddy suffer for satisfying a normal appetite? There's nothin' wrong with that man but nerves, he's sound as a dollar! And now he knows he is an' that's why he ate such a supper. He had a big load off his mind, knowin' he wasn't doomed t'—what he thought he was doomed to. . . .

MARGARET (*sadly and sweetly*): Bless his old sweet soul. . . .

BIG MAMA (*vaguely*): Yais, bless his heart, wher's Brick?

MAE: Outside.

GOOPER: —Drinkin' . . .

BIG MAMA: I know he's drinkin'. You all don't have to keep tellin' *me* Brick is drinkin'. Cain't I see he's drinkin' without you continually tellin' me that boy's drinkin'?

MARGARET: Good for you, Big Mama!

(*She applauds.*)

BIG MAMA: Other people *drink* and *have* drunk an' will *drink*, as long as they make that stuff an' put it in bottles.

MARGARET: That's the truth. I never trusted a man that didn't drink.

MAE: Gooper never drinks. Don't you trust Gooper?

MARGARET: Why, Gooper, don't you drink? If I'd known you didn't drink, I wouldn't of made that remark—

BIG MAMA: *Brick?*

MARGARET: —at least not in your presence.

(*She laughs sweetly.*)

BIG MAMA: *Brick!*

MARGARET: He's still on the gall'ry. I'll go bring him in so we can talk.

BIG MAMA (*worriedly*): I don't know what this mysterious family conference is about.

(*Awkward silence. Big Mama looks from face to face, then belches slightly and mutters, "Excuse me. . . ." She opens an ornamental fan suspended about her throat, a black lace fan to go with her black lace gown and fans her wilting corsage, sniffing nervously and looking from face to face in the uncomfortable silence as Margaret calls "Brick?" and Brick sings to the moon on the gallery.*)

I don't know what's wrong here, you all have such long faces! Open that door on the hall and let some air circulate through here, will you please, Gooper?

MAE: I think we'd better leave that door closed, Big Mama, till after the talk.

BIG MAMA: Reveren' Tooker, will *you* please open that door?!

REVEREND TOOKER: I sure will, Big Mama.

MAE: I just didn't think we ought t' take any chance of Big Daddy hearin' a word of this discussion.

BIG MAMA: *I swan!* Nothing's going to be said in Big Daddy's house that he cain't hear if he wants to!

GOOPER: Well, Big Mama, it's—

(*Mae gives him a quick, hard poke to shut him up. He glares at her fiercely as she circles before him like a burlesque ballerina, raising her skinny bare arms over her head, jangling her bracelets, exclaiming:*)

MAE: *A breeze! A breeze!*

REVEREND TOOKER: I think this house is the coolest house in the Delta.—Did you all know that Halsey Banks' widow put air-conditioning units in the church and rectory at Friar's Point in memory of Halsey?

(*General conversation has resumed; everybody is chatting so that the stage sounds like a big bird-cage.*)

GOOPER: Too bad nobody cools your church off for you. I bet you sweat in that pulpit these hot Sundays, Reverend Tooker.

REVEREND TOOKER: Yes, my vestments are drenched.

MAE (*at the same time to Dr. Baugh*): You think those vitamin B_{12} injections are what they're cracked up t' be, Doc Baugh?

DOCTOR BAUGH: Well, if you want to be stuck with something I guess they're as good to be stuck with as anything else.

BIG MAMA (*at gallery door*): *Maggie, Maggie, aren't you comin' with Brick?*

MAE (*suddenly and loudly, creating a silence*): *I have a strange feeling, I have a peculiar feeling!*

BIG MAMA (*turning from gallery*): What feeling?

MAE: That Brick said somethin' he shouldn't of said t' Big Daddy.

BIG MAMA: Now what on earth could Brick of said t' Big Daddy that he shouldn't say?

GOOPER: Big Mama, there's somethin'—

MAE: NOW, WAIT!

(*She rushes up to Big Mama and gives her a quick hug and kiss. Big Mama pushes her impatiently off as the Reverend Tooker's voice rises serenely in a little pocket of silence:*)

REVEREND TOOKER: Yes, last Sunday the gold in my chasuble faded into th' purple. . . .

GOOPER: Reveren' you must of been preachin' hell's fire last Sunday!

(*He guffaws at this witticism but the Reverend is not sincerely amused. At the same time Big Mama has crossed over to Dr. Baugh and is saying to him:*)

BIG MAMA (*her breathless voice rising high-pitched above the others*): In my day they had what they call the Keeley cure for heavy drinkers. But now I understand they just take some kind of tablets, they call them "Annie Bust" tablets. But *Brick* don't need to take *nothin'*.

(*Brick appears in gallery doors with Margaret behind him.*)

— BIG MAMA (*unaware of his presence behind her*): That boy is just broken up over Skipper's death. You know how poor Skipper died. They gave him a big, big dose of that sodium amytal stuff at his home and then they called the ambulance and give him another big, big dose of it at the hospital and that and all of the alcohol in his system fo' months an' months an' months just proved too much for his heart. . . . I'm scared of needles! I'm more scared of a needle than the knife. . . . I think more people have been needled out of this world than—

(*She stops short and wheels about.*)

OH!—here's Brick! My precious baby—

(*She turns upon Brick with short, fat arms extended, at the same time uttering a loud, short sob, which is both comic and touching.*

(*Brick smiles and bows slightly, making a burlesque gesture of gallantry for Maggie to pass before him into the room. Then he hobbles on his crutch directly to the liquor cabinet and there is absolute silence, with everybody looking at Brick as everybody has always looked at Brick when he spoke or moved or appeared. One by one he drops ice cubes in his glass, then suddenly, but not quickly, looks back over his shoulder with a wry, charming smile, and says:*)

BRICK: I'm sorry! Anyone else?

BIG MAMA (*sadly*): No, son. I *wish* you wouldn't!

BRICK: I wish I didn't have to, Big Mama, but I'm still waiting for that click in my head which makes it all smooth out!

BIG MAMA: Aw, Brick, you—BREAK MY HEART!

MARGARET (*at the same time*): Brick, go sit with Big Mama!

BIG MAMA: I just cain't *staiiiiiiii-nnnnnd*—it. . . .

(*She sobs.*)

MAE: Now that we're all assembled—

GOOPER: We kin talk. . . .

BIG MAMA: Breaks my heart. . . .

MARGARET: Sit with Big Mama, Brick, and hold her hand.

(*Big Mama sniffs very loudly three times, almost like three drum beats in the pocket of silence.*)

BRICK: You do that, Maggie. I'm a restless cripple. I got to stay on my crutch.

(*Brick hobbles to the gallery door; leans there as if waiting. (Mae sits beside Big Mama, while Gooper moves in front and sits on the end of the couch, facing her. Reverend Tooker moves nervously into the space between them; on the other side, Dr. Baugh stands looking at nothing in particular and lights a cigar. Margaret turns away.*)

BIG MAMA: Why're you all *surroundin'* me—like this? Why're you all starin' at me like this an' makin' signs at each other?

(*Reverend Tooker steps back startled.*)

MAE: Calm yourself, Big Mama.

BIG MAMA: Calm you'self, *you'self*, Sister Woman. How could I calm myself with everyone starin' at me as if big drops of blood had broken out on m'face? What's this all about, Annh! What?

(*Gooper coughs and takes a center position.*)

GOOPER: Now, Doc Baugh.

MAE: Doc Baugh?

BRICK (*suddenly*): SHHH!—

(*Then he grins and chuckles and shakes his head regretfully.*)

—Naw!—that wasn't th' click.

GOOPER: Brick, shut up or stay out there on the gallery with your liquor! We got to talk about a serious matter. Big Mama wants to know the complete truth about the report we got today from the Ochsner Clinic.

MAE (*eagerly*): —on Big Daddy's condition!

GOOPER: Yais, on Big Daddy's condition, we got to face it.

DOCTOR BAUGH: Well. . . .

BIG MAMA (*terrified, rising*): Is there? Something? Something that I? Don't—Know?

(*In these few words, this startled, very soft, question, Big Mama reviews the history of her forty-five years with Big Daddy, her great, almost embarrassingly true-hearted and simple-minded devotion to Big Daddy, who must have had something Brick has, who made himself loved so much by the "simple expedient" of not loving enough to disturb his charming detachment, also once coupled, like Brick's, with virile beauty.*

(*Big Mama has a dignity at this moment: she almost stops being fat.*)

DOCTOR BAUGH (*after a pause, uncomfortably*): Yes?—Well—

BIG MAMA: *I!!!*—want to—*knowwwwwww.* . . .

(*Immediately she thrusts her fist to her mouth as if to deny that statement.*

(*Then, for some curious reason, she snatches the withered corsage from her breast and hurls it on the floor and steps on it with her short, fat feet.*)

—*Somebody must be lyin'!*—*I want to know!*

MAE: Sit down, Big Mama, sit down on this sofa.

MARGARET (*quickly*): Brick, go sit with Big Mama.

BIG MAMA: *What is it, what is it?*

DOCTOR BAUGH: I never have seen a more thorough examination than Big Daddy Pollitt was given in all my experience with the Ochsner Clinic.

GOOPER: It's one of the best in the country.

MAE: It's *THE* best in the country—bar *none!*

(*For some reason she gives Gooper a violent poke as she goes past him. He slaps at her hand without removing his eyes from his mother's face.*)

DOCTOR BAUGH: Of course they were ninety-nine and nine-tenths percent sure before they even started.

BIG MAMA: Sure of what, sure of what, sure of—*what?*—*what!*

(*She catches her breath in a startled sob. Mae kisses her quickly. She thrusts Mae fiercely away from her, staring at the doctor.*)

MAE: Mommy, be a brave girl!

BRICK (*in the doorway, softly*):
    "By the light, by the light,
    Of the sil-ve-ry mo-ooo-n . . ."

GOOPER: Shut up!—Brick.

BRICK: —Sorry. . . .

(*He wanders out on the gallery.*)

DOCTOR BAUGH: But now, you see, Big Mama, they cut a piece off this growth, a specimen of the tissue and—

BIG MAMA: Growth? You told Big Daddy—

DOCTOR BAUGH: Now wait.

BIG MAMA (*fiercely*): You told me and Big Daddy there wasn't a thing wrong with him but—

MAE: Big Mama, they always—

GOOPER: Let Doc Baugh talk, will yuh?

BIG MAMA: —little spastic condition of—

(*Her breath gives out in a sob.*)

DOCTOR BAUGH: Yes, that's what we told Big Daddy. But we had this bit of tissue run through the laboratory and I'm sorry to say the test was positive on it. It's—well—malignant. . . .

(*Pause.*)

BIG MAMA: —Cancer?! Cancer?!

(*Dr. Baugh nods gravely.*
(*Big Mama gives a long gasping cry.*)

MAE and GOOPER: Now, now, now, Big Mama, you had to know. . . .

BIG MAMA: *WHY DIDN'T THEY CUT IT OUT OF HIM? HANH? HANH?*

DOCTOR BAUGH: Involved too much, Big Mama, too many organs affected.

MAE: Big Mama, the liver's affected and so's the kidneys, both! It's gone way past what they call a—

GOOPER: A surgical risk.

MAE: —Uh-huh. . . .

(*Big Mama draws a breath like a dying gasp.*)

REVEREND TOOKER: Tch, tch, tch, tch, tch!

DOCTOR BAUGH: Yes, it's gone past the knife.

MAE: That's why he's turned yellow, Mommy!

BIG MAMA: Git away from me, git away from me, Mae!

(*She rises abruptly.*)

I want Brick! Where's Brick? Where is my only son?

MAE: Mama! Did she say "*only* son"?

GOOPER: What does that make *me*?

MAE: A sober responsible man with five precious children!— *six!*

BIG MAMA: I want Brick to tell me! Brick! Brick!

MARGARET (*rising from her reflections in a corner*): Brick was so upset he went back out.

BIG MAMA: *Brick!*

MARGARET: Mama, let *me* tell you!

BIG MAMA: No, no, leave me alone, you're not my blood!

GOOPER: *Mama, I'm your son! Listen to me!*

MAE: Gooper's your son, Mama, he's your first-born!

BIG MAMA: Gooper never liked Daddy.

MAE (*as if terribly shocked*): *That's not TRUE!*

(*There is a pause. The minister coughs and rises.*)

REVEREND TOOKER (*to Mae*): I think I'd better slip away at this point.

MAE (*sweetly and sadly*): Yes, Doctor Tooker, you go.

REVEREND TOOKER (*discreetly*): Goodnight, goodnight, everybody, and God bless you all . . . on this place. . . .

(*He slips out.*)

DOCTOR BAUGH: That man is a good man but lacking in tact. Talking about people giving memorial windows—if he mentioned one memorial window, he must have spoke of a dozen, and saying how awful it was when somebody died intestate, the legal wrangles, and so forth.

(*Mae coughs, and points at Big Mama.*)

DOCTOR BAUGH: Well, Big Mama. . . .

(*He sighs.*)

BIG MAMA: It's all a mistake, I know it's just a bad dream.

DOCTOR BAUGH: We're gonna keep Big Daddy as comfortable as we can.

BIG MAMA: Yes, it's just a bad dream, that's all it is, it's just an awful dream.

GOOPER: In my opinion Big Daddy is having some pain but won't admit that he has it.

BIG MAMA: Just a dream, a bad dream.

DOCTOR BAUGH: That's what lots of them do, they think if they don't admit they're having the pain they can sort of escape the fact of it.

GOOPER (*with relish*): Yes, they get sly about it, they get real sly about it.

MAE: Gooper and I think—

GOOPER: Shut up, Mae!—Big Daddy ought to be started on morphine.

BIG MAMA: Nobody's going to give Big Daddy morphine.

DOCTOR BAUGH: Now, Big Mama, when that pain strikes it's going to strike mighty hard and Big Daddy's going to need the needle to bear it.

BIG MAMA: I tell you, nobody's going to give him morphine.

MAE: Big Mama, you don't want to see Big Daddy suffer, you know you—

(*Gooper standing beside her gives her a savage poke.*)

DOCTOR BAUGH (*placing a package on the table*): I'm leaving this stuff here, so if there's a sudden attack you all won't have to send out for it.

MAE: I know how to give a hypo.

GOOPER: Mae took a course in nursing during the war.

MARGARET: Somehow I don't think Big Daddy would want Mae to give him a hypo.

MAE: You think he'd want *you* to do it?

(*Dr. Baugh rises.*)

GOOPER: Doctor Baugh is goin'.

DOCTOR BAUGH: Yes, I got to be goin'. Well, keep your chin up, Big Mama.

GOOPER (*with jocularity*): She's gonna keep *both* chins up, aren't you Big Mama?

(*Big Mama sobs.*)

Now stop that, Big Mama.

MAE: Sit down with me, Big Mama.

GOOPER (*at door with Dr. Baugh*): Well, Doc, we sure do appreciate all you done. I'm telling you, we're surely obligated to you for—

(*Dr. Baugh has gone out without a glance at him.*)

GOOPER: —I guess that doctor has got a lot on his mind but it wouldn't hurt him to act a little more human. . . .

(*Big Mama sobs.*)

Now be a brave girl, Mommy.

BIG MAMA: It's not true, I know that it's just not true!

GOOPER: Mama, those tests are infallible!

BIG MAMA: Why are you so determined to see your father daid?

MAE: Big Mama!

MARGARET (*gently*): I know what Big Mama means.

MAE (*fiercely*): Oh, do you?

MARGARET (*quietly and very sadly*): Yes, I think I do.

MAE: For a newcomer in the family you sure do show a lot of understanding.

MARGARET: Understanding is needed on this place.

MAE: I guess you must have needed a lot of it in your family, Maggie, with your father's liquor problem and now you've got Brick with his!

MARGARET: Brick does not have a liquor problem at all. Brick is devoted to Big Daddy. This thing is a terrible strain on him.

BIG MAMA: Brick is Big Daddy's boy, but he drinks too much and it worries me and Big Daddy, and, Margaret, you've got to cooperate with us, you've got to cooperate with Big Daddy and me in getting Brick straightened out. Because it will break Big Daddy's heart if Brick don't pull himself together and take hold of things.

MAE: Take hold of *what* things, Big Mama?

BIG MAMA: The place.

(*There is a quick violent look between Mae and Gooper.*)

GOOPER: Big, Mama, you've had a shock.

MAE: Yais, we've all had a shock, but . . .

GOOPER: Let's be realistic—

MAE: —Big Daddy would never, would *never*, be foolish enough to—

GOOPER: —put this place in irresponsible hands!

BIG MAMA: Big Daddy ain't going to leave the place in anybody's hands; Big Daddy is *not* going to die. I want you to get that in your heads, all of you!

MAE: Mommy, Mommy, Big Mama, we're just as hopeful an' optimistic as you are about Big Daddy's prospects, we have faith in *prayer*—but nevertheless there are certain matters that have to be discussed an' dealt with, because otherwise—

GOOPER: Eventualities have to be considered and now's the time. . . . Mae, will you please get my briefcase out of our room?

MAE: Yes, honey.

(*She rises and goes out through the hall door.*)

GOOPER (*standing over Big Mama*): Now Big Mom. What you said just now was not at all true and you know it. I've always loved Big Daddy in my own quiet way. I never made a show of it, and I know that Big Daddy has always been fond of me in a quiet way, too, and he never made a show of it neither.

(*Mae returns with Gooper's briefcase.*)

MAE: Here's your briefcase, Gooper, honey.

GOOPER (*handing the briefcase back to her*): Thank you. . . . Of ca'use, my relationship with Big Daddy is different from Brick's.

MAE: You're eight years older'n Brick an' always had t'carry a bigger load of th' responsibilities than Brick ever had t'carry. He never carried a thing in his life but a football or a highball.

GOOPER: Mae, will y' let me talk, please?

MAE: Yes, honey.

GOOPER: Now, a twenty-eight thousand acre plantation's a mighty big thing t'run.

MAE: Almost singlehanded.

(*Margaret has gone out onto the gallery, and can be heard calling softly to Brick.*)

BIG MAMA: You never had to run this place! What are you talking about? As if Big Daddy was dead and in his grave, you had to run it? Why, you just helped him out with a few business details and had your law practice at the same time in Memphis!

MAE: Oh, Mommy, Mommy, Big Mommy! Let's be fair! Why, Gooper has given himself body and soul to keeping this place up for the past five years since Big Daddy's health started failing. Gooper won't say it, Gooper never thought of it as a duty, he just did it. And what did Brick do? Brick kept living in his past glory at college! Still a football player at twenty-seven!

MARGARET (*returning alone*): Who are you talking about, now? Brick? A football player? He isn't a football player and you know it. Brick is a sports announcer on TV and one of the best-known ones in the country!

MAE: I'm talking about what he was.

MARGARET: Well, I wish you would just stop talking about my husband.

GOOPER: I've got a right to discuss my brother with other members of MY OWN family which don't include *you*. Why don't you go out there and drink with Brick?

MARGARET: I've never seen such malice toward a brother.

GOOPER: How about his for me? Why, he can't stand to be in the same room with me!

MARGARET: This is a deliberate campaign of vilification for the most disgusting and sordid reason on earth, and I know what it is! It's *avarice, avarice, greed, greed!*

BIG MAMA: *Oh, I'll scream! I will scream in a moment unless this stops!*

(*Gooper has stalked up to Margaret with clenched fists at his sides as if he would strike her. Mae distorts her face again into a hideous grimace behind Margaret's back.*)

MARGARET: We only remain on the place because of Big Mom and Big Daddy. If it is true what they say about Big Daddy we are going to leave here just as soon as it's over. Not a moment later.

BIG MAMA (*sobs*): Margaret. Child. Come here. Sit next to Big Mama.

MARGARET: Precious Mommy. I'm sorry, I'm so sorry, I—!

(*She bends her long graceful neck to press her forehead to Big Mama's bulging shoulder under its black chiffon.*)

GOOPER: How beautiful, how touching, this display of devotion!

MAE: Do you know why she's childless? She's childless because that big beautiful athlete husband of hers won't go to bed with her!

GOOPER: You jest won't let me do this in a nice way, will yah? Aw right—Mae and I have five kids with another one coming! I don't give a goddam if Big Daddy likes me or don't like me or did or never did or will or will never! I'm just appealing to a sense of common decency and fair play. I'll tell you the truth. I've resented Big Daddy's partiality to Brick ever since Brick was born, and the way I've been treated like I was just barely good enough to spit on and sometimes not even good enough for that. Big Daddy is dying of cancer, and it's spread all through him and it's attacked all his vital organs including the kidneys and right now he is sinking into uremia, and you all know what uremia is, it's poisoning of the whole system due to the failure of the body to eliminate its poisons.

MARGARET (*to herself, downstage, hissingly*): Poisons, poisons! *Venomous thoughts and words! In hearts and minds!—That's poisons!*

GOOPER (*overlapping her*): I am asking for a square deal, and I expect to get one. But if I don't get one, if there's any peculiar shenanigans going on around here behind my back, or before me, well, I'm not a corporation lawyer for nothing, I know how to protect my own interests.—*OH! A late arrival!*

(*Brick enters from the gallery with a tranquil, blurred smile, carrying an empty glass with him.*)

MAE: Behold the conquering hero comes!

GOOPER: The fabulous Brick Pollitt! Remember him?—Who could forget him!

MAE: He looks like he's been injured in a game!

GOOPER: Yep, I'm afraid you'll have to warm the bench at the Sugar Bowl this year, Brick!

(*Mae laughs shrilly.*)

Or was it the Rose Bowl that he made that famous run in?

MAE: The punch bowl, honey. It was in the punch bowl, the cut-glass punch bowl!

GOOPER: Oh, that's right, I'm getting the bowls mixed up!

MARGARET: Why don't you stop venting your malice and envy on a sick boy?

BIG MAMA: *Now you two hush, I mean it, hush, all of you, hush!*

GOOPER: All right, Big Mama. A family crisis brings out the best and the worst in every member of it.

MAE: *That's* the truth.

MARGARET: *Amen!*

BIG MAMA: *I said, hush!* I won't tolerate any more catty talk in my house.

(*Mae gives Gooper a sign indicating briefcase.*

(*Brick's smile has grown both brighter and vaguer. As he prepares a drink, he sings softly:*)

BRICK:

> *Show me the way to go home,*
> *I'm tired and I wanta go to bed.*
> *I had a little drink about an hour ago—*

GOOPER (*at the same time*): Big Mama, you know it's necessary for me t'go back to Memphis in th' mornin' t'represent the Parker estate in a lawsuit.

(*Mae sits on the bed and arranges papers she has taken from the briefcase.*)

BRICK (*continuing the song*):

> *Wherever I may roam,*
> *On land or sea or foam.*

BIG MAMA: Is it, Gooper?

MAE: Yaiss.

GOOPER: That's why I'm forced to—to bring up a problem that—

MAE: Somethin' that's too important t' be put off!

GOOPER: If Brick was sober, he ought to be in on this.

MARGARET: Brick is present; we're here.

GOOPER: Well, good. I will now give you this outline my partner, Tom Bullitt, an' me have drawn up—a sort of dummy—trusteeship.

MARGARET: Oh, that's it! You'll be in charge an' dole out remittances, will you?

GOOPER: This we did as soon as we got the report on Big Daddy from th' Ochsner Laboratories. We did this thing, I mean we drew up this dummy outline with the advice and assistance of the Chairman of the Boa'd of Directors of th' Southern Plantahs Bank and Trust Company in Memphis, C. C. Bellowes, a man who handles estates for all th' prominent fam'lies in West Tennessee and th' Delta.

BIG MAMA: Gooper?

GOOPER (*crouching in front of Big Mama*): Now this is not—not final, or anything like it. This is just a preliminary outline. But it does provide a basis—a design—a—possible, feasible—*plan!*

MARGARET: Yes, I'll bet.

MAE: It's a plan to protect the biggest estate in the Delta from irresponsibility an'—

BIG MAMA: Now you listen to me, all of you, you listen here! They's not goin' to be any more catty talk in my house! And Gooper, you put that away before I grab it out of our hand and tear it right up! I don't know what the hell's in it, and I don't want to know what the hell's in it. I'm talkin' in Big Daddy's language now; I'm his *wife*, not his *widow*, I'm still his *wife*! And I'm talkin' to you in his language an'—

GOOPER: Big Mama, what I have here is—

MAE: Gooper explained that it's just a plan. . . .

BIG MAMA: I don't care what you got there. Just put it back where it came from, an' don't let me see it again, not even the outside of the envelope of it! Is that understood? Basis! Plan! Preliminary! Design! I say—what is it Big Daddy always says when he's disgusted?

BRICK (*from the bar*): Big Daddy says "crap" when he's disgusted.

BIG MAMA (*rising*): That's right—*CRAP!* I say *CRAP* too, like Big Daddy!

MAE: Coarse language doesn't seem called for in this—

GOOPER: Somethin' in me is *deeply outraged* by hearin' you talk like this.

BIG MAMA: *Nobody's goin' to take nothin'!*—till Big Daddy lets go of it, and maybe, just possibly, not—not even then! No, not even then!

BRICK:

> *You can always hear me singin' this song,*
> *Show me the way to go home.*

BIG MAMA: Tonight Brick looks like he used to look when he was a little boy, just like he did when he played wild games and used to come home all sweaty and pink-cheeked and sleepy, with his—red curls shining. . . .

(*She comes over to him and runs her fat shaky hand through his hair. He draws aside as he does from all physical contact and continues the song in a whisper, opening the ice bucket and dropping in the ice cubes one by one as if he were mixing some important chemical formula.*)

BIG MAMA (*continuing*): Time goes by so fast. Nothin' can out-run it. Death commences too early—almost before you're half-acquainted with life—you meet with the other. . . .

Oh, you know we just got to love each other an' stay to-gether, all of us, just as close as we can, especially now that such a *black* thing has come and moved into this place without invitation.

(*Awkwardly embracing Brick, she presses her head to his shoulder.*

(*Gooper has been returning papers to Mae who has restored them to briefcase with an air of severely tried patience.*)

GOOPER: Big Mama? Big Mama?

(*He stands behind her, tense with sibling envy.*)

BIG MAMA (*oblivious of Gooper*): Brick, you hear me, don't you?

MARGARET: Brick hears you, Big Mama, he understands what you're saying.

BIG MAMA: Oh, Brick, son of Big Daddy! Big Daddy does so love you! Y'know what would be his fondest dream come true? If before he passed on, if Big Daddy has to pass on, you gave him a child of yours, a grandson as much like his son as his son is like Big Daddy!

MAE (*zipping briefcase shut: an incongruous sound*): *Such a pity that Maggie an' Brick can't oblige!*

MARGARET (*suddenly and quietly but forcefully*): Everybody listen.

(*She crosses to the center of the room, holding her hands rigidly together.*)

MAE: Listen to what, Maggie?

MARGARET: I have an announcement to make.

GOOPER: A sports announcement, Maggie?

MARGARET: Brick and I are going to—*have a child!*

(*Big Mama catches her breath in a loud gasp.*)
(*Pause. Big Mama rises.*)

BIG MAMA: Maggie! Brick! This is too good to believe!

MAE: That's right, too good to believe.

BIG MAMA: Oh, my, my! This is Big Daddy's dream, his dream come true! I'm going to tell him right now before he—

MARGARET: We'll tell him in the morning. Don't disturb him now.

BIG MAMA: I want to tell him before he goes to sleep, I'm going to tell him his dream's come true this minute! And Brick! A child will make you pull yourself together and quit this drinking!

(*She seizes the glass from his hand.*)

The responsibilities of a father will—

(*Her face contorts and she makes an excited gesture; bursting into sobs, she rushes out, crying.*)

I'm going to tell Big Daddy right this minute!

    (*Her voice fades out down the hall.*
    (*Brick shrugs slightly and drops an ice cube into another glass. Margaret crosses quickly to his side, saying something under her breath, and she pours the liquor for him, staring up almost fiercely into his face.*)

BRICK (*coolly*): Thank you, Maggie, that's a nice big shot.

(*Mae has joined Gooper and she gives him a fierce poke, making a low hissing sound and a grimace of fury.*)

GOOPER (*pushing her aside*): Brick, could you possibly spare me one small shot of that liquor?

BRICK: Why, help yourself, Gooper boy.

GOOPER: I will.

MAE (*shrilly*): Of course we know that this is—

GOOPER: *Be still, Mae!*

MAE: I won't be still! I know she's made this up!

GOOPER: God damn it, I said to shut up!

MARGARET: Gracious! I didn't know that my little announcement was going to provoke such a storm!

MAE: *That* woman isn't *pregnant!*

GOOPER: Who said she was?

MAE: *She* did.

GOOPER: The doctor didn't. Doc Baugh didn't.

MARGARET: I haven't gone to Doc Baugh.

GOOPER: Then who'd you go to, Maggie?

MARGARET: One of the best gynecologists in the South.

GOOPER: Uh huh, uh huh!—I see. . . .

(*He takes out pencil and notebook.*)

—May we have his name, please?

MARGARET: No, you may not, Mister Prosecuting Attorney!

MAE: He doesn't have any name, he doesn't exist!

MARGARET: Oh, he exists all right, and so does my child, Brick's baby!

MAE: You can't conceive a child by a man that won't sleep with you unless you think you're—

(*Brick has turned on the phonograph. A scat song cuts Mae's speech.*)

GOOPER: *Turn that off!*

MAE: We know it's a lie because we hear you in here; he won't sleep with you, we hear you! So don't imagine you're going to put a trick over on us, to fool a dying man with a—

(*A long drawn cry of agony and rage fills the house. Margaret turns phonograph down to a whisper.*
(*The cry is repeated.*)

MAE (*awed*): Did you hear that, Gooper, did you hear that?

GOOPER: Sounds like the pain has struck.

MAE: Go see, Gooper!

GOOPER: Come along and leave these love birds together in their nest!

(*He goes out first. Mae follows but turns at the door, contorting her face and hissing at Margaret.*)

MAE: *Liar!*

(*She slams the door.*
(*Margaret exhales with relief and moves a little unsteadily to catch hold of Brick's arm.*)

MARGARET: Thank you for—keeping still . . .

BRICK: OK, Maggie.

MARGARET: It was gallant of you to save my face!

BRICK: —It hasn't happened yet.

MARGARET: What?

BRICK: The click. . . .

MARGARET: —the click in your head that makes you peaceful, honey?

BRICK: Uh-huh. It hasn't happened. . . . I've got to make it happen before I can sleep. . . .

MARGARET: —I—know what you—mean. . . .

BRICK: Give me that pillow in the big chair, Maggie.

MARGARET: I'll put it on the bed for you.

BRICK: No, put it on the sofa, where I sleep.

MARGARET: Not tonight, Brick.

BRICK: I want it on the sofa. That's where I sleep.

(*He has hobbled to the liquor cabinet. He now pours down three shots in quick succession and stands waiting, silent. All at once he turns with a smile and says:*)

There!

MARGARET: What?

BRICK: The *click*. . . .

(*His gratitude seems almost infinite as he hobbles out on the gallery with a drink. We hear his crutch as he swings out of sight. Then, at some distance, he begins singing to himself a peaceful song.*

(*Margaret holds the big pillow forlornly as if it were her only companion, for a few moments, then throws it on the bed. She rushes to the liquor cabinet, gathers all the bottles in her arms, turns about undecidedly, then runs out of the room with them, leaving the door ajar on the dim yellow hall. Brick is heard hobbling back along the gallery, singing his peaceful song. He comes back in, sees the pillow on the bed, laughs lightly, sadly, picks it up. He has it under his arm as Margaret returns to the room. Margaret softly shuts the door and leans against it, smiling softly at Brick.*)

MARGARET: Brick, I used to think that you were stronger than me and I didn't want to be overpowered by you. But now, since you've taken to liquor—you know what?—I guess it's bad, but now I'm stronger than you and I can love you more truly!

Don't move that pillow. I'll move it right back if you do! —Brick?

(*She turns out all the lamps but a single rose-silk-shaded one by the bed.*)

I really have been to a doctor and I know what to do and— Brick?—this is my time by the calendar to conceive!

BRICK: Yes, I understand, Maggie. But how are you going to conceive a child by a man in love with his liquor?

MARGARET: By locking his liquor up and making him satisfy my desire before I unlock it!

BRICK: Is that what you've done, Maggie?

MARGARET: Look and see. That cabinet's mighty empty compared to before!

BRICK: Well, I'll be a son of a—

(*He reaches for his crutch but she beats him to it and rushes out on the gallery, hurls the crutch over the rail and comes back in, panting.*

(*There are running footsteps. Big Mama bursts into the room, her face all awry, gasping, stammering.*)

BIG MAMA: Oh, my God, oh, my God, oh, my God, where is it?

MARGARET: Is this what you want, Big Mama?

(*Margaret hands her the package left by the doctor.*)

BIG MAMA: I can't bear it, oh, God! Oh, Brick! Brick, baby!

(*She rushes at him. He averts his face from her sobbing kisses. Margaret watches with a tight smile.*)

My son, Big Daddy's boy! Little Father!

(*The groaning cry is heard again. She runs out, sobbing.*)

MARGARET: And so tonight we're going to make the lie true, and when that's done, I'll bring the liquor back here and we'll get drunk together, here, tonight, in this place that death has come into. . . .

—What do you say?

BRICK: I don't say anything. I guess there's nothing to say.

MARGARET: Oh, you weak people, you weak, beautiful people! —who give up.—What you want is someone to—

(*She turns out the rose-silk lamp.*)

—take hold of you.—Gently, gently, with love! And—

(*The curtain begins to fall slowly.*)

I *do* love you, Brick, I *do*!

BRICK (*smiling with charming sadness*): Wouldn't it be funny if that was true?

The Curtain Comes Down

THE END

NOTE OF EXPLANATION

SOME DAY when time permits I would like to write a piece about the influence, its dangers and its values, of a powerful and highly imaginative director upon the development of a play, before and during production. It does have dangers, but it has them only if the playwright is excessively malleable or submissive, or the director is excessively insistent on ideas or interpretations of his own. Elia Kazan and I have enjoyed the advantages and avoided the dangers of this highly explosive relationship because of the deepest mutual respect for each other's creative function: we have worked together three times with a phenomenal absence of friction between us and each occasion has increased the trust.

If you don't want a director's influence on your play, there are two ways to avoid it, and neither is good. One way is to arrive at an absolutely final draft of your play before you let your director see it, then hand it to him saying, Here it is, take it or leave it! The other way is to select a director who is content to put your play on the stage precisely as you conceived it with no ideas of his own. I said neither is a good way, and I meant it. No living playwright, that I can think of, hasn't something valuable to learn about his own work from a director so keenly perceptive as Elia Kazan. It so happened that in the case of *Streetcar*, Kazan was given a script that was completely finished. In the case of *Cat*, he was shown the first typed version of the play, and he was excited by it, but he had definite reservations about it which were concentrated in the third act. The gist of his reservations can be listed as three points: one, he felt that Big Daddy was too vivid and important a character to disappear from the play except as an off-stage cry after the second act curtain; two, he felt that the character of Brick should undergo some apparent mutation as a result of the virtual vivisection that he undergoes in his interview with his father in Act Two. Three, he felt that the character of Margaret, while he understood that I sympathized with her and liked her myself, should be, if possible, more clearly sympathetic to an audience.

It was only the third of these suggestions that I embraced

wholeheartedly from the outset, because it so happened that Maggie the Cat had become steadily more charming to me as I worked on her characterization. I didn't want Big Daddy to reappear in Act Three and I felt that the moral paralysis of Brick was a root thing in his tragedy, and to show a dramatic progression would obscure the meaning of that tragedy in him and because I don't believe that a conversation, however revelatory, ever effects so immediate a change in the heart or even conduct of a person in Brick's state of spiritual disrepair.

However, I wanted Kazan to direct the play, and though these suggestions were not made in the form of an ultimatum, I was fearful that I would lose his interest if I didn't re-examine the script from his point of view. I did. And you will find included in this published script the new third act that resulted from his creative influence on the play. The reception of the playing-script has more than justified, in my opinion, the adjustments made to that influence. A failure reaches fewer people, and touches fewer, than does a play that succeeds.

It may be that *Cat* number one would have done just as well, or nearly, as *Cat* number two; it's an interesting question. At any rate, with the publication of both third acts in this volume, the reader can, if he wishes, make up his own mind about it.

Tennessee Williams

ACT THREE

Big Daddy is seen leaving as at the end of Act II.

BIG DADDY (*shouts, as he goes out DR on gallery*): ALL—LYIN'—DYIN'—LIARS! LIARS! LIARS!

(*After Big Daddy has gone, Margaret enters from DR on gallery, into room through DS door. She X to Brick at LC.*)

MARGARET: Brick, what in the name of God was goin' on in this room?

(*Dixie and Trixie rush through the room from the hall, L to gallery R, brandishing cap pistols, which they fire repeatedly, as they shout: "Bang! Bang! Bang!"*)

(*Mae appears from DR gallery entrance, and turns the children back UL, along gallery. At the same moment, Gooper, Reverend Tooker and Dr. Baugh enter from L in the hall.*)

MAE: Dixie! You quit that! Gooper, will y'please git these kiddies t'baid? Right now?

(*Gooper and Reverend Tooker X along upper gallery. Dr. Baugh holds, UC, near hall door. Reverend Tooker X to Mae near section of gallery just outside doors, R.*)

GOOPER (*urging the children along*): Mae—you seen Big Mama?
MAE: Not yet.

(*Dixie and Trixie vanish through hall, L.*)

REVEREND TOOKER (*to Mae*): Those kiddies are so full of vitality. I think I'll have to be startin' back to town.

(*Margaret turns to watch and listen.*)

MAE: Not yet, Preacher. You know we regard you as a member of this fam'ly, one of our closest an' dearest, so you just got t'be with us when Doc Baugh gives Big Mama th' actual truth about th' report from th' clinic.

(*Calls through door:*)

Has Big Daddy gone to bed, Brick?

(*Gooper has gone out DR at the beginning of the exchange between Mae and Reverend Tooker.*)

MARGARET (*replying to Mae*): Yes, he's gone to bed.

(*To Brick:*)

Why'd Big Daddy shout "liars"?
GOOPER (*off DR*): Mae!

(*Mae exits DR. Reverend Tooker drifts along upper gallery.*)

BRICK: I didn't lie to Big Daddy. I've lied to nobody, nobody but myself, just lied to myself. The time has come to put me in Rainbow Hill, put me in Rainbow Hill, Maggie, I ought to go there.
MARGARET: Over my dead body!

(*Brick starts R. She holds him.*)

Where do you think you're goin'?

(*Mae enters from DR on gallery, X to Reverend Tooker, who comes to meet her.*)

BRICK (*X below to C*): Out for some air, I want air—
GOOPER (*entering from DR to Mae, on gallery*): Now, where is that old lady?
MAE: Cantcha find her, Gooper?

(*Reverend Tooker goes out DR.*)

GOOPER (*X to Doc above hall door*): She's avoidin' this talk.
MAE: I think she senses somethin'.
GOOPER (*calls off L*): Sookey! Go find Big Mama an' tell her Doc Baugh an' the Preacher've got to go soon.
MAE: Don't let Big Daddy hear yuh!

(*Brings Dr. Baugh to R on gallery.*)

REVEREND TOOKER (*off DR, calls*): Big Mama.
SOOKEY and DAISY (*running from L to R in lawn, calling*): Miss Ida! Miss Ida!

(*They go out UR.*)

GOOPER (*calling off upper gallery*): Lacey, you look downstairs for Big Mama!

MARGARET: Brick, they're going to tell Big Mama the truth
now, an' she needs you!

(*Reverend Tooker appears in lawn area, UR, X C.*)

DOCTOR BAUGH (*to Mae, on R gallery*): This is going to be
painful.

MAE: Painful things can't always be avoided.

DOCTOR BAUGH: That's what I've noticed about 'em, Sister
Woman.

REVEREND TOOKER (*on lawn, points off R*): I see Big Mama!

(*Hurries off L. and reappears shortly in hall.*)

GOOPER (*hurrying into hall*): She's gone round the gall'ry to
Big Daddy's room. Hey, Mama!

(*Off:*)

Hey, Big Mama! Come here!

MAE (*calls*): Hush, Gooper! Don't holler, go to her!

(*Gooper and Reverend Tooker now appear together in hall.
Big Mama runs in from DR, carrying a glass of milk. She X
past Dr. Baugh to Mae, on R gallery. Dr. Baugh turns away.*)

BIG MAMA: Here I am! What d'you all want with me?

GOOPER (*steps toward Big Mama*): Big Mama, I told you we
got to have this talk.

BIG MAMA: What talk you talkin' about? I saw the light go on
in Big Daddy's bedroom an' took him his glass of milk, an'
he just shut the shutters right in my face.

(*Steps into room through R door.*)

When old couples have been together as long as me an' Big
Daddy, they, they get irritable with each other just from too
much—devotion! Isn't that so?

(*X below wicker seat to RC area.*)

MARGARET (*X to Big Mama, embracing her*): Yes, of course
it's so.

(*Brick starts out UC through hall, but sees Gooper and Reverend Tooker entering, so he hobbles through C out DS door and onto gallery.*)

BIG MAMA: I think Big Daddy was just worn out. He loves his fam'ly. He loves to have 'em around him, but it's a strain on his nerves. He wasn't himself tonight, Brick—

(*XC toward Brick. Brick passes her on his way out, DS.*)

Big Daddy wasn't himself, I could tell he was all worked up.

REVEREND TOOKER (*USC*): I think he's remarkable.

BIG MAMA: Yaiss! Just remarkable.

(*Faces US, turns, X to bar, puts down glass of milk.*)

Did you notice all the food he ate at that table?

(*XR a bit.*)

Why he ate like a hawss!

GOOPER (*USC*): I hope he don't regret it.

BIG MAMA (*turns US toward Gooper*): What! Why that man ate a huge piece of cawn bread with molassess on it! Helped himself twice to hoppin' john!

MARGARET (*X to Big Mama*): Big Daddy loves hoppin' john. We had a real country dinner.

BIG MAMA: Yais, he simply adores it! An' candied yams. Son—

(*X to DS door, looking out at Brick. Margaret X above Big Mama to her L.*)

That man put away enough food at that table to stuff a field-hand.

GOOPER: I hope he don't have to pay for it later on.

BIG MAMA (*turns US*): What's that, Gooper?

MAE: Gooper says he hopes Big Daddy doesn't suffer tonight.

BIG MAMA (*turns to Margaret, DC*): Oh, shoot, Gooper says, Gooper says! Why should Big Daddy suffer for satisfyin' a nawmal appetite? There's nothin' wrong with that man but nerves; he's sound as a dollar! An' now he knows he is, an' that's why he ate such a supper. He had a big load off his mind, knowin' he wasn't doomed to—what—he thought he was—doomed t'—

(*She wavers.*
(*Margaret puts her arms around Big Mama.*)

GOOPER (*urging Mae forward*): MAE!

(*Mae runs forward below wicker seat. She stands below Big Mama, Margaret above Big Mama. They help her to the wicker seat. Big Mama sits. Margaret sits above her. Mae stands behind her.*)

MARGARET: Bless his ole sweet soul.

BIG MAMA: Yes—bless his heart.

BRICK (*DS on gallery, looking out front*): Hello, moon, I envy you, you cool son of a bitch.

BIG MAMA: I want Brick!

MARGARET: He just stepped out for some fresh air.

BIG MAMA: Honey! I want Brick!

MAE: Bring li'l Brother in here so we cin talk.

(*Margaret rises, X through DS door to Brick on gallery.*)

BRICK (*to the moon*): I envy you—you cool son of a bitch.

MARGARET: Brick, what're you doin' out here on the gall'ry, baby?

BRICK: Admirin' an' complimentin' th' man in the moon.

(*Mae X to Dr. Baugh on R gallery. Reverend Tooker and Gooper move R UC, looking at Big Mama.*)

MARGARET (*to Brick*): Come in, baby. They're gettin' ready to tell Big Mama the truth.

BRICK: I can't witness that thing in there.

MAE: Doc Baugh, d'you think those vitamin B_{12} injections are all they're cracked up t'be?

(*Enters room to upper side, behind wicker seat.*)

DOCTOR BAUGH (*X to below wicker seat*): Well, I guess they're as good t'be stuck with as anything else.

(*Looks at watch; X through to LC.*)

MARGARET (*to Brick*): Big Mama needs you!

BRICK: I can't witness that thing in there!

BIG MAMA: What's wrong here? You all have such long faces, you sit here waitin' for somethin' like a bomb—to go off.

GOOPER: We're waitin' for Brick an' Maggie to come in for this talk.

MARGARET (*X above Brick, to his R*): Brother Man an' Mae have got a trick up their sleeves, an' if you don't go in there t'help Big Mama, y'know what I'm goin' to do—?

BIG MAMA: Talk. Whispers! Whispers!

(*Looks out DR.*)

Brick! . . .

MARGARET (*answering Big Mama's call*): Comin', Big Mama!

(*To Brick.*)

I'm goin' to take every dam' bottle on this place an' pitch it off th' levee into th' river!

BIG MAMA: Never had this sort of atmosphere here before.

MAE (*sits above Big Mama on wicker seat*): Before what, Big Mama?

BIG MAMA: This occasion. What's Brick an' Maggie doin' out there now?

GOOPER (*X DC, looks out*): They seem to be havin' some little altercation.

(*Brick X toward DS step. Maggie moves R above him to portal Dr. Reverend Tooker joins Dr. Baugh, LC.*)

BIG MAMA (*taking a pill from pill box on chain at her wrist*): Give me a little somethin' to wash this tablet down with. Smell of burnt fireworks always makes me sick.

(*Mae X to bar to pour glass of water. Dr. Baugh joins her. Gooper X to Reverend Tooker, LC.*)

BRICK (*to Maggie*): You're a live cat, aren't you?

MARGARET: You're dam' right I am!

BIG MAMA: Gooper, will y'please open that hall door—an' let some air circulate in this stiflin' room?

(*Gooper starts US, but is restrained by Mae who X through C with glass of water. Gooper turns to men DLC.*)

MAE (*X to Big Mama with water, sits above her*): Big Mama, I think we ought to keep that door closed till after we talk.

BIG MAMA: I swan!

(*Drinks water. Washes down pill.*)

MAE: I just don't think we ought to take any chance of Big Daddy hearin' a word of this discussion.

BIG MAMA (*hands glass to Mae*): What discussion of what? Maggie! Brick! Nothin' is goin' to be said in th' house of Big Daddy Pollitt that he can't hear if he wants to!

(*Mae rises, X to bar, puts down glass, joins Gooper and the two men, LC.*)

BRICK: How long are you goin' to stand behind me, Maggie?

MARGARET: Forever, if necessary.

(*Brick X US to R gallery door.*)

BIG MAMA: Brick!

(*Mae rises, looks out DS, sits.*)

GOOPER: That boy's gone t'pieces—he's just gone t'pieces.

DOCTOR BAUGH: Y'know, in my day they used to have somethin' they called the Keeley cure for drinkers.

BIG MAMA: Shoot!

DOCTOR BAUGH: But nowadays, I understand they take some kind of tablets that kill their taste for the stuff.

GOOPER (*turns to Dr. Baugh*): Call 'em anti-bust tablets.

BIG MAMA: Brick don't need to take nothin'. That boy is just broken up over Skipper's death. You know how poor Skipper died. They gave him a big, big dose of that sodium amytal stuff at his home an' then they called the ambulance an' give him another big, big dose of it at th' hospital an' that an' all the alcohol in his system fo' months an' months just proved too much for his heart an' his heart quit beatin'. I'm scared of needles! I'm more scared of a needle than th' knife—

(*Brick has entered the room to behind the wicker seat. He rests his hand on Big Mama's head. Gooper has moved a bit URC, facing Big Mama.*)

BIG MAMA: Oh! Here's Brick! My precious baby!

(*Dr. Baugh X to bar, puts down drink. Brick X below Big Mama through C to bar.*)

BRICK: Take it, Gooper!

MAE (*rising*): What?

BRICK: Gooper knows what. Take it, Gooper!

(*Mae turns to Gooper URC. Dr. Baugh X to Reverend Tooker. Margaret, who has followed Brick US on R gallery before he entered the room, now enters room, to behind wicker seat.*)

BIG MAMA (*to Brick*): You just break my heart.

BRICK (*at bar*): Sorry—anyone else?

MARGARET: Brick, sit with Big Mama an' hold her hand while we talk.

BRICK: You do that, Maggie. I'm a restless cripple. I got to stay on my crutch.

(*Mae sits above Big Mama. Gooper moves in front, below, and sits on couch, facing Big Mama. Reverend Tooker closes in to RC. Dr. Baugh XDC, faces upstage, smoking cigar. Margaret turns away to R doors.*)

BIG MAMA: Why're you all *surroundin'* me?—like this? Why're you all starin' at me like this an' makin' signs at each other?

(*Brick hobbles out hall door and X along R gallery.*)

I don't need nobody to hold my hand. Are you all crazy? Since when did Big Daddy or me need anybody—?

(*Reverend Tooker moves behind wicker seat.*)

MAE: Calm yourself, Big Mama.

BIG MAMA: Calm you'self *you'self*, Sister Woman! How could I calm myself with everyone starin' at me as if big drops of blood had broken out on m'face? What's this all about Annh! What?

GOOPER: Doc Baugh—

(*Mae rises.*)

Sit down, Mae—

(*Mae sits.*)

—Big Mama wants to know the complete truth about th' report we got today from the Ochsner Clinic!

(*Dr. Baugh buttons his coat, faces group at RC.*)

BIG MAMA: Is there somethin'—somethin' that I don't know?

DOCTOR BAUGH: Yes—well . . .

BIG MAMA (*rises*): I—want to—*knowwwwww!*

(*X to Dr. Baugh.*)

Somebody must be lyin'! *I want to know!*

(*Mae, Gooper, Reverend Tooker surround Big Mama.*)

MAE: Sit down, Big Mama, sit down on this sofa!

(*Brick has passed Margaret Xing DR on gallery.*)

MARGARET: Brick! Brick!

BIG MAMA: *What is it, what is it?*

(*Big Mama drives Dr. Baugh a bit DLC. Others follow, surrounding Big Mama.*)

DOCTOR BAUGH: I never have seen a more thorough examination than Big Daddy Pollitt was given in all my experience at the Ochsner Clinic.

GOOPER: It's one of th' best in th' country.

MAE: It's *THE* best in th' country—bar none!

DOCTOR BAUGH: Of course they were ninety-nine and nine-tenths per cent certain before they even started.

BIG MAMA: Sure of what, sure of what, sure of what—*what!?*

MAE: Now, Mommy, be a brave girl!

BRICK (*on DR gallery, covers his ears, sings*): "By the light, by the light, of the silvery moon!"

GOOPER (*breaks DR. Calls out to Brick*): Shut up, Brick!

(*Returns to group LC.*)

BRICK: Sorry . . .

(*Continues singing.*)

DOCTOR BAUGH: But now, you see, Big Mama, they cut a piece off this growth, a specimen of the tissue, an'—

BIG MAMA: Growth? You told Big Daddy—

DOCTOR BAUGH: Now, wait—

BIG MAMA: You told me an' Big Daddy there wasn't a thing wrong with him but—

MAE: Big Mama, they always—
GOOPER: Let Doc Baugh talk, will yuh?
BIG MAMA: —little spastic condition of—
REVEREND TOOKER (*throughout all this*): Shh! Shh! Shh!

(*Big Mama breaks UC, they all follow.*)

DOCTOR BAUGH: Yes, that's what we told Big Daddy. But we had this bit of tissue run through the laboratory an' I'm sorry t'say the test was positive on it. It's malignant.

(*Pause.*)

BIG MAMA: *Cancer! Cancer!*
MAE: Now now, Mommy—
GOOPER (*at the same time*): You had to know, Big Mama.
BIG MAMA: *Why didn't they cut it out of him? Hanh? Hannh?*
DOCTOR BAUGH: Involved too much, Big Mama, too many organs affected.
MAE: Big Mama, the liver's affected, an' so's the kidneys, both. It's gone way past what they call a—
GOOPER: —a surgical risk.

(*Big Mama gasps.*)

REVEREND TOOKER: Tch, tch, tch.
DOCTOR BAUGH: Yes, it's gone past the knife.
MAE: That's why he's turned yellow!

(*Brick stops singing, turns away UR on gallery.*)

BIG MAMA (*pushes Mae DS*): Git away from me, git away from me, Mae!

(*XDSR*)

I want Brick! Where's Brick! *Where's my only son?*
MAE (*a step after Big Mama*): Mama! Did she say "only" son?
GOOPER (*following Big Mama*): What does that make me?
MAE (*above Gooper*): A sober responsible man with five precious children—*six!*
BIG MAMA: I want Brick! Brick! Brick!
MARGARET (*a step to Big Mama above couch*): Mama, let *me* tell you.

BIG MAMA (*pushing her aside*): No, no, leave me alone, you're not my blood!

(*She rushes onto the DS gallery.*)

GOOPER (*X to Big Mama on gallery*): Mama! I'm your son! Listen to me!

MAE: Gooper's your son, Mama, he's your first-born!

BIG MAMA: Gooper never liked Daddy!

MAE: That's not true!

REVEREND TOOKER (*UC*): I think I'd better slip away at this point. Goodnight, goodnight everybody, and God bless you all—on this place.

(*Goes out through hall.*)

DOCTOR BAUGH (*XDR to above DS door*): Well, Big Mama—

BIG MAMA (*leaning against Gooper, on lower gallery*): It's all a mistake, I know it's just a bad dream.

DOCTOR BAUGH: We're gonna keep Big Daddy as comfortable as we can.

BIG MAMA: Yes, it's just a bad dream, that's all it is, it's just an awful dream.

GOOPER: In my opinion Big Daddy is havin' some pain but won't admit that he has it.

BIG MAMA: Just a dream, a bad dream.

DOCTOR BAUGH: That's what lots of 'em do, they think if they don't admit they're havin' the pain they can sort of escape th' fact of it.

(*Brick X US on R gallery. Margaret watches him from R doors.*)

GOOPER: Yes, they get sly about it, get real sly about it.

MAE (*X to R of Dr. Baugh*): Gooper an' I think—

GOOPER: Shut up, Mae!—Big Mama, I really do think Big Daddy should be started on morphine.

BIG MAMA (*pulling away from Gooper*): Nobody's goin't to give Big Daddy morphine!

DOCTOR BAUGH: Now, Big Mama, when that pain strikes it's goin' to strike mighty hard an' Big Daddy's goin' t'need the needle to bear it.

BIG MAMA (*X to Dr. Baugh*): I tell you, nobody's goin' to give him morphine!

MAE: Big Mama, you don't want to see Big Daddy suffer, y'know y'—

DOCTOR BAUGH (*X to bar*): Well, I'm leavin' this stuff here

(*Puts packet of morphine, etc., on bar.*)

so if there's a sudden attack you won't have to send out for it.

(*Big Mama hurries to L side bar.*)

MAE (*X C, below Dr. Baugh*): I know how to give a hypo.

BIG MAMA: Nobody's goin' to give Big Daddy morphine!

GOOPER (*X C*): Mae took a course in nursin' durin' th' war.

MARGARET: Somehow I don't think Big Daddy would want Mae t'give him a hypo.

MAE (*to Margaret*): You think he'd want *you* to do it?

DOCTOR BAUGH: Well—

GOOPER: Well, Doc Baugh is goin'—

DOCTOR BAUGH: Yes, I got to be goin'. Well, keep your chin up, Big Mama.

(*X to hall.*)

GOOPER (*as he and Mae follow Dr. Baugh into the hall*): She's goin' to keep her ole chin up, aren't you, Big Mama?

(*They go out L.*)

Well, Doc, we sure do appreciate all you've done. I'm telling you, we're obligated—

BIG MAMA: Margaret!

(*XRC.*)

MARGARET (*meeting Big Mama in front of wicker seat*): I'm right here, Big Mama.

BIG MAMA: Margaret, you've got to cooperate with me an' Big Daddy to straighten Brick out now—

GOOPER (*off L, returning with Mae*): I guess that Doctor has got a lot on his mind, but it wouldn't hurt him to act a little more human—

BIG MAMA: —because it'll break Big Daddy's heart if Brick don't pull himself together an' take hold of things here.

(*Brick XDSR on gallery.*)

MAE (*UC, overhearing*): Take hold of what things, Big Mama?

BIG MAMA (*sits in wicker chair, Margaret standing behind chair*): The place.

GOOPER (*UC*): Big Mama, you've had a shock.

MAE (*X with Gooper to Big Mama*): Yais, we've all had a shock, but—

GOOPER: Let's be realistic—

MAE: Big Daddy would not, would *never*, be foolish enough to—

GOOPER: —put this place in irresponsible hands!

BIG MAMA: Big Daddy ain't goin' t'put th' place in anybody's hands, Big Daddy is *not* goin' t'die! I want you to git that into your haids, all of you!

(*Mae sits above Big Mama, Margaret turns R to door, Gooper X L C a bit.*)

MAE: Mommy, Mommy, Big Mama, we're just as hopeful an' optimistic as you are about Big Daddy's prospects, we have faith in prayer—but nevertheless there are certain matters that have to be discussed an' dealt with, because otherwise—

GOOPER: Mae, will y'please get my briefcase out of our room?

MAE: Yes, honey.

(*Rises, goes out through hall L.*)

MARGARET (*X to Brick on DS gallery*): Hear them in there?

(*X back to R gallery door.*)

GOOPER (*stands above Big Mama. Leaning over her*): Big Mama, what you said just now was not at all true, an' you know it. I've always loved Big Daddy in my own quiet way. I never made a show of it. I know that Big Daddy has always been fond of me in a quiet way, too.

(*Margaret drifts UR on gallery. Mae returns, X to Gooper's L with briefcase.*)

MAE: Here's your briefcase, Gooper, honey.

(*Hands it to him.*)

GOOPER (*hands briefcase back to Mae*): Thank you. Of ca'use, my relationship with Big Daddy is different from Brick's.

MAE: You're eight years older'n Brick an' always had t'carry a bigger load of th' responsibilities than Brick ever had t'carry; he never carried a thing in his life but a football or a highball.

GOOPER: Mae, will y'let me talk, please?

MAE: Yes, honey.

GOOPER: Now, a twenty-eight thousand acre plantation's a mighty big thing t'run.

MAE: Almost single-handed!

BIG MAMA: You never had t'run this place, Brother Man, what're you talkin' about, as if Big Daddy was dead an' in his grave, you had to run it? Why, you just had t'help him out with a few business details an' had your law practice at the same time in Memphis.

MAE: Oh, Mommy, Mommy, Mommy! Let's be fair! Why, Gooper has given himself body an' soul t'keepin' this place up fo' the past five years since Big Daddy's health started fallin'. Gooper won't say it, Gooper never thought of it as a duty, he just did it. An' what did Brick do? Brick kep' livin' in his past glory at college!

(*Gooper places a restraining hand on Mae's leg; Margaret drifts DS in gallery.*)

GOOPER: Still a football player at twenty-seven!

MARGARET (*bursts into UR door*): Who are you talkin' about now? Brick? A football player? He isn't a football player an' you know it! Brick is a sports announcer on TV an' one of the best-known ones in the country!

MAE (*breaks UC*): I'm talkin' about what he was!

MARGARET (*X to above lower gallery door*): Well, I wish you would just stop talkin' about my husband!

GOOPER (*X to above Margaret*): Listen, Margaret, I've got a right to discuss my own brother with other members of my own fam'ly, which don't include *you*!

(*Pokes finger at her; she slaps his finger away.*)

Now, why don't you go on out there an' drink with Brick?

MARGARET: I've never seen such malice toward a brother.

GOOPER: How about his for me? Why he can't stand to be in the same room with me!

BRICK (*on lower gallery*): That's the truth!

MARGARET: This is a deliberate campaign of vilification for the most disgusting and sordid reason on earth, and I know what it is! *It's avarice, avarice, greed, greed!*

BIG MAMA: Oh, I'll scream, I will scream in a moment unless this stops! Margaret, child, come here, sit next to Big Mama.

MARGARET (*X to Big Mama, sits above her*): Precious Mommy.

(*Gooper X to bar.*)

MAE: How beautiful, how touchin' this display of devotion! Do you know why she's childless? She's childless because that big, beautiful athlete husband of hers won't go to bed with her, that's why!

(*X to L of bed, looks at Gooper.*)

GOOPER: You jest won't let me do this the nice way, will yuh? Aw right—

(*X to above wicker seat.*)

I don't give a goddam if Big Daddy likes me or don't like me or did or never did or will or will never! I'm just appealin' to a sense of common decency an' fair play! I'm tellin' you th' truth—

(*X DS through lower door to Brick on DR gallery.*)

I've resented Big Daddy's partiality to Brick ever since th' goddam day you were born, son, an' th' way I've been treated, like I was just barely good enough to spit on, an' sometimes not even good enough for that.

(*X back through room to above wicker seat.*)

Big Daddy is dyin' of cancer an' it's spread all through him an' it's attacked all his vital organs includin' the kidneys an' right now he is sinkin' into uremia, an' you all know what uremia is, it's poisonin' of the whole system due to th' failure of th' body to eliminate its poisons.

MARGARET: Poisons, poisons, venomous thoughts and words! In hearts and minds! That's poisons!

GOOPER: I'm askin' for a square deal an' by God I expect to get one. But if I don't get one, if there's any peculiar shenanigans goin' on around here behind my back, well I'm not a corporation lawyer for nothin!

(*XDS toward lower gallery door, on apex.*)

I know how to protect my own interests.

(*Rumble of distant thunder.*)

BRICK (*entering the room through DS door*): Storm comin' up.

GOOPER: Oh, a late arrival!

MAE (*X through C to below bar, LCO*): Behold, the conquerin' hero comes!

GOOPER (*X through C to bar, following Brick, imitating his limp*): The fabulous Brick Pollitt! Remember him? Who could forget him?

MAE: He looks like he's been injured in a game!

GOOPER: Yep, I'm afraid you'll have to warm th' bench at the Sugar Bowl this year, Brick! Or was it the Rose Bowl that he made his famous run in.

(*Another rumble of thunder, sound of wind rising.*)

MAE (*X to L of Brick, who has reached the bar*): The punch bowl, honey, it was the punch bowl, the cut-glass punch bowl!

GOOPER: That's right! I'm always gettin' the boy's *bowls* mixed up!

(*Pats Brick on the butt.*)

MARGARET (*rushes at Gooper, striking him*): Stop that! You stop that!

(*Thunder.*
(*Mae X toward Margaret from L. of Gooper, flails at Margaret; Gooper keeps the women apart. Lacey runs through the US lawn area in a raincoat.*)

DAISY and SOOKEY (*off UL*): Storm! Storm comin! Storm! Storm!

LACEY (*running out UR*): Brightie, close them shutters!

GOOPER (*X onto R gallery, calls after Lacey*): Lacey, put the top up on my Cadillac, will yuh?

LACEY (*off R*): Yes, sur, Mistah Pollit!

GOOPER (*X to above Big Mama*): Big Mama, you know it's goin' to be necessary for me t'go back to Memphis in th' mornin' t'represent the Parker estate in a lawsuit.

(*Mae sits on L side bed, arranges papers she removes from briefcase.*)

BIG MAMA: Is it, Gooper?

MAE: Yaiss.

GOOPER: That's why I'm forced to—to bring up a problem that—

MAE: Somethin' that's too important t'be put off!

GOOPER: If Brick was sober, he ought to be in on this. I think he ought to be present when I present this plan.

MARGARET (*UC*): Brick is present, we're present!

GOOPER: Well, good. I will now give you this outline my partner, Tom Bullit, an' me have drawn up—a sort of dummy—trusteeship!

MARGARET: Oh, that's it! You'll be in charge an' dole out remittances, will you?

GOOPER: This we did as soon as we got the report on Big Daddy from th' Ochsner Laboratories. We did this thing, I mean we drew up this dummy outline with the advice and assistance of the Chairman of the Boa'd of Directors of th' Southern Plantuhs Bank and Trust Company in Memphis, C. C. Bellowes, a man who handles estates for all th' prominent fam'lies in West Tennessee and th' Delta!

BIG MAMA: Gooper?

GOOPER (*X behind seat to below Big Mama*): Now this is not—not final, or anything like it, this is just a preliminary outline. But it does provide a—basis—a design—a—possible, feasible—*plan!*

(*He waves papers Mae has thrust into his hand, US.*)

MARGARET (*XDL*): Yes, I'll bet it's a plan!

(*Thunder rolls. Interior lighting dims.*)

MAE: It's a plan to protect the biggest estate in the Delta from irresponsibility an'—

BIG MAMA: Now you listen to me, all of you, you listen here! They's not goin' to be no more catty talk in my house! And Gooper, you put that away before I grab it out of your hand and tear it right up! I don't know what the hell's in it, and I don't want to know what the hell's in it. I'm talkin' in Big Daddy's language now, I'm his *wife*, not his *widow*, I'm still his *wife*! And I'm talkin' to you in his language an'—

GOOPER: Big Mama, what I have here is—

MAE: Gooper explained that it's just a plan . . .

BIG MAMA: I don't care what you got there, just put it back where it come from an' don't let me see it again, not even the outside of the envelope of it! Is that understood? Basis! Plan! Preliminary! Design!—I say—what is it that Big Daddy always says when he's disgusted?

(*Storm clouds race across sky.*)

BRICK (*from bar*): Big Daddy says "crap" when he is disgusted.

BIG MAMA (*rising*): That's right—*CRAPPPP!* I say *CRAP* too, like Big Daddy!

(*Thunder rolls.*)

MAE: Coarse language don't seem called for in this—

GOOPER: Somethin' in me is *deeply outraged* by this.

BIG MAMA: *Nobody's goin' to do nothin'!* till Big Daddy lets go of it, and maybe just possibly not—not even then! No, not even then!

(*Thunder clap. Glass crash, off L.*
(*Off UR, children commence crying. Many storm sounds, L and R: barnyard animals in terror, papers crackling, shutters rattling. Sookey and Daisy hurry from L to R in lawn area. Inexplicably, Daisy hits together two leather pillows. They cry, "Storm! Storm!" Sookey waves a piece of wrapping paper to cover lawn furniture. Mae exits to hall and upper gallery. Strange man runs across lawn, R to L.*
(*Thunder rolls repeatedly.*)

MAE: Sookey, hurry up an' git that po'ch fu'niture covahed; want th' paint to come off?

> (*Starts DR on gallery.*
> (*Gooper runs through hall to R gallery.*)

GOOPER (*yells to Lacey, who appears from R*): Lacey, put mah car away!

LACEY: Cain't, Mistah Pollit, you got the keys!

> (*Exit US.*)

GOOPER: Naw, you got 'em, man.

> (*Exit DR. Reappears UR, calls to Mae:*)

Where th' keys to th' car, honey?

> (*Runs C.*)

MAE (*DR on gallery*): You got 'em in your pocket!

> (*Exit DR.*
> (*Gooper exits UR. Dog howls. Daisy and Sookey sing off UR to comfort children. Mae is heard placating the children.*
> (*Storm fades away.*
> (*During the storm, Margaret X and sits on couch, DR. Big Mama X DC.*)

BIG MAMA: BRICK! Come here, Brick, I need you.

> (*Thunder distantly.*
> (*Children whimper, off L Mae consoles them. Brick X to R of Big Mama.*)

BIG MAMA: Tonight Brick looks like he used to look when he was a little boy just like he did when he played wild games in the orchard back of the house and used to come home when I hollered myself hoarse for him! all—sweaty—and pink-cheeked—an' sleepy with his curls shinin'—

> (*Thunder distantly.*
> (*Children whimper, off L. Mae consoles them. Dog howls, off.*)

Time goes by so fast. Nothin' can outrun it. Death commences too early—almost before you're half-acquainted with life—you meet with the other. Oh, you know we just got to love each other, an' stay together all of us just as close as we can, specially now that such a *black* thing has come and moved into this place without invitation.

(*Dog howls, off.*)

Oh, Brick, son of Big Daddy, Big Daddy does so love you. Y'know what would be his fondest dream come true? If before he passed on, if Big Daddy has to pass on . . .

(*Dog howls, off.*)

You give him a child of yours, a grandson as much like his son as his son is like Big Daddy. . . .

MARGARET: I know that's Big Daddy's dream.

BIG MAMA: That's his dream.

BIG DADDY (*off DR on gallery*): Looks like the wind was takin' liberties with this place.

(*Lacey appears UL, X to UC in lawn area; Brightie and Small appear UR on lawn. Big Daddy X onto the UR gallery.*)

LACEY: Evenin', Mr. Pollitt.

BRIGHTIE and SMALL: Evenin', Cap'n. Hello, Cap'n.

MARGARET (*X to R door*): Big Daddy's on the gall'ry.

BIG DADDY: Stawm crossed th' river, Lacey?

LACEY: Gone to Arkansas, Cap'n.

(*Big Mama has turned toward the hall door at the sound of Big Daddy's voice on the gallery. Now she X's DSR and out the DS door onto the gallery.*)

BIG MAMA: I can't stay here. He'll see somethin' in my eyes.

BIG DADDY (*on upper gallery, to the boys*): Stawm done any damage around here?

BRIGHTIE: Took the po'ch off ole Aunt Crawley's house.

BIG DADDY: Ole Aunt Crawley should of been settin' on it. It's time fo' th' wind to blow that ole girl away!

(*Field-hands laugh, exit, UR. Big Daddy enters room, UC, hall door.*)

Can I come in?

(Puts his cigar in ash tray on bar.
(Mae and Gooper hurry along the upper gallery and stand behind Big Daddy in hall door.)

MARGARET: Did the storm wake you up, Big Daddy?

BIG DADDY: Which stawm are you talkin' about—th' one outside or th' hullaballoo in here?

(Gooper squeezes past Big Daddy.)

GOOPER (*X toward bed, where legal papers are strewn*): 'Scuse me, sir . . .

(Mae tries to squeeze past Big Daddy to join Gooper, but Big Daddy puts his arm firmly around her.)

BIG DADDY: I heard some mighty loud talk. Sounded like somethin' important was bein' discussed. What was the powwow about?

MAE (*flustered*): Why—nothin', Big Daddy . . .

BIG DADDY (*XDLC, taking Mae with him*): What is that pregnant-lookin' envelope you're puttin' back in your briefcase, Gooper?

GOOPER (*at foot of bed, caught, as he stuffs papers into envelope*): That? Nothin', suh—nothin' much of anythin' at all . . .

BIG DADDY: Nothin'? It looks like a whole lot of nothing!

(Turns US to group:)

You all know th' story about th' young married couple—

GOOPER: Yes, sir!

BIG DADDY: Hello, Brick—

BRICK: Hello, Big Daddy.

(The group is arranged in a semi-circle above Big Daddy, Margaret at the extreme R, then Mae and Gooper, then Big Mama, with Brick at L.)

BIG DADDY: Young married couple took Junior out to th' zoo one Sunday, inspected all of God's creatures in their cages, with satisfaction.

GOOPER: Satisfaction.

BIG DADDY (*XUSC, face front*): This afternoon was a warm afternoon in spring an' that ole elephant had somethin' else on his mind which was bigger'n peanuts. You know this story, Brick?

(*Gooper nods.*)

BRICK: No, sir, I don't know it.

BIG DADDY: Y'see, in th' cage adjoinin' they was a young female elephant in heat!

BIG MAMA (*at Big Daddy's shoulder*): Oh, Big Daddy!

BIG DADDY: What's the matter, preacher's gone, ain't he? All right. That female elephant in the next cage was permeatin' the atmosphere about her with a powerful and excitin' odor of female fertility! Huh! Ain't that a nice way to put it, Brick?

BRICK: Yes, sir, nothin' wrong with it.

BIG DADDY: Brick says the's nothin' wrong with it!

BIG MAMA: Oh, Big Daddy!

BIG DADDY (*XDSC*): So this ole bull elephant still had a couple of fornications left in him. He reared back his trunk an' got a whiff of that elephant lady next door!—began to paw at the dirt in his cage an' butt his head against the separatin' partition and, first thing y'know, there was a conspicuous change in his *profile*—very *conspicuous*! Ain't I tellin' this story in decent language, Brick?

BRICK: Yes, sir, too ruttin' decent!

BIG DADDY: So, the little boy pointed at it and said, "What's that?" His Mam said, "Oh, that's—nothin'!"—His Papa said, "She's spoiled!"

(*Field-hands sing off R, featuring Sookey: "I Just Can't Stay Here by Myself," through following scene.*
(*Big Daddy X to Brick at L.*)

BIG DADDY: You didn't laugh at that story, Brick.

(*Big Mama X DRC crying. Margaret goes to her. Mae and Gooper hold URC.*)

BRICK: No, sir, I didn't laugh at that story.

(*On the lower gallery, Big Mama sobs. Big Daddy looks toward her.*)

BIG DADDY: What's wrong with that long, thin woman over there, loaded with diamonds? Hey, what's-your-name, what's the matter with you?

MARGARET (*X toward Big Daddy*): She had a slight dizzy spell, Big Daddy.

BIG DADDY (*ULC*): You better watch that, Big Mama. A stroke is a bad way to go.

MARGARET (*X to Big Daddy at C*): Oh, Brick, Big Daddy has on your birthday present to him, Brick, he has on your cashmere robe, the softest material I have ever felt.

BIG DADDY: Yeah, this is my soft birthday, Maggie. . . .
   Not my gold or my silver birthday, but my soft birthday, everything's got to be soft for Big Daddy on this soft birthday.

(*Maggie kneels before Big Daddy C. As Gooper and Mae speak, Big Mama X USRC in front of them, hushing them with a gesture.*)

GOOPER: Maggie, I hate to make such a crude observation, but there is somethin' a little indecent about your—

MAE: Like a slow-motion football tackle—

MARGARET: Big Daddy's got on his Chinese slippers that I gave him, Brick. Big Daddy, I haven't given you my big present yet, but now I will, now's the time for me to present it to you! I have an announcement to make!

MAE: What? What kind of announcement?

GOOPER: A sports announcement, Maggie?

MARGARET: Announcement of life beginning! A child is coming, sired by Brick, and out of Maggie the Cat! I have Brick's child in my body, an' that's my birthday present to Big Daddy on this birthday!

(*Big Daddy looks at Brick who X behind Big Daddy to DS portal, L.*)

BIG DADDY: Get up, girl, get up off your knees, girl.

(*Big Daddy helps Margaret rise. He X above her, to her R, bites off the end of a fresh cigar, taken from his bathrobe pocket, as he studies Margaret.*)

Uh-huh, this girl has life in her body, that's no lie!
BIG MAMA: BIG DADDY'S DREAM COME TRUE!
BRICK: *JESUS!*
BIG DADDY (*X R below wicker seat*): Gooper, I want my lawyer in the mornin'.
BRICK: Where are you goin', Big Daddy?
BIG DADDY: Son, I'm goin' up on the roof to the belvedere on th' roof to look over my kingdom before I give up my kingdom—twenty-eight thousand acres of th' richest land this side of the Valley Nile!

(*Exit through R doors, and DR on gallery.*)

BIG MAMA (*following*): Sweetheart, sweetheart, sweetheart— can I come with you?

(*Exits DR.*
(*Margaret is DSC in mirror area.*)

GOOPER (*X to bar*): Brick, could you possibly spare me one small shot of that liquor?
BRICK (*DLC*): Why, help yourself, Gooper boy.
GOOPER: I will.
MAE (*X forward*): Of course we know that this is a lie!
GOOPER (*drinks*): Be still, Mae!
MAE (*X to Gooper at bar*): I won't be still! I know she's made this up!
GOOPER: God damn it, I said to shut up!
MAE: That woman isn't pregnant!
GOOPER: Who said she was?
MAE: She did!
GOOPER: The doctor didn't. Doc Baugh didn't.
MARGARET (*X R to above couch*): I haven't gone to Doc Baugh.
GOOPER (*X through to L of Margaret*): Then who'd you go to, Maggie?

(*Offstage song finishes.*)

MARGARET: One of the best gynecologists in the South.
GOOPER: Uh-huh, I see—

(*Foot on end of couch, trapping Margaret:*)

May we have his name please?

MARGARET: No, you may not, Mister—Prosecutin' Attorney!

MAE (*X to R of Margaret, above*): He doesn't have any name, he doesn't exist!

MARGARET: He does so exist, and so does my baby, Brick's baby!

MAE: You can't conceive a child by a man that won't sleep with you unless you think you're—

> (*Forces Margaret onto couch, turns away C.*
> (*Brick starts C for Mae.*)

He drinks all the time to be able to tolerate you! Sleeps on the sofa to keep out of contact with you!

GOOPER (*X above Margaret, who lies face down on couch*): Don't try to kid us, Margaret—

MAE (*X to bed, L side, rumpling pillows*): How can you conceive a child by a man that won't sleep with you? How can you conceive? How can you? How can you!

GOOPER (*sharply*): MAE!

BRICK (*X below Mae to her R, takes hold of her*): Mae, Sister Woman, how d'you know that I don't sleep with Maggie?

MAE: We occupy the next room an' th' wall between isn't soundproof.

BRICK: Oh . . .

MAE: We hear the nightly pleadin' and the nightly refusal. So don't imagine you're goin' t'put a trick over on us, to fool a dyin' man with—a—

BRICK: Mae, Sister Woman, not everybody makes much noise about love. Oh, I know some people are huffers an' puffers, but others are silent lovers.

GOOPER (*behind seat, R*): This talk is pointless, completely.

BRICK: How d'y'know that we're not silent lovers?

Even if y'got a peep-hole drilled in the wall, how can y'tell if sometime when Gooper's got business in Memphis an' you're playin' scrabble at the country club with other ex-queens of cotton, Maggie and I don't come to some temporary agreement? How do you know that—?

> (*He X above wicker seat to above R end couch.*)

MAE: Brick, I never thought that you would stoop to her level, I just never dreamed that you would stoop to her level.

GOOPER: I don't think Brick will stoop to her level.

BRICK (*sits R of Margaret on couch*): What is your level? Tell me your level so I can sink or rise to it.

(*Rises.*)

You heard what Big Daddy said. This girl has life in her body.

MAE: That is a lie!

BRICK: No, truth is something desperate, an' she's got it. Believe me, it's somethin' desperate, an' she's got it.

(*X below seat to below bar.*)

An' now if you will stop actin' as if Brick Pollitt was dead an' buried, invisible, not heard, an' go on back to your peep-hole in the wall—I'm drunk, and sleepy—not as alive as Maggie, but still alive. . . .

(*Pours drink, drinks.*)

GOOPER (*picks up briefcase from R foot of bed*): Come on, Mae. We'll leave these love birds together in their nest.

MAE: Yeah, nest of lice! Liars!

GOOPER: Mae—Mae, you jes' go on back to our room—

MAE: Liars!

(*Exits through hall.*)

GOOPER (*DR above Margaret*): We're jest goin' to wait an' see. Time will tell.

(*X to R of bar.*)

Yes, sir, little brother, we're just goin' to wait an' see!

(*Exit, hall.*
(*The clock strikes twelve.*
(*Maggie and Brick exchange a look. He drinks deeply, puts his glass on the bar. Gradually, his expression changes. He utters a sharp exhalation.*
(*The exhalation is echoed by the singers, off UR, who commence vocalizing with "Gimme a Cool Drink of Water Fo' I Die," and continue till end of act.*)

MARGARET (*as she hears Brick's exhalation*): The click?

(*Brick looks toward the singers, happily, almost gratefully. He XR to bed, picks up his pillow, and starts toward head of couch, DR, Xing above wicker seat. Margaret seizes the pillow from his grasp, rises, stands facing C, holding the pillow close. Brick watches her with growing admiration. She moves quickly USC, throwing pillow onto bed. She X to bar. Brick counters below wicker seat, watching her. Margaret grabs all the bottles from the bar. She goes into hall, pitches the bottles, one after the other, off the platform into the UL lawn area. Bottles break, off L. Margaret re-enters the room, stands UC, facing Brick.*)

Echo Spring has gone dry, and no one but me could drive you to town for more.—

BRICK: Lacey will get me—

MARGARET: Lacey's been told not to!

BRICK: I could drive—

MARGARET: And you lost your driver's license! I'd phone ahead and have you stopped on the highway before you got halfway to Ruby Lightfoot's gin mill. I told a lie to Big Daddy, but we can make that lie come true. And then I'll bring you liquor, and we'll get drunk together, here, tonight, in this place that death has come into! What do you say? What do you say, baby?

BRICK (*X to L side bed*): I admire you, Maggie.

(*Brick sits on edge of bed. He looks up at the overhead light, then at Margaret. She reaches for the light, turns it out; then she kneels quickly beside Brick at foot of bed.*)

MARGARET: Oh, you weak, beautiful people who give up with such grace. What you need is someone to take hold of you —gently, with love, and hand your life back to you, like something gold you let go of—and I can! I'm determined to do it—and nothing's more determined than a cat on a tin roof—is there? Is there, baby?

(*She touches his cheek, gently.*)

Curtain

CHRONOLOGY

NOTE ON THE TEXTS

NOTES

Chronology

1911   Born March 26 in Columbus, Mississippi, the second
        child of Edwina Estelle Dakin Williams and Cornelius
        Coffin Williams, and christened Thomas Lanier Williams
        III. (Grandfather Thomas Lanier Williams II was an un-
        successful candidate for governor of Tennessee who later
        served as state railroad commissioner. Father, born 1879 in
        Knoxville and known as "C.C.," served in the Spanish-
        American War, worked for a telephone company as a re-
        gional manager, and then became a traveling salesman for
        a Knoxville men's clothing company. Mother, born 1884
        in Marysville, Ohio, moved between Ohio and Tennessee
        before her family settled in Mississippi in 1901. Parents
        married in 1907; their first child, Rose, was born in 1909.)
        Lives with mother, sister, and grandparents in the rectory
        of St. Paul's Church, where grandfather Walter Dakin, an
        Episcopal priest, serves as minister; father is usually away
        from home on business.

1913   Family moves to Nashville when grandfather becomes
        rector of the Church of the Advent.

1914   Father takes new job as traveling salesman for a St. Louis
        shoe company, and continues to be away from family
        most of the time.

1915   Family returns to Mississippi when grandfather becomes
        rector in Canton and then Clarksdale, town in the Missis-
        sippi Delta. Williams is read to by grandparents and
        mother and listens to animal stories told by "Ozzie," his
        African-American nurse.

1916   Develops diphtheria during summer, followed by Bright's
        disease, which leaves him confined to his house and un-
        able to walk for a year and a half. Mother reads to him
        from Dickens and Shakespeare.

1918   Father moves family in July to St. Louis, where he has
        taken a job as a branch manager with the International

Shoe Company. Williams enters Eugene Field Elementary School in September. Intimidated by his father, who calls him "Miss Nancy" because of his sensitivity and shyness.

1919   Brother Walter Dakin Williams, called Dakin, born February 21. Tension increases between his parents.

1920   Williams is sent to Clarksdale to stay with his grandparents when his mother becomes ill.

1922   Father is promoted to sales manager and moves family into better apartment. Williams enters Stix School, where he becomes friends with Hazel Kramer.

1924   Family moves into another apartment. Williams enters Ben Blewett Junior High School and begins writing on a secondhand typewriter given to him by his mother. Short story "Isolated" is printed in the school newspaper in November.

1925   Poem "Demon Smoke" appears in school yearbook. Family spends August in Elkmont, Tennessee, in the Smoky Mountains, where Williams learns to swim. Father's drinking becomes chronic problem. Rose, growing increasingly disturbed and rebellious, is sent to All Saints College in Vicksburg, Mississippi. Friendship with Hazel Kramer continues.

1926   Mother has hysterectomy. Williams enters Soldan High School in January. Family moves in June to apartment in University City just west of St. Louis. Williams enters University City High School.

1927   Wins $5 as third prize from *Smart Set* for writing an answer to the question "Can a good wife be a good sport?" Wins a prize for reviewing the film *Stella Dallas*.

1928   Short story "The Vengeance of Nitocris" published in *Weird Tales*. Rose begins to show signs of a deepening depression. Williams goes with his grandfather Dakin to New York, where they see *Show Boat* on Broadway, then sails to Europe with grandfather and a church group from Mississippi for a tour of the Continent. Visits France, Italy, Switzerland, Germany, the Netherlands, and England.

1929   Graduates from high school and enters the University of
        Missouri at Columbia, intending to study journalism.
        Pledges Alpha Tau Omega fraternity at his father's insis-
        tence. Becomes good friends with Esmeralda Mayes, who
        is also a poet.

1930   Writes one-act play *Beauty Is the Word*, for a modern
        drama class he is auditing. Submits it to the Dramatic
        Arts Club contest and wins honorable mention, the first
        freshman to be so honored.

1931   Works as typist at International Shoe Company during
        the summer. Enrolls in the University of Missouri School
        of Journalism at Columbia.

1932   Completes third year of college, but because he has failed
        ROTC, father makes him leave school and work as a clerk
        at the shoe company. Votes for Socialist candidate Nor-
        man Thomas for president.

1933   Continues writing and has poems accepted for publica-
        tion in various journals. Short story "Stella for Star"
        awarded first prize in the St. Louis Writers' Guild contest.

1935   Suffers collapse from exhaustion in January and is hospi-
        talized. Father allows him to leave the shoe company and
        spend the summer in Memphis with his Dakin grandpar-
        ents. Writes *Cairo! Shanghai! Bombay!*, which is produced
        by an amateur company in Memphis, Williams' first play
        to be staged. Begins reading the stories of Anton
        Chekhov. Returns to St. Louis in the fall and audits
        courses at Washington University.

1936   Admitted to Washington University and writes plays *The
        Magic Tower* and *Candles to the Sun* for the Mummers, a
        St. Louis drama group. Becomes friendly with a group of
        young poets, including Clark Mills McBurney, who intro-
        duces him to the work of Hart Crane. Publishes poetry in
        the university magazine. Deeply moved by seeing Alla
        Nazimova in a touring company of Ibsen's *Ghosts*.

1937   *Candles to the Sun* is performed by the Mummers in St.
        Louis in March. Rose is committed to a psychiatric ward
        in St. Louis, then moved to a Catholic convalescent

home, where she is diagnosed as having dementia praecox (schizophrenia). In the summer she is transferred to the state hospital at Farmington, Missouri, and given insulin shock treatment. Supported by the Rev. and Mrs. Dakin, Williams studies playwriting at the University of Iowa under well-known professors E. C. Mabie and E. P. Conkle. Works on a "living newspaper" drama. *The Fugitive Kind* is produced by the Mummers. Completes a draft of *Spring Storm* late in the year.

1938   Submits *Spring Storm* in March to his playwriting class at the University of Iowa, but it is not well received. Awarded B.A. degree in English by the University of Iowa. Spends summer and fall in St. Louis and submits *Spring Storm* to the Mummers, but they do not produce it. Begins writing *Not About Nightingales* in September after reading newspaper account of inmates suffocated in a steam room in a Pennsylvania prison. The St. Louis Poets' Workshop, which McBurney and William Jay Smith had established, continues to meet in the Williams home. Uses name "Tennessee Williams" for the first time on entry form for Group Theatre play contest. Goes to New Orleans in late December for the first of many stays there and is shocked by the lifestyle in the French Quarter. Soon makes friends, and becomes accustomed to and embraces the free-wheeling attitude of Quarterites.

1939   Moves January 1 to 722 Toulouse in the French Quarter, where he remains several weeks, supporting himself briefly as a waiter. Meets artists and writers, including Lyle Saxon and Roark Bradford, and attempts to secure a position with the Federal Writers' Project. Submits *Fugitive Kind* to the Project and continues work on *Not About Nightingales*. Leaves for California on February 20 with James Parrott, a musician who becomes a close friend. Wins $100 from the Group Theatre in March for one-act play collection. Engages Audrey Wood as his agent after she contacts him; she places "The Field of Blue Children" with *Story* magazine, his first publication using the name "Tennessee." Visits Frieda Lawrence in New Mexico because of his devotion to D. H. Lawrence's work. Returns to St. Louis in December, where he learns that he has been awarded a $1,000 grant from the Rockefeller Foundation.

1940   Moves to New York and enrolls in John Gassner's modern drama course at the New School for Social Research. Becomes friends with Donald Windham and Gilbert Maxwell. Lives for a while in Provincetown, Massachusetts, where he meets and falls in love with Kip Kiernan, a dancer. The Theatre Guild opens *Battle of Angels*, directed by Margaret Webster, in Boston on December 30. Becomes friends with Paul Bigelow, who works for the Guild.

1941   *Battle of Angels* closes January 11. Receives draft deferment because of his poor eyesight. Stays briefly in St. Louis, Miami, and Key West, where he meets Marion Vaccaro, who will become one of his best friends. Receives $500 advance from the Theatre Guild to rewrite *Battle of Angels*. Returns to New York and submits the revised play, which is rejected by the Guild. Hume Cronyn takes an option on one-act plays. Spends part of the summer in Provincetown. Returns to New Orleans in September and in November goes to St. Louis, where his grandmother Dakin is ill. Takes a job as a cashier at a New Orleans restaurant in December. Completes draft of a long play, *Stairs to the Roof*.

1942   Stays with friends in New York in January, working on several plays and taking a variety of odd jobs. One-act plays anthologized in *American Scenes* and *Best One-Act Plays*. Collaborates with Donald Windham on a play, *You Touched Me!*, based on a D. H. Lawrence story. Spends part of the summer in Macon, Georgia, with Paul Bigelow, and in Jacksonville, Florida, where he operates a teletype for the U.S. Engineers Office. Returns to New York, where he stays with friends and continues work on *You Touched Me!* In Texas, meets Margo Jones, a leader in the regional theater movement. Meets James Laughlin, publisher of New Directions, in December; he becomes a close friend.

1943   Rose, still confined in a mental institution, undergoes a bilateral prefrontal lobotomy in January. Williams lives in a Brooklyn hotel, then moves to the YMCA. Works briefly as elevator operator, movie theater usher, and bellhop. Returns to St. Louis, where he works on a dramatic adaptation of his story "Portrait of a Girl in

Glass" called "The Gentleman Caller." In May, at the instigation of his agent Audrey Wood, goes to Hollywood to write for MGM at $250 a week. Works on a variety of scripts, including ones for Lana Turner and Margaret O'Brien, and his own "The Gentleman Caller," but is not successful as a screenwriter. Directed by Guthrie McClintic, *You Touched Me!* opens October 13 in Cleveland, Ohio, and is later staged in Pasadena, California.

1944   Grandmother Rose Dakin dies in January in St. Louis, where he is visiting. Kip Kiernan dies from brain tumor in March. Receives a $1,000 grant from Academy of Arts and Letters and goes to Provincetown, where he rewrites "The Gentleman Caller" as a stage play. In September James Laughlin publishes 26 of his poems in *Five Young American Poets* (from this point on, New Directions will publish most of Williams' books). During rehearsals for *The Glass Menagerie*, the new title of "The Gentleman Caller," returns to St. Louis and there is interviewed by a local drama critic, William Inge, an aspiring dramatist himself. *The Glass Menagerie* opens in Chicago on December 26, with Laurette Taylor as Amanda Wingfield. The play receives excellent reviews from drama critics Claudia Cassidy and Ashton Stevens, who write about it repeatedly and are instrumental in making it a hit in Chicago.

1945   *The Glass Menagerie* opens on Broadway on March 31 to generally favorable reviews. Critics have high praise for Laurette Taylor, but some, including George Jean Nathan, have reservations about the play. Two weeks after its opening, it wins the New York Drama Critics Circle Award. Success of the play relieves Williams from the financial troubles that have burdened him; he assigns half of the royalties to his mother. Following eye surgery, goes to Mexico to work on a play called "The Moth," then renamed "Blanche's Chair in the Moon," and later "The Poker Night." New Directions publishes *27 Wagons Full of Cotton and Other One-Act Plays*. Remains in Mexico until August, when he visits Margo Jones in Dallas, then goes to Boston for rehearsals of *You Touched Me!* It debuts in New York on September 25 to generally poor reviews, and closes after 109 performances.

1946   Settles in the French Quarter in New Orleans with Pan-
        cho Rodriguez y Gonzales, whom he had met in New
        Mexico. Writes *Ten Blocks on the Camino Real*. Travels
        with Rodriguez in May to Taos, where he suffers a severe
        attack of diverticulitis that requires surgery. Goes to Nan-
        tucket for the summer and writes an appreciative letter to
        Carson McCullers, who soon joins him on the island and
        shares a house with him and Rodriguez for the summer,
        beginning an enduring friendship. Meets dramatist
        Thornton Wilder on Nantucket. Moves in the fall to St.
        Peter Street in New Orleans and works on two plays,
        "The Poker Night" and "Chart of Anatomy." Learns of
        the death of Laurette Taylor. Grandfather Dakin comes to
        New Orleans to stay with Williams and Rodriguez.

1947   In January, Hume Cronyn produces three Williams plays,
        including *Portrait of a Madonna*, starring Jessica Tandy,
        in Los Angeles. Williams travels with Rodriguez and
        grandfather Dakin to Key West, where actress Miriam
        Hopkins has a party for them. Sends finished version of
        "The Poker Night," soon renamed *A Streetcar Named
        Desire*, to Audrey Wood in March. Meets Irene Selznick,
        who will produce the play, in Charleston, South Carolina.
        Settles with Rodriguez in Provincetown, where he meets
        Frank Merlo. Rodriguez is enraged and they soon end
        their often tempestuous relationship. Dallas production of
        "Chart of Anatomy," retitled *Summer and Smoke*, opens
        July 8. Goes to Los Angeles for a month and sees Jessica
        Tandy in *Portrait of a Madonna*; she is cast as Blanche in
        Streetcar. Goes to Dallas to see Margo Jones's production
        of *Summer and Smoke*. Marlon Brando comes to
        Provincetown in August to read and is cast as Stanley. *A
        Streetcar Named Desire*, directed by Elia Kazan and star-
        ring Tandy, Brando, and Kim Hunter, opens December 3
        in New York. Williams leaves for Europe at the end of the
        year.

1948   Parents separate. *A Streetcar Named Desire* is awarded the
        Pulitzer Prize and the Drama Critics Circle Award.
        Williams stays in London, Paris, and Rome, where he
        meets Truman Capote and Gore Vidal and becomes in-
        volved with a young Italian named Salvatore. In England,
        visits Helen Hayes, who is in rehearsal for *The Glass
        Menagerie*; meets John Gielgud, Noël Coward, Laurence

Olivier, and Vivien Leigh. Becomes friends with Maria Britneva (later Lady Maria St. Just). Returns to Paris, where he meets Jean Cocteau, who wants to stage a French production of *Streetcar*. In July, his mother and brother come to London for the British opening of *The Glass Menagerie*. Returns to U.S. in September on the *Queen Mary* with Truman Capote. *One Arm and Other Stories* is published by New Directions. *Summer and Smoke*, directed by Margo Jones, opens in New York. In October Frank Merlo moves in with him, beginning the longest intimate relationship of his life. Starts work on a preliminary draft of *Sweet Bird of Youth*. Arranges for Rose to receive half the royalties from *Summer and Smoke*. Visits Paul and Jane Bowles in Tangier in December with Frank Merlo.

1949   Arranges for Rose to be transferred from the state hospital to a private sanitarium in Connecticut. Travels in January with Merlo to Italy, where they take an apartment, and later to Sicily, where they meet Merlo's family. Begins work on the novel *The Roman Spring of Mrs. Stone*. Starts to rely heavily on drugs. In March, travels with Merlo, Capote, and Jack Dunphy to Ischia. Argues frequently with Capote and others. Goes to London in April and visits with Laurence Olivier, director of the London production of *Streetcar*, and Vivien Leigh, who will star as Blanche. Returns with Merlo to New York in September, then goes to Hollywood to advise on the script of the film version of *The Glass Menagerie*. Moves with Merlo and grandfather Dakin to Key West in November. Begins work on *The Rose Tattoo*. New York production of *Streetcar* closes after two years, the longest run of any of his plays on Broadway.

1950   Goes to New York for the openings of Inge's *Come Back, Little Sheba* and Carson McCullers' stage adaptation of *The Member of the Wedding*. Returns to Key West and works on *The Rose Tattoo*, which he dedicates to Merlo. Attends a limited New York run of *Streetcar* starring Uta Hagen and Anthony Quinn and at the end of May sails with Merlo and Jane Smith to Europe. In Paris endeavors to persuade Anna Magnani to star in the stage production of *The Rose Tattoo* but she declines, feeling that she does not speak English well enough. With Merlo, again visits

Sicily, where he hopes to learn local dialect for use in *Tattoo*. They settle for a time in Rome, visit Vienna, then return to the U.S. Buys a house on Duncan Street in Key West that he had previously rented. *The Rose Tattoo* has its off-Broadway premiere in Chicago in December.

1951   *The Rose Tattoo*, starring Maureen Stapleton and Eli Wallach and produced by Cheryl Crawford, opens February 3 on Broadway and later wins Tony Award as best play. Transfers Rose to Stony Lodge, clinic near Ossining, New York, where she will spend most of the rest of her life; visits her often and on occasion takes her to visit Carson McCullers in Nyack or to shop in New York. Begins work on revision of *Battle of Angels* that will become *Orpheus Descending*. Travels with Merlo to England, Italy, Spain, Germany, and to Sweden and Denmark for the premieres of *The Rose Tattoo*. Grows increasingly dependent on alcohol and drugs. Goes to London for premiere of the play, then returns to the U.S. Elia Kazan's film of *A Streetcar Named Desire*, with Marlon Brando as Stanley and Vivien Leigh as Blanche, is released.

1952   Visits New Orleans, then goes to Key West, where he revises *Ten Blocks on the Camino Real* and a screenplay that will ultimately become *Baby Doll*. Goes to New York to see José Quintero's successful revival of *Summer and Smoke* in New York in April at Circle in the Square with Geraldine Page; is moved by the direction and acting. Elected to the National Institute of Arts and Letters. Spends summer in Europe with Merlo, with whom his relations are increasingly strained. Frequently sees Anna Magnani, Carson McCullers, and her husband, Reeves McCullers. Returns to Key West.

1953   *Camino Real* opens in New York March 19 after previews in New Haven and Philadelphia, and is not well received. William, depressed by the reviews and attacks from Walter Winchell and Ed Sullivan, returns to Key West to revise *Camino Real* for publication by New Directions. Works on *Cat on a Hot Tin Roof*. Directs Donald Windham's *The Starless Air* at the Playhouse Theatre in Houston. Argues with Windham about the play and their friendship is strained. Visits his grandfather at the Gayoso Hotel in Memphis, where the Reverend Dakin is living.

Travels extensively in Europe with Merlo and Paul Bowles in the summer. Begins work on a short story, "Man Bring This Up Road," that will ultimately become *The Milk Train Doesn't Stop Here Anymore*. Goes with Paul Bowles to Tangier in the fall. Returns to New York with Merlo in October, then goes to New Orleans, with grandfather Dakin, and spends the rest of the year there.

1954   Spends early months of the year in Key West working on *Cat on a Hot Tin Roof*. Continues work on screenplay, now called "Hide and Seek," that will become *Baby Doll*. Gives poetry reading with Carson McCullers in New York in May. Goes with Merlo a month later to Rome, where they join Maria Britneva and travel to Spain. Drinks heavily and takes increasing amounts of drugs. Returns to U.S. in September with Merlo and Anna Magnani for the filming of *The Rose Tattoo* in Key West. Continues work on revision of *Battle of Angels*. *Hard Candy*, his second collection of short stories, is published. Grandfather Dakin suffers a stroke in St. Louis.

1955   After some difficulty, Williams and agent Audrey Wood choose Elia Kazan to direct *Cat on a Hot Tin Roof*. Disagrees with Kazan on the ending of the play but eventually revises third act following Kazan's recommendation. Goes to New Orleans in mid-January to direct *27 Wagons Full of Cotton* and opera based on *Lord Byron's Love Letter* at Tulane University. Attends rehearsals of *Cat on a Hot Tin Roof* in New York. Grandfather Dakin dies February 14 in St. Louis at age 97. *Cat on a Hot Tin Roof*, starring Burl Ives, Barbara Bel Geddes, and Ben Gazzara, opens on Broadway March 24 with the revised third act and is a critical triumph. Subsequently wins the Drama Critics Circle award and the Pulitzer Prize. Film of *The Rose Tattoo* is released. Returns to Key West in April with Carson McCullers; they work together, then go to Havana briefly. In June goes again to Europe for the summer. Learns in July that Margo Jones has died. Suffering from writer's block, Williams continues to rely on drink and drugs. Attends Stockholm opening of the Swedish *Cat on a Hot Tin Roof* and visits his friend Lilla von Saher. Returns to New York to work on the screenplay of *Baby Doll*, and also works on "The Enemy: Time," which will become *Sweet Bird of Youth*.

1956   Goes with Maria Britneva and Marion Vaccaro to Miami, where Tallulah Bankhead is starring in a revival of *Streetcar*; his dissatisfaction with her performance is publicized and Williams apologizes to an angry Bankhead. *Sweet Bird of Youth*, directed by George Keathley, opens in Miami on April 16. Williams goes to Rome alone as the tension between him and Merlo increases. In November, *The Glass Menagerie* is revived in New York starring Helen Hayes as Amanda. The film *Baby Doll*, directed by Elia Kazan and starring Carroll Baker and Eli Wallach, is released; it is denounced by Cardinal Spellman, and condemned by the Catholic Legion of Decency and other groups. Goes to Key West with his mother. First collection of poetry, *In the Winter of Cities*, is published.

1957   Travels to New York for revisions and rehearsals of *Orpheus Descending*. Directed by Harold Clurman, the play opens on Broadway on March 21 and closes after two months; its negative reviews worsen Williams' depression. Father dies March 27, and Williams attends funeral in Knoxville with his brother Dakin. In June begins psychotherapy with Dr. Lawrence S. Kubie, a Freudian analyst, who, according to Williams, urges him to quit writing and to live as a heterosexual. Spends the summer in New York, visiting friends and often going to Stony Lodge to see Rose. Works on *Suddenly Last Summer*.

1958   On January 7 *Garden District*, consisting of *Suddenly Last Summer* and *Something Unspoken*, premieres Off Broadway in New York to favorable reviews. Returns to Key West to work on *Sweet Bird of Youth*. Ends his analysis with Dr. Kubie in March and leaves again for Europe. *Cat on a Hot Tin Roof* opens in London and in August the film version, directed by Richard Brooks and starring Elizabeth Taylor, Paul Newman, and Burl Ives, is released. Returns to Florida in the fall, and collaborates with Meade Roberts on script for film of *Orpheus Descending*, which is retitled *The Fugitive Kind*. Continues work on *Sweet Bird of Youth* and *Period of Adjustment*, which opens on December 29 for a brief run at the Coconut Grove Playhouse.

1959   Goes to New York in February for rehearsals of *Sweet Bird of Youth*. Directed by Elia Kazan and starring Geraldine

Page and Paul Newman, it opens on Broadway March 10. Depressed by critical response to the play, Williams leaves New York for Miami and then goes with Marion Vaccaro to Havana, where he meets Fidel Castro, an admirer of Williams' work. Returns with Vaccaro to Key West for a few weeks and in May flies with her to London for the English premiere of *Orpheus Descending*. Returns to New York in June for rehearsals of *The Fugitive Kind*. In July attends a Chicago production of *Suddenly Last Summer* with Diana Barrymore. After the play closes, returns to Havana with Vaccaro and Barrymore. Leaves in August on three-month around-the-world trip. Film of *Suddenly Last Summer*, directed by Joseph L. Mankiewicz and starring Katharine Hepburn, Elizabeth Taylor, and Montgomery Clift, is released.

1960   Settles with Merlo in Key West to work on *The Night of the Iguana* and *Period of Adjustment*. In June goes with his mother, brother Dakin, and Dakin's wife, Joyce, to Los Angeles, where they meet Elvis Presley and Mae West. Returns to Key West to work. Relations with Merlo, who shows signs of illness, are strained. *The Fugitive Kind*, film version of *Orpheus Descending*, directed by Sidney Lumet and starring Marlon Brando and Anna Magnani, is released. *The Night of the Iguana* is staged at Coconut Grove in August. *Period of Adjustment* opens on Broadway.

1961   Works in Key West on revisions of *The Night of the Iguana*. Goes with Vaccaro in January to Europe. In Rome they meet Donald Windham and Sandy Campbell, then settle in Taormina, Sicily, where he works on the play. Returns to Key West in the autumn, depressed by what he sees as his waning career and more and more dependent on liquor and pills. During previews in Detroit, Williams is hospitalized after his dog bites him. After previews in several other cities, *The Night of the Iguana*, starring Bette Davis, Margaret Leighton, and Patrick O'Neal, opens in New York on December 28.

1962   *The Night of the Iguana* wins Drama Critics Circle Award as best play. Buys a multi-story townhouse in the French Quarter in New Orleans, using income from film versions of his plays. Made lifetime member of the Ameri-

can Academy of Arts and Letters. Lucy Freeman collaborates with Williams' mother on her memoir, *Remember
Me to Tom*. The Spoleto Festival of the Two Worlds in
Italy premieres a version of *The Milk Train Doesn't Stop
Here Anymore*. Poet Frederick Nicklaus, who has moved
in with Williams and Merlo in Key West, accompanies
him to Italy. Contacted in London by Audrey Wood,
who informs him that Merlo is very ill, he flies back to
the U.S.

1963   *Milk Train* moves to New York January 16 and runs for
only two months. Merlo is diagnosed with lung cancer
and goes to Key West, then back to New York to stay
with Williams and Nicklaus. Williams begins revisions of
Milk Train in preparation for a revival. Merlo dies in September. After the funeral, Williams and Nicklaus fly to
Mexico where *Night of the Iguana* is being filmed by
John Huston, with a cast including Ava Gardner, Debo-
rah Kerr, and Richard Burton. Williams begins a period of
depression and heavy dependence on drugs that he will
call his "Stoned Age."

1964   Revival of *Milk Train*, starring Tallulah Bankhead, Tab
Hunter, Ruth Ford, and Marion Seldes opens January 1
and closes after three days. Goes to Jamaica and then to
Key West, where Nicklaus leaves him in March. Back in
New York, he begins seeing a new analyst and becomes a
patient of Dr. Max Jacobson, who provides him with am-
phetamines and barbiturates in pill and injection form.
Writes *Slapstick Tragedy*, consisting of two short plays,
The Gnädiges Fräulein and *The Mutilated*. Realizing that
he should not be alone, given his reliance on alcohol and
drugs, he hires the first of a series of paid companions,
William Glavin, to move in with him and travel with him.
Film of *The Night of the Iguana* released.

1965   *The Glass Menagerie* revived with Maureen Stapleton as
Amanda. *Milk Train* is revived again in San Francisco and
is positively received. Goes to St. Louis to visit his
mother, who has begun to suffer from delusions. Continues work on *Slapstick Tragedy*, other plays, and short
stories. *The Eccentricities of a Nightingale*, a revision of
Summer and Smoke, is published.

1966   *Slapstick Tragedy*, starring Zoe Caldwell, Margaret
            Leighton, and Kate Reid opens in New York in January
            and runs for only four days. Williams issues a public state-
            ment condemning America's involvement in Vietnam.
            Reliance on drugs grows, abetted by Dr. Jacobson, and
            his mental state becomes progressively unstable. Works on
            the film script of *Milk Train*, then goes with Glavin and
            Lester Persky, who will produce it, to London. Film of
            This Property Is Condemned, loosely based on his one-act
            play, is released.

1967   Goes with Glavin to Virgin Islands where parts of "Go-
            forth!" (soon retitled *Boom!*), based on *Milk Train*, are
            being filmed. Travels in the summer with Glavin to Eu-
            rope, visiting Sardinia where *Boom!* is now being filmed
            by director Joseph Losey with a cast including Elizabeth
            Taylor, Richard Burton, and Noël Coward. Friends such
            as Audrey Wood and Elia Kazan are increasingly con-
            cerned by his dependence on drugs and his mental state.
            Carson McCullers dies September 29 following a massive
            stroke. *The Knightly Quest: A Novella and Four Short Sto-
            ries* is published by New Directions. Attends the world
            premiere of *The Two-Character Play* in London in De-
            cember with Audrey Wood.

1968   Production of *Kingdom of Earth* with Harry Guardino,
            Estelle Parsons, and Brian Bedford premieres in February
            in Philadelphia and then opens in New York on March 27
            under the direction of José Quintero and retitled *The
            Seven Descents of Myrtle*. It runs only a month. *Boom!* is
            released to unfavorable reviews. Friend Lilla van Saher
            dies. Works on revision of *The Two-Character Play* and on
            a new play, *In the Bar of a Tokyo Hotel*. At the end of the
            year, suffering increasingly from paranoid symptoms ex-
            acerbated by drug use, goes with Glavin to Key West.

1969   Dakin, at Audrey Wood's suggestion, goes to Key West
            to check on Williams, who has grown confused and dis-
            oriented. Dakin arranges for him to be received into the
            Roman Catholic church on January 10, although
            Williams will later deny that the conversion was authen-
            tic. In the spring, assumes direction of the New York
            production of *In the Bar of a Tokyo Hotel*, which opens
            May 11 in New York and is widely condemned by critics.

Receives National Institute of Arts and Letters gold medal and an honorary doctorate from the University of Missouri at Columbia. In June, flies with actress Anne Meacham to Tokyo where they meet writer Yukio Mishima and see part of the Japanese production of *Streetcar*. Returns to Key West, where Glavin joins him, then goes to San Francisco again and to New Orleans to see Pancho Rodriguez. Becomes progressively more dependent on drugs and increasingly paranoid. In September Dakin convinces him to enter Barnes Hospital in St. Louis, where he is placed in the mental ward. Suffers seizures and two heart attacks related to withdrawal from drugs. Recovers sufficiently to return to Key West in December.

1970   Goes to New York in January for revival of *Camino Real*. Discusses his homosexuality in a television interview with David Frost. Marion Black Vaccaro dies in April. At the end of summer, travels with Oliver Evans to New Orleans and then to Hawaii, Hong Kong, Thailand, and Japan, where he meets with Yukio Mishima shortly before Mishima commits ritual suicide. *Dragon Country: A Book of Plays* is published.

1971   Attends rehearsals in Chicago of production of *Out Cry* (a revised version of *The Two-Character Play*), starring Donald Madden and Eileen Herlie. Resumes use of drugs and, in a fit of anger, dismisses his agent, Audrey Wood, who is replaced by Bill Barnes. Revises and expands *Confessional* into full-length play *Small Craft Warnings*. New Directions begins publication of the multi-volume set, *The Theatre of Tennessee Williams*. Speaks out against American involvement in the Vietnam War at a rally at the Cathedral of St. John the Divine in New York in December.

1972   Moves into an apartment in the New Orleans townhouse he had bought in 1962. *Small Craft Warnings* opens in Philadelphia in February and in New York in April. Awarded honorary degree by Purdue University. Appears in *Small Craft Warnings* as the character Doc in an attempt to boost ticket sales. Spends fall and winter in New York, Key West, and New Orleans. Completes first draft of *Memoirs*, using title "Flee, Flee This Sad Hotel." Attends the Venice Film Festival in August as a juror.

Robert Carroll becomes his companion-secretary and travels with him.

1973   *Out Cry*, with Michael York and Cara Duff-MacCormick, opens in New York March 1 and closes after twelve performances. Visits Los Angeles for a new staging of *Streetcar* and meets with Canadian television producer Harry Rasky, who has made a documentary film about him. Travels with Carroll to the Far East and then to Rome. In May Jane Bowles dies and in June William Inge commits suicide. Travels to Rome and then to Tangier to visit Paul Bowles. Works on *The Red Devil Battery Sign*. Saddened in September by the death of Anna Magnani. Awarded the first Centennial Medal of the Cathedral of St. John the Divine. Williams and Robert Carroll separate for a while.

1974   Travels extensively and visits Rose often. Works on *The Red Devil Battery Sign*. Goes to London in March for a revival of *Streetcar* with Claire Bloom. While in England, stays with Lady Maria St. Just (formerly Maria Britneva). In July *Cat on a Hot Tin Roof* is revived in New York with Elizabeth Ashley and Keir Dullea. Short story collection *Eight Mortal Ladies Possessed* is published.

1975   Receives National Arts Club's gold medal for literature in February and is given the key to the city of New York. Works on *This Is (An Entertainment)*. Second novel, *Moise and the World of Reason*, is published in May. In June, *The Red Devil Battery Sign* with Claire Bloom and Anthony Quinn opens in Boston and closes in 10 days. A successful revival of *Sweet Bird of Youth* opens in Boston and then moves to New York; there are also revivals of *Summer and Smoke* and of *The Glass Menagerie* in New York. *Memoirs* is published.

1976   *This Is (An Entertainment)* premieres in January in San Francisco, where Williams meets Lyle Leverich, whom he later selects as his biographer. Harry Rasky's documentary film *Tennessee Williams's South* appears on television. A series of young men alternate with Robert Carroll as paid companions. Returns in October to San Francisco for Leverich's production of *The Two-Character Play*. *The Eccentricities of a Nightingale* premieres in Buffalo, New

York, then moves to New York City November 23. *The Night of the Iguana* is revived in London. Inducted into the American Academy of Arts and Letters in December.

1977   *Vieux Carré* opens in May on Broadway and closes after only five performances. Goes to London in June for the premiere of *The Red Devil Battery Sign*. Second volume of poetry, *Androgyne, Mon Amour*, is published. Develops cataract on his right eye. Works on adapting the *Baby Doll* screenplay into a play, *Tiger Tail*, and writing the play *Creve Coeur*.

1978   *Tiger Tail* debuts in Atlanta but closes quickly. Returns to New Orleans for a public appearance in which he reads his poetry and fiction. The Spoleto Festival in Charleston, South Carolina, stages *Creve Coeur* (later retitled *A Lovely Sunday for Creve Coeur*). *Vieux Carré* is revived in London in August with Sylvia Miles. Mitch Douglas succeeds Bill Barnes as Williams' agent. Publishes collection of essays, *Where I Live*. Travels extensively before taking an apartment at Manhattan Plaza in New York. Brings Rose to New York for the holidays.

1979   *A Lovely Sunday for Creve Coeur* opens in New York on January 1 for a brief run. After his gardener in Key West is murdered, Williams discovers that the man had stolen manuscripts, other papers, and photographs. Works on revisions of *The Milk Train Doesn't Stop Here Anymore* and *Clothes for a Summer Hotel*. Brings Rose to Key West to live in a cottage near him, under the care of a cousin, but the arrangement proves unsatisfactory. *Kirche, Kuchen, und Kinder* opens in New York in September. In December Williams receives Kennedy Center Honors from President Jimmy Carter.

1980   In January *Will Mr. Merriwether Return from Memphis?* premieres in Key West at the opening of the Tennessee Williams Performing Arts Center. *Clothes for a Summer Hotel*, directed by José Quintero and starring Geraldine Page and Kenneth Haigh, opens in Washington, then Chicago, and in New York on March 26, his birthday, which Mayor Ed Koch declares Tennessee Williams Day; it is to be his last play on Broadway during his lifetime. Mother dies on June 1 at age 95. Travels in Europe in

June and July with artist Henry Faulkner. Works at Goodman Theatre in Chicago on three one-act plays. Appointed Distinguished Writer in Residence at the University of British Columbia in Vancouver, but does not remain for the full term. The triad of short plays, collectively called *Tennessee Laughs*, is presented at the Goodman Theatre. Spends holiday season in Key West, where he arranges for Rose to be returned to the nursing home in Ossining, New York.

1981   Works on *A House Not Meant to Stand* at Goodman. The Goodman has a party to celebrate his seventieth birthday, after which *A House Not Meant to Stand* opens. In April, former agent Audrey Wood suffers a stroke that leaves her in a coma. In the summer, works on his version of Chekhov's *The Sea Gull*, which will become *The Notebook of Trigorin*, and on *Something Cloudy, Something Clear*. The latter opens August 24 for a limited run by the Jean Cocteau Repertory, the last of his plays to debut in New York during his lifetime. In the fall, two old friends, poet Oliver Evans and artist Henry Faulkner, die. Along with Harold Pinter, he is awarded the Common Wealth Award of $11,000. Luis Sanjurjo replaces Mitch Douglas as his agent.

1982   Works in Key West on a revision of *A House Not Meant to Stand*. Travels to New York in February to receive the city's medallion of honor. *Something Cloudy, Something Clear* is revived in February by the Jean Cocteau Repertory. Goes to Chicago to discuss staging of the revised and expanded *A House Not Meant to Stand*, which opens in April for a limited run. Receives an honorary doctorate from Harvard in June. Attends staging of several of his plays at the Williamstown Theater Festival in Williamstown, Massachusetts. Works in Key West on a screenplay, then travels with Jane Smith to London and Sicily, where he works on a new play, *The Lingering Hour*. Makes last public appearance in November at the 92nd Street Y in New York. Hospitalized in Key West in December suffering from drug toxicity.

1983   In January, visits Jane Smith in New York, returns to Key West, then goes to New Orleans to arrange the sale of his townhouse. Flies to Taormina in February for a final brief visit before returning to New York. Dies on February 24; the cause of death may have been the result of an overdose of Seconal or from asphyxia caused by choking on a plastic cap of the type used on bottles of nasal spray or eyedrops. Funeral services are held at the St. Louis Cathedral on March 5; Williams is buried next to his mother in the Calvary Cemetery in St. Louis.

Note on the Texts

This volume contains 19 plays written by Tennessee Williams between 1937 and 1955. The texts printed here are taken from the first editions of the plays in book form, with the exception of *Battle of Angels*, where the text is taken from its first periodical printing.

Because Williams habitually revised his works, most of his plays exist in multiple versions. Williams revised many of them after initial book publication for editions published by Dramatists Play Service (intended for use by actors and directors), for subsequent American and English book editions, and for the collected edition *The Theatre of Tennessee Williams*, published by New Directions. Williams also rewrote two of the plays included in the present volume, *Battle of Angels* and *Summer and Smoke*, and republished them as *Orpheus Descending* and *The Eccentricities of a Nightingale*, respectively.

The acting editions of the plays are meant chiefly to aid in staging; a statement by the publisher in the Dramatists Play Service version of *The Glass Menagerie* notes that it is "intended primarily for producing groups," and stage directions "have been drastically changed in order to guide the director and the actor." The acting editions also omit prefaces and commentary that are part of the texts of the book editions.

Williams revised several of his plays relatively soon after their first book publication. The second American edition of *A Streetcar Named Desire*, published in 1950, is a substantial revision of the 1947 first edition. The first English editions of *The Glass Menagerie* and *Summer and Smoke*, published within three years of their first American editions, are also revised versions of the American editions of these plays. Williams' changes, however, are not always retained in subsequent editions of the plays, which sometimes revert to the first editions. In certain instances, Williams' revisions cause inconsistencies within a play, and occasionally he deleted or altered potentially objectionable material.

In 1971, New Directions published the first three volumes of *The Theatre of Tennessee Williams*, a collected edition of Williams' plays. Three additional volumes of this eight-volume series were published during Williams' lifetime and incorporated substantial changes in several plays. For example, the version of *Battle of Angels* printed in *The Theatre of Tennessee Williams* incorporates scenes from Williams' 1957 play *Orpheus Descending*, and the concluding act of *Cat on a*

Hot Tin Roof combines passages from the two versions of the final act that were printed in the 1955 edition.

The texts of the first book editions have been chosen for inclusion here because they are the versions of the plays Williams published for general readers immediately following the plays' composition.

Williams completed "April Is the Cruelest Month," an early draft of the play that became *Spring Storm*, in the spring of 1937, while he was enrolled in the drama school at the University of Iowa. Hoping to get the play staged, he gave a copy of it to Willard Holland, the director of the Mummers, the St. Louis company that had produced Williams' play *Candles to the Sun* in March 1937. He continued to work on the play during the 1937–38 academic year at Iowa, and he read from it to Elsworth Conkle's class in April 1938 and to E. C. Mabie's class in August of the same year. Both Conkle and Mabie responded negatively to the play. Although the Mummers announced a production in May 1938, the play was never staged. Later that year, Williams submitted his typescript to a contest sponsored by the Group Theatre in New York, which rejected it. The same typescript was submitted to MGM in 1943 for possible adaptation as a film script. The play, neither performed nor published during Williams' lifetime, was first published by New Directions in 1999 in an edition, prepared by Dan Isaac, based on the typescript sent to the Group Theatre, now at the Harry Ransom Center at the University of Texas at Austin. Isaac's edition also incorporates a scene and several speeches from earlier drafts of *Spring Storm* and emends the text in several places where the play's internal chronology is inconsistent; these alterations are listed in the notes to the present volume. The 1999 New Directions edition of *Spring Storm* is the text printed here.

Williams began writing *Not About Nightingales* in September 1938, after reading a newspaper story about inmates suffocated in a steam room in a Pennsylvania prison. He worked steadily on the play during the fall of 1938, completing three drafts by the end of the year, and sent a typescript of the finished play in February 1939 to the Group Theatre, which rejected it. The play was neither staged nor published during Williams' lifetime. The typescript sent to the Group Theatre is in the collection of the Harry Ransom Center at the University of Texas at Austin. *Not About Nightingales* was first published by New Directions in 1998 in an edition prepared by Allean Hale, based on the typescript sent to the Group Theatre but with two scenes inserted from an earlier draft of the play entitled

Hell, An Expressionistic Drama. This volume prints the text of the Group Theatre typescript as it is presented in the 1998 New Directions edition; the two scenes taken from *Hell, An Expressionistic Drama* appear in the notes to this volume.

Shortly after arriving in New York City in September 1939, Williams completed the first draft of the play that would become *Battle of Angels.* On November 31 he sent a revised draft to his agent, Audrey Wood, who submitted the play to Harold Clurman of the Group Theatre. After it became clear that the Group Theatre would not stage it, Wood sent a newly revised version of the play to the producer Guthrie McClintic, who turned it down, and to the Theatre Guild in New York, which optioned it. *Battle of Angels* began its pre-Broadway trial run in Boston on December 30, 1940, and closed two weeks later. Lawrence Langner, its producer, told Williams that *Battle of Angels* would have to be revised before the Theatre Guild would stage it in New York; after receiving a new version from Williams in May, the Guild decided not to produce the play. Williams continued to work on *Battle of Angels* in the years that followed.

Battle of Angels was published in 1945 in the first two (and only) issues of *Pharos*, a magazine distributed by New Directions, Williams' publisher. Williams eventually rewrote *Battle of Angels* and published it as a new play, *Orpheus Descending*, in 1957. The first edition of *Orpheus Descending* included a version of *Battle of Angels* that does not contain "The History of a Play (with Parentheses)" but is otherwise not significantly different from the *Pharos* version. The version of *Battle of Angels* included in Volume 1 (1971) of *The Theatre of Tennessee Williams* combines passages from *Battle of Angels* and *Orpheus Descending.* The text printed here is taken from *Pharos* 1–2, Spring 1945.

In July 1939 Williams wrote to Audrey Wood that he wanted to write a play based on the life of D. H. Lawrence, and he discussed the idea with Frieda Lawrence in August 1939. He completed *I Rise in Flame, Cried the Phœnix* in 1941, but it was not published until New Directions brought out the play in a limited edition in 1951. The acting edition published by Dramatists Play Service in 1953 contains an altered ending, as well as other changes. These revisions were retained when the play was collected in *Dragon Country: A Book of Plays* (New York: New Directions, 1970). The text printed here is taken from the 1951 New Directions edition.

The seven one-act plays in this volume that were published in *27 Wagons Full of Cotton and Other One-Act Plays* in 1946 were written between 1939 and 1945. Four of these plays had previously appeared in anthologies: "This Property Is Condemned," as part of "Landscape with Figures (Two Mississippi Plays)" in *American Scenes*, edited by William Kozlenko (New York: John Day, 1941); "The Lady of Larkspur Lotion" in *The Best One-Act Plays of 1941*, edited by Margaret Mayorga (New York: Dodd, Mead & Company, 1942); "The Last of My Solid Gold Watches" in *The Best One-Act Plays of 1942*, edited by Margaret Mayorga (New York: Dodd, Mead & Company, 1943); "27 Wagons Full of Cotton" in *The Best One-Act Plays of 1944*, edited by Margaret Mayorga (New York: Dodd, Mead & Company, 1945). *27 Wagons Full of Cotton and Other One-Act Plays* was published by New Directions on January 14, 1946. Material from "27 Wagons Full of Cotton" was used by Williams in his screenplay *Baby Doll*, published by New Directions in 1956, which in turn was the basis for his 1978 play *Tiger Tail*. Williams did not revise any of the six other plays for publication after the 1946 New Directions *27 Wagons Full of Cotton and Other One-Act Plays*. An English edition of the book was published by John Lehmann in 1947. These plays were reprinted in Volume 6 of *The Theatre of Tennessee Williams*. The texts of "27 Wagons Full of Cotton," "The Lady of Larkspur Lotion," "The Last of My Solid Gold Watches," "Portrait of a Madonna," "Auto-da-Fé," "Lord Byron's Love Letter," and "This Property Is Condemned" printed here are taken from the 1946 New Directions edition.

Williams wrote several short stories in the late 1930's and early 1940's that are related to *The Glass Menagerie*, including "If You Breathe, It Breaks," "Daughter of Revolution," and "Portrait of a Girl in Glass," which was completed in 1943 and collected in *One Arm* (New York: New Directions, 1948). In July 1943 Williams sent Audrey Wood a scenario for a film based on "Portrait of a Girl in Glass," hoping that MGM would be interested in the project. After the scenario was rejected, Williams resumed work on a stage adaptation of the story, which used the working title "The Gentleman Caller." Williams completed a draft of "The Gentleman Caller" while living in Provincetown, Massachusetts, during the summer of 1944. In October, producer Eddie Dowling agreed to stage the play, now titled *The Glass Menagerie*. Williams continued to revise the play while it was in rehearsal. *The Glass Menagerie* premiered in Chicago on December 26, 1944, and opened in New York on March 31, 1945. The book version of the play was published by Random House on July 31, 1945.

Both the acting edition (New York: Dramatists Play Service, 1948) and the English edition of *The Glass Menagerie* (London: John

Lehmann, 1948) differ from the Random House edition, and there is also variation between the Dramatists Play Service edition and the Lehmann edition. Many of the speeches, particularly those of Amanda Wingfield, are revised and often expanded in the Lehmann and Dramatists Play Service editions. The Lehmann edition also includes a preface, "The Catastrophe of Success," which appears in the notes of the present volume. The version of *The Glass Menagerie* collected in Volume I (1971) of *The Theatre of Tennessee Williams* also includes this preface but otherwise follows the text of the first American edition. The text printed here is taken from the 1945 Random House edition.

In early 1945, while in Chicago for the first run of *The Glass Menagerie*, Williams began writing a play titled first "The Moth," then "Blanche's Chair in the Moon." He returned to the play while in Mexico during the summer of 1945 but then set it aside until the fall of 1946. He worked steadily on the play, using the working title "The Poker Night," during the fall and following winter, and he sent a draft to Audrey Wood in March 1947 for submission to producers. Irene Selznick agreed in early May to stage a production, with Elia Kazan as director. Williams then changed the title to *A Streetcar Named Desire* but did not make revisions during the rehearsals before its New York premiere on December 3, 1947. *A Streetcar Named Desire* was published by New Directions on December 22, 1947; an English edition, published by John Lehmann in 1949, did not include any revisions by Williams.

A second American edition, published by New Directions in 1950, incorporates changes made by Williams, including numerous cuts and alterations of dialogue and stage directions. The Dramatists Play Service edition, published in 1953, generally follows the 1950 edition for speeches and dialogue, though the stage directions are often different. The version that appears in Volume I (1971) of *The Theatre of Tennessee Williams* follows the 1950 New Directions text. The text printed here is taken from the 1947 New Directions edition of *A Streetcar Named Desire*.

In the fall of 1945, Williams began writing "Chart of Anatomy," a play that grew out of two of his stories, "Oriflamme" and the not yet completed "The Yellow Bird." After writing a few pages, he set aside "Chart of Anatomy" until the following summer, when he worked on the play fairly continuously. In October 1946 he submitted a draft to Audrey Wood, who sent the script to potential producers. Margo Jones agreed in March 1947 to stage the play, first in Dallas and then in New York. Williams continued to revise the play, now titled *Summer and Smoke*, while living in Provincetown during the summer of 1947. He did not go to Dallas while the play was in rehearsal or in production. In preparation for the New York production, Jones traveled to Europe in the spring of 1948 to meet with Williams and to discuss his most recent version of the play. Williams made further revisions while Jones' production was in rehearsal in New York. *Summer and Smoke* opened on October 6, 1948. The play was published by New Directions on November 17, 1948.

Williams revised *Summer and Smoke* for the 1950 Dramatists Play Service edition of the play, omitting the Prologue, adding a new scene between Scenes 1 and 2, and changing stage directions. The English edition of *Summer and Smoke* was published by John Lehmann in 1952; although this edition does not incorporate many of the changes Williams made for the Dramatists Play Service edition, it is different from the 1948 New Directions edition and contains revisions not included in the Dramatists Play Service edition. *Summer and Smoke* was rewritten and published in 1965 as *The Eccentricities of a Nightingale*. Volume 2 (1971) of *The Theatre of Tennessee Williams* reprints the text of the 1948 edition. The text of *Summer and Smoke* printed here is taken from the 1948 New Directions edition.

In December 1949 Williams completed a draft of "The Eclipse of May 29, 1919," one of several working titles he used for the play that would become *The Rose Tattoo*. He continued working on the play during the winter and following spring, when Cheryl Crawford announced that she would produce the play. Williams revised the play while in Sicily during the summer of 1950, then sent additional changes to Crawford in December while the play was in rehearsal for its Chicago premiere. After it opened on December 29, 1950, Williams went to Chicago to make further revisions while the play was in production. *The Rose Tattoo* opened in New York on February 2, 1951, and was published as a book by New Directions on March 30, 1951. "The Timeless World of a Play" was first published as "Concerning the Timeless World of a Play" in *The New York Times* on January 14, 1951. Williams did not revise *The Rose Tattoo* for its Dramatists Play Service edition, the English edition, or the version that appears in Volume 2 (1971) of *The Theatre of Tennessee Williams*. The text printed here is taken from the 1951 New Directions edition of the play.

Camino Real grew out of a one-act play, "Ten Blocks on the Camino Real," written in early 1946 and first printed in *American*

Blues, a pamphlet of one-act plays published by Dramatists Play Service in 1948. Williams finished a draft of a new, expanded version of the play in January 1952. Later that year Cheryl Crawford agreed to produce *Camino Real*, with Elia Kazan as director. After working on the play while in Europe during the summer of 1952, Williams met with Kazan in September to discuss the script. Following trial runs in New Haven and Philadelphia, the play opened on Broadway on March 19, 1953. Williams altered the script during the New Haven, Philadelphia, and New York productions, and the version published by New Directions in October 1953 incorporates further revisions made after *Camino Real* closed in New York. Williams did not revise *Camino Real* for the English edition published by Secker & Warburg in 1958 or for Volume 2 (1971) of *The Theatre of Tennessee Williams*. The text printed here is taken from the 1953 New Directions edition.

"Talk to Me Like the Rain and Let Me Listen" and "Something Unspoken" first appeared in an expanded edition of *27 Wagons Full of Cotton and Other One-Act Plays,* published by New Directions in 1953. Neither play was subsequently revised by Williams. "'Something Wild'" was first published as "On the Art of Being a True Non-Conformist" in the *New York Star*, November 7, 1948. It appeared as the introduction to the 1949 second edition of *27 Wagons Full of Cotton and Other One-Act Plays* and was reprinted without changes in all subsequent editions. The texts for "'Something Wild,'" "Talk to Me Like the Rain and Let Me Listen," and "Something Unspoken" are taken from the 1953 New Directions edition of *27 Wagons Full of Cotton and Other One-Act Plays*.

Cat on a Hot Tin Roof originated in the short story "Three Players of a Summer Game," first published in *The New Yorker* on November 1, 1952. Williams then adapted the story as a play. In late 1954, the Playwrights Company agreed to produce *Cat on a Hot Tin Roof* and named Elia Kazan as director. Williams came to New York to meet with Kazan, who suggested revisions in the script and asked Williams to rewrite the third act for the Broadway premiere. The play opened on March 25, 1955, with a revised third act; when published in book form by New Directions later that year, both Williams' original version of the third act and the version performed on Broadway were included, with a "Note of Explanation" discussing the circumstances of the revision. The Dramatists Play Service edition of the play prints the revised third act and does not include Williams' original version. The English edition, published by

Secker & Warburg in 1956, and the version that appears in Volume 3 (1971) of *The Theatre of Tennessee Williams* follow the 1955 New Directions edition. For a 1973 revival of *Cat on a Hot Tin Roof* Williams wrote still another version of the third act, combining passages from the two versions of the third act presented in the 1955 edition; he also made changes in the first two acts. This version was published in 1975 by New Directions. The text printed here is taken from the 1955 New Directions edition of *Cat on a Hot Tin Roof* and includes both versions of the third act.

This volume presents the texts of the original printings chosen for inclusion here, but it does not attempt to reproduce features of their typographic design. The texts are presented without change, except for the correction of typographical errors. Spelling, punctuation, and capitalization are often expressive features and are not altered, even when inconsistent or irregular. The following is a list of typographical errors corrected, cited by page and line number: 7.2, 'an; 12.11, Arthur's; 17.13, way?; 19.8, lets; 31.23, it's; 42.7, emotion; 44.12, embarrassment.; 44.26, No.; 62.6, me?; 64.15, sharecroppers; 64.33, you; 66.33, anymore; 91.1, thing; 94.11, Aunt; 95.7, Yes,; 99.5, "Yeah,; 175.25, somthing; 187.38, Jim,; 195.2, nickles; 200.11, Yes,; 202.21, SANDRAS; 205.13, boys; 210.4, would't; 214.27, youg; 220.10, wont; 225.11, Witche's; 226.2, 'listenin'; 229.10, *Is*; 232.16, easter; 247.21, dollor; 248.37, keds; 262.22, then; 272.34, thre; 273.16, Picture; 277.40, states; 278.32, thir; 284.9, appelation; 351.25, kindergardeners; 407.28, answer—while; 407.30, Oh!"; 509.20, face; 515.6, *Blanches*; 525.15, prevue; 531.20, till I; 540.11, *Blanches*; 542.18, unforgiveable; 558.21, STELLA: Yes; 639.12, So Alma you; 662.2, *Rose*; 664.16, crooked:; 664.19, because,; 688.29, Rose; 760.8, Maître 'D'; 815.33, for; 915.14, *dam*; 916.35, *Lacy*; 956.15, Gooper don't; 982.19, Bid; 984.11, going'; 1004.12, an.

ACKNOWLEDGMENTS

The plays in this volume are published by arrangement with New Directions Publishing Corporation, New York, Publisher of the plays of Tennessee Williams, and with The University of the South, copyright proprietor of the works of Tennessee Williams.

Notes

In the notes below, the reference numbers denote page and line of this volume. No note is made for material included in standard desk-reference books such as Webster's *Collegiate*, *Biographical*, and *Geographical* dictionaries. Biblical quotations are keyed to the King James Version. Quotations from Shakespeare are keyed to *The Riverside Shakespeare*, ed. G. Blakemore Evans (Boston: Houghton Mifflin, 1974). Cast lists and production information are taken from the first book editions of the plays. For further biographical information than is contained in the Chronology, see Albert J. Devlin (ed.), *Conversations with Tennessee Williams* (Jackson: University Press of Mississippi, 1986); Ronald Hayman, *Tennessee Williams: Everyone Else Is an Audience* (New Haven: Yale University Press, 1993); Lyle Leverich, *Tom: The Unknown Tennessee Williams* (New York: W.W. Norton & Company, 1995); Harry Rasky, *Tennessee Williams: A Portrait in Laughter and Lamentation* (New York: Dodd, 1986); Donald Spoto, *The Kindness of Strangers: The Life of Tennessee Williams* (Boston: Little, Brown and Company, 1985); Dakin Williams and Shepherd Mead, *Tennessee Williams: An Intimate Biography* (New York: Arbor House, 1983); Edwina Dakin Williams as told to Lucy Freeman, *Remember Me to Tom* (New York: Putnam, 1963); Donald Windham (ed.), *Tennessee Williams' Letters to Donald Windham 1940–1965* (New York: Holt, Rinehart & Winston, 1977).

SPRING STORM

1.1   *Spring Storm*]   *Spring Storm* was first performed publicly as a staged reading in New York City on October 26 and 27, 1996, as part of the Ensemble Studio Theatre's Octoberfest 96—Sixteenth Annual Festival of Member-Initiated Plays. Curt Demptster, Artistic Director; Jamie Richards, Executive Producer. The reading was directed by Dona D. Vaughn and initiated by Dan Isaac. The stage managers were Brian George and Sherry Stregack. The cast, in order of appearance, was as follows: DICK MILES: Tristan Fitch; HEAVENLY CRITCHFIELD: Melinda Hamilton; REVEREND HOOKER: Dan Isaac; AGNES PEABODY: Catherine Campbell; ETHEL ASBURY: Carolyn Marcell; SUSAN LAMPHREY: Ina Bass-Filip; MRS. LAMPHREY: Amy Coleman; ARTHUR SHANNON: Peter Sarsgaard; HERTHA NEILSON: Diana LaMar; LILA CRITCHFIELD: Celia Weston; ESMERELDA CRITCHFIELD: Dolores Sutton; OLIVER CRITCHFIELD: Peter Maloney; MRS. DOWD: Debbie Lee Jones; MRS. BUFORD: Amy Coleman; MRS. ADAMS: Kristin Griffith; HENRY ADAMS: Chris White; FANNY: Ina Bass-Filip; MRS. KRAMER: Debbie

Lee Jones; BIRDIE SCHLAGMANN: India Cooper; MABEL: Amy Coleman; RALPH: Brian George. STAGE DIRECTIONS: Mark Johannes. This version of *Spring Storm* also includes the following characters which were not part of the version prepared for the Ensemble Studio Theatre reading: RONALD ASBURY; OZZIE; JACKSON.

5.34–35   "Swear not by the inconstant—April!] Cf. Shakespeare, *Romeo and Juliet*, II.ii.109: "O, swear not by the moon, th' inconstant moon . . . ."

7.38   *The Sheik*] Novel (1921) by Edith Maude Hull.

8.27   Heavenly!] Williams' typescript reads "Helen!" Heavenly's character was named Helen in early drafts of the play.

9.10   *Satuhday's Children?*] *Saturday's Children*, play (1927) by Maxwell Anderson that depicts the marital problems of a young couple.

14.17   Sunday?] Williams' typescript reads "tomorrow?"

24.32   Agnes] Williams' typescript reads "Birdie".

27.17   Agnes Peabody] Williams' typescript reads "Birdie Schlagmann".

28.20–27   When . . . now!] "I Shall Not Care" (1915).

30.19   Sunday night.] These words were added in the 1999 New Directions edition.

30.33–34   "—But only . . . tree!"] Final line of Joyce Kilmer's "Trees" (1914).

31.27–28   Zella Armstrong's *Southern Families*] *Notable Southern Families*, published in six volumes, 1915–33.

36.24–25   the Havilland.] A type of porcelain.

50.1–52.6   SCENE . . . *Two*] This scene, which is part of a draft of *Spring Storm* but does not appear in Williams' finished typescript, is inserted here in the 1999 New Directions edition.

50.18–19   three o'clock in the morning?] Williams' draft reads "two in the morning?"

54.21   If it does rain,] The word "rain" is added in the 1999 New Directions edition.

65.14–19   She sits . . . me!] These lines, which are part of a draft of *Sping Storm* but do not appear in Williams' finished typescript, are inserted here in the 1999 New Directions edition.

69.1–3, 8–15, 18–23   What lips . . . more.] In his typescript of *Spring Storm*, Williams did not specify a poem to be read. The 1999 New Directions edition inserts this untitled sonnet (1923) by Edna St. Vincent Millay.

69.26–27   Alcott series.]   Louisa May Alcott's novels for young readers included *Little Women* (1868–69), *An Old-Fashioned Girl* (1870), and *Little Men* (1871).

70.14   next Saturday night,]   Williams' typescript reads "tomorrow,".

75.14   nine!]   Williams' typescript reads "eleven!"

75.23   *nine*]   Williams typescript reads "*eleven*".

80.20–27   (*suddenly . . . despair*)]   These lines, which are part of a draft of *Spring Storm* but do not appear in Williams' finished typescript, are inserted here in the 1999 New Directions edition.

82.12–13   When . . . put.]   This line was spoken by Heavenly in Williams' typescript but is given to Lila in the 1999 New Directions edition.

82.34–35   the Country Club]   Williams' typescript reads "dinner".

83.6   your blue knitted suit.]   Williams' typescript reads "her white organdy". The 1999 New Directions edition also omits Mrs. Critchfield's line, "I've simply worked miracles on that dress."

83.38   you what]   Williams' typescript reads "you yesterday what".

88.28   *brilliance.*]   The 1999 New Directions edition omits the line immediately following in Williams' typescript: "*In her white organdy dress with the orchid pinned to her shoulder she is a breathtaking vision.*"

88.32   the Country Club.]   Williams' typescript reads "Lamphrey's."

NOT ABOUT NIGHTINGALES

97.1   *Not About Nightingales*]   *Not About Nightingales* was given its world première on March 5, 1998, at the Royal National Theatre, London, England. It was directed by Trevor Nunn; set design was by Richard Hoover; costume design by Karyl Newman; lighting by Chris Parry, music arrangement by Steven Edis, and sound by Christopher Shutt. Production Manager was Jo Maund and Stage Manager, Courtney Bryant. The cast, in order of speaking, was as follows: THE VOICE OF THE LORELEI: Mark Heenehan; MRS. BRISTOL: Sandra Dickinson; EVA CRANE: Sherri Parker Lee; CANARY JIM: Finbar Lynch; BOSS WHALEN, *the Warden*: Corin Redgrave; SAILOR JACK: Richard Leaf; SCHULTZ, *a guard*: Richard Ziman; BUTCH O'FALLON: James Black; THE QUEEN: Juke Akuwudike; JOE: Alex Giannini; MCBURNEY, *a guard*: Craig Pinder; OLLIE: Dion Graham; SWIFTY: Mark Dexter; GOLDIE, *an apparition*: Sandra Dickinson; SHAPIRO: Joel Leffert; MEX: Chico Andrade; KRAUSE: Daniel Stewart; ALBERTS: Noble Shropshire; CHAPLAIN: Rom Hodgkins; REVEREND HOOKER: Noble Shropshire; GUARDS, CONVICTS, TROOPERS: Mark Heenehan, Richard Leaf, Daniel Stewart, Noble Shropshire.

130.38   *Blackout*] In the 1998 New Directions edition, the following scene from "Hell, An Expressionistic Drama," an early draft of *Not About Nightinglales*, is inserted here:

Announcer: "Butch Has A Dream."
Theme up: "Roses of Picardy." Fade.
GOLDIE: Hello, Butch.
BUTCH [*half-rising on his bunk*]: Goldie!
GOLDIE: Yes, it's me.
BUTCH: How didja get in here?
GOLDIE: Walls ain't thick enough to keep us apart always, Butch.
BUTCH: You mean you walked right through? They couldn't stop you?
GOLDIE: That's right, honey.
BUTCH: It's marvelous, marvelous!
GOLDIE: Sure. I never was an ordinary bim. There was always something un-
    usual about me. You noticed that. How light I was on my feet and always
    laughing. A girl that danced like me, all night till they wrapped up the fid-
    dles and covered the drums, that never got tired, that always wanted one
    more of whatever was offered, is something kind of special. You know that,
    Butch. You don't buy us two for a quarter at the corner drug.
BUTCH: Yeah, I know that, Goldie. I always had that special feeling about
    you, kid. Honey, I used to try to find words to tell yuh what you did to
    me nights when you opened your mouth against mine and give me your
    love . . .
    Room twenty-three! That was yours. Six flights up the narrow stairs with
    brass tacks in an old red carpet and bulbs at the end of the hall. Fire-
    escape. We used to sit out there summer nights and drink iced beer till all
    we could do was giggle and then go to bed.
    Day used to come so slow and easy through the long white blinds.
    Maybe a little wind making the curtains stir. The milk wagons rattled
    along, and out on the East River the fog horns blew. I never slept, I lay and
    watched you sleeping. Your face was like the face of a little girl then. A girl
    no man ever touched. I never told you about those times I watched you
    sleeping and how I felt toward you then. Because I wasn't good at making
    speeches. But I guess you knew.
GOLDIE: Of course I knew. I knew you loved me, Butch.
BUTCH: I wonder if your face still looks like that when you're sleeping.
GOLDIE: I haven't changed. You oughta know that, Butch.
BUTCH: You don't go out with other fellows, do you?
GOLDIE: No. You know I don't. I been as true as God to you, Butch.
BUTCH: But how do you live, how do you get along now, Goldie?
GOLDIE: As good as a girl can expect. I still work days over at the Imperial
    Dry Cleaners and nights I work at the Paradise, Butch.
BUTCH: I wanted you to quit the Paradise, Goldie.
GOLDIE: What for?
BUTCH: I don't like other guys dancin' witcha.

GOLDIE: They don't mean nothing. Just pasteboard tickets, that's all they are to me, Butch. I keep the stubs an' turn 'em in for cash. And that's as far as it goes.

BUTCH: But when they hold you close sometimes when the lights go out for the waltz—you don't ever close your eyes and blow your breath on their necks like you done for me, Goldie?

GOLDIE: No. Never.

BUTCH: You wouldn't lie to me, Goldie?

GOLDIE: Of course I wouldn't. Some of the girls say one man's as good as another. They're all the same. But I'm not made like that. I give myself, I give myself for *keeps*. And time don't change me none. I'm still the same.

BUTCH: The same old Goldie, huh?

GOLDIE: The same old kid. Running my dancing slippers down at the heels. But not forgetting your love. And going home nights alone. Sleeping alone in a big brass bed. Half of it empty, Butch. And waiting for you.

BUTCH: Waiting for me!

GOLDIE: Yes! Waiting for you! [*She begins to fade into the shadows.*]

BUTCH [*reaching toward her*]: Goldie!

GOLDIE: So long, Butch. So long . . .

BUTCH [*frantically*]: Goldie! Goldie! [*She has completely disappeared.*]

JOE [*sitting up on his bunk*]: What's the matter, Butch.

QUEEN: He's talkin' in his sleep again.

BUTCH [*slowly and with terrific emphasis*]: God—*damn*!

BLACKOUT

137.29   *Blackout*] In the 1998 New Directions edition, the following scene from "Hell, An Expressionistic Drama," an early draft of *Not About Nightingales*, is inserted here:

Announcer: "Hell—an Expressionistic Interlude."
The following scene takes place on a dark stage. The shuffling of feet is heard and continues for several moments. A whistle sounds.

VOICE: TAKE PLACES AT TABLES! [*More shuffling is heard.*] Set down!
    [*Now we hear the scrape of chairs or benches as the men sit.*]

VOICE: Start eating!
    [*A low yammering commences.*]

VOICE: Start eating, I said! You heard me! Start eating!
    [*Very softly, in a whisper, voices begin to be heard, transmitting a message from table to table with rising intensity.*]

VOICES: Quit eating—quit eating—quit eating—quit eating—don't eat no more a dis slop—trow it back in deir faces—quit eating—quit eating—we don't eat crap—we're human—quit eating—QUIT EATING—
    [*The chorus grows louder, more hysterical, becomes like the roaring of animals. As the yammering swells there is a clatter of tin cups. The lights come up on Butch and others seated on benches at a table. Each has a tin cup and plate*

with which he beats time to the chorus of the Chant led by Ollie, who stands,
stage forward, in the spotlight.]

OLLIE: Devil come to meet us an' he rang on a bell,
            Twenty-five men got a ticket to hell!

CHORUS: Turn on the heat, turn on the heat,
            They're gonna give us hell when they turn on the heat.
            Turn on the heat, turn on the heat,
            They're gonna give us hell when they turn on the heat.

OLLIE: Down in Mizzoura where I was born
            I worked all day in a field of corn,
            Got pretty hot but at night it was nice
            'Cause we kept our beer in a bucket of ice.

CHORUS: Turn on the heat, turn on the heat,
            They're gonna give us hell when they turn on the heat.
            Turn on the heat, turn on the heat,
            They're gonna give us hell when they turn on the heat.

BUTCH: There's one rap that a connie can't beat
            When the Warden says, Boys, we gonna turn on the heat!

CHORUS: Turn on the heat, turn on the heat,
            They're gonna give us hell when they turn on the heat.

OLLIE: Devil come to meet us an' he rang on a bell,
            Twenty-five men got a ticket to HELL!

CHORUS: Turn on the heat, turn on the heat,
            They're gonna give us hell when they turn on the heat.
            Turn on the heat, turn on the heat,
            They're gonna give us hell when they turn on the heat.

[*The lights fade. There is a loud ringing of bells: a whistle sounds; then a sud-*
den dead silence. The lights fade and come up on Schultz and the guards, en-
tering cellblock. The prisoners are back in their cells.]

SCHULTZ: Now you boys are gonna learn a good lesson about makin' distur-
    bances in mess hall! Git one out of each cell! Keep 'em covered!

JOE [*to Butch*]: You started something all right.

QUEEN: Oh, Lord!

SCHULTZ: Ollie! Shapiro! Come on out, you're elected! Mex!

SHAPIRO: What for! Distoibance? I make no distoibance!

MEX: [*He protests volubly in Spanish.*]

OLLIE: What you want me fo', Mistuh Schultz?

SCHULTZ [*at the door of Butch's cell*]: Stand back there, Butch. [*He prods him
    with a gun.*] Who's in here with you? Joe? Queenie?

BUTCH: I started the noise.

SCHULTZ: I know you started the noise. But we're saving you, Butch. You're
    too good to waste on the Hole.

QUEEN: I didn't make any noise, Mr. Schultz. I was perfectly quiet the whole
    time.

SCHULTZ: Who's that on the bunk? Aw, the new boy. Playing Puss-in-the-
    Corner! Come on out.

QUEEN: He didn't make noise, Mr. Schultz.

SCHULTZ: Come out, boy!

SWIFTY [*shaking*]: I didn't make any noise. I was sick. I didn't want any supper. I've been sick ever since I come here.

SCHULTZ: Yes, I've heard you squawking! Git in line there.

SWIFTY: I wanta see the Warden. It makes me sick being shut up without exercise.

SCHULTZ: We'll exercise you! [*He blows a whistle.*]

SWIFTY [*wildly*]: The Hole? No! No!

SCHULTZ [*prodding him roughly with a billy*]: Git moving! Krause! Alberts!
Awright, that's all!—Two weeks in the hole, bread an' water—maybe we'll
finish off with a Turkish bath.—Step on it, Mex!

MEX: [*He swears in Spanish.*]

SHAPIRO: Distoibance? Not me. Naw.

SCHULTZ: Hep, hep, hep— [*A slow shuffling is heard as the lights begin to
dim.*]

JOE: Christ!

QUEEN: Swifty won't make it! They'll kill him down there!

[*The whistle is heard, then the distant clang of steel.*]

BUTCH [*whistles a few bars then sings out*]:

    They fly so high, nearly reach the sky
    Then like my dreams they fade an' die!
    Fawchun's always hiding—I looked ev'rywhere!

[*Theme up and dim out.*]

MEX: [*He protests in Spanish.*]

SCHULTZ: Fall in line! March! Hep, hep, hep— [*The voice diminishes as they
move, heads bent, shoulders sagging, shuffling down the corridor.*]

                BLACKOUT SLOWLY

164.4   *Jésus . . . pecados!*] Jesus—dead for our sins!

165.5–6   *Muerto . . . Sol!*] Dead—for our sins—red—with blood is—the
sun!

BATTLE OF ANGELS

189.1   *Battle of Angels*] *Battle of Angels*, a play in 2 acts and 3 scenes, was
presented by the Theatre Guild, Inc., at the Wilbur Theatre, Boston, for two
weeks, starting December 30, 1940, and ending January 11, 1941. Margaret
Webster directed, the scenery was by Cleon Throckmorton and the incidental
music was by Colin McPhee, plus Negro spiritual recordings by H. F. Chalfin.
No one is listed as lighting director in the program. *The Cast:* DOLLY BLAND:
Dorothy Peterson; BEULAH CARTWRIGHT: Edith King; PEE WEE BLAND:
Robert Emhardt; SHERIFF TALBOTT: Charles McClelland; CASSANDRA WHITE-
SIDE: Doris Dudley; VEE TALBOTT: Katherine Raht; VALENTINE XAVIER:
Wesley Addy; EVA TEMPLE: Hazel Hanna; BLANCH TEMPLE: Helen Carewe;
MYRA TORRANCE: Miriam Hopkins; JOE: Clarence Washington; SMALL BOY:
Bertram Holmes; BENNIE: Ican Lewis; JABE TORRANCE: Marshall Bradford.

229.15   *"Petty Girl"*]   Popular pin-up images drawn by illustrator George Petty (1894–1975) that first appeared in *Esquire* magazine in 1933 and were later featured in advertisements, calendars, and film posters.

234.29   Peabody Roof!]   Night club on the roof of the Peabody Hotel in Memphis.

246.21–22   hitting the sawdust trail.]   The part of a revival meeting when audience members are invited to come forward as an affirmation of faith.

I RISE IN FLAME, CRIED THE PHŒNIX

289.15   *"Forest Lawn"*]   A cemetery in Hollywood where many celebrities are buried.

292.6   Ja . . . dich.]   Yes, it is for you.

295.27   Ja . . . Ewigkeit!]   Of course! For all of eternity!

296.4   Wie du willst!]   As you wish!

27 WAGONS FULL OF COTTON AND OTHER ONE-ACT PLAYS (1946)

307.3–5   'Now . . . SAPPHO]   From Fragment 47.

312.24   dopes]   Coca-Colas.

317.7   I'm not from Missouri!]   Missouri is known as "the Show-Me State."

336.2–3   *Ce* . . . RIMBAUD]   It can only be the end of the world, moving ahead: Arthur Rimbaud, *Les Illuminations* (1886), "Enfance," IV.

336.32   Sidney Greenstreet,]   Sydney Greenstreet (1879–1954), character actor whose films included *The Maltese Falcon* (1941) and *Flamingo Road* (1949).

339.40   I.S.C.]   International Shoe Company.

341.31–32   Some people . . . to *die.*]   Reference to a tenet of the Jehovah's Witnesses.

360.31   John Abbott]   English character actor (b. 1905) whose films included *The Shanghai Gesture* (1941) and *The Mask of Dimitrios* (1944).

381.19   *Canaille!*]   Pig!

THE GLASS MENAGERIE

393.1   *The Glass Menagerie*]   *The Glass Menagerie* was first produced by Eddie Dowling and Louis J. Singer at the Playhouse Theatre, New York City, on March 31, 1945, with the following cast: THE MOTHER: Laurette Taylor; HER SON: Eddie Dowling; HER DAUGHTER: Julie Haydon; THE GENTLEMAN

CALLER: Anthony Ross. SCENERY DESIGNED AND LIGHTED by Jo Mielziner; ORIGINAL MUSIC COMPOSED by Paul Bowles; STAGED by Eddie Dowling and Margo Jones.

Later editions of *The Glass Menagerie* include the following essay, "The Catastrophe of Success," written in 1948, as a preface:

The winter marked the third anniversary of the Chicago opening of "The Glass Menagerie," an event that terminated one part of my life and began another about as different in all external circumstances as could well be imagined. I was snatched out of virtual oblivion and thrust into sudden prominence, and from the precarious tenancy of furnished rooms about the country I was removed to a suite in a first-class Manhattan hotel. My experience was not unique. Success has often come that abruptly into the lives of Americans. The Cinderella story is our favorite national myth, the cornerstone of the film industry if not of the Democracy itself. I have seen it enacted on the screen so often that I was now inclined to yawn at it, not with disbelief but with an attitude of Who Cares! Anyone with such beautiful teeth and hair as the screen protagonist of such a story was bound to have a good time one way or another, and you could bet your bottom dollar and all the tea in China that that one would not be caught dead or alive at any meeting involving a social conscience.

No, my experience was not exceptional, but neither was it quite ordinary, and if you are willing to accept the somewhat eclectic proposition that I had not been writing with such an experience in mind—and many people are not willing to believe that a playwright is interested in anything but popular success—there may be some point in comparing the two estates.

The sort of life that I had had previous to this popular success was one that required endurance, a life of clawing and scratching along a sheer surface and holding on tight with raw fingers to every inch of rock higher than the one caught hold of before, but it was a good life because it was the sort of life for which the human organism is created.

I was not aware of how much vital energy had gone into this struggle until the struggle was removed. I was out on a level plateau with my arms still thrashing and my lungs still grabbing at air that no longer resisted. This was security at last.

I sat down and looked about me and was suddenly very depressed. I thought to myself, this is just a period of adjustment. Tomorrow morning I will wake up in this first-class hotel suite above the discreet hum of an East Side boulevard and I will appreciate its elegance and luxuriate in its comforts and know that I have arrived at our American plan of Olympus. Tomorrow morning when I look at the green satin sofa I will fall in love with it. It is only temporarily that the green satin looks like slime on stagnant water.

But in the morning the inoffensive little sofa looked more revolting than the night before and I was already getting too fat for the $125 suit which a fashionable acquaintance had selected for me. In the suite things began to break accidentally. An arm came off the sofa. Cigarette burns appeared on the polished surface of the furniture. Windows were left open and a rain storm flooded the suite. But the maid always put it straight and the patience of the management was inexhaustible. Late parties could not offend them seriously. Nothing short of a demolition bomb seemed to bother my neighbors.

I lived on room service. But in this, too, there was a disenchantment. Some time between the moment when I ordered dinner over the phone and when it was rolled into my living room like a corpse on a rubber-wheeled table, I lost all interest in it. Once I ordered a sirloin steak and a chocolate sundae, but everything was so cunningly disguised on the table that I mistook the chocolate sauce for gravy and poured it over the sirloin steak.

Of course all this was the more trivial aspect of a spiritual dislocation that began to manifest itself in far more disturbing ways. I soon found myself becoming indifferent to people. A well of cynicism rose in me. Conversations all sounded as if they had been recorded years ago and were being played back on a turntable. Sincerity and kindliness seemed to have gone out of my friends' voices. I suspected them of hypocrisy. I stopped calling them, stopped seeing them. I was impatient of what I took to be inane flattery.

I got so sick of hearing people say, "I loved your play!" that I could not say thank you any more. I choked on the words and turned rudely away from the usually sincere person. I no longer felt any pride in the play itself but began to dislike it, probably because I felt too lifeless inside ever to create another. I was walking around dead in my shoes and I knew it but there were no friends I knew or trusted sufficiently, at that time, to take them aside and tell them what was the matter.

This curious condition persisted about three months, till late spring, when I decided to have another eye operation mainly because of the excuse it gave me to withdraw from the world behind a gauze mask. It was my fourth eye operation, and perhaps I should explain that I had been afflicted for about five years with a cataract on my left eye which required a series of needling operations and finally an operation on the muscle of the eye. (The eye is still in my head. So much for that.)

Well, the gauze mask served a purpose. While I was resting in the hospital the friends whom I had neglected or affronted in one way or another began to call on me and now that I was in pain and darkness, their voices seemed to have changed, or rather that unpleasant mutation which I had suspected earlier in the season had now disappeared and they sounded now as they had used to sound in the lamented days of my obscurity. Once more they were sincere and kindly voices with the ring of truth in them and that quality of understanding for which I had originally sought them out.

As far as my physical vision was concerned, this last operation was only relatively successful (although it left me with an apparently clear black pupil in the right position, or nearly so) but in another, figurative way, it had served a much deeper purpose.

When the gauze mask was removed I found myself in a readjusted world. I checked out of the handsome suite at the first-class hotel, packed my papers and a few incidental belongings and left for Mexico, an elemental country where you can quickly forget the false dignities and conceits imposed by success, a country where vagrants innocent as children curl up to sleep on the pavements and human voices, especially when their language is not familiar to the ear, are soft as birds'. My public self, that artifice of mirrors, did not exist here and so my natural being was resumed.

Then, as a final act of restoration, I settled for a while at Chapala to work on a play called "The Poker Night," which later became "A Streetcar Named Desire." It is only in his work that an artist can find reality and satisfaction, for the actual world is less intense than the world of his invention and consequently his life, without recourse to violent disorder, does not seem very substantial. The right condition for him is that in which his work is not only convenient but unavoidable.

For me a convenient place to work is a remote place among strangers where there is good swimming. But life should require a certain minimal effort. You should not have too many people waiting on you, you should have to do most things for yourself. Hotel service is embarrassing. Maids, waiters, bellhops, porters and so forth are the most embarrassing people in the world for they continually remind you of inequities which we accept as the proper thing. The sight of an ancient woman, gasping and wheezing as she drags a heavy pail of water down a hotel corridor to mop up the mess of some drunken overprivileged guest, is one that sickens and weighs upon the heart and withers it with shame for this world in which it is not only tolerated but regarded as proof positive that the wheels of Democracy are functioning as they should without interference from above or below. Nobody should have to clean up anybody else's mess in this world. It is terribly bad for both parties, but probably worse for the one receiving the service.

I have been corrupted as much as anyone else by the vast number of menial services which our society has grown to expect and depend on. We should do for ourselves or let the machines do for us, the glorious technology that is supposed to be the new light of the world. We are like a man who has bought a great amount of equipment for a camping trip, who has the canoe and the tent and the fishing lines and the axe and the guns, the mackinaw and the blankets, but who now, when all the preparations and the provisions are piled expertly together, is suddenly too timid to set out on the journey but remains where he was yesterday and the day before and the day before that, looking suspiciously through white lace curtains at the clear sky he distrusts. Our great technology is a God-given chance for adventure and for progress which we are afraid to attempt. Our ideas and our ideals remain exactly what they were and where they were three centuries ago. No. I beg your pardon. It is no longer safe for a man even to declare them!

This is a long excursion from a small theme into a large one which I did not intend to make, so let me go back to what I was saying before.

This is an oversimplification. One does not escape that easily from the seduction of an effete way of life. You cannot arbitrarily say to yourself, I will now continue my life as it was before this thing, Success, happened to me. But once you fully apprehend the vacuity of a life without struggle you are equipped with the basic means of salvation. Once you know this is true, that the heart of man, his body and his brain, are forged in a white-hot furnace for the purpose of conflict (the struggle of creation) and that with the conflict removed, the man is a sword cutting daisies, that not privation but luxury is the wolf at the door and that the fangs of this wolf are all the little vanities and conceits and laxities that Success is heir to—why, then with this knowledge you are at least in a position of knowing where danger lies.

You know, then, that the public Somebody you are when you "have a name" is a fiction created with mirrors and that the only somebody worth being is the solitary and unseen you that existed from your first breath and which is the sum of your actions and so is constantly in a state of becoming under your own violation—and knowing these things, you can even survive the catastrophe of Success!

It is never altogether too late, unless you embrace the Bitch Goddess, as William James called her, with both arms and find in her smothering caresses exactly what the homesick little boy in you always wanted, absolute protection and utter effortlessness. Security is a kind of death, I think, and it can come to you in a storm of royalty checks beside a kidney-shaped pool in Beverly Hills or anywhere at all that is removed from the conditions that made you an artist, if that's what you are or were or intended to be. Ask anyone who has experienced the kind of success I am talking about— What good is it? Perhaps to get an honest answer you will have to give him a shot of truth serum but the word he will finally groan is unprintable in genteel publications.

Then what is good? The obsessive interest in human affairs plus a certain amount of compassion and moral conviction, that first made the experience of living something that must be translated into pigment or music or bodily movement or poetry or prose or anything that's dynamic and expressive— that's what's good for you if you're at all serious in your aims. William Saroyan wrote a great play on this theme, that purity of heart is the one success worth having. "In the time of your life—live!" That time is short and it doesn't return again. It is slipping away while I write this and while you read it, and the monosyllable of the clock is Loss, loss, loss, unless you devote your heart to its opposition.

393.2-3   *Nobody . . .* Cummings]   Final line of untitled poem beginning "somewhere I have never travelled, gladly beyond" (1931).

400.27   Guernica]   Basque town bombed during the Spanish Civil War on April 26, 1937, by aircraft of the German Condor Legion, sent by Hitler to support the Nationalist forces led by General Francisco Franco. About 300 people were killed in the attack.

401.20   "ou sont les neiges."]   Cf. François Villon, "Ballade des Dames du Temps Jadis": "Où sont les neiges d'antan" ("Where are the snows of yesteryear").

433.5   *"scattering poems in the sky"*]   Cf. E. E. Cummings' untitled poem beginning "the hours rise up putting off stars and it is" (1922).

438.34   Dizzy Dean]   Pitcher for the St. Louis Cardinals.

448.15–16   Century of Progress]   Century of Progress Exposition in Chicago, 1933–34.

448.35–39   O blow, ye winds . . . away!]   Cf. the chorus in Charles Edward Caryll's "Davy and the Goblin: A Nautical Ballad" (1886).

A STREETCAR NAMED DESIRE

467.1   *A Streetcar Named Desire*]   *A Streetcar Named Desire* was presented at the Barrymore Theatre in New York on December 3, 1947, by Irene Selznick. It was directed by Elia Kazan, with the following cast: NEGRO WOMAN: Gee Gee James; EUNICE HUBBELL: Peg Hillias; STANLEY KOWALSKI: Marlon Brando; STELLA KOWALSKI: Kim Hunter; STEVE HUBBELL: Rudy Bond; HAROLD MITCHELL (MITCH): Karl Malden; MEXICAN WOMAN: Edna Thomas; TAMALE VENDOR: Richard Carlyle; BLANCHE DUBOIS: Jessica Tandy; PABLO GONZALES: Nick Dennis; A YOUNG COLLECTOR: Vito Christi; NURSE: Ann Dere; DOCTOR: Richard Garrick.

   Scenery and lighting by Jo Meilziner, costumes by Lucinda Ballard. The action of the play takes place in the spring, summer, and early fall in New Orleans. It was performed with intermissions after Scene Four and Scene Six.

   Assistant to the producer: Irving Schneider. Musical Advisor: Lehman Engel.

469.4   *The section*]   The Faubourg Marigny, just outside the French Quarter.

471.16   street-car named Desire,]   Desire, Cemeteries, and Elysian Fields were streetcar lines in and around the French Quarter until 1948. They did not connect in the manner described in the play.

474.25–27   Only . . . Weir!]   Edgar Allan Poe, "Ulalame" (1847), line 9.

497.6   Xavier Cugat!]   Popular Cuban orchestra leader of the 1940s.

498.9–11   "And . . . Browning!]   Elizabeth Barrett Browning, *Sonnets from the Portuguese* (1850), sonnet 43, lines 13–14.

521.4   owl-car.]   The last scheduled streetcar of the night.

537.17   Huey Long . . . King!"]   Long often quoted this phrase from William Jennings Bryan's "Cross of Gold" speech delivered at the 1896 Democratic National Convention, and used it as the title of his autobiography.

546.31   *Flores para los muertos.*]   Flowers for the dead.

SUMMER AND SMOKE

565.1   *Summer and Smoke*]   *Summer and Smoke* was first produced by
Margo Jones at her theater in Dallas, Texas. It was later produced and directed by Miss Jones in New York, opening at the Music Box Theater,
October 6, 1948, with Margaret Phillips and Ted Andrews in the two leading
roles; incidental music by Paul Bowles and scenery by Jo Mielziner.

565.2–4   *Who . . .* RILKE]   The opening of Rainer Maria Rilke's *Duino
Elegies*.

620.20–21   Le doy . . . cielo!]   I give her the earth, and if the earth is
not enough—I give her the sky.

630.3–4   Sophie Newcombe]   Women's college in New Orleans.

641.8–9   From the Peabody . . . Vicksburg.]   A popular description of
the limits of the Mississippi Delta.

THE ROSE TATTOO

645.1   *The Rose Tattoo*]   *The Rose Tattoo* was first produced by Cheryl
Crawford at the Erlanger Theater in Chicago on December 29, 1950. It had
its Broadway opening on February 3, 1951, at the Martin Beck Theater in
New York City, with Daniel Mann as director, setting by Boris Aronson and
music by David Diamond. Production Associate: Bea Lawrence. Assistant to
Producer: Paul Bigelow. *Cast of the New York Production*: SALVATORE:
Salvatore Mineo; VIVI: Judy Ratner; BRUNO: Salvatore Taormina; ASSUNTA:
Ludmilla Toretzka; ROSA DELLE ROSE: Phyllis Love; SERAFINA DELLE ROSE:
Maureen Stapleton; ESTRELLE HOHENGARTEN: Sonia Sorel; THE STREGA:
Daisy Belmore; GIUSEPPINA: Rossana San Marco; PEPPINA: Augusta
Merighi; VIOLETTA: Vivian Nathan; MARIELLA: Penny Santon; TERESA: Nancy
Franklin; FATHER DE LEO: Robert Carricart; A DOCTOR: Andrew Duggan;
MISS YORKE: Dorrit Kelton; FLORA: Jane Hoffman; BESSIE: Florence
Sundstrom; JACK HUNTER: Don Murray; THE SALESMAN: Eddie Hyans; AL-
VARO MANGIACAVALLO: Eli Wallach; A MAN: David Stewart; ANOTHER MAN:
Martin Balsam.

647.2–4   CARSON McCULLERS . . . world."]   "When We Are Lost,"
first published in *New Directions X* in 1948.

656.1–7   *O slinger! . . .* TRANSLATION]   Saint-John Perse, *Anabase*
(1924), translated by T. S. Eliot as *Anabasis* in 1930.

660.24–25   Stai zitta . . . Vieni qui]   Be quiet. Come here.

660.30   Che altre cose?]   What other thing?

661.20   Stai tranquilla! Calmati]   Stay quiet! Be calm!

662.30   Che bella stoffa]   What pretty material.

663.10   STREGA] Witch, sorceress.

663.27–28   Il becco della strega!] The witch's goat!

667.22–23   Ferme . . . di Dio!] Stop! Stop in the name of God!

668.29   Sicuro!] For sure!

669.21   Apri la porta!] Open the door!

669.35   Aiuto!] Help!

670.24   Smetilla,] Quit it.

671.15   Lasciami stare,] Leave me alone.

671.25   figlia . . . cosí!] Daughter, you should not talk like that!

671.28   Ecco la—chiave . . .] Here is the key.

672.33   Ho solo . . . questo mondo!] I have only you in this world!

673.12–13   'Sta fetentissima . . . maledetta!] It's the filthiest school! A cursed school!

673.25   Piantala,] Leave it.

673.32   Aspetta!] Wait!

674.6   Guardate!] Watch yourself!

685.33   Fa niente . . .] Doesn't matter.

687.30–31   Pazza . . . Finiscila!] Lunatic! Finish her.

688.3   per piacere!] If you please!

697.15   Zitta ora!] Quiet now!

704.13   Ma com'è . . . Napoletano?] But how strange! Are you from Naples?

704.19   Dov'è il gabinetto?] Where's the bathroom?

713.22   Miei . . . pomodori!] My tomatoes! Watch out for my tomatoes!

715.6   *Rondinella felice!*] Fortunate swallow!

716.29   C'è nessuno?] No one here?

726.34   Torno subito,] I'll be right back.

727.4   dove siete?] Where are you?

727.9   non voglio farlo!] I don't want to do it!

728.14   Sono . . . feroce!] I am a beast, a wild beast!

CAMINO REAL

741.1 *Camino Real*] *Camino Real* was first produced by Cheryl Crawford and Ethel Reiner, in association with Walter P. Chrysler, Jr., and following tryouts in New Haven and Philadelphia, it had its Broadway premiere on March 19, 1953, at the Martin Beck Theatre. The production was directed by Elia Kazan, with the assistance of Anna Sokolow; the scenery and costumes were designed by Lemuel Ayers; and incidental music was contributed by Bernardo Ségall. Production associate: Anderson Lawler. *Cast of the Broadway Production:* GUTMAN: Frank Silvera; SURVIVOR: Guy Thomajan; ROSITA: Aza Bard; FIRST OFFICER: Henry Silva; JACQUES CASANOVA: Joseph Anthony; LA MADRECITA DE LOS PERDIDOS: Vivian Nathan; HER SON: Rolando Valdez; KILROY: Eli Wallach; FIRST STREET CLEANER: Nehemiah Persoff; SECOND STREET CLEANER: Fred Sadoff; ABDULLAH: Ernesto Gonzalez; A BUM IN A WINDOW: Martin Balsam; A. RATT: Mike Gazzo; THE LOAN SHARK: Salem Ludwig; BARON DE CHARLUS: David J. Stewart; LOBO: Ronne Aul; SECOND OFFICER: William Lennard; A GROTESQUE MUMMER: Gluck Sandor; MARGUERITE GAUTIER: Jo Van Fleet; LADY MULLIGAN: Lucille Patton; WAITER: Page Johnson; LORD BYRON: Hurd Hatfield; NAVIGATOR OF THE FUGITIVO: Antony Vorno; PILOT OF THE FUGITIVO: Martin Balsam; MARKET WOMAN: Charlotte Jones; SECOND MARKET WOMAN: Joanna Vischer; STREET VENDOR: Ruth Volner; LORD MULLIGAN: Parker Wilson; THE GYPSY: Jennie Goldstein; HER DAUGHTER, ESMERALDA: Barbara Baxley; NURSIE: Salem Ludwig; EVA: Mary Grey; THE INSTRUCTOR: David J. Stewart; ASSISTANT INSTRUCTOR: Parker Wilson; MEDICAL STUDENT: Page Johnson; DON QUIXOTE: Hurd Hatfield; SANCHO PANZA, PRUDENCE DUVERNOY, OLYMPE: *Not in production.* Street Vendors: Aza Bard, Ernesto Gonzalez, Charlotte Jones, Gluck Sandor, Joanna Vische, Ruth Volner, Antony Vorno. Guests: Martin Balsam, Mary Grey, Lucille Patton, Joanna Vischer, Parker Wilson. Passengers: Mike Gazzo, Mary Grey, Page Johnson, Charlotte Jones, William Lennard, Salem Ludwig, Joanna Vischer, Ruth Volner. At the Fiesta: Ronne Aul, Martin Balsam, Aza Bard, Mike Gazzo, Ernesto Gonzalez, Mary Grey, Charlotte Jones, William Lennard, Nehemiah Persoff, Fred Sadoff, Gluck Sandor, Joanna Vischer, Antony Vorno, Parker Wilson.

744.38–39 Some poet . . . but be.] Archibald MacLeish, in the final lines of "Ars Poetica" (1926).

751.2 *Devoir!*] Duty!

751.16 Sus papeles! Sus documentos] Your papers! Your documents.

757.10–11 *A donde la fuente?*] Where is the fountain?

757.17 La fuente está seca!] The fountain is dry!

762.11–13 Rojo . . . de miedo!] The sun is red! The sun is red with blood! The moon is white! The moon is white with fear!

764.7   *Kilroy*]   Graffiti scrawled on walls by American soldiers during World War II.

766.11   Dulces . . . con leche!]   Sweets, sweets! Lottery! Lottery! Pastries, coffee with milk!

770.8   *Baron de Charlus,*]   A character in Marcel Proust's *A la recherche du temps perdu (Remembrance of Things Past).*

770.33   Ingreso Libero]   Free access.

773.18   the Bird Circuit.]   Reference to several gay bars in New York in the 1940's and 1950's named after birds.

779.30   Ponga selo!]   Put it on!

783.9   Recuerdos]   Souvenirs.

786.32–33   Secret Order . . . Cross!]   The Rosicrucians, an occultist secret society.

800.9   Che . . . fare!]   What can you do?

800.16   Forse . . . so!]   Perhaps, perhaps, I don't know!

821.18   Forest Lawn . . .]   See note 289.15.

836.13–14   "Humankind . . . reality."]   Cf. T. S. Eliot, *Murder in the Cathedral*, Part II.

27 WAGONS FULL OF COTTON AND OTHER ONE-ACT PLAYS (1953)

855.34   Victor Herbert]   Irish-born American composer (1859–1924) of popular operettas such as *Naughty Marietta* (1910) and *Eileen* (1917).

859.5   Mayo's.]   The Mayo Clinic in Rochester, Minnesota.

860.20–21   ça . . . petite!]   That goes without saying, my little one!

CAT ON A HOT TIN ROOF

873.1   *Cat on a Hot Tin Roof*]   *Cat on a Hot Tin Roof* was presented at the Morosco Theatre in New York on March 24, 1955, by The Playwrights' Company. It was directed by Elia Kazan; the scenery was designed by Jo Mielziner, and the costumes by Lucinda Ballard. The cast was as follows: LACEY: Maxwell Glanville; SOOKEY: Musa Williams; MARGARET: Barbara Bel Geddes; BRICK: Ben Gazzara; MAE: Madeleine Sherwood; GOOPER: Pat Hingle; BIG MAMA: Mildred Dunnock; DIXIE: Pauline Hahn; BUSTER: Darryl Richard; SONNY: Seth Edwards; TRIXIE: Janice Dunn; BIG DADDY: Burl Ives; REVEREND TOOKER: Fred Stewart; DOCTOR BAUGH: R. G.

Armstrong; DAISY: Eva Vaughan Smith; BRIGHTIE: Brownie McGhee; SMALL: Sonny Terry.

873.2–6   *And you . . .* THOMAS]   "Do Not Go Gentle Into That Good Night," lines 16–19.

876.35   my first preface to a long play.]   See pp. 275-86 in this volume.

955.23   hoppin' john.]   A southern dish of black-eyed peas, rice, and seasoning.

Library of Congress Cataloging-in-Publication Data

Williams, Tennessee, 1911–1983.
    [Plays. Selections]
    Plays / Tennessee Williams.
        p. cm. — (The Library of America 119–120)
    Selection and notes by Mel Gussow and Kenneth Holdich.
    Contents [v. 1] Plays 1937–1955: Spring storm. Not about
nightingales. Battle of angels. I rise in flame, cried the
phoenix. From 27 wagons full of cotton (1946). . . . The
glass menagerie. A streetcar named Desire. Summer and
smoke. The rose tattoo. Camino Real. From 27 Wagons full
of cotton (1953). . . . Cat on a hot tin roof—[v. 2] Plays
1957–1980: Orpheus descending. Suddenly last summer. Sweet
bird of youth. Period of adjustment. The night of the iguana.
The eccentricities of a nightingale. The milk train doesn't
stop here anymore. The mutilated. Kingdom of earth (The
seven descents of Myrtle). Small craft warnings. Out cry.
Vieux Carré. A lovely Sunday for Creve Coeur.
    ISBN 1–883011–86–8 (v. 1 : alk. paper)—ISBN 1–883011–87–6
        (v. 2 : alk. paper)
    I. Gussow, Mel.   II. Holdich, Kenneth.   III. Title.
    IV. Series.
PS3545.I5365 A6 2000
812'.54—dc21   00–030190

THE LIBRARY OF AMERICA SERIES

The Library of America helps to preserve our nation's literary heritage by publishing, and keeping permanently in print, authoritative editions of America's best and most significant writing. An independent nonprofit organization, it was founded in 1979 with seed money from the National Endowment for the Humanities and the Ford Foundation.

This book is set in 10 point Linotron Galliard,
a face designed for photocomposition by Matthew Carter
and based on the sixteenth-century face Granjon. The paper is
acid-free Ecusta Nyalite and meets the requirements for permanence
of the American National Standards Institute. The binding
material is Brillianta, a woven rayon cloth made by
Van Heek-Scholco Textielfabrieken, Holland.
The composition is by The Clarinda
Company. Printing and binding by
R.R.Donnelley & Sons Company.
Designed by Bruce Campbell.